CONSTITUTIONAL
LITIGATION UNDER § 1983

LEXISNEXIS LAW SCHOOL ADVISORY BOARD

Charles P. Craver
Freda H. Alverson Professor of Law
The George Washington University Law School

Richard D. Freer
Robert Howell Hall Professor of Law
Emory University School of Law

Craig Joyce
Andrews Kurth Professor of Law &
Co-Director, Institute for Intellectual Property and Information Law
University of Houston Law Center

Ellen S. Podgor
Professor of Law &
Associate Dean of Faculty Development and Electronic Education
Stetson University College of Law

Paul F. Rothstein
Professor of Law
Georgetown University Law Center

Robin Wellford Slocum
Professor of Law & Director,
Legal Research and Writing Program
Chapman University School of Law

Charles J. Tabb
Alice Curtis Campbell Professor of Law
University of Illinois College of Law

David I. C. Thomson
LP Professor & Director, Lawyering Process Program
University of Denver, Sturm College of Law

Judith Welch Wegner
Professor of Law
University of North Carolina School of Law

CONSTITUTIONAL LITIGATION UNDER § 1983

Second Edition

Mark R. Brown
Newton D. Baker/Baker & Hostetler Professor of Law
Capital University Law School

Kit Kinports
Professor of Law & Polisher Family Distinguished Faculty Scholar
Pennsylvania State University, The Dickinson School of Law

Library of Congress Cataloging-in-Publication Data

Brown, Mark R., 1959-
Constitutional Litigation under [section] 1983 / Mark R. Brown, Kit Kinports.—2nd ed.
p. cm.
Includes index.
ISBN 978–1–4224–2545–9 (hard cover)
1. State action (Civil rights)—United States—Cases. 2. Constitutional torts—United States—Cases. 3. Government litigation—United States—Cases. I. Kinports, Kit. II. Title.
KF1325.C58B76 2008
342.7308'8–dc22
2008034403

This publication is designed to provide accurate and authoritative information in regard to the subject matter covered. It is sold with the understanding that the publisher is not engaged in rendering legal, accounting, or other professional services. If legal advice or other expert assistance is required, the services of a competent professional should be sought.

LexisNexis, the knowledge burst logo, and Michie are trademarks of Reed Elsevier Properties Inc, used under license. Matthew Bender is a registered trademark of Matthew Bender Properties Inc.

Copyright © 2008 Matthew Bender & Company, Inc., a member of the LexisNexis Group.
All Rights Reserved.

No copyright is claimed in the text of statutes, regulations, and excerpts from court opinions quoted within this work. Permission to copy material exceeding fair use, 17 U.S.C. § 107, may be licensed for a fee of 25¢ per page per copy from the Copyright Clearance Center, 222 Rosewood Drive, Danvers, Mass. 01923, telephone (978) 750-8400.

NOTE TO USERS
To ensure that you are using the latest materials available in this area, please be sure to periodically check the LexisNexis Law School web site for downloadable updates and supplements at www.lexisnexis.com/lawschool.

Editorial Offices
744 Broad Street, Newark, NJ 07102 (973) 820-2000
201 Mission St., San Francisco, CA 94105-1831 (415) 908-3200
www.lexisnexis.com

MATTHEW⬥BENDER

DEDICATION

For Katie. MRB

For Steve, Lizzie, and Sara. KK

PREFACE

Dozens of excellent casebooks address the topics of Constitutional Law, Civil Rights, Civil Procedure, and Federal Courts. Few casebooks, however, concentrate on the intersection of these subjects — what we call Constitutional Litigation. This book is designed to fill that gap. It does not replace any of the courses presently taught at most American law schools. Indeed, it assumes that students have taken basic courses, like Constitutional Law and Civil Procedure, and prods students to take more advanced courses, like Federal Courts and Civil Rights. Its focus is the peculiar problems that arise in litigation against states, local governments and their agents under the United States Constitution. Because 42 U.S.C. § 1983 is the dominant civil mechanism for vindicating constitutional rights in America, it forms a suitable center for the text.

The book is constructed to serve as the principal reading for a two- or three-hour course. Related civil rights statutes, such as 42 U.S.C. §§ 1981 and 1982, Titles VI and IX, and Title VII, are discussed where relevant, but are not afforded the full treatment one would find in a course on, say, Employment Discrimination or Statutory Civil Rights. The reason for this is simple — time. Our intent is to convey to the student a succinct understanding of the policies, procedures, problems and precedents that surround federal litigation with government. The most efficient — and interesting — tool to this end, we believe, is the Constitution of the United States. A student versed in constitutional suits against states, local subdivisions and their agents should readily master related subjects, including direct constitutional claims against federal officials, *see, e.g., Bivens v. Six Unknown Named Agents*, 403 U.S. 388 (1971), implied statutory causes of action, *see, e.g., Cannon v. University of Chicago*, 441 U.S. 677 (1979), and the use of § 1983 to redress statutory wrongs. *See, e.g., Maine v. Thiboutot*, 448 U.S. 1 (1980). Again, these topics are addressed in the casebook, but the focus is on the subject that has received the greatest attention from the Supreme Court: constitutional claims brought under § 1983.

The text is structured to flow from beginning to end without interruption or digression. Still, instructors should not hesitate to re-organize the materials. Chapter 3's Eleventh Amendment discussion, for example, could easily be taught after Chapter 4's materials on local liability, or indeed, even at the very beginning of the course. Chapter 9's foray into attorney's fees need not be taught last — indeed, it might be best taught first! — and Chapter 5's compilation of procedural problems need not be taught in the middle. Our ordering of chapters is logical, but hardly necessary to a proper understanding of the materials or subject matter.

In order to fit the subject into a manageable number of pages, the cases have been heavily edited. Text, including footnotes and citations, is often omitted from judicial opinions without indication. We attempt to alert readers to omissions within sentences and paragraphs with ellipses; however, text that is omitted at the beginnings and ends of paragraphs is not always apparent. Footnotes are sequentially numbered in each Chapter, with the courts' original numbering included in brackets. Footnotes that we have added to opinions are enclosed in brackets and do not indicate original numbering.

The Appendix includes the text of relevant provisions of the United States Constitution, federal statutes and federal procedural rules. We have limited the Appendix to constitutional, statutory and procedural provisions that are either discussed in the cases or are directly relevant to constitutional litigation under 1983. Hence, much of the Constitution has been omitted, as has most of the United States Code and Federal Rules of Civil Procedure.

PREFACE

We trust that you will enjoy teaching and learning from the material. Having taught the course for several years from this text and others, we can attest to its resonance with students. No matter their ideologies or political persuasions, students enjoy learning about suing government.

M.R.B.
K.K.
August 2008

TABLE OF CONTENTS

Chapter 1		OFFICIAL LIABILITY FOR CONSTITUTIONAL WRONGS . 1

A. "UNDER COLOR OF" STATE LAW 1
    Monroe v. Pape 1
    Notes 8

B. "STATE ACTION" COMPARED 13
  [1]   Official Wrongdoing 13
       Almand v. DeKalb County 14
       United States v. Lanier 16
       Notes 18
  [2]   Private Wrongdoing 21
       Lugar v. Edmondson Oil Company 21
       Notes 25

C. UNAUTHORIZED CONDUCT THAT DOES NOT VIOLATE THE
    CONSTITUTION 28
    Parratt v. Taylor 28
    Notes 32
    Daniels v. Williams 34
    Davidson v. Cannon 37
    Notes 41
    Zinermon v. Burch 42
    Notes 47

D. THE PECULIAR PROBLEM OF STATE *INACTION* 53
    Deshaney v. Winnebago Department of Social Services 53
    Notes 57
    Town of Castle Rock v. Gonzales 62
    Notes 65

E. ADDITIONAL CONSTITUTIONAL AND STATUTORY VIOLATIONS ... 66
    Golden State Transit Corp. v. City of Los Angeles 66
    Notes 69

Chapter 2		OFFICIAL IMMUNITIES 75

A. ABSOLUTE IMMUNITY 75
  [1]   Legislative Immunity 75
       Bogan v. Scott-Harris 75
       Notes 78
  [2]   Judicial Immunity 80
       Stump v. Sparkman 80
       Notes 87
  [3]   Prosecutorial Immunity 90
       Buckley v. Fitzsimmons 90

TABLE OF CONTENTS

		Notes	97
B.	QUALIFIED IMMUNITY		100
		Harlow v. Fitzgerald	100
		Notes	105
		Hope v. Pelzer	112
		Notes	122

Chapter 3		**SOVEREIGN IMMUNITY**	**131**
A.	INTRODUCTION		131
		Alden v. Maine	131
		Seminole Tribe v. Florida	138
		Notes	145
B.	PROSPECTIVE INJUNCTION SUITS FILED AGAINST STATE OFFICIALS		148
		Edelman v. Jordan	148
		Notes	153
C.	WAIVER AND ABROGATION		159
		Atascadero State Hospital v. Scanlon	159
		Notes	161
		Quern v. Jordan	165
		Notes	170

Chapter 4		**LOCAL LIABILITY**	**181**
A.	HISTORICAL ANTECEDENTS		181
		Monroe v. Pape	181
		Monell v. Department of Social Services	182
		Notes	190
B.	MUNICIPAL IMMUNITY		195
		Owen v. City of Independence	195
		Notes	201
C.	AD HOC POLICIES		206
[1]	The Final Authority Analysis		206
		Pembaur v. City of Cincinnati	206
		City of St. Louis v. Praprotnik	210
		Notes	215
		McMillian v. Monroe County	218
		Notes	223
[2]	Deliberate Indifference		225
		City of Canton v. Harris	227
		Notes	231
		Board of Country Commissioners of Bryan Country v. Brown	234
		Notes	241

TABLE OF CONTENTS

D.	INNOCENT AGENTS	242
	City of Los Angeles v. Heller	243
	Notes	245
E.	USING STATE LAW TO REACH LOCAL GOVERNMENT	248
	Aldinger v. Howard	248
	Notes	250
	Wilson v. Chicago	252
	Notes	253

Chapter 5 THE RELATIONSHIP BETWEEN STATE AND FEDERAL LAW IN SECTION 1983 LITIGATION 255

A.	SECTION 1988(a), STATUTES OF LIMITATIONS, AND SURVIVORSHIP RULES	255
	Wilson v. Garcia	255
	Notes	262
B.	NOTICE-OF-CLAIM REQUIREMENTS	267
	Felder v. Casey	267
	Notes	275
C.	THE RIGHT TO JURY TRIAL IN SECTION 1983 CASES	276
	City of Monterey v. Del Monte Dunes at Monterey, Ltd.	276
	Notes	288
D.	RELEASE-DISMISSAL AGREEMENTS	289
	Town of Newton v. Rumery	289
	Notes	296

Chapter 6 REMEDIES UNDER § 1983 299

A.	COMPENSATORY DAMAGES	299
	Memphis Community School District v. Stachura	299
	Notes	302
	Hartman v. Moore	304
	Notes	309
B.	PUNITIVE DAMAGES	311
	Smith v. Wade	311
	Notes	317
	City of Newport v. Fact Concerts	322
	Notes	326
C.	PROSPECTIVE RELIEF AGAINST STATE AND LOCAL OFFICIALS	328
[1]	Article III Limitations: Standing, Ripeness, and Mootness	328
	City of Los Angeles v. Lyons	329
	Notes	335
	Northeastern Florida Chapter of Associated General Contractors of America v. City of Jacksonville	341

TABLE OF CONTENTS

	Notes	344
	U.S. Bancorp Mortgage Co. v. Bonner Mall Partnership	346
	Notes	349
	United States Parole Commission v. Geraghty	357
	Notes	359
	United Food and Commercial Workers Union Local 751 v. Brown Group, Inc.	364
	Notes	365
[2]	Statutory Limits on Prospective Relief	368
	Miller v. French	368
	Notes	372
	Hibbs v. Winn	373
	Notes	375

Chapter 7   **FEDERAL ABSTENTION IN FAVOR OF STATE PROCEEDINGS** 381

A.	AVOIDING CONSTITUTIONAL ISSUES	381
	Railroad Commission of Texas v. Pullman Co.	381
	Notes	382
B.	DEFERENCE TO PENDING STATE PROCEEDINGS	392
	Younger v. Harris	392
	Notes	397
	Ohio Civil Rights Commission v. Dayton Christian Schools	404
	Notes	408
	New Orleans Public Service, Inc. v. Council of City of New Orleans	411
	Notes	414
C.	§ 1983 CLAIMS FOR MONEY DAMAGES	416
	Deakins v. Monaghan	416
	Notes	419

Chapter 8   **PRIOR AND PARALLEL STATE PROCEEDINGS** 421

A.	PRECLUSION	421
	Migra v. Warren City School District	421
	Notes	425
[1]	Takings Claims in Federal Court	431
	San Remo Hotel L.P. v. City and County of San Francisco	432
	Notes	436
[2]	Adjudicative Decisions by State Agencies	438
	University of Tennessee v. Elliott	439
	Notes	442
[3]	Exhaustion Requirements for Prisoners	443

TABLE OF CONTENTS

		Woodford v. Ngo	444
		Notes	447
	[4]	Appealing Adjudicative Decisions	448
		City of Chicago v. International College of Surgeons	448
		Notes	453
B.		HABEAS CORPUS AND § 1983	459
	[1]	Injunctive Relief	459
		Preiser v. Rodriguez	459
		Notes	465
		Nelson v. Campbell	465
		Notes	467
	[2]	Damages	469
		Heck v. Humphrey	469
		Notes	474
	[3]	*Heck*, Accrual, and Timing	481
		Wallace v. Kato	481
		Notes	488

Chapter 9		**ATTORNEY'S FEES**	**491**
A.		PREVAILING PARTY	492
		Buckhannon Board & Care Home, Inc. v. West Virginia Department of Health and Human Resources	492
		Notes	498
B.		REASONABLE FEES	504
		City of Riverside v. Rivera	504
		Notes	508
C.		SETTLEMENTS AND CONSENT DECREES	519
		Maher v. Gagne	520
		Notes	521
D.		BARGAINING OVER FEES	524
		Marek v. Chesny	524
		Notes	529
		Evans v. Jeff D.	530
		Notes	536

Appendix	....	**App-1**
Table of Cases	....	**TC-1**
Index	....	**I-1**

Chapter 1
OFFICIAL LIABILITY FOR CONSTITUTIONAL WRONGS

> Every person who, under color of any statute, ordinance, regulation, custom, or usage, of any State or Territory or the District of Columbia, subjects, or causes to be subjected, any citizen of the United States or other person within the jurisdiction thereof to the deprivation of any rights, privileges, or immunities secured by the Constitution and laws, shall be liable to the party injured in an action at law, suit in equity, or other proper proceeding for redress, except that in any action brought against a judicial officer for an act or omission taken in such officer's judicial capacity, injunctive relief shall not be granted unless a declaratory decree was violated or declaratory relief was unavailable. For the purposes of this section, any Act of Congress applicable exclusively to the District of Columbia shall be considered to be a statute of the District of Columbia.

42 U.S.C. § 1983.

A. "UNDER COLOR OF" STATE LAW

MONROE v. PAPE
Supreme Court of the United States
365 U.S. 167 (1961)

Mr. Justice Douglas delivered the opinion of the Court.

The complaint alleges that 13 Chicago police officers broke into petitioners' home in the early morning, routed them from bed, made them stand naked in the living room, and ransacked every room, emptying drawers and ripping mattress covers. It further alleges that Mr. Monroe was then taken to the police station and detained on "open" charges for 10 hours, while he was interrogated about a two-day-old murder, that he was not taken before a magistrate, though one was accessible, that he was not permitted to call his family or attorney, that he was subsequently released without criminal charges being preferred against him. It is alleged that the officers had no search warrant and no arrest warrant and that they acted "under color of the statutes, ordinances, regulations, customs and usages" of Illinois and of the City of Chicago.

I.

Petitioners claim that the invasion of their home and the subsequent search without a warrant and the arrest and detention of Mr. Monroe without a warrant and without arraignment constituted a deprivation of their "rights, privileges, or immunities secured by the Constitution" within the meaning of [42 U.S.C. § 1983].

Section [1983] came onto the books as § 1 of the Ku Klux Act of April 20, 1871. It was one of the means whereby Congress exercised the power vested in it by § 5 of the Fourteenth Amendment to enforce the provisions of that Amendment. Senator Edmunds, Chairman of the Senate Committee on the Judiciary, said concerning this section:

> The first section is one that I believe nobody objects to, as defining the rights secured by the Constitution of the United States when they are assailed by any State law or under color of any State law, and it is merely carrying out the principles of the civil rights bill, which has since become a part of the Constitution, viz., the Fourteenth Amendment.

Its purpose is plain from the title of the legislation, "An Act to enforce the Provisions of the Fourteenth Amendment to the Constitution of the United States, and for other Purposes." Allegation of facts constituting a deprivation under color of state authority of a right guaranteed by the Fourteenth Amendment satisfies to that extent the requirement of [§ 1983]. So far petitioners are on solid ground. For the guarantee against unreasonable searches and seizures contained in the Fourth Amendment has been made applicable to the States by reason of the Due Process Clause of the Fourteenth Amendment.

II.

There can be no doubt at least since *Ex parte Virginia*, 100 U.S. 339 (1879), that Congress has the power to enforce provisions of the Fourteenth Amendment against those who carry a badge of authority of a State and represent it in some capacity, whether they act in accordance with their authority or misuse it. *See Home Tel. & Tel. Co. v. City of Los Angeles*, 227 U.S. 278 (1913). The question with which we now deal is the narrower one of whether Congress, in enacting § [1983], meant to give a remedy to parties deprived of constitutional rights, privileges and immunities by an official's abuse of his position.

It is argued that "under color of" enumerated state authority excludes acts of an official or policeman who can show no authority under state law, state custom, or state usage to do what he did. In this case it is said that these policemen, in breaking into petitioners' apartment, violated the Constitution and laws of Illinois. It is pointed out that under Illinois law a simple remedy is offered for that violation and that, so far as it appears, the courts of Illinois are available to give petitioners that full redress which the common law affords for violence done to a person; and it is earnestly argued that no "statute, ordinance, regulation, custom or usage" of Illinois bars that redress.

The Ku Klux Act grew out of a message sent to Congress by President Grant on March 23, 1871, reading:

> A condition of affairs now exists in some States of the Union rendering life and property insecure and the carrying of the mails and the collection of the revenue dangerous. The proof that such a condition of affairs exists in some localities is now before the Senate. That the power to correct these evils is beyond the control of State authorities I do not doubt; that the power of the Executive of the United States, acting within the limits of existing laws, is sufficient for present emergencies is not clear. Therefore, I urgently recommend such legislation as in the judgment of Congress shall effectually secure life, liberty, and property, and the enforcement of law in all parts of the United States.

The legislation — in particular the section with which we are now concerned — had several purposes. There are threads of many thoughts running through the debates. One who reads them in their entirety sees that the present section had three main aims.

First, it might, of course, override certain kinds of state laws. . . . Second, it provided a remedy where state law was inadequate. . . . But the purposes were much broader. The third aim was to provide a federal remedy where the state remedy, though adequate in theory, was not available in practice. The opposition to the measure complained that "It overrides the reserved powers of the States," just as they argued that the second section of the bill [now 42 U.S.C. § 1985, which is described in Note 2, *infra*] "absorb(ed) the entire jurisdiction of the States over their local and domestic affairs."

This Act of April 20, 1871, . . . was passed by a Congress that had the Klan "particularly in mind." The debates are replete with references to the lawless conditions existing in the South in 1871. There was available to the Congress during these debates a report, nearly 600 pages in length, dealing with the activities of the Klan and the inability of the state governments to cope with it. This report was drawn on by many of the speakers. It was not the unavailability of state remedies but the failure of certain States to enforce the laws with an equal hand that furnished the powerful momentum behind this "force bill." Mr. Lowe of Kansas said:

> While murder is stalking abroad in disguise, while whippings and lynchings and banishment have been visited upon unoffending American citizens, the local administrations have been found inadequate or unwilling to apply the proper corrective. Combinations, darker than the night that hides them, conspiracies, wicked as the worst of felons could devise, have gone unwhipped of justice. Immunity is given to crime, and the records of the public tribunals are searched in vain for any evidence of effective redress.

Mr. Beatty of Ohio summarized in the House the case for the bill when he said:

> [C]ertain States have denied to persons within their jurisdiction the equal protection of the laws. The proof on this point is voluminous and unquestionable. . . . (M)en were murdered, houses were burned, women were outraged, men were scourged, and officers of the law shot down; and the State made no successful effort to bring the guilty to punishment or afford protection or redress to the outraged and innocent. The State, from lack of power or inclination, practically denied the equal protection of the law to these persons.

While one main scourge of the evil — perhaps the leading one — was the Ku Klux Klan, the remedy created was not a remedy against it or its members but against those who representing a State in some capacity were unable or unwilling to enforce a state law. Senator Osborn of Florida put the problem in these terms:

> That the State courts in the several States have been unable to enforce the criminal laws of their respective States or to suppress the disorders existing, and in fact that the preservation of life and property in many sections of the country is beyond the power of the State government, is a sufficient reason why Congress should, so far as they have authority under the Constitution, enact the laws necessary for the protection of citizens of the United States. . . .

There was, it was said, no quarrel with the state laws on the books. It was their lack of enforcement that was the nub of the difficulty.

It was precisely that breadth of the remedy which the opposition emphasized. Mr. Kerr of Indiana referring to the section involved in the present litigation said:

> This section gives to any person who may have been injured in any of his rights, privileges, or immunities of person or property, a civil action for damages against the wrongdoer in the Federal courts. The offenses committed against him may be the common violations of the municipal law of his State. It may give rise to numerous vexations and outrageous prosecutions, inspired by mere mercenary considerations, prosecuted in a spirit of plunder, aided by the crimes of perjury and subornation of perjury, more reckless and dangerous to society than the alleged offenses out of which the cause of action may have arisen. It is a covert attempt to transfer another large portion of jurisdiction from the State tribunals, to which it of right belongs, to those of the United States. It is neither authorized nor expedient, and is not calculated to bring peace, or order, or domestic content and prosperity to the disturbed society of the South. The contrary will certainly be its effect.

The debates were long and extensive. It is abundantly clear that one reason the legislation was passed was to afford a federal right in federal courts because, by reason of prejudice, passion, neglect, intolerance or otherwise, state laws might not be enforced and the claims of citizens to the enjoyment of rights, privileges, and immunities guaranteed by the Fourteenth Amendment might be denied by the state agencies.

Although the legislation was enacted because of the conditions that existed in the South at that time, it is cast in general language and is as applicable to Illinois as it is to the States whose names were mentioned over and again in the debates. It is no answer that the State has a law which if enforced would give relief. The federal remedy is supplementary to the state remedy, and the latter need not be first sought and refused before the federal one is invoked. Hence the fact that Illinois by its constitution and laws outlaws unreasonable searches and seizures is no barrier to the present suit in the federal court.

We had before us in *United States v. Classic*, [313 U.S. 299 (1941),] 18 U.S.C. § 242, which provides a criminal punishment for anyone who "under color of any law, statute, ordinance, regulation, or custom" subjects any inhabitant of a State to the deprivation of "any rights, privileges, or immunities secured or protected by the Constitution or laws of the United States." Section 242 first came into the law as § 2 of the Civil Rights Act, Act of April 9, 1866. After passage of the Fourteenth Amendment, this provision was re-enacted and amended by §§ 17, 18, Act of May 31, 1870. The right involved in the *Classic* case was the right of voters in a primary to have their votes counted. The laws of Louisiana required the defendants "to count the ballots, to record the result of the count, and to certify the result of the election." But according to the indictment they did not perform their duty. In an opinion written by Mr. Justice (later Chief Justice) Stone, in which Mr. Justice Roberts, Mr. Justice Reed, and Mr. Justice Frankfurter joined, the Court ruled, "Misuse of power, possessed by virtue of state law and made possible only because the wrongdoer is clothed with the authority of state law, is action taken " 'under color of' state law." There was a dissenting opinion; but the ruling as to the meaning of "under color of" state law was not questioned.

That view of the meaning of the words "under color of" state law was reaffirmed in *Screws v. United States*, 325 U.S. 91 (1945). The acts there complained of were committed by state officers in performance of their duties, viz., making an arrest effective.

Mr. Shellabarger, reporting out the bill which became the Ku Klux Act, said of the provision with which we now deal:

> The model for it will be found in the second section of the act of April 9, 1866, known as the "civil rights act." . . . This section of this bill, on the same state of facts, not only provides a civil remedy for persons whose former condition may have been that of slaves, but also to all people where, under color of State law, they or any of them may be deprived of rights. . . .

Thus, it is beyond doubt that this phrase should be accorded the same construction in both statutes — in [§ 1983] and in 18 U.S.C. § 242.

We conclude that the meaning given "under color of" law in the *Classic* case and in the *Screws* . . . case[] was the correct one; and we adhere to it.

In the *Screws* case we dealt with a statute that imposed criminal penalties for acts "wilfully" done. We construed that word in its setting to mean the doing of an act with "a specific intent to deprive a person of a federal right." We do not think that gloss should be placed on [§ 1983] which we have here. The word "wilfully" does not appear in [§ 1983]. Moreover, [§ 1983] provides a civil remedy, while in the *Screws* case we dealt with a criminal law challenged on the ground of vagueness. Section [1983] should be read against the background of tort liability that makes a man responsible for the natural consequences of his actions.

So far, then, the complaint states a cause of action. There remains to consider only a defense peculiar to the City of Chicago. [The problem of municipal liability is discussed in Chapter 4, *infra*.]

Mr. Justice Harlan, whom Mr. Justice Stewart joins, concurring.

Were this case here as one of first impression, I would find the "under color of any statute" issue very close indeed. However, in *Classic* and *Screws* this Court considered a substantially identical statutory phrase to have a meaning which, unless we now retreat from it, requires that issue to go for the petitioners here.

From my point of view, the policy of *stare decisis*, as it should be applied in matters of statutory construction and, to a lesser extent, the indications of congressional acceptance of this Court's earlier interpretation, require that it appear beyond doubt from the legislative history of the 1871 statute that *Classic* and *Screws* misapprehended the meaning of the controlling provision, before a departure from what was decided in those cases would be justified. Since I can find no such justifying indication in that legislative history, I join the opinion of the Court.

MR. JUSTICE FRANKFURTER, dissenting.

If the question whether due process forbids this kind of police invasion were before us in isolation, the answer would be quick. If, for example, petitioners had sought damages in the state courts of Illinois and if those courts had refused redress on the ground that the official character of the respondents clothed them with civil immunity, we would be faced with the sort of situation to which the language in . . . *Wolf* [*v. Colorado*, 338 U.S. 25 (1949),] was addressed: "we have no hesitation in saying that were a State affirmatively to sanction such police incursion into privacy it would run counter to the guaranty of the Fourteenth Amendment." If that issue is not reached in this case it is not because the conduct which the record here presents can be condoned. But by bringing their action in a Federal District Court petitioners cannot rest on the Fourteenth Amendment simpliciter. They invoke the protection of a specific statute by which Congress restricted federal judicial enforcement of its guarantees to particular enumerated circumstances. They must show not only that their constitutional rights have been infringed, but that they have been infringed, "under color of (state) statute, ordinance, regulation, custom, or usage," as that phrase is used in the relevant congressional enactment.

Of course, if Congress by appropriate statutory language attempted to reach every act which could be attributed to the States under the Fourteenth Amendment's prohibition, . . . the reach of the statute would be the reach of the Amendment itself. Relevant to the enforcement of such a statute would be not only the concept of state action as this Court has developed it, but also considerations of the power of Congress, under the Amendment's Enforcement Clause, to determine what is "appropriate legislation" to protect the rights which the Fourteenth Amendment secures. Still, in this supposed case we would arrive at the question of what Congress could do only after we had determined what it was that Congress had done. So, in the case before us now, we must ask what Congress did in 1871. We must determine what Congress meant by "under color" of enumerated state authority.

Congress used that phrase not only in [§ 1983], but also in the criminal provisions of § 2 of the First Civil Rights Act of April 9, 1866 [18 U.S.C. § 242], from which is derived the present and in both cases used it with the same purpose. During the seventy years which followed these enactments, cases in this Court in which the "under color" provisions were invoked uniformly involved action taken either in strict pursuance of some specific command of state law or within the scope of executive discretion in the administration of state laws. The same is true, with two exceptions, in the lower federal courts.

A sharp change from this uniform application of seventy years was made in 1941, but without acknowledgment or indication of awareness of the revolutionary turnabout from what had been established practice. The opinion in *United States v. Classic* accomplished this. The case presented an indictment under § 242 charging certain local Commissioners of Elections with altering ballots cast in a primary held to nominate candidates for Congress. Sustaining the sufficiency of the indictment in an extensive opinion concerned principally with the question whether the right to vote in such a primary was a right secured by the Constitution, Mr. Justice Stone wrote that the alteration of the ballots was "under color" of state law. This holding was summarily announced without exposition; it had been only passingly argued.

When, however, four years later the Court was called on to review the conviction under § 242 of a Georgia County Sheriff who had beaten a Negro prisoner to death, the opinion of four of the six Justices who believed that the statute applied merely invoked *Classic* and stare decisis and did not reconsider the meaning which that case had uncritically assumed was to be attached to the language, "under color" of state authority. *Screws v. United States*[, 325 U.S. 91 (1945)].

The case of *Williams v. United States*, [341 U.S. 70 (1951),] reaffirmed *Screws* and applied it to circumstances of third-degree brutality practiced by a private detective who held a special police officer's card and was accompanied by a regular policeman.

Thus, although this Court has three times found that conduct of state officials which is forbidden by state law may be "under color" of state law for purposes of the Civil Rights Acts, it is accurate to say that that question has never received here the consideration which its importance merits.

This case squarely presents the question whether the intrusion of a city policeman for which that policeman can show no such authority at state law as could be successfully interposed in defense to a state-law action against him, is nonetheless to be regarded as "under color" of state authority within the meaning of [§ 1983]. Respondents, in breaking into the Monroe apartment, violated the laws of the State of Illinois. Illinois law appears to offer a civil remedy for unlawful searches; petitioners do not claim that none is available. Rather they assert that they have been deprived of due process of law and of equal protection of the laws under color of state law, although from all that appears the courts of Illinois are available to give them the fullest redress which the common law affords for the violence done them, nor does any "statute, ordinance, regulation, custom, or usage" of the State of Illinois bar that redress. Did the enactment by Congress of § 1 of the Ku Klux Act of 1871 encompass such a situation?

That section, it has been noted, was patterned on the similar criminal provision of § 2, Act of April 9, 1866 [18 U.S.C. § 242]. The earlier Act had as its primary object the effective nullification of the Black Codes, those statutes of the Southern legislatures which had so burdened and disqualified the Negro as to make his emancipation appear illusory. The Act had been vetoed by President Johnson, whose veto message describes contemporary understanding of its second section; the section, he wrote,

> seems to be designed to apply to some existing or future law of a State or Territory which may conflict with the provisions of the bill. . . . It provides for counteracting such forbidden legislation by imposing fine and imprisonment upon the legislators who may pass such conflicting laws, or upon the officers or agents who shall put, or attempt to put, them into execution. It means an official offense, not a common crime committed against law upon the persons or property of the black race. Such an act may deprive the black man of his property, but not of the right to hold property. It means a deprivation of the right itself, either by the State judiciary or the State Legislature.

And Senator Trumbull, then Chairman of the Senate Judiciary Committee, in his remarks urging its passage over the veto, expressed the intendment of the second section as those who voted for it read it:

> If an offense is committed against a colored person simply because he is colored, in a State where the law affords him the same protection as if he were white, this act neither has nor was intended to have anything to do with his case, because he has adequate remedies in the State courts; but if he is discriminated against under color of State laws because he is colored, then it becomes necessary to interfere for his protection.

The original text of the present § [1983] contained words, left out in the Revised Statutes, which clarified the objective to which the provision was addressed:

> That any person who, under color of any law, statute, ordinance, regulation, custom, or usage of any State, shall subject, or cause to be subjected, any person within the jurisdiction of the United States to the deprivation of any rights, privileges, or immunities secured by the Constitution of the United States, shall, any such law, statute, ordinance, regulation, custom, or usage of the State to the contrary notwithstanding, be liable to the party injured. . . .

Representative Shellabarger, reporting the section, explained it to the House as "in its terms carefully confined to giving a civil action for such wrongs against citizenship as are done under color of State laws which abridge these rights." Senator Edmunds, steering the measure through the Senate, found constitutional sanction for it in the Fourteenth Amendment, explaining that state action may consist in executive nonfeasance as well as malfeasance, so that any offenses against a citizen in a State are susceptible of federal protection "unless the criminal who shall commit those offenses is punished and the person who suffers receives that redress which the principles and spirit of the laws entitle him to have." And James A. Garfield supported the bill in the House as "so guarded as to preserve intact the autonomy of the States, the machinery of the State governments, and the municipal organizations established under State laws."

Indeed, the Ku Klux Act as a whole encountered in the course of its passage strenuous constitutional objections which focused precisely upon an assertedly unauthorized extension of federal judicial power into areas of exclusive state competence.

The general understanding of the legislators unquestionably was that, as amended, the Ku Klux Act did "not undertake to furnish redress for wrongs done by one person upon another in any of the States . . . in violation of their laws, unless he also violated some law of the United States, nor to punish one person for an ordinary assault and battery. . . . " Even those who — opposing the constitutional objectors — found sufficient congressional power in the Enforcement Clause of the Fourteenth Amendment to give this kind of redress, deemed inexpedient the exercise of any such power: "Convenience and courtesy to the States suggest a sparing use, and never so far as to supplant the State authorities except in cases of extreme necessity, and when the State governments criminally refuse or neglect those duties which are imposed upon them." Extreme Radicals, those who believed that the remedy for the oppressed Unionists in the South was a general expansion of federal judicial jurisdiction so that "loyal men could have the privilege of having their causes, civil and criminal, tried in the Federal courts," were disappointed with the Act as passed.

[A]ll the evidence converges to the conclusion that Congress by § [1983] created a civil liability enforceable in the federal courts only in instances of injury for which redress was barred in the state courts because some "statute, ordinance, regulation, custom, or usage" sanctioned the grievance complained of. This purpose, manifested even by the so-called "Radical" Reconstruction Congress in 1871, accords with the presuppositions of our federal system. The jurisdiction which Article III of the Constitution conferred on the national judiciary reflected the assumption that the state courts, not the federal courts, would remain the primary guardians of that fundamental security of person and property which the long evolution of the common law had secured to one individual as against other individuals. The Fourteenth Amendment did not alter this basic aspect of our federalism.

It follows that federal courts in actions at law under § [1983] would have to determine whether defendants' conduct is in violation of, or under color of, state law often with little guidance from earlier state decisions. Such a determination will sometimes be difficult, of course. But Federal District Courts sitting in diversity cases are often called upon to determine as intricate and uncertain questions of local law as whether official authority would cloak a given practice of the police from liability in a state-court suit. Certain fixed points of reference will be available. If a plaintiff can show that defendant is acting pursuant to the specific terms of a state statute or of a municipal ordinance, § [1983] will apply. If he can show that defendant's conduct is within the range of executive discretion in the enforcement of a state statute, or municipal ordinance, § [1983] will apply. Beyond these cases will lie the admittedly more difficult ones in which he seeks to show some "custom or usage" which has become common law.

The present case comes here from a judgment sustaining a motion to dismiss petitioners' complaint. That complaint, insofar as it describes the police intrusion, makes no allegation that that intrusion was authorized by state law. . . . In the face of Illinois decisions holding such intrusions unlawful and in the absence of more precise factual averments to support its conclusion, such a complaint fails to state a claim under § [1983].

However, the complaint does allege, as to the ten-hour detention of Mr. Monroe, that "it was, and it is now, the custom or usage of the Police Department of the City of Chicago to arrest and confine individuals in the police stations and jail cells of the said department for long periods of time on 'open' charges." . . . Such averments do present facts which, admitted as true for purposes of a motion to dismiss, seem to sustain petitioners' claim that Mr. Monroe's detention — as contrasted with the night-time intrusion into the Monroe apartment — was "under color" of state authority. Under the few relevant Illinois decisions it is impossible to say with certainty that a detention incommunicado for ten hours is unlawful per se, or that the courts of that State would hold that the lawless circumstances surrounding Mr. Monroe's arrest made his subsequent confinement illegal. On this record, then, petitioners' complaint suffices to raise the narrow issue of whether the detention incommunicado, considered alone, violates due process.

NOTES

1. Reconstruction Following the Civil War. The Thirteenth Amendment, adopted in 1865, brought an end to slavery in the United States. It did not, however, bring equality for freed slaves:

> In an attempt to curtail the market for African-American labor after the Civil War, Southern states and municipalities passed "Black Codes" that regulated African-American labor. The more severe laws practically recreated slavery for African-American agricultural workers by prescribing labor terms. South Carolina's law, for example, mandated hours of work, and specified all of the laborers' duties:
>
> [Workers] shall rise at the dawn in the morning, feed, water and care for the animals on the farm, do the usual and needful work about the premises, prepare their meals for the day, if required by the master, and begin the farm work or other work by sun-rise.

The statute specified the servants' duty of care, deduction of wages for damage to property, and even details of their personal life, such as the fact that they must "retire to rest at seasonable hours."

> States buttressed labor regulations with facially-neutral vagrancy laws that essentially prohibited temporary unemployment. South Carolina's law, for example, defined vagrants to include "all persons who have not some fixed and known place of abode, and some lawful and reputable employment. . . . " Vagrants in Mississippi had to pay a large fine or be "hired out" to a planter. African-American workers were therefore forced to stay with their employers when their contracts expired; traveling in search of a new job would leave them vulnerable to arrest for vagrancy. Republican politicians vigorously opposed these restrictions on African-American workers because they conflicted with the Republican ideology of "free labor," the primary ideological basis of the Abolitionist challenge to slavery.

The attempts by Southern states to prevent the emergence of a free labor market led to the passage of the 1866 Civil Rights Act. . . . Congress passed the Fourteenth Amendment to ensure the constitutionality of the 1866 Civil Rights Act.

David E. Bernstein, *The Law and Economics of Post-Civil War Restrictions on Interstate Migration By African-Americans*, 78 TEX. L. REV. 781, 787–88 (1998).[1]

2. Modern Descendants of the Reconstruction-era Civil Rights Statutes. Two civil provisions initially adopted as part of the Civil Rights Act of 1866 remain important today in the civil rights arena: (1) Section 1981, title 42, states that "[a]ll persons within the jurisdiction of the United States shall have the same right in every State and Territory to make and enforce contracts, to sue, be parties, give evidence, and to the full and equal benefit of all laws and proceedings for the security of persons and property as is enjoyed by white citizens, and shall be subject to like punishment, pains, penalties, taxes, licenses, and exactions of every kind, and to no other;"[2] and (2) Section 1982, title 42, provides that "[a]ll citizens of the United States shall have the same right, in every State and Territory, as is enjoyed by white citizens thereof to inherit, purchase, lease, sell, hold, and convey real and personal property." Unlike § 1983, neither statute includes an "under color of" law requirement. State involvement is thus not necessary to support actions under either § 1981 or § 1982. *See Runyon v. McCrary*, 427 U.S. 160 (1976) (holding that § 1981 applies to private school); *Jones v. Alfred H. Mayer Co.*, 392 U.S. 409 (1968) (holding that § 1982 applies to private racial discrimination in refusing to sell a home).

3. Conspiracies to Interfere with Constitutional Rights. The majority, concurring, and dissenting opinions in *Monroe* relied not only on the legislative history behind § 1983, but also that surrounding 42 U.S.C. § 1985(3). Originally drafted as section 2 of the Ku Klux Klan Act, this provision, *inter alia*, criminalized conspiracies to commit certain enumerated offenses that would be crimes if committed on federal land. Because of concerns over its breadth, however, § 1985(3) was rewritten to prohibit only conspiracies "for the purpose of depriving, either directly or indirectly, any person or class of persons of the equal protection of the laws, or of equal privileges and immunities under the laws. . . . "[3] In *Bray v. Alexandria Women's Health Clinic*, 506 U.S. 263

---

[1] © 1998 by Texas Law Review Association and David E. Bernstein. All Rights Reserved.

[2] In response to *Patterson v. McLean Credit Union*, 491 U.S. 164 (1989), which held that § 1981 was not designed to prohibit racial harassment in the workplace (as opposed to racial discrimination in the making of employment contracts), Congress in 1991 added § 1981(b), to clarify that "the term 'make and enforce contracts' includes the making, performance, modification, and termination of contracts, and the enjoyment of all benefits, privileges, terms, and conditions of the contractual relationship." *See* Stephen E. Haydon, Comment, *A Measure of Our Progress: Testing for Race Discrimination in Public Accommodations*, 44 UCLA L. REV. 1207, 1221 (1997) (observing that "the 1991 Civil Rights Act 'overruled' *Patterson*").

Section 1981a was also added to fill in any gaps between § 1981 and Title VII, 42 U.S.C. §§ 2000e-2 through e-5, which prohibits racial discrimination in the workplace. Section 1981a(a)(1) states that to the extent a "complaining party cannot recover under section 1981," he or she can still make use of Title VII. Also of note, Congress provided in § 1981(c) that "[t]he rights protected by this section are protected against impairment by nongovernmental discrimination *and impairment under color of State law*." (Emphasis added). This language responded to the Supreme Court's decision in *Jett v. Dallas Independent School District*, 491 U.S. 701 (1989) (discussed further in Chapter 4, *infra*), which had held that § 1981's protections did not extend to contracts with government. Thus, it is now clear that § 1981 applies to all contracts, be they public-sector or between private parties.

[3] A separate provision, 42 U.S.C. § 1986, which was also enacted as part of the Ku Klux Klan Act, states that "[e]very person who, having knowledge that any of the wrongs conspired to be done, and mentioned in section 1985 of this title, are about to be committed, and having power to prevent or aid in preventing the commission of the same, neglects or refuses so to do, if such wrongful act be committed, shall be liable to the party injured, or his legal representatives, for all damages caused by such wrongful act, which such person by reasonable diligence could have prevented. . . . " Section 1986 has been given little treatment by the courts.

(1993), the Court recognized that § 1985(3) applies to both private conspiracies and those "under color of" law, but limited § 1985(3)'s application to conspiracies that interfere with "class-based" rights. Conspiracies must therefore be either racially motivated, *see* Catherine E. Smith, *The Group Dangers of Race-Based Conspiracies*, 59 RUTGERS U. L. REV. 55 (2006), or (according to some lower courts) gender-motivated, *see, e.g., Lyes v. City of Riviera Beach*, 166 F.3d 1332 (11th Cir. 1999) (en banc), to be actionable under § 1985(3). Conspiracies grounded in some other objectionable motive, like interfering with access to abortions, speech or privacy, are not unlawful under § 1985(3). *See Bray* (holding that § 1985(3) does not prohibit private conspiracy to interfere with abortion rights); *Carpenters, Local 610 v. Scott*, 463 U.S. 825 (1983) (holding that a private conspiracy to infringe First Amendment rights is not actionable under § 1985(3)); *Brokaw v. Mercer Co.* 235 F.3d 1000 (7th Cir. 2000) (observing that "Due Process rights and Fourth Amendment rights are not protected against private conspiracies under Section 1985(3)").

Section 1983, which has also been applied to conspiracies, *see, e.g., Tower v. Glover*, 467 U.S. 914 (1984) (complaint properly alleged conspiracy under § 1983 between public defender and government officials),[4] differs from § 1985(3) in two important respects: (1) § 1983 requires that conspirators act under color of law; and (2) § 1983 is not limited to class-based claims. It is thus both broader and narrower than § 1985(3). *See Gray v. Laws*, 915 F. Supp. 762 (E.D.N.C. 1994) (observing that § 1983's prohibition on conspiracies involving public officials is broader than that found in § 1985(3)). Because constitutional violations generally require state action anyway, and because state action ordinarily satisfies § 1983's "under color of" requirement, *see* Section B, *infra*, § 1983 has emerged as the principal civil tool for battling governmental conspiracies. Section 1985(3)'s application to governmental conspiracies, in contrast, has proven less important. *See* Jack M. Beermann, *Why Do Plaintiffs Sue Private Parties Under Section 1983?*, 26 CARDOZO L. REV. 9 (2004) (observing that the Supreme Court's limitations on § 1985(3) have caused it to have "very little effect" in the context of civil rights).[5]

4. Section 1983's Criminal Counterpart. Section 1983 was modeled on a federal criminal provision enacted as part of the Civil Rights Act of 1866, later to become 18 U.S.C. § 242. Section 242, which criminalizes the willful deprivation of federally protected rights, is also restricted to conduct that occurs "under color of" state law. The

---

See Linda E. Fisher, *Anatomy of an Affirmative Duty to Protect: 42 U.S.C. Section 1986*, 56 WASH. & LEE L. REV. 461 (1999) (stating that while "few reported opinions discuss [§ 1986,] [e]ven fewer reported opinions have granted relief under § 1986").

[4] "To prove a 42 U.S.C. § 1983 conspiracy claim, a plaintiff must show: (1) that the defendant conspired with others to deprive him of constitutional rights; (2) that at least one of the alleged co-conspirators engaged in an overt act in furtherance of the conspiracy; and (3) that the overt act injured the plaintiff. The plaintiff is additionally required to prove a deprivation of a constitutional right or privilege in order to prevail on a § 1983 civil conspiracy claim." *White v. McKinley*, 519 F.3d 806 (8th Cir. 2008).

[5] Do the Supreme Court's limitations on private conspiracies under § 1985(3) also apply to conspiracies "under color of" law? Many lower courts have assumed that § 1985(3)'s requirements are the same for both private and governmental conspiracies. *See, e.g., Farber v. City of Paterson*, 440 F.3d 131 (3d Cir. 2006) (holding that the same limitations applied to private conspiracies under § 1985(3) also apply to governmental conspiracies; thus, no claim may be brought under § 1985(3) in the absence of race-based or gender-based discrimination); *Lyes v. City of Riviera Beach*, 166 F.3d 1332 (11th Cir. 1999) (Tjoflat, J., dissenting) ("It is abundantly clear that the presence or absence of state action is completely irrelevant to the existence of a claim under § 1985(3)."). However, the Supreme Court has left open the possibility that § 1985(3)'s requirements for governmental conspiracies differ. *See Bray v. Alexandia Women's Health Clinic*, 506 U.S. 263 (1993) (holding that § 1985(3) did not create cause of action against private persons who conspired to interfere with women's right to access abortion). Thus, one can argue that a governmental conspiracy need not involve race or gender discrimination to be actionable under § 1985(3). *Cf. Lyes v. City of Riviera Beach*, 166 F.3d 1332 (11th Cir. 1999) (en banc) (holding that sexual discrimination is actionable under § 1985(3) "where the conspiracies involve state action" and leaving open whether § 1985(3) could be applied to private conspiracies involving sexual discrimination).

Supreme Court in *United States v. Classic*, 313 U.S. 299 (1941), and *Screws v. United States*, 325 U.S. 91 (1945), interpreted the "under color of" language in § 242 to reach conduct that was not authorized by state law. The Court has continued to abide by this interpretation. *See United States v. Lanier*, 520 U.S. 259 (1997) (finding that a local judge could be held criminally liable under § 242 for extorting sexual favors from litigants).

5. *Monroe*'s Impact on Federal Litigation. *Monroe v. Pape* is credited with opening the "floodgates" of litigation under section 1983. Prior to *Monroe*, reported cases under section 1983 were few and far between. *See* JOHN C. JEFFRIES, JR., ET AL., CIVIL RIGHTS ACTIONS: ENFORCING THE CONSTITUTION 42 (2d ed. 2007) (reporting that only 21 § 1983 cases were reported between 1871 and 1920 and then only a "handful" between 1920 and 1930). In those few cases where § 1983 was used, "the acts complained of were affirmatively authorized by statute or local ordinance and thus fit even the narrowest reading of 'under color of' law." CIVIL RIGHTS ACTIONS at 43.

The frequency of § 1983 litigation skyrocketed following *Monroe*. The ensuing debate over this so-called "litigation explosion" has splintered in several different directions, including: (1) whether § 1983 encourages too much (including frivolous) litigation, *see, e.g., Hudson v. Palmer*, 468 U.S. 517, 554 n.30 (1984) (Stevens, J., concurring in part) ("I cannot help but think that the Court's holding is influenced by an unstated fear that if it recognizes that prisoners have any Fourth Amendment protection this will lead to a flood of frivolous lawsuits."); (2) whether § 1983 has caused the Supreme Court to unduly mold or modify otherwise sound doctrinal principles, *see, e.g.,* Harry A. Blackmun, *Section 1983 and Federal Protection of Individual Right — Will the Statute Remain Alive or Fade Away?*, 60 N.Y.U. L. REV. 1, 2–3 (1985) (observing that Supreme Court interpretations of section 1983 following *Monroe* "reflect a growing uneasiness with the heretofore pronounced breadth of [section 1983] and, in my view, a tendency to strain otherwise sound doctrines"); John C. Jeffries, Jr., *The Right-Remedy Gap in Constitutional Law*, 109 YALE L.J. 87 (1999) (arguing that too much remedy under § 1983 could cause the Court to limit constitutional rights); and (3) whether § 1983 is a "liberal" tool used by activist federal judges to create new constitutional rights. *See, e.g.,* Michael G. Collins, *"Economic Rights," Implied Constitutional Actions, and the Scope of Section 1983*, 77 GEO. L.J. 1493, 1493–94 (1989) (explaining the "conservative" complaint about the scope of § 1983 and the fact that § 1983 is often linked to Warren Court developments).

6. The Constitutional Litigation Explosion. Is § 1983 responsible for the emergence of new constitutional rights? *Cf.* Ann Woolhandler, *The Common Law Origins of Constitutionally Compelled Remedies*, 107 YALE L.J. 77, 80 (1997) (observing that "much of the Supreme Court's development of independent federal rights and remedies took place without reliance on either federal question jurisdiction or statutes such as § 1983, but rather under the rubric of diversity jurisdiction"). Can *Monroe*'s interpretation of § 1983 be tied to an oppressive "litigation explosion" in the United States? Consider the following:

> [T]he litigation-explosion premise is suspect, both generally and when applied to civil rights. "Explosion" suggests a sudden, surprising event. Latent and even sinister defects cause inexplicable occurrences. . . . This sinister cause may involve lawyers, an increased willingness to sue, or the liberal Congress and activist courts which have created too many rights.
>
> Elementary data ostensibly support these hypotheses. For example, in its 1995 Long Range Plan for the Federal Courts, the Judicial Conference of the United States reported that, while the "population has increased slightly more than 200% since 1904, annual civil case filings have increased 1424%, with most of that growth in the period since 1960." The five-fold difference between the rates of docket and population growth proves that people today are five times more willing to litigate (at least in federal court), they have five times more

rights now than before, or society has five-times too many lawyers. The reference to 1960 implies that much of this is due to *Monroe v. Pape*, which reinvigorated § 1983 litigation the following year.

These statistics, however, are misleading, especially given how rudimentary the comparisons are. Comparing the population and docket of the last century with those of today is like comparing apples and orchards. It is premised on the false assumption that the population and case filings should grow at the same rate: if the population triples, so should the docket. A docket increase five times larger than population growth proves that something is amiss.

Simple math impeaches the credibility of comparing population growth with the number of case filings. Because any given case involves more than one party, a better comparison is between cases and combinations. A population that increases in a linear fashion will not generate a parallel increase in the interaction of its individual members. Rather, interaction, measured by the number of possible binary combinations (or "selections" of two), increases at a factorial rate. A population of three, for example, has three binary combinations. When doubled to six, fifteen binary combinations result, which represents a five-fold increase. Tripling the population to nine causes thirty-six potential combinations, a twelve-fold increase. Quadrupling the population causes an even greater increase, and so on.

Thus a fifteen-fold increase in the number of federal cases since 1904 is not surprising when simple computation is the guide. Controlling for all other variables, including law, technology, and people's litigiousness, a nine-fold increase in federal filings should result. Although one should not dismiss this increase as trivial, a proper understanding of the numbers indicates that this increase is not alarming.

Mark R. Brown, *The Failure of Fault Under § 1983: Municipal Liability for State Law Enforcement*, 84 CORNELL L. REV. 1503, 1518–21 (1999) (footnotes omitted).[6]

7. Success under § 1983. Section 1983 litigation appears to be one of the least successful areas of private practice. In a study conducted in the early 1980s, Professors Theodore Eisenberg and Stewart Schwab discovered that "[c]onstitutional tort plaintiffs . . . obtained a money judgment or money settlement in a significantly lower percentage of cases than other plaintiffs did." THEODORE EISENBERG, CASES AND MATERIALS ON CIVIL RIGHTS LEGISLATION 158 (3d ed. 1991) (summarizing Theodore Eisenberg & Stewart Schwab, *What Shapes Perceptions of the Federal Court System?*, 56 U. CHI. L. REV. 501 (1989); Theodore Eisenberg & Stewart Schwab, *Explaining Constitutional Tort Litigation: The Influence of the Attorney Fees Statute and the Government as Defendant*, 73 CORNELL L. REV. 719 (1988); and Theodore Eisenberg & Stewart Schwab, *The Reality of Constitutional Tort Litigation*, 72 CORNELL L. REV. 641 (1987). Why is this? Is it because constitutional cases are more often frivolous than non-constitutional cases? Or is it because of legal doctrines and immunities that make it difficult for constitutional victims to succeed?

8. *Monroe*'s Continuing Debate. The Douglas-Frankfurter debate played out in *Monroe* has not subsided. In *Crawford-El v. Britton*, 523 U.S. 574 (1998), for example, discussed in Chapter 2, *infra*, Justice Scalia dissented from the Court's holding that § 1983 plaintiffs need not meet a heightened evidentiary standard:

The § 1983 that the Court created in 1961 bears scant resemblance to what Congress enacted almost a century earlier. I refer, of course, to the holding of *Monroe v. Pape*, which converted an 1871 statute covering constitutional violations committed "under color of any statute, ordinance, regulation, custom, or usage of any State," into a statute covering constitutional violations commit-

---

[6] © 1999 by Cornell Law Review and Mark R. Brown. All Rights Reserved.

ted without the authority of any statute, ordinance, regulation, custom, or usage of any State, and indeed even constitutional violations committed in stark violation of state civil or criminal law. *See Monroe* (Frankfurter, J., dissenting). . . . *Monroe* changed a statute that had generated only 21 cases in the first 50 years of its existence into one that pours into the federal courts tens of thousands of suits each year, and engages this Court in a losing struggle to prevent the Constitution from degenerating into a general tort law. (The present suit, involving the constitutional violation of misdirecting a package, is a good enough example.)

B. "STATE ACTION" COMPARED

As the majority, concurring, and dissenting opinions make clear, the outcome in *Monroe* turned on statutory interpretation. Whether Congress intended § 1983 to address *un*authorized governmental wrongdoing, it was made clear long ago that the Constitution — in particular, the Fourteenth Amendment — reaches both. Not long after holding in the *Civil Rights Cases*, 109 U.S. 3 (1883), that the Fourteenth Amendment requires "state action," the Court ruled in *Home Telephone & Telegraph v. City of Los Angeles*, 227 U.S. 278 (1913), that unauthorized governmental conduct — that is, official conduct in violation of state law — can satisfy the federal Constitution's "state action" requirement.

Home Telephone & Telegraph involved a claim that Los Angeles's local telephone rates were "confiscatory" and thus amounted to an unlawful taking under the Fifth and Fourteenth Amendments. Los Angeles responded that if this were true, then its rates necessarily violated the state constitution, too. And if the rates violated state law, Los Angeles argued, they could not be products of "state action." The Court disagreed:

> The difference between the proposition insisted upon and the true meaning of the amendment is this, that the one assumes that the amendment virtually contemplates alone wrongs authorized by a state, and gives only power accordingly, while in truth the amendment contemplates the possibility of state officers abusing the powers lawfully conferred upon them by doing wrongs prohibited by the amendment. In other words, the amendment . . . proceeds not merely upon the assumption that states acting in their governmental capacity in a complete sense may do acts which conflict with its provisions, but, also conceiving, which was more normally to be contemplated, that state powers might be abused by those who possessed them and as a result might be used as the instrument for doing wrongs, provided against all and every such possible contingency.

Monroe's interpretation of § 1983's "under color of" law requirement is, for most purposes, coextensive with *Home Telephone & Telegraph*'s reading of "state action." In constitutional cases, the Supreme Court has observed, the two issues merge into one: "It is clear that in a § 1983 action brought against a state official, the statutory requirement of action 'under color of state law' and the 'state action' requirement of the Fourteenth Amendment are identical. If the challenged conduct . . . constitutes state action . . . , then the conduct was also action under color of state law and will support a suit under § 1983." *Lugar v. Edmondson Oil Co.*, 457 U.S. 922 (1982).

[1] Official Wrongdoing

State action is clearly present where a governmental official's misconduct is expressly authorized or directed by state law. *See, e.g., Tennessee v. Garner*, 471 U.S. 1 (1985) (state law authorized police officer's use of deadly force against a non-dangerous fleeing felon). The harder cases are those like *Home Telephone & Telegraph* and *Monroe* — where officials act contrary to state law. Although *Home Telephone & Telegraph* established that unauthorized official wrongdoing *can* be state action, it did not hold that all wrongs committed by government officials necessarily are. What if, for example, a police officer commits an assault while off-duty? Consider the following cases:

ALMAND v. DEKALB COUNTY
United States Court of Appeals for the Eleventh Circuit
103 F.3d 1510 (1997)

EDMONDSON, CIRCUIT JUDGE.

This appeal . . . raises a question about when a police officer is or is not acting under color of state law for the purpose of 42 U.S.C. § 1983. We conclude that color of state law has not been shown. . . .

In July 1990, . . . Mary Almand (Almand) discovered that her daughter, Monique, was missing from home. While posting and passing out fliers near a convenience store in Atlanta, Georgia, Almand first met the defendant, Floyd Bryant (Bryant), a police officer of the DeKalb County Police Department. Bryant, who was not in uniform, approached Almand in the parking lot of the store and asked her why she was there. Almand told him that she was looking for someone, and Bryant showed her his badge. Almand then revealed that she was searching for her daughter. Bryant offered his assistance as a police officer in finding Almand's daughter on the condition that Almand go out on a date with him. Almand refused the date, but asked nonetheless for his help in finding her daughter. Bryant obtained Almand's phone number so that he could contact her if information turned up about Monique. Almand and Bryant later had several telephone conversations about Almand's daughter.

Approximately one week after her disappearance, Monique returned home with the help of the Atlanta Police Department. That same day, Almand related to Bryant what her daughter had been through. Bryant indicated that he had an idea of where Almand's daughter had been held and who had raped her.

The Atlanta Police Department later told Almand that things like those which happened to her daughter occur often in the area and that nothing could probably be done to locate the persons responsible for her daughter's rape. About one week after Monique's return home, Bryant called Almand and offered to reveal important information about the rape of her daughter, information so sensitive it could cost him his job. Bryant conditioned the disclosure on Almand's agreeing to have sex with him. Almand agreed but declined to go through with it when Bryant arrived at her apartment.

Despite Almand's rejection of his demand for sexual favors, Bryant agreed to continue helping Almand investigate her daughter's rape. This time, however, his offer was contingent upon Almand agreeing to help Bryant expose a "dirty cop," a specific DeKalb Officer. Bryant said he believed that this other police officer was — among other things — connected with the persons who raped Almand's daughter. Almand agreed to help Bryant, which she says she did.

Later, in August 1990, Bryant showed up at Almand's apartment breathing hard and sweating. He asked to come in to talk with her on urgent matters about her daughter. Almand admitted Bryant. Once inside the apartment, Bryant asked Almand why she was leading him on; and he began making sexual advances. Almand asked Bryant to leave; and although he declined at first, he eventually agreed to leave. Bryant went out the door, and Almand closed it behind him.

From outside, Bryant then forced open the closed door with such shock that wood broke off the door. Having pushed open the door, Bryant reentered Almand's apartment, physically struggled with her, and forcibly raped her. No report was made to the police at the time.

A successful section 1983 action requires that the plaintiff show she was deprived of a federal right by a person acting under color of state law. We accept that, under certain circumstances, a rape of a person by a police officer or other state actor could violate the Constitution. *See Parker v. Williams*, 862 F.2d 1471 (11th Cir. 1989) (involving rape by uniformed deputy sheriff of woman in his custody because of his representation that her bail had been revoked and that she would have to return to jail with him); *see also Dang Vang v. Vang Xiong X. Toyed*, 944 F.2d 476 (9th Cir. 1991) (upholding jury's determination that defendant acted under color of state law when he, as employee of Washington State Employment Security office, raped women looking for employment when meeting with them under the pretext of providing services pursuant to his state job). Here, however, Bryant was not acting under color of state law at the pertinent time. Almand, therefore, cannot make out the elements of her section 1983 case. . . .

A person acts under color of state law when he acts with authority possessed by virtue of his employment with the state. Not all acts by state employees are acts under color of law. "The dispositive issue is whether the official was acting pursuant to the power he/she possessed by state authority or acting only as a private individual."

Here, the assumed facts show that Bryant was acting as a private person, not a state actor under color of state law, when he forced his way into Almand's home and, overcoming her resistance by force, raped her. On the day of the rape, Bryant initially gained entry to Almand's apartment on the pretense of discussing police business with her — the progress of the investigation into Almand's daughter's rape. Bryant then made sexual comments and advances toward Almand, and she demanded that he leave her apartment.

Bryant complied with Almand's request and left her home. Almand *fully closed* the front door. Having been excluded from Almand's apartment, Bryant then burst open the front door with such force that the door was damaged; and he committed the rape inside the apartment.[7]

Bryant's initial entry into Almand's apartment probably was conducted under color of state law: he gained access to Almand's apartment because of his status as a police officer and his proffer of information about Almand's daughter.[8] But then, Almand excluded Bryant from her apartment and closed the door completely.

When Bryant reentered the apartment by forcibly breaking in, he was no different from any other ruffian. Bryant's act of breaking into the apartment and, by force, raping Almand was a private act not accomplished because of "power possessed by virtue of state law and made possible only because the wrongdoer [was] clothed with the authority of state law." Considering that Bryant gained entry to the apartment by forcibly breaking in, any thug or burglar could have committed the same violent acts. Once Bryant resorted to sheer force to break, to enter, and to rape, his status as a police officer had no bearing on his wicked behavior.

In the circumstances of this case, we draw the line at the front door of Almand's apartment. When Bryant, by physical force, broke into Almand's residence, he was not then gaining entry by virtue of any authority he might have been given by the state to act as a police officer.

ANN ALDRICH, SENIOR DISTRICT JUDGE, dissenting.

A defendant acts under color of state law when he exercises power "possessed by virtue of state law and made possible only because the wrongdoer is clothed with the

---

[7] [n.9] The extent of the force is not critical to us, but the fact of an unconsented-to entry which was accomplished by some degree of physical force against a barrier is important.

[8] [n.10] We note, by the way, that Bryant was not in uniform and was off-duty at the time of these events.

authority of state law." Hence, a defendant acts under color of state law when he abuses a position given to him by the state. Here, I believe that there is a genuine issue of material fact as to this question.

Viewing the facts in a light most favorable to Almand, it appears that Bryant was able to rape Almand only because of his abuse of his position as a police officer. As the majority notes, Bryant initially obtained access to Almand's home on the day of the rape on the pretense of discussing police business with her. Although the facts are not entirely clear on this point, it appears from Almand's deposition that she unlocked her door for Bryant and admitted him to her home. She testified that she had a double-locked door which could only be opened with a key, and that Bryant came through that door. She also testified that after Bryant entered, she put the key on top of her stereo speaker. A reasonable finder of fact could infer that she unlocked the door for Bryant. The majority concedes that if Bryant had raped Almand at that point, his actions probably would have been taken under color of state law.

Bryant did not rape Almand at that point, however. Instead, he complied with her request to leave and walked out the door. Almand shut the door behind him and turned to get the key to lock the door. At this point, *before Almand could lock the door*, Bryant slammed it open, entered, and raped her.

The majority holds that once Bryant left and then "forcibly" broke in, he was no different than "any other ruffian." If Bryant had broken through a locked door, I might accept this conclusion. If that were the case, Bryant's position as a police officer would have afforded him no advantage in his alleged rape of Almand. There is evidence, however, that Bryant merely had to open an unlocked door, which Almand had unlocked for him specifically because he was a police officer.[9] In other words, construing the evidence in Almand's favor, a reasonable finder of fact could find that Bryant's abuse of his position as a police officer induced Almand to unlock the door so that he could rape her. Thus, Bryant's abuse of his position as an officer of the state made his rape of Almand possible, and he acted under color of state law.

This case is analogous to *Dang Vang v. Vang Xiong X. Toyed*, 944 F.2d 476 (9th Cir. 1991). In *Dang Vang*, the defendant was a state employee who was responsible for interviewing Hmong refugees and finding employment for them. On the pretense of taking women job-hunting, he lured them to a motel and raped them. Of course, "any other ruffian" could have told the women he had a job for them in order to lure them to a motel and rape them. As the Ninth Circuit noted, however, the plaintiffs came into contact with the defendant because of their need for employment, and the jury could have reasonably concluded that "the defendant used his government position . . . in order to sexually assault them." Similarly, Almand came into contact with Bryant because of her need for police help, and Bryant used his position to gain access to her home in order to rape her. Again, "any other ruffian" could have raped Almand, but Bryant's status as a police officer made it possible for him to do so in a way that another could not.

UNITED STATES v. LANIER
United States Court of Appeals for the Sixth Circuit
33 F.3d 639 (1994)

MILBURN, CIRCUIT JUDGE.

[The defendant, Lanier, was an elected county judge in Tennessee. Between 1988 and 1991 Judge Lanier sexually assaulted eight women who either worked for him or

---

[9] [n.3] It is also possible, but not clear from Almand's testimony, that Bryant opened the door with such force that it did not matter that the door was not locked. If he did, then I would agree that Bryant did not act under color of state law. That fact is not clear, however, and we must resolve all factual disputes in favor of Almand.

had cases pending in his court. He was charged and convicted under § 1983's criminal counterpart, 18 U.S.C. § 242 (discussed in Section A, Note 4, *supra*) for willfully violating his victims' constitutional rights.]

Defendant argues that the government failed to prove all the necessary elements of a violation of 18 U.S.C. § 242 beyond a reasonable doubt. Specifically, he asserts that the government failed to show that he was acting under color of law when he assaulted his victims. . . .

An act is under color of law when it constitutes a " '[m]isuse of power, possessed by virtue of state law and made possible only because the wrongdoer is clothed with the authority of state law.' " "[U]nder 'color' of law [also] means under 'pretense' of law." "Acts of officers who undertake to perform their official duties are included whether they hew to the line of their authority or overstep it," but, "acts of officers in the ambit of their personal pursuits are plainly excluded." "[I]ndividuals pursuing private aims and not acting by virtue of state authority are not acting under color of law purely because they are state officers."

Defendant argues that his actions in this case were personal pursuits. However, the jury correctly concluded that defendant's actions in this case were taken under color of state law. First, all of the assaults took place in defendant's chambers during working hours, and during each assault, there was at least an aura of official authority and power. Three of the victims . . . were present in defendant's chambers because they were working for him. On the first occasion [another victim] was assaulted, she had gone to defendant's chambers to apply for a secretarial position. On the second occasion [she] was assaulted, defendant used his continuing authority to determine custody of her child to coerce her into returning to his office. Finally, [another victim] was assaulted while she was present in defendant's chambers to make a presentation about her parenting classes for juvenile offenders.

Further, there was evidence that defendant used his position to intimidate his victims into silence. Prior to the first assault, defendant told [his victim] that her father wanted to know how he could go about seeking custody of her child. Defendant was also able to coerce [the victim] back into his office a second time because he knew she needed a job in order to ensure that she would keep custody of her child.

Defendant also used his position to effectively demote [one of his victims] after he assaulted her. He told [her] that she should be afraid of him because he was a judge, and he fired her after he assaulted her. Defendant also told [another victim] that it would hurt her more than it would hurt him if she told anyone about his assault. Finally, after assaulting [another victim], defendant told her that he would see to it that she got all of the clients she needed for her parenting classes if she would come back to see him.

Consequently, the government presented sufficient evidence for a rational juror to decide that defendant was acting under color of state law and not merely for his own personal pursuits when he assaulted the victims. Moreover, contrary to defendant's assertions, the government did not establish that he acted under color of state law based merely upon the subjective impressions of his victims. The government presented considerable objective evidence, as described above, which supported the jury's conclusion that defendant acted under color of state law.

Furthermore, we wish to emphasize that this case involves much more than a defendant who is a mere public official. Rather, this case involves a state judge who committed various abhorrent and unlawful sexual acts in his chambers, oftentimes while wearing his judicial robe. We consider such egregious misconduct on the part of defendant to be shocking to the conscience of the court.

NOTES

1. ***Lanier*'s Aftermath.** The Sixth Circuit reheard Lanier's case *en banc* and overturned his convictions. *See United States v. Lanier*, 73 F.3d 1380 (6th Cir. 1996) (en banc) (*Lanier II*). In sum, the court in *Lanier II* concluded that because the relevant case law explaining that sexual assault amounted to a constitutional violation was murky at the time of Lanier's wrongs, criminal prosecution under § 242 was improper: "Such an unprecedented, selective application of the statute in this case was possible only by giving the broadest possible construction to the most ambiguous of federal criminal statutes. The indictment in this case for a previously unknown, undeclared and undefined constitutional crime cannot be allowed to stand." The Supreme Court reversed. *United States v. Lanier*, 520 U.S. 259 (1997). It concluded that the Constitution's prohibition on sexual assault by state actors was clear enough at the time of Lanier's actions to satisfy the Due Process Clause's "fair warning" requirement. *See* Chapter 2.B., *infra*. It accordingly remanded the case to the Sixth Circuit to reconsider, "to the extent the issue remains open," whether Lanier was acting "under color of" law. Because Judge Lanier fled to Mexico and thus became a fugitive from justice, the Sixth Circuit on remand never was forced to reconsider its conclusion in *Lanier I* that Judge Lanier acted "under color of" law. Lanier's fugitive status required that the court simply dismiss his appeal. *See United States v. Lanier*, 123 F.3d 945 (6th Cir. 1997). Lanier was later apprehended in Mexico and deported to the United States to serve his criminal sentence. *See United States v. Lanier*, 201 F.3d 842 (6th Cir. 2000).

2. **Police Misconduct.** "[O]ff-duty police officers who flash a badge or otherwise purport to exercise official authority generally act under color of law." *Boneberger v. Plymouth Township*, 132 F.3d 20 (3d Cir. 1997). *See also Barna v. City of Perth Amboy*, 42 F.3d 809 (3d Cir. 1994) ("Manifestations of . . . pretended [official] authority may include flashing a badge, identifying oneself as a police officer, placing an individual under arrest, or intervening in a dispute involving others pursuant to a duty imposed by police department regulations."). Applying this "show of authority" logic, courts have routinely found that misconduct by off-duty police officers constitutes state action. *See, e.g., Memphis, Tennessee Area Local American Postal Workers Union, AFL-CIO v. Memphis*, 361 F.3d 898 (6th Cir. 2004) (holding that off-duty police officers employed by a private company who harassed picketers were arguably acting under color of law); *Jocks v. Tavernier*, 316 F.3d 128 (2d Cir. 2003) (holding that off-duty police officer acted under color of law when he identified himself as a police officer and drew his gun on motorist with whom he had argument over use of roadside payphone); *Rivera v. La Porte*, 896 F.2d 691 (2d Cir. 1990) (holding that off-duty corrections officer acted under color of law when he arrested and assaulted driver following a private argument during a traffic jam).

3. ***Griffin v. City of Opa-Locka.*** The Eleventh Circuit distinguished its holding in *Almand* in *Griffin v. City of Opa-Locka*, 261 F.3d 1295 (11th Cir. 2001), where a city manager (Neal) raped a subordinate (Griffin) after taking her home from an after-hours Rotary Club meeting. Even though the meeting was not an official government function, Griffin did not have to accept a ride from Neal, and Griffin did not have to allow Neal into her home (where the rape occurred), the court still found that Neal was acting "under color of" local law:

> Neal testified that after he failed to attend one Rotary Club meeting, the Mayor made him "sternly aware" of the Club's significance, and he never again missed a meeting. Moreover, there was testimony that Griffin was at the event as a City employee. Neal himself testified that he attended the function as City Manager, that he was there "preserving his job" and "taking care of business," and that he stayed close to the Mayor or Commissioners in case they needed

anything. Neal specifically asked Griffin and other City employees to attend the meetings, the Mayor of the City was the founder of the Rotary Club chapter, and the City paid for employees, including Griffin, to join. In short, participation in the Rotary Club was a command performance for City employees.

After learning that Griffin had arranged for the City's police chief to take her home following the Rotary event due to car troubles, the evidence supports the conclusion that Neal intervened and invoked his authority as City Manager to create the opportunity to be alone with Griffin, to take her home, and then to rape her.

Although we are persuaded that the foregoing facts demonstrate that Neal utilized his authority as City Manager to facilitate the assault on Griffin and that he was therefore acting under color of law at the time of the assault, we do not believe that under the facts of this case that we are required to view the sexual assault in isolation or ignore Neal's persistent abuse of authority leading up to the assault in making our color of law determination. Rather, we believe that the entire pattern of abuse and harassment against Griffin that eventually culminated in her rape is relevant to our color of law analysis. In other words, Neal's official interactions with Griffin as her boss during and after work hours, his continual sexual harassment of her during those interactions, and the ultimate sexual assault constitute an indivisible, ongoing series of events.

It is within this context of Neal's continual exploitation of and leverage of his authority over Griffin that we find a sufficient nexus between his duties and obligations as City Manager and Griffin's boss and the abuse of that authority to facilitate his harassment and ultimate sexual assault of her.

Neal relied on *Almand* to argue that he was not engaged in state action. The court, however, distinguished *Almand* as a case "where the performance of a state actor's official duties merely facilitated the meeting of or development of a relationship between the state actor and another person; and the state actor later, on his own time and wholly independent of his official duties, commits an assault or other constitutional tort against that person." Is the court's distinction convincing? Did not the police officer in *Almand* engage in a persistent pattern of harassment?

4. Sexual Assaults by School Officials. The court in *Griffin v. City of Opa-Locka* relied in part on cases finding that teachers who sexually assaulted students were state actors: "[O]ur conclusion that Neal was acting under color of law is supported by several cases where state employees were held to be acting under color of law when they utilized their authority to create the opportunity for or to facilitate a sexual assault. For example, in *Doe v. Taylor [Independent Schools]*, 15 F.3d 443 (5th Cir. 1994), the Fifth Circuit found that there was a sufficient nexus between a teacher's duties and his sexual relationship with a student for color of law purposes where the sexual misconduct began on school grounds and where the defendant 'took full advantage of his position as [plaintiff's] teacher' to create opportunities for sexual contact, exempt her from doing schoolwork, to give her good grades, and to intervene on her behalf to get her a better grade in another class." In contrast, if a school official's misconduct occurs completely off the school's grounds and wholly outside scheduled school hours, courts have been less willing to find state action. *See, e.g., Roe v. Humke*, 128 F.3d 1213 (8th Cir. 1997) (holding that although a police officer met a student through his role as goodwill ambassador to the school, his subsequent molestation of the student at his farm while off-duty, in plain clothes and driving his personal car did not constitute state action); *Becerra v. Asher*, 105 F.3d 1042 (5th Cir. 1997) (holding that sexual assault of student by teacher five months after student left school was not official misconduct under § 1983); *D.T. v. Independent School District*, 894 F.2d 1176 (10th Cir. 1990) (holding that teacher was not acting under color of law when he molested students at his home during summer vacation).

5. Scope of Employment. Justice Brennan in *Paul v. Davis*, 424 U.S. 693 (1976) (Brennan, J., dissenting), commented that "an off-duty policeman's discipline of his own children . . . would not constitute conduct 'under color of' law." Everyone would thus seem to agree that government officials at some point — rearing their children at home, for example — shed their public authorities and become private actors. The hard question, as the previous cases make clear, is when this occurs. Can the issue best be analogized to the common "scope of employment" problem that arises under Tort Law? Generally, a "servant's conduct is within the scope of his employment if it is of the kind which he is employed to perform, occurs substantially within the authorized limits of time and space, and is actuated, at least in part, by a purpose to serve the master." See W. PAGE KEETON, DAN B. DOBBS, ROBERT E. KEETON & DAVID G. OWEN, PROSSER AND KEETON ON TORTS 502–03 (1984). Government officials who act within the scope of their employment — that is, they are on the clock doing what they are paid to do in an effort to serve their master — are state actors, even though they violate state law. *See, e.g., Monroe v. Pape*. Those who act outside the scope of their employment — either because their conduct was unusual, temporally/spatially distant, or motivated by personal gain — are not. *See, e.g., Doe v. Taylor Independent Schools*, 15 F.3d 443 (5th Cir. 1994) (en banc) (Garwood, J., dissenting) ("The physical sexual abuse principally relied on by the majority here is the sexual intercourse, and this not only was all consensual, but also took place clearly outside of school hours and not as even a purported part of any school activity. . . . None of any of this could be said to even colorably be within the course or scope of [the teacher's] employment."). Would Judge Lanier's misconduct be considered state action under this analysis? Would the city manager's misbehavior in *Griffin*? Professor Laura Oren has argued against a "scope of employment" model for § 1983: "Whether or not [officials'] actions were in the 'scope of employment,' if they abused or misused the power granted by virtue of their state positions, they are answerable in § 1983." Laura Oren, *Section 1983 and Sex Abuse in Schools: Making a Federal Case Out of It*, 72 CHI.-KENT L. REV. 747 (1997).

6. *Polk County v. Dodson*. The Supreme Court concluded in *Polk County v. Dodson*, 454 U.S. 312 (1981), that a public defender's ineffective assistance, *see* WAYNE R. LAFAVE, ET AL., CRIMINAL PROCEDURE § 11.7 (3d ed. 2000) (explaining the Sixth Amendment right to effective assistance of counsel), was not "under color of" state law and thus could not support a claim under § 1983. This was true, Justice Powell explained, even though the defender worked for the state and acted within the scope of her employment:

> First, a public defender is not amenable to administrative direction in the same sense as other employees of the State. Administrative and legislative decisions undoubtedly influence the way a public defender does his work. State decisions may determine the quality of his law library or the size of his caseload. But a defense lawyer is not, and by the nature of his function cannot be, the servant of an administrative superior.
>
> Second, and equally important, it is the constitutional obligation of the State to respect the professional independence of the public defenders whom it engages. . . . [T]he assumption [is] that counsel will be free of state control. There can be no fair trial unless the accused receives the services of an effective and independent advocate.[10]

The Supreme Court observed in *West v. Atkins*, 487 U.S. 42 (1988) (holding that a private physician hired by a prison to provide medical care was engaged in state action

---

[10] The Court cautioned, however, that "[i]n concluding that [the public defender] did not act under color of state law in exercising her independent professional judgment in a criminal proceeding," it was not "suggest[ing] that a public defender never acts in that role. In *Branti v. Finkel*, 445 U.S. 507 (1980), for example, we found that a public defender so acted when making hiring and firing decisions on behalf of the State. It may be — although the question is not present in this case — that a public defender also would act under color of state law while performing certain administrative and possibly investigative functions."

"under color of" law), that "*Polk County v. Dodson* . . . is the only case in which this Court has determined that a person who is employed by the State and who is sued under § 1983 for abusing his position in the performance of his assigned tasks was not acting under color of state law."

7. Was State Action Present in *Dodson*? The Court in *Dodson* did not address whether the public defender was engaged in state action sufficient to support a constitutional challenge. It concluded in footnote 18, however, that "an indigent prisoner retains the right to initiate . . . federal habeas corpus proceedings. For an innocent prisoner wrongly incarcerated as the result of ineffective or malicious counsel, this normally is the most important form of judicial relief."[11] Because federal habeas corpus challenges are ordinarily predicated on constitutional violations, which in turn generally demand state action, one can argue that *Dodson* implicitly recognized that the defender was engaged in state action. Understood in this fashion, is *Dodson* consistent with *Lugar v. Edmondson Oil Company*'s, 457 U.S. 922 (1982) (excerpted in Section [2], *infra*), proposition that "challenged conduct [that] constitutes state action . . . [is] also action under color of state law [that] will support a suit under § 1983"?

The Court in *Lugar* reconciled *Dodson*: "In *Polk County*, we held that a public defender's actions, when performing a lawyer's traditional functions as counsel in a state criminal proceeding, would not support a § 1983 suit. Although we analyzed the public defender's conduct in light of the requirement of action 'under color of state law,' we specifically stated that it was not necessary in that case to consider whether that requirement was identical to the 'state action' requirement of the Fourteenth Amendment." The Court in *Lugar* further explained that "§ 1983 is applicable to other constitutional provisions . . . that contain no state-action requirement. Where such a federal right is at issue, the statutory concept of action under color of state law would be a distinct element of the case not satisfied implicitly by a finding of a violation of the particular federal right." If the Sixth Amendment right to effective assistance of counsel does not demand state action, *see Cuyler v. Sullivan*, 446 U.S. 335 (1980) (holding that private defense counsel's ineffective assistance violates the Sixth Amendment), its violation would not imply that the public defender was acting "under color of" law. Hence, the Court's suggestion in *Dodson* that the victim use federal habeas corpus to redress his constitutional wrong does not necessarily imply that the public defender was engaged in state action. *See also Brentwood Academy v. Tennessee Secondary School Athletic Association*, 531 U.S. 288 (2001) ("full-time public employment would be conclusive of state action for some purposes, but not when the employee is doing a defense lawyer's primary job; then, the public defender does 'not act on behalf of the State; he is the State's adversary'").

[2] Private Wrongdoing

LUGAR v. EDMONDSON OIL COMPANY
Supreme Court of the United States
457 U.S. 922 (1982)

JUSTICE WHITE delivered the opinion of the Court.

In 1977, [Lugar], a lessee-operator of a truckstop in Virginia, was indebted to his supplier, Edmondson Oil Co., Inc. Edmondson sued on the debt in Virginia state court. Ancillary to that action and pursuant to state law, Edmondson sought prejudgment attachment of certain of [Lugar's] property. The prejudgment attachment procedure

---

[11] The Court also noted that its holding did "not disturb the theory of cases, brought under 18 U.S.C. § 242, in which public defenders have been prosecuted for extorting payment from clients' friends or relatives 'under color of . . . law. . . .'"

required only that Edmondson allege, in an ex parte petition, a belief that [Lugar] was disposing of or might dispose of his property in order to defeat his creditors. Acting upon that petition, a Clerk of the state court issued a writ of attachment, which was then executed by the County Sheriff. . . . Thirty-four days after the levy, a state trial judge ordered the attachment dismissed because Edmondson had failed to establish the statutory grounds for attachment alleged in the petition.

[Lugar] subsequently brought this action under 42 U.S.C. § 1983 against Edmondson and its president. His complaint alleged that in attaching his property [they] had acted jointly with the State to deprive him of his property without due process of law.

As a matter of substantive constitutional law the state-action requirement reflects judicial recognition of the fact that "most rights secured by the Constitution are protected only against infringement by governments."

Careful adherence to the "state action" requirement preserves an area of individual freedom by limiting the reach of federal law and federal judicial power. It also avoids imposing on the State, its agencies or officials, responsibility for conduct for which they cannot fairly be blamed.

Our cases have accordingly insisted that the conduct allegedly causing the deprivation of a federal right be fairly attributable to the State. These cases reflect a two-part approach to this question of "fair attribution." First, the deprivation must be caused by the exercise of some right or privilege created by the State or by a rule of conduct imposed by the state or by a person for whom the State is responsible. . . . Second, the party charged with the deprivation must be a person who may fairly be said to be a state actor. This may be because he is a state official, because he has acted together with or has obtained significant aid from state officials, or because his conduct is otherwise chargeable to the State. Without a limit such as this, private parties could face constitutional litigation whenever they seek to rely on some state rule governing their interactions with the community surrounding them.

Although related, these two principles are not the same. They collapse into each other when the claim of a constitutional deprivation is directed against a party whose official character is such as to lend the weight of the State to his decisions. *See Monroe v. Pape.* The two principles diverge when the constitutional claim is directed against a party without such apparent authority, i.e., against a private party.

[T]he first question is whether the claimed deprivation has resulted from the exercise of a right or privilege having its source in state authority. The second question is whether, under the facts of this case, [defendants], who are private parties, may be appropriately characterized as "state actors."

[Lugar] presented [two constitutional] counts in his complaint. . . . Count two alleged that the deprivation of property resulted from [defendants'] "malicious, wanton, willful, opressive [sic], [and] unlawful acts." By "unlawful," [Lugar] apparently meant "unlawful under state law." To say this, however, is to say that the conduct of which [Lugar] complained could not be ascribed to any governmental decision; rather, [defendants] were acting contrary to the relevant policy articulated by the State. Nor did they have the authority of state officials to put the weight of the State behind their private decision, i.e., this case does not fall within the abuse of authority doctrine recognized in *Monroe v. Pape*. That [defendants] invoked the statute without the grounds to do so could in no way be attributed to a state rule or a state decision. Count two, therefore, does not state a cause of action under § 1983 but challenges only private action.

Count one is a different matter. That count describes the procedures followed by [the defendants] in obtaining the prejudgment attachment as well as the fact that the state court subsequently ordered the attachment dismissed because [the defendants] had not met their burden under state law. [Lugar] then summarily states that this sequence of events deprived him of his property without due process. Although it is not clear whether [Lugar] is referring to the state-created procedure or the misuse of that procedure by [the defendants], we agree with the lower courts that the better reading of the complaint is that [Lugar] challenges the state statute as procedurally defective under the Fourteenth Amendment.

While private misuse of a state statute does not describe conduct that can be attributed to the State, the procedural scheme created by the statute obviously is the product of state action. This is subject to constitutional restraints and properly may be addressed in a § 1983 action, if the second element of the state-action requirement is met as well.

[W]e have consistently held that a private party's joint participation with state officials in the seizure of disputed property is sufficient to characterize that party as a "state actor" for purposes of the Fourteenth Amendment.

In summary, [Lugar] was deprived of his property through state action; [the defendants] were, therefore, acting under color of state law in participating in that deprivation. [Lugar] did present a valid cause of action under § 1983 insofar as he challenged the constitutionality of the Virginia statute; he did not insofar as he alleged only misuse or abuse of the statute.

JUSTICE POWELL, with whom JUSTICE REHNQUIST and JUSTICE O'CONNOR join, dissenting.[12]

This Court today . . . holds that [defendant], a private citizen who did no more than commence a legal action of a kind traditionally initiated by private parties, thereby engaged in "state action." This decision is as unprecedented as it is implausible.

The plain language of 42 U.S.C. § 1983 establishes that a plaintiff must satisfy two jurisdictional requisites to state an actionable claim. First, he must allege the violation of a right "secured by the Constitution and laws" of the United States. . . . Second, a § 1983 plaintiff must show that the alleged deprivation was caused by a person acting "under color" of law.

This case demonstrates why separate inquiries are required. Here it is not disputed that the Virginia Sheriff and Clerk of Court, the state officials who sequestered [Lugar's] property in the manner provided by Virginia law, engaged in state action. Yet [Lugar], while alleging constitutional injury from this action by state officials, did not sue the State or its agents.

[T]he Court's opinion inexplicably conflates the two inquiries. . . . Ignoring that this case involves two sets of actions — one by [Edmondson], who merely filed a suit and accompanying sequestration petition; another by the state officials, who issued the writ and executed the lien — it wrongly frames the question before the Court, not as whether the private [defendant] acted under color of law in filing the petition, but as "whether . . . [the defendants], who are private parties, may be appropriately characterized as 'state actors.'" It then concludes that they may, on the theory that a private party who invokes "the aid of state officials to take advantage of state-created attachment procedures" is a "joint participant" with the State and therefore a "state actor."

There are at least two fallacies in the Court's conclusion. First, . . . our cases have not established that private "joint participants" with state officials themselves necessarily become state actors. . . . Second, even when the inquiry is whether an action occurred under color of law, our cases make clear that the "joint participation" standard is not satisfied when a private citizen does no more than invoke a presumptively valid judicial process in pursuit only of legitimate private ends.

---

[12] Chief Justice Burger's dissenting opinion is omitted.

As this Court recognized in *Monroe v. Pape*, the historic purpose of § 1983 was to prevent state officials from using the cloak of their authority under state law to violate rights protected against state infringement by the Fourteenth Amendment. The Court accordingly is correct that an important inquiry in a § 1983 suit against a private party is whether there is an allegation of wrongful "conduct that can be attributed to the State." But there still remains [a] second . . . question: whether this state action fairly can be attributed to [Edmondson], whose only action was to invoke a presumptively valid attachment statute. This question, unasked by the Court, reveals the fallacy of its conclusion that [Edmondson] may be held accountable for the attachment of property because he was a "state actor." From the occurrence of state action taken by the Sheriff who sequestered petitioner's property it does not follow that [Edmondson] became a "state actor" simply because the Sheriff was. . . .

This Court of course has held that private parties are amenable to suit under § 1983 when "jointly engaged" with state officials in the violation of constitutional rights. *See Adickes v. S. H. Kress & Co.*, 398 U.S. 144 (1970).[13] Yet the Court, in advancing its "joint participation" theory, does not cite a single case in which a private decision to invoke a presumptively valid state legal process has been held to constitute state action.

Contrary to the position of the Court, our cases do not establish that a private party's mere invocation of state legal procedures constitutes "joint participation" or "conspiracy" with state officials satisfying the § 1983 requirement of action under color of law. In *Dennis v. Sparks*, 449 U.S. 24 (1980), we held that private parties acted under color of law when corruptly conspiring with a state judge in a joint scheme to defraud. In so holding, however, we explicitly stated that "merely resorting to the courts and being on the winning side of a lawsuit does not make a party a co-conspirator or a joint actor with the judge."

In *Adickes* the plaintiff sued a private restaurant under § 1983, alleging a conspiracy between the restaurant and local police to deprive her of the right to equal treatment in a place of public accommodation. Reversing the decision below, this Court upheld the cause of action. It found that the private defendant, in "conspiring" with local police to obtain official enforcement of a state custom of racial segregation, engaged in a " 'joint activity with the State or its agents' " and therefore acted under color of law within the meaning of § 1983.

[T]he Court clearly seems to have contemplated some limiting principle. A citizen summoning the police to enforce the law ordinarily would not be considered to have engaged in a "conspiracy." Nor, presumably, would such a citizen be characterized as acting under color of law and thereby risking amenability to suit for constitutional violations that subsequently might occur. Surely there is nothing in *Adickes* to indicate that the Court would have found action under color of law in cases of this kind.

The conduct in *Adickes* occurred in 1964, 10 years after *Brown v. Board of Education*, 347 U.S. 483 (1954) . . . . In view of the intense national focus on issues of racial discrimination, it is virtually inconceivable that a private citizen then could have acted in the innocent belief that the state law and customs involved in *Adickes* still were presumptively valid. . . . Construed as resting on this basis, *Adickes* establishes that a private party acts under color of law when he conspires with state officials to secure the application of a state law so plainly unconstitutional as to enjoy no presumption of validity. In such a context, the private party could be characterized as hiding behind the authority of law and as engaging in "joint participation" with the State in the deprivation of constitutional rights. Here, however, [Lugar] has alleged no conspiracy.

---

[13] [n.7] In *Adickes* the term "jointly engaged" appears to have been used specifically to connote engagement in a "conspiracy."

Nor has he even alleged that [Edmondson] was invoking the aid of a law he should have known to be constitutionally invalid.

NOTES

1. Does "Under Color of" Law Imply State Action? As explained in *Lugar*, the fact that wrongdoers act pursuant to a state statute (i.e., "under color of" law) does not necessarily mean that they are engaged in state action. A creditor who uses a state's self-help statute to repossess a car, for example, is not necessarily engaged in state action. *See Flagg Bros. v. Brooks*, 436 U.S. 149 (1978) (holding that a creditor's use of a self-help statute does not implicate Due Process Clause). Instead, something more is required than conduct "under color of" law. In the context of garnishments, prejudgment attachments and repossessions, state action has been found to exist only when state officials — such as court clerks, sheriffs or judges — assist the creditor in securing the property. *See Sniadach v. Family Finance Corp.*, 395 U.S. 337 (1969); *Fuentes v. Shevin*, 407 U.S. 67 (1972); *Mitchell v. W. T. Grant Co.*, 416 U.S. 600 (1974). This "joint participation" on the part of government officials is needed to transform the private creditor's conduct into state action. *See generally Wyatt v. Cole*, 504 U.S. 158 (1992) (holding that a judge's ministerial issuance of an attachment order renders a seizure subject to Due Process).

2. Violations of State Law by Private Parties. *Lugar* also held that the abuse or misuse of state authority by *private parties* negates liability under § 1983: "the conduct of which [Lugar] complained could not be ascribed to any governmental decision; rather, [defendants] were acting contrary to the relevant policy articulated by the State. Nor did they have the authority of state officials to put the weight of the State behind their private decision, i.e., this case does not fall within the abuse of authority doctrine recognized in *Monroe v. Pape*." Is the Court's distinction between government officials and private parties justified? Does it apply to all constitutional violations? What if a private person conspires with a police officer to seize the property of another in violation of state law (and the Fourth Amendment)? Can the private actor be held accountable under § 1983?

In *Soldal v. Cook County*, 506 U.S. 56 (1992), the manager of a trailer park enlisted the assistance of deputy sheriffs to remove a trailer from the park's premises — action that was illegal under Illinois law. The Court of Appeals concluded that because the deputies prevented the trailer's owner from using reasonable force to protect his home from the manager's private misconduct (which the officers knew to be illegal), an actionable conspiracy to violate the Fourth Amendment (and § 1983) existed between the manager and the deputies. On appeal to the Supreme Court, the defendants argued not only that their actions were lawful under the Fourth Amendment, but also that they did not act "under color of" law. Though recognizing that it had jurisdiction to address the Court of Appeals' conclusion that the defendants acted "under color of" law, the Supreme Court stated that it was "not inclined to review that holding."

The *Soldal* Court cited *Adickes v. S.H. Kress Co.*, 398 U.S. 144 (1970), to support its lack of inclination. In *Adickes*, a white woman (Adickes), in the company of several black companions, was refused service by a local restaurant. As Adickes left the restaurant, she was arrested by police for vagrancy. Adickes sued the restaurant under § 1983, alleging that the restaurant had conspired with local police to deprive her of her rights under the Fourteenth Amendment. The Supreme Court concluded that Adickes stated a claim under § 1983:

> Although this is a lawsuit against a private party, not the State or one of its officials, our cases make clear that [Adickes] will have made out a violation of her Fourteenth Amendment rights and will be entitled to relief under § 1983 if she can prove that a Kress employee, in the course of employment, and a Hattiesburg policeman somehow reached an understanding to deny Miss

Adickes service in the Kress store, or to cause her subsequent arrest because she was a white person in the company of Negroes.

Adickes establishes that where an "understanding" or conspiracy exists between a private individual and public officials, the private individual can be treated as a state actor.[14]

As the Court of Appeals' holding in *Soldal* demonstrates, this logic has also been applied in the Fourth Amendment context. Where police conspire with private actors to search and seize, for example, the private party's conduct is subject to Fourth Amendment scrutiny. Where a private party acts alone, in contrast, the Fourth Amendment is not implicated — even when evidence is turned over to police. *See, e.g., United States v. Jacobsen*, 466 U.S. 109 (1984) (holding that a private courier's opening a package and then turning its contents over to authorities does not implicate the Fourth Amendment). *See also Briscoe v. LaHue*, 460 U.S. 325 (1983) (observing that a private citizen's testimony in a criminal case is not considered state action and thus not subject to Fourth Amendment restrictions).

3. "Joint Participation." The majority noted in *Lugar* that "[c]ontrary to the suggestion of Justice Powell's dissent, we do not hold today that 'a private party's mere invocation of state legal procedures constitutes 'joint participation' or 'conspiracy' with state officials satisfying the § 1983 requirement of action under color of law.' The holding today, as the above analysis makes clear, is limited to the particular context of prejudgment attachment." As Justice Powell pointed out in dissent, simple participation on the part of public officials is not generally sufficient to convert a private party's behavior into state action. Consider the Fourteenth Amendment's Equal Protection Clause and the problem of racial discrimination. Private schools can choose to discriminate on account of race (or any other ground) free from the constraints of the Fourteenth Amendment. *See, e.g., Norwood v. Harrison*, 413 U.S. 455 (1973) ("private bias (in the admission of students to private schools) is not barred by the Constitution").[15] This remains true even when a private school enlists the aid of the state to enforce its discriminatory action.[16] Using the sheriff's office to remove a black trespasser, for example, will not transform the school into a state actor. *Cf. Shelley v. Kraemer*, 334 U.S. 1 (1948) (holding that judicial enforcement of a racially restrictive covenant amounts to state action); *Burton v. Wilmington Parking Authority*, 365 U.S. 715 (1961) (holding that a financial relationship between a state agency and private restaurant transforms the restaurant into a state actor). In the absence of some kind of preconcerted "understanding" or conspiracy, *see Adickes*, governmental participation is generally not sufficient to charge private parties with state action. *Compare Edmonson v. Leesville Concrete Co.*, 500 U.S. 614 (1991) ("our cases have found state action when

---

[14] The Court in *Adickes* also observed that § 1983's inclusion of "custom recognizes that settled practices of state officials may, by imposing sanctions or withholding benefits, transform private predilections into compulsory rules of behavior no less than legislative pronouncements." Consequently, private conduct that is directed by official custom can also be prosecuted under § 1983. For an excellent discussion of § 1983's custom language, applied in various contexts, *see* Myriam E. Gilles, *Breaking the Code of Silence: Rediscovering "Custom" in Section 1983 Municipal Liability*, 80 B.U. L. Rev. 17 (2000).

[15] Today, of course, this private citizen may run afoul of state and federal statutes, *see, e.g.*, 42 U.S.C. § 1981 (described in Note 2 following *Monroe v. Pape, supra*), but not the Constitution.

[16] In the early 1960s, prior to the adoption of the federal Civil Rights Act of 1964, the Supreme Court was forced to bend this proposition a bit to prevent the criminal prosecution of civil rights activists who used "sit-ins" to protest racial segregation in the South. *See, e.g., Bell v. Maryland*, 378 U.S. 226 (1964) (holding that trespass prosecution of black protestors who refused to leave a lunch counter violated Equal Protection). *Cf. Bray v. Alexandria Women's Health Clinic*, 506 U.S. 263, 304 n.10 (1993) (Souter, J., concurring and dissenting) (observing that "[a]lthough the question was left open in the sit-in cases . . . , government enforcement of private segregation by use of a state trespass law, rather than 'securing to all persons . . . the equal protection of the laws,' itself amounted to an unconstitutional act in violation of the Equal Protection Clause of the Fourteenth Amendment").

private parties make extensive use of state procedures with the 'overt, significant assistance of state officials' "); *cf. Brentwood Academy v. Tennessee Secondary School Athletic Association,* 531 U.S. 288 (2001) (holding that public institutions' and officials' "pervasive entwinement" converted a private athletic regulatory body into a state actor). *But see National Collegiate Athletic Association v. Tarkanian,* 488 U.S. 179 (1988) (holding that a private national athletic association is not a state actor even though it includes public institutions as members).

4. The Public Function Theory. Concerted activity is not always necessary to establish state action. State action can also be found where private actors engage in "public functions." *See, e.g., Smith v. Allwright,* 321 U.S. 649 (1944) (holding that a private party's primary elections are a public function and are governed by Fifteenth Amendment); *Marsh v. Alabama,* 326 U.S. 501 (1946) (holding that a company town is the equivalent of a municipality and is engaged in a public function); *Edmonson v. Leesville Concrete Co.,* 500 U.S. 614 (1991) (holding that jury selection is a "traditional function of government" and that private attorneys are thus prohibited from using race-based peremptory challenges).

5. Coda on State Action. It is not the purpose of this casebook to exhaustively explore state action theory. Rather, the authors wish only to provide the student with a basic understanding of the problem. A richer course on constitutional law is needed to fully explore the intricacies involved. Suffice it to say here that the Supreme Court's conclusions do not fall into an easily recognizable pattern. For an exhaustive discussion of the intersection between "under color of" law and state action, *see* Richard H.W. Maloy, *"Under Color of" — What Does It Mean?,* 56 MERCER L. REV. 565 (2005). With the caveat that what follows is a gross simplification, the authors offer the following themes and tendencies to help guide the student through the quagmire of Supreme Court opinions on state action. First, government regulation is not generally sufficient to insinuate state action into private actors' behavior. *See, e.g., Moose Lodge v. Irvis,* 407 U.S. 163 (1972) (holding that extensive regulation of a private club's dispensing alcohol does not render a club's racial discrimination the product of state action). Second, government subsidization — at least outside the context of racial discrimination, *see, e.g., Burton v. Wilmington Parking Authority,* 365 U.S. 715 (1961) (holding that a financial relationship between a state agency and a private restaurant transforms the restaurant into a state actor); *cf. Bob Jones University v. United States,* 461 U.S. 574 (1983) (avoiding the question of whether allowing tax exempt status for racially discriminatory schools would violate Equal Protection) — does not convert private conduct into state action. *See, e.g., Rendell-Baker v. Kohn,* 457 U.S. 830 (1982) (holding that regulation and public funding does not transform a private school into a state actor so that Due Process requires hearings associated with faculty dismissals); *Blum v. Yaretsky,* 457 U.S. 991 (1982) (holding that regulation and public funding does not transform a private nursing home into a state actor so that Due Process requires hearings associated with patient transfers). Third, government authorization of private activity does not transform that conduct into state action. *See, e.g., San Francisco Arts & Athletics, Inc. v. U.S. Olympic Committee,* 483 U.S. 522 (1987) (holding that government's creation of Olympic Committee and authorization to prohibit commercial use of the term "Olympic" does not implicate the First Amendment). Fourth, fulfilling constitutionally compelled obligations, such as the duty to provide medical assistance to prisoners, is a product of state action even when performed by private parties. *See, e.g., West v. Atkins,* 487 U.S. 42 (1988) (holding that a private doctor under contract with prison to provide medical assistance to inmates is a state actor even though not an employee of the prison).

C. UNAUTHORIZED CONDUCT THAT DOES NOT VIOLATE THE CONSTITUTION

Section 1983 does not create substantive rights. *See Albright v. Oliver*, 510 U.S. 266 (1994). It merely provides a remedial mechanism for federal rights established elsewhere. It is thus not sufficient that a wrongdoer is a state actor. There must also be a violation of a federally protected right. More often than not, this right is found in the Constitution — hence the focus of this book. On occasion, a constitutional protection may itself require authorized governmental conduct. When this is so, unauthorized action is simply not actionable under § 1983.

PARRATT v. TAYLOR
Supreme Court of the United States
451 U.S. 527 (1981)

JUSTICE REHNQUIST delivered the opinion of the Court.

[Taylor] is an inmate at the Nebraska Penal and Correctional Complex who ordered by mail certain hobby materials valued at $23.50. The hobby materials were lost and [Taylor] brought suit under 42 U.S.C. § 1983 to recover their value. . . . [Taylor] claimed that his property was negligently lost by prison officials in violation of his rights under the Fourteenth Amendment to the United States Constitution. More specifically, he claimed that he had been deprived of property without due process of law.[17]

[Taylor] chose to proceed in the United States District Court under . . . 42 U.S.C. § 1983, even though the State of Nebraska had a tort claims procedure which provided a remedy to persons who suffered tortious losses at the hands of the State.

Nothing in the language of § 1983 or its legislative history limits the statute solely to intentional deprivations of constitutional rights.

Section 1983, unlike its criminal counterpart, 18 U.S.C. § 242, has never been found by this Court to contain a state-of-mind requirement. The Court recognized as much in *Monroe v. Pape*, when we explained after extensively reviewing the legislative history of § 1983, that "[i]t is abundantly clear that one reason the legislation was passed was to afford a federal right in federal courts because, by reason of prejudice, passion, neglect, intolerance or otherwise, state laws might not be enforced and the claims of citizens to the enjoyment of rights, privileges and immunities guaranteed by the Fourteenth Amendment might be denied by the state agencies."

In distinguishing the criminal counterpart which had earlier been at issue in *Screws v. United States*, the *Monroe* Court stated: "In the *Screws* case we dealt with a statute that imposed criminal penalties for acts 'willfully' done. We construed that word in its setting to mean the doing of an act with 'a specific intent to deprive a person of a federal right.' We do not think that gloss should be put on [§ 1983.] The word 'willfully' does not appear in [§ 1983]. Moreover, [§ 1983] provides a civil remedy . . . [Section 1983] should be read against the background of tort liability that makes a man responsible for the natural consequences of his actions."

Accordingly, in any § 1983 action the initial inquiry must focus on whether the two essential elements to a § 1983 action are present: (1) whether the conduct complained of

---

[17] [n.1] As we explained in *Board of Regents v. Roth*, 408 U.S. 564 (1972), property interests "are not created by the Constitution. Rather, they are created and their dimensions are defined by existing rules or understandings that stem from an independent source such as state law — rules or understandings that secure certain benefits and that support claims of entitlement to those benefits." It is not contended that under Nebraska law [Taylor] does not enjoy a property interest in the hobby materials here in question.

C. UNAUTHORIZED CONDUCT THAT DOES NOT VIOLATE THE CONSTITUTION 29

was committed by a person acting under color of state law; and (2) whether this conduct deprived a person of rights, privileges, or immunities secured by the Constitution or laws of the United States.

Since this Court's decision in *Monroe v. Pape*, it can no longer be questioned that the alleged conduct by the [guards] in this case satisfies the "under color of state law" requirement. [The prison guards] were, after all, state employees in positions of considerable authority. . . . Our inquiry, therefore, must turn to the second requirement — whether [Taylor] has been deprived of any right, privilege, or immunity secured by the Constitution or laws of the United States.

Unquestionably, [Taylor's] claim satisfies three prerequisites of a valid due process claim: the [guards] acted under color of state law; the hobby kit falls within the definition of property; and the alleged loss, even though negligently caused, amounted to a deprivation. Standing alone, however, these three elements do not establish a violation of the Fourteenth Amendment. Nothing in that Amendment protects against all deprivations of life, liberty, or property by the State. The Fourteenth Amendment protects only against deprivations "without due process of law." Our inquiry therefore must focus on whether [Taylor] has suffered a deprivation of property without due process of law. In particular, we must decide whether the tort remedies which the State of Nebraska provides as a means of redress for property deprivations satisfy the requirements of procedural due process.

This Court has never directly addressed the question of what process is due a person when an employee of a State negligently takes his property. In some cases this Court has held that due process requires a predeprivation hearing before the State interferes with any liberty or property interest enjoyed by its citizens. In most of these cases, however, the deprivation of property was pursuant to some established state procedure and "process" could be offered before any actual deprivation took place. For example, in *Mullane v. Central Hanover Trust Co.*, 339 U.S. 306 (1950), the Court struck down on due process grounds a New York statute that allowed a trust company, when it sought a judicial settlement of its trust accounts, to give notice by publication to all beneficiaries even if the whereabouts of the beneficiaries were known. The Court held that personal notice in such situations was required and stated that "when notice is a person's due, process which is a mere gesture is not due process." More recently, in *Bell v. Burson*, 402 U.S. 535 (1971), we reviewed a state statute which provided for the taking of the driver's license and registration of an uninsured motorist who had been involved in an accident. We recognized that a driver's license is often involved in the livelihood of a person and as such could not be summarily taken without a prior hearing. In *Fuentes v. Shevin*, 407 U.S. 67 (1972), we struck down the Florida prejudgment replevin statute which allowed secured creditors to obtain writs in ex parte proceedings. We held that due process required a prior hearing before the State authorized its agents to seize property in a debtor's possession. In all these cases, deprivations of property were authorized by an established state procedure and due process was held to require predeprivation notice and hearing in order to serve as a check on the possibility that a wrongful deprivation would occur.

We have, however, recognized that postdeprivation remedies made available by the State can satisfy the Due Process Clause. In such cases, the normal predeprivation notice and opportunity to be heard is pretermitted if the State provides a postdeprivation remedy. In *North American Cold Storage Co. v. Chicago*, 211 U.S. 306 (1908), we upheld the right of a State to seize and destroy unwholesome food without a preseizure hearing. The possibility of erroneous destruction of property was outweighed by the fact that the public health emergency justified immediate action and the owner of the property could recover his damages in an action at law after the incident. In *Ewing v. Mytinger & Casselberry, Inc.*, 339 U.S. 594 (1950), we upheld under the Fifth Amendment Due Process Clause the summary seizure and destruction of drugs without a preseizure hearing. Similarly, in *Fahey v. Mallonee*, 332 U.S. 245

(1947), we recognized that the protection of the public interest against economic harm can justify the immediate seizure of property without a prior hearing when substantial questions are raised about the competence of a bank's management. . . . These cases recognize that either the necessity of quick action by the State or the impracticality of providing any meaningful predeprivation process, when coupled with the availability of some meaningful means by which to assess the propriety of the State's action at some time after the initial taking, can satisfy the requirements of procedural due process.

Our past cases mandate that some kind of hearing is required at some time before a State finally deprives a person of his property interests. The fundamental requirement of due process is the opportunity to be heard and it is an "opportunity which must be granted at a meaningful time and in a meaningful manner." However, as many of the above cases recognize, we have rejected the proposition that "at a meaningful time and in a meaningful manner" always requires the State to provide a hearing prior to the initial deprivation of property. This rejection is based in part on the impracticability in some cases of providing any preseizure hearing under a state-authorized procedure, and the assumption that at some time a full and meaningful hearing will be available.

The justifications which we have found sufficient to uphold takings of property without any predeprivation process are applicable to a situation such as the present one involving a tortious loss of a prisoner's property as a result of a random and unauthorized act by a state employee. In such a case, the loss is not a result of some established state procedure and the State cannot predict precisely when the loss will occur. It is difficult to conceive of how the State could provide a meaningful hearing before the deprivation takes place. The loss of property, although attributable to the State as action under "color of law," is in almost all cases beyond the control of the State. Indeed, in most cases it is not only impracticable, but impossible, to provide a meaningful hearing before the deprivation. That does not mean, of course, that the State can take property without providing a meaningful postdeprivation hearing. The prior cases which have excused the prior-hearing requirement have rested in part on the availability of some meaningful opportunity subsequent to the initial taking for a determination of rights and liabilities.

Application of the principles recited above to this case leads us to conclude [Taylor] has not alleged a violation of the Due Process Clause of the Fourteenth Amendment. Although he has been deprived of property under color of state law, the deprivation did not occur as a result of some established state procedure. Indeed, the deprivation occurred as a result of the unauthorized failure of agents of the State to follow established state procedure. There is no contention that the procedures themselves are inadequate nor is there any contention that it was practicable for the State to provide a predeprivation hearing. Moreover, the State of Nebraska has provided [Taylor] with the means by which he can receive redress for the deprivation. The State provides a remedy to persons who believe they have suffered a tortious loss at the hands of the State. Through this tort claims procedure the State hears and pays claims of prisoners housed in its penal institutions. This procedure was in existence at the time of the loss here in question but [Taylor] did not use it. It is argued that the State does not adequately protect [Taylor's] interests because it provides only for an action against the State as opposed to its individual employees, it contains no provisions for punitive damages, and there is no right to a trial by jury. Although the state remedies may not provide [Taylor] with all the relief which may have been available if he could have proceeded under § 1983, that does not mean that the state remedies are not adequate to satisfy the requirements of due process. The remedies provided could have fully compensated the respondent for the property loss he suffered, and we hold that they are sufficient to satisfy the requirements of due process.

To accept [Taylor'] argument that the conduct of the state officials in this case constituted a violation of the Fourteenth Amendment would almost necessarily result in turning every alleged injury which may have been inflicted by a state official acting under "color of law" into a violation of the Fourteenth Amendment cognizable under § 1983. It is hard to perceive any logical stopping place to such a line of reasoning. Presumably, under this rationale any party who is involved in nothing more than an automobile accident with a state official could allege a constitutional violation under § 1983. Such reasoning "would make of the Fourteenth Amendment a font of tort law to be superimposed upon whatever systems may already be administered by the States." We do not think that the drafters of the Fourteenth Amendment intended the Amendment to play such a role in our society.[18]

JUSTICE BLACKMUN [with whom JUSTICE WHITE joins], concurring.

I do not read the Court's opinion as applicable to a case concerning deprivation of life or of liberty. I also do not understand the Court to intimate that the sole content of the Due Process Clause is procedural regularity. I continue to believe that there are certain governmental actions that, even if undertaken with a full panoply of procedural protection, are, in and of themselves, antithetical to fundamental notions of due process. *See, e.g., Roe v. Wade*, 410 U.S. 113 (1973).

Most importantly, I do not understand the Court to suggest that the provision of "postdeprivation remedies" within a state system would cure the unconstitutional nature of a state official's intentional act that deprives a person of property. While the "random and unauthorized" nature of negligent acts by state employees makes it difficult for the State to "provide a meaningful hearing before the deprivation takes place," it is rare that the same can be said of intentional acts by state employees. When it is possible for a State to institute procedures to contain and direct the intentional actions of its officials, it should be required, as a matter of due process, to do so.

JUSTICE POWELL, concurring in the result.

The central question in this case is whether unintentional but negligent acts by state officials, causing [Taylor's] loss of property, are actionable under the Due Process Clause. In my view, this question requires the Court to determine whether intent is an essential element of a due process claim, just as we have done in cases applying the Equal Protection Clause and the Eighth Amendment's prohibition of "cruel and unusual punishment." The intent question cannot be given "a uniform answer across the entire spectrum of conceivable constitutional violations which might be the subject of a § 1983 action." Rather, we must give close attention to the nature of the particular constitutional violation asserted in determining whether intent is a necessary element of such a violation.

In the due process area, the question is whether intent is required before there can be a "deprivation" of life, liberty, or property. In this case, for example, the negligence of the prison officials caused respondent to lose his property. Nevertheless, I would not hold that such a negligent act, causing unintended loss of or injury to property, works a deprivation in the constitutional sense. Thus, no procedure for compensation is constitutionally required.

A "deprivation" connotes an intentional act denying something to someone, or, at the very least, a deliberate decision not to act to prevent a loss.[19] The most reasonable interpretation of the Fourteenth Amendment would limit due process claims to such active deprivations. . . . [S]uch a rule would avoid trivializing the right of action provided in § 1983. That provision was enacted to deter real abuses by state officials in the exercise of governmental powers. It would make no sense to open the federal courts

---

[18] [Editor's note: Justice Stewart's concurring opinion is omitted.]

[19] [n.4] According to Webster's New International Dictionary of the English Language (2d ed. 1945), to "deprive" is to "dispossess; bereave; divest; to hinder from possessing; debar; shut out."

to lawsuits where there has been no affirmative abuse of power, merely a negligent deed by one who happens to be acting under color of state law.[20]

The Court appears unconcerned about this prospect, probably because of an implicit belief in the availability of state tort remedies in most cases. . . . But the fact is that this rule would "make of the Fourteenth Amendment a font of tort law," whenever a State has failed to provide a remedy for negligent invasions of liberty or property interests. Moreover, despite the breadth of state tort remedies such claims will be more numerous than might at first be supposed.

Such an approach has another advantage; it avoids a somewhat disturbing implication in the Court's opinion concerning the scope of due process guarantees. The Court analyzes this case solely in terms of the procedural rights created by the Due Process Clause. Finding state procedures adequate, it suggests that no further analysis is required of more substantive limitations on state action located in this Clause. The Due Process Clause imposes substantive limitations on state action and under proper circumstances these limitations may extend to intentional and malicious deprivations of liberty and property, even where compensation is available under state law. The Court, however, fails altogether to discuss the possibility that the kind of state action alleged here constitutes a violation of the substantive guarantees of the Due Process Clause. As I do not consider a negligent act the kind of deprivation that implicates the procedural guarantees of the Due Process Clause, I certainly would not view negligent acts as violative of these substantive guarantees.[21]

NOTES

1. The Procedural Due Process Revolution. The 1970s marked a renaissance in Procedural Due Process. Beginning with *Goldberg v. Kelly*, 397 U.S. 254 (1970), the Supreme Court began to unravel arcane distinctions between rights and privileges, only the former traditionally receiving procedural protection in the courts. Instead of continuing this semantic exercise, the Court substituted the unified principle that before a state takes adverse action against a person it must afford prior process. Only a short time passed before the Court saw the need to establish limits, lest federal law swallow all of state law under the guise of due process. In a series of cases, including *Board of Regents v. Roth*, 408 U.S. 564 (1972), *Bishop v. Wood*, 426 U.S. 341 (1976), *Codd v. Velger*, 429 U.S. 624 (1977), and perhaps most significantly, *Paul v. Davis*, 424 U.S. 693 (1976), the Court scaled back the meanings of property and liberty so that not all common law torts inflicted by government officials fall within their terms. In cases like *Roth*, the Court concluded that one must have a "legitimate claim of entitlement" to have a property interest. Although this definition includes most traditional forms of property, like a person's home and auto, it excludes some modern forms of property, most importantly at-will government employment. *See Board of Regents v. Roth*, 408 U.S. 564 (1972). *Cf. Gilbert v. Homar*, 520 U.S. 924 (1997) (assuming that suspension from public-sector employment infringes property interest, but finding that a "prompt post-suspension hearing" was sufficient for purposes of Due Process Clause). In *Paul*, the Court held that there existed no liberty interest in being free from defamatory remarks made by the government. *See also Siegert v. Gilley*, 500 U.S. 226 (1991)

---

[20] [n.7] We have previously expressed concerns about the prospect that the Due Process Clause may become a vehicle for federal litigation of state torts. In *Paul v. Davis*, [424 U.S. 693 (1976),] we held that an official action damaging the reputation of a private citizen, although an actionable tort under state law, did not constitute a deprivation of "liberty" within the meaning of the Fourteenth Amendment. . . . It is clear that the hobby kit was [Taylor's] "property." But it also is clear that under state law no remedy other than tort law protects property from interferences caused by the negligence of others. The reasoning of *Paul v. Davis* would suggest, therefore, that the enjoyment of property free of negligent interference is not sufficiently "guaranteed" by state law to justify a due process claim based on official negligence.

[21] [Editor's note: Justice Marshall's opinion, concurring in part and dissenting in part, is omitted.]

C. UNAUTHORIZED CONDUCT THAT DOES NOT VIOLATE THE CONSTITUTION

(holding that defamation does not implicate liberty). Therefore, when a state injures a person's reputation, no procedural problem arises because no protected interest exists. When the state has physically injured a person, on the other hand, the Court has steadfastly found a liberty interest at stake. In *Ingraham v. Wright*, 430 U.S. 651 (1977), for example, the Court held that school paddling implicated a liberty interest: a person has a procedural right to be free from the state's infliction of "appreciable physical pain."

2. Inmates. As *Parratt* makes clear, inmates can retain property and liberty interests that entitle them to procedural protections. The Supreme Court, moreover, interpreted these interests fairly broadly in a series of cases decided in the 1970s. *See, e.g., Wolff v. McDonnell*, 418 U.S. 539 (1974) (holding that an inmate had a liberty interest created by state law in good-time credits); *Greenholtz v. Inmates of Nebraska Penal and Correctional Complex*, 442 U.S. 1 (1979) (holding that an inmate had state-created liberty interest in parole); *Hewitt v. Helms*, 459 U.S. 460 (1979) (concluding that an inmate had state-created liberty interest in remaining in general prison population and not being put into administrative segregation); *but see Meachum v. Fano*, 427 U.S. 215 (1976) (finding that an inmate had no state-created liberty interest in remaining in medium security, as opposed to maximum security, prison). Given these protected interests, states were forced to provide meaningful hearings before depriving inmates of good-time credits or parole, and before placing them in administrative segregation.

These holdings were reassessed in *Sandin v. Conner*, 515 U.S. 472 (1995), which sustained *Wolff* by holding that increasing the duration of an inmate's sentence by revoking good time credits implicates liberty, but overruled *Helms* by concluding that inmates' state-created liberty interests "will be generally limited to freedom from restraint which . . . imposes *atypical and significant hardship* on the inmate in relation to the ordinary incidents of prison life." (Emphasis added). Because being placed in administrative segregation for 30 days was not found to be an "atypical and significant hardship," the Due Process Clause did not demand pre- or post-deprivation process. *See also Young v. Harper*, 520 U.S. 143 (1997) (holding that a pre-parole program similar to parole implicates a liberty interest and must be accompanied by constitutionally sufficient procedures); *Ohio Adult Parole Authority v. Woodard*, 523 U.S. 272 (1998) (finding a "life" interest in clemency proceeding on behalf of a death row inmate, though also concluding that only "minimal procedural safeguards apply"); *Wilkinson v. Austin*, 545 U.S. 209 (2005) (holding that Ohio inmates at a "Supermax" prison suffered "atypical and significant hardship," but also concluding that Ohio's procedures, which included notice, opportunity for rebuttal, and placement review, satisfied the Due Process Clause).

3. *Hudson v. Palmer*. *Hudson v. Palmer*, 468 U.S. 517 (1984), like *Parratt*, involved a simple loss of property at the hands of prison authorities. This loss, however, was not the result of negligence but was a consequence of intentional misconduct. The prisoner alleged that during a shakedown of his cell, prison authorities purposely destroyed non-contraband property. The Court not only rejected the inmate's Fourth Amendment claim, it also extended its holding in *Parratt* to intentional deprivations of property that are "random and unauthorized." The Court concluded that both negligent and intentional wrongs are random when viewed from the state's perspective, and in neither case does the state have an opportunity to provide a predeprivation hearing. In response to the argument that the state official, who knows that he is about to destroy property, could provide a predeprivation hearing, the Court stated: "The controlling inquiry is solely whether the state is in a position to provide for predeprivation process." The Court found Virginia's remedial scheme an adequate postdeprivation procedure within the meaning of *Parratt* because the official apparently was not protected by the state's sovereign immunity, leaving the prisoner free to seek redress in the state courts.

The Aftermath of *Parratt-Hudson*. *Parratt* and *Hudson* established that where official wrongly deprives a person of property, whether with intent or through ...ice, no Procedural Due Process violation occurs absent a systemic denial of some adequate state remedy. Consequently, an illegal, *un*authorized act will not violate Procedural Due Process so long as state law redresses the violation. Consider again Justice Frankfurter's dissent in *Monroe v. Pape* (excerpted in Section A, *supra*). *Parratt-Hudson* opened a Pandora's Box of problems, the most visible being questions surrounding the adequacy of state remedies. The Court provided little guidance in either case concerning what state remedies must include to satisfy this requirement. *Parratt* did make it clear, however, that state remedies need not be equivalent to federal remedies available under § 1983. Thus, states need not provide for attorney's fees, *see* Chapter 9, *infra*, trial by jury, *see* Chapter 5, *infra*, or punitive damages, *see* Chapter 6, *infra*, all of which are available under § 1983. Furthermore, relief granted by the state need not come from the tortfeasor's pocket, but may come directly from the state's coffers. Beyond these general guidelines, the Court left the adequacy of any given remedy an open question.

Still, one principle might be drawn from *Parratt* and *Hudson*: in both cases the Court concluded that the tort victim possessed some remedy, against either the tortfeasor or the state. In *Parratt* the prisoner could receive compensation under the state's tort claims act, while in *Hudson* the tortfeasor was personally liable under state law for his intentional acts. Thus, it might be argued that both cases implicitly hold that under state law it must be possible to recover from either the state or the tortfeasor. So long as one or the other is subject to liability, the remedy is adequate. *See, e.g., Belcher v. Norton*, 497 F.3d 742 (7th Cir. 2007) ("The Supreme Court has made clear that, in order to constitute an adequate remedy, the remedy provided by state law need not be the same as that available under § 1983. Nevertheless, the relief afforded by the state remedy cannot be 'meaningless or non-existent.' "); *McNamara v. City of Rittman*, 473 F.3d 633 (6th Cir. 2007) (concluding that state law did not provide an adequate remedy to a homeowner for purposes of Procedural Due Process); *Brown v. Muhlenberg Township*, 269 F.3d 205 (3d Cir. 2001) (holding that because Pennsylvania law afforded the victim a remedy for a willful violation, an adequate remedy existed within meaning of *Parratt* and *Hudson*); *Smith v. Colorado Department of Corrections*, 23 F.3d 339 (10th Cir. 1994) (finding that Colorado law created an adequate remedy within meaning of *Parratt*).

As the following two cases demonstrate, however, not everyone agrees that *Parratt* and *Hudson* require a remedy.[22]

DANIELS v. WILLIAMS
Supreme Court of the United States
474 U.S. 327 (1986)

JUSTICE REHNQUIST delivered the opinion of the Court.

[Daniel's] claim in this case, which . . . rests on an alleged Fourteenth Amendment "deprivation" caused by the negligent conduct of a prison official, leads us to reconsider our statement in *Parratt* that "the alleged loss, even though negligently caused, amounted to a deprivation." We conclude that the Due Process Clause is simply not implicated by a negligent act of an official causing unintended loss of or injury to life, liberty, or property. In this § 1983 action, [Daniels] seeks to recover damages for back

---

[22] *See also Dykes v. Hosemann*, 776 F.2d 942, 953 (11th Cir. 1985) (Tjoflat, J., concurring in part) ("immunization of judges from suit and the corresponding absence of a tort remedy for judicial wrongs [does not] provide[] an injured party less process than he is due"); *Temple v. Marlborough Division of District Court*, 479 N.E.2d 137, 143–44 (Mass. 1985) (holding that the mere opportunity for a hearing is sufficient even if defendants are protected by absolute immunity).

C. UNAUTHORIZED CONDUCT THAT DOES NOT VIOLATE THE CONSTITUTION

and ankle injuries allegedly sustained when he fell on a prison stairway. He claims that, while an inmate at the city jail in Richmond, Virginia, he slipped on a pillow negligently left on the stairs by [Williams], a correctional deputy stationed at the jail. [William's] negligence, the argument runs, "deprived" petitioner of his "liberty" interest in freedom from bodily injury, see *Ingraham v. Wright* [, 430 U.S. 651 (1977)];[23] because [Williams] maintains that he is entitled to the defense of sovereign immunity in a state tort suit, [Daniels] is without an "adequate" state remedy. Accordingly, the deprivation of liberty was without "due process of law."

In *Parratt v. Taylor*, . . . we concluded that § 1983, unlike its criminal counterpart, 18 U.S.C. § 242, contains no state-of-mind requirement independent of that necessary to state a violation of the underlying constitutional right. We adhere to that conclusion. But in any given § 1983 suit, the plaintiff must still prove a violation of the underlying constitutional right; and depending on the right, merely negligent conduct may not be enough to state a claim. See, e.g., *Arlington Heights v. Metropolitan Housing Dev. Corp.*, 429 U.S. 252 (1977) (invidious discriminatory purpose required for claim of racial discrimination[under the Equal Protection Clause); *Estelle v. Gamble*[, 429 U.S. 97 (1976)] ("deliberate indifference" to prisoner's serious illness or injury sufficient to constitute cruel and unusual punishment under the Eighth Amendment).

In *Parratt*, before concluding that Nebraska's tort remedy provided all the process that was due, we said that the loss of the prisoner's hobby kit, "even though negligently caused, amounted to a deprivation [under the Due Process Clause]." Justice Powell, concurring in the result, criticized the majority for "pass[ing] over" this important question of the state of mind required to constitute a "deprivation" of property. He argued that negligent acts by state officials, though causing loss of property, are not actionable under the Due Process Clause. To Justice Powell, mere negligence could not "wor[k] a deprivation in the constitutional sense." Not only does the word "deprive" in the Due Process Clause connote more than a negligent act, but we should not "open the federal courts to lawsuits where there has been no affirmative abuse of power." Upon reflection, we agree and overrule *Parratt* to the extent that it states that mere lack of due care by a state official may "deprive" an individual of life, liberty, or property under the Fourteenth Amendment.

Historically, th[e] guarantee of due process has been applied to deliberate decisions of government officials to deprive a person of life, liberty, or property. No decision of this Court before *Parratt* supported the view that negligent conduct by a state official, even though causing injury, constitutes a deprivation under the Due Process Clause. This history reflects the traditional and common-sense notion that the Due Process Clause, like its forebear in the Magna Carta, was "'intended to secure the individual from the arbitrary exercise of the powers of government.'" By requiring the government to follow appropriate procedures when its agents decide to "deprive any person of life, liberty, or property," the Due Process Clause promotes fairness in such decisions. And by barring certain government actions regardless of the fairness of the procedures used to implement them, it serves to prevent governmental power from being "used for purposes of oppression."

We think that the actions of prison custodians in leaving a pillow on the prison stairs, or mislaying an inmate's property, are quite remote from the concerns just discussed. Far from an abuse of power, lack of due care suggests no more than a failure to measure up to the conduct of a reasonable person. To hold that injury caused by such conduct is a deprivation within the meaning of the Fourteenth Amendment would trivialize the centuries-old principle of due process of law.

---

[23] [Editor's note: The constitutional claim in *Ingraham* was that summary corporal punishment in public schools ran afoul of Procedural Due Process. The Supreme Court ruled that although students have a liberty interest in being free from the infliction of "appreciable physical pain," the availability of post-punishment state tort remedies against the teacher was sufficient for purposes of Due Process.]

Our Constitution deals with the large concerns of the governors and the governed, but it does not purport to supplant traditional tort law in laying down rules of conduct to regulate liability for injuries that attend living together in society. We have previously rejected reasoning that "would make of the Fourteenth Amendment a font of tort law to be superimposed upon whatever systems may already be administered by the States."

The only tie between the facts of this case and anything governmental in nature is the fact that [Williams] was a sheriff's deputy at the Richmond city jail and [Daniels] was an inmate confined in that jail. But while the Due Process Clause of the Fourteenth Amendment obviously speaks to some facets of this relationship, we do not believe its protections are triggered by lack of due care by prison officials. "Medical malpractice does not become a constitutional violation merely because the victim is a prisoner," and "false imprisonment does not become a violation of the Fourteenth Amendment merely because the defendant is a state official." Where a government official's act causing injury to life, liberty, or property is merely negligent, "no procedure for compensation is constitutionally required." *Parratt* (Powell, J., concurring in result).[24]

That injuries inflicted by governmental negligence are not addressed by the United States Constitution is not to say that they may not raise significant legal concerns and lead to the creation of protectible legal interests. The enactment of tort claim statutes, for example, reflects the view that injuries caused by such negligence should generally be redressed.[25] It is no reflection on either the breadth of the United States Constitution or the importance of traditional tort law to say that they do not address the same concerns.

[Daniels] also suggests that artful litigants, undeterred by a requirement that they plead more than mere negligence, will often be able to allege sufficient facts to support a claim of intentional deprivation. . . . What's more, requiring complainants to allege something more than negligence would raise serious questions about what "more" than negligence — intent, recklessness or "gross negligence" — is required,[26] and indeed about what these elusive terms mean. But even if accurate, [Daniels'] observations do not carry the day. In the first place, many branches of the law abound in nice distinctions that may be troublesome but have been thought nonetheless necessary. . . . More important, the difference between one end of the spectrum — negligence — and the other — intent — is abundantly clear. In any event, we decline to trivialize the Due Process Clause in an effort to simplify constitutional litigation.

Finally, [Daniels] argues that [Williams'] conduct, even if merely negligent, breached a sheriff's "special duty of care" for those in his custody. The Due Process Clause, Daniels notes, "was intended to give Americans at least the protection against governmental power that they had enjoyed as Englishmen against the power of the crown." [O]ne such protection was the right to recover against a sheriff for breach of his ministerial duty to provide for the safety of prisoners in his custody. Due process demands that the State protect those whom it incarcerates by exercising reasonable care to assure their safety and by compensating them for negligently inflicted injury.

We disagree. . . . Daniels' citation to *Ingraham v. Wright* does not support the notion that all common-law duties owed by government actors were somehow

---

[24] [n.14] Accordingly, we need not decide whether, as [Daniels] contends, the possibility of a sovereign immunity defense in a Virginia tort suit would render that remedy "inadequate" under *Parratt* and *Hudson v. Palmer*.

[25] [n.15] *See, e.g.*, the Virginia Tort Claims Act, which applies only to actions accruing on or after July 1, 1982, and hence is inapplicable to this case.

[26] [n.16] Despite his claim about what he might have pleaded, [Daniels] concedes that [Williams] was at most negligent. Accordingly, this case affords us no occasion to consider whether something less than intentional conduct, such as recklessness or "gross negligence," is enough to trigger the protections of the Due Process Clause.

C. UNAUTHORIZED CONDUCT THAT DOES NOT VIOLATE THE CONSTITUTION

constitutionalized by the Fourteenth Amendment. Jailers may owe a special duty of care to those in their custody under state tort law, see RESTATEMENT (SECOND) OF TORTS § 314A(4) (1965), but for the reasons previously stated we reject the contention that the Due Process Clause of the Fourteenth Amendment embraces such a tort law concept. . . .[27]

DAVIDSON v. CANNON
Supreme Court of the United States
474 U.S. 344 (1986)

JUSTICE REHNQUIST delivered the opinion of the Court.

[Davidson] sued prison officials seeking damages under 42 U.S.C. § 1983 for injuries he suffered when they negligently failed to protect him from another inmate [who] attacked [Davidson] with a fork, breaking his nose and inflicting other wounds to his face, neck, head, and body.

[Davidson] . . . claim[ed] that [prison officials] . . . had violated his constitutional rights under the Eighth and Fourteenth Amendments. After a bench trial, the District Court . . . found . . . that [the prison officials] "negligently failed to take reasonable steps to protect [Davison], and that he was injured as a result." [Davidson] was thereby deprived of his liberty interest in personal security, see *Ingraham v. Wright*; and because New Jersey law provides that "[n]either a public entity nor a public employee is liable for . . . any injury caused by . . . a prisoner to any other prisoner," the court concluded that the deprivation was without due process. [Davidson] was awarded compensatory damages of $2,000.

In *Daniels*, we held that the Due Process Clause of the Fourteenth Amendment is not implicated by the lack of due care of an official causing unintended injury to life, liberty or property. In other words, where a government official is merely negligent in causing the injury, no procedure for compensation is constitutionally required.

[Prison officials'] lack of due care in this case led to serious injury, but that lack of care simply does not approach the sort of abusive government conduct that the Due Process Clause was designed to prevent.

In an effort to limit the potentially broad sweep of his claim, [Davidson] emphasizes that he "does not ask this Court to read the Constitution as an absolute guarantor of his liberty from assault by a fellow prisoner, even if that assault is caused by the negligence of his jailers." Describing his claim as one of "procedural due process, pure and simple," all he asks is that New Jersey provide him a remedy. But the Fourteenth Amendment does not require a remedy when there has been no "deprivation" of a protected interest. [Davidson's] claim, based on . . . negligence, is quite different from one involving injuries caused by an unjustified attack by prison guards themselves, or by another prisoner where officials simply stood by and permitted the attack to proceed. As we held in *Daniels*, the protections of the Due Process Clause, whether procedural or substantive, are just not triggered by lack of due care by prison officials.

JUSTICE STEVENS, concurring in the judgments.

I do not agree . . . that it is necessary either to redefine the meaning of "deprive" in the Fourteenth Amendment, or to repudiate the reasoning of *Parratt v. Taylor*, to support this conclusion.

---

[27] [Editor's note: Justices Marshall concurred in the result without opinion. Justice Blackmun concurred in the judgment for the reasons stated in his dissent in the companion case of *Davidson v. Cannon*. Justice Stevens' opinion concurring in the judgments in both cases is included below with *Davidson v. Cannon*.]

We should begin by identifying the precise constitutional claims that [Davidson and Daniels] have advanced. It is not enough to note that they rely on the Due Process Clause of the Fourteenth Amendment, for that Clause is the source of three different kinds of constitutional protection. First, it incorporates specific protections defined in the Bill of Rights. Thus, the State, as well as the Federal Government, must comply with the commands in the First and Eighth Amendments; so too, the State must respect the guarantees in the Fourth, Fifth, and Sixth Amendments.

Second, it contains a substantive component, sometimes referred to as "substantive due process," which bars certain arbitrary government actions "regardless of the fairness of the procedures used to implement them." Third, it is a guarantee of fair procedure, sometimes referred to as "procedural due process": the State may not execute, imprison, or fine a defendant without giving him a fair trial, nor may it take property without providing appropriate procedural safeguards.

The type of Fourteenth Amendment interest that is implicated has important effects on the nature of the constitutional claim and the availability of § 1983 relief. If the claim is in the first category (a violation of one of the specific constitutional guarantees of the Bill of Rights), a plaintiff may invoke § 1983 regardless of the availability of a state remedy. As explained in *Monroe v. Pape*, this conclusion derives from the fact that the statute — the Ku Klux Act of 1871 — was intended to provide a federal remedy for the violation of a federal constitutional right.

Similarly, if the claim is in the second category (a violation of the substantive component of the Due Process Clause), a plaintiff may also invoke § 1983 regardless of the availability of a state remedy. For, in that category, no less than with the provisions of the Bill of Rights, if the Federal Constitution prohibits a State from taking certain actions "regardless of the fairness of the procedures used to implement them," the constitutional violation is complete as soon as the prohibited action is taken; the independent federal remedy is then authorized by the language and legislative history of § 1983.

A claim in the third category — a procedural due process claim — is fundamentally different. In such a case, the deprivation may be entirely legitimate — a State may have every right to discharge a teacher or punish a student — but the State may nevertheless violate the Constitution by failing to provide appropriate procedural safeguards. The constitutional duty to provide fair procedures gives the citizen the opportunity to try to prevent the deprivation from happening, but the deprivation itself does not necessarily reflect any "abuse" of state power. Similarly, a deprivation may be the consequence of a mistake or a negligent act, and the State may violate the Constitution by failing to provide an appropriate procedural response. In a procedural due process claim, it is not the deprivation of property or liberty that is unconstitutional; it is the deprivation of property or liberty without due process of law — without adequate procedures.

Thus, even though the State may have every right to deprive a person of his property or his liberty, the individual may nevertheless be able to allege a valid § 1983 due process claim, perhaps because a predeprivation hearing must be held, or because the state procedure itself is fundamentally flawed. So too, even though a deprivation may be unauthorized, a procedural due process claim may be raised if it challenges the State's procedures for preventing or redressing the deprivation. However, a complaint does not state a valid procedural due process objection — and a valid § 1983 claim — if it does not include a challenge to the fundamental fairness of the State's procedures. In consequence, when a predeprivation hearing is clearly not feasible, when the regime of state tort law provides a constitutionally unobjectionable system of recovery for the deprivation of property or liberty, and when there is no other challenge to the State's procedures, a valid § 1983 claim is not stated.

[Daniels' and Davidson's] claims are not of the first kind. Neither Daniels nor Davidson argues in this Court that the prison authorities' actions violated specific

C. UNAUTHORIZED CONDUCT THAT DOES NOT VIOLATE THE CONSTITUTION

constitutional guarantees incorporated by the Fourteenth Amendment. Neither now claims, for instance, that his rights under the Eighth Amendment were violated. Similarly, I do not believe [they] have raised a colorable violation of "substantive due process." Rather, their claims are of the third kind: Daniels and Davidson attack the validity of the procedures that Virginia and New Jersey, respectively, provide for prisoners who seek redress for physical injury caused by the negligence of corrections officers.

I would not reject these claims, as the Court does, by attempting to fashion a new definition of the term "deprivation" and excluding negligence from its scope. No serious question has been raised about the presence of "state action" in the allegations of negligence, and the interest in freedom from bodily harm surely qualifies as an interest in "liberty." Thus, the only question is whether negligence by state actors can result in a deprivation. "Deprivation," it seems to me, identifies, not the actor's state of mind, but the victim's infringement or loss. The harm to a prisoner is the same whether a pillow is left on a stair negligently, recklessly, or intentionally; so too, the harm resulting to a prisoner from an attack is the same whether his request for protection is ignored negligently, recklessly, or deliberately. In each instance, the prisoner is losing — being "deprived" of — an aspect of liberty as the result, in part, of a form of state action.

To prevail, [Daniels and Davidson] must demonstrate that the state procedures for redressing injuries of this kind are constitutionally inadequate. [They] must show that they contain a defect so serious that we can characterize the procedures as fundamentally unfair, a defect so basic that we are forced to conclude that the deprivation occurred without due process.

Daniels' claim is essentially the same as the claim we rejected in *Parratt*. The Court of Appeals for the Fourth Circuit determined that Daniels had a remedy for the claimed negligence under Virginia law. Although Daniels vigorously argues that sovereign immunity would have defeated his claim, the Fourth Circuit [sitting en banc] found to the contrary, and it is our settled practice to defer to the Courts of Appeals on questions of state law. It is true that *Parratt* involved an injury to "property" and that Daniels' case involves an injury to "liberty," but, in both cases, the plaintiff claimed nothing more than a "procedural due process" violation. In both cases, a predeprivation hearing was definitionally impossible. And, in both cases, the plaintiff had state remedies that permitted recovery if state negligence was established. Thus, a straightforward application of *Parratt* defeats Daniels' claim.

Davidson's claim raises a question not specifically addressed in *Parratt*. According to the Third Circuit, no state remedy was available because a New Jersey statute prohibits prisoner recovery from state employees for injuries inflicted by other prisoners. Thus, Davidson puts the question whether a state policy of noncompensability for certain types of harm, in which state action may play a role, renders a state procedure constitutionally defective. In my judgment, a state policy that defeats recovery does not, in itself, carry that consequence. Those aspects of a State's tort regime that defeat recovery are not constitutionally invalid, so long as there is no fundamental unfairness in their operation. Thus, defenses such as contributory negligence or statutes of limitations may defeat recovery in particular cases without raising any question about the constitutionality of a State's procedures for disposing of tort litigation. Similarly, in my judgment, the mere fact that a State elects to provide some of its agents with a sovereign immunity defense in certain cases does not justify the conclusion that its remedial system is constitutionally inadequate. There is no reason to believe that the Due Process Clause of the Fourteenth Amendment . . . should be construed to suggest that the doctrine of sovereign immunity renders a state procedure fundamentally unfair.[28]

---

[28] [n.20] In *Martinez v. California*, 444 U.S. 277 (1980), we held that California's immunity statute did not violate the Due Process Clause simply because it operated to defeat a tort claim arising under state law. The

JUSTICE BLACKMUN, with whom JUSTICE MARSHALL joins, dissenting.

While I concur in the judgment in *Daniels*, I do not join the Court in extending that result to this case. It is one thing to hold that a commonplace slip and fall, or the loss of a $23.50 hobby kit, *see Parratt v. Taylor*, does not rise to the dignified level of a constitutional violation. It is a somewhat different thing to say that negligence that permits anticipated inmate violence resulting in injury, or perhaps leads to the execution of the wrong prisoner, does not implicate the Constitution's guarantee of due process. When the State incarcerated Daniels, it left intact his own faculties for avoiding a slip and a fall. But the State prevented Davidson from defending himself, and therefore assumed some responsibility to protect him from the dangers to which he was exposed. In these circumstances, I feel that Davidson was deprived of liberty by the negligence of the prison officials. Moreover, the acts of the state officials in this case may well have risen to the level of recklessness. I therefore dissent.

It is well established that . . . liberty includes freedom from unjustified intrusions on personal security. *Ingraham v. Wright*. In particular, it includes a prisoner's right to safe conditions and to security from attack by other inmates. *See Youngberg v. Romeo*, 457 U.S. 307 (1982). Before a State can deprive a prisoner of the liberty he retains after imprisonment, it must afford him constitutionally adequate procedures.

I agree that mere negligent activity ordinarily will not amount to an abuse of state power. Where the Court today errs, in my view, is in elevating this sensible rule of thumb to the status of inflexible constitutional dogma. The Court declares that negligent activity can never implicate the concerns of the Due Process Clause. I see no justification for this rigid view. In some cases, by any reasonable standard, governmental negligence is an abuse of power. This is one of those cases.

It seems to me that when a State assumes sole responsibility for one's physical security and then ignores his call for help, the State cannot claim that it did not know a subsequent injury was likely to occur. Under such circumstances, the State should not automatically be excused from responsibility. In the context of prisons, this means that once the State has taken away an inmate's means of protecting himself from attack by other inmates, a prison official's negligence in providing protection can amount to a deprivation of the inmate's liberty, at least absent extenuating circumstances. Such conduct by state officials seems to me to be the "arbitrary action" against which the Due Process Clause protects. The officials' actions in such cases thus are not remote from the purpose of the Due Process Clause and § 1983.

The deprivation of Davidson's liberty interest violated the Fourteenth Amendment if it occurred "without due process of law." That condition is clearly satisfied. In both *Parratt* and *Hudson*, the Court held that where a deprivation of property was caused by a random and unauthorized act of a state official, it was impracticable for the State to provide process in advance and the State could satisfy procedural due process by a meaningful postdeprivation remedy, such as a tort suit. Even assuming the same is true for deprivations of liberty, New Jersey has failed to provide a meaningful postdeprivation remedy. By statute, the State has ruled: "Neither a public entity nor a public employee is liable for . . . any injury caused by . . . a prisoner to any other prisoner." The State acknowledges that it would have asserted the immunity statute as a defense to a state-court action and that Davidson's complaint would have been dismissed before being heard on the merits.

Conduct that is wrongful under § 1983 surely cannot be immunized by state law. A State can define defenses, including immunities, to state-law causes of action, as long as the state rule does not conflict with federal law. But permitting a state immunity

---

fact that an immunity statute does not give rise to a procedural due process claim does not, of course, mean that a State's doctrine of sovereign immunity can protect conduct that violates a federal constitutional guarantee; obviously it cannot.

defense to control in a § 1983 action "'would transmute a basic guarantee into an illusory promise; and the supremacy clause of the Constitution insures that the proper construction may be enforced.'" It is irrelevant that state immunity as applied to defeat a state-law tort claim is constitutional, and may be construed as one aspect of the State's definition of a tort claim.

Davidson has been denied "an opportunity . . . granted at a meaningful time and in a meaningful manner . . . for [a] hearing appropriate to the nature of the case." Lacking a meaningful postdeprivation remedy in state court, Davidson was deprived of his liberty without due process of law.[29]

NOTES

1. The Lower Courts' Opinions in *Daniels* and *Davidson*. The Court of Appeals for the Fourth Circuit in *Daniels* addressed both whether the *Parratt-Hudson* analysis should encompass deprivations of liberty, and assuming it does, whether an adequate state remedy exists when it appears that both the state and its tortfeasor are immune from suit. The initial three-judge panel of the court (*Daniels I*) held that *Parratt* extends to liberty interests, and that regardless of the presence of both sovereign and official immunity, there existed an adequate remedy for purposes of due process. *Daniels I* found that this remedy was simply the right to be heard, and not the right to a recovery. The matter was considered again by the Fourth Circuit (*Daniels II*), this time sitting en banc. *See* 748 F.2d 229 (4th Cir. 1985). *Daniels II* took a different tack than the original panel, though it reached the same result. First, it concluded that the guard was subject to suit under Virginia law. *See* Justice Steven's concurring opinion in *Davidson*. Next, the *Daniels II* court came to the somewhat startling conclusion — later adopted by the Supreme Court — that mere negligence on behalf of a state actor does not implicate a protected liberty interest under the Due Process Clause. Because it agreed with this conclusion, the Supreme Court did not decide whether the *Parratt-Hudson* doctrine extends to life and liberty.

In *Davidson*, meanwhile, the Third Circuit found that even if negligence were enough to support a Due Process claim, state law provided an adequate remedy. The court firmly rejected the argument that immunity rendered state process inadequate. Instead, it held that the remedy was adequate even if the state and its officials were wholly immune. Justice Stevens embraced this conclusion in his concurring opinion in *Davidson*. Justice Blackmun's dissent, in contrast, strongly suggests that liability is necessary to render any post-deprivation remedy adequate.

2. Why Did the Supreme Court Change its Mind? Assessing the adequacy of state remedies would have forced the Court to rule on the constitutionality of state immunity rules, an area of the law traditionally considered free of any difficulty. *See Martinez v. California*, 444 U.S. 277 (1980) (holding that California's immunity statute did not violate the Due Process Clause). Sovereign immunity has traditionally protected states, whereas state officials are often protected by official immunity. *See, e.g., Belcher v. Norton*, 497 F.3d 742 (7th Cir. 2007) (observing that the Indiana Tort Claims Act immunized government and police from liability for certain law enforcement functions). If § 1983 plaintiffs in such cases can raise a Due Process claim on the theory that no adequate state remedy exists, states would be placed under some pressure to modify

---

[29] [Editor's note: Justice Brennan wrote a separate dissent: "I agree with the Court that merely negligent conduct by a state official, even though causing personal injury, does not constitute a deprivation of liberty under the Due Process Clause. I do believe, however, that official conduct which causes personal injury due to recklessness or deliberate indifference, does deprive the victim of liberty within the meaning of the Fourteenth Amendment. As Justice Blackmun persuasively demonstrates in his dissent, the record in this case strongly suggests that the prison officials' failure to protect [Davidson] from attack was reckless and not merely negligent."]

their rules regarding sovereign and official immunity.[30] By changing its mind and overturning *Parratt*'s interpretation of the word "deprive," the Court avoided putting states to the choice of either abrogating their immunities or permitting the federalization of such claims as a matter of Due Process — at least in the context of simple negligence. The problem still remains, however, with reckless and intentional wrongdoing. *See, e.g., Belcher v. Norton*, 497 F.3d 742 (7th Cir. 2007) (holding that immunities for police officers and city meant that remedy was not adequate within meaning of *Parratt*); *McNamara v. City of Rittman*, 473 F.3d 633 (6th Cir. 2007) (holding that adequate remedy demanded by Procedural Due Process must provide compensation).

3. Limiting *Parratt* to Property. The Supreme Court did not have to partially overrule *Parratt* to avoid holding state immunity laws unconstitutional. It could have simply limited *Parratt* (and *Hudson*) to property interests, so that random and unauthorized deprivations of life and liberty would remain actionable under Procedural Due Process (regardless of the availability of state remedies). Why did the Court not take this latter approach? Would limiting *Parratt* to property deflect common torts away from the federal courts? In the following case the Justices unanimously agreed that *Parratt* extends to liberty.

ZINERMON v. BURCH
Supreme Court of the United States
494 U.S. 113 (1990)

JUSTICE BLACKMUN delivered the opinion of the Court.

[Burch was found wandering along a Florida highway, hurt and disoriented. He was taken to Apalachee Community Mental Health Services (ACMHS) in Tallahassee. ACMHS is a private mental health care facility[31] designated by the State to receive patients suffering from mental illness. The staff in their evaluation forms stated that, upon his arrival at ACMHS, Burch was hallucinating, confused and psychotic and believed he was "in heaven." His face and chest were bruised and bloodied, suggesting that he had fallen or had been attacked. Burch was asked to sign forms giving his consent to admission and treatment. He did so. He remained at ACMHS for three days, during which time the facility's staff diagnosed his condition as paranoid schizophrenia and gave him psychotropic medication. He was found "in need of longer-term stabilization," and was referred to Florida State Hospital (FSH), a public hospital owned and operated by the State as a mental health treatment facility. Later that day, Burch signed forms requesting admission and authorizing treatment at FSH. Burch remained at FSH for five months. During that time, no hearing was held regarding his hospitalization and treatment. After his release, Burch complained that he had been

---

[30] This is essentially what has happened with takings claims under the Fifth Amendment. *See* Note 2 following *Zinermon v. Burch, infra*. Rather than subject themselves to federal takings claims in federal courts, states tend to recognize inverse condemnation remedies. *See, e.g., River City Capital v. Board of County Commissioners*, 491 F.3d 301 (6th Cir. 2007) (holding that Ohio courts' recent decisions recognizing inverse condemnation remedy meant that taking was not without just compensation and thus could not be pursued in federal court under the Fifth Amendment); *McNamara v. City of Rittman*, 473 F.3d 633 (6th Cir. 2007) (holding that before change in Ohio's inverse condemnation laws, takings claims could be pursued under the Fifth Amendment in federal court).

[31] [Editor's note: The Eleventh Circuit assumed, without deciding, that ACMHS, a private hospital, was a state actor. *See Burch v. Apalachee Community Mental Health Services, Inc.*, 840 F.2d 797 (11th Cir. 1988). The Supreme Court did not address this issue. Four years later, in *Harvey v. Harvey*, 949 F.2d 1127 (11th Cir. 1992), the Eleventh Circuit held that private mental health facilities are not state actors for purposes of the Fourteenth Amendment. *See also Ellison v. Garbarino*, 48 F.3d 192 (6th Cir. 1995) (concluding that a privately owned mental health facility was not engaged in state action when it involuntarily committed a patient). For a discussion of state action theory, *see* Section B., *supra*.]

C. UNAUTHORIZED CONDUCT THAT DOES NOT VIOLATE THE CONSTITUTION   43

admitted inappropriately to FHS and did not remember signing a voluntary admission form. The Florida Human Rights Advocacy Committee of the State's Department of Health and Rehabilitation Services (Committee) investigated and found that Burch had signed a voluntary admission form, but was "heavily medicated and disoriented on admission and . . . probably not competent to be signing legal documents." Burch filed suit against ACMHS under § 1983 claiming that his "voluntary" admission should have included pre-commitment procedural safeguards.]

[T]he question before us is a narrow one. We decide only whether the *Parratt* rule necessarily means that Burch's complaint fails to allege any deprivation of due process, because he was constitutionally entitled to nothing more than what he received — an opportunity to sue petitioners in tort for his allegedly unlawful confinement. The broader questions of what procedural safeguards the Due Process Clause requires in the context of an admission to a mental hospital, and whether Florida's statutes meet these constitutional requirements, are not presented in this case.

Burch's complaint . . . alleges that he was admitted to and detained at FSH for five months under Florida's statutory provisions for "voluntary" admission. These provisions are part of a comprehensive statutory scheme under which a person may be admitted to a mental hospital in several different ways.

First, Florida provides for short-term emergency admission. If there is reason to believe that a person is mentally ill and likely "to injure himself or others" or is in "need of care or treatment and lacks sufficient capacity to make a responsible application on his own behalf," he may immediately be detained for up to 48 hours. . . . After 48 hours, the patient is to be released unless he "voluntarily gives express and informed consent to evaluation or treatment," or a proceeding for court-ordered evaluation or involuntary placement is initiated.

Second, under a court order a person may be detained at a mental health facility for up to five days for evaluation, if he is likely "to injure himself or others" or if he is in "need of care or treatment which, if not provided, may result in neglect or refusal to care for himself and . . . such neglect or refusal poses a real and present threat of substantial harm to his well-being." . . . After five days, the patient is to be released unless he gives "express and informed consent" to admission and treatment, or unless involuntary placement proceedings are initiated.

Third, a person may be detained as an involuntary patient, if he meets the same criteria as for evaluation, and if the facility administrator and two mental health professionals recommend involuntary placement. Before involuntary placement, the patient has a right to notice, a judicial hearing, appointed counsel, access to medical records and personnel, and an independent expert examination. . . . After six months, the facility must either release the patient, or seek a court order for continued placement.

Finally, a person may be admitted as a voluntary patient. Mental hospitals may admit for treatment any adult "making application by express and informed consent," if he is "found to show evidence of mental illness and to be suitable for treatment." "Express and informed consent" is defined as "consent voluntarily given in writing after sufficient explanation and disclosure . . . to enable the person . . . to make a knowing and willful decision without any element of force, fraud, deceit, duress, or other form of constraint or coercion."

Due process, as this Court often has said, is a flexible concept that varies with the particular situation. To determine what procedural protections the Constitution requires in a particular case, we weigh several factors: "First, the private interest that will be affected by the official action; second, the risk of an erroneous deprivation of such interest through the procedures used, and the probable value, if any, of additional or substitute procedural safeguards; and finally, the Government's interest, including the function involved and the fiscal and administrative burdens that the additional or substitute procedural requirement would entail." *Mathews v. Eldridge*, 424 U.S. 319 (1976).

Applying this test, the Court usually has held that the Constitution requires some kind of a hearing before the State deprives a person of liberty or property. In some circumstances, however, the Court has held that a statutory provision for a postdeprivation hearing, or a common-law tort remedy for erroneous deprivation, satisfies due process. *See, e.g., Ingraham v. Wright*, 430 U.S. 651 (1977) (hearing not required before corporal punishment of junior high school students); *Mitchell v. W.T. Grant Co.*, 416 U.S. 600 (1974) (hearing not required before issuance of writ to sequester debtor's property).

This is where the *Parratt* rule comes into play. *Parratt* and *Hudson* represent a special case of the general *Mathews v. Eldridge* analysis, in which postdeprivation tort remedies are all the process that is due, simply because they are the only remedies the State could be expected to provide.

[ACMHS] argue[s] that . . . as in *Parratt* and *Hudson*, the State could not possibly have provided predeprivation process to prevent the kind of "random, unauthorized" wrongful deprivation of liberty Burch alleges, so the postdeprivation remedies provided by Florida's statutory and common law necessarily are all the process Burch was due.[32]

Before turning to that issue, however, we must address a threshold question raised by Burch. He argues that *Parratt* and *Hudson* cannot apply to his situation, because those cases are limited to deprivations of property, not liberty.

Burch alleges that he was deprived of his liberty interest in avoiding confinement in a mental hospital without either informed consent[33] or the procedural safeguards of the involuntary placement process. . . . We, however, do not find support in precedent for a categorical distinction between a deprivation of liberty and one of property. In *Parratt* itself, the Court said that its analysis was "quite consistent with the approach taken" in *Ingraham v. Wright*, a liberty interest case.

It is true that *Parratt* and *Hudson* concerned deprivations of property. It is also true that Burch's interest in avoiding five months' confinement is of an order different from inmate Parratt's interest in mail-order materials valued at $23.50. But the reasoning of *Parratt* and *Hudson* emphasizes the State's inability to provide predeprivation process because of the random and unpredictable nature of the deprivation, not the fact that only property losses were at stake.

To determine whether, as [defendants] contend, the *Parratt* rule necessarily precludes § 1983 liability in this case, we must ask whether predeprivation procedural safeguards could address the risk of deprivations of the kind Burch alleges. To do this, we examine the risk involved. The risk is that some persons who come into Florida's mental health facilities will apparently be willing to sign forms authorizing admission and treatment, but will be incompetent to give the "express and informed consent" required for voluntary placement under [Florida law]. . . .

Persons who are mentally ill and incapable of giving informed consent to admission would not necessarily meet the statutory standard for involuntary placement, which

---

[32] [n.15] Burch does not dispute that he had remedies under Florida law for unlawful confinement. Florida's mental health statutes provide that a patient confined unlawfully may sue for damages. Also, a mental patient detained at a mental health facility, or a person acting on his behalf, may seek a writ of habeas corpus to "question the cause and legality of such detention and request . . . release." Finally, Florida recognizes the common-law tort of false imprisonment.

[33] [n.17] Of course, if Burch had been competent to consent to his admission and treatment at FSH, there would have been no deprivation of his liberty at all. The State simply would have been providing Burch with the care and treatment he requested. Burch alleges, however, that he was not competent, so his apparent willingness to sign the admission forms was legally meaningless.

C. UNAUTHORIZED CONDUCT THAT DOES NOT VIOLATE THE CONSTITUTION

requires either that they are likely to injure themselves or others, or that their neglect or refusal to care for themselves threatens their well-being. The involuntary placement process serves to guard against the confinement of a person who, though mentally ill, is harmless and can live safely outside an institution. Confinement of such a person not only violates Florida law, but also is unconstitutional. *O'Connor v. Donaldson*, 422 U.S. 563 (1975) (there is no constitutional basis for confining mentally ill persons involuntarily "if they are dangerous to no one and can live safely in freedom"). Thus, it is at least possible that if Burch had had an involuntary placement hearing, he would not have been found to meet the statutory standard for involuntary placement and would not have been confined at FSH.

We now consider whether predeprivation safeguards would have any value in guarding against the kind of deprivation Burch allegedly suffered. [ACMHS] urge[s] that here, as in *Parratt* and *Hudson*, such procedures could have no value at all, because the State cannot prevent its officials from making random and unauthorized errors in the admission process. We disagree.

The Florida statutes, of course, do not allow incompetent persons to be admitted as "voluntary" patients. But the statutes do not direct any member of the facility staff to determine whether a person is competent to give consent, nor to initiate the involuntary placement procedure for every incompetent patient. A patient who is willing to sign forms but incapable of informed consent certainly cannot be relied on to protest his "voluntary" admission and demand that the involuntary placement procedure be followed. The staff are the only persons in a position to take notice of any misuse of the voluntary admission process and to ensure that the proper procedure is followed.

Because [ACMHS] had state authority to deprive persons of liberty, the Constitution imposed on them the State's concomitant duty to see that no deprivation occur without adequate procedural protections.

It may be permissible constitutionally for a State to have a statutory scheme like Florida's, which gives state officials broad power and little guidance in admitting mental patients. But when those officials fail to provide constitutionally required procedural safeguards to a person whom they deprive of liberty, the state officials cannot then escape liability by invoking *Parratt* and *Hudson*.

This case, therefore, is not controlled by *Parratt* and *Hudson*, for three basic reasons: First, [ACMHS] cannot claim that the deprivation of Burch's liberty was unpredictable. Under Florida's statutory scheme, only a person competent to give informed consent may be admitted as a voluntary patient. There is, however, no specified way of determining, before a patient is asked to sign admission forms, whether he is competent. It is hardly unforeseeable that a person requesting treatment for mental illness might be incapable of informed consent. . . . Any erroneous deprivation will occur, if at all, at a specific, predictable point in the admission process — when a patient is given admission forms to sign.

This situation differs from the State's predicament in *Parratt*. While it could anticipate that prison employees would occasionally lose property through negligence, it certainly "cannot predict precisely when the loss will occur." Likewise, in *Hudson*, the State might be able to predict that guards occasionally will harass or persecute prisoners they dislike, but cannot "know when such deprivations will occur."

Second, we cannot say that predeprivation process was impossible here. Florida already has an established procedure for involuntary placement. The problem is only to ensure that this procedure is afforded to all patients who cannot be admitted voluntarily, both those who are unwilling and those who are unable to give consent.

Third, [ACMHS] cannot characterize [its] conduct as "unauthorized" in the sense the term is used in *Parratt* and *Hudson*. The State delegated to [it] the power and authority to effect the very deprivation complained of here, Burch's confinement in a mental hospital, and also delegated to [it] the concomitant duty to initiate the procedural safeguards set up by state law to guard against unlawful confinement. In *Parratt* and *Hudson*, the state employees had no similar broad authority to deprive prisoners of their personal property, and no similar duty to initiate (for persons unable to protect their own interests) the procedural safeguards required before deprivations occur. The deprivation here is "unauthorized" only in the sense that it was not an act sanctioned by state law, but, instead, was a "depriv[ation] of constitutional rights . . . by an official's abuse of his position." *Monroe*.[34]

Burch . . . was deprived of a substantial liberty interest without either valid consent or an involuntary placement hearing, by the very state officials charged with the power to deprive mental patients of their liberty and the duty to implement procedural safeguards. Such a deprivation is foreseeable, due to the nature of mental illness, and will occur, if at all, at a predictable point in the admission process.

JUSTICE O'CONNOR, with whom THE CHIEF JUSTICE, JUSTICE SCALIA, and JUSTICE KENNEDY join, dissenting.

Parratt v. Taylor and *Hudson v. Palmer* should govern this case. Only by disregarding the gist of Burch's complaint — that state actors' wanton and unauthorized departure from established practice worked the deprivation — and by transforming the allegations into a challenge to the adequacy of Florida's admissions procedures can the Court attempt to distinguish this case from *Parratt* and *Hudson*.

[ACMHS's] actions were unauthorized: [it is] alleged to have wrongly and without license departed from established state practices. Florida officials in a position to establish safeguards commanded that the voluntary admission process be employed only for consenting patients and that the involuntary hearing procedures be used to admit unconsenting patients. Yet it is alleged that [ACMHS] "with willful, wanton and reckless disregard of and indifference to" Burch's rights contravened both commands. As in *Parratt*, the deprivation "occurred as a result of the unauthorized failure of agents of the State to follow established state procedure." The wanton or reckless nature of the failure indicates it to be random. The State could not foresee the particular contravention and was hardly "in a position to provide for predeprivation process" to ensure that officials bent upon subverting the State's requirements would in fact follow those procedures. For this wrongful deprivation resulting from an unauthorized departure from established state practice, Florida provides adequate postdeprivation remedies, as two courts below concluded, and which the Court and [Burch] do not dispute.

The Court attempts to avert the force of *Parratt* and *Hudson* by characterizing [ACMHS's] alleged failures as only the routine but erroneous application of the admission process. . . . The Court's characterization omits [ACMHS's] alleged wrongful state of mind and thus the nature and source of the wrongful deprivation.

According to Burch, [ACMHS] "knew" him to be incompetent or w[as] presented with such clear evidence of his incompetence that [it] should be charged with such knowledge. [ACMHS] also knew that Florida law required [it] to provide an incompetent prospective patient with elaborate procedural safeguards. Far from alleging inadvertent or negligent disregard of duty, [Burch] alleges that [ACMHS] "acted with willful, wanton and reckless disregard of and indifference" to his rights by treating him without providing the hearing that Florida requires. That is, [ACMHS] did

---

[34] [n.20] Contrary to the dissent's view of *Parratt* and *Hudson*, those cases do not stand for the proposition that in every case where a deprivation is caused by an "unauthorized . . . departure from established practices," state officials can escape § 1983 liability simply because the State provides tort remedies. This reading of *Parratt* and *Hudson* detaches those cases from their proper role as special applications of the settled principles expressed in *Monroe* and *Mathews*.

C. UNAUTHORIZED CONDUCT THAT DOES NOT VIOLATE THE CONSTITUTION

not bumble or commit "errors" by taking Burch's "apparent willingness to be admitted at face value." Rather, [it] deliberately or recklessly subverted his rights and contravened state requirements.

The unauthorized and wrongful character of the departure from established state practice makes additional procedures an "impracticable" means of preventing this deprivation. . . . Additional safeguards designed to secure correct results in the usual case do not practically forestall state actors who flout the State's command and established practice.

Even indulging the Court's belief that the proffered safeguards would provide "some" benefit, *Parratt* and *Hudson* extend beyond circumstances in which procedural safeguards would have had "negligible" value. In *Parratt* and *Hudson* additional measures would conceivably have had some benefit in preventing the alleged deprivations. A practice of barring individual or unsupervised shakedown searches, a procedure of always pairing or monitoring guards, or a requirement that searches be conducted according to "an established policy" (the proposed measure rejected as unnecessary in *Hudson*) might possibly have helped to prevent the type of deprivation considered in *Hudson*. More sensible staffing practices, better training, or a more rigorous tracking procedure may have averted the deprivation at issue in *Parratt*. In those cases, like this one, the State knew the exact context in which the wrongful deprivation would occur. Yet the possibility of implementing such marginally beneficial measures, in light of the type of alleged deprivation, did not alter the analysis. The State's inability to foresee and to forestall the wrongful departure from established procedures renders additional predeprivation measures "impracticable" and not required by the dictates of due process.

NOTES

1. Deviations From Established State Procedures. Had the state law in *Zinermon* required Burch's detention, rather than loosely delegating the decision to ACMHS, the law itself would have been subject to constitutional scrutiny. *Parratt* would have been irrelevant. For example, in *Logan v. Zimmerman Brush Company*, 455 U.S. 422 (1982), the Supreme Court refused to extend *Parratt* to a situation where "the state system itself . . . destroys a complainant's property interest, by operation of law." In that case, Illinois had created an administrative mechanism for resolving employment discrimination claims, which under Illinois law qualified as intangible property. Claims were required to be filed with *and decided by* administrative officials within a specified period of time. Logan's claims were not decided by state officials within this specified time and were thus summarily dismissed. The Supreme Court concluded that *Parratt*'s limitations were not controlling because Logan was challenging a state law that required random deprivations, rather than an unauthorized decision by a government official.

2. Fifth Amendment Takings Claims Compared. The Fifth Amendment's prohibition on takings without just compensation is subject to a limitation similar to that found in *Parratt* and *Hudson*. Because the Fifth Amendment is only offended when a state denies compensation, states ordinarily must first be given an opportunity to pay before a Fifth Amendment claim matures. Only when the state denies relief, either administratively or through a judicial inverse condemnation action, does a Fifth Amendment claim arise. Put another way, the state must "authorize" the denial of compensation before a Fifth Amendment violation occurs. *See Williamson County Regional Planning Commission v. Hamilton Bank*, 473 U.S. 172 (1985) (holding that a takings claim is premature until a state court denies compensation for the taking of property); *San Remo Hotel, L.P. v. City and County of San Francisco*, 545 U.S. 323 (2005) (stating the general rule that property owners must first go to state court and use inverse condemnation before making a Fifth Amendment claim) (discussed in

Chapter 8.A., *infra*).[35] As a result, Fifth Amendment takings claims are most often deflected to state court to be decided under state law principles, like inverse condemnation. Fifth Amendment takings claims under § 1983 are thus relatively rare. The peculiar problems that arise with Fifth Amendment takings claims and § 1983 are discussed in greater detail in the notes that follow *International College of Surgeons v. City of Chicago*, 522 U.S. 156 (1997), which is excerpted in Chapter 8, *infra*.

   3. Substantive Due Process. Notwithstanding *Zinermon*, *Parratt-Hudson*'s authorization requirement has tended to steer § 1983 plaintiffs away from Procedural Due Process claims and toward Substantive Due Process, which falls outside the reach of *Parratt-Hudson*. See, e.g., *Cozzo v. Tangipahoa Parish Council-President Government*, 279 F.3d 273, 290 (5th Cir. 2002) ("We emphasize that only alleged violations of procedural due process may be negated by the *Parratt/Hudson* doctrine. Accordingly, violations of substantive due process rights do not fall within the doctrine's limitations."); *Doe v. Department of Public Safety*, 271 F.3d 38, 55 (2d Cir. 2001) ("*Parratt* does not apply to substantive due process claims because substantive due process violations are 'complete as soon as the prohibited action is taken' and therefore do not depend upon the adequacy of any pre- or post-deprivation remedies."). This is true for both the fundamental rights that occasionally have been recognized under the Due Process Clause, *see, e.g., Troxel v. Granville*, 530 U.S. 57, 66 (2000) (recognizing "the fundamental right of parents to make decisions concerning the care, custody, and control of their children"); *Roe v. Wade*, 410 U.S. 113 (1973) (holding that a woman has a fundamental liberty interest in choosing whether to bear or beget children), and for the more generic brand of "irrational" governmental decisions that have been found to violate Due Process. See, e.g., *Regents of University of Michigan v. Ewing*, 474 U.S. 214 (1985) (holding that arbitrary action in dismissing student from school violates Substantive Due Process, but finding no violation under the facts presented).

   4. Shocking Conduct. One way of proving a Substantive Due Process violation is to show that the government's conduct "shocks the conscience." *See Rochin v. California*, 342 U.S. 165 (1952) (holding that forcibly pumping a suspect's stomach in order to retrieve evidence "shocks the conscience" and thereby violates Due Process). This is not an easy showing, and most courts have rejected claims under this theory. In *Sacramento County v. Lewis*, 523 U.S. 833 (1998), for example, a young motorcycle passenger was killed in the course of a high speed chase by police. Although the driver of the motorcycle was suspected of nothing more than a traffic violation, police pursued him at speeds approaching 100 miles per hour. The victim's estate claimed that the police conduct violated Substantive Due Process because it "shocked the conscience" within the meaning of *Rochin*. The Supreme Court, in an opinion by Justice Souter, disagreed. As made clear by *Daniels* and *Davidson*, the Court explained, "liability for negligently inflicted harm is categorically beneath the threshold of constitutional due process." Conduct "at the other end of the culpability spectrum" — "conduct intended to injure in some way unjustifiable by any government interest" — is more "likely to rise to the conscience-shocking level." "Whether the point of the conscience-shocking is reached when injuries are produced with culpability falling within the middle range, following from something more than negligence but less than intentional conduct, such as recklessness or gross negligence, is a matter for closer calls." The Court continued:

> To be sure, we have expressly recognized the possibility that some official acts in this range may be actionable under the Fourteenth Amendment, and our cases have compelled recognition that such conduct is egregious enough to state a substantive due process claim in at least one instance. We held in *City of Revere v. Massachusetts Gen. Hospital*, [463 U.S. 239 (1983),] that "the due

---

   [35] *Contrast San Remo Hotel, L.P. v. City and County of San Francisco*, 545 U.S. 323 (2005) (Rehnquist, C.J., concurring) (arguing that *Williamson County*'s requirement that property owners first seek compensation in state court should be reconsidered) (discussed in Chapter 8.A., *infra*).

C. UNAUTHORIZED CONDUCT THAT DOES NOT VIOLATE THE CONSTITUTION

process rights of a [pretrial detainee] are at least as great as the Eighth Amendment protections available to a convicted prisoner." Since it may suffice for Eighth Amendment liability that prison officials were deliberately indifferent to the medical needs of their prisoners, see *Estelle v. Gamble*, it follows that such deliberately indifferent conduct must also be enough to satisfy the fault requirement for due process claims based on the medical needs of someone jailed while awaiting trial. Rules of due process are not, however, subject to mechanical application in unfamiliar territory. Deliberate indifference that shocks in one environment may not be so patently egregious in another, and our concern with preserving the constitutional proportions of substantive due process demands an exact analysis of circumstances before any abuse of power is condemned as conscience-shocking. What we have said of due process in the procedural sense is just as true here: "The phrase [due process of law] formulates a concept less rigid and more fluid than those envisaged in other specific and particular provisions of the Bill of Rights. Its application is less a matter of rule. Asserted denial is to be tested by an appraisal of the totality of facts in a given case. That which may, in one setting, constitute a denial of fundamental fairness, shocking to the universal sense of justice, may, in other circumstances, and in the light of other considerations, fall short of such denial."

[T]he police on an occasion calling for fast action have obligations that tend to tug against each other. Their duty is to restore and maintain lawful order, while not exacerbating disorder more than necessary to do their jobs. They are supposed to act decisively and to show restraint at the same moment, and their decisions have to be made "in haste, under pressure, and frequently without the luxury of a second chance." A police officer deciding whether to give chase must balance on one hand the need to stop a suspect and show that flight from the law is no way to freedom, and, on the other, the high-speed threat to everyone within stopping range, be they suspects, their passengers, other drivers, or bystanders. To recognize a substantive due process violation in these circumstances when only mid-level fault has been shown would be to forget that liability for deliberate indifference to inmate welfare rests upon the luxury enjoyed by prison officials of having time to make unhurried judgments, upon the chance for repeated reflection, largely uncomplicated by the pulls of competing obligations. When such extended opportunities to do better are teamed with protracted failure even to care, indifference is truly shocking. But when unforeseen circumstances demand an officer's instant judgment, even precipitate recklessness fails to inch close enough to harmful purpose to spark the shock that implicates "the large concerns of the governors and the governed." . . . Accordingly, we hold that high-speed chases with no intent to harm suspects physically or to worsen their legal plight do not give rise to liability under the Fourteenth Amendment, redressible by an action under § 1983.

Because of *Lewis*, high-speed-chase cases rarely result in liability, whether prosecuted under Substantive Due Process, see, e.g., *Meals v. City of Memphis*, 493 F.3d 720 (6th Cir. 2007) (finding no Substantive Due Process violation where high speed chase in violation of police policy resulted in the death of an innocent bystander), or the Fourth Amendment. See, e.g., *Scott v. Harris*, 127 S. Ct. 1769 (2007) (finding that a reasonable jury could not conclude that a high speed chase culminating in serious injury to the pursued driver was a product of excessive force) (discussed in Note 5, *infra*).

5. Fourth Amendment Limitations. The victim's estate in *Lewis* would have liked to have based its § 1983 claim on the Fourth Amendment's prohibition on excessive force. See *Graham v. Connor*, 490 U.S. 386 (1989) (holding that the use of excessive force by police in the course of making an arrest violates the Fourth Amendment).[36] Deadly force is excessive under the Fourth Amendment unless the arresting officer has probable cause to believe the suspect poses a significant threat of death or serious bodily injury to the officer or others. *See Tennessee v. Garner*, 471 U.S. 1 (1985) (holding that the shooting of unarmed fleeing felon not believed to be dangerous violates the Fourth Amendment). Fourth Amendment excessive force claims are not limited by *Parratt-Hudson*. However, the Fourth Amendment is only relevant when an arresting officer *intends* to stop, detain or arrest a suspect, and employs methods designed to achieve that result. Because the police did not intend to stop the victim in *Lewis* by causing the motorcycle to crash, their conduct was not subject to Fourth Amendment analysis. As *Lewis* makes clear, a high-speed chase is not subject to challenge under the Fourth Amendment when police did not intend to cause the crash. *Contrast Brower v. Inyo County*, 489 U.S. 593 (1989) (holding that police officers' use of a tractor-trailer to block a roadway around a blind curve was intended to cause the crash and was thus actionable under the Fourth Amendment).

Even assuming that police intentionally cause a crash, liability is far from certain. A jury must still find that the intentional use of force was excessive. And before the jury reaches the question, federal courts must insure that the reasonableness of the officer's force is truly at issue. For example, in *Harris v. Coweta County*, 433 F.3d 807 (11th Cir. 2005), the Eleventh Circuit sustained a District Court's denial of summary judgment to a police officer (Scott) accused of using excessive deadly force to stop a fleeing motorist: "Taking [the plaintiff's] view of the facts as given, the Court of Appeals concluded that . . . Scott's actions could constitute 'deadly force' . . . , and that the use of such force in this context 'would violate [the plaintiff's] constitutional right to be free from excessive force during a seizure.' " The Supreme Court (per Justice Scalia) relied heavily on videos of the high speed chase to conclude that "[t]he car chase that [the plaintiff] initiated in this case posed a substantial and immediate risk of serious physical injury to others . . . [and the] attempt to terminate the chase by forcing [the plaintiff] off the road was reasonable. . . . " It thus reversed the lower courts' conclusions that the arresting officer was not entitled to summary judgment. Justice Scalia described the video as portraying

> [Harris's] vehicle racing down narrow, two-lane roads in the dead of night at speeds that are shockingly fast. We see it swerve around more than a dozen other cars, cross the double-yellow line, and force cars traveling in both directions to their respective shoulders to avoid being hit. We see it run multiple red lights and travel for considerable periods of time in the occasional center left-turn-only lane, chased by numerous police cars forced to engage in the same hazardous maneuvers just to keep up. Far from being the cautious and controlled driver the lower court depicts, what we see on the video more closely resembles a Hollywood-style car chase of the most frightening sort, placing police officers and innocent bystanders alike at great risk of serious injury.

When opposing parties tell two different stories, one of which is blatantly contradicted by the record, so that no reasonable jury could believe it, a court should not adopt that version of the facts for purposes of ruling on a motion for summary judgment. That was the case here with regard to the factual issue whether respondent was driving in such fashion as to endanger human life. [The

---

[36] Prior to *Graham*, plaintiffs often pursued their excessive force claims against police officers under either Procedural or Substantive Due Process. *Graham* makes clear, however, that a police officer's use of force during an arrest or investigatory stop is properly analyzed under the Fourth Amendment's "objective reasonableness" standard, rather than Due Process. *See also Albright v. Oliver*, 510 U.S. 266 (1994) (holding that a claim that police and prosecutors lacked probable cause is properly analyzed under the Fourth Amendment). Only when a "seizure" falls outside the Fourth Amendment's threshold, as in *Lewis*, can Due Process be employed to measure its propriety. Arrests judged under this standard, as illustrated by *Lewis*, rarely prove invalid.

plaintiff's] version of events is so utterly discredited by the record that no reasonable jury could have believed him. The Court of Appeals should not have relied on such visible fiction; it should have viewed the facts in the light depicted by the videotape.[37]

6. *Miranda* Violations. Violations of *Miranda v. Arizona*, 384 U.S. 436 (1966), and the Fifth Amendment's privilege against self-incrimination are actionable under § 1983. However, "it is now clear that 'mere coercion does not violate the . . . Self-Incrimination Clause absent use of the compelled statements in a criminal case.' It is only once compelled incriminating statements are used in a criminal proceeding, as a plurality of six justices held in *Chavez v. Martinez*[, 538 U.S. 760 (2003)], that an accused has suffered the requisite constitutional injury for purposes of a § 1983 action." *McKinley v. City of Mansfield*, 404 F.3d 418, 431 (6th Cir. 2005). *See generally* Russell D. Covey, *Interrogation Warrants*, 26 Cardozo L. Rev. 1867 (2005) (discussing the problems that have emerged following the Supreme Court's decision in *Chavez*); Joel Flaxman, *Proximate Cause in Constitutional Torts: Holding Interrogators Liable for Fifth Amendment Violations at Trial*, 105 Mich. L. Rev. 1551 (2007).[38]

7. Cruel and Unusual Punishment. Today, a case like *Davidson* would likely be addressed under the Eighth Amendment, which protects inmates from cruel and unusual punishment, rather than Procedural Due Process. Parcel to this Eighth Amendment prohibition, inmates are entitled to a measure of medical care, *see, e.g., Estelle v. Gamble*, 429 U.S. 97 (1976) (holding that deliberate indifference to medical needs violates Eighth Amendment); *Perez v. Oakland County*, 466 F.3d 416 (6th Cir. 2006) (recognizing that inmates are entitled to medical care), as well as protection from guards and other inmates. *See, e.g., Farmer v. Brennan*, 511 U.S. 825 (1994) (holding that prison officials' "deliberate indifference" to a substantial risk of serious harm resulting from attacks or inadequate medical care violates the Eighth Amendment); *Mathews v. Crosby*, 480 F.3d 1265 (11th Cir. 2007) (holding that the Eighth Amendment protects inmates from attacks by guards). *But cf. Whitley v. Albers*, 475 U.S. 312 (1986) (holding that the Eighth Amendment is only violated by a "wanton" use of force in the context of prison uprisings). Similar rights have been extended to pre-trial detainees by virtue of the Due Process Clause, *see City of Revere v. Massachusetts General Hosp.*, 463 U.S. 239 (1983), as well as those individuals who have been civilly committed. *See Youngberg v. Romeo*, 457 U.S. 307 (1982).

8. Race and Gender Discrimination. As any student of Constitutional Law knows, there are "suspect" reasons behind governmental action that are almost always deemed unconstitutional. Race- and gender-discrimination, for example, are ordinarily impermissible under the Equal Protection Clause. *See, e.g., Johnson v. California*, 543 U.S. 499 (2005) ("We have held that *all* 'racial discrimination [by government] . . . must be analyzed by a reviewing court under strict scrutiny.' "); *United States v. Virginia*, 518 U.S. 515 (1996) ("The State must show 'at least that the [gender] classification serves

---

[37] [Editor's note: Only Justice Stevens dissented: "At the time of the ramming, apart from speeding and running two red lights, [the victim] was driving in a non-aggressive fashion (i.e., without trying to ram or run into the officers). Moreover, . . . [the police officer's] path on the open highway was largely clear. The videos introduced into evidence show little to no vehicular (or pedestrian) traffic, allegedly because of the late hour and the police blockade of the nearby intersections. Finally, [the police officer] issued absolutely no warning (e.g., over the loudspeaker or otherwise) prior to using deadly force."]

[38] Courts have found that many of the constitutionally-grounded procedural requirements in criminal cases are actionable under § 1983. *See, e.g., Gregory v. Louisville*, 444 F.3d 725 (6th Cir. 2006) (recognizing that violations of *Brady v. Maryland*, 373 U.S. 83 (1963) — requiring that prosecutors disclose exculpatory evidence — and *Stovall v. Denno*, 388 U.S. 293 (1967) — prohibiting unduly suggestive show-ups — are actionable under § 1983); *Yarris v. County of Delaware*, 465 F.3d 129 (3d Cir. 2006) (holding that suppression of evidence by prosecutors is subject to § 1983 action). *See generally* Leon Friedman, *Challenging Unjust Convictions Under § 1983*, 23 Touro L. Rev. 27, 49–51 (2007) (discussing the use of § 1983 to redress *Brady* violations and other procedural wrongs committed in the criminal arena).

important governmental objectives and that the discriminatory means employed are substantially related to the achievement of those objectives.'"); *cf. Nguyen v. Immigration and Naturalization Service*, 533 U.S. 53 (2001) (holding that federal law preferring mothers to fathers of illegitimate children born abroad passed intermediate scrutiny). Consequently, should government treat inmates or motorists differently on account of race or gender, the Fourteenth Amendment's Equal Protection Clause would likely be violated. This is true even though government officials do not violate the Fourth or Eighth Amendments. To use one common example, the use of racial profiling for traffic stops violates Equal Protection even though police otherwise have probable cause and do not violate the Fourth Amendment. *See, e.g., Gibson v. Superintendent of New Jersey Department of Law and Public Safety Division*, 411 F.3d 427 (3d Cir. 2005) ("it has long been a well-settled principle that the state may not selectively enforce the law against racial minorities"); *Carrasaca v. Pomeroy*, 313 F.3d 828 (3d Cir. 2002) ("The fact that there was no Fourth Amendment violation does not mean that one was not discriminatorily selected for enforcement of a law."). Had the suspect in *Lewis* been pursued because of his race, he would have had a valid Equal Protection claim even though the Fourth Amendment and Substantive Due Process were not violated.

9. Retaliation. Race- and gender-discrimination are sometimes labeled as impermissible "retaliations." Chasing or stopping motorists "because of" race, for example, can also be described as retaliating based on race. The same is true of discharging an employee because of gender; the charge can be described as retaliation based on sex. *See, e.g., Watkins v. Bowden*, 105 F.3d 1344 (11th Cir. 1997) ("to the extent [the § 1983 plaintiff] links her alleged retaliatory dismissal to her gender or race, that allegation constitutes part of her equal protection discrimination"). In order to make out a viable retaliation claim, the plaintiff must show purposeful discrimination on the part of the governmental actor. *See, e.g., Washington v. Davis*, 426 U.S. 229 (1976) (holding that standardized testing was not motivated by purposeful racial discrimination). Put another way, the suspect reason, whether race or gender, must be the cause of the government official's action. "Discriminatory purpose . . . implies more than an intent as volition or intent as awareness of consequences. It implies that the decisionmaker . . . selected . . . a particular course of action at least in part 'because of', not merely 'in spite of', its adverse effects upon an identifiable group." *Personnel Administrator v. Feeney*, 442 U.S. 256 (1979) (holding that veterans' preference in governmental hiring did not constitute gender discrimination). Causation is crucial to showing constitutional violations in these cases.

Retaliation claims can also arise in the First Amendment context. Cases involving speech-based discharges from public-sector employment, arrest, and punishment are common. As with retaliation based on race and gender, causation is critical to First Amendment retaliation claims. A § 1983 plaintiff must show that government discharged, arrested or punished him "because of" speech. *See, e.g., Mt. Healthy City School District Board of Education v. Doyle*, 429 U.S. 274 (1977) (holding that a § 1983 plaintiff must show that adverse governmental action was caused by the plaintiff's speech).

For a number of years, the courts assumed that retaliation claims under the First Amendment mirrored those under the Equal Protection Clause. Whether the government violated the Fourth Amendment, for example, was irrelevant to a charge under the First. The question was simply whether the plaintiff's speech caused the government's action — whether discharge from employment, arrest, or prosecution. *See, e.g., United States v. Wayte*, 470 U.S. 598 (1985) (holding that arrest and prosecution because of speech violated the First Amendment even though probable cause otherwise exists). Thus, a police officer's decision to make an arrest based on the suspect's speech was actionable under the First Amendment even though the police officer otherwise had probable cause (and thus did not violate the Fourth Amendment). However, the Supreme Court in *Hartman v. Moore*, 547 U.S. 250 (2006) (excerpted in Chapter 6.A., *infra*), ruled that in order to recover damages for retaliatory prosecution, a § 1983 plaintiff must show not only that speech caused his prosecution, but that the arresting officer lacked probable cause to bring the charges against him in the first place.[39] Because *Hartman* involved only retaliatory *prosecution* based on speech, it is not clear whether other forms of retaliation — like those based on race and gender, or retaliatory *arrests* based on speech — are affected. For further discussion of the differences between wrongful arrest and wrongful prosecution, *see Wallace v. Kato*, 127 S. Ct. 1091 (2007) (excerpted in Chapter 8.B.[3], *infra*) ("false imprisonment consists of detention without legal process [and] ends once the victim becomes held *pursuant to such process*" while "unlawful detention forms part of the damages for the 'entirely distinct' tort of malicious prosecution, which remedies detention accompanied, not by absence of legal process, but by *wrongful institution* of legal process").

10. Reflections on *Daniels* and *Davidson*. Were *Daniels* and *Davidson* correct to require more than simple negligence as a matter of Due Process? Justice Stevens, who concurred in *Daniels* and *Davidson*, disagreed that negligence falls outside the meaning of "deprivation:" "'Deprivation', it seems to me, identifies, not the actor's state of mind, but the victim's infringement or loss. . . . I would characterize each loss [in *Daniels* and *Davidson*] as a 'deprivation' of liberty." Are the reasons for requiring mens rea the same for both procedural and substantive guarantees? *See* Mark R. Brown, *De-Federalizing Common Law Torts: Empathy for* Parratt, Hudson *and* Daniels, 28 B.C. L. Rev. 813, 843–46 (1987) (arguing that the defendant's "mens rea is deemed relevant [with substantive guarantees] because normative choices are being made. Procedural due process, however, . . . focuses on when and how much, with the goal of minimizing the risk of substantive error.").

D. THE PECULIAR PROBLEM OF STATE *IN*ACTION

DESHANEY v. WINNEBAGO DEPARTMENT OF SOCIAL SERVICES
Supreme Court of the United States
489 U.S. 189 (1989)

CHIEF JUSTICE REHNQUIST delivered the opinion of the Court.

[Joshua DeShaney] is a boy who was beaten and permanently injured by his father, with whom he lived. [The defendants] are social workers and other local officials who received complaints that [Joshua] was being abused by his father and had reason to believe that this was the case, but nonetheless did not act to remove [Joshua] from his father's custody. [Joshua, through his personal representative,] sued [the social workers under § 1983] claiming that their failure to act deprived him of his liberty in violation of the Due Process Clause of the Fourteenth Amendment to the United States Constitution. We hold that it did not.

The facts of this case are undeniably tragic. Joshua DeShaney was born in 1979. In 1980, a Wyoming court granted his parents a divorce and awarded custody of Joshua to his father, Randy DeShaney. The father shortly thereafter moved to Neenah, a city located in Winnebago County, Wisconsin, taking the infant Joshua with him. There he entered into a second marriage, which also ended in divorce.

The Winnebago County authorities first learned that Joshua DeShaney might be a victim of child abuse in January 1982, when his father's second wife complained to the

---

[39] The Supreme Court further limited a public-sector employee's ability to recover for retaliation based on speech in *Garcetti v. Ceballos*, 547 U.S. 410 (2006). *Garcetti* holds that a public-sector employee's job-related speech is not protected by the First Amendment. *See* Sheldon H. Nahmod, *Public Employee Speech, Categorical Balancing and § 1983: A Critique of* Garcetti v. Ceballos, 42 U. Rich. L. Rev. 561, 561–62 (2008) ("*Garcetti* effectively conferred absolute immunity on public employers by excluding employer discipline based on job-required public employee speech from First Amendment scrutiny").

police, at the time of their divorce, that he had previously "hit the boy causing marks and [was] a prime case for child abuse." The Winnebago County Department of Social Services (DSS) interviewed the father, but he denied the accusations, and DSS did not pursue them further. In January 1983, Joshua was admitted to a local hospital with multiple bruises and abrasions. The examining physician suspected child abuse and notified DSS, which immediately obtained an order from a Wisconsin juvenile court placing Joshua in the temporary custody of the hospital. Three days later, the county . . . decided that there was insufficient evidence of child abuse to retain Joshua in the custody of the court.

Based on the recommendation of the [County], the juvenile court dismissed the child protection case and returned Joshua to the custody of his father. A month later, emergency room personnel called the DSS caseworker handling Joshua's case to report that he had once again been treated for suspicious injuries. The caseworker concluded that there was no basis for action. For the next six months, the caseworker made monthly visits to the DeShaney home, during which she observed a number of suspicious injuries on Joshua's head. . . . The caseworker dutifully recorded these incidents in her files, along with her continuing suspicions that someone in the DeShaney household was physically abusing Joshua, but she did nothing more. In November 1983, the emergency room notified DSS that Joshua had been treated once again for injuries that they believed to be caused by child abuse. On the caseworker's next two visits to the DeShaney home, she was told that Joshua was too ill to see her. Still DSS took no action.

In March 1984, Randy DeShaney beat 4-year-old Joshua so severely that he fell into a life-threatening coma. Emergency brain surgery revealed a series of hemorrhages caused by traumatic injuries to the head inflicted over a long period of time. Joshua did not die, but he suffered brain damage so severe that he is expected to spend the rest of his life confined to an institution for the profoundly retarded. Randy DeShaney was subsequently tried and convicted of child abuse.

[The argument is] that the State[40] deprived Joshua of his liberty interest in "free[dom] from . . . unjustified intrusions on personal security," see *Ingraham v. Wright*, by failing to provide him with adequate protection against his father's violence. The claim is one invoking the substantive rather than the procedural component of the Due Process Clause; [Joshua] do[es] not claim that the State denied [him] protection without according him appropriate procedural safeguards, but that it was categorically obligated to protect him in these circumstances, see *Youngberg v. Romeo*.[41]

But nothing in the language of the Due Process Clause itself requires the State to protect the life, liberty, and property of its citizens against invasion by private actors. The Clause is phrased as a limitation on the State's power to act, not as a guarantee of certain minimal levels of safety and security. It forbids the State itself to deprive individuals of life, liberty, or property without "due process of law," but its language cannot fairly be extended to impose an affirmative obligation on the State to ensure that those interests do not come to harm through other means. Nor does history support such an expansive reading of the constitutional text. Like its counterpart in the Fifth Amendment, the Due Process Clause of the Fourteenth Amendment was intended to prevent government "from abusing [its] power, or employing it as an instrument of

---

[40] [n.1] As used here, the term "State" refers generically to state and local governmental entities and their agents.

[41] [n.2] [Joshua] . . . also argues that the Wisconsin child protection statutes gave [him] an "entitlement" to receive protective services in accordance with the terms of the statute, an entitlement which would enjoy due process protection against state deprivation under our decision in *Board of Regents of State Colleges v. Roth*, 408 U.S. 564 (1972). But this argument is made for the first time in [Joshua's] brief to this Court: it was not pleaded in the complaint, argued to the Court of Appeals as a ground for reversing the District Court, or raised in the petition for certiorari. We therefore decline to consider it here.

oppression." Its purpose was to protect the people from the State, not to ensure that the State protected them from each other. The Framers were content to leave the extent of governmental obligation in the latter area to the democratic political processes.

Consistent with these principles, our cases have recognized that the Due Process Clauses generally confer no affirmative right to governmental aid, even where such aid may be necessary to secure life, liberty, or property interests of which the government itself may not deprive the individual. *See, e.g., Harris v. McRae*, 448 U.S. 297 (1980) (no obligation to fund abortions or other medical services) (discussing Due Process Clause of Fifth Amendment); *Lindsey v. Normet*, 405 U.S. 56 (1972) (no obligation to provide adequate housing) (discussing Due Process Clause of Fourteenth Amendment); *see also Youngberg v. Romeo* ("As a general matter, a State is under no constitutional duty to provide substantive services for those within its border"). . . . If the Due Process Clause does not require the State to provide its citizens with particular protective services, it follows that the State cannot be held liable under the Clause for injuries that could have been averted had it chosen to provide them.[42] As a general matter, then, we conclude that a State's failure to protect an individual against private violence simply does not constitute a violation of the Due Process Clause.

[Joshua] contend[s], however, that even if the Due Process Clause imposes no affirmative obligation on the State to provide the general public with adequate protective services, such a duty may arise out of certain "special relationships" created or assumed by the State with respect to particular individuals. [Joshua] argue[s] that such a "special relationship" existed here because the State knew that [he] faced a special danger of abuse at his father's hands, and specifically proclaimed, by word and by deed, its intention to protect him against that danger. Having actually undertaken to protect Joshua from this danger — which [Joshua] concede[s] the State played no part in creating — the State acquired an affirmative "duty," enforceable through the Due Process Clause, to do so in a reasonably competent fashion. Its failure to discharge that duty, so the argument goes, was an abuse of governmental power that so "shocks the conscience," *Rochin v. California*, 342 U.S. 165 (1952), as to constitute a substantive due process violation.[43]

[W]hen the State takes a person into its custody and holds him there against his will, the Constitution imposes upon it a corresponding duty to assume some responsibility for his safety and general well-being. The rationale for this principle is simple enough: when the State by the affirmative exercise of its power so restrains an individual's liberty that it renders him unable to care for himself, and at the same time fails to provide for his basic human needs — *e.g.*, food, clothing, shelter, medical care, and reasonable safety — it transgresses the substantive limits on state action set by the Eighth Amendment and the Due Process Clause. The affirmative duty to protect arises

---

[42] [n.3] The State may not, of course, selectively deny its protective services to certain disfavored minorities without violating the Equal Protection Clause. *See Yick Wo v. Hopkins*, 118 U.S. 356 (1886). But no such argument has been made here.

[43] [n.4] The genesis of this notion appears to lie in a statement in our opinion in *Martinez v. California*, 444 U.S. 277 (1980). In that case, we were asked to decide, *inter alia*, whether state officials could be held liable under the Due Process Clause of the Fourteenth Amendment for the death of a private citizen at the hands of a parolee. Rather than squarely confronting the question presented here — whether the Due Process Clause imposed upon the State an affirmative duty to protect — we affirmed the dismissal of the claim on the narrower ground that the causal connection between the state officials' decision to release the parolee from prison and the murder was too attenuated to establish a "deprivation" of constitutional rights within the meaning of § 1983. . . . Several of the Courts of Appeals have [held] that once the State learns that a third party poses a special danger to an identified victim, and indicates its willingness to protect the victim against that danger, a "special relationship" arises between State and victim, giving rise to an affirmative duty, enforceable through the Due Process Clause, to render adequate protection.

not from the State's knowledge of the individual's predicament or from its expressions of intent to help him, but from the limitation which it has imposed on his freedom to act on his own behalf.

Th[is proposition] . . . has no applicability in the present case. [Joshua] concede[s] that the harms [he] suffered occurred not while he was in the State's custody, but while he was in the custody of his natural father, who was in no sense a state actor.[44] While the State may have been aware of the dangers that Joshua faced in the free world, it played no part in their creation, nor did it do anything to render him any more vulnerable to them. That the State once took temporary custody of Joshua does not alter the analysis, for when it returned him to his father's custody, it placed him in no worse position than that in which he would have been had it not acted at all; the State does not become the permanent guarantor of an individual's safety by having once offered him shelter. Under these circumstances, the State had no constitutional duty to protect Joshua.

It may well be that, by voluntarily undertaking to protect Joshua against a danger it concededly played no part in creating, the State acquired a duty under state tort law to provide him with adequate protection against that danger. But the claim here is based on the Due Process Clause of the Fourteenth Amendment, which, as we have said many times, does not transform every tort committed by a state actor into a constitutional violation. A State may, through its courts and legislatures, impose such affirmative duties of care and protection upon its agents as it wishes. But not "all common-law duties owed by government actors were . . . constitutionalized by the Fourteenth Amendment." Because, as explained above, the State had no constitutional duty to protect Joshua against his father's violence, its failure to do so — though calamitous in hindsight — simply does not constitute a violation of the Due Process Clause.[45]

JUSTICE BRENNAN, with whom JUSTICE MARSHALL and JUSTICE BLACKMUN join, dissenting.

I would focus first on the action that Wisconsin has taken with respect to Joshua and children like him, rather than on the actions that the State failed to take. Such a method is not new to this Court. Both *Estelle v. Gamble* and *Youngberg v. Romeo* [, see Note 7, following *Zinermon* in Section C., *supra*,] began by emphasizing that the States had confined J.W. Gamble to prison and Nicholas Romeo to a psychiatric hospital. This initial action rendered these people helpless to help themselves or to seek help from persons unconnected to the government.

To put the point more directly, these cases signal that a State's prior actions may be decisive in analyzing the constitutional significance of its inaction. I thus would locate [Joshua's] claims within the framework of cases like *Youngberg* and *Estelle*, . . . by considering the actions that Wisconsin took with respect to Joshua.

Wisconsin has established a child-welfare system specifically designed to help children like Joshua. Wisconsin law places upon the local departments of social services such as respondent (DSS or Department) a duty to investigate reported instances of child abuse. While other governmental bodies and private persons are largely responsible for the reporting of possible cases of child abuse, Wisconsin law channels all

---

[44] [n.9] Had the State by the affirmative exercise of its power removed Joshua from free society and placed him in a foster home operated by its agents, we might have a situation sufficiently analogous to incarceration or institutionalization to give rise to an affirmative duty to protect. Indeed, several Courts of Appeals have held . . . that the State may be held liable under the Due Process Clause for failing to protect children in foster homes from mistreatment at the hands of their foster parents. We express no view on the validity of this analogy, however, as it is not before us in the present case.

[45] [n.10] Because we conclude that the Due Process Clause did not require the State to protect Joshua from his father, we need not address [the] alternative argument that the individual state actors lacked the requisite "state of mind" to make out a due process violation. *See Daniels v. Williams*.

such reports to the local departments of social services for evaluation and, if necessary, further action. . . . In this way, Wisconsin law invites — indeed, directs — citizens and other governmental entities to depend on local departments of social services such as respondent to protect children from abuse.

In these circumstances, a private citizen, or even a person working in a government agency other than DSS, would doubtless feel that her job was done as soon as she had reported her suspicions of child abuse to DSS. Through its child-welfare program, in other words, the State of Wisconsin has relieved ordinary citizens and governmental bodies other than the Department of any sense of obligation to do anything more than report their suspicions of child abuse to DSS. If DSS ignores or dismisses these suspicions, no one will step in to fill the gap. Wisconsin's child-protection program thus effectively confined Joshua DeShaney within the walls of Randy DeShaney's violent home until such time as DSS took action to remove him. Conceivably, then, children like Joshua are made worse off by the existence of this program when the persons and entities charged with carrying it out fail to do their jobs.

It simply belies reality, therefore, to contend that the State "stood by and did nothing" with respect to Joshua. Through its child-protection program, the State actively intervened in Joshua's life and, by virtue of this intervention, acquired ever more certain knowledge that Joshua was in grave danger. These circumstances, in my view, plant this case solidly within the tradition of cases like *Youngberg* and *Estelle*.

JUSTICE BLACKMUN, dissenting.

Like the antebellum judges who denied relief to fugitive slaves, the Court today claims that its decision, however harsh, is compelled by existing legal doctrine. On the contrary, the question presented by this case is an open one, and our Fourteenth Amendment precedents may be read more broadly or narrowly depending upon how one chooses to read them. Faced with the choice, I would adopt a "sympathetic" reading, one which comports with dictates of fundamental justice and recognizes that compassion need not be exiled from the province of judging.

Poor Joshua! Victim of repeated attacks by an irresponsible, bullying, cowardly, and intemperate father, and abandoned by [state officials] who placed him in a dangerous predicament and who knew or learned what was going on, and yet did essentially nothing except, as the Court revealingly observes, "dutifully recorded these incidents in [their] files." It is a sad commentary upon American life, and constitutional principles — so full of late of patriotic fervor and proud proclamations about "liberty and justice for all" — that this child, Joshua DeShaney, now is assigned to live out the remainder of his life profoundly retarded.

NOTES

1. **Public-Sector Employment.** The Supreme Court ruled in *Collins v. Harker Heights*, 503 U.S. 115 (1992), that public-sector employees do not enjoy any substantive right under the Due Process Clause to safe working environments. In that case, an employee (Collins) in a city's sanitation department died of asphyxia after entering a manhole to unstop a sewer line. His widow sued under § 1983 claiming violations of Due Process. Justice Stevens, writing for the Court, disagreed:

> We . . . are not persuaded that the city's alleged failure to train its employees, or to warn them about known risks of harm, was an omission that can properly be characterized as arbitrary, or conscience shocking, in a constitutional sense. [The] claim is analogous to a fairly typical state-law tort claim: The city breached its duty of care . . . by failing to provide a safe work environment. Because the Due Process Clause "does not purport to supplant traditional tort law in laying down rules of conduct to regulate liability for injuries that attend living together in society," we have previously rejected

claims that the Due Process Clause should be interpreted to impose federal duties that are analogous to those traditionally imposed by state tort law. The reasoning in those cases applies with special force to claims asserted against public employers because state law, rather than the Federal Constitution, generally governs the substance of the employment relationship.

The Due Process Clause "is not a guarantee against incorrect or ill-advised personnel decisions." Nor does it guarantee municipal employees a workplace that is free of unreasonable risks of harm.

Finally, we reject [the] suggestion that the Texas Hazard Communication Act supports [a] substantive due process claim. We assume that the Act imposed a duty on the city to warn its sanitation employees about the dangers of noxious gases in the sewers and to provide safety training and protective equipment to minimize those dangers. We also assume . . . that the Act created an entitlement that qualifies as a "liberty interest" protected by the Due Process Clause. But even with these assumptions, [the] claim must fail for . . . the deprivation of this liberty interest was [not] arbitrary in the constitutional sense. The reasons why the city's alleged failure to train and warn did not constitute a constitutionally arbitrary deprivation of Collins' life, apply a fortiori to the less significant liberty interest created by the Texas statute.

See also Lombardi v. Whitman, 485 F.3d 73 (2d Cir. 2007) (finding no governmental duty owed to workers who cleaned up the World Trade Center site following the September 2001 terrorist attacks) (discussed in Notes 2, 3, and 4, *infra*).

2. Substantive Due Process. In *DeShaney*, the Chief Justice noted that the Court was not addressing whether the county officials — assuming they had a duty to act — otherwise acted with sufficient culpability to be held liable under *Daniels v. Williams* and the Due Process Clause. *See* footnote 10. Justice Stevens in *Collins* likewise observed that Substantive Due Process is not violated by a breach of duty alone; state action must also be "arbitrary" or "shocking." In *Sacramento County v. Lewis*, 523 U.S. 833 (1998), where an innocent motorcycle passenger was killed in the course of a high speed chase by police, the Court, per Justice Souter, suggested that only intentional misconduct can prove so shocking as to violate Substantive Due Process. *See* Note 4 following *Zinermon v. Burch*, Section C., *supra*.

Lower courts in the wake of *Lewis* have demanded "an extremely high level of culpability" on the part of governmental wrongdoers before finding a Due Process violation. *See* Laura Oren, *Safari into the Snake Pit: The State-Created Danger Doctrine*, 13 Wm. & Mary Bill Rts J. 1139 (2005). For example, in *Lombardi v. Whitman*, 485 F.3d 73 (2d Cir. 2007), several injured workers who performed search, rescue and clean-up at the World Trade Center following the September 2001 terrorist attacks sued federal officials who allegedly lied about the work site's air quality. This deliberate indifference to the health of police officers, firefighters, and rescue personnel, the plaintiffs claimed, violated Substantive Due Process. The Second Circuit disagreed:

The plaintiffs do not allege that the defendants acted with an evil intent to harm; but they argue that the defendants' deliberate indifference shocks the conscience because the defendants made their decisions in an "unhurried" fashion with "hours, days, weeks and even months to contemplate, deliberate, discuss and decide what to do and say about the health hazards posed to thousands of people who were coming onto and working at Ground Zero."

Hurried or unhurried, the defendants were subjected to the "pull of competing obligations." The complaint concedes that the alleged wrongs to the plaintiffs were committed in aid of competing public goals that were not insubstantial. . . . The complaint thus recognizes what everyone knows: that one essential government function in the wake of disaster is to put the affected community on a normal footing, i.e., to avoid panic, keep order, restore services, repair infrastructure, and preserve the economy.

D. THE PECULIAR PROBLEM OF STATE *INACTION*

[T]he plaintiffs direct us to two recent district court decisions that found conduct to be conscience-shocking on facts that are in one case somewhat similar, and in the other, identical. In *Briscoe v. Potter*, 355 F.Supp.2d 30 (D.D.C. 2004), *aff'd*, 171 Fed. Appx. 850 (D.C. Cir. 2005), postal employees who had contracted anthrax alleged that their supervisors had falsely told them that it was safe to return to work after anthrax had been discovered at their facility. The district court held that the supervisors' conduct was conscience-shocking: the supervisors were "commendable for their dedication to getting the mail out but deplorable for not recognizing the potential human risk involved. . . . [T]hese alleged actions demonstrated a gross disregard for a dangerous situation in which 'actual deliberation [was] practical.'"

In *Benzman v. Whitman*, No. 04 Civ. 1888 (S.D.N.Y. 2006), the district court considered substantive due process claims arising from the same press releases at issue in this case. Citing *Briscoe, Benzman* held that if the reassuring statements made by EPA officials were made with knowledge of their falsehood, they were unquestionably conscience-shocking based on the nature of the EPA's mandate. . . .

[W]e need not decide whether *Briscoe* was correctly decided, because there is a salient ground for distinction: the need to process the mails at a single postal facility cannot be compared with the need to restore the residential, economic, educational and civic life of an entire community.

We disagree with th[e] reasoning in *Benzman*, which focuses too narrowly on the mission of a single agency [the Environmental Protection Agency (EPA)] without considering the other substantial government interests at stake.

If anything, the importance of the EPA's mission counsels against broad constitutional liability in this situation: the risk of such liability will tend to inhibit EPA officials in making difficult decisions about how to disseminate information to the public in an environmental emergency. Knowing that lawsuits alleging intentional misconduct could result from the disclosure of incomplete, confusingly comprehensive, or mistakenly inaccurate information, officials might default to silence in the face of the public's urgent need for information.

Can the goals of a government policy possibly outweigh a known risk of loss of life or bodily harm? The EPA and other federal agencies often must decide whether to regulate particular conduct by taking into account whether the risk to the potentially affected population will be acceptable. Such decisions require an exercise of the conscience, but such decisions cannot be deemed egregious, conscience-shocking, and "arbitrary in the constitutional sense," merely because they contemplate some likelihood of bodily harm.

Moreover, mass displacement, civil disorder and economic chaos in an urban area also can result in bodily harm and loss of life. The relative magnitude of such risks cannot be reliably computed, and they are in any event incommensurable. Accepting as we must the allegation that the defendants made the wrong decision by disclosing information they knew to be inaccurate, and that this had tragic consequences for the plaintiffs, we conclude that a poor choice made by an executive official between or among the harms risked by the available options is not conscience-shocking merely because for some persons it resulted in grave consequences that a correct decision could have avoided. . . . When great harm is likely to befall someone no matter what a government official does, the allocation of risk may be a burden on the conscience of the one who must make such decisions, but does not shock the contemporary conscience.

These principles apply notwithstanding the great service rendered by those who repaired New York, the heroism of those who entered the site when it was unstable and on fire, and the serious health consequences that are plausibly alleged in the complaint.

3. State-Created Dangers. The Chief Justice noted in *DeShaney* that had state officials placed Joshua in foster care, they might be held liable for harms inflicted on him by his foster parents. *See* footnote 9. More generally, the Chief Justice suggested that state officials might be held liable under Substantive Due Process where they either create a danger or render victims more vulnerable to harm. Lower courts have been reluctant to find these so-called "state-created" dangers. *See, e.g., Koulta v. Merciez*, 477 F.3d 442 (6th Cir. 2007) (finding no state-created danger where police instructed a drunk driver to get into his car and drive away); *Carver v. City of Cincinnati*, 474 F.3d 568 (6th Cir. 2007) (holding that police did not create a danger when they failed to treat an injured victim); *Jones v. Reynolds*, 438 F.3d 685 (6th Cir. 2006) (police created no actionable danger when they failed to prevent a drag race). In *Lombardi v. Whitman*, 485 F.3d 73 (2d Cir. 2007) (which is discussed in Note 2, *supra*), the Second Circuit observed that to the extent that New York City's rescue personnel "allege[d] that the [federal] defendants had an affirmative duty to prevent them from suffering exposure to environmental contaminants, their claims must fail. They cannot rely on the EPA's failure to instruct workers to wear particular equipment, its failure to explain the exact limitations of its knowledge of the health effects of the airborne substances that were present, or its failure to explain the limitations of its testing technologies."

The court in *Lombardi* further observed that while there was "some support" for the workers' argument that government officials' "affirmative assurances that the air in Lower Manhattan was safe to breathe" created an actionable danger, it was "dissimilar from the state created dangers recognized in our precedents;" in each of those cases, a third party's criminal behavior harmed the plaintiff after a government actor — always a law enforcement officer — enhanced or created the opportunity for the criminal act through some interaction or relationship with the wrongdoer:

> The closest analogy in other circuits' substantive due process case law — and it is not particularly close — is to cases in which statements by law enforcement officials give an individual a false sense of security as to the necessity of self-help. *See, e.g., Kennedy v. City of Ridgefield*, 439 F.3d 1055 (9th Cir. 2006) (holding that a complaint adequately alleged state created danger where plaintiff reported to police that her neighbor was a child molester and the police violated promises to patrol the neighborhood and to warn her before they talked to the neighbor).

The *Lombardi* court noted, however, that "[s]ome circuits have rejected factually similar claims, reasoning that whether or not an officer has expressed an intent to protect a plaintiff, the failure to provide such protection is not a substantive due process violation unless the plaintiff is restrained from acting on his own behalf." (Citing *Bright v. Westmoreland County*, 443 F.3d 276 (3d Cir. 2006) (holding that, because the plaintiff's freedom to defend his family was not impaired, there was no substantive due process violation where his daughter was murdered by a person whom the police previously assured plaintiff they would arrest); *Pinder v. Johnson*, 54 F.3d 1169 (4th Cir. 1995) (en banc) (rejecting due process claim where a policeman falsely assured plaintiff that her violent former paramour would be jailed overnight, because there was no "limitation imposed on her liberty"). *See generally* Erwin Chemerinsky, *The State-Created Danger Doctrine*, 23 Touro L. Rev. 1 (2007) (observing that "[v]arying circuits have adopted different formulations" for the state-created danger doctrine).

4. Causation. Assuming that government officials have a duty to protect because they have created a danger, causation remains a problem. The Chief Justice in *DeShaney* noted that in *Martinez v. California*, 444 U.S. 277 (1980), the Court refused to hold state officials responsible under the Fourteenth Amendment "for the death of a private citizen at the hands of a parolee." *See* footnote 4. The *Martinez* Court affirmed the dismissal of the victim's claim, the Chief Justice explained in *DeShaney*, "on the narrower ground that the causal connection between the state officials' decision to release the parolee from prison and the murder was too attenuated to establish a 'deprivation' of constitutional rights within the meaning of § 1983." In *Lombardi v. Whitman*, 485 F.3d 73 (2d Cir. 2007) (discussed in Notes 2 and 3, *supra*), the Second Circuit "assume[d] that a sufficient causal connection exist[ed] between the defendants' optimistic statements and the plaintiffs' exposure to toxic substances." "However," the court cautioned, "the point is fairly debatable" and would "raise[] difficult questions about causation and the reasonableness of [the workers'] reliance. . . . " *See also Bright v. Westmoreland County*, 443 F.3d 276 (3d Cir. 2006) (holding that a claim based on a state-created danger is only cognizable where "the harm ultimately caused was foreseeable and fairly direct").

5. Equal Protection. The Court in *DeShaney* noted an important exception to its holding. The Equal Protection Clause restricts unequal governmental inaction as well as unequal action. In *Yick Wo v. Hopkins*, 118 U.S. 356 (1886), the example cited by the Court, Chinese-Americans were *denied* permits needed to maintain commercial laundries. Governmental *inaction* — e.g., not granting a permit — is thus actionable under the Equal Protection Clause. Of course, the Equal Protection Clause has its own unique limitations. First and foremost, heightened scrutiny — either strict or intermediate — is reserved for suspect classes, quasi-suspect classes, and fundamental rights. *See Massachusetts Board of Retirement v. Murgia*, 427 U.S. 307, 312 (1976) ("equal protection analysis requires strict scrutiny of a legislative classification only when the classification impermissibly interferes with the exercise of a fundamental right or operates to the peculiar disadvantage of a suspect class"); *Craig v. Boren*, 429 U.S. 190, 197 (1976) ("[t]o withstand constitutional challenge, . . . classifications by gender must serve important governmental objectives and must be substantially related to achievement of those objectives"). Second, heightened scrutiny requires proof of intent to discriminate on the part of the defendant. *See Washington v. Davis*, 426 U.S. 229 (1976) (holding that "[d]isproportionate impact standing alone [does] not trigger the rule that racial classifications are to be subjected to the strictest scrutiny and are justifiable only by the weightiest of considerations," but that purposeful racial discrimination is subject to strict scrutiny); *Personnel Administrator of Massachusetts v. Feeney*, 442 U.S. 256 (1979) (holding that only purposeful discrimination against women is subject to intermediate scrutiny). Unintentional discrimination and discrimination against those who do not fall into a suspect or quasi-suspect class (or suffer an invasion of a fundamental right) are subject to review only under the more traditional rational basis test.

Historically, of course, rationality review has proved a death-knell for constitutional claims. However, in *Village of Willowbrook v. Olech*, 528 U.S. 562 (2000), the Supreme Court ruled that a plaintiff (Olech) who claimed that a Village arbitrarily required her to dedicate a 33-foot easement in order to receive municipal water, while it required only 15-foot easements from similarly situated homeowners, had made out an actionable Equal Protection claim:

> Our cases have recognized successful equal protection claims brought by a "class of one," where the plaintiff alleges that she has been intentionally treated differently from others similarly situated and that there is no rational basis for the difference in treatment. In so doing, we have explained that "[t]he purpose of the equal protection clause of the Fourteenth Amendment is to secure every person within the State's jurisdiction against intentional and arbitrary discrimination, whether occasioned by express terms of a statute or by its improper execution through duly constituted agents."

Consequently, one can argue that an arbitrary denial of services (or a failure to protect) violates the Equal Protection Clause, *see Olech*, but not the Due Process Clause. *See DeShaney*. Proving violations under this "class of one" theory, however, has proved difficult in practice. *See, e.g., Griffin Industries v. Irvin*, 496 F.3d 1189 (11th Cir. 2007) (finding no violation and stating that "[g]overnmental decisionmaking challenged under a 'class of one' equal protection theory must be evaluated in light of the full variety of factors that an objectively reasonable governmental decisionmaker would have found relevant in making the challenged decision [and] . . . when dissimilar governmental treatment is not the product of a one-dimensional decision . . . the 'similarly situated' requirement will be more difficult to establish"); *Cordi-Allen v. Conlon*, 494 F.3d 245 (1st Cir. 2007) (concluding that plaintiff had not proved a class-of-one violation).

The Supreme Court in *Engquist v. Oregon Department of Agriculture*, 128 S. Ct. 2146 (2008), rolled back *Olech*'s protections in the context of public-sector employment. There, a public employee argued that she was arbitrarily discharged in violation of Equal Protection. The Court concluded that *Olech*'s " 'class-of-one' theory of equal protection has no place in the public employment context."

6. Inaction and Procedural Due Process. Because of the Supreme Court's holding in *DeShaney* and lower courts' common rejections of Substantive Due Process claims based on governmental omissions, *see, e.g., Bright v. Westmoreland County*, 443 F.3d 276 (3d Cir. 2006) (described in Note 3, *supra*), victims of governmental nonfeasance turned back to Procedural Due Process for protection. The Court in *DeShaney*, after all, noted that it was not addressing denials of the procedural protections mandated by Procedural Due Process. *See* footnote 2. Can a governmental failure to protect a person's life, liberty or property violate Procedural Due Process? Can a person even have a procedurally protected interest in governmental protection? *See generally Board of Regents v. Roth*, 408 U.S. 564 (1972) (holding that a state-created entitlement demanded procedural protection under Due Process Clause).

TOWN OF CASTLE ROCK v. GONZALES
Supreme Court of the United States
545 U.S. 748 (2005)

JUSTICE SCALIA delivered the opinion for the Court.

[Police failed to enforce a restraining order that had been issued against the victim's (Gonzales's) estranged husband. Had police enforced this restraining order, Gonzales claimed, her husband could have been prevented from kidnapping and murdering their three children. The Tenth Circuit, sitting en banc, ruled that the restraining order created an entitlement under Colorado law deserving procedural protection. Because "the police never 'heard' nor seriously entertained [Gonzales's] request to enforce and protect her interests in the restraining order," moreover, the Tenth Circuit concluded that Gonzales properly stated a Procedural Due Process violation.]

We do not believe that . . . Colorado law truly made enforcement of restraining orders *mandatory*. A well established tradition of police discretion has long coexisted with apparently mandatory arrest statutes. . . . Against that backdrop, a true mandate of police action would require some stronger indication from the Colorado Legislature than "shall use every reasonable means to enforce a restraining order" (or even "shall arrest . . . or . . . seek a warrant"). That language is not perceptibly more mandatory than the Colorado statute which has long told municipal chiefs of police that they "shall pursue and arrest any person fleeing from justice in any part of the state" and that they "shall apprehend any person in the act of committing any offense . . . and, forthwith and without any warrant, bring such person before a . . . competent authority for examination and trial."

[Gonzales] does not specify the precise means of enforcement that the Colorado restraining-order statute assertedly mandated — whether her interest lay in having police arrest her husband, having them seek a warrant for his arrest, or having them "use every reasonable means, up to and including arrest, to enforce the order's terms." Such indeterminacy is not the hallmark of a duty that is mandatory. Nor can someone be safely deemed "entitled" to something when the identity of the alleged entitlement is vague.

The dissent, after suggesting various formulations of the entitlement in question, ultimately contends that the obligations under the statute were quite precise: either make an arrest or (if that is impractical) seek an arrest warrant. The problem with this is that the seeking of an arrest warrant would be an entitlement to nothing but procedure — which we have held inadequate even to support standing, see *Lujan v. Defenders of Wildlife*, 504 U.S. 555 (1992); much less can it be the basis for a property interest.

Even if the statute could be said to have made enforcement of restraining orders "mandatory" because of the domestic-violence context of the underlying statute, that would not necessarily mean that state law gave [Gonzales] an entitlement to *enforcement* of the mandate. Making the actions of government employees obligatory can serve various legitimate ends other than the conferral of a benefit on a specific class of people. The serving of public rather than private ends is the normal course of the criminal law because criminal acts, "besides the injury [they do] to individuals, . . . strike at the very being of society; which cannot possibly subsist, where actions of this sort are suffered to escape with impunity."

Even if we were to think otherwise concerning the creation of an entitlement by Colorado, it is by no means clear that an individual entitlement to enforcement of a restraining order could constitute a "property" interest for purposes of the Due Process Clause. Such a right would not, of course, resemble any traditional conception of property. Although that alone does not disqualify it from due process protection, as *Roth* and its progeny show, the right to have a restraining order enforced does not "have some ascertainable monetary value," as even our "*Roth*-type property-as-entitlement" cases have implicitly required. Perhaps most radically, the alleged property interest here arises *incidentally*, not out of some new species of government benefit or service, but out of a function that government actors have always performed — to wit, arresting people who they have probable cause to believe have committed a criminal offense.

The indirect nature of a benefit was fatal to the due process claim of the nursing-home residents in *O'Bannon v. Town Court Nursing Center*, 447 U.S. 773 (1980). We held that, while the withdrawal of "direct benefits" (financial payments under Medicaid for certain medical services) triggered due process protections, the same was not true for the "indirect benefit[s]" conferred on Medicaid patients when the Government enforced "minimum standards of care" for nursing-home facilities. "[A]n indirect and incidental result of the Government's enforcement action . . . does not amount to a deprivation of any interest in life, liberty, or property." In this case, as in *O'Bannon*, "[t]he simple distinction between government action that directly affects a citizen's legal rights . . . and action that is directed against a third party and affects the citizen only indirectly or incidentally, provides a sufficient answer to" [Gonzales's] reliance on cases that found government-provided services to be entitlements.

In light of today's decision and that in *DeShaney*, the benefit that a third party may receive from having someone else arrested for a crime generally does not trigger protections under the Due Process Clause, neither in its procedural nor in its "substantive" manifestations. This result reflects our continuing reluctance to treat the Fourteenth Amendment as "a font of tort law," *Parratt v. Taylor*, 451 U.S. 527, 544 (1981), but it does not mean States are powerless to provide victims with personally enforceable remedies.

JUSTICE SOUTER, with whom JUSTICE BREYER joins, concurring.

[Gonzales's] argument is unconventional because the state-law benefit for which it claims federal procedural protection is itself a variety of procedural regulation, a set of rules to be followed by officers exercising the State's executive power: use all reasonable means to enforce, arrest upon demonstrable probable cause, get a warrant, and so on. When her argument is understood as unconventional in this sense, a further reason appears for rejecting its call to apply *Roth*, a reason that would apply even if the statutory mandates to the police were absolute, leaving the police with no discretion when the beneficiary of a protective order insists upon its enforcement. The Due Process Clause extends procedural protection to guard against unfair deprivation by state officials of substantive state-law property rights or entitlements; the federal process protects the property created by state law. But Gonzales claims a property interest in a state-mandated process in and of itself. This argument is at odds with the rule that "[p]rocess is not an end in itself. Its constitutional purpose is to protect a substantive interest to which the individual has a legitimate claim of entitlement."

[I]n every instance of property recognized by this Court as calling for federal procedural protection, the property has been distinguishable from the procedural obligations imposed on state officials to protect it. Whether welfare benefits, *Goldberg v. Kelly*, 397 U.S. 254 (1970), attendance at public schools, *Goss v. Lopez*, 419 U.S. 565 (1975), utility services, *Memphis Light, Gas & Water Div. v. Craft*, 436 U.S. 1 (1978), public employment, *Perry v. Sindermann*, 408 U.S. 593 (1972), professional licenses, *Barry v. Barchi*, 443 U.S. 55 (1979), and so on, the property interest recognized in our cases has always existed apart from state procedural protection before the Court has recognized a constitutional claim to protection by federal process. To accede to Gonzales's argument would therefore work a sea change in the scope of federal due process, for she seeks federal process as a substitute simply for state process.

JUSTICE STEVENS, with whom JUSTICE GINSBURG joins, dissenting.

[T]he Court glosses over the dispositive question — whether the police enjoyed discretion to deny enforcement — and focuses on a different question — which "precise means of enforcement" were called for in this case. But that question is a red herring. The statute directs that, upon probable cause of a violation, "a peace officer shall arrest, or, if an arrest would be impractical under the circumstances, seek a warrant for the arrest of a restrained person." Regardless of whether the enforcement called for in this case was arrest or the seeking of an arrest warrant . . . , the crucial point is that, under the statute, the police were *required* to provide enforcement; *they lacked the discretion to do nothing.*

The Court suggests that the fact that "enforcement" may encompass different acts infects any entitlement to enforcement with "indeterminacy." But this objection is also unfounded. Our cases have never required the object of an entitlement to be some mechanistic, unitary thing. Suppose a State entitled every citizen whose income was under a certain level to receive health care at a state clinic. The provision of health care is not a unitary thing — doctors and administrators must decide what tests are called for and what procedures are required, and these decisions often involve difficult applications of judgment. But it could not credibly be said that a citizen lacks an entitlement to health care simply because the content of that entitlement is not the same in every given situation.

Police enforcement of a restraining order is a government service that is no less concrete and no less valuable than other government services, such as education. The relative novelty of recognizing this type of property interest is explained by the relative novelty of the domestic violence statutes creating a mandatory arrest duty; before this innovation, the unfettered discretion that characterized police enforcement defeated any citizen's "legitimate claim of entitlement" to this service. Novel or not, [Gonzales's] claim finds strong support in the principles that underlie our due process jurisprudence.

In this case, Colorado law *guaranteed* the provision of a certain service, in certain defined circumstances, to a certain class of beneficiaries, and [Gonzales] reasonably relied on that guarantee. . . . Surely, if [Gonzales] had contracted with a private security firm to provide her and her daughters with protection from her husband, it would be apparent that she possessed a property interest in such a contract. Here, Colorado undertook a comparable obligation, and [Gonzales] — with restraining order in hand — justifiably relied on that undertaking. . . . The fact that it is based on a statutory enactment and a judicial order entered for her special protection, rather than on a formal contract, does not provide a principled basis for refusing to consider it "property" worthy of constitutional protection.

NOTES

1. Property Interests in Police Protection. Lower courts following *Castle Rock* have been hesitant to find enforceable property interests (entitlements) in police protection, regardless of the wording of a state's statute. *See, e.g., Hudson v. Hudson*, 475 F.3d 741 (6th Cir. 2007) ("We share the Supreme Court's skepticism in *Castle Rock* that this type of entitlement could ever "constitute a 'property' interest for purposes of the Due Process Clause."); *Howard ex rel. Estate of Howard v. Bayes*, 457 F.3d 568 (6th Cir. 2006) (refusing to find entitlement in domestic violence law authorizing restraining orders). Is this interpretation of *Castle Rock* correct? *See* Alexandra Natapoff, *Underenforcement*, 75 FORDHAM L. REV. 1715 (2006) ("Together, *DeShaney* and *Gonzales* stand for the proposition that the Constitution does not mandate police protection. Even court orders and legislative enactments that call for police protection in specific instances will not give rise to constitutionally protected interests."); Note, *The Supreme Court, 2004 Term: Scope of Procedural Due Process Protection — Property Interests in Public Enforcement*, 119 HARV. L. REV. 208 (2005) (observing that "[a] particularly troubling aspect of *Castle Rock* is its strong suggestion that a state could never create a property interest in police protection from third-party harm," but arguing that this suggestion is not consistent with the Court's prior entitlement cases).

2. Governmental Failures to Protect Entitlements. What if the majority in *Castle Rock* agreed with Justice Stevens and found a protected entitlement? Would government's failure to enforce or protect the entitlement be actionable? Is Procedural Due Process different from Substantive Due Process in this regard? Or does *DeShaney* indicate that government has no duty to protect procedurally-protected rights either? Professor Erwin Chemerinsky has argued that "*Castle Rock* must be understood together with *DeShaney* as rejecting a constitutional duty to provide protection except in circumstances where the government literally creates the danger. It doesn't matter whether the claim is labeled substantive or procedural due process, the Court is unwilling to impose a constitutional duty on the government." Erwin Chemerinsky, *The End of an Era*, 8 GREENBAG 345 (2005). *See also* John C.P. Goldberg, *The Constitutional Status of Tort Law: Due Process and the Right to a Law for the Redress of Wrongs*, 115 YALE L.J. 524 (2005) ("*DeShaney* has been — and presumably *Castle Rock* now will be — treated as emblematic of a broader idea that the rights enjoyed under the Federal Constitution are negative, not affirmative."). Assuming that government has some sort of duty to enforce a police-protection entitlement, what process is required? Must government hold a hearing before deciding not to enforce the entitlement? Must it simply try to enforce the entitlement? Or must it succeed in enforcing the entitlement? *See* Martin Schwartz, *Section 1983 Cases in the October 2004 Term*, 21 TOURO L. REV. 763 (2006) ("What Jessica Gonzales presumably actually wanted was enforcement of the domestic abuse restraining order. She did want process but wanted the police to take action to protect her. The idea that her procedural due process rights were violated is a claim that does not seem to fit the factual context.").

3. "Bitter with the Sweet" Compared. Justice Souter claims in his concurring opinion in *Castle Rock* that there is a difference between constitutionally protected entitlements and a state's required process: "[I]n every instance of property recognized by this Court as calling for federal procedural protection, the property has been distinguishable from the procedural obligations imposed on state officials to protect it." Is this true? At one time the Supreme Court toyed with the idea that a state's required procedures are inseparable from substantive property interests. *See Arnette v. Kennedy*, 416 U.S. 134 (1974). In then-Justice Rehnquist's words, property owners must accept the "bitter with the sweet"; whatever else a property interest entails, it also includes the procedures created by the state to protect it. Is there tension between Justice Souter's claim and Justice Rehnquist's holding in *Arnette*? The Supreme Court eventually rejected Justice Rehnquist's "bitter with the sweet" approach to entitlements in *Cleveland Board of Education v. Loudermill*, 470 U.S. 532 (1985) ("The categories of substance and procedure are distinct. . . . 'Property' cannot be defined by the procedures provided for its deprivation any more than can life or liberty."). It is therefore clear today that although government defines the substance of property, the Constitution establishes the required procedural protections.

E. ADDITIONAL CONSTITUTIONAL AND STATUTORY VIOLATIONS

GOLDEN STATE TRANSIT CORP. v. CITY OF LOS ANGELES
Supreme Court of the United States
493 U.S. 103 (1989)

JUSTICE STEVENS delivered the opinion of the Court.

In *Golden State Transit Corp. v. Los Angeles*, 475 U.S. 608 (1986) (*Golden State I*), we held that [Los Angeles] had violated federal law by conditioning the renewal of [Golden State's] taxicab franchise on settlement of a pending labor dispute between [Golden State] and its union. On remand, the District Court enjoined the city to reinstate the franchise but concluded that 42 U.S.C. § 1983 did not authorize an award of compensatory damages. . . . We granted certiorari limited to the question whether the NLRA granted petitioner rights enforceable under § 1983.

Section 1983 provides a federal remedy for "the deprivation of any rights, privileges, or immunities secured by the Constitution and laws." As the language of the statute plainly indicates, the remedy encompasses violations of federal statutory as well as constitutional rights.

A determination that § 1983 is available to remedy a statutory or constitutional violation involves a two-step inquiry. First, the plaintiff must assert the violation of a federal right. Section 1983 speaks in terms of "rights, privileges, or immunities," not violations of federal law. In deciding whether a federal right has been violated, we have considered whether the provision in question creates obligations binding on the governmental unit or rather "does no more than express a congressional preference for certain kinds of treatment." The interest the plaintiff asserts must not be "too vague and amorphous" to be "beyond the competence of the judiciary to enforce." We have also asked whether the provision in question was "intend[ed] to benefit" the putative plaintiff.

Second, even when the plaintiff has asserted a federal right, the defendant may show that Congress "specifically foreclosed a remedy under § 1983," by providing a "comprehensive enforcement mechanis[m] for protection of a federal right." The availability of administrative mechanisms to protect the plaintiff's interests is not necessarily sufficient to demonstrate that Congress intended to foreclose a § 1983 remedy. Rather, the statutory framework must be such that "[a]llowing a plaintiff" to bring a § 1983 action "would be inconsistent with Congress' carefully tailored scheme." The burden to demonstrate that Congress has expressly withdrawn the remedy is on the defendant.

[T]he Supremacy Clause, of its own force, does not create rights enforceable under § 1983. . . . "[T]hat clause is not a source of any federal rights"; it " 'secure[s]' federal rights by according them priority whenever they come in conflict with state law." Given the variety of situations in which preemption claims may be asserted, in state court and in federal court, it would obviously be incorrect to assume that a federal right of action pursuant to § 1983 exists every time a federal rule of law pre-empts state regulatory

E. ADDITIONAL CONSTITUTIONAL AND STATUTORY VIOLATIONS

authority. Conversely, the fact that a federal statute has preempted certain state action does not preclude the possibility that the same federal statute may create a federal right for which § 1983 provides a remedy.

In all cases, the availability of the § 1983 remedy turns on whether the statute, by its terms or as interpreted, creates obligations "sufficiently specific and definite" to be within "the competence of the judiciary to enforce," is intended to benefit the putative plaintiff, and is not foreclosed "by express provision or other specific evidence from the statute itself."

The nub of the controversy between the parties is whether the NLRA creates "rights" in labor and management that are protected against governmental interference. The city does not argue, nor could it, that a § 1983 action is precluded by the existence of a comprehensive enforcement scheme. Although the National Labor Relations Board (NLRB or Board) has exclusive jurisdiction to prevent and remedy unfair labor practices by employers and unions, it has no authority to address conduct protected by the NLRA against governmental interference. There is thus no comprehensive enforcement scheme for preventing state interference with federally protected labor rights that would foreclose the § 1983 remedy. Nor can there be any substantial question that our holding in *Golden State I* that the city's conduct was preempted was within the competence of the judiciary to enforce. Rather, the city argues that it cannot be held liable under § 1983 because its conduct did not violate any rights secured by the NLRA. On the basis of our previous cases, we reject this argument. We agree with [Golden State] that it is the intended beneficiary of a statutory scheme that prevents governmental interference with the collective-bargaining process and that the NLRA gives it rights enforceable against governmental interference in an action under § 1983.

In the NLRA, Congress has not just "occupied the field" with legislation that is passed solely with the interests of the general public in mind. In such circumstances, when congressional pre-emption benefits particular parties only as an incident of the federal scheme of regulation, a private damages remedy under § 1983 may not be available. The NLRA, however, creates rights in labor and management both against one another and against the State. By its terms, the Act confers certain rights "generally on employees and not merely as against the employer." We have thus stated that "[i]f the state law regulates conduct that is actually protected by federal law, . . . pre-emption follows . . . as a matter of substantive right."

The rights protected against state interference, moreover, are not limited to those explicitly set forth in § 7 as protected against private interference. "The NLRA . . . has long been understood to protect a range of conduct against state but not private interference." And, contrary to the city's contention, " '[r]esort to economic weapons should more peaceful measures not avail' is the right of the employer as well as the employee."

The city's contrary argument, that the NLRA does not secure rights against the State because the duties of the State are not expressly set forth in the text of the statute, is not persuasive. We have held, based on the language, structure, and history of the NLRA, that the Act protects certain rights of labor and management against governmental interference. While it is true that th[is] rule . . . is not set forth in the specific text of an enumerated section of the NLRA, that might well also be said with respect to any number of rights or obligations that we have found implicit in a statute's language. A rule of law that is the product of judicial interpretation of a vague, ambiguous, or incomplete statutory provision is no less binding than a rule that is based on the plain meaning of a statute. The violation of a federal right that has been found to be implicit in a statute's language and structure is as much a "direct violation" of a right as is the violation of a right that is clearly set forth in the text of the statute.

As we held in *Golden State I*, [Los Angeles's] refusal to renew [Golden State's] franchise violated [its] right to use permissible economic tactics to withstand the strike. . . . [T]he case does not come within any recognized exception from the broad remedial scope of § 1983. . . ."

JUSTICE KENNEDY, with whom THE CHIEF JUSTICE and JUSTICE O'CONNOR join, dissenting.

The majority concludes that 42 U.S.C. § 1983 requires the city of Los Angeles to pay compensatory damages to Golden State Transit Corp. for violating the company's right under the National Labor Relations Act (NLRA), to employ economic weapons in collective bargaining without state interference.

From the earliest cases interpreting our constitutional law to the most recent ones, we have acknowledged that a private party can assert an immunity from state or local regulation on the ground that the Constitution or a federal statute, or both, allocate the power to enact the regulation to the National Government, to the exclusion of the States. A litigant has standing to contend that proper allocation of power requires a particular outcome in a dispute, and this is so whether the dispute is between individual parties, or the dispute involves a State or its subdivisions. The injured party does not need § 1983 to vest in him a right to assert that an attempted exercise of jurisdiction or control violates the proper distribution of powers within the federal system.

I submit that the Court should not interpret § 1983 to give a cause of action for damages when the only wrong committed by the State or its local entities is misapprehending the precise location of the boundaries between state and federal power.

The NLRA creates two relations which encompass different legal interests. The statute creates the first relation between Golden State and the striking union. The statute establishes duties that Golden State and the union have to each other and, as correlatives of these duties, rights that they have against each other. Under the NLRA, for example, each has a duty to bargain in good faith and, as correlatives of these duties, each has a right to have the other bargain in good faith.

The NLRA also creates a jural relation between the city and Golden State. Although the NLRA does not provide in any detailed way how a city should act when renewing an operating franchise, the statute does have a pre-emptive effect under the Supremacy Clause.

The city's lack of power gives rise to a correlative legal interest in Golden State that we did not discuss in *Golden State I*. The majority has chosen to call the interest a right. I would prefer to follow the familiar Hohfeldian terminology and say that Golden State has an immunity from the city's interference with the NLRA. *See* Hohfeld, Some Fundamental Legal Conceptions as Applied in Judicial Reasoning, 23 YALE L.J. 16, 55–58 (1913) (defining the correlative of no power as an immunity).

The preceding analysis shows that Golden State has an immunity that arose out of a relation created by the NLRA. Unlike the majority, however, I do not think that the NLRA secures this immunity. . . . Section 1983 uses the word "secure" to mean "protect" or "make certain," in the sense of securing to "any person, any individual rights." *Carter v. Greenhow*, 114 U.S. 317 (1885). The section thus distinguishes secured rights, privileges, and immunities from those interests merely resulting from the allocation of power between the State and Federal Governments.

Our cases in recent years have expanded the scope of § 1983 beyond that contemplated by the sponsor of the statute and have identified interests secured by various statutory provisions as well. *See, e.g., Wright v. Roanoke Redevelopment and Housing Authority*, 479 U.S. 418 (1987) (right to particular calculation of rent in public housing secured by the Brooke Amendment to the United States Housing Act of 1937); *Maine v. Thiboutot*, 448 U.S. 1 (1980) (right to benefits secured by the Social Security Act). None of these secured statutory interests, however, has been the sole result of a statute's pre-emptive effect, as has Golden State's immunity from the city's interference.

Golden State's immunity . . . has nothing to do with the substance of the requirement imposed on its collective bargaining. The immunity, for instance, would not prevent the United States from exercising its power under the Commerce Clause to authorize the actions taken by the city. The immunity, rather, permits the company to object only that the wrong sovereign has attempted to regulate its labor relations. Golden State's immunity does not benefit the company as an individual, but instead results from the Supremacy Clause's separate protection of the federal structure and from the division of power in the constitutional system. Federal law, as such, does not secure this immunity to Golden State within the meaning of § 1983.

NOTES

1. **The National Labor Relations Act.** The Supreme Court noted in *Golden State II* that the city "did not, and could not, violate the NLRA, or Section 8(d) specifically, since it was not a party to the collective bargaining agreement between Golden State and its [union]. . . . " "Section 8(d) of the NLRA does not create rights and obligations with respect to third parties who are not parties to a collective bargaining agreement but who, in some way, come in contact with the collective bargaining process. Rather, Section 8(d) defines the concept of collective bargaining and the obligations of the parties engaged in collective bargaining, and, in the language at issue in this case, states that the failure to make a concession during collective bargaining negotiations is not an unfair labor practice."

2. **Structural Constitutional Violations.** As made clear by *Golden State* II, structural constitutional provisions — those that separate powers between the national government and states — are actionable under § 1983. *See also Dennis v. Higgins*, 498 U.S. 439 (1991) (holding that claims under the Dormant Commerce Clause can be brought under § 1983); *Brooks v. Vassar*, 462 F.3d 341 (4th Cir. 2006) (same). Although the *Golden State II* Court was careful to emphasize that § 1983 claims do not flow directly from the Supremacy Clause, the preemptive effect of properly enacted federal statutes can be prosecuted under § 1983. The question is one of legislative intent: Did Congress intend to create individual rights or immunities under the preempting statute that can be enforced under § 1983? Factors to be considered include "whether the provision in question creates obligations binding on the governmental unit"; whether the asserted interest is "too vague and amorphous" to be judicially enforced; whether the provision was intended to benefit the plaintiff; and whether Congress "specifically foreclosed a remedy under § 1983" by providing an alternative enforcement mechanism.

Justice Kennedy's dissent in *Golden State II* relied in part on *Carter v. Greenhow*, 114 U.S. 317 (1884), which held that Article I's Contracts Clause — which can be viewed as a structural limitation on state government — was not actionable under § 1983. Subsequent developments in the law of sovereign immunity and § 1983, in particular the Court's decision in *Dennis v. Higgins*, 498 U.S. 439 (1991) (which noted that *Carter* must be given a "narrow reading"), have undermined the *Carter* Court's holding. Most lower courts today have concluded (or assumed) that the Contracts Clause is actionable under § 1983. *See, e.g., Southern California Gas Co. v. City of Santa Ana*, 336 F.3d 885 (9th Cir. 2003) (stating that "[t]he Supreme Court has explicitly given *Carter* a narrow reading"); *Smith v. City of Enid*, 149 F.3d 1151 (10th Cir. 1998); *Heart of America Grain Inspection Serv., Inc. v. Missouri Dep't of Agriculture*, 123 F.3d 1098 (8th Cir. 1997).

3. **Federal Statutory Violations.** Using an analysis similar to that employed in *Golden State II*, the Supreme Court has ruled that federal statutory violations by state and local officials can be redressed through § 1983. The seminal case in this regard is *Maine v. Thiboutot*, 448 U.S. 1 (1980), which relied on § 1983's reference to rights "secured by the Constitution *and laws*" in holding that Maine's Commissioner of

Human Services was subject to suit under § 1983 for violating the federal Social Security Act. In the twenty-plus years since *Thiboutot*, however, the Supreme Court has created two exceptions that make it difficult to prosecute federal statutory violations under § 1983. First, in *Pennhurst State School & Hospital v. Halderman*, 415 U.S. 1 (1981), the Court held that the statute at issue must have been intended to create individually enforceable rights. Second, in *Middlesex County Sewage Authority v. National Sea Clammers*, 453 U.S. 1 (1981), the Court found that where "the remedial devices provided in a particular act are sufficiently comprehensive, they may suffice to demonstrate congressional intent to preclude the remedy of suits under § 1983."

Applying this analysis, the Supreme Court in *City of Rancho Palos Verdes v. Abrams*, 544 U.S. 113 (2005), unanimously ruled that violations of the federal Communications Act of 1934, 47 U.S.C. § 332(c)(7), are not actionable under § 1983. The Court, in an opinion authored by Justice Scalia, observed that statutory rights can be enforced through § 1983 only if the plaintiff can "demonstrate that the federal statute creates an individually enforceable right in the class of beneficiaries to which he belongs," and then only if Congress intended "that remedy for [the] newly created right." Regarding the latter requirement, Justice Scalia explained that "evidence of such congressional intent may be found directly in the statute creating the right, or inferred from the statute's creation of a 'comprehensive enforcement scheme that is incompatible with individual enforcement under § 1983.'" (Justice Scalia, however, rejected the argument that "the availability of a private judicial remedy is not merely indicative of, but conclusively establishes, a congressional intent to preclude § 1983 relief.") Because the Communications Act of 1934 (as amended by the Telecommunications Act of 1996) expressly provided for expedited judicial review, Justice Scalia reasoned, Congress could not have intended § 1983 as an additional remedial vehicle. This was true even though the Communications Act's judicial review provision did not authorize damages, attorney's fees or even costs.

See also Smith v. Robinson, 468 U.S. 992 (1984) (holding that the federal Education of the Handicapped Act (EHA) cannot be remedied under § 1983); *Suter v. Artist M.*, 503 U.S. 347 (1992) (holding that the federal Adoption Assistance and Child Welfare Act of 1980 cannot be redressed under § 1983); *Blessing v. Freestone*, 520 U.S. 329 (1997) (holding that a state's compliance with Title IV-D of the federal Social Security Act cannot be challenged under § 1983); *Gonzaga University v. Doe*, 536 U.S. 273 (2002) (concluding that the Family Educational Rights and Privacy Act of 1974 confers no rights enforceable under § 1983). *Contrast Wright v. Roanoke Redevelopment and Housing Authority*, 479 U.S. 418 (1987) (holding that federal rent control legislation was subject to challenge under § 1983).

4. Replacing § 1983's Remedy for Constitutional Violations. Does the logic of federal statutory cases like *Rancho Palos Verdes* apply to *constitutional* violations that would otherwise be subject to suit under § 1983? Generally speaking, state action that violates the terms of both a federal statute and the Constitution is actionable under both the offended federal statute and § 1983. Courts have been hesitant to hold that remedies for federal statutory violations replace § 1983's remedy for a corresponding constitutional violation. Thus, a public-sector employer who purposely discharges an employee because of race is subject to suit under both Title VII's remedial mechanism (for the statutory wrong) and § 1983 (for the Equal Protection violation). Although § 1983 cannot be used to redress the Title VII violation, *see, e.g., Irby v. Sullivan*, 737 F.2d 1418 (5th Cir. 1984) (holding that Title VII offers the exclusive remedy for violations of rights created by Title VII), it can be used to remedy the separate constitutional wrong. *See, e.g., Jackson v. State Bd. of Alabama State Tenure Commission*, 405 F.3d 1276 (11th Cir. 2005) (recognizing racial discrimination claims under both § 1983 and Title VII).

The Supreme Court in *Smith v. Robinson*, 468 U.S. 922 (1984), however, concluded that the relief available under the federal Education of the Handicapped Act (EHA)

E. ADDITIONAL CONSTITUTIONAL AND STATUTORY VIOLATIONS

replaced not only § 1983's remedies for EHA violations, but also § 1983's remedies for violations of the Equal Protection Clause. Because the constitutional protections in that case were minimal — disability, after all, is not a protected class under the Equal Protection Clause — the statutory remedies mandated by the EHA seemed sufficient. But what if a suspect or quasi-suspect class were at stake? And what if the statutory protections fell short of the constitutional relief provided under § 1983? Title IX, for example, prohibits purposeful discrimination on account of gender (a quasi-suspect class) by educational institutions — including state actors — that accept federal funds. Its substance thus overlaps that of the Equal Protection Clause. Still, important remedial differences exist between Title IX and § 1983. *See generally* Michael A. Zwibelman, Comment, *Why Title IX Does Not Preclude Section 1983 Claims*, 65 U. CHI. L. REV. 1465 (1998). Whether Title IX applies to officials — as opposed to their institutional employers — is not clear. *Id.* Hence, a public-school teacher who discriminates on account of gender is susceptible to a § 1983 claim, but might not be amenable to suit under Title IX. *See, e.g., Boulahanis v. Board of Regents*, 198 F.3d 633 (7th Cir. 1999) (holding that Title IX is exclusive and does not provide actions against individual wrongdoers). Title IX's standard for institutional liability, moreover, may be more demanding than that under § 1983. *See* Chapter 4, *infra*. Given differences like these, should the relief available under Title IX replace that available under § 1983 for purposeful gender-based discrimination?

The Supreme Court in the immediate aftermath of *Rancho Palos Verdes* vacated and remanded for reconsideration a Sixth Circuit ruling that had invalidated under the Equal Protection Clause (and § 1983) Michigan's decision to schedule girls' athletic events during less desirable "off" seasons. *Michigan High School Athletic Association v. Communities for Equity*, 377 F.3d 504 (6th Cir. 2004), *vacated*, 544 U.S. 1012 (2005). Citing to *Smith v. Robinson*, Michigan authorities argued in their petition for certiorari that Title IX was meant to trump gender-based claims brought under § 1983. On remand, the Sixth Circuit (over one dissent) ruled that Title IX's remedies are not exclusive of constitutional claims under § 1983. *See Communities for Equity v. Michigan High School Athletic Association*, 459 F.3d 676 (6th Cir. 2006). Though a split in the Circuits exists on this issue, the Supreme Court denied review. *See* 127 S. Ct. 1912 (2007).

5. Implied Statutory Causes of Action. A related line of authority addresses whether federal statutes that fail to include remedial mechanisms can be read to *imply* private causes of action — i.e., suits brought directly under the federal statutes themselves rather than § 1983. The high-water mark for judicially implied private causes of action was *J.I. Case Co. v. Borak*, 377 U.S. 426 (1964), where the Court held that a private party could sue another private party under § 14(a) of the Securities Exchange Act of 1934. Courts have likewise implied direct statutory causes of action against public officials. Private remedies, for example, have been implied under Title IX. *See Davis v. Monroe County Board of Education*, 526 U.S. 629 (1999) (holding that educational institutions are liable under Title IX for deliberate indifference to sexual harassment); *Franklin v. Gwinnett County Public Schools*, 503 U.S. 60 (1992) (holding that damage remedy under Title IX is available for victim of gender discrimination by public school); *Cannon v. University of Chicago*, 441 U.S. 677 (1979) (holding that Title IX was intended to create a private cause of action on behalf of the victims of gender discrimination by private school). Similarly, Title VI, which prohibits racial discrimination by institutions receiving federal funding, creates an implied private cause of action on behalf of the victims of purposeful racial discrimination. *See Alexander v. Sandoval*, 532 U.S. 275 (2001) (recognizing an implied right of action under Title VI for purposeful discrimination).

The Supreme Court, however, has been more careful in recent years about implying remedies under federal statutes. *Cort v. Ash*, 422 U.S. 66 (1975), is an oft-cited example. There the Court developed a four-part analysis to decide whether remedies ought to be implied. *Cort*'s four factors, which include looking to whether the federal statute was enacted to benefit a special class, congressional intent, and concerns over federalism, are similar to those announced in *Golden State II*. As has proven the case with remedying federal statutory violations through § 1983, it is quite difficult today to imply private remedies and causes of action directly through federal statutes. In *Alexander v. Sandoval*, 532 U.S. 275 (2001), for example, the Court refused to recognize an implied private cause of action to enforce Title VI's prohibition of *de facto* (as opposed to purposeful) discrimination.

Once an implied statutory cause of action has been found to exist, courts commonly hold that § 1983 cannot be used to enforce the substantive prohibitions or duties found in the federal statute. Consequently, § 1983 is not available to redress statutory violations under Titles VI or IX; rather, those statutes' implied remedies are exclusive. What if the Court refuses to imply a remedy under a federal statute? Can § 1983 then be used to enforce the statute's substantive standards? In *Alexander v. Sandoval*, 532 U.S. 275 (2001), the Court left this question unanswered.

6. Implied Constitutional Causes of Action. Because § 1983 speaks to violations by persons acting "under color of any statute, ordinance, regulation, custom, or usage of any State or Territory or the District of Columbia," it does not address the wrongs of federally employed agents. The Supreme Court, for its part, has implied direct damage actions against federal officials under certain circumstances. The seminal case is *Bivens v. Six Unknown Named Agents of Federal Bureau of Narcotics*, 403 U.S. 388 (1971), which implied a direct constitutional cause of action against federal agents under the Fourth Amendment. The Court has not proven willing, however, to imply direct causes of action for each and every constitutional violation. While additional implied actions have been created to redress denials of Equal Protection, *see, e.g., Davis v. Passman*, 442 U.S. 228 (1979), and the Eighth Amendment's ban on cruel and unusual punishment, *see, e.g., Carlson v. Green*, 446 U.S. 14 (1980), the Court has relied on the existence of alternative remedies provided by Congress, or other "special factors counseling hesitation in the absence of affirmative action by Congress," in refusing to recognize implied actions for violations of Procedural Due Process, both in the context of federal employment, *see, e.g., Bush v. Lucas*, 462 U.S. 367 (1983), and federal benefits. *See, e.g., Schweiker v. Chilicky*, 487 U.S. 412 (1988). More recently, the Court has refused to imply any constitutional causes of action against federal agencies, *see FDIC v. Meyer*, 510 U.S. 471 (1994), and private organizations engaged in federal governmental action. *See Correctional Services Corp. v. Malesko*, 534 U.S. 61 (2001) (holding that a private prison acting under color of federal law is not subject to *Bivens*-type suit).

Wilkie v. Robbins, 127 S. Ct. 2588 (2007), demonstrates the Court's modern reluctance to imply damage actions directly under the Constitution. The plaintiff (Robbins) in *Wilkie* claimed that federal officials retaliated against him through a campaign of harassment and intimidation after he asserted property rights he had acquired in a ranch. The campaign commenced when Robbins refused to re-grant an easement to the federal government that federal officials had inadvertently failed to record. Robbins brought a direct, implied constitutional action (a *Bivens* action) under the Fifth Amendment against the offending officials. The Supreme Court, per Justice Souter, ruled that Robbins did not make out a proper implied constitutional claim for damages. First, Justice Souter questioned whether Robbins alleged a proper Fifth Amendment retaliation claim: "the claim against the [federal] Bureau's employees fails to fit the prior retaliation cases." "[T]rying to induce someone to grant an easement for public use is a perfectly legitimate purpose: as a landowner, the Government may have, and in this instance does have, a valid interest in getting access to neighboring lands. . . . Robbins's challenge, therefore, is not to the object the Government seeks to achieve, and for the most part his argument is not that the means the Government used were necessarily illegitimate; rather, he says that defendants simply demanded too much and went too far." Second, Justice Souter concluded that "Robbins has an administrative, and ultimately a judicial, process for vindicating virtually all of his complaints." Given these alternative remedies, Robbins could not claim a *Bivens* action even assuming a Fifth Amendment violation. In the end, Justice Souter concluded that that "any damages remedy for actions by Government employees who push too hard for the Government's benefit may come better, if at all, through legislation. 'Congress is in a far better position than a court to evaluate the impact of a new species of litigation' against those who act on the public's behalf. And Congress can tailor any remedy to the problem perceived, thus lessening the risk of raising a tide of suits threatening legitimate initiative on the part of the Government's employees." Only Justices Ginsburg and Stevens dissented.

When an implied constitutional cause of action is recognized, the problems that emerge tend to overlap those that arise under § 1983. Still, the student is well-advised to remember that *Bivens*-type claims against federal officials are distinct from those brought against state and local officials under § 1983. A *Bivens* plaintiff faces many of the same obstacles presented in a § 1983 case, e.g., qualified and absolute immunities (discussed in Chapter 2, *infra*), but does not necessarily enjoy the same benefits, e.g., shifted attorney's fees under 42 U.S.C. § 1988(b) (discussed in Chapter 9, *infra*).

Because of the many limitations that envelope § 1983, such as the prohibition on suing states and state officials in their official capacities, *see* Chapter 3, *infra*, and limitations on local liability, *see* Chapter 4, *infra*, "direct" constitutional claims might also prove a useful supplement to § 1983 causes of action. Still, "most courts have held that one cannot sue state and local officials for violation of the constitution of its own force[; o]ne must state a claim under § 1983." *Freedom Baptist Church of Delaware County v. Township of Middletown*, 204 F. Supp. 2d 857 (E.D. Pa. 2002). Although the Supreme Court has not specifically addressed the matter, it appears today that § 1983 provides the only federal, civil remedial mechanism — other than habeas corpus — for vindicating constitutional violations by state and local officials, as well as their institutional employers. Thus, there exists no *Bivens* damage remedy for constitutional violations by state agents.

Chapter 2
OFFICIAL IMMUNITIES

A. ABSOLUTE IMMUNITY

[1] Legislative Immunity

BOGAN v. SCOTT-HARRIS
Supreme Court of the United States
523 U.S. 44 (1998)

JUSTICE THOMAS delivered the opinion of the Court.

It is well established that federal, state, and regional legislators are entitled to absolute immunity from civil liability for their legislative activities. In this case, petitioners argue that they, as local officials performing legislative functions, are entitled to the same protection. They further argue that their acts of introducing, voting for, and signing an ordinance eliminating the government office held by respondent constituted legislative activities. We agree on both counts and therefore reverse the judgment below.

I

Respondent Janet Scott-Harris was administrator of the Department of Health and Human Services (DHHS) for the city of Fall River, Massachusetts, from 1987 to 1991. In 1990, respondent received a complaint that Dorothy Biltcliffe, an employee serving temporarily under her supervision, had made repeated racial and ethnic slurs about her colleagues. After respondent prepared termination charges against Biltcliffe, Biltcliffe used her political connections to press her case with several state and local officials, including petitioner Marilyn Roderick, the vice president of the Fall River City Council. The city council held a hearing on the charges against Biltcliffe and ultimately accepted a settlement proposal under which Biltcliffe would be suspended without pay for 60 days. Petitioner Daniel Bogan, the mayor of Fall River, thereafter substantially reduced the punishment.

While the charges against Biltcliffe were pending, Mayor Bogan prepared his budget proposal for the 1992 fiscal year. Anticipating a 5 to 10 percent reduction in state aid, Bogan proposed freezing the salaries of all municipal employees and eliminating 135 city positions. As part of this package, Bogan called for the elimination of DHHS, of which respondent was the sole employee. The City Council Ordinance Committee, which was chaired by Roderick, approved an ordinance eliminating DHHS. The city council thereafter adopted the ordinance by a vote of 6 to 2, with petitioner Roderick among those voting in favor. Bogan signed the ordinance into law.

Respondent then filed suit under . . . 42 U.S.C. § 1983, against the city, Bogan, Roderick, and several other city officials. She alleged that the elimination of her position was motivated by racial animus and a desire to retaliate against her for exercising her First Amendment rights in filing the complaint against Biltcliffe. . . .

The jury returned a verdict in favor of all defendants on the racial discrimination charge, but found the city, Bogan, and Roderick liable on respondent's First Amendment claim, concluding that respondent's constitutionally protected speech was a substantial or motivating factor in the elimination of her position. . . .

The United States Court of Appeals for the First Circuit set aside the verdict against the city but affirmed the judgments against Roderick and Bogan.[1] Although the court concluded that petitioners have "absolute immunity from civil liability for damages arising out of their performance of legitimate legislative activities," it held that their challenged conduct was not "legislative." Relying on the jury's finding that "constitutionally sheltered speech was a substantial or motivating factor" underlying petitioners' conduct, the court reasoned that the conduct was administrative, rather than legislative, because Roderick and Bogan "relied on facts relating to a particular individual [respondent] in the decision-making calculus." . . .

II

The principle that legislators are absolutely immune from liability for their legislative activities has long been recognized in Anglo-American law. This privilege "has taproots in the Parliamentary struggles of the Sixteenth and Seventeenth Centuries" and was "taken as a matter of course by those who severed the Colonies from the Crown and founded our Nation." *Tenney v. Brandhove*, 341 U.S. 367, 372 (1951). The Federal Constitution, the constitutions of many of the newly independent States, and the common law thus protected legislators from liability for their legislative activities.

Recognizing this venerable tradition, we have held that state and regional legislators are entitled to absolute immunity from liability under § 1983 for their legislative activities. *See Tenney v. Brandhove, supra* (state legislators); *Lake Country Estates, Inc. v. Tahoe Regional Planning Agency*, 440 U.S. 391 (1979) (regional legislators); *see also Kilbourn v. Thompson*, 103 U.S. 168, 202–204 (1881) (interpreting the federal Speech and Debate Clause, U.S. Const., Art. I, § 6, to provide similar immunity to Members of Congress). We explained that legislators were entitled to absolute immunity from suit at common law and that Congress did not intend the general language of § 1983 to "impinge on a tradition so well grounded in history and reason." *Tenney v. Brandhove, supra*, at 376. Because the common law accorded local legislators the same absolute immunity it accorded legislators at other levels of government, and because the rationales for such immunity are fully applicable to local legislators, we now hold that local legislators are likewise absolutely immune from suit under § 1983 for their legislative activities.

The common law at the time § 1983 was enacted deemed local legislators to be absolutely immune from suit for their legislative activities. New York's highest court, for example, held that municipal aldermen were immune from suit for their discretionary decisions. *Wilson v. New York*, 1 Denio 595 (N.Y. 1845). The court explained that when a local legislator exercises discretionary powers, he "is exempt from all responsibility by action for the motives which influence him, and the manner in which such duties are performed. If corrupt, he may be impeached or indicted, but the law will not tolerate an action to redress the individual wrong which may have been done." These principles, according to the court, were "too familiar and well settled to require illustration or authority."

Shortly after § 1983 was enacted, the Mississippi Supreme Court reached a similar conclusion, holding that town aldermen could not be held liable under state law for their role in the adoption of an allegedly unlawful ordinance. *Jones v. Loving*, 55 Miss. 109 (1877). The court explained that "it certainly cannot be argued that the motives of the individual members of a legislative assembly, in voting for a particular law, can be inquired into, and its supporters be made personally liable, upon an allegation that they acted maliciously towards the person aggrieved by the passage of the law." The court

---

[1] [n.2] The court held that the city was not liable because the jury could reasonably infer unlawful intent only as to two of the city council members, and municipal liability could not rest "on so frail a foundation." [Municipal liability is discussed in detail in Chapter 4, *infra*.]

thus concluded that "whenever the officers of a municipal corporation are vested with legislative powers, they hold and exercise them for the public good, and are clothed with all the immunities of government, and are exempt from all liability for their mistaken use." . . .

Even the authorities cited by respondent are consistent with the view that local legislators were absolutely immune for their legislative, as distinct from ministerial, duties. In the few cases in which liability did attach, the courts emphasized that the defendant officials lacked discretion, and the duties were thus ministerial. Respondent's heavy reliance on our decision in *Amy v. Supervisors*, 78 U.S. 136 (1871), is misguided for this very reason. In that case, we held that local legislators could be held liable for violating a court order to levy a tax sufficient to pay a judgment, but only because the court order had created a ministerial duty. *Id.* at 138 ("The rule is well settled that where the law requires absolutely a ministerial act to be done by a public officer, and he neglects or refuses to do such act, he may be compelled to respond in damages to the extent of the injury arising from his conduct"). . . .

Absolute immunity for local legislators under § 1983 finds support not only in history, but also in reason. The rationales for according absolute immunity to federal, state, and regional legislators apply with equal force to local legislators. Regardless of the level of government, the exercise of legislative discretion should not be inhibited by judicial interference or distorted by the fear of personal liability. *See Spallone v. United States*, 493 U.S. 265, 279 (1990) (noting, in the context of addressing local legislative action, that "any restriction on a legislator's freedom undermines the 'public good' by interfering with the rights of the people to representation in the democratic process"). Furthermore, the time and energy required to defend against a lawsuit are of particular concern at the local level, where the part-time citizen-legislator remains commonplace. *See Tenney v. Brandhove*, *supra*, at 377 (citing "the cost and inconvenience and distractions of a trial"). And the threat of liability may significantly deter service in local government, where prestige and pecuniary rewards may pale in comparison to the threat of civil liability.

Moreover, certain deterrents to legislative abuse may be greater at the local level than at other levels of government. Municipalities themselves can be held liable for constitutional violations, whereas States and the Federal Government are often protected by sovereign immunity. And, of course, the ultimate check on legislative abuse — the electoral process — applies with equal force at the local level, where legislators are often more closely responsible to the electorate. *Cf. Tenney*, *supra*, at 378 (stating that "self-discipline and the voters must be the ultimate reliance for discouraging or correcting such abuses").

Any argument that the rationale for absolute immunity does not extend to local legislators is implicitly foreclosed by our opinion in *Lake Country Estates*. There, we held that members of an interstate regional planning agency were entitled to absolute legislative immunity. Bereft of any historical antecedent to the regional agency, we relied almost exclusively on *Tenney*'s description of the purposes of legislative immunity and the importance of such immunity in advancing the "public good." Although we expressly noted that local legislators were not at issue in that case, we considered the regional legislators at issue to be the functional equivalents of local legislators, noting that the regional agency was "comparable to a county or municipality" and that the function of the regional agency, regulation of land use, was "traditionally a function performed by local governments." Thus, we now make explicit what was implicit in our precedents: Local legislators are entitled to absolute immunity from § 1983 liability for their legislative activities.

III

Absolute legislative immunity attaches to all actions taken "in the sphere of legitimate legislative activity." *Tenney*, *supra*, at 376. The Court of Appeals held that petitioners' conduct in this case was not legislative because their actions were specifically targeted at respondent. Relying on the jury's finding that respondent's constitutionally protected speech was a substantial or motivating factor behind petitioners' conduct, the court concluded that petitioners necessarily "relied on facts relating to a particular individual" and "devised an ordinance that targeted [respondent] and treated her differently from other managers employed by the City." Although the Court of Appeals did not suggest that intent or motive can overcome an immunity defense for activities that are, in fact, legislative, the court erroneously relied on petitioners' subjective intent in resolving the logically prior question of whether their acts were legislative.

Whether an act is legislative turns on the nature of the act, rather than on the motive or intent of the official performing it. The privilege of absolute immunity "would be of little value if [legislators] could be subjected to the cost and inconvenience and distractions of a trial upon a conclusion of the pleader, or to the hazard of a judgment against them based upon a jury's speculation as to motives." *Tenney*, 341 U.S. at 377. Furthermore, it simply is "not consonant with our scheme of government for a court to inquire into the motives of legislators." *Ibid.* We therefore held that the defendant in *Tenney* had acted in a legislative capacity even though he allegedly singled out the plaintiff for investigation in order "to intimidate and silence plaintiff and deter and prevent him from effectively exercising his constitutional rights."

This leaves us with the question whether, stripped of all considerations of intent and motive, petitioners' actions were legislative. We have little trouble concluding that they were. Most evidently, petitioner Roderick's acts of voting for an ordinance were, in form, quintessentially legislative. Petitioner Bogan's introduction of a budget and signing into law an ordinance also were formally legislative, even though he was an executive official. We have recognized that officials outside the legislative branch are entitled to legislative immunity when they perform legislative functions; Bogan's actions were legislative because they were integral steps in the legislative process.

Respondent, however, asks us to look beyond petitioners' formal actions to consider whether the ordinance was legislative in substance. We need not determine whether the formally legislative character of petitioners' actions is alone sufficient to entitle petitioners to legislative immunity, because here the ordinance, in substance, bore all the hallmarks of traditional legislation. The ordinance reflected a discretionary, policymaking decision implicating the budgetary priorities of the city and the services the city provides to its constituents. Moreover, it involved the termination of a position, which, unlike the hiring or firing of a particular employee, may have prospective implications that reach well beyond the particular occupant of the office. And the city council, in eliminating DHHS, certainly governed "in a field where legislators traditionally have power to act." *Tenney, supra,* at 379. Thus, petitioners' activities were undoubtedly legislative. . . .

NOTES

1. Evaluating the Doctrine of Legislative Immunity. The first Supreme Court opinion to recognize that some state officials enjoy absolute immunity from section 1983 suits was *Tenney v. Brandhove*, 341 U.S. 367 (1951), which conferred absolute immunity on state legislators. Unlike qualified immunity, which is discussed in Section B, *infra*, absolute immunity protects defendants even when they act unreasonably or in bad faith.

The Court reached its decision in *Tenney* despite section 1983's unqualified language — creating a cause of action against "[e]very person" acting under color of state law who violates the Constitution — and despite legislative history suggesting that "[t]he very purpose of § 1983 was . . . to protect the people from unconstitutional action under state law, 'whether that action be executive, legislative or judicial.' " *Mitchum v. Foster*, 407 U.S. 225, 242 (1972) (quoting *Ex parte Virginia*, 100 U.S. 339, 346 (1879)).

Although the doctrine of official immunities is now firmly entrenched in the Court's section 1983 jurisprudence, the immunity decisions have been criticized on the ground that they "use . . . history as a mask for . . . policymaking" and ignore "a strong counter-history," which suggests that the Reconstruction-era Congress intended section 1983 to be "a great break from the past" and assumed that it would apply to all state officials. Richard A. Matasar, *Personal Immunities Under Section 1983: The Limits of the Court's Historical Analysis*, 40 ARK. L. REV. 741, 744, 794, 780 (1987).

Note that legislative immunity, like the other absolute and qualified immunity doctrines described in this Chapter, applies only to government officials who are sued in their individual capacities. Thus, these immunity defenses are not available to governmental entities or to government officials sued in their official capacities. *See, e.g., Board of County Commissioners v. Umbehr*, 518 U.S. 668, 676 n.* (1996). *See also Owen v. City of Independence*, excerpted in Chapter 4.B., *infra*, which holds that cities are not entitled to raise an immunity defense in section 1983 cases. For a detailed discussion of the distinction between official-capacity and individual-capacity suits, *see* Note 4 following *Quern v. Jordan* in Chapter 3.C., *infra*.

2. The Functional Approach to Legislative Immunity. The Court has adopted a functional approach to absolute immunity in section 1983 cases, pursuant to which "immunity is justified and defined by the *functions* it protects and serves, not by the person to whom it attaches." *Forrester v. White*, 484 U.S. 219, 227 (1988). As applied to legislative immunity, *Bogan* notes, the functional approach immunizes defendants if they were "acting in the sphere of legitimate legislative activity." *Tenney v. Brandhove*, 341 U.S. 367, 376 (1951). *See also Gravel v. United States*, 408 U.S. 606, 625 (1972) (limiting protection afforded Members of Congress under the Speech or Debate Clause to "integral part[s] of the deliberative and communicative processes by which Members participate in committee and House proceedings with respect to the consideration and passage or rejection of proposed legislation or with respect to other matters which the Constitution places within the jurisdiction of either House"); *United States v. Brewster*, 408 U.S. 501, 512 (1972) (distinguishing between "legislative" activities covered by the Speech or Debate Clause and unprotected "political" activities).

Applying this functional approach, the Court concluded in *Supreme Court of Virginia v. Consumers Union*, 446 U.S. 719 (1980), that state supreme court justices were entitled to absolute legislative immunity because they were acting in a legislative capacity when they promulgated a code of ethical conduct governing attorneys. Likewise, as indicated in *Bogan*, the Court has extended legislative immunity to the unelected members of a regional planning agency created by California and Nevada, and charged with the task of adopting and enforcing a regional land use and conservation plan for the Lake Tahoe area. *See Lake Country Estates, Inc. v. Tahoe Regional Planning Agency*, 440 U.S. 391 (1979).

In *Forrester v. White*, 484 U.S. 219, 224 (1988), however, the Court suggested in dictum that a legislator "would not be entitled to absolute immunity, in a sex-discrimination suit filed by a personal aide whom he had fired, unless such immunity was afforded by the Speech or Debate Clause." Such personnel decisions are purely administrative, the Court noted. *See Forrester*, 484 U.S. at 229. *Cf. Fields v. Office of Eddie Bernice Johnson*, 459 F.3d 1 (D.C. Cir. 2006) (en banc) (holding that the Speech or Debate Clause did not bar congressional aide from bringing employment discrimination claim against the office of her former employer under the Congressional Accountability Act, 2 U.S.C. § 1301, because the suit did not call for evaluation of either legislative motives or conduct integral to the legislative process), *cert. dismissed sub nom. Office of Senator Mark Dayton v. Hanson*, 127 S. Ct. 2018 (2007); *Bastien v. Office of Senator Ben Nighthorse*, 390 F.3d 1301, 1318 (10th Cir. 2004) (ruling that the Speech or Debate Clause did not foreclose age discrimination claim filed under the Congressional Accountability Act because "[a] personnel decision is not a 'legislative act,'" and the case did not require that "legislative acts . . . be proved to establish the claim").

Similarly, the Supreme Court has concluded in several opinions involving Members of Congress that the Speech or Debate Clause does not protect the public distribution of legislative materials. *See Hutchinson v. Proxmire*, 443 U.S. 111, 130 (1979) (issuance of newsletters and press releases); *Doe v. McMillan*, 412 U.S. 306, 314-15 (1973) (public dissemination of committee report); *see also Bastien*, 390 F.3d at 1316 ("No Supreme Court opinion indicates that Speech or Debate Clause immunity extends to informal information gathering by individual members of Congress.").

3. Injunctive Actions. The Court made clear in *Supreme Court of Virginia v. Consumers Union*, 446 U.S. 719 (1980), that legislators enjoy absolute immunity not only from damages suits, but also from injunctive actions. Analogizing legislative immunity in section 1983 suits to the Speech or Debate Clause protection afforded Members of Congress, the Court reasoned that "'a private civil action, whether for an injunction or damages, creates a distraction and forces [legislators] to divert their time, energy, and attention from their legislative tasks to defend the litigation.'" *Consumers Union*, 446 U.S. at 732 (quoting *Eastland v. United States Servicemen's Fund*, 421 U.S. 491, 503 (1975)); *see also United States v. Rayburn Office Building*, 497 F.3d 654, 660, 662 (D.C. Cir. 2007) (concluding that the Speech or Debate Clause was violated when a search warrant was executed on the office of a Member of Congress suspected of bribery, explaining that "the legislative process is disrupted by the disclosure of legislative material, regardless of the use to which the disclosed materials are put," and the unprecedented search "denied the Congressman any opportunity to identify and assert the privilege" before the seized materials were "disclos[ed] to Executive agents"), *cert. denied*, 128 S. Ct. 1738 (2008).

4. Derivative Legislative Immunity. Interpreting the Speech or Debate Clause, the Supreme Court held in *Gravel v. United States*, 408 U.S. 606, 618 (1972), that congressional aides are also protected by absolute immunity "insofar as [their] conduct . . . would be a protected legislative act if performed by the Member himself." The Court explained that "it is literally impossible . . . for Members of Congress to perform their legislative tasks without the help of aides and assistants" and "the day-to-day work of such aides is so critical to the Members' performance that they must be treated as the latter's alter ego." *Gravel*, 408 U.S. at 616–17. Following the Supreme Court's functional approach to immunity, the federal courts have extended derivative immunity to state legislative aides sued under section 1983. *See, e.g., Romero-Barcelo v. Hernandez-Agosto*, 75 F.3d 23, 31-32 (1st Cir. 1996).

[2] Judicial Immunity

STUMP v. SPARKMAN
Supreme Court of the United States
435 U.S. 349 (1978)

Mr. Justice White delivered the opinion of the Court.

This case requires us to consider the scope of a judge's immunity from damages liability when sued under 42 U.S.C. § 1983.

I

The relevant facts underlying respondents' suit are not in dispute. On July 9, 1971, Ora Spitler McFarlin, the mother of respondent Linda Kay Spitler Sparkman, presented to Judge Harold D. Stump of the Circuit Court of DeKalb County, Ind., a document captioned "Petition To Have Tubal Ligation Performed On Minor and Indemnity Agreement." The document had been drafted by her attorney, a petitioner here. In this petition Mrs. McFarlin stated under oath that her daughter was 15 years of age and was "somewhat retarded," although she attended public school and had been promoted each year with her class. The petition further stated that Linda had been associating with "older youth or young men" and had stayed out overnight with them on several occasions. As a result of this behavior and Linda's mental capabilities, it was stated that it would be in the daughter's best interest if she underwent a tubal ligation in order "to prevent unfortunate circumstances. . . . " In the same document Mrs. McFarlin also undertook to indemnify and hold harmless Dr. John Hines, who was to perform the operation, and the DeKalb Memorial Hospital, where the operation was to take place, against all causes of action that might arise as a result of the performance of the tubal ligation.

The petition was approved by Judge Stump on the same day. . . .

On July 15, 1971, Linda Spitler entered the DeKalb Memorial Hospital, having been told that she was to have her appendix removed. The following day a tubal ligation was performed upon her. She was released several days later, unaware of the true nature of her surgery.

Approximately two years after the operation, Linda Spitler was married to respondent Leo Sparkman. Her inability to become pregnant led her to discover that she had been sterilized during the 1971 operation. As a result of this revelation, the Sparkmans filed suit in the United States District Court for the Northern District of Indiana against Mrs. McFarlin, her attorney, Judge Stump, the doctors who had performed and assisted in the tubal ligation, and the DeKalb Memorial Hospital. Respondents sought damages for the alleged violation of Linda Sparkman's constitutional rights. . . .

II

The governing principle of law is well established and is not questioned by the parties. As early as 1872, the Court recognized that it was "a general principle of the highest importance to the proper administration of justice that a judicial officer, in exercising the authority vested in him, [should] be free to act upon his own convictions, without apprehension of personal consequences to himself." *Bradley v. Fisher*, [13 Wall. 335, 347 (1872)].[2] For that reason the Court held that "judges of courts of superior or general jurisdiction are not liable to civil actions for their judicial acts, even when such acts are in excess of their jurisdiction, and are alleged to have been done maliciously or corruptly."[3] Later we held that this doctrine of judicial immunity was applicable in suits

---

[2] [n.5] Even earlier, in *Randall v. Brigham*, 7 Wall. 523 (1869), the Court stated that judges are not responsible "to private parties in civil actions for their judicial acts, however injurious may be those acts, and however much they may deserve condemnation, unless perhaps where the acts are palpably in excess of the jurisdiction of the judges, and are done maliciously or corruptly." In *Bradley* the Court reconsidered that earlier statement and concluded that "the qualifying words used were not necessary to a correct statement of the law. . . . "

[3] [n.6] In holding that a judge was immune for his judicial acts, even when such acts were performed in excess of his jurisdiction, the Court in *Bradley* stated:

> "A distinction must be here observed between excess of jurisdiction and the clear absence of all jurisdiction over the subject-matter. Where there is clearly no jurisdiction over the subject-matter any authority exercised is a usurped authority, and for the exercise of such authority, when the want of jurisdiction is known to the judge, no excuse is permissible. But where jurisdiction over the subject-matter is invested by law in the judge, or in the court which he holds, the manner and extent in which the jurisdiction shall be exercised are generally as much questions for his determination as any other questions involved in the case, although upon the correctness of his determination in these particulars the validity of his judgments may depend."

under . . . § 1983, for the legislative record gave no indication that Congress intended to abolish this long-established principle. *Pierson v. Ray*, 386 U.S. 547 (1967).

The Court of Appeals correctly recognized that the necessary inquiry in determining whether a defendant judge is immune from suit is whether at the time he took the challenged action he had jurisdiction over the subject matter before him. Because "some of the most difficult and embarrassing questions which a judicial officer is called upon to consider and determine relate to his jurisdiction . . . ," *Bradley, supra*, at 352, the scope of the judge's jurisdiction must be construed broadly where the issue is the immunity of the judge. A judge will not be deprived of immunity because the action he took was in error, was done maliciously, or was in excess of his authority; rather, he will be subject to liability only when he has acted in the "clear absence of all jurisdiction."**4**

We cannot agree that there was a "clear absence of all jurisdiction" in the DeKalb County Circuit Court to consider the petition presented by Mrs. McFarlin. As an Indiana Circuit Court Judge, Judge Stump had "original exclusive jurisdiction in all cases at law and in equity whatsoever . . . ;" jurisdiction over the settlement of estates and over guardianships, appellate jurisdiction as conferred by law, and jurisdiction over "all other causes, matters and proceedings where exclusive jurisdiction thereof is not conferred by law upon some other court, board or officer." Ind. Code § 33-4-4-3 (1975). This is indeed a broad jurisdictional grant; yet the Court of Appeals concluded that Judge Stump did not have jurisdiction over the petition authorizing Linda Sparkman's sterilization.

In so doing, the Court of Appeals noted that the Indiana statutes provided for the sterilization of institutionalized persons under certain circumstances, *see* Ind. Code §§ 16-13-13-1 through 16-13-13-4 (1973), but otherwise contained no express authority for judicial approval of tubal ligations. It is true that the statutory grant of general jurisdiction to the Indiana circuit courts does not itemize types of cases those courts may hear and hence does not expressly mention sterilization petitions presented by the parents of a minor. But in our view, it is more significant that there was no Indiana statute and no case law in 1971 prohibiting a circuit court, a court of general jurisdiction, from considering a petition of the type presented to Judge Stump. The statutory authority for the sterilization of institutionalized persons in the custody of the State does not warrant the inference that a court of general jurisdiction has no power to act on a petition for sterilization of a minor in the custody of her parents, particularly where the parents have authority under the Indiana statutes to "consent to and contract for medical or hospital care or treatment of [the minor] including surgery." Ind. Code § 16-8-4-2 (1973). . . .

The Court of Appeals also concluded that support for Judge Stump's actions could not be found in the common law of Indiana, relying in particular on the Indiana Court of Appeals' intervening decision in *A.L. v. G.R.H.*, 163 Ind. App. 636, 325 N.E.2d 501 (1975). In that case the Indiana court held that a parent does not have a common-law right to have a minor child sterilized, even though the parent might "sincerely believe the child's adulthood would benefit therefrom." The opinion, however, speaks only of the rights of the parents to consent to the sterilization of their child and does not question the jurisdiction of a circuit judge who is presented with such a petition from a parent. Although under that case a circuit judge would err as a matter of law if he were to approve a parent's petition seeking the sterilization of a child, the opinion in *A.L. v. G.R.H.* does not indicate that a circuit judge is without jurisdiction to entertain the

---

4 [n.7] In *Bradley*, the Court illustrated the distinction between lack of jurisdiction and excess of jurisdiction with the following examples: if a probate judge, with jurisdiction over only wills and estates, should try a criminal case, he would be acting in the clear absence of jurisdiction and would not be immune from liability for his action; on the other hand, if a judge of a criminal court should convict a defendant of a nonexistent crime, he would merely be acting in excess of his jurisdiction and would be immune.

petition. Indeed, the clear implication of the opinion is that, when presented with such a petition, the circuit judge should deny it on its merits rather than dismiss it for lack of jurisdiction.

Perhaps realizing the broad scope of Judge Stump's jurisdiction, the Court of Appeals stated that, even if the action taken by him was not foreclosed under the Indiana statutory scheme, it would still be "an illegitimate exercise of his common law power because of his failure to comply with elementary principles of procedural due process." This misconceives the doctrine of judicial immunity. A judge is absolutely immune from liability for his judicial acts even if his exercise of authority is flawed by the commission of grave procedural errors. The Court made this point clear in *Bradley*, where it stated: "[T]his erroneous manner in which [the court's] jurisdiction was exercised, however it may have affected the validity of the act, did not make the act any less a judicial act; nor did it render the defendant liable to answer in damages for it at the suit of the plaintiff, as though the court had proceeded without having any jurisdiction whatever. . . . "

We conclude that the Court of Appeals, employing an unduly restrictive view of the scope of Judge Stump's jurisdiction, erred in holding that he was not entitled to judicial immunity. Because the court over which Judge Stump presides is one of general jurisdiction, neither the procedural errors he may have committed nor the lack of a specific statute authorizing his approval of the petition in question rendered him liable in damages for the consequences of his actions.

The respondents argue that even if Judge Stump had jurisdiction to consider the petition presented to him by Mrs. McFarlin, he is still not entitled to judicial immunity because his approval of the petition did not constitute a "judicial" act. It is only for acts performed in his "judicial" capacity that a judge is absolutely immune, they say. We do not disagree with this statement of the law, but we cannot characterize the approval of the petition as a nonjudicial act.

Respondents themselves stated in their pleadings before the District Court that Judge Stump was "clothed with the authority of the state" at the time that he approved the petition and that "he was acting as a county circuit court judge." They nevertheless now argue that Judge Stump's approval of the petition was not a judicial act because the petition was not given a docket number, was not placed on file with the clerk's office, and was approved in an *ex parte* proceeding without notice to the minor, without a hearing, and without the appointment of a guardian *ad litem*.

This Court has not had occasion to consider, for purposes of the judicial immunity doctrine, the necessary attributes of a judicial act; but it has previously rejected the argument, somewhat similar to the one raised here, that the lack of formality involved in the Illinois Supreme Court's consideration of a petitioner's application for admission to the state bar prevented it from being a "judicial proceeding" and from presenting a case or controversy that could be reviewed by this Court. *In re Summers*, 325 U.S. 561 (1945). Of particular significance to the present case, the Court in *Summers* noted the following: "The record does not show that any process issued or that any appearance was made. . . . While no entry was placed by the Clerk in the file, on a docket, or in a judgment roll, the Court took cognizance of the petition and passed an order which is validated by the signature of the presiding officer." Because the Illinois court took cognizance of the petition for admission and acted upon it, the Court held that a case or controversy was presented.

Similarly, the Court of Appeals for the Fifth Circuit has held that a state district judge was entitled to judicial immunity, even though "at the time of the altercation [giving rise to the suit] Judge Brown was not in his judge's robes, he was not in the courtroom itself, and he may well have violated state and/or federal procedural requirements regarding contempt citations." *McAlester v. Brown*, 469 F.2d 1280, 1282

(1972).[5] Among the factors relied upon by the Court of Appeals in deciding that the judge was acting within his judicial capacity was the fact that "the confrontation arose directly and immediately out of a visit to the judge in his official capacity."[6]

The relevant cases demonstrate that the factors determining whether an act by a judge is a "judicial" one relate to the nature of the act itself, i.e., whether it is a function normally performed by a judge, and to the expectations of the parties, i.e., whether they dealt with the judge in his judicial capacity. Here, both factors indicate that Judge Stump's approval of the sterilization petition was a judicial act.[7] State judges with general jurisdiction not infrequently are called upon in their official capacity to approve petitions relating to the affairs of minors, as for example, a petition to settle a minor's claim. Furthermore, as even respondents have admitted, at the time he approved the petition presented to him by Mrs. McFarlin, Judge Stump was "acting as a county circuit court judge." We may infer from the record that it was only because Judge Stump served in that position that Mrs. McFarlin, on the advice of counsel, submitted the petition to him for his approval. Because Judge Stump performed the type of act normally performed only by judges and because he did so in his capacity as a Circuit Court Judge, we find no merit to respondents' argument that the informality with which he proceeded rendered his action nonjudicial and deprived him of his absolute immunity.[8]

---

[5] [n.9] In *McAlester* the plaintiffs alleged that they had gone to the courthouse where their son was to be tried by the defendant in order to give the son a fresh set of clothes. When they went into the defendant judge's office, he allegedly ordered them out and had a deputy arrest one of them and place him in jail for the rest of the day. Several months later, the judge issued an order holding the plaintiff in contempt of court, *nunc pro tunc*.

[6] [n.10] Other Courts of Appeals, presented with different fact situations, have concluded that the challenged actions of defendant judges were not performed as part of the judicial function and that the judges were thus not entitled to rely upon the doctrine of judicial immunity. The Court of Appeals for the Ninth Circuit, for example, has held that a justice of the peace who was accused of forcibly removing a man from his courtroom and physically assaulting him was not absolutely immune. *Gregory v. Thompson*, 500 F.2d 59 (1974). While the court recognized that a judge has the duty to maintain order in his courtroom, it concluded that the actual eviction of someone from the courtroom by use of physical force, a task normally performed by a sheriff or bailiff, was "simply not an act of a judicial nature." And the Court of Appeals for the Sixth Circuit held in *Lynch v. Johnson*, 420 F.2d 818 (1970), that the county judge sued in that case was not entitled to judicial immunity because his service on a board with only legislative and administrative powers did not constitute a judicial act.

[7] [n.11] Mr. Justice Stewart, in dissent, complains that this statement is inaccurate because it nowhere appears that judges are normally asked to approve parents' decisions either with respect to surgical treatment in general or with respect to sterilizations in particular. Of course, the opinion makes neither assertion. Rather, it is said that Judge Stump was performing a "function" normally performed by judges and that he was taking "the type of action" judges normally perform. The dissent makes no effort to demonstrate that Judge Stump was without jurisdiction to entertain and act upon the specific petition presented to him. Nor does it dispute that judges normally entertain petitions with respect to the affairs of minors. Even if it is assumed that in a lifetime of judging, a judge has acted on only one petition of a particular kind, this would not indicate that his function in entertaining and acting on it is not the kind of function that a judge normally performs. If this is the case, it is also untenable to claim that in entertaining the petition and exercising the jurisdiction with which the statutes invested him, Judge Stump was nevertheless not performing a judicial act or was engaging in the kind of conduct not expected of a judge under the Indiana statutes governing the jurisdiction of its courts.

[8] [n.12] Mr. Justice Stewart's dissent suggests that Judge Stump's approval of Mrs. McFarlin's petition was not a judicial act because of the absence of what it considers the "normal attributes of a judicial proceeding." These attributes are said to include a "case," with litigants and the opportunity to appeal, in which there is "principled decisionmaking." But under Indiana law, Judge Stump had jurisdiction to act as he did; the proceeding instituted by the petition placed before him was sufficiently a "case" under Indiana law to warrant the exercise of his jurisdiction, whether or not he then proceeded to act erroneously. That there were not two contending litigants did not make Judge Stump's act any less judicial. Courts and judges often act *ex parte*. They issue search warrants in this manner, for example, often without any "case" having been instituted,

Both the Court of Appeals and the respondents seem to suggest that, because of the tragic consequences of Judge Stump's actions, he should not be immune. For example, the Court of Appeals noted that "[t]here are actions of purported judicial character that a judge, even when exercising general jurisdiction, is not empowered to take," and respondents argue that Judge Stump's action was "so unfair" and "so totally devoid of judicial concern for the interests and well-being of the young girl involved" as to disqualify it as a judicial act. Disagreement with the action taken by the judge, however, does not justify depriving that judge of his immunity. Despite the unfairness to litigants that sometimes results, the doctrine of judicial immunity is thought to be in the best interests of "the proper administration of justice . . . [, for it allows] a judicial officer, in exercising the authority vested in him [to] be free to act upon his own convictions, without apprehension of personal consequences to himself." *Bradley v. Fisher*, 13 Wall. at 347. The fact that the issue before the judge is a controversial one is all the more reason that he should be able to act without fear of suit. . . .

The Indiana law vested in Judge Stump the power to entertain and act upon the petition for sterilization. He is, therefore, under the controlling cases, immune from damages liability even if his approval of the petition was in error. . . .

MR. JUSTICE BRENNAN took no part in the consideration or decision of this case.

MR. JUSTICE STEWART, with whom MR. JUSTICE MARSHALL and MR. JUSTICE POWELL join, dissenting.

. . . [T]he scope of judicial immunity is limited to liability for "judicial acts" and I think that what Judge Stump did on July 9, 1971, was beyond the pale of anything that could sensibly be called a judicial act.

. . . [I]f the limitations inherent in that concept have any realistic meaning at all, then I cannot believe that the action of Judge Stump in approving Mrs. McFarlin's petition is protected by judicial immunity.

The Court finds two reasons for holding that Judge Stump's approval of the sterilization petition was a judicial act. First, the Court says, it was "a function normally performed by a judge." Second, the Court says, the act was performed in Judge Stump's "judicial capacity." With all respect, I think that the first of these grounds is factually untrue and that the second is legally unsound.

When the Court says that what Judge Stump did was an act "normally performed by a judge," it is not clear to me whether the Court means that a judge "normally" is asked to approve a mother's decision to have her child given surgical treatment generally, or that a judge "normally" is asked to approve a mother's wish to have her daughter sterilized. But whichever way the Court's statement is to be taken, it is factually inaccurate. In Indiana, as elsewhere in our country, a parent is authorized to arrange for and consent to medical and surgical treatment of his minor child. Ind. Code Ann. § 16-8-4-2 (1973). And when a parent decides to call a physician to care for his sick child or arranges to have a surgeon remove his child's tonsils, he does not, "normally" or otherwise, need to seek the approval of a judge.[9] On the other hand, Indiana did in 1971

---

without any "case" ever being instituted, and without the issuance of the warrant being subject to appeal. Yet it would not destroy a judge's immunity if it is alleged and offer of proof is made that in issuing a warrant he acted erroneously and without principle.

[9] [n.3] This general authority of a parent was held by an Indiana Court of Appeals in 1975 not to include the power to authorize the sterilization of his minor child. *A.L. v. G.R.H.*, 163 Ind. App. 636, 325 N.E.2d 501.

Contrary to the Court's conclusion, that case does not in the least demonstrate that an Indiana judge is or ever was empowered to act on the merits of a petition like Mrs. McFarlin's. The parent in that case did not petition for judicial approval of her decision, but rather "filed a complaint for declaratory judgment seeking declaration of her right under the common-law attributes of the parent-child relationship to have her have statutory procedures for the sterilization of certain people who were institutionalized. But these statutes provided for administrative proceedings before a board established by the superintendent of each public hospital. Only if, after notice and an evidentiary hearing, an order of sterilization was entered in these proceedings could there be review in a circuit court. *See* Ind. Code Ann. §§ 16-13-13-1 through 16-13-13-4 (1974).[10]

In sum, what Judge Stump did on July 9, 1971, was in no way an act "normally performed by a judge." Indeed, there is no reason to believe that such an act has ever been performed by any other Indiana judge, either before or since.

When the Court says that Judge Stump was acting in "his judicial capacity" in approving Mrs. McFarlin's petition, it is not clear to me whether the Court means that Mrs. McFarlin submitted the petition to him only because he was a judge, or that, in approving it, he said that he was acting as a judge. But however the Court's test is to be understood, it is, I think, demonstrably unsound.

It can safely be assumed that the Court is correct in concluding that Mrs. McFarlin came to Judge Stump with her petition because he was a County Circuit Court Judge. But false illusions as to a judge's power can hardly convert a judge's response to those illusions into a judicial act. In short, a judge's approval of a mother's petition to lock her daughter in the attic would hardly be a judicial act simply because the mother had submitted her petition to the judge in his official capacity.

If, on the other hand, the Court's test depends upon the fact that Judge Stump said he was acting in his judicial capacity, it is equally invalid. It is true that Judge Stump affixed his signature to the approval of the petition as "Judge, De Kalb Circuit Court." But the conduct of a judge surely does not become a judicial act merely on his own say-so. A judge is not free, like a loose cannon, to inflict indiscriminate damage whenever he announces that he is acting in his judicial capacity.[11]

If the standard adopted by the Court is invalid, then what is the proper measure of a judicial act? Contrary to implications in the Court's opinion, my conclusion that what Judge Stump did was not a judicial act is not based upon the fact that he acted with informality, or that he may not have been "in his judge's robes," or "in the courtroom itself." And I do not reach this conclusion simply "because the petition was not given a docket number, was not placed on file with the clerk's office, and was approved in an *ex parte* proceeding without notice to the minor, without a hearing, and without the appointment of a guardian *ad litem*."

It seems to me, rather, that the concept of what is a judicial act must take its content from a consideration of the factors that support immunity from liability for the

---

son . . . sterilized." The Indiana Court of Appeals' decision simply established a limitation on the parent's common-law rights. It neither sanctioned nor contemplated any procedure for judicial "approval" of the parent's decision.

Indeed, the procedure followed in that case offers an instructive contrast to the judicial conduct at issue here:

> "At the outset, we thank counsel for their excellent efforts in representing a seriously concerned parent and in providing the guardian ad litem defense of the child's interest."

Id. at 638, 325 N.E.2d at 502.

[10] [n.4] These statutes were repealed in 1974.

[11] [n.5] Believing that the conduct of Judge Stump on July 9, 1971, was not a judicial act, I do not need to inquire whether he was acting in "the clear absence of all jurisdiction over the subject matter." "Jurisdiction" is a coat of many colors. I note only that the Court's finding that Judge Stump had jurisdiction to entertain Mrs. McFarlin's petition seems to me to be based upon dangerously broad criteria. Those criteria are simply that an Indiana statute conferred "jurisdiction of all . . . causes, matters and proceedings," and that there was not in 1971 any Indiana law specifically prohibiting what Judge Stump did.

performance of such an act. Those factors were accurately summarized by the Court in *Pierson v. Ray*, 386 U.S. at 554:

> "[I]t 'is . . . for the benefit of the public, whose interest it is that the judges should be at liberty to exercise their functions with independence and without fear of consequences.' . . . It is a judge's duty to decide all cases within his jurisdiction that are brought before him, including controversial cases that arouse the most intense feelings in the litigants. His errors may be corrected on appeal, but he should not have to fear that unsatisfied litigants may hound him with litigation charging malice or corruption. Imposing such a burden on judges would contribute not to principled and fearless decision-making but to intimidation."

Not one of the considerations thus summarized in the *Pierson* opinion was present here. There was no "case," controversial or otherwise. There were no litigants. There was and could be no appeal. And there was not even the pretext of principled decisionmaking. The total absence of any of these normal attributes of a judicial proceeding convinces me that the conduct complained of in this case was not a judicial act.

The petitioners' brief speaks of "an aura of deism which surrounds the bench . . . essential to the maintenance of respect for the judicial institution." Though the rhetoric may be overblown, I do not quarrel with it. But if aura there be, it is hardly protected by exonerating from liability such lawless conduct as took place here. And if intimidation would serve to deter its recurrence, that would surely be in the public interest.[12]

NOTES

1. Evaluating the Doctrine of Absolute Judicial Immunity. *Pierson v. Ray*, 386 U.S. 547 (1967), was the first Supreme Court decision to confer absolute immunity on judges in section 1983 cases. In immunizing a judge who convicted a group of ministers under an unconstitutional breach-of-the-peace statute after they peacefully entered a segregated bus terminal in Mississippi as part of a civil rights protest, the Court reasoned that "[t]he immunity of judges for acts within the judicial role is equally well established [as legislative immunity], and we presume that Congress would have specifically so provided had it wished to abolish the doctrine." *Pierson*, 386 U.S. at 554–55.

Justice Douglas's dissenting opinion in *Pierson* pointed out that Congress, when passing section 1983, "recognized that certain members of the judiciary were instruments of oppression and were partially responsible for the wrongs to be remedied," and "every member of Congress who spoke on the issue assumed that the words of the statute meant what they said and that judges would be liable." *Pierson*, 386 U.S. at 563, 562–63 (Douglas, J., dissenting). *See also* Note, *Liability of Judicial Officers Under Section 1983*, 79 YALE L.J. 322, 327 (1969) (reviewing section 1983's legislative history and concluding that "all the available evidence points to the conclusion that Congress intended to cover judges"). Moreover, judicial immunity was not a "universal" common-law doctrine at the time section 1983 was enacted; in fact, only thirteen of thirty-seven states accorded judges absolute immunity in 1871. Note, 79 YALE L.J. at 325, 326–27.

2. The Clear Absence of Jurisdiction. *Stump* recognizes two situations in which judges lose their absolute immunity. The first is when they act in "the clear absence of all jurisdiction over the subject-matter," as opposed to merely "in excess of their

---

[12] [n.6] The only question before us in this case is the scope of judicial immunity. How the absence of a "judicial act" might affect the issue of whether Judge Stump was acting "under color of" state law within the meaning of 42 U.S.C. § 1983, or the issue of whether his act was that of the State within the meaning of the Fourteenth Amendment that need not, therefore, be pursued here.

jurisdiction." Given the narrow reading the *Stump* Court gives to the concept of a clear absence of jurisdiction, however, this exception, "insofar as it applies to courts of general jurisdiction, is barely any limitation at all." Irene Merker Rosenberg, Stump v. Sparkman: *The Doctrine of Judicial Immunity*, 64 VA. L. REV. 833, 835 (1978). One of the rare cases where the exception was applied involved a town justice who issued an arrest warrant for a crime committed in a neighboring community, despite the fact that he knew he lacked subject matter jurisdiction over offenses committed outside his town. See *Maestri v. Jutkofsky*, 860 F.2d 50 (2d Cir. 1988).

3. Judicial Acts. The second exception recognized in *Stump* applies when judges are engaged in something other than a "judicial act." In *Forrester v. White*, 484 U.S. 219, 227 (1988), the Court drew a distinction between "judicial acts" and "the administrative, legislative, or executive functions that judges may on occasion be assigned by law to perform." In concluding that demoting and firing a probation officer, allegedly because of her gender, were acts taken in the judge's "administrative capacity" and thus were unprotected by absolute immunity, the Court explained that "[t]he decisions at issue . . . were not themselves judicial or adjudicative." *Forrester*, 484 U.S. at 229.

But the Court emphasized the narrow reach of the "judicial act" exception in *Mireles v. Waco*, 502 U.S. 9, 9 (1991) (per curiam), a section 1983 claim brought by a public defender who alleged that a judge ordered two police officers "to forcibly and with excessive force seize and bring [him] into [the judge's] courtroom" when he failed to appear at the morning call. In rejecting the plaintiff's contention that the judge's acts were "not taken in his judicial capacity," the Court reasoned as follows:

> A judge's direction to court officers to bring a person who is in the courthouse before him is a function normally performed by a judge. . . .
>
> Of course, a judge's direction to police officers to carry out a judicial order with excessive force is not a "function normally performed by a judge." But if only the particular act in question were to be scrutinized, then any mistake of a judge in excess of his authority would become a "nonjudicial" act, because an improper or erroneous act cannot be said to be normally performed by a judge. . . . Accordingly, as the language in *Stump* indicates, the relevant inquiry is the "nature" and "function" of the act, not the "act itself." In other words, we look to the particular act's relation to a general function normally performed by a judge, in this case the function of directing police officers to bring counsel in a pending case before the court.

Mireles, 502 U.S. at 12–13.

In dissent, Justice Stevens separated the judge's order into two components: the order to bring the plaintiff to the courtroom, which was a protected judicial act, and the order "to commit a battery," which had "no relation to a function normally performed by a judge." *Mireles*, 502 U.S. at 14 (Stevens, J., dissenting). In Justice Stevens's mind, the fact that both orders "occurred as part of the same communication" did not distinguish the case from one where "an interval of a minute or two . . . separated the two orders," thereby making it "undeniable that no immunity would attach to the latter order." *Mireles*, 502 U.S. at 15, 14.

4. The Functional Approach to Judicial Immunity. Consistent with the functional approach to immunity outlined in *Forrester v. White*, the Court has extended absolute judicial immunity to government officials who perform judicial functions. Thus, in *Butz v. Economou*, 438 U.S. 478 (1978), the Court held that administrative law judges were entitled to judicial immunity because they were " 'functionally comparable' " to judges even though they were executive-branch officials. The "special nature of their responsibilities," rather than "their particular location within the Government," was key, the Court said, concluding that "adjudication within a federal administrative agency shares enough of the characteristics of the judicial process that those who participate in such adjudication should also be immune from suits for damages." *Butz*, 438 U.S. at 511, 512–13. In so holding, the Court noted that the administrative hearings had "the safeguards built into the judicial process," thus "reduc[ing] the need for private damages actions as a means of controlling unconstitutional conduct." *Butz*, 438 U.S. at 512.

The absence of such safeguards proved critical in *Cleavinger v. Saxner*, 474 U.S. 193 (1985), where the Court held that the members of a committee presiding over prison discipline proceedings were entitled to only qualified immunity. The discipline committee was composed of members of the prison staff, rather than "professional hearing officers" who were "truly independent," the Court observed, and the hearings contained "few of the procedural safeguards" that characterized the administrative hearings at issue in *Butz*. *Cleavinger*, 474 U.S. at 203, 205. Picking up on dictum in *Cleavinger* that parole boards have traditionally been " 'neutral and detached' " and are "constitutionally required to provide greater due process protection" than prison discipline committees, *Cleavinger*, 474 U.S. at 204, most courts have held that parole board members are entitled to absolute judicial immunity. *See, e.g.*, *Holmes v. Crosby*, 418 F.3d 1256 (11th Cir. 2005); *Wilson v. Kelkhoff*, 83 F.3d 1438 (7th Cir. 1996). *Cf. Miller v. Davis*, 521 F.3d 1142 (9th Cir. 2008) (applying the functional approach and concluding that governor who reversed a grant of parole was entitled to absolute judicial immunity).

5. Derivative Judicial Immunity. Although the Supreme Court has never decided what sort of immunity attaches to government officials who execute court orders, most courts of appeals have afforded them absolute immunity. These decisions are based on the perception that it is unfair to give officials "the Hobson's choice between disobeying the court order or being haled into court to answer for damages," and inappropriate to make them a " 'lightning rod for harassing litigation aimed at judicial orders.' " *Patterson v. Von Riesen*, 999 F.2d 1235, 1240 (8th Cir. 1993) (quoting *Valdez v. City & County of Denver*, 878 F.2d 1285, 1289 (10th Cir. 1989)). *But cf. Richman v. Sheahan*, 270 F.3d 430, 435–36 (7th Cir. 2001) (noting that courts disagree whether defendants who execute a judicial order to use unreasonable force in seizing someone are entitled to absolute immunity). For a discussion of the extent to which other actors in the judicial process enjoy absolute immunity in their own right, *see* Note 5 in Section A.[3], *infra*.

6. Injunctive Actions. In *Pulliam v. Allen*, 466 U.S. 522 (1984), the Court held that judges, unlike legislators, were not absolutely immune from section 1983 suits seeking only injunctive or declaratory relief. The Court reasoned that the common law did not immunize judges from prospective relief and that "injunctive relief raises concerns different from those addressed by the protection of judges from damages awards": "[t]he limitations already imposed by the requirements for obtaining equitable relief against any defendant — a showing of an inadequate remedy at law and of a serious risk of irreparable harm — severely curtail the risk that judges will be harassed and their independence compromised by the threat of having to defend themselves against suits by disgruntled litigants." *Pulliam*, 466 U.S. at 537–38.

But *Pulliam* was severely undermined when Congress added language to section 1983 as part of the Federal Courts Improvement Act of 1996, providing that "in any action brought against a judicial officer for an act or omission taken in such officer's judicial capacity, injunctive relief shall not be granted unless a declaratory decree was violated or declaratory relief was unavailable." 42 U.S.C. § 1983. Moreover, the same bill also amended the attorney's fees statute to foreclose an award of fees "in any action brought against a judicial officer for an act or omission taken in such officer's judicial capacity . . . unless such action was clearly in excess of such officer's jurisdiction." 42 U.S.C. § 1988(b).

[3] Prosecutorial Immunity

BUCKLEY v. FITZSIMMONS
Supreme Court of the United States
509 U.S. 259 (1993)

JUSTICE STEVENS delivered the opinion of the Court.

I

Petitioner commenced this action on March 4, 1988, following his release from jail in Du Page County, Illinois. He had been incarcerated there for three years on charges growing out of the highly publicized murder of Jeanine Nicarico, an 11-year-old child, on February 25, 1983. . . .

Respondent Fitzsimmons was the duly elected Du Page County State's Attorney from the time of the Nicarico murder through December 1984, when he was succeeded by respondent Ryan, who had defeated him in a Republican primary election on March 21, 1984. Respondent Knight was an assistant state's attorney under Fitzsimmons and served as a special prosecutor in the Nicarico case under Ryan. Respondents Kilander (who came into office with Ryan) and King were assistant prosecutors, also assigned to the case.

The theory of petitioner's case is that in order to obtain an indictment in a case that had engendered "extensive publicity" and "intense emotions in the community," the prosecutors fabricated false evidence. . . .

The fabricated evidence related to a bootprint on the door of the Nicarico home apparently left by the killer when he kicked in the door. After three separate studies by experts from the Du Page County Crime Lab, the Illinois Department of Law Enforcement, and the Kansas Bureau of Identification, all of whom were unable to make a reliable connection between the print and a pair of boots that petitioner had voluntarily supplied, respondents obtained a "positive identification" from one Louise Robbins, an anthropologist in North Carolina who was allegedly well known for her willingness to fabricate unreliable expert testimony. Her opinion was obtained during the early stages of the investigation, which was being conducted under the joint supervision and direction of the sheriff and respondent Fitzsimmons, whose police officers and assistant prosecutors were performing essentially the same investigatory functions.

Thereafter, having failed to obtain sufficient evidence to support petitioner's (or anyone else's) arrest, respondents convened a special grand jury for the sole purpose of investigating the Nicarico case. After an 8-month investigation, during which the grand jury heard the testimony of over 100 witnesses, including the bootprint experts, it was still unable to return an indictment. On January 27, 1984, respondent Fitzsimmons admitted in a public statement that there was insufficient evidence to indict anyone for the rape and murder of Jeanine Nicarico. Although no additional evidence was obtained in the interim, the indictment was returned in March . . . shortly before the primary election. Petitioner was then arrested, and because he was unable to meet the bond (set at $3 million), he was held in jail.

Petitioner's trial began 10 months later, in January 1985. The principal evidence against him was provided by Robbins, the North Carolina anthropologist. Because the jury was unable to reach a verdict on the charges against petitioner, the trial judge declared a mistrial. Petitioner remained in prison for two more years, during which a third party confessed to the crime and the prosecutors prepared for petitioner's retrial. After Robbins died, however, all charges against him were dropped. He was released, and filed this action. . . .

We granted certiorari . . . limited to issues relating to prosecutorial immunity.[13] We now reverse.

III

The principles applied to determine the scope of immunity for state officials sued under [§ 1983] are by now familiar. Section 1983 on its face admits of no defense of official immunity. It subjects to liability "every person" who, acting under color of state law, commits the prohibited acts. In *Tenney v. Brandhove*, however, we held that Congress did not intend § 1983 to abrogate immunities "well grounded in history and reason." Certain immunities were so well established in 1871, when § 1983 was enacted, that "we presume that Congress would have specifically so provided had it wished to abolish" them. *Pierson v. Ray*, 386 U.S. 547, 554–555 (1967). Although we have found immunities in § 1983 that do not appear on the face of the statute, . . . "[o]ur role is to interpret the intent of Congress in enacting § 1983, not to make a freewheeling policy choice." *Malley v. Briggs*, 475 U.S. 335, 342 (1986).

. . . In most cases, qualified immunity is sufficient to "protect officials who are required to exercise their discretion and the related public interest in encouraging the vigorous exercise of official authority." *Butz v. Economou*, 438 U.S. [478, 506 (1978)].

We have recognized, however, that some officials perform "special functions" which, because of their similarity to functions that would have been immune when Congress enacted § 1983, deserve absolute protection from damages liability. "The official seeking absolute immunity bears the burden of showing that such immunity is justified for the function in question." *Burns v. Reed*, 500 U.S. at 486. Even when we can identify a common-law tradition of absolute immunity for a given function, we have considered "whether § 1983's history or purposes nonetheless counsel against recognizing the same immunity in § 1983 actions." *Tower v. Glover*, 467 U.S. [914, 920 (1984)]. Not surprisingly, we have been "quite sparing" in recognizing absolute immunity for state actors in this context. *Forrester v. White*, 484 U.S. 219, 224 (1988).

In determining whether particular actions of government officials fit within a common-law tradition of absolute immunity, or only the more general standard of qualified immunity, we have applied a "functional approach," which looks to "the nature of the function performed, not the identity of the actor who performed it," *Forrester v. White*, 484 U.S. at 229. We have twice applied this approach in determining whether the functions of contemporary prosecutors are entitled to absolute immunity.

In *Imbler v. Pachtman*, 424 U.S. 409 (1976), we held that a state prosecutor had absolute immunity for the initiation and pursuit of a criminal prosecution, including presentation of the State's case at trial. . . . We concluded that the common-law rule of immunity for prosecutors was "well settled" and that "the same considerations of public policy that underlie the common-law rule likewise countenance absolute immunity under § 1983." Those considerations[14] supported a rule of absolute immunity

---

[13] [n.3] Although petitioner also alleged that respondents violated his constitutional rights in presenting the fabricated evidence to the grand jury and his trial jury, we are not presented with any question regarding those claims. The Court of Appeals agreed with the District Court and held that those actions were protected by absolute immunity. *Buckley v. Fitzsimmons*, 919 F.2d 1230, 1243 (CA7 1990) ("The selection of evidence to present to the grand jurors, and the manner of questioning witnesses, can no more be the basis of liability than may the equivalent activities before the petit jury"). That decision was made according to traditional principles of absolute immunity under § 1983. . . .

[14] [n.4] In particular, we expressed concern that fear of potential liability would undermine a prosecutor's performance of his duties by forcing him to consider his own potential liability when making prosecutorial decisions and by diverting his "energy and attention . . . from the pressing duty of enforcing the criminal law." Suits against prosecutors would devolve into "a virtual retrial of the criminal offense [in] a new forum," and would undermine the vigorous enforcement of the law by providing a prosecutor an incentive not "to go forward with a close case where an acquittal likely would trigger a suit against him for damages." We also

for conduct of prosecutors that was "intimately associated with the judicial phase of the criminal process." In concluding that "in initiating a prosecution and in presenting the State's case, the prosecutor is immune from a civil suit for damages under § 1983," we did not attempt to describe the line between a prosecutor's acts in preparing for those functions, some of which would be absolutely immune, and his acts of investigation or "administration," which would not.

We applied the *Imbler* analysis two Terms ago in *Burns v. Reed*, 500 U.S. 478 (1991). There the § 1983 suit challenged two acts by a prosecutor: (1) giving legal advice to the police on the propriety of hypnotizing a suspect and on whether probable cause existed to arrest that suspect, and (2) participating in a probable-cause hearing. We held that only the latter was entitled to absolute immunity. Immunity for that action under § 1983 accorded with the common-law absolute immunity of prosecutors and other attorneys for eliciting false or defamatory testimony from witnesses or for making false or defamatory statements during, and related to, judicial proceedings. Under that analysis, appearing before a judge and presenting evidence in support of a motion for a search warrant involved the prosecutor's " 'role as advocate for the State.' " Because issuance of a search warrant is a judicial act, appearance at the probable-cause hearing was " 'intimately associated with the judicial phase of the criminal process.' "

We further decided, however, that prosecutors are not entitled to absolute immunity for their actions in giving legal advice to the police. We were unable to identify any historical or common-law support for absolute immunity in the performance of this function. We also noted that any threat to the judicial process from "the harassment and intimidation associated with litigation" based on advice to the police was insufficient to overcome the "absen[ce] [of] a tradition of immunity comparable to the common-law immunity from malicious prosecution, which formed the basis for the decision in *Imbler*." And though we noted that several checks other than civil litigation prevent prosecutorial abuses in advising the police, "one of the most important checks, the judicial process," will not be effective in all cases, especially when in the end the suspect is not prosecuted. In sum, we held that providing legal advice to the police was not a function "closely associated with the judicial process."

IV

In this case the Court of Appeals held that respondents are entitled to absolute immunity because the injuries suffered by petitioner occurred during criminal proceedings.[15] That holding is contrary to the approach we have consistently followed since *Imbler*. As we have noted, the *Imbler* approach focuses on the conduct for which immunity is claimed, not on the harm that the conduct may have caused or the question whether it was lawful.[16] The location of the injury may be relevant to the question whether a complaint has adequately alleged a cause of action for damages (a question that this case does not present). It is irrelevant, however, to the question whether the conduct of a prosecutor is protected by absolute immunity. . . .

Petitioner argues that *Imbler*'s protection for a prosecutor's conduct "in initiating a prosecution and in presenting the State's case" extends only to the act of initiation itself and to conduct occurring in the courtroom. This extreme position is plainly foreclosed

---

expressed concern that the availability of a damages action might cause judges to be reluctant to award relief to convicted defendants in post-trial motions.

[15] [Editor's note: The Court of Appeals thought that a prosecutor should be protected by absolute immunity if "the injury flows from the initiation or prosecution of the case," but only by qualified immunity if the "constitutional wrong is complete before the case begins." The appellate court justified this distinction on the ground that "damages remedies are unnecessary" in the former situation because "[c]ourts can curtail the costs of prosecutorial blunders . . . by cutting short the prosecution or mitigating its effects."]

[16] [Editor's note: This issue is discussed in *Hartman v. Moore* and the accompanying Notes in Chapter 6.A., *infra*.]

by our opinion in *Imbler* itself. We expressly stated that "the duties of the prosecutor in his role as advocate for the State involve actions preliminary to the initiation of a prosecution and actions apart from the courtroom," and are nonetheless entitled to absolute immunity. We noted in particular that an out-of-court "effort to control the presentation of [a] witness' testimony" was entitled to absolute immunity because it was "fairly within [the prosecutor's] function as an advocate." . . . [A]cts undertaken by a prosecutor in preparing for the initiation of judicial proceedings or for trial, and which occur in the course of his role as an advocate for the State, are entitled to the protections of absolute immunity. Those acts must include the professional evaluation of the evidence assembled by the police and appropriate preparation for its presentation at trial or before a grand jury after a decision to seek an indictment has been made.

On the other hand, as the function test of *Imbler* recognizes, the actions of a prosecutor are not absolutely immune merely because they are performed by a prosecutor. Qualified immunity " 'represents the norm' " for executive officers, *Malley v. Briggs*, 475 U.S. at 340, quoting *Harlow v. Fitzgerald*, 457 U.S. [800, 807 (1982)], so when a prosecutor "functions as an administrator rather than as an officer of the court" he is entitled only to qualified immunity. *Imbler*, 424 U.S. at 431 n.33. There is a difference between the advocate's role in evaluating evidence and interviewing witnesses as he prepares for trial, on the one hand, and the detective's role in searching for the clues and corroboration that might give him probable cause to recommend that a suspect be arrested, on the other hand. When a prosecutor performs the investigative functions normally performed by a detective or police officer, it is "neither appropriate nor justifiable that, for the same act, immunity should protect the one and not the other." *Hampton v. Chicago*, 484 F.2d 602, 608 (CA7 1973). Thus, if a prosecutor plans and executes a raid on a suspected weapons cache, he "has no greater claim to complete immunity than activities of police officers allegedly acting under his direction." 484 F.2d at 608–609.

The question, then, is whether the prosecutors have carried their burden of establishing that they were functioning as "advocates" when they were endeavoring to determine whether the bootprint at the scene of the crime had been made by petitioner's foot. A careful examination of the allegations concerning the conduct of the prosecutors during the period before they convened a special grand jury to investigate the crime provides the answer. The prosecutors do not contend that they had probable cause to arrest petitioner or to initiate judicial proceedings during that period. Their mission at that time was entirely investigative in character. A prosecutor neither is, nor should consider himself to be, an advocate before he has probable cause to have anyone arrested.[17]

---

[17] [n.5] Of course, a determination of probable cause does not guarantee a prosecutor absolute immunity from liability for all actions taken afterwards. Even after that determination, as the opinion dissenting in part points out, a prosecutor may engage in "police investigative work" that is entitled to only qualified immunity.

Furthermore, there is no "true anomaly" in denying absolute immunity for a state actor's investigative acts made before there is probable cause to have a suspect arrested just because a prosecutor would be entitled to absolute immunity for the malicious prosecution of someone whom he lacked probable cause to indict. That criticism ignores the essence of the function test. The reason that lack of probable cause allows us to deny absolute immunity to a state actor for the former function (fabrication of evidence) is that there is no common-law tradition of immunity for it, whether performed by a police officer or prosecutor. The reason that we grant it for the latter function (malicious prosecution) is that we have found a common-law tradition of immunity for a prosecutor's decision to bring an indictment, whether he has probable cause or not. By insisting on an equation of the two functions merely because a prosecutor might be subject to liability for one but not the other, the dissent allows its particular policy concerns to erase the function test it purports to respect.

In general, the dissent's distress over the denial of absolute immunity for prosecutors who fabricate evidence regarding unsolved crimes, like the holding of the Court of Appeals, seems to conflate the question whether a § 1983 plaintiff has stated a cause of action with the question whether the defendant is entitled to absolute immunity for his actions.

It was well after the alleged fabrication of false evidence concerning the bootprint that a special grand jury was empaneled. And when it finally was convened, its immediate purpose was to conduct a more thorough investigation of the crime — not to return an indictment against a suspect whom there was already probable cause to arrest. Buckley was not arrested, in fact, until 10 months after the grand jury had been convened and had finally indicted him. Under these circumstances, the prosecutors' conduct occurred well before they could properly claim to be acting as advocates. Respondents have not cited any authority that supports an argument that a prosecutor's fabrication of false evidence during the preliminary investigation of an unsolved crime was immune from liability at common law, either in 1871 or at any date before the enactment of § 1983. It therefore remains protected only by qualified immunity.

After *Burns*, it would be anomalous, to say the least, to grant prosecutors only qualified immunity when offering legal advice to police about an unarrested suspect, but then to endow them with absolute immunity when conducting investigative work themselves in order to decide whether a suspect may be arrested.[18] That the prosecutors later called a grand jury to consider the evidence this work produced does not retroactively transform that work from the administrative into the prosecutorial.[19] A prosecutor may not shield his investigative work with the aegis of absolute immunity merely because, after a suspect is eventually arrested, indicted, and tried, that work may be retrospectively described as "preparation" for a possible trial; every prosecutor might then shield himself from liability for any constitutional wrong against innocent citizens by ensuring that they go to trial. When the functions of prosecutors and detectives are the same, as they were here, the immunity that protects them is also the same. . . .

JUSTICE SCALIA, concurring.

I believe . . . that the vagueness of the "acting-as-advocate" principle may be less troublesome in practice than it seems in theory, for two reasons. First, the Court reaffirms that the defendant official bears the burden of showing that the conduct for which he seeks immunity would have been privileged at common law in 1871. Thus, if application of the principle is unclear, the defendant simply loses. Second, many claims directed at prosecutors, of the sort that are based on acts not plainly covered by the conventional malicious-prosecution and defamation privileges, are probably not actionable under § 1983, and so may be dismissed at the pleading stage without regard to immunity — undermining the dissent's assertion that we have converted absolute prosecutorial immunity into "little more than a pleading rule." I think petitioner's false-evidence claims in the present case illustrate this point. Insofar as they are based on

---

[18] [n.6] *Cf. Burns v. Reed*, 500 U.S. 478, 495 (1991): "Indeed, it is incongruous to allow prosecutors to be absolutely immune from liability for giving advice to the police, but to allow police officers only qualified immunity for following the advice. . . . Almost any action by a prosecutor, including his or her direct participation in purely investigative activity, could be said to be in some way related to the ultimate decision whether to prosecute, but we have never indicated that absolute immunity is that expansive." If the police, under the guidance of the prosecutors, had solicited the allegedly "fabricated" testimony, of course, they would not be entitled to anything more than qualified immunity.

[19] [n.7] *See Imbler v. Pachtman*, 424 U.S. 409, 431 n.33 (1976): "Preparation, both for the initiation of the criminal process and for a trial, may require the obtaining, reviewing, and evaluating of evidence. At some point, and with respect to some decisions, the prosecutor no doubt functions as an administrator rather than as an officer of the court. Drawing a proper line between these functions may present difficult questions, but this case does not require us to anticipate them." Although the respondents rely on the first sentence of this passage to suggest that a prosecutor's actions in "obtaining, reviewing, and evaluating" evidence are always protected by absolute immunity, the sentence that follows qualifies that suggestion. It confirms that some of these actions may fall on the administrative, rather than the judicial, end of the prosecutor's activities, and therefore be entitled only to qualified immunity.

respondents' supposed knowing use of fabricated evidence before the grand jury and at trial — acts which might state a claim for denial of due process — the traditional defamation immunity provides complete protection from suit under § 1983. If "reframed . . . to attack the preparation" of that evidence, the claims are unlikely to be cognizable under § 1983, since petitioner cites, and I am aware of, no authority for the proposition that the mere preparation of false evidence, as opposed to its use in a fashion that deprives someone of a fair trial or otherwise harms him, violates the Constitution.

JUSTICE KENNEDY, with whom THE CHIEF JUSTICE, JUSTICE WHITE, and JUSTICE SOUTER join, concurring in part and dissenting in part.

I

. . . I believe that the conduct relating to the expert witnesses falls on the absolute immunity side of the divide. . . . [W]hile Buckley labels the prosecutors' actions relating to the bootprint experts as "investigative," I believe it is more accurate to describe the prosecutors' conduct as preparation for trial. A prosecutor must consult with a potential trial witness before he places the witness on the stand, and if the witness is a critical one, consultation may be necessary even before the decision whether to indict. It was obvious from the outset that the bootprint was critical to the prosecution's case, and the prosecutors' consultation with experts is best viewed as a step to ensure the bootprint's admission in evidence and to bolster its probative value in the eyes of the jury.

Just as *Imbler* requires that the decision to use a witness must be insulated from liability, it requires as well that the steps leading to that decision must be free of the distortive effects of potential liability, at least to the extent that the prosecutor is engaged in trial preparation. Actions in "obtaining, reviewing, and evaluating" witness testimony are a classic function of the prosecutor as advocate. Pretrial and even preindictment consultation can be "intimately associated with the judicial phase of the criminal process." . . . Concern about potential liability arising from pretrial consultation with a witness might "hamper" a prosecutor's exercise of his judgment as to whether a certain witness should be used. . . . Moreover, "exposing the prosecutor to liability for the initial phase of his prosecutorial work could interfere with his exercise of independent judgment at every phase of his work, since the prosecutor might come to see later decisions in terms of their effect on his potential liability." *Malley v. Briggs*, 475 U.S. at 343. That distortion would frustrate the objective of accuracy in the determination of guilt or innocence.

Furthermore, the very matter the prosecutors were considering, the decision to use particular expert testimony, was "subjected to the 'crucible of the judicial process.'" *Burns v. Reed*, 500 U.S. at 496, quoting *Imbler v. Pachtman, supra,* at 440 (White, J., concurring in judgment). . . . Remedies other than prosecutorial liability, for example, a pretrial ruling of inadmissibility or a rejection by the trier of fact, are more than adequate "to prevent abuses of authority by prosecutors." *Burns v. Reed, supra,* at 496. . . .

II

The Court reaches a contrary conclusion on the issue of the bootprint evidence by superimposing a bright-line standard onto the functional approach that has guided our past decisions. . . .

. . . We were quite clear in *Imbler* that if absolute immunity for prosecutors meant anything, it meant that prosecutors were not subject to suit for malicious prosecution. Yet the central component of a malicious prosecution claim is that the prosecutor in question acted maliciously and without probable cause. If the Court means to withhold absolute immunity whenever it is alleged that the injurious actions of a prosecutor occurred before he had probable cause to believe a specified individual committed a crime, then no longer is a claim for malicious prosecution subject to ready dismissal on absolute immunity grounds, at least where the claimant is clever enough to include some actions taken by the prosecutor prior to the initiation of prosecution. . . . I also find it hard to accept any line that can be so easily manipulated by criminal defendants turned civil plaintiffs, allowing them to avoid a dismissal on absolute immunity grounds by throwing in an allegation that a prosecutor acted without probable cause.

Perhaps the Court means to draw its line at the point where an appropriate neutral third party, in this case the Illinois special grand jury, makes a determination of probable cause. This line, too, would generate anomalous results. To begin, it could have the perverse effect of encouraging prosecutors to seek indictments as early as possible in an attempt to shelter themselves from liability, even in cases where they would otherwise prefer to wait on seeking an indictment to ensure that they do not accuse an innocent person. Given the stigma and emotional trauma attendant to an indictment and arrest, promoting premature indictments and arrests is not a laudable accomplishment.

Even assuming these premature actions would not be induced by the Court's rule, . . . [i]f the false evidence or coerced confession served as the basis for the third party's determination of probable cause, as was alleged here, it is difficult to fathom why securing such a fraudulent determination transmogrifies unprotected conduct into protected conduct. Finally, the Court does not question our conclusion in *Burns* that absolute immunity attached to a prosecutor's conduct before a grand jury because it " 'perform[s] a judicial function.' " It is unclear to me, then, why preparing for grand jury proceedings, which obviously occur before an indictment is handed down, cannot be "intimately associated with the judicial phase of the criminal process" and subject to absolute immunity.

As troubling as is the line drawn by the Court, I find the [two] reasons for its line-drawing to be of equal concern. . . .

The Court's first concern, I take it, is meant to be a restatement of one of the unquestioned goals of our § 1983 immunity jurisprudence: ensuring parity in treatment among state actors engaged in identical functions. But it was for the precise reason of advancing this goal that we adopted the functional approach to absolute immunity in the first place, and I do not see a need to augment that approach by developing bright-line rules in cases where determining whether different actors are engaged in identical functions involves careful attention to subtle details. The Court, moreover, perceives a danger of disparate treatment because it assumes that before establishing probable cause, police and prosecutors perform the same functions. This assumption seem to me unwarranted. I do not understand the art of advocacy to have an inherent temporal limitation, so I cannot say that prosecutors are never functioning as advocates before the determination of probable cause. More to the point, the Court's assumption further presumes that when both prosecutors and police officers engage in the same conduct, they are of necessity engaged in the same function. With this I must disagree. Two actors can take part in similar conduct and similar inquiries while doing so for different reasons and to advance different functions. It may be that a prosecutor and a police officer are examining the same evidence at the same time, but the prosecutor is examining the evidence to determine whether it will be persuasive at trial and of assistance to the trier of fact, while the police officer examines the evidence to decide whether it provides a basis for arresting a suspect. The conduct is the same but the functions distinct.

Advancing to the second reason provided for the Court's line-drawing, I think the Court overstates the danger of allowing pre-probable-cause conduct to constitute advocacy entitled to absolute immunity. I agree with the Court that the institution of a prosecution "does not retroactively transform . . . work from the administrative into the prosecutorial," but declining to institute a prosecution likewise should not "retroactively transform" work from the prosecutorial into the administrative. In either case, the primary question, one which I have confidence the federal courts are able to answer with some accuracy, is whether a prosecutor was acting as an advocate, an investigator, or an administrator when he took the actions called into question in a subsequent § 1983 action. As long as federal courts center their attention on this question, a concern that prosecutors can disguise their investigative and administrative actions as early forms of advocacy seems to be unfounded. . . .

NOTES

1. Evaluating the Doctrine of Absolute Prosecutorial Immunity. Although *Imbler v. Pachtman*, 424 U.S. 409, 424 (1976), the first Supreme Court opinion to extend absolute immunity in section 1983 cases to prosecutors, relied on what the Court called "well settled" common law, the first American case to find prosecutors immune from malicious prosecution suits was an Indiana Supreme Court decision issued in 1896, twenty-five years after the passage of section 1983. Thus, the Court later acknowledged in *Kalina v. Fletcher*, 522 U.S. 118, 124 (1997), *Imbler*'s holding depended "even more importantly" on policy considerations.

The common-law history prompted Justice Scalia, concurring in *Kalina*, to offer the following comments:

> There was, of course, no such thing as absolute prosecutorial immunity when § 1983 was enacted. (Indeed, as the Court points out, there generally was no such thing as the modern public prosecutor.) The common law recognized a "judicial" immunity, which protected judges, jurors and grand jurors, members of courts martial, private arbitrators, and various assessors and commissioners. That immunity was absolute, but it extended only to individuals who were charged with resolving disputes between other parties or authoritatively adjudicating private rights. When public officials made discretionary policy decisions that did not involve actual adjudication, they were protected by "quasi-judicial" immunity, which could be defeated by a showing of malice, and hence was more akin to what we now call "qualified," rather than absolute, immunity. I continue to believe that "prosecutorial functions, had they existed in their modern form in 1871, would have been considered quasi-judicial."

Kalina, 522 U.S. at 132 (Scalia, J., concurring). Because the doctrine of prosecutorial immunity is so "deeply embedded in our § 1983 jurisprudence," however, Justice Scalia concurred in *Kalina* "for reasons of *stare decisis*." *Kalina*, 522 U.S. at 135.

2. The Scope of Prosecutorial Immunity. Because a prosecutor "not only prosecutes, but regularly investigates, administers, executes, and the like," defining the scope of prosecutorial immunity raises "unique" problems not found in cases involving legislators and judges. 2 SHELDON H. NAHMOD, CIVIL RIGHTS AND CIVIL LIBERTIES LITIGATION: THE LAW OF SECTION 1983 § 7:47, at 7-165 (4th ed. 2007). As noted in *Buckley*, the Court's opinion in *Imbler* indicated that prosecutors are immune for any conduct "intimately associated with the judicial phase of the criminal process." *Imbler*, 424 U.S. at 430. The Court concluded that the conduct at issue in *Imbler* — the knowing use of perjured testimony and the suppression of exculpatory evidence — met that test, as did prosecutorial decisions such as "whether to present a case to a grand jury, whether to file an information, whether and when to prosecute, whether to dismiss an indictment against particular defendants, which witnesses to call, and what other evidence to present." *Imbler*, 424 U.S. at 433 n.33.

In *Mitchell v. Forsyth*, 472 U.S. 511, 521 (1985), however, the Court held that the U.S. Attorney General was not "acting in a prosecutorial capacity" when he authorized a warrantless wiretap on the telephone of a college professor who was associated with an antiwar group suspected of conspiring to blow up federal property. *See also Mink v. Suthers*, 482 F.3d 1244, 1262–63 (10th Cir. 2007) (concluding that a prosecutor was not entitled to absolute immunity because she was "not wearing the hat of an advocate," but instead was giving "legal advice outside the courtroom to aid a nascent investigation," when she reviewed the application for a warrant to search the home of a college student being investigated on criminal libel charges in connection with his publication of an Internet-based journal that parodied a professor).

In a portion of the *Buckley* opinion omitted from the excerpt above, the Supreme Court unanimously ruled that absolute immunity did not protect allegedly false statements State's Attorney Fitzsimmons made at the press conference announcing Buckley's arrest and indictment. In so holding, the Court found that no "common-law immunity for a prosecutor's . . . out-of-court statement to the press" existed in 1871. *Buckley*, 509 U.S. at 277. Moreover, the Court concluded that "[c]omments to the media have no functional tie to the judicial process just because they are made by a prosecutor," and thus Fitzsimmons was not acting in "his role as advocate for the state" during the press conference: "[t]he conduct of a press conference does not involve the initiation of a prosecution, the presentation of the State's case in court, or actions preparatory for these functions." *Buckley*, 509 U.S. at 277–78.

In its most recent foray into this area, *Kalina v. Fletcher*, 522 U.S. 118 (1997), the Court determined that a prosecutor was acting as a complaining witness rather than an advocate — and therefore was not entitled to absolute immunity — when she made false statements of fact in an affidavit filed in support of an application for an arrest warrant. Although absolute immunity did protect the prosecutor's preparation and filing of the motion for an arrest warrant and supporting documents, it did not extend to her "personally attesting to the truth of the averments," which involved no "exercise of professional judgment." *Kalina*, 522 U.S. at 129. "Testifying about facts is the function of the witness, not of the lawyer," the Court observed. *Kalina*, 522 U.S. at 130.

It has been more than a decade since *Kalina*, and the Supreme Court has agreed to revisit the scope of prosecutorial immunity in *Van de Kamp v. Goldstein* (No. 07-854), a section 1983 suit in which a district attorney and his chief deputy allegedly failed to adequately train and supervise their subordinates to ensure they were complying with the government's constitutional obligation to disclose exculpatory material to criminal defendants. The court of appeals held that absolute immunity did not protect the two prosecutors, reasoning that the challenged conduct was "administrative and not prosecutorial in function." *Goldstein v. Long Beach*, 481 F.3d 1170, 1175 (9th Cir. 2007).

The scope of prosecutorial immunity is also likely to be a significant issue as litigation proceeds in the civil suit brought by three former Duke University lacrosse players against North Carolina prosecutor Michael Nifong. Nifong, who filed rape charges against the three students that were later dismissed for lack of evidence, subsequently lost his job and his license to practice law as a result of the case. *See* Mike Nizza, *Students Sue Prosecutor and City in Duke Case*, N.Y. TIMES, Oct. 6, 2007, at A12.

3. The Functional Approach to Prosecutorial Immunity. Pursuant to the Supreme Court's functional approach to immunity, any official who functions as a prosecutor is entitled to absolute immunity when performing the type of act that would afford a prosecutor absolute immunity. Thus, in *Butz v. Economou*, 438 U.S. 478, 515–17 (1978), the Court held that federal agency personnel who initiate administrative proceedings and present evidence at administrative hearings are entitled to the same immunity accorded to prosecutors.

4. Injunctive Actions. Prosecutors are absolutely immune from damages suits, but the Court noted in dictum in *Supreme Court of Virginia v. Consumers Union*, 446 U.S. 719, 736 (1980), that they are "natural targets for § 1983 injunctive suits." Although prosecutors are therefore not absolutely immune from injunctive relief, plaintiffs seeking injunctions against prosecutors must avoid the pitfalls of the *Younger* doctrine. *See Younger v. Harris*, 401 U.S. 37 (1971), which is discussed in Chapter 7.B., *infra*.

5. Other Actors in the Judicial Process. The Supreme Court has suggested in dictum that both grand and petit jurors are entitled to absolute immunity, *see Imbler v.*

Pachtman, 424 U.S. 409, 423 n.20 (1976); *Butz v. Economou*, 438 U.S. 478, 509–10 (1978), and the lower courts have consistently taken that view. *See* 1 JOSEPH G. COOK & JOHN L. SOBIESKI, JR., CIVIL RIGHTS ACTIONS ¶ 2.07[D] (2007).

In *Briscoe v. LaHue*, 460 U.S. 325 (1983), the Court concluded that trial witnesses who commit perjury also enjoy absolute immunity in section 1983 suits. In so holding, the Court noted that granting immunity to witnesses was "well established in English common law" and was also supported by policy considerations: the "apprehension of subsequent damages liability" might discourage witnesses from testifying and might "distort[ ]" their testimony. *Briscoe*, 460 U.S. at 331, 333. The Court refused to create an exception for testimony given by police officers, *see* 460 U.S. at 341–45, despite the fact that the police are typically entitled to only qualified immunity. *See Pierson v. Ray*, 386 U.S. 547, 555–58 (1967).

Although *Briscoe* left open the question whether absolute immunity extends to testimony at pretrial hearings, *see Briscoe*, 460 U.S. at 328 n.5, the lower courts tend to afford absolute immunity to witnesses who testify in any type of judicial proceeding. *See* 1 COOK & SOBIESKI, *supra*, ¶ 2.07[C], at 2-361 to -362. The only exception some courts recognize is for the grand jury or preliminary hearing testimony of complaining witnesses — those responsible for initiating the proceedings, *see id.* at 2-363 — on the ground that complaining witnesses were liable for malicious prosecution at common law. *See, e.g., Vakilian v. Shaw*, 335 F.3d 509, 516 (6th Cir. 2003); *Cervantes v. Jones*, 188 F.3d 805, 809–10 (7th Cir. 1999). This result seems consistent with the Court's opinions in *Kalina v. Fletcher*, described above in Note 2, and *Malley v. Briggs*, 475 U.S. 335, 340–41 (1986). In *Malley*, the Court pointed to the fact that complaining witnesses were not given absolute immunity in 1871 in support of its holding that police officers who obtain arrest warrants unsupported by probable cause are not entitled to absolute immunity. *But cf. Kalina*, 522 U.S. at 136, 134 (Scalia, J., concurring) (arguing that *Malley* "distort[ed] the term 'complaining witness,' " in the sense that the common law "did not recognize two kinds of witness; it recognized two different torts" — malicious prosecution and defamation).

In *Tower v. Glover*, 467 U.S. 914 (1984), the Court held that public defenders who allegedly conspired with various state officials to secure a client's conviction were not entitled to absolute immunity. After observing that the nineteenth-century common law did not accord absolute immunity to the counterpart of the contemporary public defender, the Court commented: "We do not have a license to establish immunities from section 1983 actions in the interest of what we judge to be sound public policy." *Tower*, 467 U.S. at 922–23. (For a discussion of public defenders and section 1983's under color of law requirement, *see Polk County v. Dodson*, 454 U.S. 312 (1981), which is described in Chapter 1. B., *supra*.)

Likewise, in *Antoine v. Byers & Anderson, Inc.*, 508 U.S. 429 (1993), the Court denied absolute immunity to a court reporter who failed to provide the plaintiff with a transcript of his criminal trial for more than two years. In so holding, the Court reasoned that "[c]ourt reporters were not among the class of persons protected by judicial immunity in the 19th century" and that, under its functional approach to immunity, "court reporters do not exercise the kind of [discretionary] judgment" that is the "touchstone" of judicial immunity. *Antoine*, 508 U.S. at 433, 437, 435.

B. QUALIFIED IMMUNITY

HARLOW v. FITZGERALD
Supreme Court of the United States
457 U.S. 800 (1982)

JUSTICE POWELL delivered the opinion of the Court.

The issue in this case is the scope of the immunity available to the senior aides and advisers of the President of the United States in a suit for damages based upon their official acts.

I

In this suit for civil damages petitioners Bryce Harlow and Alexander Butterfield are alleged to have participated in a conspiracy to violate the constitutional and statutory rights of the respondent A. Ernest Fitzgerald. Respondent avers that petitioners entered the conspiracy in their capacities as senior White House aides to former President Richard M. Nixon. . . . [Specifically, respondent alleges that the elimination of his job with the Department of the Air Force during a departmental reorganization and reduction in force constituted retaliation for his embarrassing testimony before Congress about cost-overruns on a transport plane.]

Respondent claims that Harlow joined the conspiracy in his role as the Presidential aide principally responsible for congressional relations. . . .

Disputing Fitzgerald's contentions, Harlow argues that exhaustive discovery has adduced no direct evidence of his involvement in any wrongful activity. . . . Harlow asserts he had no reason to believe that a conspiracy existed. He contends that he took all his actions in good faith.

Petitioner Butterfield also is alleged to have entered the conspiracy not later than May 1969. Employed as Deputy Assistant to the President and Deputy Chief of Staff to H.R. Haldeman, Butterfield circulated a White House memorandum in that month in which he claimed to have learned that Fitzgerald planned to "blow the whistle" on some "shoddy purchasing practices". . . . After the President had promised at a press conference to inquire into Fitzgerald's dismissal, Haldeman solicited Butterfield's recommendations. In a subsequent memorandum emphasizing the importance of "loyalty," Butterfield counseled against offering Fitzgerald another job in the administration at that time.

For his part, Butterfield denies that he was involved in any decision concerning Fitzgerald's employment status until Haldeman sought his advice in December 1969 — more than a month after Fitzgerald's termination had been scheduled and announced publicly by the Air Force. Butterfield states that he never communicated his views about Fitzgerald to any official of the Defense Department. He argues generally that nearly eight years of discovery have failed to turn up any evidence that he caused injury to Fitzgerald. . . .

II

. . . [O]ur decisions consistently have held that government officials are entitled to some form of immunity from suits for damages. As recognized at common law, public officers require this protection to shield them from undue interference with their duties and from potentially disabling threats of liability.

Our decisions have recognized immunity defenses of two kinds. For officials whose special functions or constitutional status requires complete protection from suit, we have recognized the defense of "absolute immunity." The absolute immunity of legislators, in their legislative functions, and of judges, in their judicial functions, now is well settled. Our decisions also have extended absolute immunity to certain officials of the Executive Branch. These include prosecutors and similar officials, executive officers engaged in adjudicative functions, and the President of the United States, *see Nixon v. Fitzgerald*, [457 U.S. 731 (1982)].

For executive officials in general, however, our cases make plain that qualified immunity represents the norm. In *Scheuer v. Rhodes*, 416 U.S. 232 (1974), we acknowledged that high officials require greater protection than those with less complex discretionary responsibilities. Nonetheless, we held that a governor and his aides could receive the requisite protection from qualified or good-faith immunity. In *Butz v. Economou*, [438 U.S. 478 (1978),] we extended the approach of *Scheuer* to high federal officials of the Executive Branch. Discussing in detail the considerations that also had underlain our decision in *Scheuer*, we explained that the recognition of a qualified immunity defense for high executives reflected an attempt to balance competing values: not only the importance of a damages remedy to protect the rights of citizens, but also "the need to protect officials who are required to exercise their discretion and the related public interest in encouraging the vigorous exercise of official authority." Without discounting the adverse consequences of denying high officials an absolute immunity from private lawsuits alleging constitutional violations — consequences found sufficient in *Spalding v. Vilas*, 161 U.S. 483 (1896), and *Barr v. Matteo*, 360 U.S. 564 (1959), to warrant extension to such officials of absolute immunity from [defamation] suits at common law — we emphasized our expectation that insubstantial suits need not proceed to trial. . . .

III

A

Petitioners argue that they are entitled to a blanket protection of absolute immunity as an incident of their offices as Presidential aides. In deciding this claim we do not write on an empty page. In *Butz v. Economou*, the Secretary of Agriculture — a Cabinet official directly accountable to the President — asserted a defense of absolute official immunity from suit for civil damages. We rejected his claim. In so doing we did not question the power or the importance of the Secretary's office. Nor did we doubt the importance to the President of loyal and efficient subordinates in executing his duties of office. Yet we found these factors, alone, to be insufficient to justify absolute immunity. "[The] greater power of [high] officials," we reasoned, "affords a greater potential for a regime of lawless conduct." Damages actions against high officials were therefore "an important means of vindicating constitutional guarantees." Moreover, we concluded that it would be "untenable to draw a distinction for purposes of immunity law between suits brought against state officials under [42 U.S.C.] § 1983 and suits brought directly under the Constitution against federal officials."

Having decided in *Butz* that Members of the Cabinet ordinarily enjoy only qualified immunity from suit, we conclude today that it would be equally untenable to hold absolute immunity an incident of the office of every Presidential subordinate based in the White House. Members of the Cabinet are direct subordinates of the President, frequently with greater responsibilities, both to the President and to the Nation, than White House staff. The considerations that supported our decision in *Butz* apply with equal force to this case. It is no disparagement of the offices held by petitioners to hold that Presidential aides, like Members of the Cabinet, generally are entitled only to a qualified immunity.

B

In disputing the controlling authority of *Butz*, petitioners rely on the principles developed in *Gravel v. United States*, 408 U.S. 606 (1972)[, where] we held the Speech and Debate Clause derivatively applicable to the "legislative acts" of a Senator's aide that would have been privileged if performed by the Senator himself.

Petitioners contend that the rationale of *Gravel* mandates a similar "derivative" immunity for the chief aides of the President of the United States. Emphasizing that the President must delegate a large measure of authority to execute the duties of his office, they argue that recognition of derivative absolute immunity is made essential by all the considerations that support absolute immunity for the President himself.

Petitioners' argument is not without force. Ultimately, however, it sweeps too far. If the President's aides are derivatively immune because they are essential to the functioning of the Presidency, so should the Members of the Cabinet . . . be absolutely immune. Yet we implicitly rejected such derivative immunity in *Butz*.[20] Moreover, in general our cases have followed a "functional" approach to immunity law. We have recognized that the judicial, prosecutorial, and legislative functions require absolute immunity. But this protection has extended no further than its justification would warrant. In *Gravel*, for example, we emphasized that Senators and their aides were absolutely immune only when performing "acts legislative in nature," and not when taking other acts even "in their official capacity." Our cases involving judges and prosecutors have followed a similar line. The undifferentiated extension of absolute "derivative" immunity to the President's aides therefore could not be reconciled with the "functional" approach that has characterized the immunity decisions of this Court, indeed including *Gravel* itself.[21]

C

Petitioners also assert an entitlement to immunity based on the "special functions" of White House aides. This form of argument accords with the analytical approach of our cases. For aides entrusted with discretionary authority in such sensitive areas as national security or foreign policy, absolute immunity might well be justified to protect the unhesitating performance of functions vital to the national interest. But a "special functions" rationale does not warrant a blanket recognition of absolute immunity for all Presidential aides in the performance of all their duties. This conclusion too follows from our decision in *Butz*, which establishes that an executive official's claim to absolute immunity must be justified by reference to the public interest in the special functions of his office, not the mere fact of high station.

Butz also identifies the location of the burden of proof. The burden of justifying absolute immunity rests on the official asserting the claim. . . . In order to establish entitlement to absolute immunity a Presidential aide first must show that the responsibilities of his office embraced a function so sensitive as to require a total shield

---

[20] [n.14] The Chief Justice . . . argues that senior Presidential aides work "more intimately with the President on a daily basis than does a Cabinet officer," and that *Butz* therefore is not controlling. In recent years, however, such men as Henry Kissinger and James Schlesinger have served in both Presidential advisory and Cabinet positions. Kissinger held both posts simultaneously. In our view it is impossible to generalize about the role of "offices" in an individual President's administration without reference to the functions that particular officeholders are assigned by the President. *Butz v. Economou* cannot be distinguished on this basis.

[21] [n.17] Our decision today in *Nixon v. Fitzgerald* [described in Note 2, *infra*] in no way abrogates this general rule. As we explained in that opinion, the recognition of absolute immunity for all of a President's acts in office derives in principal part from factors unique to his constitutional responsibilities and station. Suits against other officials — including Presidential aides — generally do not invoke separation-of-powers considerations to the same extent as suits against the President himself.

from liability.[22] He then must demonstrate that he was discharging the protected function when performing the act for which liability is asserted.

Applying these standards to the claims advanced by petitioners Harlow and Butterfield, we cannot conclude on the record before us that either has shown that "public policy requires [for any of the functions of his office] an exemption of [absolute] scope." *Butz*, 438 U.S., at 506. Nor, assuming that petitioners did have functions for which absolute immunity would be warranted, could we now conclude that the acts charged in this lawsuit — if taken at all — would lie within the protected area. We do not, however, foreclose the possibility that petitioners, on remand, could satisfy the standards properly applicable to their claims.

IV

Even if they cannot establish that their official functions require absolute immunity, petitioners assert that public policy at least mandates an application of the qualified immunity standard that would permit the defeat of insubstantial claims without resort to trial. We agree.

A

The resolution of immunity questions inherently requires a balance between the evils inevitable in any available alternative. In situations of abuse of office, an action for damages may offer the only realistic avenue for vindication of constitutional guarantees. It is this recognition that has required the denial of absolute immunity to most public officers. At the same time, however, it cannot be disputed seriously that claims frequently run against the innocent as well as the guilty — at a cost not only to the defendant officials, but to society as a whole. These social costs include the expenses of litigation, the diversion of official energy from pressing public issues, and the deterrence of able citizens from acceptance of public office. Finally, there is the danger that fear of being sued will "dampen the ardor of all but the most resolute, or the most irresponsible [public officials], in the unflinching discharge of their duties." *Gregoire v. Biddle*, 177 F.2d 579, 581 (CA2 1949), *cert. denied*, 339 U.S. 949 (1950).

In identifying qualified immunity as the best attainable accommodation of competing values, in *Butz*, as in *Scheuer*, we relied on the assumption that this standard would permit "[insubstantial] lawsuits [to] be quickly terminated." Yet petitioners advance persuasive arguments that the dismissal of insubstantial lawsuits without trial — a factor presupposed in the balance of competing interests struck by our prior cases — requires an adjustment of the "good faith" standard established by our decisions.

B

Qualified or "good faith" immunity is an affirmative defense that must be pleaded by a defendant official. *Gomez v. Toledo*, 446 U.S. 635 (1980).[23] Decisions of this Court have established that the "good faith" defense has both an "objective" and a "subjective" aspect. The objective element involves a presumptive knowledge of and respect for "basic, unquestioned constitutional rights." *Wood v. Strickland*, 420 U.S. 308, 322 (1975). The subjective component refers to "permissible intentions." *Ibid.* . . . Referring both to the objective and subjective elements, we have held that

---

[22] [n.20] Here as elsewhere the relevant judicial inquiries would encompass considerations of public policy, the importance of which should be confirmed either by reference to the common law or, more likely, our constitutional heritage and structure. See *Nixon v. Fitzgerald*, ante, at 747–748.

[23] [n.24] Although *Gomez* presented the question in the context of an action under 42 U.S.C. § 1983, the Court's analysis indicates that "immunity" must also be pleaded as a defense in [*Bivens*] actions under the Constitution and laws of the United States. *Gomez* did not decide which party bore the burden of proof on the issue of good faith.

qualified immunity would be defeated if an official *"knew or reasonably should have known* that the action he took within his sphere of official responsibility would violate the constitutional rights of the [plaintiff], *or* if he took the action *with the malicious intention* to cause a deprivation of constitutional rights or other injury. . . . " *Ibid.* (emphasis added).

The subjective element of the good-faith defense frequently has proved incompatible with our admonition in *Butz* that insubstantial claims should not proceed to trial. Rule 56 of the Federal Rules of Civil Procedure provides that disputed questions of fact ordinarily may not be decided on motions for summary judgment. And an official's subjective good faith has been considered to be a question of fact that some courts have regarded as inherently requiring resolution by a jury.

In the context of *Butz'* attempted balancing of competing values, it now is clear that substantial costs attend the litigation of the subjective good faith of government officials. Not only are there the general costs of subjecting officials to the risks of trial — distraction of officials from their governmental duties, inhibition of discretionary action, and deterrence of able people from public service. There are special costs to "subjective" inquiries of this kind. Immunity generally is available only to officials performing discretionary functions. In contrast with the thought processes accompanying "ministerial" tasks, the judgments surrounding discretionary action almost inevitably are influenced by the decisionmaker's experiences, values, and emotions. These variables explain in part why questions of subjective intent so rarely can be decided by summary judgment. Yet they also frame a background in which there often is no clear end to the relevant evidence. Judicial inquiry into subjective motivation therefore may entail broad-ranging discovery and the deposing of numerous persons, including an official's professional colleagues. Inquiries of this kind can be peculiarly disruptive of effective government.

Consistently with the balance at which we aimed in *Butz*, we conclude today that bare allegations of malice should not suffice to subject government officials either to the costs of trial or to the burdens of broad-reaching discovery. We therefore hold that government officials performing discretionary functions generally are shielded from liability for civil damages insofar as their conduct does not violate clearly established statutory or constitutional rights of which a reasonable person would have known.

Reliance on the objective reasonableness of an official's conduct, as measured by reference to clearly established law, should avoid excessive disruption of government and permit the resolution of many insubstantial claims on summary judgment. On summary judgment, the judge appropriately may determine, not only the currently applicable law, but whether that law was clearly established at the time an action occurred.[24] If the law at that time was not clearly established, an official could not reasonably be expected to anticipate subsequent legal developments, nor could he fairly be said to "know" that the law forbade conduct not previously identified as unlawful. Until this threshold immunity question is resolved, discovery should not be allowed. If the law was clearly established, the immunity defense ordinarily should fail, since a reasonably competent public official should know the law governing his conduct. Nevertheless, if the official pleading the defense claims extraordinary circumstances and can prove that he neither knew nor should have known of the relevant legal standard, the defense should be sustained. But again, the defense would turn primarily on objective factors.

By defining the limits of qualified immunity essentially in objective terms, we provide no license to lawless conduct. The public interest in deterrence of unlawful conduct and in compensation of victims remains protected by a test that focuses on the objective

---

[24] [n. 32] As in *Procunier v. Navarette*, 434 U.S. [555, 565 (1978)], we need not define here the circumstances under which "the state of the law" should be "evaluated by reference to the opinions of this Court, of the Courts of Appeals, or of the local District Court."

legal reasonableness of an official's acts. Where an official could be expected to know that certain conduct would violate statutory or constitutional rights, he should be made to hesitate; and a person who suffers injury caused by such conduct may have a cause of action. But where an official's duties legitimately require action in which clearly established rights are not implicated, the public interest may be better served by action taken "with independence and without fear of consequences." *Pierson v. Ray*, 386 U.S. 547, 554 (1967).[25]

C

In this case petitioners have asked us to hold that the respondent's pretrial showings were insufficient to survive their motion for summary judgment. We think it appropriate, however, to remand the case to the District Court for its reconsideration of this issue in light of this opinion. The trial court is more familiar with the record so far developed and also is better situated to make any such further findings as may be necessary. . . .

JUSTICE BRENNAN, with whom JUSTICE MARSHALL and JUSTICE BLACKMUN join, concurring.

I agree with the substantive standard announced by the Court today, imposing liability when a public-official defendant "knew or should have known" of the constitutionally violative effect of his actions. This standard would not allow the official who actually knows that he was violating the law to escape liability for his actions, even if he could not "reasonably have been expected" to know what he actually did know. Thus the clever and unusually well-informed violator of constitutional rights will not evade just punishment for his crimes. . . . I write separately only to note that given this standard, it seems inescapable to me that some measure of discovery may sometimes be required to determine exactly what a public-official defendant did "know" at the time of his actions. . . . Of course, as the Court has already noted, summary judgment will be readily available to public-official defendants whenever the state of the law was so ambiguous at the time of the alleged violation that it could not have been "known" then, and thus liability could not ensue. In my view, summary judgment will also be readily available whenever the plaintiff cannot prove, as a threshold matter, that a violation of his constitutional rights actually occurred. I see no reason why discovery of defendants' "knowledge" should not be deferred by the trial judge pending decision of any motion of defendants for summary judgment on grounds such as these.[26]

NOTES

1. Evaluating the Doctrine of Qualified Immunity for Executive-Branch Officials. The first Supreme Court opinion to mention the concept of qualified immunity was *Pierson v. Ray*, 386 U.S. 547 (1967), which held that police officials are generally entitled to only qualified immunity in section 1983 cases. When *Scheuer v. Rhodes*, 416 U.S. 232 (1974), extended *Pierson's* holding to high-ranking executive branch officials — the Governor of Ohio in *Scheuer* — the Court was largely acting as a matter of policy. As the Court subsequently acknowledged in *Wyatt v. Cole*, 504 U.S. 158, 166–67 (1992), there is no common-law basis for either the decision to afford qualified immunity to executive-branch officials or the specific elements of the qualified immunity defense the Court has adopted. In fact, there was some common-law support,

---

[25] [n.34] We emphasize that our decision applies only to suits for civil damages arising from actions within the scope of an official's duties and in "objective" good faith. We express no view as to the conditions in which injunctive or declaratory relief might be available.

[26] [Editor's note: Chief Justice Burger's dissenting opinion, which is referred to in n.14 of the majority opinion, is omitted.]

cited by the *Harlow* majority, for affording absolute immunity to at least high-ranking executive-branch officials. But the Court concluded in *Scheuer* that § 1983 would be "drained of meaning" if absolute immunity were extended to executive-branch officials. *Scheuer*, 416 U.S. at 248.

Note that the policy considerations underlying the qualified immunity defense, as detailed in *Harlow*, are similar to the policy concerns used to justify the absolute immunity given to legislators, judges, and prosecutors. Nevertheless, in *Wood v. Strickland*, 420 U.S. 308, 320 (1975), a section 1983 suit filed against members of a school board by two high school students who were expelled for spiking the punch at a school meeting, the Court explained that absolute immunity "would not sufficiently increase the ability of school officials to exercise their discretion in a forthright manner to warrant the absence of a remedy for students subjected to intentional or otherwise inexcusable deprivations." Somewhat ironically, the Court reached this conclusion after observing that school board officials "function at different times in the nature of legislators and adjudicators." *Wood*, 420 U.S. at 319. For the view that the Court has not made a convincing case for granting absolute immunity to some government officials and only qualified immunity to others, see PETER H. SCHUCK, SUING GOVERNMENT: CITIZEN REMEDIES FOR OFFICIAL WRONGS 90–91 (1983) (pointing out that "[b]ureaucrats, no less than judges, are expected and required to act objectively and without regard to personal considerations").

2. Presidential Immunity. The one executive-branch official who has been afforded absolute immunity is the President. In *Nixon v. Fitzgerald*, 457 U.S. 731, 749 (1982), the companion case to *Harlow*, the Court relied on the President's "unique position in [our] constitutional scheme" to justify this conclusion. The Court went on to define the scope of presidential immunity as extending to any "acts within the 'outer perimeter' of [the President's] official responsibility." *Nixon*, 457 U.S. at 756. Thus, in contrast to the functional approach used for other types of absolute immunity, the President's status is controlling.

Nevertheless, the Court held in *Clinton v. Jones*, 520 U.S. 681 (1997), that presidential immunity did not require staying the trial of a section 1983 claim filed against then-President Bill Clinton by Paula Jones, who alleged that Clinton had sexually harassed her while he was Governor of Arkansas. Invoking the functional approach to immunity, the Court rejected the President's "effort to construct an immunity from suit for unofficial acts grounded purely in the identity of his office." *Clinton*, 520 U.S. at 695.

3. The "Special Functions" Exception. Although *Harlow* indicated that "qualified immunity represents the norm" for other executive-branch officials, including even high-level White House aides and members of the President's cabinet, the Court left open the possibility that absolute immunity might be extended to presidential aides serving "special functions" — such as those "entrusted with discretionary authority in such sensitive areas as national security or foreign policy." But the Court has never found a case that it thought satisfied the "special functions" exception. In *Mitchell v. Forsyth*, 472 U.S. 511 (1985), the Court rejected the "special functions" argument made by the Attorney General in a suit challenging the constitutionality of a warrantless wiretap installed in the interest of domestic national security. In so holding, the Court was not convinced that "the national security functions of the Attorney General are so sensitive, so vital to the protection of our Nation's well-being, that we cannot tolerate any risk that in performing those functions he will be chilled by the possibility of personal liability for acts that may be found to impinge on the constitutional rights of citizens." *Mitchell*, 472 U.S. at 520.

4. Private Parties. In *Richardson v. McKnight*, 521 U.S. 399 (1997), the Court held that prison guards employed by a privatized correctional center were not entitled to raise a qualified immunity defense. Building on its decision five years earlier in *Wyatt v. Cole*, 504 U.S. 158 (1992), which denied qualified immunity to private parties who invoked unconstitutional state garnishment, replevin, or attachment statutes, the *Richardson* Court found no "'firmly rooted' tradition of immunity applicable to privately employed prison guards." *Richardson*, 521 U.S. at 404. Although its examination of the relevant policies was a "closer question," the Court ultimately concluded that "marketplace pressures provide the private firm with strong incentives to avoid overly timid, insufficiently vigorous, unduly fearful, or 'nonarduous' employee job performance," and "the risk of distract[ing employees from their duties] alone cannot be sufficient grounds for an immunity." *Richardson*, 521 U.S. at 407, 410, 411. The Court dismissed the defendants' argument that they performed the same function as state prison guards by noting that the functional approach is used "only to decide which type of immunity — absolute or qualified — a public officer should receive," and not "the difference between unlimited § 1983 liability and qualified immunity." *Richardson*, 521 U.S. at 408.

As it had in *Wyatt*, however, the *Richardson* Court carefully limited its holding in two respects. First, it did not "'foreclose the possibility that private defendants . . . could be entitled to an affirmative defense based on good faith and/or probable cause or that § 1983 suits against private, rather than governmental, parties could require plaintiffs to carry additional burdens.'" *Richardson*, 521 U.S. at 413 (quoting *Wyatt*, 504 U.S. at 169). Second, the Richardson Court restricted its holding to the specific facts of that case — where "a private firm, systematically organized to assume a lengthy administrative task (managing an institution) with limited direct supervision by the government, undertakes the task for profit and potentially in competition with other firms." The Court expressly left open cases involving "a private individual briefly associated with a government body, serving as an adjunct to government in an essential governmental activity, or acting under close official supervision." *Richardson*, 521 U.S. at 413.

A number of subsequent appellate court opinions have accorded private defendants a good faith defense in section 1983 cases. On remand in *Wyatt*, for example, the Fifth Circuit required the plaintiffs to establish that the defendants "failed to act in good faith in invoking the unconstitutional state procedures" — i.e., that they "either knew or should have known that [the state] statute was unconstitutional." *Wyatt v. Cole*, 994 F.2d 1113, 1115 (5th Cir. 1993).[27] *Cf. Jordan v. Fox, Rothschild, O'Brien Frankel*, 20 F.3d 1250, 1277 (3d Cir. 1994) (distinguishing the good faith defense, which "depends on [a private defendant's] subjective state of mind," from "the more demanding objective standard of reasonable belief that governs qualified immunity"). For a description of the conflict among the lower courts as to whether the private entities that employ these individuals may raise a qualified immunity defense, see Barbara Kritchevsky, *Private Parties as Defendants in Civil Rights Litigation: Civil Rights Liability of Private Entities*, 26 CARDOZO L. REV. 35 (2004).

5. Injunctive Actions. Although the Court left open, in n.34 of its opinion in *Harlow*, whether qualified immunity is available in suits seeking only injunctive relief, the defense has generally been limited to damages claims. *See, e.g., Morse v. Frederick*, 127 S. Ct. 2618, 2624 n.1 (2007).

6. Evaluating *Harlow*'s Definition of Qualified Immunity. The *Harlow* Court's decision to revise the qualified immunity defense, eliminating the subjective prong of the two-part standard articulated in *Wood v. Strickland*, 420 U.S. 308 (1975), has been criticized on the grounds that it "in large measure converted qualified immunity into the equivalent of absolute immunity." Sheldon H. Nahmod, *Constitutional Wrongs Without Remedies: Executive Official Immunity*, 62 WASH. U.L.Q. 221, 241 (1984). On the other hand, *Harlow*'s standard — albeit "quite unusual" because "ignorance of the law is virtually never an excuse" — has been characterized as "a proxy for fault," a way of

---

[27] For a discussion of how section 1983's under color of state law requirement applies in cases like *Wyatt*, see *Lugar v. Edmondson Oil Co.* which is excerpted in Chapter 1. B., *supra*.

"limiting constitutional damages liability to cases involving truly blameworthy conduct" and thereby "maintain[ing] the special status of constitutional rights in the public consciousness." Barbara E. Armacost, *Qualified Immunity: Ignorance Excused*, 51 VAND. L. REV. 583, 584, 676, 680 (1998). For the contrary argument that viewing qualified immunity as "an inquiry into the existence of wrongdoing" is "to misapprehend profoundly the nature and function" of the defense because "its primary purpose is to promote independent decisionmaking" by public officials and not to "connote wrongdoing or its absence," *see* Sheldon Nahmod, *Constitutional Damages and Corrective Justice: A Different View*, 76 VA. L. REV. 997, 1004 (1990).

With respect to *Harlow*'s recitation of the general costs of section 1983 liability and the specific costs of *Wood*'s subjective prong, some commentators have criticized the Court not only for failing to cite any empirical evidence to support its assumptions about overdeterrence, but also for ignoring studies suggesting that public officials are not unduly intimidated by the specter of section 1983 suits. *See, e.g.*, David Rudovsky, *The Qualified Immunity Doctrine in the Supreme Court: Judicial Activism and the Restriction of Constitutional Rights*, 138 U. PA. L. REV. 23, 31 n.43 (1989). Others have pointed out that the Court never considered the benefits of *Wood*'s subjective prong, noting that "if the Court is going to play the cost-benefit game, it should abide by the rules." Nahmod, 62 WASH. U.L.Q. at 249. Still others have taken the position that overdeterrence is not a cost, but rather "a societal good" because it "discourages risky conduct that might harm others in an unconstitutional fashion." Mark R. Brown, *The Failure of Fault Under § 1983: Municipal Liability for State Law Enforcement*, 84 CORNELL L. REV. 1503, 1523 (1999).

7. The Extraordinary Circumstances Exception. *Harlow* left open the possibility that even a public official who violated clearly established law could nevertheless prevail on qualified immunity grounds in a case that involved "extraordinary circumstances" such that the defendant "neither knew nor should have known of the relevant legal standard." The extraordinary circumstances exception is typically invoked in cases where the defendant relied on erroneous legal advice, *see* 2 SHELDON H. NAHMOD, CIVIL RIGHTS AND CIVIL LIBERTIES LITIGATION: THE LAW OF SECTION 1983 § 8:16 (4th ed. 2007), although some courts reject qualified immunity claims in such circumstances. *See* 1 JOSEPH G. COOK & JOHN L. SOBIESKI, JR., CIVIL RIGHTS ACTIONS ¶ 2.09[A], at 2-417 & n.10 (2007).

8. The "Threshold" Constitutional Question. On a number of occasions, the Court has cautioned that before turning to the questions surrounding the qualified immunity defense, the "threshold" issue is whether the allegations in the plaintiff's complaint demonstrate a constitutional injury. *See, e.g., Saucier v. Katz*, 533 U.S. 194, 201 (2001). *Saucier*'s instructions on this point are as follows:

> A court required to rule upon the qualified immunity issue must consider . . . this threshold question: Taken in the light most favorable to the party asserting the injury, do the facts alleged show the officer's conduct violated a constitutional right? This must be the initial inquiry. *Siegert v. Gilley*, 500 U.S. 226, 232 (1991). In the course of determining whether a constitutional right was violated on the premises alleged, a court might find it necessary to set forth principles which will become the basis for a holding that a right is clearly established. This is the process for the law's elaboration from case to case, and it is one reason for our insisting upon turning to the existence or nonexistence of a constitutional right as the first inquiry. The law might be deprived of this explanation were a court simply to skip ahead to the question whether the law clearly established that the officer's conduct was unlawful in the circumstances of the case.

Saucier, 533 U.S. at 201; *see also County of Sacramento v. Lewis*, 523 U.S. 833, 841 n.5 (1998) (indicating that this approach should "[n]ormally" be followed even when the constitutional issue is "'difficult and unresolved'"; otherwise, "standards of official conduct would tend to remain uncertain, to the detriment of both officials and individuals," because "[a]n immunity determination, with nothing more, provides no clear standard, constitutional or nonconstitutional").

The courts of appeals disagree whether the approach outlined in *Saucier* is "mandatory" or merely a description of "what the courts ordinarily should do," *Sutton v. Rasheed*, 323 F.3d 236, 250 (3d Cir. 2003), and some of the Justices have been critical of "*Saucier*'s fixed order-of-battle rule." *Scott v. Harris*, 127 S. Ct. 1769, 1780 (2007) (Breyer, J., concurring). In *Brosseau v. Haugen*, 543 U.S. 194 (2004) (per curiam), for example, Justices Breyer, Ginsburg, and Scalia expressed "concern[] that the current rule rigidly requires courts unnecessarily to decide difficult constitutional questions when there is available an easier basis for the decision (e.g., qualified immunity) that will satisfactorily resolve the case." *Brosseau*, 543 U.S. at 201 (Breyer, J., concurring). *See also Los Angeles County v. Rettele*, 127 S. Ct. 1989, 1994 (2007) (Stevens, J., concurring) (likewise advocating that the Court "disavow the unwise practice of deciding constitutional questions in advance of the necessity of doing so"). In addition to judicial economy concerns, these Justices have objected that "[s]ometimes (e.g., where the defendant loses the constitutional question but wins on qualified immunity) th[e] order-of-battle rule may immunize an incorrect constitutional ruling from review." *Scott*, 127 S. Ct. at 1780 (Breyer, J., concurring). *See also Bunting v. Mellen*, 541 U.S. 1019, 1024 (2004) (Scalia, J., dissenting from denial of certiorari) (pointing out that, "if the constitutional determination remains locked inside a § 1983 suit in which the defendant received a favorable judgment on qualified immunity grounds, then 'government defendants, as the prevailing parties, will have no opportunity to appeal for review of the newly declared constitutional right in the higher courts'"). *Saucier* has likewise come under critical scrutiny from commentators. *See* Pamela S. Karlan, *The Paradoxical Structure of Constitutional Litigation*, 75 FORDHAM L. REV. 1913, 1926 (2007) (observing that the *Saucier* approach "makes little administrative sense"); Pierre N. Leval, *Judging Under the Constitution: Dicta About Dicta*, 81 N.Y.U. L. REV. 1249, 1275 (2006) (referring to *Saucier* as "a puzzling misadventure in constitutional dictum"). Professor Karlan's prediction that *Saucier*'s "sequencing requirement may turn out to be short-lived" may soon prove true, as the Court has agreed to consider whether *Saucier* should be overruled. *See Pearson v. Callahan*, 128 S. Ct. 1702 (2008) (No. 07-751).

9. Defining "Clearly Established" Rights: Which Court Opinions Count? Although the *Harlow* Court did not attempt to apply its newly formulated qualified immunity standard to the facts at issue in that case, subsequent Supreme Court opinions have endeavored to clarify the circumstances under which a government official can be said to have "violate[d] clearly established statutory or constitutional rights of which a reasonable person would have known" within the meaning of *Harlow*. *See Malley v. Briggs*, 475 U.S. 335, 341 (1986) (holding that qualified immunity does not protect a police officer who acts in reliance on an arrest warrant issued without the requisite probable cause if, "on an objective basis, it is obvious that no reasonably competent officer would have concluded that a warrant should issue," but does apply "if officers of reasonable competence could disagree on this issue," and concluding that *Harlow* "provides ample protection to all but the plainly incompetent or those who knowingly violate the law"). Nevertheless, questions about the reach of the qualified immunity defense still remain unresolved.

For example, the Court has never definitively answered the issue left open in n.32 of *Harlow* — whether rights can be "clearly established" by lower court opinions — even though subsequent Supreme Court opinions have shed some light on that issue. In *Mitchell v. Forsyth*, 472 U.S. 511, 535 (1985), for example, the Court concluded that the Attorney General was entitled to qualified immunity for authorizing a warrantless wiretap in the interest of domestic national security because the constitutionality of such wiretaps was "an open question" at the time. In support of this conclusion, the Court observed that two district court opinions issued two and nine months before the

Attorney General acted had approved of such wiretaps and two district court rulings to the contrary were decided only after the wiretap had been terminated. *See Mitchell*, 472 U.S. at 535.

Subsequently, the Court noted in *United States v. Lanier*, 520 U.S. 259, 269 (1997), a case involving the reach of 18 U.S.C. § 242, the criminal counterpart to section 1983, that prior qualified immunity rulings issued by the Supreme Court had "referred" to appellate court decisions in analyzing whether a right was clearly established. And the Court refused to adopt "a categorical rule that decisions of the Courts of Appeals and other courts are inadequate as a matter of law" to provide fair warning to defendants. *Lanier*, 520 U.S. at 269.

Moreover, in *Wilson v. Layne*, 526 U.S. 603, 615, 617 (1999), the Court unanimously held that the Fourth Amendment prohibited a "media ride-along" — where a reporter and photographer from the *Washington Post* accompanied police officers executing an arrest warrant in Maryland — but nevertheless decided that the police were entitled to qualified immunity because the constitutionality of the practice was "by no means open and shut" and "the state of the law . . . was at best undeveloped." The Court explained that the only relevant precedents were a Wisconsin state appellate court decision and two unpublished federal district court opinions (from Ohio and California) upholding the practice and a contrary Sixth Circuit opinion that had been "decided a mere five weeks before the events of this case." *Wilson*, 526 U.S. at 616. Although the Sixth Circuit opinion "did anticipate" *Wilson*'s holding, the Supreme Court noted that the plaintiffs had been unable to find "any cases of controlling authority in their jurisdiction at the time of the incident that clearly established the rule on which they seek to rely, nor have they identified a consensus of persuasive authority such that a reasonable officer could not have believed that his actions were lawful." *Wilson*, 526 U.S. at 616, 617.

Despite these post-*Harlow* developments, the federal courts have not been able to agree which court opinions suffice to "clearly establish" a constitutional right. *See, e.g., Inouye v. Kemna*, 504 F.3d 705, 714 (9th Cir. 2007) (" '[a]bsent binding precedent, we look to all available decisional law, including the law of other circuits and district courts, to determine whether the right was clearly established,' " and " '[w]e also evaluate the likelihood that this circuit or the Supreme Court would have reached the same result' "); *Marsh v. Butler County*, 268 F.3d 1014, 1032 n.10 (11th Cir. 2001) (holding that the law can be clearly established only by decisions from the Supreme Court, the Eleventh Circuit, or "the highest court of the pertinent state," and refusing to interpret *Wilson v. Layne* as holding that a "consensus of cases of persuasive authority" from other courts suffices because "[e]ach jurisdiction has its own body of law, and . . . [w]e do not expect public officials to sort out the law of every jurisdiction"); *Anderson v. Romero*, 72 F.3d 518, 525 (7th Cir. 1995) (concluding that district court opinions "by themselves . . . cannot clearly establish the law because . . . they are not authoritative as precedent and therefore do not establish the duties of nonparties"). *See generally* 2 SHELDON H. NAHMOD, CIVIL RIGHTS AND CIVIL LIBERTIES LITIGATION: THE LAW OF SECTION 1983 § 8:22 (4th ed. 2007); Kit Kinports, *Habeas Corpus, Qualified Immunity, and Crystal Balls: Predicting the Course of Constitutional Law*, 33 ARIZ. L. REV. 115, 140–49 (1991).

10. Defining "Clearly Established" Rights: How Similar Must the Precedents Be? The Supreme Court has repeatedly rejected the contention that a public official is entitled to qualified immunity " 'unless the very action in question has previously been held unlawful.' " *Wilson v. Layne*, 526 U.S. 603, 615 (1999) (quoting *Anderson v. Creighton*, 483 U.S. 635, 640 (1987)). *See also Mitchell v. Forsyth*, 472 U.S. 511, 535 n.12 (1985) ("We do not intend to suggest that an official is always immune from liability or suit for a warrantless search merely because the warrant requirement has never explicitly been held to apply to a search conducted in identical circumstances.").

On the other hand, *Anderson v. Creighton*, 483 U.S. 635 (1987), held that qualified immunity cannot be denied simply on the grounds that it is clearly established that the Fourth Amendment prohibits warrantless searches unless the police have both probable cause to search and exigent circumstances that justify dispensing with a search warrant. "[I]f the test of 'clearly established law' were to be applied at this level of generality," the *Anderson* Court observed, "it would bear no relationship to the 'objective legal reasonableness' that is the touchstone of *Harlow*." *Anderson*, 483 U.S. at 639. Therefore, the Court held, "the right the official is alleged to have violated must have been 'clearly established' in a more particularized, and hence more relevant, sense":

> The contours of the right must be sufficiently clear that a reasonable official would understand that what he is doing violates that right. This is not to say that an official action is protected by qualified immunity unless the very action in question has previously been held unlawful, but it is to say that in the light of pre-existing law the unlawfulness must be apparent.

Anderson, 483 U.S. at 640.

As applied to the Fourth Amendment violation at issue there, the Court said, "[t]he relevant question . . . is the objective (albeit fact-specific) question whether a reasonable police officer could have believed [the] warrantless search to be lawful, in light of clearly established law and the information the searching officers possessed." Thus, if the defendant "reasonably but mistakenly" thought that there was probable cause and exigent circumstances, he was entitled to qualified immunity. *Anderson*, 483 U.S. at 641.

Anderson's "concept of probable cause to believe one has probable cause to arrest or search" has been called "metaphysical." *Boyce v. Fernandes*, 77 F.3d 946, 948 (7th Cir. 1996); *see also* Jon O. Newman, *Suing the Lawbreakers: Proposals to Strengthen the Section 1983 Damage Remedy for Law Enforcers' Misconduct*, 87 YALE L.J. 447, 460 (1978) ("Surely [an] officer could not *reasonably* believe that there was probable cause for an unlawful arrest, for an unlawful arrest is by definition an arrest for which a prudent police officer could not reasonably believe there was probable cause.").

Despite these criticisms of *Anderson*'s "particularized," "fact-specific" approach to the qualified immunity inquiry, the Supreme Court remains committed to it. Thus, in *Saucier v. Katz*, 533 U.S. 194 (2001), which involved a claim that police officers used excessive force in making an arrest, the Court rejected the appellate court's conclusion that "the qualified immunity inquiry and the merits of the Fourth Amendment excessive force claim are identical, since both concern the objective reasonableness of the officer's conduct in light of the circumstances the officer faced on the scene." *Saucier*, 533 U.S. at 199–200. Although the Supreme Court pointed out that, under the objective reasonableness standard for evaluating excessive force claims set out in *Graham v. Connor*, 490 U.S. 386 (1989), a police officer who "reasonably, but mistakenly, believed that a suspect was likely to fight back . . . would be justified in using more force than in fact was needed," the Court nevertheless concluded that "[t]he inquiries for qualified immunity and excessive force remain distinct" and "[t]he qualified immunity inquiry . . . has a further dimension." *Saucier*, 533 U.S. at 204, 205. The Court defined this "further dimension" as follows:

> The concern of the immunity inquiry is to acknowledge that reasonable mistakes can be made as to the legal constraints on particular police conduct. It is sometimes difficult for an officer to determine how the relevant legal doctrine, here excessive force, will apply to the factual situation the officer confronts. An officer might correctly perceive all of the relevant facts but have a mistaken understanding as to whether a particular amount of force is legal in those circumstances. If the officer's mistake as to what the law requires is reasonable, however, the officer is entitled to the immunity defense.

Saucier, 533 U.S. at 205. Writing on behalf of the three Justices in the minority, Justice Ginsburg criticized the majority for "[d]ouble counting 'objective reasonableness,'" arguing that "an officer whose conduct is objectively unreasonable under *Graham* should find no shelter under a sequential qualified immunity test." *Saucier*, 533 U.S. at 214 (Ginsburg, J., concurring in the judgment). (For another Supreme Court opinion applying the qualified immunity doctrine in the context of an excessive force claim, see the discussion of *Brosseau v. Haugen* in Note 2 following *Hope v. Pelzer, infra*.)

The "particularized," "fact-specific" standard mandated by *Anderson* and *Saucier* can make it difficult for plaintiffs to survive a qualified immunity motion because "[a]t the fringes, even the most well-settled doctrines lapse into vagueness and unpredictability." Mark G. Yudof, *Liability for Constitutional Torts and the Risk-Averse Public School Official*, 49 S. CAL. L. REV. 1322, 1341 (1976). In the twenty-five years since *Harlow* was decided, the federal courts have never agreed on the extent to which the plaintiff's case must be factually similar to the relevant precedents in order to support a finding that the defendant violated clearly established rights. *Compare Brokaw v. Mercer County*, 235 F.3d 1000, 1022 (7th Cir. 2000) (refusing to require plaintiffs to find "a closely analogous case" in order to avoid qualified immunity and instead recognizing the possibility that a clearly established right can exist where "the violation was so obvious that a reasonable person would have known of the unconstitutionality of the conduct at issue," noting that "in the most extreme cases, an analogous case might never arise because 'the existence of the right was so clear . . . that no one thought it worthwhile to litigate the issue' "), *and Burton v. Richmond*, 276 F.3d 973, 976 (8th Cir. 2002) (endorsing a " 'flexible standard, requiring some, but not precise factual correspondence with precedent, and demanding that officials apply general, well-developed legal principles' "), *with Hansen v. Soldenwagner*, 19 F.3d 573, 576 (11th Cir. 1994) (noting that in circumstances where the constitutional right at issue involves "a balancing of competing interests on a case-by-case basis, . . . only in the rarest of cases will reasonable government officials truly know that [their actions] violated 'clearly established' federal rights"). *See generally* 2 SHELDON H. NAHMOD, CIVIL RIGHTS AND CIVIL LIBERTIES LITIGATION: THE LAW OF SECTION 1983 §§ 8:18 & 8:20 (4th ed. 2007); Kit Kinports, *Habeas Corpus, Qualified Immunity, and Crystal Balls: Predicting the Course of Constitutional Law*, 33 ARIZ. L. REV. 115, 149–56 (1991).

Does the opinion excerpted below resolve this controversy?

HOPE v. PELZER
Supreme Court of the United States
536 U.S. 730 (2002)

JUSTICE STEVENS delivered the opinion of the Court.

I

In 1995, Alabama was the only State that followed the practice of chaining inmates to one another in work squads. It was also the only State that handcuffed prisoners to "hitching posts" if they either refused to work or otherwise disrupted work squads.[28] [Petitioner Larry Hope, a former inmate at the Limestone Prison in Alabama,] was handcuffed to a hitching post on two occasions. On May 11, 1995, while Hope was working in a chain gang near an interstate highway, he got into an argument with another inmate. Both men were taken back to the Limestone prison and handcuffed to a hitching post. Hope was released two hours later, after the guard captain determined that the altercation had been caused by the other inmate. During his two hours on the post, Hope was offered drinking water and a bathroom break every 15 minutes, and his responses to these offers were recorded on an activity log. Because he was only slightly taller than the hitching post, his arms were above shoulder height and grew tired from

---

[28] [n.1] . . . [T]he hitching post is a horizontal bar "made of sturdy, nonflexible material," placed between 45 and 57 inches from the ground. Inmates are handcuffed to the hitching post in a standing position and remain standing the entire time they are placed on the post. Most inmates are shackled to the hitching post with their two hands relatively close together and at face level.

being handcuffed so high. Whenever he tried moving his arms to improve his circulation, the handcuffs cut into his wrists, causing pain and discomfort.

On June 7, 1995, Hope was punished more severely. He took a nap during the morning bus ride to the chain gang's worksite, and when it arrived he was less than prompt in responding to an order to get off the bus. An exchange of vulgar remarks led to a wrestling match with a guard. Four other guards intervened, subdued Hope, handcuffed him, placed him in leg irons and transported him back to the prison where he was put on the hitching post. The guards made him take off his shirt, and he remained shirtless all day while the sun burned his skin.[29] He remained attached to the post for approximately seven hours. During this 7-hour period, he was given water only once or twice and was given no bathroom breaks. At one point, a guard taunted Hope about his thirst. According to Hope's affidavit: "[The guard] first gave water to some dogs, then brought the water cooler closer to me, removed its lid, and kicked the cooler over, spilling the water onto the ground."

Hope filed suit under . . . 42 U.S.C. § 1983, in the United States District Court for the Northern District of Alabama against three guards involved in the May incident, one of whom also handcuffed him to the hitching post in June. . . .

The United States Court of Appeals for the Eleventh Circuit . . . found that the use of the hitching post for punitive purposes violated the Eighth Amendment. Nevertheless, applying Circuit precedent concerning qualified immunity, the court stated that "'the federal law by which the government official's conduct should be evaluated must be preexisting, obvious and mandatory,'" and established, not by "'abstractions,'" but by cases that are "'materially similar'" to the facts in the case in front of us. The court then concluded that the facts in the two precedents on which Hope primarily relied — *Ort v. White*, 813 F.2d 318 (CA11 1987), and *Gates v. Collier*, 501 F.2d 1291 (CA5 1974) — "though analogous," were not "'materially similar' to Hope's situation." . . .

II

The threshold inquiry a court must undertake in a qualified immunity analysis is whether plaintiff's allegations, if true, establish a constitutional violation. *Saucier v. Katz*, 533 U.S. 194, 201 (2001).[30] The Court of Appeals held that "the policy and practice of cuffing an inmate to a hitching post or similar stationary object for a period of time that surpasses that necessary to quell a threat or restore order is a violation of the Eighth Amendment." The court rejected respondents' submission that Hope could have ended his shackling by offering to return to work, finding instead that the purpose of the practice was punitive,[31] and that the circumstances of his confinement created a substantial risk of harm of which the officers were aware. . . . We agree with the

---

[29] [n.2] "The most repeated complaint of the hitching post, however, was the strain it produced on inmates' muscles by forcing them to remain in a standing position with their arms raised in a stationary position for a long period of time. In addition to their exposure to sunburn, dehydration, and muscle aches, the inmates are also placed in substantial pain when the sun heats the handcuffs that shackle them to the hitching post, or heats the hitching post itself. Several of the inmates described the way in which the handcuffs burned and chafed their skin during their placement on the post." [*Austin v. Hopper*, 15 F. Supp. 2d 1210, 1248 (M.D. Ala. 1998) (a class action filed by a group of Alabama prisoners that included Hope).]

[30] [Editor's note: *Saucier*'s notion of a "threshold inquiry" is discussed in Note 8 following *Harlow v. Fitzgerald, supra*.].

[31] [n.5] In reaching this conclusion, the Court of Appeals stated: " . . . First, Hope never refused to work. . . . Therefore, it is not clear that the solution to his hitching post problem was to ask to return to work. Second, Hope was placed in a car and driven back to Limestone to be cuffed to the hitching post on both occasions. Given the facts, it is improbable that had Hope said, 'I want to go back to work,' a prison guard would have left his post at Limestone to drive Hope back to the work site. It is more likely that the guards left Hope on the post until his work detail returned to teach the other inmates a lesson."

Court of Appeals that the attachment of Hope to the hitching post under the circumstances alleged in this case violated the Eighth Amendment.

"'The unnecessary and wanton infliction of pain . . . constitutes cruel and unusual punishment forbidden by the Eighth Amendment.'" *Whitley v. Albers*, 475 U.S. 312, 319 (1986). We have said that "among 'unnecessary and wanton' inflictions of pain are those that are 'totally without penological justification.'" *Rhodes v. Chapman*, 452 U.S. 337, 346 (1981). In making this determination in the context of prison conditions, we must ascertain whether the officials involved acted with "deliberate indifference" to the inmates' health or safety. *Hudson v. McMillian*, 503 U.S. 1, 8 (1992). We may infer the existence of this subjective state of mind from the fact that the risk of harm is obvious. *Farmer v. Brennan*, 511 U.S. 825, 842 (1994).

As the facts are alleged by Hope, the Eighth Amendment violation is obvious. Any safety concerns had long since abated by the time petitioner was handcuffed to the hitching post because Hope had already been subdued, handcuffed, placed in leg irons, and transported back to the prison. He was separated from his work squad and not given the opportunity to return to work. Despite the clear lack of an emergency situation, the respondents knowingly subjected him to a substantial risk of physical harm, to unnecessary pain caused by the handcuffs and the restricted position of confinement for a 7-hour period, to unnecessary exposure to the heat of the sun, to prolonged thirst and taunting, and to a deprivation of bathroom breaks that created a risk of particular discomfort and humiliation. The use of the hitching post under these circumstances violated the "basic concept underlying the Eighth Amendment[, which] is nothing less than the dignity of man." *Trop v. Dulles*, 356 U.S. 86, 100 (1958). This punitive treatment amounts to gratuitous infliction of "wanton and unnecessary" pain that our precedent clearly prohibits.

III

Despite their participation in this constitutionally impermissible conduct, the respondents may nevertheless be shielded from liability for civil damages if their actions did not violate "clearly established statutory or constitutional rights of which a reasonable person would have known." In assessing whether the Eighth Amendment violation here met the *Harlow* test, the Court of Appeals required that the facts of previous cases be "'materially similar' to Hope's situation." This rigid gloss on the qualified immunity standard . . . is not consistent with our cases.

As we have explained, qualified immunity operates "to ensure that before they are subjected to suit, officers are on notice their conduct is unlawful." *Saucier v. Katz*, 533 U.S., at 206. For a constitutional right to be clearly established, its contours "must be sufficiently clear that a reasonable official would understand that what he is doing violates that right. This is not to say that an official action is protected by qualified immunity unless the very action in question has previously been held unlawful, see *Mitchell v. Forsyth*, 472 U.S. 511, 535 n.12 (1985); but it is to say that in the light of pre-existing law the unlawfulness must be apparent." *Anderson v. Creighton*, 483 U.S. 635, 640 (1987).

Officers sued in a civil action for damages under 42 U.S.C. § 1983 have the same right to fair notice as do defendants charged with the criminal offense defined in 18 U.S.C. § 242. Section 242 makes it a crime for a state official to act "willfully" and under color of law to deprive a person of rights protected by the Constitution. In *United States v. Lanier*, 520 U.S. 259 (1997), we held that the defendant was entitled to "fair warning" that his conduct deprived his victim of a constitutional right, and that the standard for determining the adequacy of that warning was the same as the standard for determining whether a constitutional right was "clearly established" in civil litigation under § 1983.[32]

In *Lanier*, the Court of Appeals had held that the indictment did not charge an offense under § 242 because the constitutional right allegedly violated had not been identified in any earlier case involving a factual situation " 'fundamentally similar' " to the one in issue. The Court of Appeals had assumed that the defendant in a criminal case was entitled to a degree of notice " 'substantially higher than the "clearly established" standard used to judge qualified immunity' " in civil cases under § 1983. We reversed, explaining that the "fair warning" requirement is identical under § 242 and the qualified immunity standard. We pointed out that we had "upheld convictions under § 241 or § 242 despite notable factual distinctions between the precedents relied on and the cases then before the Court, so long as the prior decisions gave reasonable warning that the conduct then at issue violated constitutional rights." We explained:

> "This is not to say, of course, that the single warning standard points to a single level of specificity sufficient in every instance. In some circumstances, as when an earlier case expressly leaves open whether a general rule applies to the particular type of conduct at issue, a very high degree of prior factual particularity may be necessary. But general statements of the law are not inherently incapable of giving fair and clear warning, and in other instances a general constitutional rule already identified in the decisional law may apply with obvious clarity to the specific conduct in question, even though 'the very action in question has [not] previously been held unlawful,' *Anderson, supra*, at 640."

Our opinion in *Lanier* thus makes clear that officials can still be on notice that their conduct violates established law even in novel factual circumstances. Indeed, in *Lanier*, we expressly rejected a requirement that previous cases be "fundamentally similar." Although earlier cases involving "fundamentally similar" facts can provide especially strong support for a conclusion that the law is clearly established, they are not necessary to such a finding. The same is true of cases with "materially similar" facts. Accordingly, pursuant to *Lanier*, the salient question that the Court of Appeals ought to have asked is whether the state of the law in 1995 gave respondents fair warning that their alleged treatment of Hope was unconstitutional. It is to this question that we now turn.

IV

The use of the hitching post as alleged by Hope "unnecessarily and wantonly inflicted pain," and thus was a clear violation of the Eighth Amendment. Arguably, the violation was so obvious that our own Eighth Amendment cases gave the respondents fair warning that their conduct violated the Constitution. Regardless, in light of binding Eleventh Circuit precedent, an Alabama Department of Corrections (ADOC) regulation, and a [U.S. Department of Justice (DOJ)] report informing the ADOC of the constitutional infirmity in its use of the hitching post, we readily conclude that the respondents' conduct violated "clearly established statutory or constitutional rights of which a reasonable person would have known."

Cases decided by the Court of Appeals for the Fifth Circuit before 1981 are binding precedent in the Eleventh Circuit today. In one of those cases, decided in 1974, the Court of Appeals reviewed a District Court decision finding a number of constitutional

---

[32] [n.10] "The object of the 'clearly established' immunity standard is not different from that of 'fair warning' as it relates to law 'made specific' for the purpose of validly applying § 242. The fact that one has a civil and the other a criminal law role is of no significance; both serve the same objective, and in effect the qualified immunity test is simply the adaptation of the fair warning standard to give officials (and, ultimately, governments) the same protection from civil liability and its consequences that individuals have traditionally possessed in the face of vague criminal statutes. To require something clearer than 'clearly established' would, then, call for something beyond 'fair warning.' " 520 U.S. 259, 270–271.

violations in the administration of Mississippi's prisons. *Gates v. Collier*, 501 F.2d 1291. That opinion squarely held that several of those "forms of corporal punishment run afoul of the Eighth Amendment [and] offend contemporary concepts of decency, human dignity, and precepts of civilization which we profess to possess." Among those forms of punishment were "handcuffing inmates to the fence and to cells for long periods of time, . . . and forcing inmates to stand, sit or lie on crates, stumps, or otherwise maintain awkward positions for prolonged periods." The fact that *Gates* found several forms of punishment impermissible does not, as respondents suggest, lessen the force of its holding with respect to handcuffing inmates to cells or fences for long periods of time. Nor, for the purpose of providing fair notice to reasonable officers administering punishment for past misconduct, is there any reason to draw a constitutional distinction between a practice of handcuffing an inmate to a fence for prolonged periods and handcuffing him to a hitching post for seven hours. The Court of Appeals' conclusion to the contrary exposes the danger of a rigid, overreliance on factual similarity. As the Government submits in its brief *amicus curiae*: "No reasonable officer could have concluded that the constitutional holding of *Gates* turned on the fact that inmates were handcuffed to fences or the bars of cells, rather than a specially designed metal bar designated for shackling. If anything, the use of a designated hitching post highlights the constitutional problem." In light of *Gates*, the unlawfulness of the alleged conduct should have been apparent to the respondents.

The reasoning, though not the holding, in a case decided by the Eleventh Circuit in 1987 sent the same message to reasonable officers in that Circuit. In *Ort v. White*, 813 F.2d 318, the Court of Appeals held that an officer's temporary denials of drinking water to an inmate who repeatedly refused to do his share of the work assigned to a farm squad "should not be viewed as punishment in the strict sense, but instead as necessary coercive measures undertaken to obtain compliance with a reasonable prison rule, i.e., the requirement that all inmates perform their assigned farm squad duties." "The officer's clear motive was to encourage Ort to comply with the rules and to do the work required of him, after which he would receive the water like everyone else." The court cautioned, however, that a constitutional violation might have been present "if later, once back at the prison, officials had decided to deny [Ort] water as punishment for his refusal to work." So too would a violation have occurred if the method of coercion reached a point of severity such that the recalcitrant prisoner's health was at risk. Although the facts of the case are not identical, *Ort*'s premise is that "physical abuse directed at [a] prisoner after he terminates his resistance to authority would constitute an actionable eighth amendment violation." This premise has clear applicability in this case. Hope was not restrained at the worksite until he was willing to return to work. Rather, he was removed back to the prison and placed under conditions that threatened his health. *Ort* therefore gave fair warning to the respondents that their conduct crossed the line of what is constitutionally permissible.

Relevant to the question whether *Ort* provided fair warning to respondents that their conduct violated the Constitution is a regulation promulgated by ADOC in 1993. The regulation authorizes the use of the hitching post when an inmate refuses to work or is otherwise disruptive to a work squad. It provides that an activity log should be completed for each such inmate, detailing his responses to offers of water and bathroom breaks every 15 minutes. Such a log was completed and maintained for petitioner's shackling in May, but the record contains no such log for the 7-hour shackling in June and the record indicates that the periodic offers contemplated by the regulation were not made. The regulation also states that an inmate "will be allowed to join his assigned squad" whenever he tells an officer "that he is ready to go to work." . . . [T]he record in this case indicate[s] that this important provision of the regulation was frequently ignored by corrections officers. If regularly observed, a requirement that would effectively give the inmate the keys to the handcuffs that attached him to the hitching post would have made this case more analogous to the practice upheld in *Ort*, rather than the kind of punishment *Ort* described as impermissible. A course of conduct that tends to prove that the requirement was merely a sham, or that respondents could ignore it with impunity, provides equally strong support for the conclusion that they were fully aware of the wrongful character of their conduct.

The respondents violated clearly established law. Our conclusion that "a reasonable person would have known" of the violation is buttressed by the fact that the DOJ specifically advised the ADOC of the unconstitutionality of its practices before the incidents in this case took place. The DOJ had conducted a study in 1994 of Alabama's use of the hitching post. Among other findings, the DOJ report noted that ADOC's officers consistently failed to comply with the policy of immediately releasing any inmate from the hitching post who agrees to return to work. The DOJ concluded that the systematic use of the restraining bar in Alabama constituted improper corporal punishment. Accordingly, the DOJ advised the ADOC to cease use of the hitching post in order to meet constitutional standards. The ADOC replied that it thought the post could permissibly be used "'to preserve prison security and discipline.'" In response, the DOJ informed the ADOC that, "'although an emergency situation may warrant drastic action by corrections staff, our experts found that the "rail" is being used systematically as an improper punishment for relatively trivial offenses. Therefore, we have concluded that the use of the "rail" is without penological justification.'" Although there is nothing in the record indicating that the DOJ's views were communicated to respondents, this exchange lends support to the view that reasonable officials in the ADOC should have realized that the use of the hitching post under the circumstances alleged by Hope violated the Eighth Amendment prohibition against cruel and unusual punishment.

The obvious cruelty inherent in this practice should have provided respondents with some notice that their alleged conduct violated Hope's constitutional protection against cruel and unusual punishment. Hope was treated in a way antithetical to human dignity — he was hitched to a post for an extended period of time in a position that was painful, and under circumstances that were both degrading and dangerous. This wanton treatment was not done of necessity, but as punishment for prior conduct. Even if there might once have been a question regarding the constitutionality of this practice, the Eleventh Circuit precedent of *Gates* and *Ort*, as well as the DOJ report condemning the practice, put a reasonable officer on notice that the use of the hitching post under the circumstances alleged by Hope was unlawful. The "fair and clear warning," *Lanier*, 520 U.S. at 271, that these cases provided was sufficient to preclude the defense of qualified immunity at the summary judgment stage.

V

In response to Justice Thomas' thoughtful dissent, we make the following . . . observations. . . .

[I]n applying the objective immunity test of what a reasonable officer would understand, the significance of federal judicial precedent is a function in part of the Judiciary's structure. The unreported District Court opinions cited by the officers are distinguishable on their own terms.[33] But regardless, they would be no match for the Circuit precedents[34] in *Gates v. Collier*, which held that "handcuffing inmates to the fence and to cells for long periods of time" was unconstitutional, and *Ort v. White*, which

---

[33] [n.12] In three of the decisions, the inmates were given the choice between working or being restrained. See *Whitson v. Gillikin* (N.D. Ala., Jan. 24, 1994); *Dale v. Murphy* (M.D. Ala., Dec. 9, 1994); *Ashby v. Dees* (N.D. Ala., Dec. 27, 1994). In others, the inmates were offered regular water and bathroom breaks. See *Lane v. Findley* (N.D. Ala., Aug. 4, 1994); *Williamson v. Anderson* (M.D. Ala., Aug. 18, 1993); *Hollis v. Folsom* (M.D. Ala., Nov. 4, 1994). Finally, in *Vinson v. Thompson* (M.D. Ala., Dec. 9, 1994), the inmate was restrained for approximately 45 minutes.

[34] [n.13] There are apparently no decisions on similar facts from other Circuits, presumably because Alabama is the only State to authorize the use of the hitching post in its prison system.

suggested that it would be unconstitutional to inflict gratuitous pain on an inmate (by refusing him water), when punishment was unnecessary to enforce on-the-spot discipline. The vitality of *Gates* and *Ort* could not seriously be questioned in light of our own decisions holding that gratuitous infliction of punishment is unconstitutional, even in the prison context, *see supra*, [Part II] (citing *Whitley v. Albers*, 475 U.S. at 319; *Rhodes v. Chapman*, 452 U.S. at 346).

JUSTICE THOMAS, with whom THE CHIEF JUSTICE and JUSTICE SCALIA join, dissenting.

The Court today subjects three prison guards to suit based on facts not alleged, law not clearly established, and its own subjective views on appropriate methods of prison discipline. Qualified immunity jurisprudence has been turned on its head. . . .

II

A

In evaluating whether it was clearly established in 1995 that respondents' conduct violated the Eighth Amendment, the Court of Appeals properly noted that "it is important to analyze the facts in [the prior cases relied upon by petitioner where courts found Eighth Amendment violations], and determine if they are materially similar to the facts in the case in front of us." The right not to suffer from "cruel and unusual punishments" is an extremely abstract and general right. In the vast majority of cases, the text of the Eighth Amendment does not, in and of itself, give a government official sufficient notice of the clearly established Eighth Amendment law applicable to a particular situation.[35] Rather, one must look to case law to see whether "the right the official is alleged to have violated [has] been 'clearly established' in a more particularized, and hence more relevant, sense: The contours of the right must be sufficiently clear that a reasonable official would understand that what he is doing violates that right." *Anderson v. Creighton*, 483 U.S. 635, 640 (1987).

In conducting this inquiry, it is crucial to look at precedent applying the relevant legal rule in similar factual circumstances. Such cases give government officials the best indication of what conduct is unlawful in a given situation. If, for instance, "various courts have agreed that certain conduct [constitutes an Eighth Amendment violation] under facts not distinguishable in a fair way from the facts presented in the case at hand," *Saucier, supra*, at 202, then a plaintiff would have a compelling argument that a defendant is not entitled to qualified immunity.

That is not to say, of course, that conduct can be "clearly established" as unlawful only if a court has already passed on the legality of that behavior under materially similar circumstances. Certain actions so obviously run afoul of the law that an assertion of qualified immunity may be overcome even though court decisions have yet to address "materially similar" conduct. Or, as the Court puts it, "officials can still be on notice that their conduct violates established law even in novel factual circumstances." . . .

B

Turning to the merits of respondents' assertion that they are entitled to qualified immunity, the relevant question is whether it should have been clear to McClaran, Pelzer, and Gates in 1995 that attaching petitioner to a restraining bar violated the Eighth Amendment. . . .

---

[35] [n.10] *Cf. Saucier v. Katz*, 533 U.S. 194, 201–202 (2001) (discounting as too general the principle that a police officer's use of force violates the Fourth Amendment if it is excessive under objective standards of reasonableness).

... [A] year before the conduct at issue in this case took place, the United States District Court for the Northern District of Alabama rejected the Eighth Amendment claim of an Alabama prisoner who was attached to a restraining bar for five hours after he refused to work and scuffled with guards. *See Lane v. Findley* (Aug. 4, 1994). The District Court reasoned that attaching the prisoner to a restraining bar "was a measured response to a potentially volatile situation and a clear warning to other inmates that refusal to work would result in immediate discipline subjecting the offending inmate to similar conditions experienced by work detail inmates rather than a return to inside the institution." The District Court therefore concluded that there was a "substantial penological justification" for attaching the plaintiff to the restraining bar. . . .

The same year that it decided *Lane*, the United States District Court for the Northern District of Alabama dismissed another complaint filed by an Alabama prisoner who was handcuffed to a restraining bar. In that case, the prisoner, after refusing to leave prison grounds with his work squad, was handcuffed to a restraining bar for eight hours. Temperatures allegedly reached 95 degrees while the prisoner was attached to the bar, and he was allegedly denied food, water, and any opportunities to use bathroom facilities. *See Whitson v. Gillikin* (Jan. 24, 1994). As a result of being handcuffed to the bar, the prisoner "suffered lacerations, pain, and swelling in his arms." The District Court, without deciding whether the defendants' conduct violated the Eighth Amendment, held that "there was no clearly established law identifying [their behavior] as unconstitutional."

Federal District Courts in five other Alabama cases decided before 1995 similarly rejected claims that handcuffing a prisoner to a restraining bar or other stationary object violated the Eighth Amendment. *See, e.g., Ashby v. Dees* (N.D. Ala., Dec. 27, 1994) (fence); *Vinson v. Thompson* (M.D. Ala., Dec. 9, 1994) (restraining bar); *Hollis v. Folsom* (M.D. Ala., Nov. 4, 1994) (fence); *Williamson v. Anderson* (M.D. Ala., Aug. 18, 1993) (fence); *Dale v. Murphy* (S.D. Ala., Feb. 4, 1986) (light pole).[36] By contrast, petitioner is unable to point to any Alabama decision issued before respondents affixed him to the restraining bar holding that a prison guard engaging in such conduct violated the Eighth Amendment.

In the face of these decisions, and the absence of contrary authority, I find it impossible to conclude that respondents either were "plainly incompetent" or "knowingly violating the law" when they affixed petitioner to the restraining bar. *Malley* [*v. Briggs*, 475 U.S. 335, 341 (1986)]. A reasonably competent prison guard attempting to obey the law is not only entitled to look at how courts have recently evaluated his colleagues' prior conduct, such judicial decisions are often the only place that a guard can look for guidance, especially in a situation where a State stands alone in adopting a particular policy.

---

[36] [n.11] The Court's attempt to distinguish away all of these decisions only serves to undermine further its qualified immunity analysis. The Court appears to suggest that affixing a prisoner to a restraining bar is not clearly unlawful so long as (1) guards provide the prisoner with water and regular bathroom breaks, or (2) the prisoner is placed on the restraining bar as a result of his refusal to work. But . . . petitioner was offered water and bathroom breaks every 15 minutes during his May 11 stay on the bar, and there has never been any allegation either that respondents McClaran and Pelzer were involved at all in the June 7 incident or that respondent Gates was responsible for denying petitioner water or bathroom breaks on that date. As a result, even under the Court's own view of the law, respondents are entitled to qualified immunity. Moreover, the Court nowhere explains how respondents were supposed to figure out in 1995 that it was permissible to affix prisoners to a restraining bar if they refused to work but it was unlawful to do so if they were disruptive while on work duty. The claim that such a distinction was clearly established in Eighth Amendment jurisprudence at that time is nothing short of incredible.

C

In concluding that respondents are not entitled to qualified immunity, the Court is understandably unwilling to hold that our Eighth Amendment jurisprudence clearly established in 1995 that attaching petitioner to a restraining bar violated the Eighth Amendment. It is far from "obvious" that respondents, by attaching petitioner to a restraining bar, acted with "deliberate indifference" to his health and safety. *Hudson v. McMillian*, 503 U.S. 1, 8 (1992). Petitioner's allegations do not come close to suggesting that respondents knew that the mere act of attaching petitioner to the restraining bar imposed "a substantial risk of serious harm" upon him. *See Farmer v. Brennan*, 511 U.S. 825, 847 (1994). If, for instance, attaching petitioner to a restraining bar amounted to the "gratuitous infliction of 'wanton and unnecessary' pain," it is curious that petitioner, while handcuffed to the bar on May 11, chose to decline most of the bathroom breaks offered to him. Respondents also affixed petitioner to the restraining bar for a legitimate penological purpose: encouraging his compliance with prison rules while out on work duty.

Moreover, if the application of this Court's general Eighth Amendment jurisprudence to the use of a restraining bar was as "obvious" as the Court claims, one wonders how Federal District Courts in Alabama could have repeatedly arrived at the opposite conclusion, and how respondents, in turn, were to realize that these courts had failed to grasp the "obvious."

D

Unable to base its holding that respondents' conduct violated "'clearly established . . . rights of which a reasonable person would have known'" on this Court's precedents, the Court instead relies upon "binding Eleventh Circuit precedent, an Alabama Department of Corrections (ADOC) regulation, and a [Department of Justice] report informing the ADOC of the constitutional infirmity in its use of the hitching post." I will address these sources in reverse order.

The Department of Justice report referenced by the Court does nothing to demonstrate that it should have been clear to respondents that attaching petitioner to a restraining bar violated his Eighth Amendment rights. To begin with, the Court concedes that there is no indication the Justice Department's recommendation that the ADOC stop using the restraining bar was ever communicated to respondents, prison guards in the small town of Capshaw, Alabama. In any event, an extraordinarily well-informed prison guard in 1995, who had read both the Justice Department's report and Federal District Court decisions addressing the use of the restraining bar, could have concluded only that there was a dispute as to whether handcuffing a prisoner to a restraining bar constituted an Eighth Amendment violation, not that such a practice was clearly unconstitutional.

The Alabama Department of Corrections regulation relied upon by the Court not only fails to provide support for its holding today, the regulation weighs in respondents' favor because it expressly authorized prison guards to affix prisoners to a restraining bar when they were "disruptive to the work squad." . . .

While the Court also observes that the regulation provides that an inmate "'will be allowed to join his assigned squad'" whenever he tells an officer "'that he is ready to go to work,'" the Court again does not explain how any of the respondents in this case failed to observe this requirement. Petitioner has never alleged that he informed respondents or any other prison guard while he was on the bar that he was ready to go to work.

Finally, the "binding Eleventh Circuit precedent" relied upon by the Court was plainly insufficient to give respondents fair warning that their alleged conduct ran afoul of petitioner's Eighth Amendment rights. The Court of Appeals held in *Ort v. White*, 813 F.2d 318 (CA11 1987), that a prison guard did not violate an inmate's Eighth

Amendment rights by denying him water when he refused to work, and the Court admits that this holding provides no support for petitioner. Instead, it claims that the "reasoning" in *Ort* "gave fair warning to the respondents that their conduct crossed the line of what is constitutionally permissible." But *Ort* provides at least as much support to respondents as it does to petitioner. For instance, *Ort* makes it abundantly clear that prison guards "have the authority to use that amount of force or those coercive measures reasonably necessary to enforce an inmate's compliance with valid prison rules" so long as such measures are not undertaken "maliciously or sadistically."

To be sure, the Court correctly notes that the Court of Appeals in *Ort* suggested that it "might have reached a different decision" had the prison officer denied the inmate water after he had returned to the prison instead of while he was out with the work squad. But the suggestion in dicta that a guard might have violated a prisoner's Eighth Amendment rights by denying him water once he returned from work duty does not come close to clearly establishing the unconstitutionality of attaching a disruptive inmate to a restraining bar after he is removed from his work squad and back within prison walls.

Admittedly, the other case upon which the Court relies, *Gates v. Collier*, 501 F.2d 1291 (CA5 1974), is more on point. Nevertheless, *Gates* is also inadequate to establish clearly the unlawfulness of respondents' alleged conduct. In *Gates*, the Court of Appeals listed "handcuffing inmates to [a] fence and to cells for long periods of time" as one of many unacceptable forms of "physical brutality and abuse" present at a Mississippi prison. Others included administering milk of magnesia as a form of punishment, depriving inmates of mattresses, hygienic materials, and adequate food, and shooting at and around inmates to keep them standing or moving. The Court of Appeals had "no difficulty in reaching the conclusion that these forms of corporal punishment run afoul the Eighth Amendment."

It is not reasonable, however, to read *Gates* as establishing a bright-line rule forbidding the attachment of prisoners to a restraining bar. For example, in referring to the fact that prisoners were handcuffed to a fence and cells "for long periods of time," the Court of Appeals did not indicate whether it considered a "long period of time" to be 1 hour, 5 hours, or 25 hours. The Court of Appeals also provided no explanation of the circumstances surrounding these incidents. The opinion does not indicate whether the handcuffed prisoners were given water and suitable restroom breaks or whether they were handcuffed in a bid to induce them to comply with prison rules. In the intervening 21 years between *Gates* and the time respondents affixed petitioner to the restraining bar, there were no further decisions clarifying the contours of the law in this area. Therefore, as another court interpreting *Gates* has noted: "There is no blanket prohibition against the use of punishment such as the hitching post in *Gates* which would signal to the Commissioner of Corrections [let alone ordinary corrections officers] that the mere use of the hitching post would be a constitutional violation." *Fountain v. Talley*, 104 F. Supp. 2d 1345, 1354 (M.D. Ala. 2000).

Moreover, Eighth Amendment law has not stood still since *Gates* was decided. In *Farmer v. Brennan*, 511 U.S. 825 (1994), this Court elucidated the proper test for measuring whether a prison official's state of mind is one of "deliberate indifference," holding that "a prison official cannot be found liable under the Eighth Amendment for denying an inmate humane conditions of confinement unless the official knows of and disregards an excessive risk to inmate health or safety; the official must both be aware of facts from which the inference could be drawn that a substantial risk of serious harm exists, and he must also draw the inference." Because the Court of Appeals in *Gates* did not consider this subjective element, *Gates* alone could not have clearly established that affixing prisoners to a restraining bar was clearly unconstitutional in 1995. Also, in the face of recent Federal District Court decisions specifically rejecting prisoners' claims that Alabama prison guards violated their Eighth Amendment rights by attaching them to a restraining bar as well as a state regulation authorizing such conduct, it seems contrary to the purpose of qualified immunity to hold that one vague sentence plucked out of a 21-year-old Court of Appeals opinion provided clear notice to respondents in 1995 that their conduct was unlawful. . . .

NOTES

1. Evaluating *Hope v. Pelzer*'s Qualified Immunity Analysis. Is it fair for the Court to analogize, as it did both in *United States v. Lanier* and *Hope v. Pelzer*, between the qualified immunity defense and the constitutional rule requiring fair warning in criminal cases? *See, e.g., Lanzetta v. New Jersey*, 306 U.S. 451, 453 (1939) (holding that "[n]o one may be required at peril of life, liberty or property to speculate as to the meaning of penal statutes" because "'a statute which either forbids or requires the doing of an act in terms so vague that men of common intelligence must necessarily guess at its meaning . . . violates the first essential of due process of law'") (quoting *Connally v. General Construction Co.*, 269 U.S. 385, 391 (1926)). Assuming the analogy is a fair one, does Justice Stevens or Justice Thomas have the better of the argument on the question whether the hitching post violated Hope's clearly established constitutional rights?

Does the Court's opinion clear up the questions that have plagued the lower courts in applying *Harlow*'s definition of qualified immunity, as outlined in the Notes preceding the *Hope v. Pelzer* excerpt? Does *Hope* undermine *Harlow*'s goal of disposing of cases on summary judgment because "whether a precedent telegraphs a reasonable warning to public officials facing discretionary decisions is entirely dependent upon what facts they confronted when they acted," and therefore it is "unlikely that *Hope* will hasten the resolution of many pretrial qualified immunity motions"? Alan K. Chen, *The Facts About Qualified Immunity*, 55 EMORY L.J. 229, 261 (2006).

2. Post-*Hope* Decisions. The Supreme Court applied *Harlow* and addressed the merits of a qualified immunity claim in two cases decided in 2004. In one they found that the government official was entitled to the defense, and they reached the opposite conclusion in the other.

***Groh v. Ramirez*, 540 U.S. 551 (2004).** In *Groh v. Ramirez*, the Court rejected a qualified immunity claim raised by a federal law enforcement official who executed a search warrant in violation of the Fourth Amendment requirement that warrants "particularly describ[e] the place to be searched, and the persons or things to be seized." Although the warrant application particularly described both the place to be searched (respondents' home) and the evidence the petitioner expected to find (automatic weapons), the actual warrant contained no description of the things to be seized. Instead, that part of the warrant — which the petitioner drafted and a magistrate signed — merely contained a description of respondents' house. Writing for the five Justices in the majority, Justice Stevens concluded, "[g]iven that the particularity requirement is set forth in the text of the Constitution, no reasonable officer could believe that a warrant that plainly did not comply with that requirement was valid." In response to the officer's argument that the search was "the product, at worst, of a lack of due care," the majority replied that "even a cursory reading of the warrant in this case — perhaps just a simple glance — would have revealed a glaring deficiency that any reasonable police officer would have known was constitutionally fatal," and therefore the warrant was "'so facially deficient . . . that the executing [officer could not] reasonably presume it to be valid.'" *Groh*, 540 U.S. at 564–65 (quoting *United States v. Leon*, 468 U.S. 897, 923 (1984)).

Two of the four dissenters in *Groh*, Justice Kennedy and then-Chief Justice Rehnquist, would have granted the petitioner qualified immunity for what they termed a "straightforward mistake of fact." These two Justices explained: "An officer who drafts an affidavit, types up an application and proposed warrant, and then obtains a judge's approval naturally assumes that he has filled out the warrant form correctly. . . . Every lawyer and every judge can recite examples of documents that they wrote, checked, and doublechecked, but that still contained glaring errors. Law enforcement officers are no different." *Groh*, 540 U.S. at 567–68 (Kennedy, J., dissenting). Likewise, Justices Thomas and Scalia thought it "inevitable that officers acting reasonably and entirely in good faith will occasionally make such errors." These two Justices also concluded that the majority "err[ed] by defining the question at too high a level of generality": "[t]he Court today points to no cases directing an officer to proofread a warrant after it has been passed on by a neutral magistrate, where the officer is already fully aware of the scope of the intended search and the magistrate gives no reason to believe that he has authorized anything other than the requested search." *Groh*, 540 U.S. at 578–79 (Thomas, J., dissenting).

***Brosseau v. Haugen*, 543 U.S. 194 (2004) (per curiam).** In the second case, *Brosseau v. Haugen*, the Court summarily reversed a Ninth Circuit decision that relied on the Supreme Court's rulings in *Tennessee v. Garner*, 471 U.S. 1 (1985), and *Graham v. Connor*, 490 U.S. 386 (1989), in denying qualified immunity to a police officer charged with an excessive use of force. The Supreme Court pointed out that "the general tests set out in *Graham* and *Garner* . . . are cast at a high level of generality." Although the Court acknowledged that, "in an obvious case, these standards can 'clearly establish' the answer, even without a body of relevant case law" (citing *Hope v. Pelzer*), the Court thought that "[t]he present case is far from the obvious one where *Graham* and *Garner* alone offer a basis for decision." Observing that the parties had identified "only a handful" of relevant lower court opinions (i.e., three appellate court decisions from other circuits), the Court noted that none of these decisions "found [a] Fourth Amendment violation when an officer shot a fleeing suspect who presented a risk to others" and therefore "[n]one of them squarely governs the case here." "These three cases taken together undoubtedly show that this area is one in which the result depends very much on the facts of each case," the Court concluded. The Court dismissed a number of other appellate court decisions that "postdate[d] the conduct in question" on the ground that they "could not have given fair notice to Brosseau and are of no use in the clearly established inquiry." Justice Stevens, the lone dissenter, thought there was "a genuine factual question as to whether a reasonably well trained officer . . . could have concluded" that Haugen posed a risk to others, and he would therefore have delegated that question to a jury. *Brosseau*, 543 U.S. at 208 (Stevens, J., dissenting).

3. Procedural Issues: Heightened Pleading Requirements and Burdens of Proof. In its pre-*Harlow* ruling in *Gomez v. Toledo*, 446 U.S. 635, 640–41 (1980), the Court unanimously held that qualified immunity is an affirmative defense, which the defendant has the burden of pleading. *See also Siegert v. Gilley*, 500 U.S. 226, 231 (1991). Although the Court observed in n.24 of its opinion in *Harlow* that *Gomez* did not determine which party has the ultimate burden of proof, most courts at that time required the defendant to shoulder the burden of proof. *See* 1 Joseph G. Cook & John L. Sobieski, Jr., Civil Rights Actions ¶ 2.06[C], at 2-301 to -302 (2007). (As explained in Note 4, *infra*, however, most jurisdictions now take a contrary position on that issue.)

Following *Harlow*, and beginning with the Fifth Circuit's opinion in *Elliott v. Perez*, 751 F.2d 1472, 1483 (5th Cir. 1985), some federal courts adopted a heightened pleading rule for complaints in section 1983 cases, requiring that they include specific, nonconclusory allegations in order to survive a pretrial motion raising a qualified immunity defense. Some years later, in *Leatherman v. Tarrant County Narcotics Intelligence & Coordination Unit*, 507 U.S. 163 (1993), the Court unanimously rejected a heightened pleading requirement for section 1983 claims alleging municipal liability. The Court found it "impossible to square the 'heightened pleading standard' . . . with the liberal system of 'notice pleading' set up by . . . Rule 8(a)(2) [of the Federal Rules of Civil Procedure, which] requires that a complaint include only 'a short and plain statement of the claim showing that the pleader is entitled to relief.'" *Leatherman*, 507 U.S. at 168. But the Court based its decision in large part on the ground that municipalities have no immunity defense and expressly declined to decide "whether our qualified immunity jurisprudence would require a heightened pleading in cases involving individual government officials." 507 U.S. at 167.

Following the Supreme Court's decision in *Leatherman*, the D.C. Circuit adopted a heightened burden of proof requirement, which mandated that section 1983 plaintiffs whose constitutional claims required proof of some impermissible motive — for example, intent to discriminate in an equal protection case or a retaliatory motive for termination in a First Amendment case — must present clear and convincing evidence of that improper motive both to defeat the defendant's motion for summary judgment and also to prevail at trial. *See Crawford-El v. Britton*, 93 F.3d 813, 821-23 (D.C. Cir. 1996) (en banc). In rejecting this requirement, the Supreme Court noted that *Harlow* made evidence of improper motive "irrelevant" to the question of qualified immunity. *Crawford-El v. Britton*, 523 U.S. 574, 589 (1998). Although the Court acknowledged that improper motive may well be "an essential component of the plaintiff's affirmative case," it observed that *Harlow* "related only to the scope of an affirmative defense" and was not meant to effect any "change in the nature of the plaintiff's burden of proving a constitutional violation." (For a description of the extent to which proof of the defendant's state of mind is a necessary element of the plaintiff's prima facie case, *see* Chapter 1. C., *supra*.)

The courts of appeals have reached a consensus that heightened pleading requirements no longer remain viable after the Court's opinion in *Crawford-El*. *See, e.g., Educadores Puertorriquenos en Accion v. Hernandez*, 367 F.3d 61, 66 (1st Cir. 2004) (concluding that "the Court has signaled its disapproval of all heightened pleading standards except those that emanate from either congressional or [Federal] Rule based authority"); *Galbraith v. County of Santa Clara*, 307 F.3d 1119, 1125 (9th Cir. 2002) (noting that "nearly all of the circuits have now disapproved any heightened pleading standard"); *Currier v. Doran*, 242 F.3d 905, 916 (10th Cir. 2001) (retreating from its heightened pleading requirement, and interpreting *Crawford-El* (particularly the language quoted in Note 4, *infra*) as allowing trial judges to require plaintiffs to make specific, nonconclusory allegations on a case-by-case basis, but forbidding appellate courts from creating special procedural rules for section 1983 cases). *See also Jones v. Bock*, 549 U.S. 199 (2007) (admonishing that "courts should generally not depart from the usual practice under the Federal Rules on the basis of perceived policy concerns," and therefore invalidating the Sixth Circuit's heightened pleading rule requiring that prisoners filing section 1983 complaints must specifically allege that they complied with the Prison Litigation Reform Act's exhaustion requirement (which is discussed in Chapter 8.A.[3], *infra*)); *Ashcroft v. Iqbal*, 128 S. Ct. 2931 (2008) (No. 07-1015) (granting review in *Bivens* suit challenging harsh detention policies implemented following the 9/11 terrorist attacks and agreeing to consider whether "a conclusory allegation that a cabinet level officer or other high ranking official knew of, condoned, or agreed to subject a plaintiff to allegedly unconstitutional acts purportedly committed by subordinate officials" suffices to survive motion to dismiss based on qualified immunity defense).

4. Procedural Issues: The Timing of Qualified Immunity Determinations and the Appropriate Decisionmaker. The heightened pleading and heightened burden of proof requirements described in the prior Note were motivated by the desire to further *Harlow*'s goal of "permit[ting] the resolution of many insubstantial claims on summary judgment" and thereby protecting government officials from "the burdens of broad-reaching discovery." "Until this threshold immunity question is resolved," the Court admonished in *Harlow*, "discovery should not be allowed." *See also Mitchell v. Forsyth*, 472 U.S. 511, 526 (1985) ("[u]nless the plaintiff's allegations state a claim of violation of clearly established law, a defendant pleading qualified immunity is entitled to dismissal before the commencement of discovery").

Nevertheless, the Court recognized in *Anderson v. Creighton*, 483 U.S. 635, 646 n.6 (1987), that its "fact-specific" formulation of the qualified immunity standard meant that discovery "tailored specifically to the question of [the defendant's] qualified immunity" may be necessary in order to resolve an immunity issue on summary judgment. Likewise, the Court noted in *Crawford-El v. Britton*, 523 U.S. 574, 593 n.14 (1998), "neither [*Harlow*] nor subsequent decisions create an immunity from *all* discovery, and . . . limited discovery may sometimes be necessary before the district court can resolve a motion for summary judgment based on qualified immunity." In the last part of its opinion, the *Crawford-El* majority discussed these concerns at some length, describing "various procedural mechanisms [that] enable trial judges to weed out baseless claims":

> When a plaintiff files a complaint against a public official alleging a claim that requires proof of wrongful motive, the trial court must exercise its discretion in a way that protects the substance of the qualified immunity defense. It must exercise its discretion so that officials are not subjected to unnecessary and burdensome discovery or trial proceedings. The district judge has two primary options prior to permitting any discovery at all. First, the court may order a reply to the defendant's or a third party's answer under Federal Rule of Civil Procedure 7(a), or grant the defendant's motion for a more definite statement under Rule 12(e). Thus, the court may insist that the plaintiff "put forward specific, nonconclusory factual allegations" that establish improper motive causing cognizable injury in order to survive a prediscovery motion for dismissal or summary judgment. *Siegert v. Gilley*, 500 U.S. 226, 236 (1991) (Kennedy, J., concurring in judgment). This option exists even if the official chooses not to plead the affirmative defense of qualified immunity. Second, if the defendant does plead the immunity defense, the district court should resolve that threshold question before permitting discovery. To do so, the court must determine whether, assuming the truth of the plaintiff's allegations, the official's conduct violated clearly established law. Because the former option of demanding more specific allegations of intent places no burden on the defendant-official, the district judge may choose that alternative before resolving the immunity question, which sometimes requires complicated analysis of legal issues.
>
> If the plaintiff's action survives these initial hurdles and is otherwise viable, the plaintiff ordinarily will be entitled to some discovery. Rule 26 vests the trial judge with broad discretion to tailor discovery narrowly and to dictate the sequence of discovery. On its own motion, the trial court
>
> "may alter the limits in [the Federal Rules] on the number of depositions and interrogatories and may also limit the length of depositions under Rule 30 and the number of requests under Rule 36. The frequency or extent of use of the discovery methods otherwise permitted under these rules . . . shall be limited by the court if it determines that . . . (iii) the burden or expense of the proposed discovery outweighs its likely benefit. . . . " Rule 26(b)(2).
>
> Additionally, upon motion the court may limit the time, place, and manner of discovery, or even bar discovery altogether on certain subjects, as required "to protect a party or person from annoyance, embarrassment, oppression, or undue burden or expense." Rule 26(c). And the court may also set the timing and sequence of discovery. Rule 26(d).
>
> These provisions create many options for the district judge. For instance, the court may at first permit the plaintiff to take only a focused deposition of the defendant before allowing any additional discovery. Alternatively, the court may postpone all inquiry regarding the official's subjective motive until discovery has been had on objective factual questions such as whether the plaintiff suffered any injury or whether the plaintiff actually engaged in protected conduct that could be the object of unlawful retaliation. The trial judge can therefore manage the discovery process to facilitate prompt and efficient resolution of the lawsuit; as the evidence is gathered, the defendant-

official may move for partial summary judgment on objective issues that are potentially dispositive and are more amenable to summary disposition than disputes about the official's intent, which frequently turn on credibility assessments.[37] Of course, the judge should give priority to discovery concerning issues that bear upon the qualified immunity defense, such as the actions that the official actually took, since that defense should be resolved as early as possible.

Beyond these procedures and others that we have not mentioned, summary judgment serves as the ultimate screen to weed out truly insubstantial lawsuits prior to trial. At that stage, if the defendant-official has made a properly supported motion,[38] the plaintiff may not respond simply with general attacks upon the defendant's credibility, but rather must identify affirmative evidence from which a jury could find that the plaintiff has carried his or her burden of proving the pertinent motive. Finally, federal trial judges are undoubtedly familiar with two additional tools that are available in extreme cases to protect public officials from undue harassment: Rule 11, which authorizes sanctions for the filing of papers that are frivolous, lacking in factual support, or "presented for any improper purpose, such as to harass"; and 28 U.S.C.A. § 1915(e)(2) (Supp. 1997), which authorizes dismissal "at any time" of *in forma pauperis* suits that are "frivolous or malicious."

It is the district judges rather than appellate judges like ourselves who have had the most experience in managing cases in which an official's intent is an element. Given the wide variety of civil rights and "constitutional tort" claims that trial judges confront, broad discretion in the management of the factfinding process may be more useful and equitable to all the parties than the categorical rule imposed by the Court of Appeals.

Crawford-El, 523 U.S. at 593, 597–601.

As implied by this excerpt from *Crawford-El*, the Supreme Court envisions qualified immunity as "a question of law, not one of 'legal facts,'" *Elder v. Holloway*, 510 U.S. 510, 516 (1994), that "ordinarily should be decided by the court long before trial." *Hunter v. Bryant*, 502 U.S. 224, 223 (1991) (per curiam) (criticizing the court of appeals for "routinely plac[ing] the question of immunity in the hands of the jury"). In *Elder*, the Court unanimously concluded that an appellate court reviewing a qualified immunity determination should consider all relevant precedents, even those that were not brought to the attention of the trial court. Although, according to one commentator, the Court's decision in *Elder* "should finally put to rest any attempts to characterize the existence of a clearly settled law issue as one implicating evidentiary and related burden of proof considerations," 2 SHELDON H. NAHMOD, CIVIL RIGHTS AND CIVIL LIBERTIES LITIGATION: THE LAW OF SECTION 1983 § 8:96, at 8-478 (4th ed. 2007), the courts of appeals continue to talk in terms of burden of proof, generally requiring the plaintiff to convince the court that the constitutional right at issue was clearly established. *See, e.g., Novitsky v. City of Aurora*, 491 F.3d 1244, 1255 (10th Cir. 2007); *Baker v. City of Hamilton*, 471 F.3d 601, 605 (6th Cir. 2006); *Sorrels v. McKee*, 290 F.3d 965, 969 (9th Cir. 2002); *St. George v. Pinellas County*, 285 F.3d 1334, 1337 (11th Cir. 2002); *Delgado v. Jones*, 282 F.3d 511,

---

[37] [n.20] The judge does, however, have discretion to postpone ruling on a defendant's summary judgment motion if the plaintiff needs additional discovery to explore "facts essential to justify the party's opposition." Rule 56(f).

[38] [n.22] "Of course, a party seeking summary judgment always bears the initial responsibility of informing the district court of the basis for its motion, and identifying those portions of 'the pleadings, depositions, answers to interrogatories, and admissions on file, together with the affidavits, if any,' which it believes demonstrate the absence of a genuine issue of material fact." *Celotex Corp. v. Catrett*, 477 U.S. 317, 323 (1986) (quoting Fed. Rule Civ. Proc. 56(c)).

516 (7th Cir. 2002). *But see DiMarco-Zappa v. Cabanillas*, 238 F.3d 25, 35 (1st Cir. 2001) (putting the burden of proof on the defendant); *Tellier v. Fields*, 280 F.3d 69, 84 (2d Cir. 2000) (same).

Similarly, despite the Supreme Court's repeated insistence that qualified immunity is a question of law, some federal courts persist in assigning the issue to the jury if it is not resolved prior to trial. *See Curley v. Klem*, 499 F.3d 199, 208–09 (3d Cir. 2007) (citing conflicting cases). *But cf.* NAHMOD, *supra*, § 8:24, at 8-115 to -118 (collecting cases which provide that if the defendants' summary judgment motion is denied because genuine issues of material fact are in dispute, the trial judge should either grant a motion for directed verdict after all the evidence is presented at trial or, if disputed issues of fact still remain, use special interrogatories or some other mechanism to enable the jury to resolve those factual issues while retaining responsibility for resolving the legal question whether the defendants reasonably believed their conduct was lawful).

Note that Justice Stevens, in his dissent in *Brosseau v. Haugen*, 543 U.S. 194 (2004) (per curiam), took the position that the qualified immunity question at issue there (described in Note 2, *supra*) involved a "quintessentially 'fact-specific' question, not a question that judges should try to answer 'as a matter of law,' " and therefore ought to be determined by the jury. *Brosseau*, 543 U.S. at 206 (Stevens, J., dissenting) (quoting *Anderson v. Creighton*, 483 U.S. 635, 641 (1987)). Justice Stevens explained that "[a]lthough it is preferable to resolve the qualified immunity question at the earliest possible stage of litigation, this preference does not give judges license to take inherently factual questions away from the jury." *See also* Alan K. Chen, *The Facts About Qualified Immunity*, 55 EMORY L.J. 229, 230–31 (2006) (arguing that "[t]he Court's continuing and fundamental failure to acknowledge the critical role of facts in qualified immunity adjudication complicates the analysis in ways that make the doctrine not only internally inconsistent, but also extraordinarily difficult and costly to administer"); Teressa E. Ravenell, *Hammering in Screws: Why the Court Should Look Beyond Summary Judgment when Resolving § 1983 Qualified Immunity Disputes*, 52 VILL. L. REV. 135, 139 (2007) (maintaining that "summary judgment is not always the most appropriate tool with which to resolve qualified immunity disputes").

5. Procedural Issues: Qualified Immunity on Appeal. In *Mitchell v. Forsyth*, 472 U.S. 511, 530 (1985), the Court held that the denial of qualified immunity on a motion for dismissal or summary judgment falls within the "collateral order" doctrine and thus, "to the extent it turns on an issue of law, is an appealable 'final decision' . . . notwithstanding the absence of a final judgment." Building on *Harlow*'s preference for early resolution of immunity questions, the *Mitchell* Court described qualified immunity as "an entitlement not to stand trial or face the other burdens of litigation" — "an *immunity from suit* rather than a mere defense to liability [that,] like an absolute immunity, . . . is effectively lost if a case is erroneously permitted to go forward." *Mitchell*, 472 U.S. at 526.[39]

In *Behrens v. Pelletier*, 516 U.S. 299 (1996), the Court expanded on *Mitchell*, interpreting it to allow defendants to file two separate interlocutory appeals — the first after being denied qualified immunity on a motion to dismiss and the second after denial of a motion for summary judgment. "[A]n unsuccessful appeal from a denial of dismissal cannot possibly render the later denial of a motion for summary judgment any *less* final," the Court reasoned. *Behrens*, 516 U.S. at 307. Although the Court recognized that allowing a second appeal might "afford[] an opportunity for abuse," it expressed confidence that "if and when abuse does occur, . . . '[i]t is well within the supervisory powers of the courts of appeals to establish summary procedures and calendars to weed out frivolous claims.' " *Behrens*, 516 U.S. at 310.

---

[39] In *Johnson v. Fankell*, 520 U.S. 911, 921 (1997), however, the Court held that the right to file an interlocutory appeal is a "federal procedural right" that does not apply to section 1983 suits filed in state courts. This case is described in Chapter 5.B., *infra*.

Moreover, *Behrens* went on to indicate that interlocutory appeals are permissible even in cases where a qualified immunity ruling in the defendants' favor will not protect them from "endur[ing] discovery and trial on . . . *separate* . . . claims." 516 U.S. at 311 (emphasis added). "The *Harlow* right to immunity is a right to immunity *from certain claims*, not from litigation in general," the Court explained. *Behrens*, 516 U.S. at 312.

In the final portion of its opinion in *Behrens*, the Court elaborated on its holding the prior year in *Johnson v. Jones*, 515 U.S. 304, 312, 307 (1995), which had refused to allow an interlocutory appeal on "a question of 'evidentiary sufficiency'" — that is, "a *fact*-related dispute about the pretrial record, namely, whether or not the evidence in the pretrial record was sufficient to show a genuine issue of fact for trial." *Johnson v. Jones* involved an excessive force claim brought against five police officers, three of whom sought summary judgment on the ground that there was no evidence that they participated in beating the plaintiff or even were present when the incident occurred. The district court denied the request for summary judgment, and the Supreme Court refused to allow the officers to file an interlocutory appeal. The Court distinguished the interlocutory appeal permitted in *Mitchell v. Forsyth*, noting that "[t]he dispute underlying the *Mitchell* appeal involved the application of 'clearly established' law to a given (for appellate purposes undisputed) set of facts." *Johnson*, 515 U.S. at 313. When a denial of qualified immunity is the subject of an interlocutory appeal, the Court explained, the appellate court is "faced with an argument that the district court mistakenly identified clearly established law [and] can simply take, as given, the facts that the district court assumed when it denied summary judgment for that (purely legal) reason." Should the lower court fail to make findings or state its assumptions, the Supreme Court continued, the court of appeals need only review the record to determine "what facts the district court, in the light most favorable to the nonmoving party, likely assumed." *Johnson*, 515 U.S. at 319.

Distinguishing *Johnson*, the *Behrens* Court explained:

> Denial of summary judgment often includes a determination that there are controverted issues of material fact, and *Johnson* surely does not mean that *every* such denial of summary judgment is nonappealable. *Johnson* held, simply, that determinations of evidentiary sufficiency are not immediately appealable merely because they happen to arise in a qualified-immunity case; if what is at issue in the sufficiency determination is nothing more than whether the evidence could support a finding that particular conduct occurred, the question decided is not truly "separable" from the plaintiff's claim, and hence there is no "final decision". . . . *Johnson* reaffirmed that summary judgment determinations *are* appealable when they resolve a dispute concerning an "abstract issue of law" relating to qualified immunity — typically, the issue whether the federal right was "clearly established."

Behrens, 516 U.S. at 312–13.

On the facts in *Behrens*, where the plaintiff alleged that he was terminated in violation of his procedural and substantive due process rights and the district court's summary judgment order denied qualified immunity "with the unadorned statement that '[m]aterial issues of fact remain,'" the Supreme Court held that an interlocutory appeal was available. *Behrens*, 516 U.S. at 304. The Court reasoned as follows: "[T]he District Court's denial of petitioner's summary judgment motion necessarily determined that certain conduct attributed to petitioner (which was controverted) constituted a violation of clearly established law. *Johnson* permits petitioner to claim on appeal that all of the conduct which the District Court deemed sufficiently supported for purposes of summary judgment met the *Harlow* standard of 'objective legal reasonableness.'" *Behrens*, 516 U.S. at 313.

Most courts of appeals read these precedents as either precluding interlocutory appellate jurisdiction over matters of factual sufficiency, or at least prohibiting independent fact finding on appeal. In *Hulen v. Yates*, 322 F.3d 1229 (10th Cir. 2003), for example, the district court denied summary judgment to defendants who allegedly violated the First Amendment by transferring a public sector employee. On interlocutory appeal, the Tenth Circuit stated that it could "not resolve Defendants' claims that [the plaintiff] cannot show any personal participation by these Defendants in the alleged retaliatory transfer.... This is an issue of evidentiary sufficiency, over which we lack jurisdiction in a qualified immunity interlocutory appeal." Similarly, in *Hamilton v. Leavy*, 322 F.3d 776 (3d Cir. 2002), a case alleging deliberate indifference to a prisoner's Eighth Amendment rights, the Third Circuit refused to review "the District Court's 'identification of the facts that are subject to genuine dispute,' but instead . . . review[ed] the legal issues in light of the facts that the District Court determined had sufficient evidentiary support for summary judgment purposes." And in *Gray-Hopkins v. Prince George's County*, 309 F.3d 224, 229 (4th Cir. 2002), an excessive force case arising under the Fourth Amendment, the Fourth Circuit stated: "to the extent that the appealing official seeks to argue the insufficiency of the evidence to raise a genuine issue of material fact — for example, that the evidence presented was insufficient to support a conclusion that the official engaged in the particular conduct alleged — we do not possess jurisdiction . . . to consider the claim."

Along these same lines, the Eleventh Circuit in *Harris v. Coweta County*, 433 F.3d 807 (11th Cir. 2005), refused on interlocutory appeal to reverse a district court's decision to deny summary judgment to a police officer (Scott) accused of using excessive force to stop a fleeing motorist (Harris). "Taking [the plaintiff's] view of the facts as given, the Court of Appeals concluded that . . . Scott's actions could constitute 'deadly force' . . . , and that the use of such force in this context 'would violate [the plaintiff's] constitutional right to be free from excessive force during a seizure.'" *Scott v. Harris*, 127 S. Ct. 1769, 1773 (2007) (quoting *Harris v. Coweta County*, 433 F.3d at 816). The Supreme Court reversed, disagreeing with the appellate court's assessment that a reasonable jury could have found that Scott used excessive force: "When opposing parties tell two different stories, one of which is blatantly contradicted by the record, so that no reasonable jury could believe it, a court should not adopt that version of the facts for purposes of ruling on a motion for summary judgment. That was the case here with regard to the factual issue whether [Harris] was driving in such fashion as to endanger human life. [Harris's] version of events is so utterly discredited by the record that no reasonable jury could have believed him. The Court of Appeals should not have relied on such visible fiction; it should have viewed the facts in the light depicted by the videotape" that showed Scott's pursuit of Harris's vehicle and the resulting crash. *Scott v. Harris*, 127 S. Ct. at 1776.

Only Justice Stevens dissented, pointing out that "the three judges on the Court of Appeals panel apparently did view the videotapes entered into evidence and described a very different version of events." "If two groups of judges can disagree so vehemently about the nature of the pursuit and the circumstances surrounding that pursuit," Justice Stevens concluded, "it seems eminently likely that a reasonable juror could disagree with this Court's characterization of events." *Scott*, 127 S. Ct. at 1785 (Stevens, J., dissenting).

In light of the Supreme Court's holding in *Johnson v. Jones*, shouldn't the Eleventh Circuit on interlocutory appeal have deferred to the district court's factual assumptions in the *Harris* case? Did the Eleventh Circuit even have jurisdiction to review the facts surrounding Scott's pursuit of Harris's vehicle? If not, should the Supreme Court have attempted to resolve the facts? Should it have considered the videotape? Did it have interlocutory appellate jurisdiction under *Johnson*? Given the Court's ruling in *Scott v. Harris*, are the lower courts' decisions in *Hulen*, *Hamilton*, and *Gray-Hopkins* now subject to question? For a discussion of *Scott v. Harris*'s impact on *Johnson v. Jones*, see Mark R. Brown, *The Fall and Rise of Qualified Immunity: From* Hope *to* Harris, ___ NEV. L.J. ___ (2008) (forthcoming). *See also* Dan M. Kahan, David A. Hoffman & Donald Braman, *Whose Eyes Are You Going to Believe?* Scott v. Harris *and the Perils of*

Cognitive Illiberalism, 122 HARV. L. REV. __ (2009) (forthcoming) (finding, after showing the *Scott v. Harris* videotape to 1,350 people, that while a majority agreed with the Supreme Court, there were "sharp differences of opinion along cultural, ideological, and other lines," and criticizing the Court's "insistence that there was only one 'reasonable' view" of the facts as "a form of bias — cognitive illiberalism — that consists in the failure to recognize the connection between perceptions of societal risk and contested visions of the ideal society").

Chapter 3
SOVEREIGN IMMUNITY

A. INTRODUCTION

The Eleventh Amendment to the Constitution provides:

> The Judicial power of the United States shall not be construed to extend to any suit in law or equity, commenced or prosecuted against one of the United States by Citizens of another State, or by Citizens or Subjects of any Foreign State.

ALDEN v. MAINE
Supreme Court of the United States
527 U.S. 706 (1999)

JUSTICE KENNEDY delivered the opinion of the Court.

[A group of probation officers filed a damages suit in state court under the Fair Labor Standards Act (FLSA), 29 U.S.C. § 201, against their employer, the State of Maine. The suit alleged that the State had violated the overtime provisions of the FLSA, which sets minimum-wage and maximum-hour rules for any employee involved in interstate commerce.]

I

The Eleventh Amendment makes explicit reference to the States' immunity from suits "commenced or prosecuted against one of the United States by Citizens of another State, or by Citizens or Subjects of any Foreign State." We have, as a result, sometimes referred to the States' immunity from suit as "Eleventh Amendment immunity." The phrase is convenient shorthand but something of a misnomer, for the sovereign immunity of the States neither derives from nor is limited by the terms of the Eleventh Amendment. Rather, as the Constitution's structure, and its history, and the authoritative interpretations by this Court make clear, the States' immunity from suit is a fundamental aspect of the sovereignty which the States enjoyed before the ratification of the Constitution, and which they retain today (either literally or by virtue of their admission into the Union upon an equal footing with the other States) except as altered by the plan of the Convention or certain constitutional Amendments.

A

Although the Constitution establishes a National Government with broad, often plenary authority over matters within its recognized competence, the founding document "specifically recognizes the States as sovereign entities." *Seminole Tribe of Fla. v. Florida,* [517 U.S. 44, 71, n. 15 (1996)]; *accord, Blatchford v. Native Village of Noatak,* 501 U.S. 775, 779 (1991) ("The States entered the federal system with their sovereignty intact"). Various textual provisions of the Constitution assume the States' continued existence and active participation in the fundamental processes of governance. The limited and enumerated powers granted to the Legislative, Executive, and Judicial Branches of the National Government, moreover, underscore the vital role reserved to the States by the constitutional design. Any doubt regarding the constitutional role of the States as sovereign entities is removed by the Tenth Amendment, which, like the other provisions of the Bill of Rights, was enacted to allay lingering concerns about the extent of the national power. The Amendment confirms the promise implicit in the original document: "The powers not delegated to the United

States by the Constitution, nor prohibited by it to the States, are reserved to the States respectively, or to the people."

The federal system established by our Constitution preserves the sovereign status of the States in two ways. First, it reserves to them a substantial portion of the Nation's primary sovereignty, together with the dignity and essential attributes inhering in that status. The States "form distinct and independent portions of the supremacy, no more subject, within their respective spheres, to the general authority than the general authority is subject to them, within its own sphere." The Federalist No. 39, p. 245 (C. Rossiter ed. 1961) (J. Madison).

Second, even as to matters within the competence of the National Government, the constitutional design secures the founding generation's rejection of "the concept of a central government that would act upon and through the States" in favor of "a system in which the State and Federal Governments would exercise concurrent authority over the people — who were, in Hamilton's words, 'the only proper objects of government.'" *Printz* [*v. United States*, 521 U.S. 898, 919–920 (1997)] (quoting The Federalist No. 15, at 109); *accord*, *New York* [*v. United States*, 505 U.S. 144, 166 (1992)] ("The Framers explicitly chose a Constitution that confers upon Congress the power to regulate individuals, not States"). . . .

The States thus retain "a residuary and inviolable sovereignty." The Federalist No. 39, at 245. They are not relegated to the role of mere provinces or political corporations, but retain the dignity, though not the full authority, of sovereignty.

B

The generation that designed and adopted our federal system considered immunity from private suits central to sovereign dignity. When the Constitution was ratified, it was well established in English law that the Crown could not be sued without consent in its own courts. *See Chisholm v. Georgia*, 2 Dall. 419, 437–446 (1793) (Iredell, J., dissenting) (surveying English practice); *cf. Nevada v. Hall*, 440 U.S. 410, 414 (1979) ("The immunity of a truly independent sovereign from suit in its own courts has been enjoyed as a matter of absolute right for centuries. Only the sovereign's own consent could qualify the absolute character of that immunity"). In reciting the prerogatives of the Crown, Blackstone — whose works constituted the preeminent authority on English law for the founding generation — underscored the close and necessary relationship understood to exist between sovereignty and immunity from suit:

> "And, first, the law ascribes to the king the attribute of sovereignty, or pre-eminence. . . . Hence it is, that no suit or action can be brought against the king, even in civil matters, because no court can have jurisdiction over him. For all jurisdiction implies superiority of power. . . . "

1 W. BLACKSTONE, COMMENTARIES ON THE LAWS OF ENGLAND 234–235 (1765).

Although the American people had rejected other aspects of English political theory, the doctrine that a sovereign could not be sued without its consent was universal in the States when the Constitution was drafted and ratified. *See Chisholm, supra*, at 434–435 (Iredell, J., dissenting) ("I believe there is no doubt that neither in the State now in question, nor in any other in the *Union*, any particular Legislative mode, authorizing a compulsory suit for the recovery of money against a State, was in being either when the Constitution was adopted, or at the time the judicial act was passed"); *Hans v. Louisiana*, 134 U.S. 1, 16 (1890) ("The suability of a State, without its consent, was a thing unknown to the law. This has been so often laid down and acknowledged by courts and jurists that it is hardly necessary to be formally asserted").

The ratification debates, furthermore, underscored the importance of the States' sovereign immunity to the American people. Grave concerns were raised by the provisions of Article III which extended the federal judicial power to controversies between States and citizens of other States or foreign nations. As we have explained:

A. INTRODUCTION

"Unquestionably the doctrine of sovereign immunity was a matter of importance in the early days of independence. Many of the States were heavily indebted as a result of the Revolutionary War. They were vitally interested in the question whether the creation of a new federal sovereign, with courts of its own, would automatically subject them, like lower English lords, to suits in the courts of the 'higher' sovereign."

Hall, supra, at 418.

The leading advocates of the Constitution assured the people in no uncertain terms that the Constitution would not strip the States of sovereign immunity. One assurance was contained in The Federalist No. 81, written by Alexander Hamilton:

"It is inherent in the nature of sovereignty not to be amenable to the suit of an individual *without its consent*. This is the general sense, and the general practice of mankind; and the exemption, as one of the attributes of sovereignty, is now enjoyed by the government of every State in the Union. Unless therefore, there is a surrender of this immunity in the plan of the convention, it will remain with the States. . . . [T]here is no color to pretend that the State governments would, by the adoption of that plan, be divested of the privilege of paying their own debts in their own way, free from every constraint but that which flows from the obligations of good faith. The contracts between a nation and individuals are only binding on the conscience of the sovereign, and have no pretensions to a compulsive force. They confer no right of action independent of the sovereign Will. To what purpose would it be to authorize suits against States for the debts they owe? How could recoveries be enforced? It is evident that it could not be done without waging war against the contracting State; and to ascribe to the federal courts, by mere implication, and in destruction of the preexisting right of the State governments, a power which would involve such a consequence, would be altogether forced and unwarrantable."

Id. at 487–488 (emphasis in original).

At the Virginia ratifying convention, James Madison echoed this theme:

"Its jurisdiction in controversies between a state and citizens of another state is much objected to, and perhaps without reason. It is not in the power of individuals to call any state into court. . . .

" . . . It appears to me that this [clause] can have no operation but this — to give a citizen a right to be heard in the federal courts, and if a state should condescend to be a party, this court may take cognizance of it."

3 J. Elliot, Debates on the Federal Constitution 533 (2d ed. 1854) (hereinafter Elliot's Debates).

When Madison's explanation was questioned, John Marshall provided immediate support:

"With respect to disputes between *a state and the citizens of another state*, its jurisdiction has been decried with unusual vehemence. I hope no Gentleman will think that a state will be called at the bar of the federal court. . . . It is not rational to suppose that the sovereign power should be dragged before a court. The intent is, to enable states to recover claims of individuals residing in other states. I contend this construction is warranted by the words. But, say they, there will be partiality in it if a state cannot be defendant. . . . It is necessary to be so, and cannot be avoided. I see a difficulty in making a state defendant, which does not prevent its being plaintiff."

Elliot's Debates at 555.

Although the state conventions which addressed the issue of sovereign immunity in their formal ratification documents sought to clarify the point by constitutional amendment, they made clear that they, like Hamilton, Madison, and Marshall, understood the Constitution as drafted to preserve the States' immunity from private suits. The Rhode Island Convention thus proclaimed that "it is declared by the Convention, that the judicial power of the United States, in cases in which a state may be a party, does not extend to criminal prosecutions, or to authorize any suit by any person against a state." The convention sought, in addition, an express amendment "to remove all doubts or controversies respecting the same." . . .

Despite the persuasive assurances of the Constitution's leading advocates and the expressed understanding of the only state conventions to address the issue in explicit terms, this Court held, just five years after the Constitution was adopted, that Article III authorized a private citizen of another State to sue the State of Georgia without its consent. *Chisholm v. Georgia*, 2 Dall. 419 (1793).[1] Each of the four Justices who concurred in the judgment issued a separate opinion. The common theme of the opinions was that the case fell within the literal text of Article III, which by its terms granted jurisdiction over controversies "between a State and Citizens of another State," and "between a State, or the Citizens thereof, and foreign States, Citizens, or Subjects." U.S. Const., Art. III, § 2. The argument that this provision granted jurisdiction only over cases in which the State was a plaintiff was dismissed as inconsistent with the ordinary meaning of "between," and with the provision extending jurisdiction to "Controversies between two or more States," which by necessity contemplated jurisdiction over suits to which States were defendants. Two Justices also argued that sovereign immunity was inconsistent with the principle of popular sovereignty established by the Constitution, *see* 2 Dall., at 454–458 (Wilson, J.); *id.* at 470–472 (Jay, C.J.); although the others did not go so far, they contended that the text of Article III evidenced the States' surrender of sovereign immunity as to those provisions extending jurisdiction over suits to which States were parties, *see id.* at 452 (Blair, J.); *id.* at 468 (Cushing, J.).

Justice Iredell dissented, relying on American history, English history, and the principles of enumerated powers and separate sovereignty. . . .

The Court's decision "fell upon the country with a profound shock." 1 C. WARREN, THE SUPREME COURT IN UNITED STATES HISTORY 96 (rev. ed. 1926). "Newspapers representing a rainbow of opinion protested what they viewed as an unexpected blow to state sovereignty. Others spoke more concretely of prospective raids on state treasuries." D. CURRIE, THE CONSTITUTION IN CONGRESS: THE FEDERALIST PERIOD 1789–1801, p. 196 (1997).

The States, in particular, responded with outrage to the decision. The Massachusetts Legislature, for example, denounced the decision as "repugnant to the first principles of a federal government," and called upon the State's Senators and Representatives to take all necessary steps to "remove any clause or article of the Constitution, which can be construed to imply or justify a decision, that, a State is compellable to answer in any suit by an individual or individuals in any Court of the United States." 15 PAPERS OF ALEXANDER HAMILTON 314 (H. Syrett & J. Cooke eds. 1969). Georgia's response was more intemperate: Its House of Representatives passed a bill providing that anyone attempting to enforce the *Chisholm* decision would be " 'guilty of felony and shall suffer death, without benefit of clergy, by being hanged.' " CURRIE, *supra*, at 196.

An initial proposal to amend the Constitution was introduced in the House of Representatives the day after *Chisholm* was announced; the proposal adopted as the Eleventh Amendment was introduced in the Senate promptly following an intervening recess. Congress turned to the latter proposal with great dispatch; little more than two months after its introduction it had been endorsed by both Houses and forwarded to the States.

---

[1] [Editor's note: *Chisholm* was an original action filed in the Supreme Court by a citizen of South Carolina. The plaintiff was the executor of the estate of another South Carolinian, who had entered into a contract to provide certain supplies to the State of Georgia during the Revolutionary period. When the State failed to pay, the executor sued to enforce the contract.]

Each House spent but a single day discussing the Amendment, and the vote in each House was close to unanimous. . . .

The text [of the Eleventh Amendment] reflects the historical context and the congressional objective in endorsing the Amendment for ratification. Congress chose not to enact language codifying the traditional understanding of sovereign immunity but rather to address the specific provisions of the Constitution that had raised concerns during the ratification debates and formed the basis of the *Chisholm* decision. Given the outraged reaction to *Chisholm*, as well as Congress' repeated refusal to otherwise qualify the text of the Amendment, it is doubtful that if Congress meant to write a new immunity into the Constitution it would have limited that immunity to the narrow text of the Eleventh Amendment:

> "Can we suppose that, when the Eleventh Amendment was adopted, it was understood to be left open for citizens of a State to sue their own state in federal courts, whilst the idea of suits by citizens of other states, or of foreign states, was indignantly repelled? Suppose that Congress, when proposing the Eleventh Amendment, had appended to it a proviso that nothing therein contained should prevent a State from being sued by its own citizens in cases arising under the Constitution or laws of the United States: can we imagine that it would have been adopted by the States? The supposition that it would is almost an absurdity on its face."

Hans, supra, at 14–15.

The more natural inference is that the Constitution was understood, in light of its history and structure, to preserve the States' traditional immunity from private suits. As the Amendment clarified the only provisions of the Constitution that anyone had suggested might support a contrary understanding, there was no reason to draft with a broader brush. . . .

Although the dissent attempts to rewrite history to reflect a different original understanding, its evidence is unpersuasive. The handful of state statutory and constitutional provisions authorizing suits or petitions of right against States only confirms the prevalence of the traditional understanding that a State could not be sued in the absence of an express waiver, for if the understanding were otherwise, the provisions would have been unnecessary. . . .

The dissent's remaining evidence cannot bear the weight the dissent seeks to place on it. The views voiced during the ratification debates by Edmund Randolph and James Wilson, when reiterated by the same individuals in their respective capacities as advocate and Justice in *Chisholm*, were decisively rejected by the Eleventh Amendment. . . . Furthermore, Randolph appears to have recognized that his views were in tension with the traditional understanding of sovereign immunity, *see* 3 Elliot's Debates, at 573 ("I think, whatever the law of nations may say, that any doubt respecting the construction that a state may be plaintiff, and not defendant, is taken away by the words *where a state shall be a party*"), and Wilson . . . expressed a radical nationalist vision of the constitutional design that not only deviated from the views that prevailed at the time but, despite the dissent's apparent embrace of the position, remains startling even today, *see post*, at 776 (quoting with approval Wilson's statement that " 'the government of each state ought to be subordinate to the government of the United States' "). . . . And, though the Court's decision in *Chisholm* may have had "champions 'every bit as vigorous in defending their interpretation of the Constitution as were those partisans on the other side of the issue,' " the vote on the Eleventh Amendment makes clear that they were decidedly less numerous.

In short, the scanty and equivocal evidence offered by the dissent establishes no more than what is evident from the decision in *Chisholm* — that some members of the founding generation disagreed with Hamilton, Madison, Marshall, Iredell, and the only state conventions formally to address the matter. The events leading to the adoption of the Eleventh Amendment, however, make clear that the individuals who believed the Constitution stripped the States of their immunity from suit were at most a small minority.

Not only do the ratification debates and the events leading to the adoption of the Eleventh Amendment reveal the original understanding of the States' constitutional immunity from suit, they also underscore the importance of sovereign immunity to the founding generation. Simply put, "The Constitution never would have been ratified if the States and their courts were to be stripped of their sovereign authority except as expressly provided by the Constitution itself." *Atascadero State Hospital v. Scanlon*, 473 U.S. 234, 239, n. 2 (1985).

C

The Court has been consistent in interpreting the adoption of the Eleventh Amendment as conclusive evidence "that the decision in *Chisholm* was contrary to the well-understood meaning of the Constitution," *Seminole Tribe*, 517 U.S. at 69, and that the views expressed by Hamilton, Madison, and Marshall during the ratification debates, and by Justice Iredell in his dissenting opinion in *Chisholm*, reflect the original understanding of the Constitution. In accordance with this understanding, we have recognized a "presumption that no anomalous and unheard-of proceedings or suits were intended to be raised up by the Constitution — anomalous and unheard of when the constitution was adopted." *Hans*, 134 U.S. at 18. As a consequence, we have looked to "history and experience, and the established order of things," *id.* at 14, rather than "adhering to the mere letter" of the Eleventh Amendment, *id.* at 13, in determining the scope of the States' constitutional immunity from suit.

Following this approach, the Court has upheld States' assertions of sovereign immunity in various contexts falling outside the literal text of the Eleventh Amendment. In *Hans v. Louisiana*, the Court held that sovereign immunity barred a citizen from suing his own State under the federal-question head of jurisdiction. The Court was unmoved by the petitioner's argument that the Eleventh Amendment, by its terms, applied only to suits brought by citizens of other States. . . . Later decisions rejected similar requests to conform the principle of sovereign immunity to the strict language of the Eleventh Amendment in holding that nonconsenting States are immune from suits brought by federal corporations, *Smith v. Reeves*, 178 U.S. 436 (1900), foreign nations, *Principality of Monaco* [*v. Mississippi*, 292 U.S. 313 (1934)], or Indian tribes, *Blatchford v. Native Village of Noatak*, 501 U.S. 775 (1991), and in concluding that sovereign immunity is a defense to suits in admiralty, though the text of the Eleventh Amendment addresses only suits "in law or equity," *Ex parte New York*, 256 U.S. 490 (1921).

These holdings reflect a settled doctrinal understanding, consistent with the views of the leading advocates of the Constitution's ratification, that sovereign immunity derives not from the Eleventh Amendment but from the structure of the original Constitution itself. The Eleventh Amendment confirmed rather than established sovereign immunity as a constitutional principle; it follows that the scope of the States' immunity from suit is demarcated not by the text of the Amendment alone but by fundamental postulates implicit in the constitutional design. . . . [A]s we have . . . recently reaffirmed:

> "Although the text of the Amendment would appear to restrict only the Article III diversity jurisdiction of the federal courts, 'we have understood the Eleventh Amendment to stand not so much for what it says, but for the presupposition . . . which it confirms.' *Blatchford v. Native Village of Noatak*, [*supra*, at 779]. That presupposition, first observed over a century ago in *Hans v. Louisiana*, has two parts: first, that each State is a sovereign entity in our federal system; and second, that " 'it is inherent in the nature of sovereignty not to be amenable to the suit of an individual without its consent,' " *id.* at 13, quoting The Federalist No. 81, p. 487. . . ."

Seminole Tribe, supra, at 54.

[The Court goes on to hold that the plaintiffs were constitutionally barred from pursuing their FLSA suit against the State even in state court. That holding is described below in Note 6 following *Quern v. Jordan* in Section C, *infra.*]

JUSTICE SOUTER, with whom JUSTICE STEVENS, JUSTICE GINSBURG, and JUSTICE BREYER join, dissenting.

In *Seminole Tribe of Fla. v. Florida*, 517 U.S. 44 (1996), a majority of this Court invoked the Eleventh Amendment to declare that the federal judicial power under Article III of the Constitution does not reach a private action against a State, even on a federal question. In the Court's conception, however, the Eleventh Amendment was understood as having been enhanced by a "background principle" of state sovereign immunity (understood as immunity to suit) that operated beyond its limited codification in the Amendment, dealing solely with federal citizen-state diversity jurisdiction. To the *Seminole Tribe* dissenters, of whom I was one, the Court's enhancement of the Amendment was at odds with constitutional history and at war with the conception of divided sovereignty that is the essence of American federalism.

Today's issue arises naturally in the aftermath of the decision in *Seminole Tribe*. The Court holds that the Constitution bars an individual suit against a State to enforce a federal statutory right under the Fair Labor Standards Act of 1938 when brought in the State's courts over its objection. In thus complementing its earlier decision, the Court of course confronts the fact that the state forum renders the Eleventh Amendment beside the point, and it has responded by discerning a simpler and more straightforward theory of state sovereign immunity than it found in *Seminole Tribe*: a State's sovereign immunity from all individual suits is a "fundamental aspect" of state sovereignty "confirmed" by the Tenth Amendment. As a consequence, *Seminole Tribe*'s contorted reliance on the Eleventh Amendment and its background was presumably unnecessary; the Tenth would have done the work with an economy that the majority in *Seminole Tribe* would have welcomed. Indeed, if the Court's current reasoning is correct, the Eleventh Amendment itself was unnecessary. Whatever Article III may originally have said about the federal judicial power, the embarrassment to the State of Georgia occasioned by attempts in federal court to enforce the State's war debt could easily have been avoided if only the Court that decided *Chisholm v. Georgia* had understood a State's inherent, Tenth Amendment right to be free of any judicial power, whether the court be state or federal, and whether the cause of action arise under state or federal law. . . .

The Court rests its decision principally on the claim that immunity from suit was "a fundamental aspect of the sovereignty which the States enjoyed before the ratification of the Constitution," an aspect which the Court understands to have survived the ratification of the Constitution in 1788 and to have been "confirmed" and given constitutional status by the adoption of the Tenth Amendment in 1791. If the Court truly means by "sovereign immunity" what that term meant at common law, its argument would be insupportable. While sovereign immunity entered many new state legal systems as a part of the common law selectively received from England, it was not understood to be indefeasible or to have been given any such status by the new National Constitution, which did not mention it. . . . I set out this position at length in my dissent in *Seminole Tribe* and will not repeat it here. . . . [Excerpts from Justice Souter's dissent in *Seminole Tribe* are included following this opinion.]

I understand the Court to rely on the Hamiltonian formulation with the object of suggesting that its conception of sovereign immunity as a "fundamental aspect" of sovereignty was a substantially popular, if not the dominant, view in the periods of Revolution and Confederation. There is, after all, nothing else in the Court's opinion that would suggest a basis for saying that the ratification of the Tenth Amendment gave this "fundamental aspect" its constitutional status and protection against any legislative tampering by Congress. . . .

[But there] is almost no evidence that the generation of the Framers thought sovereign immunity was fundamental in the sense of being unalterable. Whether one looks at the period before the framing, to the ratification controversies, or to the early republican era, the evidence is the same. Some Framers thought sovereign immunity was an obsolete royal prerogative inapplicable in a republic; some thought sovereign immunity was a common-law power defeasible, like other common-law rights, by statute; and perhaps a few thought, in keeping with a natural law view distinct from the common-law conception, that immunity was inherent in a sovereign because the body that made a law could not logically be bound by it. Natural law thinking on the part of a doubtful few will not, however, support the Court's position. . . .

SEMINOLE TRIBE v. FLORIDA
Supreme Court of the United States
517 U.S. 44 (1996)

[The majority opinion is described in Note 6 following *Quern v. Jordan* in Section C, *infra*.]

JUSTICE SOUTER, with whom JUSTICE GINSBURG and JUSTICE BREYER join, dissenting.

I

A

The doctrine of sovereign immunity comprises two distinct rules, which are not always separately recognized. The one rule holds that the King or the Crown, as the font of law, is not bound by the law's provisions; the other provides that the King or Crown, as the font of justice, is not subject to suit in its own courts. *See, e.g.,* Jaffe, *Suits Against Governments and Officers: Sovereign Immunity*, 77 HARV. L. REV. 1, 3–4 (1963).[2] The one rule limits the reach of substantive law; the other, the jurisdiction of the courts. We are concerned here only with the latter rule, which took its common-law form in the high Middle Ages. "At least as early as the thirteenth century, during the reign of Henry III (1216–1272), it was recognized that the king could not be sued in his own courts." C. Jacobs, Eleventh Amendment and Sovereign immunity 5 (1972).

The significance of this doctrine in the nascent American law is less clear, however, than its early development and steady endurance in England might suggest. While some colonial governments may have enjoyed some such immunity, the scope (and even the existence) of this governmental immunity in pre-Revolutionary America remains disputed.

Whatever the scope of sovereign immunity might have been in the Colonies, however, or during the period of Confederation, the proposal to establish a National Government under the Constitution drafted in 1787 presented a prospect unknown to the common law prior to the American experience: the States would become parts of a system in which sovereignty over even domestic matters would be divided or parcelled

---

[2] [n.2] The first of these notions rests on the ancient maxim that "the King can do no wrong." *See, e.g.,* 1 W. Blackstone, Commentaries *244. Professor Jaffe has argued this expression "originally meant precisely the contrary to what it later came to mean," that is, " 'it meant that the king must not, was not allowed, not entitled, to do wrong.' " Jaffe, 77 HARV. L. REV. at 4 (quoting L. Ehrlich, Proceedings Against the Crown (1216–1377), p. 42); *see also* 1 Blackstone, *supra*, at *246 (interpreting the maxim to mean that "the prerogative of the crown extends not to do any injury"). In any event, it is clear that the idea of the sovereign, or any part of it, being above the law in this sense has not survived in American law.

out between the States and the Nation, the latter to be invested with its own judicial power and the right to prevail against the States whenever their respective substantive laws might be in conflict. . . .

The 1787 draft [of the Constitution] in fact said nothing on the subject [of sovereign immunity], and it was this very silence that occasioned some, though apparently not widespread, dispute among the Framers and others over whether ratification of the Constitution would preclude a State sued in federal court from asserting sovereign immunity as it could have done on any matter of nonfederal law litigated in its own courts. As it has come down to us, the discussion . . . focused entirely on the limits of the judicial power provided in Article III. And although the jurisdictional bases together constituting the judicial power of the national courts under § 2 of Article III included questions arising under federal law and cases between States and individuals who are not citizens, it was only upon the latter citizen-state diversity provisions that preratification questions about state immunity from suit or liability centered.[3]

Later in my discussion I will canvass the details of the debate among the Framers and other leaders of the time; for now it is enough to say that there was no consensus on the issue. *See* Jacobs, *supra*, at 40 ("The legislative history of the Constitution hardly warrants the conclusion drawn by some that there was a general understanding, at the time of ratification, that the states would retain their sovereign immunity"). There was, on the contrary, a clear disagreement, which was left to fester during the ratification period, to be resolved only thereafter. One other point, however, was also clear: the debate addressed only the question whether ratification of the Constitution would, in diversity cases and without more, abrogate the state sovereign immunity or allow it to have some application. . . . It may have been reasonable to contend (as we will see that Madison, Marshall, and Hamilton did) that Article III would not alter States' pre-existing common-law immunity despite its unqualified grant of jurisdiction over diversity suits against States. But then, as now, there was no textual support for contending that Article III or any other provision would "constitutionalize" state sovereign immunity, and no one uttered any such contention.

B

The argument among the Framers and their friends about sovereign immunity in federal citizen-state diversity cases, in any event, was short lived and ended when this Court, in *Chisholm v. Georgia*, 2 U.S. 419, 2 Dall. 419 (1793), chose between the constitutional alternatives of abrogation and recognition of the immunity enjoyed at common law. The 4-to-1 majority adopted the reasonable (although not compelled) interpretation that the first of the two Citizen-State Diversity Clauses abrogated for purposes of federal jurisdiction any immunity the States might have enjoyed in their own courts, and Georgia was accordingly held subject to the judicial power in a common-law assumpsit action by a South Carolina citizen suing to collect a debt. . . .

. . . Justice Iredell's dissent in *Chisholm* . . . is largely devoted to stating the position taken by several federalists that state sovereign immunity was cognizable under the Citizen-State Diversity Clauses, not that state immunity was somehow invisibly codified as an independent constitutional defense. . . .

---

[3] [n.4] The one statement I have found on the subject of States' immunity in federal-question cases was an opinion that immunity would not be applicable in these cases: James Wilson, in the Pennsylvania ratification debate, stated that the federal-question clause would require States to make good on pre-Revolutionary debt owed to English merchants (the enforcement of which was promised in the Treaty of 1783) and thereby "show the world that we make the faith of treaties a constitutional part of the character of the United States; that we secure its performance no longer nominally, for the judges of the United States will be enabled to carry it into effect, let the legislatures of the different states do what they may." 2 J. Elliot, Debates on the Federal Constitution 490 (2d ed. 1836) (Elliot's Debates).

C

The Eleventh Amendment, of course, repudiated *Chisholm* and clearly divested federal courts of some jurisdiction as to cases against state parties. . . . There are two plausible readings of this provision's text. Under the first, it simply repeals the Citizen-State Diversity Clauses of Article III for all cases in which the State appears as a defendant. Under the second, it strips the federal courts of jurisdiction in any case in which a state defendant is sued by a citizen not its own, even if jurisdiction might otherwise rest on the existence of a federal question in the suit. . . .

The history and structure of the Eleventh Amendment convincingly show that it reaches only to suits subject to federal jurisdiction exclusively under the Citizen-State Diversity Clauses.[4] In precisely tracking the language in Article III providing for citizen-state diversity jurisdiction, the text of the Amendment does, after all, suggest to common sense that only the Diversity Clauses are being addressed. If the Framers had meant the Amendment to bar federal-question suits as well, they could not only have made their intentions clearer very easily, but could simply have adopted the first post-*Chisholm* proposal, introduced in the House of Representatives by Theodore Sedgwick of Massachusetts on instructions from the Legislature of that Commonwealth. Its provisions would have had exactly that expansive effect:

> "No state shall be liable to be made a party defendant, in any of the judicial courts, established, or which shall be established under the authority of the United States, at the suit of any person or persons, whether a citizen or citizens, or a foreigner or foreigners, or of any body politic or corporate, whether within or without the United States." . . .

It should accordingly come as no surprise that the weightiest commentary following the Amendment's adoption described it simply as constricting the scope of the Citizen-State Diversity Clauses. In *Cohens v. Virginia*, 19 U.S. 264 (1821), for instance, Chief Justice Marshall, writing for the Court, emphasized that the Amendment had no effect on federal courts' jurisdiction grounded on the "arising under" provision of Article III and concluded that "a case arising under the constitution or laws of the United States, is cognizable in the Courts of the Union, whoever may be the parties to that case." The point of the Eleventh Amendment, according to *Cohens*, was to bar jurisdiction in suits at common law by Revolutionary War debt creditors, not "to strip the government of the means of protecting, by the instrumentality of its courts, the constitution and laws from active violation." . . .

The good sense of this early construction of the Amendment as affecting the diversity jurisdiction and no more has the further virtue of making sense of this Court's repeated exercise of appellate jurisdiction in federal-question suits brought against States in their own courts by out-of-staters. Exercising appellate jurisdiction in these cases would have

---

[4] [n.8] The great weight of scholarly commentary agrees. *See, e.g.*, Jackson, *The Supreme Court, the Eleventh Amendment, and State Sovereign Immunity*, 98 YALE L.J. 1 (1988); Amar, *Of Sovereignty and Federalism*, 96 YALE L.J. 1425 (1987); Fletcher, *A Historical Interpretation of the Eleventh Amendment: A Narrow Construction of an Affirmative Grant of Jurisdiction Rather than a Prohibition Against Jurisdiction*, 35 STAN. L. REV. 1033 (1983); Gibbons, *The Eleventh Amendment and State Sovereign Immunity: A Reinterpretation*, 83 COLUM. L. REV. 1889 (1983); Field, *The Eleventh Amendment and Other Sovereign Immunity Doctrines: Congressional Imposition of Suit Upon the States*, 126 U. PA. L. REV. 1203 (1978). While a minority has adopted the second view set out above, *see, e.g.*, Marshall, *Fighting the Words of the Eleventh Amendment*, 102 HARV. L. REV. 1342 (1989); Massey, *State Sovereignty and the Tenth and Eleventh Amendments*, 56 U. CHI. L. REV. 61 (1989), and others have criticized the diversity theory, *see, e.g.*, Marshall, *The Diversity Theory of the Eleventh Amendment: A Critical Evaluation*, 102 HARV. L. REV. 1372 (1989), I have discovered no commentator affirmatively advocating the position taken by the Court today. As one scholar has observed, the literature is "remarkably consistent in its evaluation of the historical evidence and text of the amendment as not supporting a broad rule of constitutional immunity for states." Jackson, *supra*, at 44 n.179.

been patent error if the Eleventh Amendment limited federal-question jurisdiction, for the Amendment's unconditional language ("shall not be construed") makes no distinction between trial and appellate jurisdiction.[5] And yet, again and again we have entertained such appellate cases, even when brought against the State in its own name by a private plaintiff for money damages. The best explanation for our practice belongs to Chief Justice Marshall: the Eleventh Amendment bars only those suits in which the sole basis for federal jurisdiction is diversity of citizenship. . . .

Thus, regardless of which of the two plausible readings one adopts, . . . there is no possible argument that the Eleventh Amendment, by its terms, deprives federal courts of jurisdiction over all citizen lawsuits against the States. Not even the Court advances that proposition, and there would be no textual basis for doing so.[6] Because the plaintiffs in today's case are citizens of the State that they are suing, the Eleventh Amendment simply does not apply to them. We must therefore look elsewhere for the source of that immunity by which the Court says their suit is barred from a federal court.

II

The obvious place to look elsewhere, of course, is *Hans v. Louisiana*, 134 U.S. 1 (1890). . . . [T]he place to begin is with *Hans*'s holding that a principle of sovereign immunity derived from the common law insulates a State from federal-question jurisdiction at the suit of its own citizen. A critical examination of that case will show that it was wrongly decided, as virtually every recent commentator has concluded. It follows that the Court's further step today of constitutionalizing *Hans*'s rule against abrogation by Congress compounds and immensely magnifies the century-old mistake of *Hans* itself and takes its place with other historic examples of textually untethered elevations of judicially derived rules to the status of inviolable constitutional law.

---

[5] [n.10] We have generally rejected Eleventh Amendment challenges to our appellate jurisdiction on the specious ground that an appeal is not a "suit" for purposes of the Amendment. *See, e.g., McKesson Corp. v. Division of Alcoholic Beverages and Tobacco, Fla. Dept. of Business Regulation*, 496 U.S. 18, 27 (1990). Although *Cohens v. Virginia*, 19 U.S. 264 (1821), is cited for this proposition, that case involved a State as plaintiff. *See generally* Jackson, 98 YALE L.J., at 32–35 (rejecting the appeal/suit distinction). The appeal/suit distinction, in any case, makes no sense. Whether or not an appeal is a "suit" in its own right, it is certainly a means by which an appellate court exercises jurisdiction over a "suit" that began in the courts below.

[6] [n.12] The Court does suggest that the drafters of the Eleventh Amendment may not have had federal-question jurisdiction in mind, in the apparent belief that this somehow supports its reading. The possibility, however, that those who drafted the Eleventh Amendment intended to deal "only with the problem presented by the decision in *Chisholm*" would demonstrate, if any demonstration beyond the clear language of the Eleventh Amendment were necessary, that the Eleventh Amendment was not intended to address the broader issue of federal-question suits brought by citizens.

Moreover, the Court's point is built on a faulty foundation. The Court is simply incorrect in asserting that "the federal courts did not have federal-question jurisdiction at the time the Amendment was passed." Article III, of course, provided for such jurisdiction, and early Congresses exercised their authority pursuant to Article III to confer jurisdiction on the federal courts to resolve various matters of federal law. *Osborn v. Bank of United States*, 22 U.S. 738 (1824) (holding that federal statute conferred federal-question jurisdiction in cases involving the Bank of the United States). In fact, only six years after the passage of the Eleventh Amendment, Congress enacted a statute providing for general federal-question jurisdiction. It is, of course, true that this statute proved short lived (it was repealed by the Act of Mar. 8, 1802, 2 Stat. 132), and that Congress did not pass another statute conferring general federal jurisdiction until 1875, but the drafters of the Eleventh Amendment obviously could not have predicted such things. The real significance of the 1801 Act is that it demonstrates the awareness among the Members of the early Congresses of the potential scope of Article III. This, in combination with the pre-Eleventh Amendment statutes that conferred federal-question jurisdiction on the federal courts, cast considerable doubt on the Court's suggestion that the issue of federal-question jurisdiction never occurred to the drafters of the Eleventh Amendment; on the contrary, just because these early statutes underscore the early Congresses' recognition of the availability of federal-question jurisdiction, the silence of the Eleventh Amendment is all the more deafening.

A

The Louisiana plaintiff in *Hans* held bonds issued by that State, which, like virtually all of the Southern States, had issued them in substantial amounts during the Reconstruction era to finance public improvements aimed at stimulating industrial development. As Reconstruction governments collapsed, however, the post-Reconstruction regimes sought to repudiate these debts, and the *Hans* litigation arose out of Louisiana's attempt to renege on its bond obligations.

Hans sued the State in federal court, asserting that the State's default amounted to an impairment of the obligation of its contracts in violation of the Contract Clause. This Court affirmed the dismissal of the suit, despite the fact that the case fell within the federal court's "arising under," or federal-question, jurisdiction. Justice Bradley's opinion did not purport to hold that the terms either of Article III or of the Eleventh Amendment barred the suit, but that the ancient doctrine of sovereign immunity that had inspired adoption of the Eleventh Amendment applied to cases beyond the Amendment's scope and otherwise within the federal-question jurisdiction. Indeed, Bradley explicitly admitted that "it is true, the amendment does so read [as to permit Hans's suit], and if there were no other reason or ground for abating his suit, it might be maintainable." The Court elected, nonetheless, to recognize a broader immunity doctrine, despite the want of any textual manifestation, because of what the Court described as the anomaly that would have resulted otherwise: the Eleventh Amendment (according to the Court) would have barred a federal-question suit by a noncitizen, but the State would have been subject to federal jurisdiction at its own citizen's behest. . . .

Hans thus addressed the issue implicated (though not directly raised) in the preratification debate about the Citizen-State Diversity Clauses and implicitly settled by *Chisholm*: whether state sovereign immunity was cognizable by federal courts on the exercise of federal-question jurisdiction. According to *Hans*, and contrary to *Chisholm*, it was. But that is all that *Hans* held. Because no federal legislation purporting to pierce state immunity was at issue, it cannot fairly be said that *Hans* held state sovereign immunity to have attained some constitutional status immunizing it from abrogation.[7]

Taking *Hans* only as far as its holding, its vulnerability is apparent. The Court rested its opinion on avoiding the supposed anomaly of recognizing jurisdiction to entertain a citizen's federal question suit, but not one brought by a noncitizen. There was, however, no such anomaly at all. As already explained, federal-question cases are not touched by the Eleventh Amendment, which leaves a State open to federal-question suits by citizens and noncitizens alike. If Hans had been from Massachusetts the Eleventh Amendment would not have barred his action against Louisiana.

Although there was thus no anomaly to be cured by *Hans*, the case certainly created its own anomaly in leaving federal courts entirely without jurisdiction to enforce paramount federal law at the behest of a citizen against a State that broke it. It destroyed the congruence of the judicial power under Article III with the substantive guarantees of the Constitution, and with the provisions of statutes passed by Congress in the exercise of its power under Article I: when a State injured an individual in violation of federal law no federal forum could provide direct relief. . . .

How such a result could have been threatened on the basis of a principle not so much as mentioned in the Constitution is difficult to understand. But history provides the explanation. As I have already said, *Hans* was one episode in a long story of debt repudiation by the States of the former Confederacy after the end of Reconstruction. . . .

So it is that history explains, but does not honor, *Hans*. . . .

---

[7] [n.15] Indeed, as Justice Stevens suggests [in his separate dissenting opinion in this case], there is language in *Hans* suggesting that the Court was really construing the Judiciary Act of 1875 rather than the Constitution.

III

B

1

As I have already noted briefly, the Framers and their contemporaries did not agree about the place of common-law state sovereign immunity even as to federal jurisdiction resting on the Citizen-State Diversity Clauses. Edmund Randolph argued in favor of ratification on the ground that the immunity would not be recognized, leaving the States subject to jurisdiction.[8] Patrick Henry opposed ratification on the basis of exactly the same reading. On the other hand, James Madison, John Marshall, and Alexander Hamilton all appear to have believed that the common-law immunity from suit would survive the ratification of Article III, so as to be at a State's disposal when jurisdiction would depend on diversity. This would have left the States free to enjoy a traditional immunity as defendants without barring the exercise of judicial power over them if they chose to enter the federal courts as diversity plaintiffs or to waive their immunity as diversity defendants. [Here the dissent quotes the comments of Madison, Marshall, and Hamilton cited by the *Alden* majority.] The majority sees in these statements, and chiefly in Hamilton's discussion of sovereign immunity in The Federalist No. 81 [quoted by the *Alden* majority], an unequivocal mandate "which would preclude all federal jurisdiction over an unconsenting State." But there is no such mandate to be found.

. . . [T]he immediate context of Hamilton's discussion in Federalist No. 81 has nothing to do with federal-question cases. It addresses a suggestion "that an assignment of the public securities of one state to the citizens of another, would enable them to prosecute that state in the federal courts for the amount of those securities." Hamilton is plainly talking about a suit subject to a federal court's jurisdiction under the Citizen-State Diversity Clauses of Article III. . . .

The most that can be inferred from this is, as noted above, that in diversity cases applying state contract law the immunity that a State would have enjoyed in its own courts is carried into the federal court. When, therefore, the *Hans* Court relied in part upon Hamilton's statement, its reliance was misplaced; Hamilton was addressing diversity jurisdiction, whereas *Hans* involved federal-question jurisdiction under the Contracts Clause. No general theory of federal-question immunity can be inferred from Hamilton's discussion of immunity in contract suits. . . .

Thus, the Court's attempt to convert isolated statements by the Framers into answers to questions not before them is fundamentally misguided. The Court's difficulty is far more fundamental, however, than inconsistency with a particular quotation, for the Court's position runs afoul of the general theory of sovereignty that gave shape to the Framers' enterprise. An enquiry into the development of that concept demonstrates that American political thought had so revolutionized the concept of sovereignty itself that calling for the immunity of a State as against the jurisdiction of the national courts would have been sheer illogic.

---

[8] [n.38] *See* 3 Elliot's Debates 573 (the Constitution would "render valid and effective existing claims" against the States). *See also* 2 *id.*, at 491 (James Wilson, in the Pennsylvania ratification debate: "When a citizen has a controversy with another state, there ought to be a tribunal where both parties may stand on a just and equal footing"). Wilson, as I noted above, took a similar position in addressing the federal question, or arising under, clause, remarking that the effect of the clause would be to require States to honor pre-Revolutionary debt owed to English merchants, as had been promised in the Treaty of 1783. *See* n. 4, *supra*.

2

We said in *Blatchford v. Native Village of Noatak*, 501 U.S. 775, 779 (1991), that "the States entered the federal system with their sovereignty intact," but we surely did not mean that they entered that system with the sovereignty they would have claimed if each State had assumed independent existence in the community of nations. . . . For the adoption of the Constitution made them members of a novel federal system that sought to balance the States' exercise of some sovereign prerogatives delegated from their own people with the principle of a limited but centralizing federal supremacy. . . .

Given this metamorphosis of the idea of sovereignty in the years leading up to 1789, the question whether the old immunity doctrine might have been received as something suitable for the new world of federal-question jurisdiction is a crucial one. The answer is that sovereign immunity as it would have been known to the Framers before ratification thereafter became inapplicable as a matter of logic in a federal suit raising a federal question. The old doctrine, after all, barred the involuntary subjection of a sovereign to the system of justice and law of which it was itself the font, since to do otherwise would have struck the common-law mind from the Middle Ages onward as both impractical and absurd. *See, e.g., Kawananakoa v. Polyblank*, 205 U.S. 349, 353 (1907) (Holmes, J.) ("A sovereign is exempt from suit . . . on the logical and practical ground that there can be no legal right as against the authority that makes the law on which the right depends"). But the ratification demonstrated that state governments were subject to a superior regime of law in a judicial system established, not by the State, but by the people through a specific delegation of their sovereign power to a National Government that was paramount within its delegated sphere. When individuals sued States to enforce federal rights, the Government that corresponded to the "sovereign" in the traditional common-law sense was not the State but the National Government, and any state immunity from the jurisdiction of the Nation's courts would have required a grant from the true sovereign, the people, in their Constitution, or from the Congress that the Constitution had empowered. . . .

Given the Framers' general concern with curbing abuses by state governments, it would be amazing if the scheme of delegated powers embodied in the Constitution had left the National Government powerless to render the States judicially accountable for violations of federal rights. And of course the Framers did not understand the scheme to leave the Government powerless. In The Federalist No. 80, at 535, Hamilton observed that "no man of sense will believe that such prohibitions [running against the States] would be scrupulously regarded, without some effectual power in the government to restrain or correct the infractions of them," and that "an authority in the federal courts, to over-rule such as might be in manifest contravention of the articles of union" was the Convention's preferred remedy. By speaking in the plural of an authority in the federal "courts," Hamilton made it clear that he envisioned more than this Court's exercise of appellate jurisdiction to review federal questions decided by state courts. Nor is it plausible that he was thinking merely of suits brought against States by the National Government itself, which The Federalist's authors did not describe in the paternalistic terms that would pass without an eyebrow raised today. Hamilton's power of the Government to restrain violations of citizens' rights was a power to be exercised by the federal courts at the citizens' behest. *See also* Marshall, *Fighting the Words of the Eleventh Amendment*, 102 HARV. L. REV. 1342, 1367–1371 (1989) (discussing the Framers' concern with preserving as much state accountability as possible even in the course of enacting the Eleventh Amendment).

This sketch of the logic and objectives of the new federal order is confirmed by what we have previously seen of the preratification debate on state sovereign immunity, which in turn becomes entirely intelligible both in what it addressed and what it ignored. It is understandable that reasonable minds differed on the applicability of the immunity doctrine in suits that made it to federal court only under the original Diversity Clauses, for their features were not wholly novel. While they were, of course, in the courts of the new and, for some purposes, paramount National Government, the law that they implicated was largely the old common law (and in any case was not federal law). It was not foolish, therefore, to ask whether the old law brought the old defenses with it. But it is equally understandable that questions seem not to have been raised about state sovereign immunity in federal-question cases. The very idea of a federal question depended on the rejection of the simple concept of sovereignty from which the immunity doctrine had developed; under the English common law, the question of immunity in a system of layered sovereignty simply could not have arisen.[9] The Framers' principal objectives in rejecting English theories of unitary sovereignty, moreover, would have been impeded if a new concept of sovereign immunity had taken its place in federal-question cases, and would have been substantially thwarted if that new immunity had been held to be untouchable by any congressional effort to abrogate it.[10]

Today's majority discounts this concern. Without citing a single source to the contrary, the Court dismisses the historical evidence regarding the Framers' vision of the relationship between national and state sovereignty. . . . In the end, is it plausible to contend that the plan of the convention was meant to leave the National Government without any way to render individuals capable of enforcing their federal rights directly against an intransigent State?

NOTES

1. The Constitutional Status of Sovereign Immunity. The specific holdings in *Alden* and *Seminole Tribe* are discussed in Note 6 following *Quern v. Jordan* in Section C, *infra*. For now, these opinions are meant to highlight the controversy surrounding the extent to which the Constitution was intended to extend sovereign immunity to the states. As Justice Souter's opinion in *Seminole Tribe* notes, the great weight of academic commentary supports the views of the dissenters on this issue. Which interpretation of the constitutional language and history is more persuasive? *See also* James E. Pfander, *History and State Suability: An "Explanatory" Account of the Eleventh Amendment*, 83 CORNELL L. REV. 1269 (1998) (arguing that the Eleventh Amendment was meant to protect states from federal court suits seeking to collect debts incurred before the Constitution went into effect, but not to prevent states from being sued for actions they took in violation of federal rights after the Constitution took effect).

2. The Policy Implications of Sovereign Immunity. Putting aside questions of constitutional interpretation and history, commentators disagree — just as the Framers of the Constitution apparently did — whether the concept of sovereign immunity even makes sense in our contemporary political system. Some believe that

---

[9] [n.51] *Cf.* [Stewart Jay, *Origins of Federal Common Law: Part One*, 133 U. PA. L. REV. 1003, 1033–1034 (1985)] ("English common law might afford clues to the meaning of some terms in the Constitution, but the absence of any close federal model was recognized even at the Convention").

[10] [n.52] . . . The majority contends that state compliance with federal law may be enforced by other means, but its suggestions are all pretty cold comfort: the enforcement resources of the Federal Government itself are limited; appellate review of state court decisions is contingent upon state consent to suit in state court, and is also called into question by the majority's rationale; and the Court's decision today illustrates the uncertainty that the Court will always permit enforcement of federal law by suits for prospective relief against state officers. [The portion of the majority's decision dealing with suits seeking prospective relief against state officers is described in Note 3 following *Edelman v. Jordan* in Section B, *infra*.] Moreover, the majority's position ignores the importance of citizen suits to enforcement of federal law. *See, e.g., Alyeska Pipeline Service Co. v. Wilderness Society*, 421 U.S. 240, 263 (1975) (acknowledging that, in many instances, "Congress has opted to rely heavily on private enforcement to implement public policy"); *see also* S. Rep. No. 94-1011, p. 2 (Civil Rights Attorney's Fees Awards Act of 1976, 42 U.S.C. § 1988) (recognizing that "all of these civil rights laws depend heavily upon private enforcement"); *Pennsylvania v. Delaware Valley Citizens' Council for Clean Air*, 483 U.S. 711, 737 (1987) (Blackmun, J., dissenting) (noting importance of citizens' suits under federal environmental laws).

sovereign immunity is "an anachronistic relic" designed to serve "royal prerogatives," which "undermines [the] basic notion" of government accountability on which our country was founded. Erwin Chemerinsky, *Against Sovereign Immunity*, 53 STAN. L. REV. 1201, 1202 (2001). Others, by contrast, have praised the Eleventh Amendment's "utility in harmonizing tensions between the two levels of government." George D. Brown, *State Sovereignty Under the Burger Court — How the Eleventh Amendment Survived the Death of the Tenth: Some Broader Implications of* Atascadero State Hospital v. Scanlon, 74 GEO. L.J. 363, 363 (1985). At some level, this controversy reflects the choice between the competing policy goals of protecting state sovereignty and ensuring state compliance with federal law.

3. Who Is Barred by the Eleventh Amendment? As the Court's opinion in *Alden* indicates, the states' immunity from suit in federal court is not limited to actions brought by citizens of other states and foreign states. But the Court has long held that a state may be sued by the Federal Government or by another state. Such suits, the Court observed in *Principality of Monaco v. Mississippi*, 292 U.S. 313, 329 (1934), are "inherent in the constitutional plan," and, therefore, "[i]n ratifying the Constitution, the States consented to [such] suits." *Alden v. Maine*, 527 U.S. 706, 755 (1999). The Court explained in *Alden*:

> A suit which is commenced and prosecuted against a State in the name of the United States . . . differs in kind from the suit of an individual: While the Constitution contemplates suits among the members of the federal system as an alternative to extralegal measures, the fear of private suits against nonconsenting States was the central reason given by the Founders who chose to preserve the States' sovereign immunity.

Alden, 527 U.S. at 755–56.[11]

In addition, as Justice Souter's dissent in *Seminole Tribe* pointed out, the Supreme Court has consistently said that the Eleventh Amendment "does not constrain the appellate jurisdiction of the Supreme Court over cases arising from state courts." *McKesson Corp. v. Division of Alcoholic Beverages and Tobacco*, 496 U.S. 18, 31 (1990). Quoting from *Principality of Monaco*, the *McKesson* opinion reasoned that "it is 'inherent in the constitutional plan' that when a state court takes cognizance of a case, the State assents to appellate review by this Court of the federal issues raised in the case 'whoever may be the parties to the original suit, whether private persons, or the state itself.'" *McKesson Corp.*, 496 U.S. at 30.

4. Who Is Protected by the Eleventh Amendment? Ever since its opinion in *Lincoln County v. Luning*, 133 U.S. 529, 530 (1890), the Court has held that the Eleventh Amendment does not protect "political subdivisions such as counties and municipalities, even though such entities exercise a 'slice of state power.'" *Lake Country Estates, Inc. v. Tahoe Regional Planning Agency*, 440 U.S. 391, 401 (1979). The Court explained in *Luning* that "while the county is territorially a part of the State, yet politically it is also a corporation created by and with such powers as are given to it by the state." *Luning*, 133 U.S. at 530. The Court's Eleventh Amendment jurisprudence thus distinguishes between "an arm of the State partaking of the State's Eleventh Amendment immunity" and a "political subdivision to which the Eleventh Amendment does not extend." *Mount Healthy City School District Board of Education v. Doyle*, 429 U.S. 274, 280 (1977). *See also Northern Insurance Co. v. Chatham County*, 547 U.S. 189, 193 (2006) (unanimously

---

[11] Despite the traditional understanding recognized in *Alden*, the Court held in *Federal Maritime Commission v. South Carolina State Ports Authority*, 535 U.S. 743, 747 (2002), that sovereign immunity protected the state from a Federal Maritime Commission administrative proceeding aimed at "adjudicating a private party's complaint that a state-run port . . . violated the Shipping Act of 1984." The Court reached this conclusion even though, as it acknowledged, "the Commission's orders can only be enforced by a federal district court" — in an action that would be filed against the State *by the federal agency*. *Federal Maritime Commission*, 535 U.S. at 761–62.

rejecting the court of appeals' conclusion that " 'common law has carved out a "residual immunity," which would protect a political subdivision such as Chatham County' ").[12] For the view that this line of cases constitutes a "major exception" to the Supreme Court's usual practice of treating political subdivisions as "constitutionally indistinguishable from the state that created them," and also "frustrates" federalism because "[t]he state's right freely to delegate its powers and responsibilities in the way it deems most efficient is hampered by the fact that if it chooses to delegate power it must forego the immunity it would otherwise enjoy," see Margreth Barrett, Comment, *The Denial of Eleventh Amendment Immunity to Political Subdivisions of the States: An Unjustified Strain on Federalism*, 1979 DUKE L.J. 1042, 1042, 1062.

In concluding that the bistate regional planning agency sued in *Lake Country Estates* was a political subdivision and not an arm of the state, and therefore was not protected by the Eleventh Amendment, the Court considered a number of factors, including the following: a majority of the agency's governing members were appointed by counties and cities; the agency was funded by counties, rather than the states; the agency's obligations were not binding on either state; the agency's rules were "not subject to veto at the state level"; the agency was characterized as a "political subdivision" and a "separate legal entity" in the interstate compact that created it;[13] and "[t]he regulation of land use is traditionally a function performed by local governments." *Lake Country Estates*, 440 U.S. at 401–02.

When these various factors pointed in opposite directions in *Hess v. Port Authority Trans-Hudson Corp.*, 513 U.S. 30, 48 (1994), the Court indicated that "the vulnerability of the State's purse [is] the most salient factor in Eleventh Amendment determinations." The majority therefore held that the defendant in that case, a financially self-sufficient bistate railway authorized by interstate compact, was not protected by the Eleventh Amendment even though its commissioners were all state appointees and their actions were subject to veto by the two Governors. The four dissenters, by contrast, thought that the "critical inquiry" was "whether and to what extent the elected state government exercises oversight over the entity." *Hess*, 513 U.S. at 61 (O'Connor, J., dissenting). *See also Auer v. Robbins*, 519 U.S. 452, 456 n.1 (1997) (concluding that the St. Louis Board of Police Commissioners was not protected by the Eleventh Amendment even though the Governor appointed four of its five members, because "the city of St. Louis is responsible for the board's financial liabilities and the board is not subject to the State's direction or control in any other respect").

For a description of lower court opinions analyzing whether particular governmental entities are arms of the state or political subdivisions — though noting that "generalizations in this area of the law are somewhat treacherous" — see 1 JOSEPH G. COOK & JOHN L. SOBIESKI, JR., CIVIL RIGHTS ACTIONS ¶ 2.01[D] (2007); *see also* Alex E. Rogers, Note, *Clothing State Governmental Entities with Sovereign Immunity: Disarray in the Eleventh Amendment Arm-of-the-State Doctrine*, 92 COLUM. L. REV. 1243, 1267 (1992) (surveying the conflicting lower court cases and critiquing "the unworkable nature of the [Supreme Court's] multifactored analysis").

5. Procedural Issues. In *Puerto Rico Aqueduct & Sewer Authority v. Metcalf & Eddy, Inc.*, 506 U.S. 139 (1993), the Court invoked the collateral order exception to the

---

[12] The Court also refused to create any special Eleventh Amendment rules for "*in personam* admiralty suits that . . . aris[e] from a county's exercise of core state functions with regard to navigable waters." *Northern Insurance Co.*, 547 U.S. at 195.

[13] In *Regents of the University of California v. Doe*, 519 U.S. 425, 429 n.5 (1997), the Court noted that, even though the question whether a particular defendant "has the same kind of independent status as a county or is instead an arm of the State" entitled to Eleventh Amendment protection is "[u]ltimately . . . a question of federal law, . . . that federal question can be answered only after considering the provisions of state law that define the agency's character." *Cf. McMillian v. Monroe*, 520 U.S. 781, 786 (1997) (excerpted in Chapter 4.C., *infra*) (holding that an official's status as a state or local policymaker for purposes of assessing municipal liability is a question of state law).

final judgment rule in allowing defendants to file an interlocutory appeal challenging a district court decision that they were not an "arm" of the state entitled to Eleventh Amendment protection. Analogizing to its ruling in *Mitchell v. Forsyth*, 472 U.S. 511 (1985), that denials of qualified immunity are immediately appealable (as described in Note 5 following *Hope v. Pelzer* in Chapter 2.B., *supra*), the Court explained that the Eleventh Amendment's "withdrawal of jurisdiction effectively confers an immunity from suit," and not just "a defense to liability." *Puerto Rico Aqueduct*, 506 U.S. at 144, 145. Justice Stevens's dissenting opinion contended that the driving force behind *Mitchell* — that "the specter of a long and contentious legal proceeding in and of itself would inhibit government officials from exercising their authority with the freedom and independence necessary to serve the public interest" — was inapplicable to "a state entity claiming to be an 'arm of the State.'" *Puerto Rico Aqueduct*, 506 U.S. at 150, 149 (Stevens, J., dissenting). The majority responded as follows: "While application of the collateral order doctrine in this type of case is justified in part by a concern that the States not be unduly burdened by litigation, its ultimate justification is the importance of ensuring that the States' dignitary interests can be fully vindicated." *Puerto Rico Aqueduct*, 506 U.S. at 146.

Unlike qualified immunity, however, which is generally treated as a matter to be proven by the plaintiff (*see* Note 4 following *Hope v. Pelzer* in Chapter 2.B., *supra*), the courts of appeals tend to require the defendant to shoulder the burden of proving an entitlement to Eleventh Amendment protection. *See, e.g., ITSI TV Productions, Inc. v. Agricultural Associations*, 3 F.3d 1289, 1291 (9th Cir. 1993) (explaining that "Eleventh Amendment immunity, whatever its jurisdictional attributes, should be treated as an affirmative defense" and therefore "must be proved by the party that asserts it and would benefit from its acceptance"); *see also Christy v. Pennsylvania Turnpike Commission*, 54 F.3d 1140, 1144 (3d Cir. 1995) (same). Note that the courts disagree whether Eleventh Amendment issues must be resolved before the court turns to the merits of the case. *See Norita v. Northern Mariana Islands*, 331 F.3d 690, 691–92 & n.1 (9th Cir. 2003) (citing conflicting cases). For the Supreme Court's approach to the similar questions that arise with respect to claims of qualified immunity, *see* Note 8 following *Harlow v. Fitzgerald* in Chapter 2.B., *supra*.

B. PROSPECTIVE INJUNCTION SUITS FILED AGAINST STATE OFFICIALS

EDELMAN v. JORDAN
Supreme Court of the United States
415 U.S. 651 (1974)

Mr. Justice Rehnquist delivered the opinion of the Court.

Respondent John Jordan filed a complaint in the United States District Court for the Northern District of Illinois, individually and as a representative of a class, seeking declaratory and injunctive relief against two former directors of the Illinois Department of Public Aid, the director of the Cook County Department of Public Aid, and the comptroller of Cook County. Respondent alleged that these state officials were administering the federal-state programs of Aid to the Aged, Blind, or Disabled (AABD) in a manner inconsistent with various federal regulations and with the Fourteenth Amendment to the Constitution.

AABD is one of the categorical aid programs administered by the Illinois Department of Public Aid pursuant to the Illinois Public Aid Code. Under the Social Security Act, the program is funded by the State and the Federal Governments. The Department of Health, Education, and Welfare (HEW), which administers these payments for the Federal Government, issued regulations prescribing maximum permissible time standards within which States participating in the program had to process AABD applications. Those regulations, originally issued in 1968, required, at the time of the institution of this suit, that eligibility determinations must be made by the States within 30 days of receipt of applications for aid to the aged and blind, and within 45 days of receipt of applications for aid to the disabled. For those persons found eligible, the assistance check was required to be received by them within the applicable time period.

During the period in which the federal regulations went into effect, Illinois public aid officials were administering the benefits pursuant to their own regulations as provided in the Categorical Assistance Manual of the Illinois Department of Public Aid. Respondent's complaint charged that the Illinois defendants, operating under those regulations, were improperly authorizing grants to commence only with the month in which an application was approved and not including prior eligibility months for which an applicant was entitled to aid under federal law. The complaint also alleged that the Illinois defendants were not processing the applications within the applicable time requirements of the federal regulations; specifically, respondent alleged that his own application for disability benefits was not acted on by the Illinois Department of Public Aid for almost four months. Such actions of the Illinois officials were alleged to violate federal law and deny the equal protection of the laws. Respondent's prayer requested declaratory and injunctive relief, and specifically requested "a permanent injunction enjoining the defendants to award to the entire class of plaintiffs all AABD benefits wrongfully withheld."

In its judgment of March 15, 1972, the District Court declared § 4004 of the Illinois Manual to be invalid insofar as it was inconsistent with the federal regulations . . . , and granted a permanent injunction requiring compliance with the federal time limits for processing and paying AABD applicants. The District Court . . . also ordered the state officials to "release and remit AABD benefits wrongfully withheld to all [eligible] applicants for AABD in the State of Illinois who applied between July 1, 1968 [the date of the federal regulations] and April 16, 197[1] [the date of the preliminary injunction issued by the District Court]. . . . "

On appeal to the United States Court of Appeals for the Seventh Circuit, the Illinois officials contended, *inter alia*, that the Eleventh Amendment barred the award of retroactive benefits. . . . The Court of Appeals rejected these contentions and affirmed the judgment of the District Court. Because of an apparent conflict on the Eleventh Amendment issue with the decision of the Court of Appeals for the Second Circuit in *Rothstein v. Wyman*, 467 F.2d 226 (1972), *cert. denied*, 411 U.S. 921 (1973), we granted the petition for certiorari filed by petitioner Joel Edelman, who is the present Director of the Illinois Department of Public Aid, and successor to the former directors sued below. . . . Because we believe the Court of Appeals erred in its disposition of the Eleventh Amendment claim, we reverse that portion of the Court of Appeals decision which affirmed the District Court's order that retroactive benefits be paid by the Illinois state officials.

The historical basis of the Eleventh Amendment has been oft stated, and it represents one of the more dramatic examples of this Court's effort to derive meaning from the document given to the Nation by the Framers nearly 200 years ago. . . .

While the Amendment by its terms does not bar suits against a State by its own citizens, this Court has consistently held that an unconsenting State is immune from suits brought in federal courts by her own citizens as well as by citizens of another State. It is also well established that even though a State is not named a party to the action, the suit may nonetheless be barred by the Eleventh Amendment. In *Ford Motor Co. v. Department of Treasury*, 323 U.S. 459 (1945), the Court said:

> "When the action is in essence one for the recovery of money from the state, the state is the real, substantial party in interest and is entitled to invoke its sovereign immunity from suit even though individual officials are nominal defendants."

Thus the rule has evolved that a suit by private parties seeking to impose a liability which must be paid from public funds in the state treasury is barred by the Eleventh Amendment.

The Court of Appeals in this case, while recognizing that the *Hans* [*v. Louisiana*] line of cases permitted the State to raise the Eleventh Amendment as a defense to suit by its own citizens, nevertheless concluded that the Amendment did not bar the award of retroactive payments of the statutory benefits found to have been wrongfully withheld. The Court of Appeals held that the above-cited cases, when read in light of this Court's landmark decision in *Ex parte Young*, 209 U.S. 123 (1908), do not preclude the grant of such a monetary award in the nature of equitable restitution.

Petitioner concedes that *Ex parte Young* is no bar to that part of the District Court's judgment that prospectively enjoined petitioner's predecessors from failing to process applications within the time limits established by the federal regulations. Petitioner argues, however, that *Ex parte Young* does not extend so far as to permit a suit which seeks the award of an accrued monetary liability which must be met from the general revenues of a State, absent consent or waiver by the State of its Eleventh Amendment immunity, and that therefore the award of retroactive benefits by the District Court was improper.

Ex parte Young was a watershed case in which this Court held that the Eleventh Amendment did not bar an action in the federal courts seeking to enjoin the Attorney General of Minnesota from enforcing a statute claimed to violate the Fourteenth Amendment of the United States Constitution. This holding has permitted the Civil War Amendments to the Constitution to serve as a sword, rather than merely as a shield, for those whom they were designed to protect. But the relief awarded in *Ex parte Young* was prospective only; the Attorney General of Minnesota was enjoined to conform his future conduct of that office to the requirement of the Fourteenth Amendment. Such relief is analogous to that awarded by the District Court in the prospective portion of its order under review in this case.

But the retroactive portion of the District Court's order here, which requires the payment of a very substantial amount of money which that court held should have been paid, but was not, stands on quite a different footing. These funds will obviously not be paid out of the pocket of petitioner Edelman. Addressing himself to a similar situation in *Rothstein v. Wyman*, 467 F.2d 226 (CA2 1972), *cert. denied*, 411 U.S. 921 (1973), Judge McGowan observed for the court:

> "It is not pretended that these payments are to come from the personal resources of these appellants. Appellees expressly contemplate that they will, rather, involve substantial expenditures from the public funds of the state. . . .
>
> "It is one thing to tell the Commissioner of Social Services that he must comply with the federal standards for the future if the state is to have the benefit of federal funds in the programs he administers. It is quite another thing to order the Commissioner to use state funds to make reparation for the past. The latter would appear to us to fall afoul of the Eleventh Amendment if that basic constitutional provision is to be conceived of as having any present force."

We agree with Judge McGowan's observations. The funds to satisfy the award in this case must inevitably come from the general revenues of the State of Illinois, and thus the award resembles far more closely the monetary award against the State itself, *Ford Motor Co. v. Department of Treasury, supra*, than it does the prospective injunctive relief awarded in *Ex parte Young*.

The Court of Appeals, in upholding the award in this case, held that it was permissible because it was in the form of "equitable restitution" instead of damages, and therefore capable of being tailored in such a way as to minimize disruptions of the state program of categorical assistance. But we must judge the award actually made in this case, and not one which might have been differently tailored in a different case, and we must judge it in the context of the important constitutional principle embodied in the Eleventh Amendment.[14]

We do not read *Ex parte Young* or subsequent holdings of this Court to indicate that any form of relief may be awarded against a state officer, no matter how closely it may in practice resemble a money judgment payable out of the state treasury, so long as the relief may be labeled "equitable" in nature. The Court's opinion in *Ex parte Young* hewed to no such line. . . .

As in most areas of the law, the difference between the type of relief barred by the Eleventh Amendment and that permitted under *Ex parte Young* will not in many instances be that between day and night. The injunction issued in *Ex parte Young* was not totally without effect on the State's revenues, since the state law which the Attorney General was enjoined from enforcing provided substantial monetary penalties against railroads which did not conform to its provisions. Later cases from this Court have authorized equitable relief which has probably had greater impact on state treasuries than did that awarded in *Ex parte Young*. In *Graham v. Richardson*, 403 U.S. 365 (1971), Arizona and Pennsylvania welfare officials were prohibited from denying welfare benefits to otherwise qualified recipients who were aliens. In *Goldberg v. Kelly*, 397 U.S. 254 (1970), New York City welfare officials were enjoined from following New York State procedures which authorized the termination of benefits paid to welfare recipients without prior hearing. But the fiscal consequences to state treasuries in these cases were the necessary result of compliance with decrees which by their terms were prospective in nature. State officials, in order to shape their official conduct to the mandate of the Court's decrees, would more likely have to spend money from the state treasury than if they had been left free to pursue their previous course of conduct. Such an ancillary effect on the state treasury is a permissible and often an inevitable consequence of the principle announced in *Ex parte Young*.

But that portion of the District Court's decree which petitioner challenges on Eleventh Amendment grounds goes much further than any of the cases cited. It requires payment of state funds, not as a necessary consequence of compliance in the future with a substantive federal-question determination, but as a form of compensation to those whose applications were processed on the slower time schedule at a time when petitioner was under no court-imposed obligation to conform to a different standard. While the Court of Appeals described this retroactive award of monetary relief as a form of "equitable restitution," it is in practical effect indistinguishable in many aspects from an

---

[14] [n.11] It may be true, as stated by our Brother Douglas in dissent, that "most welfare decisions by federal courts have a financial impact on the States." But we cannot agree that such a financial impact is the same where a federal court applies *Ex parte Young* to grant prospective declaratory and injunctive relief, as opposed to an order of retroactive payments as was made in the instant case. It is not necessarily true that "whether the decree is prospective only or requires payments for the weeks or months wrongfully skipped over by the state officials, the nature of the impact on the state treasury is precisely the same." This argument neglects the fact that where the State has a definable allocation to be used in the payment of public aid benefits, and pursues a certain course of action such as the processing of applications within certain time periods as did Illinois here, the subsequent ordering by a federal court of retroactive payments to correct delays in such processing will invariably mean there is less money available for payments for the continuing obligations of the public aid system.

As stated by Judge McGowan in *Rothstein v. Wyman*, 467 F.2d 226, 235 (CA2 1972):

"The second federal policy which might arguably be furthered by retroactive payments is the fundamental goal of congressional welfare legislation — the satisfaction of the ascertained needs of impoverished persons. Federal standards are designed to ensure that those needs are equitably met; and there may perhaps be cases in which the prompt payment of funds wrongfully withheld will serve that end. As time goes by, however, retroactive payments become compensatory rather than remedial; the coincidence between previously ascertained and existing needs becomes less clear."

award of damages against the State. It will to a virtual certainty be paid from state funds, and not from the pockets of the individual state officials who were the defendants in the action. It is measured in terms of a monetary loss resulting from a past breach of a legal duty on the part of the defendant state officials.

Were we to uphold this portion of the District Court's decree, we would be obligated to overrule the Court's holding in *Ford Motor Co. v. Department of Treasury, supra.* There a taxpayer, who had, under protest, paid taxes to the State of Indiana, sought a refund of those taxes from the Indiana state officials who were charged with their collection. The taxpayer claimed that the tax had been imposed in violation of the United States Constitution. The term "equitable restitution" would seem even more applicable to the relief sought in that case, since the taxpayer had at one time had the money, and paid it over to the State pursuant to an allegedly unconstitutional tax exaction. Yet this Court had no hesitation in holding that the taxpayer's action was a suit against the State, and barred by the Eleventh Amendment. We reach a similar conclusion with respect to the retroactive portion of the relief awarded by the District Court in this case. . . .

Mr. Justice Douglas, dissenting.

In *Ex parte Young*, 209 U.S. 123, a suit by stockholders of a railroad was brought in a federal court against state officials to enjoin the imposition of confiscatory rates on the railroad in violation of the Fourteenth Amendment. The Eleventh Amendment was interposed as a defense. The Court rejected the defense, saying that state officials with authority to enforce state laws "who threaten and are about to commence proceedings, either of a civil or criminal nature, to enforce against parties affected an unconstitutional act, violating the Federal Constitution, may be enjoined by a Federal court of equity from such action." The Court went on to say that a state official seeking to enforce in the name of a State an unconstitutional act "comes into conflict with the superior authority of that Constitution, and he is in that case stripped of his official or representative character and is subjected in his person to the consequence of his individual conduct. The State has no power to impart to him any immunity from responsibility to the supreme authority of the United States."

As the complaint in the instant case alleges violations by officials of Illinois of the Equal Protection Clause of the Fourteenth Amendment, it seems that the case is governed by *Ex parte Young* so far as injunctive relief is concerned. The main thrust of the argument is that the instant case asks for relief which if granted would affect the treasury of the State.

Most welfare decisions by federal courts have a financial impact on the States. . . . The welfare cases coming here have involved ultimately the financial responsibility of the State to beneficiaries claiming they were deprived of federal rights. *King v. Smith*[, 392 U.S. 309 (1968),] required payment to children even though their mother was cohabitating with a man who could not pass muster as a "parent." *Rosado v. Wyman*, 397 U.S. 397 [(1970)], held that under this state-federal cooperative program a State could not reduce its standard of need in conflict with the federal standard. It is true that *Rosado* did not involve retroactive payments as are involved here. But the distinction is not relevant or material because the result in every welfare case coming here is to increase or reduce the financial responsibility of the participating State. In no case when the responsibility of the State is increased to meet the lawful demand of the beneficiary, is there any levy on state funds. Whether the decree is prospective only or requires payments for the weeks or months wrongfully skipped over by the state officials, the nature of the impact on the state treasury is precisely the same. . . .[15]

NOTES

1. The *Ex parte Young* Fiction. *Ex parte Young*, 209 U.S. 123 (1908), which the *Edelman* majority describes as a "landmark decision" and a "watershed case," is "clearly the most important way around the Eleventh Amendment." ERWIN CHEMERINSKY, FEDERAL JURISDICTION § 7.5, at 432 (5th ed. 2007). In holding that the Eleventh Amendment did not bar a group of railroad stockholders from suing to enjoin the Minnesota state attorney general from enforcing a state statute that set the maximum rates railroads could charge, the *Ex parte Young* Court reasoned as follows:

> The act to be enforced is alleged to be unconstitutional; and if it be so, the use of the name of the State to enforce an unconstitutional act to the injury of complainants is a proceeding without the authority of and one which does not affect the State in its sovereign or governmental capacity. It is simply an illegal act upon the part of a state official in attempting by the use of the name of the State to enforce a legislative enactment which is void because unconstitutional. If the act which the state Attorney General seeks to enforce be a violation of the Federal Constitution, the officer in proceeding under such enactment comes into conflict with the superior authority of that Constitution, and he is in that case stripped of his official or representative character and is subjected in his person to the consequences of his individual conduct.

Ex parte Young, 209 U.S. at 159-60.[16]

The injunction sought in *Ex parte Young* had the same practical impact as an injunction against the state would have had. As Justice Harlan noted in dissent, the suit was brought against Young "as, and only because he was, Attorney General of Minnesota," and its "manifest . . . object . . . was to tie the hands of the State." *Ex parte Young*, 209 U.S. at 174 (Harlan, J., dissenting) (emphasis deleted). As a result, the Court's decision has been called the "purest fiction," 17A CHARLES ALAN WRIGHT, ARTHUR R. MILLER, EDWARD H. COOPER & VIKRAM DAVID AMAR, FEDERAL PRACTICE AND PROCEDURE § 4231 at 143 (3d ed. 2007) — especially given the Court's conclusion three years later that unconstitutional behavior on the part of a state official like Minnesota Attorney General Young is nevertheless state action for purposes of the Fourteenth Amendment. *See Home Telephone & Telegraph Co. v. Los Angeles*, 227 U.S. 278 (1913) (described in Chapter 1.B., *supra*). Nevertheless, despite its fictive character, the *Ex parte Young* doctrine is considered "indispensable to the establishment of constitutional government and the rule of law." WRIGHT, MILLER, COOPER & AMAR, *supra*, at 144.

Note that the *Ex parte Young* doctrine salvages only suits filed against state officials. A complaint that names the state itself, or an arm of the state, as the defendant is barred by the Eleventh Amendment even if it seeks prospective injunctive relief. As the Court noted in *Seminole Tribe v. Florida*, 517 U.S. 44 (1996), "the relief sought by a plaintiff suing a State is *irrelevant* to the question whether the suit is barred by the Eleventh Amendment" because "[t]he Eleventh Amendment does not exist solely in order to 'preven[t] federal-court judgments that must be paid out of a State's treasury,' [but] also serves to avoid 'the indignity of subjecting a State to the coercive process of judicial tribunals at the instance of private parties.'" *Seminole Tribe*, 517 U.S. at 58 (emphasis added).

---

[15] [Editor's note: Justice Marshall, joined by Justice Blackmun, filed a separate dissenting opinion, arguing that the State had waived its Eleventh Amendment immunity by participating in the AABD program. (For further discussion of this waiver issue, *see* Section C, *infra*.) Justice Brennan also dissented based on his belief that the Eleventh Amendment did not bar suits filed against states by their own citizens.]

[16] The courts eventually upheld the constitutionality of the Minnesota statute challenged in *Ex parte Young*. *See Minnesota Rate Cases*, 230 U.S. 352 (1913).

2. Distinguishing Prospective and Retrospective Injunctions. *Edelman* held that, just as state officials cannot be sued in their official capacity for damages, *see, e.g., Ford Motor Co. v. Department of Treasury*, 323 U.S. 459, 463–64 (1945), the Eleventh Amendment bars *Ex parte Young* suits that seek retrospective injunctions. Does the Court make a persuasive argument that retrospective and prospective injunctions should be treated differently for Eleventh Amendment purposes?

In a line of cases following *Edelman*, the Court has elaborated on the difference between prospective injunctions permissible under the Eleventh Amendment and retrospective injunctions barred by the Amendment. Do these opinions create a principled and administrable distinction between prospective and retrospective injunctions?

Milliken v. Bradley, 433 U.S. 267 (1977). The first in this line of cases is *Milliken v. Bradley*, decided three years after *Edelman*. In *Milliken*, the Court upheld an injunction designed to remedy the effects of the segregated school system in Detroit. The Court concluded that the injunction was not barred by the Eleventh Amendment despite the fact that it obligated the State of Michigan to pay half the cost (to the tune of almost $6 million) of a remedial reading program, counseling and career guidance for students, racially neutral testing procedures, and a comprehensive program to train school personnel "to cope with the desegregation process." *Milliken*, 433 U.S. at 276. In characterizing this injunction as prospective, the Court reasoned as follows:

> The educational components, which the District Court ordered into effect *prospectively*, are plainly designed to wipe out continuing conditions of inequality produced by the inherently unequal dual school system long maintained by Detroit.[17]
>
> These programs were not, and as a practical matter could not be, intended to wipe the slate clean by one bold stroke, as could a retroactive award of money in *Edelman*.[18] Rather, by the nature of the antecedent violation, . . . the victims of Detroit's *de jure* segregated system will continue to experience the effects of segregation until such future time as the remedial programs can help dissipate the continuing effects of past misconduct. Reading and speech deficiencies cannot be eliminated by judicial fiat; they will require time, patience, and the skills of specially trained teachers. That the programs are also "compensatory" in nature does not change the fact that they are part of a plan that operates *prospectively* to bring about the delayed benefits of a unitary school system.

Milliken, 433 U.S. at 290 (emphasis in original). Does the *Milliken* Court convincingly distinguish the retrospective portion of the injunction sought in *Edelman*?

Hutto v. Finney, 437 U.S. 678 (1978). The following year, in *Hutto v. Finney*, the Court upheld two attorney's fee awards made to lawyers representing prisoners who had successfully challenged the constitutionality of prison conditions in Arkansas. The first award flowed from the district court's finding that state prison officials had acted in bad faith in failing to comply with its prior order requiring them to improve prison conditions. Observing that "a financial penalty may be the most effective means of insuring compliance" where "a state agency refuses to adhere to a court order," the Supreme Court approved the award of attorney's fees as an "ancillary . . . penalty imposed to enforce a prospective injunction." *Hutto*, 437 U.S. at 691, 692. The second award was made pursuant to the Civil Rights Attorney's Fees Awards Act of 1976, 42

---

[17] [n.21] Unlike the award in *Edelman*, the injunction entered here could not instantaneously restore the victims of unlawful conduct to their rightful condition. Thus, the injunction here looks to the future, not simply to presently compensating victims for conduct and consequences completed in the past.

[18] [n.22] In contrast to *Edelman*, there was no money award here in favor of respondent Bradley or any members of his class. This case simply does not involve individual citizens' conducting a raid on the state treasury for an accrued monetary liability. . . .

B. PROSPECTIVE INJUNCTION SUITS FILED AGAINST STATE OFFICIALS 155

U.S.C. § 1988(b), which allows prevailing parties in section 1983 suits to recover their attorney's fees. The Court allowed this award as well, describing it as reimbursement for "expenses incurred in litigation seeking only prospective relief," as opposed to "retroactive liability for prelitigation conduct." *Hutto*, 437 U.S. at 695. Justice Powell, joined by Chief Justice Burger, disagreed with the majority's characterization of this second fee award, observing that "[a]s with damages and restitutory relief, an award of counsel fees could impose a substantial burden on the State to make unbudgeted disbursements to satisfy an obligation stemming from past (as opposed to post-litigation) activities." *Hutto*, 437 U.S. at 708 (Powell, J., concurring in part and dissenting in part). For a detailed discussion of attorney's fees in section 1983 cases, *see* Chapter 9, *infra*.

Quern v. Jordan, 440 U.S. 332 (1979). The *Edelman* litigation returned to the Supreme Court in *Quern v. Jordan*, when Quern (who had succeeded Edelman as director of the Illinois Department of Public Aid) challenged a lower court order requiring him to send an explanatory notice to members of the plaintiff class "advising them that there is a state administrative procedure available if they desire to have the state determine whether or not they may be eligible for past benefits" that had been wrongfully withheld. *Quern*, 440 U.S. at 336. The Supreme Court upheld the notice relief as "ancillary to the prospective relief already ordered by the court," rejecting the defendant's contention that "giving the proposed notice will lead inexorably to the payment of state funds for retroactive benefits" and thus, "in effect, amounts to a monetary award":

> [T]he chain of causation which petitioner seeks to establish is by no means unbroken; it contains numerous missing links, which can be supplied, if at all, only by the State and members of the plaintiff class. . . . The notice . . . simply apprises plaintiff class members of the existence of whatever administrative procedures may already be available under state law by which they may receive a determination of eligibility for past benefits. . . . The mere sending of that notice does not trigger the state administrative machinery. Whether a recipient of notice decides to take advantage of those available state procedures is left completely to the discretion of that particular class member; the federal court plays no role in that decision. And whether or not the class member will receive retroactive benefits rests entirely with the State, its agencies, courts, and legislature, not with the federal court.

Quern, 440 U.S. at 349, 347–48.

Green v. Mansour, 474 U.S. 64 (1985). The Court reached the opposite conclusion in *Green v. Mansour*, however, finding that explanatory notice relief constitutes a retrospective award barred by the Eleventh Amendment when it is "an independent form of relief" that is not "ancillary to the grant of some other appropriate relief." *Green*, 474 U.S. at 71. In that case, the state came into compliance with the dictates of the relevant federal welfare statute as a result of congressional amendments passed while the litigation was pending. "Because there is no continuing violation of federal law to enjoin in this case, an injunction is not available," the Supreme Court explained, and therefore "notice cannot be justified as a mere case-management device that is ancillary to a judgment awarding valid prospective relief." More generally, the Court observed that "[r]emedies designed to end a continuing violation of federal law are necessary to vindicate the federal interest in assuring the supremacy of that law," whereas "compensatory or deterrence interests are insufficient to overcome the dictates of the Eleventh Amendment." 474 U.S. at 68. In response to the plaintiffs' request for a declaratory judgment that the defendant had violated "federal law in the past," the Court balked at what it termed "a partial 'end run' around our decision in *Edelman*":

> There is no claimed continuing violation of federal law, and therefore no occasion to issue an injunction. There is a dispute about the lawfulness of respondent's past actions, but the Eleventh Amendment would prohibit the award of money damages or restitution if that dispute were resolved in favor of

petitioners. We think that the award of a declaratory judgment in this situation would be useful in resolving the dispute over the past lawfulness of respondent's action only if it might be offered in state-court proceedings as res judicata on the issue of liability. . . . But the issuance of a declaratory judgment in these circumstances would have much the same effect as a full-fledged award of damages or restitution by the federal court, the latter kinds of relief being of course prohibited by the Eleventh Amendment.

Green, 474 U.S. at 71, 73.

Papasan v. Allain, 478 U.S. 265 (1986). In *Papasan v. Allain*, the Court summarized the foregoing cases as follows: the Eleventh Amendment bars "[r]elief that in essence serves to compensate a party injured in the past" or that is "tantamount to an award of damages for a past violation of federal law, even though styled as something else," but it does not prohibit "relief that serves directly to bring an end to a present violation of federal law . . . even though accompanied by a substantial ancillary effect on the state treasury." *Papasan*, 478 U.S. at 278. In that case, Native-American schoolchildren challenged the disparity between per-pupil expenditures at their schools compared to other Mississippi schools. In addition to raising an equal protection challenge, the plaintiffs argued that, by selling certain school lands and then investing the proceeds from the sale unwisely, the defendant state officials had violated their obligation to hold public school lands entrusted to the state by the federal government for the benefit of the schoolchildren. The Court held that the Eleventh Amendment barred the plaintiffs' request for an injunction requiring state officials to "meet [their] continuing federal obligation by providing the . . . schools with appropriate trust income." *Papasan*, 478 U.S. at 279. The Court "discern[ed] no substantive difference between a not-yet-extinguished liability for a past breach of trust and the continuing obligation to meet trust responsibilities": "In both cases, the trustee is required, because of the past loss of the trust corpus, to use its own resources to take the place of the corpus or the lost income from the corpus. . . . It is in substance the award, as continuing income rather than as a lump sum, of ' "an *accrued* monetary liability." ' " *Papasan*, 478 U.S. at 281 (quoting *Milliken*, 433 U.S. at 289 (quoting *Edelman*, 415 U.S. at 664)). On the other hand, the Court concluded that the plaintiffs' equal protection claim, which alleged an "ongoing constitutional violation — the unequal distribution by the State of the benefits of the State's school lands" — was not barred by the Eleventh Amendment because "[a] remedy to eliminate this current disparity, even a remedy that might require the expenditure of state funds, would ensure ' "compliance *in the future* with a substantive federal-question determination" ' rather than bestow an award for accrued monetary liability." *Papasan*, 478 U.S. at 282 (quoting *Milliken*, 433 U.S. at 289 (quoting *Edelman*, 415 U.S. at 668)).

Frew v. Hawkins, 540 U.S. 431 (2004). In the most recent of these cases, *Frew v. Hawkins*, a unanimous Supreme Court relied on *Ex parte Young* in holding that the Eleventh Amendment does not "bar[ ] enforcement of a federal consent decree entered into by state officials." *Frew*, 540 U.S. at 433. The case grew out of a suit alleging that Texas's early screening program for children violated the federal Medicaid statute. The suit was resolved by a "detailed" consent decree that "order[ed] a comprehensive plan for implementing the federal statute" and "require[d] the state officials to implement many specific procedures." *Frew*, 540 U.S. at 435. Two years after the consent decree was entered, the plaintiffs filed a motion to enforce it, alleging that the state officials had failed to comply with some of its provisions. The Fifth Circuit agreed with the defendants that "the Eleventh Amendment prevented enforcement of the decree unless the violation of the consent decree was also a statutory violation of the Medicaid Act that imposed a clear and binding obligation on the State." *Frew*, 540 U.S. at 436. The Supreme Court reversed, noting that "absent a waiver" of the Eleventh Amendment, "the state officials lacked the authority to agree to remedies [in the consent decree] beyond the scope of *Ex parte Young*" and "the state officials themselves had accepted" the consent decree. *Frew*, 540 U.S. at 438–39. The Court concluded that "[f]ederal courts are not reduced to approving consent decrees and hoping for compliance": "[o]nce entered, a consent decree may be enforced." *Frew*, 540 U.S. at 440 (citing *Hutto v. Finney*, 437 U.S. 678 (1978)).

If you find these various rulings difficult to reconcile, is that because "most remedies can be characterized either way" and therefore any attempt to draw a principled line between prospective and retrospective relief is doomed to fail? ERWIN CHEMERINSKY, FEDERAL JURISDICTION § 7.5.2, at 442 (5th ed. 2007). *But cf.* 1 JOSEPH G. COOK & JOHN L. SOBIESKI, JR., CIVIL RIGHTS ACTIONS ¶ 2.01[C], at 2-42 (2007) (surveying the lower court cases and concluding that the courts "have experienced relatively little difficulty applying the *Edelman* distinction").

3. Other Limits on *Ex parte Young*. In addition to the prospective-retrospective distinction articulated in *Edelman*, the Supreme Court has developed three other limitations on the reach of the *Ex parte Young* remedy. First, in *Pennhurst State School & Hospital v. Halderman*, 465 U.S. 89, 120 (1984), the Court held that the Eleventh Amendment's "constitutional bar applies to pendent claims as well" and, in fact, prohibits even a prospective injunction issued against state officials on pendent state-law claims. "[T]he *Young* doctrine rests on the need to promote the vindication of federal rights," the Court explained, and "[a] federal court's grant of relief against state officials on the basis of state law, whether prospective or retroactive, does not vindicate the supreme authority of federal law." *Pennhurst*, 465 U.S. at 105, 106. The four dissenters, led by Justice Stevens, pointed out that "an injunction has the same effect on the State whether it is based on federal or state law," and argued that "injunctive relief which enforces state laws and policies, if anything, enhances federal courts' respect for the sovereign prerogatives of the States." *Pennhurst*, 465 U.S. at 150, 151 (Stevens, J., dissenting). But the majority countered that "it is difficult to think of a greater intrusion on state sovereignty than when a federal court instructs state officials on how to conform their conduct to state law." *Pennhurst*, 465 U.S. at 106.

Although the *Pennhurst* ruling does not directly affect section 1983 cases — because, by definition, they involve federal constitutional or statutory claims — it does affect any pendent state-law claims a plaintiff might want to bring in conjunction with a section 1983 suit, requiring the federal courts to "examine each claim in a case to see if the court's jurisdiction over that claim is barred by the Eleventh Amendment." *Pennhurst*, 465 U.S. at 121. Moreover, if section 1983 plaintiffs choose to bifurcate their federal and state claims in order to comply with *Pennhurst*, they risk the preclusion problems discussed in Chapter 8, *infra*.

Second, in *Seminole Tribe v. Florida*, 517 U.S. 44 (1996), portions of which are excerpted above in Section A, the Court rejected the plaintiff's attempts to rely on *Ex parte Young* to authorize a prospective injunction ordering the Governor of Florida to comply with a federal statutory provision requiring states to negotiate in good faith with Native-American tribes interested in becoming involved in certain gaming activities. "[W]here Congress has prescribed a detailed remedial scheme for the enforcement against a State of a statutorily created right," the Court held, "a court should hesitate before casting aside those limitations and permitting an action against a state officer based upon *Ex parte Young*." *Seminole Tribe*, 517 U.S. at 74 (citing *Schweiker v. Chilicky*, 487 U.S. 412, 423 (1988), which declined to create a *Bivens* remedy where Congress had "provided what it considers adequate remedial mechanisms for constitutional violations" (described in Chapter 1.E., *supra*)). Noting that the federal statute at issue in *Seminole Tribe* repeatedly referred to "the State" (rather than state officials) and envisioned only a "modest set of sanctions," whereas an injunction issued under *Ex parte Young* "would expose [a state] official to the full remedial powers of a federal court," the Court concluded that "the fact that Congress chose to impose upon the State a liability that is significantly more limited than would be the liability imposed upon the state officer under *Ex parte Young* strongly indicates that Congress had no wish to create" an *Ex parte Young* remedy under the federal statute. *Seminole Tribe*, 517 U.S. at 75–76.

Third, in *Idaho v. Coeur d'Alene Tribe*, 521 U.S. 261, 281 (1997), the majority refused to apply *Ex parte Young* even though the complaint filed by the Coeur d'Alene tribe in that case, which claimed ownership of certain land located within the original boundaries of the tribe's reservation, admittedly alleged "an ongoing violation of its property rights in contravention of federal law and [sought] prospective injunctive relief." In holding the claim barred by the Eleventh Amendment under the "particular and special circumstances" of the case, the Court explained that, although "[a]n allegation of an ongoing violation of federal law where the requested relief is prospective is ordinarily sufficient to invoke the *Young* fiction, . . . this case is unusual in that the Tribe's suit is the functional equivalent of a quiet title action which implicates special sovereignty interests," and "[i]t is common ground between the parties . . . that the Tribe could not maintain a quiet title suit against Idaho in federal court, absent the State's consent." *Coeur d'Alene*, 521 U.S. at 287, 281. More generally, the Court observed:

> To interpret *Young* to permit a federal-court action to proceed in every case where prospective declaratory and injunctive relief is sought against [a state] officer . . . would be to adhere to an empty formalism and to undermine the principle . . . that Eleventh Amendment immunity represents a real limitation on a federal court's federal-question jurisdiction. The real interests served by the Eleventh Amendment are not to be sacrificed to elementary mechanics of captions and pleading. Application of the *Young* exception must reflect a proper understanding of its role in our federal system and respect for state courts instead of a reflexive reliance on an obvious fiction.

Coeur d'Alene, 521 U.S. at 270. Two members of the *Coeur d'Alene* Court (then-Chief Justice Rehnquist and Justice Kennedy) would have gone even further in undermining *Ex parte Young*. Noting that the *Young* doctrine typically applies in two types of cases — when "there is no available state forum" and when "the case calls for the interpretation of federal law" — these Justices thought that federal courts ought to conduct a case-by-case "careful balancing and accommodation of state interests" in deciding whether *Ex parte Young* applies in a particular case, considering, for example, "whether there are 'special factors counselling hesitation' before allowing a suit to proceed." 521 U.S. at 271, 274, 278, 280 (opinion of Kennedy, J.) (quoting *Bivens v. Six Unknown Named Agents*, 403 U.S. 388, 396 (1971)). The other seven members of the Court, however, refused to endorse this balancing test. See *Coeur d'Alene*, 521 U.S. at 296 (O'Connor, J., joined by Justices Scalia and Thomas, concurring in part and concurring in the judgment) (criticizing Justice Kennedy's opinion for "replac[ing] a straightforward inquiry into whether a complaint alleges an ongoing violation of federal law and seeks relief properly characterized as prospective with a vague balancing test that purports to account for a 'broad' range of unspecified factors"); *Coeur d'Alene*, 521 U.S. at 297 (Souter, J., joined by Justices Stevens, Ginsburg, and Breyer, dissenting) (noting that Justice O'Connor's opinion "wisely rejects the . . . call for federal jurisdiction contingent on case-by-case balancing").

C. WAIVER AND ABROGATION

ATASCADERO STATE HOSPITAL v. SCANLON
Supreme Court of the United States
473 U.S. 234 (1985)

JUSTICE POWELL delivered the opinion of the Court.

I

Respondent, Douglas James Scanlon, suffers from diabetes mellitus and has no sight in one eye. In November 1979, he filed this action against petitioners, Atascadero State Hospital and the California Department of Mental Health, in the United States District Court for the Central District of California, alleging that in 1978 the hospital denied him employment as a graduate student assistant recreational therapist solely because of his physical handicaps. Respondent charged that the hospital's discriminatory refusal to hire him violated § 504 of the Rehabilitation Act of 1973, 29 U.S.C. § 794, and certain state fair employment laws. Respondent sought compensatory, injunctive, and declaratory relief.

Petitioners moved for dismissal of the complaint on the ground that the Eleventh Amendment barred the federal court from entertaining respondent's claims. . . .

. . . [T]he Court of Appeals . . . held that "the Eleventh Amendment does not bar [respondent's] action because the State, if it has participated in and received funds from programs under the Rehabilitation Act, has implicitly consented to be sued as a recipient under 29 U.S.C. § 794." Although noting that the Rehabilitation Act did not expressly abrogate the States' Eleventh Amendment immunity, the court reasoned that a State's consent to suit in federal court could be inferred from its participation in programs funded by the Act. The court based its view on the fact that the Act provided remedies, procedures, and rights against "any recipient of Federal assistance" while implementing regulations expressly defined the class of recipients to include the States. Quoting our decision in *Edelman v. Jordan*, 415 U.S. 651, 672 (1974), the court determined that the "'threshold fact of congressional authorization to sue a class of defendants which literally includes [the] States'" was present in this case. . . .

II

There are . . . certain well-established exceptions to the reach of the Eleventh Amendment. For example, if a State waives its immunity and consents to suit in federal court, the Eleventh Amendment does not bar the action. *See, e.g., Clark v. Barnard*, 108 U.S. 436, 447 (1883).[19] As we said in *Edelman v. Jordan*, 415 U.S. 651, 673 (1974), "[constructive] consent is not a doctrine commonly associated with the surrender of constitutional rights, and we see no place for it here." Moreover, the Eleventh Amendment is "necessarily limited by the enforcement provisions of § 5 of the Fourteenth Amendment," that is, by Congress' power "to enforce, by appropriate legislation, the substantive provisions of the Fourteenth Amendment." *Fitzpatrick v. Bitzer*, 427 U.S. 445, 456 (1976). As a result, when acting pursuant to § 5 of the Fourteenth Amendment, Congress can abrogate the Eleventh Amendment without the States' consent.

---

[19] [n.1] A State may effectuate a waiver of its constitutional immunity by a state statute or constitutional provision, or by otherwise waiving its immunity to suit in the context of a particular federal program. In each of these situations, we require an unequivocal indication that the State intends to consent to federal jurisdiction that otherwise would be barred by the Eleventh Amendment.

But because the Eleventh Amendment implicates the fundamental constitutional balance between the Federal Government and the States, this Court consistently has held that these exceptions apply only when certain specific conditions are met. Thus, we have held that a State will be deemed to have waived its immunity "only where stated 'by the most express language or by such overwhelming implication from the text as [will] leave no room for any other reasonable construction.'" *Edelman v. Jordan*, 415 U.S. at 673, quoting *Murray v. Wilson Distilling Co.*, 213 U.S. 151, 171 (1909). Likewise, in determining whether Congress in exercising its Fourteenth Amendment powers has abrogated the States' Eleventh Amendment immunity, we have required "an unequivocal expression of congressional intent to 'overturn the constitutionally guaranteed immunity of the several States.'" *Pennhurst* [*State School and Hospital v. Halderman*, 465 U.S. 89, 99 (1984) (*Pennhurst II*)], quoting *Quern v. Jordan*, 440 U.S. 332, 342 (1979). . . .

III

Respondent argues that the State of California has waived its immunity to suit in federal court, and thus the Eleventh Amendment does not bar this suit. Respondent relies on Art. III, § 5, of the California Constitution, which provides: "Suits may be brought against the State in such manner and in such courts as shall be directed by law." In respondent's view, unless the California Legislature affirmatively imposes sovereign immunity, the State is potentially subject to suit in any court, federal as well as state.

The test for determining whether a State has waived its immunity from federal-court jurisdiction is a stringent one. Although a State's general waiver of sovereign immunity may subject it to suit in state court, it is not enough to waive the immunity guaranteed by the Eleventh Amendment. As we explained just last Term, "a State's constitutional interest in immunity encompasses not merely whether it may be sued, but where it may be sued." *Pennhurst II, supra*, at 99. Thus, in order for a state statute or constitutional provision to constitute a waiver of Eleventh Amendment immunity, it must specify the State's intention to subject itself to suit in federal court. In view of these principles, we do not believe that Art. III, § 5, of the California Constitution constitutes a waiver of the State's constitutional immunity. This provision does not specifically indicate the State's willingness to be sued in federal court. Indeed, the provision appears simply to authorize the legislature to waive the State's sovereign immunity. In the absence of an unequivocal waiver specifically applicable to federal-court jurisdiction, we decline to find that California has waived its constitutional immunity.

IV

[Part IV of the Court's opinion, which concludes that Congress did not intend to abrogate the states' Eleventh Amendment immunity when it passed the Rehabilitation Act, is considered in Note 2 following *Quern v. Jordan, infra.*]

V

Finally, we consider the position adopted by the Court of Appeals that the State consented to suit in federal court by accepting funds under the Rehabilitation Act.[20] In reaching this conclusion, the Court of Appeals relied on "the extensive provisions [of the Act] under which the states are the express intended recipients of federal assistance." It reasoned that "this is a case in which a 'congressional enactment . . . by its terms authorized suit by designated plaintiffs against a general

---

[20] [n.5] Although the Court of Appeals seemed to state that the Rehabilitation Act was adopted pursuant to § 5 of the Fourteenth Amendment, by focusing on whether the State consented to federal jurisdiction it engaged in analysis relevant to Spending Clause enactments.

class of defendants which literally included States or state instrumentalities,' and 'the State by its participation in the program authorized by Congress had in effect consented to the abrogation of that immunity.'" The Court of Appeals thus concluded that if the State "has participated in and received funds from programs under the Rehabilitation Act, [it] has implicitly consented to be sued as a recipient under 29 U.S.C. § 794."

The court properly recognized that the mere receipt of federal funds cannot establish that a State has consented to suit in federal court. [735 F.2d at 362,] citing *Florida Dept. of Health v. Florida Nursing Home Assn.*, 450 U.S. [147, 150 (1981)]; *Edelman v. Jordan, supra*, at 673. The court erred, however, in concluding that because various provisions of the Rehabilitation Act are addressed to the States, a State necessarily consents to suit in federal court by participating in programs funded under the statute. We have decided today [in Part IV of our opinion] that the Rehabilitation Act does not evince an unmistakable congressional purpose, pursuant to § 5 of the Fourteenth Amendment, to subject unconsenting States to the jurisdiction of the federal courts. The Act likewise falls far short of manifesting a clear intent to condition participation in the programs funded under the Act on a State's consent to waive its constitutional immunity. Thus, were we to view this statute as an enactment pursuant to the Spending Clause, Art. I, § 8, we would hold that there was no indication that the State of California consented to federal jurisdiction. . . .

[Justice Brennan, joined by Justices Marshall, Blackmun, and Stevens, dissented. The four dissenters disagreed with the majority on the abrogation issue, finding "unequivocal legislative history" indicating that the Rehabilitation Act was intended to abrogate the Eleventh Amendment. In addition, they urged the Court to "reexamine the [Eleventh Amendment's] historical and jurisprudential foundation" and overrule *Hans v. Louisiana*'s holding that the Amendment bars citizens from suing their own states. On the latter question, the dissenters thought that "the Framers never intended to constitutionalize the doctrine of state sovereign immunity" and thus that *Hans* "rested on misconceived history and misguided logic."]

NOTES

1. Introduction. The plaintiff's suit in *Atascadero* was in trouble on two separate counts: he was seeking retrospective relief (damages), and the named defendants were not state officials, but instead a state hospital and mental health department, clearly arms of the state entitled to Eleventh Amendment protection. Therefore, the case unquestionably fell within the Eleventh Amendment ban, unless the State had waived its Eleventh Amendment protection or Congress had abrogated that protection. (Abrogation is the subject of *Quern v. Jordan* and the Notes that follow below.)

Is the Court's recognition of the possibility that a state may waive the Eleventh Amendment "inconsistent with viewing the Eleventh Amendment as a restriction on the federal courts' subject matter jurisdiction," given that parties typically cannot waive jurisdictional limitations? ERWIN CHEMERINSKY, FEDERAL JURISDICTION § 7.6, at 453 (5th ed. 2007); *see also Seminole Tribe v. Florida*, 517 U.S. 44, 127–28 (Souter, J., dissenting) ("If it is indeed true that 'private suits against the States [are] not permitted under Article III (by virtue of the understanding represented by the Eleventh Amendment),' then it is hard to see how a State's sovereign immunity may be waived any more than it may be abrogated by Congress. After all, consent of a party is in all other instances wholly insufficient to create subject-matter jurisdiction where it would not otherwise exist.") Or should states be allowed to waive their Eleventh Amendment rights, just as individuals can waive the rights guaranteed them by the Constitution? *Cf.* Kit Kinports, *Implied Waiver After* Seminole Tribe, 82 MINN. L. REV. 793, 813 (1998) ("When a state waives its Eleventh Amendment protection, it is not seeking to waive a jurisdictional requirement and expand the court's jurisdiction — something it cannot do — but is, by virtue of its waiver, rendering the jurisdictional requirement inapplicable."); John R. Pagan, *Eleventh Amendment Analysis*, 39 ARK. L. REV. 447, 488–89 (1986) (arguing that "[w]hen a state consents to federal adjudication, it waives not the lack of subject-matter jurisdiction, which a litigant never can waive, but rather the privilege of enforcing a limitation on the exercise of jurisdiction otherwise possessed by the court").

2. Express Waiver by Virtue of State Law. The Court's opinion in *Atascadero* analyzes two separate types of waiver: express waiver and implied waiver. The plaintiff's express waiver argument rested on a provision in the California state constitution that, according to the plaintiff, explicitly waived the Eleventh Amendment. This type of waiver is a question of state law; the court must look at the state statutes consenting to suit and interpret them as a matter of state law. *See Ford Motor Co. v. Department of Treasury*, 323 U.S. 459, 467 (1945).

As the Court noted in *Atascadero*, the standard for this type of express waiver is a "stringent" one and requires that the state "specify [its] intention to subject itself to suit in *federal court*." *Atascadero*, 473 U.S. at 241 (emphasis added). Thus, a state does not expressly waive its Eleventh Amendment protection by waiving sovereign immunity and consenting to be sued in its own state courts, *see Florida Department of Health & Rehabilitative Services v. Florida Nursing Home Association*, 450 U.S. 147, 149–50 (1981) (per curiam) (finding insufficient evidence of express waiver despite state law providing that the defendant was a "'body corporate' with the capacity to 'sue and be sued'"), or even by authorizing suit in "any court of competent jurisdiction." *Kennecot Copper Corp. v. State Tax Commission*, 327 U.S. 573, 578–80 (1946).

In *Port Authority Trans-Hudson Corp. v. Feeney*, 495 U.S. 299, 306 (1990), however, the Court found sufficient evidence of express waiver even though the relevant statute contained only a very general consent to suit provision, giving "'consent to suits . . . of any form or nature at law, in equity or otherwise.'" Nevertheless, the Court reasoned that the statute's venue provision, which specifically referred to federal courts, "suffice[d] to resolve any ambiguity" and "eliminate[d] the danger . . . that federal courts may mistake a provision intended to allow suit in a State's own courts for a waiver of Eleventh Amendment immunity." *Port Authority Trans-Hudson Corp.*, 495 U.S. at 307; *see also Patsy v. Board of Regents*, 457 U.S. 496, 519 n.* (1982) (White, J., concurring in part) (taking the position that a state statute consenting to suit in "all courts of law and equity" expressly waives the Eleventh Amendment, because there is "no reason to read [such] a broad waiver . . . as meaning all but federal courts"). *But see Patsy*, 457 U.S. at 522–23 & n.5 (Powell, J., dissenting) (interpreting this statute to waive sovereign immunity only in state courts).

3. Waiver by Affirmative Invocation of Federal Jurisdiction. The Court has long held that a state also waives the Eleventh Amendment by making a voluntary appearance in federal court. *See, e.g., Clark v. Barnard*, 108 U.S. 436, 447 (1883) (state voluntarily appeared in federal court as an intervenor); *Gardner v. New Jersey*, 329 U.S. 565, 574 (1947) (state voluntarily filed a claim as a creditor in a federal bankruptcy proceeding). As the Court recently explained in *Lapides v. Board of Regents*, 535 U.S. 613, 619 (2002), in holding that a state waived the Eleventh Amendment when it removed a state-court suit to federal court:

> It would seem anomalous or inconsistent for a State both (1) to invoke federal jurisdiction, thereby contending that the "Judicial power of the United States" extends to the case at hand, and (2) to claim Eleventh Amendment immunity, thereby denying that the "Judicial power of the United States" extends to the case at hand. And a Constitution that permitted States to follow their litigation interests by freely asserting both claims in the same case could generate seriously unfair results.[21]

---

[21] The Court restricted its holding in *Lapides* to "state-law claims, in respect to which the State has explicitly waived immunity from state-court proceedings," and therefore explicitly left open cases filed in state

These principles apply, however, only when a state voluntarily appears in federal court and not, as in section 1983 cases, when it is called into federal court as a defendant.[22] Moreover, the Court has often said that a state does not waive the Eleventh Amendment by appearing in federal court as a defendant, defending the case on the merits, and then raising the Eleventh Amendment for the first time on appeal. As the Court noted in *Edelman v. Jordan*, 415 U.S. 651, 678 (1974), for example, "the Eleventh Amendment sufficiently partakes of the nature of a jurisdictional bar so that it need not be raised in the trial court." Nevertheless, the Court explained in *Patsy v. Board of Regents*, 457 U.S. 496, 516 n.19 (1982), that "because the State may, under certain circumstances, waive this defense, we have never held that it is jurisdictional in the sense that it must be raised and decided by this Court on its own motion." But cf. Jonathan R. Siegel, *Waivers of State Sovereign Immunity and the Ideology of the Eleventh Amendment*, 52 DUKE L.J. 1167, 1227 (2003) (criticizing "[t]he notion that states may assert sovereign immunity 'at any time'" as "an obvious waste of federal judicial resources" and "an invitation for states to play games with justice" by allowing a state to "litigate on the merits, knowing that if it wins, it will have a judgment that it can enforce through res judicata, while if it loses, it can still assert its immunity on appeal").

4. Implied/Constructive Waiver. The second type of waiver analyzed in *Atascadero* is the notion of implied, or constructive, waiver. The opinion most often associated with the doctrine of constructive waiver is *Parden v. Terminal Railway*, 377 U.S. 184 (1964), which held that the State of Alabama impliedly consented to be sued by injured employees under the Federal Employers' Liability Act (FELA), 45 U.S.C. § 51, when it chose to operate an interstate railroad. Noting that the FELA "conditioned the right to operate a railroad in interstate commerce upon amenability to suit in federal court," the *Parden* Court concluded that "Alabama must be taken to have accepted that condition and thus to have consented to suit" when it decided to begin operating an interstate railroad twenty years after the FELA was enacted. *Parden*, 377 U.S. at 192. Unlike express waiver, the Court indicated, the notion of constructive waiver is a matter of federal law: whether Congress extracted the state's waiver of the Eleventh Amendment as a condition of participating in some federally regulated activity or receiving some federal funds. *See Parden*, 377 U.S. at 196.

Nine years later, however, in *Employees of the Department of Public Health & Welfare v. Department of Public Health & Welfare*, 411 U.S. 279 (1973) (*Missouri Employees*), the Court distinguished *Parden* and held that employees of state health facilities in Missouri could not sue the State for failing to pay them overtime wages due under the Fair Labor Standards Act, 29 U.S.C. § 201. In concluding that the State had not constructively consented to be sued, the Court observed that *Parden* involved "a rather isolated state activity" — a "railroad business . . . operated 'for profit' . . . in [an] area where private persons and corporations normally ran the enterprise." *Employees of the Department of Public Health & Welfare*, 411 U.S. at 285, 284. *Missouri Employees*, by contrast, involved state hospitals and facilities that were not

---

court and removed to federal court that involve either federal-law claims or state-law claims "in a situation where the State's underlying sovereign immunity from suit has not been waived or abrogated in state court." *Lapides*, 535 U.S. at 617–18. Subsequent lower court opinions have disagreed on the proper reach of the ruling in *Lapides*. *Compare Meyers v. Texas*, 410 F.3d 236, 242 (5th Cir. 2005) (construing *Lapides* to "appl[y] generally to any private suit which a state removes to federal court"), *with Stewart v. North Carolina*, 393 F.3d 484, 490 (4th Cir. 2005) (distinguishing *Lapides* where the state had not waived sovereign immunity with respect to the state-law claim at issue, reasoning that "by removing the case to federal court and then invoking sovereign immunity, North Carolina did not seek to regain immunity that it had abandoned previously [but] [i]nstead . . . merely sought to have the sovereign immunity issue resolved by a federal court rather than a state court").

[22] *But cf. Sosna v. Iowa*, 419 U.S. 393, 396 n.2 (1975) (noting that under Iowa law, the State was deemed to "consent[] to suit and waive[] any defense of sovereign immunity by voluntarily appearing and defending a suit on the merits").

"proprietary," were not "conducted for profit," and were no different from "every office building in a State's governmental hierarchy." *Employees of the Department of Public Health & Welfare*, 411 U.S. at 284, 285.[23]

Later, as indicated in *Atascadero*, the Court made clear that a state does not waive the Eleventh Amendment merely by participating in a federal program or by accepting federal funds.

Instead of continuing on this course and hacking away at *Parden*, the Court ultimately overruled it in *College Savings Bank v. Florida Prepaid Postsecondary Education Expense Board*, 527 U.S. 666, 680 (1999). Describing *Parden* as "an anomaly in the jurisprudence of sovereign immunity," the Court observed that the constructive waiver doctrine could not be reconciled either with the requirement that "a State's express waiver of sovereign immunity be unequivocal" or with the law governing other constitutional provisions: "*Parden*-style waivers are simply unheard of in the context of *other* constitutionally protected privileges." *College Savings Bank*, 527 U.S. at 680, 681 (citing *Johnson v. Zerbst*'s requirement of an " 'intentional relinquishment or abandonment of a known right or privilege,' " 304 U.S. 458, 464 (1938), as "[t]he classic description of an effective waiver of a constitutional right"). "We think that the constructive-waiver experiment of *Parden* was ill conceived, and see no merit in attempting to salvage any remnant of it," the Court concluded. *College Savings Bank*, 527 U.S. at 680. *But cf.* Suzanna Sherry, *States Are People Too*, 75 NOTRE DAME L. REV. 1121, 1127 (2000) (criticizing the Court for "anthropomorphiz[ing] an abstract entity").

In recent years, however, the lower courts have resurrected the notion of implied waiver, picking up on the Court's observation in *College Savings Bank* that "Congress may, in the exercise of its spending power, condition its grant of funds to the States upon their taking certain actions that Congress could not require them to take, and [the States'] acceptance of the funds entails an agreement to the actions." *College Savings Bank*, 527 U.S. at 686 (citing *South Dakota v. Dole*, 483 U.S. 203 (1987)). "Congress has no obligation to use its Spending Clause power to disburse funds to the States," the Court explained, and while Congress may not impose "a sanction" (i.e., "exclu[de] the State from otherwise permissible activity") "if the State refuses to agree to its condition," it may "den[y] a gift or gratuity." *College Savings Bank*, 527 U.S. at 686–87. Relying on this language, a number of courts of appeals have held that states impliedly waive their Eleventh Amendment protection when they accept federal funds under a Spending Clause statute that expressly conditions the receipt of those funds on such a waiver. *See, e.g., Pace v. Bogalusa City School Board*, 403 F.3d 272 (5th Cir. 2005) (en banc); *Barbour v. Washington Metropolitan Area Transit Authority*, 374 F.3d 1161 (D.C. Cir. 2004). (For further discussion of these cases, *see* Notes 2 & 5 following the excerpt from *Quern v. Jordan, infra*.)

Even if the implied waiver theory is not viable, a plaintiff may still avoid the Eleventh Amendment bar if Congress abrogated the state's immunity from suit. That issue is the subject of the next case.

---

[23] In 1974, Congress amended the Fair Labor Standards Act, "extend[ing] the minimum wage and maximum hour provisions to almost all public employees employed by the States and their various political subdivisions." *National League of Cities v. Usery*, 426 U.S. 833, 836 (1976). (For further discussion of *National League of Cities* and the Supreme Court's Tenth Amendment analysis of the Fair Labor Standards Act, *see* n.37, *infra*.)

QUERN v. JORDAN
Supreme Court of the United States
440 U.S. 332 (1979)

Mr. Justice Rehnquist delivered the opinion of the Court.

This case is a sequel to *Edelman v. Jordan*, 415 U.S. 651 (1974), which we decided five Terms ago. In *Edelman* we held that retroactive welfare benefits awarded by a Federal District Court to plaintiffs . . . violated the Eleventh Amendment. . . .

. . . [R]espondent suggests that our decision in *Edelman* has been eviscerated by later decisions such as *Monell v. New York City Dept. of Social Services*, 436 U.S. 658 (1978)[, which, in the course of holding that a city is a "person" subject to suit under § 1983, found no "basis for concluding that the Eleventh Amendment is a bar to municipal liability."][24] . . . We disagree with respondent's suggestion. This Court's holding in *Monell* was "limited to local government units which are not considered part of the State for Eleventh Amendment purposes," and our Eleventh Amendment decisions subsequent to *Edelman* and to *Monell* have cast no doubt on our holding in *Edelman*.

. . . [A]ny doubt on that score was largely dispelled by *Alabama v. Pugh*, [438 U.S. 781 (1978),] decided just 10 days after *Hutto* [*v. Finney*, 437 U.S. 678 (1978)]. In *Pugh* the Court held, over three dissents, that the State of Alabama could not be joined as a defendant without violating the Eleventh Amendment, even though the complaint was based on 42 U.S.C. § 1983 and the claim was a violation of the Eighth and Fourteenth Amendments similar to that made in *Hutto*. The Court said:

> "There can be no doubt, however, that suit against the State and its Board of Corrections is barred by the Eleventh Amendment, unless Alabama has consented to the filing of such a suit. *Edelman v. Jordan*, 415 U.S. 651 (1974); *Ford Motor Co. v. Department of Treasury*, 323 U.S. 459 (1945); *Worcester County Trust Co. v. Riley*, 302 U.S. 292 (1937)." . . .

Mr. Justice Brennan in his opinion concurring in the judgment argues that our holding in *Edelman* that § 1983 does not abrogate the States' Eleventh Amendment immunity is "most likely incorrect." To reach this conclusion he relies on "[assumptions]" drawn from the Fourteenth Amendment, on "occasional remarks" found in a legislative history that contains little debate on § 1 of the Civil Rights Act of 1871, the precursor to § 1983, on the reference to "bodies politic" in the Act of Feb. 25, 1871, the "Dictionary Act,"[25] and, finally on the general language of § 1983 itself. But, unlike our Brother Brennan, we simply are unwilling to believe, on the basis of such slender "evidence," that Congress intended by the general language of § 1983 to override the traditional sovereign immunity of the States. . . .

There is no question that both the supporters and opponents of the Civil Rights Act of 1871 believed that the Act ceded to the Federal Government many important powers that previously had been considered to be within the exclusive province of the individual States. Many of the remarks from the legislative history of the Act quoted in Mr. Justice Brennan's opinion amply demonstrate this point. *See also Monroe v. Pape*, 365 U.S. 167, 173–176 (1961). But neither logic, the circumstances surrounding the adoption of the Fourteenth Amendment, nor the legislative history of the 1871 Act compels, or even warrants, a leap from this proposition to the conclusion that Congress intended by the

---

[24] [Editor's note: *Monell* and questions surrounding municipal liability in section 1983 cases are discussed in Chapter 4, *infra*.]

[25] [n.11] The Dictionary Act was intended to provide a "few general rules for the construction of statutes." Cong. Globe, 41st Cong., 3d Sess., 1474 (1871) (remarks of Rep. Poland). While it was enacted two months before the enactment of the 1871 Civil Rights Act, it came more than five years after passage of § 2 of the Civil Rights Act of 1866, which served as the model for the language of § 1 of the 1871 Act.

general language of the Act to overturn the constitutionally guaranteed immunity of the several States. In *Tenney v. Brandhove*, 341 U.S. 367 (1951), the Court rejected a similar attempt to interpret the word "person" in § 1983 as a withdrawal of the historic immunity of state legislators. . . . Given the importance of the States' traditional sovereign immunity, if in fact the Members of the 42d Congress believed that § 1 of the 1871 Act overrode that immunity, surely there would have been lengthy debate on this point and it would have been paraded out by the opponents of the Act along with the other evils that they thought would result from the Act. Instead, § 1 passed with only limited debate and not one Member of Congress mentioned the Eleventh Amendment or the direct financial consequences to the States of enacting § 1. We can only conclude that this silence on the matter is itself a significant indication of the legislative intent of § 1.

Our cases consistently have required a clearer showing of congressional purpose to abrogate Eleventh Amendment immunity than our Brother Brennan is able to marshal. In *Employees v. Missouri Public Health Dept.*, 411 U.S. 279 (1973), the Court concluded that Congress did not lift the sovereign immunity of the States by enacting the Fair Labor Standards Act of 1938, because of the absence of any indication "by clear language that the constitutional immunity was swept away. It is not easy to infer that Congress in legislating pursuant to the Commerce Clause, which has grown to vast proportions in its applications, desired silently to deprive the States of an immunity they have long enjoyed under another part of the Constitution." In *Fitzpatrick v. Bitzer*[, 427 U.S. 445 (1976)], the Court found present in Title VII of the Civil Rights Act of 1964, 42 U.S.C. § 2000e *et seq.*, the "threshold fact of congressional authorization" to sue the State as employer, because the statute made explicit reference to the availability of a private action against state and local governments in the event the Equal Employment Opportunity Commission or the Attorney General failed to bring suit or effect a conciliation agreement. Finally, in *Hutto v. Finney*, decided just last Term, the Court held that in enacting the Civil Rights Attorney's Fees Awards Act of 1976, 42 U.S.C. § 1988, Congress intended to override the Eleventh Amendment immunity of the States and authorize fee awards payable by the States when their officials are sued in their official capacities. Although the statutory language in *Hutto* did not separately impose liability on States in so many words,[26] the statute had "a history focusing directly on the question of state liability; Congress considered and firmly rejected the suggestion that States should be immune from fee awards." Also, the Court noted that the statute would have been rendered meaningless with respect to States if the Act did not impose liability for attorney's fees on the States. By contrast, § 1983 does not explicitly and by clear language indicate on its face an intent to sweep away the immunity of the States; nor does it have a history which focuses directly on the question of state liability and which shows that Congress considered and firmly decided to abrogate the Eleventh Amendment immunity of the States. Nor does our reaffirmance of *Edelman* render § 1983 meaningless insofar as States are concerned. *See Ex parte Young*, 209 U.S. 123 (1908). . . .

---

[26] [n.16] While *Hutto*, unlike *Fitzpatrick* and *Employees*, did not require an express statutory waiver of the State's immunity, the Court was careful to emphasize that it was concerned only with expenses incurred in litigation seeking prospective relief while the other cases involved retroactive liability for prelitigation conduct. The Court also noted that it was not concerned with a statute that imposed " 'enormous fiscal burdens on the States' " and that if it were, it might require a formal indication of Congress' intent to abrogate the States' Eleventh Amendment immunity, as did *Employees* and *Fitzpatrick*. Extending § 1983 liability to States obviously would place "enormous fiscal burdens on the States." But we need not reach the question whether an express waiver is required because neither the language of [§ 1983] nor the legislative history discloses an intent to overturn the States' Eleventh Amendment immunity by imposing liability directly upon them.

Mr. Justice Brennan, with whom Mr. Justice Marshall joins, concurring in the judgment.

I

It is deeply disturbing . . . that the Court should engage in today's gratuitous departure from customary judicial practice and reach out to decide an issue unnecessary to its holding. The Court today correctly rules that the explanatory notice approved by the Court of Appeals below is "properly viewed as ancillary to . . . prospective relief."[27] This is sufficient to sustain the Court's holding that such notice is not barred by the Eleventh Amendment. But the Court goes on to conclude, in what is patently dicta, that a State is not a "person" for purposes of 42 U.S.C. § 1983.

This conclusion is significant because, only three Terms ago, *Fitzpatrick v. Bitzer*, 427 U.S. 445 (1976), held that "Congress may, in determining what is 'appropriate legislation' for the purpose of enforcing the provisions of the Fourteenth Amendment, provide for private suits against States or state officials which are constitutionally impermissible in other contexts." If a State were a "person" for purposes of § 1983, therefore, its immunity under the Eleventh Amendment would be abrogated by the statute.[28] *Edelman v. Jordan* had held that § 1983 did not override state immunity, for the reason, as the Court later stated in *Fitzpatrick*, that "[the] Civil Rights Act of 1871, 42 U.S.C. § 1983, had been held in *Monroe v. Pape*, 365 U.S. 167, 187–191 (1961), to exclude cities and other municipal corporations from its ambit; that being the case, it could not have been intended to include States as parties defendant." 427 U.S., at 452. The premise of this reasoning was undercut last Term, however, when *Monell v. New York City Dept. of Social Services*, 436 U.S. 658 (1978), upon re-examination of the legislative history of § 1983, held that a municipality was indeed a "person" for purposes of that statute. As I stated in my concurrence in *Hutto v. Finney*, 437 U.S. 678, 703 (1978), *Monell* made it "surely at least an open question whether § 1983 properly construed does not make the States liable for relief of all kinds, notwithstanding the Eleventh Amendment." . . .

. . . [T]he question whether a State is a "person" for purposes of § 1983 is neither briefed nor argued by the parties in the instant case. Indeed, petitioner states flatly that " . . . [t]hat issue is not the issue before this Court on Petitioner's Writ for Certiorari." Respondent concurs, stating that "it is unnecessary in this case to confront directly the far-reaching question of whether Congress intended in § 1983 to provide for relief directly against States, as it did against municipalities."

Thus, the Court today decides a question of major significance without ever having had the assistance of a considered presentation of the issue, either in briefs or in arguments. The result is pure judicial fiat.

II

This fiat is particularly disturbing because it is most likely incorrect. Section 1983 was originally enacted as § 1 of the Civil Rights Act of 1871. The Act was enacted for the purpose of enforcing the provisions of the Fourteenth Amendment. That Amendment exemplifies the "vast transformation" worked on the structure of federalism in this Nation by the Civil War. *Mitchum v. Foster*, 407 U.S. 225, 242 (1972). The prohibitions of that Amendment "are directed to the States. . . . They have reference to actions of

---

[27] [Editor's note: This portion of the Court's opinion is described in Note 2 following *Edelman v. Jordan* in Section B, *supra*.]

[28] [n.3] There is no question but that § 1983 was enacted by Congress under § 5 of the Fourteenth Amendment. Section 1983 was originally the first section of an Act entitled "An Act to enforce the Provisions of the Fourteenth Amendment to the Constitution of the United States. . . . "

the political body denominated a State, by whatever instruments or in whatever modes that action may be taken." *Ex parte Virginia*, 100 U.S. 339, 346–347 (1880). The fifth section of the Amendment provides Congress with the power to enforce these prohibitions "by appropriate legislation." "Congress, by virtue of the fifth section . . . , may enforce the prohibitions whenever they are disregarded by either the Legislative, the Executive, or the Judicial Department of the State. The mode of enforcement is left to its discretion." *Virginia v. Rives*, 100 U.S. 313, 318 (1880).

The prohibitions of the Fourteenth Amendment and Congress' power of enforcement are thus directed at the States themselves, not merely at state officers. It is logical to assume, therefore, that § 1983, in effectuating the provisions of the Amendment by "[interposing] the federal courts between the States and the people, as guardians of the people's federal rights," *Mitchum v. Foster, supra*, at 242, is also addressed to the States themselves. Certainly Congress made this intent plain enough on the face of the statute.

Section 1 of the Civil Rights Act of 1871 created a federal cause of action against "any person" who, "under color of any law, statute, ordinance, regulation, custom, or usage of any State," deprived another of "any rights, privileges, or immunities secured by the Constitution of the United States." On February 25, 1871, less than two months before the enactment of the Civil Rights Act, Congress provided that "in all acts hereafter passed . . . the word 'person' may extend and be applied to bodies politic and corporate . . . unless the context shows that such words were intended to be used in a more limited sense."[29] *Monell* held that "[since] there is nothing in the 'context' of the Civil Rights Act calling for a restricted interpretation of the word 'person,' the language of that section should prima facie be construed to include 'bodies politic' among the entities that could be sued." Even the Court's opinion today does not dispute the fact that in 1871 the phrase "bodies politic and corporate" would certainly have referred to the States. Indeed, during the very debates surrounding the enactment of the Civil Rights Act, States were referred to as bodies politic and corporate. *See, e.g.,* Cong. Globe, 42d Cong., 1st Sess., 661–662 (1871) (hereinafter Globe) (Sen. Vickers) ("What is a State? Is it not a body politic and corporate?"). Thus the expressed intent of Congress, manifested virtually simultaneously with the enactment of the Civil Rights Act of 1871, was that the States themselves, as bodies corporate and politic, should be embraced by the term "person" in § 1 of that Act.

The legislative history of the Civil Rights Act of 1871 reinforces this conclusion. The Act was originally reported to the House as H.R. 320 by Representative Shellabarger. At that time Representative Shellabarger stated that the bill was meant to be remedial "in aid of the preservation of human liberty and human rights," and thus to be "liberally and beneficently construed."[30] The bill was meant to give "[full] force and effect . . . to section five" of the Fourteenth Amendment, and therefore, like the prohibitions of that Amendment, to be addressed against the States themselves.[31] It was, as Representative Kerr who opposed the bill instantly recognized, "against the rights of the States of this Union." Representative Shellabarger, in introducing the bill, made this explicit, stressing the need for "necessary affirmative legislation to enforce the personal rights which the Constitution guaranties, as between persons in the State and the State itself." Representative Bingham elaborated the point:

---

[29] [n.11] *Monell v. New York City Dept. of Social Services*, 436 U.S. 658 (1978), held that the word "may" in the Act was to be interpreted as the equivalent of "shall": "Such a mandatory use of the extended meanings of the words defined by the Act is . . . required for it to perform its intended function — to be a guide to 'rules of construction' of Acts of Congress. . . . "

[30] [n.13] . . . Senator Thurman of Ohio, who opposed the Act, stated with respect to § 1 that "there is no limitation whatsoever upon the terms that are employed, and *they are as comprehensive as can be used.*"

[31] [n.16] A view of the reach of § 1 suggested by occasional remarks in the legislative history of H.R. 320 to the effect that "[t]he Government can act only upon individuals," Globe App. 251 (Sen. Morton), was rejected last Term when *Monell* held that municipalities were "persons" for purposes of § 1983. . . .

"The powers of the States have been limited and the powers of Congress extended by the last three amendments of the Constitution. These last amendments — thirteen, fourteen, and fifteen — do, in my judgment, vest in Congress a power to *protect the rights of citizens against States*, and individuals in States, never before granted. . . .

"Why not in advance provide *against the denial of rights by States*, whether the denial be acts of omission or commission, as well as against the unlawful acts of combinations and conspiracies against the rights of the people?

"The States never had the right, though they had the power, to inflict wrongs upon free citizens by a denial of the full protection of the laws; because all State officials are by the Constitution required to be bound by oath or affirmation to support the Constitution. As I have already said, the States did deny to citizens the equal protection of the laws, they did deny the rights of citizens under the Constitution, and except to the extent of the express limitations upon the States, as I have shown, the citizen had no remedy. . . . Who dare say, now that the Constitution has been amended, that the nation cannot by law provide against all such abuses and denials of right as these in States *and by States*, or combination of persons?"[32]

H.R. 320 was necessary, as Senator Edmunds stated, to protect citizens "in the rights that the Constitution gave them . . . against any assault by any State or under any State or through the neglect of any State . . . ," and by a "State," Edmunds meant "a corporation . . . an organized thing . . . manifested, represented entirely, and fully in respect to every one of its functions, by that department of its government on which the execution of those functions is respectively devolved."

. . . Those who opposed the bill were fully aware of the major implications of such a statute. Representative Blair, for example, rested his opposition on the fact that the bill, including § 1, was aimed at the States in their "corporate and legislative capacity":

"The inhibitions in the [Thirteenth, Fourteenth, and Fifteenth] amendments against the United States and the States are against them in their corporate and legislative capacities, for the thing or acts prohibited can alone be performed by them in their corporate or legislative capacities. . . . "

"As the States have the power to violate them and not individuals, we must presume that the legislation provided for is against the States in their corporate and legislative capacity or character and those acting under their laws, and not against the individuals, as such, of the States. . . . "[33]

The answer to such arguments was, of course, that the Civil War had irrevocably and profoundly altered the balance of power between Federal and State Governments. . . .

---

[32] [n.17] Section 1 of H.R. 320 was modeled after § 2 of the Civil Rights Act of 1866, which imposed criminal penalties on "any person" who, "under color of any law, statute, ordinance, regulation, or custom," deprived "any inhabitant of any State or Territory" of "any right secured . . . by this act." As Representative Shellabarger stated: "That section [§ 2] provides a criminal proceeding in identically the same case as this one [§ 1] provides a civil remedy. . . . " Representative Bingham noted the limited application of the remedy provided by § 2:

"It is clear that if Congress do so provide by penal laws for the protection of these rights [guaranteed by the Fourteenth Amendment], those violating them must answer for the crime, and not the States. The United States punishes men, not States, for a violation of its law."

Representative Bingham was thus able to distinguish, as apparently the Court is not, *ante*, at 341 n. 11, between the reach of the word "person" in § 2 of the Civil Rights Act of 1866, and its reach in § 1 of the Civil Rights Act of 1871.

[33] [n.18] Representative Blair reached this conclusion after reasoning that if the bill were interpreted as applicable only to individuals, it would not be able to fulfill the purposes of the Reconstruction Amendments.

In the reconstructed union, national rights would be guaranteed federal protection even from the States themselves.

III

The plain words of § 1983, its legislative history and historical context, all evidence that Congress intended States to be embraced within its remedial cause of action. The Court today pronounces its conclusion in dicta by avoiding such evidence. It chooses to hear, in the eloquent and pointed legislative history of § 1983, only "silence." Such silence is in fact deafening to those who have ears to listen. But without reason to reach the question, without briefs, without argument, . . . the Court resolutely opines that a State is not a "person" for purposes of § 1983. The 42d Congress, of course, can no longer pronounce its meaning with unavoidable clarity. *Fitzpatrick*, however, cedes to the present Congress the power to rectify this erroneous misinterpretation. It need only make its intention plain.

NOTES

1. The Eleventh Amendment as a Limit on Congressional Power. On its face, the Eleventh Amendment is directed only at the courts. As Justice Brennan's plurality opinion in *Pennsylvania v. Union Gas Co.*, 491 U.S. 1, 18 (1989) noted, "[t]he language of the Eleventh Amendment gives us no hint that it limits *congressional* authority; it refers only to 'the *judicial* power' and forbids '*constru[ing]*' that power to extend to the enumerated suits — language plainly intended to rein in the Judiciary, not Congress." See also John E. Nowak, *The Scope of Congressional Power to Create Causes of Action Against State Governments and the History of the Eleventh and Fourteenth Amendments*, 75 COLUM. L. REV. 1413, 1469 (1975) (arguing that the Eleventh Amendment was intended to limit only the power of the federal courts, and thus that "Congress should be free to determine the extent of federal court jurisdiction over state governments"); Laurence H. Tribe, *Intergovernmental Immunities in Litigation, Taxation, and Regulation: Separation of Powers Issues in Controversies About Federalism*, 89 HARV. L. REV. 682 (1976) (same). But the Court has taken a contrary position, and *Union Gas* was overruled by *Seminole Tribe v. Florida*, 517 U.S. 44 (1996), which is described below in Note 6. See also Martha A. Field, *The Eleventh Amendment and Other Sovereign Immunity Doctrines: Congressional Imposition of Suit upon the States*, 126 U. PA. L. REV. 1203, 1258 (1978) (finding no support for creating a "dichotomy between congressional and judicial power").

Nevertheless, as indicated in *Quern*, the Court has ruled that Congress can abrogate the states' Eleventh Amendment protection when it enacts legislation pursuant to its power to enforce the Fourteenth Amendment. The first case to acknowledge Congress's abrogation power was *Fitzpatrick v. Bitzer*, 427 U.S. 445 (1976), which is described in *Quern*. The Court held in *Fitzpatrick* that Congress abrogated the Eleventh Amendment when it passed the 1972 amendments to Title VII, which authorized federal courts to award damages against states that were guilty of employment discrimination.

Quern did not deny Congress's power to abrogate the Eleventh Amendment, but it refused to interpret section 1983 as an exercise of that power. Is the Court's reading of section 1983's language and legislative history persuasive? One commentator finds it "anomalous that states — the entities against whom the restrictions of . . . the fourteenth amendment are specifically aimed — have been insulated from liability under the broadest measure enacted by Congress to enforce that section of the Constitution." Bruce McBirney, Note, Quern v. Jordan: *A Misdirected Bar to Section 1983 Suits Against States*, 67 CALIF. L. REV. 407, 407 (1979). *Cf. Owen v. City of Independence*, 445 U.S. 622, 651 (1980) (noting, in refusing to extend qualified immunity defense to municipalities, "[h]ow 'uniquely amiss' it would be . . . if the government itself . . . were permitted to disavow liability for the injury it has begotten"; also explaining that "[a] damages remedy against the offending party is a vital component of any scheme for vindicating cherished constitutional guarantees, and the importance of assuring its efficacy is only accentuated when the wrongdoer is the institution that has been established to protect the very rights it has transgressed"). (The Court's holding in *Owen* and municipal liability generally are discussed in detail in Chapter 4, *infra*.) *But cf.* Jesse H. Choper & John C. Yoo, *Who's Afraid of the Eleventh Amendment?*, 106 COLUM. L. REV. 213 (2006) (arguing that the Court has "only remove[d] a single tool — individual civil actions against states as entities for retroactive money damages — from the universe of options available to the federal political branches to establish uniform national policy over those areas within its constitutional competence").

2. The "Clear Statement" Rule for Abrogation. Although footnote 16 of the majority's opinion in *Quern* left open the question whether a federal statute must expressly abrogate Eleventh Amendment immunity, the Court did resolve that issue in Part IV of its opinion in *Atascadero State Hospital v. Scanlon*, 473 U.S. 234 (1985), other portions of which are excerpted above. The Court held there that "Congress may abrogate the States' constitutionally secured immunity from suit in federal court only by making its intention unmistakably clear *in the language of the statute.*" *Atascadero*, 473 U.S. at 242 (emphasis added). Four years later, the Court added in *Dellmuth v. Muth*, 491 U.S. 223 (1989), "[l]est *Atascadero* be thought to contain any ambiguity, we reaffirm today that . . . [l]egislative history generally will be *irrelevant* to a judicial inquiry into whether Congress intended to abrogate the Eleventh Amendment." *Dellmuth*, 491 U.S. at 230 (emphasis added).

The *Atascadero* majority defended its "clear statement" rule on the grounds that "'the States occupy a special and specific position in our constitutional system,'" and therefore "it is incumbent upon the federal courts to be certain of Congress's intent before finding that federal law overrides the guarantees of the Eleventh Amendment," especially where the courts are "decid[ing] whether their own jurisdiction has been expanded." *Atascadero*, 473 U.S. at 242, 243 (quoting *Garcia v. San Antonio Metropolitan Transit Authority*, 469 U.S. 528, 547 (1985)). The four *Atascadero* dissenters, on the other hand, criticized the majority for "rais[ing] formidable obstacles to congressional efforts to abrogate the States' immunity" by "put[ting] in place a series of special rules of statutory draftsmanship that Congress must obey before the Court will accord recognition to its act." *Atascadero*, 473 U.S. at 253–54 (Brennan, J., dissenting); *see also* William N. Eskridge, Jr. & Philip P. Frickey, *Quasi-Constitutional Law: Clear Statement Rules as Constitutional Lawmaking*, 45 VAND. L. REV. 593, 638, 636, 622 (1992) (condemning the Court for its "judicial haughtiness" and "backdoor" "judicial activism" in creating the clear statement rule, and also noting that the Court "played a kind of 'bait and switch' trick on Congress" by applying the clear statement rule even in interpreting older federal statutes). *But see* George D. Brown, *State Sovereignty Under the Burger Court — How the Eleventh Amendment Survived the Death of the Tenth: Some Broader Implications of* Atascadero State Hospital v. Scanlon, 74 GEO. L.J. 363, 365 (1985) (defending *Atascadero*'s clear statement rule because it "ensures thorough consideration of the states' interests at the congressional level").

On the facts of *Atascadero*, the Court concluded that section 504 of the Rehabilitation Act, 29 U.S.C. § 794, did not clearly abrogate the Eleventh Amendment even though it created remedies for "any person aggrieved by any act . . . by any recipient of Federal assistance," and the State of California was undeniably a "recipient" of federal funds. "[G]iven their constitutional role," the Court explained, "the States are not like any other class of recipients of federal aid," and therefore "[a] general authorization for suit in federal court is not the kind of unequivocal statutory language sufficient to abrogate the Eleventh Amendment." *Atascadero*, 473 U.S. at 246.

The year following the Court's decision in *Atascadero*, Congress passed the Rehabilitation Act Amendments of 1986, which provided that "[a] State shall not be immune under the Eleventh Amendment . . . from suit in Federal court for a violation of . . . any . . . Federal statute prohibiting discrimination by recipients of Federal financial assistance" (including section 504 of the Rehabilitation Act), and that the same remedies would be available to plaintiffs in such cases as are available in a "suit against any public or private entity other than a State." 42 U.S.C. § 2000d-7(a). Given this language, the courts of appeals have held that states impliedly waive the Eleventh Amendment when they accept federal funds under the Rehabilitation Act. *See, e.g., Pace v. Bogalusa City School Board*, 403 F.3d 272 (5th Cir. 2005) (en banc); *Barbour v. Washington Metropolitan Area Transit Authority*, 374 F.3d 1161 (D.C. Cir. 2004). These courts have relied on the Supreme Court's language in Part V of *Atascadero* (reprinted above) tying the clear statement requirement for abrogation to the doctrine of implied consent: "The Act likewise falls far short of manifesting a clear intent to condition participation in the programs funded under the Act on a State's consent to waive its constitutional immunity." Accordingly, the courts of appeals have held that "waiver results from participation in a Spending Clause program" only if the statute survives *Atascadero*'s clear statement hurdle. *Pace*, 403 F.3d at 279 (explaining that "the waiver condition must satisfy the clear-statement rule" in order to "ensur[e] that the state's waiver is 'knowing' "). (Implied waiver is described in Note 4 following the excerpt from *Atascadero, supra*.)

3. States as "Persons" in Section 1983 Suits. Although Justice Brennan's dissenting opinion in *Quern* accused the majority of ruling that "a State is not a 'person' for purposes of 42 U.S.C. § 1983," subsequent lower court opinions disagreed as to whether *Quern* held only that Congress had not abrogated the states' Eleventh Amendment immunity from suit *in federal court* when it enacted section 1983 or, more broadly, that the word "person" in section 1983 did not include states. In *Will v. Michigan Department of State Police*, 491 U.S. 58 (1989), the Court resolved this conflict, reaching the conclusion anticipated by Justice Brennan and holding that a state is not a "person" within the meaning of section 1983. As a result of this decision, states may not be named as defendants in section 1983 litigation even if the Eleventh Amendment does not apply — e.g., the state consents to suit or is sued in state court (as was the case in *Will*). *See also Lapides v. Board of Regents*, 535 U.S. 613, 617 (2002) (reaffirming *Will*'s holding that states are not "persons" under section 1983).

Citing *Atascadero*'s clear statement rule (despite acknowledging that *Atascadero*, as an Eleventh Amendment case, was not directly on point), the Court explained in *Will* that the language of section 1983 "[fell] far short of satisfying the ordinary rule of statutory construction that if Congress intends to alter the 'usual constitutional balance between the States and the Federal Government,' it must make its intention to do so 'unmistakably clear in the language of the statute.' " *Will*, 491 U.S. at 65. Then, piggybacking on its decision in *Quern*, the Court thought it would be odd to assume that Congress intended to subject the states to section 1983 suits in state courts — "precisely the courts Congress sought to allow civil rights claimants to avoid through § 1983" — "[g]iven that a principal purpose behind the enactment of § 1983 was to provide a federal forum for civil rights claims, and [according to *Quern*] Congress did not provide such a federal forum for civil rights claims against the States." *Will*, 491 U.S. at 66.

The *Will* majority went on to conclude that state officials sued in their official capacities are not "persons" either for purposes of section 1983. Although the Court conceded that "[o]bviously, state officials literally are persons," it noted that an official-capacity suit "is not a suit against the official but rather is a suit against the official's office" and therefore "no different from a suit against the State itself." *Will*, 491 U.S. at 71. Thus, in order to prevent "circumvent[ion]" of its ruling that states are not "persons" "by a mere pleading device," the Court extended its holding to state officials sued in their official capacity as well. But the Court then dropped a footnote, commenting that "[o]f course a state official in his or her official capacity, when sued for injunctive relief, would be a person under § 1983 because 'official-capacity actions for prospective relief are not treated as actions against the State.'" *Will*, 491 U.S. at 71 n.10 (quoting *Kentucky v. Graham*, 473 U.S. 159, 167 n.14 (1985)). *See also Hafer v. Melo*, 502 U.S. 21 (1991) (making clear that state officials who are sued in their individual capacities are "persons" within the meaning of section 1983 and that damages suits brought against them are not barred by the Eleventh Amendment).

Can the Court's conclusion in *Will* be reconciled with the language of section 1983? With its holding in *Monell v. Department of Social Services*, 436 U.S. 658 (1978), that cities are "persons" within the meaning of section 1983? (Note that the majority opinion in *Monell*, which is excerpted in Chapter 4.A., *infra*, observed that "'nothing . . . suggest[s] that the generic word "person" in § 1983 was intended to have a bifurcated application to municipal corporations depending on the nature of the relief sought'" by the plaintiff. 436 U.S. at 701 n.66.) Some commentators have pointed out that it seems "strange" that "states, historically the prime targets of the Fourteenth Amendment and § 1983, are found not to be suable persons while . . . local governments, creatures of the states, are considered such persons" — especially given that "both the Fourteenth Amendment and § 1983 were enacted by Congress against a background of profound distrust of the states." 2 SHELDON H. NAHMOD, CIVIL RIGHTS AND CIVIL LIBERTIES LITIGATION § 6.69, at 6-287 to -288 (4th ed. 2007).

4. Distinguishing Official- and Individual-Capacity Suits. *Will* and *Hafer*, discussed in the prior Note, recognize a distinction between section 1983 suits filed against state officials in their official capacity and those filed against them in their individual capacity. The distinction is often confused, but it has important ramifications for how a case develops.

An official-capacity suit is one in which the government official is named as a defendant in his or her official capacity. In essence, an official-capacity suit is a suit against the office that the defendant holds and therefore, "in all respects other than name, [is] to be treated as a suit against the entity" that employs the defendant. *Kentucky v. Graham*, 473 U.S. 159, 166 (1985). Any damages awarded to the plaintiff are paid by the defendant's employer, and, if the defendant dies or leaves office while the litigation is pending, his or her successor is automatically substituted as the defendant. *See* FED. R. CIV. P. 25(d)(1); FED R. APP. P. 43(c)(2). Given that "the real party in interest . . . is the governmental entity and not the named official," the plaintiff must satisfy *Monell*'s official policy and custom requirement for municipal liability (if the defendant is a local government official)[34] and (if the defendant is a state official) the Eleventh Amendment doctrines discussed in this Chapter come into play. *Hafer v. Melo*, 502 U.S. 21, 25 (1991). The defendant may not, however, take advantage of the absolute or qualified immunity defenses discussed in Chapter 2, *supra*. *See Hafer*, 502 U.S. at 25.

Individual-capacity (or personal-capacity) suits, on the other hand, are suits against the public employees themselves, who "come to court as individuals." *Hafer*, 502 U.S. at 27. Any damages awarded "can be executed only against the official's personal assets" (although governmental entities may choose to indemnify their employees for any such damages[35]), and, if the defendant dies while the case is pending, the plaintiff must "pursue his action against the decedent's estate." *Kentucky v. Graham*, 472 U.S. at 166

---

[34] The official policy and custom requirement for municipal liability is described in Chapter 4, *infra*. Note that, despite the Court's comments in *Hafer*, the lower courts conflict as to whether *Monell*'s official policy and custom requirement applies at all to injunctive suits, whether filed against a city or against its officials in their official capacity. *See* Note 1 following the excerpt from *Monell* in Chapter 4.A., *infra*.

[35] *See* John C. Jeffries, Jr., *In Praise of the Eleventh Amendment and Section 1983*, 84 VA. L. REV. 47, 50 (1998) (pointing out that government officials are routinely indemnified for the costs of section 1983 suits, even though "the state's readiness to defend and indemnify constitutional tort claims is a policy rather than a statutory requirement" in most jurisdictions). Note that a state's voluntary assumption of the costs of defending individual-capacity section 1983 suits does not affect the Eleventh Amendment analysis and does not

& n.11. The defendant may raise absolute or qualified immunity as a defense, but the plaintiff need not worry about *Monell*'s official policy or custom requirement or the Eleventh Amendment. *See Hafer*, 502 U.S. at 25.

The distinction between official- and individual-capacity suits should not be confused with the concept of "under color of state law," which is discussed in Chapter 1, *supra*. All section 1983 suits require proof that the defendant was acting "under color of state law," and thus in that sense even government officials who are sued in their individual capacity are still being sued for their "official conduct." But, as the Court explained in *Hafer*, "the phrase 'acting in their official capacities' is best understood as a reference to the capacity in which the . . . official is sued, not the capacity in which the officer inflict[ed] the alleged injury." *Hafer*, 502 U.S. at 26.

In *Kentucky v. Graham*, 473 U.S. at 167 n.4, the Supreme Court noted that " '[t]he course of the proceedings' . . . typically will indicate the nature of the liability sought to be imposed" in cases where "the complaint [does] not clearly specify whether the officials are sued personally, in their official capacity, or both." Citing this language, most courts have refused to require that plaintiffs "plead expressly the capacity in which [they are] suing a defendant in order to state a cause of action," preferring instead to "look to the substance of the complaint, the relief sought, and the course of proceedings to determine the nature of a plaintiff's claims." *Biggs v. Meadows*, 66 F.3d 56, 60, 58 (4th Cir. 1995); *see also Powell v. Alexander*, 391 F.3d 1, 21–22 (1st Cir. 2004) (same). Nevertheless, a few courts of appeals have created a presumption that section 1983 defendants are being sued in their official capacity unless the complaint "expressly and unambiguously" states otherwise, reasoning that "only an express statement . . . will suffice to give [government officials] proper notice" that the suit "exposes [them] to civil liability and damages." *Johnson v. Outboard Marine Corp.*, 172 F.3d 531, 535 (8th Cir. 1999). The Supreme Court recognized this conflict in *Hafer*, but declined to resolve it. *See Hafer*, 502 U.S. at 24 n.*.

Regardless of the view taken by a particular court, section 1983 plaintiffs are well-advised to specify clearly in their complaints whether any individuals named as defendants are being sued in their individual capacity, their official capacity, or both. The best approach is simply to do so in the caption: "John Doe v. Jane Roe, in her individual [personal] capacity" or "John Doe v. Jane Roe, in her official capacity." In the latter type of case, the Court has indicated that the institutional employer must be given actual notice of the suit. *See Brandon v. Holt*, 469 U.S. 464, 471–72 (1985) (noting that an official-capacity suit "imposes liability on the entity that [the defendant] represents provided, of course, the public entity received notice and an opportunity to respond"). This notice can be accomplished, for example, by mail or fax.

5. Applying the Abrogation Doctrine to Other Civil Rights Statutes. As noted in *Quern*, the Court held in *Hutto v. Finney*, 437 U.S. 678, 693–94 (1978), that the Civil Rights Attorney's Fees Awards Act of 1976, 42 U.S.C. § 1988(b), which allows prevailing parties in section 1983 suits to recover attorney's fees, was "undoubtedly intended to exercise [Congress's abrogation] power" and "to authorize fee awards payable by the States when their officials are sued in their official capacities." Even though the language of section 1988(b) did not mention states, the Court noted that the statute "contains no hint of an exception for States" and, in fact, "primarily applies to laws passed specifically to restrain state actions." *Hutto*, 437 U.S. at 694. The Court found the legislative history "equally plain," pointing out that Congress rejected efforts to amend section 1988(b) to immunize state and local governments, and that both the House and Senate Reports contained language clearly indicating that Congress envisioned fee awards would be paid by the states when their employees were sued in their official capacities for prospective relief. *See* Chapter 9.C., Note 1, *infra*.

---

turn the case into an official-capacity suit. *See* 1 Joseph G. Cook & John L. Sobieski, Jr., Civil Rights Actions ¶ 2.01[D], at 2-49 & n.150 (2007) (collecting cases).

Although *Hutto*'s reasoning does not survive *Atascadero*'s clear statement rule, the Court reaffirmed *Hutto*'s result in *Missouri v. Jenkins*, 491 U.S. 274, 278, 280 (1989):

> *Hutto v. Finney* . . . relied . . . on the distinction drawn in our earlier cases between "retroactive monetary relief" and "prospective injunctive relief." Attorney's fees, we held, belonged to the latter category, because they constituted reimbursement of "expenses incurred in litigation seeking only prospective relief," rather than "retroactive liability for prelitigation conduct." . . .[36]
>
> . . . The holding of *Hutto*, therefore, was not just that Congress had spoken sufficiently clearly to overcome Eleventh Amendment immunity in enacting § 1988, but rather that the Eleventh Amendment did not apply to an award of attorney's fees ancillary to a grant of prospective relief. That holding is unaffected by our subsequent jurisprudence concerning the degree of clarity with which Congress must speak in order to override Eleventh Amendment immunity.

In *Dellmuth v. Muth*, 491 U.S. 223 (1989), the Court concluded that the Individuals with Disabilities Education Act (IDEA), 20 U.S.C. § 1400, which guarantees a free appropriate public education to all disabled children, did not meet the clear statement rule. The Court acknowledged that the statute's "frequent reference to the States, and its delineation of the States' important role in securing an appropriate education" for disabled children made "the States, along with local agencies, logical defendants in suits alleging violations" of the Act. But it thought that "such a permissible inference, whatever its logical force, would remain just that: a permissible inference," rather than "the unequivocal declaration . . . necessary before we will determine that Congress intended to exercise its powers of abrogation." *Dellmuth*, 491 U.S. at 232. The Court noted that the IDEA's judicial review provision, which authorized "any party aggrieved by [the administrative hearing process] to bring a civil action" in any state or federal court, like the rest of the statute, contained "no reference whatsoever to either the Eleventh Amendment or the States' sovereign immunity," thereby failing to "address abrogation in even oblique terms, much less with the clarity *Atascadero* requires." *Dellmuth*, 491 U.S. at 231. As it had with *Atascadero*, Congress responded to this ruling one year later by amending the IDEA, 20 U.S.C. § 1403, to expressly condition funding on the states' waiver of their Eleventh Amendment immunity. *See, e.g., Pace v. Bogalusa City School Board*, 403 F.3d 272 (5th Cir. 2005) (en banc) (concluding that states impliedly waive the Eleventh Amendment by accepting funds under the amended version of the IDEA).

6. Abrogation Under Congress's Article I Powers. In *Seminole Tribe v. Florida*, 517 U.S. 44 (1996), the Court suggested that Congress has no power to abrogate the Eleventh Amendment when legislating under its Article I powers. Thus, even though *Atascadero*'s clear statement rule was met in that case — the Court thought that "the numerous references to the 'State' in the text of [the Indian Gaming Regulatory Act made] it indubitable that Congress intended through the Act to abrogate the States' sovereign immunity from suit" — the Court held that the statute was not "passed pursuant to a constitutional provision granting Congress the power to abrogate." *Seminole Tribe*, 517 U.S. at 57, 59. The Court explained that " 'the principle of sovereign immunity is a constitutional limitation on the federal judicial power established in Art. III' " that is "not so ephemeral as to dissipate when the subject of the suit is an area . . . that is under the exclusive control of the Federal Government." *Seminole Tribe*, 517 U.S. at 68, 72 (quoting *Pennhurst State School and Hospital v. Halderman*, 465 U.S. 89, 98 (1984)). In so ruling, the Court distinguished *Fitzpatrick v. Bitzer*'s holding that Congress may abrogate the Eleventh Amendment when legislating under section 5 of the Fourteenth Amendment on three grounds: the Fourteenth Amendment,

---

[36] [Editor's note: This portion of *Hutto*'s holding is described in Note 2 in Section B, *supra*.]

unlike Article I, was adopted "well after the adoption of the Eleventh Amendment"; the Fourteenth Amendment's prohibitions are "expressly directed at the states"; and the Fourteenth Amendment "fundamentally altered the balance of state and federal power struck by the Constitution." *Seminole Tribe*, 517 U.S. at 65, 59. *Seminole Tribe* thus overruled the plurality opinion in *Pennsylvania v. Union Gas Co.*, 491 U.S. 1, 19–20 (1989), which had concluded that "the Commerce Clause withholds power from the States at the same time as it confers it on Congress," and therefore, "to the extent that the States gave Congress the authority to regulate commerce" in ratifying the Constitution, "they also relinquished their immunity where Congress found it necessary, in exercising this authority, to render them liable." *See also* Vicki C. Jackson, *Holistic Interpretation:* Fitzpatrick v. Bitzer *and Our Bifurcated Constitution*, 53 STAN. L. REV. 1259, 1261 (2001) (criticizing *Seminole Tribe* and advocating a "holistic" approach to constitutional interpretation that construes each clause "in light of the overall constitutional structure").

In *Alden v. Maine*, 527 U.S. 706 (1999), the Court went even further, holding that Congress lacks the power under the Commerce Clause to subject the states to private damages suits in *state* court, where the Eleventh Amendment is "beside the point." *Alden*, 527 U.S. at 760 (Souter, J., dissenting). In the portion of its opinion reprinted above in Section A, *supra*, the majority observed that "the sovereign immunity of the States neither derives from nor is limited by the terms of the Eleventh Amendment." *Alden*, 527 U.S. at 713. Given its view that "the bare text of the [Eleventh] Amendment is not an exhaustive description of the States' constitutional immunity from suit," the Court thought that "our federalism requires that Congress treat the States in a manner consistent with their status as residuary sovereigns and joint participants in the governance of the Nation." *Alden*, 527 U.S. at 736, 748. "Private suits against nonconsenting States . . . present 'the indignity of subjecting a State to the coercive process of judicial tribunals at the instance of private parties' *regardless of the forum*," the Court concluded. *Alden*, 527 U.S. at 749 (emphasis added). As a result, the plaintiffs in *Alden* — a group of state employees — were foreclosed from bringing a state-court damages action alleging that the State of Maine had violated the Fair Labor Standards Act (FLSA), 29 U.S.C. § 201. Chiding the majority for "imputing immutable constitutional status to . . . a conception of state sovereign immunity that is true neither to history nor to the structure of the Constitution," the four dissenters observed that "[t]he State of Maine is not sovereign with respect to the national objectives of the FLSA," given that Congress's "legislative power under Article I . . . to extend FLSA coverage to state employees has already been decided and is not contested here." *Alden*, 527 U.S. at 814, 800 (Souter, J., dissenting) (citing *Garcia v. San Antonio Metropolitan Transit Authority*, 469 U.S. 528 (1985)).[37]

---

[37] In *Garcia*, the Court found "nothing in the overtime and minimum-wage requirements of the FLSA, as applied to [governmental employees], that is destructive of state sovereignty." 469 U.S. at 554. The Court therefore overturned its prior ruling in *National League of Cities v. Usery*, 426 U.S. 833, 851 (1976), which had held that amendments extending the FLSA to almost all state and municipal employees "impermissibly interfered with the integral governmental functions of these bodies" in violation of the Tenth Amendment. (Note that the Tenth Amendment, unlike the Eleventh, equally protects both states and municipalities.)

Although *Garcia* is still good law, the majority opinion in *Alden* (as reflected in the excerpt that appears in Section A, *supra*) cited the Tenth Amendment in support of its holding that state employees may not bring FLSA suits against the states even in state court. Even before *Alden*'s blatant strides in this direction, commentators had observed that the Court seemed to be using the Eleventh Amendment as "partial compensation for the states' loss of substantive protection" under the Tenth. George D. Brown, *State Sovereignty Under the Burger Court — How the Eleventh Amendment Survived the Death of the Tenth: Some Broader Implications of* Atascadero State Hospital v. Scanlon, 74 GEO. L.J. 363, 365 (1985). *See also* William N. Eskridge, Jr. & Philip P. Frickey, *Quasi-Constitutional Law: Clear Statement Rules as Constitutional Lawmaking*, 45 VAND. L. REV. 593, 637 (1992) (suggesting that *Atascadero*'s clear statement rule might have been intended to protect the Court from the "political heat" it would take were it to overturn *Garcia* outright).

Despite the Court's narrow reading of Congress's Article I powers in *Seminole Tribe* and *Alden*, it held in *Central Virginia Community College v. Katz*, 546 U.S. 356 (2006), that neither the Eleventh Amendment nor constitutional principles of sovereign immunity stood in the way of an action filed by a bankruptcy trustee against a state to avoid and recover preferential transfers the debtor had made to the state. The Court "acknowledge[d]" that its opinion in *Seminole Tribe* "reflected an assumption that the holding in that case would apply to the Bankruptcy Clause," Art. I, § 8, cl. 4, but explained that "[c]areful study and reflection have convinced us . . . that assumption was erroneous" and the Court was "not bound to follow our dicta in a prior case in which the point now at issue was not fully debated." On the merits, the Court reasoned that, "[i]n ratifying the Bankruptcy Clause, the States acquiesced in a subordination of whatever sovereign immunity they might otherwise have asserted in proceedings necessary to effectuate the *in rem* jurisdiction of the bankruptcy courts." Given this "'abrogation' . . . in the plan of the Convention," the Court concluded, "Congress may, at its option, either treat States in the same ways as other creditors . . . or exempt them from operation of [bankruptcy] laws." In addition, as explained above, the lower courts have held that Congress has the authority when legislating pursuant to its Article I Spending Clause powers to condition the states' receipt of federal funds on a waiver of the Eleventh Amendment. *See* Note 4 following the *Atascadero* excerpt, *supra*.

7. Limitations on Congress's Section 5 Power. Neither *Seminole Tribe* nor *Alden* undermines Congress's authority to abrogate the states' sovereign immunity in either state or federal court when acting pursuant to section 5 of the Fourteenth Amendment — which gives Congress "power to enforce [that Amendment] by appropriate legislation." When Congress legislates under its section 5 powers (as it did in enacting section 1983), the Eleventh Amendment does not prevent it from subjecting the states to suit; rather, the Eleventh Amendment question is one of statutory interpretation — whether Congress has chosen to do so. Nevertheless, at the same time as it has narrowed Congress's Article I powers, the Court has simultaneously limited congressional authority to enact legislation enforcing the Fourteenth Amendment.

In *Kimel v. Florida Board of Regents*, 528 U.S. 62 (2000), for example, the Court held that Congress's abrogation of the Eleventh Amendment in the Age Discrimination in Employment Act (ADEA), 29 U.S.C. § 621, exceeded its power under section 5 of the Fourteenth Amendment. Building on its prior decision in *City of Boerne v. Flores*, 521 U.S. 507, 519, 520 (1997), that section 5 gives Congress "the power 'to enforce,' not the power to determine what constitutes a constitutional violation" and thus requires "a congruence and proportionality between the injury to be prevented or remedied and the means adopted to that end," the Court concluded in *Kimel* that "the ADEA is not 'appropriate legislation' under § 5 of the Fourteenth Amendment." *Kimel*, 528 U.S. at 82–83. "The Act, through its broad restriction on the use of age as a discriminating factor, prohibits substantially more state employment decisions than would likely be held unconstitutional under the applicable equal protection, rational basis standard," the Court explained. *Kimel*, 528 U.S. at 86. Moreover, the legislative history of the ADEA "never identified any pattern of age discrimination by the States, much less any discrimination whatsoever that rose to the level of a constitutional violation," and "Congress' failure to uncover any significant pattern of unconstitutional discrimination . . . confirm[ed] that Congress had no reason to believe that broad prophylactic legislation was necessary in this field." *Kimel*, 528 U.S. at 89, 92.

Likewise, in *Board of Trustees v. Garrett*, 531 U.S. 356 (2001), the Court ruled that Congress lacked the power under section 5 to abrogate the Eleventh Amendment when it acted to remedy employment discrimination against the disabled in Title I of the Americans with Disabilities Act (ADA), 42 U.S.C. § 12111. Noting that the Fourteenth Amendment does not require the states "to make special accommodations for the disabled, so long as their actions toward such individuals are rational," the Court concluded that states "could quite hardheadedly — and perhaps hardheartedly — hold to job-qualification requirements which do not make allowance for the disabled."

Garrett, 531 U.S. at 367–68. As in *Kimel*, the Court found that "[t]he legislative record . . . fails to show that Congress . . . identif[ied] a pattern of irrational state discrimination in employment against the disabled." *Garrett*, 531 U.S. at 368. Although Congress had made a "general finding" that discrimination against the disabled was " 'a serious and pervasive social problem,' " the Court observed that "the great majority of these incidents do not deal with the activities of States" and that the committee reports contained language suggesting that the ADA was targeted at employment discrimination in the private sector. *Garrett*, 531 U.S. at 369, 371. Thus, the Court ruled that the ADA did not meet the "congruence" and "proportionality" requirements articulated in *City of Boerne*.

These rulings came under heavy criticism, as the work of a "new activist majority" on the Court that was "using its authority to diminish the proper role of Congress" and to "micromanag[e]" Congress "by specifying how [it] should construct a proper legislative record." Ruth Colker & James J. Brudney, *Dissing Congress*, 100 MICH. L. REV. 80, 83, 85 (2001); *see also id.* at 139 (noting that these decisions seem inconsistent with the "disdain for legislative history" reflected in other Supreme Court opinions). In its three most recent rulings in this area, however, the Court has upheld the constitutionality of federal statutes enacted pursuant to section 5 that abrogate the states' Eleventh Amendment protection.

Thus, in *Nevada Department of Human Resources v. Hibbs*, 538 U.S. 721 (2003), the Court found that Congress acted within its section 5 powers when it expressly abrogated the states' Eleventh Amendment immunity in the Family and Medical Leave Act of 1993 (FMLA), 29 U.S.C. § 2617(a)(2) (authorizing damages suits "against any employer (including a public agency) in any Federal or State court of competent jurisdiction"). Noting that " 'Congress' power "to enforce" the [Fourteenth] Amendment includes the authority both to remedy and to deter violation of rights guaranteed thereunder by prohibiting a somewhat broader swath of conduct, including that which is not itself forbidden by the Amendment's text,' " the Court observed that Congress may use its section 5 power to enact "so called prophylactic legislation that proscribes facially constitutional conduct, in order to prevent and deter unconstitutional conduct." 538 U.S. at 727–28 (quoting *Kimel*, 528 U.S. at 81). But, the Court cautioned, *City of Boerne*'s congruence and proportionality tests must be met so as distinguish section 5 legislation "reaching beyond the scope of [the Fourteenth Amendment's] actual guarantees" that is nevertheless permissible prophylactic legislation designed to provide "an appropriate remedy for identified constitutional violations" from impermissible legislation that " 'attempt[s] to substantively redefine the States' legal obligations.' " *Hibbs*, 538 U.S. at 728 (quoting *Kimel*, 528 U.S. at 88). Turning to the question whether "Congress had evidence of a pattern of constitutional violations on the part of the States in this area" when it passed the FMLA, the Court found that the congressional record indicated the states were "continu[ing] to rely on invalid gender stereotypes in the employment context, specifically in the administration of leave benefits," and the Court therefore concluded that "the States' record of unconstitutional participation in, and fostering of, gender based discrimination in the administration of leave benefits [was] weighty enough to justify the enactment of prophylactic § 5 legislation." *Hibbs*, 538 U.S. at 729, 730, 735. The Court distinguished the ADEA and ADA provisions struck down in *Kimel* and *Garrett*, noting that classifications on the basis of age and disability are subject only to rational-basis scrutiny under the Equal Protection Clause, and "[t]hus, in order to impugn the constitutionality of state discrimination against the disabled or the elderly, Congress must identify, not just the existence of age or disability based state decisions, but a 'widespread pattern' of irrational reliance on such criteria." *Hibbs*, 538 U.S. at 735 (quoting *Kimel*, 528 U.S. at 90). Given that the gender discrimination targeted by the FMLA is judged under a heightened standard of scrutiny, the Court explained, it was "easier for Congress to show a pattern of state constitutional violations." *Hibbs*, 538 U.S. at 736.

Likewise, when questions surrounding the ADA returned to the Court in *Tennessee v. Lane*, 541 U.S. 509 (2004), the Court held that Title II of the statute, 42 U.S.C. § 12132 — which prohibits denying qualified disabled persons the benefits of any "services, programs, or activities of a public entity" — was a "valid exercise" of Congress's section 5 power "as it applies to the class of cases implicating the fundamental right of access to the courts." The plaintiffs in that case, who were wheelchair-bound, alleged that they were denied access to a number of Tennessee courthouses. Writing for the five Justices in the majority, Justice Stevens noted that even though "Title II, like Title I [which the Court had struck down in *Garrett*], seeks to enforce [the constitutional] prohibition on irrational disability discrimination, . . . it also seeks to enforce a variety of other constitutional guarantees, infringements of which are subject to more searching review" — "includ[ing] some, like the right of access to the courts at issue in this case, that are protected by the Due Process Clause of the Fourteenth Amendment." *Lane*, 541 U.S. at 522–23. Examining the congressional record that led to Title II, the majority concluded that "Congress enacted Title II against a backdrop of pervasive unequal treatment in the administration of state services and programs, including systematic deprivations of fundamental rights," and "[w]ith respect to the particular services at issue in this case, Congress learned that many individuals, in many States across the country, were being excluded from courthouses and court proceedings by reason of their disabilities." *Lane*, 541 U.S. at 524, 527. The majority went on to hold that Title II satisfied *City of Boerne* because "Congress' chosen remedy" was "congruent and proportional to its object of enforcing the right of access to the courts": "Faced with considerable evidence of shortcomings of previous legislative responses, Congress was justified in concluding that this 'difficult and intractable problem' warranted 'added prophylactic measures in response,'" and the remedy was "a limited one," requiring only that the states "take reasonable measures to remove architectural and other barriers to accessibility." *Lane*, 541 U.S. at 531–32 (quoting *Hibbs*, 538 U.S. at 737).

Writing for three of the four dissenters, then-Chief Justice Rehnquist found the majority's opinion "irreconcilable" with *Garrett* because "the bulk of the Court's evidence concerns discrimination by nonstate governments, rather than the States themselves." *Lane*, 541 U.S. at 538, 542 (Rehnquist, C.J., dissenting). The Chief Justice also thought that Title II failed the congruence and proportionality standard, given that the statute was not limited to courthouses but rather "applies indiscriminately to all 'services,' 'programs,' or 'activities' of any 'public entity.'" *Lane*, 541 U.S. at 551. Justice Scalia, dissenting separately, advocated abandonment of the congruence and proportionality inquiry, describing it as a "flabby test[], . . . a standing invitation to judicial arbitrariness and policy-driven decisionmaking." *Lane*, 541 U.S. at 557–58 (Scalia, J., dissenting). Observing that section 5 merely gives Congress the power to "enforce" the Fourteenth Amendment, Justice Scalia concluded that "[s]o-called 'prophylactic legislation'" that "go[es] beyond the provisions of the Fourteenth Amendment to proscribe, prevent, or 'remedy' conduct that does not violate any provision of the Fourteenth Amendment . . . is reinforcement rather than enforcement." *Lane*, 541 U.S. at 559.

Most recently, the Court ruled in *United States v. Georgia*, 546 U.S. 151 (2006), that Title II of the ADA permissibly creates a private cause of action against states for conduct violative of the Fourteenth Amendment. In that case, a disabled prisoner sued under Title II, claiming that he was confined to his wheelchair in a small cell for almost the entire day and often was not able even to use the toilet — conditions that the state conceded, if true, would violate the Eighth and Fourteenth Amendments. Speaking for a unanimous Court, Justice Scalia concluded that "Title II validly abrogates state sovereign immunity" "insofar as [it] creates a private cause of action for damages against the State for conduct that *actually* violates the Fourteenth Amendment."

As a result of these decisions, federal statutes enacted pursuant to section 5 that abrogate the Eleventh Amendment are more likely to survive constitutional challenge if they authorize lawsuits that trigger heightened scrutiny or implicate a fundamental constitutional right. They are correspondingly less likely to survive if they create causes of action that will be resolved by the more deferential rational basis test. Does this distinction make sense? Or has the Court "offered little explanation as to why the level of scrutiny matters in determining the scope of Congress's powers" under section 5? ERWIN CHEMERINSKY, FEDERAL JURISDICTION § 7.7, at 477 (5th ed. 2007).

Chapter 4
LOCAL LIABILITY

A. HISTORICAL ANTECEDENTS

MONROE v. PAPE
Supreme Court of the United States
365 U.S. 167 (1961)

MR. JUSTICE DOUGLAS delivered the opinion of the Court.

[Parts I and II, in which the Supreme Court held that illegal and unauthorized actions can be conduct "under color of" state law for purposes of § 1983, are excerpted in Chapter 1.A., *supra*.]

III.

The City of Chicago asserts that it is not liable under § [1983]. We do not stop to explore the whole range of questions tendered us on this issue at oral argument and in the briefs. For we are of the opinion that Congress did not undertake to bring municipal corporations within the ambit of § [1983].

When the bill that became the Act of April 20, 1871, was being debated in the Senate, Senator Sherman of Ohio proposed an amendment which would have made "the inhabitants of the county, city, or parish" in which certain acts of violence occurred liable "to pay full compensation" to the person damaged or his widow or legal representative. The amendment was adopted by the Senate. The House, however, rejected it. The Conference Committee reported another version. The House rejected the Conference report. In a second conference the Sherman amendment was dropped and in its place § 6 of the Act of April 20, 1871, was substituted. This new section, which is now 42 U.S.C. § 1986, dropped out all provision for municipal liability and extended liability in damages to "any person or persons, having knowledge that any" of the specified wrongs are being committed. Mr. Poland, speaking for the House Conferees about the Sherman proposal to make municipalities liable, said: "We informed the conferees on the part of the Senate that the House had taken a stand on that subject and would not recede from it; that that section imposing liability upon towns and counties must go out or we should fail to agree."

The objection to the Sherman amendment stated by Mr. Poland was that "the House had solemnly decided that in their judgment Congress had no constitutional power to impose any obligation upon county and town organizations, the mere instrumentality for the administration of state law." The question of constitutional power of Congress to impose civil liability on municipalities was vigorously debated with powerful arguments advanced in the affirmative.

Much reliance is placed on the Act of February 25, 1871, entitled "An Act prescribing the Form of the enacting and resolving Clauses of Acts and Resolutions of Congress, and Rules for the Construction thereof." Section 2 of this Act provides that "the word 'person' may extend and be applied to bodies politic and corporate."[1] It should be noted, however, that this definition is merely an allowable, not a mandatory, one. It is said that doubts should be resolved in favor of municipal liability because private remedies

---

[1] [n.47] This Act has been described as an instance where "Congress supplies its own dictionary." Frankfurter, *Some Reflections on the Reading of Statutes*, 47 Colum. L. Rev. 527, 536. The present code provision defining "person" (1 U.S.C. § 1) does not in terms apply to bodies politic. *See* Reviser's Note, Vol. I, Rev. U.S. Stats. 1872, p. 19.

against officers for illegal searches and seizures are conspicuously ineffective, and because municipal liability will not only afford plaintiffs responsible defendants but cause those defendants to eradicate abuses that exist at the police level. We do not reach those policy considerations. Nor do we reach the constitutional question whether Congress has the power to make municipalities liable for acts of its officers that violate the civil rights of individuals.

The response of the Congress to the proposal to make municipalities liable for certain actions being brought within federal purview by the Act of April 20, 1871, was so antagonistic that we cannot believe that the word "person" was used in this particular Act to include them. Accordingly we hold that the motion to dismiss the complaint against the City of Chicago was properly granted.

MONELL v. DEPARTMENT OF SOCIAL SERVICES
Supreme Court of the United States
436 U.S. 658 (1978)

Mr. Justice Brennan delivered the opinion of the Court.

Petitioners, a class of female employees of the Department of Social Services and of the Board of Education of the city of New York, commenced this action under 42 U.S.C. § 1983 in July 1971. The gravamen of the complaint was that the Board and the Department had as a matter of official policy compelled pregnant employees to take unpaid leaves of absence before such leaves were required for medical reasons.[2] *Cf. Cleveland Board of Education v. LaFleur*, 414 U.S. 632 (1974). The suit sought injunctive relief and backpay for periods of unlawful forced leave. Named as defendants in the action were the Department and its Commissioner, the Board and its Chancellor, and the city of New York and its Mayor. In each case, the individual defendants were sued solely in their official capacities.

We granted certiorari in this case to consider "Whether local governmental officials and/or local independent school boards are 'persons' within the meaning of 42 U.S.C. § 1983 when equitable relief in the nature of back pay is sought against them in their official capacities?" . . . [W]e now overrule *Monroe v. Pape*, insofar as it holds that local governments are wholly immune from suit under § 1983.[3]

I

In *Monroe v. Pape*, we held that "Congress did not undertake to bring municipal corporations within the ambit of [§ 1983]." The sole basis for this conclusion was an inference drawn from Congress' rejection of the "Sherman amendment" to [H.R. 320,] the bill which became the Civil Rights Act of 1871, the precursor of § 1983. The Amendment would have held a municipal corporation liable for damage done to the person or property of its inhabitants by private persons "riotously and tumultuously assembled." Although the Sherman amendment did not seek to amend § 1 of the Act, which is now § 1983, and although the nature of the obligation created by that

---

[2] [n.2] The plaintiffs alleged that New York had a citywide policy of forcing women to take maternity leave after the fifth month of pregnancy unless a city physician and the head of an employee's agency allowed up to an additional two months of work. The defendants did not deny this, but stated that this policy had been changed after suit was instituted. The plaintiffs further alleged that the Board had a policy of requiring women to take maternity leave after the seventh month of pregnancy unless that month fell in the last month of the school year, in which case the teacher could remain through the end of the school term. This allegation was denied.

[3] [n.7] However, we do uphold *Monroe v. Pape*, insofar as it holds that the doctrine of respondeat superior is not a basis for rendering municipalities liable under § 1983 for the constitutional torts of their employees. See Part II, *infra*.

amendment was vastly different from that created by § 1, the Court nonetheless concluded in *Monroe* that Congress must have meant to exclude municipal corporations from the coverage of § 1 because "'the House (in voting against the Sherman amendment) had solemnly decided that in their judgment Congress had no constitutional power to impose any obligation upon county and town organizations, the mere instrumentality for the administration of state law.'" This statement, we thought, showed that Congress doubted its "constitutional power . . . to impose civil liability on municipalities," and that such doubt would have extended to any type of civil liability.[4]

A fresh analysis of the debate on the Civil Rights Act of 1871, and particularly of the case law which each side mustered in its support, shows, however, that *Monroe* incorrectly equated the "obligation" of which Representative Poland spoke with "civil liability."

The style of argument adopted by both proponents and opponents of the Sherman amendment in both Houses of Congress was largely legal, with frequent references to cases decided by this Court and the Supreme Courts of the several States. Proponents of the Sherman amendment did not, however, discuss in detail the argument in favor of its constitutionality. Nonetheless, it is possible to piece together such an argument from the debates on the first conference report and those on § 2 of the civil rights bill, which, because it allowed the Federal Government to prosecute crimes "in the States," had also raised questions of federal power. The account of Representative Shellabarger, the House sponsor of H.R. 320, is the most complete.

Shellabarger began his discussion of H.R. 320 by stating that "there is a domain of constitutional law involved in the right consideration of this measure which is wholly unexplored." There were analogies, however. With respect to the meaning of § 1 of the Fourteenth Amendment, and particularly its Privileges or Immunities Clause, Shellabarger relied on the statement of Mr. Justice Washington in *Corfield v. Coryell*, 3 F. Cas. 230, 4 Wash.C.C. 371 (CC ED Pa.1825), which defined the privileges protected by Art. IV [of the Constitution]: "'What these fundamental privileges are[,] it would perhaps be more tedious than difficult to enumerate. They may, however, be all comprehended under the following general heads: . . . protection by the Government; the enjoyment of life and liberty, with the right to acquire and possess property of every kind, and to pursue and obtain happiness and safety. . . .'"

Building on his conclusion that citizens were owed protection — a conclusion not disputed by opponents of the Sherman amendment — Shellabarger then considered Congress' role in providing that protection. Here again there were precedents:

> [Congress has always] assumed to enforce, as against the States, and also persons, every one of the provisions of the Constitution. Most of the provisions of the Constitution which restrain and directly relate to the States, such as those in [Art. I, § 10,] relate to the divisions of the political powers of the State and General Governments. . . . These prohibitions upon political powers of the States are all of such nature that they can be, and even have been, . . . enforced by the courts of the United States declaring void all State acts of encroachment on Federal powers. Thus, and thus sufficiently, has the United States 'enforced' these provisions of the Constitution. But there are some that are not of this class. These are where the court secures the rights or the liabilities of persons within the States, as between such persons and the States. These three are: first, that as to fugitives from justice [*see* U.S. Const., Art. IV, § 2, cl. 2]; second, that as to fugitives from service, (or slaves) [*see* U.S. Const.,

---

[4] [n.9] Mr. Justice Douglas, the author of *Monroe*, has suggested that the municipal exclusion might more properly rest on a theory that Congress sought to prevent the financial ruin that civil rights liability might impose on municipalities. *See City of Kenosha v. Bruno*, 412 U.S. 507 (1973). However, this view has never been shared by the Court, *see Monroe v. Pape*; *Moor v. County of Alameda*, 411 U.S. 693 (1973), and the debates do not support this position.

Art. IV, § 2, cl. 3]; third, that declaring that the "citizens of each State shall be entitled to all the privileges and immunities of citizens in the several States." [*See* U.S. Const., Art. IV, § 2, cl. 1].

Of legislation mentioned by Shellabarger, the closest analog of the Sherman amendment, ironically, was the statute implementing the fugitives from justice and fugitive slave provisions of Art. IV — the Act of Feb. 12, 1793 — the constitutionality of which had been sustained in 1842 in *Prigg v. Pennsylvania*, 10 L. Ed. 1060, 16 Pet. 539 [(1842)]. There, Mr. Justice Story, writing for the Court, held that Art. IV gave slaveowners a federal right to the unhindered possession of their slaves in whatever State such slaves might be found. Because state process for recovering runaway slaves might be inadequate or even hostile to the rights of the slaveowner, the right intended to be conferred could be negated if left to state implementation. Thus, since the Constitution guaranteed the right and this in turn required a remedy, Story held it to be a "natural inference" that Congress had the power itself to ensure an appropriate (in the Necessary and Proper Clause sense) remedy for the right.

Building on *Prigg*, Shellabarger argued that a remedy against municipalities and counties was an appropriate — and hence constitutional — method for ensuring the protection which the Fourteenth Amendment made every citizen's federal right. This much was clear from the adoption of such statutes by the several States as devices for suppressing riot.[5] Thus, said Shellabarger, the only serious question remaining was "whether, since a county is an integer or part of a State, the United States can impose upon it, as such, any obligations to keep the peace in obedience to United States laws." This he answered affirmatively, citing *Board of Comm'rs v. Aspinwall*, 24 How. 376 (1861), the first of many cases upholding the power of federal courts to enforce the Contract Clause against municipalities.

House opponents of the Sherman amendment — whose views are particularly important since only the House voted down the amendment — did not dispute Shellabarger's claim that the Fourteenth Amendment created a federal right to protection, but they argued that the local units of government upon which the amendment fastened liability were not obligated to keep the peace at state law and further that the Federal Government could not constitutionally require local governments to create police forces, whether this requirement was levied directly, or indirectly by imposing damages for breach of the peace on municipalities.

Any attempt to impute a unitary constitutional theory to opponents of the Sherman amendment is, of course, fraught with difficulties, not the least of which is that most Members of Congress did not speak to the issue of the constitutionality of the amendment. Nonetheless, [we] . . . conclude that opponents of the Sherman amendment [rejected it because they] found it unconstitutional.

[T]here was ample support for [the] view that the Sherman amendment, by putting municipalities to the Hobson's choice of keeping the peace or paying civil damages, attempted to impose obligations on municipalities by indirection that could not be imposed directly, thereby threatening to "destroy the government of the States."

If municipal liability under § 1 of the Civil Rights Act of 1871 created a similar Hobson's choice, we might conclude, as *Monroe* did, that Congress could not have intended municipalities to be among the "persons" to which that section applied. But this is not the case.

First, opponents expressly distinguished between imposing an obligation to keep the peace and merely imposing civil liability for damages on a municipality that was obligated by state law to keep the peace, but which had not in violation of the Fourteenth Amendment. Representative Poland, for example, reasoning from Contract Clause

---

[5] [n.25] Senator Sherman also observed that "[i]f a State . . . may pass a law making a county . . . responsible for a riot in order to deter such crime, then we may pass the same remedies. . . . "

precedents, indicated that Congress could constitutionally confer jurisdiction on the federal courts to entertain suits seeking to hold municipalities liable for using their authorized powers in violation of the Constitution.

Second, the doctrine of dual sovereignty apparently put no limit on the power of federal courts to enforce the Constitution against municipalities that violated it. . . . So long as federal courts were vindicating the Federal Constitution, they were providing the "positive" government action required to protect federal constitutional rights and no question was raised of enlisting the States in "positive" action. . . . It must be remembered that the . . . Court . . . vigorously enforced the Contract Clause against municipalities — an enforcement effort which included various forms of "positive" relief, such as ordering that taxes be levied and collected to discharge federal-court judgments, once a constitutional infraction was found.⁶ Thus, federal judicial enforcement of the Constitution's express limits on state power, since it was done so frequently, must- . . . have been permissible, at least so long as the interpretation of the Constitution was left in the hands of the judiciary. Since § 1 of the Civil Rights Act simply conferred jurisdiction on the federal courts to enforce § 1 of the Fourteenth Amendment — a situation precisely analogous to the grant of diversity jurisdiction under which the Contract Clause was enforced against municipalities — there is no reason to suppose that opponents of the Sherman amendment would have found any constitutional barrier to § 1 suits against municipalities.

Finally, the very votes of those Members of Congress, who opposed the Sherman amendment but who had voted for § 1, confirm that the liability imposed by § 1 was something very different from that imposed by the amendment. Section 1 without question could be used to obtain a damages judgment against state or municipal officials who violated federal constitutional rights while acting under color of law. However, . . . there was no distinction of constitutional magnitude between officers and agents — including corporate agents — of the State: Both were instrumentalities and the State could be impeded no matter over which sort of instrumentality the Federal Government sought to assert its power.

From the foregoing discussion, it is readily apparent that nothing said in debate on the Sherman amendment would have prevented holding a municipality liable under § 1 of the Civil Rights Act for its own violations of the Fourteenth Amendment. The question remains, however, whether the general language describing those to be liable under § 1 — "any person" — covers more than natural persons. An examination of the debate on § 1 and application of appropriate rules of construction show unequivocally that § 1 was intended to cover legal as well as natural persons.

Representative Bingham, for example, in discussing § 1 of the bill, explained that he had drafted § 1 of the Fourteenth Amendment with the case of *Barron v. Mayor of Baltimore*, 7 Pet. 243 (1833), especially in mind. "In [that] case the *city* had taken private property for public use, without compensation . . . , and where there was no redress for the wrong." Bingham's further remarks clearly indicate his view that such takings by cities, as had occurred in *Barron*, would be redressable under § 1 of the bill. More generally, and as Bingham's remarks confirm, § 1 of the bill would logically be the vehicle by which Congress provided redress for takings, since that section provided the only civil remedy for Fourteenth Amendment violations and that Amendment unequivocally prohibited uncompensated takings. Given this purpose, it beggars reason to

---

⁶ [n.40] Since this Court granted unquestionably "positive" relief in Contract Clause cases, it appears that the distinction between the Sherman amendment and those cases was not that the former created a positive obligation whereas the latter imposed only a negative restraint. Instead, the distinction must have been that a violation of the Constitution was the predicate for "positive" relief in the Contract Clause cases, whereas the Sherman amendment imposed damages without regard to whether a local government was in any way at fault for the breach of the peace for which it was to be held for damages. While no one stated this distinction expressly during the debates, . . . it . . . explains why everyone agreed that a state or municipal officer could constitutionally be held liable under § 1 for violations of the Constitution.

suppose that Congress would have exempted municipalities from suit, insisting instead that compensation for a taking come from an officer in his individual capacity rather than from the government unit that had the benefit of the property taken.[7]

In addition, by 1871, it was well understood that corporations should be treated as natural persons for virtually all purposes of constitutional and statutory analysis. This had not always been so. When this Court first considered the question of the status of corporations, Mr. Chief Justice Marshall, writing for the Court, denied that corporations "as such" were persons as that term was used in Art. III and the Judiciary Act of 1789. *See Bank of the United States v. Deveaux*, 5 Cranch 61 (1809). By 1844, however, the *Deveaux* doctrine was unhesitatingly abandoned: "(A) corporation created by and doing business in a particular state, is to be deemed to all intents and purposes as a person, although an artificial person, . . . capable of being treated as a citizen of that state, as much as a natural person." *Louisville R. Co. v. Letson*, 2 How. 497, 558 (1844).

And only two years before the debates on the Civil Rights Act, in *Cowles v. Mercer County*, 7 Wall. 118 (1869), the *Letson* principle was automatically and without discussion extended to municipal corporations. Under this doctrine, municipal corporations were routinely sued in the federal courts and this fact was well known to Members of Congress.

That the "usual" meaning of the word "person" would extend to municipal corporations is also evidenced by an Act of Congress which had been passed only months before the Civil Rights Act was passed. This Act provided that "in all acts hereafter passed . . . the word 'person' may extend and be applied to bodies politic and corporate . . . unless the context shows that such words were intended to be used in a more limited sense." Municipal corporations in 1871 were included within the phrase "bodies politic and corporate" and, accordingly, the "plain meaning" of § 1 is that local government bodies were to be included within the ambit of the persons who could be sued under § 1 of the Civil Rights Act.

II

Our analysis of the legislative history of the Civil Rights Act of 1871 compels the conclusion that Congress did intend municipalities and other local government units to be included among those persons to whom § 1983 applies.[8] Local governing bodies,[9] therefore, can be sued directly under § 1983 for monetary, declaratory, or injunctive relief where, as here, the action that is alleged to be unconstitutional implements or executes a policy statement, ordinance, regulation, or decision officially adopted and promulgated by that body's officers. Moreover, although the touchstone of the § 1983 action against a government body is an allegation that official policy is responsible for a

---

[7] [n.47] Indeed the federal courts found no obstacle to awards of damages against municipalities for common-law takings. *See Sumner v. Philadelphia*, 23 F. Cas. 392 (No. 13,611) (CC ED Pa. 1873) (awarding damages of $2,273.36 and costs of $346.35 against the city of Philadelphia).

[8] [n.54] There is certainly no constitutional impediment to municipal liability. "The Tenth Amendment's reservation of nondelegated powers to the States is not implicated by a federal-court judgment enforcing the express prohibitions of unlawful state conduct enacted by the Fourteenth Amendment." *Milliken v. Bradley*, 433 U.S. 267 (1977); *see Ex parte Virginia*. For this reason, *National League of Cities v. Usery*, 426 U.S. 833 (1976), is irrelevant to our consideration of this case. Nor is there any basis for concluding that the Eleventh Amendment is a bar to municipal liability. *See, e. g., Fitzpatrick v. Bitzer*, 427 U.S. 445 (1976); *Lincoln County v. Luning*, 133 U.S. 529 (1890). Our holding today is, of course, limited to local government units which are not considered part of the State for Eleventh Amendment purposes.

[9] [n.55] Since official-capacity suits generally represent only another way of pleading an action against an entity of which an officer is an agent — at least where Eleventh Amendment considerations do not control analysis — our holding today that local governments can be sued under § 1983 necessarily decides that local government officials sued in their official capacities are "persons" under § 1983 in those cases in which, as here, a local government would be suable in its own name.

deprivation of rights protected by the Constitution, local governments, like every other § 1983 "person," by the very terms of the statute, may be sued for constitutional deprivations visited pursuant to governmental "custom" even though such a custom has not received formal approval through the body's official decisionmaking channels.

On the other hand, the language of § 1983, read against the background of the same legislative history, compels the conclusion that Congress did not intend municipalities to be held liable unless action pursuant to official municipal policy of some nature caused a constitutional tort. In particular, we conclude that a municipality cannot be held liable solely because it employs a tortfeasor — or, in other words, a municipality cannot be held liable under § 1983 on a respondeat superior theory.

The . . . language [of § 1983] plainly imposes liability on a government that, under color of some official policy, "causes" an employee to violate another's constitutional rights. At the same time, that language cannot be easily read to impose liability vicariously on governing bodies solely on the basis of the existence of an employer-employee relationship with a tortfeasor. Indeed, the fact that Congress did specifically provide that A's tort became B's liability if B "caused" A to subject another to a tort suggests that Congress did not intend § 1983 liability to attach where such causation was absent.[10] See *Rizzo v. Goode*, 423 U.S. 362 (1976).

Equally important, creation of a federal law of respondeat superior would have raised all the constitutional problems associated with the obligation to keep the peace, an obligation Congress chose not to impose because it thought imposition of such an obligation unconstitutional. To this day, there is disagreement about the basis for imposing liability on an employer for the torts of an employee when the sole nexus between the employer and the tort is the fact of the employer-employee relationship. Nonetheless, two justifications tend to stand out. First is the common-sense notion that no matter how blameless an employer appears to be in an individual case, accidents might nonetheless be reduced if employers had to bear the cost of accidents. Second is the argument that the cost of accidents should be spread to the community as a whole on an insurance theory.[11]

The first justification is of the same sort that was offered for statutes like the Sherman amendment: "The obligation to make compensation for injury resulting from riot is, by arbitrary enactment of statutes, affirmatory law, and the reason of passing the statute is to secure a more perfect police regulation." This justification was obviously insufficient to sustain the amendment against perceived constitutional difficulties and there is no reason to suppose that a more general liability imposed for a similar reason would have been thought less constitutionally objectionable. The second justification was similarly put forward as a justification for the Sherman amendment: "we do not look upon [the Sherman amendment] as a punishment. . . . It is a mutual insurance." Again, this justification was insufficient to sustain the amendment.

---

[10] [n.57] Support for such a conclusion can be found in the legislative history. As we have indicated, there is virtually no discussion of § 1 of the Civil Rights Act. Again, however, Congress' treatment of the Sherman amendment gives a clue to whether it would have desired to impose respondeat superior liability. . . . Strictly speaking, of course, the fact that Congress refused to impose vicarious liability for the wrongs of a few private citizens does not conclusively establish that it would similarly have refused to impose vicarious liability for the torts of a municipality's employees. Nonetheless, when Congress' rejection of the only form of vicarious liability presented to it is combined with the absence of any language in § 1983 which can easily be construed to create respondeat superior liability, the inference that Congress did not intend to impose such liability is quite strong.

[11] [n.58] A third justification, often cited but which on examination is apparently insufficient to justify the doctrine of respondeat superior, is that liability follows the right to control the actions of a tortfeasor. By our decision in *Rizzo v. Goode*, we would appear to have decided that the mere right to control without any control or direction having been exercised and without any failure to supervise is not enough to support § 1983 liability.

We conclude, therefore, that a local government may not be sued under § 1983 for an injury inflicted solely by its employees or agents. Instead, it is when execution of a government's policy or custom, whether made by its lawmakers or by those whose edicts or acts may fairly be said to represent official policy, inflicts the injury that the government as an entity is responsible under § 1983. Since this case unquestionably involves official policy as the moving force of the constitutional violation found by the District Court, we must reverse the judgment below. In so doing, we have no occasion to address, and do not address, what the full contours of municipal liability under § 1983 may be. We have attempted only to sketch so much of the § 1983 cause of action against a local government as is apparent from the history of the 1871 Act and our prior cases, and we expressly leave further development of this action to another day.

III

[T]he constitutional defect that led to the rejection of the Sherman amendment would not have distinguished between municipalities and school boards, each of which is an instrumentality of state administration. For this reason, our cases — decided both before and after *Monroe* — holding school boards liable in § 1983 actions are inconsistent with *Monroe*, especially as *Monroe*'s immunizing principle was extended to suits for injunctive relief in *City of Kenosha v. Bruno*, 412 U.S. 507 (1973).

In the wake of our decisions, Congress not only has shown no hostility to federal-court decisions against school boards, but it has indeed rejected efforts to strip the federal courts of jurisdiction over school boards. Moreover, recognizing that school boards are often defendants in school desegregation suits, which have almost without exception been § 1983 suits, Congress has twice passed legislation authorizing grants to school boards to assist them in complying with federal-court decrees. Finally, in the Civil Rights Attorney's Fee Act of 1976 [*see* Chapter 9, *infra*], . . . Congress . . . has attempted to allow awards of attorney's fees against local governments even though *Monroe*, *City of Kenosha v. Bruno*, and *Aldinger v. Howard*, 427 U.S. 1 (1976) [discussed in Section E., *infra*], have made the joinder of such governments impossible.

[W]e hold that stare decisis does not bar our overruling of *Monroe* insofar as it is inconsistent with Parts I and II of this opinion.[12]

Mr. Justice Powell, concurring.

If . . . we continued to adhere to *Monroe*, grave doubt would be cast upon the Court's exercise of § 1983 jurisdiction over school boards. Since "the principle of blanket immunity established in *Monroe* cannot be cabined short of school boards," the conflict is squarely presented. Although there was an independent basis of jurisdiction in many of the school board cases because of the inclusion of individual public officials as nominal parties, the opinions of this Court make explicit reference to the school board party, particularly in discussions of the relief to be awarded, *see, e. g., Green v. County School Board*, 391 U.S. 430 (1968). And, as the Court points out, Congress has focused specifically on this Court's school board decisions in several statutes. Thus the exercise of § 1983 jurisdiction over school boards, while perhaps not premised on considered holdings, has been longstanding. Indeed, it predated *Monroe*.

---

[12] [n.66] No useful purpose would be served by an attempt at this late date to determine whether *Monroe* was correct on its facts. Similarly, since this case clearly involves official policy and does not involve respondeat superior, we do not assay a view on how our cases which have relied on that aspect of *Monroe* that is overruled today — *Moor v. County of Alameda*, 411 U.S. 693 (1973); *City of Kenosha v. Bruno*; and *Aldinger v. Howard* — should have been decided on a correct view of § 1983. Nothing we say today affects the conclusion reached in *Moor* that 42 U.S.C. § 1988 cannot be used to create a federal cause of action where § 1983 does not otherwise provide one, or the conclusion reached in *City of Kenosha* that "nothing . . . suggest[s] that the generic word 'person' in § 1983 was intended to have a bifurcated application to municipal corporations depending on the nature of the relief sought against them."

[I]f we continued to adhere to [*Monroe*], we could not long avoid the question whether "we should, by analogy to our decision in *Bivens v. Six Unknown Fed. Narcotics Agents*, 403 U.S. 388 (1971), imply a cause of action directly from the Fourteenth Amendment."

Mr. Justice Rehnquist, with whom The Chief Justice joins, dissenting.

[O]ur only task is to discern the intent of the 42d Congress. That intent was first expounded in *Monroe*, and it has been followed consistently ever since. This is not some esoteric branch of the law in which congressional silence might reasonably be equated with congressional indifference. Indeed, this very year, the Senate has been holding hearings on a bill which would remove the municipal immunity recognized by *Monroe*. In these circumstances, it cannot be disputed that established principles of stare decisis require this Court to pay the highest degree of deference to its prior holdings.

It is true that this Court had held that both commercial corporations and municipal corporations were "citizens" of a State within the meaning of the jurisdictional provisions of Art. III. Congress, however, also knew that this label did not apply in all contexts, since this Court in *Paul v. Virginia*, 8 Wall. 168 (1869), had held commercial corporations not to be "citizens" within the meaning of the Privileges and Immunities Clause, U.S. Const., Art. IV, § 2. Thus, the Congress surely knew that, for constitutional purposes, corporations generally enjoyed a different status in different contexts. Indeed, it may be presumed that Congress intended that a corporation should enjoy the same status under the Ku Klux Klan Act as it did under the Fourteenth Amendment, since it had been assured that § 1 "was so very simple and really reenact[ed] the Constitution." At the time § 1983 was enacted the only federal case to consider the status of corporations under the Fourteenth Amendment had concluded, with impeccable logic, that a corporation was neither a "citizen" nor a "person."

Furthermore, the state courts did not speak with a single voice with regard to the tort liability of municipal corporations. Although many Members of Congress represented States which had retained absolute municipal tort immunity, other States had adopted the currently predominant distinction imposing liability for proprietary acts as early as 1842. Nevertheless, no state court had ever held that municipal corporations were always liable in tort in precisely the same manner as other persons.

The general remarks from the floor on the liberal purposes of § 1 offer no explicit guidance as to the parties against whom the remedy could be enforced. As the Court concedes, only Representative Bingham raised a concern which could be satisfied only by relief against governmental bodies. Yet he never directly related this concern to § 1 of the Act.

The Court is probably correct that the rejection of the Sherman amendment does not lead ineluctably to the conclusion that Congress intended municipalities to be immune from liability under all circumstances. Nevertheless, it cannot be denied that the debate on that amendment, the only explicit consideration of municipal tort liability, sheds considerable light on the Congress' understanding of the status of municipal corporations in that context. Opponents of the amendment were well aware that municipalities had been subjected to the jurisdiction of the federal courts in the context of suits to enforce their contracts, but they expressed their skepticism that such jurisdiction should be exercised in cases sounding in tort.

Whatever the merits of the constitutional arguments raised against it, the fact remains that Congress rejected the concept of municipal tort liability on the only occasion in which the question was explicitly presented.

The decision in *Monroe v. Pape* was the fountainhead of the torrent of civil rights litigation of the last 17 years. Using § 1983 as a vehicle, the courts have articulated new and previously unforeseeable interpretations of the Fourteenth Amendment. At the same time, the doctrine of municipal immunity enunciated in *Monroe* has protected municipalities and their limited treasuries from the consequences of their officials' failure to predict the course of this Court's constitutional jurisprudence. None of the Members of this Court can foresee the practical consequences of today's removal of that protection. Only the Congress, which has the benefit of the advice of every segment of this diverse Nation, is equipped to consider the results of such a drastic change in the law. It seems all but inevitable that it will find it necessary to do so after today's decision.

NOTES

1. The Problem of School Desegregation. *Brown v. Board of Education* (*Brown I*), 347 U.S. 483 (1954), was decided in 1954, with its accompanying remedial decision in *Brown II*, 349 U.S. 294 (1955), coming down the following year. Notwithstanding *Monroe's* admonition in 1961 that governmental institutions are not "persons" within the meaning of § 1983, federal courts continued issuing school desegregation orders throughout the 1960s and 1970s. How could federal courts justify ordering local school boards to bus students if school boards were not "persons" within the meaning of § 1983? As pointed out by Justice Powell in his concurring opinion in *Monell*, two promising doctrinal answers found support in lower court precedent. First, one might argue by analogy to *Bivens v. Six Unknown Named Agents of Federal Bureau of Narcotics*, 403 U.S. 388 (1971) (discussed in Chapter 1.E., *supra*), that an implied, direct constitutional action exists against local school boards. *See* Jack M. Beermann, *Municipal Responsibility for Constitutional Torts*, 48 DEPAUL L. REV. 627, 637 (1999) (concluding that the "restrictions inherent in § 1983 actions might be avoided by pleading a *Bivens* action directly under the Fourteenth Amendment"). Second, one might argue that the fiction of *Ex parte Young* (discussed in Chapter 3.B., *supra*) allows injunctive relief against school officials, acting in their official capacities, even though the school boards themselves are not amenable to suit.

2. Official Capacity Claims. Prior to *Monell*, several lower courts solved the dilemma described by Justice Powell by allowing "official capacity" claims for injunctive relief against local authorities. *See, e.g., Hathaway v. Worcester City Hosp.*, 475 F.2d 701 (1st Cir. 1973) (recognizing propriety of issuing injunction against local officials rather than a city). Indeed, the Supreme Court implicitly recognized this option in *Goss v. Lopez*, 419 U.S. 565 (1975), when it approved an injunction against local school officials who violated students' due process rights. The technical problem with this "bifurcated" approach — allowing injunctive claims but not damage actions — was *City of Kenosha v. Bruno*, 412 U.S. 507 (1973), which held that local governmental entities were immune from declaratory and injunctive relief under § 1983 just as they were protected from damages: "We find nothing in the legislative history discussed in *Monroe*, or in the language actually used by Congress, to suggest that the generic word 'person' in § 1983 was intended to have a bifurcated application to municipal corporations depending on the nature of the relief sought against them." The *Monell* majority sustained *Bruno's* rejection of this "bifurcated" interpretation of § 1983, at least to the extent local governments were named as defendants. *See* footnote 66. While the Court in *Monell* did not expressly address the issue, its language and holding also seemed to reject a "bifurcated" approach to "official capacity" claims for injunctive relief under *Ex parte Young. See* footnote 55.

Lower courts have disagreed over whether *Monell* was meant to limit injunctive actions as well as damage claims against local government. Some have concluded that injunctive claims against local officials acting in their official capacities are governed by the rationale and holding of *Monell* — meaning that a local policy or custom would have to be proved to support injunctive relief (as well as monetary damages). *See, e.g., Dirrane v. Brookline Police Department*, 315 F.3d 65 (1st Cir. 2002) (holding that *Monell's* policy or custom requirement applies to official-capacity claims seeking injunctive relief); *Gernetzke v. Kenosha Unified School District No. 1*, 274 F.3d 464 (7th Cir. 2001) ("The predominant though not unanimous view is that *Monell's* holding applies regardless of the nature of the relief sought."); *Bannum, Inc. v. City of Fort Lauderdale*, 901 F.2d 989 (11th Cir. 1990) (applying *Monell* even though the plaintiff only sought declaratory and injunctive relief); *Nix v. Norman*, 879 F.2d 429 (8th Cir. 1989) (holding that a plaintiff seeking injunctive relief against an official acting in official capacity must allege and prove a "policy or custom"). Others have concluded that *Monell* is limited to damage claims against local governments. Injunctive actions against local officials acting in their official capacities — though technically proceeding against the municipal employer — need not satisfy *Monell*'s policy or custom requirement. *See, e.g., Los Angeles Police Protective League v. Gates*, 995 F.2d 1469 (9th Cir. 1993) ("a city [can be] subject to prospective injunctive relief even if the constitutional violation was not the result of an official custom or policy"); *Reynolds v. Giuliani*, 118 F. Supp. 2d 352 (S.D.N.Y 2000); *cf. Nobby Lobby, Inc. v. City of Dallas*, 970 F.2d 82 (5th Cir. 1992) (leaving open the question of "whether a plaintiff must establish a municipal policy or custom to obtain declaratory relief against a municipality").

Because the Supreme Court's Article III jurisprudence in many cases requires a governmental policy to support prospective relief anyway, *see City of Los Angeles v. Lyons*, 461 U.S. 95 (1983) (excerpted in Chapter 6.C.[1], *infra*), the matter might not have any practical significance. *See generally* Mark R. Brown, *The Failure of Fault Under § 1983: Municipal Liability for State Law Enforcement*, 84 CORNELL L. REV. 1503, 1537 (1999) ("The *Lyons* line of reasoning effectively ties injunctive relief to government policy in about the same way that damages are knotted with municipal fault."). *But see* Section C.[1], Note 3, following *McMillian v. Monroe County, infra* (discussing whether cities can be enjoined from enforcing the policies of other bodies politic — like counties and states).

3. Bifurcated Meaning of "Person" for State Liability. In contrast to *Monell*, the Supreme Court in *Will v. Michigan Department of State Police*, 491 U.S. 58 (1989) (discussed in Chapter 3.C., *supra*), adopted a bifurcated approach to *state* liability under § 1983. Officials employed by state governments are "persons" under § 1983 when sued in their "personal capacities" for damages and when sued in their "official capacities" for prospective relief (including declaratory and injunctive remedies). They are not "persons," however, when sued in their "official capacities" for damages. Justice Stevens, dissenting in *Will*, criticized the majority for "draw[ing] an illogical distinction between wrongs committed by county or municipal officials on the one hand, and those committed by state officials on the other." Does it make sense to allow state officials, acting in their official capacities, to be sued for equitable relief under § 1983 irrespective of a governmental policy or custom, but not municipal officials?

4. Was *Monell* Correct About the Meaning of "Person"? The majority and dissenting opinions in *Monell* debated the historical meaning ascribed to the term "person" in an effort to determine what the Forty-Second Congress might have meant when it passed § 1983. Given its historical meaning, the majority concluded that "person" could have been understood by the Forty-Second Congress to include municipal corporations. The Supreme Court in *Cook County v. United States ex rel. Chandler*, 538 U.S. 119 (2003), a *qui tam* action brought by a private plaintiff against Cook County under the federal False Claims Act (FCA), further elaborated on the historical meaning of "persons" amenable to suit under state and federal law. In a unanimous opinion, Justice Souter observed that when the FCA was first passed in 1863, "person" was understood to include local governments:

> While [the FCA] does not define the term "person," we have held that its meaning has remained unchanged since the original FCA was passed in 1863. There is no doubt that the term then extended to corporations, the Court in 1826 having expressly recognized the presumption that the statutory term "person" "'extends as well to persons politic and incorporate, as to natural persons whatsoever.'" This position accorded with the common understanding among contemporary commentators that corporations were "persons" in the general enjoyment of the capacity to sue and be sued. While it is true that Chief Justice

Marshall's opinion in *Bank of United States v. Deveaux*, 5 Cranch 61 (1809), declined to rely on the presumption when it decided the separate issue whether a corporation was a "citizen" for purposes of federal diversity jurisdiction, by 1844 the *Deveaux* position had been abandoned and a corporation was understood to have citizenship independent of its constituent members by virtue of its status as "a person, although an artificial person." *Louisville, C. & C.R. Co. v. Letson*, 2 How. 497 (1844).

[T]he County argues that municipal corporations were not so understood until six years later, when *Cowles v. Mercer County*, 7 Wall. 118 (1868), applied the *Letson* rule to them. *Cowles*, however, was not an extension of principle but a natural recognition of an understanding . . . that municipal corporations and private ones were simply two species of "body politic and corporate," treated alike in terms of their legal status as persons capable of suing and being sued. *See, e.g.*, W. GLOVER, A PRACTICAL TREATISE ON THE LAW OF MUNICIPAL CORPORATIONS 41 (1837) (Municipal corporations have, as an attribute "necessarily and inseparably incident to every corporation," the ability "[t]o sue or be sued, . . . and do all other acts as natural persons may"). Indeed, "[t]he archetypal American corporation of the eighteenth century [was] the municipality"; only in the early 19th century did private corporations become widespread. This history explains how the Court in *Cowles* could conclude "automatically and without discussion" that municipal corporations, like private ones, "should be treated as natural persons for virtually all purposes of constitutional and statutory analysis." *Monell*.

Justice Souter also rejected the county's claim that "full-fledged municipal corporations such as towns and cities, which were incorporated at the request of their inhabitants," should be treated differently from "'*quasi* corporations' such as counties, which were unilateral creations of the State." *See* footnote 7. "While the liability of quasi corporations at common law may have differed from that of municipal corporations, both were treated equally as legal 'persons.' Indeed, *Cowles* itself applied to an Illinois county like Cook County." It was thus clear in 1863 (and remains clear today) that counties are amenable to suit, both generally and under § 1983.

5. Did Congress Have the Power to Hold Local Governments Liable? Justice Brennan in *Monell* noted that "[t]here is certainly no constitutional impediment to municipal liability." *See* footnote 54. "'The Tenth Amendment's reservation of nondelegated powers to the States is not implicated by a federal-court judgment enforcing the express prohibitions of unlawful state conduct enacted by the Fourteenth Amendment.' For this reason, *National League of Cities v. Usery*, 426 U.S. 833 (1976), is irrelevant to our consideration of this case." Justice Brennan also rejected Eleventh Amendment concerns: "Our holding today is, of course, limited to local government units which are not considered part of the State for Eleventh Amendment purposes." (Citing *Fitzpatrick v. Bitzer*, 427 U.S. 445 (1976), and *Lincoln County v. Luning*, 133 U.S. 529 (1890). *See* Chapter 3.A., *supra* (explaining that the Eleventh Amendment does not protect "local" governments like cities, counties and school boards).

6. Respondeat Superior. Justice Stevens concurred in Parts I and III of the majority's opinion, but found Part II to be "merely advisory and . . . not necessary to explain the Court's decision." In *City of Oklahoma City v. Tuttle*, 471 U.S. 808 (1985), where a plurality concluded that a single act of deadly force by a police officer did not amount to a municipal policy or custom under *Monell*, Justice Stevens argued in dissent that respondeat superior should be the rule under § 1983:

> At the time [§ 1983] was enacted the doctrine of respondeat superior was well recognized in the common law of the several States and in England. An employer could be held liable for the wrongful acts of his agents, even when acting contrary to specific instructions, and the rule had been specifically applied to municipal corporations, and to the wrongful acts of police officers.

Because it "is always appropriate to assume that our elected representatives, like other citizens, know the law," it is equally appropriate to assume that the authors of the Civil Rights Act recognized that the rule of respondeat superior would apply to "a species of tort liability that on its face admits of no immunities." Indeed, we have repeatedly held that § 1983 should be construed to incorporate common-law doctrine "absent specific provisions to the contrary." We have consistently applied this principle of construction to federal legislation enacted in the 19th century.

The legislative history of the Ku Klux Act supports this conclusion for two reasons. First, the fact that "nobody" objected to § 1 is consistent with the view that Congress expected normal rules of tort law to be applied in enforcing it. Second, the debate on the Sherman Amendment — an amendment that would have imposed an extraordinary and novel form of absolute liability on municipalities — indicates that Congress seriously considered imposing additional responsibilities on municipalities without ever mentioning the possibility that they should have any lesser responsibility than any other person. The rejection of the Sherman Amendment sheds no light on the meaning of the statute, but the fact that such an extreme measure was even considered indicates that Congress thought it appropriate to require municipal corporations to share the responsibility for carrying out the commands of the Fourteenth Amendment.

Of greatest importance, however, is the nature of the wrong for which § 1983 provides a remedy. The Act was primarily designed to provide a remedy for violations of the United States Constitution — wrongs of the most serious kind. . . . But the conduct of an individual can be characterized as "unconstitutional" only if it is attributed to his employer. The Fourteenth Amendment does not have any application to purely private conduct. Unless an individual officer acts under color of official authority, § 1983 does not authorize any recovery against him. But if his relationship with his employer makes it appropriate to treat his conduct as state action for purposes of constitutional analysis, surely that relationship equally justifies the application of normal principles of tort law for the purpose of allocating responsibility for the wrongful state action.

Part II of *Monell* contains dicta of the least persuasive kind. . . . The commentary on respondeat superior in *Monell* was not responsive to any argument advanced by either party and was not even relevant to the Court's actual holding. . . . Having overruled its earlier — and, ironically also volunteered — misconstruction of the word "person" in *Monroe v. Pape*, in my opinion, the Court in *Monell* should simply have held that municipalities are liable for the unconstitutional activities of their agents that are performed in the course of their official duties.

[A]ll of the policy considerations that support the application of the doctrine of respondeat superior in normal tort litigation against municipal corporations apply with special force because of the special quality of the interests at stake. The interest in providing fair compensation for the victim, the interest in deterring future violations by formulating sound municipal policy, and the interest in fair treatment for individual officers who are performing difficult and dangerous work, all militate in favor of placing primary responsibility on the municipal corporation.

The Court's contrary conclusion can only be explained by a concern about the danger of bankrupting municipal corporations. That concern is surely legitimate, but it is one that should be addressed by Congress — perhaps by imposing maximum limitations on the size of any potential recovery or by requiring the purchase of appropriate liability insurance — rather than by this Court.

Justice Stevens appears to have garnered three more votes in favor of his position. *See Board of County Commissioners of Bryan County v. Brown*, 520 U.S. 397 (1997) (excerpted in Section C.[2], *infra*). *See* Eric A. Harrington, Note, *Judicial Misuse of History and § 1983: Toward a Purpose-Based Approach*, 85 TEX. L. REV. 999 (2007) (observing that *Monell* may soon be revisited). Commentators tend to endorse Justice Stevens's argument. *See, e.g.*, Paul Hoffman, *The Feds, Lies, and Videotape: The Need for an Effective Federal Role in Controlling Police Abuse in Urban America*, 66 S. CAL. L. REV. 1453, 1518 (1993) (arguing in favor of respondeat superior); Harold S. Lewis, Jr. & Theodore Y. Blumoff, *Reshaping Section 1983's Asymmetry*, 140 U. PA. L. REV. 755, 820–38 (1992) (arguing for respondeat superior against municipalities); Barbara Kritchevsky, *Reexamining* Monell: *Basing § 1983 Liability Doctrine on the Statutory Language*, 31 URBAN LAWYER 437, 478 (1999) ("A sound reading of the statute reveals that § 1983 not only does not prohibit respondeat superior liability, but it envisions direct municipal liability."); David Jacks Achtenberg, *Taking History Seriously: Municipal Liability Under 42 U.S.C. § 1983 and the Debate Over Respondeat Superior*, 73 FORDHAM L. REV. 2183, 2196 (2005) (arguing that rejection of the Sherman Amendment "was not merely consistent with the nineteenth-century rationales for respondeat superior; it was compelled by those rationales").

7. Supervisory Liability. *Rizzo v. Goode*, 423 U.S. 362 (1976), which was relied on by the majority in *Monell*, involved litigation designed to enjoin alleged abusive police practices in Philadelphia. Because *Monroe v. Pape* protected local government from § 1983 liability at that time, the plaintiffs in *Rizzo* named several high-ranking local officials as defendants rather than the city. The Supreme Court in *Rizzo* held that injunctive relief could not be issued against the municipality's supervisory officials for a number of reasons, one of which was that "the mere right to control without any control or direction having been exercised and without any failure to supervise is not enough to support § 1983 liability." Though the Court did not elaborate on what kind of participation or "affirmative link" was necessary, it ruled that the doctrine of respondeat superior could not be used to hold the city's high-ranking officials accountable for the wrongs of their subordinates. The Supreme Court's opinion in *Rizzo* is commonly cited for the proposition that supervisors cannot be held personally liable in damages for the wrongs of their subordinates without some sort of supervisory fault. Lower courts today tend to agree that proof of deliberate indifference, *see* Section C.[2], *infra* (discussing deliberate indifference in the context of municipal liability), on the supervisor's part is required for personal liability. *See generally* Kit Kinports, *The Buck Does Not Stop Here: Supervisory Liability in Section 1983 Cases*, 1997 U. ILL. L. REV. 147 (criticizing this approach and arguing in favor of a negligence standard).

The Supreme Court granted review in *Ashcroft v. Iqbal*, 128 S. Ct. 2931 (2008), to address whether high-ranking officials in the Bush Administration can be held liable for the wrongful acts of their subordinates. Although a *Bivens* action, *Iqbal* may shed light on the required level of fault for supervisory liability under § 1983.

8. Private Institutional Liability. As discussed in Chapter 1.B., *supra*, private parties can sometimes engage in unconstitutional state action that renders them liable for damages under § 1983. When private agents violate § 1983, are their principals vicariously liable? Or does *Monell* also insulate private institutions from respondeat superior? Professor Barbara Kritchevsky has found that lower courts tend to "consider private entities suable 'persons,' [but] . . . largely agree that [they] are only liable if the plaintiff satisfies the policy or custom requirement. . . . " Barbara Kritchevsky, *Civil Rights Liability of Private Entities*, 26 CARDOZO L. REV. 35, 38 (2004). For excellent discussions of the many problems surrounding private liability under § 1983, the reader is directed to the Symposium issue in which Professor Kritchevsky's article appears. *See* Jack M. Beermann, *Why Do Plaintiffs Sue Private Parties Under § 1983?*, 26 CARDOZO L. REV. 9 (2004); Myriam Gilles, *Private Parties as Defendants in Civil Rights Litigation*, 26 CARDOZO L. REV. 1 (2004); Sheldon Nahmod, *The Emerging Section*

1983 Private Party Defense, 26 CARDOZO L. REV. 81 (2004); Michael L. Wells, *Identifying State Actors in Constitutional Litigation: Reviving the Role of Substantive Content*, 26 CARDOZO L. REV. 99 (2004).

B. MUNICIPAL IMMUNITY

Monell left open the possibility that local governmental entities (like cities, counties, and school boards) might be entitled to qualified immunity, a defense discussed in detail in Chapter 2.B., *supra*. That question came to the forefront two years later.

OWEN v. CITY OF INDEPENDENCE
Supreme Court of the United States
445 U.S. 622 (1980)

MR. JUSTICE BRENNAN delivered the opinion of the Court.

[Owen, who served as chief of police, was discharged by the City of Independence under a cloud of allegations involving the management of the police department's property room. Owen filed suit under § 1983 and the Fourteenth Amendment's Due Process Clause against the City. In addition to declaratory and injunctive relief, Owen sought backpay from the date of discharge. The District Court and Court of Appeals agreed that the city's official policy was the cause of Owen's discharge. Still, both courts concluded that the City was immune. In the words of the Court of Appeals, the "Supreme Court's decisions in *Board of Regents v. Roth*, 408 U.S. 564 (1972), and *Perry v. Sindermann*, 408 U.S. 593 (1972), [which] crystallized the rule establishing the right to a name-clearing hearing for a government employee allegedly stigmatized in the course of his discharge[, were decided] two months after the discharge in the instant case. Thus, officials of the City of Independence could not have been aware of [Owen's] right to a name-clearing hearing in connection with the discharge. The City of Independence should not be charged with predicting the future course of constitutional law. . . . We hold the City not liable for actions it could not reasonably have known violated [Owen's] constitutional rights."]

By its terms, § 1983 "creates a species of tort liability that on its face admits of no immunities." Its language is absolute and unqualified; no mention is made of any privileges, immunities, or defenses that may be asserted. Rather, the Act imposes liability upon "every person" who, under color of state law or custom, "subjects, or causes to be subjected, any citizen of the United States . . . to the deprivation of any rights, privileges, or immunities secured by the Constitution and laws." And *Monell* held that these words were intended to encompass municipal corporations as well as natural "persons."

However, notwithstanding § 1983's expansive language and the absence of any express incorporation of common-law immunities, we have, on several occasions, found that a tradition of immunity was so firmly rooted in the common law and was supported by such strong policy reasons that "Congress would have specifically so provided had it wished to abolish the doctrine."

Where the immunity claimed by the defendant was well established at common law at the time § 1983 was enacted, and where its rationale was compatible with the purposes of the Civil Rights Act, we have construed the statute to incorporate that immunity. But there is no tradition of immunity for municipal corporations, and neither history nor policy supports a construction of § 1983 that would justify the qualified immunity accorded the city of Independence by the Court of Appeals. We hold, therefore, that the municipality may not assert the good faith of its officers or agents as a defense to liability under § 1983.[13]

---

[13] [n.18] The governmental immunity at issue in the present case differs significantly from the official

Since colonial times, a distinct feature of our Nation's system of governance has been the conferral of political power upon public and municipal corporations for the management of matters of local concern. As *Monell* recounted, by 1871 municipalities — like private corporations — were treated as natural persons for virtually all purposes of constitutional and statutory analysis. In particular, they were routinely sued in both federal and state courts. Local governmental units were regularly held to answer in damages for a wide range of statutory and constitutional violations, as well as for common-law actions for breach of contract. And although, as we discuss below, a municipality was not subject to suit for all manner of tortious conduct, it is clear that at the time § 1983 was enacted, local governmental bodies did not enjoy the sort of "good-faith" qualified immunity extended to them by the Court of Appeals.

As a general rule, it was understood that a municipality's tort liability in damages was identical to that of private corporations and individuals. . . . Under this general theory of liability, a municipality was deemed responsible for any private losses generated through a wide variety of its operations and functions, from personal injuries due to its defective sewers, thoroughfares, and public utilities, to property damage caused by its trespasses and uncompensated takings. Yet in the hundreds of cases from that era awarding damages against municipal governments for wrongs committed by them, one searches in vain for much mention of a qualified immunity based on the good faith of municipal officers. Indeed, where the issue was discussed at all, the courts had rejected the proposition that a municipality should be privileged where it reasonably believed its actions to be lawful.

That municipal corporations were commonly held liable for damages in tort was also recognized by the 42d Congress. For example, Senator Stevenson, in opposing the Sherman amendment's creation of a municipal liability for the riotous acts of its inhabitants, stated the prevailing law: "Numberless cases are to be found where a statutory liability has been created against municipal corporations for injuries resulting from a neglect of corporate duty." Nowhere in the debates, however, is there a suggestion that the common law excused a city from liability on account of the good faith of its authorized agents, much less an indication of a congressional intent to incorporate such an immunity into the Civil Rights Act. The absence of any allusion to a municipal immunity assumes added significance in light of the objections raised by the opponents of § 1 of the Act that its unqualified language could be interpreted to abolish the traditional good-faith immunities enjoyed by legislators, judges, governors, sheriffs, and other public officers. Had there been a similar common-law immunity for municipalities, the bill's opponents doubtless would have raised the specter of its destruction, as well.

To be sure, there were two doctrines that afforded municipal corporations some measure of protection from tort liability. The first sought to distinguish between a municipality's "governmental" and "proprietary" functions; as to the former, the city was held immune, whereas in its exercise of the latter, the city was held to the same standards of liability as any private corporation. The second doctrine immunized a municipality for its "discretionary" or "legislative" activities, but not for those which were "ministerial" in nature. A brief examination of the application and the rationale underlying each of these doctrines demonstrates that Congress could not have intended them to limit a municipality's liability under § 1983.

The governmental-proprietary distinction owed its existence to the dual nature of the municipal corporation. On the one hand, the municipality was a corporate body, capable of performing the same "proprietary" functions as any private corporation, and

---

immunities involved in our previous decisions. In those cases, various government officers had been sued in their individual capacities, and the immunity served to insulate them from personal liability for damages. Here, in contrast, only the liability of the municipality itself is at issue, not that of its officers, and in the absence of an immunity, any recovery would come from public funds.

liable for its torts in the same manner and to the same extent, as well. On the other hand, the municipality was an arm of the State, and when acting in that "governmental" or "public" capacity, it shared the immunity traditionally accorded the sovereign. But the principle of sovereign immunity — itself a somewhat arid fountainhead for municipal immunity — is necessarily nullified when the State expressly or impliedly allows itself, or its creation, to be sued. Municipalities were therefore liable not only for their "proprietary" acts, but also for those "governmental" functions as to which the State had withdrawn their immunity. And, by the end of the 19th century, courts regularly held that in imposing a specific duty on the municipality either in its charter or by statute, the State had impliedly withdrawn the city's immunity from liability for the nonperformance or misperformance of its obligation. Thus, despite the nominal existence of an immunity for "governmental" functions, municipalities were found liable in damages in a multitude of cases involving such activities.

That the municipality's common-law immunity for "governmental" functions derives from the principle of sovereign immunity also explains why that doctrine could not have served as the basis for the qualified privilege [the] city claims under § 1983. First, because sovereign immunity insulates the municipality from unconsented suits altogether, the presence or absence of good faith is simply irrelevant. The critical issue is whether injury occurred while the city was exercising governmental, as opposed to proprietary, powers or obligations — not whether its agents reasonably believed they were acting lawfully in so conducting themselves.[14] More fundamentally, however, the municipality's "governmental" immunity is obviously abrogated by the sovereign's enactment of a statute making it amenable to suit. Section 1983 was just such a statute. By including municipalities within the class of "persons" subject to liability for violations of the Federal Constitution and laws, Congress — the supreme sovereign on matters of federal law — abolished whatever vestige of the State's sovereign immunity the municipality possessed.

The second common-law distinction between municipal functions — that protecting the city from suits challenging "discretionary" decisions — was grounded not on the principle of sovereign immunity, but on a concern for separation of powers. A large part of the municipality's responsibilities involved broad discretionary decisions on issues of public policy — decisions that affected large numbers of persons and called for a delicate balancing of competing considerations. For a court or jury, in the guise of a tort suit, to review the reasonableness of the city's judgment on these matters would be an infringement upon the powers properly vested in a coordinate and coequal branch of government.

Although many, if not all, of a municipality's activities would seem to involve at least some measure of discretion, the influence of this doctrine on the city's liability was not as significant as might be expected. For just as the courts implied an exception to the municipality's immunity for its "governmental" functions, here, too, a distinction was made that had the effect of subjecting the city to liability for much of its tortious conduct. While the city retained its immunity for decisions as to whether the public interest required acting in one manner or another, once any particular decision was made, the city was fully liable for any injuries incurred in the execution of its judgment. Thus municipalities remained liable in damages for a broad range of conduct implementing their discretionary decisions.

Once again, an understanding of the rationale underlying the common-law immunity for "discretionary" functions explains why that doctrine cannot serve as the foundation for a good-faith immunity under § 1983. That common-law doctrine merely prevented

---

[14] [n.29] The common-law immunity for governmental functions is thus more comparable to an absolute immunity from liability for conduct of a certain character, which defeats a suit at the outset, than to a qualified immunity, which "depends upon the circumstances and motivations of [the official's] actions, as established by the evidence at trial."

courts from substituting their own judgment on matters within the lawful discretion of the municipality. But a municipality has no "discretion" to violate the Federal Constitution; its dictates are absolute and imperative. And when a court passes judgment on the municipality's conduct in a § 1983 action, it does not seek to second-guess the "reasonableness" of the city's decision nor to interfere with the local government's resolution of competing policy considerations. Rather, it looks only to whether the municipality has conformed to the requirements of the Federal Constitution and statutes.

Our rejection of a construction of § 1983 that would accord municipalities a qualified immunity for their good-faith constitutional violations is compelled both by the legislative purpose in enacting the statute and by considerations of public policy.

How "uniquely amiss" it would be . . . if the government itself — "the social organ to which all in our society look for the promotion of liberty, justice, fair and equal treatment, and the setting of worthy norms and goals for social conduct" — were permitted to disavow liability for the injury it has begotten. A damages remedy against the offending party is a vital component of any scheme for vindicating cherished constitutional guarantees, and the importance of assuring its efficacy is only accentuated when the wrongdoer is the institution that has been established to protect the very rights it has transgressed. Yet owing to the qualified immunity enjoyed by most government officials, many victims of municipal malfeasance would be left remediless if the city were also allowed to assert a good-faith defense. Unless countervailing considerations counsel otherwise, the injustice of such a result should not be tolerated.[15]

Moreover, § 1983 was intended not only to provide compensation to the victims of past abuses, but to serve as a deterrent against future constitutional deprivations, as well. The knowledge that a municipality will be liable for all of its injurious conduct, whether committed in good faith or not, should create an incentive for officials who may harbor doubts about the lawfulness of their intended actions to err on the side of protecting citizens' constitutional rights. Furthermore, the threat that damages might be levied against the city may encourage those in a policymaking position to institute internal rules and programs designed to minimize the likelihood of unintentional infringements on constitutional rights. Such procedures are particularly beneficial in preventing those "systemic" injuries that result not so much from the conduct of any single individual, but from the interactive behavior of several government officials, each of whom may be acting in good faith.

Our previous decisions conferring qualified immunities on various government officials are not to be read as derogating the significance of the societal interest in compensating the innocent victims of governmental misconduct. Rather, in each case we concluded that overriding considerations of public policy nonetheless demanded that the official be given a measure of protection from personal liability. The concerns that justified those decisions, however, are less compelling, if not wholly inapplicable, when the liability of the municipal entity is at issue.

[The Court has] identified the two "mutually dependent rationales" on which the doctrine of official immunity rested: "(1) the injustice, particularly in the absence of bad faith, of subjecting to liability an officer who is required, by the legal obligations of his position, to exercise discretion; (2) the danger that the threat of such liability would deter his willingness to execute his office with the decisiveness and the judgment required by the public good."[16] The first consideration is simply not implicated when

---

[15] [n.33] The absence of any damages remedy for violations of all but the most "clearly established" constitutional rights could also have the deleterious effect of freezing constitutional law in its current state of development, for without a meaningful remedy aggrieved individuals will have little incentive to seek vindication of those constitutional deprivations that have not previously been clearly defined.

[16] [n.38] *Wood v. Strickland*, 420 U.S. 308 (1975), mentioned a third justification for extending a qualified

the damages award comes not from the official's pocket, but from the public treasury. It hardly seems unjust to require a municipal defendant which has violated a citizen's constitutional rights to compensate him for the injury suffered thereby. Indeed, Congress enacted § 1983 precisely to provide a remedy for such abuses of official power. Elemental notions of fairness dictate that one who causes a loss should bear the loss.

It has been argued, however, that revenue raised by taxation for public use should not be diverted to the benefit of a single or discrete group of taxpayers, particularly where the municipality has at all times acted in good faith. On the contrary, . . . it is the public at large which enjoys the benefits of the government's activities, and it is the public at large which is ultimately responsible for its administration. Thus, even where some constitutional development could not have been foreseen by municipal officials, it is fairer to allocate any resulting financial loss to the inevitable costs of government borne by all the taxpayers, than to allow its impact to be felt solely by those whose rights, albeit newly recognized, have been violated.[17]

The second rationale . . . loses its force when it is the municipality, in contrast to the official, whose liability is at issue. At the heart of this justification for a qualified immunity for the individual official is the concern that the threat of personal monetary liability will introduce an unwarranted and unconscionable consideration into the decisionmaking process, thus paralyzing the governing official's decisiveness and distorting his judgment on matters of public policy. The inhibiting effect is significantly reduced, if not eliminated, however, when the threat of personal liability is removed. First, as an empirical matter, it is questionable whether the hazard of municipal loss will deter a public officer from the conscientious exercise of his duties; city officials routinely make decisions that either require a large expenditure of municipal funds or involve a substantial risk of depleting the public fisc. More important, though, is the realization that consideration of the municipality's liability for constitutional violations is quite properly the concern of its elected or appointed officials. Indeed, a decisionmaker would be derelict in his duties if, at some point, he did not consider whether his decision comports with constitutional mandates and did not weigh the risk that a violation might result in an award of damages from the public treasury.

Mr. Justice Powell, with whom The Chief Justice, Mr. Justice Stewart, and Mr. Justice Rehnquist join, dissenting.

Until two years ago, municipal corporations enjoyed absolute immunity from § 1983 claims. *Monroe v. Pape.* But *Monell* held that local governments are "persons" within the meaning of the statute, and thus are liable in damages for constitutional violations inflicted by municipal policies.

After today's decision, municipalities will have gone in two short years from absolute immunity under § 1983 to strict liability. As a policy matter, I believe that strict municipal liability unreasonably subjects local governments to damages judgments for actions that were reasonable when performed. It converts municipal governance into a

---

immunity to public officials: the fear that the threat of personal liability might deter citizens from holding public office. Such fears are totally unwarranted, of course, once the threat of personal liability is eliminated.

[17] [n.39] *Monell* . . . indicated that the principle of loss-spreading was an insufficient justification for holding the municipality liable under § 1983 on a respondeat superior theory. Here of course, quite a different situation is presented. [Owen] does not seek to hold the city responsible for the unconstitutional actions of an individual official "solely because it employs a tortfeasor." Rather, liability is predicated on a determination that "the action that is alleged to be unconstitutional implements or executes a policy statement, ordinance, regulation, or decision officially adopted and promulgated by that body's officers." In this circumstance — when it is the local government itself that is responsible for the constitutional deprivation — it is perfectly reasonable to distribute the loss to the public as a cost of the administration of government, rather than to let the entire burden fall on the injured individual.

hazardous slalom through constitutional obstacles that often are unknown and unknowable.

Important public policies support the extension of qualified immunity to local governments. First, as recognized by the doctrine of separation of powers, some governmental decisions should be at least presumptively insulated from judicial review. Mr. Chief Justice Marshall wrote in *Marbury v. Madison* that "[t]he province of the court is . . . not to inquire how the executive, or executive officers, perform duties in which they have a discretion." Marshall stressed the caution with which courts must approach "[q]uestions, in their nature political, or which are, by the constitution and laws, submitted to the executive." The allocation of public resources and the operational policies of the government itself are activities that lie peculiarly within the competence of executive and legislative bodies. When charting those policies, a local official should not have to gauge his employer's possible liability under § 1983 if he incorrectly — though reasonably and in good faith — forecasts the course of constitutional law. Excessive judicial intrusion into such decisions can only distort municipal decisionmaking and discredit the courts.

Because today's decision will inject constant consideration of § 1983 liability into local decisionmaking, it may restrict the independence of local governments and their ability to respond to the needs of their communities.

The Court now argues that local officials might modify their actions unduly if they face personal liability under § 1983, but that they are unlikely to do so when the locality itself will be held liable. This contention denigrates the sense of responsibility of municipal officers, and misunderstands the political process. Responsible local officials will be concerned about potential judgments against their municipalities for alleged constitutional torts. Moreover, they will be accountable within the political system for subjecting the municipality to adverse judgments. If officials must look over their shoulders at a strict municipal liability for unknowable constitutional deprivations, the resulting degree of governmental paralysis will be little different from that caused by fear of personal liability.[18]

In addition, basic fairness requires a qualified immunity for municipalities. . . . Constitutional law is what the courts say it is, and — as demonstrated by today's decision and its precursor, *Monell* — even the most prescient lawyer would hesitate to give a firm opinion on matters not plainly settled. Municipalities, often acting in the utmost good faith, may not know or anticipate when their action or inaction will be deemed a constitutional violation.

The Court nevertheless suggests that, as a matter of social justice, municipal corporations should be strictly liable even if they could not have known that a particular action would violate the Constitution. After all, the Court urges, local governments can "spread" the costs of any judgment across the local population. The Court neglects, however, the fact that many local governments lack the resources to withstand substantial unanticipated liability under § 1983. Even enthusiastic proponents of municipal liability have conceded that ruinous judgments under the statute could imperil local governments. By simplistically applying the theorems of welfare economics and ignoring the reality of municipal finance, the Court imposes strict liability on the level of government least able to bear it.[19] For some municipalities, the result could be a severe limitation on their ability to serve the public.

---

[18] [n.9] The Court's argument is not only unpersuasive, but also is internally inconsistent. The Court contends that strict liability is necessary to "create an incentive for officials . . . to err on the side of protecting citizens' constitutional rights." Yet the Court later assures us that such liability will not distort municipal decisionmaking because "[t]he inhibiting effect is significantly reduced, if not eliminated . . . when the threat of personal liability is removed." Thus, the Court apparently believes that strict municipal liability is needed to modify public policies, but will not have any impact on those policies anyway.

[19] [n.12] Ironically, the State and Federal Governments cannot be held liable for constitutional depriva-

The Court's decision also runs counter to the common law in the 19th century, which recognized substantial tort immunity for municipal actions. Nineteenth-century courts generally held that municipal corporations were not liable for acts undertaken in their "governmental," as opposed to their "proprietary," capacity. Most States now use other criteria for determining when a local government should be liable for damages. Still, the governmental/proprietary distinction retains significance because it was so widely accepted when § 1983 was enacted. It is inconceivable that a Congress thoroughly versed in current legal doctrines would have intended through silence to create the strict liability regime now imagined by this Court.

More directly relevant to this case is the common-law distinction between the "discretionary" and "ministerial" duties of local governments. This Court wrote in *Harris v. District of Columbia*, 256 U.S. 650 (1921): "[W]hen acting in good faith municipal corporations are not liable for the manner in which they exercise discretionary powers of a public or legislative character." The rationale for this immunity derives from the theory of separation of powers.

That reasoning, frequently applied in the 19th century, parallels the theory behind qualified immunity under § 1983. This Court has recognized the importance of preserving the autonomy of executive bodies entrusted with discretionary powers. . . . Strict municipal liability can only undermine that discretion.[20]

Today's decision also conflicts with the current law in 44 States and the District of Columbia. All of those jurisdictions provide municipal immunity at least analogous to a "good faith" defense against liability for constitutional torts. Thus, for municipalities in almost 90% of our jurisdictions, the Court creates broader liability for constitutional deprivations than for state-law torts.

This disregard of precedent and policy is especially unfortunate because suits under § 1983 typically implicate evolving constitutional standards. A good-faith defense is much more important for those actions than in those involving ordinary tort liability. The duty not to run over a pedestrian with a municipal bus is far less likely to change than is the rule as to what process, if any, is due the bus driver if he claims the right to a hearing after discharge. The right of a discharged government employee to a "name clearing" hearing was not recognized until our decision in *Roth*. That ruling was handed down 10 weeks after Owen was discharged and 8 weeks after the city denied his request for a hearing. By stripping the city of any immunity, the Court punishes it for failing to predict our decision in *Roth*. As a result, local governments and their officials will face the unnerving prospect of crushing damages judgments whenever a policy valid under current law is later found to be unconstitutional. I can see no justice or wisdom in that outcome.

NOTES

1. Is Governmental Immunity "Uniquely Amiss"? Justice Brennan opines "[h]ow 'uniquely amiss' it would be" if government were afforded immunity. But this is exactly what the Supreme Court has done for *state*, as opposed to local, government. Can Justice Brennan's comments be reconciled with the Court's decisions in *Quern v.*

---

tions. The Federal Government has not waived its sovereign immunity against such claims, and the States are protected by the Eleventh Amendment.

[20] [n.18] The Court cannot wish away these extensive municipal immunities. . . . The Court takes some solace in the absence in the 19th century of a qualified immunity for local governments. That absence, of course, was due to the availability of absolute immunity for governmental and discretionary acts. There is no justification for discovering strict municipal liability in § 1983 when that statute was enacted against a background of extensive municipal immunity. The Court also points out that municipalities were subject to suit for some statutory violations and neglect of contractual obligations imposed by State or Federal Constitutions. That amenability to suit is simply irrelevant to the immunity available in tort actions, which controls the immunity available under § 1983.

Jordan, 440 U.S. 332 (1979), and *Will v. Michigan Department of State Police*, 491 U.S. 58 (1989), discussed in Chapter 3.C., *supra*?

2. The Problem of Prospectivity. Beginning with the Warren Court revolution in constitutional criminal procedure, courts agonized over the consequences of applying new principles of law to past governmental actions. Both the Warren and Burger Courts explored an ad hoc, prospective approach in an effort to avoid flooding lower courts with habeas corpus petitions. *See, e.g., Linkletter v. Walker*, 381 U.S. 618 (1965); *see generally* Sam Kamin, *Harmless Error and the Rights/Remedies Split*, 88 VA. L. REV. 1, 28 (2002) ("[T]he Court [in *Linkletter*] held it would weigh the 'merits and demerits' of retroactive application on a rule-by-rule basis. Only where that balancing favored the retroactive application of new constitutional rules would the law be applied other than prospectively."); Kit Kinports, *Habeas Corpus, Qualified Immunity, and Crystal Balls: Predicting the Course of Constitutional Law*, 33 ARIZ. L. REV. 115, 172 (1991) ("The *Linkletter* test required examination of the purposes of the new rule, the extent to which law enforcement authorities had relied on the prior doctrine, and the effect of retroactive application on the administration of justice."). The Court did not abandon this experiment until William Rehnquist's tenure as Chief Justice, when, in *Griffith v. Kentucky*, 479 U.S. 314 (1987), and *Teague v. Lane*, 489 U.S. 288 (1989), it opted for a bright line distinction between direct appeals and collateral attacks on convictions. Under *Griffith* and *Teague*, courts must apply new principles of constitutional law in all cases on direct review not yet final, but generally not in cases proceeding under habeas corpus.

A new-law exception, not unlike that found in the pre-*Teague* criminal context, was also developed in the context of civil litigation. In *Chevron Oil Co. v. Huson*, 404 U.S. 97 (1971), the Court outlined an equitable approach that considered three factors: (1) whether a "new principle of law" was at issue; (2) whether retroactive application served the purpose of the new principle; and (3), whether equity favored prospective application. Even private defendants, who generally have no immunities, could escape civil liability under *Huson*'s three-pronged formula.

The Court applied the *Huson* exception to a constitutional claim in *American Trucking Ass'ns v. Smith*, 496 U.S. 167 (1990). The substantive issue in *Smith* was whether an Arkansas tax discriminated against out-of-state commerce in violation of the Commerce Clause. Before final judgment in *Smith*, but after the filing of the complaint, the Court applied the Commerce Clause to invalidate a nearly identical Pennsylvania law in *American Trucking Ass'ns v. Scheiner*, 483 U.S. 266 (1987). Justice O'Connor, writing for a plurality in *Smith*, relied on *Huson* to hold that *Scheiner* should not be applied retroactively to the facts of *Smith*. She concluded that, in light of precedent that upheld similar taxes, *Scheiner* established a new principle of law. Because *Scheiner* was new and unpredictable, Justice O'Connor further concluded that applying it retroactively would serve neither the purpose of the Commerce Clause nor the principle of deterrence. Because the state had reasonably relied on precedent, moreover, the inequity of retroactive application was "apparent."

The Court revisited *Huson*'s application to constitutional law in *Harper v. Virginia Department of Taxation*, 509 U.S. 86 (1993), another case involving state taxation.[21] A bare five-to-four majority overruled *Smith* and held that courts must apply new constitutional rules retroactively in civil litigation as well as criminal prosecutions. Putting practicalities aside and harkening back to the jurisprudential philosophy of Oliver Wendell Holmes, the Court, per Justice Thomas, decided that retrospective application of the law should prove the rule, just as it has been "for near a thousand

---

[21] In *Harper*, Virginia had exempted state and local, but not federal, retirement benefits from its state income tax. The Court had found a similar Michigan law invalid four years earlier in *Davis v. Michigan Department of Treasury*, 489 U.S. 803 (1989).

years." *See also Reynoldsville Casket Co. v. Hyde*, 514 U.S. 749 (1995) (holding that Commerce Clause ruling was to be applied retroactively).[22]

The Supreme Court's decision to revisit *Smith* was not surprising. First, *Smith* was a plurality decision that hinged on an ambivalent concurrence by Justice Scalia. (Justice Scalia had joined the plurality's result in *Smith* despite protesting that nonretroactive decisionmaking proves inconsistent with Article III judicial power.) Second, Justice O'Connor's realist observation in *Smith* that courts sometimes make law contradicted the Court's prior conceptualist approach in *Griffith v. Kentucky*, which held that new constitutional principles must apply retroactively in criminal cases. An explanation for this philosophical difference seemed in order. Third, *Smith* appeared to contradict *Owen*, at least in the context of constitutional wrongdoing. Although some have argued that *Owen* and *Smith* can be reconciled, *see, e.g.*, Richard H. Fallon, Jr. & Daniel J. Meltzer, *New Law, Non-Retroactivity, and Constitutional Remedies*, 104 HARV. L. REV. 1733, 1796 (1991), the tension is apparent. *See generally* Ronald M. Levin, *"Vacation" at Sea: Judicial Remedies and Equitable Discretion in Administrative Law*, 53 DUKE L.J. 291 (2003) (discussing the Supreme Court's holdings in *Huson* and *Harper*).[23]

3. Threat to the Public Fisc. Justice Powell's dissent in *Owen* complained that governmental treasuries are placed at risk by the potential for large monetary judgments. Justice O'Connor expressed similar sentiments in dissent in *Harper*.[24] Is there convincing proof that § 1983 threatens municipal bankruptcy?

For the 1980–1981 fiscal year, Professors Theodore Eisenberg and Stewart Schwab studied three dense federal districts, the Eastern District of Pennsylvania, the Northern District of Georgia, and the Central District of California, none of which had ever recognized qualified immunity for local municipalities. *See* THEODORE EISENBERG, CASES AND MATERIALS ON CIVIL RIGHTS LEGISLATION 158 (3rd ed. 1991) (summarizing Theodore Eisenberg & Stewart Schwab, *What Shapes Perceptions of the Federal Court System?*, 56 U. CHI. L. REV. 501 (1989); Theodore Eisenberg & Stewart Schwab, *Explaining Constitutional Tort Litigation: The Influence of the Attorney Fees Statute and the Government as Defendant*, 73 CORNELL L. REV. 719 (1988); and Theodore

---

[22] What about private institutions that are subject to suit under § 1983? *See* Chapter 1.B., *supra*. Are they entitled to qualified immunity? *See* Barbara Kritchevsky, *Civil Rights Liability of Private Entities*, 26 CARDOZO L. REV. 35, 38 (2004) (finding that lower courts "do not agree on whether private entities may claim immunity"). Is prospectivity under *Huson* still an option?

[23] Does *Harper* bar "pure" prospectivity in constitutional cases, that is, holding that a new constitutional principle does not apply to any actions — even those of the parties — that occurred before the date of decision? Professor Levin has noted that Justice Thomas's opinion in *Harper*, read in light of the Court's plurality opinion in *James B. Beam Distilling Co. v. Georgia*, 501 U.S. 529 (1991), can be read to bar only selective prospectivity, that is, applying a new ruling to some (like the parties before the Court) but not others. Levin, *supra*, at 355–56. Lower courts have disagreed over the matter. *Contrast Crowe v. Bolduc*, 365 F.3d 86 (1st Cir. 2004) ("A court in a civil case may apply a decision purely prospectively, binding neither the parties before it nor similarly situated parties in other pending cases. . . . Selective prospectivity, however, is not permissible; if a new rule is applied to the parties in the rule-creating case, then it must be applied retroactively to similarly situated parties in all pending cases."); *and Glazner v. Glazner*, 347 F.3d 1212 (11th Cir. 2003) ("The Supreme Court has retreated from, but has not abandoned, prospectivity in civil cases. . . . The main principle for which *Harper* . . . stand[s] is that once a court applies a newly announced rule to the parties before it, all other courts must apply that rule to all pending cases."), *with Hulin v. Fibreboard Corp.*, 178 F.3d 316 (5th Cir. 1999) (stating that *Harper* leaves only "an indistinct possibility of the application of pure prospectivity in an extremely unusual and unforeseeable case"); *and Fairfax Covenant Church v. Fairfax County School Board*, 17 F.3d 703 (4th Cir. 1994) ("Though the precise issue in *Harper* was so-called 'selective prospectivity,' every indication in the opinion of the Court is that its logic would also forbid all types of prospectivity.").

[24] Although this fiscal concern failed to carry a majority in *Owen*, it garnered majority support in *City of Newport v. Fact Concerts*, 453 U.S. 247 (1981) (excerpted in Chapter 6.B., *infra*), where the Court held that municipalities cannot be held liable for punitive damages under § 1983.

Eisenberg & Stewart Schwab, *The Reality of Constitutional Tort Litigation*, 72 CORNELL L. REV. 641 (1987)). Professors Eisenberg and Schwab concluded that constitutional tort litigation under § 1983, even in the absence of qualified immunity for local government, has only a limited impact on municipal budgets. Specifically, Eisenberg and Schwab found that money damages awarded under § 1983 comprised only 0.02% of the studied governmental entities' budgets. They therefore concluded that additional limitations on constitutional tort suits against municipalities were not needed. *See also* Barbara Kritchevsky, *Is There a Cost Defense? Budgetary Constraints as a Defense in Civil Rights Litigation*, 35 RUTGERS L.J. 483, 565 (2004) (arguing that "courts should continue to recognize that budgetary constraints rarely justify inaction. A defendant can almost always do something to stop or prevent constitutional violations by reallocating spending priorities or adjusting internal policies."); Lawrence Rosenthal, *A Theory of Governmental Damages Liability: Torts, Constitutional Torts, and Takings*, 9 U. PA. J. CONST. L. 797 (2007) (discussing financial repercussions of damage awards against government).

4. A Loss to Taxpayers? Even assuming that § 1983 cases consume a significant portion of municipal resources, are tax dollars that pay § 1983 judgments a total loss? "The public . . . is not throwing its tax dollars to the wind. It gets something in return: more responsible government. The private attorneys general that § 1983 created are an important check on state and local government. The Department of Justice does not have the resources to investigate and prosecute every constitutional violation." Mark R. Brown, *The Failure of Fault Under Section 1983: Municipal Liability for State Law Enforcement*, 84 CORNELL L. REV. 1503, 1529–30 (1999); *see also* Myriam E. Gilles, *Reinventing Structural Reform Litigation: Deputizing Private Citizens in the Enforcement of Civil Rights*, 100 COLUM. L. REV. 1384 (2000) (arguing that citizens should be given even more power to sue government). Would police departments abide by the Constitution in the absence of § 1983 litigation? *See* Barbara Armacost, *Organizational Culture and Police Misconduct*, 72 GEO. WASH. U. L. REV. 453, 454 (2004) (arguing that "[r]eal reform requires police organizations to accept collective responsibility, not only for heroism, but for police brutality and corruption as well"); David Rudovsky, *Running in Place: The Paradox of Expanding Rights and Restricted Remedies*, 2005 U. ILL. L. REV. 1199, 1231–32 ("Studies and investigations of law enforcement practices and organizational structures by government agencies, independent auditors, and litigants in court proceedings have documented the 'us vs. them' attitudes of law enforcement officers, the pervasiveness of the code of silence in many departments, the unwritten policies and practices of using extra-legal measures to increase crime control and order maintenance, and the lack of management controls and accountability for abusive conduct.").

5. Fairness, Reliance and Corrective Justice. Justices Brennan and Powell also argue over "fairness" in *Owen*. Is it unfair to force government to pay for constitutional wrongs when it could not foresee the development of the underlying right? Is "fairness" another term for "reliance"? Is reliance unique to government? *See* Mark R. Brown, *The Demise of Constitutional Prospectivity: New Life for* Owen?, 79 IOWA L. REV. 273, 291–93 (1994) ("Citizens also have expectations and concomitant reliance interests. When performing everyday functions like driving to work, shopping, or speaking to neighbors, for instance, people order their affairs in accord with principles of constitutional law. They assume their government's powers and discretions are limited.") Does fairness also implicate morality and corrective justice? Is holding government strictly accountable under *Owen* consistent with corrective justice? *See* John C. Jeffries, Jr., *Compensation for Constitutional Torts: Reflections on the Significance of Fault*, 88 MICH. L. REV. 82, 94 (1989). Dean Jeffries argues that corrective justice teaches that governments should be held liable only when they are at fault — when "government wrongdoing . . . causes individual injury." *Id.* Contrast Harold S. Lewis, Jr., & Theodore Y. Blumoff, *Reshaping Section 1983's Asymmetry*,

140 U. Pa. L. Rev. 755, 834 (1992) (arguing that because cities do not think, "the search for entity 'fault' is literally futile").

6. Constitutional Evolution. Justice Brennan worries in footnote 33 to his majority opinion in *Owen* that affording qualified immunity to local governments as well as their officials could "freeze" the development of constitutional law.[25] Contrary to Justice Brennan's concern that qualified immunity could deter constitutional evolution, Dean Jeffries worries that its absence might discourage judicial innovation: "liability in money damages (plus attorney's fees) for all constitutional violations would exert a baleful influence on the definition of rights." John C. Jeffries, Jr., *In Praise of the Eleventh Amendment and Section 1983*, 84 Va. L. Rev. 47, 78 (1998). According to Jeffries, imposing liability on government risks having courts define rights "with one eye on damages liability" and the other on the Constitution's proper meaning. *Id.* If Jeffries is correct, courts could render bad constitutional decisions to avoid subjecting local governments to financial liability. Jeffries cites to *Miranda v. Arizona*, 384 U.S. 436 (1966), which established the famous warnings due criminal suspects before custodial questioning, as "[a]n important example" of how "nonretroactivity facilitated the creation of new rights by reducing the costs of innovation." Jeffries, *supra*, at 79. He argues that "[i]t is hard to imagine that *Miranda v. Arizona* would ever have been decided if every confessed criminal then in custody had to be set free," adding that "[t]he Court's ability to avoid that result was simultaneously a curtailment of the *Miranda* right and a necessary precondition of its birth." *See also* John C. Jeffries, Jr., *The Right-Remedy Gap in Constitutional Law*, 109 Yale L.J. 87, 90 (1999) (arguing that the "curtailment of damages liability for constitutional violations has deep structural advantages for American constitutionalism. Put simply, limiting money damages for constitutional violations fosters the development of constitutional law").[26]

Assuming that Jeffries is correct about *Miranda* and the Warren Court's other criminal procedure rulings — i.e., that the Supreme Court felt free to expand the rights of criminal defendants because of its ability to limit remedies — does this logic support limiting the remedial reach of constitutional decisions in civil cases? At the time of *Miranda*, for example, remedial concerns were paramount because all prisoners, regardless of the dates of their convictions, could take advantage of changes in constitutional law using federal habeas corpus. The same is not true in civil litigation, where claim and issue preclusion, *see* Chapter 8.A., *infra*, as well as statutes of limitations, *see* Chapter 5.A., *infra*, limit the ability of plaintiffs to make retroactive use of new precedents.

7. Can Government Be Deterred? Most commentators agree that the principal aims of § 1983 are deterrence and compensation. Holding municipalities liable, they argue, insures compensation (which otherwise might not be forthcoming given government officials' shallow pockets) and deters future governmental wrongdoing. Is this thesis sound? Can government be deterred by damages? *Contrast* Darryl J. Levinson, *Making Government Pay: Markets, Politics, and the Allocation of Constitutional*

---

[25] The Supreme Court eventually solved this problem in the context of qualified immunity by instructing courts to first declare the constitutional rights at stake, and next decide whether the errant government official should enjoy immunity. *See, e.g., Hope v. Pelzer*, 536 U.S. 730 (2002). The Court's solution, however, has created its own unique problems. *See* Chapter 2.B., *supra*.

[26] Does the Supreme Court need encouragement to make constitutional law? *See* Mark R. Brown, *The Failure of Fault Under Section 1983: Municipal Liability for State Law Enforcement*, 84 Cornell L. Rev. 1503, 1534-35 (1999) ("The natural tendency to aggrandize power should be sufficient incentive for the Court to make constitutional law. Allowing the judiciary the luxury of remediless, prospective decision making cedes too much government authority."). Is the Supreme Court's development of constitutional law always "good"? *See* Jack M. Beermann, *The Supreme Court's Narrow View on Civil Rights*, 1993 Sup. Ct. Rev. 199, 243 ("It is a political reality . . . that judicial independence at the Supreme Court has not overall served the cause of civil rights well. . . . Rather than be part of the Reconstruction-era and later Congress's solution to the problem of civil rights, the Court has been part of the problem.").

Costs, 67 U. CHI. L. REV. 345 (2000) (arguing that government, which is not like a private entrepreneur, might not be deterred by money damages), *with* Mark R. Brown, *Deterring Bully Government: A Sovereign Dilemma*, 76 TULANE L. REV. 149 (2001) (arguing that government can be deterred by money damages); Myriam E. Gilles, *In Defense of Making Government Pay: The Deterrent Effect of Constitutional Tort Remedies*, 35 GA. L. REV. 845, 847–48 (2001) (arguing that "there are tangible and salutary effects to a constitutional damages regime, including deterrence"); Lawrence Rosenthal, *A Theory of Governmental Damages Liability: Torts, Constitutional Torts, and Takings*, 9 U. PA. J. CONST. L. 797, 800 (2007) (arguing that money damages can deter and that "[t]he Constitution does not leave its enforcement to the political process; accordingly, political accountability is never an adequate remedy for a constitutional violation").

C. AD HOC POLICIES

Monell opened the door to local liability under § 1983, but then limited liability to cases involving official policies and customs. Judged under its own terms, *Monell* was an easy case. The city had adopted an express policy requiring maternity leave after five months, a policy that was facially unconstitutional under *Cleveland Board of Education v. LaFleur*, 414 U.S. 632 (1974) (holding that mandated maternity leave constitutes an unconstitutional irrebuttable presumption under the Due Process Clause). Government, however, rarely passes facially unconstitutional laws that are invalid in all of their applications. *See United States v. Salerno*, 481 U.S. 739 (1987) ("[a] facial challenge to a legislative Act is, of course, the most difficult challenge to mount successfully, since the challenger must establish that no set of circumstances exists under which the Act would be valid"). More often, governments enact policies that are generally valid, but suffer unconstitutional applications. A city, for example, might hand out guns to its police officers and direct them to arrest suspected criminals. Gun use by police officers is facially valid. It only becomes a constitutional problem when police use their weapons to shoot suspects who are not dangerous within the meaning of *Tennessee v. Garner*, 471 U.S. 1 (1985) (holding that the use of deadly force to seize non-dangerous fleeing felon violates the Fourth Amendment). Can local government be held financially accountable for a police officer's wrong under these circumstances? More generally, can local government be held liable in the absence of a facially unconstitutional policy?

[1] The Final Authority Analysis

PEMBAUR v. CITY OF CINCINNATI
Supreme Court of the United States
475 U.S. 469 (1986)

JUSTICE BRENNAN delivered the opinion of the Court, [except as to Part II-B, which is joined by JUSTICES WHITE, MARSHALL and BLACKMUN].

I

During [an] investigation, [a] grand jury issued subpoenas for the appearance of two of Pembaur's employees. When these employees failed to appear as directed, the Prosecutor obtained capiases for their arrest and detention.[27]

On May 19, 1977, two Hamilton County Deputy Sheriffs attempted to serve the capiases at Pembaur's [office]. . . . Pembaur . . . closed the door, which

---

[27] [n.1] A capias is a writ of attachment commanding a county official to bring a subpoenaed witness who has failed to appear before the court to testify and to answer for civil contempt.

automatically locked from the inside, and wedged a piece of wood between it and the wall. . . . Pembaur refused to let them enter, claiming that the police had no legal authority to be there and requesting that they leave. . . . The Deputy Sheriffs then telephoned [Assistant Prosecutor] Whalen and informed him of the situation. Whalen conferred with County Prosecutor Leis, who told Whalen to instruct the Deputy Sheriffs to "go in and get [the witnesses]." Whalen in turn passed these instructions along to the Deputy Sheriffs [who then forcibly entered the premises].

Pembaur filed [this § 1983] action . . . against the city of Cincinnati, the County of Hamilton, . . . Assistant Prosecutor Whalen, and nine city and county police officers. . . . His theory was that, absent exigent circumstances, the Fourth Amendment prohibits police from searching an individual's home or business without a search warrant even to execute an arrest warrant for a third person. We agreed with that proposition in *Steagald v. United States*, 451 U.S. 204 (1981), decided the day after Pembaur filed this lawsuit.

The District Court . . . agreed that the entry and search of Pembaur's clinic violated the Fourth Amendment under *Steagald*, but held *Steagald* inapplicable since it was decided nearly four years after the incident occurred. Because it construed the law in . . . 1977 to permit law enforcement officials to enter the premises of third persons to serve capiases, the District Court held that the individual municipal officials were all immune under *Harlow v. Fitzgerald*.

The claims against the county and the city were dismissed on the ground that the individual officers were not acting pursuant to the kind of "official policy" that is the predicate for municipal liability under *Monell*. . . . [The Court of Appeals affirmed, holding that a single unconstitutional act cannot give rise to municipal liability.]

II

A

As we read its opinion, the Court of Appeals held that a single decision to take particular action, although made by municipal policymakers, cannot establish the kind of "official policy" required by *Monell* as a predicate to municipal liability under § 1983.[28] However, examination of the opinion in *Monell* clearly demonstrates that the Court of Appeals misinterpreted its holding.

The "official policy" requirement was intended to distinguish acts of the municipality from acts of employees of the municipality, and thereby make clear that municipal liability is limited to action for which the municipality is actually responsible. *Monell* reasoned that recovery from a municipality is limited to acts that are, properly speaking, acts "of the municipality" — that is, acts which the municipality has officially sanctioned or ordered.

With this understanding, it is plain that municipal liability may be imposed for a single decision by municipal policymakers under appropriate circumstances. No one has ever doubted, for instance, that a municipality may be liable under § 1983 for a single decision by its properly constituted legislative body — whether or not that body had taken similar action in the past or intended to do so in the future — because even a

---

[28] [n.6] The opinion below also can be read as holding that municipal liability cannot be imposed for a single incident of unconstitutional conduct by municipal employees whether or not that conduct is pursuant to municipal policy. Such a conclusion is unsupported by either the language or reasoning of *Monell*, or by any of our subsequent decisions. As we explained last Term in *Oklahoma City v. Tuttle*, 471 U.S. 808 (1985), once a municipal policy is established, "it requires only one application . . . to satisfy fully *Monell*'s requirement that a municipal corporation be held liable only for constitutional violations resulting from the municipality's official policy." The only issue before us, then, is whether petitioner satisfied *Monell*'s requirement that the tortious conduct be pursuant to "official municipal policy."

single decision by such a body unquestionably constitutes an act of official government policy. But the power to establish policy is no more the exclusive province of the legislature at the local level than at the state or national level.

Indeed, any other conclusion would be inconsistent with the principles underlying § 1983. To be sure, "official policy" often refers to formal rules or understandings — often but not always committed to writing — that are intended to, and do, establish fixed plans of action to be followed under similar circumstances consistently and over time. That was the case in *Monell* itself, which involved a written rule requiring pregnant employees to take unpaid leaves of absence before such leaves were medically necessary. However, . . . a government frequently chooses a course of action tailored to a particular situation and not intended to control decisions in later situations. If the decision to adopt that particular course of action is properly made by that government's authorized decisionmakers, it surely represents an act of official government "policy" as that term is commonly understood.

B

[N]ot every decision by municipal officers automatically subjects the municipality to § 1983 liability. Municipal liability attaches only where the decisionmaker possesses final authority to establish municipal policy with respect to the action ordered.[29] The fact that a particular official — even a policymaking official — has discretion in the exercise of particular functions does not, without more, give rise to municipal liability based on an exercise of that discretion. The official must also be responsible for establishing final government policy respecting such activity before the municipality can be held liable.[30] Authority to make municipal policy may be granted directly by a legislative enactment or may be delegated by an official who possesses such authority, and of course, whether an official had final policymaking authority is a question of state law. . . . We hold that municipal liability under § 1983 attaches where — and only where — a deliberate choice to follow a course of action is made from among various alternatives by the official or officials responsible for establishing final policy with respect to the subject matter in question.

C

[The County] argues that the County Prosecutor lacked authority to establish municipal policy respecting law enforcement practices because only the County Sheriff may establish policy respecting such practices. [The County] suggests that the County Prosecutor was merely rendering "legal advice" when he ordered the Deputy Sheriffs to "go in and get" the witnesses.

---

[29] [n.10] Section 1983 also refers to deprivations under color of a state "custom or usage," and the Court in *Monell* noted accordingly that "local governments, like every other § 1983 'person,' . . . may be sued for constitutional deprivations visited pursuant to governmental 'custom' even though such a custom has not received formal approval through the body's official decisionmaking channels." A § 1983 plaintiff thus may be able to recover from a municipality without adducing evidence of an affirmative decision by policymakers if able to prove that the challenged action was pursuant to a state "custom or usage." . . . [T]his aspect of *Monell* is not at issue in this case.

[30] [n.11] Thus, for example, the County Sheriff may have discretion to hire and fire employees without also being the county official responsible for establishing county employment policy. If this were the case, the Sheriff's decisions respecting employment would not give rise to municipal liability, although similar decisions with respect to law enforcement practices, over which the Sheriff is the official policymaker, would give rise to municipal liability. Instead, if county employment policy was set by the Board of County Commissioners, only that body's decisions would provide a basis for county liability. This would be true even if the Board left the Sheriff discretion to hire and fire employees and the Sheriff exercised that discretion in an unconstitutional manner; the decision to act unlawfully would not be a decision of the Board. However, if the Board delegated its power to establish final employment policy to the Sheriff, the Sheriff's decisions would represent county policy and could give rise to municipal liability.

We might be inclined to agree with [the county] if we thought that the Prosecutor had only rendered "legal advice." However, the Court of Appeals concluded, based upon its examination of Ohio law, that both the County Sheriff and the County Prosecutor could establish county policy under appropriate circumstances, a conclusion that we do not question here. . . . In ordering the Deputy Sheriffs to enter [Pembaur's] clinic the County Prosecutor was acting as the final decisionmaker for the county, and the county may therefore be held liable under § 1983.

JUSTICE WHITE, concurring.[31]

The forcible entry made in this case was not then illegal under federal, state, or local law. . . . Further, the county officials who had the authority to approve or disapprove such entries opted for the forceful entry, a choice that was later held to be inconsistent with the Fourth Amendment. Vesting discretion in its officers to use force and its use in this case sufficiently manifested county policy to warrant reversal of the judgment below.

This does not mean that every act of municipal officers with final authority to effect or authorize arrests and searches represents the policy of the municipality. It would be different if *Steagald* had been decided when the events at issue here occurred, if the State Constitution or statutes had forbidden forceful entries without a warrant, or if there had been a municipal ordinance to this effect. Local law enforcement officers are expected to obey the law and ordinarily swear to do so when they take office. Where the controlling law places limits on their authority, they cannot be said to have the authority to make contrary policy. Had the Sheriff or Prosecutor in this case failed to follow an existing warrant requirement, it would be absurd to say that he was nevertheless executing county policy in authorizing the forceful entry in this case and even stranger to say that the county would be liable if the Sheriff had secured a warrant and it turned out that he and the Magistrate had mistakenly thought there was probable cause for the warrant. If deliberate or mistaken acts like this, admittedly contrary to local law, expose the county to liability, it must be on the basis of respondeat superior and not because the officers' acts represent local policy.

JUSTICE POWELL, with whom THE CHIEF JUSTICE and JUSTICE REHNQUIST join, dissenting.

[Justice Powell first argued that *Steagald* should not be applied retroactively under the equitable analysis of *Chevron Oil Co. v. Huson*, 404 U.S. 97 (1971), discussed in Section B., note 2, following *Owen v. City of Independence, supra*.]

Even if *Steagald* is applied retroactively, [Pembaur] has failed to demonstrate the existence of an official policy for which Hamilton County can be liable.

The Court['s] reasoning is circular: it contends that policy is what policymakers make, and policymakers are those who have authority to make policy. . . . Thus, the Court's test for determining the existence of policy focuses only on whether a decision was made "by the official or officials responsible for establishing final policy with respect to the subject matter in question." In my view, the question whether official policy — in any normal sense of the term — has been made in a particular case is not answered by explaining who has final authority to make policy. The question here is not "could the County Prosecutor make policy?" but rather, "did he make policy?" By

---

[31] Justice O'Connor wrote a short concurring opinion agreeing with Justice White: "As the city of Cincinnati freely conceded, forcible entry of third-party property to effect an arrest was standard operating procedure in May 1977. Given that this procedure was consistent with federal, state, and local law at the time the case arose, it seems fair to infer that [the] county's policy was no different." Justice Stevens also wrote a concurring opinion arguing that "there can be no doubt that the Congress that enacted the Ku Klux Act of 1871 intended the statute to authorize a recovery in a case of this kind."

focusing on the authority granted to the official under state law, the Court's test fails to answer the key federal question presented. The Court instead turns the question into one of state law.

Today's decision finds that policy is established because a policymaking official made a decision on the telephone that was within the scope of his authority. The Court ignores the fact that no business organization or governmental unit makes binding policy decisions so cavalierly. The Court provides no mechanism for distinguishing those acts or decisions that cannot fairly be construed to create official policy from the normal process of establishing an official policy that would be followed by a responsible public entity. Thus, the Court has adopted in part what it rejected in *Monell*: local government units are now subject to respondeat superior liability, at least with respect to a certain category of employees, *i.e.*, those with final authority to make policy.

In my view, proper resolution of the question whether official policy has been formed should focus on two factors: (i) the nature of the decision reached or the action taken, and (ii) the process by which the decision was reached or the action was taken.

Focusing on the nature of the decision distinguishes between policies and mere ad hoc decisions. Such a focus also reflects the fact that most policies embody a rule of general applicability. . . . The clear implication is that policy is created when a rule is formed that applies to all similar situations — a "governing principle [or] plan."

Another factor indicating that policy has been formed is the process by which the decision at issue was reached. Formal procedures that involve, for example, voting by elected officials, prepared reports, extended deliberation, or official records indicate that the resulting decisions taken "may fairly be said to represent official policy."

Applying these factors to the instant case demonstrates that no official policy was formulated. Certainly, no rule of general applicability was adopted. . . . Nothing about the Prosecutor's response to the inquiry over the phone, nor the circumstances surrounding the response, indicates that such a rule of general applicability was formed.

CITY OF ST. LOUIS v. PRAPROTNIK
Supreme Court of the United States
485 U.S.112 (1988)

JUSTICE O'CONNOR announced the judgment of the Court and delivered an opinion, in which THE CHIEF JUSTICE, JUSTICE WHITE, and JUSTICE SCALIA join.[32]

[Praprotnik, a city employee, allegedly was laterally transferred and ultimately terminated by his immediate supervisors for exercising his First Amendment rights. At trial, the jury returned a verdict in favor of the officials who allegedly made the employment decisions affecting Praprotnik, but also rendered a verdict against their municipal employer. The Eighth Circuit affirmed the judgment against the City, concluding that the supervisors' employment decisions were final because they were not subject to de novo review by the City's Civil Service Commission.]

Two Terms ago, in *Pembaur*, we undertook to define more precisely when a decision on a single occasion may be enough to establish an unconstitutional municipal policy. Although the Court was unable to settle on a general formulation, . . . a majority of the Court agreed [on four propositions]. First, . . . municipalities may be held liable under § 1983 only for acts for which the municipality itself is actually responsible, "that is, acts which the municipality has officially sanctioned or ordered." Second, only those municipal officials who have "final policymaking authority" may by their actions subject the government to § 1983 liability. Third, whether a particular official has "final

---

[32] [Editor's note: Justice Kennedy did not participate in the case.]

policymaking authority" is a question of state law. Fourth, the challenged action must have been taken pursuant to a policy adopted by the official or officials responsible under state law for making policy in that area of the city's business.

[T]he identification of policymaking officials is not a question of federal law, and it is not a question of fact in the usual sense. The States have extremely wide latitude in determining the form that local government takes, and local preferences have led to a profusion of distinct forms. Among the many kinds of municipal corporations, political subdivisions, and special districts of all sorts, one may expect to find a rich variety of ways in which the power of government is distributed among a host of different officials and official bodies. Without attempting to canvass the numberless factual scenarios that may come to light in litigation, we can be confident that state law (which may include valid local ordinances and regulations) will always direct a court to some official or body that has the responsibility for making law or setting policy in any given area of a local government's business.

We are not, of course, predicting that state law will always speak with perfect clarity. We have no reason to suppose, however, that federal courts will face greater difficulties here than those that they routinely address in other contexts. We are also aware that there will be cases in which policymaking responsibility is shared among more than one official or body. In the case before us, for example, it appears that the Mayor and Aldermen are authorized to adopt such ordinances relating to personnel administration as are compatible with the City Charter. The Civil Service Commission, for its part, is required to "prescribe . . . rules for the administration and enforcement of the provisions of this article, and of any ordinance adopted in pursuance thereof, and not inconsistent therewith." Assuming that applicable law does not make the decisions of the Commission reviewable by the Mayor and Aldermen, or vice versa, one would have to conclude that policy decisions made either by the Mayor and Aldermen or by the Commission would be attributable to the city itself. In any event, however, a federal court would not be justified in assuming that municipal policymaking authority lies somewhere other than where the applicable law purports to put it. And certainly there can be no justification for giving a jury the discretion to determine which officials are high enough in the government that their actions can be said to represent a decision of the government itself.

As the plurality in *Pembaur* recognized, special difficulties can arise when it is contended that a municipal policymaker has delegated his policymaking authority to another official. If the mere exercise of discretion by an employee could give rise to a constitutional violation, the result would be indistinguishable from respondeat superior liability. If, however, a city's lawful policymakers could insulate the government from liability simply by delegating their policymaking authority to others, § 1983 could not serve its intended purpose. It may not be possible to draw an elegant line that will resolve this conundrum, but certain principles should provide useful guidance.

First, whatever analysis is used to identify municipal policymakers, egregious attempts by local governments to insulate themselves from liability for unconstitutional policies are precluded by a separate doctrine. Relying on the language of § 1983, the Court has long recognized that a plaintiff may be able to prove the existence of a widespread practice that, although not authorized by written law or express municipal policy, is "so permanent and well settled as to constitute a 'custom or usage' with the force of law." That principle, which has not been affected by *Monell* or subsequent cases, ensures that most deliberate municipal evasions of the Constitution will be sharply limited.

Second, as the *Pembaur* plurality recognized, the authority to make municipal policy is necessarily the authority to make final policy. When an official's discretionary decisions are constrained by policies not of that official's making, those policies, rather than the subordinate's departures from them, are the act of the municipality. Similarly, when a subordinate's decision is subject to review by the municipality's authorized policymakers, they have retained the authority to measure the official's conduct for conformance with their policies. If the authorized policymakers approve a subordinate's decision and the basis for it, their ratification would be chargeable to the municipality because their decision is final.

[Praprotnik] contends that the record can be read to establish that his supervisors [retaliated against him for exercising his First Amendment rights.] Even if one assumes that all this was true, it says nothing about the actions of those whom the law established as the makers of municipal policy in matters of personnel administration. The Mayor and Aldermen enacted no ordinance designed to retaliate against [Praprotnik] or against similarly situated employees. On the contrary, the city established an independent Civil Service Commission and empowered it to review and correct improper personnel actions. . . . [T]he Civil Service Commission never so much as hinted that retaliatory transfers or layoffs were permissible.

The Court of Appeals concluded that "appointing authorities," . . . who had the authority to initiate transfers and layoffs, were municipal "policymakers." The court based this conclusion on its findings (1) that the decisions of these employees were not individually reviewed for "substantive propriety" by higher supervisory officials; and (2) that the Civil Service Commission decided appeals from such decisions, if at all, in a circumscribed manner that gave substantial deference to the original decisionmaker.

Simply going along with discretionary decisions made by one's subordinates, however, is not a delegation to them of the authority to make policy. It is equally consistent with a presumption that the subordinates are faithfully attempting to comply with the policies that are supposed to guide them. It would be a different matter if a particular decision by a subordinate was cast in the form of a policy statement and expressly approved by the supervising policymaker. It would also be a different matter if a series of decisions by a subordinate official manifested a "custom or usage" of which the supervisor must have been aware. In both those cases, the supervisor could realistically be deemed to have adopted a policy that happened to have been formulated or initiated by a lower-ranking official. But the mere failure to investigate the basis of a subordinate's discretionary decisions does not amount to a delegation of policymaking authority, especially where (as here) the wrongfulness of the subordinate's decision arises from a retaliatory motive or other unstated rationale.

We nowhere say or imply . . . that "a municipal charter's precatory admonition against discrimination or any other employment practice not based on merit and fitness effectively insulates the municipality from any liability based on acts inconsistent with that policy." Rather, we would respect the decisions, embodied in state and local law, that allocate policymaking authority among particular individuals and bodies. Refusals to carry out stated policies could obviously help to show that a municipality's actual policies were different from the ones that had been announced. If such a showing were made, we would be confronted with a different case than the one we decide today.

Nor do we believe that we have left a "gaping hole" in § 1983 that needs to be filled with the vague concept of "de facto final policymaking authority." Except perhaps as a step towards overruling *Monell* and adopting the doctrine of respondeat superior, ad hoc searches for officials possessing such "de facto" authority would serve primarily to foster needless unpredictability in the application of § 1983.[33]

---

[33] [Editor's note: Justice O'Connor found it unnecessary to decide whether the First Amendment was violated, whether there was sufficient evidence in the record to support Praprotnik's claims, or whether "the jury verdict exonerating the individual defendants" could be "reconciled with the verdict against the city." She instead remanded the case to Eighth Circuit for further proceedings. This last issue — whether the jury's verdict against the city but in favor of its officials could be reconciled — is the subject of *City of Los Angeles v. Heller*, which appears in Section D., *infra*.]

JUSTICE BRENNAN, with whom JUSTICE MARSHALL and JUSTICE BLACKMUN join, concurring in the judgment.

In my view, *Pembaur* controls this case. As an "appointing authority," [the supervisor] was empowered under the City Charter to initiate [employment decisions] such as the one challenged here, subject to the approval of both the Director of Personnel and the appointing authority of the . . . agency. The Charter, however, nowhere confers upon agency heads any authority to establish city policy, final or otherwise, with respect to such [decisions]. . . . Instead, the evidence discloses but one . . . decision — the one involving [Praprotnik] — which [his supervisor] ostensibly undertook pursuant to a citywide program of fiscal restraint and budgetary reductions. At most, then, the record demonstrates that [the supervisor] had the authority to determine how best to effectuate a policy announced by his superiors, rather than the power to establish that policy. Like the hypothetical Sheriff in *Pembaur* . . . , [the supervisor] had discretionary authority to [make personnel decisions]; that he may have used this authority to punish [Praprotnik] for the exercise of his First Amendment rights does not, without more, render the city liable for [Praprotnik's] resulting constitutional injury.[34]

These determinations, it seems to me, are sufficient to dispose of this case, and I therefore think it unnecessary to decide, as the plurality does, who the actual policymakers in St. Louis are.

In any case in which the policymaking authority of a municipal tortfeasor is in doubt, state law will naturally be the appropriate starting point, but ultimately the factfinder must determine where such policymaking authority actually resides, and not simply "where the applicable law purports to put it." . . . [A]lthough I agree with the plurality that juries should not be given open-ended "discretion to determine which officials are high enough in the government that their actions can be said to represent a decision of the government itself," juries can and must find the predicate facts necessary to a determination whether a given official possesses final policymaking authority. While the jury instructions in this case were regrettably vague, the plurality's solution tosses the baby out with the bath water. The identification of municipal policymakers is an essentially factual determination "in the usual sense," and is therefore rightly entrusted to a properly instructed jury.

Nor does the "custom or usage" doctrine adequately compensate for the inherent inflexibility of a rule that leaves the identification of policymakers exclusively to state statutory law. That doctrine, under which municipalities and States can be held liable for unconstitutional practices so well settled and permanent that they have the force of law, has little if any bearing on the question whether a city has delegated de facto final policymaking authority to a given official. A city practice of delegating final policymaking authority to a subordinate or mid-level official would not be unconstitutional in and of itself, and an isolated unconstitutional act by an official entrusted with such authority would obviously not amount to a municipal "custom or usage." Under *Pembaur*, of course, such an isolated act should give rise to municipal liability. Yet a case such as this would fall through the gaping hole the plurality's construction leaves in § 1983, because state statutory law would not identify the municipal actor as a policymaking official, and a single constitutional deprivation, by definition, is not a well-settled and permanent municipal practice carrying the force of law.

---

[34] [n.4] While the Court of Appeals erred to the extent it equated the authority to act on behalf of a city with the power to establish municipal policy, in my view the lower court quite correctly concluded that the CSC's highly circumscribed and deferential review of [the supervisor's] decisions in no way rendered those decisions less than final. Moreover, the facts of this case reveal that the CSC believed it lacked the authority to review lateral transfers. Accordingly, had [the supervisor] actually possessed policymaking authority with respect to such decisions, I would have little difficulty concluding that such authority was final.

For these same reasons, I cannot subscribe to the plurality's narrow and overly rigid view of when a municipal official's policymaking authority is "final." Attempting to place a gloss on *Pembaur*'s finality requirement, the plurality suggests that whenever the decisions of an official are subject to some form of review — however limited — that official's decisions are nonfinal. Under the plurality's theory, therefore, even where an official wields policymaking authority with respect to a challenged decision, the city would not be liable for that official's policy decision unless reviewing officials affirmatively approved both the "decision and the basis for it." Reviewing officials, however, may as a matter of practice never invoke their plenary oversight authority, or their review powers may be highly circumscribed. Under such circumstances, the subordinate's decision is in effect the final municipal pronouncement on the subject. Certainly a § 1983 plaintiff is entitled to place such considerations before the jury, for the law is concerned not with the niceties of legislative draftsmanship but with the realities of municipal decisionmaking, and any assessment of a municipality's actual power structure is necessarily a factual and practical one.

Finally, I think it necessary to emphasize that despite certain language in the plurality opinion suggesting otherwise, the Court today need not and therefore does not decide that a city can only be held liable under § 1983 where the plaintiff "prove[s] the existence of an unconstitutional municipal policy." Just last Term, we left open for the second time the question whether a city can be subjected to liability for a policy that, while not unconstitutional in and of itself, may give rise to constitutional deprivations. *See Springfield v. Kibbe*, 480 U.S. 257 (1987). That question is certainly not presented by this case, and nothing we say today forecloses its future consideration.

JUSTICE STEVENS, dissenting.

I believe that affirmance is required by this Court's precedents.[35] In *Monell* we held that municipal corporations are "persons" within the meaning of 42 U.S.C. § 1983. Since a corporation is incapable of doing anything except through the agency of human beings, that holding necessarily gave rise to the question of what human activity undertaken by agents of the corporation may create municipal liability in § 1983 litigation.[36] Both *Pembaur* and the plurality and concurring opinions today acknowledge that a high official who has ultimate control over a certain area of city government can bind the city through his unconstitutional actions even though those actions are not in the form of formal rules or regulations. Although the Court has explained its holdings by reference to the nonstatutory term "policy," it plainly has not embraced the standard understanding of that word as covering a rule of general applicability. Instead it has used that term to include isolated acts not intended to be binding over a class of situations. But when one remembers that the real question in cases such as this is not "what constitutes city policy?" but rather "when should a city be liable for the acts of its agents?", the inclusion of single acts by high officials makes sense, for those acts bind a municipality in a way that the misdeeds of low officials do not.

---

[35] [n.1] This would, of course, be an easy case if the Court disavowed its dicta in Part II of the opinion in *Monell*. Like many commentators who have confronted the question, I remain convinced that Congress intended the doctrine of respondeat superior to apply in § 1983 litigation. Given the Court's reiteration of the contrary ipse dixit in *Monell* and subsequent opinions, however, I shall join the Court's attempt to draw an intelligible boundary between municipal agents' actions that bind and those that do not.

[36] [n.19] The "theme" of *Monell* — "that some basis for government liability other than vicarious liability for the acts of individuals must be found" — has proved to be a "difficult" one largely because "there is no obvious way to distinguish the acts of a municipality from the acts of the individuals whom it employs." In other words, every time a municipality is held liable in tort, even in a case like *Monell*, actions of its human agents are necessarily involved. Accordingly, our task is not to draw a line between the actions of the city and the actions of its employees, but rather to develop a principle for determining which human acts should bind a municipality.

Every act of a high official constitutes a kind of "statement" about how similar decisions will be carried out; the assumption is that the same decision would have been made, and would again be made, across a class of cases. Lower officials do not control others in the same way. Since their actions do not dictate the responses of various subordinates, those actions lack the potential of controlling governmental decisionmaking; they are not perceived as the actions of the city itself. If a County police officer had broken down Dr. Pembaur's door on the officer's own initiative, this would have been seen as the action of an overanxious officer, and would not have sent a message to other officers that similar actions would be countenanced. One reason for this is that the County Prosecutor himself could step forward and say "that was wrong"; when the County Prosecutor authorized the action himself, only a self-correction would accomplish the same task, and until such time his action would have countywide ramifications. Here, the Mayor, those working for him, and the agency heads are high-ranking officials; accordingly, we must assume that their actions have citywide ramifications, both through their similar response to a like class of situations, and through the response of subordinates who follow their lead.

[H]olding St. Louis liable in this case is supported by both *Pembaur* and *Owen*. We hold a municipality liable for the decisions of its high officials in large part because those decisions, by definition, would be applied across a class of cases. Just as we assume in *Pembaur* that the County Prosecutor (or his subordinates) would issue the same break-down-the-door order in similar cases, and just as we assume in *Owen* that the City Council (or those following its lead) would fire an employee without notice of reasons or opportunity to be heard in similar cases, so too must we assume that whistleblowers like [Praprotnik] would be dealt with in similar retaliatory fashion if they offend the Mayor, his staff, and relevant agency heads, or if they offend those lower ranking officials who follow the example of their superiors.

NOTES

1. *Praprotnik* on Remand. Justice O'Connor concluded that remand to the Eighth Circuit was necessary in *Praprotnik* so that the lower courts could apply the correct legal standard. On remand, the Eighth Circuit concluded that "the supervisors responsible for Praprotnik's transfer and layoff . . . were not vested with final policymaking authority for making municipal policy in the area of personnel administration and layoffs. At most, these officials were entrusted with the authority for making discretionary personnel decisions in their departments. . . . [I]t appears that the Commission possesses primary policymaking authority for making general personnel policy and for making final decisions as to individual employees. Its decisions in these respects can fairly be said to be decisions of the city. The mayor and aldermen's policymaking authority, on the other hand, appears to be limited to personnel matters of a more broad, all-encompassing nature (e.g., compensation rates, retirement plans, department appropriations). As a general rule, decisions of the mayor and aldermen which specifically address and adversely affect individual employees are not 'final' for purposes of § 1983 because those decisions are subject to review by the Commission." *Praprotnik*, 879 F.2d 1573 (8th Cir. 1989).

2. Conduct Subject to Review. *Pembaur* and *Praprotnik* make clear that an ad hoc unconstitutional decision can be a "custom or policy" within the meaning of *Monell*. The question is whether the conduct is that of, or is directly caused by, a "policymaker" with "final authority." Both *Pembaur* and *Praprotnik* deny that the mere delegation of discretionary power to a governmental official will make that official a "final" authority. The plurality in *Praprotnik* took this one step farther and held that an official's action is not final so long as it is subject to review, even when review is of a limited nature. In light of this development, would a county be wise to adopt the following policy: "All decisions of any and all employees and agents of the municipality are subject to review by the County Commission"? Would this insulate the county from liability for decisions made by anyone other than the county commissioners?

3. Is "Final Authority" a Factual Issue? A majority of Justices in *Praprotnik* agreed that whether an official is a "final authority" is primarily a function of state law. The Court divided, however, over whether juries should play a role in resolving this issue, or whether it should be answered by judges alone. The following year, a majority in *Jett v. Dallas Independent School District*, 491 U.S. 701 (1989), concluded that "the identification of those officials whose decisions represent the official policy of the local governmental unit is itself a legal question to be resolved by the trial judge before the case is submitted to the jury." The trial judge should "[r]eview[] the relevant legal materials, including state and local positive law, as well as 'custom or usage having the force of law,' [to] . . . identify those officials or governmental bodies who speak with final policymaking authority."

4. Clearly Established Constitutional Law. Justice White's concurring opinion in *Pembaur* states that where federal law clearly renders certain acts illegal, no local official — no matter how high in the chain of command — can authorize subordinates' violations. If *Steagald*, for example, had been decided before the deputies broke down Pembaur's office door, Justice White would not have held the County liable for its Prosecutor's directions. Hence, local government under Justice White's proposal would *not* be liable when federal law clearly prohibited the conduct at issue. Is this position consistent with the Court's rejection of qualified immunity for municipalities in *Owen* (an opinion that Justice White joined)? In *Owen* the city argued that it could only be held liable when federal law was clearly established at the time of the wrong.

5. Retaliation in Public-Sector Employment. Justice Brennan's plurality opinion in *Pembaur* hypothesized that had the "County Sheriff [been granted] discretion to hire and fire employees without also being the county official responsible for establishing county employment policy . . . the Sheriff's decisions respecting employment would not give rise to municipal liability, although similar decisions with respect to law enforcement practices, over which the Sheriff is the official policymaker, would. . . . " "[I]f county employment policy was set by the Board of County Commissioners, only that body's decisions would provide a basis for county liability. This would be true even if the Board left the Sheriff discretion to hire and fire employees and the Sheriff exercised that discretion in an unconstitutional manner. . . . " *See* footnote 11 in *Pembaur, supra*. Because of this footnote and Justice O'Connor's plurality opinion in *Praprotnik*, lower courts have often rejected § 1983 retaliation claims — whether based on speech, race or gender — brought against municipalities. *See, e.g., Davison v. City of Minneapolis*, 490 F.3d 648 (8th Cir. 2007) (holding that the City was not liable for its Fire Chief's First Amendment violation even though the Chief "had the authority to select particular individuals for promotion and even to design the procedures governing promotions within his department"); *Beattie v. Madison County School District*, 254 F.3d 595 (5th Cir. 2001) (finding that retaliation by a school superintendent would not result in a school district's liability because the board had authority to review the superintendent's personnel decisions); *Jett v. Dallas Independent School District*, 7 F.3d 1241 (5th Cir. 1994) (holding that a school superintendent's retaliatory personnel decision was not that of a final authority because "[u]nder Texas law such policymaking authority rested exclusively with the [school district's] board of trustees"). *Cf. Jeffes v. Barnes*, 208 F.3d 49 (2d Cir. 2000) (where a code of silence was imposed by sheriff and retaliation went "far beyond . . . routine classes of personnel actions within the domain of a civil service commission," the sheriff was treated as a final authority even though the civil service commission technically had power to review the sheriff's decisions).

6. Custom. *Praprotnik*'s various opinions leave open the possibility that municipal liability for retaliation in public-sector employment can be based on municipal custom as well as the final authority analysis. "Showing a 'longstanding practice or custom which constitutes the "standard operating procedure" of the local government entity' is one way to establish municipal liability." *Ulrich v. City and County of San Francisco*, 308 F.3d 968 (9th Cir. 2002). Hence, the fact that a retaliatory personnel decision is not formally rendered by a recognized final authority, such as a Civil Service Commission, does not mean that a municipality necessarily escapes liability. A pattern of similar incidents can be used to prove a municipal custom of wrongdoing. *See, e.g., Baron v. Suffolk County Sheriff's Department*, 402 F.3d 225 (1st Cir. 2005) (finding a municipal "custom" of retaliation against deputies who spoke out against — or "ratted" on — other deputies); *Garza v. City of Omaha*, 814 F.3d 553 (8th Cir. 1987) (finding municipal liability where a supervisors' retaliation amounted to a custom spread out over a number of years); *see also City of Canton v. Harris*, 489 U.S. 378 (1989) (O'Connor, J., concurring and dissenting) (observing that a city could be liable for deliberate indifference where "policymakers were aware of, and acquiesced in, a pattern of constitutional violations involving the exercise of police discretion") (excerpted in Section C.[2], *infra*); *Jett v. Dallas Independent School District*, 491 U.S. 701 (1989) (observing that a municipality is not liable where "there is no evidence that [the school superintendent's] decision . . . 'manifested a "custom or usage" of which the' [school] board 'must have been aware' "). Professor Myriam Gilles has lamented, however, that these "custom" claims have not been overly successful in the lower courts. Myriam E. Gilles, *Breaking the Code of Silence: Rediscovering "Custom" in Section 1983 Municipal Liability*, 80 B.U. L. REV. 17, 61 (2001) (reporting that few custom cases have proved successful).

7. Ratification. Lower courts have also found municipal liability where policymakers ratify subordinates' unconstitutional personnel decisions. For example, in *Ulrich v. City and County of San Francisco*, 308 F.3d 968 (9th Cir. 2002), the Ninth Circuit concluded that even if a hospital administrator responsible for retaliating against a physician (Dr. Ulrich) was not a final authority within the meaning of *Praprotnik*, the municipality could still be held liable if the administrator's "decisions were ratified by officials with final policymaking authority." "It may . . . be possible to infer from [the administrator's] consultations with Dr. Welch and others about her decision . . . that her actions were ratified by policymaking officials." *See also Jett v. Dallas Independent School District*, 491 U.S. 701 (1989) (observing that a school district could be found liable if its superintendent's retaliatory decision "was cast in the form of a policy statement and expressly approved by the [school] board"); Jack C. Hanssen, Note, *Municipal Liability Under 42 U.S.C. § 1983 and the Ratification Theory of City of St. Louis v. Praprotnik: An Analysis of Federal Court Treatment*, 27 J. LEGIS. 361, 367 (2001) ("all circuits agree that if there is evidence that the reviewing final policymaker ratified the subordinate's decision and the basis for it prior to the infliction of the injury or contemporaneously with the infliction, the municipality may incur § 1983 liability"). What the lower court have not agreed upon, however, is what "ratification" requires. Most courts demand more than simple review or consideration; rather, they require that the policymakers embrace the retaliatory reason. *Id.*

8. Decisions Made by Councils, Commissions and Boards. What must a § 1983 plaintiff prove to hold a municipality liable for the actions of multi-member bodies, like commissions, boards, and councils? Is it enough to show that one of the members acted with improper animus? Must the plaintiff prove a majority acted with improper animus? In *Scarbrough v. Morgan City Board of Education*, 470 F.3d 250 (6th Cir. 2006), the plaintiff (Scarbrough) alleged that a School Board retaliated against him based on his speech. He could only prove, however, that three of the seven board members acted with the improper motive. Because two additional members supported Scarbrough, the court still concluded that the improper motive shared by these three board members could have changed the outcome and thus could support municipal liability:

> Circuits are split on how to determine if a board, as opposed to its individual members, acts with improper motive. The Second, Third, and Ninth Circuits have implied that a board is liable for actions that it would not have taken "but for" members acting with improper motive. *See LaVerdue v. County of Montgomery*, 324 F.3d 123 (3d Cir. 2003) (no municipal liability because board

voted unanimously and only one member had improper motive); *Jeffries v. Harleston*, 52 F.3d 9 (2d Cir. 1995) ("[T]he nine votes based on legitimate grounds constitute a superseding cause breaking the causal chain between the tainted motives . . . and the decision"); *Kawaoka v. City of Arroyo Grande*, 17 F.3d 1227 (9th Cir. 1994) (no municipal liability because board acted unanimously and only one member had improper motive). Thus, where improperly motivated members supply the deciding margin, the board itself is liable.

Applying the "but for" approach here, Scarbrough has submitted enough evidence to hold the Board itself liable. He has submitted evidence showing [three] voted with improper motivation. The Board would not have taken the action it did were it not for their votes. Thus, the Board is not entitled to summary judgment on this issue.[37]

9. Law Enforcement. As demonstrated in *Pembaur*, law enforcement decisions are rarely made by commissions, boards, or councils. They are ordinarily made either by police officers on the scene, by supervisors, by chiefs and sheriffs, or on occasion (as in *Pembaur*) by prosecutors. Lower courts following *Pembaur* and *Praprotnik* often held municipalities liable for law enforcement decisions made or directed by local chiefs of police and county sheriffs. *See, e.g., Dotson v. Chester*, 937 F.2d 920 (4th Cir. 1991) (holding that a Maryland sheriff was a county's final authority for purposes of prison conditions); *Turner v. Upton County*, 915 F.2d 133 (5th Cir. 1990) (finding that a Texas sheriff was a county's final authority for law enforcement purposes); *cf. Weber v. Dell*, 804 F.2d 796 (2d Cir. 1986) (holding that a New York sheriff was a county's final authority even for personnel decisions). Is it always clear, however, that sheriffs work for counties? What if the sheriff works for the state?

McMILLIAN v. MONROE COUNTY
Supreme Court of the United States
520 U.S. 781 (1997)

CHIEF JUSTICE REHNQUIST delivered the opinion of the Court.

[McMillian was convicted of capital murder and spent six years in prison based on false evidence allegedly manufactured by Tate, the Sheriff of Monroe County, Alabama. Following the reversal of his conviction by the Alabama Court of Criminal Appeals, McMillian brought suit under § 1983 against the Sheriff of Monroe County, acting in his official capacity, for damages.]

If the sheriff's actions constitute county "policy," then the county is liable for them. The parties agree that the sheriff is a "policymaker" for § 1983 purposes, but they disagree about whether he is a policymaker for Monroe County or for the State of Alabama.

In deciding this dispute, our inquiry is guided by two principles. First, the question is not whether Sheriff Tate acts for Alabama or Monroe County in some categorical, "all or nothing" manner. Our cases on the liability of local governments under § 1983 instruct us to ask whether governmental officials are final policymakers for the local government in a particular area, or on a particular issue. Thus, we are not seeking to make a characterization of Alabama sheriffs that will hold true for every type of official

---

[37] The Sixth Circuit rejected the approach taken in *Scott-Harris v. City of Fall River*, 134 F.3d 427 (1st Cir. 1997), *rev'd on other grounds sub nom. Bogan v. Scott-Harris*, 523 U.S. 44 (1998) (excerpted in Chapter 2.A.[1], *supra*). The Sixth Circuit reasoned that in *Scott-Harris*, "board liability only existed where the plaintiff established both: '(a) bad motive on the part of at least a significant block of legislators, and (b) circumstances suggesting the probable complicity of others.' That approach would be difficult to apply, because it leaves many questions unanswered. Among the most important of these is what constitutes a 'significant bloc of legislators' or 'circumstances suggesting the probable complicity of others.'" Note that individual board or commission members can be cloaked with absolute legislative immunity. *See* Chaper 2.A.[1], *supra*.

action they engage in. We simply ask whether Sheriff Tate represents the State or the county when he acts in a law enforcement capacity.

Second, our inquiry is dependent on an analysis of state law. This is not to say that state law can answer the question for us by, for example, simply labeling as a state official an official who clearly makes county policy. But our understanding of the actual function of a governmental official, in a particular area, will necessarily be dependent on the definition of the official's functions under relevant state law.

We begin with the Alabama Constitution, "the supreme law of the state." We agree with the Court of Appeals[38] that the constitutional provisions concerning sheriffs, the historical development of those provisions, and the interpretation given them by the Alabama Supreme Court strongly support Monroe County's contention that sheriffs represent the State, at least for some purposes. Alabama's Constitution, adopted in 1901, states that "[t]he executive department shall consist of a governor, lieutenant governor, attorney-general, state auditor, secretary of state, state treasurer, superintendent of education, commissioner of agriculture and industries, and a sheriff for each county." This designation is especially important for our purposes, because although every Alabama Constitution has included sheriffs as constitutional officers and has provided for their election by county voters, sheriffs have not always been explicitly listed as members of the state "executive department." Thus, the 1867 Constitution listed only the "governor, lieutenant governor, secretary of state, auditor, treasurer, and attorney general" as constituting "the executive department." This changed with the 1875 Constitution, when sheriffs and the superintendent of education were added to the list.

The framers of the 1901 Constitution took two significant steps in an attempt to solidify the place of sheriffs in the executive department, and to clarify that sheriffs were acting for the State when exercising their law enforcement functions. First, faced with reports that sheriffs were allowing mobs to abduct prisoners and lynch them, the framers made such "neglect" by sheriffs an impeachable offense.

Second, authority to impeach sheriffs was moved from the county courts to the State Supreme Court, because of "[t]he failure of county courts to punish sheriffs for neglect of duty." One of the primary purposes of this change, proposed by ex-Governor Thomas Goode Jones at the 1901 Convention, was "to augment the power of the Governor." After this change, the Governor could order the State Supreme Court, rather than the county court, to begin impeachment proceedings against a wayward sheriff, and would not have to worry that local support for the sheriff would annul his effort at centralized control. Thus, sheriffs now share the same impeachment procedures as state legal officers and lower state court judges, rather than county and municipal officers.

Critically for our case, [an] Alabama Supreme Court [opinion] has interpreted these provisions and their historical background as evidence of "the framers' intent to ensure that sheriffs be considered executive officers of the state." Based primarily on this understanding of the State Constitution, the court [in that case] held unequivocally that sheriffs are state officers, and that tort claims brought against sheriffs based on their official acts therefore constitute suits against the State, not suits against the sheriff's county.[39] Thus, Alabama counties are not liable under a theory of respondeat superior for a sheriff's official acts that are tortious. . . . The [Alabama Supreme Court's] . . . decision is . . . strong evidence . . . that sheriffs act on behalf of the State, rather than the county, when acting in their law enforcement capacity.

---

[38] [Editor's note: The Chief Justice observed that "[s]ince the jurisdiction of the Court of Appeals includes Alabama, we defer considerably to that court's expertise in interpreting Alabama law."]

[39] [n.5] As a result of this holding and the State Constitution's sovereign immunity provision, the Alabama Supreme Court has held that a sheriff is absolutely immune from all suits for damages based on his official acts.

Turning from the Alabama Constitution to the Alabama Code, the relevant provisions are less compelling, but still support th[is] conclusion . . . to some extent. . . . First, a sheriff must "attend upon" the state courts in his county, must "obey the lawful orders and directions" of those courts, and must "execute and return the process and orders" of any state court, even those outside his county. Thus, judges (who are state officers) may order the sheriff to take certain actions, even if the judge sits in a distant county. And . . . the presiding circuit judge "exercise[s] a general supervision" over the county sheriffs in his circuit,[40] just as if the sheriffs are normal "court [i.e., state] employees."

Second, the sheriff must give to the county treasurer a sworn written statement detailing the funds he has received for the county since his last statement, and must pay these funds to the treasurer. In contrast to the state judges, however, the county treasurer does not appear to have any statutory authority to direct the sheriff to take specific actions.

Third and most importantly, "[i]t shall be the duty of sheriffs in their respective counties, by themselves or deputies, to ferret out crime, to apprehend and arrest criminals and, insofar as within their power, to secure evidence of crimes in their counties and to present a report of the evidence so secured to the district attorney or assistant district attorney for the county." By this mandate, sheriffs are given complete authority to enforce the state criminal law in their counties. In contrast, the "powers and duties" of the counties themselves — creatures of the State who have only the powers granted to them by the State — do not include any provision in the area of law enforcement. Thus, the "governing body" of the counties — which in every Alabama county is the county commission — cannot instruct the sheriff how to ferret out crime, how to arrest a criminal, or how to secure evidence of a crime. And when the sheriff does secure such evidence, he has an obligation to share this information not with the county commission, but with the district attorney (a state official).

While the county commission thus has no direct control over how the sheriff fulfills his law enforcement duty, the Governor and the attorney general do have this kind of control. [T]hey can direct the sheriff to investigate "any alleged violation of law in their counties." And after "proceed[ing] promptly" to complete this investigation, the sheriff must "promptly" write a report to the state official in charge of the investigation, stating his findings, listing the witnesses he has secured, and summarizing what the witnesses can prove. In addition, the salaries of all sheriffs are set by the state legislature, not by the county commissions.

To all of this, [McMillian] counters with four important provisions that cut in favor of the conclusion that sheriffs are county officials. First, the sheriff's salary is paid "out of the county treasury." Second, the county provides the sheriff with equipment (including cruisers), supplies, lodging, and reimbursement for expenses, to the extent "reasonably needed for the proper and efficient conduct of the affairs of the sheriff's office." Third, the sheriff's jurisdiction is limited to the borders of his county. Fourth, the sheriff is elected locally by the voters in his county (as he has been since Alabama's 1819 Constitution).

We do not find these provisions sufficient to tip the balance in favor of [McMillian]. The county's payment of the sheriff's salary does not translate into control over him, since the county neither has the authority to change his salary nor the discretion to refuse payment completely. The county commissions do appear to have the discretion to deny funds to the sheriffs for their operations beyond what is "reasonably necessary." But at most, this discretion would allow the commission to exert an attenuated and indirect influence over the sheriff's operations.

---

[40] [n.6] Seventeen of the forty judicial circuits in Alabama contain more than one county, including the circuit in which Monroe County sits.

[McMillian's] contention that sheriffs are county officials because "state policymakers" typically make policy for the entire State (without limits on their jurisdiction) and are typically elected on a statewide (not local) basis, surely has some force. But district attorneys and state judges are often considered (and in Alabama are considered) state officials, even though they, too, have limited jurisdictions and are elected locally. These characteristics are therefore consistent with an understanding of the 67 Alabama sheriffs as state officials who have been locally placed throughout the State, with an element of control granted to the officials and residents of the county that receives the sheriff's services.

[McMillian] argues that this conclusion will create a lack of uniformity in Alabama and throughout the country. First, he argues that it is anomalous to have 67 different "state policymakers" in the person of Alabama's 67 county sheriffs, all of whom may have different "state law enforcement policies" in their counties. Second, he points out that most Federal Courts of Appeals have found county sheriffs to be county, not state, officials, and he implies that our affirmance of the Court of Appeals will either call those decisions into question or create an unacceptable patchwork of rulings as to § 1983 liability of counties for the acts of their sheriffs. We reject both arguments: The first ignores the history of sheriffs, and the second ignores our Nation's federal nature. English sheriffs (or "shire-reeves") were the King's "reeves" (officers or agents) in the "shires" (counties), at least after the Norman Conquest in 1066.

As the basic forms of English government were transplanted in our country, it also became the common understanding here that the sheriff, though limited in jurisdiction to his county and generally elected by county voters, was in reality an officer of the State, and ultimately represented the State in fulfilling his duty to keep the peace.

This historical sketch indicates that the common law itself envisioned the possibility that state law enforcement "policies" might vary locally, as particular sheriffs adopted varying practices for arresting criminals or securing evidence. Thus, [McMillian's] disagreement with the concept that "county sheriffs" may actually be state officials is simply a disagreement with the ancient understanding of what it has meant to be a sheriff.

[McMillian's] second concern is that under our holding here, sheriffs will be characterized differently in different States. But while it might be easier to decide cases arising under § 1983 and *Monell* if we insisted on a uniform, national characterization for all sheriffs, such a blunderbuss approach would ignore a crucial axiom of our government: the States have wide authority to set up their state and local governments as they wish. Understandably, then, the importance of counties and the nature of county government have varied historically from region to region, and from State to State.

The final concern of [McMillian] and his *amici* is that state and local governments will manipulate the titles of local officials in a blatant effort to shield the local governments from liability. But such efforts are already foreclosed by our decision in *Praprotnik* ("[E]gregious attempts by local governments to insulate themselves from liability for unconstitutional policies are precluded" by allowing plaintiffs to prove that "a widespread practice" has been established by " 'custom or usage' with the force of law"). And there is certainly no evidence of such manipulation here; indeed, the Alabama provisions that cut most strongly against petitioner's position predate our decision in *Monell* by some time.

JUSTICE GINSBURG, with whom JUSTICE STEVENS, JUSTICE SOUTER, and JUSTICE BREYER join, dissenting.

Alabama has 67 county sheriffs, each elected, paid, and equipped locally, each with countywide, not statewide, authority. Unlike judges who work within the State's judicial hierarchy, or prosecutors who belong to a prosecutorial corps superintended by the State's Attorney General, sheriffs are not part of a state command and serve under no "State Sheriff General."

Alabama law does not consistently designate sheriffs as "executive department" officers; instead, Alabama law in several instances refers to sheriffs as county officials. Moreover, designations Alabama attaches to sheriffs in its laws and decisions are not dispositive of a court's assessment of Sheriff Tate's status for § 1983 purposes. If a State's designation sufficed to answer the federal question at issue, "States would then be free to nullify for their own people the legislative decisions that Congress has made on behalf of all the People." Nor are the 1901 impeachment measures secure indicators that a sheriff acts on behalf of the State, not the county. As the Court explains, the impeachment amendments were intended to provide a state check on county sheriffs in view of their glaring lapses in acquiescing to abductions and lynchings in the late 1800's. However, making an officer eligible for impeachment, by itself, does not change the governmental unit to which the officer belongs. And transferring impeachment proceedings from county courts to the State Supreme Court is sensibly seen as an acknowledgment of the power wielded by sheriffs within their own counties, and the consequent need for placement of removal authority outside a sheriff's bailiwick. Furthermore, impeachment of sheriffs is not a power reserved exclusively to state officials; "five resident taxpayers" of the sheriff's county can initiate an impeachment. Impeachment, in sum, provides an ultimate check on flagrant behavior, but does not serve as a tight control rein.

The prime controllers of a sheriff's service are the county residents, the people who select their sheriff at quadrennial elections. Sheriff Tate owes his position as chief law enforcement officer of Monroe County to the county residents who elected him, and who can unseat him. On the ballot, candidates for the office of sheriff are grouped with candidates for other county offices, and are not listed with state office candidates. Traditionally, Alabama sheriffs have had autonomy to formulate and execute law enforcement policy within the geographic confines of their counties. Under Alabama law, "[i]t shall be the duty of sheriffs in their respective counties . . . to ferret out crime, to apprehend and arrest criminals and . . . to secure evidence of crimes."

Monroe County pays Sheriff Tate's salary, and the sheriff operates out of an office provided, furnished, and equipped by the county. The obligation to fully equip the sheriff is substantial, requiring a county commission to furnish the sheriff with the necessary quarters, books, stationery, office equipment, supplies, postage and other conveniences and equipment, including automobiles and necessary repairs, maintenance and all expenses incidental thereto." These obligations are of practical importance, for they mean that purse strings can be pulled at the county level; a county is obliged to provide a sheriff only what is "reasonably needed for the proper and efficient conduct of the affairs of the sheriff's office." How generously the sheriff will be equipped is likely to influence that officer's day-to-day conduct to a greater extent than the remote prospect of impeachment.

Sheriff Tate, in short, is in vital respects a county official. Indeed, one would be hard pressed to think of a single official who more completely represents the exercise of significant power within a county.[41]

If the Court means to suggest that Sheriff Tate should be classified as a state actor because he is enforcing state (as opposed to county or municipal) law, the Court proves far too much. Because most criminal laws are of statewide application, relying on whose law the sheriff enforces yields an all-state categorization of sheriffs, despite the Court's recognition that such blanket classification is inappropriate.

---

[41] [n.2] The majority of Courts of Appeals to have addressed this question have similarly concluded that sheriffs, when engaged in a variety of activities, are county actors.

The Court also suggests that because the Governor can direct a sheriff to investigate a violation of law in the county, an Alabama sheriff must be a state, not a county, official. It is worth noting that a group of county citizens can likewise trigger an investigation by the sheriff. . . . Monroe County did not inform us whether the Governor directs county sheriffs to conduct investigations with any regularity. More important, there is no suggestion that Sheriff Tate was proceeding under the Governor's direction when Tate pursued the investigation that led to McMillian's Death Row confinement. If Sheriff Tate were acting on instruction from the Governor, this would be a very different case. But the bare possibility that a Governor might sometime direct a sheriff's law enforcement activities does not lessen the sheriff's authority, as the final county policymaker, in the general run of investigations the sheriff undertakes.

The Court's reliance on "the ancient understanding of what it has meant to be a sheriff" is no more persuasive than its interpretation of Alabama law. This emphasis on the historical understanding of the office of sheriff implies, again, an all-state categorization of sheriffs throughout the Nation; but because the Court expressly disclaims such a "blunderbuss" approach, that cannot be what this history lesson is intended to convey. In England, it is true, the sheriff did perform "the king's business in the county." But the English sheriff, as Blackstone described him, was far closer to the crown than his contemporary counterpart is to the central state government. While sheriffs were for a time chosen locally, "[t]his election," according to Blackstone, "was in all probability not absolutely vested in the [inhabitants of the counties], but required the royal approbation." Eventually, the king chose the sheriff from a list proposed by the judges and other great officers.

Whatever English history may teach, "[t]hroughout U.S. history, the sheriff has remained the principal law enforcement officer in the county." In the United States, "[i]n order to reserve control over the sheriff's department and its police functions, the people made the sheriff an elective officer." It is this status as the county's law enforcement officer chosen by the county's residents that is at the root of the contemporary understanding of the sheriff as a county officer.

The Court's Alabama-specific approach . . . assures that today's immediate holding is of limited reach. The Court does not appear to question that an Alabama sheriff may still be a county policymaker for some purposes, such as hiring the county's chief jailor. And, as the Court acknowledges, under its approach sheriffs may be policymakers for certain purposes in some States and not in others. The Court's opinion does not call into question the numerous Court of Appeals decisions, some of them decades old, ranking sheriffs as county, not state, policymakers. Furthermore, the Court's recognition of the historic reasons why Alabama listed sheriffs as members of the State's "executive department" should discourage endeavors to insulate counties and municipalities from *Monell* liability by change-the-label devices. Thus, the Court's opinion, while in my view misguided, does little to alter § 1983 county and municipal liability in most jurisdictions.

NOTES

1. Can a State Convert All Local Officials into State Employees? Remember that the final authority analysis relies on state law for answers. Can a state convert all local officials into state employees by simply amending its constitution? Is it sufficient to simply pass a law asserting that local actors are state employees? How important is the fact that the Alabama Constitution antedated *Monroe* and *Monell*? Can a state convert cities and counties into state agencies? Does *McMillian* vastly expand the scope of Eleventh Amendment immunity? See Chapter 3.A., *supra*.

2. *McMillian*'s Functional Analysis. As the majority in *McMillian* makes clear, whether an official works for the state or a local governmental entity is not an all-or-nothing issue. It varies not only between states, but also between functions. A sheriff might be deemed a state official when engaged in law enforcement, *see, e.g., McMillian*, but a local official when administering jails. *See, e.g., Parker v. Williams*, 855 F.2d 763

(11th Cir. 1988) (holding that an Alabama sheriff worked for a county when administering its jail), *overruled by Turquitt v. Jefferson County*, 137 F.3d 1285 (11th Cir. 1998) (en banc) (relying on *McMillian* to hold that an Alabama sheriff is state official even in that context); *Jeffes v. Barnes*, 208 F.3d 49 (2d Cir. 2000) (holding that a sheriff was final authority for a county in the context of personnel decisions at a jail). The converse could also prove true. *See, e.g., Strickler v. Waters*, 989 F.2d 1375 (4th Cir. 1993) (holding that a sheriff is a state official for purposes of administering a jail); *Thompson v. Duke*, 882 F.2d 1180 (7th Cir. 1989) (concluding that a sheriff is a state official for purposes of setting jail policies). As noted by Justice Ginsburg's dissent, prior to *McMillian* most lower courts held that sheriffs were local officials, regardless of the nature of their actions. After *McMillian*, lower courts have reached mixed results. *Contrast Grech v. Clayton County*, 335 F.3d 1326 (11th Cir. 2003) (en banc) (holding that a Georgia sheriff acted for the state in a law enforcement context), *with Brewster v. Shasta County*, 275 F.3d 803 (9th Cir. 2001) (holding that a California sheriff is a local official when investigating crime).

3. Chiefs of Police, Prosecutors, and Judges. Lower courts have generally concluded that municipal chiefs of police are local (and not state) law enforcement officials, no matter their tasks. *See, e.g., Dill v. City of Edmond*, 155 F.3d 1193 (10th Cir. 1998) (holding that a city is liable under the final authority analysis for personnel actions of its chief of police); *Grech v. Clayton County*, 335 F.3d 1326 (11th Cir. 2003) (en banc) (observing that a county police department, as opposed to a sheriff's office, was a local actor). *But see Abbott v. Village of Winthrop Harbor*, 205 F.3d 976 (7th Cir. 2000) (holding that a police chief was not a final policymaker implicating municipal liability for purposes of wire tapping). Prosecutors have often been found to be state officials when engaged in prosecutorial activities, *see, e.g., Ying Jing Gan v. City of New York*, 996 F.2d 522 (2d Cir. 1993) (holding that a New York county district attorney is a state policymaker when prosecuting); *Weiner v. San Diego County*, 210 F.3d 1025 (9th Cir. 2000) (holding that a California District Attorney worked for the state), but have also been deemed to be local officials. *See, e.g., Gobel v. Maricopa County*, 867 F.2d 1201 (9th Cir. 1989) (holding that an Arizona county attorney was a county policymaker when acting as a prosecutor); *Crane v. Texas*, 766 F.2d 193 (5th Cir. 1985) (holding that a Texas district attorney was a county policymaker when issuing misdemeanor capiases); *Hudson v. City of New Orleans*, 174 F.3d 677 (5th Cir. 1999) (holding that a New Orleans District Attorney was a local official and not protected by the Eleventh Amendment). Prosecutors have likewise been treated as both state and local officials when engaged in administrative tasks. *See, e.g., Coleman v. Kaye*, 87 F.3d 1491 (3d Cir. 1996) (holding that a New Jersey prosecutor made policy for a county in personnel context); *Bibbs v. Newman*, 997 F. Supp. 1174 (S.D. Ind. 1998) (holding that an Indiana prosecutor acted as a state official when hiring and firing a deputy prosecutor). Judges, meanwhile, have been generally deemed state agents, at least when they are engaged in judicial business. *See, e.g., Eggar v. City of Livingston*, 40 F.3d 312 (9th Cir. 1994) (finding that a municipal judge is a state official under § 1983); *Duvall v. County of Kitsap*, 260 F.3d 1124 (9th Cir. 2001) (holding that a county could not control a judge and was thus not accountable for his wrongs).

4. State Law Enforcement. Justice Ginsburg's dissent in *McMillian* complains that "[i]f the Court means to suggest that Sheriff Tate should be classified as a state actor because he is enforcing state (as opposed to county or municipal) law, the Court proves far too much. Because most criminal laws are of statewide application, relying on whose law the sheriff enforces yields an all-state categorization of sheriffs, despite the Court's recognition that such blanket classification is inappropriate." Does this suggestion prove too much? *See* Jessica R. Manley, Comment, *Common Field of Vision: Municipal Liability For State Law Enforcement and Principles of Federalism in Section 1983 Cases*, 100 Nw. U. L. Rev. 967, 997 (2006) (arguing that the Court should "extend Eleventh Amendment sovereign immunity to municipalities in their enforcement of state law"). What if a state law supplies the unconstitutional policy or custom or directs a local policymaker's actions? In *Bethesda Lutheran Homes & Services, Inc. v. Leean*, 154 F.3d 716 (7th Cir. 1998), for example, a home for disabled adults brought a § 1983 damages suit against Jefferson County, Wisconsin, challenging the constitutionality of a residence requirement imposed on its patients. The Seventh Circuit ruled that "while a county does not have the shield of the Eleventh Amendment, it cannot be held liable under section 1983 for acts that it did under the command of state or federal law." Because state law demanded the residence requirement, the county could not be held financially accountable. Judge Posner explained that while this result "admittedly is anomalous from the standpoint of conventional tort law, in which obedience to a superior's orders is not a defense to liability . . . [t]he logic of our position . . . is rooted in the principle (firmly established though often criticized . . .) that a municipality is not vicariously liable under 42 U.S.C. § 1983 for the torts of its employees."[42] Section 1983 plaintiffs, Posner observed, "must be able to trace the action of the employees who actually injured him to a policy or other action of the municipality itself. When the municipality is acting under compulsion of state or federal law, it is the policy contained in that state or federal law, rather than anything devised or adopted by the municipality, that is responsible for the injury." Moreover, this "position has the virtue of minimizing the occasions on which federal constitutional law, enforced through section 1983, puts local government at war with state government."[43] *See also Brotherton v. Cleveland*, 173 F.3d 552 (6th Cir. 1999) ("Where county officials are sued simply for complying with state mandates that afford no discretion, they act as an arm of the State.").

The Seventh Circuit in *Leann* distinguished *Garner v. Memphis Police Department*, 8 F.3d 358 (6th Cir. 1993), where a divided panel ruled that Memphis could be held financially liable for a police officer's use of deadly force, even though the officer's actions were authorized by a state statute. "The [city was] bound to follow the statute in that [it] could not adopt a more permissive deadly force policy. . . . [It] did not, however, prevent the [city] from adopting a more restrictive deadly force policy. In fact, [the city] did exercise [its] freedom to choose a more restrictive policy, refusing to authorize use of deadly force to apprehend certain non-violent felony suspects such as embezzlers and frauds. [The city's] decision to authorize use of deadly force to apprehend nondangerous fleeing burglary suspects was, therefore, a deliberate choice from among various alternatives under *Pembaur*."

[2] Deliberate Indifference

Pembaur, Praprotnik, and *McMillian* recognize that local government *can* be held liable for isolated decisions — so long as the relevant decisionmaker is cloaked with final, policymaking authority for the local government. But "[m]ost § 1983 municipal liability cases do not fit [this] . . . approach. In most cases, the plaintiff cannot show that a policymaker has engaged in or ordered an unconstitutional act." Barbara Kritchevsky, *Reexamining* Monell: *Basing § 1983 Municipal Liability Doctrine on the Statutory Language*, 31 URBAN LAWYER 437 (1999). What then about these discrete

---

[42] Criminal law likewise holds joint participants in a crime equally responsible. *See, e.g.,* MODEL PENAL CODE §§ 2.06 (1) & (3)(a)(ii) (1985) ("A person is guilty of an offense if it is committed by his own conduct or by the conduct of another person . . . [when he] aids or agrees or attempts to aid such other person in planning or committing it."); WAYNE R. LAFAVE, CRIMINAL LAW § 13.1, at 663–64 (4th ed. 2003).

[43] Although the District Court in *Leean* rejected damages, it awarded the plaintiff injunctive relief. Can local government be enjoined under § 1983 from enforcing a state policy, like that codified in a state criminal law? Is a city a "person" within the meaning of § 1983 when it enforces a policy not its own? *Contrast Minnesota Dog Clubs v. City of Minneapolis*, 540 N.W.2d 903, 906 (Minn. Ct. App. 1996) (holding that a city's policy of enforcing state law is insufficient to support injunction against city under § 1983), *with McLaughlin v. City of Canton*, 947 F. Supp. 954 (S.D. Miss.1995) (holding that municipal defendants who enforced a state statute were not liable in damages, but "remain subject to the declaratory and injunctive powers of the court"). Is a negative answer consistent with *Ex parte Young*, discussed in Chapter 3.B., *supra*?

decisions made by front-line officials without advice or direction from policymaking supervisors? The Supreme Court first addressed this issue in *City of Oklahoma City v. Tuttle*, 471 U.S. 808 (1985), where the widow of a man shot to death by an Oklahoma City police officer brought suit under § 1983 against both the officer and the city. The claim against the city was premised on its alleged policy of inadequately training its police force. This policy differed from that in *Monell* in two fundamental ways. First, it was not expressed in a code or regulation. Second, it was passive, speaking not to what the city did, but what it failed to do.

The specific question presented to the Supreme Court in *Tuttle* was whether a single act of police misconduct could alone justify holding a municipality liable for a policy of inadequately training its police force. Although the Court concluded that the single incident at issue in *Tuttle* was not sufficient to support municipal liability, it avoided the larger issue of whether a single wrong could ever satisfy *Monell*'s policy requirement. Then-Justice Rehnquist, speaking for a plurality, offered the following thoughts:

> [T]he word "policy" generally implies a course of action consciously chosen from among various alternatives; it is therefore difficult in one sense even to accept the submission that someone pursues a "policy" of "inadequate training," unless evidence be adduced which proves that the inadequacies resulted from conscious choice — that is, proof that the policymakers deliberately chose a training program which would prove inadequate.

Justice Rehnquist further stated that "some limitation must be placed on establishing municipal liability through policies that are not themselves unconstitutional, or the test set out in *Monell* will become a dead letter." He ended by "express[ing] no opinion on whether a policy that itself is not unconstitutional, such as the general 'inadequate training' alleged here, can ever meet the 'policy' requirement of *Monell*."

Subsequent to *Tuttle*, lower courts understandably struggled with municipal liability. Still, despite Justice Rehnquist's suggestion to the contrary in *Tuttle*, they uniformly recognized that municipalities could be subjected to liability under § 1983 for ad hoc decisions by non-policymaking officials, at least under certain circumstances. Most of these courts, in turn, relied on passive municipal behavior, like failing to properly train police officers, to supply the needed *Monell* policy. The rule that emerged was that inadequate training — like improper training — could furnish the policy necessary to support municipal liability under § 1983. The question that remained was under what circumstances?

In search of an answer, many courts turned to the causation language found in § 1983. Causation then led these courts to fault, with the question becoming whether negligence, recklessness, or deliberate indifference was sufficient to support liability. Regardless of the precise level of scienter required, fault became a proxy for causation.

The Supreme Court granted certiorari to address the problem of inadequate training in *City of Springfield v. Kibbe*, 475 U.S. 1064 (1986). Specifically, two related questions were raised: (1) whether "a municipality can be held liable under 42 U.S.C. § 1983 for inadequate training of its employees"; and (2) whether "more than negligence in training is required in order to establish such liability." Although the Court later dismissed certiorari because the issues were not properly preserved, 480 U.S. 257 (1987), Justice O'Connor (speaking for herself and three other Justices) wrote an opinion addressing the merits. She argued that municipal liability should be limited to those situations "where the failure to train amounts to a reckless disregard for or deliberate indifference to the rights of persons within the city's domain." Justice O'Connor reasoned that the existence of a causal connection between inadequate training, an omission, and an unconstitutional act is "largely a matter of speculation and conjecture." A stricter fault requirement is justified in such cases, she explained, because "the law has been willing to trace more distant causation where there is a cognitive component to the defendant's fault rather than where the defendant's conduct results from simple or heightened negligence." The Court found her reasoning convincing two years later in *City of Canton v. Harris*.

CITY OF CANTON v. HARRIS
Supreme Court of the United States
489 U.S. 378 (1989)

JUSTICE WHITE delivered the opinion of the Court.

[Harris was arrested by officers working for the Canton Police Department. After she arrived at the police station, Harris became incoherent and slumped to the floor of her cell. No medical attention was provided. When she was released one hour later, her family had her taken to a local hospital where she was diagnosed as suffering from several emotional ailments. Harris remained hospitalized for one week and received subsequent outpatient treatment for an additional year. Harris filed a § 1983 action against the City of Canton and its officials, claiming that her right to medical assistance under the Due Process Clause had been violated. She presented evidence that, pursuant to a municipal regulation, shift commanders were authorized to determine, in their sole discretion, whether detainees required medical care. In addition, she argued that that the city's shift commanders were not provided with any special training (beyond first-aid training) in making determinations as to when to summon medical care for injured detainees. The jury ruled in favor of Harris and against the city.]

In this case, we are asked to determine if a municipality can ever be liable under 42 U.S.C. § 1983 for constitutional violations resulting from its failure to train municipal employees. We hold that, under certain circumstances, such liability is permitted by the statute.

[O]ur first inquiry in any case alleging municipal liability under § 1983 is the question whether there is a direct causal link between a municipal policy or custom and the alleged constitutional deprivation. The inquiry is a difficult one; one that has left this Court deeply divided in a series of cases that have followed *Monell*; one that is the principal focus of our decision again today.

Based on the difficulty that this Court has had defining the contours of municipal liability in these circumstances, [the city] urges us to adopt the rule that a municipality can be found liable under § 1983 only where "the policy in question [is] itself unconstitutional." Whether such a rule is a valid construction of § 1983 is a question the Court has left unresolved. Under such an approach, the outcome here would be rather clear: we would have to reverse and remand the case with instructions that judgment be entered for [the City].[44] There can be little doubt that on its face the city's policy regarding medical treatment for detainees is constitutional. The policy states that the city jailer "shall . . . have [a person needing medical care] taken to a hospital for medical treatment, with permission of his supervisor. . . . " It is difficult to see what constitutional guarantees are violated by such a policy.

Nor, without more, would a city automatically be liable under § 1983 if one of its employees happened to apply the policy in an unconstitutional manner, for liability would then rest on respondeat superior. The claim in this case, however, is that if a concededly valid policy is unconstitutionally applied by a municipal employee, the city is liable if the employee has not been adequately trained and the constitutional wrong has

---

[44] [n.5] In this Court, in addition to suggesting that the city's failure to train its officers amounted to a "policy" that resulted in the denial of medical care to detainees, [Harris] also contended the city had a "custom" of denying medical care to those detainees suffering from emotional or mental ailments. As [Harris] described it in her brief, and at argument, this claim of an unconstitutional "custom" appears to be little more than a restatement of her "failure-to-train as policy" claim. However, to the extent that this claim poses a distinct basis for the city's liability under § 1983, we decline to determine whether [Harris's] contention that such a "custom" existed is an alternative ground for affirmance.

been caused by that failure to train. For reasons explained below, we conclude, as have all the Courts of Appeals that have addressed this issue, that there are limited circumstances in which an allegation of a "failure to train" can be the basis for liability under § 1983. Thus, we reject petitioner's contention that only unconstitutional policies are actionable under the statute.

[W]e cannot agree that the District Court's jury instructions on this issue were proper. . . . Unlike the question whether a municipality's failure to train employees can ever be a basis for § 1983 liability — on which the Courts of Appeals have all agreed — there is substantial division among the lower courts as to what degree of fault must be evidenced by the municipality's inaction before liability will be permitted. We hold today that the inadequacy of police training may serve as the basis for § 1983 liability only where the failure to train amounts to deliberate indifference to the rights of persons with whom the police come into contact.[45] This rule is most consistent with our admonition in *Monell* . . . that a municipality can be liable under § 1983 only where its policies are the "moving force [behind] the constitutional violation." Only where a municipality's failure to train its employees in a relevant respect evidences a "deliberate indifference" to the rights of its inhabitants can such a shortcoming be properly thought of as a city "policy or custom" that is actionable under § 1983.

Monell's rule that a city is not liable under § 1983 unless a municipal policy causes a constitutional deprivation will not be satisfied by merely alleging that the existing training program for a class of employees, such as police officers, represents a policy for which the city is responsible.[46] That much may be true. The issue in a case like this one, however, is whether that training program is adequate; and if it is not, the question becomes whether such inadequate training can justifiably be said to represent "city policy." It may seem contrary to common sense to assert that a municipality will actually have a policy of not taking reasonable steps to train its employees. But it may happen that in light of the duties assigned to specific officers or employees the need for more or different training is so obvious, and the inadequacy so likely to result in the violation of constitutional rights, that the policymakers of the city can reasonably be said to have been deliberately indifferent to the need.[47] In that event, the failure to

---

[45] [n.8] The "deliberate indifference" standard we adopt for § 1983 "failure to train" claims does not turn upon the degree of fault (if any) that a plaintiff must show to make out an underlying claim of a constitutional violation. For example, this Court has never determined what degree of culpability must be shown before the particular constitutional deprivation asserted in this case — a denial of the due process right to medical care while in detention — is established. Indeed, in *Revere v. Massachusetts General Hospital*, 463 U.S. 239 (1983), we reserved decision on the question whether something less than the Eighth Amendment's "deliberate indifference" test may be applicable in claims by detainees asserting violations of their due process right to medical care while in custody. We need not resolve here the question left open in *Revere* for two reasons. First, [the city] has conceded that, as the case comes to us, we must assume that [Harris's] constitutional right to receive medical care was denied by city employees — whatever the nature of that right might be. Second, the proper standard for determining when a municipality will be liable under § 1983 for constitutional wrongs does not turn on any underlying culpability test that determines when such wrongs have occurred.

[46] [n.9] The plurality opinion in *Tuttle* explained why this must be so: "Obviously, if one retreats far enough from a constitutional violation some municipal 'policy' can be identified behind almost any . . . harm inflicted by a municipal official; for example, [a police officer] would never have killed Tuttle if Oklahoma City did not have a 'policy' of establishing a police force. But *Monell* must be taken to require proof of a city policy different in kind from this latter example before a claim can be sent to a jury on the theory that a particular violation was 'caused' by the municipal 'policy.'"

[47] [n.10] For example, city policymakers know to a moral certainty that their police officers will be required to arrest fleeing felons. The city has armed its officers with firearms, in part to allow them to accomplish this task. Thus, the need to train officers in the constitutional limitations on the use of deadly force, *see Tennessee v. Garner* [discussed in Chapter 1.C., *supra*], can be said to be "so obvious," that failure to do so could properly be characterized as "deliberate indifference" to constitutional rights. It could also be that the police, in exercising their discretion, so often violate constitutional rights that the need for further training must have been plainly obvious to the city policymakers, who, nevertheless, are "deliberately indifferent" to the need.

provide proper training may fairly be said to represent a policy for which the city is responsible, and for which the city may be held liable if it actually causes injury.[48]

In resolving the issue of a city's liability, the focus must be on adequacy of the training program in relation to the tasks the particular officers must perform. That a particular officer may be unsatisfactorily trained will not alone suffice to fasten liability on the city, for the officer's shortcomings may have resulted from factors other than a faulty training program. It may be, for example, that an otherwise sound program has occasionally been negligently administered. Neither will it suffice to prove that an injury or accident could have been avoided if an officer had had better or more training, sufficient to equip him to avoid the particular injury-causing conduct. Such a claim could be made about almost any encounter resulting in injury, yet not condemn the adequacy of the program to enable officers to respond properly to the usual and recurring situations with which they must deal. And plainly, adequately trained officers occasionally make mistakes; the fact that they do says little about the training program or the legal basis for holding the city liable.

Moreover, for liability to attach in this circumstance the identified deficiency in a city's training program must be closely related to the ultimate injury. Thus in the case at hand, [Harris] must still prove that the deficiency in training actually caused the police officers' indifference to her medical needs. Would the injury have been avoided had the employee been trained under a program that was not deficient in the identified respect? Predicting how a hypothetically well-trained officer would have acted under the circumstances may not be an easy task for the factfinder, particularly since matters of judgment may be involved, and since officers who are well trained are not free from error and perhaps might react very much like the untrained officer in similar circumstances. But judge and jury, doing their respective jobs, will be adequate to the task.

To adopt lesser standards of fault and causation would open municipalities to unprecedented liability under § 1983. In virtually every instance where a person has had his or her constitutional rights violated by a city employee, a § 1983 plaintiff will be able to point to something the city "could have done" to prevent the unfortunate incident. Thus, permitting cases against cities for their "failure to train" employees to go forward under § 1983 on a lesser standard of fault would result in de facto respondeat superior liability on municipalities — a result we rejected in *Monell*. It would also engage the federal courts in an endless exercise of second-guessing municipal employee-training programs. This is an exercise we believe the federal courts are ill suited to undertake, as well as one that would implicate serious questions of federalism.

Consequently, while claims such as [Harris's] — alleging that the city's failure to provide training to municipal employees resulted in the constitutional deprivation she suffered — are cognizable under § 1983, they can only yield liability against a municipality where that city's failure to train reflects deliberate indifference to the constitutional rights of its inhabitants.

The final question here is whether this case should be remanded for a new trial, or whether, as [the city] suggests, we should conclude that there are no possible grounds on which [Harris] can prevail. It is true that the evidence in the record now does not meet the standard of § 1983 liability we have set forth above. But, the standard of proof the District Court ultimately imposed on [Harris] . . . was a lesser one than the one we adopt today. Whether [Harris] should have an opportunity to prove her case under

---

[48] [n.11] The record indicates that [the] city did train its officers and that its training included first-aid instruction. [The city] argues that it could not have been obvious to the city that such training was insufficient to administer the written policy, which was itself constitutional. This is a question to be resolved on remand.

the "deliberate indifference" rule we have adopted is a matter for the Court of Appeals to deal with on remand.[49]

JUSTICE O'CONNOR, with whom JUSTICE SCALIA and JUSTICE KENNEDY join, concurring in part and dissenting in part.

I join . . . the Court's opinion except footnote 11.

Where, as here, a claim of municipal liability is predicated upon a failure to act, the requisite degree of fault must be shown by proof of a background of events and circumstances which establish that the "policy of inaction" is the functional equivalent of a decision by the city itself to violate the Constitution. Without some form of notice to the city, and the opportunity to conform to constitutional dictates both what it does and what it chooses not to do, the failure to train theory of liability could completely engulf *Monell*, imposing liability without regard to fault. Moreover, absent a requirement that the lack of training at issue bear a very close causal connection to the violation of constitutional rights, the failure to train theory of municipal liability could impose "prophylactic" duties on municipal governments only remotely connected to underlying constitutional requirements themselves.

In my view, it could be shown that the need for training was obvious in one of two ways. First, a municipality could fail to train its employees concerning a clear constitutional duty implicated in recurrent situations that a particular employee is certain to face. As the majority notes [in footnote 10], the constitutional limitations established by this Court on the use of deadly force by police officers present one such situation. The constitutional duty of the individual officer is clear, and it is equally clear that failure to inform city personnel of that duty will create an extremely high risk that constitutional violations will ensue.

The claim in this case — that police officers were inadequately trained in diagnosing the symptoms of emotional illness — falls far short of the kind of "obvious" need for training that would support a finding of deliberate indifference to constitutional rights on the part of the city. As the Court's opinion observes, this Court has not yet addressed the precise nature of the obligations that the Due Process Clause places upon the police to seek medical care for pretrial detainees who have been physically injured while being apprehended by the police. There are thus no clear constitutional guideposts for municipalities in this area, and the diagnosis of mental illness is not one of the "usual and recurring situations with which [the police] must deal." The lack of training at issue here is not the kind of omission that can be characterized, in and of itself, as a "deliberate indifference" to constitutional rights.

Second, I think municipal liability for failure to train may be proper where it can be shown that policymakers were aware of, and acquiesced in, a pattern of constitutional violations involving the exercise of police discretion. In such cases, the need for training may not be obvious from the outset, but a pattern of constitutional violations could put the municipality on notice that its officers confront the particular situation on a regular basis, and that they often react in a manner contrary to constitutional requirements. The lower courts that have applied the "deliberate indifference" standard we adopt today have required a showing of a pattern of violations from which a kind of "tacit authorization" by city policymakers can be inferred.

[Harris] presented no testimony from any witness indicating that there had been past incidents of "deliberate indifference" to the medical needs of emotionally disturbed detainees or that any other circumstance had put the city on actual or constructive notice of a need for additional training in this regard. . . . There is quite simply nothing in this record to indicate that the city of Canton had any reason to suspect that

---

[49] [Editor's note: Justice Brennan concurred with the understanding that the Court of Appeals could remand for a new trial.]

failing to provide this kind of training would lead to injuries of any kind, let alone violations of the Due Process Clause. None of the Courts of Appeals that already apply the standard we adopt today would allow [Harris] to take her claim to a jury based on the facts she adduced at trial.

Allowing an inadequate training claim such as this one to go to the jury based upon a single incident would only invite jury nullification of *Monell*. . . . [T]he resources of local government are not inexhaustible. The grave step of shifting those resources to particular areas where constitutional violations are likely to result through the deterrent power of § 1983 should certainly not be taken on the basis of an isolated incident. If § 1983 and the Constitution require the city of Canton to provide detailed medical and psychological training to its police officers, or to station paramedics at its jails, other city services will necessarily suffer, including those with far more direct implications for the protection of constitutional rights.

NOTES

1. Scienter Under *City of Canton*. The *City of Canton* Court's deliberate indifference standard demands more than gross negligence or recklessness. The Court of Appeals in *City of Canton* ruled that municipal liability could attach where the city acted intentionally, recklessly, or with gross negligence. The Supreme Court described this standard as a "lesser one than the one we adopt today." Still, as the Court made clear in *Farmer v. Brennan*, 511 U.S. 825 (1994) (holding that the Eighth Amendment is violated only by "deliberate indifference" to threatened harm), (discussed in Chapter 1.C., *supra*), *City of Canton*'s fault standard, unlike the Eighth Amendment's deliberate indifference requirement, is objective:[50]

> In *Canton* . . . we held that a municipality can be liable for failure to train its employees when the municipality's failure shows "a deliberate indifference to the rights of its inhabitants." In speaking to the meaning of the term, we said that "it may happen that in light of the duties assigned to specific officers or employees the need for more or different training is so obvious, and the inadequacy so likely to result in the violation of constitutional rights, that the policymakers of the city can reasonably be said to have been deliberately indifferent to the need." It would be hard to describe the *Canton* understanding of deliberate indifference, permitting liability to be premised on obviousness or constructive notice, as anything but objective.

Consequently, the *City of Canton* standard would not appear to be as demanding as the Eighth Amendment's subjective scienter requirement. *See, e.g., Howard v. Grinage*, 82 F.3d 1343 (6th Cir. 1996) ("the [*City of Canton*] Court . . . held that 'deliberate indifference' . . . was an objective standard, imposing on prison officials 'actual or constructive notice' of the 'obvious[ness]' of an alleged violation"); *Hare v. City of Corinth*, 74 F.3d 633 (5th Cir. 1996) ("To succeed in holding a municipality accountable . . . the [plaintiff] must show that the municipal employee's act resulted from a municipal policy or custom adopted or maintained with objective deliberate indifference to the detainee's constitutional rights.").

2. Patterns of Wrongdoing. Justice O'Connor explained in her concurring opinion in *City of Canton* that municipal liability is proper "where it can be shown that policymakers were aware of, and acquiesced in, a pattern of constitutional violations. . . . " Lower courts have uniformly relied on this language to hold that "[d]eliberate indifference may be established by a pattern of constitutional violations." *Bruce v. Beary*, 498 F.3d 1232 (11th Cir. 2007). Indeed, "proving deliberate indifference

---

[50] In footnote 8 to the majority's opinion in *City of Canton*, the Court distinguished the state of mind required to prove a particular constitutional violation, *see* Chapter 1.C., *supra* (discussing scienter requirements for various constitutional provisions), from the deliberate indifference required in order to subject a municipality to liability for inadequate training.

in the absence of such a pattern is a difficult task." *Carswell v. Borough of Homestead*, 381 F.3d 235 (3d Cir. 2004); *see also Board of County Commissioners of Bryan County v. Brown*, 520 U.S. 397 (1997) (excerpted below) (finding that a single hiring decision by a final authority was not sufficient to support municipal liability). The troubling question that emerges is one of quantity: how many similar wrongs are needed to create an actionable pattern? In *Lytle v. Doyle*, 326 F.3d 463 (4th Cir. 2003), for example, the Fourth Circuit stated that "'isolated incidents' of unconstitutional conduct by subordinate employees are not sufficient to establish a custom or practice for § 1983 purposes. Rather, there must be 'numerous particular instances' of unconstitutional conduct in order to establish a custom or practice." *See, e.g., Young v. City of Providence ex rel. Napolitano*, 404 F.3d 4 (1st Cir. 2005) (stating that there must be "some evidence" of a pattern that a jury can rely upon to hold a city liable); *Bordanaro v. McLeod*, 871 F.2d 1151 (1st Cir. 1989) (finding that twenty to sixty incidents over twenty-four years was sufficient to create a jury question). Two additional incidents, apparently, are not sufficient. *See, e.g., Morais v. City of Philadelphia*, F. Supp. 2d (E.D. Pa. 2007) (holding that two additional violations of rights of mentally ill were not sufficient to establish a pattern). Assuming "numerous" and similar wrongs on behalf of either the wrongdoer or other officials working for the municipality, a jury question is presented over whether a municipality's failures amount to deliberate indifference to the pattern.

3. Causation. Deliberate indifference must also cause the violation at issue for a municipality to be held liable. Where more or better training could not avoid a violation, municipal liability is not proper. In *Grazier ex rel. White v. City of Philadephia*, 328 F.3d 120 (3d Cir. 2003), for example, the court concluded that Philadelphia could not be liable for its police officers' shooting of a motorist during a traffic stop "even if plaintiffs could show deliberate indifference." The plaintiffs, the court observed, would "also have to prove that the City's inadequate training policies were the 'moving force' behind their injuries." "In this case, plaintiffs cannot point to evidence that the officers cut them off and shot at their car because they were trained to do so. To the contrary, the [city's] directives instruct officers to follow different procedures." *See also Young v. City of Providence ex rel. Napolitano*, 404 F.3d 4 (1st Cir. 2005) (observing that although the issue was "close," "[a] jury could find that training would have made a difference here, unlike in other situations where it would have been unlikely to stop unconstitutional conduct"); *contrast Barney v. Pulsipher*, 143 F.3d 1299 (10th Cir. 1998) (holding that a claim of deliberately indifferent training failed because more or better training would not likely have stopped a jailer from sexually assaulting inmates). *See generally Board of County Commissioners of Bryan County v. Brown*, 520 U.S. 397 (1997) (excerpted in Section 3.[2], *infra*) (stating that a § 1983 "plaintiff must also demonstrate that, through its deliberate conduct, the municipality was the 'moving force' behind the injury alleged. That is, a plaintiff must show that the municipal action was taken with the requisite degree of culpability and must demonstrate a direct causal link between the municipal action and the deprivation of federal rights.").

4. Deliberate Indifference to Obvious Rights. The Supreme Court in *City of Canton* observed that "obvious" constitutional rights can give rise to municipal liability even in the absence of express policies or ignored patterns. It offered *Tennessee v. Garner*, 471 U.S. 1 (1985), which limited the use of deadly force when making arrests, as an illustration: "the need to train officers in the constitutional limitations on the use of deadly force can be said to be 'so obvious', that failure to do so could properly be characterized as 'deliberate indifference' to constitutional rights." *See* footnote 10. Under this approach, is it enough that a city consciously disregards a risk of harm to the victim? Or does the Court's standard mean that the city must disregard the risk of an obvious *constitutional* violation? Under the facts of *City of Canton*, must the city have understood that Harris had a constitutional right to medical care (as opposed to merely ignoring her medical needs)?

In *Szabla v. City of Brooklyn Park*, 486 F.3d 385 (7th Cir. 2007), a homeless man (Szabla) sued a city under § 1983 after being bitten by a police dog. Szabla argued that police "used excessive force by commanding the dog to 'track,' or bite and hold, without first providing a warning," and that the city was responsible for this Fourth Amendment violation because it did not train its canine unit to the contrary. On appeal, the Seventh Circuit ruled that although the city was not entitled to qualified immunity, it could not be held liable if the right to a warning was not clearly established at the time of the incident:

> In this case, a constitutional requirement that an officer in Baker's situation give advance warning before commanding a canine to bite and hold a suspect was not clearly established as of August 2000. The need for training or other safeguards relating to warnings, therefore, was not so obvious at the time of this incident that Brooklyn Park's actions can properly be characterized as deliberate indifference to Szabla's constitutional rights. While a municipality does not enjoy qualified immunity from damages liability that results from a policy that is itself unconstitutional or from an unconstitutional decision by municipal policymakers, we agree with the Second Circuit and several district courts that a municipal policymaker cannot exhibit fault rising to the level of deliberate indifference to a constitutional right when that right has not yet been clearly established. *Townes v. City of New York*, 176 F.3d 138 (2d Cir. 1999).
>
> This conclusion is not inconsistent with the Supreme Court's decisions in *Owen* and *Pembaur* because neither of those cases involved an alleged municipal policy of deliberate indifference. . . . [T]he municipality was liable in each case because a particular municipal action *itself* violated federal law. Fault and causation were obvious in each case.
>
> Where the municipality has not directly inflicted an injury, however, "rigorous standards of culpability and causation must be applied," and a showing of deliberate indifference is required. The absence of clearly established constitutional rights — what Justice O'Connor called "clear constitutional guideposts" — undermines the assertion that a municipality *deliberately* ignored an *obvious* need for additional safeguards to augment its facially constitutional policy. This is not an application of qualified immunity for liability flowing from an unconstitutional policy. Rather, the lack of clarity in the law precludes a finding that the municipality had an unconstitutional policy at all, because its policymakers cannot properly be said to have exhibited a policy of deliberate indifference to constitutional rights that were not clearly established.[51]

Is *Szabla*'s standard requiring conscious disregard of an established constitutional right consistent with the Court's rejection of qualified immunity in *Owen*? See Mark R. Brown, *Correlating Municipal Liability and Official Immunity Under Section 1983*, 1989 U. ILL. L. REV. 625, 654–55 (arguing that in order to achieve consistency with *Owen* "[t]he better approach, if fault is to be used at all, is to ask only whether the city consciously disregarded the risk of harm, and not the risk of a constitutional violation"). The Seventh Circuit in *Szabla* relied on *Board of County Commissioners of Bryan County v. Brown*, 520 U.S. 397 (1997) (excerpted below), for support.

---

[51] [n.4] That the Supreme Court in *City of Canton* remanded the case for further proceedings does not mean the Court rejected Justice O'Connor's view that clear constitutional duties and guideposts are vital to a showing of deliberate indifference. While the precise obligations of city employees to pre-trial detainees under the Due Process Clause were unsettled when *City of Canton* was decided, it was clearly established that a detainee was entitled to protections *at least* as great as those available to convicted prisoners under the Eighth Amendment. The Court relied on a concession by the city, for purposes of the decision, that its employees had violated the plaintiff's constitutional rights under the Eighth Amendment's clearly-established "deliberate indifference" standard, so the absence of clear constitutional duties and guideposts was not a basis for directing entry of judgment as a matter of law.

BOARD OF COUNTRY COMMISSIONERS OF BRYAN COUNTRY v. BROWN
Supreme Court of the United States
520 U.S. 397 (1997)

JUSTICE O'CONNOR delivered the opinion of the Court.

[Brown alleged that a Bryan County deputy sheriff (Stacy Burns) used excessive force in the course of making an arrest. She claimed that Bryan County was liable based on its Sheriff's (B.J. Moore) decision to hire Burns, who was a son of Moore's nephew. Specifically, Brown argued that Sheriff Moore failed to adequately review Burns's background, which included a history of driving infractions and misdemeanors, including assault and battery, resisting arrest, and public drunkenness.]

The jury concluded that Stacy Burns had arrested [Brown] without probable cause and had used excessive force, and therefore found him liable for [her] injuries. It also found that the "hiring policy" and the "training policy" of Bryan County "in the case of Stacy Burns as instituted by its policymaker, B.J. Moore," were each "so inadequate as to amount to deliberate indifference to the constitutional needs of the Plaintiff [Brown]." The District Court entered judgment for [Brown] on the issue of Bryan County's § 1983 liability. [The Court of Appeals affirmed.]

The parties join issue on whether, under *Monell* and subsequent cases, a single hiring decision by a county sheriff can be a "policy" that triggers municipal liability. Relying on our decision in *Pembaur*, [Brown] claims that a single act by a decisionmaker with final authority in the relevant area constitutes a "policy" attributable to the municipality itself. So long as a § 1983 plaintiff identifies a decision properly attributable to the municipality, [Brown] argues, there is no risk of imposing *respondeat superior* liability. Whether that decision was intended to govern only the situation at hand or to serve as a rule to be applied over time is immaterial.

As our § 1983 municipal liability jurisprudence illustrates, however, it is not enough for a § 1983 plaintiff merely to identify conduct properly attributable to the municipality. The plaintiff must also demonstrate that, through its deliberate conduct, the municipality was the "moving force" behind the injury alleged. That is, a plaintiff must show that the municipal action was taken with the requisite degree of culpability and must demonstrate a direct causal link between the municipal action and the deprivation of federal rights.

In relying heavily on *Pembaur*, [Brown] blurs the distinction between § 1983 cases that present no difficult questions of fault and causation and those that do. To the extent that we have recognized a cause of action under § 1983 based on a single decision attributable to a municipality, we have done so only where the evidence that the municipality had acted and that the plaintiff had suffered a deprivation of federal rights also proved fault and causation. For example, *Owen v. Independence* involved [a] formal decision[] of [a] municipal legislative bod[y]. In *Owen*, the city council allegedly censured and discharged an employee without a hearing. [The decision did not] reflect[] implementation of a generally applicable rule. But we did not question that [the] decision, duly promulgated by city lawmakers, could trigger municipal liability if the decision itself were found to be unconstitutional. Because fault and causation were obvious . . . , proof that the municipality's decision was unconstitutional would suffice to establish that the municipality itself was liable for the plaintiff's constitutional injury.

Similarly, *Pembaur v. Cincinnati* concerned a decision by a county prosecutor, acting as the county's final decisionmaker, to direct county deputies to forcibly enter petitioner's place of business to serve capiases upon third parties. . . . [W]e concluded that a final decisionmaker's adoption of a course of action "tailored to a particular situation and not intended to control decisions in later situations" may, in some circumstances, give rise to municipal liability under § 1983. In *Pembaur*, it was not disputed that the prosecutor had specifically directed the action resulting in the deprivation of petitioner's rights. The conclusion that the decision was that of a final municipal decisionmaker and was therefore properly attributable to the municipality established municipal liability. No questions of fault or causation arose.

Claims not involving an allegation that the municipal action itself violated federal law, or directed or authorized the deprivation of federal rights, present much more difficult problems of proof. That a plaintiff has suffered a deprivation of federal rights at the hands of a municipal employee will not alone permit an inference of municipal culpability and causation; the plaintiff will simply have shown that the employee acted culpably. We recognized these difficulties in *Canton*, [where we concluded] . . . that an "inadequate training" claim could be the basis for § 1983 liability in "limited circumstances." We spoke, however, of a deficient training "program," necessarily intended to apply over time to multiple employees. Existence of a "program" makes proof of fault and causation at least possible in an inadequate training case. If a program does not prevent constitutional violations, municipal decisionmakers may eventually be put on notice that a new program is called for. Their continued adherence to an approach that they know or should know has failed to prevent tortious conduct by employees may establish the conscious disregard for the consequences of their action — the "deliberate indifference" — necessary to trigger municipal liability. In addition, the existence of a pattern of tortious conduct by inadequately trained employees may tend to show that the lack of proper training, rather than a one-time negligent administration of the program or factors peculiar to the officer involved in a particular incident, is the "moving force" behind the plaintiff's injury.

Before trial, counsel for Bryan County stipulated that Sheriff Moore "was the policy maker for Bryan County regarding the Sheriff's Department." . . . Accepting the county's representations below, then, this case presents no difficult questions concerning whether Sheriff Moore has final authority to act for the municipality in hiring matters. [Brown] does not claim that she can identify any pattern of injuries linked to Sheriff Moore's hiring practices. Indeed, [Brown] does not contend that Sheriff Moore's hiring practices are generally defective. The only evidence on this point at trial suggested that Sheriff Moore had adequately screened the backgrounds of all prior deputies he hired. [Brown] instead seeks to trace liability to what can only be described as a deviation from Sheriff Moore's ordinary hiring practices.

In *Canton*, we did not foreclose the possibility that evidence of a single violation of federal rights, accompanied by a showing that a municipality has failed to train its employees to handle recurring situations presenting an obvious potential for such a violation, could trigger municipal liability. [Brown] purports to rely on *Canton*, arguing that Burns' use of excessive force was the plainly obvious consequence of Sheriff Moore's failure to screen Burns' record. In essence, [Brown] claims that this showing of "obviousness" would demonstrate both that Sheriff Moore acted with conscious disregard for the consequences of his action and that the Sheriff's action directly caused her injuries, and would thus substitute for the pattern of injuries ordinarily necessary to establish municipal culpability and causation.

The proffered analogy between failure-to-train cases and inadequate screening cases is not persuasive. In leaving open in *Canton* the possibility that a plaintiff might succeed in carrying a failure-to-train claim without showing a pattern of constitutional violations, we simply hypothesized that, in a narrow range of circumstances, a violation of federal rights may be a highly predictable consequence of a failure to equip law enforcement officers with specific tools to handle recurring situations. The likelihood that the situation will recur and the predictability that an officer lacking specific tools to handle that situation will violate citizens' rights could justify a finding that policymakers' decision not to train the officer reflected "deliberate indifference" to the obvious consequence of the policymakers' choice — namely, a violation of a specific constitutional or statutory right. The high degree of predictability may also support an inference of causation — that the municipality's indifference led directly to the very consequence that was so predictable.

Where a plaintiff presents a § 1983 claim premised upon the inadequacy of an official's review of a prospective applicant's record, however, there is a particular danger that a municipality will be held liable for an injury not directly caused by a deliberate action attributable to the municipality itself. Every injury suffered at the hands of a municipal employee can be traced to a hiring decision in a "but-for" sense: But for the municipality's decision to hire the employee, the plaintiff would not have suffered the injury. To prevent municipal liability for a hiring decision from collapsing into respondeat superior liability, a court must carefully test the link between the policymaker's inadequate decision and the particular injury alleged.

In attempting to import the reasoning of *Canton* into the hiring context, [Brown] ignores the fact that predicting the consequence of a single hiring decision, even one based on an inadequate assessment of a record, is far more difficult than predicting what might flow from the failure to train a single law enforcement officer as to a specific skill necessary to the discharge of his duties. As our decision in *Canton* makes clear, "deliberate indifference" is a stringent standard of fault, requiring proof that a municipal actor disregarded a known or obvious consequence of his action. Unlike the risk from a particular glaring omission in a training regimen, the risk from a single instance of inadequate screening of an applicant's background is not "obvious" in the abstract; rather, it depends upon the background of the applicant.

We assume that a jury could properly find in this case that Sheriff Moore's assessment of Burns' background was inadequate. Sheriff Moore's own testimony indicated that he did not inquire into the underlying conduct or the disposition of any of the misdemeanor charges reflected on Burns' record before hiring him. But this showing of an instance of inadequate screening is not enough to establish "deliberate indifference." In layman's terms, inadequate screening of an applicant's record may reflect "indifference" to the applicant's background. For purposes of a legal inquiry into municipal liability under § 1983, however, that is not the relevant "indifference." A plaintiff must demonstrate that a municipal decision reflects deliberate indifference to the risk that a violation of a particular constitutional or statutory right will follow the decision. Only where adequate scrutiny of an applicant's background would lead a reasonable policymaker to conclude that the plainly obvious consequence of the decision to hire the applicant would be the deprivation of a third party's federally protected right can the official's failure to adequately scrutinize the applicant's background constitute "deliberate indifference."

Neither the District Court nor the Court of Appeals directly tested the link between Burns' actual background and the risk that, if hired, he would use excessive force. The District Court instructed the jury on a theory analogous to that reserved in *Canton*. The court required respondent to prove that Sheriff Moore's inadequate screening of Burns' background was "so likely to result in violations of constitutional rights" that the Sheriff could "reasonably [be] said to have been deliberately indifferent to the constitutional needs of the Plaintiff." The court also instructed the jury, without elaboration, that [Brown] was required to prove that the "inadequate hiring . . . policy directly caused [Brown's] injury."

As discussed above, a finding of culpability simply cannot depend on the mere probability that any officer inadequately screened will inflict any constitutional injury. Rather, it must depend on a finding that *this* officer was highly likely to inflict the *particular* injury suffered by the plaintiff. The connection between the background of the particular applicant and the specific constitutional violation alleged must be strong.

Even assuming without deciding that proof of a single instance of inadequate screening could ever trigger municipal liability, the evidence in this case was insufficient to support a finding that, in hiring Burns, Sheriff Moore disregarded a known or obvious risk of injury. To test the link between Sheriff Moore's hiring decision and respondent's injury, we must ask whether a full review of Burns' record reveals that Sheriff Moore should have concluded that Burns' use of excessive force would be a plainly obvious consequence of the hiring decision.[52] On this point, [Brown's] showing was inadequate. To be sure, Burns' record reflected various misdemeanor infractions. [Brown] claims that the record demonstrated such a strong propensity for violence that Burns' application of excessive force was highly likely. The primary charges on which [Brown] relies, however, are those arising from a fight on a college campus where Burns was a student. In connection with this single incident, Burns was charged with assault and battery, resisting arrest, and public drunkenness.[53] In January 1990, when he pleaded guilty to those charges, Burns also pleaded guilty to various driving-related offenses, including nine moving violations and a charge of driving with a suspended license. In addition, Burns had previously pleaded guilty to being in actual physical control of a vehicle while intoxicated.

The fact that Burns had pleaded guilty to traffic offenses and other misdemeanors may well have made him an extremely poor candidate for reserve deputy. Had Sheriff Moore fully reviewed Burns' record, he might have come to precisely that conclusion. But unless he would necessarily have reached that decision because Burns' use of excessive force would have been a plainly obvious consequence of the hiring decision, Sheriff Moore's inadequate scrutiny of Burns' record cannot constitute "deliberate indifference" to [Brown's] federally protected right to be free from a use of excessive force.

Because there was insufficient evidence on which a jury could base a finding that Sheriff Moore's decision to hire Burns reflected conscious disregard of an obvious risk that a use of excessive force would follow, the District Court erred in submitting [Brown's] inadequate screening claim to the jury.

JUSTICE SOUTER, with whom JUSTICE STEVENS and JUSTICE BREYER join, dissenting.

While . . . [*Monell's*] policy requirement may be satisfied in more than one way, there are in fact three alternatives discernible in our prior cases. It is certainly met when the appropriate officer or entity promulgates a generally applicable statement of policy and the subsequent act complained of is simply an implementation of that policy. *Monell* exemplified these circumstances, where city agencies had issued a rule requiring pregnant employees to take unpaid leaves of absence before any medical need arose. We have also held the policy requirement satisfied where no rule has been announced as "policy" but federal law has been violated by an act of the policymaker itself. In this situation, the choice of policy and its implementation are one, and the first

---

[52] [n.1] In suggesting that our decision complicates this Court's § 1983 municipal liability jurisprudence by altering the understanding of culpability, Justice Souter and Justice Breyer misunderstand our approach. We do not suggest that a plaintiff in an inadequate screening case must show a higher degree of culpability than the "deliberate indifference" required in *Canton*; we need not do so, because, as discussed below, [Brown] has not made a showing of deliberate indifference here. Furthermore, in assessing the risks of a decision to hire a particular individual, we draw no distinction between what is "so obvious" or "so likely to occur" [— language used in *City of Canton* —] and what is "plainly obvious." The difficulty with the lower courts' approach is that it fails to connect the background of the particular officer hired in this case to the particular constitutional violation [Brown] suffered. Ensuring that lower courts link the background of the officer to the constitutional violation alleged does not complicate our municipal liability jurisprudence with degrees of "obviousness," but seeks to ensure that a plaintiff in an inadequate screening case establishes a policymaker's deliberate indifference — that is, conscious disregard for the known and obvious consequences of his actions.

[53] [n.2] Justice Souter implies that Burns' record reflected assault and battery charges arising from more than one incident. There has never been a serious dispute that a single misdemeanor assault and battery conviction arose out of a single campus fight. . . . In fact, [Brown's] own expert witness testified that Burns' record reflected a single assault conviction. . . . Involvement in a single fraternity fracas does not demonstrate "a proclivity to violence against the person."

or only action will suffice to ground municipal liability simply because it is the very policymaker who is acting. *See Pembaur; Owen v. Independence.*

We have, finally, identified a municipal policy in a third situation, even where the policymaker has failed to act affirmatively at all, so long as the need to take some action to control the agents of the government "is so obvious, and the inadequacy [of existing practice] so likely to result in the violation of constitutional rights, that the policymake[r] . . . can reasonably be said to have been deliberately indifferent to the need." *Canton v. Harris.*

Deliberate indifference is thus treated, as it is elsewhere in the law, as tantamount to intent, so that inaction by a policymaker deliberately indifferent to a substantial risk of harm is equivalent to the intentional action that setting policy presupposes.

Under this prior law, Sheriff Moore's failure to screen out his 21-year-old great-nephew Burns on the basis of his criminal record, and the decision instead to authorize Burns to act as a deputy sheriff, constitutes a policy choice attributable to Bryan County under § 1983. . . . [I]t was open to the jury to find that the sheriff knew of the record of his nephew's violent propensity, but hired him in deliberate indifference to the risk that he would use excessive force on the job, as in fact he later did. That the sheriff's act did not itself command or require commission of a constitutional violation (like the order to perform an unlawful entry and search in *Pembaur*) is not dispositive under § 1983, for we have expressly rejected the contention that "only unconstitutional policies are actionable" under § 1983, and have never suggested that liability under the statute is otherwise limited to policies that facially violate other federal law. The sheriff's policy choice creating a substantial risk of a constitutional violation therefore could subject the county to liability under existing precedent.[54]

At the level of theory, at least, the Court does not disagree, and it assumes for the sake of deciding the case that a single, facially neutral act of deliberate indifference by a policymaker could be a predicate to municipal liability if it led to an unconstitutional injury inflicted by subordinate officers. At the level of practice, however, the tenor of the Court's opinion is decidedly different: it suggests that the trial court insufficiently appreciated the specificity of the risk to which such indifference must be deliberate in order to be actionable; it expresses deep skepticism that such appreciation of risk could ever reasonably be attributed to the policymaker who has performed only a single unsatisfactory, but not facially unconstitutional, act; and it finds the record insufficient to make any such showing in this case.

The Court is certainly correct in emphasizing the need to show more than mere negligence on the part of the policymaker, for at the least the element of deliberateness requires both subjective appreciation of a risk of unconstitutional harm, and a risk substantial enough to justify the heightened responsibility that deliberate indifference generally entails. The Court goes a step further, however, in requiring that the "particular" harmful consequence be "plainly obvious" to the policymaker, a characterization of deliberate indifference adapted from dicta set forth in . . . footnote [10] in *Canton*. While we speculated in *Canton* that "[i]t could . . . be that the police, in exercising their discretion, so often violate constitutional rights that the need for further training must have been plainly obvious to the city policymakers, who, nevertheless, are 'deliberately indifferent' to the need," we did not purport to be defining the fault of deliberate indifference universally as the failure to act in relation to a "plainly obvious consequence" of harm. Nor did we, in addressing the requisite risk

---

[54] [n.2] Given the sheriff's position as law enforcement policymaker, it is simply off the point to suggest, as the Court does, that there is some significance in either the fact that Sheriff Moore's failure to screen may have been "a deviation" from his ordinary hiring practices or that a pattern of injuries resulting from his past practices is absent. *Pembaur* made clear that a single act by a designated policymaker is sufficient to establish a municipal policy, and *Canton* explained, as the Court recognizes, that evidence of a single violation of federal rights can trigger municipal liability under § 1983.

that constitutional violations will occur, suggest that the deliberate indifference necessary to establish municipal liability must be, as the Court says today, indifference to the particular constitutional violation that in fact occurred.

The Court's formulation that deliberate indifference exists only when the risk of the subsequent, particular constitutional violation is a plainly obvious consequence of the hiring decision, while derived from *Canton*, is thus without doubt a new standard. As to the "particular" violation, the Court alters the understanding of deliberate indifference as set forth in *Canton*, where we spoke of constitutional violations generally.[55] As to "plainly obvious consequence," the Court's standard appears to be somewhat higher, for example, than the standard for "reckless" fault in the criminal law, where the requisite indifference to risk is defined as that which "consciously disregards a substantial and unjustifiable risk that the material element exists or will result . . . [and] involves a gross deviation from the standard of conduct that a law-abiding person would observe in the actor's situation." *See* AMERICAN LAW INSTITUTE, MODEL PENAL CODE § 2.02(2)(c) (1985).

[But] even under the "plainly obvious consequence" rule the evidence here would support the verdict.

At trial, [the County's] expert witness stated during cross-examination that Burns's rap sheet listed repeated traffic violations, including driving while intoxicated and driving with a suspended license, resisting arrest, and more than one charge of assault and battery. The witness further testified that Burns pleaded guilty to assault and battery and other charges 16 months before he was hired by Sheriff Moore. [Brown's] expert witness testified that Burns's arrest record showed a "blatant disregard for the law and problems that may show themselves in abusing the public or using excessive force," and [the County's] own expert agreed that Burns's criminal history should have caused concern. When asked if he would have hired Burns, he replied that it was "doubtful." On this evidence, the jury could have found that the string of arrests and convictions revealed "that Burns had [such] a propensity for violence and a disregard for the law" that his subsequent resort to excessive force was the plainly obvious consequence of hiring him as a law enforcement officer authorized to employ force in performing his duties.

The county escapes from liability through the Court's untoward application of an enhanced fault standard to a record of inculpatory evidence showing a contempt for constitutional obligations as blatant as the nepotism that apparently occasioned it. The novelty of this escape shows something unsuspected (by me, at least) until today. Despite arguments that *Monell*'s policy requirement was an erroneous reading of § 1983, *see Oklahoma City v. Tuttle* (Stevens, J., dissenting), I had not previously thought that there was sufficient reason to unsettle the precedent of *Monell*. Now it turns out, however, that *Monell* is hardly settled. That being so, Justice Breyer's powerful call to reexamine § 1983 municipal liability afresh finds support in the Court's own readiness to rethink the matter.

JUSTICE BREYER, with whom JUSTICE STEVENS and JUSTICE GINSBURG join, dissenting.

I believe that the legal prerequisites for reexamination of an interpretation of an important statute are present here. The soundness of the original principle is doubtful. The original principle has generated a body of interpretive law that is so complex that the law has become difficult to apply. Factual and legal changes have divorced the law from the distinction's apparent original purposes. And there may be only a handful of

---

[55] [n.3] The Court's embellishment on the deliberate indifference standard is, in any case, no help in resolving this case because there has never been any suggestion that Deputy Burns's criminal background, including charges of assault and battery, indicated that he would commit a constitutional violation different from the one he in fact committed.

individuals or groups that have significantly relied upon perpetuation of the original distinction. If all this is so, later law has made the original distinction, not simply wrong, but obsolete and a potential source of confusion.

First, consider *Monell*'s original reasoning. The *Monell* "no vicarious liability" principle rested upon a historical analysis of § 1983 and upon § 1983's literal language — language that imposes liability upon (but only upon) any "person." Justice Stevens has clearly explained why neither of these rationales is sound.

Second, *Monell*'s basic effort to distinguish between vicarious liability and liability derived from "policy or custom" has produced a body of law that is neither readily understandable nor easy to apply. Today's case provides a good example. The District Court in this case told the jury it must find (1) Sheriff Moore's screening "so likely to result in violations of constitutional rights" that he could "reasonably [be] said to have been deliberately indifferent to the constitutional needs of the Plaintiff" and (2) that the "inadequate hiring . . . policy directly caused the Plaintiff's injury." This instruction comes close to repeating this Court's language in *Canton v. Harris*.

The majority says that the [lower courts] did not look closely enough at the specific facts of this case. It also adds that the harm must be a "plainly obvious consequence" of the "decision to hire" Burns. But why elaborate *Canton*'s instruction in this way? The Court's verbal formulation is slightly different; and that being so, a lawyer or judge will ignore the Court's precise words at his or her peril. Yet those words, while adding complexity, do not seem to reflect a difference that significantly helps one understand the difference between "vicarious" liability and "policy." Even if the Court means only that the record evidence does not meet *Canton*'s standard, it will be difficult for juries, and for judges, to understand just why that is so. It will be difficult for them to apply today's elaboration of *Canton* — except perhaps in the limited context of police force hiring decisions that are followed by a recruit's unconstitutional conduct.

Consider some of the other distinctions that this Court has had to make as it has sought to distinguish liability based upon policymaking from liability that is "vicarious." It has proved necessary, for example, to distinguish further, between an exercise of policymaking authority and an exercise of delegated discretionary policy-implementing authority. . . . But the distinction is not a clear one. It requires federal courts to explore state and municipal law that distributes different state powers among different local officials and local entities. That law is highly specialized; it may or may not say just where policymaking authority lies, and it can prove particularly difficult to apply in light of the Court's determination that a decision can be "policymaking" even though it applies only to a single instance. It is not surprising that results have sometimes proved inconsistent.

Nor does the location of "policymaking" authority pose the only conceptually difficult problem. Lower courts must also decide whether a failure to make policy was "deliberately indifferent," rather than "grossly negligent." And they must decide, for example, whether it matters that some such failure occurred in the officer-training, rather than the officer-hiring, process. Given the basic *Monell* principle, these distinctions may be necessary, for without them, the Court cannot easily avoid a "municipal liability" that "collaps[es] into *respondeat superior*." But a basic legal principle that requires so many such distinctions to maintain its legal life may not deserve such longevity.

Finally, relevant legal and factual circumstances may have changed in a way that affects likely reliance upon *Monell*'s liability limitation. The legal complexity just described makes it difficult for municipalities to predict just when they will be held liable based upon "policy or custom."

Moreover, their potential liability is, in a sense, greater than that of individuals, for they cannot assert the "qualified immunity" defenses that individuals may raise. *Owen v. Independence*. Further, many States have statutes that appear to, in effect, mimic respondeat superior by authorizing indemnification of employees found liable under

§ 1983 for actions within the scope of their employment. These statutes — valuable to government employees as well as to civil rights victims — can provide for payments from the government that are similar to those that would take place in the absence of *Monell*'s limitations. To the extent that they do so, municipal reliance upon the continuation of *Monell*'s "policy" limitation loses much of its significance.

Any statement about reliance, of course, must be tentative, as we have not heard argument on the matter. We do not know the pattern of indemnification: how often, and to what extent, States now indemnify their employees, and which of their employees they indemnify. I also realize that there may be other reasons, constitutional and otherwise, that I have not discussed that argue strongly for reaffirmation of *Monell*'s holding.

Nonetheless, for the reasons I have set forth, I believe the case for reexamination is a strong one. Today's decision underscores this need. Consequently, I would ask for further argument that would focus upon the continued viability of *Monell*'s distinction between vicarious municipal liability and municipal liability based upon policy and custom.

NOTES

1. Improper Hiring and Fault. *Bryan County*, unlike *City of Canton*, focused on inadequate screening — or more generally stated, improper hiring. Does the Court hold that a single hiring decision simply cannot support municipal liability? Or can the decision be read more narrowly as only a refinement of *City of Canton*'s fault standard in the context of hiring? *See Crete v. City of Lowell*, 418 F.3d 54 (1st Cir. 2005) (stating that "it is unnecessary for us to reach the issue of whether a single hiring decision can make the City susceptible to section 1983 liability" because the evidence was not otherwise sufficient). Regardless of the answer, it appears clear that a general indifference to harm or constitutional rights is insufficient to hold a municipality liable for improper hiring. Rather, "deliberate indifference to the risk that a violation of a *particular* constitutional . . . right will follow the decision" is needed. Applying this standard, it was not enough that Sheriff Moore was deliberately indifferent to a risk that Deputy Burns might violate the Constitution. It had to be established that Moore was deliberately indifferent to the risk that Burns might use excessive force in violation of the Fourth Amendment. Is this a sensible position? Given the facts of *Bryan County*, did the jury not realize that the deliberate indifference it found related directly to Burns's use of excessive force? Does this mean that Sheriff Moore had to understand that excessive force violated the Fourth Amendment? *Compare Szabla v. City of Brooklyn Park*, 486 F.3d 385 (7th Cir. 2007) (holding that right must be clearly established for city to be held liable under deliberate indifference standard) (excerpted in Note 4 following *City of Canton, supra)*.

2. Insufficient Evidence. Because the District Court in *Bryan County* improperly instructed the jury, should not the case have been remanded for a new trial with proper instructions? Why did the Supreme Court proceed in the first instance to address the sufficiency of Brown's evidence under its new standard? In *City of Canton*, remember, the Court remanded for further proceedings under its newly announced deliberate indifference standard. Would not this have been the better approach in *Bryan County*? Or is *Bryan County* authority for a more rigorous assessment of proof in improper hiring cases? Lower courts in the aftermath of *Bryan County* have often found "insufficient evidence" to support sending improper hiring cases to juries. *See, e.g., Crete v. City of Lowell*, 418 F.3d 54 (1st Cir. 2005) (finding insufficient evidence to support finding that a city's hiring of a convicted criminal as a police officer amounted to deliberate indifference to the risk that he might use excessive force); *Morris v. Crawford County*, 299 F.3d 919 (8th Cir. 2002); *Gros v. City of Grand Prairie*, 209 F.3d 431 (5th Cir. 2000).

3. Inadequate Training Revisited. Does *Bryan County*'s revised fault standard apply to claims of municipal liability based on inadequate or improper training? Does *Bryan County* mean that constitutional rights must be clearly established for § 1983 plaintiffs to recover for inadequate training? *See Szabla v. City of Brooklyn Park*, 486 F.3d 385 (7th Cir. 2007) (holding that a right must be clearly established for a city to be held liable for inadequate training) (excerpted in Note 4 following *City of Canton, supra*). The jury in *Bryan County* held the county liable both for improperly hiring Burns and for inadequately training him. The Court of Appeals initially reversed the latter finding, concluding that "we do not find the training practices inadequate." *Bryan County*, 53 F.3d 1410, 1425 (5th Cir. 1995). Following rehearing, however, the Court of Appeals omitted any discussion of the city's inadequate training and affirmed the judgment based on the city's improper hiring. *See* 67 F.3d 1174 (5th Cir. 1995). Only the "improper hiring" theory of liability was challenged before the Supreme Court. Following the Supreme Court's reversal, the Fifth Circuit remanded the case to the District Court to reexamine the jury's conclusion that Moore inadequately trained Burns. 117 F.3d 239 (5th Cir. 1997). The District Court sustained the jury's verdict in favor of Brown on this theory, and the Fifth Circuit once again affirmed. 219 F.3d 450 (5th Cir. 2000). The Supreme Court denied review. 532 U.S. 1007 (2001).

The jury instructions in *Bryan County*, which quoted extensively from *City of Canton*, did not distinguish between improper hiring and inadequate training. Although the Supreme Court invalidated these instructions in the context of improper hiring, the Fifth Circuit sustained them in the context of inadequate training. Assuming the Fifth Circuit is correct, the Supreme Court's more rigorous *Bryan County* standard thus applies only to claims of municipal liability premised on improper hiring, and not inadequate training. *See Young v. City of Providence ex rel. Napolitano*, 404 F.3d 4 (1st Cir. 2005) ("It is much harder for a *Monell* plaintiff to succeed on a hiring claim than a failure to train claim. This is because it is especially difficult, with a hiring claim, to find both causation (that the hiring decision caused the constitutional deprivation of the plaintiff in a particularized sense) and fault (that the hiring decision reflected deliberate indifference to the particular constitutional right at issue of the plaintiff)."). *Cf. Gold v. City of Miami*, 151 F.3d 1346, 1354 (11th Cir. 1998) (apparently applying *Bryan County*'s standard to an inadequate training claim).

D. INNOCENT AGENTS

In *City of St. Louis v. Praprotnik*, 485 U.S. 112 (1988), which is excerpted in Section C.[1], *supra*, government officials responsible for firing a public-sector employee (Praprotnik) were exonerated at trial. How could the City be held liable for a constitutional violation that never occurred? The Eighth Circuit resolved this difficulty by finding that the jury could have concluded that the named defendants "were not the supervisors directly causing the lay off, when the actual damages arose." Instead, the jury could have concluded that certain unnamed supervisors were responsible, and that the City in turn was responsible for these unnamed supervisors' actions. The Supreme Court did not address this issue in *Praprotnik*. In the absence of individual liability, should local government be excused?

CITY OF LOS ANGELES v. HELLER
Supreme Court of the United States
475 U.S. 796 (1986)

PER CURIAM.[56]

[Heller sued the city of Los Angeles and two police officers under the Fourth Amendment and § 1983 for excessive force and unlawful arrest.]

The District Court held a bifurcated trial, and first heard [Heller's] claims against one of the individual police officers.[57] The jury was instructed that Heller would make out his constitutional claim if he were arrested without reasonable cause, or if he were arrested with "unreasonable force" that exceeded the force necessary under the circumstances to effect arrest. The jury was not instructed on any affirmative defenses that might have been asserted by the individual police officer. The jury returned a verdict for the defendant police officer and against [Heller]. The District Court then dismissed the action against [Los Angeles], concluding that if the police officer had been exonerated by the jury there could be no basis for assertion of liability against the city or the persons constituting its Police Commission.[58]

[Heller] appealed to the Court of Appeals for the Ninth Circuit, and that court reversed the judgment of the District Court dismissing [Heller's] case against [Los Angeles] even though it did not disturb the verdict for the defendant police officer. [Heller] urged, and the Court of Appeals apparently agreed, that "the jury could have believed that [Officer] Bushey, having followed Police Department regulations, was entitled in substance to a defense of good faith. Such a belief would not negate the existence of a constitutional injury."

The difficulty with this position is that the jury was not charged on any affirmative defense such as good faith which might have been availed of by the individual police officer. [Heller] contends in his brief in opposition to certiorari that even though no issue of qualified immunity was presented to the jury, the jury might nonetheless have considered evidence which would have supported a finding of such immunity. But the theory under which jury instructions are given by trial courts and reviewed on appeal is that juries act in accordance with the instructions given them, and that they do not consider and base their decisions on legal questions with respect to which they are not charged. We think that the Court of Appeals' search for ambiguity in the verdict was unavailing; as that court itself noted later in its opinion, "[b]ecause the instructions required a verdict for [Heller] if either the due process or the excessive force claim was found, the jury's verdict for the defendant required a negative finding on both claims." This negative, it seems to us, was conclusive not only as to Officer Bushey, but also as to the city and its Police Commission. They were sued only because they were thought legally responsible for Bushey's actions; if the latter inflicted no constitutional injury on [Heller], it is inconceivable that [they] could be liable to [Heller].

[T]his was an action for damages, and neither *Monell* nor any other of our cases authorizes the award of damages against a municipal corporation based on the actions of one of its officers when in fact the jury has concluded that the officer inflicted no constitutional harm. If a person has suffered no constitutional injury at the hands of the

---

[56] [Editor's note: Justice Brennan did not participate in the case.]

[57] [n.*] The second of the two police officers named as defendants was granted summary judgment by the District Court.

[58] [Editor's note: Several lower courts have concluded that police departments and sheriff's offices are not "persons" under § 1983 and thus are not proper parties to constitutional litigation. *See, e.g., Manders v. Lee*, 285 F.3d 983 (11th Cir. 2002) (leaving open the possibility that state law might make police departments or sheriff's offices suable entities under § 1983).]

individual police officer, the fact that the departmental regulations might have authorized the use of constitutionally excessive force is quite beside the point.

JUSTICE STEVENS, with whom JUSTICE MARSHALL joins, dissenting.

It is undisputed that Ronald Heller crashed through a plate-glass window after some kind of an altercation with Officer Bushey. He had been stopped on suspicion of driving while intoxicated and given sobriety tests.[59] In his claim against the municipal entities, Heller contended that the city and the Police Department had adopted a policy of condoning excessive force in making arrests, that the policy was unlawful, and that he had been injured by the application of that policy at the time of his arrest. In his claim against Officer Bushey, Heller contended that his constitutional rights were violated because Officer Bushey had employed "unreasonable force" in arresting him.

On the day before trial, the District Judge bifurcated the trial into two phases — the first against Officer Bushey and the second against the municipal entities. The record contains no explanation for this decision, but it does reveal that Heller's counsel opposed bifurcation.

In the proceeding against Officer Bushey, considerable evidence of the Los Angeles Police Department's policy and custom on the use of force was introduced. An expert witness testified regarding Los Angeles' officially sanctioned use of "escalating force," culminating in the use of the notorious "chokehold." Officer Bushey himself testified that Heller's flight through the window resulted from his attempt to impose a chokehold, and that he was carefully following official Police Department policy.

In submitting the claim against Officer Bushey to the jury, the trial judge gave an instruction that simply stated that whether or not the force used in making an arrest is unreasonable "is an issue to be determined in the light of all the surrounding circumstances." After deliberating several hours, the jury returned a general verdict in favor of the officer.

Thus, despite the majority's summary assertion to the contrary, it is perfectly obvious that the general verdict rejecting the excessive force claim against Officer Bushey did not necessarily determine the constitutionality of the city's "escalating force" policy — a subject on which the jury had received no instructions at all. The verdict merely determined that the officer's action was not unreasonable "in the light of all the surrounding circumstances" — which, of course, included the evidence that Officer Bushey was merely obeying orders and following established Police Department policy.

In view of the fact that the Court of Appeals correctly concluded that there was no necessary inconsistency between a verdict exonerating Officer Bushey and a verdict holding the city and Police Department liable for the "escalating force" policy, it did not have to consider the appropriate response to a possible inconsistency in the context of a bifurcated trial.

Inconsistent verdicts are, of course, a familiar phenomenon. In a criminal case, a jury's apparently inconsistent verdict is allowed to stand. In a civil case, the rule is less clear. Nevertheless, in contrast to the Court's blithe assumption today, it is far from certain that the District Court's action — the dismissal — was an appropriate response, even if somehow a verdict against the municipal entities might have created an inconsistency. First, the Court ignores the fact that, in certain circumstances, a court retains the authority, even in a civil case, to allow an apparently inconsistent verdict to stand. Second, the Court ignores the fact that, when faced with an apparently inconsistent verdict, a court has a duty to attempt to read the verdict in a manner that

---

[59] [n.2] After the altercation, Heller was given an alcohol level test, and was found to have one-tenth the level of alcohol in his body necessary for a finding of driving while intoxicated under California law. Heller was never charged with driving while intoxicated.

will resolve inconsistencies. Third, the Court ignores the fact that, upon receiving an apparently inconsistent verdict, the trial judge has the responsibility, not to retain half of the verdict, but to resubmit the question to the jury. Finally, the Court ignores the fact that, if verdicts are genuinely inconsistent and if the evidence might support either of the "inconsistent" verdicts, the appropriate remedy is ordinarily, not simply to accept one verdict and dismiss the other, but to order an entirely new trial.

Although the Court fails to address it, the question this case raises (if, in fact, the initial view of inevitable inconsistency is accepted) is whether a different set of principles should apply in a bifurcated trial — more narrowly, in a trial that was bifurcated over the objection of the plaintiff. Because the question has not been argued, I do not foreclose the possibility that bifurcation should make a difference, but it is not immediately apparent to me why it should.

If the Court's unprecedented, ill-considered, and far-reaching decision happens to be correct, defendants as a class have been presented with a tactical weapon of great value. By persuading trial judges to bifurcate trials in which both the principal and its agents are named as defendants, and to require the jury to bring in its verdict on the individual claim first, they may obtain the benefit of whatever intangible factors have prompted juries to bring in a multitude of inconsistent verdicts in past years; defendants will no longer have to abide the mechanisms that courts have used to mitigate and resolve apparent inconsistencies. Perhaps that is an appropriate response to the current widespread concern about the potential liabilities of our municipalities, but I doubt it.

NOTES

1. Bifurcated Trials. Bifurcated trials like that in *Heller* are not uncommon in § 1983 litigation. *See* Douglas L. Colbert, *Bifurcation of Civil Rights Defendants: Undermining* Monell *in Police Brutality Cases*, 44 HASTINGS L.J. 499 (1993) (discussing the use of bifurcated trials in § 1983 litigation); *see also* Steven S. Gensler, *Bifurcation Unbarred*, 75 WASH. L. REV. 705 (2000) (discussing the use of bifurcated trials in civil litigation). Is this approach wise for the defense? For the plaintiff? Is it fair? *See* Lars Noah, *Civil Jury Nullification*, 86 IOWA L. REV. 1601, 1654–55 (2001) ("Studies of the procedure demonstrate that defendants prevail in bifurcated trials more often than in unitary trials, which suggests that jury nullification occurs more often in unitary trials and argues for the value of issue separation. A survey of trial judges found support for the belief that bifurcation improves fairness, and 'there is evidence that jurors hearing bifurcated cases are less likely to trade off weak causal evidence against strong evidence on liability or damages.' ").

2. Innocent Agents in Criminal Proceedings. Criminal law has struggled with the problem of "innocent agents" for some time. *See* JOHN KAPLAN & ROBERT WEISBERG, CRIMINAL LAW: CASES AND MATERIALS 613–14 (2d ed. 1991). At common law, a would-be accomplice who used a child, or other agent who was by definition incompetent, to commit a crime was treated as a principal and convicted of the crime on that basis. "Perpetration by means," as it was called, ensured punishment for the would-be accomplice. *Id.* at 614; *see, e.g., State v. McCarthy*, 425 A.2d 924 (Conn. 1979) (holding that a criminal defendant who directed a drug-dependent follower to commit a murder could be convicted even if the follower could not form an intent to kill because of her drug consumption); MODEL PENAL CODE § 2.06(2)(a) ("[a] person is legally accountable for the conduct of another person when . . . acting with the kind of culpability that is sufficient for the commission of the offense, he causes an innocent or irresponsible person to engage in such conduct").

Where the agent is not by definition "innocent," but is not guilty on the facts of the particular case, criminal courts have experienced more difficulty extending liability to a would-be accomplice. For example, in one well-known case, *State v. Hayes*, 16 S.W.2d 514 (Mo. 1891), a principal (Hill) attempted to trick his accomplice (Hayes) into committing burglary by feigning agreement to steal bacon from a store. Although Hayes helped Hill into the store (and thus for all intents and purposes appeared to be an accomplice), the court concluded Hayes could not be convicted of burglary because no burglary had been committed by Hill. Hill, after all, never intended to steal anything, and thus was not a true burglar. "Philosophical concerns . . . make extension of the 'perpetration by means' doctrine problematic. Because the principle of free will is prominent in the law, chains of causation involving human beings make us uneasy." KAPLAN & WEISBERG, *supra*, at 614.[60] Does causation likewise make us uneasy about holding Los Angeles liable for the acts of its innocent police officers? Can *Heller* be best explained in terms of causation?

3. Innocent Agents and Tort Law. Tort law addresses the problem of innocent agents through the doctrines of negligent supervision and negligent entrustment. Even if an employee's conduct is not itself actionable, his or her employer can be held liable under either a negligent supervision or negligent entrustment theory. *See* JAMES A. BRANCH, JR., NEGLIGENT HIRING PRACTICE MANUAL 16–17 (1988); *see also Robinson v. Moore*, 512 S.W.2d 573 (Tenn. Ct. App. 1974) (holding an employer but not its employee liable for the employee's conduct); *Wise v. Fiberglass Systems, Inc.*, 718 P.2d 1178 (Idaho 1986) (describing differences between negligent entrustment and respondeat superior). Should a similar "deliberately indifferent supervision and/or entrustment" approach be followed under § 1983? *See Hopkins v. Andaya*, 958 F.2d 881 (9th Cir. 1992) ("the police chief and city might be held liable for improper training or improper procedure even if [the police officer who allegedly used excessive force] is exonerated, since they put an officer on the street who is so badly trained and instructed he lets his baton be taken away from him and then has to kill an unarmed civilian to save his own life").

4. *Heller* Applied. A majority of lower courts have read *Heller* as a per se constitutional rule that precludes municipal liability when the named individual defendant escapes liability. Without a constitutional violation on the part of the alleged perpetrator, they reason, there can be no § 1983 action against a municipal employer. *See, e.g., Ewolski v. City of Brunswick*, 287 F.3d 492 (6th Cir. 2002) ("Where, as here, a municipality's liability is alleged on the basis of the unconstitutional actions of its employees, it is necessary to show that the employees inflicted a constitutional harm."); *Curley v. Village of Suffern*, 268 F.3d 65 (2d Cir. 2001) ("a municipality cannot be liable for inadequate training or supervision when the officers involved in making an arrest did not violate the plaintiff's constitutional rights"); *Quintanilla v. City of Downey*, 84 F.3d 353 (9th Cir. 1996) (same); *Johnson v. City of Lincoln Park*, 434 F. Supp. 2d 467 (E.D. Mich. 2006) (same). *But see Hopkins v. Andaya*, 958 F.2d 881 (9th Cir. 1992) (suggesting that a city could be liable for negligent entrustment even though its officer was not guilty of using excessive force); *Fagan v. City of Vineland*, 22 F.3d 1283 (3d Cir. 1994) (holding that in "a substantive due process case arising out of a police pursuit, an underlying constitutional tort can still exist even if no individual police officer violated the Constitution").[61] Municipal liability, however, can be proper "even in the absence of individual liability, at least so long as the injuries complained of are not solely attributable to the actions of named individual defendants." *Barrett v. Orange County Human Rights Commission*, 194 F.3d 341 (2d Cir. 1999). The theory behind this latter approach is that an unnamed official might have violated the plaintiff's rights.

---

[60] Should a city's corporate nature play a part in the analysis? "Corporations have been convicted of crimes requiring knowledge on the basis of the 'collective knowledge' of the employees as a group, even though no single employee possessed sufficient information to know that the crime was being committed." *Developments in the Law — Corporate Crime: Regulating Corporate Behavior Through Criminal Sanctions*, 92 HARV. L. REV. 1227, 1248 (1979).

[61] The Third Circuit in *Brown v. Commonwealth of Pennsylvania, Department of Health Emergency Medical Services Training Institute*, 318 F.3d 473 (3d Cir. 2003), noted that most of its sister Circuits, and one of its own panels, disagreed with the conclusion in *Vineland*.

See, e.g., Young v. City of Providence ex rel. Napolitano, 404 F.3d 4 (1st Cir. 2005) (holding that a voluntary dismissal of named wrongdoers does not prevent a city from being held liable so long as the plaintiff can prove a constitutional violation on behalf of some municipal agent).

5. Constitutional Duties. Can government be held liable for failing to live up to a constitutional duty — like providing medical assistance to pretrial detainees, *see* Chapter 1.C., *supra* — when no single official is responsible? In *Fairley v. Luman*, 281 F.3d 913 (9th Cir. 2002), the plaintiff (Fairley) was erroneously arrested and held for twelve days under a warrant for the arrest of his twin brother. Fairley sued the city and the arresting officers under § 1983 for both excessive force and wrongful detention. Following a jury trial, the arresting officers were exonerated on both counts. The Ninth Circuit concluded that because the officers were exonerated, *Heller* precluded municipal liability for excessive force. In contrast, the court found that *Heller* had "no bearing on [Fairley's] Fourth and Fourteenth Amendment claims against the City for arrest without probable cause and deprivation of liberty without due process. These alleged constitutional deprivations were not suffered as a result of actions of the individual officers, but as a result of the collective inaction of the Long Beach Police Department." The court explained:

> [D]etention pursuant to a valid warrant but in the face of repeated protests of innocence will, after a lapse of time, deprive the accused of a constitutional "liberty." "[A]n individual has a liberty interest in being free from incarceration absent a criminal conviction." Indeed, we have stated freedom from incarceration is the "paradigmatic liberty interest" under the due process clause.
>
> [Fairley] had a liberty interest in being free from a twelve-day incarceration without any procedural safeguard in place to verify the warrant he was detained on was his and in the face of his repeated protests of innocence. In light of the importance of [Fairley's] liberty interest, the significant risk of deprivation of that interest through the City's warrant procedures, and the minimum burden to the City of instituting readily available procedures for decreasing the risk of erroneous detention, the procedures afforded by the City to [Fairley] failed to provide him due process under the Fourteenth Amendment.
>
> [The City's] decision not to instigate any procedures to alleviate the problem of detaining individuals on the wrong warrant could constitute a policy. . . . [W]here the city failed to implement internal procedures for tracking inmate arraignments, the policy was one of inaction: wait and see if someone complains.

Similarly, the Seventh Circuit in *Gibson v. City of Chicago*, 910 F.2d 1510, 1519–21 (7th Cir. 1990), held that Chicago could be held liable for failing to retrieve a weapon from a police officer who had been relieved of duty and who subsequently shot an innocent bystander, even though the officer could not be held liable for using excessive force because he was not acting "under color of" law. The court reasoned that "the municipality itself is the state actor and its action in maintaining the alleged policy at issue supplies the 'color of law' requirement under § 1983. In short, under this theory of liability, Gibson contends that the City's policy of allowing a deranged police officer to retain his service revolver and bullets is the state action that deprived him of his life."

6. Exoneration Because of Qualified Immunity. As suggested in *Heller*, most lower courts allow institutional liability when an official escapes liability only because of qualified or absolute immunity. *See, e.g., International Ground Transportation v. Mayor and City Council of Ocean City*, 475 F.3d 214 (4th Cir. 2007) ("when a jury, which has been instructed on a qualified immunity defense as to the individual defendants, returns a general verdict in favor of the individual defendants but against the municipality, the verdict is consistent and liability will lie against the municipality (assuming the verdict is proper in all other respects)"); *Curley v. Village of Suffern*, 268 F.3d 65 (2d Cir. 2001) ("*Heller* will not save a defendant municipality from liability where an individual officer is found not liable because of qualified immunity"). Immunity protects the official from liability but does not deny that a constitutional wrong took place. Therefore, the governmental employer, which is not protected by immunity, *see Owen v. City of Independence* (excerpted in Section B, *supra*), can still be held accountable.

7. Can *Heller* Be Squared with Constitutional Precedent? On a number of occasions before *Heller*, the Supreme Court recognized that institutional responsibility for constitutional wrongs need not be premised on any given individual's liability. In particular, school desegregation cases often found institutional responsibility without searching for individual wrongdoers. *See, e.g., Swann v. Charlotte-Mecklenburg Bd. of Educ.*, 402 U.S. 1 (1971); *cf.* Christina B. Whitman, *Government Responsibility for Constitutional Torts*, 85 MICH. L. REV. 225, 257 (1986) (noting that the school desegregation cases can be explained under the traditional theory that requires one individual to be responsible, but that the cases also suggest a possible movement away from the individual model). School desegregation, of course, is only one application of the Supreme Court's Equal Protection jurisprudence. Viewed more broadly, the Court on a number of occasions has recognized governmental wrongdoing under the Equal Protection Clause without insisting on a single, culpable wrongdoer. *See* Whitman, *supra*, at 261. The same is true in the context of Procedural Due Process. In *Owen v. City of Independence*, for example, a municipal employee (Owen) was allegedly discharged and defamed in violation of Procedural Due Process. *See, e.g., Board of Regents v. Roth*, 408 U.S. 564 (1972) (holding that public-sector employees with legitimate expectation of continued employment are entitled to hearing before discharge). The supervisor responsible for the discharge (the City Manager) did not defame Owen; rather, members of the City Council did. The City Council, meanwhile, did not discharge Owen, the City Manager did. Thus, neither the City Manager who discharged Owen, nor the members of the City Council who defamed him, satisfied both Due Process requirements for this particular constitutional violation. Though the Court in *Owen* never made clear whether either the City Manager or the members of the City Council individually violated the Constitution, it recognized a violation of the Due Process Clause. Is this aspect of *Owen* consistent with *Heller*? Do both Equal Protection and Procedural Due Process impose constitutional duties? *See* Note 5, *supra*.

E. USING STATE LAW TO REACH LOCAL GOVERNMENT

ALDINGER v. HOWARD
Supreme Court of the United States
427 U.S. 1 (1976)

MR. JUSTICE REHNQUIST delivered the opinion of the Court.

[Aldinger claimed that she was discharged from her job with Spokane County by Howard, the county treasurer, in violation of the First Amendment and Procedural Due Process. Not only did she seek damages from Howard under § 1983, Aldinger also joined the County as a defendant in federal court.]

In [*United Mine Workers v. Gibbs*, 383 U.S. 715 (1966)], the respondent brought an action in federal court against petitioner UMW, asserting parallel claims — a federal statutory claim and a claim under the common law of Tennessee arising out of alleged concerted union efforts to deprive him of contractual and employment relationships with the coal mine's owners. Though the federal claim was ultimately dismissed after trial, and though diversity was absent, the lower courts sustained jurisdiction over the state-law claim, and affirmed the damages award based thereon. . . . [This Court held that] in a federal-question case, where the federal claim is of sufficient substance, and the factual relationship between "that claim and the state claim permits the conclusion that the entire action before the court comprises but one constitutional 'case,'" pendent jurisdiction extends to the state claim. The Court, in the second aspect of the *Gibbs* formulation, went on to enumerate the various factors bearing on a district court's discretionary decision whether the power should be exercised in a given parallel-claims case, emphasizing that "pendent jurisdiction is a doctrine of discretion, not of plaintiff's right."

The situation with respect to the joining of a new party . . . strikes us as being both factually and legally different from the situation facing the Court in *Gibbs* and its predecessors. From a purely factual point of view, it is one thing to authorize two parties, already present in federal court by virtue of a case over which the court has jurisdiction, to litigate in addition to their federal claim a state-law claim over which there is no independent basis of federal jurisdiction. But it is quite another thing to permit a plaintiff, who has asserted a claim against one defendant with respect to which there is federal jurisdiction, to join an entirely different defendant on the basis of a state-law claim over which there is no independent basis of federal jurisdiction, simply because his claim against the first defendant and his claim against the second defendant "derive from a common nucleus of operative fact." True, the same considerations of judicial economy would be served insofar as plaintiff's claims "are such that he would ordinarily be expected to try them all in one judicial proceeding. . . . " But the addition of a completely new party would run counter to the well-established principle that federal courts, as opposed to state trial courts of general jurisdiction, are courts of limited jurisdiction marked out by Congress.

There is also a significant legal difference. In . . . *Gibbs* Congress was silent on the extent to which the defendant, already properly in federal court under a statute, might be called upon to answer nonfederal questions or claims; the way was thus left open for the Court to fashion its own rules under the general language of Art. III. But the extension of *Gibbs* to this kind of "pendent party" jurisdiction bringing in an additional defendant at the behest of the plaintiff presents rather different statutory jurisdictional considerations.

[Aldinger] does not, and indeed could not, contest the fact that as to § 1983, counties are excluded from the "person[s]" answerable to the plaintiff "in an action at law [or] suit in equity" to redress the enumerated deprivations [under this Court's holding in *Monroe v. Pape*]. [Aldinger] must necessarily argue that in spite of the language emphasized above Congress left it open for the federal courts to fashion a jurisdictional doctrine under the general language of Art. III enabling them to circumvent this exclusion, as long as the civil rights action and the state-law claim arise from a "common nucleus of operative fact." . . . Parties such as counties, whom Congress excluded from liability in § 1983, . . . can argue with a great deal of force that the scope of that "civil action" over which the district courts have been given statutory jurisdiction should not be broadly read as to bring them back within that power merely because the facts also give rise to an ordinary civil action against them under state law. In short, as against a plaintiff's claim of additional power over a "pendent party," the reach of the statute conferring jurisdiction should be construed in light of the scope of the cause of action as to which federal judicial power has been extended by Congress.

Resolution of a claim of pendent-party jurisdiction, therefore, calls for careful attention to the relevant statutory language. As we have indicated, we think a fair reading of the . . . scope of § 1983 . . . requires a holding that the joinder of a municipal corporation, like the county here, for purposes of asserting a state-law claim not within federal diversity jurisdiction, is without the statutory jurisdiction of the district court.

We conclude that in this case Congress has by implication declined to extend federal jurisdiction over a party such as Spokane County.[62]

NOTES

1. *Aldinger*'s Continuing Validity. *Aldinger* involved a § 1983 plaintiff who sought to join a county in federal court using a state law that held municipalities vicariously liable for the wrongs of their agents. *Monroe* had yet to be overruled by *Monell*, and consequently § 1983 could not be used as a predicate for federal jurisdiction. Because diversity was lacking, no independent basis of federal jurisdiction could be established. The Court rejected pendent party jurisdiction by relying on Congress's intent under § 1983, which at the time was interpreted to foreclose local government liability. The specific reasoning in *Aldinger* — that a local governmental entity could not be joined because of the Forty-Second Congress's decision to insulate municipalities — was overruled by the Supreme Court two years later in *Monell*. The Supreme Court in *Monell*, however, did not hold that a state-law claim against a municipality can be brought in federal court simply because the claim is pendent to a § 1983 action against a municipal official. *See* footnote 66 to the majority's opinion in *Monell* (excerpted in Section A, *supra*). Does *Aldinger* survive *Monell*?

2. *Jett v. Dallas Independent School District*. In *Jett v. Dallas Independent School District*, 491 U.S. 701 (1989), a white football coach (Jett) sued the Dallas Independent School District and the principal of his former high school claiming that he was fired because of his race. The suit was filed both under § 1983 and 42 U.S.C. § 1981, which prohibits racial discrimination in the making and enforcement of contracts. (Section 1981 is described more fully in Chapter 1.A., *supra*.) Jett tried to avoid *Monell*'s official policy or custom requirement by arguing that § 1981, unlike § 1983, authorized respondeat superior. The Supreme Court avoided this latter issue by holding that public-sector employees, like high school football coaches, must use § 1983 rather than § 1981 to prosecute claims of racial discrimination against their employers.[63]

The Court in *Jett* also rejected the argument that Texas's law of respondeat superior could be "borrowed" under 42 U.S.C. § 1988(a), which (as discussed more fully in Chapter 5.A., *infra*) authorizes federal courts to use "the common law, as modified and changed by the constitution and the statutes of the State wherein the court having jurisdiction of such civil or criminal cause is held," when federal law is otherwise "deficient in the provisions necessary to furnish suitable remedies and punish offenses against law":

> Far from supporting [Jett's] call for the creation or implication of a damages remedy broader than that provided by § 1983, we think the plain language of § 1988 supports the result we reach here. As we noted in *Moor v. County of Alameda*, 411 U.S. 693 (1973), in rejecting an argument similar to [Jett's] contention here: "[Section 1988] expressly limits the authority granted federal

---

[62] [Editor's note: Justices Brennan, Marshall, and Blackmun dissented.]

[63] Was this aspect of *Jett* changed by the Civil Rights Restoration Act of 1991, which among other things added § 1981(c): "The rights protected by this section are protected against impairment by nongovernmental discrimination *and impairment under color of State law*." (Emphasis added). *See Federation of African-American Contractors v. Oakland*, 96 F.3d 1204 (9th Cir. 1996) (holding that § 1981(c) overturned *Jett*). Notwithstanding § 1981(c), courts have continued to hold that local governments are not subject to suit under § 1981 for racial discrimination. *See, e.g., Butts v. County of Volusia*, 222 F.3d 891 (11th Cir. 2000) ("We conclude the amendments did not change § 1981 and § 1983 contains the sole cause of action against state actors for violations of § 1981."); *Bolden v. City of Topeka*, 441 F.3d 1129 (10th Cir. 2006) (agreeing with *Butts*). Those courts that have concluded otherwise have also rejected respondeat superior as a basis of liability under § 1981 in suits against local government. *See, e.g., Federation of African-American Contractors v. Oakland*, 96 F.3d 1204 (9th Cir. 1996) (holding that a policy or custom must be established under § 1981). Section 1981 suits against private defendants, in contrast, can proceed under a respondeat superior theory of liability. Does disparate treatment for public and private employers make sense?

courts to look to the common law, as modified by state law, to instances in which that law 'is not inconsistent with the Constitution and laws of the United States.'" As we indicated in *Moor*, "Congress did not intend, as a matter of federal law, to impose vicarious liability on municipalities for violations of federal civil rights by their employees."

As it did in *Aldinger*, the *Jett* Court refused to allow the use of state attribution rules to define the terms of municipal liability under § 1983. Unlike *Aldinger*, *Jett* was decided after *Monell*. Does *Jett* suggest that *Aldinger* survived *Monell*?

3. Pendent Claims Between 1978 and 1990. After *Monell*, lower federal courts continued to dismiss claims against municipalities based on state laws creating vicarious liability that were joined with § 1983 actions against local officials. *See, e.g., Mathis v. Parks*, 741 F. Supp. 567, 575 (E.D.N.C. 1990) (dismissing a state claim based on respondeat superior brought against a local government because of *Aldinger*); *Grier v. Galinac*, 740 F. Supp. 338, 340 (M.D. Pa. 1990) (same); *Vacca v. Barletta*, 753 F. Supp. 400, 402 (D. Mass. 1990) (noting that *Monell* partially overruled *Aldinger*, but the "basic holding of *Aldinger* . . . is still good law"), *aff'd*, 933 F.2d 31 (1st Cir. 1991). *See generally* Peter Cassat, Note, *Statutory Indemnification in Section 1983 Actions Based on Police Misconduct: Choosing a Forum*, 1988 WIS. L. REV. 605, 615–17. On the other hand, many federal courts entertained pendent state-law claims against local governments where the complaints raised "colorable or plausible" claims under *Monell*. *See, e.g., Ismail v. Cohen*, 899 F.2d 183, 187 (2d Cir. 1990). All of this apparently changed, however, with the passage of 28 U.S.C. § 1367(a) ("Supplemental Jurisdiction") in 1990.

4. The Arrival of Supplemental Jurisdiction. In *Finley v. United States*, 490 U.S. 545 (1989), the Supreme Court held that state-law claims against pendent parties could *not* be joined in federal court with claims brought under the Federal Tort Claims Act. Congress responded to *Finley* in October of 1990 by adding 28 U.S.C. § 1367(a), which allows pendent-party jurisdiction over state claims that "are so related to claims in the action within the district court's original jurisdiction that they form part of the same case or controversy under Article III of the United States Constitution." *See generally* Patrick D. Murphy, *A Federal Practitioner's Guide to Supplemental Jurisdiction Under 28 U.S.C. § 1367*, 78 MARQ. L. REV. 973 (1995). Section 1367(a) overturns the Court's holding in *Finley*, *see Exxon Mobil Corp. v. Allapattah Services, Inc.*, 545 U.S. 546 (2005) ("[a]ll parties to this litigation and all courts to consider the question agree that § 1367 overturned the result in *Finley*"), and would also appear to lift *Aldinger*'s bar to pendent-party jurisdiction in § 1983 cases. *See Brown v. Grabowski*, 922 F.2d 1097 (3d Cir. 1990) (suggesting that § 1367(a) solves *Aldinger*'s jurisdictional problem); Note, *Defining the Parameters of Supplemental Jurisdiction After 28 U.S.C. § 1367*, 43 DRAKE L. REV. 391, 404 (1994) ("[w]ith this grant of supplemental jurisdiction, Congress clearly overruled *Finley* and *Aldinger*").[64] Assuming *United Mine Workers v. Gibbs* provides the proper standard, joining a state-law vicarious liability claim against a municipality should not prove problematic in the § 1983 context, since it would necessarily arise from the same facts supporting the federal claim against the local official.

---

[64] Note that § 1367(c) grants district courts discretion to decline pendent-party jurisdiction if: (1) the state claim is "novel or complex," (2) the state claim "substantially predominates over the federal claim," (3) the federal claim has been dismissed, or (4) other "compelling reasons" exist. For further discussion of § 1367, *see City of Chicago v. International College of Surgeons*, 522 U.S. 156 (1997) (excerpted in Chapter 8.A.[4], *infra*).

WILSON v. CHICAGO
United States Court of Appeals for the Seventh Circuit
120 F.3d 681 (7th Cir. 1997)

Before POSNER, CHIEF JUDGE, and COFFEY AND EASTERBROOK, CIRCUIT JUDGES.

POSNER, CHIEF JUDGE.

[Wilson brought suit under § 1983 against a Chicago police officer, Burge, and the City of Chicago claiming that Burge had used torture to extract a confession. The jury found for both the City and Burge. On appeal, the Seventh Circuit affirmed the judgment in favor of the City, but reversed the judgment in favor of Burge and remanded for a new trial. On remand, Wilson amended his complaint to add an indemnity claim against the City under Illinois's Tort Immunity Act, which provides that cities are "directed to pay any tort judgment or settlement for compensatory damages for which it or an employee while acting within the scope of his employment is liable." After the jury returned a judgment against Burge for $50,000 in compensatory damages, the city claimed that it was improperly joined as a defendant in federal court.]

The City argues that there is no federal jurisdiction over Wilson's claim against it because that claim rests entirely on the state statute that we have cited and diversity of citizenship is absent. It cites *Peacock v. Thomas*, 516 U.S. 349 (1996), for the proposition that a suit to enforce a federal judgment is not within federal jurisdiction merely by virtue of the judgment. What is correct is that once a judgment becomes final and the court has relinquished jurisdiction, a new suit requires a new basis of federal jurisdiction. So if it is a suit claiming a violation of a settlement agreement resolving a federal case, it cannot be brought in federal court merely by virtue of its origin in that case. *Kokkonen v. Guardian Life Ins. Co.*, 511 U.S. 375 (1994). But that has nothing necessarily to do with the present case. This is not a new suit against the City; the City was brought in (or rather brought back in, after being dismissed on the authority of *Monell*, as an alleged violator of Wilson's constitutional rights) before the suit against Burge was over, as a party derivatively liable for any judgment against him. If it was proper to bring the City back into the suit in this way, there was no new suit and *Peacock* is inapposite.

The joinder of an additional party against whom the plaintiff has a state claim closely related to the claim on which federal jurisdiction is based, as is a state claim advanced in order to enable the collection of a judgment against the original defendant, is expressly authorized by the statute conferring supplemental jurisdiction on the federal district courts. 28 U.S.C. § 1367(a). But that statute is applicable only to suits that began after November 30, 1990, and this suit began before. The main purpose and effect of the statute were to codify the ancillary and pendent jurisdiction of the federal district courts as it existed before *Finley v. United States* put the kibosh on pendent party jurisdiction, in which a plaintiff adds a defendant against whom he has a claim related to his main claim but unsupported by an independent ground of federal jurisdiction. *Finley* did not, however, sweep away the whole of the ancillary jurisdiction. It recognized the continued validity of that jurisdiction when "necessary to give effect to the court's judgment," and gave the example of adding as a defendant a person alleged to have received a fraudulent conveyance from an insolvent original party. Subsequent cases recognized the limited impact of *Finley*.

The nonstatutory ancillary jurisdiction that survived *Finley* embraces not only postjudgment collection proceedings but also what in this case is tantamount to a prejudgment collection proceeding, an effort to bring into the case a solvent party to pay the judgment against an insolvent one. What is more, Burge had impleaded the City, seeking indemnity (under state and local provisions discussed later in this opinion) of the judgment rendered against him (*see* Fed. R. Civ. P. 14(a)) and thus bringing the

City back into the case on an unexceptionable application of the post-*Finley* but prestatutory concept of ancillary jurisdiction.

The City argues that the state statute on which Wilson relied in bringing the City back into the case comes into play only when a judgment is formally entered against its employee; so Wilson jumped the gun. This would not affect the district court's jurisdiction over his claim against the City; it would just show that the claim lacked merit (more precisely, as we shall see, that it was premature). So let us turn to the merits. There is surely something to the City's argument; the City cannot be made to pay a judgment while the liability of its employee is still in question, and we do not . . . mean that Wilson could have sued the City directly without proceeding against Burge. It does not follow that Wilson could not proceed under [state law against the City] until the judgment against Burge became final. The City concedes as it must that if it disobeys the direction in the [Tort Immunity Act] (assuming the statute is applicable to the City), the plaintiff can obtain a judgment against it. Once it became clear, therefore, as it did shortly after we remanded the case, that the City would not pay a judgment when and if one was entered against its employee, the plaintiff, in order to expedite the collection of the judgment, could ask the court to enter a judgment against the City that would take effect when and if a judgment against Burge was entered and no longer contestable.

In effect Wilson was asking the court to enter a declaratory judgment against the City, a typical move when an insurer (as the City in effect is of the judgment against Burge) is in the picture, and one not invalidated by its conditional character. In fact Wilson asked for just this kind of declaratory relief, and the omission to describe it in these terms in the judgment that the district court entered is a detail.

We would be more sympathetic to the City's argument if we could see any benefit from forcing Wilson to wait until a final judgment was entered against Burge and made incontestable by exhaustion of his appellate remedies. It would still be possible for Wilson to seek to collect the judgment by ancillary proceedings against the City. Fed. R. Civ. P. 69(a).[65] All that would be involved would be delay and maybe a little more paperwork.

Last and least, the City argues that to allow Wilson to use [the Tort Immunity Act] to affix liability to it violates the Rules Enabling Act, 28 U.S.C. § 2072(b), by giving substantive force to a rule of procedure, namely Fed. R. Civ. P. 69(a). The City was held not to be liable to Wilson under 42 U.S.C. § 1983 because it had not been complicit in his wrongdoing; by using Rule 69(a) in conjunction with the state statute, Wilson has succeeded, the City argues, in overturning the judgment exonerating it. Not so. At most the rule is merely the vehicle by which Wilson is able to litigate a state claim in federal law. He could just as well have sued the City in state court. Rule 69(a) affected only the choice of forum, not his substantive rights against the City. But for completeness we add that Rule 69(a) may not even be in play in this case, for it specifies the procedures for collecting a judgment after the judgment has been rendered. Authority to bring the City back into the case and obtain a judgment against it simultaneous with the judgment against Burge was based on the ancillary jurisdiction of the federal courts interpreted in light of settled principles of declaratory relief. Rule 69(a) is based ultimately on ancillary jurisdiction, but it has a narrower office.

NOTES

1. Collection From Local Governments. *Wilson* makes clear that a successful § 1983 plaintiff can pursue a local governmental "insurer" under state law after winning a federal judgment. The question is whether this must take place in state court after

---

[65] [Editor's note: The Seventh Circuit later agreed with Judge Posner's suggestion and ruled in *Yang v. City of Chicago*, 137 F.3d 522 (7th Cir. 1998), that Rule 69(a) allows judgment creditors to pursue insurers — like the City in Wilson — in ancillary proceedings in federal court following judgment.]

the federal judgment is handed down or whether it can be joined with the underlying federal action. *Wilson* holds that neither *Aldinger* nor *Finley* prevents a federal district court from joining a local governmental insurer as a pendent party in a § 1983 case. If *Wilson* is correct, local government can be joined under 28 U.S.C. § 1367(a), at least if it has agreed (or is required) to indemnify its employees. Because indemnity arrangements are quite common in the public sector today, *see* Howard M. Wasserman, *Civil Rights Plaintiffs and John Doe Defendants: A Study in Section 1983 Precedents*, 25 CARDOZO L. REV. 793, 827 (2003) ("the officer likely can count on the government providing his counsel and defense and indemnifying him for any judgment entered against him"), the dictates of *Monell* can often be avoided. *See* David F. Hamilton, *The Importance and Overuse of Policy and Custom Claims: A View from One Trench*, 48 DEPAUL L. REV. 723 (1999) (observing that § 1983 plaintiffs too often ignore indemnity arrangements in favor of pursuing cities directly under *Monell*). *Contrast* David Rudovsky, *Running in Place: The Paradox of Expanding Rights and Restricted Remedies*, 2005 U. ILL. L. REV. 1199, 1229 ("in cases in which the official's conduct was particularly egregious, the state will often refuse indemnification, thus creating the anomalous situation of denying compensation in the most serious cases").

2. Reconciling *Jett*. *Jett v. Dallas Independent School District*, 491 U.S. 701 (1989) (discussed in Note 2 following *Aldinger*, *supra*), refused to allow federal courts to "borrow" state vicarious liability rules under 42 U.S.C. § 1988(a) (discussed in Chapter 5.A., *infra*) to hold local governments liable for the wrongs of their employees. *Wilson*, in contrast, allows state-law insurance and indemnification claims against cities to be joined with § 1983 claims in federal court against their insured officials, either under 28 U.S.C. § 1367(a) or Rule 69. Are these two cases reconcilable? Are insurance claims different from those premised on vicarious liability?Did Congress's adoption of supplemental jurisdiction in 1990 overrule the result in *Jett*?

Chapter 5
THE RELATIONSHIP BETWEEN STATE AND FEDERAL LAW IN SECTION 1983 LITIGATION

A. SECTION 1988(a), STATUTES OF LIMITATIONS, AND SURVIVORSHIP RULES

42 U.S.C. § 1988(a) provides:

> The jurisdiction in civil and criminal matters conferred on the district courts by the provisions of [§ 1983, as well as §§ 1981, 1982, 1985, and 1986, among others], for the protection of all persons in the United States in their civil rights, and for their vindication, shall be exercised and enforced in conformity with the laws of the United States, so far as such laws are suitable to carry the same into effect; but in all cases where they are not adapted to the object, or are deficient in the provisions necessary to furnish suitable remedies and punish offenses against law, the common law, as modified and changed by the constitution and statutes of the State wherein the court having jurisdiction of such civil or criminal cause is held, so far as the same is not inconsistent with the Constitution and laws of the United States, shall be extended to and govern the said courts in the trial and disposition of the cause, and if it is of a criminal nature, in the infliction of punishment on the party found guilty.

WILSON v. GARCIA
Supreme Court of the United States
471 U.S. 261 (1985)

JUSTICE STEVENS delivered the opinion of the Court.

In this case we must determine the most appropriate state statute of limitations to apply to claims enforceable under . . . 42 U.S.C. § 1983.

On January 28, 1982, respondent brought this § 1983 action in the United States District Court for the District of New Mexico seeking "money damages to compensate him for the deprivation of his civil rights guaranteed by the Fourth, Fifth and Fourteenth Amendments to the United States Constitution and for the personal injuries he suffered which were caused by the acts and omissions of the [petitioners] acting under color of law." The complaint alleged that on April 27, 1979, petitioner Wilson, a New Mexico State Police officer, unlawfully arrested the respondent, "brutally and viciously" beat him, and sprayed his face with tear gas; that petitioner Vigil, the Chief of the New Mexico State Police, had notice of Officer Wilson's allegedly "violent propensities," and had failed to reprimand him for committing other unprovoked attacks on citizens; and that Vigil's training and supervision of Wilson was seriously deficient.

The respondent's complaint was filed two years and nine months after the claim purportedly arose. Petitioners moved to dismiss on the ground that the action was barred by the 2-year statute of limitations [for tort actions brought against governmental entities or employees] contained in § 41-4-15(A) of the New Mexico Tort Claims Act. The petitioners' motion was supported by a decision of the New Mexico Supreme Court which squarely held that the Tort Claims Act provides "the most closely analogous state cause of action" to § 1983, and that its 2-year statute of limitations is therefore applicable to actions commenced under § 1983 in the state courts. *DeVargas v. New Mexico*, 642 P.2d 166 (1982). In addition to the 2-year statute of limitations in the Tort Claims Act, two other New Mexico statutes conceivably could apply to § 1983 claims: § 37-1-8, which provides a 3-year limitation period for actions "for an injury to the person or reputation of any person"; and § 37-1-4, which provides a 4-year limitation period for "all other actions not herein otherwise provided for." If either of these longer statutes applies to the respondent's § 1983 claim, the complaint was timely filed. . . .

I

The Reconstruction Civil Rights Acts do not contain a specific statute of limitations governing § 1983 actions — "a void which is commonplace in federal statutory law." *Board of Regents v. Tomanio*, 446 U.S. 478, 483 (1980). When Congress has not established a time limitation for a federal cause of action, the settled practice has been to adopt a local time limitation as federal law if it is not inconsistent with federal law or policy to do so.[1] In 42 U.S.C. § 1988, Congress has implicitly endorsed this approach with respect to claims enforceable under the Reconstruction Civil Rights Acts.

The language of § 1988 directs the courts to follow "a three-step process" in determining the rules of decision applicable to civil rights claims:

> "First, courts are to look to the laws of the United States 'so far as such laws are suitable to carry [the civil and criminal civil rights statutes] into effect.' [42 U.S.C. § 1988.] If no suitable federal rule exists, courts undertake the second step by considering application of state 'common law, as modified and changed by the constitution and statutes' of the forum state. *Ibid.* A third step asserts the predominance of the federal interest: courts are to apply state law only if it is not 'inconsistent with the Constitution and laws of the United States.' *Ibid.*"

Burnett v. Grattan, 468 U.S. 42, 47–48 (1984).

This case principally involves the second step in the process: the selection of "the most appropriate," or "the most analogous" state statute of limitations to apply to this § 1983 claim.

In order to determine the most "most appropriate" or "most analogous" New Mexico statute to apply to the respondent's claim, we must answer three questions. We must first consider whether state law or federal law governs the characterization of a § 1983 claim for statute of limitations purposes. If federal law applies, we must next decide whether all § 1983 claims should be characterized in the same way, or whether they should be evaluated differently depending upon the varying factual circumstances and legal theories presented in each individual case. Finally, we must characterize the essence of the claim in the pending case, and decide which state statute provides the most appropriate limiting principle. Although the text of neither § 1983 nor § 1988 provides a pellucid answer to any of these questions, all three parts of the inquiry are, in final analysis, questions of statutory construction.

II

Our identification of the correct source of law properly begins with the text of § 1988. Congress' first instruction in the statute is that the law to be applied in adjudicating civil rights claims shall be in "conformity with the laws of the United States, so far as such laws are suitable." This mandate implies that resort to state law — the second step in the process — should not be undertaken before principles of federal law are exhausted. The characterization of § 1983 for statute of limitations purposes is derived from the elements of the cause of action, and Congress' purpose in providing it. These, of course, are matters of federal law. Since federal law is available to decide the question, the language of § 1988 directs that the matter of characterization should be treated as a

---

[1] [n.12] *See, e.g., Runyon v. McCrary*, 427 U.S. 160, 180–182 (1976); *Auto Workers v. Hoosier Cardinal Corp.*, 383 U.S. 696, 704 (1966); *Chattanooga Foundry & Pipe Works v. Atlanta*, 203 U.S. 390, 397–398 (1906); *McClaine v. Rankin*, 197 U.S. 154, 158 (1905); *Campbell v. Haverhill*, 155 U.S. 610, 617 (1895).

federal question. Only the length of the limitations period, and closely related questions of tolling and application, are to be governed by state law.

This interpretation is also supported by Congress' third instruction in § 1988: state law shall only apply "so far as the same is not inconsistent with" federal law. This requirement emphasizes "the predominance of the federal interest" in the borrowing process, taken as a whole. *Burnett v. Grattan*, 468 U.S. at 48. Even when principles of state law are borrowed to assist in the enforcement of this federal remedy, the state rule is adopted as "a federal rule responsive to the need whenever a federal right is impaired." *Sullivan v. Little Hunting Park, Inc.*, 396 U.S. 229, 240 (1969). The importation of the policies and purposes of the States on matters of civil rights is not the primary office of the borrowing provision in § 1988; rather, the statute is designed to assure that neutral rules of decision will be available to enforce the civil rights actions, among them § 1983. Congress surely did not intend to assign to state courts and legislatures a conclusive role in the formative function of defining and characterizing the essential elements of a federal cause of action.

. . . [H]ere, the federal interest in uniformity and the interest in having "firmly defined, easily applied rules," *see Chardon* [*v. Fumero Soto*, 462 U.S. 650, 667 (1983)] (Rehnquist, J., dissenting), support the conclusion that Congress intended the characterization of § 1983 to be measured by federal rather than state standards. The Court of Appeals was therefore correct in concluding that it was not bound by the New Mexico Supreme Court's holding in *DeVargas*.

III

. . . [I]n considering whether all § 1983 claims should be characterized in the same way for limitations purposes, it is useful to recall that § 1983 provides "a uniquely federal remedy against incursions under the claimed authority of state law upon rights secured by the Constitution and laws of the Nation." *Mitchum v. Foster*, 407 U.S. 225, 239 (1972). The high purposes of this unique remedy make it appropriate to accord the statute "a sweep as broad as its language." Because the § 1983 remedy is one that can "override certain kinds of state laws," *Monroe v. Pape*, 365 U.S. 167, 173 (1961), and is, in all events, "supplementary to any remedy any State might have," *McNeese v. Board of Education*, 373 U.S. 668, 672 (1963), it can have no precise counterpart in state law. *Monroe v. Pape*, 365 U.S. at 196 n.5 (Harlan, J., concurring). Therefore, it is "the purest coincidence," *ibid.*, when state statutes or the common law provide for equivalent remedies; any analogies to those causes of action are bound to be imperfect.

In this light, practical considerations help to explain why a simple, broad characterization of all § 1983 claims best fits the statute's remedial purpose. The experience of the courts that have predicated their choice of the correct statute of limitations on an analysis of the particular facts of each claim demonstrates that their approach inevitably breeds uncertainty and time-consuming litigation that is foreign to the central purposes of § 1983. Almost every § 1983 claim can be favorably analogized to more than one of the ancient common-law forms of action, each of which may be governed by a different statute of limitations. In the case before us, for example, the respondent alleges that he was injured by a New Mexico State Police officer who used excessive force to carry out an unlawful arrest. This § 1983 claim is arguably analogous to distinct state tort claims for false arrest, assault and battery, or personal injuries. Moreover, the claim could also be characterized as one arising under a statute, or as governed by the special New Mexico statute authorizing recovery against the State for the torts of its agents.

. . . If the choice of the statute of limitations were to depend upon the particular facts or the precise legal theory of each claim, counsel could almost always argue, with considerable force, that two or more periods of limitations should apply to each § 1983 claim. Moreover, under such an approach different statutes of limitations would be applied to the various § 1983 claims arising in the same State, and multiple periods of limitations would often apply to the same case.² There is no reason to believe that Congress would have sanctioned this interpretation of its statute.

When § 1983 was enacted, it is unlikely that Congress actually foresaw the wide diversity of claims that the new remedy would ultimately embrace. The simplicity of the admonition in § 1988 is consistent with the assumption that Congress intended the identification of the appropriate statute of limitations to be an uncomplicated task for judges, lawyers, and litigants, rather than a source of uncertainty, and unproductive and ever-increasing litigation. Moreover, the legislative purpose to create an effective remedy for the enforcement of federal civil rights is obstructed by uncertainty in the applicable statute of limitations, for scarce resources must be dissipated by useless litigation on collateral matters.

Although the need for national uniformity "has not been held to warrant the displacement of state statutes of limitations for civil rights actions," *Board of Regents v. Tomanio*, 446 U.S. at 489, uniformity within each State is entirely consistent with the borrowing principle contained in § 1988. We conclude that the statute is fairly construed as a directive to select, in each State, the one most appropriate statute of limitations for all § 1983 claims. The federal interests in uniformity, certainty, and the minimization of unnecessary litigation all support the conclusion that Congress favored this simple approach.

IV

After exhaustively reviewing the different ways that § 1983 claims have been characterized in every Federal Circuit, the Court of Appeals concluded that the tort action for the recovery of damages for personal injuries is the best alternative available. We agree that this choice is supported by the nature of the § 1983 remedy, and by the federal interest in ensuring that the borrowed period of limitations not discriminate against the federal civil rights remedy.

The specific historical catalyst for the Civil Rights Act of 1871 was the campaign of violence and deception in the South, fomented by the Ku Klux Klan, which was denying decent citizens their civil and political rights. The debates on the Act chronicle the alarming insecurity of life, liberty, and property in the Southern States, and the refuge that local authorities extended to the authors of these outrageous incidents. . . .

The atrocities that concerned Congress in 1871 plainly sounded in tort. Relying on this premise we have found tort analogies compelling in establishing the elements of a cause of action under § 1983, *Monroe v. Pape*, 365 U.S. at 187, and in identifying the immunities available to defendants, *City of Newport v. Fact Concerts, Inc.*, 453 U.S. 247, 258 (1981); *Pierson v. Ray*, 386 U.S. 547, 553–557 (1967). As we have noted, however, the § 1983 remedy encompasses a broad range of potential tort analogies, from injuries to property to infringements of individual liberty.

Among the potential analogies, Congress unquestionably would have considered the remedies established in the Civil Rights Act to be more analogous to tort claims for personal injury than, for example, to claims for damages to property or breach of contract. . . .

Relying on the language of the statute, the Court of Appeals for the Fourth Circuit has succinctly explained why this analogy is persuasive:

"In essence, § 1983 creates a cause of action where there has been injury, under color of state law, to the person or to the constitutional or federal

---

² [n.33] For example, in *Polite v. Diehl*, 507 F.2d 119 (CA3 1974) (en banc), the plaintiff alleged that police officers unlawfully arrested him, beat him and sprayed him with mace, coerced him into pleading guilty to various offenses, and had his automobile towed away. The court held that a 1-year false arrest statute of limitations applied to the arrest claim, a 2-year personal injuries statute applied to the beating and coerced-plea claims, and a 6-year statute for actions seeking the recovery of goods applied to the towing claim.

statutory rights which emanate from or are guaranteed to the person. In the broad sense, every cause of action under § 1983 which is well-founded results from 'personal injuries.'"

Almond v. Kent, 459 F.2d 200, 204 (1972).[3]

Had the 42d Congress expressly focused on the issue decided today, we believe it would have characterized § 1983 as conferring a general remedy for injuries to personal rights.

The relative scarcity of statutory claims when § 1983 was enacted makes it unlikely that Congress would have intended to apply the catchall periods of limitations for statutory claims that were later enacted by many States. Section 1983, of course, is a statute, but it only provides a remedy and does not itself create any substantive rights. *Chapman v. Houston Welfare Rights Organization*, 441 U.S. 600, 617–618 (1979). Although a few § 1983 claims are based on statutory rights, *Maine v. Thiboutot*, 448 U.S. 1, 4–8 (1980), most involve much more. . . .

Finally, we are satisfied that Congress would not have characterized § 1983 as providing a cause of action analogous to state remedies for wrongs committed by public officials. It was the very ineffectiveness of state remedies that led Congress to enact the Civil Rights Acts in the first place. Congress therefore intended that the remedy provided in § 1983 be independently enforceable whether or not it duplicates a parallel state remedy. *Monroe v. Pape*, 365 U.S. at 173. The characterization of all § 1983 actions as involving claims for personal injuries minimizes the risk that the choice of a state statute of limitations would not fairly serve the federal interests vindicated by § 1983. General personal injury actions, sounding in tort, constitute a major part of the total volume of civil litigation in the state courts today, and probably did so in 1871 when § 1983 was enacted. It is most unlikely that the period of limitations applicable to such claims ever was, or ever would be, fixed in a way that would discriminate against federal claims, or be inconsistent with federal law in any respect.

V

In view of our holding that § 1983 claims are best characterized as personal injury actions, the Court of Appeals correctly applied the 3-year statute of limitations governing actions "for an injury to the person or reputation of any person." . . .

JUSTICE POWELL took no part in the consideration or decision of this case.

JUSTICE O'CONNOR, dissenting.

. . . Characterization of § 1983 claims is, I agree, a matter of federal law. But I see no justification, given our longstanding interpretation of 42 U.S.C. § 1988 and Congress' awareness of it, for abandoning the rule that courts must identify and apply the statute of limitations of the state claim most closely analogous to the particular § 1983 claim. . . .

I

The rule that a federal court adjudicating rights under § 1983 will adopt the state statute of limitations of the most closely analogous state-law claim traces its lineage to *M'Cluny v. Silliman*, 3 Pet. 270 (1830), *Campbell v. Haverhill*, 155 U.S. 610 (1895), and *O'Sullivan v. Felix*, 233 U.S. 318 (1914). These opinions held that where "Congress . . . could have, by specific provision, prescribed a limitation, but no specific provision [was]

---

[3] [n.38] *Cf. Runyon v. McCrary*, 427 U.S. 160, 179–182 (1976) (affirming Court of Appeals' reliance on statute of limitations for "personal injuries" actions in 42 U.S.C. § 1981 claim).

adduced," "Congress . . . intended to subject such action to the general laws of the State applicable to actions of a similar nature" and "intended that the remedy should be enforced in the manner common to like actions within the same jurisdiction." With respect to the borrowing of state law in § 1983 claims, . . . [t]his Court has consistently interpreted § 1988 as instructing that the rule applicable to the analogous state claim shall furnish the rule of decision "so far as the same is not inconsistent with the Constitution and the laws of the United States." *See, e.g., Board of Regents v. Tomanio,* 446 U.S. 478 (1980); *Robertson v. Wegmann,* 436 U.S. 584 (1978); *Johnson v. Railway Express Agency, Inc.,* 421 U.S. 454 (1975).

In *Johnson v. Railway Express Agency,* the Court described the policies behind Congress' decision to borrow the most appropriate state limitations period:

> "Although any statute of limitations is necessarily arbitrary, the length of the period allowed for instituting suit inevitably reflects a value judgment concerning the point at which the interests in favor of protecting valid claims are outweighed by the interests in prohibiting prosecution of stale ones. . . . In borrowing a state period of limitation for application to a federal cause of action, a federal court is relying on the State's wisdom in setting a limit . . . on the prosecution of a closely analogous claim."

Plainly the legislative judgment to which this Court has traditionally deferred is not some purely arbitrary imposition of a conveniently uniform time limit. For example, a legislature's selection of differing limitations periods for a claim sounding in defamation and one based on a written contract is grounded in its evaluation of the characteristics of those claims relevant to the realistic life expectancy of the evidence and the adversary's reasonable expectations of repose.

Despite vocal criticism of the "confusion" created by individualized statutes of limitations, most Federal Courts of Appeals and state courts have continued the settled practice of seeking appropriate factual analogies for each genus of § 1983 claim. As these courts have recognized:

> "The variety of possible claims that might be brought under section 1983 is unlimited, ranging from simple police brutality to school desegregation cases. To impose one statute of limitations for actions so diverse would be to disregard the unanimous judgments of the states that periods of limitations should vary with the subject matter of the claim. While the present system of reference to these many state limits is not perfect in operation, it surely preserves some of the judgments that have been made about what appropriate periods of limitation should be for causes of action diverse in nature."

Note, *Choice of Law Under Section 1983,* 37 U. CHI. L. REV. 494, 504 (1970).

II

The majority concedes that "[by] adopting the statute governing an analogous cause of action under state law, federal law incorporates the State's judgment on the proper balance between the policies of repose and the substantive policies of enforcement embodied in the state cause of action." Yet the Court posits, without any serious attempt at explanation, that a § 1983 claim differs so fundamentally from a state-law cause of action that "any analogies to those causes of action are bound to be imperfect." The only fundamental differences the Court identifies — § 1983's "uniqueness," its "high purposes," its "supplementary" nature — in no way explain the determination that a single inflexible analogy should govern what the Court concedes is the "wide diversity" of claims the § 1983 remedy embraces. . . .

The Court's all-purpose analogy is appealing; after all, every compensable injury, whether to constitutional or statutory rights, through violence, deception, or broken promises, to the person's pocketbook, person, or dignity, might plausibly be described as a "personal injury." But so sweeping an analogy is no analogy at all. In all candor, the

A. SECTION 1988(a), STATUTES OF LIMITATIONS, AND SURVIVORSHIP RULES 261

Court has perceived a need for uniformity and has simply seized the opportunity to legislate it. The Court takes this step even though a number of bills proposed to recent Congresses to standardize § 1983 limitations periods have failed of enactment, a fact that the Court would normally interpret as a persuasive indication that Congress does not agree that concerns for uniformity dictate a unitary rule. *See Robertson v. Wegmann*, 436 U.S. at 593 & n.11 [pointing out that "whatever the value of nationwide uniformity in areas of civil rights enforcement where Congress has not spoken, in the areas to which § 1988 is applicable Congress has provided direction, indicating that state law will often provide the content of the federal remedial rule [and thus] there will not be nationwide uniformity on these issues"].

As well as co-opting federal legislation, the Court's decision effectively forecloses legislative creativity on the part of the States. Were a State now to formulate a detailed statutory scheme setting individualized limitations periods for various § 1983 claims, drawing upon policies regarding the timeliness of suits for assault, libel, written contract, employment disputes, and so on, the Supremacy Clause would dictate that the blunt instrument announced today must supersede such legislative fine-tuning. Presumably, today's decision would pre-empt such legislation even if the State's limitations period in a given case were more generous than the tort rule that the Court today mandates invariably shall apply. In the case of *Blake v. Katter*, 693 F.2d 677 (CA7 1982), for example, a plaintiff who claimed deprivation of liberty through false arrest enjoyed the benefit of Indiana's generous 5-year statute for claims against public officials. The same plaintiff would now find his § 1983 cause of action foreclosed by the comparatively meager 2-year statute governing injuries to the person.

In exchange for the accrued, collective wisdom of many legislatures, the Court gains only a half measure of uniformity. The Court has heretofore wisely disavowed uniformity as a value not warranting "displacement of state statutes of limitations for civil rights actions." *See Board of Regents v. Tomanio*, 446 U.S. at 489; *Robertson v. Wegmann, supra*, at 584–585 & n.11. True, the Court's decision means that all § 1983 claims in a given State must be brought within a single set period. Yet even the promise of uniformity within each State is illusory. In achieving statewide symmetry among civil rights claims the Court creates fresh problems of asymmetry that are of far greater moment to the local practitioner. Any lawyer knows that § 1983 claims do not occur in splendid isolation; they are usually joined with claims under state tort or contract law arising out of the same facts. In the end, today's decision saves neither judges nor local practitioners any headaches, since for 150 years characterization of the state law claims with reference to the relevant facts has been a routine prerequisite to establishing the applicable statute of limitations. . . . For example, under the newly revised Pennsylvania statutory scheme . . . , a state law claim for libel or slander will be stale in one year, but a § 1983 claim based on the same facts can still be filed after two years. More puzzling still, a § 1983 claim for violation of constitutional rights arising out of a breach of contract will be foreclosed in two years but its state law counterpart based on the identical breach will remain fresh and litigable at six years. This sort of half-baked uniformity is a poor substitute for the careful selection of the appropriate state law analogy.

Today's decision does not so much resolve confusion as banish it to the lower courts. The Court's new analogy lacks any magical power to conjure uniformity where diversity is the natural order. In fact, the rule the Court adopts failed in application literally before the ink of the Tenth Circuit's decision was dry. The decision of the Court of Appeals for the Tenth Circuit in this case, affirmed today, was only one of four handed down on the same day in a valiant attempt to fix limitations periods for the entire Tenth Circuit. Kansas law conveniently supplied a 2-year statute for "injury to the rights of another," *see Hamilton v. City of Overland Park*, 730 F.2d 613 (1984); but Utah law contained no such provision, *see Mismash v. Murray City*, 730 F.2d 1366 (1984) (selecting Utah's 4-year residuary statute, absent any statute for personal injury). Colorado law defied the newly minted rule by supplying not one but two periods that govern various injuries to personal rights. *McKay v. Hammock*, 730 F.2d 1367 (1984). The Tenth Circuit resolved its dilemma by declaring both limitations periods "irrelevant" and instead selecting Colorado's 3-year residuary statute. As these cases demonstrate, there is no guarantee state law will obligingly supply a limitations period to match an abstract analogy that may have little relevance to the forum State's limitations scheme.

. . . Though the task of characterization is admittedly not "uncomplicated," it is nevertheless a routine feature of state procedural law, a task that is handled daily by the same judges, lawyers, and litigants as rely on § 1983, often in the same actions. It was Congress' choice in 1866, when it incorporated by reference "the common law, as modified . . . by . . . the statutes of the [forum] State," to forgo legislating a simplistic rule and to entrust judges with the task of integrating a federal remedy into a federal system.

Therefore, I would reverse the Court of Appeals' scholarly but ultimately flawed attempt to impose a single state limitations period for all § 1983 claims. Because I would apply the statute of limitations New Mexico applies to state claims directly analogous to the operative facts of this case, I respectfully dissent.

NOTES

1. Section 1988(a). Although section 1988(a) instructs the federal courts to look to state law whenever federal law is "deficient," much of the Supreme Court's section 1983 jurisprudence has been developed without any mention of section 1988(a) or any consideration of state law. Consider, for example, the Court's rulings creating the doctrines of absolute and qualified immunity (Chapter 2, *supra*), refusing to require exhaustion of state administrative remedies (Chapter 8.A., *infra*), articulating the official policy or custom requirement for suits filed against local governments (Chapter 4, *supra*), and defining the damages that may be awarded in section 1983 suits (Chapter 6, *infra*). Although section 1983 is silent on all of these issues, none of the Court's rulings in these areas turned on an application of section 1988(a) or considered what the relevant state law rule would have been. Instead, the Court treated each issue as one to be governed by a uniform federal rule. *See, e.g., Smith v. Wade*, 461 U.S. 30, 91 n.17 (1983) (Rehnquist, J., dissenting) (noting that the majority articulated a federal standard for awarding punitive damages in section 1983 cases rather than looking to state law under section 1988(a), apparently because it "conclud[ed] *sub silentio*" that federal law was "suitable"); *Carey v. Piphus*, 435 U.S. 247, 258 n.13 (1978) (citing section 1988(a), but looking to "the common law of torts" generally, rather than the applicable rules in Illinois, in determining how damages for procedural due process violations should be assessed); *Sullivan v. Little Hunting Park, Inc.*, 396 U.S. 229, 239–40 (1969) (interpreting section 1988(a), in a case claiming the denial of property rights under 42 U.S.C. § 1982, as giving federal courts a choice between "federal and state rules on damages . . . , whichever better serves the policies expressed in the federal statutes"). Can these opinions be reconciled with *Wilson*? *See* Jack M. Beerman, *A Critical Approach to Section 1983 with Specific Attention to Sources of Law*, 42 STAN. L. REV. 51, 101 (1989) (criticizing "[t]he indeterminacy of the Court's choice of law rules," and arguing that "[t]he Court's manipulation of text, legislative history and policy is transparent . . . when it jumps merrily from one source of law to another").

2. Alternative Interpretations of Section 1988(a). Several commentators have argued that the Court's whole approach to section 1988(a) is fundamentally misguided. According to Professor Theodore Eisenberg, for example, section 1988(a) was meant to apply only in cases that were removed from state to federal court and thus has no applicability to run-of-the-mill section 1983 suits initiated in federal court. *See* Theodore Eisenberg, *State Law in Federal Civil Rights Cases: The Proper Scope of Section 1988*, 128 U. PA. L. REV. 499 (1980). Eisenberg derives support for this theory from the historical context of section 1988(a), which was originally passed as part of section 3 of the Civil Rights Act of 1866 just following a sentence (now codified as 28 U.S.C. § 1443) that allowed state-court defendants to remove a case to federal court when the rights guaranteed to them by section 1 of the 1866 Act[4] were being denied in state court.

Pointing out that "[i]t requires an incongruous historical vision to picture the Reconstruction Congress establishing the local law of the recently-rebelling states as the linchpin of an avowedly nationalist enforcement program," Professor Seth Kreimer has likewise advanced a competing theory of section 1988(a) based on its historical context. Seth F. Kreimer, *The Source of Law in Civil Rights Actions: Some Old Light on Section 1988*, 133 U. PA. L. REV. 601, 616 (1985). Kreimer observes that section 1988(a) was passed more than seventy years before *Swift v. Tyson*, 41 U.S. (16 Pet.) 1 (1842), was overruled by *Erie Railroad Co. v. Tompkins*, 304 U.S. 64 (1938), and he therefore maintains that section 1988(a) ought to be interpreted in light of *Swift v. Tyson*. Under *Swift v. Tyson*'s (now discredited) view, section 1988(a)'s reference to "the laws of the United States" would pertain only to federal statutes, and its reference to "the common law" would mean, not the common law of a particular state, but the common law created by the federal courts and applied in diversity cases. Thus, according to Kreimer, "the norm is uniformity": "[i]n areas not directly governed by federal statute, a uniform 'general common law' should be the centerpiece of enforcement," unless that common law has been modified by a specific state statute. Kreimer, *supra*, at 620.

3. Limitations Periods for Section 1983 Suits. As *Wilson* indicates, the federal courts have traditionally borrowed state limitations periods for federal causes of action — even in the absence of a federal statute like section 1988(a). Congress did not enact a residual statute of limitations until 1990, and even then it applies only to statutes enacted after that date. *See* 28 U.S.C. § 1658 (creating a four-year limitations period for "civil action[s] arising under an Act of Congress" "[e]xcept as otherwise provided by law"); *see also City of Rancho Palos Verdes v. Abrams*, 544 U.S. 113, 124 (2005) (suggesting that section 1658's four-year limitations period "would seem to apply" to section 1983 suits brought under *Maine v. Thiboutot*, 448 U.S. 1 (1980) (described in Chapter 1.E., *supra*), and predicated on violations of federal statutes enacted after 1990); *Jones v. R.R. Donnelley & Sons Co.*, 541 U.S. 369 (2004) (concluding that section 1658 applies to hostile environment and other claims brought under the 1991 amendments to 42 U.S.C. § 1981 (which are described in Chapter 1.A., *supra*)).

In the wake of the Court's decision in *Wilson* that the state limitations period applicable to personal injury actions governs section 1983 cases, a conflict arose among the courts of appeals in cases where a state had more than one such limitations period. The Court resolved that conflict in *Owens v. Okure*, 488 U.S. 235 (1989), a section 1983 suit in which the plaintiff claimed that he had been unlawfully arrested and beaten by two police officers. A unanimous Court applied the state's three-year "residual statute of limitations for claims of personal injury not embraced by specific statutes of limitations," rather than the one-year statute that covered certain intentional torts, including assault, battery, and false imprisonment. *Owens*, 488 U.S. at 238. "[W]here state law provides multiple statutes of limitations for personal injury actions," the Court held, "courts considering § 1983 claims should borrow the general or residual statute for personal injury actions." *Owens*, 488 U.S. at 250. But the Court made clear that it was not retreating from its rejection of New Mexico's four-year residual limitations period on the facts of *Wilson*, instructing courts to look "in the first instance" to the state's personal injury limitations period and to "resort to residual statutes of limitations only where state law provides multiple statutes of limitations for personal injury actions and the residual one embraces, either explicitly or by judicial construction, unspecified personal injury actions." *Owens*, 488 U.S. at 250 n.12.

---

[4] The surviving provisions of section 1 of the 1866 Act are the contract and property rights now contained in 42 U.S.C. §§ 1981–1982, which are described in Chapter 1.A., *supra*.

Pursuant to the rules outlined in *Wilson* and *Owens*, the statute of limitations for section 1983 suits is now fairly well settled and, in most states, is two or three years. *See* 3 SHELDON H. NAHMOD, CIVIL RIGHTS AND CIVIL LIBERTIES LITIGATION: THE LAW OF SECTION 1983 §§ 9:16–9:29 (4th ed. 2007) (surveying the lower court case law). *But cf. Larson v. Snow College*, 189 F. Supp. 2d 1286, 1295, 1298 (D. Utah 2000) (building on the decision in *Arnold v. Duchesne County*, 26 F.3d 982, 986 (10th Cir. 1994), which found two-year statute of limitations created specifically for section 1983 cases in Utah "inconsistent" with federal law, and likewise refusing to apply amended Utah statute creating two-year limitations period that "specifically and exclusively target[ed] federal civil rights actions in general," on the grounds that it "circumvented the entire process and purpose of borrowing the most appropriate state limitations period").

4. Tolling Rules. As the Court indicates in *Wilson*, state law governs not only the limitations period for section 1983 suits, but also the rules determining when that statute of limitations is tolled. Invoking section 1988(a), the Court so held in *Board of Regents v. Tomanio*, 446 U.S. 478 (1980), concluding that the plaintiff's section 1983 suit was time-barred because New York law did not toll the limitations period while she was challenging the defendant's decision to deny her a chiropractor's license in state court. The Supreme Court likewise refused to find the New York rule "inconsistent" with federal law within the meaning of section 1988(a), noting that section 1983's policies of deterrence and compensation were not "significantly affected by this rule of limitations since plaintiffs can still readily enforce their claims, thereby recovering compensation and fostering deterrence, simply by commencing their actions within three years." 446 U.S. at 488. *See also Chardon v. Fumero Soto*, 462 U.S. 650 (1983) (holding that state law governs the tolling rules for class action section 1983 suits as well); *Hardin v. Straub*, 490 U.S. 536 (1989) (concluding that state provision tolling the limitations period for prisoners applies to section 1983 suits).

Despite these rulings, the federal courts have occasionally suggested that a federal doctrine of equitable tolling may toll the limitations period in section 1983 suits. *See, e.g., Mitchell v. Donchin*, 286 F.3d 447 (7th Cir. 2002); *Ashafa v. City of Chicago*, 146 F.3d 459, 464 n.1 (7th Cir. 1998) (citing conflicting Seventh Circuit opinions); *Bell v. Fowler*, 99 F.3d 262, 266–67 & n.3 (8th Cir. 1996) (noting conflict among the circuits).

The Supreme Court expressly declined to rule on the propriety of a federal tolling doctrine in *Heck v. Humphrey*, 512 U.S. 477, 489 (1994) (excerpted in Chapter 8.B.[2], *infra*). But in *Wallace v. Kato*, 127 S. Ct. 1091, 1099 (2007) (excerpted in Chapter 8.B.[3]), the Court indicated that it was not "inclined to adopt a federal tolling rule" that would extend the limitations period for the false arrest claim at issue there. Noting that "[w]e have generally referred to state law for tolling rules, just as we have for the length of statutes of limitation," the Court observed that the plaintiff "has not brought to our attention, nor are we aware of, Illinois cases providing tolling in even remotely comparable circumstances." *Wallace*, 127 S. Ct. at 1098–99. Justice Breyer, joined by Justice Ginsburg, dissented. Given the procedural complications created by *Heck v. Humphrey*, the dissenters thought that "[t]he use of [federal principles of] equitable tolling in cases of potential temporal conflict between civil § 1983 and related criminal proceedings is consistent with, indeed, it would further, § 1983's basic purposes." Therefore, the dissent concluded, "[i]f a given state court lacks the necessary tolling provision, [§ 1983] permits the federal courts to devise and impose such principles." *Wallace*, 127 S. Ct. at 1103 (Breyer, J., dissenting).

5. Accrual Rules. Even though section 1983 borrows state statutes of limitations and tolling rules, the related question of when a plaintiff's cause of action accrues is "a question of federal law that is *not* resolved by reference to state law." *Wallace v. Kato*, 127 S. Ct. 1091, 1095 (2007). Looking to "common-law tort principles," the Court noted that " 'the standard rule [is] that [accrual occurs] when the plaintiff has "a complete and present cause of action," ' that is, when 'the plaintiff can file suit and obtain relief.' " Applying that standard to the false arrest claim brought there, the Court observed that the plaintiff "could have filed suit as soon as the allegedly wrongful arrest occurred." Nevertheless, in light of the fact that "the victim may not be able to sue while he is still imprisoned," the Court held that the limitations period for false arrest claims " 'begin[s] to run . . . when the alleged false imprisonment ends,' " i.e., "once the victim becomes held *pursuant to [lawful] process* — when, for example, he is bound over by a magistrate or arraigned on charges." *Wallace*, 127 S. Ct. at 1095–96.

For examples of other section 1983 cases in which accrual questions have arisen, see *Heck v. Humphrey*, 512 U.S. 477 (1994) (deciding that section 1983 suits implicating the validity of a conviction or prison sentence — for example, malicious prosecution claims — do not accrue until the conviction (or sentence) has been reversed, expunged, or otherwise declared invalid) (excerpted in Chapter 8.B.[2], *infra*); *Chardon v. Fernandez*, 454 U.S. 6, 8 (1981) (per curiam) (holding that a section 1983 suit challenging termination from a government job accrued on the date of the alleged "*discriminatory*" act, not the point at which the *consequences* of the act bec[a]me painful") (relying on *Delaware State College v. Ricks*, 449 U.S. 250 (1980), which reached a similar conclusion in an employment discrimination suit filed under Title VII and section 1981).

6. Accrual, Statutes of Limitations, and Prospective Actions. Statutes of limitations typically apply only to actions seeking damages, and not those seeking injunctive relief. As the Supreme Court observed in *Holmberg v. Armbrecht*, 327 U.S. 392, 396 (1946), "[t]raditionally and for good reasons, statutes of limitation are not controlling measures of equitable relief. Such statutes have been drawn upon by equity solely for the light they may shed in determining that which is decisive for the chancellor's intervention, namely, whether the plaintiff has inexcusably slept on his rights so as to make a decree against the defendant unfair." *See also United States v. Telluride*, 146 F.3d 1241, 1245 (10th Cir. 1998) (reaffirming that "historically, statutes of limitations are not controlling measures of equitable relief"). This same practice has commonly been followed in civil rights actions. *See, e.g., Anderson v. Cornejo*, 199 F.R.D. 228, 245 (N.D. Ill. 2000) (noting that "as to the class claims for injunctive relief, the most pertinent time period is prospective," and therefore "[a] statute of limitations does not necessarily apply to a claim for prospective, injunctive relief").

Nevertheless, relying in part on *Wallace v. Kato*, 127 S. Ct. 1091 (2007), the Sixth Circuit ruled in *Cooey v. Strickland*, 479 F.3d 412 (6th Cir. 2007), that even though a death-row inmate sought only prospective relief in his section 1983 action challenging the constitutionality of execution by means of lethal injection, his claim was time-barred by Ohio's two-year statute of limitations. The court of appeals recognized that "[s]etting an accrual date at the point when actual harm is inflicted, i.e., at the point of execution, is problematic in this context because the death-sentenced inmate's claim would not accrue until he was executed, at which time it would be simultaneously moot." Thus, the court held, a challenge to a method of execution accrues "upon conclusion of direct review in the state court or the expiration of time for seeking such review." Using this standard, however, Cooey's claim accrued two years before Ohio first began using lethal injection and ten years before it became the state's sole method of execution. But the Sixth Circuit noted that "even under the later date, . . . Cooey's claim exceeds the two-year statute of limitations deadline." In dissent, Judge Gilman took the position that Cooey's claim did not accrue "until his execution date became imminent," observing that "[u]nder the majority's rationale, . . . virtually every death-sentenced litigant will be barred from bringing a § 1983 action challenging the constitutionality of the method of execution chosen by the State." *Cf. McNair v. Allen*, 515 F.3d 1168 (11th Cir. 2008) (finding that method-of-execution claim accrues either on the date the "death sentence becomes final following direct appeal," or "the date on which the capital litigant becomes subject to a new or substantially changed execution protocol," whichever is later, and therefore the claim there was barred by the two-year limitations period generally applicable to section 1983 suits). Should these courts have relied on a state statute of limitations to defeat a purely prospective claim for relief under section

1983? (For further discussion of section 1983 suits challenging methods of execution, *see Nelson v. Campbell*, 541 U.S. 637 (2004), excerpted in Chapter 8.B.[1], *infra*.)

7. Survivorship and Wrongful Death. The Supreme Court's current approach to section 1988(a) can be traced to its opinion in *Robertson v. Wegmann*, 436 U.S. 584 (1978). The original plaintiff in that case (Clay Shaw) died four years after filing a section 1983 suit alleging that he had been prosecuted in bad faith, and the question facing the Court was whether to apply a Louisiana survivorship statute that prevented the executor of Shaw's estate, Edward Wegmann, from being substituted as plaintiff. Under the state's survivorship statute, a suit other than one alleging damage to property survived only in favor of the plaintiff's spouse, children, parents, and siblings, and Shaw's action abated with his death because he had no such living relatives. Concluding that the case was governed by section 1988(a) and finding federal law "deficient" on questions involving the survival of section 1983 suits, the Court held that the Louisiana statute was not "inconsistent" with federal law within the meaning of section 1988(a). The Court observed that "[a] state statute cannot be considered 'inconsistent' with federal law merely because the statute causes the plaintiff to lose the litigation" because, under that theory, "there would be no reason at all to look to state law, for the appropriate rule would then always be the one favoring the plaintiff." 436 U.S. at 593. Turning to the specifics of the Louisiana survivorship provision, the Court explained:

> Despite the broad sweep of § 1983, we can find nothing in the statute or its underlying policies to indicate that a state law causing abatement of a particular action should invariably be ignored in favor of a rule of absolute survivorship. . . . No claim is made here that Louisiana's survivorship laws are in general inconsistent with [§ 1983's] policies [of compensation and deterrence], and indeed most Louisiana actions survive the plaintiff's death. . . . [S]urely few persons are not survived by one of these close relatives, and in any event no contention is made here that Louisiana's decision to restrict certain survivorship rights in this manner is an unreasonable one.

Robertson, 436 U.S. at 590–92. Emphasizing that its decision was a "narrow one," the Court left open the possibility that it might reach a different conclusion under other circumstances: where "state law generally is inhospitable to survival of § 1983 actions" or has an "independent adverse effect on the policies underlying § 1983"; where "state law 'did not provide for survival of any tort actions' or . . . significantly restricted the types of actions that survive"; or where the "deprivation of federal rights caused [the plaintiff's] death." *Robertson*, 436 U.S. at 594.

In dissent, Justice Blackmun, joined by Justices Brennan and White, was critical of the Court's reliance on state law, noting that prior Supreme Court opinions setting forth the damages and immunity rules applicable in section 1983 litigation had relied on general common law principles rather than a particular state's law. *See Robertson*, 436 U.S. at 596–97 (Blackmun, J., dissenting) (citing *Carey v. Piphus*, 435 U.S. 247 (1978) (measuring damages for procedural due process violations), and *Imbler v. Pachtman*, 424 U.S. 409 (1976) (granting absolute immunity to prosecutors)). Citing the importance of "uniformity," the dissenters also endorsed "[a] federal rule of survivorship," such that section 1983 "[l]itigants identically aggrieved in their federal civil rights, residing in geographically adjacent States, will not have differing results due to the vagaries of state law." *Robertson*, 436 U.S. at 602.

Two years later, in *Carlson v. Green*, 446 U.S. 14 (1980), the Court refused to follow the applicable state survivorship rule in a *Bivens* suit alleging constitutional violations in connection with the death of a federal prisoner.[5] Concluding that "only a uniform

---

[5] *Bivens* actions — civil suits filed against federal officials who act unconstitutionally — are described in Chapter 1.E., *supra*. Note that, despite the Supreme Court's ruling in *Carlson*, the federal courts tend to apply *Wilson v. Garcia*'s holding to *Bivens* claims, so that the statute of limitations is the same for both section 1983

federal rule of survivorship will suffice to redress the constitutional deprivation here alleged and . . . protect against repetition of such conduct," the Court distinguished *Robertson v. Wegmann* on two grounds: first, "Section 1988 does not in terms apply to *Bivens* actions" filed against federal officials, where "[n]o state interests are implicated"; and, second, "the plaintiff's death [in *Robertson*] was not caused by the acts of the defendants upon which the suit was based." *Carlson*, 446 U.S. at 23, 24 & n.11.

Because most section 1983 claims do survive under the applicable state survivorship rules, there is little authority on when those rules will be deemed "inconsistent" with federal law. *See* 2 JOSEPH G. COOK & JOHN L. SOBIESKI, JR., CIVIL RIGHTS ACTIONS ¶ 4.05, at 4-83 n.13 (2007). But the few lower court opinions that do exist agree with *Carlson*'s implication that section 1983 actions must survive if the defendant's constitutional violation led to the plaintiff's death. *See id.* at 4-86. *Cf. Evans v. Twin Falls County*, 796 P.2d 87, 94 (Idaho 1990) (holding that Idaho law providing that "personal causes of action do not survive the death of the injured party" applies to section 1983 suits where the defendant did not cause the plaintiff's death).

The lower courts conflict, however, on the applicability of state rules limiting the amount or type of damages that can be recovered either when a survivor litigates the original plaintiff's constitutional claims (thus seeking to redress the decedent's injuries) or in a wrongful death suit (where survivors request compensation for the losses *they* suffered as a result of the decedent's death). *See, e.g., Frontier Insurance Co. v. Blaty*, 454 F.3d 590 (6th Cir. 2006) (citing conflicting cases); *Carringer v. Rodgers*, 331 F.3d 844, 850 n.9 (11th Cir. 2003) (same). The Supreme Court has twice agreed to consider this question, but on both occasions ultimately dismissed the writ of certiorari without reaching the merits. *See Jefferson v. City of Tarrant*, 522 U.S. 75 (1997); *Jones v. Hildebrant*, 432 U.S. 183 (1977) (per curiam). *See generally* Steven H. Steinglass, *Wrongful Death Actions and Section 1983*, 60 IND. L.J. 559 (1985).

B. NOTICE-OF-CLAIM REQUIREMENTS

FELDER v. CASEY
Supreme Court of the United States
487 U.S. 131 (1988)

JUSTICE BRENNAN delivered the opinion of the Court.

I

On July 4, 1981, Milwaukee police officers stopped petitioner Bobby Felder for questioning while searching his neighborhood for an armed suspect. The interrogation proved to be hostile and apparently loud, attracting the attention of petitioner's family and neighbors, who succeeded in convincing the police that petitioner was not the man they sought. According to police reports, the officers then directed petitioner to return home, but he continued to argue and allegedly pushed one of them, thereby precipitating his arrest for disorderly conduct. Petitioner alleges that in the course of this arrest the officers beat him about the head and face with batons, dragged him across the ground, and threw him, partially unconscious, into the back of a paddy wagon face first, all in full view of his family and neighbors. Shortly afterwards, in response to complaints from these neighbors, a local city alderman and members of the Milwaukee Police Department arrived on the scene and began interviewing witnesses to the arrest. Three days later, the local alderman wrote directly to the chief of police requesting a full investigation into the incident. Petitioner, who is black, alleges that various

---

and *Bivens* suits. *See, e.g., King v. One Unknown Federal Correctional Officer*, 201 F.3d 910, 913 (7th Cir. 2000); *Kelly v. Serna*, 87 F.3d 1235, 1238 (11th Cir. 1996).

members of the Police Department responded to this request by conspiring to cover up the misconduct of the arresting officers, all of whom are white. The Department took no disciplinary action against any of the officers, and the city attorney subsequently dropped the disorderly conduct charge against petitioner.

Nine months after the incident, petitioner filed this action in the Milwaukee County Circuit Court against the city of Milwaukee and certain of its police officers, alleging that the beating and arrest were unprovoked and racially motivated, and violated his rights under the Fourth and Fourteenth Amendments to the United States Constitution. He sought redress under 42 U.S.C. § 1983, as well as attorney's fees pursuant to 42 U.S.C. § 1988. The officers moved to dismiss the suit based on petitioner's failure to comply with the State's notice-of-claim statute. That statute provides that no action may be brought or maintained against any state governmental subdivision, agency, or officer unless the claimant either provides written notice of the claim within 120 days of the alleged injury, or demonstrates that the relevant subdivision, agency, or officer had actual notice of the claim and was not prejudiced by the lack of written notice. Wis. Stat. § 893.80(1)(a). The statute further provides that the party seeking redress must also submit an itemized statement of the relief sought to the governmental subdivision or agency, which then has 120 days to grant or disallow the requested relief. Finally, claimants must bring suit within six months of receiving notice that their claim has been disallowed.

The trial court granted the officers' motion as to all state-law causes of action but denied the motion as to petitioner's remaining federal claims. . . . The Wisconsin Supreme Court, however, reversed. Passing on the question for the first time, the court reasoned that while Congress may establish the procedural framework under which claims are heard in federal courts, States retain the authority under the Constitution to prescribe the rules and procedures that govern actions in their own tribunals. Accordingly, a party who chooses to vindicate a congressionally created right in state court must abide by the State's procedures. Requiring compliance with the notice-of-claim statute, . . . the court reasoned, . . . advances the State's legitimate interests in protecting against stale or fraudulent claims, facilitating prompt settlement of valid claims, and identifying and correcting inappropriate conduct by governmental employees and officials. Turning to the question of compliance in this case, the court concluded that the complaints lodged with the local police by petitioner's neighbors and the letter submitted to the police chief by the local alderman failed to satisfy the statute's actual notice standard, because these communications neither recited the facts giving rise to the alleged injuries nor revealed petitioner's intent to hold the defendants responsible for those injuries. . . .

II

No one disputes the general and unassailable proposition relied upon by the Wisconsin Supreme Court below that States may establish the rules of procedure governing litigation in their own courts. By the same token, however, where state courts entertain a federally created cause of action, the "federal right cannot be defeated by the forms of local practice." *Brown v. Western R. Co. of Alabama*, 338 U.S. 294, 296 (1949). The question before us today, therefore, is essentially one of preemption: is the application of the State's notice-of-claim provision to § 1983 actions brought in state courts consistent with the goals of the federal civil rights laws? . . .

A

Any assessment of the applicability of a state law to federal civil rights litigation . . . must be made in light of the purpose and nature of the federal right. This is so whether the question of state-law applicability arises in § 1983 litigation brought in state courts, which possess concurrent jurisdiction over such actions, or in federal-court litigation, where, because the federal civil rights laws fail to provide certain rules of decision thought essential to the orderly adjudication of rights, courts are occasionally called upon to borrow state law. *See* 42 U.S.C. § 1988. Accordingly, we have held that a state law that immunizes government conduct otherwise subject to suit under § 1983 is preempted, even where the federal civil rights litigation takes place in state court, because the application of the state immunity law would thwart the congressional remedy, *see Martinez v. California*, 444 U.S. 277, 284 (1980), which of course already provides certain immunities for state officials. Similarly, in actions brought in federal courts, we have disapproved the adoption of state statutes of limitation that provide only a truncated period of time within which to file suit, because such statutes inadequately accommodate the complexities of federal civil rights litigation and are thus inconsistent with Congress' compensatory aims. *Burnett* [*v. Grattan*, 468 U.S. 42, 50–55 (1984)]. . . .

Although we have never passed on the question, the lower federal courts have all, with but one exception, concluded that notice-of-claim provisions are inapplicable to § 1983 actions brought in federal court. These courts have reasoned that, unlike the lack of statutes of limitations in the federal civil rights laws, the absence of any notice-of-claim provision is not a deficiency requiring the importation of such statutes into the federal civil rights scheme. Because statutes of limitation are among the universally familiar aspects of litigation considered indispensable to any scheme of justice, it is entirely reasonable to assume that Congress did not intend to create a right enforceable in perpetuity. Notice-of-claim provisions, by contrast, are neither universally familiar nor in any sense indispensable prerequisites to litigation, and there is thus no reason to suppose that Congress intended federal courts to apply such rules, which "significantly inhibit the ability to bring federal actions."

While we fully agree with this near-unanimous conclusion of the federal courts, that judgment is not dispositive here, where the question is not one of adoption but of preemption. . . .

B

. . . [T]he central purpose of the Reconstruction-Era laws is to provide compensatory relief to those deprived of their federal rights by state actors. Section 1983 accomplishes this goal by creating a form of liability that, by its very nature, runs only against a specific class of defendants: government bodies and their officials. Wisconsin's notice-of-claim statute undermines this "uniquely federal remedy" in several inter-related ways. First, it conditions the right of recovery that Congress has authorized, and does so for a reason manifestly inconsistent with the purposes of the federal statute: to minimize governmental liability. Nor is this condition a neutral and uniformly applicable rule of procedure; rather, it is a substantive burden imposed only upon those who seek redress for injuries resulting from the use or misuse of governmental authority. Second, the notice provision discriminates against the federal right. While the State affords the victim of an intentional tort two years to recognize the compensable nature of his or her injury, the civil rights victim is given only four months to appreciate that he or she has been deprived of a federal constitutional or statutory right. Finally, the notice provision operates, in part, as an exhaustion requirement, in that it forces claimants to seek satisfaction in the first instance from the governmental defendant. We think it plain that Congress never intended that those injured by governmental wrongdoers could be required, as a condition of recovery, to submit their claims to the government responsible for their injuries.

(1)

Wisconsin's notice-of-claim statute is part of a broader legislative scheme governing the rights of citizens to sue the State's subdivisions. The statute, both in its earliest and current forms, provides a circumscribed waiver of local governmental immunity that limits the amount recoverable in suits against local governments and imposes the notice requirements at issue here. Although the Wisconsin Supreme Court has held that the statutory limits on recovery are preempted in federal civil rights actions, and thus recognizes that partial immunities inconsistent with § 1983 must yield to the federal right, it concluded in the present case that the notice and exhaustion conditions attached to the waiver of such immunities may nevertheless be enforced in federal actions. The purposes of these conditions, however, mirror those of the judicial immunity the statute replaced. Such statutes "are enacted primarily for the benefit of governmental defendants," and enable those defendants to "investigate early, prepare a stronger case, and perhaps reach an early settlement." Moreover, where the defendant is unable to obtain a satisfactory settlement, the Wisconsin statute forces claimants to bring suit within a relatively short period after the local governing body disallows the claim, in order to "assure prompt initiation of litigation." *Gutter v. Seamandel*, 103 Wis. 2d 1, 22, 308 N.W.2d 403, 413 (1981). To be sure, the notice requirement serves the additional purpose of notifying the proper public officials of dangerous physical conditions or inappropriate and unlawful governmental conduct, which allows for prompt corrective measures. This interest, however, is clearly not the predominant objective of the statute. Indeed, the Wisconsin Supreme Court has emphasized that the requisite notice must spell out both the amount of damages the claimant seeks and his or her intent to hold the governing body responsible for those damages precisely because these requirements further the State's interest in minimizing liability and the expenses associated with it.

In sum, as respondents explain, the State has chosen to expose its subdivisions to large liability and defense costs, and, in light of that choice, has made the concomitant decision to impose conditions that "assis[t] municipalities in controlling those costs." Brief for Respondents 12. The decision to subject state subdivisions to liability for violations of federal rights, however, was a choice that Congress, not the Wisconsin Legislature, made, and it is a decision that the State has no authority to override. Thus, however understandable or laudable the State's interest in controlling liability expenses might otherwise be, it is patently incompatible with the compensatory goals of the federal legislation, as are the means the State has chosen to effectuate it. . . .

This burdening of a federal right, moreover, is not the natural or permissible consequence of an otherwise neutral, uniformly applicable state rule. Although it is true that the notice-of-claim statute does not discriminate between state and federal causes of action against local governments, the fact remains that the law's protection extends only to governmental defendants and thus conditions the right to bring suit against the very persons and entities Congress intended to subject to liability. . . . This defendant-specific focus of the notice requirement serves to distinguish it, rather starkly, from rules uniformly applicable to all suits, such as rules governing service of process or substitution of parties, which respondents cite as examples of procedural requirements that penalize noncompliance through dismissal. That state courts will hear the entire § 1983 cause of action once a plaintiff complies with the notice-of-claim statute, therefore, in no way alters the fact that the statute discriminates against the precise type of claim Congress has created.

(2)

. . . In *Wilson*, we held that, for purposes of choosing a limitations period for § 1983 actions, federal courts must apply the state statute of limitations governing personal injury claims because it is highly unlikely that States would ever fix the limitations period applicable to such claims in a manner that would discriminate against the federal right. Here, the notice-of-claim provision most emphatically does discriminate in a manner detrimental to the federal right: only those persons who wish to sue governmental defendants are required to provide notice within such an abbreviated time period. Many civil rights victims, however, will fail to appreciate the compensable nature of their injuries within the 4-month window provided by the notice-of-claim provision, and will thus be barred from asserting their federal right to recovery in state court unless they can show that the defendant had actual notice of the injury, the circumstances giving rise to it, and the claimant's intent to hold the defendant responsible — a showing which, as the facts of this case vividly demonstrate, is not easily made in Wisconsin.

(3)

Finally, the notice provision imposes an exhaustion requirement on persons who choose to assert their federal right in state courts, inasmuch as the § 1983 plaintiff must provide the requisite notice of injury within 120 days of the civil rights violation, then wait an additional 120 days while the governmental defendant investigates the claim and attempts to settle it. In *Patsy v. Board of Regents of Florida*, 457 U.S. 496 (1982), we held that plaintiffs need not exhaust state administrative remedies before instituting § 1983 suits in federal court. . . . [A]s we noted in *Patsy*, Congress enacted § 1983 in response to the widespread deprivations of civil rights in the Southern States and the inability or unwillingness of authorities in those States to protect those rights or punish wrongdoers. Although it is true that the principal remedy Congress chose to provide injured persons was immediate access to federal courts, it did not leave the protection of such rights exclusively in the hands of the federal judiciary, and instead conferred concurrent jurisdiction on state courts as well. Given the evil at which the federal civil rights legislation was aimed, there is simply no reason to suppose that Congress meant "to provide these individuals immediate access to the federal courts notwithstanding any provision of state law to the contrary," yet contemplated that those who sought to vindicate their federal rights in state courts could be required to seek redress in the first instance from the very state officials whose hostility to those rights precipitated their injuries. . . .

C

Respondents and their supporting *amici* urge that we approve the application of the notice-of-claim statute to § 1983 actions brought in state court as a matter of equitable federalism. . . . Litigants who choose to bring their civil rights actions in state courts presumably do so in order to obtain the benefit of certain procedural advantages in those courts, or to draw their juries from urban populations. Having availed themselves of these benefits, civil rights litigants must comply as well with those state rules they find less to their liking.

However equitable this bitter-with-the-sweet argument may appear in the abstract, it has no place under our Supremacy Clause analysis. Federal law takes state courts as it finds them only insofar as those courts employ rules that do not "impose unnecessary burdens upon rights of recovery authorized by federal laws." *Brown v. Western R. Co. of Alabama*, 338 U.S. at 298–299; *see also Monessen Southwestern R. Co. v. Morgan*, 486 U.S. 330, 336 (1988) (state rule designed to encourage settlement cannot limit recovery in federally created action). . . .

Under *Erie R. Co. v. Tompkins*, 304 U.S. 64 (1938), when a federal court exercises diversity or pendent jurisdiction over state-law claims, "the outcome of the litigation in the federal court should be substantially the same, so far as legal rules determine the outcome of a litigation, as it would be if tried in a State court." *Guaranty Trust Co. v. York*, 326 U.S. 99, 109 (1945). Accordingly, federal courts entertaining state-law claims against Wisconsin municipalities are obligated to apply the notice-of-claim provision. Just as federal courts are constitutionally obligated to apply state law to state claims, so too the Supremacy Clause imposes on state courts a constitutional duty "to proceed in such manner that all the substantial rights of the parties under controlling federal law [are] protected."

. . . Wisconsin . . . may not alter the outcome of federal claims it chooses to entertain in its courts by demanding compliance with outcome-determinative rules that are inapplicable when such claims are brought in federal court, for " '[w]hatever springes the State may set for those who are endeavoring to assert rights that the State confers, the assertion of federal rights, when plainly and reasonably made, is not to be defeated under the name of local practice.' " *Brown v. Western R. Co. of Alabama, supra,* at 298–299. The state notice-of-claim statute is more than a mere rule of procedure: as we discussed above, the statute is a substantive condition on the right to sue governmental officials and entities, and the federal courts have therefore correctly recognized that the notice statute governs the adjudication of state-law claims in diversity actions. In *Guaranty Trust, supra,* we held that, in order to give effect to a State's statute of limitations, a federal court could not hear a state-law action that a state court would deem time-barred. Conversely, a state court may not decline to hear an otherwise properly presented federal claim because that claim would be barred under a state law requiring timely filing of notice. State courts simply are not free to vindicate the substantive interests underlying a state rule of decision at the expense of the federal right.

Finally, in *Wilson,* we characterized § 1983 suits as claims for personal injuries because such an approach ensured that the same limitations period would govern all § 1983 actions brought in any given State, and thus comported with Congress' desire that the federal civil rights laws be given a uniform application within each State. A law that predictably alters the outcome of § 1983 claims depending solely on whether they are brought in state or federal court within the same State is obviously inconsistent with this federal interest in intrastate uniformity. . . .

JUSTICE WHITE, concurring.

It cannot be disputed that, if Congress had included a statute of limitations in 42 U.S.C. § 1983, any state court that entertained a § 1983 suit would have to apply that statute of limitations. . . .

Similarly, where the Court has determined that a particular state statute of limitations ought to be borrowed in order to effectuate the congressional intent underlying a federal cause of action that contains no statute of limitations of its own, any state court that entertains the same federal cause of action must apply the same state statute of limitations. We made such a determination in *Wilson v. Garcia,* 471 U.S. 261 (1985), which held that § 1983 suits must as a matter of federal law be governed by the state statute of limitations applicable to tort suits for the recovery of damages for personal injuries. . . .

It has since been assumed that *Wilson v. Garcia* governs the timeliness of § 1983 suits brought in state as well as federal court. [Here, Justice White cites opinions issued by ten state courts.]

The Wisconsin Supreme Court likewise assumed that *Wilson v. Garcia* governed which statute of limitations should apply to petitioner's § 1983 claim. The court then effectively truncated the applicable limitations period, however, by dismissing petitioner's § 1983 suit for failure to file a notice of claim within 120 days. . . . Hence, petitioner was allowed only about four months in which to investigate whether the facts and the law would support any claim against respondents (or retain a lawyer who would do so), and to notify respondents of his claim, rather than the two or three years that he would have been allowed under Wisconsin law had he sought to assert a similar personal-injury claim against a private party. It is also unlikely that any other State would apply a 120-day limitations period — or, indeed, a limitations period of less than one year — to such a personal-injury claim. This reflects a generally accepted belief among state policymakers that individuals who have suffered injuries to their personal rights cannot fairly be expected to seek redress within so short a period of time.

The application of the Wisconsin notice-of-claim statute to bar petitioner's § 1983 suit . . . thus undermines the purposes of *Wilson v. Garcia* to promote "[t]he federal interests in uniformity, certainty, and the minimization of unnecessary litigation," and assure that state procedural rules do not "discriminate against the federal civil rights remedy." I therefore agree that in view of the adverse impact of Wisconsin's notice-of-claim statute on the federal policies articulated in *Wilson v. Garcia*, the Supremacy Clause proscribes the statute's application to § 1983 suits brought in Wisconsin state courts.

JUSTICE O'CONNOR, with whom THE CHIEF JUSTICE joins, dissenting.

"A state statute cannot be considered 'inconsistent' with federal law merely because the statute causes the plaintiff to lose the litigation." *Robertson v. Wegmann*, 436 U.S. 584, 593 (1978). Disregarding this self-evident principle, the Court today holds that Wisconsin's notice of claim statute is pre-empted by federal law as to actions under 42 U.S.C. § 1983 filed in state court. This holding is not supported by the statute whose pre-emptive force it purports to invoke, or by our precedents. Relying only on its own intuitions about "the goals of the federal civil rights laws," the Court fashions a new theory of pre-emption that unnecessarily and improperly suspends a perfectly valid state statute. . . .

Wisconsin's notice of claim statute, which imposes a limited exhaustion of remedies requirement on those with claims against municipal governments and their officials, serves at least two important purposes apart from providing municipal defendants with a special affirmative defense in litigation. First, the statute helps ensure that public officials will receive prompt notice of wrongful conditions or practices, and thus enables them to take prompt corrective action. Second, it enables officials to investigate claims in a timely fashion, thereby making it easier to ascertain the facts accurately and to settle meritorious claims without litigation. These important aspects of the Wisconsin statute bring benefits to governments and claimants alike, and it should come as no surprise that 37 other States have apparently adopted similar notice of claim requirements. Without some compellingly clear indication that Congress has forbidden the States to apply such statutes in their own courts, there is no reason to conclude that they are "pre-empted" by federal law. Allusions to such vague concepts as "the compensatory aims of the federal civil rights laws," which are all that the Court actually relies on, do not provide an adequate substitute for the statutory analysis that we customarily require of ourselves before we reach out to find statutory pre-emption of legitimate procedures used by the States in their own courts.

. . . [T]he original version of § 1983 provided that the federal courts would have exclusive jurisdiction of actions arising under it. This fact is conclusive proof that the "Congress which enacted § 1983 over 100 years ago" could not possibly have meant thereby to alter the operation of state courts in any way or to "pre-empt" them from using procedural statutes like the one at issue today.

State courts may now entertain § 1983 actions if a plaintiff chooses a state court over the federal forum that is always available as a matter of right. *See, e.g., Martinez v. California*, 444 U.S. 277, 283 & n.7 (1980). Abandoning the rule of exclusive federal jurisdiction over § 1983 actions, and thus restoring the tradition of concurrent jurisdiction, however, "did not leave behind a pre-emptive grin without a statutory cat." Congress has never given the slightest indication that § 1983 was meant to replace state procedural rules with those that apply in the federal courts. The majority does not, because it cannot, cite any evidence to the contrary.

In an effort to remedy this fatal defect in its position, the majority engages in an extended discussion of *Patsy v. Board of Regents of Florida*. *Patsy*, however, actually undermines the majority's conclusion. In that case, the Court concluded that state exhaustion of remedies requirements were not to be applied in § 1983 actions brought in *federal court*. The Court relied on legislative history indicating that § 1983 was meant to provide a federal forum with characteristics *different* from those in the state courts, and it came only to the limited and hesitant conclusion that "it seems fair to infer that the 1871 Congress did not intend that an individual be compelled *in every case* to exhaust state administrative remedies before filing an action under [§ 1983]," [457 U.S.] at 507 (emphasis added). Even this limited conclusion, the Court admitted, was "somewhat precarious," which would have made no sense if the Court had been able to rely on the more general proposition — from which the holding in *Patsy* follows *a fortiori* — that it adopts today. . . .

For similar reasons, *Brown v. Western R. Co. of Alabama*, 338 U.S. 294 (1949), which is repeatedly quoted by the majority, does not control the present case. In *Brown*, which arose under the Federal Employers' Liability Act (FELA), this Court refused to accept a state court's interpretation of allegations in a complaint asserting a federal statutory right. Concluding that the state court's interpretation of the complaint operated to "detract from 'substantive rights' granted by Congress in FELA cases," the Court "simply h[e]ld that under the facts alleged it was error to dismiss the complaint and that [the claimant] should be allowed to try his case." In the case before us today, by contrast, the statute at issue does not diminish or alter any substantive right cognizable under § 1983. As the majority concedes, the Wisconsin courts "will hear the entire § 1983 cause of action once a plaintiff complies with the notice-of-claim statute."

Unable to find support for its position in § 1983 itself, or in its legislative history, the majority suggests that the Wisconsin statute somehow "discriminates against the federal right." The Wisconsin statute, however, applies to all actions against municipal defendants, whether brought under state or federal law. The majority is therefore compelled to adopt a new theory of discrimination, under which the challenged statute is said to "conditio[n] the right to bring suit against the very persons and entities [viz., local governments and officials] Congress intended to subject to liability." This theory, however, is untenable. First, the statute erects no barrier at all to a plaintiff's right to bring a § 1983 suit against anyone. Every plaintiff has the option of proceeding in federal court, and the Wisconsin statute has not the slightest effect on that right. Second, if a plaintiff chooses to proceed in the Wisconsin state courts, those courts stand ready to hear the entire federal cause of action, as the majority concedes. Thus, the Wisconsin statute "discriminates" only against a right that Congress has never created: the right of a plaintiff to have the benefit of selected federal court procedures after the plaintiff has rejected the federal forum and chosen a state forum instead. . . .

The Court also suggests that there is some parallel between this case and cases that are tried in federal court under the doctrine of *Erie R. Co. v. Tompkins*, 304 U.S. 64 (1938). Quoting the "outcome-determinative" test of *Guaranty Trust Co. v. York*, 326 U.S. 99, 109 (1945), the Court opines today that state courts hearing federal suits are obliged to mirror federal procedures to the same extent that federal courts are obliged to mirror state procedures in diversity suits. This suggestion seems to be based on a sort of upside-down theory of federalism, which the Court attributes to Congress on the basis of no evidence at all. Nor are the implications of this "reverse-*Erie*" theory quite clear. If the Court means the theory to be taken seriously, it should follow that defendants, as well as plaintiffs, are entitled to the benefit of all federal court procedural rules that are "outcome determinative." If, however, the Court means to create a rule that benefits only plaintiffs, then the discussion of *Erie* principles is simply an unsuccessful effort to find some analogy, no matter how attenuated, to today's unprecedented holding.

"Borrowing" cases under 42 U.S.C. § 1988, which the Court cites several times, have little more to do with today's decision than does *Erie*. Under that statute and those cases, we are sometimes called upon to fill in gaps in federal law by choosing a state procedural rule for application in § 1983 actions brought in federal court. The congressionally imposed necessity of *supplementing* federal law with state procedural rules might well caution us against *supplanting* state procedural rules with federal gaps, but it certainly offers no support for what the Court does today.

Finally, Justice White's concurrence argues that Wisconsin's notice of claim statute is in the nature of a statute of limitations, and that the principles articulated in *Wilson v. Garcia* preclude its application to any action under § 1983. Assuming, *arguendo*, that state courts must apply the same statutes of limitations that federal courts borrow under § 1988, the concurrence is mistaken in treating this notice of claim requirement as a statute of limitations. As the concurrence acknowledges, the 120-day claim period established by the Wisconsin statute does not apply if the local government had actual notice of the claim and has not been prejudiced by the plaintiff's delay. The concurrence suggests that the Wisconsin statute nonetheless is equivalent to a statute of limitations because the present case demonstrates that "the 'actual notice' requirement is difficult to satisfy." I agree that a sufficiently burdensome notice of claim requirement could effectively act as a statute of limitations. The facts of this case, however, will not support such a characterization of the Wisconsin law. The court below said that no "detailed claim for damages" need be submitted; rather, the injured party need only "recit[e] the facts giving rise to the injury and [indicate] an intent . . . to hold the city responsible for any damages resulting from the injury." It has not been suggested that petitioner tried to comply with this requirement but encountered difficulties in doing so. Indeed, it would have been easier to file the required notice of claim than to file this lawsuit, which petitioner proved himself quite capable of doing. Far from encountering "difficulties" in complying with the notice of claim statute, petitioner never tried.

As I noted at the outset, the majority correctly characterizes the issue before us as one of statutory pre-emption. In order to arrive at the result it has chosen, however, the Court is forced to search for "inconsistencies" between Wisconsin's notice of claim statute and some ill-defined federal policy that Congress has never articulated, implied, or suggested, let alone enacted. Nor is there any difficulty in explaining the absence of congressional attention to the problem that the Court wrongly imagines it is solving. A plaintiff who chooses to bring a § 1983 action in state court necessarily rejects the federal courts that Congress has provided. Virtually the only conceivable reason for doing so is to benefit from procedural advantages available exclusively in state court. Having voted with their feet for state procedural systems, such plaintiffs would hardly be in a position to ask Congress for a new type of forum that combines the advantages that Congress gave them in the federal system with those that Congress did not give them, and which are only available in state courts. Fortunately for these plaintiffs, however, Congress need not be consulted. The concept of statutory pre-emption takes on new meaning today, and it is one from which I respectfully dissent.

NOTES

1. Notice-of-Claim Requirements. The issue addressed by the Court in *Felder* is the extent to which federal law preempts state law in section 1983 suits brought in state court. Because Felder filed his complaint in state court, section 1988(a) did not govern his case. Nevertheless, the majority relies on principles similar to those appearing in its opinions interpreting section 1988(a) in holding that a state's notice-of-claim requirement cannot be used to foreclose a section 1983 claim brought in state court.

Does the majority make a persuasive case for refusing to require Felder to comply with Wisconsin's notice-of-claim provision? Would doing so effectively impose an exhaustion requirement, in conflict with the Court's conclusion in *Patsy v. Board of Regents*, 457 U.S. 496 (1982), that plaintiffs need not exhaust their administrative remedies before bringing a section 1983 suit in federal court? (*Patsy*'s no-exhaustion rule is described in Chapter 8.A.[2], *infra*.) Or does Justice O'Connor have the stronger argument that Felder "voted with [his] feet" by choosing to file his section 1983 claim in state court and therefore ought to be bound by the dictates of state law?

Consistent with the dictum in *Felder*, the federal courts have refused to apply state notice-of-claim requirements to section 1983 suits filed in federal court. *See* 2 JOSEPH G. COOK & JOHN L. SOBIESKI, JR., CIVIL RIGHTS ACTIONS ¶ 4.01[B], at 4-21 to -22 & n.83 (2007) (citing cases).

2. Section 1983 Suits in State Courts. Although an increasing number of section 1983 cases are brought in state court, most such claims continue to be filed in federal court. *See* 1 SHELDON H. NAHMOD, CIVIL RIGHTS AND CIVIL LIBERTIES LITIGATION: THE LAW OF SECTION 1983 § 1:58 (4th ed. 2007).

3. Subsequent Preemption Cases. Two years after *Felder*, the Supreme Court relied on its decision in that case in unanimously holding that the Supremacy Clause prevented a state court from applying state sovereign immunity rules to bar a section 1983 claim filed against a local school board. *See Howlett v. Rose*, 496 U.S. 356 (1990). The Court noted that, while states could "apply their own neutral procedural rules to federal claims," they could not do so if "those rules [were] pre-empted by federal law." *Howlett*, 496 U.S. at 372 (citing *Felder*). In this case, the Court concluded, Florida's sovereign immunity doctrine could not override "[f]ederal law mak[ing] governmental defendants that are not arms of the State, such as municipalities, liable for their constitutional violations." *Howlett*, 496 U.S. at 377 (citing *Monell*).

Subsequently, however, in *Johnson v. Fankell*, 520 U.S. 911 (1997), the Court unanimously refused to pre-empt an Idaho appellate rule that did not allow section 1983 defendants to file an interlocutory appeal challenging the denial of their qualified immunity defense — even though such an interlocutory appeal is available in section 1983 suits filed in federal court under the Court's ruling in *Mitchell v. Forsyth*, 472 U.S. 511 (1985) (described in Note 5 following *Hope v. Pelzer* in Chapter 2.B., *supra*). Distinguishing both *Felder* and *Howlett v. Rose*, the Court described the Idaho rule as "a neutral state rule regarding the administration of the state courts" that did not "target civil rights claims against the State." *Johnson*, 520 U.S. at 918 & n.9. Moreover, the Court said, the Idaho rule was not outcome-determinative in the sense in which that term was used in *Felder* because it did not control "the ultimate disposition of the case": "the postponement of the appeal until after final judgment will not affect the ultimate outcome of the case," the Court explained. *Johnson*, 520 U.S. at 921.

The Supreme Court has granted review in *Haywood v. Drown*, 128 S. Ct. 2938 (2008) (No. 07-10374), a preemption case involving a New York statute that bars the state courts from entertaining damages suits filed against state prison officials in their individual capacities. The New York courts upheld the constitutionality of the statute on the grounds that it "does not discriminate" against section 1983 suits, but rather "creates a neutral jurisdictional barrier to all claims," whether state or federal. *Haywood v. Drown*, 881 N.E.2d 180, 184-85 (N.Y. 2007).

C. THE RIGHT TO JURY TRIAL IN SECTION 1983 CASES

CITY OF MONTEREY v. DEL MONTE DUNES AT MONTEREY, LTD.
Supreme Court of the United States
526 U.S. 687 (1999)

JUSTICE KENNEDY delivered the opinion of the Court, except as to Part IV-A-2.

This case began with attempts by the respondent, Del Monte Dunes, and its predecessor in interest to develop a parcel of land within the jurisdiction of the petitioner, the city of Monterey. The city, in a series of repeated rejections, denied proposals to develop the property, each time imposing more rigorous demands on the developers. Del Monte Dunes brought suit in the United States District Court for the Northern District of California, under 42 U.S.C. § 1983. After protracted litigation, the case was submitted to the jury on Del Monte Dunes' theory that the city effected a

C. THE RIGHT TO JURY TRIAL IN SECTION 1983 CASES   277

regulatory taking or otherwise injured the property by unlawful acts, without paying compensation or providing an adequate postdeprivation remedy for the loss. . . . [In addition to its takings claim, Del Monte Dunes alleged violations of equal protection and substantive due process. The District Court submitted the equal protection claim to the jury along with the takings claim, but reserved the substantive due process claim for itself.]

At the close of argument, the District Court instructed the jury it should find for Del Monte Dunes [on the takings claim] if it found either that Del Monte Dunes had been denied all economically viable use of its property or that "the city's decision to reject the plaintiff's 190 unit development proposal did not substantially advance a legitimate public purpose." . . .

The jury delivered a general verdict for Del Monte Dunes on its takings claim, a separate verdict for Del Monte Dunes on its equal protection claim, and a damages award of $1.45 million. After the jury's verdict, the District Court ruled for the city on the substantive due process claim, stating that its ruling was not inconsistent with the jury's verdict on the equal protection or the takings claim. . . .

The Court of Appeals affirmed [on the takings claim]. . . . Because upholding the verdict on the regulatory takings claim was sufficient to support the award of damages, the court did not address the equal protection claim. . . .

IV

[The city alleges that it was not] proper for the District Court to submit the question of liability on Del Monte Dunes' regulatory takings claim to the jury. (Before the District Court, the city agreed it was proper for the jury to assess damages.) As the Court of Appeals recognized, the answer depends on whether Del Monte Dunes had a statutory or constitutional right to a jury trial, and, if it did, the nature and extent of the right. Del Monte Dunes asserts the right to a jury trial is conferred by § 1983 and by the Seventh Amendment.

Under our precedents, "before inquiring into the applicability of the Seventh Amendment, we must 'first ascertain whether a construction of the statute is fairly possible by which the [constitutional] question may be avoided.'" *Feltner v. Columbia Pictures Television, Inc.*, 523 U.S. 340, 345 (1998) (quoting *Tull v. United States*, 481 U.S. 412, 417 n.3 (1987)); accord *Curtis v. Loether*, 415 U.S. 189, 192 n.6 (1974).

The character of § 1983 is vital to our Seventh Amendment analysis, but the statute does not itself confer the jury right. Section 1983 authorizes a party who has been deprived of a federal right under the color of state law to seek relief through "an action at law, suit in equity, or other proper proceeding for redress." Del Monte Dunes contends that the phrase "action at law" is a term of art implying a right to a jury trial. We disagree, for this is not a necessary implication.

In *Lorillard v. Pons*, 434 U.S. 575, 583 (1978), we found a statutory right to a jury trial in part because the statute authorized "legal . . . relief." Our decision, however, did not rest solely on the statute's use of the phrase but relied as well on the statute's explicit incorporation of the procedures of the Fair Labor Standards Act, which had been interpreted to guarantee trial by jury in private actions. We decline, accordingly, to find a statutory jury right under § 1983 based solely on the authorization of "an action at law."

As a consequence, we must reach the constitutional question. The Seventh Amendment provides that "in Suits at common law, where the value in controversy shall exceed twenty dollars, the right of trial by jury shall be preserved. . . ." Consistent with the textual mandate that the jury right be preserved, our interpretation of the Amendment has been guided by historical analysis comprising two principal inquiries. "We ask, first, whether we are dealing with a cause of action that either was tried at law at the time of the founding or is at least analogous to one that was." *Markman v. Westview Instruments, Inc.*, 517 U.S. 370, 376 (1996). "If the action in question belongs in the law category, we then ask whether the particular trial decision must fall to the jury in order to preserve the substance of the common-law right as it existed in 1791." *Ibid.*

A

With respect to the first inquiry, we have recognized that "suits at common law" include "not merely suits, which the common law recognized among its old and settled proceedings, but [also] suits in which legal rights were to be ascertained and determined, in contradistinction to those where equitable rights alone were recognized, and equitable remedies were administered." *Parsons v. Bedford*, 3 Peters 433, 447 (1830). The Seventh Amendment thus applies not only to common-law causes of action but also to statutory causes of action "'analogous to common-law causes of action ordinarily decided in English law courts in the late 18th century, as opposed to those customarily heard by courts of equity or admiralty.'" *Feltner, supra*, at 348.

1

Del Monte Dunes brought this suit pursuant to § 1983 to vindicate its constitutional rights. We hold that a § 1983 suit seeking legal relief is an action at law within the meaning of the Seventh Amendment. Justice Scalia's concurring opinion presents a comprehensive and convincing analysis of the historical and constitutional reasons for this conclusion. We agree with his analysis and conclusion.

It is undisputed that when the Seventh Amendment was adopted there was no action equivalent to § 1983, framed in specific terms for vindicating constitutional rights. It is settled law, however, that the Seventh Amendment jury guarantee extends to statutory claims unknown to the common law, so long as the claims can be said to "sound basically in tort," and seek legal relief. *Curtis*, 415 U.S. at 195–196.

As Justice Scalia explains, there can be no doubt that claims brought pursuant to § 1983 sound in tort. Just as common-law tort actions provide redress for interference with protected personal or property interests, § 1983 provides relief for invasions of rights protected under federal law. Recognizing the essential character of the statute, "'we have repeatedly noted that 42 U.S.C. § 1983 creates a species of tort liability,'" *Heck v. Humphrey*, 512 U.S. 477, 483 (1994) (quoting *Memphis Community School Dist. v. Stachura*, 477 U.S. 299, 305 (1986)), and have interpreted the statute in light of the "background of tort liability," *Monroe v. Pape*, 365 U.S. 167, 187 (1961). Our settled understanding of § 1983 and the Seventh Amendment thus compel the conclusion that a suit for legal relief brought under the statute is an action at law.

Here Del Monte Dunes sought legal relief. It was entitled to proceed in federal court under § 1983 because, at the time of the city's actions, the State of California did not provide a compensatory remedy for temporary regulatory takings. The constitutional injury alleged, therefore, is not that property was taken but that it was taken without just compensation. Had the city paid for the property or had an adequate postdeprivation remedy been available, Del Monte Dunes would have suffered no constitutional injury from the taking alone. Because its statutory action did not accrue until it was denied just compensation, in a strict sense Del Monte Dunes sought not just compensation per se but rather damages for the unconstitutional denial of such compensation. Damages for a constitutional violation are a legal remedy. *See, e.g., Teamsters v. Terry*, 494 U.S. 558, 570 (1990) ("Generally, an action for money damages was 'the traditional form of relief offered in the courts of law'") (quoting *Curtis, supra*, at 196).

Even when viewed as a simple suit for just compensation, we believe Del Monte Dunes' action sought essentially legal relief. "We have recognized the 'general rule' that monetary relief is legal." *Feltner*, 523 U.S. at 352 (quoting *Teamsters v. Terry, supra,* at

570). Just compensation, moreover, differs from equitable restitution and other monetary remedies available in equity, for in determining just compensation, "the question is what has the owner lost, not what has the taker gained." *Boston Chamber of Commerce v. Boston*, 217 U.S. 189, 195 (1910). As its name suggests, then, just compensation is, like ordinary money damages, a compensatory remedy. The Court has recognized that compensation is a purpose "traditionally associated with legal relief." *Feltner, supra*, at 352. Because Del Monte Dunes' statutory suit sounded in tort and sought legal relief, it was an action at law.

2

In an attempt to avoid the force of this conclusion, the city urges us to look not to the statutory basis of Del Monte Dunes' claim but rather to the underlying constitutional right asserted. At the very least, the city asks us to create an exception to the general Seventh Amendment rule governing § 1983 actions for claims alleging violations of the Takings Clause of the Fifth Amendment. Because the jury's role in estimating just compensation in condemnation proceedings was inconsistent and unclear at the time the Seventh Amendment was adopted, this Court has said "that there is no constitutional right to a jury in eminent domain proceedings." *United States v. Reynolds*, 397 U.S. 14, 18 (1970). The city submits that the analogy to formal condemnation proceedings is controlling, so that there is no jury right here.

As Justice Scalia notes, we have declined in other contexts to classify § 1983 actions based on the nature of the underlying right asserted, and the city provides no persuasive justification for adopting a different rule for Seventh Amendment purposes. Even when analyzed not as a § 1983 action *simpliciter*, however, but as a § 1983 action seeking redress for an uncompensated taking, Del Monte Dunes' suit remains an action at law.

Although condemnation proceedings spring from the same Fifth Amendment right to compensation which, as incorporated by the Fourteenth Amendment, is applicable here, a condemnation action differs in important respects from a § 1983 action to redress an uncompensated taking. Most important, when the government initiates condemnation proceedings, it concedes the landowner's right to receive just compensation and seeks a mere determination of the amount of compensation due. Liability simply is not an issue. As a result, even if condemnation proceedings were an appropriate analogy, condemnation practice would provide little guidance on the specific question whether Del Monte Dunes was entitled to a jury determination of liability. . . .

Our conclusion is confirmed by precedent. Early authority finding no jury right in a condemnation proceeding did so on the ground that condemnation did not involve the determination of legal rights because liability was undisputed. . . .

(Although Justice Souter's dissenting opinion takes issue with this distinction, its arguments are unpersuasive. . . . [I]t correctly notes that when the government initiates formal condemnation procedures, a landowner may question whether the proposed taking is for public use. The landowner who raises this issue, however, seeks not to establish the government's liability for damages, but to prevent the government from taking his property at all. As the dissent recognizes, the relief desired by a landowner making this contention is analogous not to damages but to an injunction; it should be no surprise, then, that the landowner is not entitled to a jury trial on his entitlement to a remedy that sounds not in law but in equity. . . .)

In these circumstances, we conclude the cause of action sounds in tort and is most analogous to the various actions that lay at common law to recover damages for interference with property interests. . . .

The city argues that because the Constitution allows the government to take property for public use, a taking for that purpose cannot be tortious or unlawful. We reject this conclusion. Although the government acts lawfully when, pursuant to proper authorization, it takes property and provides just compensation, the government's action is lawful solely because it assumes a duty, imposed by the Constitution, to provide just compensation. When the government repudiates this duty, either by denying just compensation in fact or by refusing to provide procedures through which compensation may be sought, it violates the Constitution. In those circumstances the government's actions are not only unconstitutional but unlawful and tortious as well.

(The argument that an uncompensated taking is not tortious because the landowner seeks just compensation rather than additional damages for the deprivation of a remedy reveals the same misunderstanding. Simply put, there is no constitutional or tortious injury until the landowner is denied just compensation. That the damages to which the landowner is entitled for this injury are measured by the just compensation he has been denied is neither surprising nor significant.)

B

Having decided that Del Monte Dunes' § 1983 suit was an action at law, we must determine whether the particular issues of liability were proper for determination by the jury. *See Markman v. Westview Instruments, Inc.*, 517 U.S. 370 (1996). . . . We look to history to determine whether the particular issues, or analogous ones, were decided by judge or by jury in suits at common law at the time the Seventh Amendment was adopted. Where history does not provide a clear answer, we look to precedent and functional considerations.

Just as no exact analogue of Del Monte Dunes' § 1983 suit can be identified at common law, so also can we find no precise analogue for the specific test of liability submitted to the jury in this case. We do know that in suits sounding in tort for money damages, questions of liability were decided by the jury, rather than the judge, in most cases. This allocation preserved the jury's role in resolving what was often the heart of the dispute between plaintiff and defendant. Although these general observations provide some guidance on the proper allocation between judge and jury of the liability issues in this case, they do not establish a definitive answer.

We look next to our existing precedents. Although this Court has decided many regulatory takings cases, none of our decisions has addressed the proper allocation of liability determinations between judge and jury in explicit terms. This is not surprising. Most of our regulatory takings decisions have reviewed suits against the United States, or suits seeking only injunctive relief. It is settled law that the Seventh Amendment does not apply in these contexts. . . .

In actions at law predominantly factual issues are in most cases allocated to the jury. The allocation rests on a firm historical foundation, and serves "to preserve the right to a jury's resolution of the ultimate dispute," *Markman, supra*, at 377. . . .

In accordance with these pronouncements, we hold that the issue whether a landowner has been deprived of all economically viable use of his property is a predominantly factual question. . . . [I]n actions at law otherwise within the purview of the Seventh Amendment, this question is for the jury.

The jury's role in determining whether a land-use decision substantially advances legitimate public interests within the meaning of our regulatory takings doctrine presents a more difficult question. Although our cases make clear that this inquiry involves an essential factual component, it no doubt has a legal aspect as well, and is probably best understood as a mixed question of fact and law.

In this case, the narrow question submitted to the jury was whether, when viewed in light of the context and protracted history of the development application process, the city's decision to reject a particular development plan bore a reasonable relationship to its proffered justifications. As the Court of Appeals recognized, this question was "essentially fact-bound [in] nature." Under these circumstances, we hold that it was proper to submit this narrow, fact-bound question to the jury.

C

We note the limitations of our Seventh Amendment holding. We do not address the jury's role in an ordinary inverse condemnation suit. The action here was brought under § 1983, a context in which the jury's role in vindicating constitutional rights has long been recognized by the federal courts. A federal court, moreover, cannot entertain a takings claim under § 1983 unless or until the complaining landowner has been denied an adequate postdeprivation remedy. . . . Our decision is also circumscribed in its conceptual reach. The posture of the case does not present an appropriate occasion to define with precision the elements of a temporary regulatory takings claim; although the city objected to submitting issues of liability to the jury at all, it approved the instructions that were submitted to the jury and therefore has no basis to challenge them.

For these reasons, we do not attempt a precise demarcation of the respective provinces of judge and jury in determining whether a zoning decision substantially advances legitimate governmental interests. The city and its *amici* suggest that sustaining the judgment here will undermine the uniformity of the law and eviscerate state and local zoning authority by subjecting all land-use decisions to plenary, and potentially inconsistent, jury review. Our decision raises no such specter. Del Monte Dunes did not bring a broad challenge to the constitutionality of the city's general land-use ordinances or policies, and our holding does not extend to a challenge of that sort. In such a context, the determination whether the statutory purposes were legitimate, or whether the purposes, though legitimate, were furthered by the law or general policy, might well fall within the province of the judge. Nor was the gravamen of Del Monte Dunes' complaint even that the city's general regulations were unreasonable as applied to Del Monte Dunes' property; we do not address the proper trial allocation of the various questions that might arise in that context. Rather, to the extent Del Monte Dunes' challenge was premised on unreasonable governmental action, the theory argued and tried to the jury was that the city's denial of the final development permit was inconsistent not only with the city's general ordinances and policies but even with the shifting ad hoc restrictions previously imposed by the city. Del Monte Dunes' argument, in short, was not that the city had followed its zoning ordinances and policies but rather that it had not done so. As is often true in § 1983 actions, the disputed questions were whether the government had denied a constitutional right in acting outside the bounds of its authority, and, if so, the extent of any resulting damages. These were questions for the jury. . . .

JUSTICE SCALIA, concurring in part and concurring in the judgment.

I join all except Part IV-A-2 of Justice Kennedy's opinion. In my view, all § 1983 actions must be treated alike insofar as the Seventh Amendment right to jury trial is concerned; that right exists when monetary damages are sought; and the issues submitted to the jury in the present case were properly sent there.

I

The fundamental difference between my view of this case and Justice Souter's is that I believe § 1983 establishes a unique, or at least distinctive, cause of action, in that the legal duty which is the basis for relief is ultimately defined not by the claim-creating statute itself, but by an extrinsic body of law to which the statute refers, namely "federal rights elsewhere conferred." In this respect § 1983 is, so to speak, a prism through which many different lights may pass. Unlike Justice Souter, I believe that, in analyzing this cause of action for Seventh Amendment purposes, the proper focus is on the prism itself, not on the particular ray that happens to be passing through in the present case.

The Seventh Amendment inquiry looks first to the "nature of the statutory action." *Feltner v. Columbia Pictures Television, Inc.*, 523 U.S. 340, 348 (1998). The only "statutory action" here is a § 1983 suit. The question before us, therefore, is not what common-law action is most analogous to some generic suit seeking compensation for a Fifth Amendment taking, but what common-law action is most analogous *to a § 1983 claim*. The fact that the breach of duty which underlies the particular § 1983 claim at issue here — a Fifth Amendment takings violation — may give rise to *another* cause of action besides a § 1983 claim, namely a so-called inverse condemnation suit, which is (according to Part IV-A-2 of Justice Kennedy's opinion) or is not (according to Justice Souter's opinion) entitled to be tried before a jury, seems to me irrelevant. The central question remains whether a *§ 1983 suit* is entitled to a jury. . . .

This is exactly the approach we took in *Wilson v. Garcia*, 471 U.S. 261 (1985) — an opinion whose analysis is so precisely in point that it gives this case a distinct quality of *déjà vu*. *Wilson* required us to analogize § 1983 actions to common-law suits . . . to identify the relevant statute of limitations. Since no federal limitations period was provided, the Court had to apply 42 U.S.C. § 1988(a). . . . In applying this provision, the Court . . . concluded (as I do here) that all § 1983 claims should be characterized in the same way. It said (as I have) that § 1983 was "a uniquely federal remedy," and that it is "the purest coincidence . . . when state statutes or the common law provide for equivalent remedies; any analogies to those causes of action are bound to be imperfect." And the Court was affected (as I am here) by the practical difficulties of the other course, which it described as follows:

> "Almost every § 1983 claim can be favorably analogized to more than one of the ancient common-law forms of action, each of which may be governed by a different statute of limitations. . . . "

For these reasons the Court concluded that all § 1983 actions should be characterized as "tort actions for the recovery of damages for personal injuries." . . .

II

To apply this methodology to the present case: There is no doubt that the cause of action created by § 1983 is, and was always regarded as, a tort claim. Thomas Cooley's treatise on tort law, which was published roughly contemporaneously with the enactment of § 1983, tracked Blackstone's view, *see* 3 W. Blackstone, Commentaries on the Laws of England 115–119 (1768), that torts are remedies for invasions of certain rights, such as the rights to personal security, personal liberty, and property. T. COOLEY, LAW OF TORTS 2–3 (1880). Section 1983 assuredly fits that description. . . .

This Court has confirmed in countless cases that a § 1983 cause of action sounds in tort. . . . We have commonly described it as creating a "constitutional tort". . . . *See Crawford-El v. Britton*, 523 U.S. 574, 600–601 (1998); *St. Louis v. Praprotnik*, 485 U.S. 112, 121 (1988); *Daniels v. Williams*, 474 U.S. 327, 329 (1986); *Monell v. New York City Dept. of Social Servs.*, 436 U.S. 658, 691 (1978). In *Wilson v. Garcia*, we explicitly identified § 1983 as a personal-injury tort, stating that "[a] violation of [§ 1983] is an injury to the individual rights of the person," and that "Congress unquestionably would have considered the remedies established in the Civil Rights Act [of 1871] to be more analogous to tort claims for personal injury than, for example, to claims for damages to property or breach of contract."

. . . We have also used § 1983's character as a tort cause of action to determine the scope of immunity, *Kalina v. Fletcher*, 522 U.S. 118, 124–125 (1997), the recoverable damages, *Heck, supra*, at 483; *Memphis Community School Dist.*, 477 U.S. 299, 305, and the scope of liability, *Monroe v. Pape*, 365 U.S. 167, 187 (1961). . . .

... It is clear from our cases that a tort action for money damages is entitled to jury trial under the Seventh Amendment. *See Curtis v. Loether*, 415 U.S. 189, 195 (1974) (according jury trial because "[a] damages action under [Title VIII of the Civil Rights Act of 1968] sounds basically in tort — the statute merely defines a new legal duty, and authorizes the courts to compensate a plaintiff for the injury caused by the defendant's wrongful breach").

A number of lower courts have held that a § 1983 damages action — without reference to what might have been the most analogous common-law remedy for violation of the particular federal right at issue — must be tried to a jury. [Here Justice Scalia cites decisions issued by the First, Third, Fourth, Sixth, Tenth, and Eleventh Circuits, as well as several district court opinions.] ...

III

To say that respondents had the right to a jury trial on their § 1983 claim is not to say that they were entitled to have the jury decide every issue. The precise scope of the jury's function is the second Seventh Amendment issue before us here — and there again, as we stated in *Markman v. Westview Instruments, Inc.*, 517 U.S. 370, 377 (1996), history is our guide. I agree with the Court's methodology, which, in the absence of a precise historical analogue, recognizes the historical preference for juries to make primarily factual determinations and for judges to resolve legal questions. That fact-law dichotomy is routinely applied by the lower courts in deciding § 1983 cases. For instance, in cases alleging retaliatory discharge of a public employee in violation of the First Amendment, judges determine whether the speech that motivated the termination was constitutionally protected speech, while juries find whether the discharge was caused by that speech. And in cases asserting municipal liability for harm caused by unconstitutional policies, judges determine whether the alleged policies were unconstitutional, while juries find whether the policies in fact existed and whether they harmed the plaintiff.

In the present case, the question of liability for a Takings Clause violation was given to the jury to determine by answering two questions. ... I concur in the Court's assessment that the "economically viable use" issue presents primarily a question of fact appropriate for consideration by a jury. The second question — whether the taking "substantially advances [a] legitimate public interest"[6] — seems to me to break down (insofar as is relevant to the instructions here) into two subquestions: (1) Whether the government's asserted basis for its challenged action represents a legitimate state interest. That was a question of law for the court. (2) Whether that legitimate state interest is substantially furthered by the challenged government action. I agree with the Court that at least in the highly particularized context of the present case, involving the denial of a single application for stated reasons, that was a question of fact for the jury. ...

JUSTICE SOUTER, with whom JUSTICE O'CONNOR, JUSTICE GINSBURG, and JUSTICE BREYER join, concurring in part and dissenting in part.

I

... I ... join the Court in thinking the statutory language "an action at law" insufficient to provide a jury right under 42 U.S.C. § 1983, with the consequence that *Markman v. Westview Instruments, Inc.*, 517 U.S. 370 (1996), must provide the appropriate questions in passing on the issue of a constitutional guarantee of jury trial. ... The Court soundly concedes that at the adoption of the Seventh Amendment

---

[6] [n.2] As the Court explains, petitioner forfeited any objection to this standard, and I express no view as to its propriety.

there was no action like the modern inverse condemnation suit for obtaining just compensation when the government took property without invoking formal condemnation procedures. Like the Court, I am accordingly remitted to a search for any analogy that may exist and a consideration of any implication going to the substance of the jury right that the results of that enquiry may raise. But this common launching ground is where our agreement ends.

II

The city's proposed analogy of inverse condemnation proceedings to direct ones is intuitively sensible, given their common Fifth Amendment constitutional source and link to the sovereign's power of eminent domain.

The intuition is borne out by closer analysis of the respective proceedings. The ultimate issue is identical in both direct and inverse condemnation actions: a determination of "the fair market value of the property [taken] on the date it is appropriated," as the measure of compensation required by the Fifth Amendment. It follows, as Justice Brandeis said in *Hurley v. Kincaid*, 285 U.S. 95 (1932), that "the compensation which [a property owner] may obtain in [an inverse condemnation] proceeding will be the same as that which he might have been awarded had the [government] instituted . . . condemnation proceedings." . . . As we said in *First English Evangelical Lutheran Church of Glendale v. County of Los Angeles*, 482 U.S. 304 (1987):

> " 'The fact that condemnation proceedings were not instituted and that the right was asserted in suits by the owners does not change the essential nature of the claim. The form of the remedy did not qualify the right. It rested upon the Fifth Amendment.' "

. . . Thus, the analogy between direct and inverse condemnation is apparent whether we focus on the underlying Fifth Amendment right or the common remedy of just compensation.

The strength of the analogy is fatal to respondents' claim to a jury trial as a matter of right. Reaffirming what was already a well-established principle, the Court explained over a century ago that "the estimate of the just compensation for property taken for the public use, under the right of eminent domain, is not required to be made by a jury," *Bauman v. Ross*, 167 U.S. 548, 593 (1897), and we have since then thought it "long . . . settled that there is no constitutional right to a jury in eminent domain proceedings." *United States v. Reynolds*, 397 U.S. 14, 18 (1970).

The reason that direct condemnation proceedings carry no jury right is not that they fail to qualify as "Suits at common-law" within the meaning of the Seventh Amendment's guarantee, for we may assume that they are indeed common law proceedings, *see Kohl v. United States*, 91 U.S. 367, 376 (1876) ("The right of eminent domain always was a right at common law"). The reason there is no right to jury trial, rather, is that the Seventh Amendment "preserve[s]" the common law right where it existed at the time of the framing, but does not create a right where none existed then. There is no jury right, then, because condemnation proceedings carried "no uniform and established right to a common law jury trial in England or the colonies at the time . . . the Seventh Amendment was adopted." . . .

In sum, at the time of the framing the notion of regulatory taking or inverse condemnation was yet to be derived, the closest analogue to the then-unborn claim was that of direct condemnation, and the right to compensation for such direct takings carried with it no right to a jury trial, just as the jury right is foreign to it in the modern era. On accepted Seventh Amendment analysis, then, there is no reason to find a jury right either by direct analogy or for the sake of preserving the substance of any jury practice known to the law at the crucial time. Indeed, the analogy with direct condemnation actions is so strong that there is every reason to conclude that inverse condemnation should implicate no jury right.

III

The plurality avoids this obvious conclusion in two alternative ways. One way is to disparage the comparison of inverse to direct taking, on the grounds that litigation of the former involves proof of liability that the latter does not and is generally more onerous to the landowner. The disparagement is joined with adoption of a different analogy, between inverse condemnation proceedings and actions for tortious interference with property interests, the latter of which do implicate a right to jury trial. . . .

A

1

The plurality's argument that no jury is required in a direct condemnation proceeding because the government's liability is conceded, leaving only the issue of damages to be assessed, rests on a premise that is only partially true. The part that is true, of course, is that the overwhelming number of direct condemnation cases join issue solely on the amount of damages, that is, on the just compensation due the landowner. But that is not true always. Now and then a landowner will fight back by denying the government's right to condemn, claiming that the object of the taking was not a public purpose or was otherwise unauthorized by statute. *See, e.g., Hawaii Housing Authority v. Midkiff*, 467 U.S. 229, 240 (1984) ("There is . . . a role for courts to play in reviewing a legislature's judgment of what constitutes a public use, even . . . [if] it is an 'extremely narrow' one"). . . .

. . . Just as significantly, the plurality's new rationale is absent from any of our precedents, including those underlying the *Reynolds* decision.[7]

. . . [T]he absence of the plurality's rationale from our prior discussions of the matter most probably reflects the fact that the want of a liability issue in most condemnation cases says nothing to explain why no jury ought to be provided on the question of damages that always is before the courts. The dollars-and-cents issue is about as "factual" as one can be (to invoke a criterion of jury suitability emphasized by the Court in another connection), and no dispute about liability provokes more contention than the price for allowing the government to put a landowner out of house and home. If an emphasis on factual issues vigorously contested were a sufficient criterion for identifying something essential to the preservation of the Seventh Amendment jury right, there ought to be a jury right in direct condemnation cases as well as the inverse ones favored by the plurality. . . .

2

Just as the plurality's efforts to separate direct from inverse condemnation actions thus break down, so does its proposal to analogize inverse condemnation to property damage torts. . . .

The plurality introduces its claimed analogue of tort actions for property damage by emphasizing what it sees as a real difference between the action of the government in direct condemnations, and those inverse condemnations, at least, that qualify for litigation under § 1983. Whereas in eminent domain proceedings the government admits its liability for the value of the taking, in the inverse condemnation cases litigated under

---

[7] [n.5] Moreover, if presence of a liability issue were crucial, then the jury right presumably would be lost in every tort case with liability conceded, which goes to trial on damages alone. Such, of course, is not the practice. *See, e.g., Blazar v. Perkins*, 463 A.2d 203, 207 (R.I. 1983) ("The fact that prior to trial, defendants admitted liability, thereby removing one issue from the consideration of the jury, does not alter the application of the principle [that plaintiffs cannot waive a jury trial on the issue of damage when defendants have demanded a jury trial]").

§ 1983, it refuses to do so inasmuch as it denies the landowner any state process (or effective process) for litigating his claim. . . . According to the plurality, it is the taking of property without providing compensation or a mechanism to obtain it that is tortious and subject to litigation under § 1983. By this reasoning, the plurality seeks to distinguish such a § 1983 action from a direct condemnation action and possibly from "an ordinary inverse condemnation suit," as well, by which the plurality presumably means a suit under a state law providing a mechanism for redress of regulatory taking claims. . . .

. . . [But] this very assumption that liability flows from wrongful or unauthorized conduct is at odds with the modern view of acts effecting inverse condemnation as being entirely lawful.[8] Unlike damages to redress a wrong . . . , a damages award in an inverse condemnation action orders payment of the "just compensation" required by the Constitution for payment of an obligation lawfully incurred. . . .

If the chosen tort analogy were not already too weak to sustain the plurality's position, it would be rendered so by the plurality's inability to identify any tort recovery . . . for the government's sin of omission in failing to provide a process of compensation (which the plurality finds at the heart of the § 1983 claim), as distinct from the acts of interfering with use or enjoyment of land. . . . When an inverse condemnation claim is brought under § 1983, the "provision" of law that is thereby enforced is the Fifth Amendment Just Compensation Clause and no other. There is no separate cause of action for withholding process, and respondents in the instant case do not claim otherwise; they simply seek just compensation for their land, subject to the usual rules governing § 1983 liability and damages awards.[9]

Finally, it must be said that even if the tort analogue were not a failure, it would prove too much. For if the comparison to inverse condemnation were sound, it would be equally sound as to direct condemnation and so require recognition of the very jury right that we have previously denied. . . .

B

In addition to the plurality's direct tort analogy, it pursues a different analytical approach in adopting Justice Scalia's analogy [to all § 1983 actions and] to § 1983 actions seeking legal relief. . . . The analogy to the broad class of § 1983 actions is put forward as serving the undoubted virtues of simplicity and uniformity in treating various actions that may be brought under a single remedial statute. . . . Th[e] subclass of § 1983 actions [brought to recover money damages, Justice Scalia] quite correctly notes, has been treated as tortlike in character and thus as much entitled to jury trial as tort actions have been at common law. For two independent reasons, however, I think the analogy with § 1983 actions, either as a class or as a subclass of damages actions, is inadequate.

---

[8] [n.7] When an inverse condemnee seeks an injunction (as when a direct condemnee challenges the taking, or a plaintiff claims a substantive due process violation), there is a claim of wrong in the sense of lack of authority. But this is not so in the usual case where damages are sought.

[9] [n.10] Respondents in this case sought damages for the fair market value of the property, interim damages for a temporary taking, holding costs, interest, attorney's fees, costs, and other consequential damages. . . . Respondents thus sought no incremental "damages" (beyond just compensation) for denial of state compensation procedures. Indeed, the only "damages" available in inverse condemnation cases is the just compensation measured by the value of the land. The fact that no further element of damages is recognized confirms rejection of the tort analogy, for it would be a peculiar tort indeed that did not recognize its concomitant injury in damages.

1

First, . . . trial by jury is not a uniform feature of § 1983 actions. The statute provides not only for actions at law with damages remedies where appropriate, but for "suits in equity, or other proper proceedings for redress." Accordingly, rights passing through the § 1983 prism may in proper cases be vindicated by injunction, by orders of restitution, and by declaratory judgments, none of which implicate, or always implicate, a right to jury trial. Comparing inverse condemnation actions to the class of § 1983 actions that are treated like torts does not, therefore, preserve a uniformity in jury practice under § 1983 that would otherwise be lost. Justice Scalia's metaphor is, indeed, an apt one: § 1983 is a prism, not a procrustean bed.

Nor, as I have already mentioned, is there a sound basis for treating inverse condemnation as providing damages for a tort. . . .

2

Even if an argument for § 1983 simplicity and uniformity were sustainable, however, it would necessarily be weaker than the analogy with direct condemnation actions. That analogy rests on two elements that are present in each of the two varieties of condemnation actions: a Fifth Amendment constitutional right and a remedy specifically mandated by that same amendment. Because constitutional values are superior to statutory values, uniformity as between different applications of a given constitutional guarantee is more important than uniformity as between different applications of a given statute. If one accepts that proposition as I do, a close analogy between direct and inverse condemnation proceedings is necessarily stronger than even a comparably close resemblance between two statutory actions.

IV

Were the results of the analysis to this point uncertain, one final anomaly of the Court's position would point up its error. The inconsistency of recognizing a jury trial right in inverse condemnation, notwithstanding its absence in condemnation actions, appears the more pronounced on recalling that . . . one theory of recovery in inverse condemnation cases is that the taking makes no substantial contribution to a legitimate governmental purpose. This issue includes not only a legal component that may be difficult to resolve, but one so closely related to similar issues in substantive due process property claims, that this Court cited a substantive due process case when recognizing the theory under the rubric of inverse condemnation. *See Agins* [*v. City of Tiburon*, 447 U.S. 255, 260 (1980)] (citing *Nectow v. Cambridge*, 277 U.S. 183, 188 (1928)). Substantive due process claims are, of course, routinely reserved without question for the court. *See, e.g., County of Sacramento v. Lewis*, 523 U.S. 833, 853–855 (1998); *FM Properties Operating Co. v. Austin*, 93 F.3d 167, 172 n.6 (CA5 1996) (rational relationship to legitimate government interest for purposes of substantive due process a question of law for the court). Thus, it would be far removed from usual practice to charge a jury with the duty to assess the constitutional legitimacy of the government's objective or the constitutional adequacy of its relationship to the government's chosen means.

The usual practice makes perfect sense. While juries are not customarily called upon to assume the subtleties of deferential review, courts apply this sort of limited scrutiny in all sorts of contexts and are routinely accorded institutional competence to do it. Scrutinizing the legal basis for governmental action is "one of those things that judges often do and are likely to do better than juries unburdened by training in exegesis." *Markman*, 517 U.S. at 388. It therefore should bring no surprise to find that in the takings cases a question whether regulatory action substantially advances a legitimate public aim has more often than not been treated by the federal courts as a legal issue. These practices point up the great gulf between the practical realities of takings litigation, and the Court's reliance on the assertion that "in suits sounding in tort for money damages, questions of liability were decided by the jury, rather than the judge, in most cases."

Perhaps this is the reason that the Court apparently seeks to distance itself from the ramifications of today's determination [in Part IV(C) of its opinion]. . . . But the Court's reticence is cold comfort simply because it rests upon distinctions that withstand analysis no better than the tort-law analogies on which the Court's conclusion purports to rest. The narrowness of the Court's intentions cannot, therefore, be accepted as an effective limit on the consequences on its reasoning, from which I respectfully dissent.

NOTES

1. The Right to Jury Trial in Section 1983 Cases. Although Justice Scalia finds support in the Court's decision in *Wilson v. Garcia* for his conclusion that all section 1983 damages claims should be treated alike with respect to the right to jury trial, *City of Monterey* views the scope of the right to jury trial in section 1983 cases strictly as a matter of federal law. None of the Justices suggest that section 1988(a) is implicated in analyzing this issue.

City of Monterey was the first Supreme Court opinion to expressly address the applicability of the Seventh Amendment's right to jury trial in section 1983 cases. Although the Justices disagree about the scope of that right as applied to regulatory takings claims like that at issue in *City of Monterey*, all of them seem to presume that the right to jury trial extends to run-of-the mill section 1983 damages claims. (For a discussion of the constitutional principles governing takings claims, see Chapter 8.A.[1], *infra*.)

Note that the Seventh Amendment does not apply in section 1983 cases seeking only equitable relief. In a portion of Justice Scalia's opinion omitted above, however, he points out that the right to jury trial is not lost simply "by virtue of the fact that, under our modern unified system, the equitable relief of an injunction is also sought." If one of the parties requests a jury trial in a case involving claims for both damages and injunctive relief, the Constitution requires that the legal claims be determined by a jury. *See Ross v. Bernhard*, 396 U.S. 531, 537–38 (1970).

Even though the constitutional right to jury trial extends to most section 1983 damages actions, the various opinions in *City of Monterey* make clear that the Seventh Amendment does not mandate that the jury resolve every issue in the case. Traditionally, questions of fact have been determined by the jury, legal questions by the judge. Part III of Justice Scalia's opinion illustrates how this distinction has been applied in some section 1983 cases. Other examples of issues arising in section 1983 litigation that the Supreme Court considers questions of law to be determined by the judge are whether a defendant is entitled to qualified immunity (*see* Note 4 following *Hope v. Pelzer* in Chapter 2.B., *supra*), and which local officials are final policymakers within the meaning of *Monell*'s official policy or custom requirement (*see* Note 3 following *City of St. Louis v. Praprotnik* in Chapter 4.C.[1], *supra*).

2. The Right to Jury Trial in State Court. Unlike most of the rights guaranteed in the Bill of Rights, the Seventh Amendment right to jury trial does not apply to the states. *See Minneapolis & St. Louis R.R. Co. v. Bombolis*, 241 U.S. 211 (1916). Thus, in *State ex rel. Cherry v. Burns*, 602 N.W.2d 477, 482 (Neb. 1999), the Nebraska Supreme Court relied on *City of Monterey*'s holding that section 1983 itself does not confer a right to jury trial in concluding that state law governs the scope of the jury trial right in section 1983 cases filed in state court.

3. Waiving the Right to Jury Trial. The Seventh Amendment guarantees a right to jury trial to both parties in a civil case. *See, e.g., Curtis v. Loether*, 415 U.S. 189, 192 (1974). Under Federal Rule of Civil Procedure 38(d), however, a jury trial is deemed to be waived if neither party files a timely request.

The following case is one in which the plaintiff waived, not merely the right to a jury trial, but the right to pursue a section 1983 claim altogether.

D. RELEASE-DISMISSAL AGREEMENTS

TOWN OF NEWTON v. RUMERY
Supreme Court of the United States
480 U.S. 386 (1987)

JUSTICE POWELL announced the judgment of the Court and delivered the opinion of the Court with respect to Parts I, II, III-A, IV, and V, and an opinion with respect to Part III-B, in which THE CHIEF JUSTICE, JUSTICE WHITE, and JUSTICE SCALIA join.

The question in this case is whether a court properly may enforce an agreement in which a criminal defendant releases his right to file an action under 42 U.S.C. § 1983 in return for a prosecutor's dismissal of pending criminal charges.

I

In 1983, a grand jury in Rockingham County, New Hampshire, indicted David Champy for aggravated felonious sexual assault. Respondent Bernard Rumery, a friend of Champy's, read about the charges in a local newspaper. Seeking information about the charges, he telephoned Mary Deary, who was acquainted with both Rumery and Champy. Coincidentally, Deary had been the victim of the assault in question and was expected to be the principal witness against Champy. The record does not reveal directly the date or substance of this conversation between Rumery and Deary, but Deary apparently was disturbed by the call. On March 12, according to police records, she called David Barrett, the Chief of Police for the town of Newton. She told him that Rumery was trying to force her to drop the charges against Champy. Rumery talked to Deary again on May 11. The substance of this conversation also is disputed. Rumery claims that Deary called him and that she raised the subject of Champy's difficulties. According to the police records, however, Deary told Chief Barrett that Rumery had threatened that, if Deary went forward on the Champy case, she would "end up like" two women who recently had been murdered in Lowell, Massachusetts. Barrett arrested Rumery and accused him of tampering with a witness . . . , a Class B felony.

Rumery promptly retained Stephen Woods, an experienced criminal defense attorney. Woods contacted Brian Graf, the Deputy County Attorney for Rockingham County. He warned Graf that he "had better [dismiss] these charges, because we're going to win them and after that we're going to sue." After further discussions, Graf and Woods reached an agreement, under which Graf would dismiss the charges against Rumery if Rumery would agree not to sue the town, its officials, or Deary for any harm caused by the arrest. All parties agreed that one factor in Graf's decision not to prosecute Rumery was Graf's desire to protect Deary from the trauma she would suffer if she were forced to testify. . . .

Woods drafted an agreement in which Rumery agreed to release any claims he might have against the town, its officials, or Deary if Graf agreed to dismiss the criminal charges (the release-dismissal agreement). After Graf approved the form of the agreement, Woods presented it to Rumery. Although Rumery's recollection of the events was quite different, the District Court found that Woods discussed the agreement with Rumery in his office for about an hour and explained to Rumery that he would forgo all civil actions if he signed the agreement. Three days later, on June 6, 1983, Rumery returned to Woods' office and signed the agreement. The criminal charges were dropped.

Ten months later, on April 13, 1984, Rumery filed an action under § 1983 in the Federal District Court for the District of New Hampshire. He alleged that the town and its officers had violated his constitutional rights by arresting him, defaming him, and imprisoning him falsely. The defendants filed a motion to dismiss, relying on the release-dismissal agreement as an affirmative defense. . . .

II

We begin by noting the source of the law that governs this case. The agreement purported to waive a right to sue conferred by a federal statute. The question whether the policies underlying that statute may in some circumstances render that waiver unenforceable is a question of federal law. We resolve this question by reference to traditional common-law principles, as we have resolved other questions about the principles governing § 1983 actions. *E.g., Pulliam v. Allen*, 466 U.S. 522, 539–540 (1984). The relevant principle is well established: a promise is unenforceable if the interest in its enforcement is outweighed in the circumstances by a public policy harmed by enforcement of the agreement.[10]

III

The Court of Appeals concluded that the public interests related to release-dismissal agreements justified a per se rule of invalidity. . . . [A]lthough we agree that in some cases these agreements may infringe important interests of the criminal defendant and of society as a whole, we do not believe that the mere possibility of harm to these interests calls for a per se rule.

A

Rumery's first objection to release-dismissal agreements is that they are inherently coercive. He argues that it is unfair to present a criminal defendant with a choice between facing criminal charges and waiving his right to sue under § 1983. We agree that some release-dismissal agreements may not be the product of an informed and voluntary decision. The risk, publicity, and expense of a criminal trial may intimidate a defendant, even if he believes his defense is meritorious. But this possibility does not justify invalidating all such agreements. In other contexts criminal defendants are required to make difficult choices that effectively waive constitutional rights. For example, it is well settled that plea bargaining does not violate the Constitution even though a guilty plea waives important constitutional rights.[11] We see no reason to believe that release-dismissal agreements pose a more coercive choice than other situations we have accepted. *E.g., Corbitt v. New Jersey*, 439 U.S. 212 (1978) (upholding a statute that imposed higher sentences on defendants who went to trial than on those who entered guilty pleas). As Justice Harlan explained:

> "The criminal process, like the rest of the legal system, is replete with situations requiring 'the making of difficult judgments' as to which course to follow. Although a defendant may have a right, even of constitutional dimen-

---

[10] [n.2] *Cf.* RESTATEMENT (SECOND) OF CONTRACTS § 178(1) (1981). *See also Crampton v. Ohio*, decided with *McGautha v. California*, 402 U.S. 183, 213 (1971) ("The threshold question is whether compelling [a defendant to decide whether to waive constitutional rights] impairs to an appreciable extent any of the policies behind the rights involved").

[11] [n.3] We recognize that the analogy between plea bargains and release-dismissal agreements is not complete. The former are subject to judicial oversight. Moreover, when the State enters a plea bargain with a criminal defendant, it receives immediate and tangible benefits, such as promptly imposed punishment without the expenditure of prosecutorial resources. Also, the defendant's agreement to plead to some crime tends to ensure some satisfaction of the public's interest in the prosecution of crime and confirms that the prosecutor's charges have a basis in fact. The benefits the State may realize in particular cases from release-dismissal agreements may not be as tangible, but they are not insignificant.

sions, to follow whichever course he chooses, the Constitution does not by that token always forbid requiring him to choose."

Crampton v. Ohio, decided with *McGautha v. California*, 402 U.S. 183, 213 (1971).

In many cases a defendant's choice to enter into a release-dismissal agreement will reflect a highly rational judgment that the certain benefits of escaping criminal prosecution exceed the speculative benefits of prevailing in a civil action. Rumery's voluntary decision to enter this agreement exemplifies such a judgment. Rumery is a sophisticated businessman. He was not in jail and was represented by an experienced criminal lawyer, who drafted the agreement. Rumery considered the agreement for three days before signing it. The benefits of the agreement to Rumery are obvious: he gained immunity from criminal prosecution in consideration of abandoning a civil suit that he may well have lost.

Because Rumery voluntarily waived his right to sue under § 1983, the public interest opposing involuntary waiver of constitutional rights is no reason to hold this agreement invalid. Moreover, we find that the possibility of coercion in the making of similar agreements [is] insufficient by itself to justify a per se rule against release-dismissal bargains. If there is such a reason, it must lie in some external public interest necessarily injured by release-dismissal agreements.

B

. . . It is true, of course, that § 1983 actions to vindicate civil rights may further significant public interests. But it is important to remember that Rumery had no public duty to institute a § 1983 action merely to further the public's interest in revealing police misconduct. Congress has confined the decision to bring such actions to the injured individuals, not to the public at large. Thus, we hesitate to elevate more diffused public interests above Rumery's considered decision that he would benefit personally from the agreement.

We also believe the Court of Appeals misapprehended the range of public interests arguably affected by a release-dismissal agreement. The availability of such agreements may threaten important public interests. They may tempt prosecutors to bring frivolous charges, or to dismiss meritorious charges, to protect the interests of other officials.[12] But a per se rule of invalidity fails to credit other relevant public interests and improperly assumes prosecutorial misconduct.[13]

The vindication of constitutional rights and the exposure of official misconduct are not the only concerns implicated by § 1983 suits. No one suggests that all such suits are meritorious. Many are marginal and some are frivolous. Yet even when the risk of ultimate liability is negligible, the burden of defending such lawsuits is substantial. Counsel may be retained by the official, as well as the governmental entity. Preparation for trial, and the trial itself, will require the time and attention of the defendant officials, to the detriment of their public duties. In some cases litigation will extend over a period of years. This diversion of officials from their normal duties and the inevitable expense of defending even unjust claims is distinctly not in the public interest. To the extent release-dismissal agreements protect public officials from the burdens of defending such unjust claims, they further this important public interest.

---

[12] [n.4] Actions taken for these reasons properly have been recognized as unethical. *See* ABA MODEL CODE OF PROFESSIONAL RESPONSIBILITY, Disciplinary Rule 7-105 (1980).

[13] [n.5] Prosecutors themselves rarely are held liable in § 1983 actions. *See Imbler v. Pachtman*, 424 U.S. 409 (1976) (discussing prosecutorial immunity). Also, in many States and municipalities — perhaps in most — prosecutors are elected officials and are entirely independent of the civil authorities likely to be defendants in § 1983 suits. There may be situations, of course, when a prosecutor is motivated to protect the interests of such officials or of police. But the constituency of an elected prosecutor is the public, and such a prosecutor is likely to be influenced primarily by the general public interest.

A per se rule invalidating release-dismissal agreements also assumes that prosecutors will seize the opportunity for wrongdoing. In recent years the Court has considered a number of claims that prosecutors have acted improperly. Our decisions in those cases uniformly have recognized that courts normally must defer to prosecutorial decisions as to whom to prosecute. The reasons for judicial deference are well known. Prosecutorial charging decisions are rarely simple. In addition to assessing the strength and importance of a case, prosecutors also must consider other tangible and intangible factors, such as government enforcement priorities. Finally, they also must decide how best to allocate the scarce resources of a criminal justice system that simply cannot accommodate the litigation of every serious criminal charge. Because these decisions "are not readily susceptible to the kind of analysis the courts are competent to undertake," we have been "properly hesitant to examine the decision whether to prosecute."

. . . Indeed, the merit of this view is illustrated by this case, where the only evidence of prosecutorial misconduct is the agreement itself. . . .

IV

Turning to the agreement presented by this case, we conclude that the District Court's decision to enforce the agreement was correct. As we have noted, it is clear that Rumery voluntarily entered the agreement. Moreover, in this case the prosecutor had an independent, legitimate reason to make this agreement directly related to his prosecutorial responsibilities. The agreement foreclosed both the civil and criminal trials concerning Rumery, in which Deary would have been a key witness. She therefore was spared the public scrutiny and embarrassment she would have endured if she had had to testify in either of those cases. Both the prosecutor and the defense attorney testified in the District Court that this was a significant consideration in the prosecutor's decision.

In sum, we conclude that this agreement was voluntary, that there is no evidence of prosecutorial misconduct, and that enforcement of this agreement would not adversely affect the relevant public interests.[14]

V

We reverse the judgment of the Court of Appeals and remand the case to the District Court for dismissal of the complaint.

JUSTICE O'CONNOR, concurring in part and concurring in the judgment.

I join in Parts I, II, III-A, IV, and V of the Court's opinion. . . . I agree with the Court that a case-by-case approach appropriately balances the important interests on both sides of the question of the enforceability of these agreements, and that on the facts of this particular case Bernard Rumery's covenant not to sue is enforceable. I write separately, however, . . . to emphasize that it is the burden of those relying upon such covenants to establish that the agreement is neither involuntary nor the product of an abuse of the criminal process.

---

[14] [n.10] We note that two Courts of Appeals have applied a voluntariness standard to determine the enforceability of agreements entered into after trial, in which the defendants released possible § 1983 claims in return for sentencing considerations. See *Bushnell v. Rossetti*, 750 F.2d 298 (CA4 1984); *Jones v. Taber*, 648 F.2d 1201 (CA9 1981). We have no occasion in this case to determine whether an inquiry into voluntariness alone is sufficient to determine the enforceability of release-dismissal agreements. We also note that it would be helpful to conclude release-dismissal agreements under judicial supervision. Although such supervision is not essential to the validity of an otherwise-proper agreement, it would help ensure that the agreements did not result from prosecutorial misconduct.

As the Court shows, there are substantial policy reasons for permitting release-dismissal bargains to be struck in appropriate cases. . . . [P]rosecutors may legitimately believe that, though the police properly defused a volatile situation by arresting a minor misdemeanant, the public interest in further prosecution is outweighed by the cost of litigation. Sparing the local community the expense of litigation associated with some minor crimes for which there is little or no public interest in prosecution may be a legitimate objective of a release-dismissal agreement.

On the other hand, . . . the availability of the release option may tempt officials to ignore their public duty by dropping meritorious criminal prosecutions in order to avoid the risk, expense, and publicity of a § 1983 suit. . . . By introducing extraneous considerations into the criminal process, the legitimacy of that process may be compromised. . . .

As the Court indicates, a release-dismissal agreement is not directly analogous to a plea bargain. The legitimacy of plea bargaining depends in large measure upon eliminating extraneous considerations from the process. No court would knowingly permit a prosecutor to agree to accept a defendant's plea to a lesser charge in exchange for the defendant's cash payment to the police officers who arrested him. Rather, the prosecutor is permitted to consider only legitimate criminal justice concerns in striking his bargain — concerns such as rehabilitation, allocation of criminal justice resources, the strength of the evidence against the defendant, and the extent of his cooperation with the authorities. The central problem with the release-dismissal agreement is that public criminal justice interests are explicitly traded against the private financial interest of the individuals involved in the arrest and prosecution. Moreover, plea bargaining takes place only under judicial supervision, an important check against abuse. Release-dismissal agreements are often reached between the prosecutor and defendant with little or no judicial oversight.

Nevertheless, the dangers of the release-dismissal agreement do not preclude its enforcement in all cases. The defendants in a § 1983 suit may establish that a particular release executed in exchange for the dismissal of criminal charges was voluntarily made, not the product of prosecutorial overreaching, and in the public interest. But they must prove that this is so; the courts should not presume it as I fear portions of Part III-B of the plurality opinion may imply. . . .

Close examination of all the factors in this case leads me to concur in the Court's decision that this covenant not to sue is enforceable. There is ample evidence in the record concerning the circumstances of the execution of this agreement. Testimony of the prosecutor, defense counsel, and Rumery himself leave little doubt that the agreement was entered into voluntarily. While the charge pending against Rumery was serious — subjecting him to up to seven years in prison — it is one of the lesser felonies under New Hampshire law, and a long prison term was probably unlikely given the absence of any prior criminal record and the weaknesses in the case against Rumery.[15] Finally, as the Court correctly notes, the prosecutor had a legitimate reason to enter into this agreement directly related to his criminal justice function. . . . Mary Deary's emotional distress, her unwillingness to testify against Rumery, presumably in later civil as well as criminal proceedings, and the necessity of her testimony in the pending sexual assault case against David Champy all support the prosecutor's judgment that the charges against Rumery should be dropped if further injury to Deary, and therefore the Champy case, could thereby be avoided.

Against the convincing evidence that Rumery voluntarily entered into the agreement and that it served the public interest, there is only Rumery's blanket claim that agreements such as this one are inherently coercive. While it would have been

---

[15] [Editor's note: Earlier in her opinion, Justice O'Connor expressed the view that "[t]he nature of the criminal charges that are pending is also important, for the greater the charge, the greater the coercive effect."]

preferable, and made this an easier case, had the release-dismissal agreement been concluded under some form of judicial supervision, I concur in the Court's judgment, and all but Part III-B of its opinion, that Rumery's § 1983 suit is barred by his valid, voluntary release.

JUSTICE STEVENS, with whom JUSTICE BRENNAN, JUSTICE MARSHALL, and JUSTICE BLACKMUN join, dissenting.

I

A few days before respondent was scheduled for a probable-cause hearing on the charge of witness tampering, respondent's attorney advised him to sign [the release-dismissal agreement]. The advice was predicated on the lawyer's judgment that the value of a dismissal outweighed the harmful consequences of an almost certain indictment on a felony charge together with the risk of conviction in a case in which the outcome would depend on the jury's assessment of the relative credibility of respondent and his alleged victim. The lawyer correctly advised respondent that even if he was completely innocent, there could be no guarantee of acquittal. He therefore placed a higher value on his client's interest in terminating the criminal proceeding promptly than on the uncertain benefits of pursuing a civil remedy against the town and its police department. After delaying a decision for three days, respondent reluctantly followed his lawyer's advice.

From respondent's point of view, it is unquestionably true that the decision to sign the release-dismissal agreement was, as the Court emphasizes, "voluntary, deliberate, and informed." . . . I submit, however, that the deliberate and rational character of respondent's decision is not a sufficient reason for concluding that the agreement is enforceable. Otherwise, a promise to pay a state trooper $20 for not issuing a ticket for a traffic violation, or a promise to contribute to the police department's retirement fund in exchange for the dismissal of a felony charge, would be enforceable. Indeed, I would suppose that virtually all contracts that courts refuse to enforce nevertheless reflect perfectly rational decisions by the parties who entered into them. . . .

The "voluntary, deliberate, and informed" character of a defendant's decision generally provides an acceptable basis for upholding the validity of a plea bargain. But it is inappropriate to assume that the same standard determines the validity of a [release-dismissal] agreement. . . .

The net result of every plea bargain is an admission of wrongdoing by the defendant and the imposition of a criminal sanction with its attendant stigma. Although there may be some cases in which an innocent person pleads guilty to a minor offense to avoid the risk of conviction on a more serious charge, it is reasonable to presume that such cases are rare and represent the exception rather than the rule. See Fed. Rule Crim. Proc. 11(f) (court may not enter judgment on a guilty plea unless it is satisfied the plea has a factual basis). Like a plea bargain, an agreement by the suspect to drop § 1983 charges and to pay restitution to the victim in exchange for the prosecutor's termination of criminal proceedings involves an admission of wrongdoing by the defendant. The same cannot be said about an agreement that completely exonerates the defendant. Not only is such a person presumptively innocent as a matter of law; as a factual matter the prosecutor's interest in obtaining a covenant not to sue will be strongest in those cases in which he realizes that the defendant was innocent and was wrongfully accused. Moreover, the prosecutor will be most willing — indeed, he is ethically obligated — to drop charges when he believes that probable cause as established by the available, admissible evidence is lacking.

. . . By simultaneously establishing and limiting the defendant's criminal liability, plea bargains delicately balance individual and social advantage. This mutuality of advantage does not exist in release-dismissal agreements. A defendant entering a release-dismissal agreement is forced to waive claims based on official conduct under color of state law, in exchange merely for the assurance that the State will not prosecute him for conduct for which he has made no admission of wrongdoing. The State is spared the necessity of going to trial, but its willingness to drop the charge completely indicates that it might not have proceeded with the prosecution in any event. No social interest in the punishment of wrongdoers is satisfied; the only interest vindicated is that of resolving once and for all the question of § 1983 liability. . . .

The plurality assumes that many § 1983 suits "are marginal and some are frivolous." Whether that assumption is correct or incorrect, the validity of each ought to be tested by the adversary process. . . .

II

When the prosecutor negotiated the agreement with respondent, he represented three potentially conflicting interests. . . .

If we view the problem from the standpoint of the prosecutor's principal client, the State of New Hampshire, it is perfectly clear that the release-dismissal agreement was both unnecessary and unjustified. For both the prosecutor and the State of New Hampshire enjoy absolute immunity from common-law and § 1983 liability arising out of a prosecutor's decision to initiate criminal proceedings. The agreement thus gave the State and the prosecutor no protection that the law did not already provide.

The record in this case indicates that an important reason for obtaining the covenant was "[to] protect the police department." There is, however, an obvious potential conflict between the prosecutor's duty to enforce the law and his objective of protecting members of the Police Department who are accused of unlawful conduct. The public is entitled to have the prosecutor's decision to go forward with a criminal case, or to dismiss it, made independently of his concerns about the potential damages liability of the Police Department. It is equally clear that this separation of functions cannot be achieved if the prosecutor may use the threat of criminal prosecution as a weapon to obtain a favorable termination of a civil claim against the police. . . .

At bottom, the Court's holding in this case seems to rest on concerns related to the potential witness, Mary Deary. As is true with the prosecutor's concerns for police liability, there is a potential conflict between the public interest represented by the prosecutor and the private interests of a recalcitrant witness. As a general matter there is no reason to fashion a rule that either requires or permits a prosecutor always to defer to the interests of a witness. The prosecutor's law enforcement responsibilities will sometimes diverge from those interests; there will be cases in which the prosecutor has a plain duty to obtain critical testimony despite the desire of the witness to remain anonymous or to avoid a courtroom confrontation with an offender. There may be other cases in which a witness has given false or exaggerated testimony for malicious reasons. It would plainly be unwise for the Court to hold that a release-dismissal agreement is enforceable simply because it affords protection to a potential witness. . . .

The need for Deary's testimony in the pending sexual assault case against Champy simply cannot justify denying this respondent a remedy for a violation of his Fourth Amendment rights. Presumably, if there had been an actual trial of the pending charge against Champy,[16] that trial would have concluded long before Deary would have been required to testify in any § 1983 litigation. . . .

---

[16] [n.21] Champy pleaded guilty to a lesser included offense and the felony charge against him was dismissed without a trial.

III

Because this is the first case of this kind that the Court has reviewed, I am hesitant to adopt an absolute rule invalidating all such agreements.[17] I am, however, persuaded that the federal policies reflected in the enactment and enforcement of § 1983 mandate a strong presumption against the enforceability of such agreements and that the presumption is not overcome in this case by the facts or by any of the policy concerns discussed by the plurality. . . . The interest in vindication of constitutional violations unquestionably outweighs the interest in avoiding the expense and inconvenience of defending unmeritorious claims. Paradoxically, the plurality seems more sensitive to that burden than to the cost to the public and the individual of denying relief in meritorious cases. . . . Unless [§ 1983 is repealed,] however, we should respect the congressional decision to attach greater importance to the benefits associated with access to a federal remedy than to the burdens of defending these cases. . . .

NOTES

1. The Validity of Release-Dismissal Agreements. Analogizing to the discussion of absolute judicial immunity in *Pulliam v. Allen* (which is described in Chapter 2.A.[2], *supra*), the Court held that the validity of the release-dismissal agreement at issue in *Rumery* was a question of federal law, and not one governed by state law or section 1988(a).

Although the *Rumery* majority purported to resolve the case by looking to the "well established" common-law principle that "a promise is unenforceable if the interest in its enforcement is outweighed in the circumstances by a public policy harmed by enforcement of the agreement," one commentator has argued that "[t]he common law fairly bristles with other appropriate starting points for analysis, most of which would point to the per se voidability of release-dismissal bargains." Seth F. Kreimer, *Releases, Redress, and Police Misconduct: Reflections on Agreements to Waive Civil Rights Actions in Exchange for Dismissal of Criminal Charges*, 136 U. PA. L. REV. 851, 861 (1988). By way of example, Kreimer offers the following illustrations:

> Contracts induced by threats of prosecution are voidable at common law, and duress by imprisonment can prevent the enforcement of releases. At common law, obtaining items of value under color of public office constituted the crime of extortion, and the common law offense of "compounding a crime" punished agreements not to prosecute a crime in exchange for payment.

Kreimer, supra, at 861–62. In addition, Kreimer concludes, based on the "relevant empirical literature and interviews with prosecutors and defense attorneys in twenty jurisdictions," that release-dismissal agreements are "widely disapproved by prosecutors" and "unreliable mechanisms for screening out 'unjust' civil rights actions," and that the prosecutors who do use them "appear to do so primarily as a means of routinely eliminating civil rights claims and accommodating police and municipal claims departments." *Kreimer, supra*, at 853.

Note that Part III(B) of the opinion in *Rumery*, which was joined by only a plurality of the Court, cited as some of the advantages of release-dismissal agreements the same

---

[17] [n.22] It seems likely, however, that the costs of having courts determine the validity of release-dismissal agreements will outweigh the benefits that most agreements can be expected to provide. . . . This inquiry will occupy a significant amount of the court's and the parties' time, and will subject prosecutorial decisionmaking to judicial review. . . . [P]rosecutors already enjoy absolute immunity, and . . . police have been afforded qualified immunity. Thus, the vast majority of "marginal or frivolous" § 1983 suits can be dismissed under existing standards with little more burden on the defendants than is entailed in defending a release-dismissal agreement. . . . In most cases, if social and judicial resources are to be expended at all, they would seem better spent on an evaluation of the merits of the § 1983 claim rather than on a detour into the enforceability of a release-dismissal agreement.

policies used to justify the immunity doctrines: preventing the diversion of public officials from their duties, reducing the costs of defending section 1983 suits, and weeding out meritless claims. Are these arguments persuasive, or does using them to justify both the immunity defenses and release-dismissal agreements smack of double-counting?

2. Subsequent Lower Court Case Law. *Rumery* requires a determination of the validity of release-dismissal agreements on a case-by-case basis, and most of the decisions issued since *Rumery* have upheld such agreements. But in *Hall v. Ochs*, 817 F.2d 920 (1st Cir. 1987), the court struck down a release-dismissal agreement obtained by a police officer on a preprinted form, which the plaintiff signed in jail — despite initially refusing to do so — after being told that the charges would be dropped if he signed the form. "Not surprisingly," the court noted, "after three refusals and well over an hour in jail, his resolve buckled." "No waiver executed under such circumstances can be called voluntary," the court concluded. *Hall*, 817 F.2d at 924. Likewise, in *Vallone v. Lee*, 7 F.3d 196, 199 (11th Cir. 1993), where the plaintiff signed a release-dismissal agreement after spending seven months in jail because he could not make bail following his arrest on misdemeanor charges, the court thought that he had presented sufficient evidence of "coercion stemm[ing] from the threat of continuing and unjustified incarceration pending his trial, . . . to justify the district court's submission to the jury the question whether [he] voluntarily assented to the agreement."

Note that there is some disagreement among the courts of appeals as to the standard of proof to be used in determining the validity of release-dismissal agreements. *Compare Gonzalez v. Kokot*, 314 F.3d 311, 318–19 (7th Cir. 2002) (adopting a preponderance standard), *with Livingstone v. North Belle Vernon Borough*, 91 F.3d 515, 535–36 (3d Cir. 1996) (requiring proof by clear and convincing evidence).

Although footnote 10 of the majority's opinion in *Rumery* left open the question whether the voluntariness of a release-dismissal agreement is sufficient to justify its enforcement, some courts have required in addition a finding that "enforcement [of the release-dismissal agreement] is in the public interest." *Lynch v. City of Alhambra*, 880 F.2d 1122, 1126 (9th Cir. 1989); *see also Livingstone v. North Belle Vernon Borough*, 91 F.3d 515, 527 (3d Cir. 1996) (likewise requiring, not only evidence of voluntariness, but also proof that enforcement of the agreement " 'would advance the public interest,' " and interpreting that latter standard to include both an objective element — that " 'the facts known to the prosecutor when the agreement was reached' must have sufficed to support the prosecutor's proffered public interest reason for concluding the agreement, and that this public-interest reason be a legitimate one" — and a subjective element — that " 'the public interest reason proffered by the prosecutor must be the prosecutor's *actual reason* for seeking the release' ") (quoting *Cain v. Darby Borough*, 7 F.3d 377, 380–81 (3d Cir. 1993) (en banc)).

Chapter 6
REMEDIES UNDER § 1983

A. COMPENSATORY DAMAGES

MEMPHIS COMMUNITY SCHOOL DISTRICT v. STACHURA
Supreme Court of the United States
477 U.S. 299 (1986)

JUSTICE POWELL delivered the opinion of the Court.

Stachura is a tenured teacher in the Memphis, Michigan, public schools. When the events that led to this case occurred, [Stachura] taught seventh-grade life science, using a textbook that had been approved by the School Board. The textbook included a chapter on human reproduction. During the 1978–1979 school year, [Stachura] spent six weeks on this chapter. As part of their instruction, students were shown pictures of [Stachura's] wife during her pregnancy. [Stachura] also showed the students two films concerning human growth and sexuality. These films were provided by the County Health Department, and the Principal of [Stachura's] school had approved their use. Both films had been shown in past school years without incident.

After the showing of the pictures and the films, a number of parents complained to school officials about [Stachura's] teaching methods. These complaints, which appear to have been based largely on inaccurate rumors about the allegedly sexually explicit nature of the pictures and films, were discussed at an open School Board meeting held on April 23, 1979. Following the advice of the School Superintendent, [Stachura] did not attend the meeting, during which a number of parents expressed the view that [Stachura] should not be allowed to teach in the Memphis school system. The day after the meeting, [Stachura] was suspended with pay. The School Board later confirmed the suspension, and notified [Stachura] that an "administration evaluation" of his teaching methods was underway. No such evaluation was ever made. [Stachura] was reinstated the next fall, after filing this lawsuit.

[Stachura] sued the School District, the Board of Education, various Board members and school administrators, and two parents . . . [for] depriv[ing] him of both liberty and property without due process of law and violat[ing] his First Amendment right to academic freedom. [Stachura] sought compensatory and punitive damages under 42 U.S.C. § 1983 for these constitutional violations.

At the close of trial on these claims, the District Court instructed the jury as to the law governing the asserted bases for liability. Turning to damages, the court instructed the jury that on finding liability it should award a sufficient amount to compensate [Stachura] for the injury caused by [the defendants'] unlawful actions:

> You should consider in this regard any lost earnings; loss of earning capacity; out-of-pocket expenses; and any mental anguish or emotional distress that you find the Plaintiff to have suffered as a result of conduct by the Defendants depriving him of his civil rights.

Finally, at [Stachura's] request and over [the defendants'] objection, the court charged that damages also could be awarded based on the value or importance of the constitutional rights that were violated:

> If you find that the Plaintiff has been deprived of a Constitutional right, you may award damages to compensate him for the deprivation. Damages for this type of injury are more difficult to measure than damages for a physical injury or injury to one's property. There are no medical bills or other expenses by which you can judge how much compensation is appropriate. In one sense, no

monetary value we place upon Constitutional rights can measure their importance in our society or compensate a citizen adequately for their deprivation. However, just because these rights are not capable of precise evaluation does not mean that an appropriate monetary amount should not be awarded. The precise value you place upon any Constitutional right which you find was denied to Plaintiff is within your discretion. You may wish to consider the importance of the right in our system of government, the role which this right has played in the history of our republic, [and] the significance of the right in the context of the activities which the Plaintiff was engaged in at the time of the violation of the right.

The jury found [the defendants'] liable, and awarded a total of $275,000 in compensatory damages and $46,000 in punitive damages. The District Court entered judgment notwithstanding the verdict as to one of the defendants, reducing the total award to $266,750 in compensatory damages and $36,000 in punitive damages.

[T]he damages instructions plainly authorized — in addition to punitive damages — two distinct types of "compensatory" damages: one based on [Stachura's] actual injury according to ordinary tort law standards, and another based on the "value" of certain rights.

We have repeatedly noted that 42 U.S.C. § 1983 creates "'a species of tort liability' in favor of persons who are deprived of 'rights, privileges, or immunities secured' to them by the Constitution." *Carey v. Piphus*, 435 U.S. 247 (1978). Accordingly, when § 1983 plaintiffs seek damages for violations of constitutional rights, the level of damages is ordinarily determined according to principles derived from the common law of torts.

Punitive damages aside,[1] damages in tort cases are designed to provide "*compensation* for the injury caused to plaintiff by defendant's breach of duty." To that end, compensatory damages may include not only out-of-pocket loss and other monetary harms, but also such injuries as "impairment of reputation . . . , personal humiliation, and mental anguish and suffering." *Gertz v. Robert Welch, Inc.*, 418 U.S. 323, 350 (1974). *See also Carey v. Piphus* (mental and emotional distress constitute compensable injury in § 1983 cases). Deterrence is also an important purpose of this system, but it operates through the mechanism of damages that are *compensatory* — damages grounded in determinations of plaintiffs' actual losses.

Carey v. Piphus represents a straightforward application of these principles. *Carey* involved a suit by a high school student suspended for smoking marijuana; the student claimed that he was denied procedural due process because he was suspended without an opportunity to respond to the charges against him. . . . We . . . held that the student could recover compensatory damages only if he proved actual injury caused by the denial of his constitutional rights. We noted: "Rights, constitutional and otherwise, do not exist in a vacuum. Their purpose is to protect persons from injuries to particular interests. . . . " Where no injury was present, no "compensatory" damages could be awarded.

The instructions at issue here cannot be squared with *Carey*, or with the principles of tort damages on which *Carey* and § 1983 are grounded. The jurors in this case were told that, in determining how much was necessary to "compensate [Stachura] for the

---

[1] [n.9] The purpose of punitive damages is to punish the defendant for his willful or malicious conduct and to deter others from similar behavior. In *Smith v. Wade*, 461 U.S. 30 (1983) [excerpted in Section B., *infra*], the Court held that punitive damages may be available in a proper § 1983 case. . . . [Stachura] does not, and could not reasonably, contend that the separate instructions authorizing damages for violation of constitutional rights were equivalent to punitive damages instructions. In these separate instructions, the jury was authorized to find damages for constitutional violations without any finding of malice or ill will. Moreover, the jury instructions separately authorized punitive damages, and the District Court expressly labeled the "constitutional rights" damages compensatory. The instructions concerning damages for constitutional violations are thus impermissible unless they reasonably could be read as authorizing *compensatory* damages.

deprivation" of his constitutional rights, they should place a money value on the "rights" themselves by considering such factors as the particular right's "importance . . . in our system of government," its role in American history, and its "significance . . . in the context of the activities" in which [Stachura] was engaged. These factors focus, not on compensation for provable injury, but on the jury's subjective perception of the importance of constitutional rights as an abstract matter. *Carey* establishes that such an approach is impermissible. The constitutional right transgressed in *Carey* — the right to due process of law — is central to our system of ordered liberty. We nevertheless held that *no* compensatory damages could be awarded for violation of that right absent proof of actual injury. *Carey* thus makes clear that the abstract value of a constitutional right may not form the basis for § 1983 damages.²

[Stachura] nevertheless argues that *Carey* does not control here, because in this case a *substantive* constitutional right — [Stachura's] First Amendment right to academic freedom — was infringed. The argument misperceives our analysis in *Carey*. That case does not establish a two-tiered system of constitutional rights, with substantive rights afforded greater protection than "mere" procedural safeguards. We did acknowledge in *Carey* that "the elements and prerequisites for recovery of damages" might vary depending on the interests protected by the constitutional right at issue. But we emphasized that, whatever the constitutional basis for § 1983 liability, such damages must always be designed "to *compensate injuries* caused by the [constitutional] deprivation."³ That conclusion simply leaves no room for non-compensatory damages measured by the jury's perception of the abstract "importance" of a constitutional right.

Nor do we find such damages necessary to vindicate the constitutional rights that § 1983 protects. Section 1983 presupposes that damages that compensate for actual harm ordinarily suffice to deter constitutional violations. Moreover, damages based on the "value" of constitutional rights are an unwieldy tool for ensuring compliance with the Constitution. History and tradition do not afford any sound guidance concerning the precise value that juries should place on constitutional protections. Accordingly, were such damages available, juries would be free to award arbitrary amounts without any evidentiary basis, or to use their unbounded discretion to punish unpopular defendants. Such damages would be too uncertain to be of any great value to plaintiffs, and would inject caprice into determinations of damages in § 1983 cases.

[Stachura] further argues that the challenged instructions authorized a form of "presumed" damages — a remedy that is both compensatory in nature and traditionally part of the range of tort law remedies.

[The] argument has [no] merit. Presumed damages are a *substitute* for ordinary compensatory damages, not a *supplement* for an award that fully compensates the alleged injury. When a plaintiff seeks compensation for an injury that is likely to have occurred but difficult to establish, some form of presumed damages may possibly be appropriate. *See Gertz v. Robert Welch, Inc.* In those circumstances, presumed damages may roughly approximate the harm that the plaintiff suffered and thereby compensate for harms that may be impossible to measure.⁴ Moreover, no rough substitute for

---

² [n.11] We did approve an award of nominal damages for the deprivation of due process in *Carey*. Our discussion of that issue makes clear that nominal damages, and not damages based on some undefinable "value" of infringed rights, are the appropriate means of "vindicating" rights whose deprivation has not caused actual, provable injury.

³ [n.13] *Carey* recognized that "the task . . . of adapting common-law rules of damages to provide fair compensation for injuries caused by the deprivation of a constitutional right" is one "of some delicacy." We also noted that "the elements and prerequisites for recovery of damages appropriate to compensate injuries caused by the deprivation of one constitutional right are not necessarily appropriate to compensate injuries caused by the deprivation of another." This "delicate" task need not be undertaken here.

⁴ [n.14] For the same reason, *Nixon v. Herndon*, 273 U.S. 536 (1927), and similar cases do not support the challenged instructions. In *Nixon*, the Court held that a plaintiff who was illegally prevented from voting in

compensatory damages was required in this case, since the jury was fully authorized to compensate [Stachura] for both monetary and nonmonetary harms caused by [the defendants'] conduct.

JUSTICE MARSHALL, with whom JUSTICE BRENNAN, JUSTICE BLACKMUN, and JUSTICE STEVENS join, concurring in the judgment.

I write separately to emphasize that the violation of a constitutional right, in proper cases, may itself constitute a compensable injury.

Following *Carey*, the Courts of Appeals have recognized that invasions of constitutional rights sometimes cause injuries that cannot be redressed by a wooden application of common-law damages rules. In *Hobson v. Wilson*, 737 F.2d 1 (D.C. Cir. 1984), . . . plaintiffs claimed that defendant Federal Bureau of Investigation agents had invaded their First Amendment rights to assemble for peaceable political protest, to associate with others to engage in political expression, and to speak on public issues free of unreasonable government interference. The District Court found that the defendants had succeeded in diverting plaintiffs from, and impeding them in, their protest activities. The Court of Appeals for the District of Columbia Circuit held that that injury to a First Amendment-protected interest could itself constitute compensable injury wholly apart from any "emotional distress, humiliation and personal indignity, emotional pain, embarrassment, fear, anxiety and anguish" suffered by plaintiffs. The court warned, however, that that injury could be compensated with substantial damages only to the extent that it was "reasonably quantifiable"; damages should not be based on "the so-called inherent value of the rights violated."

I believe that the *Hobson* court correctly stated the law. When a plaintiff is deprived, for example, of the opportunity to engage in a demonstration to express his political views, "[i]t is facile to suggest that no damage is done."

The instructions given the jury in this case were improper because they did not require the jury to focus on the loss actually sustained by [Stachura]. . . . These instructions invited the jury to speculate on matters wholly detached from the real injury occasioned [Stachura] by the deprivation of the right.

NOTES

1. Nominal Damages. *Carey v. Piphus*, 435 U.S. 247 (1978), involved a Procedural Due Process challenge to a high school principal's decision to summarily suspend a student (Piphus) for allegedly smoking marijuana. Because Piphus could not show that he would have prevailed at a pre-suspension hearing — and thus would not have been suspended — the Supreme Court concluded that he was not entitled to compensatory damages. Still, the Court observed that "[b]ecause the right to procedural due process is 'absolute' in the sense that it does not depend upon the merits of a claimant's substantive assertions, and because of the importance to organized society that procedural due process be observed, we believe that the denial of procedural due process should be actionable for nominal damages [that is, $1] without proof of actual injury." Courts have relied on *Carey* to award nominal damages for both substantive and procedural constitutional violations. *See, e.g., Edwards v. Balisok*, 520 U.S. 641 (1997) (noting that an inmate was entitled to nominal damages for a prison's violation of Procedural Due Process in the context of a disciplinary proceeding) (discussed in

---

a state primary election suffered compensable injury. This holding did not rest on the "value" of the right to vote as an abstract matter; rather, the Court recognized that the plaintiff had suffered a particular injury — his inability to vote in a particular election — that might be compensated through substantial money damages. *Nixon* followed a long line of cases authorizing substantial money damages as compensation for persons deprived of their right to vote in particular elections. Although these decisions sometimes speak of damages for the value of the right to vote, their analysis shows that they involve nothing more than an award of presumed damages for a nonmonetary harm that cannot easily be quantified.

Chapter 8.B.[2], *infra*); *Farrar v. Hobby*, 506 U.S. 103 (1992) (observing that § 1983 plaintiff was awarded nominal damages for malicious prosecution) (discussed in Chapter 9.B., *infra*). Assuming that a § 1983 plaintiff proves a constitutional violation, are nominal damages mandatory? See Mark T. Morrell, Comment, *Who Wants Nominal Damages Anyway? The Impact of an Automatic Entitlement to Nominal Damages Under § 1983*, 13 REGENT U. L. REV. 225, 234 (2000–2001) (discussing various approaches and arguing that "nominal damages as an automatic award should be available to plaintiffs suffering from constitutional violations"). If not, are they limited to "grave" or constitutional violations or "important" rights? See *Brandt v. Board of Education of City of Chicago*, 480 F.3d 460 (7th Cir. 2007) ("It is true that nominal damages can be awarded for a constitutional violation, as is sometimes true for other intentionally tortious conduct as well. But such an award presupposes a violation of sufficient gravity to merit a judgment, even if significant damages cannot be proved; and this is not such a case.").

2. Presumed Damages. The Court in *Stachura* observed that presumed damages might still be recovered in appropriate cases — that is, where compensation is sought "for an injury that is likely to have occurred but difficult to establish." The Court in footnote 14 of *Stachura, supra*, described one such instance, a denial of the right to vote. Thus, "if . . . you are illegally prevented from voting . . . you can seek substantial compensatory damages without laying any proof of injury before the jury, provided that you do not ask for heavy damages on the ground that the constitutional right invaded was 'important.' " *Hessel v. O'Hearn*, 977 F.2d 299 (7th Cir. 1992). Lower courts have also sometimes allowed presumed damages "if your home is illegally invaded or you are illegally prevented from . . . speaking," *id.*, though there are few cases supporting these propositions. See Michael L. Wells, *Section 1983, the First Amendment, and Public Employee Speech: Shaping the Right to Fit the Remedy*, 35 GA. L. REV. 939, 974 (2001) ("While a few cases have allowed awards of presumed damages, most plaintiffs receive only damages they can prove, typically for lost pay and emotional distress."); *Norwood v. Bain*, 143 F.3d 843, 856 (4th Cir. 1998) (refusing to allow presumed damages "where the specific right claimed to have been violated is one whose violation will, if it results in any actual harm, present no difficulty in proving either the harm or its extent"); *Trevino v. Gates*, 99 F.3d 911, 921 (9th Cir. 1996) (refusing to allow presumed damages for the illegal use of excessive force).[5]

3. Causation. Can *Carey v. Piphus* be best understood in terms of causation? The school principal's procedural violation, after all, caused Piphus no substantive harm; he would have been suspended with or without a hearing. For this reason, several lower courts prior to *Stachura* limited *Carey*'s holding to procedural constitutional challenges. *Stachura* makes clear, however, that compensatory damages for substantive wrongs must also be supported by tangible injuries. In terms of causation, actual injury must be directly linked to a substantive wrong. If the injury would have occurred anyway, it is not compensable under § 1983.

This principle is perhaps best-illustrated in the public-sector employment context, where retaliation claims based on race, gender, and speech are more commonly made. In *Mt. Healthy City School District v. Doyle*, 429 U.S. 274 (1977), for example, a public-school teacher suffered retaliatory discharge based on his speech. The Supreme Court

---

[5] Congress is always free to limit, or even deny, the availability of monetary relief. For example, 47 U.S.C. § 555a(a) offers cable television franchising authorities (like cities and counties) protection from monetary liability under § 1983: "In any court proceeding pending on or initiated after October 5, 1992, involving any claim against a franchising authority or other governmental entity, or any official, member, employee, or agent of such authority or entity, arising from the regulation of cable service or from a decision of approval or disapproval with respect to a grant, renewal, transfer, or amendment of a franchise, any relief, to the extent such relief is required by any other provision of Federal, State, or local law, shall be limited to injunctive relief and declaratory relief." Section 555a(c) provides an exception "to the extent such claim involves discrimination on the basis of race, color, sex, age, religion, national origin, or handicap."

established the following analysis to determine whether money damages are appropriate: "Initially, . . . the burden [i]s properly placed upon [the plaintiff] to show that his conduct was constitutionally protected, and that this conduct was a 'substantial factor,' or to put it in other words, that it was a 'motivating factor,' in the Board's decision not to rehire him. [Plaintiff] having carried that burden . . . the District Court should . . . go[] on to determine whether the [defendant] had shown by a preponderance of the evidence that it would have reached the same decision as to [plaintiff's] reemployment even in the absence of the protected conduct." Where the same result would have obtained anyway, damages cannot be recovered.

This same result has also been reached in other doctrinal areas. In *Texas v. Lesage*, 528 U.S. 18 (1999), to use another example, a white plaintiff (Lesage) applied for admission to a Ph.D. program at the University of Texas. Lesage's application was denied, and he subsequently brought a § 1983 action challenging Texas's affirmative action admissions policy under the Fourteenth Amendment. The Supreme Court ruled that even if Texas's affirmative action policy proved unconstitutional, Lesage could not prove that he would have been admitted under a race-neutral policy. He thus had no cognizable § 1983 claim for compensatory damages:

> [E]ven if the government has considered an impermissible criterion in making a decision adverse to the plaintiff, it can nonetheless defeat liability by demonstrating that it would have made the same decision absent the forbidden consideration. Our previous decisions on this point have typically involved alleged retaliation for protected First Amendment activity rather than racial discrimination, but that distinction is immaterial. The underlying principle is the same: The government can avoid liability by proving that it would have made the same decision without the impermissible motive. Simply put, where a plaintiff challenges a discrete governmental decision as being based on an impermissible criterion and it is undisputed that the government would have made the same decision regardless, there is no cognizable injury warranting relief under § 1983.[6]

Does this approach — i.e., that government officials are liable if their actions are causally connected to constitutionally impermissible motives — apply to the conduct of police officers?

HARTMAN v. MOORE
Supreme Court of the United States
547 U.S. 250 (2006)

JUSTICE SOUTER delivered the opinion of the Court.

This is a *Bivens* action against criminal investigators for inducing prosecution in retaliation for speech. The question is whether the complaint states an actionable

---

[6] Should the plaintiff in *Lesage* have recovered nominal damages? *See* Note 1, *supra*. Did she suffer a constitutional violation if she would not have been admitted anyway? Litigation surrounding Boston's school choice program holds not. There, two plaintiffs who successfully challenged Boston's student assignment program and who could demonstrate that they would have been placed in their preferred schools were awarded nominal damages by the District Court, while several other students who could not make such a showing were not. The trial court relied on *Lesage* for its distinction. The First Circuit affirmed and refused to award nominal damages to any other students because "*Lesage* makes no distinction among the classes of damages that become unavailable upon defendants' showing that they would have reached the same admissions result even in the absence of an unconstitutional use of race." *Anderson ex rel. Dowd v. City of Boston*, 375 F.3d 71 (1st Cir. 2004). *Contrast Johnson v. Board of Regents of University of Georgia*, 263 F.3d 1234 (11th Cir. 2001) (District Court awards nominal damages to the challengers of affirmative action plan even though they could not show they would have been admitted and even though they were not entitled to prospective relief).

violation of the First Amendment without alleging an absence of probable cause to support the underlying criminal charge.

In the 1980's, respondent William G. Moore, Jr., was the chief executive of Recognition Equipment Inc. (REI), which manufactured a multiline optical character reader for interpreting multiple lines of text. Although REI had received some $50 million from the United States Postal Service to develop this technology for reading and sorting mail, the Postmaster General and other top officials of the Postal Service were urging mailers to use nine-digit zip codes (Zip + 4), which would provide enough routing information on one line of text to allow single-line scanning machines to sort mail automatically by reading just that line.

Besides Moore, who obviously stood to gain financially from the adoption of multiline technology, some Members of Congress and Government research officers had reservations about the Postal Service's Zip + 4 policy and its intended reliance on single-line readers. Critics maligned single-line scanning technology, objected to the foreign sources of single-line scanners, decried the burden of remembering the four extra numbers, and echoed the conclusion reached by the United States Office of Technology Assessment, that use of the single-line scanners in preference to multiliners would cost the Postal Service $1 million a day in operational losses.

The campaign succeeded, and in July 1985 the Postal Service made what it called a "mid-course correction" and embraced multiline technology. But the change of heart did not extend to Moore and REI, for the Service's ensuing order of multiline equipment, valued somewhere between $250 million and $400 million went to a competing firm.

Not only did REI lose out on the contract, but Moore and REI were soon entangled in two investigations by Postal Service inspectors. The first looked into the purported payment of kickbacks . . . ; the second sought to document REI's possibly improper role in the search for a new Postmaster General. Notwithstanding very limited evidence linking Moore and REI to any wrongdoing, an Assistant United States Attorney decided to bring criminal charges against them, and in 1988 the grand jury indicted Moore, REI, and REI's vice president. At the close of the Government's case, after six weeks of trial, however, the District Court concluded that there was a "complete lack of direct evidence" connecting the defendants to any of the criminal wrongdoing alleged, and it granted the REI defendants' motion for judgment of acquittal.

Moore then brought an action . . . under *Bivens*,[7] against the prosecutor and the five postal inspectors. . . . His complaint raised five causes of action, only one of which is relevant here, the claim that the prosecutor and the inspectors had engineered his criminal prosecution in retaliation for criticism of the Postal Service, thus violating the First Amendment. In the course of these proceedings Moore has argued, among other things, that the postal inspectors launched a criminal investigation against him well before they had any inkling of either of the two schemes mentioned above, that the inspectors targeted him for his lobbying activities, and that they pressured the United States Attorney's Office to have him indicted. . . . The District Court dismissed the claims against the Assistant United States Attorney in accordance with the absolute immunity for prosecutorial judgment. [*See* Chapter 2.A.[3], *supra*.]

[T]he inspectors moved for summary judgment, urging that because the underlying criminal charges were supported by probable cause they were entitled to qualified immunity from a retaliatory-prosecution suit.

---

[7] [n.2] "*Bivens* established that the victims of a constitutional violation by a federal agent have a right to recover damages against the official in federal court despite the absence of any statute conferring such a right." Though more limited in some respects not relevant here, a *Bivens* action is the federal analog to suits brought against state officials under . . . § 1983. [*See* Chapter 1.E., supra.]

Official reprisal for protected speech "offends the Constitution [because] it threatens to inhibit exercise of the protected right," and the law is settled that as a general matter the First Amendment prohibits government officials from subjecting an individual to retaliatory actions, including criminal prosecutions, for speaking out. Some official actions adverse to such a speaker might well be unexceptionable if taken on other grounds, but when nonretaliatory grounds are in fact insufficient to provoke the adverse consequences, we have held that retaliation is subject to recovery as the but-for cause of official action offending the Constitution. When the vengeful officer is federal, he is subject to an action for damages on the authority of *Bivens*.

[T]he issue before us is straightforward: whether a plaintiff in a retaliatory-prosecution action must plead and show the absence of probable cause for pressing the underlying criminal charges.

The inspectors argue on two fronts that absence of probable cause should be an essential element. Without such a requirement, they first say, the *Bivens* claim is too readily available. A plaintiff can afflict a public officer with disruption and expense by alleging nothing more, in practical terms, than action with a retaliatory animus, a subjective condition too easy to claim and too hard to defend against. In the inspectors' view, some "objective" burden must be imposed on these plaintiffs, simply to filter out the frivolous. The second argument complements the first, for the inspectors believe that the traditional tort of malicious prosecution tells us what the objective requirement should be. In an action for malicious prosecution after an acquittal, a plaintiff must show that the criminal action was begun without probable cause for charging the crime in the first place; the inspectors see retaliatory prosecution under *Bivens* as a close cousin of malicious prosecution under common law, making the latter's no-probable-cause requirement a natural feature of the constitutional tort. *See Heck v. Humphrey*, 512 U.S. 477 (1994) [excerpted in Chapter 8.B.[2], *infra*].

In fact, we think there is a fair argument for what the inspectors call an "objective" fact requirement in this type of case, but the nub of that argument differs from the two they set out, which we will deal with only briefly. As for the invitation to rely on common-law parallels, we certainly are ready to look at the elements of common-law torts when we think about elements of actions for constitutional violations, but the common law is best understood here more as a source of inspired examples than of prefabricated components of *Bivens* torts. And in this instance we could debate whether the closer common-law analog to retaliatory prosecution is malicious prosecution (with its no-probable-cause element) or abuse of process (without it).

Nor is there much leverage in the fear that without a filter to screen out claims federal prosecutors and federal courts will be unduly put upon by the volume of litigation. The basic concern is fair enough, but the slate is not blank. Over the past 25 years fewer than two dozen damages actions for retaliatory prosecution under *Bivens* or § 1983 have come squarely before the Federal Courts of Appeals, and there is no disproportion of those cases in Circuits that do not require showing an absence of probable cause.[8]

It is, instead, the need to prove a chain of causation from animus to injury, with details specific to retaliatory-prosecution cases, that provides the strongest justification for the no-probable-cause requirement espoused by the inspectors. Although a *Bivens* (or § 1983) plaintiff must show a causal connection between a defendant's retaliatory animus and subsequent injury in any sort of retaliation action, the need to demonstrate causation in the retaliatory-prosecution context presents an additional difficulty that can be understood by comparing the requisite causation in ordinary retaliation claims, where the government agent allegedly harboring the animus is also the individual allegedly taking the adverse action, with causation in a case like this one.

---

[8] [n.6] In fact, many of the appellate challenges have been brought in the Second, Fifth, and Eleventh Circuits, all of which require plaintiffs to show an absence of probable cause.

Take the example of a public employee's claim that he was fired for speech criticizing the government. While the employee plaintiff obviously must plead and prove adverse official action in retaliation for making the statements, our discussions of the elements of the constitutional tort do not specify any necessary details about proof of a connection between the retaliatory animus and the discharge, which will depend on the circumstances. The cases have simply taken the evidence of the motive and the discharge as sufficient for a circumstantial demonstration that the one caused the other. It is clear, moreover, that the causation is understood to be but-for causation, without which the adverse action would not have been taken; we say that upon a prima facie showing of retaliatory harm, the burden shifts to the defendant official to demonstrate that even without the impetus to retaliate he would have taken the action complained of (such as firing the employee). If there is a finding that retaliation was not the but-for cause of the discharge, the claim fails for lack of causal connection between unconstitutional motive and resulting harm, despite proof of some retaliatory animus in the official's mind. It may be dishonorable to act with an unconstitutional motive and perhaps in some instances be unlawful, but action colored by some degree of bad motive does not amount to a constitutional tort if that action would have been taken anyway.

When the claimed retaliation for protected conduct is a criminal charge, however, a constitutional tort action will differ from this standard case in two ways. Like any other plaintiff charging official retaliatory action, the plaintiff in a retaliatory-prosecution claim must prove the elements of retaliatory animus as the cause of injury, and the defendant will have the same opportunity to respond to a prima facie case by showing that the action would have been taken anyway, independently of any retaliatory animus. What is different about a prosecution case, however, is that there will always be a distinct body of highly valuable circumstantial evidence available and apt to prove or disprove retaliatory causation, namely evidence showing whether there was or was not probable cause to bring the criminal charge. Demonstrating that there was no probable cause for the underlying criminal charge will tend to reinforce the retaliation evidence and show that retaliation was the but-for basis for instigating the prosecution, while establishing the existence of probable cause will suggest that prosecution would have occurred even without a retaliatory motive. This alone does not mean, of course, that a *Bivens* or § 1983 plaintiff should be required to plead and prove no probable cause, but it does mean that litigating probable cause will be highly likely in any retaliatory-prosecution case, owing to its powerful evidentiary significance.

The second respect in which a retaliatory-prosecution case is different also goes to the causation that a *Bivens* plaintiff must prove; the difference is that the requisite causation between the defendant's retaliatory animus and the plaintiff's injury is usually more complex than it is in other retaliation cases, and the need to show this more complex connection supports a requirement that no probable cause be alleged and proven. A *Bivens* (or § 1983) action for retaliatory prosecution will not be brought against the prosecutor, who is absolutely immune from liability for the decision to prosecute.[9] Instead, the defendant will be a non-prosecutor, an official, like an inspector here, who may have influenced the prosecutorial decision but did not himself make it, and the cause of action will not be strictly for retaliatory prosecution, but for successful retaliatory inducement to prosecute.[10] The consequence is that a plaintiff like Moore

---

[9] [n.8] An action could still be brought against a prosecutor for conduct taken in an investigatory capacity, to which absolute immunity does not extend. *See Buckley v. Fitzsimmons*, 509 U.S. 259 (1993) (no absolute immunity when prosecutor acts in administrative capacity); *Burns v. Reed*, 500 U.S. 478 (1991) (absolute immunity does not attach when a prosecutor offers legal advice to the police regarding interrogation practices) [discussed in Chapter 2.A.[3], *supra*]. In fact, Moore's complaint charged the prosecutor with acting in an investigative as well as in a prosecutorial capacity, but dismissal of the complaint as against the prosecutor was affirmed [by the D.C. Circuit], and no claim against him is before us now.

[10] [n.9] No one here claims that simply conducting a retaliatory investigation with a view to promote a prosecution is a constitutional tort. That is not part of Moore's complaint. Whether the expense or other

must show that the nonprosecuting official acted in retaliation, and must also show that he induced the prosecutor to bring charges that would not have been initiated without his urging.

Thus, the causal connection required here is not merely between the retaliatory animus of one person and that person's own injurious action, but between the retaliatory animus of one person and the action of another.

Herein lies the distinct problem of causation in cases like this one. Evidence of an inspector's animus does not necessarily show that the inspector induced the action of a prosecutor who would not have pressed charges otherwise. Moreover, to the factual difficulty of divining the influence of an investigator or other law enforcement officer upon the prosecutor's mind, there is an added legal obstacle in the longstanding presumption of regularity accorded to prosecutorial decisionmaking. And this presumption that a prosecutor has legitimate grounds for the action he takes is one we do not lightly discard, given our position that judicial intrusion into executive discretion of such high order should be minimal, *see Wayte v. United States*, 470 U.S. 598 (1985).

Some sort of allegation, then, is needed both to bridge the gap between the nonprosecuting government agent's motive and the prosecutor's action, and to address the presumption of prosecutorial regularity. And at the trial stage, some evidence must link the allegedly retaliatory official to a prosecutor whose action has injured the plaintiff. The connection, to be alleged and shown, is the absence of probable cause.

It would be open to us, of course, to give no special prominence to an absence of probable cause in bridging the causal gap, and to address this distinct causation concern at a merely general level, leaving it to such pleading and proof as the circumstances allow. A prosecutor's disclosure of retaliatory thinking on his part, for example, would be of great significance in addressing the presumption and closing the gap. So would evidence that a prosecutor was nothing but a rubber stamp for his investigative staff or the police. In fact, though, these examples are likely to be rare and consequently poor guides in structuring a cause of action. In most cases, for instance, it would be unrealistic to expect a prosecutor to reveal his mind even to the degree that this record discloses, with its reported statement by the prosecutor that he was not galvanized by the merits of the case, but sought the indictment against Moore because he wanted to attract the interest of a law firm looking for a tough trial lawyer.[11]

Accordingly, the significance of probable cause or the lack of it looms large, being a potential feature of every case, with obvious evidentiary value. True, it is not necessarily dispositive: showing an absence of probable cause may not be conclusive that the inducement succeeded, and showing its presence does not guarantee that inducement was not the but-for fact in a prosecutor's decision. But a retaliatory motive on the part of an official urging prosecution combined with an absence of probable cause supporting the prosecutor's decision to go forward are reasonable grounds to suspend the presumption of regularity behind the charging decision, and enough for a prima facie inference that the unconstitutionally motivated inducement infected the prosecutor's decision to bring the charge.

Our sense is that the very significance of probable cause means that a requirement to plead and prove its absence will usually be cost free by any incremental reckoning. The

---

adverse consequences of a retaliatory investigation would ever justify recognizing such an investigation as a distinct constitutional violation is not before us.

[11] [n.10] Some may suggest that we should structure a cause of action in the alternative, dispensing with a requirement to show no probable cause when a plaintiff has evidence of a direct admission by a prosecutor that, irrespective of probable cause, the prosecutor's sole purpose in initiating a criminal prosecution was to acquiesce to the inducements of other government agents, who themselves harbored retaliatory animus. But this would seem a little like proposing that retirement plans include the possibility of winning the lottery. Unambiguous admissions of successful inducement are likely to be rare, and hassles over the adequacy of admissions will be the predictable result, if any exemption to a no-probable-cause requirement is allowed.

issue is so likely to be raised by some party at some point that treating it as important enough to be an element will be a way to address the issue of causation without adding to time or expense. In this case, for example, Moore cannot succeed in the retaliation claim without showing that the Assistant United States Attorney was worse than just an unabashed careerist, and if he can show that the prosecutor had no probable cause, the claim of retaliation will have some vitality.

In sum, the complexity of causation in a claim that prosecution was induced by an official bent on retaliation should be addressed specifically in defining the elements of the tort. Probable cause or its absence will be at least an evidentiary issue in practically all such cases. Because showing an absence of probable cause will have high probative force, and can be made mandatory with little or no added cost, it makes sense to require such a showing as an element of a plaintiff's case, and we hold that it must be pleaded and proven.[12]

JUSTICE GINSBURG, with whom JUSTICE BREYER joins, dissenting.

The Court of Appeals, reviewing the record so far made, determined that "[t]he evidence of retaliatory motive [came] close to the proverbial smoking gun." The record also indicated that the postal inspectors engaged in "unusual prodding," strenuously urging a reluctant U.S. Attorney's Office to press charges against Moore.

I would assign to the postal inspectors who urged the prosecution the burden of showing that, had there been no retaliatory motive and importuning, the U.S. Attorney's Office nonetheless would have pursued the case.

Under the Court's proof burden allocation, which saddles plaintiff — the alleged victim — with the burden to plead and prove lack of probable cause, only entirely "baseless prosecutions" would be checked. So long as the retaliators present evidence barely sufficient to establish probable cause and persuade a prosecutor to act on their thin information, they could accomplish their mission cost free. Their victim, on the other hand, would incur not only the costs entailed in mounting a defense, he likely would sustain a reputational loss as well, and neither loss would be compensable under federal law. Under the D.C. Circuit's more speech-protective formulation, "[a] *Bivens* . . . recovery remains possible . . . in those rare cases where strong motive evidence combines with weak probable cause to support a finding that the [investigation and ensuing] prosecution would not have occurred but for the [defending] officials' retaliatory animus." That such situations "are likely to be rare," it seems to me, does not warrant "structuring a cause of action," that precludes relief when they do arise.

NOTES

1. Retaliatory Searches and Arrests. Does *Hartman* apply to retaliatory *searches* and *arrests*[13] as well as retaliatory prosecutions? Even though warrantless arrests and searches can proceed without either a prosecutor's or judge's assistance — "there are differences between wrongful arrest and malicious prosecution" — "there is an obvious similarity in that 'the significance of probable cause or the lack of it looms large.'" *Leonard v. Robinson*, 477 F.3d 347 (6th Cir. 2007) (concluding that it need not decide whether *Hartman* applies to retaliatory warrantless arrests). The Circuits are presently split over *Hartman*'s application to warrantless searches and arrests claimed

---

[12] [Editor's note: neither the Chief Justice (Roberts) nor Justice Alito participated in the case.]

[13] For a discussion of the differences between wrongful arrest and wrongful prosecution in the Fourth Amendment context, see *Wallace v. Kato*, 127 S. Ct. 1091 (2007) ("false imprisonment consists of detention without legal process [and] ends once the victim becomes held *pursuant to such process*," while "unlawful detention forms part of the damages for the 'entirely distinct' tort of malicious prosecution, which remedies detention accompanied, not by absence of legal process, but by *wrongful institution* of legal process") (excerpted in Chapter 8.B.[3], *infra*).

to violate the First Amendment. *Contrast Williams v. City of Carl Junction*, 480 F.3d 871 (8th Cir. 2007) (holding that "the Supreme Court's holding in *Hartman* is broad enough to apply even where intervening actions by a prosecutor are not present"), *with Skoog v. County of Clackamas*, 469 F.3d 1221 (9th Cir. 2006) (holding that *Hartman* does not apply to a retaliatory search and seizure even when a warrant is first obtained).

What about searches and arrests that are supported by warrants? Does prior approval by a judge or grand jury liken the causation problem to that in *Hartman*? In *Skoog v. County of Clackamas*, 469 F.3d 1221 (9th Cir. 2006), where the plaintiff's (Skoog) office was searched by a police officer (Royster) with a warrant, the Ninth Circuit concluded that *Hartman* did not control:

> In *Hartman*, the Supreme Court was careful to explain that the practical problems of establishing causation in retaliatory prosecution actions motivated its decision, not any need to provide additional protection to government officials.
>
> Pleading and proving the absence of probable cause is necessary in retaliatory prosecution cases, the Court reasoned, because of the complexity of causation in such cases. Retaliatory prosecution claims are really "for successful retaliatory *inducement* to prosecute" because they can only be maintained against officials, such as investigators, who may persuade prosecutors to act. To prove causation, then, a plaintiff must show not only that the defendant official harbored retaliatory animus and thus sought to induce prosecution, but also that the official succeeded — that is, that the "prosecutor [] would not have pressed charges otherwise." A plaintiff's task is particularly difficult, the Court noted, due to the "long-standing presumption of regularity accorded to prosecutorial decisionmaking" which courts may not "lightly discard."
>
> We conclude that the retaliation claim in this case does not involve multi-layered causation as did the claim in *Hartman*. To be sure, one aspect of the situation in this case is somewhat analogous to that in *Hartman* — a second party (the magistrate judge in this case; the prosecutor in *Hartman*) found probable cause based on the defendant's affidavit and the evidence that was used is readily available. However, an important fact distinguishes the situation in this case from that in *Hartman:* Royster retained control over the allegedly retaliatory action (the search and seizure) after the second party (the magistrate judge) found probable cause. Causation thus turns on his actions alone and no "bridge" between motive and action is necessary. Thus, the rationale for requiring the pleading of no probable cause in *Hartman* is absent here. This case presents an "ordinary" retaliation claim.

Contrast Barnes v. Wright, 449 F.3d 709 (6th Cir. 2006) (holding that a retaliatory arrest by a conservation officer based on a grand jury indictment is subject to the rule announced in *Hartman*).

2. Prosecutors' Investigations. The *Hartman* Court in footnote 8 observed that prosecutors do not have absolute immunity when acting as investigators. Consequently, a prosecutor can be charged under § 1983 (or *Bivens*) for retaliatory searches and seizures, as well as prosecutions, when actively investigating cases. *See, e.g., Yarris v. County of Delaware*, 465 F.3d 129 (3d Cir. 2006) (holding that prosecutors can be held liable under § 1983 for suppressing evidence). *See generally* Leon Friedman, *Challenging Unjust Convictions Under § 1983*, 23 TOURO L. REV. 27, 49–51 (2007) (discussing using § 1983 to redress procedural wrongs committed in the criminal arena by prosecutors). Would a § 1983 plaintiff have to show an absence of probable cause in a retaliatory action brought against a prosecutor? The Court in *Hartman* did not entertain the issue because the prosecutor prevailed in the lower courts and "and no claim against him is before us now." *See* footnote 8.

3. Selective Enforcement Based on Race. Does *Hartman* apply to selective enforcement of criminal laws based on race? What if a police officer arrested or induced the prosecution of Moore, for example, for racial reasons? Would Moore have to show that the police lacked probable cause?[14] "[I]t has long been a well-settled principle that the state may not selectively enforce the law against racial minorities." *Gibson v. Superintendent of New Jersey Department of Law and Public Safety Division*, 411 F.3d 427 (3d Cir. 2005). "The fact that there was no Fourth Amendment violation does not mean that one was not discriminatorily selected for enforcement of a law." *Carrasca v. Pomeroy*, 313 F.3d 828 (3d Cir. 2002). Consequently, before *Hartman* courts generally did not require that a plaintiff prove the absence of probable cause in a race-based selective enforcement case. *See, e.g, Vakillan v. Shaw*, 335 F.3d 509 (6th Cir. 2003) ("an officer's reasonable belief that probable cause exists for arrest does not affect the availability of a separate selective enforcement claim under the Equal Protection Clause"); *United States v. Avery*, 137 F.3d 343 (6th Cir. 1997) ("[t]he Equal Protection Clause of the Fourteenth Amendment provides citizens a degree of protection independent of the Fourth Amendment protection against unreasonable searches and seizures").

4. Prospective Relief. Do *Carey, Stachura, Mt. Healthy,* and *Hartman* limit a § 1983 plaintiff's ability to recover non-monetary relief, such as an injunction or declaratory judgment? In *Texas v. Lesage*, 528 U.S. 18 (1999), which challenged an affirmative action program, the Court ruled that although the plaintiff could not recover damages she could still seek non-monetary prospective relief: "a plaintiff who challenges an ongoing race-conscious program and seeks forward-looking relief need not affirmatively establish that he would receive the benefit in question if race were not considered. The relevant injury in such cases is 'the inability to compete on an equal footing.'" (Citing *Northeastern Florida Chapter of Associated General Contractors of America v. City of Jacksonville*, 508 U.S. 656 (1993) (holding that § 1983 plaintiff can recover prospective relief against municipal defendant even though it could not win money damages for lack of injury) (excerpted in Section C.[1], *infra*)). The problem in the context of non-monetary relief is one of Article III standing. Quite often, the victim of a constitutional tort cannot establish the Article III standing needed to support future-looking relief (like an injunction or declaratory judgment). *See, e.g., City of Los Angeles v. Lyons*, 461 U.S. 95 (1983) (holding that a victim of excessive force in violation of the Fourth Amendment does not have standing to challenge city's chokehold policy) (excerpted in Section C.[1], *infra*).

B. PUNITIVE DAMAGES

SMITH v. WADE
Supreme Court of the United States
461 U.S. 30 (1983)

JUSTICE BRENNAN delivered the opinion of the Court.

William H. Smith, is a [prison] guard. . . . Daniel R. Wade was assigned to [the prison] as an inmate in 1976. In the summer of 1976 Wade voluntarily checked into [the prison's] protective custody unit. Because of disciplinary violations during his stay in

---

[14] The Supreme Court in *Whren v. United States*, 517 U.S. 806 (1996), ruled that police officers' subjective motivations are not relevant in the context of the Fourth Amendment. The presence of probable cause thus defeats a Fourth Amendment challenge to an otherwise proper warrantless search regardless of a police officer's pretextual motive. Lower courts, however, have agreed that *Whren* does not apply to Equal Protection claims. *See, e.g., Marshall v. Columbia Lea Regional Hospital*, 345 F.3d 1157 (10th Cir. 2003) ("the right to equal protection may be violated even if the actions of the police are acceptable under the Fourth Amendment").

protective custody, Wade was given a short term in punitive segregation and then transferred to administrative segregation. On the evening of Wade's first day in administrative segregation, he was placed in a cell with another inmate. Later, when Smith came on duty in Wade's dormitory, he placed a third inmate in Wade's cell. According to Wade's testimony, his cellmates harassed, beat, and sexually assaulted him.

Wade brought suit under 42 U.S.C. § 1983 against Smith . . . , alleging that his Eighth Amendment rights had been violated. At trial his evidence showed that he had placed himself in protective custody because of prior incidents of violence against him by other inmates. The third prisoner whom Smith added to the cell had been placed in administrative segregation for fighting. Smith had made no effort to find out whether another cell was available; in fact there was another cell in the same dormitory with only one occupant. Further, only a few weeks earlier, another inmate had been beaten to death in the same dormitory during the same shift, while Smith had been on duty. Wade asserted that Smith and the other defendants knew or should have known that an assault against him was likely under the circumstances.

During trial, . . . the judge instructed the jury that Wade could recover only if [Smith was] guilty of "gross negligence" (defined as "a callous indifference or a thoughtless disregard for the consequences of one's act or failure to act") or "egregious failure to protect" Wade (defined as "a flagrant or remarkably bad failure to protect"). He reiterated that Wade could not recover on a showing of simple negligence.

The district judge also charged the jury that it could award punitive damages on a proper showing:

> In addition to actual damages, the law permits the jury, under certain circumstances, to award the injured person punitive and exemplary damages, in order to punish the wrongdoer for some extraordinary misconduct, and to serve as an example or warning to others not to engage in such conduct.
>
> If you find the issues in favor of the plaintiff, and if the conduct of one or more of the defendants is shown to be *a reckless or callous disregard of, or indifference to, the rights or safety of others*, then you may assess punitive or exemplary damages in addition to any award of actual damages.
>
> The amount of punitive or exemplary damages assessed against any defendant may be such sum as you believe will serve to punish that defendant and to deter him and others from like conduct.

The jury . . . found Smith liable . . . and awarded $25,000 in compensatory damages and $5,000 in punitive damages.

Smith correctly concedes that "punitive damages are available in a 'proper' § 1983 action. . . . " *Carlson v. Green*, 446 U.S. 14 (1980). Although there was debate about the theoretical correctness of the punitive damages doctrine in the latter part of the last century, the doctrine was accepted as settled law by nearly all state and federal courts, including this Court. It was likewise generally established that individual public officers were liable for punitive damages for their misconduct on the same basis as other individual defendants. Further, although the precise issue of the availability of punitive damages under § 1983 has never come squarely before us, we have had occasion more than once to make clear our view that they are available; indeed, we have rested decisions on related questions on the premise of such availability.[15]

---

[15] [n.5] In *Newport v. Fact Concerts, Inc.*, 453 U.S. 247 (1981) [excerpted, *infra*], for example, we held that a municipality (as opposed to an individual defendant) is immune from liability for punitive damages under § 1983. A significant part of our reasoning was that deterrence of constitutional violations would be adequately accomplished by allowing punitive damage awards directly against the responsible individuals. Similarly, in *Carlson v. Green*, 446 U.S. 14 (1980), we stated that punitive damages would be available in an action against federal officials directly under the Eighth Amendment, partly on the reasoning that since such damages are

Smith argues, nonetheless, that this was not a "proper" case in which to award punitive damages. More particularly, he attacks the instruction that punitive damages could be awarded on a finding of reckless or callous disregard of or indifference to Wade's rights or safety. Instead, he contends that the proper test is one of actual malicious intent — "ill will, spite, or intent to injure." He offers two arguments for this position: first, that actual intent is the proper standard for punitive damages in all cases under § 1983; and second, that even if intent is not always required, it should be required here because the threshold for punitive damages should always be higher than that for liability in the first instance.

Smith does not argue that the common law, either in 1871 or now, required or requires a showing of actual malicious intent for recovery of punitive damages.

Perhaps not surprisingly, there was significant variation (both terminological and substantive) among American jurisdictions in the latter nineteenth century on the precise standard to be applied in awarding punitive damages — variation that was exacerbated by the ambiguity and slipperiness of such common terms as "malice" and "gross negligence." Most of the confusion, however, seems to have been over the degree of negligence, recklessness, carelessness, or culpable indifference that should be required — not over whether actual intent was essential. On the contrary, the rule in a large majority of jurisdictions was that punitive damages (also called exemplary damages, vindictive damages, or smart money) could be awarded without a showing of actual ill will, spite, or intent to injure.

The same rule applies today. The RESTATEMENT (SECOND) OF TORTS (1977), for example, states: "Punitive damages may be awarded for conduct that is outrageous, because of the defendant's evil motive *or his reckless indifference to the rights of others.*" Most cases under state common law, although varying in their precise terminology, have adopted more or less the same rule, recognizing that punitive damages in tort cases may be awarded not only for actual intent to injure or evil motive, but also for recklessness, serious indifference to or disregard for the rights of others, or even gross negligence.

The remaining question is whether the policies and purposes of § 1983 itself require a departure from the rules of tort common law. As a general matter, we discern no reason why a person whose federally guaranteed rights have been violated should be granted a more restrictive remedy than a person asserting an ordinary tort cause of action.

Smith's argument, which he offers in several forms, is that an actual intent standard is preferable to a recklessness standard because it is less vague. He points out that punitive damages, by their very nature, are not awarded to compensate the injured party. He concedes, of course, that deterrence of future egregious conduct is a primary purpose of both § 1983, and of punitive damages. But deterrence, he contends, cannot be achieved unless the standard of conduct sought to be deterred is stated with sufficient clarity to enable potential defendants to conform to the law and to avoid the proposed sanction. Recklessness or callous indifference, he argues, is too uncertain a standard to achieve deterrence rationally and fairly. A prison guard, for example, can be expected to know whether he is acting with actual ill will or intent to injure, but not whether he is being reckless or callously indifferent.

Smith's argument, if valid, would apply to ordinary tort cases as easily as to § 1983 suits; hence, it hardly presents an argument for adopting a different rule under § 1983. In any event, the argument is unpersuasive.

Smith's argument for certainty in the interest of deterrence overlooks the distinction between a standard for punitive damages and a standard of liability in the first instance. Smith seems to assume that prison guards and other state officials look mainly to the

---

available under § 1983, it would be anomalous to allow punitive awards against state officers but not federal ones.

standard for punitive damages in shaping their conduct. We question the premise; we assume, and hope, that most officials are guided primarily by the underlying standards of federal substantive law — both out of devotion to duty, and in the interest of avoiding liability for compensatory damages. At any rate, the conscientious officer who desires clear guidance on how to do his job and avoid lawsuits can and should look to the standard for actionability in the first instance. The need for exceptional clarity in the standard for punitive damages arises only if one assumes that there are substantial numbers of officers who will not be deterred by compensatory damages; only such officers will seek to guide their conduct by the punitive damages standard. The presence of such officers constitutes a powerful argument *against* raising the threshold for punitive damages.

Smith contends that even if § 1983 does not ordinarily require a showing of actual malicious intent for an award of punitive damages, such a showing should be required in this case. He argues that the deterrent and punitive purposes of punitive damages are served only if the threshold for punitive damages is higher in every case than the underlying standard for liability in the first instance. In this case, while the district judge did not use the same precise terms to explain the standards of liability for compensatory and punitive damages, the parties agree that there is no substantial difference between the showings required by the two instructions; both apply a standard of reckless or callous indifference to Wade's rights. Hence, Smith argues, the district judge erred in not requiring a higher standard for punitive damages, namely, actual malicious intent.

This argument incorrectly assumes that, simply because the instructions specified the same *threshold* of liability for punitive and compensatory damages, the two forms of damages were equally available to the plaintiff. The argument overlooks a key feature of punitive damages — that they are never awarded as of right, no matter how egregious the defendant's conduct.

Moreover, the rules of ordinary tort law are once more against Smith's argument. There has never been any general common-law rule that the threshold for punitive damages must always be higher than that for compensatory liability.

This common-law rule makes sense in terms of the purposes of punitive damages. Punitive damages are awarded in the jury's discretion "to punish [the defendant] for his outrageous conduct and to deter him and others like him from similar conduct in the future." The focus is on the character of the tortfeasor's conduct — whether it is of the sort that calls for deterrence and punishment over and above that provided by compensatory awards. If it is of such a character, then it is appropriate to allow a jury to assess punitive damages; and that assessment does not become less appropriate simply because the plaintiff in the case faces a more demanding standard of actionability.

As with his first argument, Smith gives us no good reason to depart from the common-law rule in the context of § 1983. He argues that too low a standard of exposure to punitive damages in cases such as this threatens to undermine the policies of his qualified immunity as a prison guard. . . . Smith overstates the extent of his immunity. Smith is protected from liability for mere negligence because of the need to protect his use of discretion in his day-to-day decisions in the running of a correctional facility. But the immunity on which Smith relies is coextensive with the interest it protects. The very fact that the privilege is qualified reflects a recognition there is no societal interest in protecting those uses of a prison guard's discretion that amount to reckless or callous indifference to the rights and safety of the prisoners in his charge. Once the protected sphere of privilege is exceeded, we see no reason why state officers should not be liable for their reckless misconduct on the same basis as private tortfeasors.

JUSTICE REHNQUIST, with whom THE CHIEF JUSTICE and JUSTICE POWELL join, dissenting.

A fundamental premise of our legal system is the notion that damages are awarded to *compensate* the victim — to redress the injuries that he or she *actually* has suffered. In sharp contrast to this principle, the doctrine of punitive damages permits the award of "damages" beyond even the most generous and expansive conception of actual injury to the plaintiff. This anomaly is rationalized principally on three grounds. First, punitive damages "are assessed for the avowed purpose of visiting *a punishment* upon the defendant." Second, the doctrine is rationalized on the ground that it deters persons from violating the rights of others. Third, punitive damages are justified as a "bounty" that encourages private lawsuits seeking to assert legal rights.

Despite these attempted justifications, the doctrine of punitive damages has been vigorously criticized throughout the Nation's history. Countless cases remark that such damages have never been "a favorite in the law." The year after § 1983 was enacted, the New Hampshire Supreme Court declared, "The idea of [punitive damages] is wrong. It is a monstrous heresy. It is an unsightly and unhealthy excrescence, deforming the symmetry of the body of the law." *Fay v. Parker*, 53 N.H. 342, 382 (1872).

Until today, the Court has adhered, with some fidelity, to the scarcely controversial principle that its proper role in interpreting § 1983 is determining what the 42d Congress intended. . . . The Court's opinion purports to pursue an inquiry into legislative intent, yet relies heavily upon state court decisions decided well after the 42d Congress adjourned. I find these cases unilluminating, at least in part because I am unprepared to attribute to the 42d Congress the truly extraordinary foresight that the Court seems to think it had. The reason our earlier decisions interpreting § 1983 have relied upon common law decisions is simple: members of the 42d Congress were lawyers, familiar with the law of their time. In resolving ambiguities in the enactments of that Congress, as with other Congresses, it is useful to consider the legal principles and rules that shaped the thinking of its members. The decisions of state courts decided well after 1871, while of some academic interest, are largely irrelevant to what members of the 42d Congress intended by way of a standard for punitive damages.

[T]he decisions rendered by state courts in the years preceding and immediately following the enactment of § 1983 attest to the fact that a solid majority of jurisdictions took the view that the standard for an award of punitive damages included a requirement of ill will. To be sure, a few jurisdictions followed a broader standard; a careful review of the decisions at the time uncovers a number of decisions that contain some reference to "recklessness." And equally clearly, in more recent years many courts have adopted a standard including "recklessness" as the minimal degree of culpability warranting punitive damages.

Most clear of all, however, is the fact that at about the time § 1983 was enacted a considerable number of the 37 States then belonging to the Union required some showing of wrongful intent before punitive damages could be awarded. . . . [I]t is but a statement of the obvious that "evil motive" was the general standard for punitive damages in many states at the time of the 42d Congress.

In deciding whether Congress heeded such advice, it is useful to consider the language of § 1983 itself — which should, of course, be the starting point for any inquiry into legislative intent. . . . Plainly, the statutory language itself provides absolutely no support for the cause of action for punitive damages that the Court reads into the provision. Indeed, it merely creates "liab[ility] to the party injured . . . for redress." "Redress" means "reparation of, satisfaction or compensation for, a wrong sustained or the loss resulting from this." And, as the Court concedes, punitive damages are not "reparation" or "compensation"; their very purpose is to punish, not to compensate. If Congress meant to create a right to recover punitive damages, then it chose singularly inappropriate words: both the reference to injured parties and to redress suggests compensation, and not punishment.

Other statutes roughly contemporaneous with § 1983 illustrate that if Congress wanted to subject persons to a punitive damages remedy, it did so explicitly. For example, in . . . [1870,] . . . Congress created express punitive damages remedies for various types of commercial misconduct. Likewise, the False Claims Act (1863) provided a civil remedy of double damages and a $2,000 civil forfeiture penalty for certain misstatements to the government.

Finally, even if the evidence of congressional intent were less clearcut, I would be persuaded to resolve any ambiguity in favor of an actual malice standard. It scarcely needs repeating that punitive damages are not a "favorite in the law," owing to the numerous persuasive criticisms that have been leveled against the doctrine.

Moreover, notwithstanding the Court's inability to discern them, there are important distinctions between a right to damages under § 1983 and a similar right under state tort law. A leading rationale seized upon by proponents of punitive damages to justify the doctrine is that "the award is . . . a covert response to the legal system's overt refusal to provide financing for litigation." Yet, § 1988[16] provides not just a "covert response" to plaintiffs' litigation expenses but an explicit provision for an award to the prevailing party in a § 1983 action of "a reasonable attorney's fee as part of the costs." By permitting punitive damages *as well as* attorney's fees, § 1983 plaintiffs, unlike state tort law plaintiffs, get not just one windfall but two — one for them, and one for their lawyer.

The staggering effect of § 1983 claims upon the workload of the federal courts has been decried time and again. The torrent of frivolous claims under that section threatens to incapacitate the judicial system's resolution of claims where true injustice is involved; those claims which truly warrant redress are in a very real danger of being lost in a sea of meritless suits. Yet, apparently oblivious to this, the Court today reads into the silent, inhospitable terms of § 1983 a remedy that is designed to serve as a "bounty" to encourage private litigation. In a time when the courts are flooded with suits that do not raise colorable claims, in large part because of the existing incentives for litigation under § 1983, it is regrettable that the Court should take upon itself, in apparent disregard for the likely intent of the 42d Congress, the legislative task of encouraging yet more litigation. There is a limit to what the federal judicial system can bear.

Finally, by unquestioningly transferring the standard of punitive damages in *state* tort actions to *federal* § 1983 actions, the Court utterly fails to recognize the fundamental difference that exists between an award of punitive damages by a federal court, acting under § 1983, and a similar award by a state court acting under prevailing local laws. . . . When federal courts enforce punitive damage awards against local officials they intrude into sensitive areas of sovereignty of coordinate branches of our nation, thus implicating the most basic values of our system of federalism. Moreover, by yet further distorting the incentives that exist for litigating claims against local officials in federal court, as opposed to state courts, the Court's decision makes it even more difficult for state courts to attempt to conform the conduct of state officials to the Constitution.

JUSTICE O'CONNOR, dissenting.

Once it is established that the common law of 1871 provides us with no real guidance . . . , we should turn to the policies underlying § 1983 to determine which rule best accords with those policies. . . . [W]e [have] identified the purposes of § 1983 as preeminently to compensate victims of constitutional violations and to deter further violations. The conceded availability of compensatory damages, particularly when coupled with the availability of attorney's fees under § 1988, completely fulfills the goal

---

[16] [Editor's note: § 1988's fee-shifting provision is discussed in Chapter 9, *infra*.]

of compensation, leaving only deterrence to be served by awards of punitive damages. We must then confront the close question whether a standard permitting an award of unlimited punitive damages on the basis of recklessness will chill public officials in the performance of their duties more than it will deter violations of the Constitution, and whether the availability of punitive damages for reckless violations of the Constitution in addition to attorney's fees will create an incentive to bring an ever-increasing flood of § 1983 claims, threatening the ability of the federal courts to handle those that are meritorious. . . . I am persuaded that the policies counseling against awarding punitive damages for the recklessness of public officials outweigh the desirability of any incremental deterrent effect that such awards may have.

NOTES

1. Intent of the Forty-Second Congress. Notwithstanding Justice Rehnquist's dissent in *Smith*, Justice Scalia pointed out in *Pacific Mutual Life Insurance Co. v. Haslip*, 499 U.S. 1 (1991) (Scalia, concurring), that "[i]n 1868 . . . when the Fourteenth Amendment was adopted, punitive damages were undoubtedly an established part of the American common law of torts. . . . Even fierce opponents of the doctrine acknowledged that it was a firmly established feature of American law." The only real question following the Civil War (when § 1983 was enacted) was *when* to allow punitive damages. On this point, Justices Brennan and Rehnquist disagreed. Justice Brennan's majority opinion in *Smith* claimed that the rule in a "large majority of jurisdictions" focused on something less than specific intent. Justice Rehnquist countered that a "solid majority of jurisdictions took the view that the standard for an award of punitive damages included a requirement of ill will." Can these two historical interpretations be reconciled? Justice Brennan noted "in passing" that

> it appears quite uncertain whether . . . Justice Rehnquist's dissent ultimately [is] . . . that "ill will, spite, or intent to injure" should be required to allow punitive damages awards. Justice Rehnquist consistently confuses, and attempts to blend together, the quite distinct concepts of *intent to cause* injury, on one hand, and *subjective consciousness* of risk of injury (or of unlawfulness) on the other. For instance, his dissent purports to base its analysis on the "fundamental distinction" between "wrongful motive, actual intention to inflict harm *or intentional doing of an act known to be unlawful*," versus "very careless or negligent conduct." Yet in the same paragraph, the dissent inaccurately recharacterizes the first element of this distinction as "acts that are intentionally harmful," requiring "inquiry into the actor's subjective motive and purpose." Consciousness of consequences or of wrongdoing, of course, does not require injurious intent or motive; it is equally consistent with indifference toward or disregard for consequences. This confusion of standards continues throughout the opinion. Justice Rehnquist's dissent frequently uses such phrases as "intent to injure" or "evil motive"; yet at several points it refers more broadly to "subjective mental state" or like phrases, and expressly includes consciousness (as opposed to intent) in its reasoning. More telling, perhaps, is its citation of cases and treatises, which frequently and consistently includes authority supporting (at most) a consciousness requirement rather than the "actual intent" standard for which the opinion purports to argue elsewhere.

For the majority in *Smith*, then, history held that the required level of scienter, whether deemed "ill will," "intent to injure," or "evil motive," could be met by the modern-day equivalents of "recklessness," "consciousness of consequences," and "deliberate indifference."

2. Policy. Justice Rehnquist's three policy arguments against punitive damages — that they are "monstrous," encourage frivolous litigation and threaten federalism — are reminiscent of those made against both official liability, *see* Chapter 1.A., *supra* (discussing the "litigation explosion" that followed *Monroe v. Pape*), and local governments' liability for the wrongs of their agents. *See* Chapter 4.A., *supra* (discussing Congress's power to impose liability on local government); Chapter 4.B., *supra* (discussing fairness of denying municipalities qualified immunity). Justice O'Connor's concern that the availability of punitive damages might deter governmental officials from performing needed tasks also harkens back to policy discussions had in the context of both official and municipal liability. *See* Chapter 2, *supra* (discussing the need for official immunities); Chapter 4.B., *supra* (discussing whether municipal immunity is needed). Do Justices Rehnquist and O'Connor add anything new to the debate?

3. Constitutional Constraints on Punitive Damages. In *Browning-Ferris Industries of Vermont, Inc. v. Kelco Disposal, Inc.*, 492 U.S. 257 (1989), the Supreme Court considered whether the Eighth Amendment's Excessive Fines Clause limited awards of punitive damages. After rejecting that argument, the Court ruled in a series of cases that the Fourteenth Amendment's Due Process Clause limits punitive awards: "[p]unitive damages pose an acute danger of arbitrary deprivation of property. Jury instructions typically leave the jury with wide discretion in choosing amounts, and the presentation of evidence of a defendant's net worth creates the potential that juries will use their verdicts to express biases against big businesses, particularly those without strong local presences." *Honda Motor, Ltd. v. Oberg*, 512 U.S. 415 (1994). In *BMW of North America v. Gore*, 517 U.S. 559 (1996), for example, the plaintiff (Gore) was not told that a new $40,000 automobile he purchased had been previously damaged. This non-disclosure led a jury to award Gore $2 million in punitive damages. The Court found this award grossly excessive in violation of Due Process. The *Gore* Court used three "guideposts" to measure the constitutional propriety of the award: "[1] the degree of reprehensibility of the nondisclosure; [2] the disparity between the harm or potential harm suffered by . . . Gore and his punitive damages award; and [3] the difference between this remedy and the civil penalties authorized or imposed in comparable cases." *See also Cooper Industries, Inc. v. Leatherman Tool Group, Inc.*, 532 U.S. 424, 434 (2001) ("The Due Process Clause of its own force . . . prohibits the States from imposing 'grossly excessive' punishments on tortfeasors."). In *State Farm Mutual Automobile Insurance Co. v. Campbell*, 538 U.S. 408 (2003), which reversed a $25 million punitive award where compensatory damages totaled only $1 million, the Court further observed that "in practice, few awards exceeding a single-digit ratio between punitive and compensatory damages, to a significant degree, will satisfy due process." More recently, the Court imposed procedural limitations on awards of punitive damages: "the Constitution's Due Process Clause forbids a State to use a punitive damages award to punish a defendant for injury that it inflicts upon nonparties or those whom they directly represent, i.e., injury that it inflicts upon those who are, essentially, strangers to the litigation." *Philip Morris USA v. Williams*, 549 U.S. 346 (2007) (reversing and remanding $32 million punitive award against tobacco company). *See also* Exxon Shipping Co. v. Baker, 128 S. Ct. 2605 (2008) (holding that federal maritime law limits punitive damages "to an amount equal to compensatory damages").

These limitation have been applied to § 1983 claims litigated in both state and federal court.[17] Because compensatory awards in § 1983 cases tend to be smaller than in other comparable civil contexts, however, courts have been more willing to sustain relatively large punitive damage awards under § 1983 in the face of Due Process challenges. In *Romanski v. Detroit Entertainment*, 428 F.3d 629 (6th Cir. 2005), for example, a casino patron (Romanski) won only $279.05 in compensatory damages for false arrest — she was detained and ejected for "slot-walking," i.e., taking a five-cent token from a slot machine's tray — but was awarded $875,000 in punitive damages in her § 1983 action

---

[17] The Supreme Court's limitations under the Fourteenth Amendment Due Process Clause in cases like *Gore, State Farm*, and *Philip Morris* were applied to punitive awards in state courts. Still, federal courts have "recognized that the principles announced in *Gore* are equally applicable to [the] review of punitive damages awarded in a federal district court." *Patterson v. Balsamico*, 440 F.3d 104 (2d Cir. 2006).

against a casino.[18] Applying the Supreme Court's instructions in *Gore* and *State Farm*, the court refused to overturn the award; it instead offered to remit it to $600,000. Finding the casino's misconduct "inexplicable and egregious" — "[t]his is not a case of mistaken identity, nor one in which a law enforcement officer reasonably misread the circumstances" — the court went on to address whether it exceeded *State Farms*' prescribed "single-digit" ratio and awards in comparable cases:

> When considered against the broad spectrum of civil cases, the ratio in this case (3,135 to 1) is unusually high and the compensatory damages award is unusually low. But this is a § 1983 case in which the basis for the punitive damages award was the plaintiff's unlawful arrest and the plaintiff's economic injury was so minimal as to be essentially nominal. The Supreme Court's cases on the ratio component of the excessiveness inquiry — which involved substantial compensatory damages awards for economic and measurable noneconomic harm — are therefore of limited relevance.
>
> This Court and other courts have recognized that where "injuries are without a ready monetary value," such as invasions of constitutional rights unaccompanied by physical injury or other compensable harm, higher ratios between the compensatory or nominal award and the punitive award are to be expected. Indeed, . . . in cases where the compensatory award is very low or nominal, "*any* appreciable exemplary award would produce a ratio that would appear excessive by this measure."
>
> Consistent with these principles, we think that to determine whether the punitive award in this case is within constitutional limits, the best approach is to compare it to punitive awards examined by courts "in other civil rights cases to find limits and proportions."
>
> We know of only one prior case in which we considered the constitutionality of a punitive damages award assessed pursuant to a finding of liability under § 1983. The case, *Gregory v. Shelby County*, 220 F.3d 433 (6th Cir. 2000), is quite distinguishable, however, because the plaintiff "suffered severe physical abuse, endured long hours of conscious pain and suffering, and ultimately died as a result [of a police officer's] actions." Furthermore, the compensatory award in *Gregory* was $778,000, so the $2.2 million punitive award easily satisfied *Gore*'s ratio guidepost.
>
> In *Lee v. Edwards*, 101 F.3d 805 (2d Cir. 1996), the plaintiff was awarded nominal compensatory damages and the Second Circuit concluded that the malicious prosecution verdict against the defendant, a police officer, would support a punitive damages award of no more than $75,000; the jury had awarded $200,000.
>
> In *Dean v. Olibas*, 129 F.3d 1001 (8th Cir. 1997), the Eighth Circuit sustained a $70,000 punitive award against a bail bondsman after the jury found him liable for causing the police to wrongfully arrest and book the plaintiff. . . . Finally, in *Williams v. Kaufman County*, 352 F.3d 994 (5th Cir. 2003), the Fifth Circuit sustained a $15,000 per-plaintiff punitive award against a police officer for having conducted illegal strip searches of the plaintiffs.
>
> Our decision in *Gregory* and our review of these cases from other circuits leads us to two important conclusions: First, substantial punitive awards in § 1983 cases, not surprisingly, tend to accompany conduct that results in physical or psychological harm. Second, in the typical § 1983 case in which punitive damages are awarded, the defendant is an individual police officer, not

---

[18] Because the casino's security guard who detained the patron was licensed to act as police officer by state law, the Court of Appeals concluded that she acted "under color of" law. *See* Chapter 1.B., *supra* (discussing private actors who are subject to suit under § 1983).

the police department or municipality[19] (which, odds are, have deeper pockets than the officer), let alone a deeply pocketed company, which the casino indisputably is. We have not found a case in which punitive damages were awarded based exclusively on a finding that the defendant unlawfully arrested the plaintiff and the award was challenged as unconstitutionally excessive.

Because her suit was against a private casino, which "yielded a daily intake of nearly $1,000,000," the court felt that a substantial punitive award was justified. "[I]t was entirely appropriate for the jury to craft a punitive damages award that was sensitive to the casino's financial position." "Under the totality of the circumstanc-es, . . . we think an award of no greater than $600,000 — sixty per cent of the casino's daily intake at the time of the verdict — would satisfy the demands of the due process clause. . . . [A] $600,000 award is comfortably within the ballpark of the punitive damages awards in the civil rights cases we have canvassed; the less reprehensible conduct in this case being counteracted by the need to make the award large enough." *See also Hardeman v. City of Albuquerque*, 377 F.3d 1106 (10th Cir. 2004) (sustaining a post-remittitur punitive damages award of $625,000 that was twenty times larger than compensatory award in a racial discrimination case); *Davis v. Rennie*, 264 F.3d 86 (1st Cir. 2001) (sustaining a $1 million punitive damage award that was ten times larger than the compensatory damages); *Nydam v. Lennerton*, 948 F.2d 808 (1st Cir. 1991) (affirming two awards of $100,000 each in punitive damages for an excessive force claim); *Gutierrez-Rodriguez v. Soto*, 882 F.2d 553 (1st Cir. 1989) (affirming a total award of $600,000 in punitive damages for a police shooting).

4. Remittitur. As illustrated by *Romanski*, federal courts retain a large measure of discretion to remit punitive awards even if when they satisfy *Gore*. *See generally* 11 CHARLES ALAN WRIGHT, ET AL., FEDERAL PRACTICE AND PROCEDURE § 2815 (2d ed. 1995). In *Patterson v. Balsamico*, 440 F.3d 104 (2d Cir. 2006), for example, the court observed that the "inquiry does not end . . . with the *Gore* factors. Rather, we must also consider [the defendant's] personal financial situation. . . . This Court will not . . . affirm punitive damages awards that 'result in the financial ruin of the defendant' or 'constitute a disproportionately large percentage of the defendant's net worth.' " "[C]onventional remittitur . . . requires giving the plaintiff a choice between accepting a reduced damage award and a new trial."[20] *Bisbal-Ramos v. City of Mayaguez*, 467 F.3d 16 (1st Cir. 2006) (reversing a reduction of a punitive award in a § 1983 case because the court did not give the plaintiff a choice).

Mathie v. Fries, 121 F.3d 808 (2d Cir. 1997), where a sexual abuse victim (Mathie) was awarded $250,000 and $500,000 in compensatory and punitive damages, respectively, provides a useful illustration of remittitur. Although the Court of Appeals found the punitive award consistent with the limitations set out in *Gore* — "Fries's sexual abuse of an inmate in his custody was reprehensible in the extreme and involved violence and malice, the two-to-one ratio between the punitive and compensatory awards is not unreasonable, and the civil and criminal penalties potentially applicable to Fries's conduct are not more lenient than the $500,000 punitive damages award" — it still remitted:

> That task requires comparison with awards approved in similar cases, to determine, as with compensatory awards, whether the punitive award is "so high as to shock the judicial conscience and constitute a denial of jus-

---

[19] [Editor's note: As explained in *City of Newport v. Fact Concerts*, 453 U.S. 247 (1981) (excerpted, *infra*), municipalities cannot be sued under § 1983 for punitive damages.]

[20] Reduction under the Due Process Clause, in contrast, does not require affording the plaintiff any choice. *See Bisbal-Ramos v. City of Mayaguez*, 467 F.3d 16 (1st Cir. 2006) ("Whether an award of punitive damages is excessive under the Due Process Clause is a constitutional question that we review *de novo*. We . . . may simply ascertain the amount of punitive award that would be appropriate and order the district court to enter judgment in such amount.").

tice." . . . We consider punitive awards in cases involving both sexual assaults by private individuals and assaultive and other misconduct by law enforcement officers.

sexual assaults by private individuals:

— $500,000 awarded to each of two plaintiffs, aged seven and ten, who were repeatedly raped, sodomized, and otherwise sexually abused.

— $200,000 awarded to a plaintiff who was raped at knife-point by an acquaintance who also slashed her face and clothes.

— $100,000, reduced from $275,000, awarded to a plaintiff who was sexually touched as a child by her stepfather.

misconduct by law enforcement officers:

— $500,000, reduced from $1,250,000, awarded to each plaintiff whom police officers shot at, assaulted, denied medical care, and maliciously prosecuted.

— $350,000 to a plaintiff who was the victim of police harassment.

— $185,000 awarded to a plaintiff who was beaten by police officers while handcuffed.

— $150,000 to a plaintiff who was severely beaten by a police officer, placed in jail for 60 hours, and wrongly charged with several offenses.

— $150,000, reduced from $250,000, to a plaintiff held in pre-trial detention for two months at Rikers Island as a result of a malicious prosecution.

— $75,000, reduced from $200,000, to a plaintiff who was a victim of a police assault and a malicious prosecution.

Fries's conduct was . . . "an outrageous abuse of power and authority." A substantial punitive award was clearly merited. . . . Nevertheless, . . . [b]earing in mind both the outrageousness of Fries's conduct and our own appellate responsibilities, we conclude that the punitive damages award in this case may not exceed $200,000.

5. Punitive Damages Without Actual Injury. Lower courts have sometimes held that § 1983 plaintiffs can recover punitive damages even though they cannot establish sufficient injury to justify an award of actual damages. In *Provost v. City of Newburgh*, 262 F.3d 146 (2d Cir. 2001), for example, the court sustained a $10,000 punitive award even though the plaintiff won only nominal damages. *See also Patterson v. Balsamico*, 440 F.3d 104 (2d Cir. 2006) (holding that a $10,000 punitive award would be proper notwithstanding an award of nominal damages and observing that "in a § 1983 case in which the compensatory damages are nominal, . . . the use of a multiplier to assess punitive damages is not the best tool"); *Williams v. Kaufman County*, 352 F.3d 994 (5th Cir. 2003) (sustaining a punitive award and observing that "any punitive damages-to-*compensatory* damages 'ratio analysis' cannot be applied effectively in cases where only nominal damages have been awarded"). Would a punitive damage award be proper in the absence of at least an award of nominal damages? In *Alexander v. Riga*, 208 F.3d 419, 430 (3d Cir. 2000), the court stated that "beyond a doubt, punitive damages can be awarded in a civil rights case where a jury finds a constitutional violation, even when the jury has not awarded compensatory or nominal damages." *Contrast* Christy Lynn McQuality, Note, *No Harm, No Foul? An Argument for the Allowance of Punitive Damages Without Compensatory Damages Under 42 U.S.C. § 1981a*, 59 WASH. & LEE L. REV. 643, 658 (2002) ("Many courts will not award punitive damages unless the plaintiff proves actual damage."). *Cf. Louisiana Acorn Housing v. LeBlanc*, 211 F.3d 298 (5th Cir. 2000) (holding that punitive damages cannot be recovered under the Fair Housing Act unless there is also an award of nominal or compensatory damages). Is an award of punitive damages in the absence of compensatory damages consistent with the Supreme Court's decision in *Texas v. Lesage*, 528 U.S. 18 (1999) (holding that damages cannot be recovered in the absence of proof that unconstitutional conduct caused actual injury) (described in Section A, Note 3 following *Stachura, supra*)?

CITY OF NEWPORT v. FACT CONCERTS
Supreme Court of the United States
453 U.S. 247 (1981)

JUSTICE BLACKMUN delivered the opinion of the Court.

Fact Concerts, Inc., is a Rhode Island corporation organized for the purpose of promoting musical concerts. In 1975, it received permission from the Rhode Island Department of Natural Resources to present several summer concerts at Fort Adams, a state park located in the city of Newport. In securing approval for the final concerts, to be held August 30 and 31, [Fact Concerts] sought and obtained an entertainment license from [the] city of Newport. Under their written contract, [Fact Concerts] retained control over the choice of performers and the type of music to be played while the city reserved the right to cancel the license without liability if "in the opinion of the City the interests of public safety demand."

[Fact Concerts] engaged a number of well-known jazz music acts to perform during the final August concerts. Shortly before the dates specified, the group Blood, Sweat and Tears was hired as a replacement for a previously engaged performer who was unable to appear. Members of the Newport City Council, including the Mayor, became concerned that Blood, Sweat and Tears, which they characterized as a rock group rather than as a jazz band, would attract a rowdy and undesirable audience to Newport. Based on this concern, the Council attempted to have Blood, Sweat and Tears removed from the program.

[Following failed negotiations, the] Council . . . voted to cancel the contract because [Fact Concerts] had not "lived up to all phases" of the agreement. The Council offered [Fact Concerts] a new contract for the same dates, specifically excluding Blood, Sweat and Tears.

[Fact Concerts sued the city and several officials under § 1983, arguing] that the license cancellation amounted to content-based censorship, and that its constitutional rights to free expression and due process had been violated under color of state law. . . . [Fact Concerts] sought compensatory and punitive damages against the city. . . . The jury returned verdicts for [Fact Concerts] on both counts, awarding compensatory damages of $72,910 and punitive damages of $275,000; of the punitive damages, $75,000 was spread among the seven individual officials and $200,000 was awarded against the city.

It is by now well settled that the tort liability created by § 1983 cannot be understood in a historical vacuum. . . . Congress . . . expressed no intention to do away with the immunities afforded state officials at common law, and the Court consistently has declined to construe the general language of § 1983 as automatically abolishing such traditional immunities by implication. Instead, the Court has recognized immunities of varying scope applicable to different officials sued under the statute. One important assumption underlying the Court's decisions in this area is that members of the 42d Congress were familiar with common-law principles, including defenses previously recognized in ordinary tort litigation, and that they likely intended these common-law principles to obtain, absent specific provisions to the contrary.

At the same time, the Court's willingness to recognize certain traditional immunities as affirmative defenses has not led it to conclude that Congress incorporated all immunities existing at common law. Indeed, because the 1871 Act was designed to expose state and local officials to a new form of liability, it would defeat the promise of the statute to recognize any preexisting immunity without determining both the policies that it serves and its compatibility with the purposes of § 1983. Only after careful inquiry into considerations of both history and policy has the Court construed § 1983 to incorporate a particular immunity defense.

By the time Congress enacted what is now § 1983, the immunity of a municipal corporation from punitive damages at common law was not open to serious question. It was generally understood by 1871 that a municipality, like a private corporation, was to be treated as a natural person subject to suit for a wide range of tortious activity, but this understanding did not extend to the award of punitive or exemplary damages. Indeed, the courts that had considered the issue prior to 1871 were virtually unanimous in denying such damages against a municipal corporation. Judicial disinclination to award punitive damages against a municipality has persisted to the present day in the vast majority of jurisdictions.

In general, courts viewed punitive damages as contrary to sound public policy, because such awards would burden the very taxpayers and citizens for whose benefit the wrongdoer was being chastised. The courts readily distinguished between liability to compensate for injuries inflicted by a municipality's officers and agents, and vindictive damages appropriate as punishment for the bad-faith conduct of those same officers and agents. Compensation was an obligation properly shared by the municipality itself, whereas punishment properly applied only to the actual wrongdoers. The courts thus protected the public from unjust punishment, and the municipalities from undue fiscal constraints.[21]

Given that municipal immunity from punitive damages was well established at common law by 1871, we proceed on the familiar assumption that "Congress would have specifically so provided had it wished to abolish the doctrine." Nothing in the legislative debates suggests that, in enacting § [1983], the 42d Congress intended any such abolition. Indeed, the limited legislative history relevant to this issue suggests the opposite.

Because there was virtually no debate on § [1983], the Court has looked to Congress' treatment of the amendment to the Act introduced by Senator Sherman as indicative of congressional attitudes toward the nature and scope of municipal liability.[22] Initially, it is significant that the Sherman amendment as proposed contemplated the award of no more than compensatory damages for injuries inflicted by mob violence. The

---

[21] [n.23] In the face of this history, [Fact Concerts] acknowledged at oral argument that in 1871 the common law did not contemplate the imposition of punitive damages against municipalities, but contended that the functional equivalent was achieved through the respondeat superior liability to which municipalities were, and still are, exposed. Apparently, [Fact Concerts] argues that because municipalities were liable for the conduct of their agents, including conduct over which their executive officials had no actual responsibility or knowledge, it would have been unnecessary to expose them to punitive damages with regard to the same conduct. This argument, however, does not alter the persuasiveness of the prevalent common-law immunity; if anything, it goes to the soundness of the common-law defense at that time and now. Moreover, the respondeat superior doctrine did not cover all instances in which the municipality could assert immunity in its own capacity.

[22] [n.24] Briefly, the Sherman amendment was a proposed addition to the statute, and was defended by its sponsor as an attempt to enlist the aid of persons of property in suppressing the lawless violence of the Ku Klux Klan. In its initial form, the amendment imposed liability on any inhabitant of a municipality for damage inflicted by persons "riotously and tumultuously assembled." That version was passed by the Senate but overwhelmingly rejected by the House. A first conference substitute was then proposed. The substitute version placed liability directly on the local government, regardless of whether the municipality had had notice of the impending riot, had made reasonable efforts to stop it, or was even authorized under state law to exercise police power. The conference substitute also created a lien which ran against "all moneys in the treasury," thus permitting execution against public property such as jails and courthouses. It was generally understood that the extent of the proposed public liability went beyond what was contemplated under § [1983]. After much debate, the amendment passed the Senate but was again rejected by the House. It is from the debate over the first conference substitute that we glean "clue[s]" as to Congress' views on municipal liability. *Monell*, [discussed *supra* in Chapter 4].

amendment would not have exposed municipal governments to punitive damages; rather, it proposed that municipalities "shall be liable to pay full compensation to the person or persons damnified" by mob violence.

That the exclusion of punitive damages was no oversight was confirmed by Representative Butler, one of the amendment's chief supporters, when he responded to a critical inquiry on the floor of the House:

> The invalidity of the gentleman's argument is that he looks upon [the amendment] as a punishment for the county. Now, we do not look upon it as a punishment at all. It is a mutual insurance. We are there a community, and if there is any wrong done by our community, or by the inhabitants of our community, we will indemnify the injured party for that wrong. . . .

We doubt that a Congress having no intention of permitting punitive awards against municipalities in the explicit context of the Sherman amendment would have meant to expose municipal bodies to such novel liability sub silentio under § [1983].

Notwithstanding the compensatory focus of the amendment, its proposed extension of municipal liability met substantial resistance in Congress, resulting in its defeat on two separate occasions. In addition to the constitutional reservations broached by legislators, which the Court has discussed at some length in *Monell*, [excerpted and discussed in Chapter 4.A., *supra*], Members of both Chambers also expressed more practical objections. Notably, supporters as well as opponents of § [1983] voiced concern that this extension of public liability might place an unmanageable financial burden on local governments. Legislators also expressed apprehension that innocent taxpayers would be unfairly punished for the deeds of persons over whom they had neither knowledge nor control. . . . We see no reason to believe that Congress' opposition to punishing innocent taxpayers and bankrupting local governments would have been less applicable with regard to the novel specter of punitive damages against municipalities.

Finding no evidence that Congress intended to disturb the settled common-law immunity, we now must determine whether considerations of public policy dictate a contrary result.

Punitive damages by definition are not intended to compensate the injured party, but rather to punish the tortfeasor whose wrongful action was intentional or malicious, and to deter him and others from similar extreme conduct. Regarding retribution, it remains true that an award of punitive damages against a municipality "punishes" only the taxpayers, who took no part in the commission of the tort. These damages are assessed over and above the amount necessary to compensate the injured party. Thus, there is no question here of equitably distributing the losses resulting from official misconduct. Indeed, punitive damages imposed on a municipality are in effect a windfall to a fully compensated plaintiff, and are likely accompanied by an increase in taxes or a reduction of public services for the citizens footing the bill. Neither reason nor justice suggests that such retribution should be visited upon the shoulders of blameless or unknowing taxpayers.[23]

If a government official acts knowingly and maliciously to deprive others of their civil rights, he may become the appropriate object of the community's vindictive sentiments. A municipality, however, can have no malice independent of the malice of its officials. Damages awarded for punitive purposes, therefore, are not sensibly assessed against the governmental entity itself.

To the extent that the purposes of § 1983 have any bearing on this punitive rationale, they do not alter our analysis. The Court previously has indicated that punitive damages might be awarded in appropriate circumstances in order to punish violations of

---

[23] [n.29] It is perhaps possible to imagine an extreme situation where the taxpayers are directly responsible for perpetrating an outrageous abuse of constitutional rights. Nothing of that kind is presented by this case. Moreover, such an occurrence is sufficiently unlikely that we need not anticipate it here.

constitutional rights, but it never has suggested that punishment is as prominent a purpose under the statute as are compensation and deterrence. Whatever its weight, the retributive purpose is not significantly advanced, if it is advanced at all, by exposing municipalities to punitive damages.

The other major objective of punitive damages awards is to prevent future misconduct. [Fact Concerts] argues vigorously that deterrence is a primary purpose of § 1983, and that because punitive awards against municipalities for the malicious conduct of their policymaking officials will induce voters to condemn official misconduct through the electoral process, the threat of such awards will deter future constitutional violations. . . . For several reasons, however, we conclude that the deterrence rationale of § 1983 does not justify making punitive damages available against municipalities.

First, it is far from clear that municipal officials, including those at the policymaking level, would be deterred from wrongdoing by the knowledge that large punitive awards could be assessed based on the wealth of their municipality. Indemnification may not be available to the municipality under local law, and even if it were, officials likely will not be able themselves to pay such sizable awards. Thus, assuming arguendo, that the responsible official is not impervious to shame and humiliation, the impact on the individual tortfeasor of this deterrence in the air is at best uncertain.

There also is no reason to suppose that corrective action, such as the discharge of offending officials who were appointed and the public excoriation of those who were elected, will not occur unless punitive damages are awarded against the municipality. . . . "The more reasonable assumption is that responsible superiors are motivated not only by concern for the public fisc but also by concern for the Government's integrity." This assumption is no less applicable to the electorate at large. And if additional protection is needed, the compensatory damages that are available against a municipality may themselves induce the public to vote the wrongdoers out of office.

Moreover, there is available a more effective means of deterrence. By allowing juries and courts to assess punitive damages in appropriate circumstances against the offending official, based on his personal financial resources, the statute directly advances the public's interest in preventing repeated constitutional deprivations.[24] In our view, this provides sufficient protection against the prospect that a public official may commit recurrent constitutional violations by reason of his office. . . . [A] damages remedy recoverable against individuals is more effective as a deterrent than the threat of damages against a government employer. We see no reason to depart from that conclusion here, especially since the imposition of additional penalties would most likely fall upon the citizen-taxpayer.

Finally, although the benefits associated with awarding punitive damages against municipalities under § 1983 are of doubtful character, the costs may be very real. . . . [M]unicipalities and other units of state and local government face the possibility of having to assure compensation for persons harmed by abuses of governmental authority covering a large range of activity in everyday life. To add the burden of exposure for the malicious conduct of individual government employees may create a serious risk to the financial integrity of these governmental entities.

The Court has remarked elsewhere on the broad discretion traditionally accorded to juries in assessing the amount of punitive damages. Because evidence of a tortfeasor's wealth is traditionally admissible as a measure of the amount of punitive damages that should be awarded, the unlimited taxing power of a municipality may have a prejudicial impact on the jury, in effect encouraging it to impose a sizable award. The impact of such

---

[24] [n.30] A number of state statutes requiring municipal corporations to indemnify their employees for adverse judgments rendered as a result of performance of governmental duties specifically exclude indemnification for malicious or willful misconduct by the employees.

a windfall recovery is likely to be both unpredictable and, at times, substantial, and we are sensitive to the possible strain on local treasuries and therefore on services available to the public at large.

[W]e hold that a municipality is immune from punitive damages under 42 U.S.C. § 1983.

JUSTICE BRENNAN, with whom JUSTICE MARSHALL and JUSTICE STEVENS join, dissenting.

[Justice Brennan first argued that because the city did not object to the District Court's instructions on punitive damages, it waived its challenge to the punitive damages awarded by the jury.]

Because I conclude that the Court of Appeals should be affirmed on a procedural ground, I need not consider th[e] additional argument [that punitive damages are authorized against cities under § 1983]. . . . The Court . . . relies on 19th-century case law for the proposition that municipalities may not be held liable for punitive damages, without distinguishing between the common situation in which municipal liability is predicated on a theory of respondeat superior, and the more unusual situation in which the violation is committed in accordance with official governmental policy. Only in the latter situation have we held that a municipality may be sued under § 1983. It is in the latter context that the Court's cited precedent is least relevant, and that its concern for "blameless or unknowing taxpayers" is least compelling. Indeed, when the elected representatives of the people adopt a municipal policy that violates the Constitution, it seems perfectly reasonable to impose punitive damages on those ultimately responsible for the policy — the citizens."]

NOTES

1. Immunity from Punitive Damages in 1871. The Court in *Monell* and *Owen* (both of which are excerpted at length in Chapters 4.A. & 4.B., respectively, *supra*) refused to recognize immunities for municipalities. Why then are cities immune from punitive damage awards? As Justice Blackmun makes clear, the common law refused to countenance punitive damage awards against government. *See also Cook County v. United States ex rel. Chandler*, 538 U.S. 119 (2003) ("Although it was well established in 1863 'that a municipality, like a private corporation, was to be treated as a natural person subject to suit for a wide range of tortious activity, . . . this understanding did not extend to the award of punitive or exemplary damages.'"). *See also* Ronen Perry, *The Role of Retributive Justice in the Common Law of Torts: A Descriptive Theory*, 73 TENN. L. REV. 177, 229 (2006) ("Another feature of the law of punitive damages which can also be explained in retributive terms is the common law's consistent and express refusal to award punitive damages against municipalities"). But by 1871, as Justice Brennan points out in dissent, cities were held liable under respondeat superior for punitive damages assessed against their agents. Given this reality, is Justice Blackmun's historical discussion convincing? If cities were traditionally liable on a respondeat superior basis for punitive damages awarded against their agents anyway, would it matter that they were immune from punitive liability for their own wrongs? Were there gaps between liability under respondeat superior and direct municipal responsibility that might have made this distinction meaningful in 1871? *See* footnote 23 in *City of Newport*. *Compare* Chapter 4.D., *supra* (discussing the problem of innocent agents).

2. Private Institutions. Private firms do not necessarily share municipalities' protection from punitive damage awards. The Second Restatement of Agency and Second Restatement of Torts, for example, both authorize imputing punitive damages from agents to private principals when

(a) the principal authorized the doing and the manner of the act, or

(b) the agent was unfit and the principal was reckless in employing him, or

(c) the agent was employed in a managerial capacity and was acting in the scope of employment, or

(d) the principal or a managerial agent of the principal ratified or approved the act.

RESTATEMENT (SECOND) OF AGENCY § 217C; *see also* RESTATEMENT (SECOND) OF TORTS § 909 (same). Some states, moreover, authorize respondeat superior liability on the part of private principals for punitive damage awards assessed against their agents. *See* 2 J. GHIARDI & J. KIRCHER, PUNITIVE DAMAGES: LAW AND PRACTICE § 24.01 (1998) (discussing disagreement among states); Ronen Perry, *The Role of Retributive Justice in the Common Law of Torts: A Descriptive Theory*, 73 TENN. L. REV. 177, 230 (2006) (discussing the law of punitive damages).

As pointed out in Chapter 1.B., *supra*, private actors can engage in unconstitutional state action that renders them liable for damages under § 1983. *See, e.g., Lugar v. Edmondson Oil Co.*, 457 U.S. 922 (1982) (holding that a private party can be liable under § 1983 for unconstitutionally invoking a state prejudgment attachment statute); *Adickes v. S.H. Kress Co.*, 398 U.S. 144 (1970) (holding that a private party can be held liable under § 1983 when it acted "in concert" with a public official). Assuming liability under § 1983, can a private firm be held liable for its agent's punitive damages? Most lower courts have concluded that *Monell*'s "policy or custom" requirement applies to private institutions; thus, there can be no respondeat superior liability under § 1983 even with private defendants. *See* Barbara Kritchevsky, *Civil Rights Liability of Private Entities*, 26 CARDOZO L. REV. 35, 38 (2004) (observing that courts tend to hold "that private entities are only liable if the plaintiff satisfies the policy or custom requirement"). Assuming a policy or custom is established, however, "plaintiffs have succeeded in obtaining such damages" from private institutions. *Id.* Does it make sense to expose private institutions to punitive damage awards when governmental institutions — otherwise subject to the same policy or custom requirement — are not? *See* Perry, *supra*, at 231 (observing that "the municipality/private-corporation distinction in the law of punitive damages seems somewhat anomalous").

3. Footnote 29. Justice Blackmun states in footnote 29 in *City of Newport* that "an extreme situation" might be imagined "where the taxpayers are directly responsible for perpetrating an outrageous abuse of constitutional rights." Are punitive damages against a city authorized in this situation? Does footnote 29 leave open a possibility that punitive damages can be imposed on a municipality? The Second Circuit in *Ciraolo v. City of New York*, 216 F.3d 236 (2d Cir. 2000), ruled that footnote 29 creates an exception only "for cases in which the taxpayers are directly responsible — in their role as voters — for the adoption of an unconstitutional municipal policy, rather than an exception for especially outrageous abuses of constitutional rights." "If, for example, a town adopted, by a unanimous vote, a referendum establishing an unconstitutional rule, we can see no reason in the policies discussed in *Newport* why punitive damages ought not to be awarded." Outside this peculiar context, however, it would seem that municipalities simply cannot be held liable under § 1983 for punitive damages. *See* Gloria Jean Rottell, *Paying the Price: It's Time to Hold Municipalities Liable for Punitive Damages Under 42 U.S.C. § 1983*, 10 J. L. & POL'Y REV. 189, 191 (2001) ("A number of courts have considered footnote 29; none have opted to uphold an award of punitive damages against a municipality.").

4. Indemnity. Justice Blackmun notes that many municipal corporations will not indemnify their employees for "malicious or willful misconduct," *see* footnote 30 in *City of Newport*, which in turn limits their liability — via indemnification — for their employees' punitive damages. What if a municipality agreed to indemnify its employees for all their wrongs, including those that generate awards of punitive damages? *See* Martin A. Schwartz, *Should Juries be Informed the Municipality Will Indemnify Officer's § 1983 Liability for Constitutional Wrongdoing?*, 86 IOWA L. REV. 1209, 1219 (2001) ("Some state and local indemnification policies authorize indemnification of an officer's punitive damages."). Can a municipality be held liable for a § 1983 punitive damage award against one of its agents? *See, e.g., Saldana-Sanchez v. Lopez-Gerena*, 256 F.3d 1 (1st Cir. 2001) (holding that a city could be liable for punitive damages awarded against its mayor under a state indemnification rule notwithstanding *Newport*); *Bell v. Clackamas County*, 341 F.3d 858 (9th Cir. 2003) ("Although municipal defendants are immune from liability for punitive damages under § 1983, municipalities may pay punitive damages in some circumstances") (citing CAL. GOV'T CODE § 825(b) as "authorizing a public entity to pay a punitive damages award against an employee if the employee acted in good faith and within the scope of his or her public employment")). *See generally Wilson v. Chicago*, 120 F.3d 681 (7th Cir. 1997) (excerpted in Chapter 4.E., *supra*) (discussing use of state indemnification rules to recover § 1983 damages from cities).

5. Title VII Compared. The Supreme Court in *Kolstad v. American Dental Association*, 527 U.S. 526 (1999), ruled that "in the punitive damages context, an employer may not be vicariously liable for the discriminatory employment decisions of managerial agents where these decisions are contrary to the employer's 'good-faith efforts to comply with Title VII.' " Put another way, private employers can be held liable under Title VII for punitive damage awards leveled against their employees — at least when they do not make good faith efforts to comply with Title VII. Although governmental employers are subject to compensatory damages under Title VII, punitive damages against governmental institutions are precluded by 42 U.S.C. § 1981a(b)(1) ("[a] complaining party may recover punitive damages under this section [Title VII] against a respondent (*other than a government, government agency or political subdivision*) if the complaining party demonstrates that the respondent engaged in a discriminatory practice or discriminatory practices with malice or with reckless indifference to the federally protected rights of an aggrieved individual") (emphasis added). *See Cross v. New York City Transit Authority*, 417 F.3d 241 (2d Cir. 2005) (stating that Title VII precludes punitive awards against governmental employers).

C. PROSPECTIVE RELIEF AGAINST STATE AND LOCAL OFFICIALS

[1] Article III Limitations: Standing, Ripeness, and Mootness

As discussed in Chapter 3.A., *supra*, § 1983 has been interpreted to foreclose suits against states in either state or federal court. However, under the fiction of *Ex parte Young*, 209 U.S. 123 (1908) (discussed in Chapter 3.B., *supra*), a § 1983 plaintiff can win prospective relief (both declaratory and injunctive) against a state official, and this relief will effectively operate against the state itself. Local governments and their officials can likewise be sued for prospective relief, perhaps under the logic of *Ex parte Young* and certainly under *Monell v. New York Department of Social Services*, 436 U.S. 658 (1978) (excerpted in Chapter 4.A., *supra*). *See Truth v. Kent School District*, 499 F.3d 999 (9th Cir. 2007) (holding that prospective actions can be brought against municipal officials under *Ex parte Young* without satisfying *Monell*'s "policy or custom" requirement). As a result, one can obtain prospective relief against state and local governments under § 1983 notwithstanding classical sovereign immunity.

Unlike litigation with the federal government, *see generally* ALFRED C. AMAN, JR. & WILLIAM T. MAYTON, ADMINISTRATIVE LAW 422 (2d ed. 2001); GREGORY C. SISK, LITIGATION WITH THE FEDERAL GOVERNMENT (2000), § 1983 suits against state and local officials seeking prospective relief ordinarily need not await the outcome of administrative proceedings. "Exhaustion" of state administrative remedies, as it is often called, is generally not required under § 1983.[25] Indeed, § 1983 does not ordinarily require that

---

[25] In 1996, Congress passed a general exhaustion requirement for inmates challenging conditions of

any state remedial processes, whether administrative or judicial, be used. *See Patsy v. Florida Board of Regents*, 457 U.S. 496 (1982) (described in Note 3 following *University of Tennessee v. Elliott* in Chapter 8.A.[2], *infra*). Instead, a § 1983 plaintiff can proceed directly to court — state[26] or federal.

Last, but not least, "[t]raditionally and for good reasons, statutes of limitation are not controlling measures of equitable relief. Such statutes have been drawn upon by equity solely for the light they may shed in determining that which is decisive for the chancellor's intervention, namely, whether the plaintiff has inexcusably slept on his rights so as to make a decree against the defendant unfair." *Holmberg v. Armbrecht*, 327 U.S. 392 (1946). Consequently, § 1983 plaintiffs seeking prospective relief ordinarily need not worry about state statutes of limitations. *See* Chapter 5.A., *supra*. Indeed, because prospective actions are designed to prevent harm from occurring in the future, there rarely is a decisive past wrong to identify when the action accrued.[27]

Notwithstanding their forward-looking character, prospective claims under § 1983 continue to experience timing problems. In particular, Article III's "case" or "controversy" requirement raises unique timing problems for plaintiffs seeking prospective relief in federal court.[28]

CITY OF LOS ANGELES v. LYONS
Supreme Court of the United States
461 U.S. 95 (1983)

JUSTICE WHITE delivered the opinion of the Court.

The issue here is whether respondent Lyons satisfied the prerequisites for seeking injunctive relief in the federal district court.

This case began on February 7, 1977, when . . . Adolph Lyons filed a complaint for damages, injunction, and declaratory relief in [federal court against] . . . the City of Los Angeles and four of its police officers. The complaint alleged that on October 6, 1976, at 2 a.m., Lyons was stopped by the defendant officers for a traffic or vehicle code violation and that although Lyons offered no resistance or threat whatsoever, the officers, without provocation or justification, seized Lyons and applied a "chokehold" — either the "bar arm control" hold or the "carotid-artery control" hold or both — rendering him unconscious and causing damage to his larynx. Counts I through IV of the complaint sought damages against the officers and the City. Count V, with which we are principally concerned here, sought a preliminary and permanent injunction against the City barring the use of the control holds.

---

confinement. Section 1997e(a) of title 42 now states: "No action shall be brought with respect to prison conditions under section 1983 of this title, or any other Federal law, by a prisoner confined in any jail, prison, or other correctional facility until such administrative remedies as are available are exhausted." This requirement is discussed in Chapter 8.B., *infra*.

[26] *See, e.g., Howlett v. Rose*, 496 U.S. 356 (1990) (holding that state courts of general jurisdiction cannot refuse to entertain § 1983 claims) (discussed in Chapter 5.B., *supra*).

[27] *But see Cooey v. Strickland*, 479 F.3d 412 (6th Cir. 2007) (ruling that even though a death-row inmate sought only prospective relief in his § 1983 action challenging the constitutionality of execution by lethal injection, *see Hill v. McDonough*, 547 U.S. 573 (2006) (discussed in Chapter 8.B.[1], *infra*), his claim was time-barred by Ohio's two-year statute of limitations). Should the *Cooey* court have relied on Ohio's statute of limitations to defeat a purely prospective claim for relief under § 1983? *See Jones v. Allen*, 483 F. Supp. 2d 1142 (M.D. Ala. 2007) (criticizing *Cooey* and concluding that "because the execution itself is the event Jones claims would violate his constitutional rights, it defies logic, and is contrary to the common law of torts, to conclude that the statute of limitations has already run on a suit to prevent an unconstitutional act that has not yet occurred"), *aff'd*, 485 F.3d 635 (11th Cir. 2007).

[28] Plaintiffs in federal courts seeking retrospective relief (e.g., money damages) must also satisfy Article III's "standing" requirement. Article III's demands, however, are routinely met when plaintiffs seek money damages for past injuries they have suffered. *See Richmond v. J.A. Croson Co.*, 488 U.S. 469, 478 n.1 (1989).

The District Court found that Lyons had been stopped for a traffic infringement and that without provocation or legal justification the officers involved had applied a "department-authorized chokehold which resulted in injuries to the plaintiff." The court further found that the department authorizes the use of the holds in situations where no one is threatened by death or grievous bodily harm, that officers are insufficiently trained, that the use of the holds involves a high risk of injury or death as then employed, and that their continued use in situations where neither death nor serious bodily injury is threatened "is unconscionable in a civilized society." The court concluded that such use violated Lyons' substantive due process rights under the Fourteenth Amendment. A preliminary injunction was entered enjoining "the use of both the carotid-artery and bar arm holds under circumstances which do not threaten death or serious bodily injury."

Since our grant of certiorari, circumstances pertinent to the case have changed. Originally, Lyons' complaint alleged that at least two deaths had occurred as a result of the application of chokeholds by the police. His first amended complaint alleged that 10 chokehold-related deaths had occurred. By May, 1982, there had been five more such deaths. On May 6, 1982, the Chief of Police in Los Angeles prohibited the use of the bar-arm chokehold in any circumstances. A few days later, on May 12, 1982, the Board of Police Commissioners imposed a six-month moratorium on the use of the carotid-artery chokehold except under circumstances where deadly force is authorized.

Based on these events, on June 3, 1982, the City filed in this Court a Memorandum Suggesting a Question of Mootness, reciting the facts but arguing that the case was not moot.

Lyons [argues] . . . that in light of changed conditions, an injunctive decree is now unnecessary because he is no longer subject to a threat of injury. He urges that the preliminary injunction should be vacated. The City, on the other hand, while acknowledging that subsequent events have significantly changed the posture of this case, again asserts that the case is not moot because the moratorium is not permanent and may be lifted at any time.

We agree with the City that the case is not moot, since the moratorium by its terms is not permanent. Intervening events have not "irrevocably eradicated the effects of the alleged violation." We nevertheless hold, for another reason, that the federal courts are without jurisdiction to entertain Lyons' claim for injunctive relief.

It goes without saying that those who seek to invoke the jurisdiction of the federal courts must satisfy the threshold requirement imposed by Article III of the Constitution by alleging an actual case or controversy. Plaintiffs must demonstrate a "personal stake in the outcome" in order to "assure that concrete adverseness which sharpens the presentation of issues" necessary for the proper resolution of constitutional questions. Abstract injury is not enough. The plaintiff must show that he "has sustained or is immediately in danger of sustaining some direct injury" as the result of the challenged official conduct and the injury or threat of injury must be both "real and immediate," not "conjectural" or "hypothetical."

In *O'Shea v. Littleton*, 414 U.S. 488 (1974), we dealt with a case brought by a class of plaintiffs claiming that they had been subjected to discriminatory enforcement of the criminal law. Among other things, a county magistrate and judge were accused of discriminatory conduct in various respects, such as sentencing members of plaintiff's class more harshly than other defendants. . . . Although it was claimed in that case that particular members of the plaintiff class had actually suffered from the alleged unconstitutional practices, we observed that "[p]ast exposure to illegal conduct does not in itself show a present case or controversy regarding injunctive relief . . . if unaccompanied by any continuing, present adverse effects." Past wrongs were evidence bearing on "whether there is a real and immediate threat of repeated injury." But the prospect of future injury rested "on the likelihood that [plaintiffs] will again be arrested for and charged with violations of the criminal law and will again be subjected to bond proceedings, trial, or sentencing before petitioners." The most that could be said for plaintiffs' standing was "that *if* [plaintiffs] proceed to violate an unchallenged law and *if* they are charged, held to answer, and tried in any proceedings before petitioners, they will be subjected to the discriminatory practices that petitioners are alleged to have followed." We could not find a case or controversy in those circumstances: the threat to the plaintiffs was not "sufficiently real and immediate to show an existing controversy simply because they anticipate violating lawful criminal statutes and being tried for their offenses. . . . " It was to be assumed "that [plaintiffs] will conduct their activities within the law and so avoid prosecution and conviction as well as exposure to the challenged course of conduct said to be followed by [the government]."

We further observed that case or controversy considerations "obviously shade into those determining whether the complaint states a sound basis for equitable relief," and went on to hold that even if the complaint presented an existing case or controversy, an adequate basis for equitable relief against [the government] had not been demonstrated:

> [Plaintiffs] have failed, moreover, to establish the basic requisites of the issuance of equitable relief in these circumstances — the likelihood of substantial and immediate irreparable injury, and the inadequacy of remedies at law. We have already canvassed the necessarily conjectural nature of the threatened injury to which [plaintiffs] are allegedly subjected. And if any of the [plaintiffs] are ever prosecuted and face trial, or if they are illegally sentenced, there are available state and federal procedures which could provide relief from the wrongful conduct alleged.

Another relevant decision for present purposes is *Rizzo v. Goode*, 423 U.S. 362 (1976), a case in which plaintiffs alleged widespread illegal and unconstitutional police conduct aimed at minority citizens and against City residents in general. The Court reiterated the holding in *O'Shea* that past wrongs do not in themselves amount to that real and immediate threat of injury necessary to make out a case or controversy. The claim of injury rested upon "what one or a small, unnamed minority of policemen might do to them in the future because of that unknown policeman's perception" of departmental procedures. This hypothesis was "even more attenuated than those allegations of future injury found insufficient in *O'Shea* to warrant [the] invocation of federal jurisdiction." The Court also held that plaintiffs' showing at trial of a relatively few instances of violations by individual police officers, without any showing of a deliberate policy on behalf of the named defendants, did not provide a basis for equitable relief.

No extension of *O'Shea* and *Rizzo* is necessary to hold that respondent Lyons has failed to demonstrate a case or controversy with the City that would justify the equitable relief sought.[29] Lyons' standing to seek the injunction requested depended on whether he was likely to suffer future injury from the use of the chokeholds by police officers. Count V of the complaint alleged the traffic stop and choking incident five months before. That Lyons may have been illegally choked by the police on October 6, 1976, while presumably affording Lyons standing to claim damages against the individual officers and perhaps against the City, does nothing to establish a real and immediate threat that he would again be stopped for a traffic violation, or for any other offense, by an officer or officers who would illegally choke him into unconsciousness without any provocation or resistance on his part. The additional allegation in the complaint that the police in Los Angeles routinely apply chokeholds in situations where they are not threatened by the use of deadly force falls far short of the allegations that would be necessary to establish a case or controversy between these parties.

---

[29] [n.6] The City states in its brief that . . . "the parties agreed and advised the district court that [Lyons's] damages claim could be severed from his effort to obtain equitable relief." [Lyons] does not suggest otherwise. This case, therefore, as it came to us, is on all fours with *O'Shea* and should be judged as such.

In order to establish an actual controversy in this case, Lyons would have had not only to allege that he would have another encounter with the police but also to make the incredible assertion either, (1) that *all* police officers in Los Angeles *always* choke any citizen with whom they happen to have an encounter, whether for the purpose of arrest, issuing a citation or for questioning or, (2) that the City ordered or authorized police officers to act in such manner. Although Count V alleged that the City authorized the use of the control holds in situations where deadly force was not threatened, it did not indicate why Lyons might be realistically threatened by police officers who acted within the strictures of the City's policy. If, for example, chokeholds were authorized to be used only to counter resistance to an arrest by a suspect, or to thwart an effort to escape, any future threat to Lyons from the City's policy or from the conduct of police officers would be no more real than the possibility that he would again have an encounter with the police and that either he would illegally resist arrest or detention or the officers would disobey their instructions and again render him unconscious without any provocation.[30]

Under *O'Shea* and *Rizzo*, these allegations were an insufficient basis to provide a federal court with jurisdiction to entertain Count V of the complaint.

[E]ven assuming that Lyons would again be stopped for a traffic or other violation in the reasonably near future, it is untenable to assert, and the complaint made no such allegation, that strangleholds are applied by the Los Angeles police to every citizen who is stopped or arrested regardless of the conduct of the person stopped. We cannot agree that the "odds," that Lyons would not only again be stopped for a traffic violation but would also be subjected to a chokehold without any provocation whatsoever are sufficient to make out a federal case for equitable relief. We note that five months elapsed between October 6, 1976, and the filing of the complaint, yet there was no allegation of further unfortunate encounters between Lyons and the police. Of course, it may be that among the countless encounters between the police and the citizens of a great city such as Los Angeles, there will be certain instances in which strangleholds will be illegally applied and injury and death unconstitutionally inflicted on the victim. As we have said, however, it is no more than conjecture to suggest that in every instance of a traffic stop, arrest, or other encounter between the police and a citizen, the police will act unconstitutionally and inflict injury without provocation or legal excuse. And it is surely no more than speculation to assert either that Lyons himself will again be involved in one of those unfortunate instances, or that he will be arrested in the future and provoke the use of a chokehold by resisting arrest, attempting to escape, or threatening deadly force or serious bodily injury.

The Court of Appeals also asserted that Lyons "had a live and active claim" against the City "if only for a period of a few seconds" while the stranglehold was being applied to him and that for two reasons the claim had not become moot so as to disentitle Lyons

---

[30] [n.7] The centerpiece of Justice Marshall's dissent is that Lyons had standing to challenge the City's policy because to recover damages he would have to prove that what allegedly occurred on October 6, 1976, was pursuant to City authorization. We agree completely that for Lyons to succeed in his damages action, it would be necessary to prove that what happened to him — that is, as alleged, he was choked without any provocation or legal excuse whatsoever — was pursuant to a City policy. For several reasons, however, it does not follow that Lyons had standing to seek the injunction prayed for in Count V. First, Lyons['s] alleg[ation was that the City authorized] the use of chokeholds "in situations where [the officers] are threatened by far less than deadly force." This is not equivalent to the unbelievable assertion that the City either orders or authorizes application of the chokeholds where there is no resistance or other provocation. . . . [E]ven if the complaint must be read as containing an allegation that officers are authorized to apply the chokeholds where there is no resistance or other provocation, it does not follow that Lyons has standing to seek an injunction against the application of the restraint holds in situations that he has not experienced, as for example, where the suspect resists arrest or tries to escape but does not threaten the use of deadly force. . . . [I]n any event, to have a case or controversy with the City that could sustain Count V, Lyons would have to credibly allege that he faced a realistic threat from the future application of the City's policy. Justice Marshall nowhere confronts this requirement — the necessity that Lyons demonstrate that he, himself, will not only again be stopped by the police but will be choked without any provocation or legal excuse.

to injunctive relief: First, because under normal rules of equity, a case does not become moot merely because the complained of conduct has ceased; and second, because Lyons' claim is "capable of repetition but evading review" and therefore should be heard. We agree that Lyons had a live controversy with the City. Indeed, he still has a claim for damages against the City that appears to meet all Article III requirements. Nevertheless, the issue here is not whether that claim has become moot but whether Lyons meets the preconditions for asserting an injunctive claim in a federal forum. The equitable doctrine that cessation of the challenged conduct does not bar an injunction is of little help in this respect, for Lyons' lack of standing does not rest on the termination of the police practice but on the speculative nature of his claim that he will again experience injury as the result of that practice even if continued.

The rule that a claim does not become moot where it is capable of repetition, yet evades review, is likewise inapposite. Lyons' claim that he was illegally strangled remains to be litigated in his suit for damages; in no sense does that claim "evade" review. Furthermore, the capable-of-repetition doctrine applies only in exceptional situations, and generally only where the named plaintiff can make a reasonable showing that he will again be subjected to the alleged illegality. *DeFunis v. Odegaard*, 416 U.S. 312 (1974). As we have indicated, Lyons has not made this demonstration. . . . There was no finding that Lyons faced a real and immediate threat of again being illegally choked. The City's policy was described as authorizing the use of the strangleholds "under circumstances where no one is threatened with death or grievous bodily harm." That policy was not further described, but the record before the court contained the department's existing policy with respect to the employment of chokeholds. Nothing in that policy, contained in a Police Department manual, suggests that the chokeholds, or other kinds of force for that matter, are authorized absent some resistance or other provocation by the arrestee or other suspect. On the contrary, police officers were instructed to use chokeholds only when lesser degrees of force do not suffice and then only "to gain control of a suspect who is violently resisting the officer or trying to escape."

Lyons fares no better if it be assumed that his pending damages suit affords him Article III standing to seek an injunction as a remedy for the claim arising out of the October 1976 events. The equitable remedy is unavailable absent a showing of irreparable injury, a requirement that cannot be met where there is no showing of any real or immediate threat that the plaintiff will be wronged again — a "likelihood of substantial and immediate irreparable injury." The speculative nature of Lyons' claim of future injury requires a finding that this prerequisite of equitable relief has not been fulfilled.

Nor will the injury that Lyons allegedly suffered in 1976 go unrecompensed; for that injury, he has an adequate remedy at law. Contrary to the view of the Court of Appeals, it is not at all "difficult" under our holding "to see how anyone can ever challenge police or similar administrative practices." The legality of the violence to which Lyons claims he was once subjected is at issue in his suit for damages and can be determined there.

Absent a sufficient likelihood that he will again be wronged in a similar way, Lyons is no more entitled to an injunction than any other citizen of Los Angeles; and a federal court may not entertain a claim by any or all citizens who no more than assert that certain practices of law enforcement officers are unconstitutional.[31]

---

[31] [Editor's note: Justice White also observed that "state courts need not impose the same standing or remedial requirements that govern federal court proceedings. The individual states may permit their courts to use injunctions to oversee the conduct of law enforcement authorities on a continuing basis."]

JUSTICE MARSHALL, with whom JUSTICE BRENNAN, JUSTICE BLACKMUN and JUSTICE STEVENS join, dissenting.

The District Court found that the City of Los Angeles authorizes its police officers to apply life-threatening chokeholds to citizens who pose no threat of violence, and that . . . Adolph Lyons, was subjected to such a chokehold. The Court today holds that a federal court is without power to enjoin the enforcement of the City's policy, no matter how flagrantly unconstitutional it may be. Since no one can show that he will be choked in the future, no one — not even a person who, like Lyons, has almost been choked to death — has standing to challenge the continuation of the policy. The City is free to continue the policy indefinitely as long as it is willing to pay damages for the injuries and deaths that result.

There is plainly a "case or controversy" concerning the constitutionality of the City's chokehold policy. The constitutionality of that policy is directly implicated by Lyons' claim for damages against the City. The complaint clearly alleges that the officer who choked Lyons was carrying out an official policy, and a municipality is liable under 42 U.S.C. § 1983 for the conduct of its employees only if they acted pursuant to such a policy. Lyons therefore has standing to challenge the City's chokehold policy and to obtain whatever relief a court may ultimately deem appropriate. None of our prior decisions suggests that his requests for particular forms of relief raise any additional issues concerning his standing.

Although the City instructs its officers that use of a chokehold does not constitute deadly force, since 1975 no less than 16 persons have died following the use of a chokehold by an LAPD police officer. Twelve have been Negro males. The evidence submitted to the District Court established that for many years it has been the official policy of the City to permit police officers to employ chokeholds in a variety of situations where they face no threat of violence. In reported "altercations" between LAPD officers and citizens the chokeholds are used more frequently than any other means of physical restraint. Between February 1975 and July 1980, LAPD officers applied chokeholds on at least 975 occasions, which represented more than three-quarters of the reported altercations.

Although there has been no occasion to determine the precise contours of the City's chokehold policy, the evidence submitted to the District Court provides some indications. LAPD training officer Terry Speer testified that an officer is authorized to deploy a chokehold whenever he "*feels* that there's about to be a bodily attack made on him." A training bulletin states that "[c]ontrol holds . . . allow officers to subdue *any* resistance by the suspects." In the proceedings below the City characterized its own policy as authorizing the use of chokeholds "to gain control of a suspect who is violently resisting the officer *or trying to escape*," to "subdue *any* resistance by suspects," and to permit an officer, "where . . . resisted, but *not necessarily threatened with serious bodily harm or death*, . . . to subdue a suspect who forcibly resists an officer."

There is no basis for the Court's assertion that Lyons has failed to allege "that the City either orders or authorizes application of the chokeholds where there is no resistance or other provocation." . . . The Court apparently finds Lyons' complaint wanting because, although it alleges that he was choked without provocation and that the officers acted pursuant to an official policy, it fails to allege *in haec verba* that the City's policy authorizes the choking of suspects without provocation. I am aware of no case decided since the abolition of the old common law forms of action, and the Court cites none, that in any way supports this crabbed construction of the complaint. A federal court is capable of concluding for itself that two plus two equals four.

In sum, it is absolutely clear that Lyons' requests for damages and for injunctive relief call into question the constitutionality of the City's policy concerning the use of chokeholds. If he does not show that that policy is unconstitutional, he will be no more entitled to damages than to an injunction.

As the Court recognized in *O'Shea*, standing under Article III is established by an allegation of "threatened *or* actual injury." Because the plaintiffs in *O'Shea* [and] *Rizzo* . . . did not seek to redress past injury, their standing to sue depended entirely on the risk of future injury they faced. Apart from the desire to eliminate the possibility of future injury, the plaintiffs in those cases had no other personal stake in the outcome of the controversies.

By contrast, Lyons' request for prospective relief is coupled with his claim for damages based on past injury. In addition to the risk that he will be subjected to a chokehold in the future, Lyons has suffered past injury. Because he has a live claim for damages, he need not rely solely on the threat of future injury to establish his personal stake in the outcome of the controversy. In the cases relied on by the majority, the Court simply had no occasion to decide whether a plaintiff who has standing to litigate a dispute must clear a separate standing hurdle with respect to each form of relief sought.[32]

The Court's decision removes an entire class of constitutional violations from the equitable powers of a federal court. It immunizes from prospective equitable relief any policy that authorizes persistent deprivations of constitutional rights as long as no individual can establish with substantial certainty that he will be injured, or injured again, in the future. The Chief Justice asked in *Bivens v. Six Unknown Fed. Narcotics Agents*, 403 U.S. 388 (1971) (dissenting opinion), "what would be the judicial response to a police order authorizing 'shoot to kill' with respect to every fugitive?" His answer was that it would be "easy to predict our collective wrath and outrage." We now learn that wrath and outrage cannot be translated into an order to cease the unconstitutional practice, but only an award of damages to those who are victimized by the practice and live to sue and to the survivors of those who are not so fortunate. Under the view expressed by the majority today, if the police adopt a policy of "shoot to kill," or a policy of shooting one out of ten suspects, the federal courts will be powerless to enjoin its continuation.

NOTES

1. Injuries. Article III of the United States Constitution requires that federal courts confine themselves to "cases" or "controversies." This "standing" inquiry, according to the Supreme Court, divides into three questions: (1) whether the plaintiff has experienced "injury-in-fact"; (2) whether this injury is fairly traceable to the defendant's complained-of conduct; and (3) whether the injury is likely to be redressed by judicial intervention. *See Lujan v. Defenders of Wildlife*, 504 U.S. 555 (1992). Commentators have often noted that the indeterminate nature of this three-part test renders "the Court's standing jurisprudence one of the most manipulated, result-oriented arenas of constitutional law." Gene R. Nichol, Jr., *Standing for Privilege: The Failure of Injury Analysis*, 82 B.U. L. Rev. 301, 339 (2002).

Regarding the injury-in-fact requirement, several observations are in order:

  a) As made clear in *Lyons*, personal injuries (e.g., physical and emotional harm) qualify as injuries-in-fact for purposes of Article III;

---

[32] [n.17] The Court's reliance on *Rizzo* is misplaced for another reason. In *Rizzo* the Court concluded that the evidence presented at trial failed to establish an "affirmative link between the occurrence of various incidents of police misconduct and the adoption of any plan or policy by [defendants]." Because the misconduct being challenged was, in the Court's view, the result of the behavior of unidentified officials not named as defendants rather than any policy of the named defendants — the City Managing Director, and the Police Commissioner — the Court had "serious doubts" whether a case or controversy existed between the plaintiffs and those defendants. Here, by contrast, Lyons has clearly established a case or controversy between himself and the City concerning the constitutionality of the City's policy. In *Rizzo* the Court specifically distinguished those cases where a case or controversy was found to exist because of the existence of an official policy responsible for the past or threatened constitutional deprivations.

b) Economic harms satisfy Article III's injury-in-fact requirement. *See, e.g., General Motors Corp. v. Tracy*, 519 U.S. 278 (1997) (finding that economic injury to consumers of natural gas, who would have to pay higher prices because of state sales taxes, was sufficient to confer standing to pursue a challenge under the Dormant Commerce Clause);

c) Injury-in-fact includes interference with virtually any statutory or common-law rights, like those bound up in real estate, *see, e.g., Duke Power Co. v. Carolina Environmental Study Group*, 438 U.S. 59 (1978) (holding that potential thermal pollution of several lakes in the vicinity of a proposed nuclear power plant provided standing to surrounding property owners), and business. *See, e.g., Association of Data Processing Service Organizations, Inc. v. Camp*, 397 U.S. 150 (1970) (finding that the prospect of greater competition caused by a change in federal regulations was sufficient injury-in-fact);[33] and

d) Interference with one's constitutional rights, like the right to speak or the right to be treated equally, can give rise to a direct injury-in-fact. *See, e.g., Elrod v. Burns*, 427 U.S. 347 (1976) (Brennan, J.) ("[t]he loss of First Amendment freedoms, for even minimal periods of time, unquestionably constitutes irreparable injury"); *Northeastern Florida Chapter of Associated General Contractors of America v. City of Jacksonville*, 508 U.S. 656 (1993) (holding that the denial of equal treatment constitutes an actionable injury) (excerpted, *infra*).

As demonstrated by *Lyons*, however, the existence of a past injury-in-fact does not mean that a constitutional victim is entitled to prospective relief. Lyons's personal injuries presumably entitled him to monetary damages, but he was not entitled to an injunction. The converse can also prove true; one who suffered an injury-in-fact because of a constitutional violation might be entitled to forward-looking relief, but not monetary damages for the past wrong. In *Northeastern Florida Chapter of Associated General Contractors of America v. City of Jacksonville*, 508 U.S. 656 (1993) (excerpted, *infra*), for example, white-owned businesses challenged a Jacksonville minority set-aside program under the Equal Protection Clause. Even though the white-owned businesses could not demonstrate any economic injury — that is, they could not show that they would have been awarded any construction projects but for the set-aside program — the Court concluded they could win prospective relief:

> When the government erects a barrier that makes it more difficult for members of one group to obtain a benefit than it is for members of another group, a member of the former group seeking to challenge the barrier need not

---

[33] Note that where an alleged right (and concomitant injury-in-fact) is a creature of federal statute or regulation, the Supreme Court employs an additional "prudential" standing test to insure that the right falls within the "zone of interests" protected by the federal law. *See, e.g., Barlow v. Collins*, 397 U.S. 159 (1970) (finding that tenant farmers' alleged right not to be compelled to finance their farm needs through their landlords fell within the "zone of interests" protected by Food and Agriculture Act of 1965). This prudential analysis is most often encountered in the context of federal administrative law, since the Court has concluded that the "zone of interests" test was incorporated by language contained in the Administrative Procedure Act (APA), 5 U.S.C. § 702, which provides that "[a] person suffering legal wrong because of agency action, or adversely affected or aggrieved by agency action within the meaning of a relevant statute, is entitled to judicial review thereof." *See Association of Data Processing Service Organizations v. Camp*, 397 U.S. 150 (1970). Because § 1983 litigation involves primarily *constitutional* rights, the prudential "zone of interests" test has little application. *See Clarke v. Securities Industry Association*, 479 U.S. 388 (1987) ("The principal cases in which the 'zone of interest' test has been applied are those involving claims under the APA, and the test is most usefully understood as a gloss on the meaning of § 702."). *But see National Solid Waste Management Association v. Pine Belt Regional Solid Waste Management Authority*, 389 F.3d 491 (5th Cir. 2004) (applying a zone-of-interest test to a Dormant Commerce Clause challenge). Professor Mank has criticized the result in *Pine Belt*: "it makes little sense to impose 'zone of interests' barriers in constitutional cases because the Supreme Court has never provided a clear test for when a plaintiff has a relevant interest." Bradford C. Mank, *Prudential Standing and the Dormant Commerce Clause: Why the "Zone of Interests" Test Should Not Apply to Constitutional Cases*, 48 Ariz. L. Rev. 23, 24 (2006).

allege that he would have obtained the benefit but for the barrier in order to establish standing. The "injury in fact" in an equal protection case of this variety is the denial of equal treatment resulting from the imposition of the barrier, not the ultimate inability to obtain the benefit. And in the context of a challenge to a set-aside program, the "injury in fact" is the inability to compete on an equal footing in the bidding process, not the loss of a contract. To establish standing, therefore, a party challenging a set-aside program like Jacksonville's need only demonstrate that it is able and ready to bid on contracts and that a discriminatory policy prevents it from doing so on an equal basis.

As later made clear in *Texas v. Lesage*, 528 U.S. 18, 21 (1999) (discussed in Note 3 following *Stachura* in Section A, *supra*), however, the plaintiffs in *Northeastern Florida* could not have won money damages. In *Lesage*, the Supreme Court ruled that applicants who successfully challenged Texas's affirmative action program were not entitled to monetary damages because they could not show they would have been admitted to the educational program, but for the illegal admission policy, to which they had applied.

2. Threatened Injury. *Lyons* demonstrates that *threatened* injury can satisfy Article III, subject to two conditions: first, the actual injury itself (were it to occur) must otherwise satisfy Article III's injury-in-fact requirement; and second, the threat must be real and not merely speculation. *See Steffel v. Thompson*, 415 U.S. 452 (1974) (holding that a reasonable fear of prosecution confers standing) (discussed in Chapter 7.B., *infra*); *Doran v. Salem Inn, Inc.*, 422 U.S. 922 (1975) (same). "*Steffel* held that a reasonable threat of prosecution for conduct allegedly protected by the Constitution gives rise to a sufficiently ripe controversy." *Ohio Civil Rights Commission v. Dayton Christian Schools*, 477 U.S. 619 (1986) (excerpted in Chapter 7.B., *infra*). Following cases like *Steffel*, *Doran*, and *Dayton Christian Schools*, ripeness is not a particularly difficult hurdle to clear in constitutional litigation. Still, as *Lyons* demonstrates, a mere threat of future interaction with government officials is not sufficient to confer standing; there must be a reasonable likelihood of future harm.

3. Likelihood of Redress. *Lyons* focused on the third requirement of Article III, that is, whether judicial intervention would provide the victim (Lyons) any relief. As the opinion in *Lyons* demonstrates, this third prong sometimes overlaps the injury-in-fact requirement. Because Lyons' future injury was speculative, any relief ordered by a federal court was deemed unlikely to offer redress. The question in *Lyons* was whether the risk of Lyons's being choked again (the threatened injury) was sufficient to justify judicial intervention. If there was no chance of Lyons being choked again, then an injunction preventing the use of chokeholds would afford him no relief. The Court found the threat to Lyons speculative for two reasons: first, he could not demonstrate that he would be stopped or arrested by police in the future; and second, if stopped, he could not prove that he would be choked again. As for the former, the Court cited *O'Shea v. Littleton* for the assumption that people "will conduct their activities within the law and so avoid prosecution and conviction as well as exposure to the challenged course of conduct." Regarding the latter, in the absence of the incredible claim that "*all* police officers in Los Angeles *always* choke any citizen with whom they happen to have an encounter," or at least that "the City ordered or authorized police officers to act in such a manner," the Court concluded that Lyons could not establish a realistic threat of being choked again. The fact that police had a measure of discretion when (and when not) to use chokeholds, in effect, defeated Lyons's standing.

4. Multiple Past Encounters with Government Officials. The fact that Lyons was once arrested was relevant as an evidentiary matter to his cause for prospective relief, but was not by itself sufficient to establish a likelihood of future injury. Multiple arrests, however, have sometimes been found to establish a sufficient likelihood of future arrest to support Article III standing. *See, e.g., City of Houston v. Hill*, 482 U.S. 451 (1987) (finding standing to assert an overbreadth challenge to a criminal ordinance prohibiting interrupting a police officer where the plaintiff expressed a willingness to engage in the prohibited activity again and had "already been arrested four times under the ordinance").

5. Plaintiff's Inability to Control Future Encounters. Courts have also found *Lyons* inapplicable in cases where a plaintiff cannot control or determine future encounters with government officials. In *Lyons*, remember, the Court assumed that normal law-abiding citizens would seek to avoid arrest, minimizing the likelihood of future encounters with police. In *Honig v. Doe*, 484 U.S. 305 (1988), by contrast, an emotionally disabled child was allowed to prospectively challenge procedures employed by school authorities to remove disruptive students from the classroom. Because the nature of the child's disability prevented him from controlling his behavior, there was a greater likelihood of interaction with school officials and future removal from the classroom. *See also Church v. City of Huntsville*, 30 F.3d 1332 (11th Cir. 1994) (finding that homeless persons had standing to prospectively challenge a city policy of arrest and harassment "because the plaintiffs here are far more likely to have future encounters with the police than was Lyons"); *Jones v. City of Los Angeles*, 444 F.3d 1118 (9th Cir. 2006) (holding that homeless persons had standing to challenge a city's application of a criminal provision prohibiting sleeping in public).

6. Policies Mandating Challenged Action. Had Los Angeles mandated chokeholds in the context of every arrest, whether or not the suspect resisted, Lyons would have had a much better argument for Article III standing. A city policy clearly directing official action not only improves a plaintiff's probability of success against the city in an action at law for money damages, *see* Chapter 4, it also adds to the plaintiff's potential standing. Accordingly, courts sometimes distinguish *Lyons* as not involving a challenge to an established policy or procedure. *See, e.g., Lynch v. Baxley*, 744 F.2d 1452 (11th Cir. 1984) (finding that an involuntarily committed detainee had standing to prospectively challenge Alabama's commitment procedures and distinguishing *Lyons* and *O'Shea*, on the ground that in those cases "[t]here was a notable absence of allegations about the unconstitutionality of the statute on its face or as applied"). Where the constitutional challenge is directed at a law or policy, as opposed to an *ad hoc* decision (as in *Lyons*), "courts routinely entertain suits to declare statutes unconstitutional." DOUGLAS LAYCOCK, MODERN AMERICAN REMEDIES 498 (2d ed. 1994).

7. Third Party Standing. As a prudential matter, third parties are generally precluded from asserting the rights of others. *See, e.g., Allen v. Wright*, 468 U.S. 737 (1984) (one of the Court's "self-imposed limits . . . is a general prohibition on a litigant's raising another person's legal rights"). Exceptions exist in various contexts, such as health care providers asserting the rights of patients, *see, e.g., City of Revere v. Massachusetts General Hospital*, 463 U.S. 239 (1983), and schools asserting the rights of parents. *See, e.g., Pierce v. Society of Sisters*, 268 U.S. 510 (1925) (holding that a school may assert the Substantive Due Process right of parents to send children to private school). Assuming the third party has suffered some injury-in-fact — for instance, in *Pierce* the school's attendance and thus its revenue declined — the decision to allow the third party to assert the constitutional right of another depends on three factors: (1) the ability of the other party to bring suit to assert its own rights; (2) the nature of the relationship between the right holder and the third party; and (3) the extent to which the complained-of conduct materially impairs the right holder's exercise of its constitutional rights. *Cf. Sprint Communications v. APCC Services*, 128 S. Ct. 2531 (2008) (holding that an assignee of a legal claim is not a third party and thus is not governed by this prudential doctrine).

Elk Grove Unified School District v. Newdow, 542 U.S. 1 (2004), illustrates the flexible nature of this prudential inquiry. There, California law required that public elementary schools begin their days with "appropriate patriotic exercises," which can include recitation of the Pledge of Allegiance. Because of the Pledge's inclusion of the words, "under God," an unwed father (Newdow) of a public elementary school student sued under § 1983 and the First Amendment's Establishment Clause to enjoin this requirement. The Court, per Justice Stevens, sidestepped the merits of the case by holding that Newdow, who had "joint legal custody" of his daughter but who had not been awarded "next-friend" status by the California courts, did not have prudential standing to challenge the Pledge's use in California's public schools. Because the child's mother disagreed with the father over the propriety of the Pledge, the Court felt it best not to entertain the matter: "it is improper for the federal courts to entertain a claim by a plaintiff whose standing to sue is founded on family law rights that are in dispute when prosecution of the lawsuit may have an adverse effect on the person who is the source of the plaintiff's claimed standing. When hard questions of domestic relations are sure to affect the outcome, the prudent course is for the federal court to stay its hand rather than reach out to resolve a weighty question of federal constitutional law."[34]

The Court also used these prudential concerns in *Kowalski v. Tesmer*, 543 U.S. 125 (2004),[35] to deny standing to criminal defense attorneys who challenged Michigan's practice of denying appellate representation to indigents who had pleaded guilty. The Supreme Court, per the Chief Justice (Rehnquist), held that the attorneys, who only sought to represent indigents on appeal (but who had no actual clients, contrast *Caplin & Drysdale v. United States*, 491 U.S. 617 (1989) (holding that a lawyer can assert the constitutional rights of a client)), were not proper third-party plaintiffs. First, they had no existing relationships with any criminal defendants being denied appellate counsel. Second, the lawyers could not establish any " 'hindrance' to the indigents' advancing their own constitutional rights against the Michigan scheme."[36]

8. Taxpayer Standing. The Supreme Court held in *Frothingham v. Mellon*, 262 U.S. 447 (1923), that federal taxpayers cannot use that status as a basis for standing to challenge federal expenditures. Even though a taxpayer may suffer some injury-in-fact, it is one "shared with millions of others; is comparatively minute and indeterminate; and the effect upon future taxation . . . so remote . . . that no basis is afforded for an appeal to the preventive power of a court of equity." In *DaimlerChrysler Corp. v. Cuno*, 547 U.S. 332 (2006), the Court (in a unanimous opinion by the Chief Justice) extended *Frothingham* to preclude challenges directed at state tax credits by state taxpayers: "This logic is equally applicable to taxpayer challenges to expenditures that deplete the treasury, and to taxpayer challenges to so-called 'tax expenditures,' which reduce amounts available to the treasury by granting tax credits or exemptions." Moreover, the *Frothingham* "rationale for rejecting federal taxpayer standing applies with undiminished force to state taxpayers. . . . The allegations of injury that [the state taxpayers] make in their complaint furnish no better basis for finding standing than those made in the cases where federal taxpayer standing was denied."

The lone exception to the rule prohibiting federal-taxpayer standing was established in *Flast v. Cohen*, 392 U.S. 83 (1968), where the Court refused to extend *Frothingham* to suits brought under the Establishment Clause to enjoin congressional expenditures

---

[34] The Chief Justice (Rehnquist), joined by Justices O'Connor and Thomas, dissented on the standing issue. Reaching the merits, the Chief Justice concluded that California's use of the Pledge did not violate the Establishment Clause. Justice Scalia did not participate in the case.

[35] The Chief Justice also invoked the policies supporting federal abstention (which is discussed in Chapter 7.B., *infra*): "It is a fair inference that the attorneys and the three indigent plaintiffs that filed this § 1983 action did not want to allow the state process to take its course. Rather, they wanted a federal court to short-circuit the State's adjudication of this constitutional question. . . . The doctrine of *Younger v. Harris*, 401 U.S. 37 (1971) [excerpted in Chapter 7.B., *infra*], reinforces our federal scheme by preventing a state criminal defendant from asserting ancillary challenges to ongoing state criminal procedures in federal court. In this case, the three indigent criminal defendants who were originally plaintiffs in this § 1983 action were appropriately dismissed under *Younger*. . . . An unwillingness to allow the *Younger* principle to be thus circumvented is an additional reason to deny the attorneys third-party standing."

[36] The Supreme Court later in the Term ruled that Michigan's practice violated the equality principle laid down in *Douglas v. California*, 372 U.S. 353 (1963). *See Halbert v. Michigan*, 545 U.S. 605 (2005).

for religious purposes. The Court there reasoned that taxpayer standing was permissible because there existed "a logical nexus between the status asserted and the claim sought to be adjudicated." This "nexus," the Court stated, "has two aspects to it":

> First, the taxpayer must establish a logical link between that status and the type of legislative enactment attacked. Thus, a taxpayer will be a proper party to allege the unconstitutionality only of exercises of congressional power under the taxing and spending clause. . . . It will not be sufficient to allege an incidental expenditure of tax funds in the administration of an essentially regulatory statute. . . . Secondly, the taxpayer must establish a nexus between that status and the precise nature of the constitutional infringement alleged. Under this requirement, the taxpayer must show that the challenged enactment exceeds specific constitutional limitations imposed upon the exercise of the congressional taxing and spending power and not simply that the enactment is generally beyond the powers delegated to Congress by Art. I, § 8. When both nexuses are established, the litigant will have shown a taxpayer's stake in the outcome of the controversy and will be a proper and appropriate party to invoke a federal court's jurisdiction.

The Court has extended this rationale to state- and local-taxpayers challenging state and local expenditures under the Establishment Clause. *See School District of City of Grand Rapids v. Ball*, 473 U.S. 373 (1985) (finding "numerous cases in which we have adjudicated Establishment Clause challenges by state taxpayers to programs for aiding nonpublic schools"). Indeed, the Court in *Frothingham* recognized that because municipal taxpayers are different from federal-taxpayers — they are fewer and, the Court stated, have a "peculiar relation . . . to the [municipal] corporation" — they can sue local government as taxpayers in any constitutional setting. Local-taxpayer standing, however, cannot support challenges to *state* expenditures (outside the Establishment Clause context). *See DaimlerChrysler Corp. v. Cuno*, 547 U.S. 332 (2006) (holding that local taxpayers did not have standing to challenge state expenditures).[37]

9. Mootness. Assuming that Lyons possessed standing in the first instance to challenge the city's use of chokeholds, he faced an additional problem: mootness. The city had placed a moratorium on the use of chokeholds. The Supreme Court found that this *temporary* change did not moot Lyons's case. What if the change, however, was permanent? Consider the following case.

---

[37] What about federal *executive* expenditures that allegedly violate the Establishment Clause? Are they subject to taxpayer suits? In *Hein v. Freedom of Religion Foundation, Inc.*, 127 S. Ct. 2553 (2007), the Court (in a plurality opinion authored by Justice Alito and joined by the Chief Justice and Justice Kennedy) ruled that *Flast* does not apply to federal-taxpayer suits challenging *executive* expenditures under the Establishment Clause. Because "[n]o congressional legislation specifically authorized" the executive programs; "[r]ather, they were 'created entirely within the executive branch . . . by Presidential executive order,'" Justice Alito concluded that *Flast* did not control: "in the four decades since its creation, the *Flast* exception has largely been confined to its facts. We have declined to lower the taxpayer standing bar in suits alleging violations of any constitutional provision apart from the Establishment Clause." Because it had otherwise "consistently held that [a taxpayer's] interest is too generalized and attenuated to support Article III standing," Justice Alito refused to extend *Flast* to cover executive expenditures. Concurring in the result, Justice Scalia, joined by Justice Thomas, argued that *Flast* should be overturned: "*Flast* is wholly irreconcilable with the Article III restrictions on federal-court jurisdiction that this Court has repeatedly confirmed are embodied in the doctrine of standing." Justice Souter, joined by Justices Stevens, Ginsburg and Breyer, dissented.

NORTHEASTERN FLORIDA CHAPTER OF ASSOCIATED GENERAL CONTRACTORS OF AMERICA v. CITY OF JACKSONVILLE
Supreme Court of the United States
508 U.S. 656 (1993)

JUSTICE THOMAS delivered the opinion of the Court.

In 1984, Jacksonville enacted an ordinance entitled "Minority Business Enterprise Participation," which required that 10% of the amount spent on city contracts be set aside each fiscal year for so-called "Minority Business Enterprises" (MBE's). An MBE was defined as a business whose ownership was at least 51% "minority" or female, and a "minority" was in turn defined as a person who is or considers himself to be black, Spanish-speaking, Oriental, Indian, Eskimo, Aleut, or handicapped. Once projects were earmarked for MBE bidding by the city's chief purchasing officer, they were "deemed reserved for minority business enterprises only." Under the ordinance, "[m]athematical certainty [was] not required in determining the amount of the set aside," but the chief purchasing officer was required to "make every attempt to come as close as possible to the ten percent figure." The ordinance also provided for waiver or reduction of the 10% set-aside under certain circumstances.

[T]he Northeastern Florida Chapter of the Associated General Contractors of America (AGC), is an association of individuals and firms in the construction industry. [AGC] members do business in Jacksonville, and most of them do not qualify as MBE's under the city's ordinance. On April 4, 1989, [AGC] filed an action, pursuant to 42 U.S.C. § 1983, against the city . . . in the United States District Court for the Middle District of Florida. Claiming that Jacksonville's ordinance violated the Equal Protection Clause of the Fourteenth Amendment (both on its face and as applied), [AGC] sought declaratory and injunctive relief.

On October 27, 1992, 22 days after our grant of certiorari, the city repealed its MBE ordinance and replaced it with an ordinance entitled "African-American and Women's Business Enterprise Participation," which became effective the next day. This ordinance differs from the repealed ordinance in three principal respects. First, unlike the prior ordinance, which applied to women and members of seven different minority groups, the new ordinance applies only to women and blacks. Second, rather than a 10% "set aside," the new ordinance has established "participation goals" ranging from 5 to 16%, depending upon the type of contract, the ownership of the contractor, and the fiscal year in which the contract is awarded. Third, the new ordinance provides not one but five alternative methods for achieving the "participation goals." Which of these methods the city will use is decided on a "project by project basis," but one of them, the "Sheltered Market Plan," is (apart from the percentages) virtually identical to the prior ordinance's "set aside." Under this plan, certain contracts are reserved "for the exclusive competition" of certified black- and female-owned businesses. Claiming that there was no longer a live controversy with respect to the constitutionality of the repealed ordinance, respondents filed a motion to dismiss the case as moot on November 18, 1992.

[T]he mootness question is controlled by *City of Mesquite v. Aladdin's Castle, Inc.*, 455 U.S. 283 (1982), where we applied the "well settled" rule that "a defendant's voluntary cessation of a challenged practice does not deprive a federal court of its power to determine the legality of the practice." Although the challenged statutory language at issue in *City of Mesquite* had been eliminated while the case was pending in the Court of Appeals, we held that the case was not moot, because the defendant's "repeal of the objectionable language would not preclude it from reenacting precisely the same provision if the District Court's judgment were vacated."

This is an *a fortiori* case. There is no mere risk that Jacksonville will repeat its allegedly wrongful conduct; it has already done so. Nor does it matter that the new ordinance differs in certain respects from the old one. *City of Mesquite* does not stand for the proposition that it is only the possibility that the *selfsame* statute will be enacted that prevents a case from being moot; if that were the rule, a defendant could moot a case by repealing the challenged statute and replacing it with one that differs only in some insignificant respect. The gravamen of [AGC's] complaint is that its members are disadvantaged in their efforts to obtain city contracts. The new ordinance may disadvantage them to a lesser degree than the old one, but insofar as it accords preferential treatment to black- and female-owned contractors — and, in particular, insofar as its "Sheltered Market Plan" is a "set aside" by another name — it disadvantages them in the same fundamental way.[38]

We hold that the case is not moot.

JUSTICE O'CONNOR, with whom JUSTICE BLACKMUN joins, dissenting.

Earlier this Term, the Court reaffirmed the longstanding rule that a case must be dismissed as moot "if an event occurs [pending review] that makes it impossible for the court to grant 'any effectual relief whatever' to a prevailing party." *Church of Scientology of Cal. v. United States*, 506 U.S. 9 (1992). That principle applies to challenges to legislation that has expired or has been repealed, where the plaintiff has sought only prospective relief. If the challenged statute no longer exists, there ordinarily can be no real controversy as to its continuing validity, and an order enjoining its enforcement would be meaningless. In such circumstances, it is well settled that the case should be dismissed as moot.

The analysis varies when the challenged statute is amended or is repealed but replaced with new legislation. I agree with the Court that a defendant cannot moot a case simply by altering the law "in some insignificant respect." We have recognized, however, that material changes may render a case moot. *See, e.g., Princeton Univ. v. Schmid*, 455 U.S. 100 (1982) *(per curiam)* ("substantia[l] amend[ment]" of challenged regulation mooted controversy over its validity). It seems clear, for example, that when the challenged law is revised so as plainly to cure the alleged defect, or in such a way that the law no longer applies to the plaintiff, there is no live controversy for the Court to decide. Such cases functionally are indistinguishable from those involving outright repeal: Neither a declaration of the challenged statute's invalidity nor an injunction against its future enforcement would benefit the plaintiff, because the statute no longer can be said to affect the plaintiff.

A more difficult question is presented when, after we have granted review of a case, the challenged statute is replaced with new legislation that, while not obviously or completely remedying the alleged infirmity in the original act, is more narrowly drawn. The new law ultimately may suffer from the same legal defect as the old. But the statute may be sufficiently altered so as to present a substantially different controversy from the one the District Court originally decided. In such cases, this Court typically has exercised caution and treated the case as moot.

In *Diffenderfer v. Central Baptist Church of Miami, Inc.*, 404 U.S. 412 (1972) *(per curiam)*, for example, plaintiffs challenged a Florida statute that exempted from taxation certain church property used in part as a commercial parking lot as violative of the Religion Clauses of the First Amendment. After this Court noted probable

---

[38] [n.3] At bottom, the dissent differs with us only over the question whether the new ordinance is sufficiently similar to the repealed ordinance that it is permissible to say that the challenged conduct continues — or, as the dissent puts it, whether the ordinance has been "sufficiently altered so as to present a substantially different controversy from the one the District Court originally decided." We believe that the ordinance has not been "sufficiently altered"; the dissent disagrees. As for the merits of that disagreement, the short answer to the dissent's argument that this case is controlled by *Diffenderfer v. Central Baptist Church of Miami, Inc.*, 404 U.S. 412 (1972) *(per curiam)*, and *Fusari v. Steinberg*, 419 U.S. 379 (1975) — both of which predate *City of Mesquite* — is that the statutes at issue in those cases were changed substantially, and that there was therefore no basis for concluding that the challenged conduct was being repeated.

jurisdiction, the Florida Legislature repealed the statute and replaced it with new legislation exempting from taxation only church property used predominantly for religious purposes. Observing that the church property in question might not be entitled to an exemption under the new law, we concluded that the controversy before us was moot.

Recognizing that the plaintiffs might wish to challenge the newly enacted legislation, we declined simply to order dismissal, as is our practice when a controversy becomes moot pending a decision by this Court. *See United States v. Munsingwear, Inc.*, 340 U.S. 36 (1950). Instead, we vacated the lower court's judgment and remanded with leave to the plaintiffs to amend their pleadings.

The Court took a similar approach in *Fusari v. Steinberg*, 419 U.S. 379 (1975), in which plaintiffs challenged Connecticut's procedures for determining continuing eligibility for unemployment compensation. A three-judge District Court held that the scheme violated due process because it failed to provide an adequate hearing and because administrative review of the hearing examiner's decision took an unreasonably long time. After this Court noted probable jurisdiction, the state legislature amended the relevant statutes, establishing additional procedural protections at the hearing stage and altering the structure of administrative review to make it quicker and fairer. Because these changes "[might] alter significantly the character of the system considered by the District Court," and because it was unclear how the new procedures would operate, we vacated the lower court's judgment and remanded for reconsideration in light of the intervening changes in state law.

These precedents establish that, where a challenged statute is replaced with more narrowly drawn legislation pending our review, and the plaintiff seeks only prospective relief, we generally should decline to decide the case. The controversy with respect to the old statute is moot, because a declaration of its invalidity or an injunction against the law's future enforcement would not benefit the plaintiff. Where we cannot be sure how the statutory changes will affect the plaintiff's claims, dismissal avoids the possibility that our decision will prove advisory.

Like *Diffenderfer*, this case concerns a law that was repealed and replaced after this Court granted review. [AGC's] complaint requests only declaratory and injunctive relief from a set-aside ordinance that no longer exists.

The new ordinance clearly was written to remedy the constitutional defects that [AGC] alleged and the District Court found in the original program.

Whether or not the new ordinance survives scrutiny under the Fourteenth Amendment — a question on which I express no view — I cannot say that these changes are "insignificant" to [AGC's] equal protection claim. The majority avoids this difficulty by characterizing petitioner's complaint in the most general terms possible: "The gravamen of petitioner's complaint is that its members are disadvantaged in their efforts to obtain city contracts." We did not undertake such a generalized approach in *Diffenderfer* or our other cases involving more narrowly drawn statutory changes. There, as here, any challenge to the new law "presents a different case," and the proper course therefore is to decline to render a decision.

I believe the wiser course, and the one most consistent with our precedents, would be to follow *Diffenderfer*. On the authority of that case, I would vacate the Court of Appeals' judgment and remand to that court with instructions to remand the case to the District Court to permit the petitioner to challenge the new ordinance.

I also cannot agree with the majority's assertion that *City of Mesquite* "control[s]" this case. I understand *City of Mesquite* to have created a narrow exception to the general principles I have described — an exception that clearly is inapplicable here.

The plaintiff in *City of Mesquite* challenged a licensing ordinance governing coin-operated amusement establishments. One of the factors considered in determining whether to grant a license under the ordinance was whether the applicant has "connections with criminal elements." The District Court held that this phrase was unconstitutionally vague, and the Court of Appeals affirmed. While the case was pending before the Court of Appeals, however, the contested language was eliminated from the ordinance.

When the case came before us, we concluded that it need not be dismissed as moot. We relied on the voluntary-cessation doctrine, which provides that "a defendant's voluntary cessation of a challenged practice does not deprive a federal court of its power to determine the legality of the practice." If it did, defendants forever could avoid judicial review simply by ceasing the challenged practice, only to resume it after the case was dismissed. In such cases, we have said that the defendant, to establish mootness, bears a heavy burden of "demonstrat[ing] that there is no reasonable expectation that the wrong will be repeated." *United States v. W.T. Grant Co.*, 345 U.S. 629 (1953). In *City of Mesquite*, we decided to reach the merits of the plaintiff's claim because "the city's repeal of the objectionable language would not preclude it from reenacting precisely the same provision if the District Court's judgment were vacated." We expressly noted that the city in fact had announced an intention to do exactly that, just as it already had eliminated and then reinstated another aspect of the same ordinance in the course of the same litigation, obviously in response to prior judicial action. These circumstances made it virtually impossible to say that there was "no reasonable expectation" that the city would reenact the challenged language.

City of Mesquite did not purport to overrule the long line of cases in which we have found repeal of a challenged statute to moot the case. Significantly, we have not referred to the voluntary-cessation doctrine in any other case involving a statute repealed or materially altered pending review. The reason seems to me obvious. Unlike in *City of Mesquite*, in the ordinary case it is not at all reasonable to suppose that the legislature has repealed or amended a challenged law simply to avoid litigation and that it will reinstate the original legislation if given the opportunity. This is especially true where, as here, the law has been replaced — no doubt at considerable effort and expense — with a more narrowly drawn version designed to cure alleged legal infirmities. We ordinarily do not presume that legislative bodies act in bad faith. That is why, other than in *City of Mesquite*, we have not required the government to establish that it cannot be expected to reenact repealed legislation before we will dismiss the case as moot.

At most, I believe *City of Mesquite* stands for the proposition that the Court has discretion to decide a case in which the statute under review has been repealed or amended. The Court appropriately may render judgment where circumstances demonstrate that the legislature likely will reinstate the old law — which would make a declaratory judgment or an order enjoining the law's enforcement worthwhile. But such circumstances undoubtedly are rare.

NOTES

1. Changes to Challenged Policies and Practices. As illustrated by *Princeton University v. Schmid*, 455 U.S. 100 (1982), a substantial change to a challenged law can render a controversy moot. *See also* footnote 3 in *Northeastern Florida*. However, as made clear by both *Northeastern Florida* and *City of Mesquite v. Aladdin's Castle, Inc.*, 455 U.S. 283 (1982), voluntary cessation of allegedly unlawful conduct on the part of a governmental defendant need not render a controversy moot. Because the governmental defendant can return to its illegal practices once the case is dismissed, courts should be careful to consider the risk that cessation proves fleeting or temporary. Where the defendant has already enacted similar legislation, *see, e.g., Northeastern Florida*,[39] threatens to do so in the future, *see, e.g., City of Mesquite*, or

---

[39] Professor Girardeau Sprann criticizes *Northeastern Florida* on this point: "The voluntary cessation exception seems inapplicable to *Northeastern Florida*. Application of the exception might have made sense if

merely announces that it will not enforce a challenged policy, *see, e.g., City of Los Angeles v. Lyons* (excerpted, *supra*); *American Civil Liberties Union v. National Security Agency*, 493 F.3d 644 (6th Cir. 2007) (holding that government's announcement that it would no longer engage in electronic surveillance without the assistance of the FISA Court does not moot controversy), the controversy will most often not be rendered moot and can proceed to judgment.

What if the governmental defendant repeals a challenged policy and has not either enacted a similar measure, as in *Northeastern Florida*, or announced its intent to do so, as in *City of Mesquite*? In his concurring opinion in *City of Mesquite*, Justice White distinguished *Princeton University v. Schmid*, 455 U.S. 100 (1982), as a situation where the challenged regulations had been "substantially amended" and the defendant "gave no indication that it desired to return to the original regulatory scheme and would do so absent a judicial barrier." In contrast, "Mesquite 'has announced just such an intention.' . . . [I]t is on this basis that our disposition of the two cases is consistent." *See* Michael Ashton, Note, *Recovering Attorney's Fees with the Voluntary Cessation Exception to Mootness Doctrine After* Buckhannon Board and Care Home, Inc. v. West Virginia Department of Health and Human Resources, 2002 WIS. L. REV. 965, 988 (stating that the "Supreme Court has yet to hold, in a case in which the issue was squarely presented, that legislative repeal or amendment of a challenged law falls within the voluntary cessation exception").

In the absence of either an announced intention to re-enact a similar law or an actual re-enactment, most lower courts have refused to find continuing live controversies. *See, e.g., Worth v. Jackson*, 451 F.3d 854 (D.C. Cir. 2006) ("the Supreme Court has occasionally addressed challenges to laws no longer in force, but it has done so only when the statute or ordinance in question has been replaced by a substantially similar enactment, or where the governing body expressed an intent to re-enact the allegedly defective law"). In *Chemical Producers and Distributors Ass'n v. Helliker*, 463 F.3d 871 (9th Cir. 2006), for example, the court noted the confusion surrounding *City of Mesquite*'s and *Northeastern Florida*'s application, but stated: "we have been clear in refining the voluntary cessation exception for state legislative enactments that otherwise moot a controversy. In that circumstance the exception is narrow: 'A statutory change . . . is usually enough to render a case moot, even if the legislature possesses the power to reenact the statute after the lawsuit is dismissed. As a general rule, if a challenged law is repealed or expires, the case becomes moot. The exceptions to this general line of holdings are rare and typically involve situations where it is virtually certain that the repealed law will be reenacted.'" *See also D.H.L Associates v. O'Gorman*, 199 F.3d 50 (1st Cir. 1999) (applying *Diffenderfer* and finding controversy moot because the government had not expressed an intention to re-enact the challenged law). *See generally* Ashton, *supra*, at 988 ("[T]he lower courts have not followed the dicta in *City of Mesquite* and *Northeastern Florida*. Instead, they continue to hold that government action falls within the voluntary cessation exception only in exceptional circumstances.").

2. Attorney's Fees. Mootness can have profound consequences on the availability of plaintiffs' attorneys' ability to recover their fees from governmental defendants. As described more fully in Chapter 9.A., *infra*, attorney fee-shifting is a common practice in § 1983 litigation. To win attorney's fees from the losing defendant, however, the plaintiff must "prevail" on the merits. Mootness denies the plaintiff the opportunity to achieve this "prevailing party" status. If a case becomes moot in the District Court, the plaintiff cannot prevail and cannot force the defendant to pay its attorney's fees. Much of the litigation surrounding mootness today is a function of this attorney's fees problem.

---

there were some danger that the city of Jacksonville would re-institute the old set-aside program once the litigation was dismissed on mootness grounds. But there was no such danger." Girardeau A. Sprann, *Color-Coded Standing*, 80 CORNELL L. REV. 1422, 1443 (1995).

3. Mootness on Appeal. The event that allegedly mooted the challenger's case in *Northeastern Florida* occurred while the case was pending on appeal in the Supreme Court. What would the Supreme Court have done with the case had it agreed with the City and found the matter moot?

U.S. BANCORP MORTGAGE CO. v. BONNER MALL PARTNERSHIP
Supreme Court of the United States
513 U.S. 18 (1994)

JUSTICE SCALIA delivered the opinion of the Court.

The question in this case is whether appellate courts in the federal system should vacate civil judgments of subordinate courts in cases that are settled after appeal is filed or certiorari sought.

After we granted the petition [for certiorari] and received briefing on the merits, Bancorp and Bonner stipulated to . . . a settlement that mooted the case. Bancorp, however, also requested that we exercise our power under 28 U.S.C. § 2106 to vacate the judgment [against it entered by] the Court of Appeals. Bonner opposed the motion.

[Bonner] questions our power to entertain [Bancorp's] motion to vacate, suggesting that the limitations on the judicial power conferred by Article III, see U.S. Const., Art. III, § 1, "may, at least in some cases, prohibit an act of vacatur when no live dispute exists due to a settlement that has rendered a case moot." The statute that supplies the power of vacatur provides:

> The Supreme Court or any other court of appellate jurisdiction may affirm, modify, vacate, set aside or reverse any judgment, decree, or order of a court lawfully brought before it for review, and may remand the cause and direct the entry of such appropriate judgment, decree, or order, or require such further proceedings to be had as may be just under the circumstances.

28 U.S.C. § 2106.

Of course, no statute could authorize a federal court to decide the merits of a legal question not posed in an Article III case or controversy. For that purpose, a case must exist at all the stages of appellate review. But reason and authority refute the quite different notion that a federal appellate court may not take any action with regard to a piece of litigation once it has been determined that the requirements of Article III no longer are (or indeed never were) met. That proposition is contradicted whenever an appellate court holds that a district court lacked Article III jurisdiction in the first instance, vacates the decision, and remands with directions to dismiss. In cases that become moot while awaiting review, [Bonner's] logic would hold the Court powerless to award costs, or even to enter an order of dismissal.

Article III does not prescribe such paralysis. "If a judgment has become moot [while awaiting review], this Court may not consider its merits, but may make such disposition of the whole case as justice may require." *Walling v. James Reuter, Co., Inc.*, 321 U.S. 671 (1944). As with other matters of judicial administration and practice "reasonably ancillary to the primary, dispute-deciding function" of the federal courts, Congress may authorize us to enter orders necessary and appropriate to the final disposition of a suit that is before us for review.

The leading case on vacatur is *United States v. Munsingwear, Inc.*, 340 U.S. 36 (1950), in which the United States sought injunctive and monetary relief for violation of a price control regulation. The damages claim was held in abeyance pending a decision on the injunction. The District Court held that [Munsingwear's] prices complied with the regulations and dismissed the complaint. While the United States' appeal was pending, the commodity at issue was decontrolled; at [Munsingwear's] request, the case was dismissed as moot, a disposition in which the United States acquiesced. [Munsingwear] then obtained dismissal of the damages action on the ground of res judicata, and we took the case to review that ruling. The United States protested the unfairness of according preclusive effect to a decision that it had tried to appeal but could not. We saw no such unfairness, reasoning that the United States should have asked the Court of Appeals to vacate the District Court's decision before the appeal was dismissed. We stated that "[t]he established practice of the Court in dealing with a civil case from a court in the federal system which has become moot while on its way here or pending our decision on the merits is to reverse or vacate the judgment below and remand with a direction to dismiss." We explained that vacatur "clears the path for future relitigation of the issues between the parties and eliminates a judgment, review of which was prevented through happenstance." Finding that the United States had "slept on its rights," we affirmed.

The parties in the present case agree that vacatur must be decreed for those judgments whose review is, in the words of *Munsingwear*, "prevented through happenstance" — that is to say, where a controversy presented for review has "become moot due to circumstances unattributable to any of the parties." They also agree that vacatur must be granted where mootness results from the unilateral action of the party who prevailed in the lower court. The contested question is whether courts should vacate where mootness results from a settlement.

The principles that have always been implicit in our treatment of moot cases counsel against extending *Munsingwear* to settlement. From the beginning we have disposed of moot cases in the manner "'most consonant to justice' . . . in view of the nature and character of the conditions which have caused the case to become moot." The principal condition to which we have looked is whether the party seeking relief from the judgment below caused the mootness by voluntary action. The reference to "happenstance" in *Munsingwear* must be understood as an allusion to this equitable tradition of vacatur. A party who seeks review of the merits of an adverse ruling, but is frustrated by the vagaries of circumstance, ought not in fairness be forced to acquiesce in the judgment.⁴⁰ The same is true when mootness results from unilateral action of the party who prevailed below. Where mootness results from settlement, however, the losing party has voluntarily forfeited his legal remedy by the ordinary processes of appeal or certiorari, thereby surrendering his claim to the equitable remedy of vacatur. The judgment is not unreviewable, but simply unreviewed by his own choice. The denial of vacatur is merely one application of the principle that "[a] suitor's conduct in relation to the matter at hand may disentitle him to the relief he seeks."

In these respects the case stands no differently than it would if jurisdiction were lacking because the losing party failed to appeal at all. In *Karcher v. May*, 484 U.S. 72 (1987), two state legislators, acting in their capacities as presiding officers of the legislature, appealed from a federal judgment that invalidated a state statute on constitutional grounds. After the jurisdictional statement was filed the legislators lost their posts, and their successors in office withdrew the appeal. Holding that we lacked jurisdiction for want of a proper appellant, we dismissed. The legislators then argued that the judgments should be vacated under *Munsingwear*. But we denied the request, noting that "[t]his controversy did not become moot due to circumstances unattributable to any of the parties. The controversy ended when the losing party — the [State] Legislature — declined to pursue its appeal. Accordingly, the *Munsingwear* procedure is inapplicable to this case." So, too, here.

---

⁴⁰ [n.3] We thus stand by *Munsingwear*'s dictum that mootness by happenstance provides sufficient reason to vacate. Whether that principle was correctly applied to the circumstances of that case is another matter. The suit for injunctive relief in *Munsingwear* became moot on appeal because the regulations sought to be enforced by the United States were annulled by Executive Order. We express no view on *Munsingwear*'s implicit conclusion that repeal of administrative regulations cannot fairly be attributed to the Executive Branch when it litigates in the name of the United States.

It is true, of course, that [Bonner] agreed to the settlement that caused the mootness. [Bancorp] argues that vacatur is therefore fair to [Bonner], and seeks to distinguish our prior cases on that ground. But that misconceives the emphasis on fault in our decisions. That the parties are jointly responsible for settling may in some sense put them on even footing, but [Bancorp's] case needs more than that. [Bonner] won below. It is [Bancorp's] burden, as the party seeking relief from the status quo of the appellate judgment, to demonstrate not merely equivalent responsibility for the mootness, but equitable entitlement to the extraordinary remedy of vacatur. [Bancorp's] voluntary forfeiture of review constitutes a failure of equity that makes the burden decisive, whatever [Bonner's] share in the mooting of the case might have been.

As always when federal courts contemplate equitable relief, our holding must also take account of the public interest. "Judicial precedents are presumptively correct and valuable to the legal community as a whole. They are not merely the property of private litigants and should stand unless a court concludes that the public interest would be served by a vacatur." Congress has prescribed a primary route, by appeal as of right and certiorari, through which parties may seek relief from the legal consequences of judicial judgments. To allow a party who steps off the statutory path to employ the secondary remedy of vacatur as a refined form of collateral attack on the judgment would — quite apart from any considerations of fairness to the parties — disturb the orderly operation of the federal judicial system. *Munsingwear* establishes that the public interest is best served by granting relief when the demands of "orderly procedure" cannot be honored; we think conversely that the public interest requires those demands to be honored when they can.

A final policy justification urged by [Bancorp] is the facilitation of settlement, with the resulting economies for the federal courts. But while the availability of vacatur may facilitate settlement after the judgment under review has been rendered and certiorari granted (or appeal filed), it may deter settlement at an earlier stage. Some litigants, at least, may think it worthwhile to roll the dice rather than settle in the district court, or in the court of appeals, if, but only if, an unfavorable outcome can be washed away by a settlement-related vacatur. And the judicial economies achieved by settlement at the district-court level are ordinarily much more extensive than those achieved by settlement on appeal. We find it quite impossible to assess the effect of our holding, either way, upon the frequency or systemic value of settlement.

Although the case before us involves only a motion to vacate, by reason of settlement, the judgment of a court of appeals (with, of course, the consequential vacation of the underlying judgment of the district court), it is appropriate to discuss the relevance of our holding to motions at the court-of-appeals level for vacatur of district-court judgments. Some opinions have suggested that vacatur motions at that level should be more freely granted, since district-court judgments are subject to review as of right. Obviously, this factor does not affect the primary basis for our denying vacatur. Whether the appellate court's seizure of the case is the consequence of an appellant's right or of a petitioner's good luck has no bearing upon the lack of equity of a litigant who has voluntarily abandoned review. If the point of the proposed distinction is that district-court judgments, being subject to review as of right, are more likely to be overturned and hence presumptively less valid: We again assert the inappropriateness of disposing of cases, whose merits are beyond judicial power to consider, on the basis of judicial estimates regarding their merits. Moreover, . . . the reversal rate for cases in which this Court grants certiorari (a precondition for our vacatur) is over 50% — more than double the reversal rate for appeals to the courts of appeals.

We hold that mootness by reason of settlement does not justify vacatur of a judgment under review. This is not to say that vacatur can never be granted when mootness is produced in that fashion. As we have described, the determination is an equitable one, and exceptional circumstances may conceivably counsel in favor of such a course. It should be clear from our discussion, however, that those exceptional circumstances do not include the mere fact that the settlement agreement provides for vacatur — which neither diminishes the voluntariness of the abandonment of review nor alters any of the policy considerations we have discussed.

NOTES

1. Vacatur. A case that becomes moot in a district court is dismissed for want of subject matter jurisdiction. A case that becomes moot on appeal forces an additional question:[41] what should the appellate court do with the judgment (or order) below?[42] *See* RICHARD H. FALLON, ET AL., HART AND WECHSLER'S THE FEDERAL COURTS AND THE FEDERAL SYSTEM 224–25 (4th ed. 1996). Assuming mootness, a federal appellate court will not have the constitutional authority to address the merits of the case. That much is understood. Disposition of the lower court's judgment — which can carry with it important legal ramifications, such as claim preclusion, *see* Chapter 8.A., *infra*, value as legal precedent, *see* Note 5, *infra*, costs, *see, e.g., Slagenweit v. Slagenweit*, 63 F.3d 719 (8th Cir. 1995) (observing that vacatur following mootness by happenstance should result in the denial of costs), and attorney-fee-shifting, *see* Note 10, *infra*; Chapter 9.A., *infra* — depends on the reasons the case became moot while on appeal:

a) Where mootness is caused by happenstance, that is, through no fault of either party, the lower court's judgment must be vacated; *see Arizonans for Official English v. Arizona*, 520 U.S. 43 (1997) ("When a civil case becomes moot . . . '[t]he established practice . . . is to reverse or vacate the judgment below and remand with a direction to dismiss.' "); *Chemical Producers and Distributors Association v. Helliker*, 463 F.3d 871 (9th Cir. 2006) ("Where mootness was caused not by the 'voluntary action' of the party seeking vacatur but by 'happenstance' or the 'vagaries of circumstance,' we direct vacatur."); *Dow Jones, Inc. v. Kaye*, 256 F.3d 1251 (11th Cir. 2001) ("where a case becomes moot after the district court enters judgment but before the appellate court has issued a decision, the appellate court must dismiss the appeal, vacate the district court's judgment, and remand with instructions to dismiss as moot");

b) Where mootness is caused by the conduct of the losing party in the court below (the appellant or petitioner), the judgment is ordinarily allowed to stand, *see, e.g., Karcher v. May*, 484 U.S. 72 (1987) ("The controversy ended when the losing party — the New Jersey Legislature — declined to pursue its appeal."); *but see Arizonans for Official English v. Arizona*, 520 U.S. 43 (1997) (finding an extraordinary reason for vacating the lower courts' judgments even though the state, which had lost below, appeared to acquiesce in the judgment and forfeit its appeal) (discussed in Note 8, *infra*); *Wyoming v. U.S. Dept. of Agriculture*,

---

[41] The assumption here is that the case is proceeding in the federal court system. Because state courts are not bound by Article III of the United States Constitution, "the decision as to whether state courts can render advisory opinions is a state law issue, not a federal question." 1 RONALD D. ROTUNDA & JOHN E. NOWAK, TREATISE ON CONSTITUTIONAL LAW — SUBSTANCE & PROCEDURE § 2.13 (3d ed. 1999). "Consequently, if the case, originally brought in the state court, becomes moot on appeal to the U.S. Supreme Court, or the U.S. Supreme Court cannot take the appeal because it determines that there never was a 'case or controversy' within the meaning of Article III of the Constitution, then the U.S. Supreme Court will dismiss the appeal, but it will not require the state court to vacate the judgment or dismiss the complaint." *Id.*

[42] The *vacatur* principles spelled out in *Bonner Mall* apply equally to orders as well as judgments. *See Anderson v. Green*, 513 U.S. 1995 (1995) (applying *Bonner Mall* to vacate a district court's *order* (short of judgment) granting preliminary injunctive relief); *Select Milk Producers v. Johanns*, 400 F.3d 939 (D.C. Cir. 2005) ("when a losing party is blocked from appealing an adverse judgment or order because the case becomes moot due to happenstance, the court will vacate the disputed judgment or order"). Courts have vacated preliminary orders (both awarding and denying relief) that have been mooted by intervening events. *See, e.g., Watkins v. Mabus*, 502 U.S. 954 (1991) (per curiam) (vacating a District Court order based on a claim to preliminary relief in an election case); *Van Wie v. Pataki*, 267 F.3d 109 (2d Cir. 2001) (vacating a District Court order refusing preliminary relief following an intervening election).

414 U.S. 1207 (10th Cir. 2005) (vacating a lower court's preliminary injunction even though the government — which lost below — mooted the order on appeal), the theory being that the losing party has voluntarily relinquished its right to appeal;

c) Where mootness is caused by the conduct of the prevailing party below (the appellee or respondent), the lower court's judgment must be vacated, the theory being that the winning party should not be allowed to prevent the loser's appeal; *see, e.g., Shelby v. Superperformance Intern, Inc.*, 435 F.3d 42 (1st Cir. 2006) ("Vacatur is ordinarily appropriate when mootness results from vagarious circumstance or the unilateral act of the prevailing party."); and

d) Where mootness is caused by joint conduct of the appellant/petitioner and appellee/respondent, such as a settlement, the judgment below will not be vacated in the absence of "exceptional circumstances." *See Bonner Mall* (excerpted *supra*). *But see Wal-Mart Sores v. Rodriguez*, 322 F.3d 747 (1st Cir. 2003) (vacating a preliminary injunction even though the parties settled on appeal). Note that the Supreme Court in *Bonner Mall* concluded that "those exceptional circumstances do not include the mere fact that the settlement agreement provides for vacatur."[43]

2. Happenstance. What constitutes happenstance? Consider three examples from the Supreme Court: In *Karcher v. May*, 484 U.S. 72 (1987), two state legislative leaders (Karcher and Orechio) sought to appeal an adverse ruling declaring unconstitutional a New Jersey law mandating a moment of silence in school. While their appeal was pending, Karcher and Orechio were replaced in office; the new legislative leaders refused to press the appeal. The Supreme Court concluded that "[t]his case did not become unreviewable when Karcher and Orechio left office. Rather, under Federal Rule of Appellate Procedure 43(c)(1), the authority of Karcher and Orechio to pursue the appeal on behalf of the legislature passed to their successors in office." Consequently, "[t]his controversy did not become moot due to circumstances unattributable to any of the parties. The controversy ended when the losing party — the New Jersey Legislature — declined to pursue its appeal." Because the appeal's demise was attributable to the losing party, it was not a matter of happenstance and would not support vacatur.

In *Anderson v. Green*, 513 U.S. 557 (1995), California officials appealed a District Court judgment ruling California's durational residence requirement for welfare benefits unconstitutional. While that appeal was pending, the Court of Appeals in a separate proceeding ruled that the federal government had improperly approved the California program. Because of this separate ruling, California's requirement could not take effect. The Supreme Court concluded that the case was moot and the District Court's judgment in *Anderson* had to be vacated: "in deciding whether to disturb prior judgments in a case rendered nonjusticiable, we have inquired, pivotally, 'whether the party seeking relief from the judgment below caused the [nonjusticiability] by voluntary action.' Unlike settlement . . . California's loss of the federal approval necessary to implement its program was not voluntary."

In *Harper ex rel. Harper v. Poway Unified School District*, 127 S. Ct. 1484 (2007), a student was denied a preliminary injunction against a school district that disciplined him because of a controversial t-shirt. After the Ninth Circuit affirmed the denial of preliminary relief, *see* 445 F.3d 1166 (9th Cir. 2006), the District Court rendered final judgment. The Supreme Court in a memorandum opinion granted certiorari to vacate

---

[43] Note that these same considerations can be applied in the District Court under Rule 60(b) — which authorizes District Courts to order relief from final judgments — when mootness comes after final judgment but before appeal. *See Valero Terrestrial Corp. v. Paige*, 211 F.3d 112 (4th Cir. 2000) (observing that a court of appeals is also free to remand for the district court to consider vacatur under Rule 60(b)). According to the Fourth Circuit in *Paige*, the standards for vacatur are identical whether employed in the District Court or the Court of Appeals.

the Ninth Circuit's opinion. The Supreme Court found that the District Court's final judgment not only mooted the plaintiff's claim to preliminary relief, it was happenstance that required vacatur down the line.

Lower courts tend to agree that an intervening election — to the extent it moots election challenges — constitutes happenstance that requires vacatur. Thus, in *Van Wie v. Pataki*, 267 F.3d 109 (2d Cir. 2001), the Second Circuit vacated a District Court's dismissal of a constitutional challenge to New York's primary election restrictions because the intervening election was not the fault of the challengers.[44] Student's graduations that moot challenges to school policies are also commonly treated as happenstance. *See, e.g., Murphy v. Fort Worth Independent School District*, 334 F.3d 470 (5th Cir. 2003) (per curiam) (vacating because the losing party's graduation was "happenstance").

3. Death. The death of a governmental defendant in a § 1983 case seeking only prospective relief does not ordinarily matter. Where a governmental defendant (sued in her official capacity) passes away, Federal Rule of Appellate Procedure 43(c)(2) states that "the action does not abate" and directs the automatic substitution of the official's successor. *See also* FED. R. CIV. P. 25(a)(1) (providing for the substitution of a party at death "where claim is not thereby extinguished"). Because a prospective action under these circumstances is against the office, and not the officer, death has no Article III significance and vacatur does not become an issue. *See Karcher v. May*, 484 U.S. 72 (1987) (discussed in Note 2, *supra*). *See also Goldin v. Bartholow*, 166 F.3d 710 (5th Cir. 1999) ("The classic cases of mootness due to changed circumstances involve *plaintiffs* whose relations to the case have changed. Because of the liberal allowance for substitution in the federal rules, cases in which a defendant's change in status leads to mootness are rare.").

The death of a § 1983 plaintiff, in contrast, will ordinarily moot a claim to personal prospective relief[45] — whether the case is in the District Court or in the Court of Appeals at the time of death.[46] *See, e.g., Hubbard v. Taylor*, 399 F.3d 150 (3d Cir. 2005) (holding that an inmate's death on appeal moots a prospective claim under the Americans with Disabilities Act); *Crowder v. Housing Authority of City of Atlanta*, 908 F.2d 843 (11th Cir. 1990) (dismissing an appeal after the death of a civil rights plaintiff/appellant where she only sought injunctive relief). The difficult question on appeal, assuming mootness, is one of vacatur. If the deceased § 1983 plaintiff won in the

---

[44] *Contrast Blankenship v. Blackwell*, 429 F.3d 254 (6th Cir. 2005) (holding that an intervening election was not happenstance and did not entitle Ralph Nader's campaign to vacatur of a District Court's order denying Nader ballot access because the campaign's delay in bringing the action "contributed to the[] case's becoming moot").

[45] The Supreme Court in *Tory v. Cochran*, 544 U.S. 734 (2005), ruled that famed-attorney Johnnie Cochran's death did not moot Cochran's successful injunctive action under California law against a disgruntled client (Tory) who had picketed Cochran's law office: "Despite Johnnie Cochran's death, the injunction remains in effect. Nothing in its language says to the contrary. . . . The parties have not identified, nor have we found, any source of California law that says the injunction here *automatically* becomes invalid upon Cochran's death, not even the portion personal to Cochran. Counsel also points to the 'value of' Cochran's 'law practice' and adds that his widow has an interest in enforcing the injunction." Were the case deemed moot by the Supreme Court, note that vacatur of the California state courts' decisions would not have been an option under Article III. *See* footnote 41, *supra*. The Supreme Court, however, vacated the state courts' injunction under the First Amendment's doctrine against prior restraints and remanded to the state courts for further consideration.

[46] Contrast claims to monetary damages, where the deceased plaintiff's personal representative can be substituted under either Civil Rule 25(a)(1), Appellate Rule 43(a), or Supreme Court Rule 35 and a state's relevant survivorship statute. *See Robertson v. Wegman*, 436 U.S. 584 (1978) (discussed in Chapter 5.A., *supra*). Claims to monetary damages are not rendered moot by the death of the plaintiff when the decedent's estate can be properly substituted as a party. *See, e.g., Consolidated Rail Corp. v. Darrone*, 465 U.S. 624 (1984) (holding that a claim to back pay under federal Rehabilitation Act is not mooted by the death of the plaintiff).

lower court and is the appellee/respondent, it appears clear that vacatur of the lower court's judgment is required. *See, e.g., McMann v. Richardson*, 397 U.S. 759 (1970) (dismissing the government's appeal as moot where a habeas petitioner had died and vacating the lower court proceedings resolved in the habeas petitioner's favor); *McMann v. Ross*, 396 U.S. 118 (1969) (memorandum opinion) (same); *Hall v. Unum Life Insurance Company of America*, 300 F.3d 1197 (10th Cir. 2002) (vacating declaratory relief under ERISA following a successful plaintiff's death on appeal). After all, whether treated as happenstance or attributed to the § 1983 plaintiff (the prevailing party), vacatur down the line is the rule. *Cf. Padgett v. Nicholson*, 473 F.3d 1364 (Fed. Cir. 2007) (stating that the general approach is to vacate an underlying judgment where a successful plaintiff passes away on appeal).[47] What if the § 1983 plaintiff lost in the lower court? If considered happenstance, of course, the appellant/petitioner's death will result in vacatur of the judgment below. This is the approach commonly taken in criminal proceedings, *see, e.g., United States v. Koblan*, 478 F.3d 1324 (11th Cir. 2007) ("[w]hen a defendant dies pending direct appeal of his criminal conviction, the Court will dismiss the appeal as moot with respect to that defendant and remand the case to the district court to vacate the judgment and dismiss the indictment"), and has been followed by civil courts. *See, e.g., Wojewski v. Rapid City Regional Hospital*, 450 F.3d 368 (8th Cir. 2006) (vacating a District Court's judgment for the defendant in a civil rights case where the unsuccessful plaintiff died during appeal); *Griffey v. Lindsey*, 349 F.3d 1157 (9th Cir. 2003) (vacating the denial of habeas relief following an inmate's death during appeal). If the death is somehow attributed to the § 1983 appellant/petitioner, however, the underlying judgment could be allowed to stand. *See* Note 4, *infra*. Although this would appear to be a minority view, there is some precedent for this approach in practice. *See, e.g, Jackson v. Leavitt*, 209 Fed. Appx. 681 (9th Cir. 2006) (court dismisses appeal but does not vacate the judgment against an appellant who died while the appeal was pending).

4. Conduct of the Losing Party. When a losing party does not appeal, its appellate rights, along with its complaints about the underlying judgment, are forfeited. *See, e.g., Karcher v. May*, 484 U.S. 72 (1987) (holding that a state's abandonment of appeal terminated the case). One might say the appeal is moot, yet the underlying judgment remains. To the extent the losing party's actions are the equivalent of acquiescing in the judgment or abandoning the appeal, courts have had little difficulty refusing vacatur. In *Staley v. Harris County*, 485 F.3d 305 (5th Cir. 2007) (en banc), for example, the court refused to vacate an injunction against a religious display outside a Texas courthouse after the defendant-county voluntarily removed it. *See also Sierra Club v. Glickman*, 156 F.3d 606 (5th Cir. 1998) (refusing to vacate because the appellant mooted the case by voluntarily complying with the District Court's judgment).

A losing party's contribution to mootness need not be the only cause or even the proximate cause to defeat vacatur. The Sixth Circuit in *Blankenship v. Blackwell*, 429 F.3d 254 (6th Cir. 2005), for example, concluded that Ralph Nader's delay in challenging Ohio's ballot access laws during the 2004 presidential election contributed to the mootness of his case and thus defeated his claim to vacatur. Nader's name was placed

---

[47] What if a § 1983 plaintiff dies after the full submission of an appellate case but before an opinion is handed down by the appellate court? Is the case moot? If so, must the lower court judgment be vacated? In *Padgett v. Nicholson*, 473 F.3d 1364 (Fed. Cir. 2007), the court observed that "[w]here a party dies after his case is submitted, but before the opinion issues, and the case would otherwise be rendered moot, the Supreme Court has consistently entered judgment nunc *pro tunc* to the date of the party's death." Thus, "where the delay in rendering a judgment or a decree arises from the act of the court, that is, . . . cause not attributable to the laches of the parties, the judgment or the decree may be entered retrospectively, as of a time when it should or might have been entered up." None of the Supreme Court cases cited by the *Padgett* court, however, were prospective proceedings. Hence, it would seem doubtful that this practice is acceptable to avoid mootness in prospective proceedings that do not involve money damages. *See* Chapter 5.A., *supra* (discussing borrowing state laws to substitute plaintiffs in cases seeking monetary relief).

on Ohio' ballot on September 8, 2004, only to be removed following an official protest by Democratic challengers on September 28, 2004. *See* Mark R. Brown, *Policing Ballot Access: Lessons from Nader's 2004 Run for President*, 35 CAPITAL U. L. REV. 165, 182–83 (2006). Nader's campaign then sued under § 1983 and the First Amendment on October 6, 2004, seeking both an injunction placing his name back on Ohio's ballot and a declaration that Ohio's election law (requiring that the circulators of a presidential candidate's petitions be registered voters and state residents) was unconstitutional. The District Court denied relief and dismissed Nader's complaint on October 12. *Id.* Nader then moved for an expedited appeal and asked the Sixth Circuit to award preliminary relief restoring his name to the ballot before the November election. On October 18, the Sixth Circuit refused to expedite the appeal and refused preliminary relief. Following the election — which proceeded without Nader's name on the 2004 ballot — the Sixth Circuit dismissed Nader's appeal as moot. It also refused to vacate the District Court's order denying Nader injunctive relief, *see Blankenship v. Blackwell*, 341 F. Supp. 2d 911 (S.D. Ohio 2004):

> [W]e cannot conclude that [Nader is] entitled to the extraordinary equitable remedy of vacatur. First, given the fixed date of the 2004 election, [Nader] could and should have acted more expeditiously in asserting [his] legal rights to ensure that [his] case was resolved prior to that election. Although [his] complaint is based in part on the 8,009 signatures invalidated by the local election boards, a decision that was completed by September 3, 2004, [Nader] nonetheless waited until October 6 — a delay of 33 days — to file [his] complaint in federal district court. Also, [Nader's] circulators began gathering signatures in June 2004 and should have been aware of Ohio's residency requirements for circulators at that time. Most damning of all is the fact that Ralph Nader announced his run for the presidency in mid-February of 2004, some eight and a half months before the election, at which time [he] should have known of [his] interest in the application of Ohio's circulator-residency requirements. There is simply no excuse for [Nader's] waiting more than seven months to bring [his] declaratory judgment claim and leaving the federal courts less than a month before the election to resolve it.
>
> In light of [Nader's] refusal to challenge Ohio's circulator-residency requirement until more than seven months after Nader announced his candidacy . . . we cannot say that [he is a] mere victim[ ] of the "vagaries of circumstance." Because at least some of the blame for the mootness of this case lies with [Nader], we cannot grant [him] the extraordinary equitable remedy of vacating the district court's judgment.

Who (or what) was responsible for Nader's challenge becoming moot?[48] Nader did not challenge the state's ballot access laws until after he was removed from the ballot on September 28, just six weeks before the election. Could he have filed suit seeking ballot access sooner?[49] Did the state's belated removal of Nader's name from the ballot contribute to the mootness problem? Was the Court of Appeals' refusal to grant an emergency hearing before the election a factor? *Contrast Watkins v. Mabus*, 502 U.S. 954 (1991) (per curiam) (finding that an intervening election mooted a prospective

---

[48] Was not Nader's challenge to the constitutionality of Ohio's election laws "capable of repetition, yet evading review"? *See United States Parole Commission v. Geraghty*, 445 U.S. 388 (1980) (excerpted, *infra*). Though Nader argued that his challenge to Ohio's election law qualified under the capable-of-repetition exception to mootness, *see* Brown, *supra*, at 187 n.60, the Sixth Circuit did not mention the doctrine in its opinion.

[49] Note that because ballots are not generally established until just weeks before elections, ballot access challenges are notoriously filed on the eves of elections. *See, e.g., Suster v. Marshall*, 149 F.3d 523 (6th Cir. 1998) (observing that the ballot access challenge was filed three months before the election); *Brown v. Chote*, 411 U.S. 452 (1973) (challenge filed just before election); *Moore v. Ogilvie*, 394 U.S. 814 (1969) (same).

candidate's claim to emergency relief and "vacat[ing] that portion of the judgment below [addressing the election] with instructions to dismiss the relevant part of the complaint").

5. Precedent and Preclusion. Why was Nader interested in having the District Court's judgment vacated? After all, he was not going to win ballot access for an election that had long since passed. In *Munsingwear*, remember, the federal government discovered after mooting its appeal that the District Court's judgment was to be given preclusive effect. Vacatur prevents this from happening.[50] Moreover, even if a judgment has no preclusive effect, it might still have value as a precedent. Again, vacatur ordinarily drains a judgment of its value as a precedent. *But see* Charles A. Sullivan, *On Vacation*, 43 HOUSTON L. REV. 1143 (2006) (reporting that some courts afford vacated decisions precedential value).

Consider the facts of *Bunting v. Mellen*, 541 U.S. 1019 (2004), where two cadets at the Virginia Military Institute (VMI) challenged the practice of organized prayer at the college's Supper Roll Call ceremony under the Establishment Clause. The cadets sued the Superintendent of VMI (Bunting) seeking both nominal damages and prospective relief. The District Court ruled in favor of the cadets, which precipitated an appeal to the Fourth Circuit on behalf of VMI and Bunting. While the appeal was pending the cadets graduated and Bunting retired. The Fourth Circuit held that the cadets' graduations mooted their claims for prospective relief and required vacatur of this portion of their judgment under *Bonner Mall*. *See Mellen v. Bunting*, 327 F.3d 355 (4th Cir. 2003). Their claim for damages against Bunting in his individual capacity, however, remained alive; it was not mooted by either the cadets' graduations or by Bunting's retirement. In this regard, the Fourth Circuit ruled that although the VMI practice violated the Establishment Clause, Bunting was protected by qualified immunity. Bunting consequently won his appeal.

Bunting and his VMI successor (Peay) thereafter petitioned the Supreme Court to review the Fourth Circuit's conclusion that VMI's prayer violated the Establishment Clause. The Court denied certiorari. Five Justices joined in writing to explain and complain about the Court's refusal to take up the case. In an opinion joined by Justices Ginsburg and Breyer, Justice Stevens noted that certiorari was not justified because Bunting had retired and "will suffer no direct injury if VMI is unable to continue the prayer." The cadets, meanwhile, did not appeal the award of qualified immunity in Bunting's favor, which meant that "there no longer is a live controversy between Bunting [the petitioner] and respondents [the cadets] regarding the constitutionality of the prayer." Justice Scalia (joined by the Chief Justice) dissented from the denial of certiorari. He argued that the Supreme Court should consider abandoning its requirement that constitutional issues be addressed before qualified immunity, *see* Chapter 2.B., *supra*, or allow appeals by governmental defendants who prevail because of qualified immunity. Otherwise, Justice Scalia complained, constitutional decisions in the District Courts and Courts of Appeals could be insulated from appellate review. Not only should the Court take the case to "clarify the ordinary availability of appeal," Justice Scalia noted, it should take the case "to specify that, in the unusual situation such as this where lack of standing precludes appeal, resolution of the constitutional question does not have *stare decisis* effect."

---

[50] It is not clear that a judgment mooted on appeal but not vacated under *Bonner Mall* must be given preclusive effect. *See Remus Joint Venture v. McAnally*, 116 F.3d 180 (6th Cir. 1997) (holding that a refusal to vacate does not mean the judgment is entitled to preclusive effect; it "is up to the [subsequent] courts, applying federal preclusion principles, to determine the preclusive effect of that decision"); *see generally* 18 C. WRIGHT, A. MILLER & E. COOPER, FEDERAL PRACTICE AND PROCEDURE § 4421 (2d ed. 2002) (observing that findings that are not subject to "the appellate procedure ordinarily available" might not have preclusive effect). Preclusion is discussed in greater detail in Chapter 8.A., *infra*.

Was it fair to VMI — which could not appeal — to let the Fourth Circuit's decision stand? Was it fair to Nader — whose appeal was moot — to let the District Court's decision stand?

6. Government's Repeal of Challenged Legislation. "It goes without saying that disputes concerning repealed legislation are generally moot." *Houston Chronicle Publishing Co. v. City of League City*, 488 F.3d 613 (5th Cir. 2007). But what if the repeal comes after judgment in favor of one challenging the legislation? What if it comes after the government succeeds in defending the legislation? Does vacatur matter whether the government won or lost in the court below? In *Houston Chronicle Publishing Co. v. City of League City*, 488 F.3d 613 (5th Cir. 2007), where newspapers successfully challenged local ordinances restricting their circulation efforts, the Court of Appeals refused to vacate the lower court's judgment following the city's repeal of the offensive ordinances: "[T]he equitable factors in the instant case weigh against vacating the district court's injunction. . . . [T]he mootness-causing action did not result from typical progression of events, such as a student graduating from school. . . . [T]he City has not shown its repealing the Ordinance provisions was not in response to the district court judgment. . . . [T]he newspapers obtained full relief in district court *before* League City repealed most of the Ordinance. Moreover, the Ordinance has been applied exclusively against the newspapers, rather than non-parties to this litigation." Had the City won in the court below and then repealed the challenged Ordinances to moot the newspapers' appeal, however, vacatur would likely have been in order to clear the way for future litigation. *See* Note 8, *infra* (discussing mootness caused by prevailing parties).

7. Lack of Responsibility for Repealed Legislation. The Court in *Munsingwear* assumed that the federal government could have successfully appealed to have the lower court's judgment vacated, thus draining it of any *res judicata* (claim preclusion) effect. But in order to do this, the federal government (which lost below) could not have been responsible for the mooting event — deregulation by the Executive Branch — which it plainly was under the facts of *Munsingwear*. Justice Scalia in *Bonner Mall* observed in footnote 3 that while the Court would "stand by" the principles announced in *Munsingwear*, it "express[ed] no view on *Munsingwear*'s implicit conclusion that repeal of administrative regulations cannot fairly be attributed to the Executive Branch when it litigates in the name of the United States." Note that if the *Munsingwear* Court were correct on this point, i.e., a legislative or executive repeal of a challenged law can not be imputed to the government's litigators, a losing government can both cause mootness and win vacatur on appeal. This is precisely what happened in *Brooks v. Vassar*, 462 F.3d 341 (4th Cir. 2006), where, following its defeat in the District Court, Virginia's legislature repealed a challenged law and then moved for vacatur of the District Court's judgment in the Court of Appeals. The Fourth Circuit ruled that because a legislative change in "a challenged law is not 'voluntary cessation' attributable to the State's executive officials defending a challenge to that law," the losing state officials had not caused the mootness and vacatur of the District Court's judgment was required.

Contrary to the position taken in *Brooks*, most courts follow Justice Scalia's suggestion in *Bonner Mall* and hold governmental litigators accountable for the actions of their lawmakers. *See, e.g., Houston Chronicle Publishing Co. v. City of League City*, 488 F.3d 613 (5th Cir. 2007) (holding a city accountable for the repeal of challenged ordinance). However, where the government's lawmakers cannot control the repeal, courts have not held them strictly accountable. Thus, in *AT&T Communications of Southwest v. City of Austin*, 235 F.3d 241 (5th Cir. 2000), the court vacated a judgment due to mootness when the challenged local ordinance was superseded by a Texas state law. Likewise, when a governmental defendant convinces the appellate court that its repeal was not related to the unfavorable judgment, courts have sometimes treated the intervening mootness as an independent event supporting vacatur. *See Khodra Envi-*

ronmental, Inc. v. Beckman, 237 F.3d 186 (3d Cir. 2001) (awarding vacatur where no evidence suggested the mootness-causing legislation was a response to the unfavorable judgment).[51]

8. Conduct of the Prevailing Party. In *Arizonans for Official English v. Arizona*, 520 U.S. 43 (1997), the plaintiff (Yniguez) won a judgment against Arizona (through its Governor as the lone official defendant) holding the state's "English Only" requirement for government workers unconstitutional. Two and one-half months after the judgment, but while an appeal was pending, Yniguez resigned her governmental employment and went to work in the private sector. The Supreme Court, per Justice Ginsburg, observed that "[v]acatur is in order when mootness occurs through happenstance — circumstances not attributable to the parties — or relevant here, the 'unilateral action of the party who prevailed in the lower court.' " Because "Yniguez's changed circumstances — her resignation from public sector employment to pursue work in the private sector — mooted the case stated in her complaint," Justice Ginsburg explained, vacatur was required. *See also Goldin v. Bartholow*, 166 F.3d 710 (5th Cir. 1999) (vacating because the appellees caused mootness by failing to substitute a proper defendant).

9. Exceptional Circumstances. The Court in *Bonner Mall* stated that a losing party's complicity in causing mootness — such as joining in a settlement — ordinarily defeats vacatur. "Exceptional circumstances" are needed to overcome this rule. In *Arizonans for Official English*, discussed in Note 8, *supra*, the plaintiff (Yniguez), who left her public-sector employment after winning a judgment, argued that she was not alone responsible for the case becoming moot on appeal. The lone defendant (the Governor), she pointed out, had failed to properly appeal before the case was rendered moot. The state, she argued, thus acquiesced in the judgment and was not entitled to vacatur. Justice Ginsburg responded that because "Yniguez did not tell the Court of Appeals that she had left the State's employ," the state's Attorney General had sought to defend the state's law in the appellate proceedings, timely notice of her departure could have resulted in vacatur earlier in the appellate proceedings, and the "extraordinary course of this litigation," "exceptional circumstances" justified "vacatur down the line [a]s the equitable solution."

10. Attorney's Fees. As observed in Note 2 following *Northeastern Florida*, *supra*, mootness can defeat a § 1983 plaintiff's claim to recover attorney's fees from a governmental defendant. Where mootness occurs on appeal, the logic of *Bonner Mall* controls the attorney's fee inquiry. Thus, if mootness occurs by happenstance or because of the prevailing party's actions, the judgment below will be vacated and the (formerly) prevailing party's right to attorney's fees will be lost. If mootness is caused by the losing party, however, the judgment below will not be vacated and the prevailing party will still be entitled to fees under § 1988(b) for its victory in the lower court. Because attorney-fee-shifting ordinarily only benefits § 1983 plaintiffs (and not governmental defendants), this problem generally arises when the § 1983 plaintiff has won in the lower court and seeks to defend its victory on appeal.

11. Avoiding Mootness. Mootness, whether in the District Court or on appeal, can be avoided by adding a claim for money damages. *See, e.g., McKinley v. Kaplan*, 177 F.3d 1253 (11th Cir. 1999) (holding that the District Court abused its discretion by not allowing the plaintiff to amend her complaint to include a claim for money damages once her prospective claims became moot). Of course, there are peculiar obstacles to winning monetary relief, like official immunities, *see* Chapter 2, *supra*, Eleventh Amendment immunity, *see* Chapter 3.A., *supra*, and limitations on municipal liability. *See* Chapter

---

[51] When government repeals legislation *before* judgment, the case is rendered moot and any needed vacatur is automatic. *See, e.g., National Black Police Association v. District of Columbia*, 108 F.3d 346 (D.C. Cir. 1997) (vacating judgment as moot when challenged campaign-contribution limits were removed *before* the district court enjoined them); *Goldin v. Bartholow*, 166 F.3d 710 (5th Cir. 1999) ("If mootness occurred prior to the rendering of final judgment by the district court, *vacatur* and dismissal is automatic.").

4.B., *supra*. Hence, a plaintiff seeking prospective relief might also want to consider class certification, *see United States Parole Commission v. Geraghty*, 445 U.S. 388 (1980) (excerpted, *infra*), or joining a membership association as an additional plaintiff. *See United Food and Commercial Workers Union Local 751 v. Brown Group, Inc.*, 517 U.S. 544 (1996) (excerpted, *infra*).

UNITED STATES PAROLE COMMISSION v. GERAGHTY
Supreme Court of the United States
445 U.S. 388 (1980)

MR. JUSTICE BLACKMUN delivered the opinion of the Court.

[Geraghty, a federal prison inmate, challenged various changes to the federal government's parole policies. He sought certification of a class of "all federal prisoners who are or will become eligible for release on parole." The District Court denied Geraghty's request for class certification and granted summary judgment for the Parole Commission on all his claims. Geraghty appealed both the denial of class certification and the District Court's decision on the merits. While this appeal was pending, and before any brief had been filed in the Court of Appeals, Geraghty was released from prison. The government then moved to dismiss the appeal as moot.]

Article III of the Constitution limits federal "Judicial Power," that is, federal-court jurisdiction, to "Cases" and "Controversies." This case-or-controversy limitation serves "two complementary" purposes. It limits the business of federal courts to "questions presented in an adversary context and in a form historically viewed as capable of resolution through the judicial process," and it defines the "role assigned to the judiciary in a tripartite allocation of power to assure that the federal courts will not intrude into areas committed to the other branches of government." Likewise, mootness has two aspects: "when the issues presented are no longer 'live' or the parties lack a legally cognizable interest in the outcome."

It is clear that the controversy over the validity of the Parole Release Guidelines is still a "live" one between [the government] and at least some members of the class [Geraghty] seeks to represent. This is demonstrated by the fact that prisoners currently affected by the guidelines have moved to be substituted, or to intervene, as "named" respondents in this Court. We therefore are concerned here with the second aspect of mootness, that is, the parties' interest in the litigation. The Court has referred to this concept as the "personal stake" requirement.

On several occasions the Court has considered the application of the "personal stake" requirement in the class-action context. In *Sosna v. Iowa*, 419 U.S. 393 (1975), it held that mootness of the named plaintiff's individual claim after a class has been duly certified does not render the action moot. It reasoned that "even though appellees . . . might not again enforce the Iowa durational residency requirement against [the class representative], it is clear that they will enforce it against those persons in the class that appellant sought to represent and that the District Court certified." The Court stated specifically that an Art. III case or controversy "may exist . . . between a named defendant and a member of the class represented by the named plaintiff, even though the claim of the named plaintiff has become moot."

Although one might argue that *Sosna* contains at least an implication that the critical factor for Art. III purposes is the timing of class certification, other cases, applying a "relation back" approach, clearly demonstrate that timing is not crucial. When the claim on the merits is "capable of repetition, yet evading review," the named plaintiff may litigate the class certification issue despite loss of his personal stake in the outcome of the litigation. *E.g., Gerstein v. Pugh*, 420 U.S. 103 (1975). The "capable of repetition, yet evading review" doctrine, to be sure, was developed outside the class-action context. But it has been applied where the named plaintiff does have a personal stake at the outset of the lawsuit, and where the claim may arise again with respect to that plaintiff;

the litigation then may continue notwithstanding the named plaintiff's current lack of a personal stake. *See, e.g., Roe v. Wade*, 410 U.S. 113 (1973). Since the litigant faces some likelihood of becoming involved in the same controversy in the future, vigorous advocacy can be expected to continue.

When, however, there is no chance that the named plaintiff's expired claim will reoccur, mootness still can be avoided through certification of a class prior to expiration of the named plaintiff's personal claim. Some claims are so inherently transitory that the trial court will not have even enough time to rule on a motion for class certification before the proposed representative's individual interest expires. The Court considered this possibility in *Gerstein v. Pugh*, . . . an action challenging pretrial detention conditions. The Court assumed that the named plaintiffs were no longer in custody awaiting trial at the time the trial court certified a class of pretrial detainees. There was no indication that the particular named plaintiffs might again be subject to pretrial detention. Nonetheless, the case was held not to be moot because:

> The length of pretrial custody cannot be ascertained at the outset, and it may be ended at any time by release on recognizance, dismissal of the charges, or a guilty plea, as well as by acquittal or conviction after trial. It is by no means certain that any given individual, named as plaintiff, would be in pretrial custody long enough for a district judge to certify the class. Moreover, in this case the constant existence of a class of persons suffering the deprivation is certain. The attorney representing the named respondents is a public defender, and we can safely assume that he has other clients with a continuing live interest in the case.

In two different contexts the Court has stated that the proposed class representative who proceeds to a judgment on the merits may appeal denial of class certification. First, this assumption was "an important ingredient" in the rejection of interlocutory appeals, "as of right," of class certification denials. *Coopers & Lybrand v. Livesay*, 437 U.S. 463 (1978).[52] The Court reasoned that denial of class status will not necessarily be the "death knell" of a small-claimant action, since there still remains "the prospect of prevailing on the merits and reversing an order denying class certification."

Second, in *United Airlines, Inc. v. McDonald*, 432 U.S. 385 (1977), the Court held that a putative class member may intervene, for the purpose of appealing the denial of a class certification motion, after the named plaintiffs' claims have been satisfied and judgment entered in their favor. Underlying that decision was the view that "refusal to certify was subject to appellate review after final judgment at the behest of the named plaintiffs." And today, the Court holds that named plaintiffs whose claims are satisfied through entry of judgment over their objections may appeal the denial of a class certification ruling. *Deposit Guaranty Nat. Bank v. Roper*, 445 U.S. 326.

Gerstein, McDonald, and *Roper* are all examples of cases found not to be moot, despite the loss of a "personal stake" in the merits of the litigation by the proposed class representative. The interest of the named plaintiffs in *Gerstein* was precisely the same as that of Geraghty here. Similarly, after judgment had been entered in their favor, the named plaintiffs in *McDonald* had no continuing narrow personal stake in the outcome of the class claims. And in *Roper* the Court points out that an individual controversy is rendered moot, in the strict Art. III sense, by payment and satisfaction of a final judgment. These cases demonstrate the flexible character of the Art. III mootness doctrine.

---

[52] [Editor's note: Rule 23(f), added in 1998, amends the Court's decision in *Coopers & Lybrand* rejecting interlocutory appeals from denials of class certification. Rule 23(f) states that "[a] court of appeals may in its discretion permit an appeal from an order of a district court granting or denying class action certification under this rule if application is made to it within ten days after entry of the order." Fed. R. Civ. P. 23(f). *See Newton v. Merrill, Lynch, Pierce, Fenner & Smith, Inc.*, 259 F.3d 154 (3d Cir. 2001) (describing when courts of appeals should entertain interlocutory appeals under Rule 23(f)).]

A plaintiff who brings a class action presents two separate issues for judicial resolution. One is the claim on the merits; the other is the claim that he is entitled to represent a class. "The denial of class certification stands as an adjudication of one of the issues litigated.

[T]he purpose of the "personal stake" requirement is to assure that the case is in a form capable of judicial resolution. The imperatives of a dispute capable of judicial resolution are sharply presented issues in a concrete factual setting and self-interested parties vigorously advocating opposing positions. We conclude that these elements can exist with respect to the class certification issue notwithstanding the fact that the named plaintiff's claim on the merits has expired. The question whether class certification is appropriate remains as a concrete, sharply presented issue.

We therefore hold that an action brought on behalf of a class does not become moot upon expiration of the named plaintiff's substantive claim, even though class certification has been denied.[53] The proposed representative retains a "personal stake" in obtaining class certification sufficient to assure that Art. III values are not undermined. If the appeal results in reversal of the class certification denial, and a class subsequently is properly certified, the merits of the class claim then may be adjudicated pursuant to the holding in *Sosna*.

Our holding is limited to the appeal of the denial of the class certification motion. A named plaintiff whose claim expires may not continue to press the appeal on the merits until a class has been properly certified. If, on appeal, it is determined that class certification properly was denied, the claim on the merits must be dismissed as moot.

Our conclusion that the controversy here is not moot does not automatically establish that the named plaintiff is entitled to continue litigating the interests of the class. "[I]t does shift the focus of examination from the elements of justiciability to the ability of the named representative to 'fairly and adequately protect the interests of the class.'" We hold only that a case or controversy still exists. The question of who is to represent the class is a separate issue.

JUSTICE POWELL, with whom THE CHIEF JUSTICE, JUSTICE STEWART, and JUSTICE REHNQUIST, join, dissenting.

Art. III contains no exception for class actions. Thus, we have held that a putative class representative who alleges no individual injury "may [not] seek relief on behalf of himself or any other member of the class." Only after a class has been certified in accordance with Rule 23 [of the Federal Rules of Civil Procedure] can it "acquir[e] a legal status separate from the interest asserted by [the named plaintiff]." "Given a properly certified class," the live interests of unnamed but identifiable class members may supply the personal stake required by Art. III when the named plaintiff's individual claim becomes moot.

This case presents a fundamentally different situation. No class has been certified, and the lone plaintiff no longer has any personal stake in the litigation.

In any realistic sense, the only persons before this Court who appear to have an interest are the defendants and a lawyer who no longer has a client.

NOTES

1. Class Certification. *Sosna v. Iowa*, 419 U.S. 393 (1975), establishes that mootness can be avoided by certifying a named plaintiff to represent a class of similarly situated victims under Federal Rule of Civil Procedure 23(b). *See also Gratz v. Bollinger*, 539

---

[53] [n.10] We intimate no view as to whether a named plaintiff who settles the individual claim after denial of class certification may, consistent with Art. III, appeal from the adverse ruling on class certification. *See United Airlines, Inc. v. McDonald*, 432 U.S. 385 (1977).

U.S. 244 (2003) (finding that a class action seeking prospective relief was still alive even though the named plaintiffs had graduated). The assumption underlying *Sosna*'s conclusion is that the named plaintiff had standing when the action was filed, *see Simon v. Eastern Kentucky Welfare Rights Organization*, 426 U.S. 26 (1976) ("named plaintiffs who represent a class 'must allege and show that they personally have been injured, not that injury has been suffered by other, unidentified members of the class to which they belong and which they purport to represent'"), and was qualified under Article III to seek the requested relief. *See Blum v. Yaretsky*, 457 U.S. 991 (1982) ("a plaintiff who has been subject to injurious conduct of one kind [does not] possess by virtue of that injury the necessary stake in litigating conduct of another kind, although similar"). While not yet answered by the Supreme Court, a majority of lower courts have held that the named plaintiff's claim must still be alive (i.e., not moot) at the time the district court certifies the class. *See, e.g., Cruz v. Farquharson*, 252 F.3d 530 (1st Cir. 2001) ("Despite the fact that a case is brought as a putative class action, it ordinarily must be dismissed as moot if no decision on class certification has occurred by the time that the individual claims of all named plaintiffs have been fully resolved."); *In re Eaton Vance Corporation Securities Litigation*, 220 F.R.D. 162 (D. Mass. 2004) (holding that mootness before class certification requires dismissal). Should the named plaintiff's claim become moot before certification,[54] the case ordinarily must be dismissed under Article III for lack of subject matter jurisdiction, subject to an exception for claims that are "capable of repetition, yet evading review," which is discussed in Note 2, *infra*.

Assuming the District Court reaches the plaintiff's certification motion before plaintiff's claim becomes moot, *Geraghty* establishes that the named plaintiff has a separate procedural interest in certification. Should the District Court deny class certification, the named plaintiff has a sufficient interest for purposes of Article III to appeal the denial of class certification even after its interest in the merits has become moot. Reversal on the denial of class certification by the appellate court then "relates back" to the time certification was initially denied, which means that the plaintiff can challenge the defendant's conduct on the merits in the District Court following remand as a class representative under Rule 23(b) and the logic of *Sosna*.

2. Capable of Repetition, Yet Evading Review. *Geraghty* speaks to another avenue around mootness. Actions that are "capable of repetition, yet evading review" are not mooted by the plaintiff's loss of a stake in the merits of the controversy, regardless of whether the plaintiff is certified as a class representative under Rule 23(b)(2). *Geraghty* cites *Roe v. Wade*, 410 U.S. 113 (1973), the famous abortion rights decision, as an example. A preliminary issue in *Roe* was whether Jane Roe, one of the named plaintiffs, continued to possess Article III standing once her pregnancy ended. The Court stated:

> The usual rule in federal cases is that an actual controversy must exist at stages of appellate or certiorari review, and not simply at the date the action is initiated. But when, as here, pregnancy is a significant fact in the litigation, the normal 266-day human gestation period is so short that the pregnancy will come to term before the usual appellate process is complete. If that termination makes a case moot, pregnancy litigation seldom will survive much beyond the trial stage, and appellate review will be effectively denied. Our law should not be that rigid. Pregnancy often comes more than once to the same woman, and in the general population, if man is to survive, it will always be with us. Pregnancy provides a classic justification for a conclusion of nonmootness. It truly could be "capable of repetition, yet evading review."

---

[54] The Third Circuit has liberalized this rule to protect plaintiffs who move for certification before mootness: "So long as a class representative has a live claim at the time he *moves* for class certification, neither a pending motion nor a certified class action need be dismissed if his individual claim subsequently becomes moot." *Holmes v. Pension Plan of Bethlehem Steel Corp.*, 213 F.3d 124 (3d Cir. 2000) (emphasis added).

C. PROSPECTIVE RELIEF AGAINST STATE AND LOCAL OFFICIALS 361

In order to avail itself of the "capable of repetition, yet evading review" exception, the plaintiff must satisfy three requirements: First, the plaintiff must prove that it had standing, i.e., an extant injury, when the case was filed. *See* 1 RONALD D. ROTUNDA & JOHN E. NOWAK, TREATISE ON CONSTITUTIONAL LAW — SUBSTANCE & PROCEDURE § 2.13 (2001).[55] Second, the plaintiff must show that the injury is one that qualifies under the exception, i.e., it is capable of repetition yet evades review. Professors Nowak and Rotunda divide these cases into two categories, one where the government's challenged act is too short in duration to be challenged in federal court, *see, e.g., Gerstein v. Pugh*, 420 U.S. 103 (1975) (holding that suspects held without warrants are entitled to post-arrest judicial review without unreasonable delay, and that they have standing after their release to bring a federal challenge); *County of Riverside v. McLaughlin*, 500 U.S. 44 (1991) (same), and the other where unique factual circumstances make it difficult or impossible to complete federal review before the controversy dies. *See, e.g., Roe v. Wade*, 410 U.S. 113 (1973).

Elections present a useful example of the timing problem. In *Norman v. Reed*, 502 U.S. 279 (1992), a new political party in Illinois challenged the state's ballot restrictions under the First Amendment. Following the party's administrative success, a state trial court ruled that the party had not properly qualified and removed the party from the state's ballot. Following an unsuccessful appeal to the state's supreme court, the United States Supreme Court on October 29, 1990, granted a stay, which effectively restored the party to the ballot. Following its grant of certiorari in May of 1991, the Supreme Court was asked to dismiss the controversy on mootness grounds, since the November election was over. The Court, citing *Moore v. Ogilvie*, 394 U.S. 814 (1969) (holding an election challenge capable of repetition yet evading review), denied the motion, finding "every reason to expect the same parties to generate a similar, future controversy subject to identical time constraints if we should fail to resolve the constitutional issues that arose in 1990." *See also Davis v. Federal Election Commission*, 128 S. Ct. 2759 (2008) (holding that a challenge to campaign finance restrictions was capable of repetition and hence not moot); *Meyer v. Grant*, 486 U.S. 414 (1988) (holding that a challenged to Colorado's ban on paid circulators was not mooted by the election that spawned the controversy); *Storer v. Brown*, 415 U.S. 724 (1974) (holding that an "as applied" challenge to various California election laws was not mooted by an election); *Democratic Party v. Wisconsin ex rel. La Follette*, 450 U.S. 107 (1981) (finding that an election challenge was not mooted by election); *Brown v. Chote*, 411 U.S. 452 (1973) (same); *Rosario v. Rockefeller*, 410 U.S. 752 (1973) (same).

Following *Ogilvie* and *Norman*, lower courts have routinely concluded that intervening elections do not moot constitutional challenges to election laws, including ballot restrictions. *See, e.g., ACLU of Ohio v. Taft*, 385 F.3d 641 (6th Cir. 2004) (holding that a governor's refusal to call a special election to replace a member of Congress was capable of repetition yet evading review even though time for the election had passed); *Libertarian Party of Ohio v. Blackwell*, 462 F.3d 579 (6th Cir. 2006) ("Legal disputes involving election laws almost always take more time to resolve than the election cycle

---

[55] There exists some contrary authority for claims that become moot before the plaintiff has an adequate opportunity to file suit in federal court. The Eleventh Circuit in *Lynch v. Baxley*, 744 F.2d 1452 (11th Cir. 1984), for example, found standing in a *Gerstein*-type case even though the plaintiff did not file suit until after he was released from custody. Similarly, in *Church v. City of Huntsville*, 30 F.3d 1332 (11th Cir. 1994), where a number of homeless persons challenged their harassment and arrest at the hands of local police, the Eleventh Circuit found standing without mentioning whether the plaintiffs were in custody when the suit was filed. *See also Dionne v. Bouley*, 757 F.2d 1344 (1st Cir. 1985) (finding standing on behalf of a plaintiff challenging post-judgment attachment procedures even though the creditor released attachment prior to the plaintiff's filing suit). *Pulliam v. Allen*, 466 U.S. 522 (1984), arguably supports this result. *Pulliam* involved a challenge to Virginia's practice of preliminarily detaining criminal suspects for offenses that (upon conviction) carried no jail time. Even though the plaintiffs had been "tried, found guilty, fined, and released" prior to filing suit, the District Court enjoined the practice. The Supreme Court affirmed, though it did not speak to the plaintiffs' standing.

permits."); *Lawrence v. Blackwell*, 430 F.3d 368 (6th Cir. 2005) (holding that a challenge to ballot access laws was capable of repetition, yet evading review).[56]

Third, the plaintiff must establish a "reasonable expectation" or a "demonstrable probability" that it (the plaintiff) will be subjected to the complained-of governmental conduct in the future. This reasonable expectation, however, need not rise to the same level as that needed to establish standing in the first instance. In *Libertarian Party of Ohio v. Blackwell*, 462 F.3d 579 (6th Cir. 2006), for example, the court observed that the repetition requirement for the exception is "somewhat relaxed" and is "easily satisfie[d]" in election cases. *See generally Honig v. Doe*, 484 U.S. 305 (1988) ("Our concern . . . in all [cases] involving potentially moot claims [is] whether the controversy [is] capable of repetition and not . . . whether the claimant had demonstrated that a recurrence of the dispute was more probable than not").

3. Certification Requirements. Rule 23(b)(2) is commonly used in civil rights cases seeking declaratory or injunctive relief, as opposed to money damages.[57] It was "added specifically to . . . facilitate civil rights class actions." *See Alexander v. Fulton County*, 207 F.3d 1303 (11th Cir. 2000). By its terms, Rule 23(b)(2) provides for certification where "the party opposing the class has acted or refused to act on grounds generally applicable to the class, thereby making appropriate final injunctive relief or corresponding declaratory relief with respect to the class as a whole." Fed. R. Civ. P. 23(b)(2). Rule 23(b)(2) also demands that the requirements of Rule 23(a) be met. Consequently, class certification under Rule 23(b) is appropriate only if (1) the class is so numerous that joinder of all members is impracticable, (2) there are questions of law or fact common to the class, (3) the claims or defenses of the representative parties are typical of the claims or defenses of the class, and (4) the representative parties will fairly and adequately protect the interests of the class. *See* Fed. R. Civ. P. 23(a).

Class certification under Rule 23(b) is largely subject to the discretion of the district court, *see e.g., Powers v. Hamilton County Public Defender Commission*, 501 F.3d 592 (6th Cir. 2007) ("We review a class-certification determination for an abuse of discretion."), though the requirements of Rule 23(b) are ultimately controlling. The most frequently litigated class certification problems involve numerosity, commonality and typicality. "Generally, courts will find that the numerosity requirement has been satisfied when the class comprises forty or more members." *Monaco v. Stone*, 187 F.R.D. 50 (E.D.N.Y. 1999) (finding that class consisted of roughly 300 individuals). However, forty is not a magic number. Where forty or more individuals can be easily joined as plaintiffs, courts have been hesitant to certify a class. *See, e.g., Pruitt v. City of Chicago*, 472 F.3d 925 (7th Cir. 2006) ("Sometimes 'even' 40 plaintiffs would be unmanageable, but plaintiffs do not contend that this is one of those occasions."). Moreover, "[c]ourts have not required evidence of the exact class size or identity of class members to satisfy the numerosity requirement. Instead, a good faith estimate is sufficient when the exact number of class members is not readily ascertainable."

---

[56] Not all orders or issues that naturally expire before completion of litigation qualify under the capable-of-repetition-yet-evading-review exception. Challenges brought by students in the educational context, for example, often expire because the students graduate before litigation can be completed. Still, courts — including the Supreme Court — have been hesitant to recognize these cases as "capable of repetition, yet evading review." *See, e.g., DeFunis v. Odegaard*, 416 U.S. 312 (1974) (finding a challenge to an affirmative action admission policy moot because the petitioner graduated and hence "will never again be required to run the gauntlet of the Law School's admission process"); *Adler v. Duval County School District*, 112 F.3d 1475, 1478 (11th Cir. 1997) ("Because the complaining students have graduated from high school, there is no reasonable expectation that they will be subjected to the same injury again") (citing *Weinstein v. Bradford*, 423 U.S. 147 (1975) (per curiam)).

[57] Achieving class certification in actions seeking monetary judgments is more complex and difficult than in actions seeking only prospective relief. For a lucid description of problems encountered in class actions where plaintiffs seek monetary judgments, see Linda S. Mullenix, *Abandoning the Federal Class Action Ship: Is There Smoother Sailing for Class Actions in Gulf Waters?*, 74 Tul. L. Rev. 1709 (2000).

Monaco v. Stone, 187 F.R.D. 50 (E.D.N.Y. 1999). Additional considerations in determining whether the numerosity requirement is met include "judicial economy arising from the avoidance of a multiplicity of actions, geographic dispersion of class members, financial resources of class members, the ability of claimants to institute individual suits, and requests for prospective injunctive relief which would involve future class members." *Id.*[58]

The related concerns of commonality and typicality "serve[] to ensure that the claims of the class members are so interrelated that the interests of absent class members will be protected." *Kutschbach v. Davies*, 885 F. Supp. 1079 (E.D. Ohio 1995). The more general the plaintiff's challenge, the more likely its claim will be deemed common to and typical of members of the class. For instance, in *Kutschbach*, the plaintiff's husband took her car without her permission and was arrested for driving without a license. The car and license plates were duly seized pursuant to Ohio law. The plaintiff [Kutschbach] challenged the seizure as violating Procedural Due Process, since she was not given timely notice of how she might regain possession of the car and plates. The District Court certified Kutschbach to represent a class of "vehicle owners whose vehicles and/or license plates have been or will be seized, pursuant to [Ohio law], while their vehicles are being driven by third persons, or will be retained after such seizure." The Court found Kutschbach's claim common because it targeted a general policy rather than specific applications: "The commonality requirement is satisfied 'as long as the members of the class have allegedly been affected by a general policy of the defendant, and the general policy is the focus of the litigation.'" Her claim was typical because it resulted from application of the challenged policy.

Likewise, in *Morel v. Giuliani*, 927 F. Supp. 622 (S.D.N.Y. 1995), recipients of AFDC benefits challenged New York's failure to provide timely process following the termination of benefits. The Court certified a class of "all residents of New York City who have received, receive, or will receive AFDC, Food Stamp or Home Relief benefits who have requested, are requesting, or will request a fair hearing in response to an action by the City agency to discontinue, suspend, reduce or restrict benefits and are entitled to aid continuing." Commonality and typicality were established because the plaintiffs challenged a policy applicable to a large group and had themselves been subjected to the policy. "Minor factual differences in the circumstances of each class representative and the class members are not determinative, so long as they share the ultimate issues of entitlement to and denial of timely aid continuing." *Id. See also Monaco v. Stone*, 187 F.R.D. 50 (E.D.N.Y. 1999) ("A single common question of law is sufficient to satisfy the commonality requirement."); *Hiatt v. County of Adams*, 155 F.R.D. 605, 609 (S.D. Ohio 1994) (commonality is established "as long as the members of the class have allegedly been affected by a general policy of the defendant, and the general policy is the focus of the litigation"; typicality is established because "the named Plaintiffs suffered the same alleged injuries as those claimed for all class members").

Class certification also demands that the plaintiff be an adequate representative. "Adequate representation depends on two factors: (a) the plaintiff's attorney must be qualified, experienced, and generally able to conduct the proposed litigation, and (b) the plaintiff must not have interests antagonistic to those of the class." *New Directions Treatment Services v. City of Reading*, 490 F.3d 293 (3d Cir. 2007).[59] "A class representative need only possess 'a minimal degree of knowledge necessary to meet the

---

[58] Applying these factors, the court in *Stone*, which involved a constitutional challenge brought by a purported class of mentally ill plaintiffs, found certification appropriate. The mental condition of those in the purported class made "individual suits . . . difficult to pursue." Moreover, "the fluidity of the class [made] certification particularly appropriate." *See also Hiatt v. County of Adams*, 155 F.R.D. 605 (S.D. Ohio 1994) (certifying a class in a challenge brought by pre-trial detainees because of the fluidity of the class).

[59] The indigence of putative class members can also be a factor favoring certification under Rule 23(b)(2). *See, e.g., Kutschbach v. Davies*, 885 F. Supp. 1079, 1085 (S.D. Ohio 1995) ("the financial disincentives to initiating a lawsuit such as this one create a significant hardship for prospective plaintiffs and warrant the

adequacy standard.'" *Id.* "Conflicts of interest are rare in Rule 23(b)(2) class actions seeking only declaratory and injunctive relief," and the fact that "individual plaintiffs seek damages . . . for themselves" does not ordinarily affect the decision to certify prospective class action. *Id.*

4. Associational Standing. Class certification is only one form of "representative" standing. "Associational standing" offers another option.

UNITED FOOD AND COMMERCIAL WORKERS UNION LOCAL 751 v. BROWN GROUP, INC.
Supreme Court of the United States
517 U.S. 544 (1996)

JUSTICE SOUTER delivered the opinion of the Court.

[An unincorporated union, Local 751, filed suit against an employer, Brown Group, alleging that Brown Group closed its plant and laid off union members before giving the union notice as required by the federal Worker Adjustment and Retraining Notification Act. The union sought backpay for each of its affected members. The District Court and the Court of Appeals concluded that the union lacked standing to represent its members in a suit seeking money damages.]

The Worker Adjustment and Retraining Notification Act (WARN Act or Act) obligates certain employers to give workers or their union 60 days' notice before a plant closing or mass layoff. If an employer fails to give the notice, the employees may sue for backpay for each day of the violation, and, in the alternative, the union is ostensibly authorized to sue on their behalf.

Permitting a union to sue under the Act on behalf of its employee-members raises a question of standing. In *Hunt v. Washington State Apple Advertising Comm'n*, 432 U.S. 333 (1977), we described a three-prong test for an association's standing to sue based on injury to one of its members. [Under the *Hunt* test, "an association has standing to bring suit on behalf of its members when: (a) its members would otherwise have standing to sue in their own right; (b) the interests it seeks to protect are germane to the organization's purpose; and (c) neither the claim asserted nor the relief requested requires the participation of individual members in the lawsuit."] *Hunt* held that "individual participation" is not normally necessary when an association seeks prospective or injunctive relief for its members, but indicated that such participation would be required in an action for damages to an association's members, thus suggesting that an association's action for damages running solely to its members would be barred for want of the association's standing to sue.

The questions presented here are whether, in enacting the WARN Act, Congress intended to abrogate this otherwise applicable standing limitation so as to permit the union to sue for damages running to its workers, and, if it did, whether it had the constitutional authority to do so. We answer yes to each question.

Th[e] . . . primary question in the case [is] whether the union has standing to bring this action on behalf of its members. . . . Supplementing the[] constitutional requirements [of Article III is] the prudential doctrine of standing [which] has come to encompass "several judicially self-imposed limits on the exercise of federal jurisdiction." The question here is whether a bar to the union's suit found in the test for so-called associational standing is constitutional and absolute, or prudential and malleable by Congress.

The notion that an organization might have standing to assert its members' injury has roots in *NAACP v. Alabama ex rel. Patterson*, 357 U.S. 449 (1958), where the Court noted that for the purpose of determining the scope of the National Association for the

---

conclusion that the questioned statutes would go unchallenged were a class not certified").

Advancement of Colored People's (NAACP's) rights as a litigant, the association "and its members are in every practical sense identical." The Court accordingly permitted the NAACP to rely on violations of its members' First Amendment associational rights in suing to bar the State of Alabama from compelling disclosure of the association's membership lists.

There are two ways in which *Hunt* addresses the Article III requirements of injury in fact, causal connection to the defendant's conduct, and redressability. First and most obviously, it guarantees the satisfaction of these elements by requiring an organization suing as representative to include at least one member with standing to present, in his or her own right, the claim (or the type of claim) pleaded by the association. . . . *Hunt*'s second prong is, at the least, complementary to the first, for its demand that an association plaintiff be organized for a purpose germane to the subject of its member's claim raises an assurance that the association's litigators will themselves have a stake in the resolution of the dispute, and thus be in a position to serve as the defendant's natural adversary. But once an association has satisfied *Hunt*'s first and second prongs assuring adversarial vigor in pursuing a claim for which member Article III standing exists, it is difficult to see a constitutional necessity for anything more. To see *Hunt*'s third prong as resting on less than constitutional necessity is not, of course, to rob it of its value. It may well promote adversarial intensity. It may guard against the hazard of litigating a case to the damages stage only to find the plaintiff lacking detailed records or the evidence necessary to show the harm with sufficient specificity. And it may hedge against any risk that the damages recovered by the association will fail to find their way into the pockets of the members on whose behalf injury is claimed. But these considerations are generally on point whenever one plaintiff sues for another's injury.

Circumstantial evidence of the prudential nature of this requirement is seen in the wide variety of other contexts in which a statute, federal rule, or accepted common-law practice permits one person to sue on behalf of another, even where damages are sought. "[R]epresentative damages litigation is common — from class actions under Fed. R. Civ. P. 23(b)(3) to suits by trustees representing hundreds of creditors in bankruptcy to parens patriae actions by state governments to litigation by and against executors of decedents' estates." In addition, § 706(f)(1) of Title VII of the Civil Rights Act of 1964 expressly authorizes the Equal Employment Opportunity Commission to sue for backpay on behalf of employees who are victims of employment discrimination, and the Fair Labor Standards Act of 1938 contains a comparable provision permitting the Secretary of Labor to sue for the recovery of unpaid minimum wages and overtime compensation. If these provisions for representative actions were generally resulting in nonadversarial actions that failed to resolve the claims of the individuals ultimately interested, their disservice to the core Article III requirements would be no secret. There is no reason to expect that union actions under the WARN Act portend any greater Article III incursions.

Because Congress authorized the union to sue for its members' damages, and because the only impediment to that suit is a general limitation, judicially fashioned and prudentially imposed, there is no question that Congress may abrogate the impediment.

NOTES

1. Benefits of Associational Standing. The Supreme Court in *International Union v. Brock*, 477 U.S. 274 (1986), observed that associational standing is "advantageous both to the individuals represented and to the judicial system as a whole." "[A]n association suing to vindicate the interests of its members can draw upon a pre-existing reservoir of expertise and capital. 'Besides financial resources, organizations often have specialized expertise and research resources relating to the subject matter of the lawsuit that individual plaintiffs lack.' These resources can assist both courts and plaintiffs." Like class certification, associational standing also allows plaintiffs to avoid mootness. So long as an association has at least one member with Article III standing,[60] its case can continue even though other members forfeit theirs. *See, e.g., United States v. Comprehensive Drug Testing, Inc.*, 473 F.3d 915 (9th Cir. 2006) (holding that a players' association can assert the Fourth Amendment rights of members who individually have standing); *Lopez-Torres v. New York State Board of Elections*, 462 F.3d 161 (2d Cir. 2006) (holding that Common Cause can assert the First Amendment rights of its members), *rev'd on other grounds*, 128 S. Ct. 791 (2008). Unlike with class actions, associations need not satisfy the technical requirements of, and difficulties associated with, certification. Numerosity, typicality and commonality are not concerns with associational standing.

Still, associational standing is not a panacea. It requires that at least one member of the association maintain a live controversy throughout the course of the litigation — which is not always possible to prove. *See, e.g., National Park Hospitality Association v. Department of Interior*, 538 U.S. 803 (2003) (Stevens, J., concurring) (arguing that because a trade association did not plead or prove "a specific incident in which the Park Service's regulation caused a [member injury] . . . [the association] has no standing to pursue its claim"); *Clark v. Burger King Corp.*, 255 F. Supp. 2d 334 (D.N.J. 2003) (holding that an association must plead and prove which of its members have individual standing). Perhaps more importantly, it is not available for claims to money damages under § 1983.

2. Members' Privacy. Associational standing can be used to help insure secrecy and confidentiality. Plaintiffs are sometimes hesitant to come forward lest they be penalized by government and/or members of their community. Naming an association as the plaintiff can shield the identities of members who otherwise might not be willing to press suit. In *Forum for Academic and Institutional Rights v. Rumsfeld*, 291 F. Supp. 2d 269 (D.N.J. 2003), *rev'd on other grounds*, 390 F.3d 219 (3d Cir. 2004), *rev'd on other grounds*, 547 U.S. 47 (2006), for example, several law school faculties joined an association (the Forum for Academic and Institutional Rights or FAIR) to challenge the federal Solomon Amendment, which threatened schools that resisted military recruiters with a loss of federal funding. The District Court observed that "FAIR membership is kept secret to allay members' fears of retaliatory efforts on behalf of the government and private actors if the law schools were to participate as named plaintiffs in a legal challenge. . . . They also fear that they and their sister institutions will be singled out for virulent and unfair attacks by politicians and in the press, attacks that have already materialized in such mainstream media outlets as the Wall Street Journal, The Legal Times, and Fox News. Such attacks, unfairly mischaracterizing the lawsuit and the interests of FAIR's members in the lawsuit, expose FAIR's members and their sister institutions to the loss of students, the anger of alumni, and the loss of donations." *See also* Emily M. Calhoun, *Academic Freedom: Disciplinary Lessons from Hogwarts*, 77 U. COLO. L. REV. 843, 877 n.157 (2006) ("The FAIR plaintiffs creatively constructed a formal corporate entity to represent academic interests not because corporate status is a prerequisite to holding or defining associational rights, but because certain law schools and professors desired litigation anonymity."). Thus, the District Court ruled, "FAIR need not reveal its membership list at the pleading stage in order to bring suit on its members' behalf." *See also Doe v. Stincer*, 175 F.3d 879 (11th Cir. 1999) (holding

---

[60] Can the Supreme Court's prudential limitations on third-party standing be applied to the individual members' injuries? For example, what if a medical association asserts the rights of its members, who individually would assert the rights of their patients? *See, e.g., Pennsylvania Psychiatric Society v. Green Springs Health Services, Inc.*, 280 F.3d 278 (3d Cir. 2002) (finding that association has standing to assert its members' rights). *See generally* Tracy F. Flint, Comment, *A New Brand of Representational Standing*, 70 U. CHI. L. REV. 1037, 1038 (2003) (observing that "[t]he Court has not specified whether the members' standing must be first-party (in other words, the members must have standing to assert claims on their own behalf) or whether it may be third-party (in other words, the members may assert claims on others' behalf)").

that an Advocacy Center for the mentally ill was not required to "name the members on whose behalf suit is brought").[61] The District Court noted in *FAIR*, however, that it was not "reach[ing] the issue of whether First Amendment rights of association will protect FAIR from revealing its membership list later in this litigation." (citing *Brown v. Socialist Workers '74 Campaign Committee*, 459 U.S. 87 (1982); *Shelton v. Tucker*, 364 U.S. 479 (1960); *NAACP v. Alabama ex rel. Patterson*, 357 U.S. 449 (1958)).

3. Connection Between Organization's Objective and Litigation. *Hunt v. Washington State Apple Advertising Commission*, 432 U.S. 333 (1977), stated that associational standing requires that the interest the association seeks to protect through litigation be "germane" to the organization's purpose. In practice, this requirement has not proven debilitating, since an organization is always free to define its purpose. *See Boy Scouts of America v. Dale*, 530 U.S. 640 (2000) (deferring to the Boy Scouts' description of its mission). In *Forum for Academic and Institutional Rights v. Rumsfeld*, 291 F. Supp. 2d 269 (D.N.J. 2003), *rev'd on other grounds*, 390 F.3d 219 (3d Cir. 2004), *rev'd on other grounds*, 547 U.S. 47 (2006), for example, the District Court concluded that FAIR's stated mission, "to promote academic freedom, support educational institutions in opposing discrimination and vindicate the rights of institutions of higher education," was germane to "[t]he interests FAIR seeks to protect in this suit — the right of law schools to adhere to their non-discrimination policies."

4. Membership Organizations. The associational standing test applied in *Brown Group* has generally been limited to *membership* organizations, like trade associations and environmental groups, regardless of how the organization is constituted under state law. Generally, these organizations are voluntary, though this need not be the case. In *Hunt v. Washington State Apple Advertising Commission*, 432 U.S. 333 (1977), for example, the organization acting as plaintiff was created by the state, while its members (apple growers and dealers) were required by state law to join and pay dues. Still, the Supreme Court found the requisite "indicia of membership" to support associational standing: "The Commission, while admittedly a state agency, for all practical purposes, performs the functions of a traditional trade association representing the Washington apple industry." "[W]hile the apple growers and dealers are not 'members' of the Commission in the traditional trade association sense," the Court observed, "they possess all of the indicia of membership in an organization. They alone elect the members of the Commission; they alone may serve on the Commission; they alone finance its activities, including the costs of this lawsuit, through assessments levied upon them." The Court dismissed the fact that membership was compulsory, since "[m]embership in a union, or its equivalent, is often required." To use another example, the Court pointed out that "membership in a bar association, which may also be an agency of the State, is often a prerequisite to the practice of law. Yet in neither instance would it be reasonable to suggest that such an organization lacked standing to assert the claims of its constituents."

Must organizations allow their membership to control their policies through voting to take advantage of *Hunt*? Many modern advocacy organizations, fearing hostile takeovers, deny voting rights to their constituents. Should these groups be prevented from asserting their "members'" rights? *See* Karl S. Coplan, *Is Voting Necessary? Organization Standing and Non-Voting Members of Environmental Advocacy*

---

[61] The use of pseudonymous plaintiffs in § 1983 litigation to protect the identities of constitutional challengers is not uncommon, even outside the associational context. *See, e.g., Roe v. Wade*, 410 U.S. 113 (1973) (challenger to Texas abortion statute uses pseudonym of "Jane Roe"); *Santa Fe Independent School District v. Doe*, 530 U.S. 290 (2000) (plaintiff who challenged prayer at football game is allowed to proceed anonymously). Still, because "most state and federal courts are reluctant to permit plaintiffs to proceed pseudonymously," Jayne S. Ressler, *Privacy, Plaintiffs, and Pseudonyms: The Anonymous Doe Plaintiff in the Information Age*, 53 U. KAN. L. REV. 195, 213 (2004), associational standing may prove to be the only workable mechanism to insure privacy.

Organizations, 14 SOUTHEASTERN ENVT'L L.J. 47, 58 (2005) ("Some courts have rejected any claim to representational standing on behalf of persons lacking voting membership rights, while other courts have found there to be 'de facto' membership with little or no discussion of the extent of members' voting rights.").

Should non-membership organizations — like for-profit businesses — be allowed to assert the rights of clients, patients and contributors? Some courts have steadfastly answered "no." *See, e.g., Fund Democracy, LLC v. S.E.C.*, 278 F.3d 21 (D.C. Cir. 2002) (holding that a non-membership organization could not assert associational standing); *Region 8 Forest Service Timber Purchasers Council v. Alcock*, 993 F.2d 800 (11th Cir. 1993) (refusing to extend *Hunt* to a for-profit corporation attempting to assert the rights of its employees). Others have been more receptive to associational standing on behalf of groups with constituents who prove to be the functional equivalent of members. *See, e.g., Friends of the Earth, Inc. v. Chevron Chemical Co.*, 129 F.3d 826 (5th Cir. 1997) (applying a functional analysis to determine whether a group's constituents had interests similar to those of members).

[2] Statutory Limits on Prospective Relief

MILLER v. FRENCH
Supreme Court of the United States
530 U.S. 327 (2000)

JUSTICE O'CONNOR delivered the opinion of the Court.

The Prison Litigation Reform Act of 1995 (PLRA) establishes standards for the entry and termination of prospective relief in civil actions challenging prison conditions. If prospective relief under an existing injunction does not satisfy these standards, a defendant or intervenor is entitled to "immediate termination" of that relief. And under the PLRA's "automatic stay" provision, a motion to terminate prospective relief "shall operate as a stay" of that relief during the period beginning 30 days after the filing of the motion (extendable to up to 90 days for "good cause") and ending when the court rules on the motion.

This litigation began in 1975, when four inmates at what is now the Pendleton Correctional Facility brought a class action under § 1983, on behalf of all persons who were, or would be, confined at the facility against the predecessors in office of petitioners (hereinafter State). After a trial, the District Court found that living conditions at the prison violated both state and federal law, including the Eighth Amendment's prohibition against cruel and unusual punishment, and the court issued an injunction to correct those violations. . . . [These violations included] overcrowding and double celling, the use of mechanical restraints, staffing, and the quality of food and medical services. . . . This ongoing injunctive relief has remained in effect ever since.

In 1996, Congress enacted the PLRA. As relevant here, the PLRA establishes standards for the entry and termination of prospective relief in civil actions challenging conditions at prison facilities. Specifically, a court "shall not grant or approve any prospective relief unless the court finds that such relief is narrowly drawn, extends no further than necessary to correct the violation of a Federal right, and is the least intrusive means necessary to correct the violation of the Federal right." 18 U.S.C. § 3626(a)(1)(A). The same criteria apply to existing injunctions, and [under § 3626(b)(2)] a defendant or intervenor may move to terminate prospective relief that does not meet this standard.

A court may not terminate prospective relief, however, if it "makes written findings based on the record that prospective relief remains necessary to correct a current and ongoing violation of the Federal right, extends no further than necessary to correct the violation of the Federal right, and that the prospective relief is narrowly drawn and the

C. PROSPECTIVE RELIEF AGAINST STATE AND LOCAL OFFICIALS   369

least intrusive means necessary to correct the violation." § 3626(b)(3). The PLRA also requires courts to rule "promptly" on motions to terminate prospective relief, with mandamus available to remedy a court's failure to do so.

Section 3626(e)(2) states that a motion to terminate prospective relief "*shall operate as a stay during*" the specified time period from 30 (or 90) days after the filing of the § 3626(b) motion *until* the court rules on that motion. Thus, not only does the statute employ the mandatory term "shall," but it also specifies the points at which the operation of the stay is to begin and end. In other words, § 3626(e)(2) unequivocally mandates that the stay "shall operate *during*" this specific interval. To allow courts to exercise their equitable discretion to prevent the stay from "operating" during this statutorily prescribed period would be to contradict § 3626(e)(2)'s plain terms.

[T]he Government finds support for its view [that § 3626(e)(2) allows the court to "stay the stay"] in § 3626(e)(3). That provision authorizes an extension, for "good cause," of the starting point for the automatic stay, from 30 days after the § 3626(b) motion is filed until 90 days after that motion is filed. The Government explains that, by allowing the court to prevent the entry of the stay for up to 60 days under the relatively generous "good cause" standard, Congress by negative implication has preserved courts' discretion to suspend the stay *after* that time under the more stringent standard for injunctive relief. [We disagree.] When §§ 3626(e)(2) and (3) are read together, it is clear that the district court cannot enjoin the operation of the automatic stay. The § 3626(b) motion "shall operate as a stay during" a specific time period. Section 3626(e)(3) only adjusts the starting point for the stay, and it merely permits that starting point to be delayed. Once the 90-day period has passed, the § 3626(b) motion "shall operate as a stay" until the court rules on the § 3626(b) motion. During that time, any attempt to enjoin the stay is irreconcilable with the plain language of the statute.

The Constitution enumerates and separates the powers of the three branches of Government in Articles I, II, and III, and it is this "very structure" of the Constitution that exemplifies the concept of separation of powers. While the boundaries between the three branches are not " 'hermetically' sealed," the Constitution prohibits one branch from encroaching on the central prerogatives of another. . . . As we explained in *Plaut v. Spendthrift Farm, Inc.*, 514 U.S. 211 (1995), Article III "gives the Federal Judiciary the power, not merely to rule on cases, but to *decide* them, subject to review only by superior courts in the Article III hierarchy."

[The] prisoners contend that § 3626(e)(2) encroaches on the central prerogatives of the Judiciary and thereby violates the separation of powers doctrine. It does this, the prisoners assert, by legislatively suspending a final judgment of an Article III court in violation of *Plaut* and *Hayburn's Case*, 2 Dall. 409 (1792).

Hayburn's Case arose out of a 1792 statute that authorized pensions for veterans of the Revolutionary War. The statute provided that the circuit courts were to review the applications and determine the appropriate amount of the pension, but that the Secretary of War had the discretion either to adopt or reject the courts' findings. Although this Court did not reach the constitutional issue in *Hayburn's Case*, the opinions of five Justices, sitting on Circuit Courts, were reported, and we have since recognized that the case "stands for the principle that Congress cannot vest review of the decisions of Article III courts in officials of the Executive Branch." As we recognized in *Plaut*, such an effort by a coequal branch to "annul a final judgment" is " 'an assumption of Judicial power' and therefore forbidden."

Unlike the situation in *Hayburn's Case*, § 3626(e)(2) does not involve the direct review of a judicial decision by officials of the Legislative or Executive Branches. Nonetheless, the prisoners suggest that § 3626(e)(2) falls within *Hayburn's* prohibition against an indirect legislative "suspension" or reopening of a final judgment, such as that addressed in *Plaut*. In *Plaut*, we held that a federal statute that required federal courts to reopen final judgments that had been entered before the statute's enactment was unconstitutional on separation of powers grounds. The plaintiffs had brought a civil securities fraud action seeking money damages. While that action was pending, we ruled . . . that such suits must be commenced within one year after the discovery of the facts constituting the violation and within three years after such violation. In light of this intervening decision, the *Plaut* plaintiffs' suit was untimely, and the District Court accordingly dismissed the action as time barred. After the judgment dismissing the case had become final, Congress enacted a statute providing for the reinstatement of those actions, including the *Plaut* plaintiffs', that had been dismissed . . . but that would have been timely under the previously applicable statute of limitations.

We concluded that this retroactive command that federal courts reopen final judgments exceeded Congress' authority. The decision of an inferior court within the Article III hierarchy is not the final word of the department (unless the time for appeal has expired), and "[i]t is the obligation of the last court in the hierarchy that rules on the case to give effect to Congress's latest enactment, even when that has the effect of overturning the judgment of an inferior court, since each court, at every level, must 'decide according to existing laws.'" But once a judicial decision achieves finality, it "becomes the last word of the judicial department." And because Article III "gives the Federal Judiciary the power, not merely to rule on cases, but to *decide* them, subject to review only by superior courts in the Article III hierarchy," the "judicial Power is one to render dispositive judgments," and Congress cannot retroactively command Article III courts to reopen final judgments.

Plaut, however, was careful to distinguish the situation before the Court in that case — legislation that attempted to reopen the dismissal of a suit seeking money damages — from legislation that "altered the prospective effect of injunctions entered by Article III courts." We emphasized that "nothing in our holding today calls . . . into question" Congress' authority to alter the prospective effect of previously entered injunctions. Prospective relief under a continuing, executory decree remains subject to alteration due to changes in the underlying law.

[T]he automatic stay of § 3626(e)(2) does not unconstitutionally "suspend" or reopen a judgment of an Article III court. Section 3626(e)(2) does not by itself "tell judges when, how, or what to do." Instead, § 3626(e)(2) merely reflects the change implemented by § 3626(b), which does the "heavy lifting" in the statutory scheme by establishing new standards for prospective relief.

By establishing new standards for the enforcement of prospective relief in § 3626(b), Congress has altered the relevant underlying law. The PLRA has restricted courts' authority to issue and enforce prospective relief concerning prison conditions, requiring that such relief be supported by findings and precisely tailored to what is needed to remedy the violation of a federal right. We note that the constitutionality of § 3626(b) is not challenged here; we assume, without deciding, that the new standards it pronounces are effective. As *Plaut* . . . instruct[s], when Congress changes the law underlying a judgment awarding prospective relief, that relief is no longer enforceable to the extent it is inconsistent with the new law. Although the remedial injunction here is a "final judgment" for purposes of appeal, it is not the "last word of the judicial department." The provision of prospective relief is subject to the continuing supervisory jurisdiction of the court, and therefore may be altered according to subsequent changes in the law. Prospective relief must be "modified if, as it later turns out, one or more of the obligations placed upon the parties has become impermissible under federal law."

For the same reasons, § 3626(e)(2) does not violate the separation of powers principle articulated in *United States v. Klein*, 13 Wall. 128 (1871). In that case, Klein, the executor of the estate of a Confederate sympathizer, sought to recover the value of property seized by the United States during the Civil War, which by statute was recoverable if Klein could demonstrate that the decedent had not given aid or comfort to the rebellion. In *United States v. Padelford*, 9 Wall. 531 (1869), we held that a Presidential pardon satisfied the burden of proving that no such aid or comfort had been given. While Klein's case was pending, Congress enacted a statute providing that a pardon would instead be taken as proof that the pardoned individual had in fact aided the enemy, and if the claimant offered proof of a pardon the court must dismiss the case for lack of jurisdiction. We concluded that the statute was unconstitutional because it purported to "prescribe rules of decision to the Judicial Department of the government in cases pending before it."

Here, the prisoners argue that Congress has similarly prescribed a rule of decision because, for the period of time until the district court makes a final decision on the merits of the motion to terminate prospective relief, § 3626(e)(2) mandates a particular outcome: the termination of prospective relief. As we noted in *Plaut*, however, "[w]hatever the precise scope of *Klein*, . . . later decisions have made clear that its prohibition does not take hold when Congress 'amend[s] applicable law.'" The prisoners concede this point but contend that, because § 3626(e)(2) does not itself amend the legal standard, *Klein* is still applicable. As we have explained, however, § 3626(e)(2) must be read not in isolation, but in the context of § 3626 as a whole. Section 3626(e)(2) operates in conjunction with the new standards for the continuation of prospective relief; if the new standards of § 3626(b)(2) are not met, then the stay "shall operate" unless and until the court makes the findings required by § 3626(b)(3). Rather than prescribing a rule of decision, § 3626(e)(2) simply imposes the consequences of the court's application of the new legal standard.

Finally, the prisoners assert that, even if § 3626(e)(2) does not fall within the recognized prohibitions of *Hayburn's Case, Plaut,* or *Klein*, it still offends the principles of separation of powers because it places a deadline on judicial decisionmaking, thereby interfering with core judicial functions. Congress' imposition of a time limit in § 3626(e)(2), however, does not in itself offend the structural concerns underlying the Constitution's separation of powers. For example, if the PLRA granted courts 10 years to determine whether they could make the required findings, then certainly the PLRA would raise no apprehensions that Congress had encroached on the core function of the Judiciary to decide "cases and controversies properly before them." Respondents' concern with the time limit, then, must be its relative brevity. But whether the time is so short that it deprives litigants of a meaningful opportunity to be heard is a due process question, an issue that is not before us. We leave open, therefore, the question whether this time limit, particularly in a complex case, may implicate due process concerns.

JUSTICE SOUTER, with whom JUSTICE GINSBURG joins, concurring in part and dissenting in part.

I agree that § 3626(e)(2) is unambiguous. . . . I also agree that applying the automatic stay may raise the due process issue, of whether a plaintiff has a fair chance to preserve an existing judgment that was valid when entered. But I believe that applying the statute may also raise a serious separation-of-powers issue if the time it allows turns out to be inadequate for a court to determine whether the new prerequisite to relief is satisfied in a particular case.

JUSTICE BREYER, with whom JUSTICE STEVENS joins, dissenting.

It is . . . possible . . . that the statute, as the majority reads it, would sometimes terminate a complex system of orders entered over a period of years by a court familiar with the local problem — perhaps only to reinstate those orders later, when the termination motion can be decided. Such an automatic termination could leave constitutionally prohibited conditions unremedied, at least temporarily. Alternatively, the threat of termination could lead a district court to abbreviate proceedings that fairness would otherwise demand. At a minimum, the mandatory automatic stay would provide a recipe for uncertainty, as complex judicial orders that have long governed the administration of particular prison systems suddenly turn off, then (perhaps selectively) back on. So read, the statute directly interferes with a court's exercise of its traditional equitable authority, rendering temporarily ineffective pre-existing remedies aimed at correcting past, and perhaps ongoing, violations of the Constitution. That interpretation, as the majority itself concedes, might give rise to serious constitutional problems.

NOTES

1. Congressional Power. As *Miller* makes clear, Congress not only has a large measure of authority to change rules of decision, it also has a great deal of authority to restrict the jurisdiction and remedial power of the federal courts. Congress thus can withdraw previously granted jurisdiction from federal courts, *see, e.g.*, *Ex parte McCardle*, 74 U.S. (7 Wall.) 506 (1869) (sustaining congressional power to remove appellate jurisdiction from the Supreme Court even while a case is still pending), can both prospectively and retroactively alter substantive rules of decision, *see, e.g.*, *I.N.S. v. St. Cyr*, 533 U.S. 289, 315 (2001) ("Despite the dangers inherent in retroactive legislation, it is beyond dispute that, within constitutional limits, Congress has the power to enact laws with retrospective effect."), and can restrict (or change) the courts' ability to render forward-looking relief. *See, e.g.*, *Miller*; Tax Injunction Act of 1937, 28 U.S.C. § 1341 (discussed in Note 3, *infra*).

An Article III limitation on this almost boundless congressional power was expressed in *Plaut v. Spendthrift Farms*, 514 U.S. 211 (1995), where the Supreme Court held that Congress cannot force federal courts to reconsider *final* judgments. *Plaut*, however, involved a claim to money damages under the federal securities laws. Because the judgment in *Plaut* was final, i.e., the case had reached judgment in the District Court and the time to appeal had expired, subsequent changes in federal law could not be applied to the case. Nor could the District Court be ordered by Congress to re-open the judgment. Article III, one might say, demands closure.

Because ongoing prospective relief is never final, *see Miller*, the Article III limitation found in *Plaut* proves irrelevant in the context of forward-looking remedies. Consequently, the remedial standards imposed by §§ 3626(a) and (b) of the Prison Litigation Reform Act — i.e., that a court "shall not grant or approve any prospective relief unless the court finds that such relief is narrowly drawn, extends no further than necessary to correct the violation of a Federal right, and is the least intrusive means necessary to correct the violation of the Federal right" — can constitutionally be applied to existing injunctions. Constitutional limitations must be found outside Article III, presumably in the Bill of Rights or Civil War Amendments.[62] The questions that arise in cases seeking prospective relief are therefore primarily statutory — *did* Congress authorize judicial action? — rather than constitutional.

2. Additional Limitations in the Prison Litigation Reform Act. The Prison Litigation Reform Act creates several unique obstacles for "prisoners"[63] who challenge the conditions of their confinement or who otherwise seek redress under § 1983. In addition to the limitations on injunctive relief discussed in *Miller v. French*, prisoners must first exhaust their administrative remedies, 42 U.S.C. § 1997e(a) (discussed in Chapter 8.A.[3], *infra*), are subject to *sua sponte* dismissal for failure to state a proper claim, *id.* § 1997e(c), and can recover only limited attorney's fees. *Id.* § 1997e(d)

---

[62] The Supreme Court in *Miller* did not address whether the remedial standards enacted by Congress violated some other constitutional right or prohibition. Do they violate the Eighth Amendment? *See Lewis v. Casey*, 518 U.S. 343 (1994) (holding that injunctive relief in the prison conditions context must be "limited to the inadequacy that produced the injury in fact that the plaintiff has established"). Do the remedial standards violate Procedural Due Process? Do they provide the benefactors of the prior injunction a "fair chance" to challenge any change?

[63] The statute defines the term "prisoner" to include "any person incarcerated or detained in any facility who is accused of, convicted of, sentenced for, or adjudicated delinquent for, violations of criminal law or the terms and conditions of parole, probation, pretrial release, or diversionary program." 42 U.S.C. § 1997e(h).

(discussed in Chapter 9.B., *infra*). In addition, § 1997e(e) states that "[n]o Federal civil action may be brought by a prisoner confined in a jail, prison, or other correctional facility, for mental or emotional injury suffered while in custody without a prior showing of physical injury." Lower courts have held, however, that this last limitation does not apply to claims seeking prospective relief. *See, e.g., Dawes v. Walker*, 239 F.3d 489 (2d Cir. 2001) (holding that a prisoner seeking injunctive relief need not allege a prior physical injury).

3. The Tax Injunction Act. The Tax Injunction Act of 1937 was intended to protect state (and local)[64] treasuries from the excesses of *Ex parte Young* (described in Chapter 3.B., *supra*), by preventing federal courts from enjoining the collection of state and local taxes. *See* RICHARD H. FALLON, DANIEL J. MELTZER & DAVID L. SHAPIRO, HART & WECHSLER'S FEDERAL COURTS AND THE FEDERAL SYSTEM 1212–17 (4th ed. 1996). So long as adequate state remedies exist, federal courts are not to interfere. Consequently, disgruntled taxpayers cannot reduce their tax bills by obtaining a federal court order under § 1983 (or any other statute) prohibiting state and local taxing agencies from collecting taxes. *See also National Private Truck Council v. Oklahoma Tax Commission*, 515 U.S. 582 (1995) (extending the Tax Injunction Act to § 1983 actions brought in state court) (discussed in Chapter 8.A.[1], *infra*). The taxpayer must make use of state-law and state-court remedial mechanisms instead.[65] What if the state's taxing scheme is racially discriminatory in violation of the Equal Protection Clause?

HIBBS v. WINN
Supreme Court of the United States
542 U.S. 88 (2004).

JUSTICE GINSBURG delivered the opinion for the Court.

[The challengers, Arizona taxpayers, filed suit in federal court under the Establishment Clause seeking to enjoin income-tax credits that Arizona law made available to taxpayers who donated money to nonprofit "school tuition organizations" (STOs). The District Court concluded that the Tax Injunction Act barred the suit. The Ninth Circuit reversed.]

The question presented is whether the Tax Injunction Act (TIA or Act), [28 U.S.C. § 1341,] which prohibits a lower federal court from restraining "the assessment, levy or collection of any tax under State law," bars th[is] suit. [The challengers] do not contest their own tax liability. Nor do they seek to impede Arizona's receipt of tax revenues. Their suit, we hold, is not the kind [the Act] proscribes.

In decisions spanning a near half century, courts in the federal system, including this Court, have entertained challenges to tax credits authorized by state law, without conceiving of § 1341 as a jurisdictional barrier. On this first occasion squarely to confront the issue, we confirm the authority federal courts exercised in those cases.

---

[64] State taxation includes local taxation under the Tax Injunction Act. *See* 17 C. WRIGHT, A. MILLER, & E. COOPER, FEDERAL PRACTICE AND PROCEDURE § 4237 (2d ed. 1988).

[65] This is also true of refund actions. While the Tax Injunction Act precludes prospective relief — assuming, of course, the existence of an adequate state remedy — actions for monetary relief are precluded by *Fair Assessment in Real Estate Ass'n v. McNary*, 454 U.S. 100 (1981) (using comity principles to prevent federal courts from ordering refunds of state and local taxes) (discussed in Chapter 8.A.[1], *infra*). Section 1983, of course, cannot be used to seek tax refunds in state courts from state agencies because of *Will v. Michigan Dep't of State Police*, 491 U.S. 58 (1989) (holding that states and their official-capacity agents (sued for money damages) are not "persons" for purposes of § 1983 when sued in state court) (discussed in Chapter 3.C., *supra*). Nor have lower courts allowed § 1983 to be used to collect tax refunds from local taxing agencies. *See* Chapter 8.A.[1], *infra*. The practical result is that § 1983 is not useful as a tool for taxpayers to avoid paying unconstitutionally charged taxes — be they state or local. State remedies instead must be pursued in state courts.

It is hardly ancient history that States, once bent on maintaining racial segregation in public schools, and allocating resources disproportionately to benefit white students to the detriment of black students, fastened on tuition grants and tax credits as a promising means to circumvent *Brown v. Board of Education*, 347 U.S. 483 (1954). The federal courts, this Court among them, adjudicated the ensuing challenges, instituted under 42 U.S.C. § 1983, and upheld the Constitution's equal protection requirement. *See, e.g., Griffin v. School Bd. of Prince Edward Cty.*, 377 U.S. 218 (1964) (faced with unconstitutional closure of county public schools and tuition grants and tax credits for contributions to private segregated schools, District Court could require county to levy taxes to fund nondiscriminatory public schools).

In the instant case, [the Director of the Arizona Department of Revenue argues that] . . . we and other federal courts were wrong in those civil-rights cases. The TIA, petitioner maintains, trumps § 1983; the Act, according to [the Director], bars all lower federal-court interference with state tax systems, even when the challengers are not endeavoring to avoid a tax imposed on them, and no matter whether the State's revenues would be raised or lowered should the plaintiffs prevail. The alleged jurisdictional bar, which petitioner asserts has existed since the TIA's enactment in 1937, was not even imagined by the jurists in the pathmarking civil-rights cases just cited, or by the defendants in those cases, litigants with every interest in defeating federal-court adjudicatory authority. Our prior decisions command no respect, petitioner urges, because they constitute mere "sub silentio holdings." We reject that [argument].

The understanding of the Act's purposes and legislative history . . . underpins this Court's previous applications of the TIA. In *California v. Grace Brethren Church*, 457 U.S. 393 (1982), for example, we recognized that the principal purpose of the TIA was to "limit drastically" federal-court interference with "the collection of [state] taxes." . . . The complainants in *Grace Brethren Church* were several California churches and religious schools. They sought federal-court relief from an unemployment compensation tax that state law imposed on them. Their federal action, which bypassed state remedies, was exactly what the TIA was designed to ward off.

The Director invokes several other decisions alleged to keep matters of "state tax administration" entirely free from lower federal-court "interference." Like *Grace Brethren Church*, all of them fall within § 1341's undisputed compass: All involved plaintiffs who mounted federal litigation to avoid paying state taxes (or to gain a refund of such taxes). Federal-court relief, therefore, would have operated to reduce the flow of state tax revenue.[66]

In sum, this Court has interpreted and applied the TIA only in cases Congress wrote the Act to address, i.e., cases in which state taxpayers seek federal-court orders enabling them to avoid paying state taxes. We have read harmoniously the § 1341 instruction conditioning the jurisdictional bar on the availability of "a plain, speedy and efficient remedy" in state court. The remedy inspected in our decisions was not one designed for the universe of plaintiffs who sue the State. Rather, it was a remedy tailor-made for taxpayers.

In a procession of cases not rationally distinguishable from this one, no Justice or member of the bar of this Court ever raised a § 1341 objection that, according to the [Director] in this case, should have caused us to order dismissal of the action for want of jurisdiction. *See Mueller v. Allen*, 463 U.S. 388 (1983) (state tax deduction for parents

---

[66] [n.8] [The Director] urges, and the dissent agrees, that the TIA safeguards another vital state interest: the authority of state courts to determine what state law means. [The challengers], however, have not asked the District Court to interpret any state law — there is no disagreement as to the meaning of [Arizona law], only about whether, as applied, the State's law violates the Federal Constitution. That is a question federal courts are no doubt equipped to adjudicate.

who send their children to parochial schools does not violate Establishment Clause). Consistent with the decades-long understanding prevailing on this issue, [this] suit may proceed without any TIA impediment.

JUSTICE STEVENS, concurring.

Justice Kennedy observes that "years of unexamined habit by litigants and the courts" do not lessen this Court's obligation correctly to interpret a statute. It merits emphasis, however, that prolonged congressional silence in response to a settled interpretation of a federal statute provides powerful support for maintaining the status quo. In statutory matters, judicial restraint strongly counsels waiting for Congress to take the initiative in modifying rules on which judges and litigants have relied. In a contest between the dictionary and the doctrine of *stare decisis*, the latter clearly wins. The Court's fine opinion, which I join without reservation, is consistent with these views.

JUSTICE KENNEDY, with whom the CHIEF JUSTICE and JUSTICES SCALIA and THOMAS join, dissenting.

[T]the TIA's literal text bars district courts from enjoining, suspending, or restraining a State's recording of taxpayer liability on its tax rolls, whether the recordings are made by self-reported taxpayer filing forms or by a State's calculation of taxpayer liability. . . . To order the Director not to record . . . would be to bar the Director from recording the correct taxpayer liability. The TIA's language bars this relief and so bars this suit.

[T]he legislative history of the Tax Injunction Act demonstrates that Congress worried not so much about the form of relief available in the federal courts, as about divesting the federal courts of jurisdiction to interfere with state tax administration.

The Act is designed to respect not only the administration of state tax systems but also state court authority to say what state law means. . . . The TIA protects the responsibility of the States and their courts to administer their own tax systems and to be accountable to the citizens of the State for their policies and decisions.

Th[e] unfortunate result [of the majority's decision] deprives state courts of the first opportunity to hear [tax-credit] cases and to grant the relief the Constitution requires.[67]

NOTES

1. Taxes for TIA Purposes. What qualifies as a tax for purposes of the Tax Injunction Act? In *Henderson v. Stalder*, 407 F.3d 351 (5th Cir. 2005), the plaintiffs sued to enjoin a Louisiana specialty license plate program under the First Amendment. Specifically, they argued that the state's allowing "Choose Life" plates, while not allowing specialty plates with competing views, violated the First Amendment's Free Speech Clause. Louisiana officials responded that the charges for the specialty plates constituted taxes for purposes of the Tax Injunction Act. The Fifth Circuit agreed:

---

[67] [Editor's note: The Supreme Court in *DaimlerChrysler Corp. v. Cuno*, 547 U.S. 332 (2006), ruled that state- and local-taxpayers do not have standing "as taxpayers" to challenge a state's tax credits. The Court in *Hein v. Freedom of Religion Foundation, Inc.*, 127 S. Ct. 2553 (2007), ruled that federal taxpayers lacked standing to challenge Executive expenditures under the Establishment Clause. *See* Note 8 following *City of Los Angeles v. Lyons* (excerpted in Section C.[1], *supra*). Do these cases mean that the local taxpayers in *Hibbs* lack Article III standing to challenge Arizona's tax credits? *Cf. Doe v. Tangipahoa Parish School Board*, 494 F.3d 494 (5th Cir. 2007) (en banc) (holding that local taxpayers did not have standing to challenge prayer events sponsored by a public school).]

[A] broad construction of "tax" is necessary to honor Congress's goals in promulgating the TIA, including that of preventing federally-based delays in the collection of public revenues by state and local governments.

A few brief examples flesh out the distinction between a TIA-covered tax and regulatory fees. In *Hager v. City of West Peoria*, 84 F.3d 865 (7th Cir. 1996), the Seventh Circuit held that graduated fees on the weight of truckloads had been legislated to discourage heavy trucks from using a particular road and thus "were passed to control certain activities, not to raise revenue." This court has, on the other hand, routinely characterized local improvement assessments imposed on a selected class of business as taxes, not fees, in line with the understanding that a "tax" "embraces any extraction of property from a private person by a sovereign for its use."

Neinast v. Texas, 217 F.3d 275 (5th Cir. 2000), . . . found no TIA bar to adjudicating handicapped persons' challenge to a Texas statutory fee for obtaining handicapped parking placards. Revenue obtained from the fee was paid into the state highway fund for the purpose of defraying the cost of the handicapped placards. The court characterized fees, exempt from the TIA, as charges imposed "(1) by an agency, not the legislature; (2) upon those it regulates, not the community as a whole; and (3) for the purpose of defraying regulatory costs, not simply for general revenue-raising purposes." While the first two criteria tugged in opposite directions, the court held that the fee was tagged "for the benefit of the program itself," i.e., to reimburse the costs of the placards.

[Here], the fees for Louisiana specialty plates are directly set by the legislature, even though they are collected by a state agency's motor vehicle unit. . . . Second, the fact that specialty plate charges are paid by some, though not all, purchasers, much less all license plate purchasers, . . . suggest[s] . . . that the charge . . . represented in this respect a fee rather than a tax. On the other hand, this court has held that special assessments imposed on a limited subgroup of the population, were TIA "taxes" because their revenue was used for community improvements.

Finally, [the] argument that specialty plate fees cannot be taxes because they do not serve the general community welfare, inasmuch as they are earmarked for special recipient organizations, is unpersuasive. The fees in question exceed the ordinary motor vehicle registration fees (which are based on a vehicle's value) and an additional handling charge; they are not tied to vehicle regulation as such. . . . [T]he question is not where the money is deposited, but the purpose of the assessment. The Louisiana legislature decreed that the excess charges would be used for a number of purposes, ranging from (but not limited to) park development to university education to adoption support. None of these purposes is "regulatory" as to the specialty plate purchasers.

The voluntariness of the vehicle owner's payment constitutes, in our view, at most a superficial distinction for purposes of the TIA. . . . Any party who pays special assessments to the government does so "voluntarily" in order to engage in particular activity, whether that activity is homebuilding, engaging in a regulated industry, or obtaining permission to park in handicapped spots. . . . A taxpayer "voluntarily" pays the state's ordinary vehicle registration tax for the privilege of legally owning a car, yet that charge is indisputably a tax. It is thus not the taxpayer's motivation but the government's purpose in exacting the charge . . . that distinguishes taxes from non-TIA-covered regulatory fees.

A dominant feature of the program, evidenced in over half of the provisions authorizing specialty license plates, is to raise revenue. Given the TIA's broad purpose to prevent federal courts from interfering with challenges to state and local revenue-raising measures, and the correspondingly narrow and focused exception that has been carved out for regulatory fees that defray the costs of a particular regulatory regime, we are unwilling to mischaracterize the Louisiana legislature's appropriations measures as "fees" in order to achieve federal jurisdiction.

Eight judges sitting on the Fifth Circuit disagreed with the panel's conclusion. Writing a dissent from the denial of rehearing en banc, *see* 434 F.3d 352 (5th Cir. 2005) (Davis, J., dissenting), Judge Davis explained his disagreement:

> The panel concludes that because the charges do not "constitute regulatory fees, we are persuaded that the additional charges must be characterized as taxes." . . . But it is simply not the law that all payments to the state must be regarded as either taxes or regulatory fees.
>
> [T]he relevant question is whether this charge is a tax and if the answer to this question is no, the TIA does not apply regardless of whether the charge is characterized as a regulatory fee, a charitable donation or something else.
>
> The charge at issue here has none of the attributes of a tax. . . . First, the payment in question does not "sustain the essential flow of revenue to the government" because in most cases the funds collected are not retained by the state. Second, the charge is not "imposed" by the legislature; because it is entirely optional and voluntary on the part of Louisiana citizens electing to pay the extra charge for a specialty plate. Third, the payment does not provide a "benefit for the entire community" because the fee from most specialty license plates is dedicated entirely to the specific organization or cause identified on the selected license plate.

The Sixth Circuit in *American Civil Liberties Union v. Bredesen*, 441 F.3d 370 (6th Cir. 2006), which involved a First Amendment challenge to Tennessee's "prestige" license plate program, agreed with Judge Davis's dissent in *Stalder*:

> [T]he payments are most closely analogous to payments for simple purchases from the government. Ordinary purchase payments are not taxes under the TIA, and neither is the extra payment for a specialty license plate.
>
> "Generally speaking, a tax is a pecuniary burden laid upon individuals or property for the purpose of supporting the Government. . . . It is required to be paid. . . . The amount is fixed by the statute, . . . and capable of being enforced by action against the will of the taxpayer."
>
> "Taxes are not debts. . . . Debts are obligations for the payment of money founded upon contract, express or implied."
>
> In this case, Tennessee's sale of specialty plates creates contractual debts to pay but imposes no tax. Instead of using its sovereign power to coerce sales, Tennessee induces willing purchases as would any ordinary market participant. The government confers all the same driving privileges on people who forgo specialty plates to buy standard-issue plates. Drivers' only motive for buying such plates, therefore, must rest with the attractiveness of the "Choose Life" message as Tennessee has marketed it, not a desire to obey Tennessee's will.
>
> We recognize that there is some case law to the effect that cases like this one are precluded by the Tax Injunction Act. *See Henderson v. Stalder*, 407 F.3d 351 (5th Cir. 2005). These cases proceed on the questionable assumption that the applicable test is the one for differentiating between a regulatory fee and a tax.
>
> In contrast, a purchase price cannot be said to be "imposed by an agency upon those subject to its regulation." Instead it is merely a contract price. The test for determining which compelled exactions are taxes and which are fees cannot logically be used to determine whether a payment is a compelled exaction in the first place.

2. Forcing Others to Pay. The Supreme Court in *Hibbs* distinguished between challenges that seek to relieve the challenger from paying a tax (which are covered by the TIA) and those that seek to force others to pay a tax (which are not). In *Henderson v. Stalder*, 407 F.3d 351 (5th Cir. 2005), the court concluded that a challenge to Louisiana's specialty license plate program fell into the former category and was thus precluded by the TIA. Even though the challenger did not want to avoid the tax, the court held, the fact that she sought to prevent others from paying it doomed her suit under the TIA:

> *Hibbs* opened the federal courthouse doors slightly notwithstanding the limits of the TIA, but it did so only where (1) a third party (not the taxpayer) files suit, and (2) the suit's success will enrich, not deplete, the government entity's coffers.
>
> [The] First Amendment attack on Louisiana's prestige license plate program satisfies only the first part of *Hibbs*. [The challenger's] success, however, flies in the face of *Hibbs*'s second prong: in enjoining the program's operation, [the challenger's] judgment has placed the federal courts in the position of reducing state tax revenues.
>
> [I]n other cases in which a plaintiff has objected to her exclusion from a state-sponsored forum, the Supreme Court's remedy has not been to close down the forum and censor the speech of others, but to approve injunctions opening up the forum to the plaintiff. Had [the challenger] sought such forum-opening relief, . . . the proper relief would have entailed an increase of state revenues and would not conflict with *Hibbs* or the TIA.

Contrast American Civil Liberties Union v. Bredesen, 441 F.3d 370 (6th Cir. 2006) ("Plaintiffs in this case are . . . not seeking to avoid paying for a 'Choose Life' license plate, and it is therefore at least questionable whether the TIA would apply even if the payment for the license plates were a 'tax.' ").

3. The Johnson Act. The Johnson Act of 1934, 28 U.S.C. § 1342, is similar to the Tax Injunction Act in that it deprives federal courts of jurisdiction to enjoin state ratemaking proceedings, so long as the ratemaking proceedings do not interfere with interstate commerce, are not pre-empted by federal law, *see, e.g., IBEW v. Public Service Commission*, 614 F.2d 206 (9th Cir. 1980), and adequate state remedies otherwise exist. *See generally New Orleans Public Services, Inc. v. Council of City of New Orleans*, 491 U.S. 350 (1989) (excerpted in Chapter 7.B., *infra*). Both the Tax Injunction Act and Johnson Act were responses to federal courts' perceived abuse of *Ex parte Young* (described in Chapter 3.B., *supra*), which holds that the Eleventh Amendment does not bar the issuance of prospective relief against state officials who act unconstitutionally. *See* RICHARD H. FALLON, DANIEL J. MELTZER & DAVID L. SHAPIRO, HART & WECHSLER'S FEDERAL COURTS AND THE FEDERAL SYSTEM 1212–17 (4th ed. 1996).

4. The Anti-Injunction Act. The Anti-Injunction Act, 28 U.S.C. § 2283, states: "A court of the United States may not grant an injunction to stay proceedings in a State court except as expressly authorized by Act of Congress, or where necessary in aid of its jurisdiction, or to protect or effectuate its judgments." The Supreme Court ruled in *Mitchum v. Foster*, 407 U.S. 225, 242 (1972), that § 1983 "expressly authorized" federal injunctions staying proceedings in state courts:

> Th[e] legislative history makes evident that Congress clearly conceived that it was altering the relationship between the states and the nation with respect to the protection of federally created rights; it was concerned that state instrumentalities could not protect those rights; it realized that state officers might, in fact, be antipathetic to the vindication of those rights; and it believed that these failings extended to the state courts.

Notwithstanding the Court's decision in *Mitchum*, the abstention doctrine articulated in *Younger v. Harris*, 401 U.S. 37 (1971) (excerpted and discussed at length in Chapter

7.B., *infra*), creates a significant stumbling block by preventing federal courts from enjoining ongoing state proceedings under certain circumstances.

Chapter 7
FEDERAL ABSTENTION IN FAVOR OF STATE PROCEEDINGS

A. AVOIDING CONSTITUTIONAL ISSUES

RAILROAD COMMISSION OF TEXAS v. PULLMAN CO.
Supreme Court of the United States
312 U.S. 496 (1941)

Mr. Justice Frankfurter delivered the opinion of the Court.

In those sections of Texas where the local passenger traffic is slight, trains carry but one sleeping car. These trains, unlike trains having two or more sleepers, are without a Pullman conductor; the sleeper is in charge of a porter who is subject to the train conductor's control. As is well known, porters on Pullmans are colored and conductors are white. Addressing itself to this situation, the Texas Railroad Commission after due hearing ordered that "no sleeping car shall be operated on any line of railroad in the State of Texas . . . unless such cars are continuously in the charge of an employee . . . having the rank and position of Pullman conductor." Thereupon, the Pullman Company and the railroads affected brought this action in a federal district court to enjoin the Commission's order. Pullman porters were permitted to intervene as complainants, and Pullman conductors entered the litigation in support of the order.

The Pullman Company and the railroads assailed the order as unauthorized by Texas law as well as violative of the Equal Protection, the Due Process and the Commerce Clauses of the Constitution. The intervening porters adopted these objections but mainly objected to the order as a discrimination against Negroes in violation of the Fourteenth Amendment.

The complaint of the Pullman porters undoubtedly tendered a substantial constitutional issue. It is more than substantial. It touches a sensitive area of social policy upon which the federal courts ought not to enter unless no alternative to its adjudication is open. Such constitutional adjudication plainly can be avoided if a definitive ruling on the state issue would terminate the controversy. It is therefore our duty to turn to a consideration of questions under Texas law.

The Commission found justification for its order in a Texas statute which we quote in the margin.[1] It is common ground that if the order is within the Commission's authority its subject matter must be included in the Commission's power to prevent "unjust discrimination . . . and to prevent any and all other abuses" in the conduct of railroads. Whether arrangements pertaining to the staffs of Pullman cars are covered by the Texas concept of "discrimination" is far from clear. What practices of the railroads may be deemed to be "abuses" subject to the Commission's correction is equally doubtful. Reading the Texas statutes and the Texas decisions as outsiders

---

[1] [n.1] Vernon's Anno. Texas Civil Statutes, Article 6445:

> Power and authority are hereby conferred upon the Railroad Commission of Texas over all railroads . . . and it is hereby made the duty of the said Commission to adopt all necessary rates, charges and regulations, to govern and regulate such railroads, . . . and to correct abuses and prevent unjust discrimination in the rates, charges and tolls of such railroads, . . . and to fix division of rates, charges and regulations between railroads and other utilities and common carriers where a division is proper and correct, and to prevent any and all other abuses in the conduct of their business and to do and perform such other duties and details in connection therewith as may be provided by law.

without special competence in Texas law, we would have little confidence in our independent judgment regarding the application of that law to the present situation. The lower court did deny that the Texas statutes sustained the Commission's assertion of power. . . . Had we . . . no choice in the matter but to decide what is the law of the state, we should hesitate long before rejecting their forecast of Texas law. But no matter how seasoned the judgment of the district court may be, it cannot escape being a forecast rather than a determination. The last word on the meaning of Article 6445 of the Texas Civil Statutes, and therefore the last word on the statutory authority of the Railroad Commission in this case, belongs neither to us nor to the district court but to the supreme court of Texas. In this situation a federal court of equity is asked to decide an issue by making a tentative answer which may be displaced tomorrow by a state adjudication. The reign of law is hardly promoted if an unnecessary ruling of a federal court is thus supplanted by a controlling decision of a state court. The resources of equity are equal to an adjustment that will avoid the waste of a tentative decision as well as the friction of a premature constitutional adjudication.

An appeal to the chancellor, as we had occasion to recall only the other day, is an appeal to the "exercise of the sound discretion, which guides the determination of courts of equity." The history of equity jurisdiction is the history of regard for public consequences in employing the extraordinary remedy of the injunction. There have been as many and as variegated applications of this supple principle as the situations that have brought it into play. Few public interests have a higher claim upon the discretion of a federal chancellor than the avoidance of needless friction with state policies, whether the policy relates to the enforcement of the criminal law, or the administration of a specialized scheme for liquidating embarrassed business enterprises, or the final authority of a state court to interpret doubtful regulatory laws of the state. These cases reflect a doctrine of abstention appropriate to our federal system whereby the federal courts, "exercising a wise discretion," restrain their authority because of "scrupulous regard for the rightful independence of the state governments" and for the smooth working of the federal judiciary. This use of equitable powers is a contribution of the courts in furthering the harmonious relation between state and federal authority without the need of rigorous congressional restriction of those powers.

Regard for these important considerations of policy in the administration of federal equity jurisdiction is decisive here. If there was no warrant in state law for the Commission's assumption of authority there is an end of the litigation; the constitutional issue does not arise. The law of Texas appears to furnish easy and ample means for determining the Commission's authority. Article 6453 of the Texas Civil Statutes gives a review of such an order in the state courts. Or, if there are difficulties in the way of this procedure of which we have not been apprised, the issue of state law may be settled by appropriate action on the part of the State to enforce obedience to the order. In the absence of any showing that these obvious methods for securing a definitive ruling in the state courts cannot be pursued with full protection of the constitutional claim, the district court should exercise its wise discretion by staying its hands.

We therefore remand the cause to the district court, with directions to retain the bill pending a determination of proceedings, to be brought with reasonable promptness, in the state court in conformity with this opinion.

NOTES

1. *Pullman* Basics. An "important reason for abstention is to avoid unwarranted determination of federal constitutional questions. When federal courts interpret state statutes in a way that raises federal constitutional questions, 'a constitutional determination is predicated on a reading of the statute that is not binding on state courts and may be discredited at any time — thus essentially rendering the federal-court decision advisory and the litigation underlying it meaningless'." *Pennzoil Co. v. Texaco, Inc.*, 481 U.S. 1 (1987). *See also Addiction Specialists, Inc. v. Township of Hampton*, 411 F.3d 399 (3d Cir. 2005) ("[T]he Supreme Court's decision in [*Pullman*] counsels against deciding unsettled issues of state law where it is not necessary to do so."). Thus, *Pullman* abstention is "appropriate only when three concurrent criteria are satisfied: (1) the federal plaintiff's complaint must require resolution of a sensitive question of federal constitutional law; (2) that question must be susceptible to being mooted or narrowed by a definitive ruling on state law issues; and (3) the possibly determinative state law must be unclear." *United States v. Morros*, 268 F.3d 695 (9th Cir. 2001) (refusing to apply *Pullman* to a preemption problem). *See also Propper v. Clark*, 337 U.S. 472 (1949) (holding that *Pullman* abstention is not proper to avoid decision of nonconstitutional federal questions).[2]

2. Ambiguous State Laws. *Pullman* abstention is not justified when state law is clear. In *City of Houston v. Hill*, 482 U.S. 451 (1987), for example, a Houston ordinance that made it a crime "to assault, strike or in any manner oppose, molest, abuse or interrupt any policeman in the execution of his duty" was challenged under the First Amendment. The Supreme Court ruled that abstention was not proper: "This ordinance is not susceptible to a limiting construction because, as both courts below agreed, its language is plain and its meaning unambiguous." Rejecting the city's proposed limiting constructions, the Court observed that "it is doubtful that even 'a remarkable job of plastic surgery upon the face of the ordinance' could save it." *See also United States v. Morros*, 268 F.3d 695 (9th Cir. 2001) (holding that *Pullman* abstention is not proper when "there is no unclear state law issue that would moot the preemption question if resolved by a state court").

3. Forcing State Court Proceedings. Justice Frankfurter concluded in *Pullman* that the plaintiffs were required to file a claim in state court to resolve the meaning of Texas law, rather than join their state claim with their federal claim in the proceedings in federal court. *Pullman* abstention is thus proper regardless of whether state court proceedings are pending, and irrespective of the plaintiffs' desire to file an action in state court. In fact, *Pullman* abstention can be invoked by the federal court even when the governmental defendant agrees that the state law is clear or otherwise seeks to have the matter addressed by the federal court. *See, e.g., Ohio Bureau of Employment Services v. Hodory*, 431 U.S. 471 (1977) ("*Pullman* abstention, where deference to the state process may result in elimination or material alteration of the constitutional issue, surely does not require that this Court defer to the wishes of the parties concerning adjudication."); *Kendall-Jackson Winery, Ltd. v. Bransen*, 212 F.3d 995 (7th Cir. 2000) ("*Hodory* observes that states cannot *compel* federal courts to adjudicate a tough constitutional point when state courts may construe the statute in a way that obviates the need.").

4. *Pullman* and *Pennhurst*. The challengers in *Pullman* raised state-law claims for prospective relief in federal court. Because of the Eleventh Amendment and the Supreme Court's decision in *Pennhurst State School and Hospital v. Halderman*, 465 U.S. 89 (1984) (discussed in Note 3 following *Edelman v. Jordan* in Chapter 3.B., *supra*), federal courts today cannot award prospective relief under state law against state officials. Were *Pullman* to arise today, then, a federal court would clearly be prohibited from awarding the plaintiffs prospective relief under Texas law. For this reason, it is not uncommon for plaintiffs to avoid pleading state law in federal court when seeking injunctive relief from state officials.

In part because of *Pennhurst*, most *Pullman* settings today involve a challenged state law that is itself ambiguous. The meaning of state law is necessary to the federal

---

[2] The Supreme Court extended *Pullman* to § 1983 actions in *Harrison v. NAACP*, 360 U.S. 167 (1959). *See also Bellotti v. Baird*, 428 U.S. 132 (1976) (holding that abstention was proper in a § 1983 case involving a constitutional challenge).

constitutional challenge, but cannot itself justify a federal court's order enjoining the governmental defendant's action. What about a situation where a challenged state law is itself clear, but is perhaps subject to challenge under a higher state law — like the Texas enabling statute in *Pullman* or perhaps a state constitutional provision? Either kind of challenge would appear to be unnecessary to the federal constitutional question, and *Pennhurst* would in any event prevent the challengers from joining them with their federal challenge. Can the plaintiffs still be forced to file an original action in state court challenging this otherwise clear state law under state law? In *Askew v. Hargrave*, 401 U.S. 476 (1971), a class action challenging Florida's school financing program under the Equal Protection Clause, the Supreme Court invoked *Pullman* abstention and remanded the case so that the lower federal court could consider staying its hand in favor of an ongoing challenge under the Florida Constitution in state court. Success in the Florida courts under the Florida Constitution, after all, would "obviate the necessity of determining the [Equal Protection] question." Professors Fallon, Meltzer and Shapiro, in their authoritative treatise on federal jurisdiction, ask: "Is it reasonable to compel plaintiffs, at their own expense, to make state law claims they do not wish to make in a forum in which they do not wish to litigate, when resolution of the state claim is not *necessary* to consideration of the federal claim?" RICHARD H. FALLON, DANIEL J. MELTZER & DAVID L. SHAPIRO, HART & WECHSLER'S FEDERAL COURTS AND THE FEDERAL SYSTEM 1239 (4th ed. 1996).

5. Supplemental Jurisdiction. Supplemental state-law claims for prospective relief directed at *local* officials and governments are not barred by the Eleventh Amendment. *See Lincoln County v. Luning*, 133 U.S. 529 (1890) (discussed in Note 4 following *Seminole Tribe* in Chapter 3.A., *supra*). Assuming these claims otherwise fall within a federal court's subject matter jurisdiction, the Constitution does not prohibit federal courts from addressing them. Federal jurisdiction over state claims in a non-diversity setting is provided by 28 U.S.C. § 1367(a), the federal supplemental jurisdiction statute, which states that "in any civil action of which the district courts have original jurisdiction, the district courts shall have supplemental jurisdiction over all other claims that are so related to claims in the action within such original jurisdiction that they form part of the same case or controversy under Article III of the United States Constitution." *See also United Mine Workers v. Gibbs*, 383 U.S. 715 (1966) (holding that federal jurisdiction is proper over state claims so long as they arise from "common nucleus of operative fact" supporting the federal claims).

District Courts have a large measure of discretion under this supplemental jurisdiction statute to dismiss state law claims — those seeking prospective relief as well as money damages — that would otherwise fall under federal jurisdiction. Section 1367(c) states:

> The district courts may decline to exercise supplemental jurisdiction over a claim under subsection (a) if—
>
> (1) the claim raises a novel or complex issue of State law,
>
> (2) the claim substantially predominates over the claim or claims over which the district court has original jurisdiction,
>
> (3) the district court has dismissed all claims over which it has original jurisdiction, or
>
> (4) in exceptional circumstances, there are other compelling reasons for declining jurisdiction.

Remember that a federal court that invokes *Pullman* abstention deflects state-law issues to state court and stays its hand, but still retains jurisdiction over the properly pleaded federal claims.[3] Section 1367(c), in contrast, envisions a federal court's

---

[3] *But cf. Harris County Commissioners v. Moore*, 420 U.S. 77 (1975) (instructing the District Court to dismiss federal claims under *Pullman* without prejudice because the state supreme court had ruled that it

proceeding with its federal claims after dismissing the supplemental state-law claims. *Pullman*, moreover, has not historically been applied to challenges seeking money damages. *See, e.g., Bad Frog Brewery Inc. v. New York State Liquor Authority*, 134 F.3d 87 (2d Cir. 1998) (observing that *Pullman* abstention was not proper but declining to entertain a state-law damage claims under § 1367). *Pullman* also has a broader scope than § 1367 in that it does not require that state law claims even be pleaded. For further discussion of § 1367, *see City of Chicago v. International College of Surgeons*, 522 U.S. 156 (1997) (remanding to lower courts to consider abstention under either *Pullman* or § 1367) (excerpted in Chapter 8.A.[4], *infra*).

6. Appeal of *Pullman* Decisions. A District Court's interlocutory decision to abstain under *Pullman* is immediately appealable, *see Moses H. Cone Memorial Hospital v. Mercury Construction Co.*, 460 U.S. 1 (1983), while its decision *not* to abstain is not. *See Gulfstream Aerospace v. Mayacamas*, 485 U.S. 271 (1988). The proper standard of review on interlocutory appeal is subject to dispute. Several Circuits have held that a District Court's decision to abstain is subject to *de novo* review on appeal, as opposed to the more lenient "abuse of discretion" standard. *See, e.g., Planned Parenthood of Dutchess-Ulster v. Steinhaus*, 60 F.3d 122 (2d Cir. 1995) ("There is little, if any, discretion to abstain in a case which does not meet the requirements of a particular abstention principle."); *Cedar Shake and Shingle Bureau v. City of Los Angeles*, 997 F.2d 620 (9th Cir. 1993) ("A district court has no discretion to abstain where the abstention requirements are not met; whether those requirements are met is reviewed de novo."). Others have expressed a more deferential standard toward the District Court's abstention decision. *See, e.g., Stone v. Wall*, 135 F.3d 1438 (11th Cir. 1998) ("We reverse a district court's decision to abstain when there is an abuse of discretion.").

A District Court's decision not to abstain is ordinarily not subject to interlocutory appeal. *See, e.g., Hi Tech Trans LLC v. New Jersey*, 382 F.3d 295 (3d Cir. 2004) ("The prevailing view now is 'that for all of the abstention doctrines, a federal court's decision to abstain is immediately appealable, but its refusal to abstain is not appealable until there is a final judgment.'"). Once appealed, moreover, a decision not to abstain is subject to review only for abuse of discretion. *See, e.g., Hartford Courant Co. v. Pelligrino*, 380 F.3d 83 (2d Cir. 2004) ("Decisions involving both *Pullman* and *Burford* abstention are . . . reviewed for abuse of discretion, although the abuse of discretion inquiry is somewhat more searching in the abstention context."); *Cedar Shake and Shingle Bureau v. City of Los Angeles*, 997 F.2d 620 (9th Cir. 1993) ("We review the district court's decision not to abstain for an abuse of discretion."); *Louisiana Debating and Literary Ass'n v. City of New Orleans*, 42 F.3d 1483 (5th Cir. 1995). This reflects the fact that a District Court is not legally required to abstain whenever it might; rather, assuming abstention is legally proper, there is still room for discretion.

Like the District Courts, appellate courts can invoke *Pullman* abstention on their own motions. *See Nicholson v. Scoppetta*, 344 F.3d 154 (2d Cir. 2003) ("Although the parties do not appeal that determination, we have an independent obligation to consider whether *Pullman* abstention is appropriate. Indeed, abstention could not serve its proper function if the parties could, by their own decisions, force us to confront an otherwise avoidable constitutional question."); *Columbia Basin Apartment Association v. City of Pasco*, 268 F.3d 791 (9th Cir. 2001) (reversing sua sponte a District Court's failure to abstain).

7. Attorney's Fees. Given that a fee-shifting statute, 42 U.S.C. § 1988(b) (discussed in Chapter 9.A., *infra*) accompanies § 1983, a feature not often found under state laws, can a state-law ruling by a state court duplicate the relief available under federal law? What if the Texas state court in *Pullman*, for example, ruled that Texas's law prohibited the discriminatory order? Presumably the discriminatory order would be declared invalid or otherwise enjoined under state law. But the successful plaintiffs would likely not be

---

could not afford relief while federal claim was pending in federal court).

entitled to recover their attorney's fees from the losing defendants under state law. Are they entitled to return to federal court and force a ruling on the federal constitutional issue under § 1983? If the plaintiff only seek prospective relief, is not the case now moot? *See* Chapter 6.C., *supra* (discussing mootness). If the case is not moot, are the plaintiffs otherwise precluded from litigating the federal issues involved in federal court? *See England v. Louisiana Board of Medical Examiners*, 375 U.S. 411 (1964) (holding that federal plaintiffs are not barred from litigating federal issues in federal court following *Pullman* abstention so long as they properly reserve their claims for the federal court) (excerpted in Note 6 following *Migra* in Chapter 8.A., *infra*). If they can return to federal court, are the plaintiffs allowed to recover attorney's fees under § 1988(b) for the time invested in the state court proceedings? *See, e.g., Schneider v. Colegio de Abrogadas de Puerto Rico*, 187 F.3d 30 (1st Cir. 1999) (Lipez, J., concurring) ("Under certain conditions, federal courts have held that hours expended in state court proceedings are compensable under § 1988. We have, for example, held that hours expended in state court proceedings are compensable where those state proceedings were initiated and pursued solely because of a federal court's *Pullman* abstention subsequent to the initial filing of a federal claim in the federal forum."). *Cf. Webb v. Board of Education*, 471 U.S. 234 (1985) (holding that attorney's hours devoted to "optional" administrative proceedings are not compensable as being necessary to successful § 1983 litigation).

8. **Certification to State Courts.** Many states have adopted certification procedures authorizing their supreme courts to entertain state-law questions directed to them by federal courts. Florida, for example, authorizes certification by the Supreme Court or any United State Court of Appeals:

> On either its own motion or that of a party, the Supreme Court of the United States or a United States court of appeals may certify a question of law to the Supreme Court of Florida if the answer is determinative of the cause and there is no controlling precedent of the Supreme Court of Florida.

FLA. R. APP. P. 9.150(a). *See Clay v. Sun Insurance Office, Ltd.*, 363 U.S. 207 (1960). Arizona law likewise permits the State's highest court to

> answer questions of law certified to it by the supreme court of the United States, a court of appeals of the United States, a United States district court or a tribal court . . . if there are involved in any proceedings before the certifying court questions of [Arizona law] which may be determinative of the cause then pending in the certifying court and as to which it appears to the certifying court there is no controlling precedent in the decisions of the supreme court and the intermediate appellate courts of this state.

ARIZ. REV. STAT. ANN. § 12-1861 (1994).

Is certification preferable to *Pullman* abstention? Arizona's certification procedure was addressed at length by the Supreme Court in *Arizonans for Official English v. Arizona*, 520 U.S. 43 (1997), where a state constitutional provision declaring English to be "the official language of the State" was challenged on First Amendment grounds. Because the case was moot, the Court did not rule on the constitutionality of the provision. *See* Note 8 following *U.S. Bancorp Mortgage Co.* in Chapter 6.C.[1], *supra*. Still, it took the opportunity, in an opinion by Justice Ginsburg, to trumpet the merits of certification:

> Certification today covers territory once dominated by a deferral device called "Pullman abstention," after the generative case, *Railroad Comm'n of Tex. v. Pullman Co.* Designed to avoid federal-court error in deciding state-law questions antecedent to federal constitutional issues, the *Pullman* mechanism remitted parties to the state courts for adjudication of the unsettled state-law issues. If settlement of the state-law question did not prove dispositive of the case, the parties could return to the federal court for decision of the federal issues. Attractive in theory because it placed state-law questions in courts

equipped to rule authoritatively on them, *Pullman* abstention proved protracted and expensive in practice, for it entailed a full round of litigation in the state court system before any resumption of proceedings in federal court. Certification procedure, in contrast, allows a federal court faced with a novel state-law question to put the question directly to the State's highest court, reducing the delay, cutting the cost, and increasing the assurance of gaining an authoritative response. Most States have adopted certification procedures. Arizona's statute permits the State's highest court to consider questions certified to it by federal district courts, as well as courts of appeals and this Court.

Both lower federal courts in this case refused to invite the aid of the Arizona Supreme Court because they found the language of [the state law] "plain," and the Attorney General's limiting construction unpersuasive. Furthermore, the Ninth Circuit suggested as a proper price for certification a concession by the Attorney General that [the state law] "would be unconstitutional if construed as [plaintiff Yniguez] contended it should be." Finally, the Ninth Circuit acknowledged the pendency of a case similar to Yniguez's in the Arizona court system, but found that litigation no cause for a stay of the federal-court proceedings.

A more cautious approach was in order. Through certification of novel or unsettled questions of state law for authoritative answers by a State's highest court, a federal court may save "time, energy, and resources and hel[p] build a cooperative judicial federalism." It is true . . . that in our decision certifying questions in *Virginia v. American Booksellers Assn., Inc.*, 484 U.S. 383 (1988), we noted the State's concession that the statute there challenged would be unconstitutional if construed as plaintiffs contended it should be. But neither in that case nor in any other did we declare such a concession a condition precedent to certification.

The District Court and the Court of Appeals ruled out certification primarily because they believed [the state law] was not fairly subject to a limiting construction. . . . Nevertheless, the Court of Appeals understood that the ballot initiative proponents themselves at least "partially endorsed the Attorney General's reading." Given the novelty of the question and its potential importance to the conduct of Arizona's business, plus the views of the Attorney General and those of [the state law's] sponsors, the certification requests merited more respectful consideration than they received in the proceedings below.

Blending abstention with certification, the Ninth Circuit found "no unique circumstances in this case militating in favor of certification." Novel, unsettled questions of state law, however, not "unique circumstances," are necessary before federal courts may avail themselves of state certification procedures. Those procedures do not entail the delays, expense, and procedural complexity that generally attend abstention decisions. Taking advantage of certification made available by a State may "greatly simplif[y]" an ultimate adjudication in federal court.

As observed by the Court in *Arizonans for Official English*, certification can be a useful tool to answer troubling state-law issues. *See* Kathryn A. Watts, *Adapting to Administrative Law's* Erie *Doctrine*, 101 Nw. U. L. Rev. 997, 1021 (2007) ("certification enabled the federal courts to interact and communicate with state courts in the wake of *Erie* rather than blindly imposing their own interpretations on unclear state law"). All that is required is a state law that is ambiguous or "'fairly susceptible' to a narrowing construction," *Stenberg v. Carhart*, 545 U.S. 748 (2005); *see also City of Houston v. Hill*, 482 U.S. 451 (1987) (refusing to certify a question because the statute was not subject to narrowing), a state rule authorizing certification, and a state court willing to entertain the certified issues. *See, e.g., Friery v. Los Angeles Unified School District*, 448 F.3d

1146 (9th Cir. 2006) (observing that the California Supreme Court refused to answer its certified questions). As illustrated by the Florida and Arizona approaches, states do not agree on a single, uniform procedure. Nebraska, for instance, requires that the certified question be "determinative of the cause." See NEB. REV. STAT. § 24-219 (1995).[4] But most follow the simple pattern laid down by Florida and Arizona. Notwithstanding the Court's encouragement in *Arizonans for Official English* and the streamlined procedures often available under state laws, federal courts remain somewhat hesitant to certify state law questions. Many have opted for abstention instead. See, e.g., *Currie v. Group Insurance Commission*, 290 F.3d 1 (1st Cir. 2002) ("Certification would interrupt the normal state appellate processes. Moreover, it would put the decisions of the state law issue directly to the state's highest court on a record developed to address federal, not state, issues. Finally, it is unclear whether the [state court] would accept certification where, as here, the state court's decision on state issues would not be dispositive of the federal issue, but would merely render it moot.").

Although courts need not await a motion or request to certify — rather, they can do so on their own motions and over the objections of the parties, *see, e.g., Elkins v. Moreno*, 435 U.S. 647 (1978) (Supreme Court certifying question *sua sponte* to state's highest court); *Nicholson v. Scoppetta*, 344 F.3d 154 (2d Cir. 2003) (certifying state-law questions to New York Court of Appeals even though neither party requested it) — the fact that certification has not been requested is relevant to the certification decision. *See, e.g., Town of Castle Rock v. Gonzales*, 545 U.S. 748 (2005) (refusing to certify a question in part because neither party requested it); *Stenberg v. Carhart*, 545 U.S. 748 (2005) (observing that the state did not request certification). In the end, assuming an ambiguous state law and a state certification procedure, whether to use the certification procedure is left to the discretion of the federal court.

9. *Burford* Abstention. Abstention doctrines pepper federal court jurisprudence. Together with *Pullman* abstention, one that often arises in the context of constitutional litigation is abstention under *Younger v. Harris*, 401 U.S. 37 (1971), which forms the basis of Section B., *infra*. Before proceeding to *Younger*, however, it is useful to consider two additional abstention doctrines that occasionally emerge in constitutional cases. The first can be traced to the Supreme Court's opinion in *Burford v. Sun Oil Co.*, 319 U.S. 315 (1943), which is succinctly explained by Justice Scalia in *New Orleans Public Service, Inc. v. Council of City of New Orleans*, 491 U.S. 350 (1989) *(NOPSI)*:

> In *Burford v. Sun Oil Co.*, a Federal District Court sitting in equity was confronted with a Fourteenth Amendment challenge to the reasonableness of the Texas Railroad Commission's grant of an oil drilling permit. The constitutional challenge was of minimal federal importance, involving solely the question whether the commission had properly applied Texas' complex oil and gas conservation regulations. Because of the intricacy and importance of the regulatory scheme, Texas had created a centralized system of judicial review of commission orders, which "permit[ted] the state courts, like the Railroad Commission itself, to acquire a specialized knowledge" of the regulations and industry. We found the state courts' review of commission decisions "expeditious and adequate," and, because the exercise of equitable jurisdiction by comparatively unsophisticated Federal District Courts alongside state-court review had repeatedly led to "[d]elay, misunderstanding of local law, and needless federal conflict with the state policy," we concluded that "a sound respect for the independence of state action requir[ed] the federal equity court to stay its hand."
>
> From th[is] case[ ], and others on which [it] relied, we have distilled the principle now commonly referred to as the "*Burford* doctrine." Where timely

---

[4] The Court in *Stenberg v. Carhart*, 545 U.S. 748 (2005), used this as one reason to deny certification over the meaning of Nebraska's partial-birth abortion statute.

and adequate state-court review is available, a federal court sitting in equity must decline to interfere with the proceedings or orders of state administrative agencies: (1) when there are "difficult questions of state law bearing on policy problems of substantial public import whose importance transcends the result in the case then at bar"; or (2) where the "exercise of federal review of the question in a case and in similar cases would be disruptive of state efforts to establish a coherent policy with respect to a matter of substantial public concern."

The Court in *NOPSI* concluded that *Burford* does not require abstention when a federal challenge is premised on the meaning of federal, as opposed to state, law:

> While *Burford* is concerned with protecting complex state administrative processes from undue federal interference, it does not require abstention whenever there exists such a process, or even in all cases where there is a "potential for conflict" with state regulatory law or policy. Here, [the] primary claim is that the [City] Council is prohibited by federal law from refusing to provide reimbursement [to an electric utility] for [federally]-allocated wholesale costs. Unlike a claim that a state agency has misapplied its lawful authority or has failed to take into consideration or properly weigh relevant state-law factors, federal adjudication of this sort of pre-emption claim would not disrupt the State's attempt to ensure uniformity in the treatment of an "essentially local problem."
>
> That *Burford* abstention is not justified in these circumstances is strongly suggested by our decision in *Public Util. Comm'n of Ohio v. United Fuel Gas Co.*, 317 U.S. 456 (1943), decided just four months prior to *Burford*, in which a District Court had enjoined on federal pre-emption grounds a State's attempt to fix interstate gas rates. After determining that the State's order impinged on the authority Congress had vested solely in the Federal Power Commission, we addressed the State's contention that the District Court had nonetheless abused its discretion by granting injunctive relief: "It is perhaps unnecessary at this late date to repeat the admonition that the federal courts should be wary of interrupting the proceedings of state administrative tribunals by use of the extraordinary writ of injunction. But this, too, is a rule of equity and not to be applied in blind disregard of fact. And what are the commanding circumstances of the present case? First, and most important, the orders of the state Commission are on their face plainly invalid. No inquiry beyond the orders themselves and the undisputed facts which underlie them is necessary in order to discover that they are in conflict with the federal Act."
>
> Similarly in the case at bar, no inquiry beyond the four corners of the Council's retail rate order is needed to determine whether it is facially pre-empted. . . . Such an inquiry would not unduly intrude into the processes of state government or undermine the State's ability to maintain desired uniformity. It may, of course, result in an injunction against enforcement of the rate order, but "there is . . . no doctrine requiring abstention merely because resolution of a federal question may result in the overturning of a state policy."

Burford abstention differs from *Pullman* abstention in several ways. First, unlike *Pullman* abstention, *Burford* abstention is not limited to cases involving federal constitutional issues. *See* James C. Rehnquist, *Taking Comity Seriously: How to Neutralize the Abstention Doctrine*, 46 STAN. L. REV. 1049, 1077 (1994). Second, it does not require an unsettled or ambiguous state law. *Id.* Third, courts have sometimes applied *Burford* to claims seeking money damages. *See* Steven Plitt & Joshua D. Rogers, *Charting a Course for Federal Removal Through the Abstention Doctrine: A Titanic Experience in the Sargossa Sea of Jurisdictional Manipulation*, 56 DEPAUL L. REV. 107, 134 & n.230 (2006) (collecting cases). *Contrast Quackenbush v. Allstate Insurance Co.*, 517 U.S. 706 (1996) (holding that *Burford* abstention does not apply to claims for money damages) (cited in Note 11, *infra*). Notwithstanding this greater breadth, *Burford* abstention — as illustrated by *NOPSI* — has been used sparingly by the Supreme Court. "The Supreme Court has considered *Burford* abstention in several subsequent cases, but has only once[, in *Alabama Public Service Commission v. Southern Railway*, 341 U.S. 341 (1951),] applied *Burford* directly." Rehnquist, *supra*, at 1078. Lower courts, however, continue to apply *Burford* when they fear that federal intervention might disrupt important state policies. *Id. See also* Gordon G. Young, *Federal Court Abstention and State Administrative Law from* Burford *to* Ankenbrandt: *Fifty Years of Judicial Federalism Under* Burford v. Sun Oil Co. *and Kindred Doctrines*, 42 DePaul L. Rev. 859, 866 (1993) ("[*NOPSI*] clarifies *Burford* abstention in some respects, seriously shrinking its domain of operation, but it clouds the doctrine in other ways. Confusion over the scope of *Burford* abounds, both in Supreme Court opinions and in those of the lower courts.").[5] The better view after *NOPSI* seems to be that *Burford* has little application to constitutional challenges filed in federal court under § 1983. *See, e.g., Harper v. Public Service Commission of West Virginia*, 396 F.3d 348 (4th Cir. 2005) (holding that *Burford* did not apply to a § 1983 challenge brought under the Dormant Commerce Clause against a state licensing agency). *Contrast Martin v. Stewart*, 499 F.3d 360 (4th Cir. 2007) (Wilkinson, J., dissenting) ("there is a basic divide between those who believe *Burford* abstention has some modest utility in the face of constitutional challenges to state regulatory regimes and those who do not").

10. *Colorado River Water District* Abstention. The second form of abstention that is occasionally used in constitutional cases is the oft-misunderstood doctrine of *Colorado River Water District v. United States*, 424 U.S. 800 (1976). Once thought to afford federal courts a large measure of discretion to abstain in favor of parallel state court proceedings, regardless of the basis for federal jurisdiction and the underlying federal claim, *Colorado River Water District* today seems quite limited. As explained by Justice Brennan, speaking for the Court in *Moses H. Cone Memorial Hospital v. Mercury Construction Corp.*, 460 U.S. 1 (1983):

> *Colorado River* involved the effect of the McCarran Amendment on the existence and exercise of federal-court jurisdiction to adjudicate federal water rights. The Amendment waives the [Federal] Government's sovereign immunity to permit the joinder of the United States in some state-court suits for the adjudication of water rights. In *Colorado River*, however, the Government proceeded in Federal District Court, bringing suit against some 1,000 nonfederal water users, seeking a declaration of the water rights of certain federal entities and Indian tribes. Shortly thereafter, a defendant in that suit sought to join the United States in a state-court proceeding for the comprehensive adjudication and administration of all water rights within the river system that was the subject of the federal-court suit. The District Court dismissed the federal suit, holding that the abstention doctrine required deference to the state-court proceedings. . . .
>
> [W]e held that the District Court's dismissal was proper . . . resting not on considerations of state-federal comity or on avoidance of constitutional decisions, as does abstention, but on "considerations of '[w]ise judicial administration, giving regard to conservation of judicial resources and comprehensive disposition of litigation.' " We noted that "the pendency of an action in the state court is no bar to proceedings concerning the same matter in the Federal court having jurisdiction," and that the federal courts have a "virtually unflagging obligation . . . to exercise the jurisdiction given them."

---

[5] Despite its modern aversion to *Burford*, the Court in *Ankenbrandt v. Richards*, 504 U.S. 689 (1992), stated that "[i]t is not inconceivable . . . that in certain circumstances, the abstention principles developed in *Burford v. Sun Oil Co.* might be relevant in a case involving elements of the domestic relationship. . . . Such might well be the case if a federal suit were filed prior to effectuation of a divorce, alimony, or child custody decree, and the suit depended on a determination of the status of the parties."

> Given this obligation, and the absence of weightier considerations of constitutional adjudication and state-federal relations, the circumstances permitting the dismissal of a federal suit due to the presence of a concurrent state proceeding for reasons of wise judicial administration are considerably more limited than the circumstances appropriate for abstention. The former circumstances, though exceptional, do nevertheless exist.
>
> It has been held, for example, that the court first assuming jurisdiction over property may exercise that jurisdiction to the exclusion of other courts. . . . In assessing the appropriateness of dismissal in the event of an exercise of concurrent jurisdiction, a federal court may also consider such factors as the inconvenience of the federal forum; the desirability of avoiding piecemeal litigation; and the order in which jurisdiction was obtained by the concurrent forums. No one factor is necessarily determinative; a carefully considered judgment taking into account both the obligation to exercise jurisdiction and the combination of factors counseling against that exercise is required. Only the clearest of justifications will warrant dismissal.
>
> [T]he decision whether to dismiss a federal action because of parallel state-court litigation does not rest on a mechanical checklist, but on a careful balancing of the important factors as they apply in a given case, with the balance heavily weighted in favor of the exercise of jurisdiction. The weight to be given to any one factor may vary greatly from case to case, depending on the particular setting of the case. *Colorado River* itself illustrates this principle in operation. By far the most important factor in our decision to approve the dismissal there was the "clear federal policy . . . [of] avoidance of piecemeal adjudication of water rights in a river system," as evinced in the McCarran Amendment. . . . In addition, we noted that other factors in the case tended to support dismissal — the absence of any substantial progress in the federal-court litigation; the presence in the suit of extensive rights governed by state law; the geographical inconvenience of the federal forum; and the Government's previous willingness to litigate similar suits in state court.

The parties in *Moses H. Cone*, a hospital and a contractor, had entered into a construction contract that included an arbitration clause. The hospital sued the contractor in state court seeking to have its rights declared under the contract and also seeking to prevent the contractor from proceeding to arbitration. The contractor then filed a diversity action in federal court to compel arbitration under the federal Arbitration Act, 9 U.S.C. § 4. Applying *Colorado River Water District*'s various factors, the Supreme Court found federal deference to the state proceedings to be improper. First, "[t]he Hospital concede[d] that . . . [t]here was no assumption by either court of jurisdiction over any res or property, nor is there any contention that the federal forum was any less convenient to the parties than the state forum." Nor did the remaining factors — "avoidance of piecemeal litigation, and the order in which jurisdiction was obtained by the concurrent forums" — support staying the federal proceeding.

More importantly, the Court concluded that "the fact that federal law provides the rule of decision on the merits" counseled against abstention. "The state-versus-federal-law factor was of ambiguous relevance in *Colorado River*," whereas the principal issues in *Moses H. Cone* were federal. The Court noted the exceptional nature of *Colorado River* in this context: "Although in some rare circumstances the presence of state-law issues may weigh in favor of that surrender, the presence of federal-law issues must always be a major consideration weighing against surrender." As a result of *Moses H. Cone*, "today a federal court's ability to abstain in favor of a parallel state litigation is rather limited. This is particularly true in situations in which federal law provides the basis for the litigation." Martin H. Redish, *Intersystemic Redundancy and Federal Power: Proposing a Zero Tolerance Solution to the Duplicative Litigation Problem*, 75 NOTRE DAME L. REV. 1347, 1356 (2000). *See also* Carl E. Brody, Jr., *Abstention in the*

Federal Courts: A Suggested Bifurcated Standard of Review to Create Procedural Reliance Where States and Localities Regulate Constitutionally Protected Activity, 13 ST. THOMAS L. REV. 539 (2001); Rex E. Lee, *An Analysis of Supplemental Jurisdiction and Abstention with Recommendations of Legislative Action*, 1990 B.Y.U. L. REV. 321.

Because *Pullman* abstention, unlike the abstention doctrines found in *Burford* and *Colorado River Water District*, is specifically designed to avoid forcing federal courts to rule on constitutional issues, it has overshadowed the other two abstention doctrines in constitutional litigation.[6] This is not to say that *Burford* and *Colorado River Water District* are irrelevant; but they rarely can be properly applied to § 1983 cases in federal court raising federal constitutional issues. *See, e.g., Chase Brexton Health Services v. Maryland*, 411 F.3d 457 (4th Cir. 2005) (refusing to apply *Colorado River Water District* to a § 1983 claim).

11. Law Versus Equity. Abstention principles, like that applied in *Pullman*, are generally understood to apply only to equitable actions (i.e., those seeking prospective relief) and not claims for money damages. *See, e.g., Quackenbush v. Allstate Insurance Co.*, 517 U.S. 706 (1996) (holding that *Burford* abstention cannot be applied to claims seeking money damages). The reason for this limitation rests in the nature of equity, which is limited, never final, and left to the discretion of the District Court. *See* Martha A. Field, *Abstention in Constitutional Cases: The Scope of the* Pullman *Abstention Doctrine*, 122 U. PA. L. REV. 1071 (1974). Still, the Supreme Court has applied its abstention doctrines, including that in *Pullman*, in a handful of cases seeking money damages. *See, e.g., Clay v. Sun Insurance Office, Ltd.*, 363 U.S. 207 (1960).

B. DEFERENCE TO PENDING STATE PROCEEDINGS

YOUNGER v. HARRIS
Supreme Court of the United States
401 U.S. 37 (1971)

MR. JUSTICE BLACK delivered the opinion of the Court.

John Harris, Jr., was indicted in a California state court, [and] charged with violation of the . . . California Criminal Syndicalism Act . . . [which prohibited "advocating . . . the commission of crime . . . as a means of accomplishing a change in industrial ownership or control, or effecting any political change."] He then filed a complaint in the Federal District Court, asking that court to enjoin . . . Younger, the District Attorney of Los Angeles County, from prosecuting him, and alleging that the prosecution and even the presence of the Act inhibited him in the exercise of his rights of free speech and press, rights guaranteed him by the First and Fourteenth Amendments. A three-judge Federal District Court, convened pursuant to 28 U.S.C. § 2284, held that it had jurisdiction and power to restrain the District Attorney from prosecuting, held that the State's Criminal Syndicalism Act was void for vagueness and overbreadth in violation of the First and Fourteenth Amendments, and accordingly restrained the District Attorney from "further prosecution of the currently pending action against plaintiff Harris for alleged violation of the Act."

Without regard to . . . the constitutionality of the state law, we have concluded that the judgment of the District Court, enjoining . . . Younger from prosecuting under

---

[6] Although *Pullman* abstention appears to be inapplicable to diversity actions — the doctrine was designed, after all, to help federal courts avoid federal constitutional issues that presumably are not present in simple diversity matters — the Supreme Court has applied *Pullman* abstention in a handful of these cases. *See, e.g., Fornaris v. Ridge Tool Co.*, 400 U.S. 41 (1970). It has also developed abstention doctrines similar to that established in *Pullman* for diversity actions. *See, e.g., Louisiana Power & Light Co. v. City of Thibodaux*, 360 U.S. 25 (1959) (holding that a federal court should have abstained in a diversity action that sounded in eminent domain).

these California statutes, must be reversed as a violation of the national policy forbidding federal courts to stay or enjoin pending state court proceedings except under special circumstances.[7] We express no view about the circumstances under which federal courts may act when there is no prosecution pending in state courts at the time the federal proceeding is begun.

Since the beginning of this country's history Congress has, subject to few exceptions, manifested a desire to permit state courts to try state cases free from interference by federal courts. In 1793 an Act unconditionally provided: "(N)or shall a writ of injunction be granted to stay proceedings in any court of a state. . . . " A comparison of the 1793 Act with 28 U.S.C. § 2283, its present-day successor, graphically illustrates how few and minor have been the exceptions granted from the flat, prohibitory language of the old Act. During all this lapse of years from 1793 to 1970 the statutory exceptions to the 1793 congressional enactment have been only three: (1) "except as expressly authorized by Act of Congress;" (2) "where necessary in aid of its jurisdiction;" and (3) "to protect or effectuate its judgments." In addition, a judicial exception to the longstanding policy evidenced by the statute has been made where a person about to be prosecuted in a state court can show that he will, if the proceeding in the state court is not enjoined, suffer irreparable damages. *See Ex parte Young*, 209 U.S. 123 (1908).

The precise reasons for this longstanding public policy against federal court interference with state court proceedings have never been specifically identified but the primary sources of the policy are plain. One is the basic doctrine of equity jurisprudence that courts of equity should not act, and particularly should not act to restrain a criminal prosecution, when the moving party has an adequate remedy at law and will not suffer irreparable injury if denied equitable relief. The doctrine may originally have grown out of circumstances peculiar to the English judicial system and not applicable in this country, but its fundamental purpose of restraining equity jurisdiction within narrow limits is equally important under our Constitution, in order to prevent erosion of the role of the jury and avoid a duplication of legal proceedings and legal sanctions where a single suit would be adequate to protect the rights asserted. This underlying reason for restraining courts of equity from interfering with criminal prosecutions is reinforced by an even more vital consideration, the notion of "comity," that is, a proper respect for state functions, a recognition of the fact that the entire country is made up of a Union of separate state governments, and a continuance of the belief that the National Government will fare best if the States and their institutions are left free to perform their separate functions in their separate ways. This, perhaps for lack of a better and clearer way to describe it, is referred to by many as "Our Federalism," and one familiar with the profound debates that ushered our Federal Constitution into existence is bound to respect those who remain loyal to the ideals and dreams of "Our Federalism." The concept does not mean blind deference to "States' Rights" any more than it means centralization of control over every important issue in our National Government and its courts. The Framers rejected both these courses. What the concept does represent is a system in which there is sensitivity to the legitimate interests of both State and National Governments, and in which the National Government, anxious though it may be to vindicate and protect federal rights and federal interests, always endeavors to do so in ways that will not unduly interfere with the legitimate activities of the States. It should never be forgotten that this slogan, "Our Federalism," born in the early struggling days of our Union of States, occupies a highly important place in our Nation's history and its future.

---

[7] [n.2] [Harris] did not explicitly ask for a declaratory judgment in [his] complaint. [He] did, however, ask the District Court to grant "such other and further relief as to the Court may seem just and proper," and the District Court in fact granted a declaratory judgment. For the reasons stated in our opinion today in *Samuels v. Mackell*, 401 U.S. 66 (1971), we hold that declaratory relief is also improper when a prosecution involving the challenged statute is pending in state court at the time the federal suit is initiated.

This brief discussion should be enough to suggest some of the reasons why it has been perfectly natural for our cases to repeat time and time again that the normal thing to do when federal courts are asked to enjoin pending proceedings in state courts is not to issue such injunctions. In *Fenner v. Boykin*, 271 U.S. 240 (1926), suit had been brought in the Federal District Court seeking to enjoin state prosecutions under a recently enacted state law that allegedly interfered with the free flow of interstate commerce. The Court, in a unanimous opinion made clear that such a suit, even with respect to state criminal proceedings not yet formally instituted, could be proper only under very special circumstances. . . .

[T]he Court stressed the importance of showing irreparable injury, the traditional prerequisite to obtaining an injunction. In addition, however, the Court also made clear that in view of the fundamental policy against federal interference with state criminal prosecutions, even irreparable injury is insufficient unless it is "both great and immediate." Certain types of injury, in particular, the cost, anxiety, and inconvenience of having to defend against a single criminal prosecution, could not by themselves be considered "irreparable" in the special legal sense of that term. Instead, the threat to the plaintiff's federally protected rights must be one that cannot be eliminated by his defense against a single criminal prosecution.

This is where the law stood when the Court decided *Dombrowski v. Pfister*, 380 U.S. 479 (1965), and held that an injunction against the enforcement of certain state criminal statutes could properly issue under the circumstances presented in that case.[8] In *Dombrowski*, unlike many of the earlier cases denying injunctions, the complaint made substantial allegations that: "the threats to enforce the statutes against appellants are not made with any expectation of securing valid convictions, but rather are part of a plan to employ arrests, seizures, and threats of prosecution under color of the statutes to harass appellants and discourage them and their supporters from asserting and attempting to vindicate the constitutional rights of Negro citizens of Louisiana."

The appellants in *Dombrowski* had offered to prove that their offices had been raided and all their files and records seized pursuant to search and arrest warrants that were later summarily vacated by a state judge for lack of probable cause. They also offered to prove that despite the state court order quashing the warrants and suppressing the evidence seized, the prosecutor was continuing to threaten to initiate new prosecutions of appellants under the same statutes, was holding public hearings at which photostatic copies of the illegally seized documents were being used, and was threatening to use other copies of the illegally seized documents to obtain grand jury indictments against the appellants on charges of violating the same statutes. These circumstances, as viewed by the Court sufficiently establish the kind of irreparable injury, above and beyond that associated with the defense of a single prosecution brought in good faith, that had always been considered sufficient to justify federal intervention. Indeed, after quoting the Court's statement in *Douglas* [*v. City of Jeannette*, 319 U.S. 157 (1943),] concerning the very restricted circumstances under which an injunction could be justified, the Court in *Dombrowski* went on to say: "But the allegations in this complaint depict a situation in which defense of the State's criminal prosecution will not assure adequate vindication of constitutional rights. They suggest that a substantial loss of or impairment of freedoms of expression will occur if

---

[8] [n.4] [T]he cases dealing with standing to raise claims of vagueness or overbreadth, *e.g.*, *Thornhill v. Alabama*, 310 U.S. 88 (1940), [have not] changed the basic principles governing the propriety of injunctions against state criminal prosecutions. In the standing cases we allowed attacks on overly broad or vague statutes in the absence of any showing that the defendant's conduct could not be regulated by some properly drawn statute. But in each of these cases the statute was not merely vague or overly broad "on its face"; the statute was held to be vague or overly broad as construed and applied to a particular defendant in a particular case. If the statute had been too vague as written but sufficiently narrow as applied, prosecutions and convictions under it would ordinarily have been permissible.

appellants must await the state court's disposition and ultimate review in this Court of any adverse determination. These allegations, if true, clearly show irreparable injury."

It is against the background of these principles that we must judge the propriety of an injunction under the circumstances of the present case. Here a proceeding was already pending in the state court, affording Harris an opportunity to raise his constitutional claims. There is no suggestion that this single prosecution against Harris is brought in bad faith or is only one of a series of repeated prosecutions to which he will be subjected. In other words, the injury that Harris faces is solely "that incidental to every criminal proceeding brought lawfully and in good faith," and therefore under the settled doctrine we have already described he is not entitled to equitable relief "even if such statutes are unconstitutional."

The District Court, however, thought that the *Dombrowski* decision substantially broadened the availability of injunctions against state criminal prosecutions and that under that decision the federal courts may give equitable relief, without regard to any showing of bad faith or harassment, whenever a state statute is found "on its face" to be vague or overly broad, in violation of the First Amendment. We recognize that there are some statements in the *Dombrowski* opinion that would seem to support this argument. But, as we have already seen, such statements were unnecessary to the decision of that case, because the Court found that the plaintiffs had alleged a basis for equitable relief under the long-established standards. In addition, we do not regard the reasons adduced to support this position as sufficient to justify such a substantial departure from the established doctrines regarding the availability of injunctive relief. It is undoubtedly true, as the Court stated in *Dombrowski*, that "(a) criminal prosecution under a statute regulating expression usually involves imponderables and contingencies that themselves may inhibit the full exercise of First Amendment freedoms." But this sort of "chilling effect," as the Court called it, should not by itself justify federal intervention. In the first place, the chilling effect cannot be satisfactorily eliminated by federal injunctive relief. . . . The chilling effect can, of course, be eliminated by an injunction that would prohibit any prosecution whatever for conduct occurring prior to a satisfactory rewriting of the statute. But the States would then be stripped of all power to prosecute even the socially dangerous and constitutionally unprotected conduct that had been covered by the statute, until a new statute could be passed by the state legislature and approved by the federal courts in potentially lengthy trial and appellate proceedings.

Moreover, the existence of a "chilling effect," even in the area of First Amendment rights, has never been considered a sufficient basis, in and of itself, for prohibiting state action. Where a statute does not directly abridge free speech, but — while regulating a subject within the State's power — tends to have the incidental effect of inhibiting First Amendment rights, it is well settled that the statute can be upheld if the effect on speech is minor in relation to the need for control of the conduct and the lack of alternative means for doing so.

Beyond all this is another, more basic consideration. Procedures for testing the constitutionality of a statute "on its face" in the manner apparently contemplated by *Dombrowski*, and for then enjoining all action to enforce the statute until the State can obtain court approval for a modified version, are fundamentally at odds with the function of the federal courts in our constitutional plan. The power and duty of the judiciary to declare laws unconstitutional is in the final analysis derived from its responsibility for resolving concrete disputes brought before the courts for decision; a statute apparently governing a dispute cannot be applied by judges, consistently with their obligations under the Supremacy Clause, when such an application of the statute would conflict with the Constitution. *Marbury v. Madison*, 5 U.S. (1 Cranch) 137 (1803). But this vital responsibility, broad as it is, does not amount to an unlimited power to survey the statute books and pass judgment on laws before the courts are called upon to enforce them. Ever since the Constitutional Convention rejected a proposal for having members of the Supreme Court render advice concerning pending legislation it has been clear that, even when suits of this kind involve a "case or controversy" sufficient to satisfy the requirements of Article III of the Constitution, the task of analyzing a proposed statute, pinpointing its deficiencies, and requiring correction of these deficiencies before the statute is put into effect, is rarely if ever an appropriate task for the judiciary. The combination of the relative remoteness of the controversy, the impact on the legislative process of the relief sought, and above all the speculative and amorphous nature of the required line-by-line analysis of detailed statutes ordinarily results in a kind of case that is wholly unsatisfactory for deciding constitutional questions, whichever way they might be decided. In light of this fundamental conception of the Framers as to the proper place of the federal courts in the governmental processes of passing and enforcing laws, it can seldom be appropriate for these courts to exercise any such power of prior approval or veto over the legislative process.

For these reasons, fundamental not only to our federal system but also to the basic functions of the Judicial Branch of the National Government under our Constitution, we hold that the *Dombrowski* decision should not be regarded as having upset the settled doctrines that have always confined very narrowly the availability of injunctive relief against state criminal prosecutions. We do not think that opinion stands for the proposition that a federal court can properly enjoin enforcement of a statute solely on the basis of a showing that the statute "on its face" abridges First Amendment rights. There may, of course, be extraordinary circumstances in which the necessary irreparable injury can be shown even in the absence of the usual prerequisites of bad faith and harassment.

Other unusual situations calling for federal intervention might also arise, but there is no point in our attempting now to specify what they might be. It is sufficient for purposes of the present case to hold, as we do, that the possible unconstitutionality of a statute "on its face" does not in itself justify an injunction against good-faith attempts to enforce it, and that . . . Harris has failed to make any showing of bad faith, harassment, or any other unusual circumstance that would call for equitable relief. Because our holding rests on the absence of the factors necessary under equitable principles to justify federal intervention, we have no occasion to consider whether 28 U.S.C. § 2283, which prohibits an injunction against state court proceedings "except as expressly authorized by Act of Congress" would in and of itself be controlling under the circumstances of this case.[9]

Mr. Justice Douglas, dissenting.

Whatever the balance of the pressures of localism and nationalism prior to the Civil War, they were fundamentally altered by the war. The Civil War Amendments made civil rights a national concern. Those Amendments, especially § 5 of the Fourteenth Amendment, cemented the change in American federalism brought on by the war. Congress immediately commenced to use its new powers to pass legislation. Just as the first Judiciary Act and the "anti- injunction" statute represented the early views of American federalism, the Reconstruction statutes, including the enlargement of federal jurisdiction, represent a later view of American federalism.

A state law enforcement officer is someone acting under "color of law" even though he may be misusing his authority. *Monroe v. Pape.* And prosecution under a patently unconstitutional statute is a "deprivation of . . . rights, privileges, or immunities secured by the Constitution." "Suit(s) in equity" obviously includes injunctions.

---

[9] [Editor's note: Justice Brennan, joined by Justices White and Marshall, wrote an opinion concurring in the result. Justice Stewart, joined by Justice Harlan, also wrote a concurring opinion.]

I hold to the view that § 1983 is included in the "expressly authorized" exception to § 2283. . . . There is no more good reason for allowing a general statute dealing with federalism passed at the end of the 18th century to control another statute also dealing with federalism, passed almost 80 years later, than to conclude that the early concepts of federalism were not changed by the Civil War.

NOTES

1. Historical Antecedents. Courts sitting in equity have historically refused to enjoin criminal prosecutions. *See* RICHARD H. FALLON, DANIEL J. MELTZER & DAVID L. SHAPIRO, HART & WECHSLER'S FEDERAL COURTS AND THE FEDERAL SYSTEM 1265 (4th ed. 1996). Equitable remedies like injunctive relief, moreover, have traditionally been limited to cases where there is no adequate remedy at law, leaving the plaintiff threatened with irreparable injury. "Because the legal remedy of defending a criminal proceeding was ordinarily considered adequate, the irreparable injury requirement also established a barrier to injunctions against criminal proceedings." *Id.* In *Ex parte Young*, 209 U.S. 123 (1908), which held that the Eleventh Amendment does not bar suits filed against state officials that seek only prospective relief (*see* Chapter 3.B., *supra*), the Court also drew a distinction between suits seeking to enjoin *future*, as opposed to *pending*, prosecutions: "a Federal court [which has] first obtained jurisdiction over the subject matter [of the case] has the right, in both civil and criminal cases, to hold and maintain such jurisdiction, to the exclusion of all other courts . . . . But the Federal court cannot, of course, interfere in a case where the proceedings were already pending in a state court."[10]

2. Declaratory Relief. In a companion case, *Samuels v. Mackell*, 401 U.S. 66 (1971),[11] the Court, per Justice Black, extended *Younger's* logic to § 1983 claims[12] for declaratory relief under 28 U.S.C. § 2201:[13]

> In our opinion in the *Younger* case, we set out in detail the historical and practical basis for the settled doctrine of equity that a federal court should not enjoin a state criminal prosecution begun prior to the institution of the federal suit except in very unusual situations, where necessary to prevent immediate irreparable injury. The question presented here is whether under ordinary circumstances the same considerations that require the withholding of injunctive relief will make declaratory relief equally inappropriate. The question is not, however, a novel one. It was presented and fully considered by this Court in *Great Lakes Dredge & Dock Co. v. Huffman*, 319 U.S. 293 (1943), [where] . . . the Court made clear that a suit for declaratory judgment was . . . "essentially an equitable cause of action," and was "analogous to the equity jurisdiction in

---

[10] By way of contrast, state courts can never restrain federal proceedings, regardless of when the federal proceedings are filed. *See General Atomic Co. v. Felter*, 434 U.S. 12 (1977); *Donovan v. City of Dallas*, 377 U.S. 408 (1964).

[11] In another companion case, *Perez v. Ledesma*, 401 U.S. 82 (1971), the Court vacated a federal injunction blocking the use of illegally seized evidence in a state criminal prosecution: "The propriety of arrests and the admissibility of evidence in state criminal prosecutions are ordinarily matters to be resolved by state tribunals, subject, of course, to review by certiorari or appeal in this Court, or, in a proper case, on federal habeas corpus."

[12] *Younger* has also been applied to federal habeas corpus claims that attempt to abort state prosecutions. *See, e.g., Hughes v. Attorney General of Florida*, 377 F.3d 1258 (11th Cir. 2004) ("When a petitioner seeks federal habeas relief prior to a pending state criminal trial the petitioner must satisfy the '*Younger* abstention hurdles' before the federal courts can grant such relief.").

[13] The federal Declaratory Judgment Act authorizes federal courts to award declaratory relief "[i]n a case of actual controversy within its jurisdiction . . . upon the filing of an appropriate pleading . . . whether or not further relief is or could be sought. Any such declaration shall have the force and effect of a final judgment or decree and shall be reviewable as such." 28 U.S.C. § 2201. As the Sixth Circuit observed in *Davis v. United States*, 499 F.3d 590 (6th Cir. 2007), however, "§ 2201 does not create an independent cause of action."

suits quia timet or for a decree quieting title." In addition, the legislative history of the Federal Declaratory Judgment Act of 1934, as amended, 28 U.S.C. § 2201, showed that Congress had explicitly contemplated that the courts would decide to grant or withhold declaratory relief on the basis of traditional equitable principles. Accordingly, the Court held that in an action for a declaratory judgment, "the district court was as free as in any other suit in equity to grant or withhold the relief prayed, upon equitable grounds."

In both situations deeply rooted and long-settled principles of equity have narrowly restricted the scope for federal intervention, and ordinarily a declaratory judgment will result in precisely the same interference with and disruption of state proceedings that the longstanding policy limiting injunctions was designed to avoid. This is true for at least two reasons. In the first place, the Declaratory Judgment Act provides that after a declaratory judgment is issued the district court may enforce it by granting "(f)urther necessary or proper relief," 28 U.S.C. § 2202, and therefore a declaratory judgment issued while state proceedings are pending might serve as the basis for a subsequent injunction against those proceedings to "protect or effectuate" the declaratory judgment, 28 U.S.C. § 2283, and thus result in a clearly improper interference with the state proceedings. Secondly, even if the declaratory judgment is not used as a basis for actually issuing an injunction, the declaratory relief alone has virtually the same practical impact [under preclusion principles] as a formal injunction would. . . . We therefore hold that, in cases where the state criminal prosecution was begun prior to the federal suit, the same equitable principles relevant to the propriety of an injunction must be taken into consideration by federal district courts in determining whether to issue a declaratory judgment, and that where an injunction would be impermissible under these principles, declaratory relief should ordinarily be denied as well.

We do not mean to suggest that a declaratory judgment should never be issued in cases of this type if it has been concluded that injunctive relief would be improper. There may be unusual circumstances in which an injunction might be withheld because, despite a plaintiff's strong claim for relief under the established standards, the injunctive remedy seemed particularly intrusive or offensive; in such a situation, a declaratory judgment might be appropriate and might not be contrary to the basic equitable doctrines governing the availability of relief. Ordinarily, however, the practical effect of the two forms of relief will be virtually identical, and the basic policy against federal interference with pending state criminal prosecutions will be frustrated as much by a declaratory judgment as it would be by an injunction.

Samuels makes clear that a plaintiff cannot avoid the dictates of *Younger* by seeking only declaratory relief in federal court. But what if *Younger* does not apply? Even then, federal courts have a large measure of discretion to deny declaratory relief. The federal Declaratory Judgment Act, 28 U.S.C. § 2201, states that a federal court "*may* declare the rights and other legal relations of any interested party." In *Wilton v. Seven Falls Co.*, 515 U.S. 277 (1995), a federal diversity action, the Supreme Court ruled that the permissive language of the Declaratory Judgment Act affords federal courts discretion to withhold declaratory relief in favor of ongoing state proceedings. In *Wilton* the federal diversity action was filed before the state proceedings commenced. *See* Note 6, *infra* (discussing the impact of subsequently filed state criminal proceedings). Still, the Court found that the District Court had discretion to withhold declaratory relief and allow the state court proceedings to go forward. *See also Brillhart v. Excess Insurance Co.*, 316 U.S. 491 (1942) (holding that a federal court should abstain from issuing declaratory relief where a parallel action was in state court). *See generally* Steven Plitt & Joshua D. Rogers, *Charting a Course for Federal Removal Through the Abstention Doctrine: A Titanic Experience in the Sargossa Sea of Jurisdictional Manipulation*, 56 DEPAUL L. REV. 107, 144 (2006) ("*Wilton* provide[s] a broad power of abstention over federal declaratory judgment actions where there are pending parallel state actions"). In the wake of *Wilton*, the decision to award declaratory relief in spite of pending state proceedings is left to the District Court's discretion. *See, e.g., Rossi v. Gemma*, 489 F.3d 26 (1st Cir. 2007) ("Insofar as the [complaint] sought a declaratory judgment that [the] lien was invalid under state law, we review the district court's dismissal for something akin to abuse of discretion."). Does *Wilton* apply to federal question cases, particularly those filed under § 1983? *See, e.g., Chase Brexton Health Services v. Maryland*, 411 F.3d 457 (4th Cir. 2005) (assuming that *Wilton* can be applied to a § 1983 claim for declaratory relief but denying a stay); *Clay Regional Water v. City of Spirit Lake*, 193 F. Supp. 2d 1129 (N.D. Iowa 2002) (holding that *Wilton* applies to a § 1983 claim seeking declaratory relief).

3. Declaratory Relief Where Prosecution is Threatened. *Younger* adhered to the distinction between pending and future prosecutions. The Court in *Steffel v. Thompson*, 415 U.S. 452 (1974), in an opinion authored by Justice Brennan, reiterated this distinction in the context of declaratory judgments:

> [W]hile [Steffel] and other individuals were distributing handbills protesting American involvement in Vietnam on an exterior sidewalk of the North DeKalb Shopping Center, shopping center employees asked them to stop handbilling and leave. They declined to do so, and police officers were summoned. The officers told them that they would be arrested if they did not stop handbilling. The group then left to avoid arrest. Two days later [Steffel] and a companion returned to the shopping center and again began handbilling. The manager of the center called the police, and [Steffel] and his companion were once again told that failure to stop their handbilling would result in their arrests. [Steffel] left to avoid arrest. His companion stayed, however, continued handbilling, and was arrested and subsequently arraigned on a charge of criminal trespass in violation of [Georgia law]. [Steffel] alleged in his complaint that, although he desired to return to the shopping center to distribute handbills, he had not done so because of his concern that he, too, would be arrested for violation of [Georgia law]. [T]he parties stipulated that, if [Steffel] returned and refused upon request to stop handbilling, a warrant would be sworn out and he might be arrested and charged with a violation of the Georgia statute.
>
> When no state criminal proceeding is pending at the time the federal complaint is filed, federal intervention does not result in duplicative legal proceedings or disruption of the state criminal justice system; nor can federal intervention, in that circumstance, be interpreted as reflecting negatively upon the state court's ability to enforce constitutional principles. In addition, while a pending state prosecution provides the federal plaintiff with a concrete opportunity to vindicate his constitutional rights, a refusal on the part of the federal courts to intervene when no state proceeding is pending may place the hapless plaintiff between the Scylla of intentionally flouting state law and the Charybdis of forgoing what he believes to be constitutionally protected activity in order to avoid becoming enmeshed in a criminal proceeding.
>
> When no state proceeding is pending and thus considerations of equity, comity, and federalism have little vitality, the propriety of granting federal declaratory relief may properly be considered independently of a request for injunctive relief. Here, the Court of Appeals held that, because injunctive relief would not be appropriate since [Steffel] failed to demonstrate irreparable injury — a traditional prerequisite to injunctive relief — it followed that declaratory relief was also inappropriate. Even if the Court of Appeals correctly viewed injunctive relief as inappropriate — a question we need not reach today since [Steffel] has abandoned his request for that remedy — the court erred in treating the requests for injunctive and declaratory relief as a single issue.

The subject matter jurisdiction of the lower federal courts was greatly expanded in the wake of the Civil War. A pervasive sense of nationalism led to enactment of [§ 1983], empowering the lower federal courts to determine the constitutionality of actions, taken by persons under color of state law, allegedly depriving other individuals of rights guaranteed by the Constitution and federal law. Four years later, in the Judiciary Act of March 3, 1875, Congress conferred upon the lower federal courts, for but the second time in their nearly century-old history, general federal question jurisdiction subject only to a jurisdictional-amount requirement, *see* 28 U.S.C. § 1331. With this latter enactment, the lower federal courts "ceased to be restricted tribunals of fair dealing between citizens of different states and became the primary and powerful reliances for vindicating every right given by the Constitution, the laws, and treaties of the United States." These two statutes, together with the Court's decision in *Ex parte Young*, have "established the modern framework for federal protection of constitutional rights from state interference."

A "storm of controversy" raged in the wake of *Ex parte Young*, focusing principally on the power of a single federal judge to grant ex parte interlocutory injunctions against the enforcement of state statutes. This uproar was only partially quelled by Congress' passage of legislation requiring the convening of a three-judge district court before a preliminary injunction against enforcement of a state statute could issue, and providing for direct appeal to this Court from a decision granting or denying such relief. From a State's viewpoint the granting of injunctive relief — even by these courts of special dignity — "rather clumsily" crippled state enforcement of its statutes pending further review. Furthermore, plaintiffs were dissatisfied with this method of testing the constitutionality of state statutes, since it placed upon them the burden of demonstrating the traditional prerequisites to equitable relief — most importantly, irreparable injury.

To dispel these difficulties, Congress in 1934 enacted the Declaratory Judgment Act, 28 U.S.C. §§ 2201–2202. That Congress plainly intended declaratory relief to act as an alternative to the strong medicine of the injunction and to be utilized to test the constitutionality of state criminal statutes in cases where injunctive relief would be unavailable is amply evidenced by the legislative history of the Act.

It was this history that formed the backdrop to our decision in *Zwickler v. Koota*, 389 U.S. 241 (1967), where a state criminal statute was attacked on grounds of unconstitutional overbreadth and no state prosecution was pending against the federal plaintiff. There, we found error in a three-judge district court's considering, as a single question, the propriety of granting injunctive and declaratory relief. Although we noted that injunctive relief might well be unavailable under principles of equity jurisprudence . . . , we held that "a federal district court has the duty to decide the appropriateness and the merits of the declaratory request irrespective of its conclusion as to the propriety of the issuance of the injunction." Only one year ago, we reaffirmed the *Zwickler v. Koota* holding in *Roe v. Wade*, 410 U.S. 113, and *Doe v. Bolton*, 410 U.S. 179 (1973). In those two cases, we declined to decide whether the District Courts had properly denied to the federal plaintiffs, against whom no prosecutions were pending, injunctive relief restraining enforcement of the Texas and Georgia criminal abortion statutes; instead, we affirmed the issuance of declaratory judgments of unconstitutionality, anticipating that these would be given effect by state authorities.

The "different considerations" entering into a decision whether to grant declaratory relief have their origins in the preceding historical summary. First, as Congress recognized in 1934, a declaratory judgment will have a less intrusive effect on the administration of state criminal laws. . . . Second, engrafting upon the Declaratory Judgment Act a requirement that all of the traditional equitable prerequisites to the issuance of an injunction be satisfied before the issuance of a declaratory judgment is considered would defy Congress' intent to make declaratory relief available in cases where an injunction would be inappropriate.

The only occasions where this Court has disregarded these "different considerations" and found that a preclusion of injunctive relief inevitably led to a denial of declaratory relief have been cases in which principles of federalism militated altogether against federal intervention in a class of adjudications. *See Samuels v. Mackell.* In the instant case, principles of federalism not only do not preclude federal intervention, they compel it. Requiring the federal courts totally to step aside when no state criminal prosecution is pending against the federal plaintiff would turn federalism on its head. When federal claims are premised on 42 U.S.C. § 1983 . . . we have not required exhaustion of state judicial or administrative remedies, recognizing the paramount role Congress has assigned to the federal courts to protect constitutional rights. But exhaustion of state remedies is precisely what would be required if both federal injunctive and declaratory relief were unavailable in a case where no state prosecution had been commenced.

[Georgia officials], however, . . . argue that, although it may be appropriate to issue a declaratory judgment when no state criminal proceeding is pending and the attack is upon the facial validity of a state criminal statute, such a step would be improper where, as here, the attack is merely upon the constitutionality of the statute as applied, since the State's interest in unencumbered enforcement of its laws outweighs the minimal federal interest in protecting the constitutional rights of only a single individual. We reject the argument.

Indeed, the State's concern with potential interference in the administration of its criminal laws is of lesser dimension when an attack is made upon the constitutionality of a state statute as applied. A declaratory judgment of a lower federal court that a state statute is invalid in toto — and therefore incapable of any valid application — or is overbroad or vague — and therefore no person can properly be convicted under the statute until it is given a narrowing or clarifying construction — will likely have a more significant potential for disruption of state enforcement policies than a declaration specifying a limited number of impermissible applications of the statute. While the federal interest may be greater when a state statute is attacked on its face, since there exists the potential for eliminating any broad ranging deterrent effect on would-be actors, we do not find this consideration controlling. The solitary individual who suffers a deprivation of his constitutional rights is no less deserving of redress than one who suffers together with others.[14]

We therefore hold that, regardless of whether injunctive relief may be appropriate, federal declaratory relief is not precluded when no state prosecution is pending and a federal plaintiff demonstrates a genuine threat of enforcement of a disputed state criminal statute, whether an attack is made on the constitutionality of the statute on its face or as applied.[15]

---

[14] [n.21] Abstention, a question "entirely separate from the question of granting declaratory or injunctive relief," might be more appropriate when a challenge is made to the state statute as applied, rather than upon its face, since the reach of an uncertain state statute might, in that circumstance, be more susceptible of a limiting or clarifying construction that would avoid the federal constitutional question.

[15] [Editor's note: *Steffel*'s conclusion that the criminal prosecution of one does not necessarily prevent federal relief due another was reaffirmed in *Doran v. Salem Inn*, 422 U.S. 922 (1975), where three bar owners challenged a local ban on topless dancing on First Amendment grounds. The day after the § 1983 complaint

4. Injunctive Relief Where Prosecution is Threatened. Although *Steffel* made much of the distinction between declaratory judgments and injunctions, subsequent cases have not. In *Wooley v. Maynard*, 430 U.S. 705 (1977) (Burger, C.J.), for example, the Court sustained a permanent injunction barring enforcement of a state law that made it criminal to "obscure" the state's motto — "Live Free or Die" — on state license plates. The plaintiff there (Maynard) had been convicted three times under the statute, but sought only to prevent *future* prosecutions. For this reason, *Younger* was found to not be a bar. As a result, even though injunctive relief is more difficult to obtain, it is not precluded by *Younger* so long as it is directed only at future, and not pending, state criminal proceedings.

In light of the Supreme Court's holdings in *Steffel* and *Wooley*, would it have been proper for Younger's attorney — who was not charged with a criminal offense — to file a § 1983 action on his own behalf in federal court challenging California's syndicalism statute? Would the attorney have had Article III standing? Is an attorney barred from litigating a client's constitutional claims by prudential standing doctrines? In *Kowalski v. Tesmer*, 543 U.S. 125 (2004), the Supreme Court ruled that defense attorneys who sought to challenge Michigan's denial of public counsel on appeal to indigents who pleaded guilty[16] were not proper third-party plaintiffs under § 1983 in federal court. In addition to holding that the absence of established attorney-client relationships counseled against third-party standing, the Court concluded that *Younger v. Harris* justified dismissal: "In this case, the three indigent criminal defendants who were originally plaintiffs in this § 1983 action were appropriately dismissed under *Younger*. . . . An unwillingness to allow the *Younger* principle to be thus circumvented is an additional reason to deny the attorneys third-party standing."

5. Exhaustion of State Appellate Remedies. The Supreme Court concluded in *Younger* that criminal defendants cannot simultaneously challenge a state's criminal laws in both state and federal courts. Instead, federal courts must abstain in favor of state proceedings. Nor can losing criminal defendants simultaneously appeal their convictions and pursue parallel equitable relief under § 1983 in federal court. Again, federal courts that are asked to upset criminal convictions must abstain in favor of ongoing state appellate proceedings. Can losing criminal defendants avoid or abort state appellate mechanisms in order to challenge their convictions in federal court under § 1983? The Court in *Huffman v. Pursue, Ltd.*, 420 U.S. 592 (1975), said no. To the extent losing criminal defendants seek to challenge or upset their convictions, they must first exhaust their state appellate remedies. One who chooses not to exhaust, moreover, forfeits any equitable challenges to the conviction that might have otherwise been available in federal court under § 1983.[17] *Cf. Heck v. Humphrey*, 512 U.S. 477 (1994) (excerpted in Chapter 8.B.[3], *infra*) (holding that a § 1983 claim for money damages that would upset a prior state court conviction does not arise until the conviction has been set aside on appeal, by executive order, or through habeas corpus). Once exhaustion is complete, *Younger*'s bar to federal review is lifted. *See, e.g, Taliaferro v.*

---

was filed in federal court, one of the plaintiffs resumed topless dancing, and a criminal prosecution was immediately filed against it in state court. The other two plaintiffs, however, refrained from topless dancing. Faced with the argument that the criminal prosecution should bar any federal challenge, the Supreme Court stated that prospective plaintiffs ought not "be thrown into the same hopper for *Younger*" purposes. Although there "may be some circumstances in which legally distinct parties are so closely related that they should all be subjected to the *Younger* considerations which govern any one of them, this is not such a case." The Court thus affirmed an award of preliminary injunctive relief on behalf of the two bar owners who had not been criminally charged.]

[16] The Supreme Court ruled in *Halbert v. Michigan*, 545 U.S. 605 (2005), that Michigan's practice violated the equality principle laid down in *Douglas v. California*, 372 U.S. 353 (1963).

[17] In contrast, one who does not challenge her conviction, but seeks only future relief from further prosecution, need not exhaust available state remedies. *See, e.g., Wooley v. Maynard*, 430 U.S. 705 (1977) (discussed in Note 4, *supra*).

Darby Township Zoning Board, 458 F.3d 181 (3d Cir. 2006) (holding that *Younger* no longer barred federal review of a zoning decision because state appellate review had been exhausted). However, preclusion principles could inevitably defeat any subsequent federal action. *See* Chapter 8.A., *infra* (discussing preclusion).

What exactly does exhaustion entail? Must a convicted defendant take a discretionary appeal to the state's supreme court? Must a convicted defendant use a state's collateral relief mechanism? In *Tesmer v. Granholm*, 333 F.3d 683 (6th Cir. 2003) (en banc), *rev'd on other grounds sub nom. Kowalski v. Tesmer*, 543 U.S. 125 (2004), the Sixth Circuit, sitting en banc, ruled that *Huffman's* exhaustion requirement extends to collateral relief mechanisms available under state law. *Younger* was thus found to preclude federal judicial involvement under § 1983 until *after* the defendant had exhausted both direct appeals and collateral challenges afforded by state law.[18]

6. Subsequently Filed Charges. In *Doran v. Salem Inn*, 422 U.S. 922 (1975), three bar owners challenged a local ban on topless dancing on First Amendment grounds. The day after the § 1983 complaint was filed in federal court, one of the bar owners resumed topless dancing and a criminal prosecution was immediately lodged against it in state court. The Supreme Court ruled that the *Younger* doctrine prohibited this bar owner from pressing its federal challenge even though the criminal charges were filed *after* its commencement of the federal suit. This result also obtained in *Hicks v. Miranda*, 422 U.S. 332 (1975): "where state criminal proceedings are begun against federal plaintiffs after the federal complaint is filed but before any proceedings of substance on the merits have taken place in the federal court, the principles of *Younger v. Harris* should apply in full force." The *Hicks* Court sustained the dismissal of a federal complaint filed on November 29 because criminal charges were filed the following January 15, before the defendant had filed its answer and "prior to any proceedings whatsoever before [the district court]." *See also Stroman Realty v. Martinez*, 505 F.3d 658 (7th Cir. 2007) (holding that *Younger* applied where state proceedings were filed after the federal complaint). *Cf. Hawaii Housing Authority v. Midkiff*, 467 U.S. 229 (1984) (finding that a "proceeding of substance on the merits" had occurred where the district court had issued a preliminary injunction).

7. Exceptions to *Younger*. The *Younger* Court suggested two exceptions where a federal court might be permitted to enjoin pending criminal proceedings in state court. The first of these is the so-called "bad faith" exception. Bad faith exists when prosecutions are commenced "with no expectation of convictions but only to discourage exercise of protected rights." *Cameron v. Johnson*, 390 U.S. 611 (1968). In practice, this argument has rarely been persuasive. *See* Brian Stagner, *Avoiding Abstention: The* Younger *Exceptions*, 29 TEX. TECH L. REV. 137, 157 (1998) ("[T]he bad faith/harassment exception has aptly been described as 'a virtually empty universe.' Applications of the exception are sporadic and inconsistent at best."). The second exception suggested in *Younger* involves "a statute [that is] flagrantly and patently violative of express constitutional prohibitions in every clause, sentence and paragraph, and in whatever manner and against whomever an effort might be made to apply it." Again, however, this argument has rarely been successful. *See, e.g., Hughes v. Attorney General of Florida*, 377 F.3d 1258 (11th Cir. 2004) (refusing to use this exception where pilots claimed that local prosecution for flying while intoxicated was clearly pre-empted by federal law); Stagner, *supra*, at 159 ("[T]here is not a single instance in which the Supreme Court has invoked the patently unconstitutional exception to justify federal interference. Instead, much like bad faith/harassment, the Court has tended to treat the exception as more symbolic than real."). Though lacking clear textual support in *Younger*, a third exception has also emerged for constitutional challenges directed at the adequacy of state fora. In

---

[18] Note that any equitable federal challenge under § 1983 to the conviction *after* exhaustion of state remedies is likely precluded by the availability of federal habeas corpus. *See Preiser v. Rodriguez*, 411 U.S. 475 (1973) (excerpted in Chapter 8.B.[1], *infra*).

Gibson v. Berryhill, 411 U.S. 564 (1973), for example, the Court concluded that federal intervention may be appropriate under the "inadequate state forum" exception when a state agency appears biased. Use of this exception appears more difficult, however, when the focus of the federal challenge is state *judicial* proceedings. *See* Stagner, *supra*, at 167–68.

8. The Anti-Injunction Act. As noted in *Younger*, the federal Anti-Injunction Act, 28 U.S.C. § 2283, prohibits federal courts from staying state court proceedings "except as expressly authorized by Act of Congress, or where necessary in aid of its jurisdiction, or to protect or effectuate its judgments." The year following its decision in *Younger*, the Court ruled in *Mitchum v. Foster*, 407 U.S. 225 (1972), that § 1983 fell within the first exception to the Anti-Injunction Act because it expressly authorizes federal courts to employ equitable remedies. The Anti-Injunction Act is thus not an impediment to § 1983 claims seeking prospective relief. Rather, limitations on federal injunctive relief must be found in the principles of comity and federalism recognized in *Younger*.

9. *Pullman* Compared. *Younger* and *Pullman* abstention are similar in that they deflect litigation from federal to state court. However, they have important differences. First, *Pullman* abstention results only in a stay of the federal proceeding; it assumes that the matter may return to federal court. *Younger*, in contrast, requires dismissal of the federal action. Second, *Pullman* is premised on ambiguity or uncertainty in state law rather than deference to state courts. Indeed, no state action need be pending. *Younger*, on the other hand, requires a pending (or at least soon-to-be-filed) action in state court. Third, *Pullman* applies generally, so that any uncertainty in the law — be it civil or criminal — can result in abstention. By its terms, *Younger* is limited to criminal laws that are being enforced in the state's criminal courts. As the following case demonstrates, however, this last distinction has lost some of its significance.

OHIO CIVIL RIGHTS COMMISSION v. DAYTON CHRISTIAN SCHOOLS
Supreme Court of the United States
477 U.S. 619 (1986)

JUSTICE REHNQUIST delivered the opinion of the Court.

Dayton Christian Schools, Inc. (Dayton), and various individuals brought an action in the United States District Court for the Southern District of Ohio under 42 U.S.C. § 1983, seeking to enjoin a pending state administrative proceeding brought against Dayton by [the] Ohio Civil Rights Commission (Commission). Dayton asserted that the Free Exercise and Establishment Clauses of the First Amendment prohibited the Commission from exercising jurisdiction over it or from punishing it for engaging in employment discrimination.

Dayton is a private nonprofit corporation that provides education at both the elementary and secondary school levels. It was formed by two local churches, the Patterson Park Brethren Church and the Christian Tabernacle, and it is regarded as a "nondenominational" extension of the Christian education ministries of these two churches. Dayton's corporate charter establishes a board of directors (board) to lead the corporation in both spiritual and temporal matters. The charter also includes a section entitled "Statement of Faith," which serves to restrict membership on the board and the educational staff to persons who subscribe to a particular set of religious beliefs. The Statement of Faith requires each board or staff member to be a born-again Christian and to reaffirm his or her belief annually in the Bible, the Trinity, the nature and mission of Jesus Christ, the doctrine of original sin, the role of the Holy Ghost, the resurrection and judgment of the dead, the need for Christian unity, and the divine creation of human beings.

The board has elaborated these requirements to include a belief in the internal resolution of disputes through the "Biblical chain of command." The core of this doctrine, rooted in passages from the New Testament, is that one Christian should not take another Christian into courts of the State. Teachers are expected to present any grievance they may have to their immediate supervisor, and to acquiesce in the final authority of the board, rather than to pursue a remedy in civil court. The board has sought to ensure compliance with this internal dispute resolution doctrine by making it a contractual condition of employment.

Linda Hoskinson was employed as a teacher at Dayton during the 1978–1979 school year. She subscribed to the Statement of Faith and expressly agreed to resolve disputes internally through the Biblical chain of command. In January 1979, she informed her principal, James Rakestraw, that she was pregnant. After consulting with his superiors, Rakestraw informed Hoskinson that her employment contract would not be renewed at the end of the school year because of Dayton's religious doctrine that mothers should stay home with their preschool age children. Instead of appealing this decision internally, Hoskinson contacted an attorney who sent a letter to Dayton's superintendent, Claude Schindler, threatening litigation based on state and federal sex discrimination laws if Dayton did not agree to rehire Hoskinson for the coming school year. Upon receipt of this letter, Schindler informed Hoskinson that she was suspended immediately for challenging the nonrenewal decision in a manner inconsistent with the internal dispute resolution doctrine. The board reviewed this decision and decided to terminate Hoskinson. It stated that the sole reason for her termination was her violation of the internal dispute resolution doctrine, and it rescinded the earlier nonrenewal decision because it said that she had not received adequate prior notice of the doctrine concerning a mother's duty to stay home with her young children.

Hoskinson filed a complaint with [the Commission], alleging that Dayton's nonrenewal decision constituted sex discrimination, in violation of Ohio [law], and that its termination decision penalized her for asserting her rights, [also] in violation of Ohio [law]. . . . The Commission eventually determined that there was probable cause to believe that Dayton had discriminated against Hoskinson based on her sex and had retaliated against her for attempting to assert her rights in violation of [Ohio law]. . . . [I]t sent Dayton a proposed Conciliation Agreement and Consent Order that would have required Dayton to reinstate Hoskinson with backpay, and would have prohibited Dayton from taking retaliatory action against any employee for participating in the preliminary investigation. The Commission warned Dayton that failure to accede to this proposal or an acceptable counteroffer would result in formal administrative proceedings being initiated against it. When Dayton failed to respond, the Commission initiated administrative proceedings against it by filing a complaint. Dayton answered the complaint by asserting that the First Amendment prevented the Commission from exercising jurisdiction over it since its actions had been taken pursuant to sincerely held religious beliefs.

While these administrative proceedings were pending, Dayton filed this action against the Commission in the United States District Court for the Southern District of Ohio under 42 U.S.C. § 1983, seeking a permanent injunction against the state proceedings on the ground that any investigation of Dayton's hiring process or any imposition of sanctions for Dayton's nonrenewal or termination decisions would violate the Religion Clauses of the First Amendment.

We conclude that the District Court should have abstained from adjudicating this case under *Younger v. Harris*, and later cases.[19] The Commission urged such

---

[19] [n.2] We think that any ripeness challenge to appellees' complaint is foreclosed by *Steffel v. Thompson*, 415 U.S. 452 (1974), and *Doran v. Salem Inn, Inc.*, 422 U.S. 922 (1975). *Steffel* held that a reasonable threat of prosecution for conduct allegedly protected by the Constitution gives rise to a sufficiently ripe controversy. If a reasonable threat of prosecution creates a ripe controversy, we fail to see how the actual filing of the administrative action threatening sanctions in this case does not. It is true that the administrative body may rule completely or partially in appellees' favor; but it was equally true that the plaintiffs in *Steffel* and *Doran* may have prevailed had they in fact been prosecuted.

abstention in the District Court, and on oral argument here. Dayton has filed a postargument brief urging that the Commission has waived any claim to abstention because it had stipulated in the District Court that that court had jurisdiction of the action. We think, however, that this argument misconceives the nature of *Younger* abstention. It does not arise from lack of jurisdiction in the District Court, but from strong policies counseling against the exercise of such jurisdiction where particular kinds of state proceedings have already been commenced. A State may of course voluntarily submit to federal jurisdiction even though it might have had a tenable claim for abstention. *See Brown v. Hotel Employees*, 468 U.S. 491, 500, n.9 (1984); *Ohio Bureau of Employment Services v. Hodory*, 431 U.S. 471 (1977); *Sosna v. Iowa*, 419 U.S. 393 (1975). But in each of these cases the State expressly urged this Court or the District Court to proceed to an adjudication of the constitutional merits. We think there was no similar consent or waiver here, and we therefore address the issue of whether the District Court should have abstained from deciding the case.

In *Younger v. Harris* we held that a federal court should not enjoin a pending state criminal proceeding except in the very unusual situation that an injunction is necessary to prevent great and immediate irreparable injury. We justified our decision both on equitable principles and on the "more vital consideration" of the proper respect for the fundamental role of States in our federal system. Because of our concerns for comity and federalism, we thought that it was "perfectly natural for our cases to repeat time and time again that the *normal* thing to do when federal courts are asked to enjoin pending proceedings in state courts is not to issue such injunctions."

We have since recognized that our concern for comity and federalism is equally applicable to certain other pending state proceedings. We have applied the *Younger* principle to civil proceedings in which important state interests are involved. *Huffman v. Pursue, Ltd.*, 420 U.S. 592 (1975); *Juidice v. Vail*, 430 U.S. 327 (1977); *Trainor v. Hernandez*, 431 U.S. 434 (1977); *Moore v. Sims*, 442 U.S. 415 (1979). We have also applied it to state administrative proceedings in which important state interests are vindicated, so long as in the course of those proceedings the federal plaintiff would have a full and fair opportunity to litigate his constitutional claim. We stated in *Gibson v. Berryhill*, 411 U.S. 564 (1973), that "administrative proceedings looking toward the revocation of a license to practice medicine may in proper circumstances command the respect due court proceedings." Similarly, we have held that federal courts should refrain from enjoining lawyer disciplinary proceedings initiated by state ethics committees if the proceedings are within the appellate jurisdiction of the appropriate State Supreme Court. *Middlesex County Ethics Committee v. Garden State Bar Assn.*, 457 U.S. 423 (1982). Because we found that the administrative proceedings in *Middlesex* were "judicial in nature" from the outset, it was not essential to the decision that they had progressed to state-court review by the time we heard the federal injunction case.[20]

We think the principles enunciated in these cases govern the present one. We have no doubt that the elimination of prohibited sex discrimination is a sufficiently important state interest to bring the present case within the ambit of the cited authorities. We also have no reason to doubt that Dayton will receive an adequate opportunity to raise its constitutional claims. Dayton contends that the mere exercise of jurisdiction over it by the state administrative body violates its First Amendment rights. But we have repeatedly rejected the argument that a constitutional attack on state procedures

---

[20] [n.3] Of course, if state law expressly indicates that the administrative proceedings are not even "judicial in nature," abstention may not be appropriate. *See Hawaii Housing Authority v. Midkiff*, 467 U.S. 229 (1984). The application of the *Younger* principle to pending state administrative proceedings is fully consistent with *Patsy v. Florida Board of Regents*, 457 U.S. 496 (1982), which holds that litigants need not exhaust their administrative remedies prior to bringing a § 1983 suit in federal court. *Cf. Huffman v. Pursue, Ltd.*, 420 U.S. 592 (1975). Unlike *Patsy*, the administrative proceedings here are coercive rather than remedial, began before any substantial advancement in the federal action took place, and involve an important state interest.

themselves "automatically vitiates the adequacy of those procedures for purposes of the *Younger-Huffman* line of cases." Even religious schools cannot claim to be wholly free from some state regulation. *Wisconsin v. Yoder*, 406 U.S. 205 (1972). We therefore think that however Dayton's constitutional claim should be decided on the merits, the Commission violates no constitutional rights by merely investigating the circumstances of Hoskinson's discharge in this case, if only to ascertain whether the ascribed religious-based reason was in fact the reason for the discharge.

Dayton also contends that the administrative proceedings do not afford the opportunity to level constitutional challenges against the potential sanctions for the alleged sex discrimination. In its reply brief in this Court, the Commission cites several rulings to demonstrate that religious justifications for otherwise illegal conduct are considered by it. Dayton in turn relies on a decision of the Supreme Court of Ohio, *Mobil Oil Corp. v. Rocky River*, 38 Ohio St. 2d 23, 26, 309 N.E.2d 900, 902 (1974), in which that court held that a local zoning commission could not consider constitutional claims. But even if Ohio law is such that the Commission may not consider the constitutionality of the statute under which it operates, it would seem an unusual doctrine, and one not supported by the cited case, to say that the Commission could not construe its own statutory mandate in the light of federal constitutional principles. In any event, it is sufficient under *Middlesex* that constitutional claims may be raised in state-court judicial review of the administrative proceeding. [Ohio law] provides that any "respondent claiming to be aggrieved by a final order of the commission . . . may obtain judicial review thereof." Dayton cites us to no Ohio authority indicating that this provision does not authorize judicial review of claims that agency action violates the United States Constitution.

JUSTICE STEVENS, with whom JUSTICE BRENNAN, JUSTICE MARSHALL, and JUSTICE BLACKMUN join, concurring in the judgment.

Like the majority, I agree . . . that neither the investigation of certain charges nor the conduct of a hearing on those charges is prohibited by the First Amendment. . . . I further agree . . . that any challenge to a possibly intrusive remedy is premature at this juncture. As the majority points out, the Commission recognizes religious justifications for conduct that might otherwise be illegal. Thus, although [Ohio law] forbids discrimination on the basis of religion, the Commission has dismissed complaints alleging religious discrimination by religious educational institutions, and in particular has dismissed complaints by teachers against sectarian schools for limiting employment to instructors who subscribe to the appropriate faith. It bears emphasis that the Commission dismissed these complaints only *after* investigating charges of discrimination, finding probable cause that the statute had been violated, and holding a hearing on the complaint. It therefore follows that the Commission's finding of probable cause and decision to schedule a hearing in this case does not also mean that the Commission intends to impose *any* sanction, let alone a sanction in derogation of the First Amendment's Religion Clauses. In view of this fact, the District Court was entirely correct in concluding that [Dayton's] constitutional challenge to the remedial provisions of the Ohio statute is not ripe for review.[21]

---

[21] [n.4] I fully agree with the majority's general statement that "a reasonable threat of prosecution for conduct allegedly protected by the Constitution gives rise to a sufficiently ripe controversy." Thus, when the constitutional challenge is to the arrest and initiation of criminal proceedings — as was the case with the pamphleteer in *Steffel v. Thompson* and the operators of the bars in *Doran* — a "reasonable threat" of arrest and prosecution is sufficient to make the controversy ripe for judicial review. For purposes of this case, it follows from *Steffel* and *Doran* that appellees' First Amendment challenge to the Commission's decision to investigate and adjudicate a charge of sex discrimination against the School is ripe, because the investigation has been completed and the matter set for hearing. However, it does not follow that a challenge to whatever *remedy* might ultimately be fashioned (should liability be established and relief ordered) is ripe merely upon a showing of a "reasonable threat" that proceedings will commence. *Doran* and *Steffel* do not suggest this

Accordingly, I concur in the judgment.[22]

NOTES

1. *Younger* in the Civil Context. As demonstrated by *Dayton Christian Schools*, the *Younger* abstention doctrine has been extended to civil cases to which the state is a party, so long as "important state interests" are at stake. The Court cites several examples, including *Huffman v. Pursue, Ltd.*, 420 U.S. 592 (1975), a civil nuisance abatement proceeding filed against a theater, *Juidice v. Vail*, 430 U.S. 327 (1977), a civil contempt proceeding (prosecuted by the state) that arose in a collection case between private parties, *Trainor v. Hernandez*, 431 U.S. 434 (1977), a civil enforcement action brought by the state to recover welfare payments allegedly obtained by fraud, and *Moore v. Sims*, 442 U.S. 415 (1979), a child custody proceeding initiated by the state to remove children from their parents' home. The key to these decisions was that proceedings in state courts had been commenced by government officials against the would-be § 1983 plaintiffs. *See Ankenbrandt v. Richards*, 504 U.S. 689 (1992) ("Absent any *pending* proceeding in state tribunals, . . . application by the lower courts of *Younger* abstention was clearly erroneous.").

In an apparent extension of the principles applied in the foregoing cases, the Court concluded in *Pennzoil Co. v. Texaco, Inc.*, 481 U.S. 1 (1987), that *Younger* barred a § 1983 suit in federal court challenging a state bonding requirement that effectively precluded a losing party from appealing an adverse judgment in state court. Pennzoil obtained an $11 billion judgment against Texaco in a Texas state court. State law required that in order to avoid execution of the judgment, Texaco was required to post a bond in the amount of the judgment. The District Court issued a preliminary injunction restraining collection of the bond because it found that it would force Texaco into bankruptcy, prevent its taking an appeal, and thereby deprive it of due process of law. The Supreme Court, in an opinion authored by Justice Powell, reversed: "[T]he State's interests in the proceeding are so important that exercise of the federal judicial power would disregard the comity between the States and the National Government." *Pennzoil* appears to have extended *Younger* because Texas was not responsible for initiating the state-court proceedings. Justice Stevens noted in his concurring opinion that when applying *Younger* the Court has "invariably required that the State have a *substantive* interest in the ongoing proceeding, an interest that goes beyond its interest as adjudicator of wholly private disputes." Notwithstanding *Pennzoil*, courts have been hesitant to invoke *Younger* abstention when government is not party to ongoing state-court proceedings. *See, e.g., AmerisourceBergen Corp. v. Roden*, 495 F.3d 1143 (9th Cir. 2007) (holding that the state did not have an important interest for *Younger* purposes in merely adjudicating disputes and enforcing state-court judgments); *Rio Grande Community Health Center, Inc. v. Rullan*, 397 F.3d 56 (1st Cir. 2005) (refusing to abstain under *Younger* because the action was "not an enforcement proceeding brought by the state or an agency" and did not involve "fundamental workings of the state's judicial system (like its contempt process or method of enforcing judgments)").

---

result, for they did not address the constitutionality of possible remedies for the conduct prosecuted in those cases. In view of the absence of any finding of liability in this case, and the Commission's demonstrated willingness to tailor remedies to accommodate the exercise of religious freedoms, there is plainly no "reasonable threat" that an overly intrusive remedy will trench on [Dayton's] First Amendment rights.

[22] [n.5] I do not agree with the majority that the doctrine of abstention associated with *Younger v. Harris* required the District Court to dismiss [Dayton's] complaint. That disposition would presumably deny the School a federal forum to adjudicate the constitutionality of a provisional administrative remedy, such as reinstatement pending resolution of the complainant's charges, even though the constitutional issues have become ripe for review by the Commission's entry of a coercive order and the Commission refuses to address the merits of the constitutional claims. *Younger* abstention has never been applied to subject a federal-court plaintiff to an allegedly unconstitutional state administrative order when the constitutional challenge to that order can be asserted, if at all, only in state-court judicial review of the administrative proceeding.

2. Important State Interests. The Supreme Court has not been overly demanding when searching for "important state interests" to justify abstention under *Younger*. Nor has it been willing to "sneak a peek" at the merits of a controversy to decide whether a state's interest is more important than the interest underlying the federal challenge. In *New Orleans Public Service, Inc. v. Council of City of New Orleans*, 491 U.S. 350 (1989) (*NOPSI*) (excerpted *infra*), a federal challenge brought by a power company (NOPSI) against a local ratemaking body, the power company argued that *Younger* abstention was not required "in the face of a substantial claim that the challenged state action is completely pre-empted by federal law." "Such a claim," NOPSI argued, "calls into question the prerequisite of *Younger* abstention that the State have a legitimate, substantial interest in its pending proceedings." NOPSI thus claimed that a federal court "presented with a pre-emption-based request for equitable relief should take a quick look at the merits; and if upon that look the claim appears substantial, the court should endeavor to resolve it." The Supreme Court, per Justice Scalia, disagreed:

> There is no greater federal interest in enforcing the supremacy of federal statutes than in enforcing the supremacy of explicit constitutional guarantees, and constitutional challenges to state action, no less than pre-emption-based challenges, call into question the legitimacy of the State's interest in its proceedings reviewing or enforcing that action. Yet it is clear that the mere assertion of a substantial constitutional challenge to state action will not alone compel the exercise of federal jurisdiction. That is so because when we inquire into the substantiality of the State's interest in its proceedings we do not look narrowly to its interest in the *outcome* of the particular case — which could arguably be offset by a substantial federal interest in the opposite outcome. Rather, what we look to is the importance of the generic proceedings to the State. In *Younger*, for example, we did not consult California's interest in prohibiting John Harris from distributing handbills, but rather its interest in "carrying out the important and necessary task" of enforcing its criminal laws. Similarly, in [*Dayton Christian Schools*] we looked not to Ohio's specific concern with Dayton Christian Schools' firing of Linda Hoskinson, but to its more general interest in preventing employers from engaging in sex discrimination. Because pre-emption-based challenges merit a similar focus, the appropriate question here is not whether Louisiana has a substantial, legitimate interest in reducing NOPSI's retail rate below that necessary to recover its wholesale costs, but whether it has a substantial, legitimate interest in regulating intrastate retail rates. It clearly does.

Still, not every state interest must qualify under *Younger*. In *Harper v. Public Service Commission of West Virginia*, 396 F.3d 348 (4th Cir. 2005), for example, the Fourth Circuit distinguished *NOPSI* and ruled that a state's interest in refusing to license an out-of-state waste disposal company was not important enough to justify *Younger* abstention. The challenger (Harper) argued that West Virginia had created a monopoly in favor of local companies in violation of the Dormant Commerce Clause. Notwithstanding that Harper was party to an administrative action proceeding before the state's licensing commission, the Fourth Circuit refused to abstain:

> Many interests beyond criminal law are core sources of state authority. For instance, enforcing state court judgments cuts to the state's ability to operate its own judicial system, a vital interest for *Younger* purposes. States have always held primary sway over education; likewise, its close cousin "[f]amily relations [is] a traditional area of state concern." Similarly, property law concerns, such as land use and zoning questions, are frequently "important" state interests justifying *Younger* abstention. Further, the law of probate, trusts, and estates — allocating the personal property of citizens — remains an important interest of the states for *Younger* purposes.

Matters relating to public health are not infrequently under the purview of the states, and may justify abstaining under *Yonger.* Similarly, the regulation and licensing of health care professionals may be an important interest under the states' residual police powers and bear on the abstention decision.

Corporate law, too, often reveals state interests important in *Younger* analysis. Charitable trusts and corporations, like other corporations, have traditionally been creatures of the states. In addition, certain businesses have historically been subject to the oversight of state government, a factor which bears on abstention decisions.

Because the interest advanced here is one that *by its very nature* serves to impede interstate commerce, we must evaluate the effect of the dormant Commerce Clause upon the decision to abstain. Although we do not reach the merits of the underlying claim, we conclude that the interest West Virginia advances through the state action SOD challenges is insufficient to warrant abstention.

The commerce power plays a role in abstention analysis quite different from many of the other provisions of the Constitution. The dormant Commerce Clause demonstrates a difference of kind, not merely of degree. By its very nature, it implicates interstate interests. . . . Recognizing that there is a peculiarly national interest — and therefore, more limited state interest — in no way threatens the kind of comity that has always underpinned the *Younger* doctrine.

In short, the commerce power itself justifies a narrower view of state interests in the abstention context.

[A] state interest that on its face implicates the Commerce Clause is seldom an important state interest for *Younger* purposes. . . .

Contrast Stroman Realty v. Martinez, 505 F.3d 658 (7th Cir. 2007) (distinguishing *Harper* and holding that abstention was proper where the Dormant Commerce Clause challenge was made to a state real estate licensing decision).

3. Administrative Proceedings. *Dayton Christian Schools* also demonstrates that state administrative proceedings of a judicial nature can be the proper subject of *Younger* abstention. *See also Middlesex County Ethics Committee v. Garden State Bar Ass'n*, 457 U.S. 423 (1982) (applying *Younger* to prevent a lawyer from interrupting an ongoing disciplinary proceeding filed against him by a local ethics committee). So long as the state is enforcing an "important" interest and the agency is acting in a judicial capacity, the Court ruled, *Younger* applies. The school in *Dayton Christian Schools* argued that because it could not raise its constitutional claims before the Commission, it had no adequate remedy at law under *Younger.* The Supreme Court in *Dayton Christian Schools* disagreed, explaining that, even if the school was right, it could raise its constitutional claims "in state-court judicial review of the administrative proceeding." Can this holding be reconciled with *Patsy v. Board of Regents*, 457 U.S. 496 (1982) (discussed in Note 3 following *Elliott* in Chapter 8.A.[3], *infra*), where the Court ruled that exhaustion of state administrative remedies is ordinarily unnecessary before proceeding under § 1983? *Patsy* involved a state university that allegedly discriminated against an employee (Patsy) based on her race and gender. Rather than make use of available state administrative procedures, Patsy filed suit under § 1983. The Court, per Justice Marshall, ruled that regardless of whether state remedies mirrored those available under federal law, exhaustion of administrative remedies was not a necessary predicate to suit under § 1983. The Court in *Dayton Christian Schools* distinguished the cases this way: "Unlike *Patsy,* the administrative proceedings here are coercive rather than remedial, began before any substantial advancement in the federal action took place, and involve an important state interest." Hence, when a state forces a would-be § 1983 plaintiff into a state administrative proceeding, *Younger* abstention — and the exhaustion it entails — can be proper. Should a § 1983 plaintiff choose to make use of state administrative proceedings, in contrast, *Younger* abstention is not warranted and exhaustion is not required.

4. Waiver and Appeal. The Court in *Dayton Christian Schools* found that *Younger* abstention, unlike *Pullman* abstention, can be waived by the state: "A State may of course voluntarily submit to federal jurisdiction even though it might have had a tenable claim for abstention." Because *Younger* abstention causes dismissal of federal proceedings, dismissed plaintiffs are entitled to take immediate appeals of the adverse final judgments. See 28 U.S.C. § 1291 (providing for appeal from final judgments of District Courts). The standard of review applied to dismissals based on *Younger's* abstention doctrine is *de novo*. See, e.g., *Joseph A. v. Ingram*, 275 F.3d 1253 (10th Cir. 2002) ("In general, we review de novo a district court's application of the *Younger* abstention doctrine."). Should the District Court refuse to abstain under *Younger*, however, a defendant can not take an interlocutory appeal as a matter of right. See, e.g., *Hi Tech Trans LLC v. New Jersey*, 382 F.3d 295 (3d Cir. 2004) ("The prevailing view now is 'that for all of the abstention doctrines, a federal court's decision to abstain is immediately appealable, but its refusal to abstain is not appealable until there is a final judgment.' "); *Robinson v. Kansas*, 295 F.3d 1183 (10th Cir. 2002) ("[it] is not even clear that we would have jurisdiction to consider a *Younger* claim such as that presented in this case on interlocutory appeal"). The District Court is always free to certify an appeal under 28 U.S.C. § 1292(b) if it is "of the opinion that such order involves a controlling question of law as to which there is substantial ground for difference of opinion and that an immediate appeal from the order may materially advance the ultimate termination of the litigation," but this is not an appeal as of right. See, e.g., *Dababnah v. West Virginia Bd. of Medicine*, 57 F. Supp. 2d 355 (S.D. W. Va. 1999) (certifying for interlocutory appeal the denial of a motion to dismiss based on *Younger*). Should the District Court reject *Younger* abstention and preliminarily enjoin state proceedings, an immediate appeal as of right is available under 28 U.S.C. § 1292(a) (authorizing appeals from District Court orders "granting, continuing, modifying, refusing or dissolving injunctions, or refusing to dissolve or modify injunctions"). See, e.g., *Diamond "D" Const. Corp. v. McGowan*, 282 F.3d 191 (2d Cir. 2002) (entertaining the *Younger* doctrine on interlocutory appeal from an award of a preliminary injunction). Assuming that an interlocutory appeal can be taken from a District Court's refusal to employ *Younger*, the standard of review is *de novo*, rather than the abuse of discretion standard commonly applied to decisions not to abstain. See, e.g., *Hartford Courant Co. v. Pelligrino*, 380 F.3d 83 (2d Cir. 2004) ("We evaluate a district court's determination not to abstain under *Younger* . . . *de novo*, because it implicates the court's subject matter jurisdiction.").

5. Quasi-Legislative and -Executive Agency Action. Does *Dayton Christian Schools* insulate all state agency decision-making from federal review?

NEW ORLEANS PUBLIC SERVICE, INC. v. COUNCIL OF CITY OF NEW ORLEANS
Supreme Court of the United States
491 U.S. 350 (1989)

JUSTICE SCALIA delivered the opinion of the Court.

New Orleans Public Service, Inc. (NOPSI), a producer, wholesaler, and retailer of electricity that provides retail electrical service to the city of New Orleans, [agreed to participate in the construction and operation of] two 1250 megawatt nuclear reactors, Grand Gulf 1 and 2, in return for the right to the reactors' electrical output. The estimated cost of completing the two reactors was $1.2 billion.

During the late 1970's, consumer demand turned out to be far lower than expected, and regulatory delays, enhanced construction requirements, and high inflation led to spiraling costs. As a result, construction of Grand Gulf 2 was suspended, and the cost of completing Grand Gulf 1 alone eventually exceeded $3 billion. Not surprisingly, the cost of the electricity produced by the reactor greatly exceeded that of power generated by . . . conventional facilities.

Acting pursuant to its exclusive regulatory authority over interstate wholesale power transactions, FERC [the Federal Energy Regulatory Commission] . . . concluded that, because the planned nuclear reactors had been designed "to meet overall System needs and objectives," . . . 17 percent of Grand Gulf costs (approximately $13 million per month) [should be allocated] to NOPSI.

When NOPSI sought from the New Orleans City Council (Council) — the local ratemaking body with final authority over the utility's retail rates — a rate increase to cover the increase in wholesale rates resulting from FERC's allocation of Grand Gulf costs, the Council denied an immediate rate adjustment. . . . NOPSI responded by filing an action for injunctive and declaratory relief in the United States District Court for the Eastern District of Louisiana, asserting that federal law required the Council to allow it to recover, through an increase in retail rates, its FERC-allocated share of the Grand Gulf expenses.

The District Court granted the Council's motion to dismiss, holding that pursuant to the Johnson Act, 28 U.S.C. § 1342,[23] it had no jurisdiction to entertain the action, and that even if it had jurisdiction it would be compelled by *Burford v. Sun Oil Co.*, 319 U.S. 315 (1943), to abstain. On appeal, the Fifth Circuit [in *NOPSI I*] initially reversed on both grounds, but later, on its own motion, vacated its earlier opinion in part and held that abstention was proper both under *Burford* and under *Younger v. Harris*.

By resolution of October 10, 1985, while *NOPSI I* was still pending before the Fifth Circuit, the Council initiated an investigation into the prudence of NOPSI's involvement in Grand Gulf 1.

In November 1985, NOPSI filed a second suit in the United States District Court for the Eastern District of Louisiana, seeking to preclude the Council from requiring NOPSI or its shareholders to absorb any of NOPSI's FERC — allocated share of the Grand Gulf costs. The District Court dismissed the suit as unripe, but held in the alternative that abstention was appropriate. On appeal, the Fifth Circuit affirmed the judgment on ripeness grounds. *NOPSI II*.

The Council completed its prudence review on February 4, 1988, and immediately entered a final order disallowing $135 million of the Grand Gulf costs.

Upon receipt of the Council's decree, NOPSI turned once again to the District Court for the Eastern District of Louisiana, seeking declaratory and injunctive relief on the ground that, in light of this Court's recent decision in *Nantahala Power & Light Co. v. Thornburg*, 476 U.S. 953 (1986), the Council's rate order was pre-empted by federal law. Although the District Court expressed considerable doubt as to the merits of the Council's position on the pre-emption question, it concluded that . . . it should still abstain from deciding the suit.

Anticipating that the District Court might again abstain, NOPSI had filed a petition for review of the Council's order in [state court]. As filed, NOPSI's petition raised only state-law claims and federal due process and takings claims, but NOPSI informed the state court by letter that it would amend to raise its federal pre-emption claim if the federal court once again dismissed its complaint. When that happened, it did so.

---

[23] [Editor's note: The Johnson Act precludes federal courts from enjoining the operation of state rate-making agencies when "a plain, speedy and efficient remedy may be had in the courts of such a state." *See* Note 3 following *Hibbs* in Chapter 6.C.[2], *supra*. The Act does not, however, protect rate-making orders that "interfere with interstate commerce," 28 U.S.C. § 1342(2), nor does it govern challenges based on federal preemption. *See id.* § 1342(1); *e.g., IBEW v. Public Serv. Comm'n*, 614 F.2d 206 (9th Cir. 1980). The Fifth Circuit ruled in *NOPSI I* that because of the challengers' preemption argument, the Johnson Act did not apply. That ruling was not appealed to the Supreme Court.]

In the parallel federal proceedings, the Fifth Circuit affirmed the District Court's dismissal, agreeing that the case was effectively controlled by *NOPSI I*, i.e., that *Burford* and *Younger* abstention applied.[24]

NOPSI's challenge must stand or fall upon the answer to the question whether the Louisiana court action is the type of proceeding to which *Younger* applies. Viewed in isolation, it plainly is not. Although our concern for comity and federalism has led us to expand the protection of *Younger* beyond state criminal prosecutions, to civil enforcement proceedings, and even to civil proceedings involving certain orders that are uniquely in furtherance of the state courts' ability to perform their judicial functions, see *Juidice v. Vail* (civil contempt order); *Pennzoil Co. v. Texaco Inc.* (requirement for the posting of bond pending appeal), it has never been suggested that *Younger* requires abstention in deference to a state judicial proceeding reviewing legislative or executive action. Such a broad abstention requirement would make a mockery of the rule that only exceptional circumstances justify a federal court's refusal to decide a case in deference to the States.

In asserting that *Younger* is applicable, however, [the Council] focus[es] not upon the Louisiana court action in isolation, but upon that action as a mere continuation of the Council proceeding. The[] contention is that "[t]he Council's own ratemaking and prudence inquiry, even though complete, constitutes an 'ongoing proceeding' because it is subject to state judicial review." The proper question . . . is whether the Council proceeding qualified for *Younger* treatment — because if it did, the proceeding is not complete until judicial review is concluded. [The Council] argue[s] by analogy to the treatment of court proceedings, for *Younger* purposes, as an uninterruptible whole. When, in a proceeding to which *Younger* applies, a state trial court has entered judgment, the losing party cannot, of course, pursue equitable remedies in federal district court while concurrently challenging the trial court's judgment on appeal. For *Younger* purposes, the State's trial-and-appeals process is treated as a unitary system, and for a federal court to disrupt its integrity by intervening in mid-process would demonstrate a lack of respect for the State as sovereign. For the same reason, a party may not procure federal intervention by terminating the state judicial process prematurely — forgoing the state appeal to attack the trial court's judgment in federal court. "[A] necessary concomitant of *Younger* is that a party [wishing to contest in federal court the judgment of a state judicial tribunal] must exhaust his state appellate remedies before seeking relief in the District Court." *Huffman v. Pursue, Ltd.* [The Council] urge[s] that these principles apply equally where the initial adjudicatory tribunal is an agency — i.e., that the litigation, from agency through courts, is to be viewed as a unitary process that should not be disrupted, so that federal intervention is no more permitted at the conclusion of the administrative stage than during it.

We will assume, without deciding, that this is correct.[25] [The Council's] case for abstention still requires, however, that the Council proceeding be the sort of proceeding entitled to *Younger* treatment. We think it is not. While we have expanded *Younger*

---

[24] [Editor's note: The Supreme Court first concluded that abstention was not required by *Burford v. Sun Oil Co.*, because "NOPSI's primary claim is that the Council is prohibited by federal law from refusing to provide reimbursement for FERC — allocated wholesale costs. Unlike a claim that a state agency has misapplied its lawful authority or has failed to take into consideration or properly weigh relevant state-law factors, federal adjudication of this sort of pre-emption claim would not disrupt the State's attempt to ensure uniformity in the treatment of an essentially local problem.' " See Note 9 following *Pullman* in Section A, *supra.*]

[25] [n.4] In *Dayton Christian Schools*, we held that the *Younger* doctrine prevented an injunction against an on-going sex discrimination proceeding before the Ohio Civil Rights Commission. . . . The fact that *Dayton Christian Schools* relied, as an alternative argument, upon the fact that the federal challenge could be made upon appeal to the state courts suggests, perhaps, that an administrative proceeding to which *Younger* applies cannot be challenged in federal court even after the administrative action has become final. But we have never squarely faced the question.

beyond criminal proceedings, and even beyond proceedings in courts, we have never extended it to proceedings that are not "judicial in nature."

[R]atemaking is an essentially legislative act. Thus, the Council's proceedings here were plainly legislative.

That characterization does not, however, end the inquiry. . . . [I]n the present case, if the Louisiana courts' review of Council ratemaking was legislative in nature, NOPSI's challenge to the Council's order should have been dismissed as unripe.

There is no contention here that the Louisiana courts' review involves anything other than a judicial act — that is, not "the making of a rule for the future," but the declaration of NOPSI's rights vis a vis the Council "on present or past facts and under laws supposed already to exist." Nor does there seem to be room for such a contention. Since the state-court review is not an extension of the legislative process, NOPSI's preemption claim was ripe for federal review when the Council's order was entered.

As a challenge to completed legislative action, NOPSI's suit represents neither the interference with ongoing judicial proceedings against which *Younger* was directed, nor the interference with an ongoing legislative process against which our ripeness holding[s] [are] directed. It is, insofar as our policies of federal comity are concerned, no different in substance from a facial challenge to an allegedly unconstitutional statute or zoning ordinance — which we would assuredly not require to be brought in state courts. It is true, of course, that the federal court's disposition of such a case may well affect, or for practical purposes pre-empt, a future — or, as in the present circumstances, even a pending — state-court action. But there is no doctrine that the availability or even the pendency of state judicial proceedings excludes the federal courts. Viewed, as it should be, as no more than a state-court challenge to completed legislative action, the Louisiana suit comes within none of the exceptions that *Younger* and later cases have established.

CHIEF JUSTICE REHNQUIST, concurring in [part] and concurring in the judgment.

Nothing in the Court's opinion curtails our prior application of *Younger* to certain administrative proceedings which are "judicial in nature," nor does it alter our prior case law indicating that such proceedings should be regarded as "ongoing" for the purposes of *Younger* abstention until state appellate review is completed. . . .

JUSTICE BLACKMUN, concurring in the judgment.[26]

I am not entirely persuaded that this Court's decisions applying *Younger* abstention to administrative proceedings that are judicial in nature leave open the question whether abstention must continue through the judicial review process. In my view, the majority's observations on these questions are not necessary to the result or to the legal standard the majority has adopted.

NOTES

1. Non-Judicial Administrative Action. *NOPSI* established that *Younger* does not require "abstention in deference to a state judicial proceeding reviewing legislative or executive action." George D. Brown, *When Federalism and Separation of Powers Collide — Rethinking* Younger *Abstention*, 59 GEO. WASH. L. REV. 114, 149 (1990). *See, e.g., Rio Grande Community Health Center, Inc. v. Rullan*, 397 F.3d 56 (1st Cir. 2005) (holding that *Younger* does not apply to "judicial review of executive action, rather than an enforcement proceeding"); *Blankenship v. Blackwell*, 341 F. Supp. 2d 911 (S.D. Ohio 2004) (holding *Younger* did not apply to Ralph Nader's challenge in federal court to the

---

[26] [Editor's note: Justices Brennan and Marshall also concurred, but voiced their continuing disagreement with *Younger*'s extension to civil proceedings.]

Ohio Secretary of State's decision to remove his name from the presidential ballot even though that decision was also being reviewed in state court), *dismissed as moot*, 429 F.3d 254 (6th Cir. 2005). If it were any other way, Professor Fallon explains, "it would virtually always be possible for state officials sued for declaratory or injunctive relief in federal court effectively to remove the dispute to state court by filing a declaratory judgment suit in a state forum." Richard H. Fallon, Jr., *The "Conservative" Paths of the Rehnquist Court's Federalism Decisions*, 69 U. CHI. L. REV. 429, 473 (2002). *NOPSI*, some might say, thus put the breaks on *Pennzoil*'s expansion of *Younger* abstention. "The *Younger* doctrine does not require abstention merely because a federal plaintiff, alleging a constitutional violation in federal court, filed a claim under state law, in state court, on the same underlying facts." *Wexler v. Lepore*, 385 F.3d 1336 (11th Cir. 2004).

Federal review of state executive and legislative agency action, however, is subject to a distinct limitation. Where state court review is an extension of the legislative process, as opposed to being judicial in nature, a federal challenge will not be ripe until the state court completes its review. *See* Clinton A. Vince & John S. Moot, *Energy Federalism, Choice of Forum, and State Utility Regulations*, 42 ADMIN. L. REV. 323, 363 (1990). In these relatively rare cases — few, if any, are reported — a federal court would not be able to review the government's action until after the state court's review. Whether state court review is deemed legislative or judicial, moreover, appears to be a question of state law.

2. Quasi-Judicial Administrative Action. As explained in *NOPSI*, ratemaking is a form of rulemaking; it thus is generally considered a legislative function. License revocation, in contrast, is ordinarily deemed quasi-adjudicative, which means that it is judicial for purposes of *Younger* abstention. *See, e.g., Stroman Realty v. Martinez*, 505 F.3d 658 (7th Cir. 2007) ("It is uncontested that the state proceeding at issue is judicial in nature, as the motivating factor behind the Department's filing of its complaint was to enforce its real estate licensing requirements against Stroman."). Condemnation proceedings have also been held to be judicial for purposes of *Younger* abstention, *see, e.g., Aaron v. Target Corp.*, 357 F.3d 768 (8th Cir. 2004) (relying on Missouri law to hold that a "state court action in which private property is condemned for a public use is judicial in nature"), as have enforcement proceedings in the zoning context. *See, e.g., Forty-One News, Inc. v. County of Lake*, 491 F.3d 662 (7th Cir. 2007) (holding that a zoning enforcement proceeding supported *Younger* abstention); *JMM, Corp. v. District of Columbia*, 378 F.3d 1117 (D.C. Cir. 2004) (holding that an administrative enforcement action in the context of zoning adult businesses justified *Younger* abstention). Of course, the *Younger* abstention doctrine assumes an agency *hearing*. An initial administrative denial of a license, permit or variance — coupled with a right to seek either administrative or judicial review — might not be enough to implicate *Younger*. *See, e.g., Executive Arts Studio, Inc. v. City of Grand Rapids*, 391 F.3d 783 (6th Cir. 2004) (observing a difference between the simple denial of a land use permit, which causes no *Younger* problem, and the enforcement of a denial, which does); *Nader v. Keith*, 385 F.3d 729 (7th Cir. 2004) (holding that the state's denial of ballot access which was being challenged in state court did not justify *Younger* abstention). Should an enforcement action follow the denial of a license, permit, or variance, of course, then *Younger* abstention would appear warranted.[27]

3. Ongoing Proceedings. The Court in *NOPSI* did not decide whether a federal court must abstain under *Younger* pending completion of state court review of a state

---

[27] Can state or local government transform an executive decision into a quasi-judicial proceeding by surrounding it with the trappings of a courtroom? In *Blankenship v. Blackwell*, 341 F. Supp. 2d 911 (S.D. Ohio 2004), *dismissed as moot*, 429 F.3d 254 (6th Cir. 2005), for example, Ohio's Secretary of State held a contested administrative hearing before deciding that Ralph Nader's name should not appear on Ohio's ballot. That decision was then challenged by Nader directly in the Ohio Supreme Court and in an original proceeding filed in federal district court. The latter refused to abstain under *Younger*, finding that the Secretary's decision was an executive one notwithstanding its quasi-judicial attributes.

agency's "judicial" decision. *See* James C. Rehnquist, *Taking Comity Seriously: How to Neutralize the Abstention Doctrine*, 46 STAN. L. REV. 1049, 1109 (1994). Chief Justice Rehnquist, in his concurring opinion, assumed this to be the case, as have lower courts in *NOPSI*'s wake. *See, e.g., Harper v. Public Service Commission of West Virginia*, 396 F.3d 348 (4th Cir. 2005) (observing that the availability of discretionary review of a state agency decision in West Virginia's high court might qualify as "ongoing judicial proceedings" barring federal judicial action under *Younger*).

One legal wrinkle that has emerged, post-*NOPSI*, in the context of quasi-adjudicative administrative decisions involves cross-system appeals. The Supreme Court in *City of Chicago v. International College of Surgeons*, 522 U.S. 156 (1997) (excerpted in Chapter 8.A.[4], *infra*), ruled that a local zoning board's denial of a request for a variance can be "appealed" to federal court as well as state court; at least there is no federal jurisdictional bar. Armed with *International College of Surgeons*, one can arguably bypass state appellate processes and appeal directly to federal court (assuming the presence of a federal question or some other jurisdictional hook). Whether *Younger* directs that a federal district court should abstain in favor of a state's available appellate processes in such a setting remains an open question. If the underlying administrative proceeding were coercive, like that in *Dayton Christian Schools*, it would seem that a strong argument could be made that *Younger* requires deference to the state's appellate processes. *Cf. Nader v. Keith*, 385 F.3d 729 (7th Cir. 2004) (holding that a state's denial of ballot access, which was being challenged in state court, did not justify *Younger* abstention because the state proceeding was not coercive). Assuming that one must exhaust state appellate remedies before proceeding to federal court, the next question is what state appellate remedies qualify under the "ongoing judicial proceedings" label. All agree that appeals-as-of-right qualify, but what about discretionary appeals? *See, e.g., Harper v. Public Service Commission of West Virginia*, 396 F.3d 348 (4th Cir. 2005) (observing that the availability of discretionary review of a state agency decision in West Virginia's high court might qualify as an "ongoing judicial proceedings" barring federal judicial action under *Younger*).

C. § 1983 CLAIMS FOR MONEY DAMAGES

Younger, like *Pullman*, is generally understood to apply only to federal actions seeking *equitable* relief. What if a federal plaintiff files an action for money damages while a state criminal charge is pending?

DEAKINS v. MONAGHAN
Supreme Court of the United States
484 U.S. 193 (1988)

JUSTICE BLACKMUN delivered the opinion of the Court.

William Monaghan, Theodore DeSantis, and John James are in the construction business together. They jointly own . . . Foundations & Structures, Inc. (F & S), and MJD Construction Company, Inc., New Jersey corporations, and William E. Monaghan Associates, a New Jersey general partnership. On October 4, 1984, . . . Albert G. Palentchar, a criminal investigator for the State of New Jersey, applied to the Honorable Samuel T. Lenox, Jr., the "assignment judge" of the Superior Court for Mercer County with supervisory authority over the state grand jury, for a warrant to search the Tuckahoe, N.J., premises of F & S for evidence of theft, bribery, records tampering, and other criminal activities that were the subject of an ongoing state grand jury investigation. Judge Lenox found probable cause and issued a warrant authorizing the seizure of documents, including contracts, minutes, site logs, invoices, correspondence, memoranda, deeds, canceled checks, and bank statements. The validity of this warrant has not been contested.

The following morning, Palentchar and eight other New Jersey law enforcement officers . . . executed the warrant. The search lasted approximately eight hours. . . . [I]n addition to seizing hundreds of documents, [the police officers] barricaded the sole exit from the premises, searched all departing vehicles, recorded the serial numbers on F & S machinery, detained in one room all persons on the premises at the time of the search until they produced identification, threatened to tear apart respondents' homes if the documents were not discovered, and engaged in a number of other unlawful activities. The execution of the warrant gave rise to the federal litigation now before us.

On December 27, . . . [Monaghan, DeSantis and James] instituted this civil rights action under 42 U.S.C. § 1983 in the United States District Court for the District of New Jersey. [They] sought equitable relief, including the return of all documents seized, and, as well, compensatory and punitive damages for the alleged violations of their rights under the Fourth, Fifth, Sixth, and Fourteenth Amendments, and attorney's fees. . . . Prior to filing an answer, [the police officers] moved to dismiss the complaint, arguing that the existence of an ongoing state grand jury investigation required the federal court to abstain from adjudicating disputes arising out of that investigation.

Several months later, on August 6, 1985, the District Court granted [the] motion to dismiss on abstention grounds.

[Subsequently], the state grand jury returned an indictment against . . . Monaghan, DeSantis, and F & S — and against others not parties to the present federal action. None of the seized documents had ever been submitted to the indicting grand jury, and the contested documents were . . . under seal at the time the indictment was returned. The Superior Court of New Jersey, Law Division, Cumberland County, to which the indictment was assigned for trial, took jurisdiction over [the] equitable claims for the return of the seized documents. . . . In light of these developments, [Monaghan, DeSantis and James], through common counsel, [assert] that they do not wish to pursue their claims for equitable relief in federal court. They wish to withdraw these claims from their federal complaint and seek injunctive relief exclusively in the state proceedings initiated by the indictment. [They] also represent that, if the complaint were remanded to the District Court, they would seek a stay of all federal proceedings on the damages claims pending resolution of the state proceedings.

[The police officers] argue that the *Younger* doctrine — which requires a federal court to abstain where a plaintiff's federal claims could be adjudicated in a pending state judicial proceeding — applies to complaints seeking only monetary relief. [They] further argue that it is within the District Court's discretion to dismiss rather than stay a federal complaint for damages and fees where abstention is required. We need not decide the extent to which the *Younger* doctrine applies to a federal action seeking only monetary relief, however, because even if the *Younger* doctrine requires abstention here, the District Court has no discretion to dismiss rather than to stay claims for monetary relief that cannot be redressed in the state proceeding.

In reversing the District Court's dismissal of the claims for damages and attorney's fees, the Court of Appeals applied the Third Circuit rule that requires a District Court to stay rather than dismiss claims that are not cognizable in the parallel state proceeding. The Third Circuit rule is sound. It allows a parallel state proceeding to go forward without interference from its federal sibling, while enforcing the duty of federal courts "to assume jurisdiction where jurisdiction properly exists."[28] This Court repeatedly has stated that the federal courts have a "virtually unflagging obligation" to

---

[28] [n.7] [T]he Court of Appeals recognized that unless it retained jurisdiction during the pendency of the state proceeding, a plaintiff could be barred permanently from asserting his claims in the federal forum by the running of the applicable statute of limitations.

exercise their jurisdiction except in those extraordinary circumstances "where the order to the parties to repair to the State court would clearly serve an important countervailing interest."

We are unpersuaded by [the] suggestion that this case presents such extraordinary circumstances. [The police officers'] speculation that the District Court, if allowed to retain jurisdiction, would "hover" about the state proceeding, ready to lift the stay whenever it concluded that things were proceeding unsatisfactorily, is groundless. [They] seem to assume that the District Court would not hold up its end of the comity bargain — an assumption as inappropriate as the converse assumption that the States cannot be trusted to enforce federal rights with adequate diligence.

Finally, [the police officers] argue that allowing the District Court to dismiss the complaint will prevent the piecemeal litigation of the dispute between the parties. But the involvement of the federal courts cannot be blamed for the fragmentary nature of the proceedings in this litigation. Because the state criminal proceeding can provide only equitable relief, any action for damages would necessarily be separate.

JUSTICE WHITE, with whom JUSTICE O'CONNOR joins, concurring.

My difficulty with the Court's opinion is that, while approving the Court of Appeals' decision to stay and not dismiss the damages claim, it does not adequately explain why the federal courts must or may stay, rather than proceed to adjudicate, the federal constitutional claims for damages.

The Third Circuit rule, which the Court endorses, appears to rest on "prudential considerations" and not on the view that *Younger* requires that a damages action be stayed when there is a parallel state criminal (or "quasi-criminal") proceeding underway. But we have never held that in all cases where there are parallel state and federal proceedings involving a federal constitutional issue, the federal court should hold its hand and allow the state court to proceed first.

To affirm the Court of Appeals' judgment ordering a stay requires a more substantial basis than "prudential consideration," and that basis is not difficult to find: it is that *Younger* requires, not only dismissal of the equitable claim in this case, but also that the damages action not go forward. Several times before this Court has declined to state that *Younger* applies to damages actions. *E.g., Tower v. Glover*, 467 U.S. 914 (1984); *Juidice v. Vail*, 430 U.S. 327 (1977). In the absence of direction from this Court, it now appears that a plurality of the Circuits apply the *Younger* doctrine — in some fashion — to damages claims like [that here].

The reasons for such an approach are obvious. As the *Younger* decision itself recognized, it has long been the rule that the federal courts should not interfere with or pre-empt the progress of state criminal proceedings. A judgment in the federal damages action may decide several questions at issue in the state criminal proceeding. It may determine, for example, that certain evidence was seized contrary to the Fourth Amendment, or that an interrogation was conducted in violation of the Sixth Amendment, or that Fifth Amendment rights were somehow violated. . . . If the claims the Court remands today were disposed of on the merits by the District Court, this decision would presumably be owed res judicata effect in the forthcoming state criminal trial. . . .

In light of the developments in this case and our decisions in *Younger* and *Samuels*, it is clear that the District Court should not dismiss the damages claims, yet must not proceed to judgment on them either. Consequently, I would couple our remand of this case with a holding that, pursuant to *Younger*, the lower courts *may not* adjudicate . . . damages claims until the conclusion of the pending state criminal proceedings.

NOTES

1. Grand Jury Proceedings. The Supreme Court in *Deakins* did not decide whether *Younger* abstention is an appropriate form of deference toward state grand jury proceedings. Language in recent Supreme Court opinions suggests the Justices remain ambivalent about the matter. In *Morales v. TWA, Inc.*, 504 U.S. 374 (1992), for example, the Court described *Younger* in dictum as "impos[ing] heightened requirements for an injunction to restrain an already-pending or an about-to-be-pending state criminal action." In *Ankenbrandt v. Richards*, 504 U.S. 689 (1992), the Court stated that it has never applied the notions of comity so critical to *Younger*'s 'Our Federalism' when no state proceeding was pending." The lower federal courts, too, are of different minds on the matter. *Contrast Texas Association of Business v. Earle*, 388 F.3d 515 (5th Cir. 2004) (holding that *Younger* applies to state grand jury proceedings); *Potomac Electric Power Co. v. Sachs*, 802 F.2d 1527 (4th Cir. 1986) ("the *Younger* doctrine applies to state initiated grand jury proceedings"); *Kaylor v. Fields*, 661 F.2d 1177 (8th Cir. 1981) (same), *with Monaghan v. Deakins*, 798 F.2d 632 (3d Cir. 1986) (holding that *Younger* does not apply to grand jury proceedings). Surprisingly, very little litigation since the Supreme Court's decision in *Deakins* has addressed the question.

2. Parallel State Litigation. Parallel proceedings in state and federal court are not improper and are not uncommon. *See Exxon Mobil Corp. v. Saudi Basic Industries Corp.*, 544 U.S. 280 (2005) (observing that "[t]here is nothing necessarily inappropriate" with multiple actions proceeding in state and federal court) (excerpted in Note 2 following *International College of Surgeons* in Chapter 8.A.[4], *infra*). Generally, federal courts will not defer to state court proceedings, even when the state court proceedings involve the same transaction and the same parties. Similarly, state courts are not expected to defer to federal proceedings. In the absence of an abstention doctrine (like that found in *Younger*), the result is a race to judgment with the first decision often having preclusive effect. *See* Chapter 8.A., *infra*.

3. Money Damages. Federal abstention, like that found in *Pullman* and *Younger*, constitutes an exception rather than the rule. Ordinarily, the various abstention doctrines have been confined to federal actions sounding in equity. Hence, it would seem that *Younger* abstention has no application in the context of § 1983 claims seeking money damages. Still, as made clear by Justice Blackmun's and Justice White's remarks in *Deakins*, most of the Courts of Appeals have "in some fashion" applied a *Younger*-like doctrine to abate damage actions under § 1983 when state criminal proceedings have been commenced. The Supreme Court in *Deakins* ultimately avoided the issue, ruling only that *if Younger* applies, federal district courts still only have the authority to stay, rather than dismiss the damage claims. *See also Quackenbush v. Allstate Insurance Co.*, 517 U.S. 706 (1996) ("We have held that federal courts may stay actions for damages based on abstention principles, we have not held that those principles support the outright dismissal or remand of damages actions."). *See generally* James C. Rehnquist, *Taking Comity Seriously: How to Neutralize the Abstention Doctrine*, 46 STAN. L. REV. 1049, 1108 (1994) ("The Supreme Court . . . has twice refused to decide whether *Younger* is limited to cases seeking injunctive relief, and the question remains open.").

While the Circuits remain split on the precise question of whether *Younger* technically applies to § 1983 claims for monetary relief, *contrast Amerson v. Iowa*, 94 F.3d 510 (8th Cir. 1996) (holding that *Younger* applies), *with Rivers v. McLeod*, 252 F.3d 99 (2d Cir. 2001) ("application of the *Younger* doctrine is inappropriate where the litigant seeks money damages for an alleged violation of § 1983"), they appear today to agree that § 1983 claims for money damages should be stayed in the face of ongoing state criminal proceedings that would otherwise justify *Younger* abstention. *See Rossi v. Gemma*, 489 F.3d 26 (1st Cir. 2007) ("we think that abstention is appropriate on the § 1983 damages claims, in addition to the abstention on the § 1983 equitable claims"); *AmerisourceBergen Corp. v. Roden*, 495 F.3d 1143 (9th Cir. 2007) ("although *Younger* principles apply to actions at law as well as for injunctive or declaratory relief . . . , federal courts should not dismiss actions where damages are at issue; rather, damages actions should be *stayed* until the state proceedings are completed"). Under this approach, assuming that the state proceedings have no preclusive effect, § 1983 damage claims can resume and proceed to judgment once the state-court proceedings are complete.

4. Statutes of Limitations. Unlike claims to prospective relief, § 1983 claims for money damages encounter timing problems under states' statutes of limitations. *See* Chapter 5.A., *supra*. The Court in *Deakins* observed in footnote 7 that "unless [the District Court] retained jurisdiction during the pendency of the state proceeding, a plaintiff could be barred permanently from asserting his claims in the federal forum by the running of the applicable statute of limitations." It appeared following the Supreme Court's decision in *Heck v. Humphrey*, 512 U.S. 477 (1994) (excerpted in Chapter 8.B.[2], *infra*), which held that § 1983 claims for money damages that necessarily conflicted with a state-court criminal conviction could not arise until the conviction was somehow set aside, that the timing problem alluded to in *Deakins* would in practice prove non-existent. *See* RICHARD H. FALLON, DANIEL J. MELTZER & DAVID L. SHAPIRO, HART & WECHSLER'S FEDERAL COURTS AND THE FEDERAL SYSTEM 1305 n.9 (4th ed. 1996) (suggesting that *Heck* "disposed of most if not all of the general problems presented by § 1983 damages actions that necessarily require testing the validity of a state criminal conviction"). After all, were the criminal defendants in *Deakins* convicted, their § 1983 claims challenging the search of their businesses would likely never arise within the meaning of *Heck*.

In the years following *Heck*, however, the lower federal courts discovered that state statutes of limitations still posed technical difficulties in the context of parallel state and federal proceedings. It was not always obvious, for example, that a § 1983 plaintiff's ultimate success in federal court would necessarily contradict a yet-to-be-resolved state court criminal proceeding, at least not within the meaning of *Heck*. Thus, *Deakins*-type stays have emerged as a preferred method of preserving § 1983 claims to money damages under state statutes of limitations. The Supreme Court in *Wallace v. Kato*, 549 U.S. 384 (2007) (excerpted in Chapter 8.B.[3], *infra*), endorsed this practice: "If a plaintiff files a false arrest claim before he has been convicted (or files any other claim related to rulings that will likely be made in a pending or anticipated criminal trial), it is within the power of the district court, and in accord with common practice, to stay the civil action until the criminal case or the likelihood of a criminal case is ended."

Chapter 8
PRIOR AND PARALLEL STATE PROCEEDINGS

The abstention doctrines discussed in Chapter 7, *supra*, demonstrate that litigants can sometimes be forced to use state remedial mechanisms before turning to federal court and § 1983. Plaintiffs, moreover, may voluntarily choose to pursue state-created remedies before proceeding to federal court. What effect do state court judgments have on subsequent or pending § 1983 proceedings in federal court? Are preclusion principles (i.e., collateral estoppel and res judicata) relevant? Can a § 1983 plaintiff "appeal" an adverse state-agency decision to federal court? Does the availability of an alternative federal remedy (i.e., federal habeas corpus) preclude (or delay) proceeding under § 1983? These questions are explored in the following sections.

A. PRECLUSION

MIGRA v. WARREN CITY SCHOOL DISTRICT
Supreme Court of the United States
465 U.S. 75 (1984)

JUSTICE BLACKMUN delivered the opinion of the Court.

This case raises issues concerning the claim preclusive effect[1] of a state-court judgment in the context of a subsequent suit, under 42 U.S.C. §§ 1983 and 1985[2] in federal court.

Dr. Ethel D. Migra, was employed by the Warren [Ohio] City School District Board of Education from August 1976 to June 1979. She served as supervisor of elementary education. Her employment was on an annual basis under written contracts for successive school years.

On April 17, 1979, at a regularly scheduled meeting, the Board, with all five of its members present, unanimously adopted a resolution renewing Dr. Migra's employment as supervisor for the 1979–1980 school year. Being advised of this, she accepted the renewed appointment by letter dated April 18 delivered to a member of the Board on April 23. Early the following morning her letter was passed on to the Superintendent of Schools and to the Board's President.

The Board, however, held a special meeting, called by its President, on the morning of April 24. Although there appear to have been some irregularities about the call, four

---

[1] [n.1] The preclusive effects of former adjudication are discussed in varying and, at times, seemingly conflicting terminology, attributable to the evolution of preclusion concepts over the years. These effects are referred to collectively by most commentators as the doctrine of "res judicata." *See* RESTATEMENT (SECOND) OF JUDGMENTS, Introductory Note before ch. 3 (1982); 18 C. WRIGHT, A. MILLER, & E. COOPER, FEDERAL PRACTICE AND PROCEDURE § 4402 (1981). Res judicata is often analyzed further to consist of two preclusion concepts: "issue preclusion" and "claim preclusion." Issue preclusion refers to the effect of a judgment in foreclosing relitigation of a matter that has been litigated and decided. This effect also is referred to as direct or collateral estoppel. Claim preclusion refers to the effect of a judgment in foreclosing litigation of a matter that never has been litigated, because of a determination that it should have been advanced in an earlier suit. Claim preclusion therefore encompasses the law of merger and bar. This Court on more than one occasion has used the term "res judicata" in a narrow sense, so as to exclude issue preclusion or collateral estoppel. *See e.g., Allen v. McCurry*, 449 U.S. 90 (1980); *Brown v. Felsen*, 442 U.S. 127 (1979). When using that formulation, "res judicata" becomes virtually synonymous with "claim preclusion." In order to avoid confusion resulting from the two uses of "res judicata," this opinion utilizes the term "claim preclusion" to refer to the preclusive effect of a judgment in foreclosing relitigation of matters that should have been raised in an earlier suit.

[2] [Editor's note: Section 1985(3) creates a civil cause of action based on conspiracies that interfere with civil rights. *See* Note 3 following *Monroe* in Chapter 1.A., *supra*.]

of the five members of the Board were present. The President first read Dr. Migra's acceptance letter. Then, after disposing of other business, a motion was made and adopted, by a vote of three to one, not to renew [her] employment for the 1979–1980 school year. Dr. Migra was given written notice of this nonrenewal and never received a written contract of employment for that year. The Board's absent member, James Culver, learned of the special meeting and of Dr. Migra's termination after he returned from Florida on April 25 where he had attended a National School Boards Convention.

[Dr. Migra] brought suit in the Court of Common Pleas of Trumbull County, Ohio, against the Board and its three members who had voted not to renew her employment. The complaint, although in five counts, presented what the parties now accept as essentially two causes of action, namely, breach of contract by the Board, and wrongful interference by the individual members with [Dr. Migra's] contract of employment. The state court, after a bench trial, "reserved and continued" the "issue of conspiracy" and did not reach the question of the individual members' liability. It ruled that under Ohio law [Migra] had accepted the employment proffered for 1979–1980, that this created a binding contract between her and the Board, and that the Board's subsequent action purporting not to renew the employment relationship had no legal effect. The court awarded Dr. Migra reinstatement to her position and compensatory damages. Thereafter, [Dr. Migra] moved the state trial court to dismiss without prejudice "the issue of the conspiracy and individual board member liability." That motion was granted. The Ohio Court of Appeals, Eleventh District, in an unreported opinion, affirmed the judgment of the Court of Common Pleas. Review was denied by the Supreme Court of Ohio.[3]

In July 1980, Dr. Migra filed the present action in the United States District Court for the Northern District of Ohio against the Board, its then individual members, and the Superintendent of Schools. Her complaint alleged that [she] had become the director of a commission appointed by the Board to fashion a voluntary plan for the desegregation of the District's elementary schools; that she had prepared a social studies curriculum; that the individual defendants objected to and opposed the curriculum and resisted the desegregation plan; that hostility and ill will toward [Dr. Migra] developed; and that, as a consequence, the individual defendants determined not to renew [Dr. Migra's] contract of employment. Many of the alleged facts had been proved in the earlier state-court litigation. Dr. Migra claimed that the Board's actions were intended to punish her for the exercise of her First Amendment rights. . . . [D]efendants moved for summary judgment on the basis of res judicata.

The Constitution's Full Faith and Credit Clause[4] is implemented by the Federal Full Faith and Credit Statute, 28 U.S.C. § 1738. That statute reads in pertinent part:

> Such Acts, records and judicial proceedings or copies thereof, so authenticated, shall have the same full faith and credit in every court within the United States and its Territories and Possessions as they have by law or usage in the courts of such State, Territory or Possession from which they are taken.

It is now settled that a federal court must give to a state-court judgment the same preclusive effect as would be given that judgment under the law of the State in which the judgment was rendered. In *Allen v. McCurry*, 449 U.S. 90 (1980), this Court said:

---

[3] [n.2] It is apparent, from the foregoing recital of facts and of events that took place in the state court litigation, that the cause of action for reinstatement and for damages was brought to a conclusion in the Ohio courts, but that the cause of action sounding in tort, that is, for wrongful interference with [Dr. Migra's] contract of employment, was not. Instead, that cause of action was "reserved and continued," evidently by the state trial court sua sponte, and was eventually dismissed without prejudice upon [Migra's] motion. This dismissal was subsequent to the entry of judgment on the breach of contract cause of action.

[4] [n.3] "Full Faith and Credit shall be given in each State to the public Acts, Records, and judicial Proceedings of every other State. And the Congress may by general Laws prescribe the Manner in which such Acts, Records and Proceedings shall be proved, and the Effect thereof." U.S. Const., Art. IV, § 1.

Indeed, though the federal courts may look to the common law or to the policies supporting res judicata and collateral estoppel in assessing the preclusive effect of decisions of other federal courts, Congress has specifically required all federal courts to give preclusive effect to state-court judgments whenever the courts of the State from which the judgments emerged would do so. . . .

In *Allen*, the Court considered whether 42 U.S.C. § 1983 modified the operation of § 1738 so that a state-court judgment was to receive less than normal preclusive effect in a suit brought in federal court under § 1983. In that case, the [§ 1983 plaintiff] had been convicted in a state-court criminal proceeding. In that proceeding, the [§ 1983 plaintiff] sought to suppress certain evidence against him on the ground that it had been obtained in violation of the Fourth Amendment. The trial court denied the motion to suppress. [He] then brought a § 1983 suit in federal court against the officers who had seized the evidence. The District Court held the suit barred by collateral estoppel (issue preclusion) because the issue of a Fourth Amendment violation had been resolved against [him] by the denial of his suppression motion in the criminal trial. The Court of Appeals reversed. That court concluded that, because a § 1983 suit was [his] only route to a federal forum for his constitutional claim,[5] and because one of § 1983's underlying purposes was to provide a federal cause of action in situations where state courts were not adequately protecting individual rights, the [§ 1983 plaintiff] should be allowed to proceed to trial in federal court unencumbered by collateral estoppel. This Court, however, reversed the Court of Appeals, explaining:

> [N]othing in the language of § 1983 remotely expresses any congressional intent to contravene the common-law rules of preclusion or to repeal the express statutory requirements of the predecessor of 28 U.S.C. § 1738. . . . Section 1983 creates a new federal cause of action. It says nothing about the preclusive effect of state-court judgments. Moreover, the legislative history of § 1983 does not in any clear way suggest that Congress intended to repeal or restrict the traditional doctrines of preclusion. . . . [T]he legislative history as a whole . . . lends only the most equivocal support to any argument that, in cases where the state courts have recognized the constitutional claims asserted and provided fair procedures for determining them, Congress intended to override § 1738 or the common-law rules of collateral estoppel and res judicata. Since repeals by implication are disfavored . . . much clearer support than this would be required to hold that § 1738 and the traditional rules of preclusion are not applicable to § 1983 suits.

Allen therefore made clear that issues actually litigated in a state-court proceeding are entitled to the same preclusive effect in a subsequent federal § 1983 suit as they enjoy in the courts of the State where the judgment was rendered.

The Court in *Allen* left open the possibility, however, that the preclusive effect of a state-court judgment might be different as to a federal issue that a § 1983 litigant could have raised but did not raise in the earlier state-court proceeding. That is the central issue to be resolved in the present case. [Dr. Migra] did not litigate her § 1983 claim in state court, and she asserts that the state-court judgment should not preclude her suit in federal court simply because her federal claim could have been litigated in the state-court proceeding. Thus, [Dr. Migra] urges this Court to interpret the interplay of § 1738 and § 1983 in such a way as to accord state-court judgments preclusive effect in § 1983 suits only as to issues actually litigated in state court.

It is difficult to see how the policy concerns underlying § 1983 would justify a distinction between the issue preclusive and claim preclusive effects of state-court

---

[5] [n.4] The [§ 1983 plaintiff] had not asserted that the state courts had denied him a "full and fair opportunity" to litigate his search and seizure claim; he therefore was barred by *Stone v. Powell*, 428 U.S. 465 (1976), from seeking a writ of habeas corpus in federal district court.

judgments. The argument that state-court judgments should have less preclusive effect in § 1983 suits than in other federal suits is based on Congress' expressed concern over the adequacy of state courts as protectors of federal rights. *Allen* recognized that the enactment of § 1983 was motivated partially out of such concern, but *Allen* nevertheless held that § 1983 did not open the way to relitigation of an issue that had been determined in a state criminal proceeding. Any distrust of state courts that would justify a limitation on the preclusive effect of state judgments in § 1983 suits would presumably apply equally to issues that actually were decided in a state court as well as to those that could have been. If § 1983 created an exception to the general preclusive effect accorded to state-court judgments, such an exception would seem to require similar treatment of both issue preclusion and claim preclusion. Having rejected in *Allen* the view that state-court judgments have no issue preclusive effect in § 1983 suits, we must reject the view that § 1983 prevents the judgment in [Dr. Migra's] state-court proceeding from creating a claim preclusion bar in this case.

[Dr. Migra] suggests that to give state-court judgments full issue preclusive effect but not claim preclusive effect would enable litigants to bring their state claims in state court and their federal claims in federal court, thereby taking advantage of the relative expertise of both forums. Although such a division may seem attractive from a plaintiff's perspective, it is not the system established by § 1738. That statute embodies the view that it is more important to give full faith and credit to state-court judgments than to ensure separate forums for federal and state claims. This reflects a variety of concerns, including notions of comity, the need to prevent vexatious litigation, and a desire to conserve judicial resources.

In the present litigation, [Dr. Migra] does not claim that the state court would not have adjudicated her federal claims had she presented them in her original suit in state court. Alternatively, [Dr. Migra] could have obtained a federal forum for her federal claim by litigating it first in a federal court.[6] Section 1983, however, does not override state preclusion law and guarantee [Dr. Migra] a right to proceed to judgment in state court on her state claims and then turn to federal court for adjudication of her federal claims. We hold, therefore, that [Dr. Migra's] state-court judgment in this litigation has the same claim preclusive effect in federal court that the judgment would have in the Ohio state courts.

JUSTICE WHITE, with whom THE CHIEF JUSTICE and JUSTICE POWELL join, concurring.

In *Union & Planters' Bank v. Memphis*, 189 U.S. 71 (1903), this Court held that a federal court "can accord [a state judgment] no greater efficacy" than would the judgment-rendering state. . . . The Court has also indicated that the states are bound by a similar rule under the full faith and credit clause. *Public Works v. Columbia College*, 17 Wall. 521 (1873). The Court is thus justified in this case to rule that preclusion in this case must be determined under state law, even if there would be preclusion under federal standards.

This construction of § 1738 and its predecessors is unfortunate. In terms of the purpose of that section, which is to require federal courts to give effect to state-court judgments, there is no reason to hold that a federal court may not give preclusive effect to a state judgment simply because the judgment would not bar relitigation in the state courts. If the federal courts have developed rules of res judicata and collateral estoppel that prevent relitigation in circumstances that would not be preclusive in state courts, the federal courts should be free to apply them, the parties then being free to relitigate

---

[6] [n.7] The author of this opinion was in dissent in *Allen*. The rationale of that dissent, however, was based largely on the fact that the § 1983 plaintiff in that case first litigated his constitutional claim in state court in the posture of his being a defendant in a criminal proceeding. In this case, [Dr. Migra] was in an offensive posture in her state court proceeding, and could have proceeded first in federal court had she wanted to litigate her federal claim in a federal forum.

in the state courts. The contrary construction of § 1738 is nevertheless one of long standing, and Congress has not seen fit to disturb it, however justified such an action might have been.

NOTES

1. Claim Preclusion. As Justice Blackmun points out in footnote 1, res judicata (claim preclusion) and collateral estoppel (issue preclusion) have experienced a long and tortured history in the American legal system. Briefly, claim preclusion bars claims that were *or should have* been raised in prior litigation between the parties, or those in privity with them. Generally speaking, in order for a judgment to have res judicata effect, four requirements must be satisfied: "First, the prior judgment must be valid in that it was rendered by a court of competent jurisdiction and in accordance with the requirements of due process. Second the judgment must be final and on the merits. Third, there must be identity of both parties or their privies. Fourth, the later proceeding must involve the same cause of action as involved in the earlier proceeding." *In re Atlanta Retail*, 456 F.3d 1277 (11th Cir. 2006). Res judicata is generally an affirmative defense that must be pleaded and proved by the defendant. *See* Fed. R. Civ. P. 8(c); *Exxon Mobil Corp. v. Saudi Basic Industries Corp.*, 544 U.S. 280, 293 (2005) (noting that res judicata is an affirmative defense); *Harris v. Ford Motor Co.*, 852 N.E.2d 750 (Ohio App. 2006) (observing that claim preclusion is an affirmative defense under Ohio law).

A court lacking subject matter jurisdiction over a controversy cannot render a preclusive judgment. Generally speaking, however, a court's rendering judgment in a contested action will conclusively establish that it was competent to take jurisdiction. *See* 1 Restatement (Second) of Judgments § 12 (1982). The rendering court's jurisdiction is thus ordinarily not subject to attack in subsequent collateral proceedings. *See, e.g., Marshall v. Marshall*, 547 U.S. 293 (2006) (stating that a rendering court's conclusion about its jurisdiction is generally entitled to preclusive effect); *Kontrick v. Ryan*, 540 U.S. 443 (2004) ("Even subject-matter jurisdiction, however, may not be attacked collaterally."). *But see* 1 Restatement (Second) of Judgments § 12 (1982) (stating that a court "plainly lacking" jurisdiction or incapable of rendering an informed decision about its jurisdiction can not bind subsequent courts that inquire of its competence).

Finality for purposes of res judicata generally refers to the final conclusion of the trial court. *See* 1 Restatement (Second) of Judgments § 13 (1982). Thus, although there is substantial disagreement over the matter, the "better view" is that a trial court's judgment is entitled to preclusive effect even though the appellate process is not yet complete. *Id.* comment f. *See Clay v. United States*, 537 U.S. 522 (2003) ("Typically, a federal judgment becomes final for appellate review and claim preclusion purposes when the district court disassociates itself from the case, leaving nothing to be done at the court of first instance save execution of the judgment."). Should the preclusive judgment be set aside on appeal, then its continuing preclusive effect can be addressed by those courts that recognized the judgment. *See* 1 Restatement (Second) of Judgments § 16 (1982). Because they lack finality, orders granting or denying preliminary injunctive relief ordinarily will not be given preclusive effect. *See, e.g., Overstreet v. Lexington-Fayette Urban County Government*, 305 F.3d 566 (6th Cir. 2002) (observing that a preliminary injunction pending appeal "has no *res judicata* effect because it does not constitute a final adjudication of the merits of an issue").[7]

---

[7] A preliminary proceeding might prove full and fair enough on some matters to justify issue preclusion. But then the question is whether the preliminary adjudication provided sufficient procedural safeguards to justify confidence in the outcome. *See* 1 Restatement (Second) of Judgments § 13 (1982) ("for purposes of issue preclusion (as distinguished from merger and bar), 'final judgment' includes any prior adjudication of an issue in another action that is determined to be sufficiently firm to be accorded conclusive effect").

Denial of permanent declaratory or injunctive relief, in contrast, can give rise to claim preclusion, but only if the denial constitutes a decision on the merits. *See, e.g., Remus Joint Venture v. McAnally*, 116 F.3d 180 (6th Cir. 1997) ("when a district court's ruling rests on alternative grounds, at least one of which is based on the inability of the court to reach the merits, the judgment should not act as a bar in a future action"). Denials and dismissals based on abstention, equitable discretion, lack of subject matter jurisdiction or mootness are generally not final decisions on the merits. *See, e.g., Florida Public Interest Research Group Citizen Lobby, Inc. v. EPA*, 386 F.3d 1070 (11th Cir. 2004) (holding that "mootness is jurisdictional" and that "[a]ny decision on the merits of a moot case would be an impermissible advisory opinion"); *Pujol v. Shearson/American Express, Inc.*, 829 F.2d 1201 (1st Cir. 1987) (action "was dismissed as moot and accordingly has no *res judicata* effect"); *District of Columbia Hosp. Ass'n v. District of Columbia*, 73 F. Supp. 2d 8 (D.D.C. 1999) (stating that where a previous suit was dismissed as moot, a subsequent suit is not barred by res judicata since the merits of the claims were never tested); *see also* 1 RESTATEMENT (SECOND) OF JUDGMENTS § 20(1)(A) ("A personal judgment for the defendant, although valid and final, does not bar another action by the plaintiff on the same claim . . . [w]hen the judgment is one of dismissal for lack of jurisdiction").

"Final decision in an action for permanent injunctive or other equitable relief commands full preclusion effects, unless some rare circumstance invokes the special rules that once were required by the separation of law and equity." CHARLES A. WRIGHT, ET AL., FEDERAL PRACTICE & PROCEDURE § 4445 (2007). Similarly, "[a] valid and final judgment in an action brought to declare rights or other legal relations of the parties is conclusive in a subsequent action between them as to the matters declared." 1 RESTATMENT (SECOND) JUDGMENTS § 33.[8]

"A person is in privity with another person if he has 'a close relationship, bordering on near identity.'" *United States v. Gurley*, 43 F.3d 1188 (8th Cir. 1994). Examples include close contractual relationships, *see, e.g., E.W. Audet & Sons v. Firemen's Fund Ins.*, 635 A.2d 1181 (R.I. 1994) (relationship between construction contractor and subcontractor); *Bates v. Township of Van Buren*, 459 F.3d 731 (6th Cir. 2006) (finding that a topless dancer and a club owner were in privity under Michigan law for purposes of a subsequent § 1983 challenge to an ordinance banning nude dance), derivative property rights, *see, e.g., Doe v. Mitchell*, 244 N.W.2d 827, 861 (Mich. 1976) (observing that privity is commonly satisfied by succession to another's property interest), and parens patriae claims brought by states on behalf of their citizens. *See, e.g., Lance v. Dennis*, 546 U.S. 459 (2006) (observing that the lower court found privity under *Washington v. Washington State Commercial PassengerFishing Vessel Ass'n*, 443 U.S. 658 (1979), and *Tacoma v. Taxpayers of Tacoma*, 357 U.S. 320 (1958), because "when a state government litigates a matter of public concern, that state's citizens will be deemed to be in privity with the government for preclusion purposes").

---

[8] However, because decisions issuing prospective declaratory or injunctive relief are not "as final" as judgments rendering retrospective relief, *see, e.g.*, Chapter 6.C.[2], *supra* (discussing Congress's ability to reopen judgments issuing injunctions), they can be modified or set aside more readily than damage judgments. In *Agostini v. Felton*, 521 U.S. 203 (1997), for example, government officials were able to use Rule 60(b) of the Federal Rules of Civil Procedure to reopen (and ultimately overturn) a final judgment enjoining them from sending public school teachers into parochial schools to teach remedial courses twelve years after the initial decision was handed down by the Supreme Court. The Court stated that "it is appropriate to grant a Rule 60(b)(5) motion when the party seeking relief from an injunction or consent decree can show a 'significant change either in factual conditions or in law.'" *See also Miller v. French*, 530 U.S. 327 (2000) ("Prospective relief under a continuing, executory decree remains subject to alteration due to changes in the underlying law."). Generally, this kind of relief from judgment must be initiated in the court that rendered the judgment. *See* 5 RESTATMENT (SECOND) JUDGMENTS § 78. *See generally* James P. George, *Parallel Litigation*, 51 BAYLOR L. REV. 769 (1999) (discussing effects of state court injunctions on parallel federal proceedings).

In regard to the fourth requirement, i.e., that the second case must involve the same cause of action as the first, most modern courts speak in terms of "transactions" rather than "claims" or "causes of actions." *See* 1 RESTATEMENT (SECOND) OF JUDGMENTS § 24(1) ("[T]he claim extinguished includes all rights . . . with respect to all or any part of the transaction, or series of connected transactions, out of which the action arose."). Consequently, distinct legal claims that arise from a single transaction are generally barred regardless of whether they are actually litigated. If a claim should have been raised in the first proceeding under the state's procedural rules, it is likely subject to preclusion in subsequent proceedings. Whether a claim should have been raised in a prior state court proceeding is a question of the rendering state's law.

2. Issue Preclusion. Collateral estoppel (issue preclusion) bars parties from relitigating issues (factual and legal) that were actually resolved in a prior judicial proceeding. *See* 1 RESTATEMENT (SECOND) OF JUDGMENTS § 27 (stating that an issue of fact or law, actually litigated and resolved by a valid final judgment, is binding on the parties in a subsequent action). Formal finality is not necessary; rather, it is enough that the decision "be sufficiently firm to be accorded conclusive effect." 1 RESTATEMENT (SECOND) OF JUDGMENTS § 13. This bar is effective in litigation involving third persons as well as in renewed litigation between the parties. Thus, were A to lose an issue, call it x, to B, A would not only be precluded from relitigating x against B, but would also be precluded from challenging x in litigation against a third person, C.

At one time, courts often required "mutuality of estoppel" before allowing C, who was not privy to the original proceeding, to make use of issue preclusion against a losing party, like A. Thus, C could only use A's defeat against it if A — had it won — were allowed to use its success against C. Because C was not privy to the original proceeding, however, A would generally not be allowed to use any of its successes against C. After all, collateral estoppel assumes that the party to be estopped had a previous opportunity to contest the issue. Faced with a lack of mutuality, some courts will not allow a third party, like C, to invoke issue preclusion against someone like A, who had an opportunity to contest the issue but lost in a prior proceeding. *See, e.g., Goodson v. McDonough Power Equipment, Inc.*, 443 N.E.2d 978 (Ohio 1983). However, most states have rejected the mutuality of estoppel requirement, as have federal courts for purposes of the preclusive effect of federal judgments. *See Parklane Hosiery Co. v. Shore*, 439 U.S. 322 (1979). Thus, the majority rule today is that even though A cannot assert its victory against C, who was not party to or privy to the prior proceeding, C can take advantage of A's loss in a subsequent suit.

3. Full Faith and Credit. Article IV's Full Faith and Credit Clause provides that "Full Faith and Credit shall be given in each State to the public Acts, Records, and Judicial Proceedings of every other State." *See* U.S. CONST., ART. IV, § 1. The Federal Full Faith and Credit Statute, 28 U.S.C. § 1738, states that the "Acts, records and judicial proceedings [of a State] shall have the same full faith and credit in every court within the United States and its Territories and Possessions as they have by law or usage in the courts of such State, Territory or Possession from which they are taken." Together, these provisions mean that both federal and state courts must provide prior state court judgments the same preclusive effect they would receive in the rendering state. The rendering state's law provides the rule of decision. By way of contrast, federal law determines the preclusive effect due federal court judgments grounded in federal law (including, of course, claims made under § 1983). *See Deposit Bank v. Frankfort*, 191 U.S. 499 (1903); 5 RESTATEMENT (SECOND) OF JUDGMENTS § 87. When a federal court exercises jurisdiction over a state-law claim, the preclusive effect of a judgment on that claim is left to the law of the state that provided the substantive rule of decision. *See, e.g., Dupasseur v. Rochereau*, 88 U.S. (21 Wall.) 130 (1874).

4. Full and Fair Opportunity. Both Article IV and § 1738 have been interpreted to require that parties be afforded a "full and fair opportunity to litigate" for preclusion principles to apply. This requires that state proceedings at least satisfy the minimum procedural requirements of the Fourteenth Amendment's Due Process Clause. *Kremer v. Chemical Construction Corp.*, 456 U.S. 461 (1982). Perhaps most importantly, this means that one not a party to a judgment ordinarily cannot be subjected to the bars of either res judicata or collateral estoppel in subsequent proceedings. *See, e.g., Martin v. Wilks*, 490 U.S. 755 (1989). To use a common example in the § 1983 context, police officers cannot ordinarily be precluded from relitigating search and seizure issues that have been resolved against a prosecutor in prior criminal proceedings filed against a suspect the police officers arrested. Police, after all, are not generally parties to these criminal proceedings. A state criminal court's conclusion that a search was unreasonable will thus not ordinarily preclude the officers from litigating the reasonableness and lawfulness of their search in subsequent proceedings under § 1983. *See, e.g., Jenkins v. City of New York*, 478 F.3d 76 (2d Cir. 2007) (holding that a ruling in a New York state criminal proceeding that the defendant's arrest was not supported by probable cause did not collaterally estop the police officers from relitigating the question when the criminal defendant sued them under § 1983); *Bilida v. McCleod*, 211 F.3d 166 (1st Cir. 2000) ("[T]he interests and incentives of the individual police [officers] . . . are not identical to those of the state, and the officers normally have little control over the conduct of a criminal proceeding.").

5. *Allen v. McCurry*. In *Allen v. McCurry*, 449 U.S. 90 (1980), the Court held that a state's preclusion principles apply to actions brought under 42 U.S.C. § 1983. *Allen* involved a criminal defendant (McCurry) who lost in state criminal court and then brought a § 1983 suit in federal court challenging the constitutionality of evidence seized by police. Because McCurry had unsuccessfully raised his Fourth Amendment claims in the state criminal proceedings, the majority in *Allen* had little trouble applying the state's preclusion principle in the subsequent federal proceeding.[9] Left open by the Court in *Allen* was the question presented in *Migra*: Whether general rules of res judicata (claim preclusion) bar civil rights victims from subsequently bringing § 1983 claims in federal court that were not raised in prior state court proceedings. The Court in *Migra* found that nothing in § 1983 prevents a federal court from giving preclusive effect to a prior state court judgment that could have addressed the federal claims. State courts of general jurisdiction, after all, must entertain § 1983 claims. *See Howlett v. Rose*, 496 U.S. 356 (1990) (discussed in Note 3 following *Felder v. Casey* in Chapter 5.B., *supra*). The question is simply whether state preclusion rules would bar further litigation in the state's courts. If so, federal courts must respect that bar.

6. The Peculiar Problem of *Pullman* Abstention. Litigants who are forced into state court by *Railroad Commission of Texas v. Pullman*, 312 U.S. 496 (1941) (excerpted in Chapter 7.A., *supra*), face potential preclusion problems upon their return to federal court. What if the state court resolves both the state and federal claims? Should a state court's resolution of federal claims bind the parties to the federal proceeding where abstention was ordered? The Supreme Court, per Justice Brennan, answered these two questions in *England v. Louisiana State Board of Medical Examiners*, 375 U.S. 411 (1964), a case involving a Fourteenth Amendment challenge to limits placed on chiropractors:

---

[9] Note that preclusion principles do not ordinarily prevent a convicted criminal from arguing the same defenses that were rejected in subsequent criminal proceedings involving different transactions, and do not prohibit a convicted criminal from suing to prevent future applications of the very criminal statute under which he was convicted. *See, e.g., Stanton v. District of Columbia Court of Appeals*, 127 F.3d 72 (D.C. Cir. 1997). Compare *Maynard v. Wooley*, 406 F.Supp. 1381 (D.N.H.1976), *aff'd*, 430 U.S. 705 (1977) (discussed in Note 4 following *Younger* in Chapter 7.B., *supra*) (recognizing that the *Younger* abstention doctrine does not preclude a subsequent prospective action). Thus, criminal defendants are free to renew their previously rejected constitutional arguments in subsequent criminal proceedings and can raise the same constitutional arguments in § 1983 suits for prospective relief. *See also Interoceanica Corp. v. Sound Pilots, Inc.*, 107 F.3d 86 (2d Cir. 1997) (holding that claim preclusion does not bar suit for declaration that New York statute was unconstitutional even though the plaintiff could have raised the issue as a defense in a prior criminal proceeding).

There are fundamental objections to any conclusion that a litigant who has properly invoked the jurisdiction of a Federal District Court to consider federal constitutional claims can be compelled, without his consent and through no fault of his own, to accept instead a state court's determination of those claims. Such a result would be at war with the unqualified terms in which Congress, pursuant to constitutional authorization, has conferred specific categories of jurisdiction upon the federal courts. . . . The right of a party plaintiff to choose a Federal court where there is a choice cannot be properly denied. Nor does anything in the abstention doctrine require or support such a result. Abstention is a judge-fashioned vehicle for according appropriate deference to the respective competence of the state and federal court systems. Its recognition of the role of state courts as the final expositors of state law implies no disregard for the primacy of the federal judiciary in deciding questions of federal law. Accordingly, we have on several occasions explicitly recognized that abstention does not, of course, involve the abdication of federal jurisdiction, but only the postponement of its exercise.

It is true that, after a post-abstention determination and rejection of his federal claims by the state courts, a litigant could seek direct review in this Court. But such review, even when available by appeal rather than only by discretionary writ of certiorari, is an inadequate substitute for the initial District Court determination . . . to which the litigant is entitled in the federal courts. This is true as to issues of law; it is especially true as to issues of fact. Limiting the litigant to review here would deny him the benefit of a federal trial court's role in constructing a record and making fact findings. How the facts are found will often dictate the decision of federal claims. . . . Thus in cases where, but for the application of the abstention doctrine, the primary fact determination would have been by the District Court, a litigant may not be unwillingly deprived of that determination. The possibility of appellate review by this Court of a state court determination may not be substituted, against a party's wishes, for his right to litigate his federal claims fully in the federal courts.

But we see no reason why a party, after unreservedly litigating his federal claims in the state courts although not required to do so, should be allowed to ignore the adverse state decision and start all over again in the District Court. Such a rule would not only countenance an unnecessary increase in the length and cost of the litigation; it would also be a potential source of friction between the state and federal judiciaries. . . . We now explicitly hold that if a party freely and without reservation submits his federal claims for decision by the state courts, litigates them there, and has them decided there, then — whether or not he seeks direct review of the state decision in this Court — he has elected to forgo his right to return to the District Court.

This rule requires clarification of our decision in *Government & Civic Employees Organizing Committee, C.I.O. v. Windsor*, 353 U.S. 364 [1957]. . . . The plaintiffs in *Windsor* had submitted to the state courts only the question whether the state statute they challenged applied to them, and had not "advanced" or "presented" to those courts their contentions against the statute's constitutionality. We held that "the bare adjudication by the Alabama Supreme Court that the (appellant) union is subject to this Act does not suffice, since that court was not asked to interpret the statute in light of the constitutional objections presented to the District Court. If appellants' freedom-of-expression and equal-protection arguments had been presented to the state court, it might have construed the statute in a different manner." . . . The District Court [in the present case] thought that under *Windsor* a party is required to litigate his federal question in the state courts and "dare not restrict his state court case to local law issues." Others have read *Windsor* the same way. It should not be so read. The case does not mean that a party must litigate his federal claims in the state courts, but only that he must inform those courts what his federal claims are, so that the state statute may be construed "in light of" those claims. Thus mere compliance with *Windsor* will not support a conclusion, much less create a presumption, that a litigant has freely and without reservation litigated his federal claims in the state courts and so elected not to return to the District Court.

We recognize that in the heat of litigation a party may find it difficult to avoid doing more than is required by *Windsor*. This would be particularly true in the typical case, such as the instant one, where the state courts are asked to construe a state statute against the backdrop of a federal constitutional challenge. The litigant denying the statute's applicability may be led not merely to state his federal constitutional claim but to argue it, for if he can persuade the state court that application of the statute to him would offend the Federal Constitution, he will ordinarily have persuaded it that the statute should not be construed as applicable to him. In addition, the parties cannot prevent the state court from rendering a decision on the federal question if it chooses to do so; and even if such a decision is not explicit, a holding that the statute is applicable may arguably imply, in view of the constitutional objections to such a construction, that the court considers the constitutional challenge to be without merit.

Despite these uncertainties arising from application of *Windsor* a party may readily forestall any conclusion that he has elected not to return to the District Court. He may . . . inform the state courts that he is exposing his federal claims there only for the purpose of complying with *Windsor*, and that he intends, should the state courts hold against him on the question of state law, to return to the District Court for disposition of his federal contentions. Such an explicit reservation is not indispensable; the litigant is in no event to be denied his right to return to the District Court unless it clearly appears that he voluntarily did more than *Windsor* required and fully litigated his federal claims in the state courts. When the reservation has been made, however, his right to return will in all events be preserved.[10]

Lower courts have continued to struggle over the preclusion principles that should be applied to state court factual findings following a federal court's *Pullman* abstention order. It is clear that a proper *England* reservation precludes a claim preclusion defense. Thus, a federal court that has abstained under *Pullman* can still entertain the action on its return from state court. Issue preclusion, however, is more problematic. "Normally, when the federal court abstains pursuant to *Pullman* and the federal litigant reserves his rights as required by *England*, issue preclusion applies only to the state law question decided by the state court. Upon return to federal court, the federal plaintiff may fully litigate his federal claims, including the factual issues that may be identical to those underlying the state law question." *Ivy Club v. Edwards*, 943 F.2d 270 (3d Cir. 1991). However, a state court's resolution of factual issues necessary to a state-law claim can under certain circumstances still be given preclusive effect. See, e.g., *San Remo Hotel L.P. v. City and County of San Francisco*, 364 F.3d 1088 (9th Cir. 2004) ("To the extent that they fully litigated a necessary issue in the course of the state proceedings that is identical to an issue before the federal court, the [plaintiffs] are precluded from taking a second bite of the apple [in federal court]."); *Instructional Systems, Inc. v. Computer Curriculum Corp.*, 35 F.3d 813 (3d Cir. 1994) (recognizing that "modified" preclusion principles may apply to "factual findings necessary to" a state law claim). When factual determinations must be given preclusive effect is not clear.

---

[10] Justice Brennan noted in *England* that "[t]he reservation may be made by any party to the litigation. Usually the plaintiff will have made the original choice to litigate in the federal court, but the defendant also, by virtue of the removal jurisdiction, has a right to litigate the federal question there. Once issue has been joined in the federal court, no party is entitled to insist, over another's objection, upon a binding state court determination of the federal question."

[1] Takings Claims in Federal Court

Putting *Pullman* abstention aside, constitutional doctrines can sometimes require that a plaintiff first resort to a state's administrative or judicial machinery. For instance, as seen in Chapter 1.C., *supra*, Procedural Due Process violations are predicated on a denial of either pre- or post-deprivation process. This process may take the form of either pre-deprivation administrative hearings, *see, e.g., Cleveland Board of Education v. Loudermill*, 470 U.S. 532 (1985) (holding that public sector employees are entitled to hearings before discharge), or post-deprivation judicial proceedings. *See, e.g., Parratt v. Taylor*, 451 U.S. 527 (1981) (holding that an accidental loss of property can be redressed through post-loss state law claims).

The same is true of takings claims under the Fifth Amendment. Generally speaking, the Fifth Amendment requires that government provide compensation for takings of private property. *See* Richard H. Seamon, *The Asymmetry of State Sovereign Immunity*, 76 WASH. L. REV. 1067 (2001) (arguing that the Supreme Court has yet to expressly hold that the Fifth Amendment's Takings Clause overcomes state sovereign immunity, but still concluding that in order to comply with the Fifth Amendment's terms states must provide some sort of compensation). In *Williamson County Regional Planning Commission v. Hamilton Bank*, 473 U.S. 172 (1985), the Supreme Court ruled that Fifth Amendment claims do not ripen until property owners who have suffered takings[11] at the hands of state or local officials are denied compensation in the state's courts. In *Williamson County*, a landowner challenged a retroactive zoning law under the Fifth Amendment. Because Tennessee recognized suits for inverse condemnation,[12] the Court ruled that the landowner was required to first exhaust that procedural avenue of potential relief. Only after the state's courts refused to provide relief would a landowner have a claim under the Fifth Amendment.[13]

Can a property owner who has lost an inverse condemnation proceeding in state court sue in federal court under the Fifth Amendment for the alleged uncompensated taking? Will the property owner be precluded by either res judicata or collateral estoppel? *See, e.g., Rockstead v. City of Crystal Lake*, 486 F.3d 963 (7th Cir. 2007) ("The litigation in state court is the end of the road, *see* 28 U.S.C. § 1738, unless the state itself

---

[11] *Williamson County* further established that in the context of zoning a ripe taking also depends on state or local authorities' denial of an application for a variance. Thus, landowners who claim that takings have occurred through land-use regulations must ordinarily seek variances to ripen their Fifth Amendment claims. *See, e.g., Palazzolo v. Rhode Island*, 533 U.S. 606 (2001) (noting that the "central question in resolving the ripeness issue . . . is whether petitioner obtained a final decision from the Council determining the permitted use for the land"); *Urban Developers LLC v. City of Jackson*, 468 F.3d 281 (5th Cir. 2006) (observing that a landowner must use available state procedures for seeking permits or variances).

[12] What if rather than recognizing a statutory or common law inverse condemnation claim, a state recognizes only a constitutional taking claim under its state constitution? Is this an available state procedure requiring exhaustion for purposes of *Williamson County*? *See, e.g., Asociacion De Subscripcion Conjunta Del Seguro De Responsabilidad Obligatorio v. Galarza*, 484 F.3d 1 (1st Cir. 2007) (holding that Puerto Rico's constitutional taking claim need not be exhausted under *Williamson County*). *Contrast* Scott Keller, *Judicial Jurisdiction Stripping Masquerading as Ripeness: Eliminating the Williamson County State Litigation Requirements for Regulatory Takings Claims*, 85 TEX. L. REV. 199, 204–05 (2006) (observing that federal takings plaintiffs need to pursue any available state takings claim, among other procedures, to meet the *Willaimson County* requirement).

[13] Note that a state's failure to offer *any* avenue of relief to property owners who have experienced takings, like those claiming oppressive land-use regulations, allows the property owners to proceed directly to federal court under the Fifth Amendment (and § 1983). *See City of Monterey v. Del Monte Dunes at Monterey*, 526 U.S. 687 (1999) (observing that California had not provided a compensatory remedy for temporary regulatory takings and thus land owners could proceed directly under federal law in federal court); *Washington Legal Foundation v. Legal Foundation of Washington*, 271 F.3d 835 (9th Cir. 2001) (holding that *Williamson* does not direct Fifth Amendment challengers to state courts when state law expressly forbids compensation), *affirmed sub nom. on other grounds, Brown v. Legal Foundation of Washington*, 538 U.S. 216 (2003) (concluding that state IOLTA program was not an unconstitutional taking).

allows relitigation of the constitutional question."). Recognizing these looming difficulties, property owners in the wake of *Williamson County* sometimes filed *England* reservations in state courts in an effort to preserve their Fifth Amendment claims in subsequent federal proceedings. Most Circuits recognized this tactic in the context of claim preclusion. *See, e.g., DLX, Inc. v. Kentucky*, 381 F.3d 511 (6th Cir. 2004) ("We join our sister circuits in holding that a party's *England* reservation of federal takings claims in a state takings action will suffice to defeat claim preclusion in a subsequent federal action."). Others, like the Second Circuit in *Santini v. Connecticut Hazardous Waste Management Services*, 342 F.3d 118 (2d Cir. 2003), went so far as to rule that a proper *England* reservation even insulated the property owner from issue preclusion in subsequent federal proceedings for the claimed taking. The Supreme Court addressed the matter in the following case.

SAN REMO HOTEL L.P. v. CITY AND COUNTY OF SAN FRANCISCO
Supreme Court of the United States
545 U.S. 323 (2005)

JUSTICE STEVENS delivered the opinion of the Court.

[Because of a housing shortage, San Francisco in 1979 placed a moratorium on conversions of "residential hotels" — those that housed local residents — to ones serving tourists. Although San Francisco relaxed this moratorium in later years, it still closely regulated conversions. Permits were required, and these "could be obtained only by constructing new residential units, rehabilitating old ones, or paying an 'in lieu' fee into the City's Residential Hotel Preservation Fund Account." In 1993, the city's Planning Commission granted the San Remo Hotel a conversion permit, but conditioned the permit on the payment of a $567,000 "in lieu" fee. The Hotel immediately petitioned the California Superior Court for mandamus. While this state-court action was pending, the Hotel filed a § 1983 action in federal court arguing, *inter alia*, both facial and as-applied violations of the Fifth Amendment Takings Clause. Applying *Williamson County Regional Planning Commission v. Hamilton Bank*, 473 U.S. 172 (1985), the District Court concluded that the Hotel's as-applied challenge was not ripe and its facial challenge was barred by California's statute of limitations. On appeal, the Ninth Circuit agreed that the as-applied challenge was not ripe for federal review, but rather than relying on the statute of limitations decided to abstain from deciding the Hotel's *facial* Takings claim under *Railroad Comm'n of Tex. v. Pullman Co.*, 312 U.S. 496 (1941).

Upon its return to state court, the Hotel attempted to "reserve" its facial Takings challenge to the federal forum under *England v. Louisiana Board of Medical Examiners*, 375 U.S. 411 (1964), but ultimately presented the state courts with a state-law claim using "language that sounded in the rules and standards established and refined by [the Supreme] Court's takings jurisprudence." The Hotel argued, for example, "that imposition of the fee fail[ed] to substantially advance a legitimate government interest and that [t]he amount of the fee imposed [was] not roughly proportional to the impact of the proposed tourist use of the San Remo Hotel." Following several years of litigation, the California Supreme Court ruled against the Hotel. Although the California Supreme Court noted that the Hotel had reserved its federal causes of action and sought no relief under the Federal Constitution, it applied "congruent" federal precedents in denying the Hotel's state-law takings claims.

Following its loss in state court, the Hotel returned to federal court in an effort to litigate both its facial and as-applied Takings claims. The former, it argued, was protected by its *England* reservation. Regarding the latter, it argued, the court ought to fashion an exception to the federal full faith and credit statute, 28 U.S.C. § 1738, to allow it to proceed. The District Court and United States Court of Appeals for the Ninth Circuit rejected both claims.]

The essence of [the Hotel's] argument is as follows: because no claim that a state agency has violated the federal Takings Clause can be heard in federal court until the property owner has "been denied just compensation" through an available state compensation procedure, "federal courts [should be] required to disregard the decision of the state court" in order to ensure that federal takings claims can be "considered on the merits in . . . federal court." Therefore, the argument goes, whenever plaintiffs reserve their claims under *England v. Louisiana Bd. of Medical Examiners*, 375 U.S. 411 (1964), federal courts should review the reserved federal claims *de novo*, regardless of what issues the state court may have decided or how it may have decided them.

"Typical" *England* cases generally involve federal constitutional challenges to a state statute that can be avoided if a state court construes the statute in a particular manner. In such cases, the purpose of abstention is not to afford state courts an opportunity to adjudicate an issue that is functionally identical to the federal question. To the contrary, the purpose of *Pullman* abstention in such cases is to avoid resolving the federal question by encouraging a state-law determination that may moot the federal controversy. Additionally, our opinion made it perfectly clear that the effective reservation of a federal claim was dependent on the condition that plaintiffs take no action to broaden the scope of the state court's review beyond decision of the antecedent state-law issue.

Our holding in *England* does not support [the Hotel's] attempt to relitigate issues resolved by the California courts. With respect to [the Hotel's] facial takings claims, the Court of Appeals invoked *Pullman* abstention after determining that a ripe federal question existed — namely "the facial takings challenge to the [ordinance]."[14] It did so because "land use planning is a sensitive area of social policy" and because [the Hotel's] pending state mandamus action had the potential of mooting [its] facial challenge . . . by overturning the City's original classification of the San Remo Hotel as a "residential" property. Thus, [the Hotel was] entitled to insulate from preclusive effect one federal issue — their facial constitutional challenge to the [ordinance] — while [it] returned to state court to resolve [its] petition for writ of mandate.

[The Hotel], however, chose to advance broader issues than the limited issues contained within [its] state petition for writ of administrative mandamus on which the Ninth Circuit relied when it invoked *Pullman* abstention. In [its] state action, [it] advanced not only [its] request for a writ of administrative mandate, but also [its] various claims that the [law] was unconstitutional on its face and as applied for (1) its failure to substantially advance a legitimate interest, (2) its lack of a nexus between the required fees and the ultimate objectives sought to be achieved via the ordinance, and (3) its imposition of an undue economic burden on individual property owners. By broadening [its] state action beyond the mandamus petition to include [its] "substantially advances" claims, [the Hotel] effectively asked the state court to resolve the same federal issues [it] asked it to reserve. *England* does not support the exercise of any such right.

[The Hotel's] as-applied takings claims fare no better. As an initial matter, the Court of Appeals did not abstain with respect to those claims. Instead, the court found that they were unripe under *Williamson County*. The court therefore affirmed the district court's dismissal of those claims. Unlike [its] "substantially advances" claims, [the Hotel's] as-applied claims were never properly before the District Court, and there was

---

[14] [n. 23] [The Hotel's] facial challenges to the [ordinance] were ripe, of course, under *Yee v. Escondido*, 503 U.S. 519, 534 (1992), in which we held that facial challenges based on the 'substantially advances' test need not be ripened in state court — the claims do "not depend on the extent to which petitioners are deprived of the economic use of their particular pieces of property or the extent to which these particular petitioners are compensated."

no reason to expect that they could be relitigated in full if advanced in the state proceedings. In short, our opinion in *England* does not support [the Hotel's] attempt to circumvent § 1738.

[The Hotel's] ultimate submission, however, does not rely on *England* alone. Rather, [it argues] that federal courts simply should not apply ordinary preclusion rules to state-court judgments when a case is forced into state court by the ripeness rule of *Williamson County*. [We disagree.]

First, [the Hotel] . . . ultimately depend[s] on an assumption that plaintiffs have a right to vindicate their federal claims in a federal forum. We have repeatedly held, to the contrary, that issues actually decided in valid state-court judgments may well deprive plaintiffs of the "right" to have their federal claims relitigated in federal court. This is so even when the plaintiff would have preferred not to litigate in state court, but was required to do so by statute or prudential rules. The relevant question in such cases is not whether the plaintiff has been afforded access to a federal forum; rather, the question is whether the state court actually decided an issue of fact or law that was necessary to its judgment.

As in *Allen*[*v. McCurry*, 449 U.S. 90 (1980)], we are presently concerned only with issues *actually decided* by the state court that are dispositive of federal claims raised under § 1983. And, also as in *Allen*, it is clear that [the Hotel] would have preferred not to have been forced to have [its] federal claims resolved by issues decided in state court. Unfortunately for [the Hotel], it is entirely *unclear* why [its] preference for a federal forum should matter for constitutional or statutory purposes.

The only distinction between this case and *Allen* that is possibly relevant is the fact that [the Hotel] here originally invoked the jurisdiction of a Federal District Court, which abstained on *Pullman* grounds while [the Hotel] returned to state court. But [the Hotel's] as-applied takings claims were never properly before the District Court because they were unripe. And, as we have already explained, the Court of Appeals invoked *Pullman* abstention only with respect to [the Hotel's] "substantially advances" takings challenge, which [the Hotel] then gratuitously presented to the state court. At a bare minimum, with respect to the facial takings claim, [the Hotel was] "in an offensive posture in [its] state court proceeding, and could have proceeded first in federal court had [it] wanted to litigate [its 'substantially advances'] federal claim in a federal forum." Thus, the only distinction between this case and *Allen* is a distinction of no relevant significance.

The second reason we find [the Hotel's] argument unpersuasive is that it assumes that courts may simply create exceptions to 28 U.S.C. § 1738 wherever courts deem them appropriate. Even conceding, *arguendo*, the laudable policy goal of making federal forums available to deserving litigants, we have expressly rejected [its] view. Our cases have therefore made plain that "an exception to § 1738 will not be recognized unless a later statute contains an express or implied partial repeal." Even when the plaintiff's resort to state court is involuntary and the federal interest in denying finality is robust, we have held that Congress "must 'clearly manifest' its intent to depart from § 1738."

Third, [the Hotel has] overstated the reach of *Williamson County* throughout this litigation. [The Hotel was] never required to ripen the heart of [its] complaint — the claim that the [ordinance] was facially invalid because it failed to substantially advance a legitimate state interest — in state court. *See Yee v. Escondido*, 503 U.S. 519, 534 (1992). [The Hotel] therefore could have raised most of [its] facial takings challenges, which by their nature requested relief distinct from the provision of "just compensation," directly in federal court.[15]

---

[15] [n.25] In all events, [the Hotel] may no longer advance such claims given our recent holding that the "'substantially advances' formula is not a valid takings test, and indeed . . . has no proper place in our

Alternatively, [the Hotel] had the option of reserving [its] facial claims while pursuing [its] as-applied claims along with [its] petition for writ of administrative mandamus. [The Hotel] did not have the right, however, to seek state review of the same substantive issues [it] sought to reserve. The purpose of the *England* reservation is not to grant plaintiffs a second bite at the apple in their forum of choice.

With respect to those federal claims that did require ripening, we reject [the Hotel's] contention that *Williamson County* forbids plaintiffs from advancing their federal claims in state courts. The requirement that aggrieved property owners must seek "compensation through the procedures the State has provided for doing so," does not preclude state courts from hearing simultaneously a plaintiff's request for compensation under state law and the claim that, in the alternative, the denial of compensation would violate the Fifth Amendment of the Federal Constitution. Reading *Williamson County* to preclude plaintiffs from raising such claims in the alternative would erroneously interpret our cases as requiring property owners to "resort to piecemeal litigation or otherwise unfair procedures."

It is hardly a radical notion to recognize that, as a practical matter, a significant number of plaintiffs will necessarily litigate their federal takings claims in state courts. [T]here is scant precedent for the litigation in federal district court of claims that a state agency has taken property in violation of the Fifth Amendment's takings clause. To the contrary, most of the cases in our takings jurisprudence, including nearly all of the cases on which [the Hotel] rel[ies], came to us on writs of certiorari from state courts of last resort.

Moreover, this is not the only area of law in which we have recognized limits to plaintiffs' ability to press their federal claims in federal courts. *See, e.g., Fair Assessment in Real Estate Assn., Inc. v. McNary*, 454 U.S. 100, 116 (1981) (holding that taxpayers are "barred by the principle of comity from asserting § 1983 actions against the validity of state tax systems in federal courts"). State courts are fully competent to adjudicate constitutional challenges to local land-use decisions. Indeed, state courts undoubtedly have more experience than federal courts do in resolving the complex factual, technical, and legal questions related to zoning and land-use regulations.

CHIEF JUSTICE REHNQUIST, with whom JUSTICE O'CONNOR, JUSTICE KENNEDY, and JUSTICE THOMAS join, concurring in the judgment.

It is not clear to me that *Williamson County* was correct in demanding that, once a government entity has reached a final decision with respect to a claimant's property, the claimant must seek compensation in state court before bringing a federal takings claim in federal court. The Court in *Williamson County* purported to interpret the Fifth Amendment in divining this state-litigation requirement. More recently, we have referred to it as merely a prudential requirement. *Suitum v. Tahoe Regional Planning Agency*, 520 U.S. 725, 733–734 (1997). It is not obvious that either constitutional or prudential principles require claimants to utilize all state compensation procedures before they can bring a federal takings claim. Cf. *Patsy v. Board of Regents of Fla.*, 457 U.S. 496, 516 (1982) (holding that plaintiffs suing under § 1983 are not required to have exhausted state administrative remedies).[16]

Finally, *Williamson County*'s state-litigation rule has created some real anomalies, justifying our revisiting the issue. For example, our holding today ensures that litigants

---

takings jurisprudence." *Lingle* [*v. Chevron U.S.A.*, 544 U.S. 528 (2005) (holding that the claim that government action does not "substantially advance" a legitimate interest sounds in Due Process rather than Takings jurisprudence)].

[16] [n.1] In creating the state-litigation rule, the Court, in addition to relying on the Fifth Amendment's text, analogized to *Ruckelshaus v. Monsanto Co.*, 467 U.S. 986 (1984), and *Parratt v. Taylor*, 451 U.S. 527 (1981). [T]hose cases provided limited support for the state-litigation requirement.

who go to state court to seek compensation will likely be unable later to assert their federal takings claims in federal court. . . . *Williamson County* all but guarantees that claimants will be unable to utilize the federal courts to enforce the Fifth Amendment's just compensation guarantee. The basic principle that state courts are competent to enforce federal rights and to adjudicate federal takings claims is sound, and would apply to any number of federal claims. But that principle does not explain why federal takings claims in particular should be singled out to be confined to state court, in the absence of any asserted justification or congressional directive.[17]

I joined the opinion of the Court in *Williamson County*. But further reflection and experience lead me to think that the justifications for its state-litigation requirement are suspect, while its impact on takings plaintiffs is dramatic. Here, no court below has addressed the correctness of *Williamson County*, neither party has asked us to reconsider it, and resolving the issue could not benefit petitioners. In an appropriate case, I believe the Court should reconsider whether plaintiffs asserting a Fifth Amendment takings claim based on the final decision of a state or local government entity must first seek compensation in state courts.

NOTES

1. Facial Takings Claims. The San Remo Hotel argued that San Francisco's moratorium on conversions was facially invalid under the Fifth Amendment because it did not "substantially advance" a legitimate governmental interest. As noted by the Court in *San Remo*, *see* footnote 23, this sort of claim does not seek compensation and is not subject to *Williamson County*'s ripening requirement. *See Yee v. Escondido*, 503 U.S. 519 (1992) (holding that facial challenges based on the "substantially advances" test need not be ripened in state court). And because these facial challenges can proceed directly under § 1983 and the Fifth Amendment in federal court, *Pullman* abstention, together with *England* reservations, can be proper. Under the facts in *San Remo Hotel*, however, the Court found that a proper *England* reservation was not made. Rather, the Hotel voluntarily presented its facial challenge to the California courts, thereby relinquishing its reservation and opening itself to preclusion defenses upon its return to federal court.

What if the Hotel had not voluntarily presented its facial claim to California's courts? Would its *England* reservation allow it to relitigate, de novo, its facial claim and surrounding factual issues in federal court? Note that the Supreme Court in effectively disposed of this problem in the Takings context in *Lingle v. Chevron U.S.A.*, 544 U.S. 528 (2005), which held that the Fifth Amendment's Takings Clause does not include a facial "substantially advances" challenge. *See* footnote 25 to the majority's opinion in *San Remo*. Facial challenges like that in *San Remo Hotel* must now be brought under the Fourteenth Amendment's Due Process Clause, which only requires that government action be rationally related to a legitimate governmental interest. Fifth Amendment Takings claims, then, will ordinarily be directed to state court and will likely give rise to preclusion problems upon return to federal court. *See, e.g., Torromeo v. Town of Fremont*, 438 F.3d 113 (1st Cir. 2006) (holding that res judicata applied to a federal takings claim that was actually litigated to a final judgment on the merits in the state court). *See generally* J. David Breemer, *You Can Check Out But You Can Never Leave: The Story of* San Remo Hotel — *the Supreme Court Relegates Federal Takings*

---

[17] [n.2] Indeed, in some States the courts themselves apply the state-litigation requirement from *Williamson County*, refusing to entertain any federal takings claim until the claimant receives a final denial of compensation through all the available state procedures. This precludes litigants from asserting their federal takings claim even in *state* court. The Court tries to avoid this anomaly by asserting that, for plaintiffs attempting to raise a federal takings claim in state court as an alternative to their state claims, *Williamson County* does not command that the state courts themselves impose the state-litigation requirement. But that is so only if *Williamson County*'s state-litigation requirement is merely a prudential rule, and not a constitutional mandate, a question that the Court today conspicuously leaves open.

Claims to State Courts Under a Rule Intended to Ripen the Claims for Federal Review, 33 B.C. ENVTL AFF. L. REV. 247 (2006) (discussing exhaustion and preclusion problems generated by Fifth Amendment takings claims).

2. As-Applied Takings Claims. The *San Remo Hotel* majority recognized that as-applied takings claims under the Fifth Amendment must generally be ripened under *Williamson County* through state-law proceedings in state court. The end result is that takings claims can only rarely be heard by a federal court (other than the Supreme Court). *But see* footnote 13, preceding *San Remo Hotel supra* (noting that federal courts are appropriate where states provide no remedial mechanism for uncompensated taking). The Chief Justice's concurring opinion, in contrast, deemed the *Williamson County* rule a prudential requirement that might be discarded or reconsidered. Its requirements, after all, not only preclude takings plaintiffs from litigating their claims in federal court, but in some states prevent them from litigating their federal claims in state court as well. *See* footnote 2 to the Chief Justice's concurring opinion, *supra*. Notwithstanding the Chief Justice's concerns, lower federal courts have continued to apply *Williamson County* as if it is a constitutionally-grounded doctrine. *See, e.g., Peters v. Village of Clifton*, 498 F.3d 727 (7th Cir. 2007) ("*Williamson County's* ripeness requirements are prudential in nature. The prudential character of the *Williamson County* requirements do not, however, give the lower federal courts license to disregard them.").

3. Tax Claims Under § 1983. In *McKesson Corp. v. Division of Alcoholic Beverages and Tobacco*, 496 U.S. 18 (1990), a wholesale liquor distributor (McKesson) filed suit in state court claiming that a tax scheme which allowed tax preferences for alcoholic beverages manufactured from certain products grown in Florida violated the Dormant Commerce Clause. The Florida Supreme Court ruled in McKesson's favor, but refused to order a refund of the improperly collected taxes. The Supreme Court disagreed. It held that where a state penalizes taxpayers for failing to remit taxes in a timely fashion, thus requiring them to pay first and obtain review of the tax's validity later in a refund action, the Due Process Clause requires that the state supply a meaningful post-payment remedy.

Following *McKesson*, states are put to a choice: they can either provide predeprivation process — for example, "by authorizing taxpayers to bring suit to enjoin imposition of a tax prior to its payment, or by allowing taxpayers to withhold payment and then interpose their objections as defenses in a tax enforcement proceeding initiated by the State" — or they can provide retrospective relief as part of a postdeprivation procedure. If a state chooses the latter option, however, and allows a post-payment refund action, it "must provide taxpayers . . . not only a fair opportunity to challenge the accuracy and legal validity of their tax obligation, but also a 'clear and certain remedy' for any erroneous or unlawful tax collection."

Rather than using this state-created "clear and certain remedy," can a taxpayer go directly to federal court under § 1983 to recover unconstitutionally collected taxes? Assuming that *McKesson* is satisfied, a disgruntled taxpayer would not have a Procedural Due Process complaint to support a § 1983 claim. But it could be that some other constitutional provision, the Dormant Commerce Clause, for example, *see, e.g., Dennis v. Higgins*, 498 U.S. 439 (1991) (holding that Dormant Commerce Clause claims are actionable under § 1983), might support a § 1983 suit notwithstanding the state's procedural compliance with *McKesson*. Can the taxpayer ignore the state's remedy and proceed directly to federal court on this claim under § 1983?

Section 1983, of course, cannot be used (in either state or federal court) to seek tax refunds from state agencies because of *Will v. Michigan Dep't of State Police*, 491 U.S. 58 (1989) (discussed in Note 3 following *Quern v. Jordan* in Chapter 3.C., *supra*), which held that states and their official-capacity agents are not "persons" for purposes of § 1983 when sued for money damages. Local taxing agencies, in contrast, are not protected by *Will* and thus are amenable to suit under § 1983. Still, the Supreme Court in *Fair Assessment in Real Estate Ass'n, Inc. v. McNary*, 454 U.S. 100 (1981), held that principles of comity and federalism peculiar to taxation preclude federal courts from hearing tax refund claims under § 1983 when state law otherwise furnishes an "adequate legal remedy." Hence, regardless of the constitutional challenge, the state-refund proceedings mandated by *McKesson* will have to be employed to win a tax refund. Following this state-created round of litigation, preclusion principles will then likely prohibit the taxpayer from proceeding to federal court. The end result is that § 1983 cannot be used in federal court to obtain tax refunds from either state or local governments.

Can § 1983 be used in state court to obtain a tax refund from local government? The Nebraska Supreme Court in *Francis v. City of Columbus*, 676 N.W.2d 346 (Neb. 2004), ruled that § 1983 is not available in state court: "Although *Fair Assessment* was limited only to § 1983 claims in federal court, its concerns apply with equal force to § 1983 claims brought in state court. If such suits were allowed, litigants in state courts could use a federal remedy to grind to a halt state and local taxation schemes." The California Court of Appeal reached the same result in *Union Oil Company of California v. City of Los Angeles*, 79 Cal. App. 4th 383, 94 Cal. Rptr. 2d 81 (2000), as did the Pennsylvania Commonwealth Court in *Murtagh v. County of Berks*, 715 A.2d 548 (Pa. Comm. Ct. 1998). Is this position sound? *McNary* was premised on abstention principles, which direct federal judicial deference toward state courts. Does this reasoning apply to an action in state court? In his concurring opinion in *San Remo Hotel*, the Chief Justice complained about using *McNary* to support *Williamson County*:

> The Court today attempts to shore up the state-litigation requirement by referring to *Fair Assessment in Real Estate Assn., Inc. v. McNary*, 454 U.S. 100 (1981). There, we held that the principle of comity (reflected in the Tax Injunction Act, 28 U.S.C. § 1341) bars taxpayers from asserting § 1983 claims against the validity of state tax systems in federal courts. Our decision that such suits must be brought in state court was driven by the unique and sensitive interests at stake when federal courts confront claims that States acted impermissibly in administering their own tax systems. Those historically grounded, federalism-based concerns had led to a longstanding, "fundamental principle of comity between federal courts and state governments . . ., particularly in the area of state taxation," a principle which predated the enactment of § 1983 itself.

If the Chief Justice is correct about *McNary*, should not § 1983 be available in refund actions against local taxing authorities in state courts? The Court in *National Private Truck Council v. Oklahoma Tax Commission*, 515 U.S. 582 (1995) (discussed in Note 3 following *Miller v. French* in Chapter 6.C.[2], *supra*), held that § 1983 cannot be used to obtain prospective relief from state courts in cases alleging the unconstitutional collection of state and local taxes. The Court reasoned that so long as adequate remedies exist under state law, the policies that motivated the federal Tax Injunction Act, 28 U.S.C. § 1341 (prohibiting federal courts from enjoining the collection of state and local taxes, assuming adequate state remedies), also preclude state courts from providing prospective relief under § 1983. Does *National Private Truck Council* support a rule prohibiting § 1983 from being used to win refunds? The practical effect of cases like *Williamson County*, *McKesson*, *McNary*, and *National Private Truck* is that plaintiffs lose the tactical advantages that surround § 1983. First and foremost is fee-shifting under 42 U.S.C. § 1988(b). *See* Chapter 9, *infra*.

[2] Adjudicative Decisions by State Agencies

Section 1738 literally speaks to the respect federal courts must afford state *judicial* proceedings. *Allen*, *Migra* and *San Remo Hotel* all dealt with state-court judgments. What about the determinations and decisions handed down by state agencies? Consider the following case.

UNIVERSITY OF TENNESSEE v. ELLIOTT
Supreme Court of the United States
478 U.S. 788 (1986)

JUSTICE WHITE delivered the opinion of the Court.

A state Administrative Law Judge determined that [the] University of Tennessee (hereafter . . . University) was not motivated by racial prejudice in seeking to discharge [Elliott, a black employee of the University's Agricultural Extension Service]. The question presented is whether this finding is entitled to preclusive effect in federal court, where [Elliott] has raised discrimination claims under various civil rights laws, including Title VII of the Civil Rights Act of 1964, and 42 U.S.C. § 1983.

In 1981, [the University] informed [Elliott] . . . that he would be discharged for inadequate work performance and misconduct on the job. [Elliott] requested a hearing under the Tennessee Uniform Administrative Procedures Act to contest his proposed termination. Prior to the start of the hearing, [Elliott] also filed suit in the United States District Court for the Western District of Tennessee, alleging that his proposed discharge was racially motivated and seeking relief under Title VII and other civil rights statutes, including 42 U.S.C. § 1983. The relief sought included damages, an injunction prohibiting [Elliott's] discharge, and classwide relief from alleged patterns of discrimination by petitioner.

The District Court initially entered a temporary restraining order prohibiting the University from taking any job action against respondent, but later lifted this order and permitted the state administrative proceeding to go forward. There followed a hearing at which an administrative assistant to the University's Vice President for Agriculture presided as an Administrative Law Judge (ALJ). The focus of the hearing was on 10 particular charges that the University gave as grounds for [Elliott's] discharge. [Elliott] denied these charges, which he contended were motivated by racial prejudice, and also argued that the University's subjecting him to the charges violated his rights under the Constitution, Title VII, and other federal statutes. The ALJ held that he lacked jurisdiction to adjudicate [Elliott's] federal civil rights claims, but did allow [Elliott] to present, as an affirmative defense, evidence that the charges against him were actually motivated by racial prejudice and hence not a proper basis for his proposed discharge.

After hearing extensive evidence, the ALJ found that the University had proved some but not all of the charges against [Elliott], and that the charges were not racially motivated. Concluding that the proposed discharge of [Elliott] was too severe a penalty, the ALJ ordered him transferred to a new assignment with supervisors other than those with whom he had experienced conflicts. [Elliott] appealed to the University's Vice President for Agriculture, who affirmed the ALJ's ruling. The Vice President stated that his review of the record persuaded him that the proposed discharge of [Elliott] had not been racially motivated.

[Elliott] did not seek review of these administrative proceedings in the Tennessee courts; instead, he returned to federal court to pursue his civil rights claims. There, [the University] moved for summary judgment on the ground that [Elliott's] suit was an improper collateral attack on the ALJ's ruling, which [the University] contended was entitled to preclusive effect. The District Court agreed, holding that the civil rights statutes on which [Elliott] relied "were not intended to afford the plaintiff a means of relitigating what plaintiff has heretofore litigated over a five-month period."

[Elliott] appealed to the . . . Sixth Circuit, which reversed the District Court's judgment. As regards [Elliott's] Title VII claim, the Court of Appeals looked for guidance to our decision in *Kremer v. Chemical Construction Corp.*, 456 U.S. 461 (1982).[18] While *Kremer* teaches that final state-court judgments are entitled to full faith

---

[18] [n.3] In *Kremer*, an employee filed a Title VII discrimination charge with the Equal Employment

and credit in Title VII actions, it indicates that unreviewed determinations by state agencies stand on a different footing.

Title 28 U.S.C. § 1738 governs the preclusive effect to be given the judgments and records of state courts, and is not applicable to the unreviewed state administrative factfinding at issue in this case. However, we have frequently fashioned federal common-law rules of preclusion in the absence of a governing statute. Although § 1738 is a governing statute with regard to the judgments and records of state courts, because § 1738 antedates the development of administrative agencies it clearly does not represent a congressional determination that the decisions of state administrative agencies should not be given preclusive effect.

Under 42 U.S.C. § 2000e-5(b), the Equal Employment Opportunity Commission (EEOC), in investigating discrimination charges, must give "substantial weight to final findings and orders made by State or local authorities in proceedings commenced under State or local [employment discrimination] law." As we noted in *Kremer*, it would make little sense for Congress to write such a provision if state agency findings were entitled to preclusive effect in Title VII actions in federal court.

Moreover, our decision in *Chandler v. Roudebush*, 425 U.S. 840 (1976), strongly supports [Elliott's] contention that Congress intended one in his position to have a trial de novo on his Title VII claim. In *Chandler*, we held that a federal employee whose discrimination claim was rejected by her employing agency after an administrative hearing was entitled to a trial de novo in federal court on her Title VII claim.

Like the plaintiff in *Chandler*, [Elliott] . . . pursued his Title VII action following an administrative proceeding at which the employing agency rejected a discrimination claim. It would be contrary to the rationale of *Chandler* to apply res judicata to deny [Elliott] a trial de novo on his Title VII claim.

On the basis of our analysis in *Kremer* and *Chandler* of the language and legislative history of Title VII, we conclude that . . . Congress did not intend unreviewed state administrative proceedings to have preclusive effect on Title VII claims.[19]

This Court has held that § 1738 requires that state-court judgments be given both issue and claim preclusive effect in subsequent actions under 42 U.S.C. § 1983. *Allen v. McCurry* (issue preclusion); *Migra v. Warren City School District Board of Education* (claim preclusion). Those decisions are not controlling in this case, where § 1738 does not apply; nonetheless, they support the view that Congress, in enacting the Reconstruction civil rights statutes, did not intend to create an exception to general rules of preclusion.

We also see no reason to suppose that Congress, in enacting the Reconstruction civil rights statutes, wished to foreclose the adaptation of traditional principles of preclusion to such subsequent developments as the burgeoning use of administrative adjudication in the 20th century.

We have previously recognized that it is sound policy to apply principles of issue preclusion to the factfinding of administrative bodies acting in a judicial capacity. . . . [G]iving preclusive effect to administrative factfinding serves the value underlying general principles of collateral estoppel: enforcing repose. This value, which encompasses both the parties' interest in avoiding the cost and vexation of repetitive

---

Opportunity Commission, which pursuant to 42 U.S.C. § 2000e-5 referred the case to the New York State Division of Human Rights, the agency charged with administering the State's employment discrimination laws. The state agency rejected the employee's discrimination claim, a judgment that was affirmed both at the agency appellate level and by a reviewing state court. The employee then brought a Title VII action, in which the employer raised a res judicata defense. This Court held that under 28 U.S.C. § 1738 the state court's judgment affirming the state agency's finding of no discrimination was entitled to preclusive effect in the employee's Title VII action.

[19] [n.5] The fact that [Elliott] requested the administrative hearing rather than being compelled to participate in it does not weigh in favor of preclusion.

litigation and the public's interest in conserving judicial resources, is equally implicated whether factfinding is done by a federal or state agency. Having federal courts give preclusive effect to the factfinding of state administrative tribunals also serves the value of federalism.

Significantly, all of the opinions in *Thomas v. Washington Gas Light Co.*, 448 U.S. 261 (1980), express the view that the Full Faith and Credit Clause compels the States to give preclusive effect to the factfindings of an administrative tribunal in a sister State. The Full Faith and Credit Clause is of course not binding on federal courts, but we can certainly look to the policies underlying the Clause in fashioning federal common-law rules of preclusion. "Perhaps the major purpose of the Full Faith and Credit Clause is to act as a nationally unifying force,"and this purpose is served by giving preclusive effect to state administrative factfinding rather than leaving the courts of a second forum, state or federal, free to reach conflicting results.[20] Accordingly, we hold that when a state agency "acting in a judicial capacity . . . resolves disputed issues of fact properly before it which the parties have had an adequate opportunity to litigate," federal courts must give the agency's factfinding the same preclusive effect to which it would be entitled in the State's courts.[21]

JUSTICE STEVENS, with whom JUSTICE BRENNAN and JUSTICE BLACKMUN join, concurring in part and dissenting in part.

[T]he Court concludes that the findings of [an] administrative assistant may bar [Elliott's] claims under 42 U.S.C. § 1983 and other of the Reconstruction-era Civil Rights Acts. Although its reading of the legislative history of the 1964 Civil Rights Act persuades the Court that it should not interpose a judicially created bar to the cause of action authorized by that statute, it creates such a bar to claims authorized by the earlier Civil Rights Acts without even mentioning the concerns that prompted their enactment. As a consequence, the Court's analysis is incomplete and ultimately unconvincing.

Preclusion of claims brought under the post-Civil War Acts does not advance the objectives typically associated with finality or federalism. In the employment setting which concerns us here, precluding civil rights claims based on the Reconstruction-era statutes fails to conserve the resources of either the litigants or the courts, because the complainant's companion Title VII claim will still go to federal court under today's decision. Nor does preclusion show respect for state administrative determinations, because litigants apprised of this decision will presumably forgo state administrative determinations for the same reason they currently forgo state judicial review of those determinations — to protect their entitlement to a federal forum.

Needless to say, there is nothing in the legislative history of the post-Civil War legislation remotely suggesting that Congress intended to give binding effect to unreviewed rulings by state administrators in litigation arising under that statute. Quite the contrary, as we explained in *Monroe v. Pape*: "It is abundantly clear that one reason the legislation was passed was to afford a federal right in federal courts because, by reason of prejudice, passion, neglect, intolerance or otherwise, state laws might not be enforced and the claims of citizens to the enjoyment of rights, privileges, and immunities guaranteed by the Fourteenth Amendment might be denied by the state agencies." Due respect for the intent of the Congress that enacted the Civil Rights Act

---

[20] [n.7] Congress of course may decide, as it did in enacting Title VII, that other values outweigh the policy of according finality to state administrative factfinding.

[21] [Editor's note: Justice Marshall took no part in the consideration or decision of this case.]

of 1871, as revealed in the voluminous legislative history of that Act, should preclude the Court from creating a judge-made rule that bars access to the express legislative remedy enacted by Congress.

NOTES

1. Title VII. Title VII, codified at 42 U.S.C. §§ 2000e, *et seq.*, is a federal measure designed to rectify discrimination on account of race, ethnicity, religion, gender and pregnancy in the nation's workplace. It applies to both private- and public-sector employers with 15 or more employees. It has a comparatively short statute-of-limitations, ranging from 180 to 300 days, requires administrative exhaustion, *see* Note 2, *infra*, allows jury trials, authorizes equitable back pay for two years, and provides for compensatory and punitive damages covering pecuniary loss, emotional distress, mental anguish, and "loss of enjoyment of life." Compensatory and punitive damages, however, are limited: $300,000 for employers with over 500 employees; $200,000 for employers with more than 200 employees; $100,000 for employers with more than 100 employees; and $50,000 for employers with more than 14 employees.

Because Title VII prohibits gender- and race-based discrimination in public-sector employment, its remedies often overlap with those available under § 1983 for violations of the Equal Protection Clause. As in *Elliott*, public-sector employees often combine racial and gender discrimination claims under Title VII and § 1983. Evidentiary standards, however, differ markedly under the two statutes. For example, while the Equal Protection Clause demands proof of purposeful discrimination on account of race or gender, *see, e.g., Washington v. Davis*, 426 U.S. 229 (1976), Title VII liability can be premised on disparate impact alone. *See, Griggs v. Duke Power Co.*, 401 U.S. 424 (1971) (construing Title VII to proscribe "not only overt discrimination but also practices that are fair in form but discriminatory in practice").[22]

2. Procedures Under Title VII. The Equal Employment Opportunity Commission (EEOC) is a federal agency charged, *inter alia*, with enforcing Title VII. The EEOC has no adjudicative authority; rather, it is an investigative agency delegated executive powers. Unlike courts (and a host of other federal agencies), it cannot adjudicate disputes between workers and their employers. It can mediate, which sometimes leads to settlements, but ultimately the parties have the right to trials de novo. In order to proceed under Title VII, aggrieved employees must first "exhaust" their administrative remedies by affording the EEOC an opportunity to investigate and perhaps mediate. Because of its demanding workload, the EEOC has negotiated time-share arrangements with various state agencies around the country. As a result, employees' complaints often are referred by the EEOC to one of these state agencies for investigation. On occasion, as was the case in *Elliott*, the state agency may (unlike the EEOC) possess adjudicative authority. If so, its decision may be entitled to judicial deference or outright preclusion under state law in state court proceedings. Notwithstanding state-law rules of this nature, *Elliott* holds that Title VII entitles the parties to de novo judicial proceedings. In short, the administrative determinations, even if rendered in an adjudicative setting, are not entitled to deference and will not preclude the parties from relitigating the issues under Title VII.

---

[22] There is also overlap between § 1981, which prohibits racial discrimination in the making and terms of contracts, *see* Note 2 following *Monroe v. Pape* in Chapter 1.A., *supra*, and Title VII. *See generally* Harold S. Lewis, Jr. & Elizabeth J. Norman, Civil Rights Law and Practice 16 (2004). Section 1981a attempts to separate the two statutes somewhat by stating that a complaining party can recover for unlawful intentional discrimination in employment under Title VII only if he or she cannot recover under § 1981. *See* 42 U.S.C. § 1981a(a)(1). Still, there are good reasons for a plaintiff to use both statutes to redress racial discrimination in employment. *See* Lewis & Norman, *supra*, at 17–19. Title VII is quite complex, as is § 1981, and the intricacies of both fall beyond the contours of this book.

3. Exhaustion Under § 1983. Section 1983 has no general exhaustion requirement. In *Patsy v. Board of Regents*, 457 U.S. 496 (1982), a state university employee (Patsy) filed a § 1983 claim against her employer asserting race and gender discrimination. The District Court dismissed based on Patsy's failure to pursue her administrative remedies. The Supreme Court reversed, holding that § 1983 does not require exhaustion. Hence, one need *not* ordinarily resort to federal or state agencies before filing a claim under § 1983. However, if an administrative claim is filed and decided by a state agency sitting in an adjudicatory capacity, *Elliott* establishes that the agency's decision must be given the same preclusive effect in a subsequent § 1983 action that it would be given in later state court proceedings. Consequently, public-sector employees who experience workplace discrimination are put at some risk should they choose to file administrative claims for relief. An adverse decision by a state adjudicatory agency could preclude further litigation under § 1983. What if the state agency offers something less than an adversarial hearing? Should *Elliott* apply? *See* Ann Woolhandler & Michael Collins, *Judicial Federalism and the Administrative State*, 87 CAL. L. REV. 613, 694–96 (1999) (arguing that *Elliott* should not apply to state administrative proceedings that are not truly adjudicative).

[3] Exhaustion Requirements for Prisoners

The Prison Litigation Reform Act of 1995, 42 U.S.C. § 1997e(a), requires that prisoners who file § 1983 suits challenging "prison conditions" exhaust "available" administrative remedies. *See* 42 U.S.C. § 1997e(a). *See Porter v. Nussle*, 534 U.S. 516 (2002) (holding that the Prison Litigation Reform Act's exhaustion requirement also applies to single instances of excessive force). In *Booth v. Churner*, 532 U.S. 731 (2001), the Court ruled that exhaustion is required even when the prisoner seeks relief, like money damages, that cannot be provided administratively. "[S]o long as some remedy remains available, failure to exhaust is not excused." *Ruggiero v. County of Orange*, 467 F.3d 170 (2d Cir. 2006). Prison remedies, moreover, need not meet any minimal federal standards and need not be "plain, speedy, and effective." *See generally* Lynn S. Branham, *The Prison Litigation Reform Act's Enigmatic Exhaustion Requirement: What It Means and What Congress, Courts and Correctional Officials Can Learn from It*, 86 CORNELL L. REV. 483, 547 (2001) (suggesting modifications to correct Congress' "shoddy work" in drafting the exhaustion requirement).[23]

Exhaustion requirements commonly come with so-called "procedural bars." Federal habeas corpus, for example, requires that inmates first exhaust state judicial remedies before proceeding to federal court. Inmates who cannot exhaust their state judicial remedies because they fail to meet deadlines or preserve objections are often procedurally barred from raising their challenges in a federal habeas court. *See, e.g., Coleman v. Thompson*, 501 U.S. 722 (1991) (observing that procedural bars are merged into federal habeas corpus's exhaustion requirement). Procedural bars have also been commonly joined with exhaustion requirements in administrative settings, *see* ALFRED C. AMAN, JR. & WILLIAM T. MAYTON, ADMINISTRATIVE LAW 428 (2d ed. 2001), though exceptions can be found in various civil rights statutes. Title VII, for instance, requires exhaustion on the part of claimants but has been held not to impose procedural bars. *See EEOC v. Commercial Office Products Co.*, 486 U.S. 107 (1988) (holding that a Title VII claimant's untimely grievance filed with a state agency was irrelevant in determining whether she could proceed in federal court). *See also Oscar Mayer & Co. v. Evans*, 441 U.S. 750 (1979) (finding that the ADEA does not impose a procedural bar on those who fail to timely exhaust age discrimination claims). What about the Prison Litigation Reform Act? Does it impose procedural bars?

---

[23] The remedies available to prisoners under § 1983 have also been restricted by the Prison Litigation Reform Act, *see Miller v. French*, 530 U.S. 327 (2000) (excerpted in Chapter 6.C.[2], *supra*), as has their entitlement to attorney's fees. *See* Note 10 following *Rivera* in Chapter 9.B., *infra*.

WOODFORD v. NGO
Supreme Court of the United States
548 U.S. 81 (2006)

JUSTICE ALITO delivered the opinion of the Court.

This case presents the question whether a prisoner can satisfy the Prison Litigation Reform Act's exhaustion requirement, 42 U.S.C. § 1997e(a), by filing an untimely or otherwise procedurally defective administrative grievance or appeal. We hold that proper exhaustion of administrative remedies is necessary.

[Ngo] is a prisoner who was convicted for murder and is serving a life sentence in the California prison system. In October 2000, [Ngo] was placed in administrative segregation for allegedly engaging in "inappropriate activity" in the prison chapel. Two months later, [Ngo] was returned to the general population, but [Ngo] claims that he was prohibited from participating in "special programs," including a variety of religious activities. Approximately six months after that restriction was imposed, [Ngo] filed a grievance with prison officials challenging that action. That grievance was rejected as untimely because it was not filed within 15 working days of the action being challenged.

"The doctrine of exhaustion of administrative remedies is well established in the jurisprudence of administrative law." . . . Exhaustion of administrative remedies serves two main purposes. First, exhaustion protects "administrative agency authority." Exhaustion gives an agency "an opportunity to correct its own mistakes with respect to the programs it administers before it is haled into federal court," and it discourages "disregard of [the agency's] procedures."

Second, exhaustion promotes efficiency. Claims generally can be resolved much more quickly and economically in proceedings before an agency than in litigation in federal court. In some cases, claims are settled at the administrative level, and in others, the proceedings before the agency convince the losing party not to pursue the matter in federal court. "And even where a controversy survives administrative review, exhaustion of the administrative procedure may produce a useful record for subsequent judicial consideration."

Because exhaustion requirements are designed to deal with parties who do not want to exhaust, administrative law creates an incentive for these parties to do what they would otherwise prefer not to do, namely, to give the agency a fair and full opportunity to adjudicate their claims. Administrative law does this by requiring proper exhaustion of administrative remedies, which "means using all steps that the agency holds out, and doing so *properly* (so that the agency addresses the issues on the merits)." This Court has described the doctrine as follows: "[A]s a general rule . . . courts should not topple over administrative decisions unless the administrative body not only has erred, *but has erred against objection made at the time appropriate under its practice*."

Requiring proper exhaustion . . . gives prisoners an effective incentive to make full use of the prison grievance process and accordingly provides prisons with a fair opportunity to correct their own errors. . . . Proper exhaustion reduces the quantity of prisoner suits because some prisoners are successful in the administrative process, and others are persuaded by the proceedings not to file an action in federal court. Finally, proper exhaustion improves the quality of those prisoner suits that are eventually filed because proper exhaustion often results in the creation of an administrative record that is helpful to the court. When a grievance is filed shortly after the event giving rise to the grievance, witnesses can be identified and questioned while memories are still fresh, and evidence can be gathered and preserved.

[Ngo] . . . suggests that the PLRA exhaustion requirement was patterned on . . . the Age Discrimination in Employment Act of 1967, and . . . Title VII of the Civil Rights Act of 1964, but these are implausible models. Neither of these provisions makes reference to the concept of exhaustion, and neither is in any sense an exhaustion provision.

[T]he ADEA . . . provides that, if a State has an agency to redress state-law age-related employment-discrimination claims, an ADEA claim may not be brought in federal court "before the expiration of sixty days *after proceedings have been commenced* under the State law." (Emphasis added). This provision makes no reference to the exhaustion of state remedies, only to the "commence[ment]" of state proceedings, and this provision leaves no doubt that proper commencement of those proceedings is not required.

Title VII is also fundamentally different from the PLRA exhaustion provision. As interpreted by this Court, [under Title VII] a complainant who "initially institutes proceedings with a state or local agency with authority to grant or seek relief from the practice charged" must "file a charge" with that agency, or "have the EEOC refer the charge to that agency, within 240 days of the alleged discriminatory event. . . . " [W]e [have] held that this filing requirement did not demand that the charge submitted to the state or local authority be filed in compliance with the authority's time limit. Because . . . Title VII refers only to the filing of a charge with a state or local agency and not to the exhaustion of remedies, [it] cannot be viewed as a model for the PLRA exhaustion provision.

[Ngo] maintains that his interpretation of the PLRA exhaustion provision is bolstered by another PLRA provision, 42 U.S.C. § 1997e(c)(2), that permits a district court to dismiss certain prisoner claims "without first requiring the exhaustion of administrative remedies." According to [Ngo], this provision shows that Congress thought that, at the point when a district court might make such a ruling (which would typically be well after the filing of the complaint), a prisoner might still have the opportunity to exhaust administrative remedies. Because short administrative filing deadlines would make this impossible, [Ngo] contends, Congress cannot have thought that a prisoner's failure to comply with those deadlines would preclude litigation in federal court.

[Ngo's] argument is unconvincing for at least two reasons. First, [Ngo] has not shown that Congress had reason to believe that every prison system would have relatively short and categorical filing deadlines. Indeed, [Ngo] asserts that most grievance systems give administrators the discretion to hear untimely grievances. Second, even if dismissals under § 1997e(c)(2) typically occur when the opportunity to pursue administrative remedies has passed, § 1997e(c)(2) still serves a useful function by making it clear that the PLRA exhaustion requirement is not jurisdictional, and thus allowing a district court to dismiss plainly meritless claims without first addressing what may be a much more complex question, namely, whether the prisoner did in fact properly exhaust available administrative remedies.

[Ngo] contends that requiring proper exhaustion will lead prison administrators to devise procedural requirements that are designed to trap unwary prisoners and thus to defeat their claims. [Ngo] does not contend, however, that anything like this occurred in his case, and it is speculative that this will occur in the future. Corrections officials concerned about maintaining order in their institutions have a reason for creating and retaining grievance systems that provide — and that are perceived by prisoners as providing — a meaningful opportunity for prisoners to raise meritorious grievances. And with respect to the possibility that prisons might create procedural requirements for the purpose of tripping up all but the most skillful prisoners, while Congress repealed the "plain, speedy, and effective" standard, we have no occasion here to decide how such situations might be addressed.

[Ngo] argues that requiring proper exhaustion is harsh for prisoners, who generally are untrained in the law and are often poorly educated. This argument overlooks the informality and relative simplicity of prison grievance systems like California's, as well as the fact that prisoners who litigate in federal court generally proceed *pro se* and are forced to comply with numerous unforgiving deadlines and other procedural requirements.

JUSTICE BREYER, concurring in the judgment.

I agree with the Court that, in enacting the Prison Litigation Reform Act (PLRA),Congress intended the term "exhausted" to "mean what the term means in administrative law, where exhaustion means proper exhaustion." I do not believe that Congress desired a system in which prisoners could elect to bypass prison grievance systems without consequences. Administrative law, however, contains well established exceptions to exhaustion. *See generally* II R. PIERCE, ADMINISTRATIVE LAW TREATISE § 15 (4th ed.2002). Moreover, habeas corpus law, which contains an exhaustion requirement that is "substantively similar" to administrative law's and which informs the Court's opinion, also permits a number of exceptions.

At least two Circuits that have interpreted the statute in a manner similar to that which the Court today adopts have concluded that the PLRA's proper exhaustion requirement is not absolute. In my view, on remand, the lower court should similarly consider any challenges that [Ngo] may have concerning whether his case falls into a traditional exception that the statute implicitly incorporates.

JUSTICE STEVENS, with whom JUSTICE SOUTER and JUSTICE GINSBURG join, dissenting.

The waiver doctrine in administrative law is "largely [a] creatur[e] of statute." In other words, many statutes explicitly prohibit courts from considering claims "that ha[ve] not been urged' " before the administrative agency. It is important to emphasize that statutory waiver requirements always mandate, by their plain terms, that courts shall not consider arguments not properly raised before the agency; we have never suggested that the word "exhaustion," standing alone, imposes a statutory waiver requirement.

In the federal administrative law context we have also imposed waiver requirements even in the absence of explicit statutory directive. This judge-made rule, discussed extensively by the majority, however, is based on "an analogy to the rule that appellate courts will not consider arguments not raised before trial courts." [T]his is because, in the context of such appellate review proceedings, procedural errors in the course of exhaustion naturally create bars to review because the decision under review rests on a procedural ground.

Applying these principles, it is clear that ordinary principles of administrative law do not justify engrafting procedural default into the PLRA. The purpose of a § 1983 action such as that filed by [Ngo] is not to obtain direct review of an order entered in the grievance procedure, but to obtain redress for an alleged violation of federal law committed by state corrections officials.

In sum, because federal district court proceedings in prison condition litigation bear no resemblance to appellate review of lower court decisions, the administrative law precedent cited by the majority makes clear that we should not engraft a judge-made procedural default sanction into the PLRA.

Finally, the majority's invocation of judge-made administrative law principles fails for an entirely separate reason: An "established exception" to the judge-made doctrine of procedural default in review of administrative proceedings permits individuals to raise constitutional complaints for the first time in federal court, even if they failed to raise those claims properly before the agency. Because [Ngo] has raised constitutional claims, under our precedent, the Court may not, as a matter of federal common law, apply an extrastatutory waiver requirement against him.

NOTES

1. Exceptions. Justice Breyer observed in his concurring opinion in *Ngo* that administrative law ordinarily recognizes exceptions to the procedural-bar requirement attached to exhaustion. Constitutional claims, for example, cannot generally be considered by agencies and thus are not forfeited when not specifically raised before an agency. *See, e.g., Mathews v. Eldridge*, 424 U.S. 319 (1976) (noting that constitutional claims that are not raised before federal agencies are not barred in subsequent review proceedings in federal court). Administrative law also recognizes a "futility" exception, which commonly holds that administrative proceedings need not be exhausted when the agency lacks the authority to render the requested relief, *see, e.g., McCarthy v. Madigan*, 503 U.S. 140 (1992) (finding that the agency was not competent to award damages), has already decided the matter, *see, e.g., Brand v. Lewis*, 784 F.2d 1515 (11th Cir. 1986) (holding that because a state court had already decided the matter, a federal habeas court did not have to await exhaustion), or is unduly biased. *See, e.g., Gibson v. Berryhill*, 411 U.S. 564 (1973) (holding that the agency was comprised in violation of Due Process). Because the Prison Litigation Reform Act states that prisoners challenging prison conditions must exhaust "administrative remedies as are available," however, it appears clear that this particular "futility" exception will not save an inmate's claim. A prison's inability to award any particular form of relief cannot itself excuse bypassing the prison's procedures. *See Booth v. Churner*, 532 U.S. 731 (2001) (holding that the substance of a claim must first be exhausted even though the prison cannot pay money damages).

Undue prejudice and hardship have also been recognized as exceptions to the usual exhaustion requirements. *See, e.g., McKart v. United States*, 395 U.S. 185 (1969) (observing that a procedural bar would place undue hardship on a draftee who sought to challenge his selective service classification in a criminal proceeding). In particular, lengthy or indefinite administrative delays and timeframes have been found to cause undue prejudice. *See, e.g., Gibson v. Berryhill*, 411 U.S. 564 (1973) (observing that administrative remedies are deemed inadequate "[m]ost often . . . because of delay by the agency"). Justice Stevens, dissenting in *Ngo*, pointed out that federal habeas law also recognizes exceptions to its exhaustion requirement: habeas "petitioners [can] overcome procedural defaults if they can show that the procedural rule is not firmly established and regularly followed, if they can demonstrate cause and prejudice to overcome a procedural default, or if enforcing the procedural default rule would result in a miscarriage of justice."

2. Heightened Pleading for Inmates. The Supreme Court in *Jones v. Bock*, 549 U.S. 199 (2007), in an opinion by the Chief Justice, unanimously ruled that the Prison Litigation Reform Act's exhaustion requirement creates an affirmative defense that must be raised by the defendant rather than pleaded by the prisoner-plaintiff. The Court rejected the charge that "policy concerns" justified saddling inmates with a heightened pleading requirement; absent an express change by Congress, "the usual practice should be followed." The Supreme Court also rejected a Sixth Circuit rule requiring that inmates specifically identify in their administrative complaints all defendants later charged under § 1983: "The PLRA requires exhaustion of 'such administrative remedies as are available,' but nothing in the statute imposes a 'name all defendants' requirement along the lines of the Sixth Circuit's judicially created rule." Because exhaustion's demands are a function of available local remedies, "[t]he level of detail necessary in a grievance to comply with the grievance procedures will vary from system to system and claim to claim. . . . [B]ut . . . exhaustion is not *per se* inadequate simply because an individual later sued was not named in the grievances." As a final matter, the Supreme Court in *Jones v. Bock* overturned the Sixth Circuit's "total exhaustion" rule, which required the dismissal of an inmate's entire complaint when any claim had not been properly exhausted: "we have never heard of an entire complaint being thrown out simply because one of several discrete claims was barred by the statute of limitations, and it is hard to imagine what purpose such a rule would serve." "As a general matter, if a complaint contains both good and bad claims, the court proceeds with the good and leaves the bad."

3. Former Inmates. Lower courts have unanimously agreed that the PLRA's exhaustion requirement does not apply to § 1983 challenges filed by *former* inmates, even when the challenge is based on prison conditions. *See, e.g., Michau v. Charleston County*, 434 F.3d 725 (4th Cir. 2006); *Nerness v. Johnson*, 401 F.3d 874 (8th Cir. 2005).

[4] Appealing Adjudicative Decisions

Most state administrative mechanisms provide that an adjudicative agency's decision can be appealed to a state court. If not appealed, the agency's decision then becomes final, conclusive, and otherwise subject to preclusion. Should an appeal be taken, state law commonly instructs the court to defer to the agency's fact-finding. Either way, a state reviewing court is to some extent bound by the agency's decision. Is this true of a federal district court acting under § 1983? Can one even "appeal" a state adjudicative agency's decision to the federal court system? The next case sheds light on these questions.

CITY OF CHICAGO v. INTERNATIONAL COLLEGE OF SURGEONS
Supreme Court of the United States
522 U.S. 156 (1997)

JUSTICE O'CONNOR delivered the opinion of the Court.

[The] International College of Surgeons and the United States Section of the International College of Surgeons (jointly ICS) own two properties on North Lake Shore Drive in the city of Chicago. In July 1988, the Chicago Landmarks Commission made a preliminary determination that seven buildings on Lake Shore Drive, including two mansions on ICS' properties, qualified for designation as a landmark district under the city's Landmarks Ordinance. In June 1989, the city council enacted an ordinance (the Designation Ordinance) designating the landmark district.

In February 1989, after the Commission's preliminary determination, ICS executed a contract for the sale and redevelopment of its properties. The contract called for the developer, whose interest has since been acquired by respondent Robin Construction Company, to demolish all but the facades of the two mansions and to construct a high-rise condominium tower. In October 1990, ICS applied to the Landmarks Commission for the necessary permits to allow demolition of a designated landmark. The Commission denied the permit applications, finding that the proposed demolition would "adversely affect and destroy significant historical and architectural features of the [landmark] district." ICS then reapplied for the permits under a provision of the Landmarks Ordinance allowing for exceptions in cases of economic hardship. The Commission again denied the applications, finding that ICS did not qualify for the hardship exception.

Following each of the Commission's decisions, ICS filed actions for judicial review in the Circuit Court of Cook County pursuant to the Illinois Administrative Review Law. Both of ICS' complaints raised a number of federal constitutional claims, including that the Landmarks and Designation Ordinances, both on their face and as applied, violate the Due Process and Equal Protection Clauses and effect a taking of property without just compensation under the Fifth and Fourteenth Amendments, and that the manner in which the Commission conducted its administrative proceedings violated ICS' rights to due process and equal protection. The complaints also sought relief under the Illinois

Constitution as well as administrative review of the Commission's decisions denying the permits.

The defendants (collectively City) . . . removed both lawsuits to the District Court for the Northern District of Illinois on the basis of federal question jurisdiction. The District Court consolidated the cases. After dismissing some of the constitutional claims and exercising supplemental jurisdiction over the state law claims, the court granted summary judgment in favor of the City, ruling that the Landmarks and Designation Ordinances and the Commission's proceedings were consistent with the Federal and State Constitutions, and that the Commission's findings were supported by the evidence in the record and were not arbitrary and capricious.

The Court of Appeals for the Seventh Circuit reversed and remanded the case to state court, concluding that the District Court was without jurisdiction.

We granted certiorari to address whether a case containing claims that local administrative action violates federal law, but also containing state law claims for on-the-record review of the administrative findings, is within the jurisdiction of federal district courts.

We have reviewed on several occasions the circumstances in which cases filed initially in state court may be removed to federal court. As a general matter, defendants may remove to the appropriate federal district court "any civil action brought in a State court of which the district courts of the United States have original jurisdiction." 28 U.S.C. § 1441(a).[24] The propriety of removal thus depends on whether the case originally could have been filed in federal court. The district courts have original jurisdiction under the federal question statute over cases "arising under the Constitution, laws, or treaties of the United States." § 1331. "It is long settled law that a cause of action arises under federal law only when the plaintiff's well-pleaded complaint raises issues of federal law."

In this case, there can be no question that ICS' state court complaints raised a number of issues of federal law in the form of various federal constitutional challenges to the Landmarks and Designation Ordinances, and to the manner in which the Commission conducted the administrative proceedings. It is true, as ICS asserts, that the federal constitutional claims were raised by way of a cause of action created by state law, namely, the Illinois Administrative Review Law. *See Howard v. Lawton*, 22 Ill.2d 331, 333, 175 N.E.2d 556, 557 (1961) (constitutional claims may be raised in a complaint for administrative review). As we have explained, however, "[e]ven though state law creates [a party's] causes of action, its case might still 'arise under' the laws of the United States if a well-pleaded complaint established that its right to relief under state law requires resolution of a substantial question of federal law." ICS' federal constitutional claims, which turn exclusively on federal law, unquestionably fit within this rule. Accordingly, ICS errs in relying on the established principle that a plaintiff, as master of the complaint, can "choose to have the cause heard in state court." By raising several claims that arise under federal law, ICS subjected itself to the possibility that the City would remove the case to the federal courts.

As for ICS' accompanying state law claims, this Court has long adhered to principles of pendent and ancillary jurisdiction by which the federal courts' original jurisdiction

---

[24] [Editor's note: In addition, 28 U.S.C. § 1441(b) authorizes removal from state to federal court of "[a]ny civil action of which the district courts have original jurisdiction founded on a claim or right arising under the Constitution, treaties or laws of the United States. . . . " Section 1441(c), in turn, authorizes the removal of otherwise "non-removable" claims joined with removable federal questions. Section 1441 is commonly used to remove federal claims, including those under § 1983, from state to federal court. Unlike in diversity cases, moreover, a defendant's domicile is not relevant to whether a federal question case can be removed from state to federal court. While a separate removal statute, 28 U.S.C. § 1443, exists for civil rights claims, it "has received narrow constructions from the Supreme Court . . . and is rarely used successfully." HOWARD P. FINK, ET. AL, FEDERAL COURTS IN THE 21ST CENTURY: CASES AND MATERIALS 430 (1996).]

over federal questions carries with it jurisdiction over state law claims that "derive from a common nucleus of operative fact," such that "the relationship between [the federal] claim and the state claim permits the conclusion that the entire action before the court comprises but one constitutional 'case.'" *Mine Workers v. Gibbs*, 383 U.S. 715, 725 (1966). Congress has codified those principles in the supplemental jurisdiction statute, which combines the doctrines of pendent and ancillary jurisdiction under a common heading. 28 U.S.C. § 1367. The statute provides, "in any civil action of which the district courts have original jurisdiction, the district courts shall have supplemental jurisdiction over all other claims that are so related to claims in the action within such original jurisdiction that they form part of the same case or controversy under Article III of the United States Constitution." § 1367(a). That provision applies with equal force to cases removed to federal court as to cases initially filed there; a removed case is necessarily one "of which the district courts . . . have original jurisdiction." *See* § 1441(a).

Here, . . . the state and federal claims "derive from a common nucleus of operative fact," namely, ICS' unsuccessful efforts to obtain demolition permits from the Chicago Landmarks Commission. That is all the statute requires to establish supplemental jurisdiction (barring an express statutory exception, see § 1367(a)).

ICS, urging us to adopt the reasoning of the Court of Appeals, argues that the District Court was without jurisdiction over its actions because they contain state law claims that require on-the-record review of the Landmarks Commission's decisions. A claim that calls for deferential judicial review of a state administrative determination, ICS asserts, does not constitute a "civil action . . . of which the district courts of the United States have original jurisdiction" under 28 U.S.C. § 1441(a).

That reasoning starts with an erroneous premise. Because this is a federal question case, the relevant inquiry is not, as ICS submits, whether its state claims for on-the-record review of the Commission's decisions are "civil actions" within the "original jurisdiction" of a district court: The District Court's original jurisdiction derives from ICS' federal claims, not its state law claims. Those federal claims suffice to make the actions "civil actions" within the "original jurisdiction" of the district courts for purposes of removal. § 1441(a).

The dissent [argues] . . . that federal jurisdiction would lie over ICS' federal claims if they had been brought under 42 U.S.C. § 1983, because review would then range beyond the administrative record; but ICS deliberately confined review of its claims to the administrative record by raising them under the Illinois Administrative Review Law, thereby assuring itself a state forum. The essential premise of [this] argument is that [ICS's] actions arise solely under state law and so are not within the district courts' federal question jurisdiction, and that § 1367(a) — which presupposes a "civil action of which the district courts have original jurisdiction" — is thus inapplicable.

That reasoning is incorrect because ICS in fact raised claims not bound by the administrative record (its facial constitutional claims), and because, as we have explained, the facial and as-applied federal constitutional claims raised by ICS "arise under" federal law for purposes of federal question jurisdiction. *See New Orleans Public Service, Inc. v. Council of City of New Orleans*, 491 U.S. 350, 372 (1989) ("[A] facial challenge to an allegedly unconstitutional . . . zoning ordinance" is a claim "which we would assuredly not require to be brought in state courts").

There is nothing in the text of § 1367(a) that indicates an exception to supplemental jurisdiction for claims that require on-the-record review of a state or local administrative determination. Instead, the statute generally confers supplemental jurisdiction over "all other claims" in the same case or controversy as a federal question, without reference to the nature of review. Congress could of course establish an exception to supplemental jurisdiction for claims requiring deferential review of state administrative decisions, but the statute, as written, bears no such construction.

After all, district courts routinely conduct deferential review pursuant to their original jurisdiction over federal questions, including on-the-record review of federal administrative action. See *Califano v. Sanders*, 430 U.S. 99, 105–107 (1977). Nothing in § 1367(a) suggests that district courts are without supplemental jurisdiction over claims seeking precisely the same brand of review of local administrative determinations.

The dissent disagrees with our conclusion that 28 U.S.C. § 1367(a) encompasses state law claims for on-the-record review of local administrative action, but it is unclear exactly why, for the dissent never directly challenges our application of that statute to ICS' claims. In fact, the dissent only makes passing reference to the terms of § 1367(a), which, in our view, resolve the case. In this light, the dissent's candid misgivings about attempting to square its position with the text of the jurisdictional statutes are understandable. And the failure to come to grips with the text of § 1367(a) explains the dissent's repeated assumption that the jurisdictional analysis of diversity cases would be no different. But to decide that state law claims for on-the-record review of a local agency's decision fall within the district courts' "supplemental" jurisdiction under § 1367(a), does not answer the question, nor do we, whether those same claims, if brought alone, would substantiate the district courts' "original" jurisdiction over diversity cases under § 1332. Ultimately, the dissent never addresses this case as it is presented: a case containing federal questions within the meaning of § 1331 and supplemental state law claims within the meaning of § 1367(a).

Of course, to say that the terms of § 1367(a) authorize the district courts to exercise supplemental jurisdiction over state law claims for on-the-record review of administrative decisions does not mean that the jurisdiction must be exercised in all cases. Our decisions have established that pendent jurisdiction "is a doctrine of discretion, not of plaintiff's right," *Gibbs*, 383 U.S., at 726, and that district courts can decline to exercise jurisdiction over pendent claims for a number of valid reasons. . . . The supplemental jurisdiction statute codifies these principles.

In addition to their discretion under § 1367(c), district courts may be obligated not to decide state law claims (or to stay their adjudication) where one of the abstention doctrines articulated by this Court applies. Those doctrines embody the general notion that "federal courts may decline to exercise their jurisdiction, in otherwise exceptional circumstances, where denying a federal forum would clearly serve an important countervailing interest, for example where abstention is warranted by considerations of proper constitutional adjudication, regard for federal-state relations, or wise judicial administration." *Quackenbush v. Allstate Ins. Co.*, 517 U.S. 706, 716 (1996).

The District Court properly recognized that it could exercise supplemental jurisdiction over ICS' state law claims, including the claims for on-the-record administrative review of the Landmarks Commission's decisions. ICS contends that abstention principles required the District Court to decline to exercise supplemental jurisdiction, and also alludes to its contention below that the District Court should have refused to exercise supplemental jurisdiction under 28 U.S.C. § 1367(c). We express no view on those matters, but think it the preferable course to allow the Court of Appeals to address them in the first instance.

JUSTICE GINSBURG, with whom JUSTICE STEVENS joins, dissenting.

This now-federal case originated as an appeal in state court from a municipal agency's denials of demolition permits. The review that state law provides is classically appellate in character — on the agency's record, not de novo. Nevertheless, the Court decides today that this standard brand of appellate review can be shifted from the appropriate state tribunal to a federal court of first instance at the option of either party — plaintiff originally or defendant by removal. The Court approves this enlargement of district court authority explicitly in federal-question cases, and by inescapable implication in diversity cases, satisfied that "neither the jurisdictional statutes nor our prior decisions suggest that federal jurisdiction is lacking."

The Court's authorization of cross-system appeals qualifies as a watershed decision. After today, litigants asserting federal-question or diversity jurisdiction may routinely lodge in federal courts direct appeals from the actions of all manner of local (county and municipal) agencies, boards, and commissions. Exercising this cross-system appellate authority, federal courts may now directly superintend local agencies by affirming, reversing, or modifying their administrative rulings.

Until now it has been taken almost for granted that federal courts of first instance lack authority under §§ 1331 and 1332 to displace state courts as forums for on-the-record review of state and local agency actions. . . . Cross-system appellate authority is entrusted to this Court, we said in *Rooker v. Fidelity Trust Co.*, 263 U.S. 413 (1923), but it is outside the domain of the lower federal courts. Interpreting the statutory predecessors of 28 U.S.C. §§ 1331 and 1257, we held in *Rooker* that a federal district court could not modify a decision of the Indiana Supreme Court, for only this Court could exercise such authority.

Today, the Court holds that Congress, by enacting § 1367, has authorized federal district courts to conduct deferential, on-the-record review of local agency decisions whenever a federal question is pended to the agency review action. Dismissing, as irrelevant to jurisdiction, the distinction between de novo and deferential review, the Court also provides easy access to federal court whenever the dissatisfied party in a local agency proceeding has the requisite diverse citizenship. The Court does all this despite the overwhelming weight of lower federal court decisions disclaiming cross-system appellate authority, and without even a hint from Congress that so startling a reallocation of power from state courts to federal courts was within the national lawmakers' contemplation.[25]

Until today, federal habeas corpus proceedings were the closest we had come to cross-system appellate review. *See* 28 U.S.C. §§ 2241–2254. Unlike the jurisdictional reallocation the Court now endorses, habeas corpus jurisdiction does not entail direct review of a state or local authority's decision. Notably, in providing for federal habeas corpus review, Congress has taken great care to avoid interrupting or intruding upon state-court processes. *See, e.g.*, 28 U.S.C. § 2254(b)(1) (requiring exhaustion of state remedies before filing a federal petition for writ of habeas corpus). The Court's holding in this "Chicago" case, however, permits the federal court to supplant the State's entire scheme for judicial review of local administrative actions.

When a local actor or agency violates a person's federal right, it is indeed true that the aggrieved party may bring an action under 42 U.S.C. § 1983 without first exhausting state remedies. *See Patsy v. Board of Regents of Fla.*, 457 U.S. 496 (1982). But such an action involves no disregard, as the cross-system appeal does, of the separateness of state and federal adjudicatory systems. In a § 1983 action, a federal (or state) court inquires whether a person, acting under color of state law, has subjected another "to the deprivation of any rights, privileges, or immunities secured by the Constitution and [federal] laws." The court exercises original, not appellate, jurisdiction; it proceeds independently, not as substantial evidence reviewer on a nonfederal agency's record.

If, as the Court reasons today, the distinction between de novo and deferential review is inconsequential, then a district court may, indeed must, entertain cross-

---

[25] [n.3] The Court's holding can embrace the decisions of state, as opposed to local, agencies, only if the State consents to the district court's jurisdiction. In *Pennhurst State School and Hospital v. Halderman*, 465 U.S. 89 (1984), the Court held it would violate the Eleventh Amendment for a federal court to entertain, without the State's consent, "a claim that state officials violated state law in carrying out their official responsibilities." The Court further held that "this principle applies as well to state-law claims brought into federal court under pendent jurisdiction." Notably, the Court commented in *Pennhurst*: "[I]t is difficult to think of a greater intrusion on state sovereignty than when a federal court instructs state officials on how to conform their conduct to state law."

system, on-the-record appeals from local agency decisions — without regard to the presence or absence of any federal question — whenever the parties meet the diversity-of-citizenship requirement of § 1332. The Court so confirms by noting that, in accord with *Califano v. Sanders*, 430 U.S. 99 (1977), "district courts routinely conduct deferential review [of federal administrative action] pursuant to their original jurisdiction over federal questions." Just as routinely, it now appears, district courts must "conduct deferential review [of local administrative action] pursuant to their original jurisdiction over [diversity cases]."

Statutes like the Illinois Administrative Review Law explicitly provide for state-court judicial review of state and local agency decisions. Unlike the federal picture the Court confronted in *Sanders*, there is no void to fill. The gap to which *Sanders* attended — the absence of any forum for "nonstatutory" review of federal agency decisions unless § 1331 provided one — simply does not exist in a case brought under a state measure like the Illinois Administrative Review Law.

ICS acknowledged that it might have chosen to bypass on-the-record administrative review in state court, invoking federal jurisdiction under § 1983 instead, without exhausting state remedies. Had ICS done so, review would have been "plenary in its scope" and would not have been "confined by the administrative record." But ICS did not take that path. It proceeded under the Illinois Administrative Review Law seeking resolution of both state-law and federal constitutional issues "in the context of on-the-record administrative review."

In *Ankenbrandt v. Richards*, 504 U.S. 689 (1992), we addressed the question whether civil actions for divorce, alimony, or child custody fall within § 1332 when the parties are of diverse citizenship. Nothing in the text of the Constitution or in the words of § 1332 excluded parties from bringing such "civil actions" in federal court. Historically, however, decrees terminating marriages had been considered wholly within the State's domain. That understanding, we noted in *Ankenbrandt*, had prevailed "for nearly a century and a half."

History and policy tug strongly here as well. There surely has been no "expression of congressional dissatisfaction" with the near-unanimous view of the Circuits that federal courts may not engage in cross-system appellate review, and "the elaboration of [state] administrative law" is a "prim[e] responsibilit[y] of the state judiciary."

NOTES

1. Revisiting the Eleventh Amendment. The Eleventh Amendment, remember, protects state agencies from claims to money damages in federal court. *See* Chapter 3.A., *supra*. Consequently, private claims for money damages against state agencies are barred from federal court, whether they are premised on § 1983, *see Edelman v. Jordan*, excerpted in Chapter 3.B., *supra*, or state law. *See Raygor v. Regents of the University of Minnesota*, 534 U.S. 533 (2002) ("we hold that § 1367(a)'s grant of [supplemental] jurisdiction does not extend to claims against nonconsenting state defendants"). The most a private plaintiff can win from a state agency in federal court is prospective relief (*e.g.*, an injunction or declaratory judgment) *under federal law*. *See Ex parte Young*, 209 U.S. 123 (1908) (discussed in Note 1 following *Edelman* in Chapter 3.B., *supra*).

As noted by Justice Ginsburg in footnote 3 to her dissenting opinion, the Eleventh Amendment also prohibits private plaintiffs from pursuing prospective relief against state agencies *under state law* in federal court. *See Pennhurst State School and Hospital v. Halderman*, 465 U.S. 89 (1984) (discussed in Note 1 following *Edelman* in Chapter 3.B., *supra*). Because local government does not share the state's protections, *see Lincoln County v. Luning*, 133 U.S. 529 (1890) (discussed in Note 4 following *Seminole Tribe* in Chapter 3.A., *supra*), claims for damages and prospective relief, whether under federal or state law, do not pose a problem under the Eleventh Amendment. Claims challenging a state adjudicative agency decision would thus appear to be limited to prospective relief under federal law should a cross-system appeal be taken into federal court. In contrast, claims against a local agency, like that in *International College of Surgeons*, pose no Eleventh Amendment difficulties.

2. *Rooker-Feldman*. Justice Ginsburg's dissent cites *Rooker v. Fidelity Trust Co.*, 263 U.S. 413 (1923), for the proposition that "[c]ross-system appellate authority is entrusted to [the Supreme Court], . . . but is outside the domain of the lower federal courts." The gist of *Rooker*, and its more recent manifestation, *District of Columbia Court of Appeals v. Feldman*, 460 U.S. 462 (1983), which held that lower federal courts have no jurisdiction to hear "challenges to state court decisions in particular cases arising out of judicial proceedings" or issues "inextricably intertwined" with state court judgments), is that the lower federal courts do not have the authority to hear "appeals" from state courts.

The precise rationale for the *Rooker-Feldman* doctrine is not overly clear. It appears to be a function of a lack of statutory support for appellate review of state court judgments by lower federal courts,[26] federal respect for state courts (*e.g.*, *Younger v. Harris*, 401 U.S. 37 (1971) (excerpted in Chapter 7.B., *supra*)), and a judicial preference for closure (*e.g.*, claim and issue preclusion). *See* HOWARD P. FINK, LINDA S. MULLENIX, THOMAS D. ROWE, JR., & MARK V. TUSHNET, FEDERAL COURTS IN THE 21ST CENTURY 868 (1996). Professor Suzanna Sherry has reported that between 1983 and 1999, the Supreme Court did not use the *Rooker-Feldman* doctrine once to bar a case from federal court. *See* Suzanna Sherry, *Judicial Federalism in the Trenches: The* Rooker-Feldman *Doctrine in Action*, 74 NOTRE DAME L. REV. 1085, 1087–88 (1999). During this same time frame, however, *Rooker-Feldman* experienced "explosive growth in the lower courts." *Id.* Notwithstanding its tenuous justification, *Rooker-Feldman* became a darling of the lower federal courts. Indeed, some lower federal courts used *Rooker-Feldman* to justify dismissal whenever there was a prior or parallel state-court proceeding involving the same subject matter. Far from just preventing appeals from state court to federal district court, *Rooker-Feldman* became a substitute for abstention and preclusion doctrines.

The Supreme Court sought to correct this abuse of *Rooker-Feldman* in *Exxon Mobil Corp. v. Saudi Basic Industries Corp.*, 544 U.S. 280 (2005), a suit between parties to a polyethylene production/sales agreement. Following a dispute over royalties, Saudi Basic (SABIC) preemptively sued ExxonMobil in Delaware Superior Court seeking a declaratory judgment that it had complied with the terms of the agreement. Two weeks later, ExxonMobil sued SABIC in federal district court alleging breach of contract.[27] Following the Delaware court's entry of judgment in favor of ExxonMobil, the Third Circuit (which had taken the case on appeal) invoked the *Rooker-Feldman* doctrine on its own motion to dismiss the case. In an opinion by Justice Ginsburg, the Supreme Court unanimously reversed:

> The *Rooker-Feldman* doctrine, we hold today, is confined to cases of the kind from which the doctrine acquired its name: cases brought by state-court losers complaining of injuries caused by state-court judgments rendered before the district court proceedings commenced and inviting district court review and rejection of those judgments. *Rooker-Feldman* does not otherwise override or supplant preclusion doctrine or augment the circumscribed doctrines that allow federal courts to stay or dismiss proceedings in deference to state-court actions.

---

[26] Section 1257 of title 28 of the United States Code, by way of contrast, authorizes the Supreme Court to review final decisions "rendered by the highest court of a State in which a decision could be had." By negative implication, the argument goes, this precludes lower federal courts from hearing appeals from state courts.

[27] Exxon claimed federal jurisdiction was proper because SABIC was an arm of the Saudi government. *See* 28 U.S.C. § 1330 (authorizing federal jurisdiction over actions against foreign states).

In *Rooker v. Fidelity Trust*, the parties defeated in state court turned to a Federal District Court for relief. Alleging that the adverse state-court judgment was rendered in contravention of the Constitution, they asked the federal court to declare it "null and void."

Sixty years later, the Court decided *District of Columbia Court of Appeals v. Feldman*. The two plaintiffs in that case, Hickey and Feldman, neither of whom had graduated from an accredited law school, petitioned the District of Columbia Court of Appeals to waive a court Rule that required D.C. bar applicants to have graduated from a law school approved by the American Bar Association. After the D.C. court denied their waiver requests, Hickey and Feldman filed suits in the United States District Court for the District of Columbia.

Recalling *Rooker*, this Court's opinion in *Feldman* observed first that the District Court lacked authority to review a final judicial determination of the D.C. high court. "Review of such determinations," the *Feldman* opinion reiterated, "can be obtained only in this Court." The "crucial question," the Court next stated, was whether the proceedings in the D.C. court were "judicial in nature."

In applying the accreditation Rule to the Hickey and Feldman waiver petitions, this Court determined, the D.C. court had acted judicially. As to that adjudication, *Feldman* held, this Court alone among federal courts had review authority.[28]

Since *Feldman*, this Court has never applied *Rooker-Feldman* to dismiss an action for want of jurisdiction.

Rooker and *Feldman* exhibit the limited circumstances in which this Court's appellate jurisdiction over state-court judgments . . . precludes a United States district court from exercising subject-matter jurisdiction in an action it would otherwise be empowered to adjudicate under a congressional grant of authority. In both cases, the losing party in state court filed suit in federal court after the state proceedings ended, complaining of an injury caused by the state-court judgment and seeking review and rejection of that judgment. Plaintiffs in both cases, alleging federal-question jurisdiction, called upon the District Court to overturn an injurious state-court judgment. Because § 1257, as long interpreted, vests authority to review a state court's judgment solely in this Court, the District Courts in *Rooker* and *Feldman* lacked subject-matter jurisdiction.[29]

When there is parallel state and federal litigation, *Rooker-Feldman* is not triggered simply by the entry of judgment in state court. This Court has repeatedly held that "the pendency of an action in the state court is no bar to proceedings concerning the same matter in the Federal court having jurisdiction." Comity or abstention doctrines [*see* Chapter 7, *supra*] may, in various circumstances, permit or require the federal court to stay or dismiss the federal action in favor of the state-court litigation. But neither *Rooker* nor *Feldman* supports the notion that properly invoked concurrent jurisdiction vanishes if a state court reaches judgment on the same or related question while the case remains *sub judice* in a federal court.

---

[28] [Editor's note: Justice Ginsburg observed, however, that *Feldman* would not prevent the same plaintiffs from turning to federal court to challenge the facial validity of the District of Columbia's bar rule. "The Rule could be contested in federal court, this Court held [in *Feldman*], so long as plaintiffs did not seek review of the Rule's application in a particular case."]

[29] [n.8] Congress, if so minded, may explicitly empower district courts to oversee certain state-court judgments and has done so, most notably, in authorizing federal habeas review of state prisoners' petitions.

Disposition of the federal action, once the state-court adjudication is complete, would be governed by preclusion law. . . . In parallel litigation, a federal court may be bound to recognize the claim- and issue-preclusive effects of a state-court judgment, but federal jurisdiction over an action does not terminate automatically on the entry of judgment in the state court.

ExxonMobil plainly has not repaired to federal court to undo the Delaware judgment in its favor. Rather, it appears ExxonMobil filed suit in Federal District Court (only two weeks after SABIC filed in Delaware and well before any judgment in state court) to protect itself in the event it lost in state court on grounds (such as the state statute of limitations) that might not preclude relief in the federal venue.[30] *Rooker-Feldman* did not prevent the District Court from exercising jurisdiction when ExxonMobil filed the federal action, and it did not emerge to vanquish jurisdiction after ExxonMobil prevailed in the Delaware courts.

The Court reiterated *Exxon Mobil*'s caution about *Rooker-Feldman* in *Lance v. Dennis*, 546 U.S. 459 (2006), a redistricting challenge filed in federal court on the heals of a Colorado Supreme Court ruling that a court-ordered plan took precedence over a new plan drafted by the state's General Assembly. The three-judge District Court dismissed the federal claim based on *Rooker-Feldman*, holding that the challengers were necessarily "in privity" for purposes of *Rooker-Feldman* with the General Assembly which unsuccessfully defended its action before the Colorado Supreme Court. Their subsequent action before the three-judge District Court was therefore, in effect, an impermissible "appeal" of the General Assembly's loss in the Colorado Supreme Court. The Supreme Court reversed in a brief *per curiam* opinion:

> The District Court erroneously conflated preclusion law with *Rooker-Feldman*. Whatever the impact of privity principles on preclusion rules, *Rooker-Feldman* is not simply preclusion by another name. The doctrine applies only in limited circumstances, where a party in effect seeks to take an appeal of an unfavorable state-court decision to a lower federal court. The *Rooker-Feldman* doctrine does not bar actions by nonparties to the earlier state-court judgment simply because, for purposes of preclusion law, they could be considered in privity with a party to the judgment. . . . Congress has directed federal courts to look principally to *state* law in deciding what effect to give state-court judgments. Incorporation of preclusion principles into *Rooker-Feldman* risks turning that limited doctrine into a uniform *federal* rule governing the preclusive effect of state-court judgments, contrary to the Full Faith and Credit Act.

3. Terri Schiavo. The well-publicized death of Terri Schiavo in the spring of 2005 raised several doctrinal and procedural problems under § 1983. Schiavo suffered cardiac arrest, fell into a persistent vegetative state, and was placed on artificial life support (which included the insertion of nutrition and hydration tubes) in 1990. *See Bush v. Schiavo*, 885 So. 2d 321 (Fla. 2004). In 1998, a Florida judge found that clear and convincing evidence demonstrated that Schiavo did not want artificial assistance to remain alive. Over her parents' objections, the judge ordered the removal of her feeding tubes. Following years of legal wrangling between Schiavo's husband and her parents — including an ultimately unsuccessful resort to Florida's legislature[31] — the judge again ordered removal of Schiavo's nutrition and hydration tubes in 2004.

---

[30] [n.9] The Court of Appeals criticized ExxonMobil for pursuing its federal suit as an "insurance policy" against an adverse result in state court. There is nothing necessarily inappropriate, however, about filing a protective action.

[31] The Florida legislature in October 2003 passed a private bill authorizing Florida's Governor, Jeb Bush, to override a local judge's order to remove Schiavo's feeding and hydration tubes. The Florida Supreme Court

Once it became clear that they had exhausted all avenues of relief available under Florida law, Schiavo's parents turned to Congress for assistance. In March 2005 Congress passed, and the President signed, a private bill granting Schiavo's parents standing to challenge the Florida judge's order, awarding the United States District Court for the Middle District of Florida jurisdiction over the subject matter of a "suit or claim by or on behalf of Theresa Marie Schiavo for the alleged violation of any right of Theresa Marie Schiavo under the Constitution or laws of the United States relating to the withholding or withdrawing of food, fluids, or medical treatment necessary to sustain her life," and instructing the Middle District to "determine de novo any claim of a violation of any right of Theresa Marie Schiavo within the scope of this Act, notwithstanding any prior State court determination and regardless of whether such a claim has previously been raised, considered, or decided in State court proceedings . . . without any delay or abstention in favor of State court proceedings, and regardless of whether remedies available in the State courts have been exhausted." *See Schiavo ex rel. Schindler v. Schiavo*, 404 F.3d 1277 (11th Cir. 2005) (denying rehearing en banc) (quoting Pub. L. 109-3).

The District Court conducted two emergency hearings before denying the parents' requested emergency relief. *See Schiavo ex rel. Schindler v. Schiavo*, 357 F. Supp. 2d 1378 (M.D. Fla. 2005); *Schiavo ex rel. Schindler v. Schiavo*, 358 F. Supp. 2d 1161 (M.D. Fla. 2005). In sum, the District Court concluded that the parents could not show that they were likely to prevail on the merits of their constitutional claims; their daughter had been afforded all the substantive and procedural process due her under the Fourteenth Amendment; she was not likely denied equal protection; no state actor had infringed her First Amendment religious rights; and she was not being punished in violation of the Eighth Amendment. Both the Eleventh Circuit, *see* 403 F.3d 1223 (11th Cir. 2005); 403 F.3d 1289 (11th Cir. 2005); 403 F.3d 1261 (11th Cir. 2005) (denying rehearing en banc); 403 F.3d 1270 (11th Cir. 2005) (denying rehearing en banc), and the Supreme Court refused to intervene. *See* 544 U.S. 947 (2005) (denying stay and certiorari). Schiavo died a short time later. *See* Jack M. Beerman, *Federal Court Self-Preservation and Terri Schiavo*, 54 BUFF. L. REV. 553 (2006) (chronicling the Schiavo matter and arguing that the federal courts ultimately refused to intervene, in part, because they did not want to be put in a position of having to order the withdraw of life support).

Was the Schiavo legislation necessary? Although it would appear that constitutional arguments existed to support a credible complaint under § 1983 prior to the private bill's enactment, any suit on Schiavo's behalf in federal court would likely have run into preclusion problems, as well as difficulties under standing doctrine (*see* Chapter 6.C.[1], *supra*), abstention principles (*see* Chapter 7.B., *supra*), and *Rooker-Feldman* (*see* note 2, *supra*) precedents.[32] The Schiavo legislation was specifically designed with these hurdles in mind. Was the Schiavo legislation constitutional? Judge Birch concluded in his concurring opinion in *Schiavo ex rel. Schindler v. Schiavo*, 404 F.3d 1277 (11th Cir. 2005) (denying rehearing en banc) (Birch, J., concurring), that it was not. In addition to concluding that it violated basic separation-of-powers principles, Judge Birch suggested that it impermissibly contradicted the *Rooker-Feldman* doctrine. Judge Tjoflat disagreed. *See Schiavo ex rel. Schindler v. Schiavo*, 404 F.3d 1277 (11th Cir. 2005) (denying rehearing en banc) (Tjoflat, J., dissenting). He concluded that the Schiavo legislation did not violate separation of powers, nor did it unconstitutionally trump *Rooker-Feldman*. Is

---

concluded that this law violated Florida's constitutional separation-of-powers. *See Bush v. Schiavo*, 885 So.2d 321 (Fla. 2004).

[32] Additionally, the state court judge would likely have been immune from immediate injunctive relief under § 1983. *See* Federal Courts Improvement Act of 1996 (amending 42 U.S.C. § 1983 to insulate state judges from injunctive relief "unless a declaratory decree was violated or declaratory relief was unavailable") (discussed in Chapter 2.A., *supra*).

Rooker-Feldman a constitutionally designed doctrine? Consider footnote 8 to Justice Ginsburg's opinion in *Exxon Mobil* (discussed in Note 2 *supra*).

4. Appealing Agency Action. Putting the hurdles of *Rooker-Feldman* and the Eleventh Amendment aside, five alternative routes appear to exist for challenging an adjudicative agency's decision following *International College of Surgeons*:

(1) an "appellate" action can be filed in state court challenging the agency's state-law determinations and also alleging federal constitutional violations under either § 1983 or some state-law remedial analog, like the Illinois Administrative Review Law used in *International College of Surgeons*;

(2) an "original" action can be filed in federal district court alleging federal constitutional violations under § 1983 and challenging the agency's state-law determinations under the federal supplemental jurisdiction statute;[33]

(3) an "appellate" action can be filed in state court challenging only the agency's state-law conclusions;

(4) an "original" action can be filed in federal district court alleging only federal constitutional violations under § 1983; or

(5) an "appellate" action can be filed in state court challenging the agency's state-law determinations along with a parallel "original" action in federal district court alleging federal constitutional violations under § 1983. See, e.g., *New Orleans Public Service, Inc. v. Council of City of New Orleans*, 491 U.S. 350 (1989) (excerpted in Chapter 7.B., *supra*).

Should one choose to "split" state-law and federal-law claims between state- and federal-court actions, the risk of preclusion is severe.[34] Because state courts are generally required to entertain federal constitutional claims, *see, e.g., Howlett v. Rose*, 496 U.S. 356 (1990), a failure to join a federal claim under the third alternative will likely prevent its being subsequently raised in federal court. See, e.g., *Migra v. Warren City School District*, 465 U.S. 75 (1984) (excerpted in Section A.,*supra*). Similarly, a failure to raise state-law claims in a federal proceeding could preclude further litigation in state court. Splitting claims between federal and state courts, moreover, invites federal abstention, which could delay resolution of the federal claims. See, e.g., *Time Warner Cable v. Doyle*, 66 F.3d 867 (7th Cir. 1995) (holding that a pending agency action justified abstention under *Pullman*); contrast *City of Chicago v. International College of Surgeons*, 153 F.3d 356 (7th Cir. 1998) (refusing on remand from the Supreme Court to abstain in favor of a state court appeal). See generally *New Orleans Public Service, Inc. v. Council of City of New Orleans*, 491 U.S. 350 (1989) (excerpted in Chapter 7.B., *supra*)

---

[33] When a *local* agency is involved, federal claims could also be pursued through a state-law remedial analog, like that in *International College of Surgeons*. See, e.g., *Royal Towing, Inc. v. City of Harvey*, 350 F. Supp. 2d 750 (N.D. Ill. 2004) ("In *City of Chicago* the Court determined that federal district courts can exercise supplemental jurisdiction for claims requiring on-the-record review of state or local administrative decisions."). Because *states* are protected by the Eleventh Amendment, use of a state-law remedial mechanism in federal court against a state agency to redress state-law violations might cause problems under *Pennhurst*. See Note 1, *supra*. When a state agency removes a case to federal court, on the other hand, a federal court can entertain state law claims against the state agency. This is because a state agency's removal of a state-law claim to federal court acts as a waiver of its Eleventh Amendment immunity. See *Lapides v. Board of Regents*, 535 U.S. 613 (2002) (which is described in Note 3 following *Scanlon* in Chapter 3.C., *supra*). Note that the Supreme Court in *Lapides* did not hold that a state agency's removal waives its immunity from suit under § 1983: "we have held that a State is not a 'person' against whom a § 1983 claim for money damages might be asserted."

[34] Assuming federal and state claims are joined in a single federal proceeding, preclusion may still be a problem in modified form. Professors Woolhander and Collins observe that *University of Tennessee v. Elliott*, 478 U.S. 788 (1986) (excerpted, *supra*), likely requires that a federal court afford state agency fact-finding "the same deference or finality that the state courts would on direct review." See Ann Woolhandler & Michael G. Collins, *Judicial Federalism and the Administrative States*, 87 CAL. L. REV. 613, 697 (1999).

(holding that abstention was not proper where a parallel challenge to a state agency's rulemaking decision was pending in state court, but acknowledging that abstention may be proper where the state agency decision is adjudicative in nature); *cf. Harper v. Public Service Commission of West Virginia*, 396 F.3d 348 (4th Cir. 2005) (noting that federal abstention in favor of a state-court appeal of a state agency decision would have been proper if the state had an important interest within the meaning of *Younger*). There is thus good reason for joining state and federal claims in a single proceeding — whether in state or federal court.[35]

5. Statutes of Limitations. Assuming that one chooses to appeal an adverse agency decision to federal court using § 1983, unique timing problems may be presented. Generally speaking, § 1983 "borrows" a forum state's personal injury period of limitations. *See Wilson v. Garcia*, 471 U.S. 261 (1985) (excerpted in Chapter 5.A., *supra*). Those limitations periods commonly stretch for two, three or even four years. Appeals from administrative awards or orders, however, must ordinarily be taken to state court within a much shorter period of time, often within weeks or days. *See, e.g.*, FLORIDA ADMINISTRATIVE PROCEDURE ACT, § 120.68(2)(a) (requiring that judicial review be sought within 30 days). Failure to appeal within this shorter time period could preclude subsequent judicial proceedings. *See University of Elliott*, 478 U.S. 788 (1986) (excerpted in Section A.[2], *supra*).[36]

B. HABEAS CORPUS AND § 1983

[1] Injunctive Relief

PREISER v. RODRIGUEZ
Supreme Court of the United States
411 U.S. 475 (1973)

MR. JUSTICE STEWART delivered the opinion of the Court.

[State prisoners who were deprived of good-conduct-time credits by the New York State Department of Correctional Services as a result of disciplinary proceedings brought a § 1983 action in federal district courtseeking injunctive relief to compel restoration of credits.]

The question before us is whether state prisoners seeking such redress may obtain equitable relief under [§ 1983], even though the federal habeas corpus statute, 28 U.S.C. § 2254, clearly provides a specific federal remedy.

The question is of considerable practical importance. For if a remedy under [§ 1983] is available, a plaintiff need not first seek redress in a state forum. *Monroe v. Pape*, 365 U.S. 167 (1961). If, on the other hand, habeas corpus is the exclusive federal remedy in

---

[35] Where a local agency is involved, as in *International College of Surgeons*, it would seem that one has a true choice between state and federal court. But where a state agency's action is at issue, Eleventh Amendment concerns might effectively force a challenger into state court. *See Raygor v. Regents*, 534 U.S. 533 (2002) (Stevens, J., dissenting) (observing that "many litigants with such mixed claims against state entities may decide to file their entire suits in state court").

[36] Note that the supplemental jurisdiction statute, 28 U.S.C. § 1367(d), tolls the statutes of limitations for supplemental state-law claims that are joined with federal claims in federal court but which are ultimately dismissed without prejudice by the District Court. Section 1367(d) thus provides additional time to re-file these state-law claims that otherwise might be time-barred in state court. *See, e.g., Jinks v. Richland County*, 538 U.S. 456 (2003) (holding that this tolling mechanism applies to state-law claims made against a local government that were dismissed by a federal court under § 1367). Primarily because of Eleventh Amendment concerns, however, the Supreme Court ruled in *Raygor v. Regents*, 534 U.S. 533 (2002), that this tolling mechanism does not apply to state-law claims made against states and their agencies.

these circumstances, then a plaintiff cannot seek the intervention of a federal court until he has first sought and been denied relief in the state courts, if a state remedy is available and adequate. 28 U.S.C. § 2254(b).

[For example,] Rodriguez, having been convicted in a New York state court of perjury and attempted larceny, was sentenced to imprisonment for an indeterminate term of from one and one-half to four years. Under New York Correction Law a prisoner serving an indeterminate sentence may elect to participate in a conditional-release program by which he may earn up to 10 days per month good-behavior-time credit toward reduction of the maximum term of his sentence. Rodriguez elected to participate in this program. Optimally, such a prisoner may be released on parole after having served approximately two-thirds of his maximum sentence (20 days out of every 30); but accrued good-behavior credits so earned may at any time be withdrawn, in whole or in part, for bad behavior or for violation of the institutional rules.

Rodriguez was charged in two separate disciplinary action reports with possession of contraband material in his cell. The deputy warden determined that as punishment, 120 days of Rodriguez' earned good-conduct-time credits should be canceled, and that Rodriguez should be placed in segregation, where he remained for more than 40 days.

Rodriguez then filed in the District Court a complaint pursuant to § 1983, combined with a petition for a writ of habeas corpus. He asserted . . . that he had received no notice or hearing on the charges for which he had ostensibly been punished. Thus, he contended that he had been deprived of his good-conduct-time credits without due process of law.

[T]he essence of habeas corpus is an attack by a person in custody upon the legality of that custody, and . . . the traditional function of the writ is to secure release from illegal custody.

The original view of a habeas corpus attack upon detention under a judicial order was a limited one. The relevant inquiry was confined to determining simply whether or not the committing court had been possessed of jurisdiction. But, over the years, the writ of habeas corpus evolved as a remedy available to effect discharge from any confinement contrary to the Constitution or fundamental law, even though imposed pursuant to conviction by a court of competent jurisdiction. Thus, whether the [Rodriguez's] challenge to his custody is that the statute under which he stands convicted is unconstitutional, that he has been imprisoned prior to trial on account of a defective indictment against him, that he is unlawfully confined in the wrong institution, that he was denied his constitutional rights at trial, that his guilty plea was invalid, that he is being unlawfully detained by the Executive or the military, or that his parole was unlawfully revoked, causing him to be reincarcerated in prison — in each case his grievance is that he is being unlawfully subjected to physical restraint, and in each case habeas corpus has been accepted as the specific instrument to obtain release from such confinement.[37]

In the case before us, the . . . suits in the District Court fell squarely within this traditional scope of habeas corpus. They alleged that the deprivation of their good-conduct-time credits was causing or would cause them to be in illegal physical confinement, i.e., that once their conditional-release date had passed, any further

---

[37] [n.7] It was not until quite recently that habeas corpus was made available to challenge less obvious restraints. In 1963, the Court held that a prisoner released on parole from immediate physical confinement was nonetheless sufficiently restrained in his freedom as to be in custody for purposes of federal habeas corpus. *Jones v. Cunningham*, 371 U.S. 236. In *Carafas v. LaVallee*, 391 U.S. 234 (1968), the Court for the first time decided that once habeas corpus jurisdiction has attached, it is not defeated by the subsequent release of the prisoner. And just this Term, in *Hensley v. Municipal Court*, 411 U.S. 345 (1973), we held that a person, who, after conviction, is released on bail or on his own recognizance, is "in custody" within the meaning of the federal habeas corpus statute. But those cases marked no more than a logical extension of the traditional meaning and purpose of habeas corpus-to effect release from illegal custody.

detention of them in prison was unlawful; and they sought restoration of those good-time credits, which, by the time the District Court ruled on their petitions, meant their immediate release from physical custody.

Even if the restoration of the[ir] credits would not have resulted in their immediate release, but only in shortening the length of their actual confinement in prison, habeas corpus would have been their appropriate remedy. For recent cases have established that habeas corpus relief is not limited to immediate release from illegal custody, but that the writ is available as well to attack future confinement and obtain future releases. In *Peyton v. Rowe*, 391 U.S. 54 (1968), the Court held that a prisoner may attack on habeas the second of two consecutive sentences while still serving the first. . . . So, even if restoration of respondents' good-time credits had merely shortened the length of their confinement, rather than required immediate discharge from that confinement, their suits would still have been within the core of habeas corpus in attacking the very duration of their physical confinement itself.

Although conceding that they could have proceeded by way of habeas corpus, the [prisoners] argue that . . . they were nonetheless entitled to bring their suits under § 1983 so as to avoid the necessity of first seeking relief in a state forum. Pointing to the broad language of § 1983, they argue that since their complaints plainly came within the literal terms of that statute, there is no justifiable reason to exclude them from the broad remedial protection provided by that law.

The broad language of § 1983, however, is not conclusive of the issue before us. The statute is a general one, and, despite the literal applicability of its terms, the question remains whether the specific federal habeas corpus statute, explicitly and historically designed to provide the means for a state prisoner to attack the validity of his confinement, must be understood to be the exclusive remedy available in a situation like this where it so clearly applies. . . . [A] state prisoner challenging his underlying conviction and sentence on federal constitutional grounds in a federal court is limited to habeas corpus. It was conceded that he cannot bring a § 1983 action, even though the literal terms of § 1983 might seem to cover such a challenge, because Congress has passed a more specific act to cover that situation, and, in doing so, has provided that a state prisoner challenging his conviction must first seek relief in a state forum, if a state remedy is available. It is clear to us that the result must be the same in the case of a state prisoner's challenge to the fact or duration of his confinement, based, as here, upon the alleged unconstitutionality of state administrative action. Such a challenge is just as close to the core of habeas corpus as an attack on the prisoner's conviction, for it goes directly to the constitutionality of his physical confinement itself and seeks either immediate release from that confinement or the shortening of its duration.

In amending the habeas corpus laws in 1948, Congress clearly required exhaustion of adequate state remedies as a condition precedent to the invocation of federal judicial relief under those laws. It would wholly frustrate explicit congressional intent to hold that the [prisoners] in the present case could evade this requirement by the simple expedient of putting a different label on their pleadings. In short, Congress has determined that habeas corpus is the appropriate remedy for state prisoners attacking the validity of the fact or length of their confinement, and that specific determination must override the general terms of § 1983.

In the [prisoners'] view, the whole purpose of the exhaustion requirement, now codified in § 2254(b), is to give state courts the first chance at remedying their own mistakes, and thereby to avoid "the unseemly spectacle of federal district courts trying the regularity of proceedings had in courts of coordinate jurisdiction." This policy, the [prisoners'] contend, does not apply when the challenge is not to the action of a state court, but, as here, to the action of a state administrative body. In that situation, they say, the concern with avoiding unnecessary interference by one court with the courts of another sovereignty with concurrent powers, and the importance of giving state courts the first opportunity to correct constitutional errors made by them, do not apply; and hence the purpose of the exhaustion requirement of the habeas corpus statute is inapplicable.

We cannot agree. . . . The rule of exhaustion in federal habeas corpus actions is rooted in considerations of federal-state comity. That principle was defined in *Younger v. Harris*, 401 U.S. 37 (1971), as "a proper respect for state functions," and it has as much relevance in areas of particular state administrative concern as it does where state judicial action is being attacked.

It is difficult to imagine an activity in which a State has a stronger interest, or one that is more intricately bound up with state laws, regulations, and procedures, than the administration of its prisons. The relationship of state prisoners and the state officers who supervise their confinement is far more intimate than that of a State and a private citizen. For state prisoners, eating, sleeping, dressing, washing, working, and playing are all done under the watchful eye of the State, and so the possibilities for litigation under the Fourteenth Amendment are boundless. What for a private citizen would be a dispute with his landlord, with his employer, with his tailor, with his neighbor, or with his banker becomes, for the prisoner, a dispute with the State. Since these internal problems of state prisons involve issues so peculiarly within state authority and expertise, the States have an important interest in not being bypassed in the correction of those problems. Moreover, because most potential litigation involving state prisoners arises on a day-to-day basis, it is most efficiently and properly handled by the state administrative bodies and state courts, which are, for the most part, familiar with the grievances of state prisoners and in a better physical and practical position to deal with those grievances.

Requiring exhaustion in situations like that before us means, of course, that a prisoner's state remedy must be adequate and available, as indeed § 2254(b) provides. The [prisoners'] in this case concede that New York provided them with an adequate remedy for the restoration of their good-time credits, through [a state statute] which explicitly provides for injunctive relief to a state prisoner "for improper treatment where such treatment constitutes a violation of his constitutional rights."

But while conceding the availability in the New York courts of an opportunity for equitable relief, the [prisoners'] contend that confining state prisoners to federal habeas corpus, after first exhausting state remedies, could deprive those prisoners of any damages remedy to which they might be entitled for their mistreatment, since damages are not available in federal habeas corpus proceedings, and New York provides no damages remedy at all for state prisoners. In the [prisoners'] view, if habeas corpus is the exclusive federal remedy for a state prisoner attacking his confinement, damages might never be obtained, at least where the State makes no provision for them. They argue that even if such a prisoner were to bring a subsequent federal civil rights action for damages, that action could be barred by principles of *res judicata* where the state courts had previously made an adverse determination of his underlying claim, even though a federal habeas court had later granted him relief on habeas corpus.

The answer to this contention is that the [prisoners] here sought no damages, but only equitable relief — restoration of their good-time credits — and our holding today is limited to that situation. If a state prisoner is seeking damages, he is attacking something other than the fact or length of his confinement, and he is seeking something other than immediate or more speedy release — the traditional purpose of habeas corpus. In the case of a damages claim, habeas corpus is not an appropriate or available federal remedy. Accordingly, as [the State] concede[s], a damages action by a state prisoner could be brought under [§ 1983] in federal court without any requirement of prior exhaustion of state remedies.

Principles of *res judicata* are, of course, not wholly applicable to habeas corpus proceedings. Hence, a state prisoner in the [prisoners'] situation who has been denied relief in the state courts is not precluded from seeking habeas relief on the same claims in federal court. On the other hand, *res judicata* has been held to be fully applicable to a civil rights action brought under § 1983. Accordingly, there would be an inevitable incentive for a state prisoner to proceed at once in federal court by way of a civil rights action, lest he lose his right to do so. This would have the unfortunate dual effect of denying the state prison administration and the state courts the opportunity to correct the errors committed in the State's own prisons, and of isolating those bodies from an understanding of and hospitality to the federal claims of state prisoners in situations such as those before us. Federal habeas corpus, on the other hand, serves the important function of allowing the State to deal with these peculiarly local problems on its own, while preserving for the state prisoner an expeditious federal forum for the vindication of his federally protected rights, if the State has denied redress.

The [prisoners] place a great deal of reliance on our recent decisions upholding the right of state prisoners to bring federal civil rights actions to challenge the conditions of their confinement. *Cooper v. Pate*, 378 U.S. 546 (1964); *Houghton v. Shafer*, 392 U.S. 639 (1968); *Wilwording v. Swenson*, 404 U.S. 249 (1971); *Haines v. Kerner*, 404 U.S. 519 (1972). But none of the state prisoners in those cases was challenging the fact or duration of his physical confinement itself, and none was seeking immediate release or a speedier release from that confinement — the heart of habeas corpus. In *Cooper*, the prisoner alleged that, solely because of his religious beliefs, he had been denied permission to purchase certain religious publications and had been denied other privileges enjoyed by his fellow prisoners. In *Houghton*, the prisoner's contention was that prison authorities had violated the Constitution by confiscating legal materials which he had acquired for pursuing his appeal, but which, in violation of prison rules, had been found in the possession of another prisoner. In *Wilwording*, the prisoners' complaints related solely to their living conditions and disciplinary measures while confined in maximum security. And in *Haines*, the prisoner claimed that prison officials had acted unconstitutionally by placing him in solitary confinement as a disciplinary measure, and he sought damages for claimed physical injuries sustained while so segregated. It is clear, then, that in all those cases, the prisoners' claims related solely to the States' alleged unconstitutional treatment of them while in confinement. None sought, as did the [prisoners] here, to challenge the very fact or duration of the confinement itself. Those cases, therefore, merely establish that a § 1983 action is a proper remedy for a state prisoner who is making a constitutional challenge to the conditions of his prison life, but not to the fact or length of his custody. Upon that understanding, we reaffirm those holdings.[38]

This is not to say that habeas corpus may not also be available to challenge such prison conditions. When a prisoner is put under additional and unconstitutional restraints during his lawful custody, it is arguable that habeas corpus will lie to remove the restraints making the custody illegal.

But we need not in this case explore the appropriate limits of habeas corpus as an alternative remedy to a proper action under § 1983. That question is not before us. What is involved here is the extent to which § 1983 is a permissible alternative to the traditional remedy of habeas corpus. Upon that question, we hold today that when a state prisoner is challenging the very fact or duration of his physical imprisonment, and the relief he seeks is a determination that he is entitled to immediate release or a speedier release from that imprisonment, his sole federal remedy is a writ of habeas corpus.

---

[38] [n.14] If a prisoner seeks to attack both the conditions of his confinement and the fact or length of that confinement, his latter claim, under our decision today, is cognizable only in federal habeas corpus, with its attendant requirement of exhaustion of state remedies. But, consistent with our prior decisions, that holding in no way precludes him from simultaneously litigating in federal court, under § 1983, his claim relating to the conditions of his confinement.

MR. JUSTICE BRENNAN, with whom MR. JUSTICE DOUGLAS and MR. JUSTICE MARSHALL join, dissenting.

At bottom, the Court's holding today rests on an understandable apprehension that the no-exhaustion rule of § 1983 might, in the absence of some limitation, devour the exhaustion rule of the habeas corpus statute. The problem arises because the two statutes necessarily overlap. Indeed, every application by a state prisoner for federal habeas corpus relief against his jailers could, as a matter of logic and semantics, be viewed as an action under [§ 1983] to obtain injunctive relief against "the deprivation," by one acting under color of state law, "of any rights, privileges, or immunities secured by the Constitution and laws" of the United States. To prevent state prisoners from nullifying the habeas corpus exhaustion requirement by invariably styling their petitions as pleas for relief under § 1983, the Court today devises an ungainly and irrational scheme that permits some prisoners to sue under § 1983, while others may proceed only by way of petition for habeas corpus. And the entire scheme operates in defiance of the purposes underlying both the exhaustion requirement of habeas corpus and the absence of a comparable requirement under § 1983.

At the outset, it is important to consider the nature of the line that the Court has drawn. . . . [E]ven under the Court's approach, there are undoubtedly some instances where a prisoner has the option of proceeding either by petition for habeas corpus or by suit under § 1983.

Putting momentarily to one side the grave analytic shortcomings of the Court's approach, it seems clear that the scheme's unmanageability is sufficient reason to condemn it. For the unfortunate but inevitable legacy of today's opinion is a perplexing set of uncertainties and anomalies. And the nub of the problem is the definition of the Court's new-found and essentially ethereal concept, the "core of habeas corpus."

A prisoner is unlucky enough to have his action fall within the core of habeas corpus whenever he challenges the fact or duration of his confinement. For example, an attack on the validity of conviction or sentence is plainly directed at the fact or duration of confinement, and the prisoner can therefore proceed only by petition for habeas corpus.

At the opposite end of the spectrum from an attack on the conviction itself or on the deprivation of good-time credits is a prisoner's action for monetary damages against his jailers. "If a state prisoner is seeking damages," the Court makes clear, . . . "a damages action . . . could be brought under (§ 1983) in federal court without any requirement of prior exhaustion of state remedies."

Between a suit for damages and an attack on the conviction itself or on the deprivation of good-time credits are cases where habeas corpus is an appropriate and available remedy, but where the action falls outside the "core of habeas corpus" because the attack is directed at the conditions of confinement, not at its fact or duration. Notwithstanding today's decision, a prisoner may challenge, by suit under § 1983, prison living conditions and disciplinary measures, or confiscation of legal materials, or impairment of the right to free exercise of religion, even though federal habeas corpus is available as an alternative remedy. It should be plain enough that serious difficulties will arise whenever a prisoner seeks to attack in a single proceeding both the conditions of his confinement and the deprivation of good-time credits. And the addition of a plea for monetary damages exacerbates the problem.

If a prisoner's sole claim is that he was placed in solitary confinement pursuant to an unconstitutional disciplinary procedure, he can obtain federal injunctive relief and monetary damages in an action under § 1983. The unanswered question is whether he loses the right to proceed under § 1983 if, as punishment for his alleged misconduct, his jailers have not only subjected him to unlawful segregation and thereby inflicted an injury that is compensable in damages, but have compounded the wrong by improperly depriving him of good-time credits.

The concern that § 1983 not be used to nullify the habeas corpus exhaustion doctrine is, of course, legitimate. But our effort to preserve the integrity of the doctrine must rest on an understanding of the purposes that underlie it. In my view, the Court misapprehends these fundamental purposes and compounds the problem by paying insufficient attention to the reasons why exhaustion of state remedies is not required in suits under § 1983. As a result, the Court mistakenly concludes that allowing suit under § 1983 would jeopardize the purposes of the exhaustion rule.

Exhaustion of state remedies is not required [by § 1983] precisely because such a requirement would jeopardize the purposes of the Act. For that reason, the imposition of such a requirement, even if done indirectly by means of a determination that jurisdiction under § 1983 is displaced by an alternative remedial device, must be justified by a clear statement of congressional intent, or, at the very least, by the presence of the most persuasive considerations of policy. In my view, no such justification can be found.

NOTES

1. **Habeas and Prison Conditions.** As made clear by *Rodriguez*, state and local inmates *must* use the federal habeas corpus statute, 28 U.S.C. § 2554, rather than § 1983, to challenge the "fact or duration" of their confinements. By way of contrast, state prisoners who challenge the conditions or nature of their confinement *can* use § 1983. See, e.g., *Farmer v. Brennan*, 511 U.S. 825 (1994) (addressing an Eighth Amendment challenge brought by a prisoner who was attacked by other inmates); *Sandin v. Conner*, 515 U.S. 472 (1995) (addressing a Procedural Due Process challenge brought by a prisoner placed in administrative segregation). *Can* inmates use the federal habeas corpus statute to challenge anything less than the "fact or duration" of their confinement? *Can* they use habeas corpus to challenged administrative discipline, like being placed in solitary confinement? *Can* they use habeas corpus to challenge prison conditions? In *Muhammad v. Close*, 540 U.S. 749 (2004) (discussed in Note 4 following *Heck* in Section B.[2], *infra*), where an inmate was placed in "special detention" following a dispute with a guard, the Supreme Court observed that it "has never followed the speculation in *Preiser* . . . that . . . a prisoner subject to 'additional and unconstitutional restraint' [beyond that established by the conviction and sentence] might have a habeas claim independent of § 1983." Does this mean that federal habeas corpus cannot be used to challenge prison conditions? *See* Margo Schlanger, *Inmate Litigation*, 116 Harv. L. Rev. 1555, 1637 & n.277 (2003) (noting that the Supreme Court has not decided whether federal habeas corpus jurisdiction can be invoked by inmates to challenge the specific conditions of their confinement).

2. **Exhaustion for Inmates' Suits.** As illustrated by *Woodford v. Ngo*, 548 U.S. 81 (2006) (excerpted in Section A.[3], *supra*), exhaustion of a state's "available" administrative remedies is now a prerequisite under § 1997e(a) before inmates may sue under § 1983 for unlawful prison conditions. Does this recent Congressional enactment alleviate Justice Brennan's concerns in *Preiser*? Note that exhaustion requirements for federal habeas corpus are in many ways more demanding than those required by § 1997e for § 1983. Is this the reason inmates, especially those sentenced to death, would rather use § 1983? Consider the following case.

NELSON v. CAMPBELL
Supreme Court of the United States
541 U.S. 637 (2004)

JUSTICE O'CONNOR delivered the opinion of the Court.

[An Alabama death row inmate (Nelson) attempted to use § 1983 to challenge the use of a "cut-down" procedure designed to facilitate lethal injection. The United States Court of Appeals for the Eleventh Circuit treated his § 1983 claim as the functional equivalent of a petition for habeas corpus and ruled that it was barred by habeas law's "successive" petition prohibition, which acts as a procedural bar should an inmate not properly press his constitutional challenges in the first habeas petition. *See* 28 U.S.C. § 2244(b) (prohibiting "successive" petitions for habeas corpus).]

Due to years of drug abuse, [Nelson] has severely compromised peripheral veins, which are inaccessible by standard techniques for gaining intravenous access, such as a needle. Upon confirming that [Nelson] had compromised veins, Warden Culliver informed [Nelson] that prison personnel would cut a 0.5-inch incision in [Nelson's] arm and catheterize a vein 24 hours before the scheduled execution. At a second meeting . . . the warden dramatically altered the prognosis: prison personnel would now make a 2-inch incision in [Nelson's] arm or leg; the procedure would take place one hour before the scheduled execution; and only local anesthesia would be used. There was no assurance that a physician would perform or even be present for the procedure.

[T]hree days before his scheduled execution, [Nelson] filed the present § 1983 action alleging that the so-called "cut-down" procedure constituted cruel and unusual punishment and deliberate indifference to his serious medical needs in violation of the Eighth Amendment.

We have not yet had occasion to consider whether civil rights suits seeking to enjoin the use of a particular method of execution — *e.g.*, lethal injection or electrocution — fall within the core of federal habeas corpus or, rather, whether they are properly viewed as challenges to the conditions of a condemned inmate's death sentence. Neither the "conditions" nor the "fact or duration" label is particularly apt. A suit seeking to enjoin a particular means of effectuating a sentence of death does not directly call into question the "fact" or "validity" of the sentence itself — by simply altering its method of execution, the State can go forward with the sentence. On the other hand, imposition of the death penalty presupposes a means of carrying it out. In a State such as Alabama, where the legislature has established lethal injection as the preferred method of execution, a constitutional challenge seeking to permanently enjoin the use of lethal injection may amount to a challenge to the fact of the sentence itself. A finding of unconstitutionality would require statutory amendment or variance, imposing significant costs on the State and the administration of its penal system. And while it makes little sense to talk of the "duration" of a death sentence, a State retains a significant interest in meting out a sentence of death in a timely fashion.

We need not reach here the difficult question of how to categorize method-of-execution claims generally. [The state] at oral argument conceded that § 1983 would be an appropriate vehicle for an inmate who is not facing execution to bring a "deliberate indifference" challenge to the constitutionality of the cut-down procedure if used to gain venous access for purposes of providing medical treatment. We see no reason on the face of the complaint to treat petitioner's claim differently solely because he has been condemned to die.

If as a legal matter the cut-down were a statutorily mandated part of the lethal injection protocol, or if as a factual matter [Nelson] were unable or unwilling to concede acceptable alternatives for gaining venous access, respondents might have a stronger argument that success on the merits, coupled with injunctive relief, would call into question the death sentence itself. But [Nelson] has been careful throughout these proceedings, in his complaint and at oral argument, to assert that the cut-down, as well as the warden's refusal to provide reliable information regarding the cut-down protocol, are *wholly unnecessary* to gaining venous access. [Nelson] has alleged alternatives that, if they had been used, would have allowed the State to proceed with the execution as scheduled. No Alabama statute requires use of the cut-down, and [the state has] offered no duly-promulgated regulations to the contrary.

If on remand and after an evidentiary hearing the District Court concludes that use of the cut-down procedure as described in the complaint is necessary for administering the lethal injection, the District Court will need to address the broader question, left open here, of how to treat method-of-execution claims generally.

[The state] argue[s] that [authorizing use of § 1983] would open the floodgates to all manner of method-of-execution challenges, as well as last minute stay requests. But, because we do not here resolve the question of how to treat method-of-execution claims generally, our holding is extremely limited.

A stay is an equitable remedy, and "[e]quity must take into consideration the State's strong interest in proceeding with its judgment and . . . attempt[s] at manipulation." Thus, before granting a stay, a district court must consider not only the likelihood of success on the merits and the relative harms to the parties, but also the extent to which the inmate has delayed unnecessarily in bringing the claim. Given the State's significant interest in enforcing its criminal judgments, there is a strong equitable presumption against the grant of a stay where a claim could have been brought at such a time as to allow consideration of the merits without requiring entry of a stay.

Finally, the ability to bring a § 1983 claim, rather than a habeas application, does not entirely free inmates from substantive or procedural limitations. The Prison Litigation Reform Act of 1995 (Act) imposes limits on the scope and duration of preliminary and permanent injunctive relief, including a requirement that, before issuing such relief, "[a] court shall give substantial weight to any adverse impact on . . . the operation of a criminal justice system caused by the relief." 18 U.S.C. § 3626(a)(1); accord § 3626(a)(2). It [also] requires that inmates exhaust available state administrative remedies before bringing a § 1983 action challenging the conditions of their confinement. 42 U.S.C. § 1997e(a).

NOTES

1. *Hill v. McDonough*. The Court revisited this issue in *Hill v. McDonough*, 547 U.S. 573 (2006), where a death row inmate challenged Florida's protocol for lethal injection. Acting pursuant to Florida law, which does not mandate any particular lethal-injection procedure, the Florida Department of Corrections implemented a three-drug injection sequence: the first drug injected, sodium pentothal, anesthetizes the subject; the second and third drugs injected, pancuronium bromide and potassium chloride, paralyze the subject's lungs and induce a fatal heart attack. The plaintiff (Hill) filed suit under § 1983 four days before his scheduled execution to challenge Florida's protocol under the Eighth Amendment. Specifically, Hill asserted that Florida's three-drug procedure carried a risk of continued consciousness and severe pain should the anesthetic prove insufficient. Both the District Court and Eleventh Circuit agreed that Hill's § 1983 claim was the functional equivalent of a petition for writ of habeas corpus. Because Hill had previously filed an unsuccessful habeas petition, his claim (like the one in *Nelson*) constituted an improper "successive" petition which had to be dismissed under 28 U.S.C. § 2244(b). In a unanimous opinion by Justice Kennedy, the Court reversed under the logic of *Nelson*. The Court also warned, however, that § 1983 litigation should not be tolerated as a means of delaying execution:

> [Florida and its *amici*] contend that the legal distinction between habeas corpus and § 1983 actions must account for the practical reality of capital litigation tactics: Inmates file these actions intending to forestall execution, and *Nelson*'s emphasis on whether a suit challenges something "necessary" to the execution provides no endpoint to piecemeal litigation aimed at delaying the execution. Viewed in isolation, no single component of a given execution procedure may be strictly necessary, the argument goes, and a capital litigant may put off execution by challenging one aspect of a procedure after another. The *amici* States point to *Nelson*'s aftermath as a cautionary example, contending that on remand the District Court allowed Nelson to amend his complaint and that litigation over the constitutionality of Alabama's adopted alternative — one that Nelson had previously proposed — continues to this day.

[W]e agree courts should not tolerate abusive litigation tactics.

Filing an action that can proceed under § 1983 does not entitle the complainant to an order staying an execution as a matter of course. Both the State and the victims of crime have an important interest in the timely enforcement of a sentence. Our conclusions today do not diminish that interest, nor do they deprive federal courts of the means to protect it.

We state again, as we did in *Nelson*, that a stay of execution is an equitable remedy. It is not available as a matter of right, and equity must be sensitive to the State's strong interest in enforcing its criminal judgments without undue interference from the federal courts. Thus, like other stay applicants, inmates seeking time to challenge the manner in which the State plans to execute them must satisfy all of the requirements for a stay including a showing of a significant possibility of success on the merits. A court considering a stay must also apply "a strong equitable presumption against the grant of a stay where a claim could have been brought at such a time as to allow consideration of the merits without requiring entry of a stay."

After *Nelson* a number of federal courts have invoked their equitable powers to dismiss suits they saw as speculative or filed too late in the day. Although the particular determinations made in those cases are not before us, we recognize that the problem they address is significant. Repetitive or piecemeal litigation presumably would raise similar concerns. The federal courts can and should protect States from dilatory or speculative suits, but it is not necessary to reject *Nelson* to do so.

2. Benefits of § 1983. As the Court's opinions in *Nelson* and *Hill* make clear, § 1983 challenges to death sentences need not be treated as the functional equivalents of applications for habeas corpus. This does not mean, however, that § 1983 challenges are devoid of limitations. Exhaustion is required by the Prison Litigation Reform Act, stays are not a matter of right, and federal courts have a good deal of power to manage inmates' claims. The doctrine of laches, in particular, has been used to deny emergency stays in § 1983 challenges to death sentences. *See, e.g., Hill v. McDonough*, 464 F.3d 1246 (11th Cir. 2006) (denying a stay based on equitable principles). *Compare Cooey v. Strickland*, 479 F.3d 412 (6th Cir. 2007) (using Ohio's statute of limitations to deny stay) (discussed in Note 6 following *Wilson v. Garcia* in Chapter 5.A., *supra*).

Given these limitations, what advantages are to be gained by challenging executions under § 1983? In both *Nelson* and *Hill*, remember, the Eleventh Circuit concluded that the inmates could not use habeas corpus because they had "abused" the writ of habeas corpus through successive petitions. *See generally Gonzalez v. Crosby*, 545 U.S. 524 (2005) (describing limitations on successive petitions for writs of habeas corpus). Given habeas corpus's limitation on "successive" petitions, § 1983 may supply capital inmates their only remaining federal option. *See generally* Note, *A New Test for Evaluating Eighth Amendment Challenges to Lethal Injections*, 120 HARV. L. REV. 1301 (2007).[39]

---

[39] The Supreme Court in *Baze v. Rees*, 128 S. Ct. 1520 (2008), upheld Kenttucky's lethal injection procedure under the Eighth Amendment. The constitutional challenge in *Baze* was filed in state court under Kentucky's declaratory judgment act, KY. REV. STAT. § 418.040, rather than § 1983.

[2] Damages

HECK v. HUMPHREY
Supreme Court of the United States
512 U.S. 477 (1994)

JUSTICE SCALIA delivered the opinion of the Court.

This case presents the question whether a state prisoner may challenge the constitutionality of his conviction in a suit for damages under 42 U.S.C. § 1983.

Roy Heck was convicted in Indiana state court of voluntary manslaughter for the killing of Rickie Heck, his wife, and is serving a 15-year sentence in an Indiana prison. While the appeal from his conviction was pending, [Heck], proceeding *pro se*, filed this suit in Federal District Court under 42 U.S.C. § 1983, naming as defendants ... James Humphrey and Robert Ewbank, Dearborn County prosecutors, and Michael Krinoph, an investigator with the Indiana State Police. The complaint alleged that [these defendants], acting under color of state law, had engaged in an "unlawful, unreasonable, and arbitrary investigation" leading to petitioner's arrest; "knowingly destroyed" evidence "which was exculpatory in nature and could have proved [Heck's] innocence"; and caused "an illegal and unlawful voice identification procedure" to be used at [Heck's] trial. The complaint sought, among other things, compensatory and punitive monetary damages. It did not ask for injunctive relief, and [Heck] has not sought release from custody in this action.

[The Indiana Supreme Court upheld Heck's conviction on direct appeal. Heck's petitions for writs of habeas corpus in federal court were denied. Heck conceded that his § 1983 claim "challeng[ed] the legality of his conviction."]

This case lies at the intersection of the two most fertile sources of federal-court prisoner litigation — [§ 1983] and the federal habeas corpus statute. Both of these provide access to a federal forum for claims of unconstitutional treatment at the hands of state officials, but they differ in their scope and operation. In general, exhaustion of state remedies "is *not* a prerequisite to an action under § 1983," *Patsy v. Board of Regents of Fla.*, 457 U.S. 496, 501 (1982) (emphasis added), even an action by a state prisoner. The federal habeas corpus statute, by contrast, requires that state prisoners first seek redress in a state forum.

Preiser v. Rodriguez considered the potential overlap between these two provisions, and held that habeas corpus is the exclusive remedy for a state prisoner who challenges the fact or duration of his confinement and seeks immediate or speedier release, even though such a claim may come within the literal terms of § 1983. We emphasize that *Preiser* did *not* create an exception to the "no exhaustion" rule of § 1983; it merely held that certain claims by state prisoners are not *cognizable* under that provision, and must be brought in habeas corpus proceedings, which do contain an exhaustion requirement.

This case is clearly not covered by the holding of *Preiser*, for [Heck] seeks not immediate or speedier release, but monetary damages, as to which he could not "have sought and obtained fully effective relief through federal habeas corpus proceedings."

[T]he question posed by § 1983 damages claims that ... call into question the lawfulness of conviction or confinement remains open. To answer that question correctly, we see no need to abandon ... our teaching that § 1983 contains no exhaustion requirement beyond what Congress has provided. The issue with respect to monetary damages challenging conviction is not, it seems to us, exhaustion; but rather, the same as the issue was with respect to injunctive relief challenging conviction in *Preiser*: whether the claim is cognizable under § 1983 at all. We conclude that it is not.

The common-law cause of action for malicious prosecution provides the closest analogy to claims of the type considered here because, unlike the related cause of action for false arrest or imprisonment, it permits damages for confinement imposed pursuant to legal process. "If there is a false arrest claim, damages for that claim cover the time of detention up until issuance of process or arraignment, but not more." W. KEETON, D. DOBBS, R. KEETON, & D. OWEN, PROSSER AND KEETON ON LAW OF TORTS 888 (5th ed. 1984). But a successful malicious prosecution plaintiff may recover, in addition to general damages, "compensation for any arrest or imprisonment, including damages for discomfort or injury to his health, or loss of time and deprivation of the society."

One element that must be alleged and proved in a malicious prosecution action is termination of the prior criminal proceeding in favor of the accused. This requirement "avoids parallel litigation over the issues of probable cause and guilt . . . and it precludes the possibility of the claimant [*sic*] succeeding in the tort action after having been convicted in the underlying criminal prosecution, in contravention of a strong judicial policy against the creation of two conflicting resolutions arising out of the same or identical transaction." Furthermore, "to permit a convicted criminal defendant to proceed with a malicious prosecution claim would permit a collateral attack on the conviction through the vehicle of a civil suit."[40] We think the hoary principle that civil tort actions are not appropriate vehicles for challenging the validity of outstanding criminal judgments applies to § 1983 damages actions that necessarily require the plaintiff to prove the unlawfulness of his conviction or confinement, just as it has always applied to actions for malicious prosecution.

We hold that, in order to recover damages for allegedly unconstitutional conviction or imprisonment, or for other harm caused by actions whose unlawfulness would render a conviction or sentence invalid,[41] a § 1983 plaintiff must prove that the conviction or sentence has been reversed on direct appeal, expunged by executive order, declared invalid by a state tribunal authorized to make such determination, or called into question by a federal court's issuance of a writ of habeas corpus. A claim for damages bearing that relationship to a conviction or sentence that has *not* been so invalidated is not cognizable under § 1983. Thus, when a state prisoner seeks damages in a § 1983 suit, the district court must consider whether a judgment in favor of the plaintiff would necessarily imply the invalidity of his conviction or sentence; if it would, the complaint must be dismissed unless the plaintiff can demonstrate that the conviction or sentence has already been invalidated. But if the district court determines that the plaintiff's

---

[40] [n.4] Justice Souter criticizes our reliance on malicious prosecution's favorable termination requirement as illustrative of the common-law principle barring tort plaintiffs from mounting collateral attacks on their outstanding criminal convictions. Malicious prosecution is an inapt analogy, he says, because "[a] defendant's conviction, under Reconstruction-era common law, dissolved his claim for malicious prosecution because the conviction was regarded as irrebuttable evidence that the prosecution never lacked probable cause." (Citing T. COOLEY, LAW OF TORTS 185 (1879)). Chief Justice Cooley no doubt intended merely to set forth the general rule that a conviction defeated the malicious prosecution plaintiff's allegation (essential to his cause of action) that the prior proceeding was without probable cause. But this was not an absolute rule in all jurisdictions, and early on it was recognized that there must be exceptions to the rule in cases involving circumstances such as fraud, perjury, or mistake of law. Some cases even held that a "conviction, although it be afterwards reversed, is *prima facie* evidence — and that only — of the existence of probable cause." . . . Yet even if Justice Souter were correct in asserting that a prior conviction, although reversed, "dissolved [a] claim for malicious prosecution," our analysis would be unaffected. It would simply demonstrate that *no* common-law action, *not even* malicious prosecution, would permit a criminal proceeding to be impugned in a tort action, *even after* the conviction had been reversed. That would, if anything, strengthen our belief that § 1983, which borrowed general tort principles, was not meant to permit such collateral attack.

[41] [n.6] An example of this latter category — a § 1983 action that does not seek damages directly attributable to conviction or confinement but whose successful prosecution would necessarily imply that the plaintiff's criminal conviction was wrongful — would be the following: A state defendant is convicted of and sentenced for the crime of resisting arrest, defined as intentionally preventing a peace officer from effecting a *lawful* arrest. (This is a common definition of that offense.) He then brings a § 1983 action against the arresting officer, seeking damages for violation of his Fourth Amendment right to be free from unreasonable seizures. In order to prevail in this § 1983 action, he would have to negate an element of the offense of which he has been convicted. Regardless of the state law concerning res judicata, the § 1983 action will not lie.

action, even if successful, will *not* demonstrate the invalidity of any outstanding criminal judgment against the plaintiff, the action should be allowed to proceed,[42] in the absence of some other bar to the suit.[43]

[The defendants] had urged us to adopt a rule that was in one respect broader than this: Exhaustion of state remedies should be required, they contended, not just when success in the § 1983 damages suit would necessarily show a conviction or sentence to be unlawful, but whenever "judgment in a § 1983 action would resolve a necessary element to a likely challenge to a conviction, even if the § 1983 court [need] not determine that the conviction is invalid." Such a broad sweep was needed, [they] contended, lest a judgment in a prisoner's favor in a federal-court § 1983 damages action claiming, for example, a Fourth Amendment violation, be given preclusive effect as to that subissue in a subsequent state-court postconviction proceeding. Preclusion might result, they asserted, if the State exercised sufficient control over the officials' defense in the § 1983 action. While we have no occasion to rule on the matter at this time, it is at least plain that preclusion will not necessarily be an automatic, or even a permissible, effect.[44]

In another respect, however, our holding sweeps more broadly than the approach [the defendants] had urged. We do not engraft an exhaustion requirement upon § 1983, but rather deny the existence of a cause of action. Even a prisoner who has fully exhausted available state remedies has no cause of action under § 1983 unless and until the conviction or sentence is reversed, expunged, invalidated, or impugned by the grant of a writ of habeas corpus.[45]

---

[42] [n.7] For example, a suit for damages attributable to an allegedly unreasonable search may lie even if the challenged search produced evidence that was introduced in a state criminal trial resulting in the § 1983 plaintiff's still-outstanding conviction. Because of doctrines like independent source and inevitable discovery, and especially harmless error, such a § 1983 action, even if successful, would not *necessarily* imply that the plaintiff's conviction was unlawful. In order to recover compensatory damages, however, the § 1983 plaintiff must prove not only that the search was unlawful, but that it caused him actual, compensable injury, which, we hold today, does *not* encompass the "injury" of being convicted and imprisoned (until his conviction has been overturned).

[43] [n.8] For example, if a state criminal defendant brings a federal civil-rights lawsuit during the pendency of his criminal trial, appeal, or state habeas action, abstention may be an appropriate response to the parallel state-court proceedings. Moreover, we do not decide whether abstention might be appropriate in cases where a state prisoner brings a § 1983 damages suit raising an issue that also could be grounds for relief in a state-court challenge to his conviction or sentence.

[44] [n.9] State courts are bound to apply federal rules in determining the preclusive effect of federal-court decisions on issues of federal law. The federal rules on the subject of issue and claim preclusion, unlike those relating to exhaustion of state remedies, are "almost entirely judge-made." And in developing them the courts can, and indeed should, be guided by the federal policies reflected in congressional enactments. Thus, the court-made preclusion rules may, as judicial application of the categorical mandate of § 1983 may *not*, see *Patsy v. Board of Regents of Fla.*, 457 U.S. 496, 509 (1982), take account of the policy embodied in § 2254(b)'s exhaustion requirement that state courts be given the first opportunity to review constitutional claims bearing upon state prisoners' release from custody.

[45] [n.10] Justice Souter also adopts the common-law principle that one cannot use the device of a civil tort action to challenge the validity of an outstanding criminal conviction, but thinks it necessary to abandon that principle in those cases (of which no real-life example comes to mind) involving former state prisoners who, because they are no longer in custody, cannot bring postconviction challenges. We think the principle barring collateral attacks — a longstanding and deeply rooted feature of both the common law and our own jurisprudence — is not rendered inapplicable by the fortuity that a convicted criminal is no longer incarcerated. Justice Souter opines that disallowing a damages suit for a former state prisoner framed by Ku Klux Klan — dominated state officials is "hard indeed to reconcile . . . with the purpose of § 1983." But if, as Justice Souter appears to suggest, the goal of our interpretive enterprise under § 1983 were to provide a remedy for all conceivable invasions of federal rights that freedmen may have suffered at the hands of officials of the former States of the Confederacy, the entire landscape of our § 1983 jurisprudence would look very different. We would not, for example, have adopted the rule that judicial officers have absolute immunity from

Applying these principles to the present action, in which both courts below found that the damages claims challenged the legality of the conviction, we find that the dismissal of the action was correct.

JUSTICE THOMAS, concurring.

I write separately to note that it is we who have put § 1983 and the habeas statute on what Justice Souter appropriately terms a "collision course." It has long been recognized that we have expanded the prerogative writ of habeas corpus and § 1983 far beyond the limited scope either was originally intended to have. Expanding the two historic statutes brought them squarely into conflict in the context of suits by state prisoners, as we made clear in *Preiser*. Given that the Court created the tension between the two statutes, it is proper for the Court to devise limitations aimed at ameliorating the conflict, provided that it does so in a principled fashion. Because the Court today limits the scope of § 1983 in a manner consistent both with the federalism concerns undergirding the explicit exhaustion requirement of the habeas statute, and with the state of the common law at the time § 1983 was enacted, I join the Court's opinion.

JUSTICE SOUTER, with whom JUSTICE BLACKMUN, JUSTICE STEVENS, and JUSTICE O'CONNOR join, concurring in the judgment.

While I do not object to referring to the common law when resolving the question this case presents, I do not think that the existence of the tort of malicious prosecution alone provides the answer. Common-law tort rules can provide a "starting point for the inquiry under § 1983," *Carey v. Piphus*, 435 U.S. 247, 258 (1978), but we have relied on the common law in § 1983 cases only when doing so was thought to be consistent with ordinary rules of statutory construction.

In addition to proving favorable termination, a plaintiff in a malicious-prosecution action, according to the same sources the Court relies upon, must prove the "[a]bsence of probable cause for the proceeding" as well as " '[m]alice,' or a primary purpose other than that of bringing an offender to justice." W. KEETON, D. DOBBS, R. KEETON, & D. OWEN, PROSSER AND KEETON ON LAW OF TORTS 871 (5th ed. 1984). As § 1983 requirements, however, these elements would mean that even a § 1983 plaintiff whose conviction was invalidated as unconstitutional (premised, for example, on a confession coerced by an interrogation-room beating) could not obtain damages for the unconstitutional conviction and ensuing confinement if the defendant police officials (or perhaps the prosecutor) had probable cause to believe the plaintiff was guilty and intended to bring him to justice. Absent an independent statutory basis for doing so, importing into § 1983 the malicious-prosecution tort's favorable-termination requirement but not its probable-cause requirement would be particularly odd since it is from the latter that the former derives.

Furthermore, . . . [a] defendant's conviction, under Reconstruction-era common law, dissolved his claim for malicious prosecution because the conviction was regarded as irrebuttable evidence that the prosecution never lacked probable cause. Thus the definition of "favorable termination" with which the framers of § 1983 were aware (if they were aware of any definition) included none of the events relevant to the type of § 1983 claim involved in this case ("revers[al] on direct appeal, expunge[ment] by executive order, [a] declar[ation] [of] invalid[ity] by a state tribunal authorized to make such determination, or [the] call[ing] into question by a federal court's issuance of a writ of habeas corpus,") and it is easy to see why the analogy to the tort of malicious prosecution in this context has escaped the collective wisdom of the many courts and

---

liability for damages under § 1983, a rule that would prevent recovery by a former slave who had been tried and convicted before a corrupt state judge in league with the Ku Klux Klan.

commentators to have addressed the issue, previously, as well as the parties to this case. Indeed, relying on the tort of malicious prosecution to dictate the outcome of this case would logically drive one to the position, untenable as a matter of statutory interpretation (and, to be clear, disclaimed by the Court), that conviction of a crime wipes out a person's § 1983 claim for damages for unconstitutional conviction or postconviction confinement.[46]

We are not, however, in any such strait, for our enquiry in this case may follow the interpretive methodology employed in *Preiser v. Rodriguez*, [where] we read the "general" § 1983 statute in light of the "specific federal habeas corpus statute," which applies only to "person[s] in custody," and the habeas statute's policy, embodied in its exhaustion requirement, that state courts be given the first opportunity to review constitutional claims bearing upon a state prisoner's release from custody. Though in contrast to *Preiser* the state prisoner here seeks damages, not release from custody, the distinction makes no difference when the damages sought are for unconstitutional conviction or confinement. . . . Whether or not a federal-court § 1983 damages judgment against state officials in such an action would have preclusive effect in later litigation against the State, mounting damages against the defendant-officials for unlawful confinement (damages almost certainly to be paid by state indemnification) would, practically, compel the State to release the prisoner. Because allowing a state prisoner to proceed directly with a federal-court § 1983 attack on his conviction or sentence "would wholly frustrate explicit congressional intent" as declared in the habeas exhaustion requirement, the statutory scheme must be read as precluding such attacks. This conclusion flows not from a preference about how the habeas and § 1983 statutes ought to have been written, but from a recognition that "Congress has determined that habeas corpus is the appropriate remedy for state prisoners attacking the validity of the fact or length of their confinement, [a] specific determination [that] must override the general terms of § 1983."

That leaves the question of how to implement what statutory analysis requires. It is at this point that the malicious-prosecution tort's favorable-termination requirement becomes helpful, not in dictating the elements of a § 1983 cause of action, but in suggesting a relatively simple way to avoid collisions at the intersection of habeas and § 1983. A state prisoner may seek federal-court § 1983 damages for unconstitutional conviction or confinement, but only if he has previously established the unlawfulness of his conviction or confinement, as on appeal or on habeas. This has the effect of requiring a state prisoner challenging the lawfulness of his confinement to follow habeas's rules before seeking § 1983 damages for unlawful confinement in federal court, and it is ultimately the Court's holding today. It neatly resolves a problem that has bedeviled lower courts, legal commentators, and law students (some of whom doubtless have run up against a case like this in law-school exams).

It may be that the Court's analysis takes it no further than I would thus go, and that any objection I may have to the Court's opinion is to style, not substance. . . . The

---

[46] [n.3] Some of the traditional common-law requirements appear to have liberalized over the years, strengthening the analogy the Court draws. But surely the Court is not of the view that a single tort in its late 20th-century form can conclusively (and retroactively) dictate the requirements of a 19th-century statute for a discrete category of cases. Defending the historical analogy, the Court suggests that Chief Justice Cooley did not mean what he clearly said and that, despite the Cooley treatise, the Reconstruction-era common law recognized a limited exception to the rule denying a malicious-prosecution plaintiff the benefit of the invalidation of his conviction: an exception for convictions "obtained by some type of fraud." Even if such a narrow exception existed, however, the tort of malicious prosecution as it stood during the mid-19th century would still make for a weak analogy to a statutory action under which, as even the Court accepts, defendants whose convictions were reversed as violating "any righ[t] . . . secured by the Constitution" may obtain damages for the unlawful confinement associated with the conviction (assuming, of course, no immunity bar). Nor, of course, would the existence of such an exception explain how one element of a malicious-prosecution action may be imported into § 1983, but not the others.

Court's opinion can be read as saying nothing more than that now, after enactment of the habeas statute and because of it, prison inmates seeking § 1983 damages in federal court for unconstitutional conviction or confinement must satisfy a requirement analogous to the malicious-prosecution tort's favorable-termination requirement.

That would be a sensible way to read the opinion, in part because the alternative would needlessly place at risk the rights of those outside the intersection of § 1983 and the habeas statute, individuals not "in custody" for habeas purposes. If these individuals (people who were merely fined, for example, or who have completed short terms of imprisonment, probation, or parole, or who discover (through no fault of their own) a constitutional violation after full expiration of their sentences), like state prisoners, were required to show the prior invalidation of their convictions or sentences in order to obtain § 1983 damages for unconstitutional conviction or imprisonment, the result would be to deny any federal forum for claiming a deprivation of federal rights to those who cannot first obtain a favorable state ruling. The reason, of course, is that individuals not "in custody" cannot invoke federal habeas jurisdiction, the only statutory mechanism besides § 1983 by which individuals may sue state officials in federal court for violating federal rights. That would be an untoward result.

It is one thing to adopt a rule that forces prison inmates to follow the federal habeas route with claims that fall within the plain language of § 1983 when that is necessary to prevent a requirement of the habeas statute from being undermined. . . . A prisoner caught at the intersection of § 1983 and the habeas statute can still have his attack on the lawfulness of his conviction or confinement heard in federal court, albeit one sitting as a habeas court; and, depending on the circumstances, he may be able to obtain § 1983 damages.

It would be an entirely different matter, however, to shut off federal courts altogether to claims that fall within the plain language of § 1983. . . . Consider the case of a former slave framed by Ku Klux Klan-controlled law-enforcement officers and convicted by a Klan-controlled state court of, for example, raping a white woman; and suppose that the unjustly convicted defendant did not (and could not) discover the proof of unconstitutionality until after his release from state custody. If it were correct to say that § 1983 independently requires a person not in custody to establish the prior invalidation of his conviction, it would have been equally right to tell the former slave that he could not seek federal relief even against the law-enforcement officers who framed him unless he first managed to convince the state courts that his conviction was unlawful. That would be a result hard indeed to reconcile either with the purpose of § 1983 or with the origins of what was "popularly known as the Ku Klux Act."

Nor do I see any policy reflected in a congressional enactment that would justify denying to an individual today federal damages (a significantly less disruptive remedy than an order compelling release from custody) merely because he was unconstitutionally fined by a State, or to a person who discovers after his release from prison that, for example, state officials deliberately withheld exculpatory material. And absent such a statutory policy, surely the common law can give us no authority to narrow the "broad language" of § 1983.

NOTES

1. Exhaustion Under the PLRA? Assuming that Heck's claim were to arise today, would he first have to exhaust his administrative remedies? Note that the Prison Litigation Reform Act, 42 U.S.C. § 1997e, applies to claims by prisoners challenging "prison conditions," not the wrongs of prosecutors and police who make the initial arrest. See, e.g., Linares v. Jones, No. 04-0247 (D.D.C. 2007) ("it is very doubtful whether the PLRA's exhaustion requirement applies to the circumstances surrounding Plaintiff's arrest and initial police custody").

2. Preclusion following *Heck*. *Heck* announced a federal rule that bars a § 1983 claim for money damages when its substance is inconsistent with a standing criminal conviction. This rule did not replace state rules of issue preclusion, which must also be applied by federal courts following state criminal convictions. *See Allen v. McCurry* (1980) (discussed in Note 5 following *Migra* in Section A, *supra*). Even assuming that *Heck* allows a § 1983 claim to go forward, issue preclusion under state law can still hamper (or even defeat) a plaintiff's claim. *See, e.g., Davis v. Schifone*, 185 F. Supp. 2d 95 (D. Mass. 2002) ("a party to a civil action against a former criminal defendant may invoke the doctrine of collateral estoppel to preclude the criminal defendant from relitigating an issue decided in the criminal prosecution"); *Smith v. Jackson*, 463 F. Supp. 2d 72 (D. Me. 2006) (applying Maine's preclusion principles to a § 1983 claim challenging police conduct following a conviction).

When § 1983 plaintiffs succeed in having their convictions set aside, on the other hand, issue preclusion presents less of a problem. A conviction that is reversed on direct appeal ordinarily has no preclusive effect. *See* RESTATEMENT (SECOND) JUDGMENTS § 16 (1982). Similarly, a criminal conviction that is set aside by a collateral reviewing court, whether state or federal, generally loses any preclusive authority — at least to the extent the former is inconsistent with the latter. *See id.* § 15 (stating that when two judgments are inconsistent the later in time is given preclusive effect). Although a § 1983 plaintiff may not always be able to use a favorable collateral decision as a sword — the § 1983 defendants, for example, may not have been parties to the collateral action — the prior conviction can no longer be used as defensive shield, either.

3. Fundamental Unconstitutional Procedures. The Court left open in footnote 7 the possibility of challenging police procedures — such as unlawful searches and seizures — that do not necessarily imply the invalidity of convictions. *See, e.g., Ove v. Gwinn*, 264 F.3d 817 (9th Cir. 2001) (holding that a § 1983 challenge to the taking of blood to prove DUI was not barred by a DUI conviction). Some procedural challenges, however, involve principles that are so fundamental their violations necessarily impeach the integrity of convictions. In *Edwards v. Balisok*, 520 U.S. 641 (1997), for example, an inmate (Balisok) at the Washington State Penitentiary in Walla Walla was found guilty of four prison infractions and sentenced to ten days' solitary confinement, twenty days in segregation, and loss of thirty days' good-time credit. Balisok thereafter filed a § 1983 action challenging the procedures used at his disciplinary hearing. He requested a declaration that the procedures violated Due Process as well as compensatory and punitive damages. Because of *Preiser v. Rodriguez*, 411 U.S. 475 (1973), which held that the sole federal remedy for a prisoner seeking restoration of good-time credits is a writ of habeas corpus, Balisok's complaint did not request restoration of any lost good-time credits. Still, Justice Scalia ruled for the Court that Balisok's claim was precluded by Heck:

> [Balisok] . . . limited his request to damages for depriving him of good-time credits *without due process*, not for depriving him of good-time credits *undeservedly* as a substantive matter. That is to say, his claim posited that the procedures were wrong, but not necessarily that the result was. The distinction between these two sorts of claims is clearly established in our case law, as is the plaintiff's entitlement to recover at least nominal damages under § 1983 if he proves the former one without also proving the latter one. *See Carey v. Piphus*, 435 U.S. 247 (1978).
>
> [However, Balisok is] incorrect in asserting that a claim seeking damages only "for using the wrong procedure, not for reaching the wrong result," would never be subject to the limitation announced in *Heck*.
>
> The principal procedural defect complained of by [Balisok] would, if established, necessarily imply the invalidity of the deprivation of his good-time credits. His claim is, first of all, that he was completely denied the opportunity to put on a defense through specifically identified witnesses who possessed exculpatory evidence. It appears that all witness testimony in his defense was excluded. This is an obvious procedural defect, and state and federal courts have

reinstated good-time credits (absent a new hearing) when it is established. [Balisok's] claim . . . goes even further, asserting that the cause of the exclusion of the exculpatory evidence was the deceit and bias of the hearing officer himself. He contends that the hearing officer lied about the nonexistence of witness statements, and thus "intentionally denied" him the right to present the extant exculpatory evidence. A criminal defendant tried by a partial judge is entitled to have his conviction set aside, no matter how strong the evidence against him.

We conclude, therefore, that [Balisok's] claim for declaratory relief and money damages, based on allegations of deceit and bias on the part of the decisionmaker that necessarily imply the invalidity of the punishment imposed, is not cognizable under § 1983.

4. Administrative Discipline. Both *Preiser* (excerpted in Section B.[1], *supra*) and *Edwards v. Balisok* (discussed in Note 3, *supra*) involved deprivations of inmates' good-time credits. Consequently, the prisons' disciplinary proceedings in those cases necessarily affected the inmates' lengths of confinement. What if an inmate were to challenge punishment other than a deprivation of good-time credits? *Must* inmates (pursuant to *Heck*) first use federal habeas corpus to overturn their administrative punishments before turning to § 1983? The Supreme Court addressed this question in *Muhammad v. Close*, 540 U.S. 749 (2004) (per curiam), a § 1983 suit that "grew out of a confrontation between [an inmate], Muhammad, . . . and [a] Michigan prison official, Close." Following the confrontation, Close charged Muhammad with "Threatening Behavior" requiring immediate special detention. At the prison disciplinary hearing, Muhammad was acquitted of "Threatening Behavior," but was convicted of a lesser offense, "Insolence," which did not require immediate pre-hearing detention. As a result, Muhammad was required to serve seven additional days of detention and was deprived of prison privileges for thirty days. He did not forfeit good-time credits.

Muhammad challenged his pre-hearing detention under § 1983, claiming that the initial charge filed by Close was in retaliation for prior lawsuits and grievance proceedings Muhammad had filed against him. Muhammad sought compensatory and punitive damages totaling $10,000. He did not challenge his conviction for insolence, his subsequent punishment, nor seek to expunge his record. Rather, he focused solely on the alleged damage caused by his wrongful pre-hearing detention. The Court, in a per curiam opinion, concluded that *Heck* did not apply:

Heck's requirement to resort to state litigation and federal habeas before § 1983 is not . . . implicated by a prisoner's challenge that threatens no consequence for his conviction or the duration of his sentence.**⁴⁷** There is no need to preserve the habeas exhaustion rule and no impediment under *Heck* in such a case, of which this is an example.**⁴⁸**

The decision of the Court of Appeals was flawed as a matter of fact and as a matter of law. Its factual error was the assumption that Muhammad sought to expunge the misconduct charge from his prison record. The court simply overlooked the amended complaint that sought no such relief.

---

⁴⁷ [n.1] The assumption is that the incarceration that matters under *Heck* is the incarceration ordered by the original judgment of conviction, not special disciplinary confinement for infraction of prison rules. This Court has never followed the speculation in *Preiser v. Rodriguez* that such a prisoner subject to "additional and unconstitutional restraint" might have a habeas claim independent of § 1983, and the contention is not raised by the State here.

⁴⁸ [n.2] Members of the Court have expressed the view that unavailability of habeas for other reasons may also dispense with the *Heck* requirement. This case is no occasion to settle the issue. [Editor's note: Consider note 5, *infra*, which discusses the various opinions in *Spencer v. Kemna*, 523 U.S. 1 (1998).]

The factual error was compounded by following the mistaken view . . . that *Heck* applies categorically to all suits challenging prison disciplinary proceedings.

But these administrative determinations do not as such raise any implication about the validity of the underlying conviction, and although they may affect the duration of time to be served (by bearing on the award or revocation of good-time credits) that is not necessarily so. The effect of disciplinary proceedings on good-time credits is a matter of state law or regulation, and in this case, the [District Court] expressly found or assumed that no good-time credits were eliminated by the prehearing action Muhammad called in question. His § 1983 suit challenging this action could not therefore be construed as seeking a judgment at odds with his conviction or with the State's calculation of time to be served in accordance with the underlying sentence. That is, he raised no claim on which habeas relief could have been granted on any recognized theory, with the consequence that *Heck*'s favorable termination requirement was inapplicable.

Footnote 1 makes clear that *Heck*'s concern is with § 1983 challenges that might upset court-ordered incarceration, and "not special disciplinary confinement for infraction of disciplinary rules." It is also strongly suggested in this same footnote that inmates cannot use federal habeas corpus to challenge disciplinary confinement.

5. Unavailability of Habeas Corpus. Justice Souter complained in his *Heck* concurrence that Justice Scalia's position could prevent convicted defendants who had completed their sentences from ever bringing a federal challenge to his conviction. Moreover, some constitutional violations — like searches and seizures in violation of the Fourth Amendment — simply cannot be redressed through federal habeas corpus. *See Stone v. Powell*, 428 U.S. 465 (1976) (holding that so long as the state provides a full and fair opportunity to contest a search and seizure, federal habeas cannot be used). Does this mean that convicted criminals who have completed their sentences are not subject to *Heck*? Does it mean that illegal searches and seizures that fall outside the purview of federal habeas corpus *never* present problems under *Heck*?

This problem surfaced in *Spencer v. Kemna*, 523 U.S. 1 (1998), where an inmate (Spencer) attempted to use federal habeas corpus proceedings to challenge the revocation of his parole. While his petition for habeas corpus was pending in federal district court, Spencer completed his sentence and was released. The Court, per Justice Scalia, concluded that because Spencer could not demonstrate any concrete adverse consequences supporting standing, his habeas claim was mooted by his release. In particular, Justice Scalia rejected Spencer's claim that because he fell within *Heck* (and could not file a § 1983 claim for money damages) he suffered a continuing injury:

> This is a great non sequitur, unless one believes (as we do not) that a § 1983 action for damages must always and everywhere be available. It is not certain, in any event, that a § 1983 damages claim would be foreclosed. If, for example, petitioner were to seek damages "for using the wrong procedures, not for reaching the wrong result," and if that procedural defect did not "necessarily imply the invalidity of" the [parole] revocation, then *Heck* would have no application all.

Justice Souter (joined by Justices O'Connor, Ginsburg and Breyer, concurred) echoing his prior misgivings about *Heck*:

> I join the Court's opinion as well as the judgment, though I do so for an added reason that the Court does not reach, but which I spoke to while concurring in a prior case. One of Spencer's arguments for finding his present interest adequate to support continuing standing despite his release from custody is, as he says, that he may not now press his claims of constitutional injury by action against state officers under § 1983. He assumes that *Heck v. Humphrey* held or entails that conclusion, with the result that holding his habeas claim moot would

leave him without any present access to a federal forum to show the unconstitutionality of his parole revocation. If Spencer were right on this point, his argument would provide a reason, whether or not dispositive, to recognize continuing standing to litigate his habeas claim. But he is wrong; *Heck* did not hold that a released prisoner in Spencer's circumstances is out of court on a § 1983 claim, and for reasons explained in my *Heck* concurrence, it would be unsound to read either *Heck* or the habeas statute as requiring any such result. For all that appears here, then, Spencer is free to bring a § 1983 action, and his corresponding argument for continuing habeas standing falls accordingly.

To be sure, the majority opinion in *Heck* can be read to suggest that [the] favorable-termination requirement is an element of any § 1983 action alleging unconstitutional conviction, whether or not leading to confinement and whether or not any confinement continued when the § 1983 action was filed. Indeed, although *Heck* did not present such facts, the majority acknowledged the possibility that even a released prisoner might not be permitted to bring a § 1983 action implying the invalidity of a conviction or confinement without first satisfying the favorable-termination requirement.

Concurring in the judgment in *Heck*, I . . . thought it important to read the Court's . . . opinion as subjecting only inmates seeking § 1983 damages for unconstitutional conviction or confinement to "a requirement analogous to the malicious-prosecution tort's favorable-termination requirement," lest the plain breadth of § 1983 be unjustifiably limited at the expense of persons not "in custody" within the meaning of the habeas statute. The subsequent case of *Edwards v. Balisok* was, like *Heck* itself, a suit by a prisoner and so for present purposes left the law where it was after *Heck*. Now, as then, we are forced to recognize that any application of the favorable-termination requirement to § 1983 suits brought by plaintiffs not in custody would produce a patent anomaly: a given claim for relief from unconstitutional injury would be placed beyond the scope of § 1983 if brought by a convict free of custody (as, in this case, following service of a full term of imprisonment), when exactly the same claim could be redressed if brought by a former prisoner who had succeeded in cutting his custody short through habeas.

The better view, then, is that a former prisoner, no longer "in custody," may bring a § 1983 action establishing the unconstitutionality of a conviction or confinement without being bound to satisfy a favorable-termination requirement that it would be impossible as a matter of law for him to satisfy. Thus, the answer to Spencer's argument that his habeas claim cannot be moot because *Heck* bars him from relief under § 1983 is that *Heck* has no such effect. After a prisoner's release from custody, the habeas statute and its exhaustion requirement have nothing to do with his right to any relief.

Justice Ginsburg added her own concurring remarks: "Mindful of 'real-life example[s],' among them this case, I have come to agree with Justice Souter's reasoning: Individuals without recourse to the habeas statute because they are not 'in custody' (people merely fined or whose sentences have been fully served, for example) fit within § 1983's 'broad reach.' " Justice Stevens also concurred, stating that "it is perfectly clear, as Justice Souter explains, that [Spencer] may bring an action under 42 U.S.C. § 1983." A majority of Justices therefore appear to agree that *Heck* does not preclude a § 1983 claim when the plaintiff is unable to make use of federal habeas corpus because of release from confinement.[49] *See, e.g., Powers v. Hamilton County Public Defender*

---

[49] What about habeas challenges that are precluded by *Stone v. Powell*? *See Wallace v. Kato*, 549 U.S. 384 (2007) (Stevens, J., concurring) (arguing that "*Heck* cannot postpone" a challenge to police procedures that could not be pursued through federal habeas corpus because of *Stone v. Powell*) (excerpted in Section B.[3], *infra*).

Commission, 501 F.3d 592 (6th Cir. 2007) (holding that a one-day sentence was too short to facilitate habeas and thus that *Heck* did not apply); *Nonette v. Small*, 316 F.3d 872 (9th Cir. 2002) (observing that *Spencer* allows a released prisoner to bring a § 1983 challenge notwithstanding *Heck*); *Jenkins v. Harbert*, 179 F.3d 19 (2d Cir. 1999) (same). *But see Figerora v. Rivera*, 147 F.3d 77 (1st Cir. 1998) (refusing to recognize dicta in *Kemna* and holding that *Heck* applies regardless of whether a habeas petition is possible).

In contrast, where habeas corpus was available but was not properly pursued, *Heck* remains a bar to proceeding under § 1983. *See, e.g., Cunningham v. Gates*, 312 F.3d 1148 (9th Cir. 2002) (refusing to waive *Heck* where a habeas claim was merely time-barred). Concurring in *Wilkinson v. Dotson*, 544 U.S. 74 (2005) (discussed in Note 6, *infra*), Justice Scalia explained that "a prisoner who wishes to challenge the length of his confinement, but who cannot obtain federal habeas relief because of the statute of limitations or the restrictions on successive petitions cannot use the unavailability of federal habeas relief in his individual case as grounds for proceeding under § 1983."

6. Challenging Parole Decisions. The plaintiff in *Spencer* attempted to use federal habeas corpus to challenge the revocation of his parole. Can habeas corpus be used to challenge an initial decision not to parole an inmate? Justice Scalia opined in his concurrence in *Wilkinson v. Dotson*, 544 U.S. 74 (2005), that habeas ought not be used to challenge denials of parole, since a grant of the writ in the context of parole ordinarily would "neither terminate[] custody, accelerate[] the future date of release from custody, nor reduce[] the level of custody." Justice Kennedy disagreed, taking the position that "[c]hallenges to parole proceedings are cognizable in habeas."

Whether or not habeas corpus is available to challenge a denial of parole, the majority in *Wilkinson v. Dotson*, 544 U.S. 74 (2005) (per Justice Breyer), ruled that § 1983 can be used and that *Heck* was not a problem. The inmates in *Dotson* simply requested new parole hearings under what they claimed to be proper procedures. They did not demand release. Because they did not seek early release, their success under § 1983 would not necessarily contradict their confinement:

> Ohio points out that the inmates in these cases attack their parole-eligibility proceedings . . . only because they believe that victory on their claims will lead to speedier release from prison. Consequently, Ohio argues, the prisoners' lawsuits, in effect, collaterally attack the *duration* of their confinement; hence, such a claim may only be brought through a habeas corpus action, not through § 1983.
>
> The problem with Ohio's argument lies in its jump from a true premise (that in all likelihood the prisoners hope these actions will help bring about earlier release) to a faulty conclusion (that habeas is their sole avenue for relief). A consideration of this Court's case law makes clear that the connection between the constitutionality of the prisoners' parole proceedings and release from confinement is too tenuous here to achieve Ohio's legal door-closing objective.
>
> The Court initially addressed the relationship between § 1983 and the federal habeas statutes in *Preiser v. Rodriguez*. . . . In *Wolf v. McDonnell*, 418 U.S. 539 (1974), the Court elaborated the contours of this habeas corpus "core." As in *Preiser*, state prisoners brought a § 1983 action challenging prison officials' revocation of good-time credits by means of constitutionally deficient disciplinary proceedings. The Court held that the prisoners could not use § 1983 to obtain restoration of the credits because *Preiser* had held that "an injunction restoring good time improperly taken is foreclosed."
>
> But the inmates *could* use § 1983 to obtain a declaration ("as a predicate to" their requested damages award) that the disciplinary procedures were invalid. They could also seek "by way of ancillary relief[,] an otherwise proper injunction enjoining the *prospective* enforcement of invalid prison regulations." In neither case would victory for the prisoners necessarily have meant immediate release

or a shorter period of incarceration; the prisoners attacked only the "wrong procedures, not . . . the wrong result (i.e., [the denial of] good-time credits)."

In *Heck* the Court considered a different, but related, circumstance. A state prisoner brought a § 1983 action for damages, challenging the conduct of state officials who, the prisoner claimed, had unconstitutionally caused his conviction by improperly investigating his crime and destroying evidence. The Court . . . held that where "establishing the basis for the damages claim necessarily demonstrates the invalidity of the conviction," a § 1983 action will not lie "unless . . . the conviction or sentence has already been invalidated."

Finally, in *Edwards v. Balisok*, the Court returned to the prison disciplinary procedure context of the kind it had addressed previously in *Preiser* and *Wolff*. . . . Applying *Heck*, the Court found that habeas was the sole vehicle for the inmate's constitutional challenge insofar as the prisoner sought declaratory relief and money damages, because the "principal procedural defect complained of," namely deceit and bias on the part of the decisionmaker, "would, if established, necessarily imply the invalidity of the deprivation of [Balisok's] good-time credits." Hence, success on the prisoner's claim for money damages (and the accompanying claim for declaratory relief) would "necessarily imply the invalidity of the punishment imposed." Nonetheless, the prisoner's claim for an injunction barring *future* unconstitutional procedures did *not* fall within habeas' exclusive domain. That is because "[o]rdinarily, a prayer for such prospective relief will not 'necessarily imply' the invalidity of a previous loss of good-time credits."

Throughout the legal journey from *Preiser* to *Balisok*, the Court has focused on the need to ensure that state prisoners use only habeas corpus (or similar state) remedies when they seek to invalidate the duration of their confinement — either *directly* through an injunction compelling speedier release or *indirectly* through a judicial determination that necessarily implies the unlawfulness of the State's custody. . . . These cases, taken together, indicate that a state prisoner's § 1983 action is barred (absent prior invalidation) — no matter the relief sought (damages or equitable relief), no matter the target of the prisoner's suit (state conduct leading to conviction or internal prison proceedings) — *if* success in that action would necessarily demonstrate the invalidity of confinement or its duration.

Applying these principles to the present case, we conclude that [the inmates'] claims are cognizable under § 1983, i.e., they do not fall within the implicit habeas exception. [The inmates] seek relief that will render invalid the state procedures used to deny parole eligibility. . . . Neither [inmate] seeks an injunction ordering his immediate or speedier release into the community. . . . Success . . . does not mean immediate release from confinement or a shorter stay in prison; it means at most new eligibility review, which at most will speed *consideration* of a new parole application. Success . . . means at most a new parole hearing at which Ohio parole authorities may, in their discretion, decline to shorten his prison term. Because neither prisoner's claim would necessarily spell speedier release, neither lies at "the core of habeas corpus." Finally, the prisoners' claims for *future* relief (which, if successful, will not necessarily imply the invalidity of confinement or shorten its duration) are yet more distant from that core.

Ohio points to language in *Heck* indicating that a prisoner's § 1983 damages action cannot lie where a favorable judgment would "necessarily imply the invalidity of his conviction *or sentence*." Ohio then argues that its parole proceedings are part of the prisoners' "sentence[s]" — indeed, an aspect of the "sentence[s]" that the § 1983 claims, if successful, will invalidate.

We do not find this argument persuasive. In context, *Heck* uses the word "sentence" to refer not to prison procedures, but to substantive determinations as to the length of confinement. See *Muhammad v. Close (per curiam)* ("[T]he incarceration that matters under *Heck* is the incarceration ordered by the original judgment of conviction"). *Heck* uses the word "sentence" interchangeably with such other terms as "continuing confinement" and "imprisonment." So understood, *Heck* is consistent with other cases permitting prisoners to bring § 1983 challenges to prison administrative decisions. Indeed, this Court has repeatedly permitted prisoners to bring § 1983 actions challenging the conditions of their confinement — conditions that, were Ohio right, might be considered part of the "sentence."

7. Excessive Force. As the *Heck* majority points out, a Fourth Amendment claim for false arrest — i.e., that the police lacked probable cause to make the arrest — is ordinarily precluded by a state court conviction. *See, e.g., Wells v. Bonner*, 45 F.3d 90, 95 (5th Cir. 1995) (holding that *Heck* barred a plaintiff's Fourth Amendment claim for false arrest following his conviction). The same is not necessarily true of a Fourth Amendment claim predicated on excessive force, even when a § 1983 plaintiff is convicted of resisting arrest. The question in this sort of case is whether the criminal conviction for resisting arrest necessarily implies the reasonableness or lawfulness of the officer's use of force. Where the state's resisting arrest statute requires a "lawful arrest" — that is, the defendant is guilty only if he or she resists the use of lawful force — conviction will ordinarily bar a Fourth Amendment excessive force claim under § 1983. *See Heck* (footnote 6), *supra*. Where the state criminalizes resisting *any* arrest, however, a conviction would not necessarily imply a reasonable or lawful use of force on the part of the arresting officer. A Fourth Amendment claim grounded in excessive force would then not be precluded by *Heck*. *See, e.g., Nelson v. Jashurek*, 109 F.3d 142 (3d Cir. 1997) (holding that an excessive force claim was proper notwithstanding a prior conviction for resisting arrest).[50]

[3] *Heck*, Accrual, and Timing

WALLACE v. KATO
Supreme Court of the United States
549 U.S. 384 (2007)

JUSTICE SCALIA delivered the opinion of the Court.

[Wallace] filed suit under . . . 42 U.S.C. § 1983, seeking damages for an arrest that violated the Fourth Amendment. We decide whether his suit is timely.

On January 17, 1994, John Handy was shot to death in the city of Chicago. Sometime around 8 p.m. two days later, Chicago police officers located [Wallace], then 15 years of age, and transported him to a police station for questioning. After interrogations that lasted into the early morning hours the next day, [Wallace] agreed to confess to Handy's murder. An assistant state's attorney prepared a statement to this effect, and [Wallace] signed it, at the same time waiving his Miranda rights.

Prior to trial in the Circuit Court of Cook County, [Wallace] unsuccessfully attempted to suppress his station house statements as the product of an unlawful

---

[50] Likewise, if the officer's challenged force is not responsive to a § 1983 plaintiff's resistance, or is otherwise divorced from the criminal charges brought against him, the conviction might not imply the lawfulness or reasonableness of the complained-of conduct. In *Martinez v. City of Albuquerque*, 184 F.3d 1123 (10th Cir. 1999), for example, the plaintiff's conviction for resisting arrest was based on his flight from police officers. His Fourth Amendment excessive force claim, meanwhile, was predicated on the force *subsequently* employed by police officers during the course of his arrest. The Tenth Circuit concluded that the plaintiff's conviction did not prevent his § 1983 claim premised on the subsequent use of excessive force.

arrest. He was convicted of first-degree murder and sentenced to 26 years in prison. On direct appeal, the Appellate Court of Illinois held that officers had arrested [Wallace] without probable cause, in violation of the Fourth Amendment. According to that court (whose determination we are not reviewing here), even assuming [Wallace] willingly accompanied police to the station, his presence there "escalated to an involuntary seizure prior to his formal arrest." After another round of appeals, the Appellate Court concluded on August 31, 2001, that the effect of [Wallace's] illegal arrest had not been sufficiently attenuated to render his statements admissible, *see Brown v. Illinois*, 422 U.S. 590 (1975), and remanded for a new trial. On April 10, 2002, prosecutors dropped the charges against [Wallace].

On April 2, 2003, [Wallace] filed this § 1983 suit against the city of Chicago and several Chicago police officers, seeking damages arising from, inter alia, his unlawful arrest. . . . According to the Seventh Circuit, [Wallace]'s § 1983 suit was time barred because his cause of action accrued at the time of his arrest, and not when his conviction was later set aside.

Section 1983 provides a federal cause of action, but in several respects relevant here federal law looks to the law of the State in which the cause of action arose. This is so for the length of the statute of limitations: It is that which the State provides for personal-injury torts. The parties agree that under Illinois law, this period is two years. Thus, if the statute on [Wallace's] cause of action began to run at the time of his unlawful arrest, or even at the time he was ordered held by a magistrate, his § 1983 suit was plainly dilatory, even according him tolling for the two-plus years of his minority. But if, as the dissenting judge argued below, the commencement date for running of the statute is governed by this Court's decision in *Heck v. Humphrey*, 512 U.S. 477 (1994), that date may be the date on which [Wallace's] conviction was vacated, in which case the § 1983 suit would have been timely filed.

While we have never stated so expressly, the accrual date of a § 1983 cause of action is a question of federal law that is not resolved by reference to state law. . . . There can be no dispute that [Wallace] could have filed suit as soon as the allegedly wrongful arrest occurred, subjecting him to the harm of involuntary detention, so the statute of limitations would normally commence to run from that date.

There is, however, a refinement to be considered, arising from the common law's distinctive treatment of the torts of false arrest and false imprisonment, "[t]he . . . cause[s] of action [that] provid[e] the closest analogy to claims of the type considered here." False arrest and false imprisonment overlap; the former is a species of the latter. "Every confinement of the person is an imprisonment, whether it be in a common prison or in a private house, or in the stocks, or even by forcibly detaining one in the public streets; and when a man is lawfully in a house, it is imprisonment to prevent him from leaving the room in which he is." We shall thus refer to the two torts together as false imprisonment. That tort provides the proper analogy to the cause of action asserted against the present respondents for the following reason: The sort of unlawful detention remediable by the tort of false imprisonment is detention without legal process, and the allegations before us arise from [the] detention of [Wallace] without legal process in January 1994. They did not have a warrant for his arrest.

The running of the statute of limitations on false imprisonment is subject to a distinctive rule — dictated, perhaps, by the reality that the victim may not be able to sue while he is still imprisoned: "Limitations begin to run against an action for false imprisonment when the alleged false imprisonment ends." Thus, to determine the beginning of the limitations period in this case, we must determine when [Wallace's] false imprisonment came to an end.

Reflective of the fact that false imprisonment consists of detention without legal process, a false imprisonment ends once the victim becomes held pursuant to such process — when, for example, he is bound over by a magistrate or arraigned on charges. Thereafter, unlawful detention forms part of the damages for the "entirely distinct" tort of malicious prosecution, which remedies detention accompanied, not by absence of legal process, but by wrongful institution of legal process.[51] "If there is a false arrest claim, damages for that claim cover the time of detention up until issuance of process or arraignment, but not more. From that point on, any damages recoverable must be based on a malicious prosecution claim and on the wrongful use of judicial process rather than detention itself." Thus, [Wallace's] contention that his false imprisonment ended upon his release from custody, after the State dropped the charges against him, must be rejected. It ended much earlier, when legal process was initiated against him, and the statute would have begun to run from that date, but for its tolling by reason of [Wallace's] minority.[52]

[Wallace] asserts that the date of his release from custody must be the relevant date in the circumstances of the present suit, since he is seeking damages up to that time. The theory of his complaint is that the initial Fourth Amendment violation set the wheels in motion for his subsequent conviction and detention: The unlawful arrest led to the coerced confession, which was introduced at his trial, producing his conviction and incarceration. As we have just explained, at common law damages for detention after issuance of process or arraignment would be attributable to a tort other than the unlawful arrest alleged in petitioner's complaint — and probably a tort chargeable to defendants other than th[ose] here. Even assuming, however, that all damages for detention pursuant to legal process could be regarded as consequential damages attributable to the unlawful arrest, that would not alter the commencement date for the statute of limitations. "Under the traditional rule of accrual . . . the tort cause of action accrues, and the statute of limitations commences to run, when the wrongful act or omission results in damages. The cause of action accrues even though the full extent of the injury is not then known or predictable." Were it otherwise, the statute would begin to run only after a plaintiff became satisfied that he had been harmed enough, placing the supposed statute of repose in the sole hands of the party seeking relief.

We conclude that the statute of limitations on [Wallace's] § 1983 claim commenced to run when he appeared before the examining magistrate and was bound over for trial. Since more than two years elapsed between that date and the filing of this suit — even leaving out of the count the period before he reached his majority — the action was time barred.

This would end the matter, were it not for [Wallace's] contention that *Heck v. Humphrey* compels the conclusion that his suit could not accrue until the State dropped its charges against him.

[T]he *Heck* rule for deferred accrual is called into play only when there exists "a conviction or sentence that has not been . . . invalidated," that is to say, an "outstanding criminal judgment." It delays what would otherwise be the accrual date of a tort action until the setting aside of an extant conviction which success in that tort action would impugn. We assume that, for purposes of the present tort action, the *Heck* principle would be applied not to the date of accrual but to the date on which the statute of limitations began to run, that is, the date [Wallace] became held pursuant to legal process. Even at that later time, there was in existence no criminal conviction that the cause of action would impugn; indeed, there may not even have been an indictment.

What [Wallace] seeks, in other words, is the adoption of a principle that goes well beyond *Heck*: that an action which would impugn an anticipated future conviction

---

[51] [n.2] We have never explored the contours of a Fourth Amendment malicious-prosecution suit under § 1983, *see Albright v. Oliver*, 510 U.S. 266 (1994) (plurality opinion), and we do not do so here. Assuming without deciding that such a claim is cognizable under § 1983, [Wallace] has not made one.

[52] [n.3] This is not to say, of course, that [Wallace] could not have filed suit immediately upon his false arrest. While the statute of limitations did not begin to run until [Wallace] became detained pursuant to legal process, he was injured and suffered damages at the moment of his arrest, and was entitled to bring suit at that time.

cannot be brought until that conviction occurs and is set aside. The impracticality of such a rule should be obvious. In an action for false arrest it would require the plaintiff (and if he brings suit promptly, the court) to speculate about whether a prosecution will be brought, whether it will result in conviction, and whether the pending civil action will impugn that verdict — all this at a time when it can hardly be known what evidence the prosecution has in its possession. And what if the plaintiff (or the court) guesses wrong, and the anticipated future conviction never occurs, because of acquittal or dismissal? Does that event (instead of the *Heck*-required setting aside of the extant conviction) trigger accrual of the cause of action? Or what if prosecution never occurs — what will the trigger be then?

We are not disposed to embrace this bizarre extension of *Heck*. If a plaintiff files a false arrest claim before he has been convicted (or files any other claim related to rulings that will likely be made in a pending or anticipated criminal trial), it is within the power of the district court, and in accord with common practice, to stay the civil action until the criminal case or the likelihood of a criminal case is ended. If the plaintiff is ultimately convicted, and if the stayed civil suit would impugn that conviction, *Heck* will require dismissal; otherwise, the civil action will proceed, absent some other bar to suit.

There is, however, one complication that we must address here. It arises from the fact that § 1983 actions, unlike the tort of malicious prosecution which *Heck* took as its model, sometimes accrue before the setting aside of — indeed, even before the existence of — the related criminal conviction. That of course is the case here, and it raises the question whether, assuming that the *Heck* bar takes effect when the later conviction is obtained, the statute of limitations on the once valid cause of action is tolled as long as the *Heck* bar subsists. In the context of the present case: If [Wallace's] conviction on April 19, 1996, caused the statute of limitations on his (possibly) impugning but yet-to-be-filed cause of action to be tolled until that conviction was set aside, his filing here would have been timely.

We have generally referred to state law for tolling rules, just as we have for the length of statutes of limitation. [Wallace] has not brought to our attention, nor are we aware of, Illinois cases providing tolling in even remotely comparable circumstances. . . . Nor would we be inclined to adopt a federal tolling rule to this effect. Under such a regime, it would not be known whether tolling is appropriate by reason of the *Heck* bar until it is established that the newly entered conviction would be impugned by the not-yet-filed, and thus utterly indeterminate, § 1983 claim.[53] It would hardly be desirable to place the question of tolling *vel non* in this jurisprudential limbo, leaving it to be determined by those later events, and then pronouncing it retroactively. Defendants need to be on notice to preserve beyond the normal limitations period evidence that will be needed for their defense; and a statute that becomes retroactively extended, by the action of the plaintiff in crafting a conviction-impugning cause of action, is hardly a statute of repose.[54]

---

[53] [n.4] Had [Wallace] filed suit upon his arrest and had his suit then been dismissed under *Heck*, the statute of limitations, absent tolling, would have run by the time he obtained reversal of his conviction. If under those circumstances he were not allowed to refile his suit, *Heck* would produce immunity from § 1983 liability, a result surely not intended. Because in the present case petitioner did not file his suit within the limitations period, we need not decide, had he done so, how much time he would have had to refile the suit once the *Heck* bar was removed.

[54] [n.5] Justice Stevens reaches the same result by arguing that, under *Stone v. Powell*, 428 U.S. 465 (1976), the *Heck* bar can never come into play in a § 1983 suit seeking damages for a Fourth Amendment violation, so that "a habeas remedy was never available to [Wallace] in the first place." This reads *Stone* to say more than it does. Under *Stone*, Fourth Amendment violations are generally not cognizable on federal habeas, but they are cognizable when the State has failed to provide the habeas petitioner "an opportunity for full and fair litigation of a Fourth Amendment claim." Federal habeas petitioners have sometimes succeeded in arguing that *Stone*'s general prohibition does not apply. At the time of a Fourth Amendment wrong, and at the time

Justice Breyer argues in dissent that equitable tolling should apply "so long as the issues that [a § 1983] claim would raise are being pursued in state court." We know of no support (nor does the dissent suggest any) for the far-reaching proposition that equitable tolling is appropriate to avoid the risk of concurrent litigation. As best we can tell, the only rationale for such a rule is the concern that "[Wallace] would have had to divide his attention between criminal and civil cases." But when has it been the law that a criminal defendant, or a potential criminal defendant, is absolved from all other responsibilities that the law would otherwise place upon him? If a defendant has a breach-of-contract claim against the prime contractor for his new home, is he entitled to tolling for that as well while his criminal case is pending? Equitable tolling is a rare remedy to be applied in unusual circumstances, not a cure-all for an entirely common state of affairs. Besides its never-heard-of-before quality, the dissent's proposal suffers from a more ironic flaw. Although the dissent criticizes us for having to develop a system of stays and dismissals, it should be obvious that the omnibus tolling solution will require the same. Despite the existence of the new tolling rule, some (if not most) plaintiffs will nevertheless file suit before or during state criminal proceedings. How does the dissent propose to handle such suits? Finally, the dissent's contention that law enforcement officers would prefer the possibility of a later § 1983 suit to the more likely reality of an immediate filing, is both implausible and contradicted by those who know best. As no fewer than 11 States have informed us in this litigation, "States and municipalities have a strong interest in timely notice of alleged misconduct by their agents."

We hold that the statute of limitations upon a § 1983 claim seeking damages for a false arrest in violation of the Fourth Amendment, where the arrest is followed by criminal proceedings, begins to run at the time the claimant becomes detained pursuant to legal process. Since in the present case this occurred (with appropriate tolling for the plaintiff's minority) more than two years before the complaint was filed, the suit was out of time.

JUSTICE STEVENS, with whom JUSTICE SOUTER, joins, concurring in the judgment.

While I do not disagree with the Court's conclusion, I reach it by a more direct route.

Unlike the majority, my analysis would not depend on any common-law tort analogies. Instead, I would begin where all nine Justices began in *Heck*. That case, we unanimously agreed, required the Court to reconcile § 1983 with the federal habeas corpus statute. In concluding that *Heck*'s damages claim was not cognizable under § 1983, we found that the writ of habeas corpus, and not § 1983, affords the " 'appropriate remedy for state prisoners attacking the validity of the fact or length of their confinement.' " Given our holding in *Stone v. Powell*, 428 U.S. 465 (1976), however, that writ cannot provide a remedy for [Wallace]. And because a habeas remedy was never available to him in the first place, *Heck* cannot postpone the accrual of [Wallace's] § 1983 Fourth Amendment claim.[55] So while it may well be appropriate to stay the trial

---

of conviction, it cannot be known whether a prospective § 1983 plaintiff will receive a full and fair opportunity to litigate his Fourth Amendment claim. It thus remains the case that a conflict with the federal habeas statute is possible, that a Fourth Amendment claim can necessarily imply the invalidity of a conviction, and that if it does it must, under *Heck*, be dismissed. Insofar as Justice Stevens simply suggests that *Heck* has no bearing here because [Wallace] received a full and fair opportunity to litigate his Fourth Amendment claim in state court, the argument is equally untenable. At the time that [Wallace] became detained pursuant to legal process, it was impossible to predict whether this would be true. And even at the point when his limitations period ended, state proceedings on his conviction were ongoing; full and fair opportunity up to that point was not enough. *Stone* requires full and fair opportunity to litigate a Fourth Amendment claim "at trial and on direct review."

55 [n.3] *See Spencer v. Kemna*, 523 U.S. 1 (1998).

of claims of this kind until after the completion of state proceedings, I am aware of no legal basis for holding that the cause of action has not accrued once the Fourth Amendment violation has been completed.

The Court regrettably lets the perfect become the enemy of the good. It eschews my reasoning because "[f]ederal habeas petitioners have sometimes succeeded in arguing that Stone's general prohibition does not apply." However, in the vast run of cases, a State will provide a habeas petitioner with "an opportunity for full and fair litigation of a Fourth Amendment claim," and *Heck* will not apply. It is always possible to find aberrant examples in the law, but we should not craft rules for the needle rather than the haystack in an area like this.

JUSTICE BREYER, with whom JUSTICE GINSBURG joins, dissenting.

I agree with the Court that the accrual date of a 42 U.S.C. § 1983 claim is not postponed by the presence of a possible bar to suit under *Heck*. I also agree with the rest of the Court and with Justice Stevens that had [Wallace] timely filed his § 1983 case, the Federal District Court might have found it appropriate to stay the trial of his claims until the completion of state proceedings. In the absence of a stay, a litigant like [Wallace] would have had to divide his attention between criminal and civil cases with attendant risks of loss of time and energy as well as of inconsistent findings.

The Court's holding, however, simply leads to the question of what is to happen when, for example, the possibility of a *Heck* problem prevents the court from considering the merits of a § 1983 claim. And I disagree with the Court's insistence upon a rule of law that would require immediate filing, followed by an uncertain system of stays, dismissals, and possible refiling. I disagree because there is a well-established legal tool better able to deal with the problems presented by this type of suit.

Where a "plaintiff because of disability, irremediable lack of information, or other circumstances beyond his control just cannot reasonably be expected to sue in time," courts have applied a doctrine of "equitable tolling." The doctrine tolls the running of the limitations period until the disabling circumstance can be overcome. (This is why the limitations period does not run against a falsely arrested person until his false imprisonment ends. His action has certainly accrued because, as the majority recognizes, he can file his claim immediately if he is able to do so.)

In particular, equitable tolling could apply where a § 1983 plaintiff reasonably claims that the unlawful behavior of which he complains was, or will be, necessary to a criminal conviction. It could toll the running of the limitations period: (1) from the time charges are brought until the time they are dismissed or the defendant is acquitted or convicted, and (2) thereafter during any period in which the criminal defendant challenges a conviction (on direct appeal, on state collateral challenge, or on federal habeas) and reasonably asserts the behavior underlying the § 1983 action as a ground for overturning the conviction.

I find it difficult to understand why the Court rejects the use of "equitable tolling" in regard to typical § 1983 plaintiffs. The Court's alternative — file all § 1983 claims (including potentially *Heck*-barred claims) at once and then seek stays or be subject to dismissal and refiling — suffers serious practical disadvantages. For one thing, that approach would force all potential criminal defendants to file all potential § 1983 actions soon lest they lose those claims due to protracted criminal proceedings. For another, it would often require a federal court, seeking to determine whether to dismiss an action as *Heck* barred or to grant a stay, to consider issues likely being litigated in the criminal proceeding (Was the Constitution violated? Was the violation-related evidence necessary for conviction?). The federal court's decision as to whether a claim was *Heck* barred (say, whether the alleged constitutional violation was central to the state criminal conviction) might later bind a state court on conviction review. Because of this, even a claim without a likely *Heck* bar might linger on a federal docket because the federal court (or the plaintiff who has been forced to early file) wishes to avoid interfering with any state proceedings and therefore must postpone reaching, not only the merits of the § 1983 claim, but the threshold *Heck* inquiry as well.

Principles of equitable tolling avoid these difficulties. Since equitable tolling obviates the need for immediate filing, it permits the criminal proceedings to winnow the constitutional wheat from chaff, and thereby increase the likelihood that the constitutionally meritless claims will never (in a § 1983 action) see the light of day. Moreover, an appropriate equitable tolling principle would apply not only to state criminal proceedings as here, but also to state appellate proceedings, state collateral attacks, and federal habeas proceedings.

Of course, § 1983 ordinarily borrows its limitations principles from state law. And I do not know whether or which States have comparable equitable tolling principles in place. If a given state court lacks the necessary tolling provision, however, § 1983, in my view, permits the federal courts to devise and impose such principles.

The use of equitable tolling in cases of potential temporal conflict between civil § 1983 and related criminal proceedings is consistent with, indeed, it would further, § 1983's basic purposes. It would provide for orderly adjudication, minimize the risk of inconsistent legal determinations, avoid clogging the courts with potentially unnecessary "protective" filings, and, above all, assure a plaintiff who possesses a meritorious § 1983 claim that his pursuit of criminal remedies designed to free him from unlawful confinement will not compromise his later ability to obtain civil § 1983 redress as well.

The Court is wrong in concluding that the principle I have described would "place" the tolling "question" in "jurisprudential limbo." Under the approach I propose, a potential § 1983 plaintiff knows his claim is being tolled so long as the issues that claim would raise are being pursued in state court. Such a rule is prophylactic (it will sometimes toll claims that would not be barred by *Heck*), but under such an approach neither the plaintiff, nor the defendant, nor the federal court need speculate as to whether the claims are in any way barred until the state court has had the opportunity to consider the claims in the criminal context.

A tolling principle certainly seems to me to create greater order than the rule the majority sets out, whereby all criminal defendants must file their § 1983 suits immediately, some will be stayed, some dismissed, and then some may be refiled and entitled to tolling. The majority acknowledges that tolling may be necessary to protect the plaintiff who previously filed and was dismissed. Why not simply apply that tolling principle across the board?

The majority is also wrong when it suggests that the proposed equitable tolling rule would create a significant problem of lack of notice. Because the rule would toll only while the potential § 1983 plaintiff is challenging the alleged misconduct in a state court, the State itself would have notice of the plaintiff's claims. For similar reasons, the potential individual § 1983 defendants, the state officers, would also likely have notice of the charge. But even if they do not, I believe that many would prefer to forgo immediate notice, for it comes with a pricetag attached — the price consists of being immediately sued by the filing of a § 1983 lawsuit, rife with stays and delays, which otherwise, in the course of time (as claims are winnowed in state court) might never have been filed.

The Court's suggested limitations system, like an equitable tolling rule, will produce some instances in which a plaintiff will file a § 1983 lawsuit at an initially uncertain future date. And, under both approaches, in the many § 1983 suits that do not involve any *Heck* bar, a defendant can and will file immediately and his suit would proceed (for there is no tolling unless the potential § 1983 plaintiff is asserting in a conviction challenge that a constitutional violation did impugn his conviction). My problem with the Court's approach lies in its insistence that all potential plaintiffs (including those whose suits may be *Heck* barred) file immediately — even though their suits cannot then proceed. With tolling, only rarely would a plaintiff choose to file a potentially *Heck*-barred § 1983 suit while his criminal case is pending; and in those cases the district court could, if it wished, stay the action, or simply dismiss the suit without prejudice, secure in the knowledge that the suit could be timely filed at a later date.

The Court's refusal to admit the equitable tolling possibility means that large numbers of defendants will be sued immediately by all potential § 1983 plaintiffs with arguable *Heck* issues, no matter how meritless the claims; these suits may be endlessly stayed or dismissed and then, at some point in the future, some defendants will also be sued again. With equitable tolling, however, defendants will be sued once, in suits with constitutional claims that a state court has not already found meritless, at a time when the suit can be promptly litigated. Given the practical difficulties of the Court's approach, I would not rule out now, in advance, the use of an equitable tolling rule along the lines I have described.

NOTES

1. Applying *Heck* Before Conviction. Several circuits following *Heck* ruled that *Heck* applied not only to § 1983 suits challenging convictions, but also to those that potentially contradicted pending criminal charges. *See, e.g., Shamaeizadeh v. Cunigan,* 182 F.3d 391 (6th Cir. 1999) ("we hold that the reasoning of *Heck* applies pre-conviction, [and] requires that a § 1983 plaintiff show that a decision in his favor would not imply the invalidity of a future conviction"); *Covington v. City of New York,* 171 F.3d 117 (2d Cir. 1999) (same); *Uboh v. Reno,* 141 F.3d 1000 (11th Cir. 1998) (same); *Washington v. Summerville,* 127 F.3d 552 (7th Cir. 1997) (same); *Smith v. Holtz,* 87 F.3d 108 (3d Cir. 1996) (same). Under this approach, § 1983 actions filed before a criminal defendant's successful termination of criminal proceedings would be dismissed as not yet ripe. Only if a § 1983 plaintiff prevailed in state criminal court would he or she be allowed to file a § 1983 claim, and the local statute of limitations would run from the date criminal charges were defeated. *See, e.g., Shamaeizadeh v. Cunigan,* 182 F.3d 391 (6th Cir. 1999).

For its part, the Supreme Court in *Deakins v. Monaghan,* 484 U.S. 193 (1988) (excerpted in Chapter 7.C., *supra*), recommended a different approach: analogizing to *Younger*'s abstention principle, *see* Chapter 7.B., *supra*, the Supreme Court in *Deakins* ruled that District Courts are authorized to *stay* § 1983 claims seeking damages pending the outcome of state criminal proceedings. The Court in *Wallace v. Kato,* 549 U.S. 384 (2007), endorsed this approach, though it did not hold that it was mandatory or preferred over outright dismissal. It instead seemed to punt the choice back to the lower federal courts, stating that "it is within the power of the district court, and in accord with common practice, to stay the civil action until the criminal case or the likelihood of a criminal case is ended," while also noting that District Courts might dismiss instead. *See* footnote 4, *supra*. *But see Eidson v. State of Tennessee Department of Children Services,* 510 F.3d 631 (6th Cir. 2007) ("In *Wallace*, the court specifically held that *Heck* is not to be extended into the pre-conviction arena. The *Wallace* court recognized that deferred-accrual reasoning was unnecessary and inappropriate in the pre-conviction setting because the common abstention practice of staying the § 1983 action would afford adequate protection to the plaintiff.").

2. Dismissal Before Conclusion of Criminal Proceedings. Assume that Wallace had filed his § 1983 claim for false arrest before the conclusion of the state's criminal proceedings and within Illinois's two-year statute of limitations. What would happen if the District Court dismissed his § 1983 claim because of *Heck* (i.e., the court concluded that the § 1983 claim necessarily contradicted the pending criminal charges)? Would Wallace be allowed to refile his § 1983 action several years later following a successful appeal of his conviction? Or would his § 1983 claim be barred by Illinois's two-year statute of limitations? Would equitable tolling be appropriate? Justice Scalia noted in *Kato* that "if under those circumstances [Wallace] were not allowed to refile his suit,

Heck would produce immunity from § 1983 liability, a result surely not intended." *See* footnote 4. How else could Justice Scalia avoid this unintended consequence? Is Justice Breyer correct that equitable tolling will necessarily be used in this instance?

3. *Heck*, Accrual and Equitable Tolling. Before *Kato*, lower courts commonly took a wait-and-see approach in the context of accrual. If, as things turned out, a criminal conviction was impugned by a § 1983 claim, then *Heck* applied and the cause of action could not accrue until the conviction was set aside. *See, e.g., Swiecicki v. Delgado*, 463 F.3d 489 (6th Cir. 2006) (holding that false arrest and excessive force claims contradicted convictions and thus did not arise until convictions were overturned). If the § 1983 claim did not contradict the conviction, on the other hand, the accrual date was that of the initial injury. *See, e.g., Gauger v. Hendle*, 349 F.3d 354 (7th Cir. 2003) ("an arrest [that] violated the Fourth Amendment does not undermine the defendant's conviction and therefore the claim arises, and the statute of limitations begins to run, when the arrest is made").

Because of the uncertainty presented by this wait-and-see approach, some courts experimented with equitable tolling. So long as the § 1983 plaintiff had a reasonable belief that *Heck* applied, he or she could devote attention to defeating or upsetting the criminal conviction and not worry about losing the § 1983 claim to the statute of limitations. Judge Posner, for example, proposed this solution in *Heck v. Humphrey*, 997 F.3d 355 (7th Cir. 1993), and reiterated it (unsuccessfully) in *Wallace v. City of Chicago*, 440 F.3d 921 (7th Cir. 2006) (Posner, J., dissenting from denial of rehearing en banc). Justice Breyer embraced this approach in *Kato*: "equitable tolling could apply where a § 1983 plaintiff reasonably claims that the unlawful behavior of which he complains was, or will be, necessary to a criminal conviction." The Supreme Court in *Heck*, however, found Judge Posner's proposal to be unnecessary — "Under our analysis the statute of limitations poses no difficulty while the state challenges are being pursued, since the § 1983 claim has not yet arisen" — and concluded it was unwise in *Kato* — "Equitable tolling is a rare remedy to be applied in unusual circumstances, not a cure-all for an entirely common state of affairs."

4. Malicious Prosecution. As noted in *Kato*, the Supreme Court has "never explored the contours of a Fourth Amendment malicious-prosecution suit under § 1983." *See* footnote 2. Still, the Court in *Heck* generally explained the cause of action's demands. First, the Fourth Amendment version of malicious prosecution requires that the plaintiff show a lack of probable cause for the prosecution. *Compare Hartman v. Moore*, 547 U.S. 250 (2006) (excerpted in Chapter 6.A., *supra*) (holding that a First Amendment claim against a police officer for inducing prosecution is also predicated on an absence of probable cause). Second, it requires a favorable termination of the criminal proceedings in the plaintiff's favor. Assuming that these two elements are satisfied, "a successful malicious prosecution plaintiff may recover, in addition to general damages, 'compensation for any arrest or imprisonment, including damages for discomfort or injury to his health, or loss of time and deprivation of the society.'" In contrast, a false arrest claim requires only proof of a lack of probable cause; there need be no showing of a favorable criminal outcome. The false arrest plaintiff can then recover only damages that "cover the time of detention up until issuance of process or arraignment, but not more." *See* W. KEETON, D. DOBBS, R. KEETON, & D. OWEN, PROSSER AND KEETON ON LAW OF TORTS 888 (5th ed. 1984).

Because *Heck* specifically ruled that no § 1983 claim for malicious prosecution exists "while the state challenges are being pursued, since the § 1983 claim has not yet arisen," a claim for malicious prosecution would appear to accrue only when the criminal defendant ultimately prevails. In *Kato*, however, the Court broadly stated that *Heck* simply does not apply to § 1983 cases involving "anticipated future convictions." Does this leave open the possibility that a § 1983 claim for malicious prosecution could exist before conviction? If so, does a malicious prosecution claim accrue with the onset of criminal proceedings? Can a § 1983 malicious prosecution claim be filed before criminal proceedings are completed?

Before *Kato*, lower courts commonly dismissed § 1983 claims for malicious prosecution (as well as false arrest) when criminal charges were pending. The logic behind these dismissals was that a malicious prosecution claim cannot accrue until criminal proceedings are terminated in the plaintiff's favor. In footnote 3 to his majority opinion in *Kato*, however, Justice Scalia observed that Wallace could have filed suit for false arrest before his claim actually accrued: "While the statute of limitations did not begin to run until [Wallace] became detained pursuant to legal process, he was injured and suffered damages at the moment of his arrest, and was entitled to bring suit at that time." Does this suggest that a malicious prosecution claim can be properly filed before it actually accrues? If so, what should a District Court do with a § 1983 claim for malicious prosecution that is filed before the completion of criminal proceedings? What should it do when the § 1983 plaintiff is convicted? *See, e.g., Eidson v. State of Tennessee Department of Children's Services*, 510 F.3d 631 (6th Cir. 2007) ("What made *Heck*'s malicious-prosecution-type § 1983 claims materially unique was the fact that proof of the invalidity of Heck's conviction was essential or at least integral to (1) proving his claims and (2) recovering damages for the unlawful conviction."); *Fox v. DeSoto*, 489 F.3d 227 (6th Cir. 2007) (suggesting that malicious prosecution claims are different from those for false arrest for purposes of *Heck* and *Kato*).

5. Applying *Kato* Across-the-Board. Does *Kato* apply to Fourth Amendment claims for excessive force? *See, e.g., Graham v. Connor*, 490 U.S. 386 (1989) (describing contours of Fourth Amendment excessive force claims) (discussed in Note 5 following *Zinerman* in Chapter 1.C., *supra*). Is *Kato* limited to Fourth Amendment claims? Note that *Heck* has been applied to a wide range of constitutional claims, *see, e.g., Edwards v. Balisok*, 520 U.S. 641 (1997) (applying *Heck* to a bar claim under the Due Process Clause) (discussed in Note 3 following *Heck* in Section B.[2], *supra*); the question under *Heck* is simply whether the constitutional challenge — whatever it might be — contradicts the plaintiff's conviction. At least one Circuit has applied *Kato* outside the Fourth Amendment arena, *see, e.g., Eidson v. State of Tennessee Department of Children's Services*, 510 F.3d 631 (6th Cir. 2007) (applying *Kato* to a Procedural Due Process claim brought by a parent against social workers who removed his daughter), and it would seem that *Kato* has no logical stopping place (possibly short of malicious prosecution).

Chapter 9
ATTORNEY'S FEES

Modern civil litigation in America generally proceeds under the assumption that plaintiffs and defendants must pay their own lawyers. This "American Rule," as it is called, remains a cornerstone of private rights resolution. Whether the action involves a contract, a tort, or real estate, parties ordinarily retain and pay their own lawyers.

Contrary to the American practice, English courts historically required that losing parties compensate winners' lawyers. Borrowing from this practice, American law today often applies a modified "English Rule" fee-shifting principle to public rights[1] — that is, rights, privileges, and immunities that protect individuals from government. Under this approach, successful civil rights plaintiffs recover their attorney's fees from governmental defendants; successful governmental defendants, however, only rarely recover their fees from civil rights plaintiffs. *See* Charles Silver, *Unloading the Lodestar: Toward a New Fee Award Procedure*, 70 TEX. L. REV. 865, 877 (1992). By modifying the English approach in this way, the number of "private attorneys general" policing the constitutional landscape is set at a near-maximal level. Plaintiffs' lawyers are encouraged to accept risky § 1983 cases as well as those that promise only small judgments.

Toward this end, the Civil Rights Attorney's Fee Awards Act of 1976,[2] 42 U.S.C. § 1988(b), states in relevant part:

> In any action or proceeding to enforce a provision of section[ ] . . . 1983 . . . of this title, the court, in its discretion, may allow the prevailing party, other than the United States, a reasonable attorney's fee as part of the costs, except that in any action brought against a judicial officer for an act or omission taken in such officer's judicial capacity such officer shall not be held liable for any costs, including attorney's fees, unless such action was clearly in excess of such officer's jurisdiction.[3]

Though its language is murky, the history behind § 1988(b) proves that it was intended to encourage plaintiffs' lawyers to take cases. It was not intended to compensate defense lawyers. *See* Armand Derfner, *Background and Origin of the Civil Rights Attorney's Fee Awards Act of 1976*, 37 URB. LAW. 653 (2005). A prevailing *defendant* is therefore only entitled to attorney's fees under § 1988(b) if it can prove that a plaintiff's claims were frivolous, groundless or vexatious. *See Christiansburg Garment Co. v. EEOC*, 434 U.S. 412, 421 (1978) ("a district court may in its discretion award attorney's fees to a prevailing defendant in a Title VII case upon a finding that the plaintiff's action was frivolous, unreasonable, and without foundation, even though not brought in subjective bad faith"); *Hughes v. Rowe*, 449 U.S. 5 (1980) (adopting this same standard for successful § 1983 defendants). *Cf. Scarborough v. Principi*, 541 U.S. 401 (2004) (observing that the federal Equal Access to Justice Act (EAJA) requires that the

---

[1] Fee-shifting has also been legislatively adopted in some private-right settings in America, including Title VII litigation, 42 U.S.C. § 2000e-5(k), and cases proceeding under both the Securities Act of 1933, 15 U.S.C. § 77k, and the Securities Exchange Act of 1934, 15 U.S.C. § 78j. Private parties are also free to contractually agree to fee-shifting. *See, e.g., Double Oak Construction Co. v. Cornerstone Development*, 97 P.3d 140 (Colo. Ct. App. 2003) (observing that a contract can shift attorney's fees). However, these instances are exceptional.

[2] Section 1988 was amended in 1991, so that the portion addressing attorney's fees is now § 1988(b). The last clause of § 1988(b), which creates an exception for suits against judicial officers, was added as part of the Federal Courts Improvement Act of 1996.

[3] In addition to authorizing fee-shifting under § 1983, § 1988(b) offers fee shifting to successful plaintiffs under §§ 1981, 1982, 1985, and 1986 of title 42, as well as Titles VI, VII and IX, the Religious Freedom Restoration Act, the Religious Land Use and Institutionalized Persons Act, and the Violence Against Women Act. Several other federal civil rights statutes, including the Americans with Disabilities Act (ADA) and the federal Fair Housing Amendments Act of 1988 (FHAA), employ similar, "English" fee-shifting principles. A host of environmental statutes also adopt modified versions of the English rule.

federal government pay a successful adversary's attorney's fees only when the government's position in litigation was not "substantially justified"). Governmental defendants often prevail, but they rarely win attorney's fees.

Attorney's fees due under fee-shifting statutes, like § 1988(b), belong in the first instance to the client — not the lawyer. *See, e.g., Evans v. Jeff D.*, 475 U.S. 717 (1986) (excerpted in Section D., *infra*). A lawyer therefore must enter into a contract with the § 1983 plaintiff and should obtain an assignment of the right to recover the fee. *See, e.g., Gilbrook v. City of Westminster*, 177 F.3d 839 (9th Cir. 1999) ("In the absence of a contractual assignment to counsel, § 1988 requires that attorney fee awards be made directly to the prevailing party, with the ultimate disposition of the award dependent on the contract between the lawyer and the client.").

Before § 1983 plaintiffs can claim an award of attorney's fees under § 1988(b), they must "prevail" in their suits. The first and most important question that arises under § 1988(b), then, focuses on the meaning of "prevailing party."

A. PREVAILING PARTY

BUCKHANNON BOARD & CARE HOME, INC. v. WEST VIRGINIA DEPARTMENT OF HEALTH AND HUMAN RESOURCES
Supreme Court of the United States
532 U.S. 598 (2001)

CHIEF JUSTICE REHNQUIST delivered the opinion of the Court.

Numerous federal statutes allow courts to award attorney's fees and costs to the "prevailing party." The question presented here is whether this term includes a party that has failed to secure a judgment on the merits or a court-ordered consent decree, but has nonetheless achieved the desired result because the lawsuit brought about a voluntary change in the defendant's conduct. We hold that it does not.

Buckhannon Board and Care Home, Inc., which operates care homes that provide assisted living to their residents, failed an inspection by the West Virginia Office of the State Fire Marshal because some of the residents were incapable of "self-preservation" as defined under state law. On October 28, 1997, after receiving cease and desist orders requiring the closure of its residential care facilities within 30 days, Buckhannon Board and Care Home, Inc., on behalf of itself and other similarly situated homes and residents . . . , brought suit . . . seeking declaratory and injunctive relief that the "self-preservation" requirement violated the Fair Housing Amendments Act of 1988 (FHAA) and the Americans with Disabilities Act of 1990 (ADA).

[West Virginia] agreed to stay enforcement of the cease and desist orders pending resolution of the case and the parties began discovery. In 1998, the West Virginia Legislature enacted two bills eliminating the "self-preservation" requirement, and [West Virginia] moved to dismiss the case as moot. The District Court granted the motion, finding that the 1998 legislation had eliminated the allegedly offensive provisions and that there was no indication that the West Virginia Legislature would repeal the amendments.

[Buckhannon] requested attorney's fees as the "prevailing party" under the FHAA and ADA. . . . [It] argued that [it was] entitled to attorney's fees under the "catalyst theory," which posits that a plaintiff is a "prevailing party" if it achieves the desired result because the lawsuit brought about a voluntary change in the defendant's conduct.

In the United States, parties are ordinarily required to bear their own attorney's fees — the prevailing party is not entitled to collect from the loser. Under this "American Rule," we follow "a general practice of not awarding fees to a prevailing party absent explicit statutory authority." Congress, however, has authorized the award of attorney's fees to the "prevailing party" in numerous statutes in addition to those at issue here, such as the Civil Rights Act of 1964, the Voting Rights Act Amendments of 1975, and the Civil Rights Attorney's Fees Awards Act of 1976, 42 U.S.C. § 1988.[4]

In designating those parties eligible for an award of litigation costs, Congress employed the term "prevailing party," a legal term of art. Black's Law Dictionary 1145 (7th ed. 1999) defines "prevailing party" as "[a] party in whose favor a judgment is rendered, regardless of the amount of damages awarded . . . . — Also termed *successful party.*" This view that a "prevailing party" is one who has been awarded some relief by the court can be distilled from our prior cases.

In *Hanrahan v. Hampton*, 446 U.S. 754 (1980) (per curiam), we reviewed the legislative history of § 1988 and found that "Congress intended to permit the interim award of counsel fees only when a party has prevailed on the merits of at least some of his claims." Our "[r]espect for ordinary language requires that a plaintiff receive at least some relief on the merits of his claim before he can be said to prevail." We have held that even an award of nominal damages suffices under this test. *See Farrar v. Hobby*, 506 U.S. 103 (1992).[5]

In addition to judgments on the merits, we have held that settlement agreements enforced through a consent decree may serve as the basis for an award of attorney's fees. *See Maher v. Gagne*, 448 U.S. 122 (1980). Although a consent decree does not always include an admission of liability by the defendant, it nonetheless is a court-ordered "chang[e] [in] the legal relationship between [the plaintiff] and the defendant."[6] These decisions, taken together, establish that enforceable judgments on the merits and court-ordered consent decrees create the "material alteration of the legal relationship of the parties" necessary to permit an award of attorney's fees.

We think, however, the "catalyst theory" falls on the other side of the line from these examples. It allows an award where there is no judicially sanctioned change in the legal relationship of the parties. Even under a limited form of the "catalyst theory," a plaintiff could recover attorney's fees if it established that the "complaint had sufficient merit to withstand a motion to dismiss for lack of jurisdiction or failure to state a claim on which relief may be granted." This is not the type of legal merit that our prior decisions, based upon plain language and congressional intent, have found necessary. Indeed, we [have] held . . . that an interlocutory ruling that reverses a dismissal for failure to state a claim "is not the stuff of which legal victories are made."

The dissenters chide us for upsetting "long-prevailing Circuit precedent." But, as Justice Scalia points out in his concurrence, several Courts of Appeals have relied upon dicta in our prior cases in approving the "catalyst theory." Now that the issue is squarely presented, it behooves us to reconcile the plain language of the statutes with our prior holdings. We have only awarded attorney's fees where the plaintiff has received a judgment on the merits, or obtained a court-ordered consent decree — we have not awarded attorney's fees where the plaintiff has secured the reversal of a directed verdict, or acquired a judicial pronouncement that the defendant has violated the Constitution unaccompanied by "judicial relief." Never have we awarded attorney's

---

[4] [n.4] We have interpreted these fee-shifting provisions consistently, *see Hensley v. Eckerhart*, 461 U.S. 424, 433, n. 7 (1983), and so approach the nearly identical provisions at issue here.

[5] [n.6] However, in some circumstances such a "prevailing party" should still not receive an award of attorney's fees. *See Farrar v. Hobby* [described in Note 3, following *Rivera* in Section B.,*infra*].

[6] [n.7] We have subsequently characterized the *Maher* opinion as also allowing for an award of attorney's fees for private settlements. *See Farrar v. Hobby.* But this dicta ignores that *Maher* only "held that fees may be assessed . . . after a case has been settled by the entry of a consent decree." *Evans v. Jeff D.*, 475 U.S. 717 (1986). Private settlements do not entail the judicial approval and oversight involved in consent decrees. And federal jurisdiction to enforce a private contractual settlement will often be lacking unless the terms of the agreement are incorporated into the order of dismissal. *See Kokkonen v. Guardian Life Ins. Co. of America*, 511 U.S. 375 (1994).

fees for a nonjudicial "alteration of actual circumstances." While urging an expansion of our precedents on this front, the dissenters would simultaneously abrogate the "merit" requirement of our prior cases and award attorney's fees where the plaintiff's claim "was at least colorable" and "not . . . groundless." We cannot agree that the term "prevailing party" authorizes federal courts to award attorney's fees to a plaintiff who, by simply filing a nonfrivolous but nonetheless potentially meritless lawsuit (it will never be determined), has reached the "sought-after destination" without obtaining any judicial relief.

[Buckhannon] nonetheless argue[s] that the legislative history of the Civil Rights Attorney's Fees Awards Act supports a broad reading of "prevailing party" which includes the "catalyst theory." We doubt that legislative history could overcome what we think is the rather clear meaning of "prevailing party" — the term actually used in the statute. Since we resorted to such history in [prior cases], however, we do likewise here.

The House Report to § 1988 states that "[t]he phrase 'prevailing party' is not intended to be limited to the victor only after entry of a final judgment following a full trial on the merits," while the Senate Report explains that "parties may be considered to have prevailed when they vindicate rights through a consent judgment or without formally obtaining relief." "[Buckhannon] argue[s] that these Reports and their reference to a 1970 decision from the Court of Appeals for the Eighth Circuit, *Parham v. Southwestern Bell Telephone Co.*, 433 F.2d 421 (CA8 1970), indicate Congress' intent to adopt the "catalyst theory."[7] We think the legislative history cited by petitioners is at best ambiguous as to the availability of the "catalyst theory" for awarding attorney's fees. Particularly in view of the "American Rule" that attorney's fees will not be awarded absent "explicit statutory authority," such legislative history is clearly insufficient to alter the accepted meaning of the statutory term.

[Buckhannon] finally assert[s] that the "catalyst theory" is necessary to prevent defendants from unilaterally mooting an action before judgment in an effort to avoid an award of attorney's fees. [It] also claim[s] that the rejection of the "catalyst theory" will deter plaintiffs with meritorious but expensive cases from bringing suit.

[Buckhannon] discount[s] the disincentive that the "catalyst theory" may have upon a defendant's decision to voluntarily change its conduct, conduct that may not be illegal. "The defendants' potential liability for fees in this kind of litigation can be as significant as, and sometimes even more significant than, their potential liability on the merits," and the possibility of being assessed attorney's fees may well deter a defendant from altering its conduct.

And [Buckhannon's] fear of mischievous defendants only materializes in claims for equitable relief, for so long as the plaintiff has a cause of action for damages, a defendant's change in conduct will not moot the case. Even then, it is not clear how often courts will find a case mooted: "It is well settled that a defendant's voluntary cessation of a challenged practice does not deprive a federal court of its power to determine the legality of the practice" unless it is "absolutely clear that the allegedly wrongful behavior could not reasonably be expected to recur." *Friends of Earth, Inc. v. Laidlaw Environmental Services (TOC), Inc.*, 528 U.S. 167 (2000). If a case is not found

---

[7] [n.9] Although the Court of Appeals in *Parham* awarded attorney's fees to the plaintiff because his "lawsuit acted as a catalyst which prompted the [defendant] to take action . . . seeking compliance with the requirements of Title VII," it did so only after finding that the defendant had acted unlawfully. Thus, consistent with our holding in *Farrar*, *Parham* stands for the proposition that an enforceable judgment permits an award of attorney's fees. And like the consent decree in *Maher v. Gagne*, 448 U.S. 122 (1980), the Court of Appeals in *Parham* ordered the District Court to "retain jurisdiction over the matter for a reasonable period of time to insure the continued implementation of the appellee's policy of equal employment opportunities." Clearly *Parham* does not support a theory of fee shifting untethered to a material alteration in the legal relationship of the parties as defined by our precedents.

to be moot, and the plaintiff later procures an enforceable judgment, the court may of course award attorney's fees. Given this possibility, a defendant has a strong incentive to enter a settlement agreement, where it can negotiate attorney's fees and costs.

We have also stated that "[a] request for attorney's fees should not result in a second major litigation," and have accordingly avoided an interpretation of the fee-shifting statutes that would have "spawn[ed] a second litigation of significant dimension." Among other things, a "catalyst theory" hearing would require analysis of the defendant's subjective motivations in changing its conduct, an analysis that "will likely depend on a highly factbound inquiry and may turn on reasonable inferences from the nature and timing of the defendant's change in conduct." Although we do not doubt the ability of district courts to perform the nuanced "three thresholds" test required by the "catalyst theory" [and explained by the dissent,] it is clearly not a formula for "ready administrability."

For the reasons stated above, we hold that the "catalyst theory" is not a permissible basis for the award of attorney's fees under the FHAA and ADA.

JUSTICE SCALIA, with whom JUSTICE THOMAS joins, concurring.

"Prevailing party" is not some newfangled legal term invented for use in late-20th-century fee-shifting statutes. "[B]y the long established practice and universally recognized rule of the common law, in actions at law, the prevailing party is entitled to recover a judgment for costs . . . ." *Mansfield, C. & L. M. R. Co. v. Swan*, 111 U.S. 379 (1884).

At the time 42 U.S.C. § 1988 was enacted, I know of no case, state or federal, in which — either under a statutory invocation of "prevailing party," or under the common-law rule — the "catalyst theory" was enunciated as the basis for awarding costs. Indeed, the dissent cites only one case in which (although the "catalyst theory" was not expressed) costs were awarded for a reason that the catalyst theory would support, but today's holding of the Court would not: *Baldwin v. Chesapeake & Potomac Tel. Co.*, 156 Md. 552, 557, 144 A. 703, 705 (1929). . . . And that case is irrelevant to the meaning of "prevailing party," because it was a case in equity. While, as *Mansfield* observed, costs were awarded in actions at law to the "prevailing party," an equity court could award costs "as the equities of the case might require." The other state or state-law cases the dissent cites as awarding costs despite the absence of a judgment all involve a judicial finding — or its equivalent, an acknowledgment by the defendant — of the merits of plaintiff's case. Moreover, the dissent cites not a single case in which this Court — or even any other federal court applying federal law prior to enactment of the fee-shifting statutes at issue here — has regarded as the "prevailing party" a litigant who left the courthouse emptyhanded. If the term means what the dissent contends, that is a remarkable absence of authority.

The dissent distorts the term "prevailing party" beyond its normal meaning for policy reasons, but even those seem to me misguided. . . . As the dissent would have it, by giving the term its normal meaning the Court today approves the practice of denying attorney's fees to a plaintiff with a proven claim of discrimination, simply because the very merit of his claim led the defendant to capitulate before judgment. That is not the case. To the contrary, the Court approves the result in *Parham v. Southwestern Bell Tel. Co.*, 433 F.2d 421 (CA8 1970), where attorney's fees were awarded "after [a] finding that the defendant had acted unlawfully." What the dissent's stretching of the term produces is something more, and something far less reasonable: an award of attorney's fees when the merits of plaintiff's case remain unresolved — when, for all one knows, the defendant only "abandon[ed] the fray" because the cost of litigation — either financial or in terms of public relations — would be too great. In such a case, the plaintiff may have "prevailed" as Webster's defines that term — "gain[ed] victory by virtue of strength or superiority." But I doubt it was greater strength in financial resources, or superiority in media manipulation, rather than superiority in legal merit, that Congress intended to reward.

It could be argued, perhaps, that insofar as abstract justice is concerned, there is little to choose between the dissent's outcome and the Court's: If the former sometimes rewards the plaintiff with a phony claim (there is no way of knowing), the latter sometimes denies fees to the plaintiff with a solid case whose adversary slinks away on the eve of judgment. But it seems to me the evil of the former far outweighs the evil of the latter. There is all the difference in the world between a rule that denies the extraordinary boon of attorney's fees to some plaintiffs who are no less "deserving" of them than others who receive them, and a rule that causes the law to be the very instrument of wrong — exacting the payment of attorney's fees to the extortionist.

The dissent points out that [Buckhannon's] object in bringing [its] suit was not to obtain "a judge's approbation," but to "stop enforcement of a [West Virginia] rule." True enough. But not even the dissent claims that if a plaintiff accumulated attorney's fees in preparing a threatened complaint, but never filed it prior to the defendant's voluntary cessation of its offending behavior, the wannabe-but-never-was plaintiff could recover fees; that would be countertextual, since the fee-shifting statutes require that there be an "action" or "proceeding" — which in legal parlance (though not in more general usage) means a lawsuit. . . . My point is not that it would take no more twisting of language to produce prelitigation attorney's fees than to produce the decreeless attorney's fees that the dissent favors (though that may well be true). My point is that the departure from normal usage that the dissent favors cannot be justified on the ground that it establishes a regime of logical evenhandedness. There must be a cutoff of seemingly equivalent entitlements to fees — either the failure to file suit in time or the failure to obtain a judgment in time. The term "prevailing party" suggests the latter rather than the former. One does not prevail in a suit that is never determined.

The dissent's ultimate worry is that today's opinion will "impede access to court for the less well-heeled." But, of course, the catalyst theory also harms the "less well-heeled," putting pressure on them to avoid the risk of massive fees by abandoning a solidly defensible case early in litigation. Since the fee-shifting statutes at issue here allow defendants as well as plaintiffs to receive a fee award, we know that Congress did not intend to maximize the quantity of "the enforcement of federal law by private attorneys general." Rather, Congress desired an appropriate level of enforcement — which is more likely to be produced by limiting fee awards to plaintiffs who prevail "on the merits," or at least to those who achieve an enforceable "alteration of the legal relationship of the parties," than by permitting the open-ended inquiry approved by the dissent.

JUSTICE GINSBURG, with whom JUSTICE STEVENS, JUSTICE SOUTER, and JUSTICE BREYER join, dissenting.

The Court's insistence that there be a document filed in court — a litigated judgment or court-endorsed settlement — upsets long-prevailing Circuit precedent applicable to scores of federal fee-shifting statutes.

Prior to 1994, every Federal Court of Appeals . . . concluded that plaintiffs . . . could obtain a fee award if their suit acted as a "catalyst" for the change they sought, even if they did not obtain a judgment or consent decree.

The array of federal court decisions applying the catalyst rule suggested three conditions necessary to a party's qualification as "prevailing" short of a favorable final judgment or consent decree. A plaintiff first had to show that the defendant provided "some of the benefit sought" by the lawsuit. Under most Circuits' precedents, a plaintiff had to demonstrate as well that the suit stated a genuine claim, i.e., one that was at least "colorable," not "frivolous, unreasonable, or groundless." Plaintiff finally had to establish that her suit was a "substantial" or "significant" cause of defendant's action providing relief. In some Circuits, to make this causation showing, plaintiff had to satisfy the trial court that the suit achieved results "by threat of victory," not "by dint of nuisance and threat of expense."

It is altogether true, as the concurring opinion points out, that litigation costs other than attorney's fees traditionally have been allowed to the "prevailing party," and that a judgment winner ordinarily fits that description. It is not true, however, that precedent on costs calls for the judgment requirement the Court ironly adopts today for attorney's fees.

There are . . . enlightening analogies. In multiple instances, state high courts have regarded plaintiffs as prevailing, for costs taxation purposes, when defendants' voluntary conduct, mooting the suit, provided the relief that plaintiffs sought. The concurring opinion labors unconvincingly to distinguish these state law cases.[8] A similar federal practice has been observed in cases governed by Federal Rule of Civil Procedure 54(d), the default rule allowing costs "to the prevailing party unless the court otherwise directs."

In short, there is substantial support, both old and new, federal and state, for a costs award, "in [the court's] discretion," to the plaintiff whose suit prompts the defendant to provide the relief plaintiff seeks.

The catalyst rule stemmed from modern legislation extending civil rights protections and enforcement measures. The Civil Rights Act of 1964 included provisions for fee awards to "prevailing parties" in Title II (public accommodations) and Title VII (employment), but not in Title VI (federal programs). The provisions' central purpose was "to promote vigorous enforcement" of the laws by private plaintiffs; although using the two-way term "prevailing party," Congress did not make fees available to plaintiffs and defendants on equal terms.

Once the 1964 Act came into force, courts commenced to award fees regularly under the statutory authorizations, and sometimes without such authorization. *See Alyeska Pipeline Service Co. v. Wilderness Society*, 421 U.S. 240 (1975). In *Alyeska*, this Court reaffirmed the "American rule" that a court generally may not award attorney's fees without a legislative instruction to do so. To provide the authorization *Alyeska* required for fee awards under Title VI of the 1964 Civil Rights Act, as well as under Reconstruction Era civil rights legislation, 42 U.S.C. §§ 1981–1983, 1985, 1986, and certain other enactments, Congress passed the Civil Rights Attorney's Fees Awards Act of 1976, 42 U.S.C. § 1988.

As explained in the Reports supporting § 1988, civil rights statutes vindicate public policies "of the highest priority," yet "depend heavily on private enforcement." Persons who bring meritorious civil rights claims, in this light, serve as "private attorneys general." Such suitors, Congress recognized, often "cannot afford legal counsel." They therefore experience "severe hardshi[p]" under the "American Rule." Congress enacted § 1988 to ensure that nonaffluent plaintiffs would have "effective access" to the Nation's courts to enforce civil rights laws. That objective accounts for the fee-shifting provisions before the Court in this case, prescriptions of the FHAA and the ADA modeled on § 1988.

The Court declines to look beneath the surface of these arguments, placing its reliance, instead, on a meaning of "prevailing party" that other jurists would scarcely

---

[8] [n.8] The concurrence urges that *Baldwin* [*v. Chesapeake & Potomac Tel. Co.*, 156 Md. 552, 144 A. 703 (1929),] is inapposite because it was an action "in equity," and equity courts could award costs as the equities required. The catalyst rule becomes relevant, however, only when a party seeks relief of a sort traditionally typed equitable, i.e., a change of conduct, not damages. There is no such thing as an injunction at law, and therefore one cannot expect to find long-ago plaintiffs who quested after that mythical remedy and received voluntary relief. By the concurrence's reasoning, the paucity of precedent applying the catalyst rule to "prevailing parties" is an artifact of nothing more "remarkable" than the historic law-equity separation.

recognize as plain. Had the Court inspected the "policy arguments" listed in its opinion, I doubt it would have found them impressive.

In opposition to the argument that defendants will resist change in order to stave off an award of fees, one could urge that the catalyst rule may lead defendants promptly to comply with the law's requirements: the longer the litigation, the larger the fees. Indeed, one who knows noncompliance will be expensive might be encouraged to conform his conduct to the legal requirements before litigation is threatened. No doubt, a mootness dismissal is unlikely when recurrence of the controversy is under the defendant's control. But, as earlier observed, why should this Court's fee-shifting rulings drive a plaintiff prepared to accept adequate relief, though out-of-court and unrecorded, to litigate on and on? And if the catalyst rule leads defendants to negotiate not only settlement terms but also allied counsel fees, is that not a consummation to applaud, not deplore?

Might not one conclude overall, as Courts of Appeals have suggested, that the catalyst rule "saves judicial resources" by encouraging "plaintiffs to discontinue litigation after receiving through the defendant's acquiescence the remedy initially sought"?

The concurring opinion adds another argument against the catalyst rule: That opinion sees the rule as accommodating the "extortionist" who obtains relief because of "greater strength in financial resources, or superiority in media manipulation, rather than superiority in legal merit." This concern overlooks both the character of the rule and the judicial superintendence Congress ordered for all fee allowances. The catalyst rule was auxiliary to fee-shifting statutes whose primary purpose is "to promote the vigorous enforcement" of the civil rights laws. To that end, courts deemed the conduct-altering catalyst that counted to be the substance of the case, not merely the plaintiff's atypically superior financial resources, media ties, or political clout. And Congress assigned responsibility for awarding fees not to automatons unable to recognize extortionists, but to judges expected and instructed to exercise "discretion." So viewed, the catalyst rule provided no berth for nuisance suits or "thinly disguised forms of extortion."

NOTES

1. History and Effect of § 1988(b). Titles II and VII of the Civil Rights Act of 1964 authorized attorney's fees awards to successful plaintiffs in order to insure proper enforcement of emerging anti-discrimination policies. *See* Armand Derfner, *Background and Origin of the Civil Rights Attorney's Fee Awards Act of 1976*, 37 URB. LAW. 653 (2005) ("Congress knew enforcement of these new national policies would depend heavily on private litigation"). Relying on this development, federal courts began awarding attorney's fees in other kinds of civil rights cases, particularly suits brought to enforce the Supreme Court's "one-person-one-vote" mandate (handed down in *Reynolds v. Sims*, 377 U.S. 533 (1964)). *See* Derfner, *supra*, at 656. "All this came to a screeching halt in May 1975," *id.*, when the Supreme Court handed down *Alyeska Pipe Line Service v. Wilderness Society*, 421 U.S. 240 (1975). *Alyeska Pipe* held that federal courts can not award attorney's fees without statutory authorization. Congress responded almost immediately with the Civil Rights Attorney's Fee Awards Act (now § 1988(b)). Derfner, *supra*, at 657–58.

As expected, § 1988(b) opened the courthouse door to constitutional victims who otherwise could not seek redress. Lawyers who could not afford to take cases under ordinary contingent-fee arrangements were provided the needed incentive to prosecute a host of constitutional violations, even those that would not generate large damage awards. *See Hudson v. Michigan*, 547 U.S. 586 (2006) ("The number of public-interest law firms and lawyers who specialize in civil-rights grievances has greatly expanded [since the adoption of § 1988(b)].").

2. Discretionary Fees? Although § 1988(b) states that a "court, in its discretion, may allow the prevailing party . . . a reasonable attorney's fee as part of the costs," an award of attorney's fees to a prevailing *plaintiff* is ordinarily required. *See Newman v. Piggie Park Enterprises, Inc.*, 390 U.S. 400 (1968) (holding that award of attorney's fees to prevailing plaintiff under 1964 Civil Rights Act, on which § 1988(b) was modeled, was mandatory absent "special circumstances"). The court's discretion is limited to the amount of the award. However, as the Chief Justice observed in footnote 6 to his majority opinion in *Buckhannon*, this discretion over the amount of the fee can "in some circumstances" mean that "a 'prevailing party' should still not receive an award of attorney's fees. *See Farrar v. Hobby* [discussed in Note 3 following *Rivera* in Section B., *infra*]."

3. Intermediate Success. What if a plaintiff succeeds on appeal in obtaining a reversal of a District Court's final judgment in favor of the defendant? Does this make the plaintiff, now an appellant, a prevailing party in the court of appeals? Is the appellant entitled to fees under § 1988(b) for the time invested in the successful appeal? The Supreme Court in *Hanrahan v. Hampton*, 446 U.S. 754 (1980) (per curiam), answered that a successful reversal, by itself, does not ordinarily entitle an appellant to an award of attorney's fees under § 1988. *Hanrahan*, as explained by the Court, "arose from the execution in 1969 of a judicial warrant to search for and seize illegal weapons within an apartment in Chicago occupied by nine members of the Black Panther Party. In the course of the search two of the apartment's occupants were killed by gunfire, and four others were wounded. The police seized various weapons and arrested the seven surviving occupants of the apartment. The survivors were indicted by a state grand jury on charges of attempted murder and aggravated battery, but the indictments ultimately were dismissed." The victims of the police raid sued under § 1983, only to have the District Court dismiss. On appeal, the Seventh Circuit reversed, finding that the plaintiffs had made out a prima facie case against most of the defendants. It thus remanded the case to the District Court for a new trial and also ordered the trial court to consider reopening discovery. Further, the Seventh Circuit ordered the defendants to pay to the plaintiffs the attorney's fees they incurred on appeal. The Supreme Court in a short per curiam opinion reversed the award of attorney's fees:

> [T]he Court of Appeals was authorized to award to the [plaintiffs] the attorney's fees attributable to their appeal only if, by reason of obtaining a partial reversal of the trial court's judgment, they "prevailed" within the meaning of § 1988. . . . While the [plaintiffs] did prevail on these matters in the sense that the Court of Appeals overturned several rulings against them by the District Court, they were not, we have concluded, "prevailing" parties in the sense intended by 42 U.S.C. § 1988.
>
> The legislative history of the Civil Rights Attorney's Fees Awards Act of 1976 indicates that a person may in some circumstances be a "prevailing party" without having obtained a favorable "final judgment following a full trial on the merits." Thus, for example, "parties may be considered to have prevailed when they vindicate rights through a consent judgment or without formally obtaining relief."
>
> It is evident also that Congress contemplated the award of fees *pendente lite* in some cases. But it seems clearly to have been the intent of Congress to permit such an interlocutory award only to a party who has established his entitlement to some relief on the merits of his claims, either in the trial court or on appeal. The congressional Committee Reports described what were considered to be appropriate circumstances for such an award by reference to two cases — *Bradley v. Richmond School Board*, 416 U.S. 696 (1974), and *Mills v. Electric Auto-Lite Co.*, 396 U.S. 375 (1970). In each of those cases the party to whom fees were awarded had established the liability of the opposing party, although final remedial orders had not been entered. The House Committee Report, more-

over, approved the standard suggested by this Court in *Bradley*, that "the entry of any order that determines substantial rights of the parties may be an appropriate occasion upon which to consider the propriety of an award of counsel fees. . . . " Similarly, the Senate Committee Report explained that the award of counsel fees *pendente lite* would be "especially appropriate where a party has prevailed on an important matter in the course of litigation, even when he ultimately does not prevail on all issues." It seems apparent from these passages that Congress intended to permit the interim award of counsel fees only when a party has prevailed on the merits of at least some of his claims. For only in that event has there been a determination of the "substantial rights of the parties," which Congress determined was a necessary foundation for departing from the usual rule in this country that each party is to bear the expense of his own attorney.

The [plaintiffs] have of course not prevailed on the merits of any of their claims. The Court of Appeals held only that the[y] were entitled to a trial of their cause. As a practical matter they are in a position no different from that they would have occupied if they had simply defeated the defendants' motion for a directed verdict in the trial court. . . . Nor may they fairly be said to have "prevailed" by reason of the Court of Appeals' other interlocutory dispositions, which affected only the extent of discovery. As is true of other procedural or evidentiary rulings, these determinations may affect the disposition on the merits, but were themselves not matters on which a party could "prevail" for purposes of shifting his counsel fees to the opposing party under § 1988.

4. Mootness and Attorney's Fees. As *Hampton* makes clear, a plaintiff's intermediate success will not ordinarily justify an award of attorney's fees under § 1988(b). Instead, a plaintiff must *finally* prevail to win attorney's fees. What if, however, something beyond the plaintiff's control prevents ultimate success? What if the plaintiff is poised to win in federal court, for example, but cannot because of mootness? In *Buckhannon*, the majority observed that a case that becomes moot in the District Court cannot proceed to judgment in the plaintiff's favor. It thus cannot support an award of attorney's fees under § 1988(b). *See also Rhodes v. Stewart*, 488 U.S. 1 (1988) (holding that a judgment that is moot when entered cannot create a prevailing party for purposes of § 1988).

Mootness, however, is not automatic. The majority reiterated in *Buckhannon* that "a defendant's voluntary cessation of a challenged practice does not deprive a federal court of its power to determine the legality of the practice unless it is absolutely clear that the allegedly wrongful behavior could not reasonably be expected to recur." *See Northeastern Florida Chapter of Associated General Contractors of America v. City of Jacksonville*, 508 U.S. 656 (1993) (holding that the defendant's voluntary repeal of minority set-aside program did not moot claim for declaratory and injunctive relief) (excerpted in Chapter 6.C.[1], *supra*); *Friends of the Earth, Inc. v. Laidlaw*, 528 U.S. 167 (2000) (observing that voluntary conduct on the part of a defendant does not ordinarily moot a case and that plaintiffs might still be entitled to recover attorney's fees even when defendants voluntarily cause mootness). Thus, a governmental defendant's attempt to moot a case in the District Court could prove unsuccessful. Because of this risk under *Northeastern Florida*, governmental defendants will have, the Chief Justice observed in *Buckhannon*, a "strong incentive" to settle claims seeking declaratory and injunctive relief.[9] Thus, *Buckhannon*'s rejection of the catalyst theory, if one believes the Chief Justice, may prove less important than initially thought.[10]

---

[9] Note also that a voluntary change in the defendant's behavior cannot moot a claim for money damages. *See Richmond v. J.A. Croson Co.*, 488 U.S. 469, 478 n.1 (1989).

[10] Because lower courts have been reluctant to use *Northeastern Florida* to save cases that are mooted by legislative changes, could it be that the Chief Justice's assumption about incentives is wrong? *See, e.g., Outdoor*

What about a case that becomes moot on appeal? Further, what if the plaintiff prevailed in the District Court and was there awarded attorney's fees? The Supreme Court has made it clear that "[a]n [appellate] order vacating the judgment on grounds of mootness would deprive [the plaintiff] of its claim for attorney's fees under 42 U.S.C. § 1988 . . . because such fees are available only to a party that 'prevails' by winning the relief it seeks." *Lewis v. Continental Bank Corp.*, 494 U.S. 472 (1990). Thus, where appellate mootness leads to vacatur of the judgment below, any award of attorney's fees to the plaintiff under § 1988(b) must also be vacated. Where the lower court's judgment is not vacated, however, an award of attorney's fees will stand. Remember that the Supreme Court in *U.S. Bancorp Mortgage Co. v. Bonner Mall Partnership*, 513 U.S. 18 (1994) (excerpted in Chapter 6.C.[1], *supra*), ruled that while a lower court judgment must be vacated on appeal if the case has become moot by happenstance or by conduct attributable to the prevailing party below, the lower court's judgment ordinarily should not be vacated if the appeal was mooted by the losing party. Thus, if a losing governmental defendant moots its appeal by, say, repealing the law that is being challenged, the lower court's judgment against that defendant will not be vacated and an award of attorney's fees will be allowed to stand.

5. Preliminary Relief and Attorney's Fees. Left unclear by the Supreme Court in *Buckhannon* is whether and to what extent an award of attorney's fees can be based on an award of preliminary relief. Most lower courts prior to *Buckhannon* interpreted *Hanrahan v. Hampton* (discussed in Note 3, *supra*) to authorize an award of attorney's fees under § 1988(b) (either immediately or at the close of the litigation) when the plaintiff obtained a preliminary injunction.[11] Many lower courts extended this practice to cases where defendants *agreed to* or *acquiesced in* preliminary relief, *see, e.g., Smith v. Thomas*, 725 F.2d 354 (5th Cir. 1984) (awarding attorney's fees where the defendant agreed to abide by a preliminary order); *Martin v. Heckler*, 773 F.2d 1145 (11th Cir. 1985) (awarding attorney's fees where the defendant assured the court that challenged policies would shortly be rescinded, thereby leading the court to defer ruling on the motion for preliminary injunction), regardless of whether the court found, or the defendant admitted, wrongdoing. *See Armstrong v. Asarco, Inc.*, 138 F.3d 382 (8th Cir. 1998) (plaintiffs awarded fees even though the District Court did not address the merits of the motion for preliminary injunction).

Preliminary relief in the form of an injunction proves relatively unimportant (in terms of attorney's fees) when a case matures to final judgment. Should the plaintiff ultimately prevail — as is typically true when a preliminary injunction is granted — the ensuing fee award will include compensation for the time spent obtaining the preliminary relief. If the defendant happens to win in the end, on the other hand, preliminary relief will usually dissolve and the plaintiff will forfeit its right to attorney's fees.[12]

Preliminary relief proves highly important under § 1988(b), however, when mootness prevents the case from proceeding to final judgment. In such cases, should the defendant be forced to pay the plaintiff's attorney's fees based on the award of preliminary relief? Lower courts prior to *Buckhannon* had little difficulty holding defendants accountable for plaintiffs' attorney's fees when the mooting event was caused

---

Media Group v. City of Beaumont, 506 F.3d 895 (9th Cir. 2007) ("A statutory change, however, is usually enough to render a case moot, even if the legislature possesses the power to reenact the statute after the lawsuit is dismissed."). *See generally* Note 1 following *Northeastern Florida* in Chapter 6.C.[1], *supra*.

[11] Courts have proved less willing, however, to award fees based solely on the issuance of temporary restraining orders. *See, e.g., Foreman v. Dallas County*, 193 F.3d 314 (5th Cir. 1999) (refusing to award attorney's fees for temporary restraining order).

[12] Indeed, when the defendant ultimately prevails on the merits in the district court (or on appeal), any interim fees paid to the plaintiff must usually be refunded. *See, e.g., Pottgen v. Missouri State High School Activities Association*, 103 F.3d 720 (8th Cir. 1997) (holding that a preliminary injunction that is reversed on appeal cannot support an award of attorney's fees); *LaRouche v. Kezer*, 20 F.3d 68 (2d Cir. 1994) (holding that a preliminary injunction upset by a final judgment cannot support an award of attorney's fees).

by the defendant. *See, e.g., Coalition for Basic Human Needs v. King*, 691 F.2d 597 (1st Cir. 1982) (holding that plaintiffs who won an injunction pending appeal were entitled to an award of attorney's fees). Where the defendant moots the case, after all, it can hardly be heard to complain about not having an opportunity to challenge the award.[13]

The present ambiguity as to whether fee awards based on preliminary injunctions remain viable arises not so much because of *Buckhannon*'s holding as its facts. The defendants in *Buckhannon*, according to the majority, "agreed to stay enforcement of the cease and desist orders [closing Buckhannon] pending resolution of the case." Justice Ginsburg elaborated in dissent, explaining that "at a hearing on plaintiffs' request for a temporary restraining order, defendants agreed to the entry of an interim order allowing Buckhannon to remain open." Because the case was eventually mooted by the defendants, and because the agreement not to close Buckhannon during the pendency of the litigation was included in a court order, this agreement would have supported an award of attorney's fees in most circuits (with or without the catalyst theory). Are these cases still good law?

Smyth v. Rivero, 282 F.3d 268 (4th Cir. 2002), where a governmental defendant mooted a case by voluntarily changing its challenged practices following an award of preliminary relief to the plaintiff, holds that they are not:

> A preliminary injunction . . . is closely analogous . . . to the examples of judicial relief deemed insufficient in *Buckhannon*. While granting such an injunction does involve an inquiry into the merits of a party's claim, and is, like any court order, "enforceable," the merits inquiry in the preliminary injunction context is necessarily abbreviated. . . . At the most, a party seeking a preliminary injunction may have to demonstrate "a 'strong showing of likelihood of success' or a 'substantial likelihood of success' by 'clear and convincing evidence'" in order to obtain relief." A district court's determination that such a showing has been made is best understood as a prediction of a probable, but necessarily uncertain, outcome. The fact that a preliminary injunction is granted in a given circumstance, then, by no means represents a determination that the claim in question will or ought to succeed ultimately; that determination is to be made upon the "deliberate investigation" that follows the granting of the preliminary injunction.

The District of Columbia Circuit Court of Appeals disagreed with *Smyth* in *Select Milk Producers v. Johanns*, 400 F.3d 939 (D.C. Cir. 2005). At issue in *Milk Producers*, an action brought against the federal Secretary of Agriculture under the Agricultural Marketing Agreement Act ("AMAA"), 7 U.S.C. § 601, *et seq.* (2000), was whether the Equal Access to Justice Act (EAJA)[14] authorized an award of attorney's fees to plaintiffs ("Milk Producers") who had won a preliminary injunction against the federal government. As in *Smyth*, the federal government mooted the case in the District Court by repealing the challenged rule following the award of preliminary relief. The court found that the plaintiffs were still entitled to an attorney's fee award:

---

[13] What if mootness is either caused by the plaintiff or comes about through happenstance? While there is precedent for awarding fees in these situations, *see, e.g., Smith v. Thomas*, 725 F.2d 354 (5th Cir. 1984); *Coalition for Basic Needs v. King*, 691 F.2d 597 (1st Cir. 1982), the Supreme Court's decision in *U.S. Bancorp Mortgage Co. v. Bonner Mall Partnership*, 513 U.S. 18 (1994), strongly suggests that an award of fees would be improper. As explained in Note 4, *supra*, and described in greater detail in Chapter 6.C.[1], *supra*, the Court in *Bonner Mall* ruled that judgments that become moot on appeal through "happenstance" — that is, "due to circumstances unattributable to any of the parties" — or through actions attributable to the prevailing party, must be vacated. Without a preliminary injunction to support it, an award of attorney's fees would also have to be vacated.

[14] The EAJA, which applies to litigation with the federal government, provides that "a court shall award to a prevailing party . . . fees and other expenses . . . incurred by that party in any civil action . . . unless the court finds that the position of the United States was substantially justified or that special circumstances make an award unjust." 28 U.S.C. § 2412(d)(1)(A).

Although *Buckhannon* decisively rejected the "catalyst theory," . . . the decision . . . left no doubt that a plaintiff need not obtain a judicial determination on the merits in order to be considered a "prevailing party." . . . Therefore, *Buckhannon* surely does not endorse a *per se* rule that a preliminary injunction can *never* transform a party in whose favor the injunction is issued into a "prevailing party" under EAJA.

We also note that our decision comports with the well-recognized principle that, normally, when a losing party is blocked from appealing an adverse judgment or order because the case becomes moot due to happenstance, the court will vacate the disputed judgment or order. *See U.S. Bancorp Mortgage Co. v. Bonner Mall P'ship*, 513 U.S. 18 (1994). . . . Just as it is not unfair to deny the remedy of vacatur to a party whose voluntary action moots a case, it is not somehow unfair here to conclude that Milk Producers were "prevailing parties" when the Government voluntarily forfeited its right to appeal the injunction and voluntarily elected to moot the case *after* judicial action was taken against the Government.

See also Dubuc v. Green Oak Township, 312 F.3d 736 (6th Cir. 2002) (holding that a preliminary injunction supported a fee award); *Watson v. County of Riverside*, 300 F.3d 1092 (9th Cir. 2003) (same).

6. *Sole v. Wyner*. The Supreme Court granted review in *Sole v. Wyner*, 127 S. Ct. 2188 (2007), to resolve the split between *Smyth* and *Johanns* and decide whether "a preliminary injunction is relief on the merits . . . for prevailing party status." In *Sole*, the § 1983 plaintiff (Wyner) had won a preliminary injunction allowing her to put on a nude protest in a public park. Following a full hearing on the merits, however, the District Court denied Wyner's request for permanent relief. Still, the District Court awarded Wyner attorney's fees based on her preliminary success, and the Eleventh Circuit affirmed. The Supreme Court reversed in a unanimous decision by Justice Ginsburg. Because the "eventual ruling on the merits for defendants, after both sides considered the case fit for final adjudication, superseded the preliminary ruling," Justice Ginsburg avoided the broader issue of whether preliminary injunctions can ever support fee awards. Instead, she concluded that where a final judgment contradicts a preliminary injunction, as in *Sole*, the plaintiff cannot be a prevailing party: "Wyner is not a prevailing party, we conclude, for her initial victory was ephemeral. A plaintiff who 'secur[es] a preliminary injunction, then loses on the merits as the case plays out and judgment is entered against [her],' has '[won] a battle but los[t] the war.'" Justice Ginsburg observed in closing that the Court "express[ed] no view on whether, in the absence of a final decision on the merits of a claim for permanent injunctive relief, success in gaining a preliminary injunction may sometimes warrant an award of counsel fees." Thus, when final judgment cannot be reached because of mootness, a plaintiff who has won a preliminary injunction might still be considered a prevailing party. The split between *Smyth* and *Johanns* remains undecided.

7. Prison Litigation Reform Act. Justice Ginsburg observed in her dissent in *Buckhannon* that "[t]he Prison Litigation Reform Act of 1995 . . . directs that fee awards to prisoners under § 1988 be 'proportionately related to the *court ordered relief* for the violation.' That statute, by its express terms, forecloses an award to a prisoner on a catalyst theory." It is therefore clear, irrespective of *Buckhannon*, that inmates cannot recover attorney's fees based on a catalyst theory. Even though one can argue that the PLRA's "court ordered relief" language is more restrictive than § 1988(b)'s "prevailing party" requirement, courts after *Buckhannon* have tended to apply the same prevailing party analysis to inmates and non-inmates alike. *See, e.g., Cody v. Hillard*, 304 F.3d 767 (8th Cir. 2002) (holding that a consent decree supported an award of attorney's fees to inmates). *See also* Note 10 following *Rivera* in Section B., Note 10, *infra* (discussing further limitations on inmates' ability to recover attorney's fees).

B. REASONABLE FEES

Assuming that a party prevails, the next attorney's fees question focuses on quantity: how much should the prevailing party's attorney be paid? Should the fee be a percentage of the recovery? Must it be proportional to relief? Should the amount be quantified on an hourly basis, a common legal practice across America?

CITY OF RIVERSIDE v. RIVERA
Supreme Court of the United States
477 U.S. 561 (1986)

JUSTICE BRENNAN announced the judgment of the Court and delivered an opinion in which JUSTICE MARSHALL, JUSTICE BLACKMUN, and JUSTICE STEVENS join.

[Eight plaintiffs recovered a total of $33,350 from the City of Riverside and five of its police officers in a suit alleging that the police acted unconstitutionally by entering a home without a warrant and using excessive force to break up a party. Notwithstanding that 25 police officers were exonerated, the District Court awarded the plaintiffs' attorneys $245,456.25 in fees. The District Court came to this conclusion by multiplying the number of hours the plaintiffs' lawyers had spent on the litigation — almost 2000 hours — by a $125 hourly rate, and then adding 84.5 hours expended by law clerks multiplied by $25 per hour. The District Court determined that $125 per hour was the "rate typical of the prevailing market rate for similar services by lawyers of comparable skill, experience and reputation within the Central District at the time these services were performed," and that "[t]he rate of $25 per hour, which counsel seeks as compensation for the time expended by two law clerks, was lower than the customary hourly rate for such services at the time those services were performed."]

The issue presented in this case is whether an award of attorney's fees under 42 U.S.C. § 1988 is per se "unreasonable" within the meaning of the statute if it exceeds the amount of damages recovered by the plaintiff in the underlying civil rights action.

While the [Civil Rights Attorney's Fees Awards Act of 1976, 42 U.S.C. § 1988] itself does not explain what constitutes a reasonable fee, both the House and Senate Reports accompanying § 1988 expressly endorse the analysis set forth in *Johnson v. Georgia Highway Express, Inc.*, 488 F.2d 714 (5th Cir. 1974). *Johnson* identifies 12 factors to be considered in calculating a reasonable attorney's fee.[15]

"[T]he most useful starting point for determining the amount of a reasonable fee is the number of hours reasonably expended on the litigation multiplied by a reasonable hourly rate." This figure, commonly referred to as the "lodestar," is presumed to be the reasonable fee contemplated by § 1988.

[O]ther considerations . . . might lead the district court to adjust the lodestar figure upward or downward, including the "important factor of the 'results obtained.'" . . . [W]here a prevailing plaintiff has succeeded on only some of his claims, an award of fees for time expended on unsuccessful claims may not be appropriate. In these situations, . . . the judge should consider whether or not the plaintiff's unsuccessful claims were related to the claims on which he succeeded, and whether the plaintiff achieved a level of success that makes it appropriate to award attorney's fees for hours reasonably expended on unsuccessful claims.

---

[15] [n.3] These factors are: (1) the time and labor required; (2) the novelty and difficulty of the questions; (3) the skill requisite to perform the legal service properly; (4) the preclusion of employment by the attorney due to acceptance of the case; (5) the customary fee; (6) whether the fee is fixed or contingent; (7) time limitations imposed by the client or the circumstances; (8) the amount involved and the results obtained; (9) the experience, reputation, and ability of the attorneys; (10) the "undesirability" of the case; (11) the nature and length of the professional relationship with the client; and (12) awards in similar cases.

"In [some] cases the plaintiff's claims for relief will involve a common core of facts or will be based on related legal theories. Much of counsel's time will be devoted generally to the litigation as a whole, making it difficult to divide the hours expended on a claim-by-claim basis. Such a lawsuit cannot be viewed as a series of discrete claims. Instead the district court should focus on the significance of the overall relief obtained by the plaintiff in relation to the hours reasonably expended on the litigation."

"[W]here a plaintiff has obtained excellent results, his attorney should recover a fully compensatory fee," and . . . "the fee award should not be reduced simply because the plaintiff failed to prevail on every contention raised in the lawsuit."

The District Court carefully considered the results obtained by [the plaintiffs] . . . and concluded that [they] were entitled to recover attorney's fees for all hours expended on the litigation. First, the court found that "[t]he amount of time expended by counsel in conducting this litigation was reasonable and reflected sound legal judgment under the circumstances."[16] The court also determined that counsel's excellent performances in this case entitled them to be compensated at prevailing market rates, even though they were relatively young when this litigation began. *See Johnson*, 488 F.2d at 718–19 ("If a young attorney demonstrates the skill and ability, he should not be penalized for only recently being admitted to the bar").

The District Court then concluded that it was inappropriate to adjust [the plaintiffs'] fee award downward to account for the fact that [plaintiffs] had prevailed only on some of their claims, and against only some of the defendants. The court first determined that "it was never actually clear what officer did what until we had gotten through with the whole trial," so that "[u]nder the circumstances of this case, it was reasonable for plaintiffs initially to name thirty-one individual defendants . . . as well as the City of Riverside as defendants in this action."

The District Court also considered the amount of damages recovered, and determined that the size of the damages award did not imply that [plaintiffs'] success was limited: "[T]he size of the jury award resulted from (a) the general reluctance of jurors to make large awards against police officers, and (b) the dignified restraint which the plaintiffs exercised in describing their injuries to the jury. For example, although some of the actions of the police would clearly have been insulting and humiliating to even the most insensitive person and were, in the opinion of the Court, intentionally so, plaintiffs did not attempt to play up this aspect of the case."

Finally, the District Court "focus[ed] on the significance of the overall relief obtained by [plaintiffs] in relation to the hours reasonably expended on the litigation." The court concluded that [they] had "achieved a level of success in this case that makes the total number of hours expended by counsel a proper basis for making the fee award:" "Counsel for plaintiffs achieved excellent results for their clients, and their accomplishment in this case was outstanding. The amount of time expended by counsel in conducting this litigation was reasonable and reflected sound legal judgment under the circumstances."

Based on our review of the record, we agree . . . that the District Court's findings were not clearly erroneous. We conclude that the District Court correctly calculate[ed] plaintiffs' fee award, and that the court did not abuse its discretion in awarding attorney's fees for all time reasonably spent litigating the case.

[Defendants], joined by the United States as amicus curiae, maintain that [the] lodestar approach is inappropriate in civil rights cases where a plaintiff recovers only

---

[16] [n.4] [A] fee applicant should "exercise 'billing judgment' with respect to hours worked." . . . "Counsel for the prevailing party should make a good-faith effort to exclude from a fee request hours that are excessive, redundant, or otherwise unnecessary. . . . " In this case, the District Court found that the number of hours expended by respondents' counsel was reasonable. Thus, counsel did, in fact, exercise . . . "billing judgment" . . . . [A] fee applicant should [also] "maintain billing time records in a manner that will enable a reviewing court to identify distinct claims."

monetary damages. In these cases, so the argument goes, use of the lodestar may result in fees that exceed the amount of damages recovered and that are therefore unreasonable. Likening such cases to private tort actions, [defendants] and the United States submit that attorney's fees in such cases should be proportionate to the amount of damages a plaintiff recovers. Specifically, they suggest that fee awards in damages cases should be modeled upon the contingent-fee arrangements commonly used in personal injury litigation. In this case, assuming a 33% contingency rate, this would entitle [plaintiffs] to recover approximately $11,000 in attorney's fees.

The amount of damages a plaintiff recovers is certainly relevant to the amount of attorney's fees to be awarded under § 1988. It is, however, only one of many factors that a court should consider in calculating an award of attorney's fees. We reject the proposition that fee awards under § 1988 should necessarily be proportionate to the amount of damages a civil rights plaintiff actually recovers.

As an initial matter, we reject the notion that a civil rights action for damages constitutes nothing more than a private tort suit benefiting only the individual plaintiffs whose rights were violated. Unlike most private tort litigants, a civil rights plaintiff seeks to vindicate important civil and constitutional rights that cannot be valued solely in monetary terms. And, Congress has determined that "the public as a whole has an interest in the vindication of the rights conferred by the statutes enumerated in § 1988, over and above the value of a civil rights remedy to a particular plaintiff. . . . " Regardless of the form of relief he actually obtains, a successful civil rights plaintiff often secures important social benefits that are not reflected in nominal or relatively small damages awards. In this case, for example, the District Court found that many of [the] unlawful acts were "motivated by a general hostility to the Chicano community," and that this litigation therefore served the public interest.

In addition, the damages a plaintiff recovers contributes significantly to the deterrence of civil rights violations in the future. This deterrent effect is particularly evident in the area of individual police misconduct, where injunctive relief generally is unavailable.

Congress expressly recognized that a plaintiff who obtains relief in a civil rights lawsuit " 'does so not for himself alone but also as a 'private attorney general,' vindicating a policy that Congress considered of the highest importance.' "

Because damages awards do not reflect fully the public benefit advanced by civil rights litigation, Congress did not intend for fees in civil rights cases, unlike most private law cases, to depend on obtaining substantial monetary relief. Rather, Congress made clear that it "intended that the amount of fees awarded under [§ 1988] be governed by the same standards which prevail in other types of equally complex Federal litigation, such as antitrust cases and not be reduced because the rights involved may be nonpecuniary in nature." . . . The Senate Report specifically approves of the fee awards made in cases [where] counsel received substantial attorney's fees despite the fact the plaintiffs sought no monetary damages. Thus, Congress recognized that reasonable attorney's fees under § 1988 are not conditioned upon and need not be proportionate to an award of money damages.

A rule that limits attorney's fees in civil rights cases to a proportion of the damages awarded would seriously undermine Congress' purpose in enacting § 1988. Congress enacted § 1988 specifically because it found that the private market for legal services failed to provide many victims of civil rights violations with effective access to the judicial process. As the House Report states: "[W]hile damages are theoretically available under the statutes covered by [§ 1988], it should be observed that, in some cases, immunity doctrines and special defenses, available only to public officials, preclude or severely limit the damage remedy. Consequently, awarding counsel fees to prevailing plaintiffs in such litigation is particularly important and necessary if Federal civil and constitutional rights are to be adequately protected."

Congress enacted § 1988 specifically to enable plaintiffs to enforce the civil rights laws even where the amount of damages at stake would not otherwise make it feasible for them to do so.

A rule of proportionality would make it difficult, if not impossible, for individuals with meritorious civil rights claims but relatively small potential damages to obtain redress from the courts. This is totally inconsistent with Congress' purpose in enacting § 1988. Congress recognized that private-sector fee arrangements were inadequate to ensure sufficiently vigorous enforcement of civil rights. In order to ensure that lawyers would be willing to represent persons with legitimate civil rights grievances, Congress determined that it would be necessary to compensate lawyers for all time reasonably expended on a case.[17]

JUSTICE POWELL, concurring in the judgment.

For me affirmance — quite simply — is required by the District Court's detailed findings of fact, which were approved by the Court of Appeals. On its face, the fee award seems unreasonable. But I find no basis for this Court to reject the findings made and approved by the courts below.

Federal Rule of Civil Procedure 52(a) provides that "[f]indings of fact [by a district court] shall not be set aside unless clearly erroneous. . . . " The Court of Appeals did not disagree with any of the foregoing findings by the District Court. I see no basis on which this Court now could hold that these findings are clearly erroneous.

[D]espite serious doubts as to the fairness of the fees awarded in this case, I cannot conclude that the detailed findings made by the District Court, and accepted by the Court of Appeals, were clearly erroneous, or that the District Court abused its discretion in making this fee award.[18]

CHIEF JUSTICE BURGER, dissenting.

I write only to add that it would be difficult to find a better example of legal nonsense than the fixing of attorney's fees by a judge at $245,456.25 for the recovery of $33,350 damages.

The two attorneys receiving this nearly quarter-million-dollar fee graduated from law school in 1973 and 1974; they brought this action in 1975, which resulted in the $33,350 jury award in 1980. Their total professional experience when this litigation began consisted of Gerald Lopez' 1-year service as a law clerk to a judge and Roy Cazares' two years' experience as a trial attorney in the Defenders' Program of San Diego County. For their services the District Court found that an hourly rate of $125 per hour was reasonable.

---

[17] [n.9] Of course, we do not mean to suggest that private-sector comparisons are irrelevant to fee calculations under § 1988. We have suggested that in determining an appropriate hourly rate for a lawyer's services, "the rates charged in private representations may afford relevant comparisons." We have also indicated that "[c]ounsel for a prevailing party should make a good-faith effort to exclude from a fee request hours that are excessive, redundant, or otherwise unnecessary, just as a lawyer in private practice ethically is obligated to exclude such hours from his fee submission." However, while private-market considerations are not irrelevant, Congress clearly rejected the notion that attorney's fees under § 1988 should be based on private-sector fee arrangements.

[18] [n.4] [T]he plurality emphasizes that a primary purpose of § 1988 was to assure the availability of counsel in civil rights cases. This was an expressed and proper purpose of Congress when § 1988 was enacted a decade ago. Although the tables in the Annual Report of the Director of the Administrative Office are not explicit in this respect, it is clear that the increased filings of civil rights cases that began following *Monroe v. Pape*, particularly § 1983 cases, have continued and even accelerated since 1976. These facts suggest that § 1988 is serving well Congress' purpose to assure availability of counsel, and that this purpose does not justify more generous fee awards than otherwise would be viewed as fair and reasonable.

Can anyone doubt that no private party would ever have dreamed of paying these two novice attorneys $125 per hour in 1975, which, considering inflation, would represent perhaps something more nearly a $250 per hour rate today?

The Court's result will unfortunately only add fuel to the fires of public indignation over the costs of litigation.

JUSTICE REHNQUIST, with whom THE CHIEF JUSTICE, JUSTICE WHITE, and JUSTICE O'CONNOR join, dissenting.

A brief look at the history of this case reveals just how "unreasonable" it was for [plaintiffs'] lawyers to spend so much time on it. [Plaintiffs] filed their initial complaint in 1976, seeking injunctive and declaratory relief and compensatory and punitive damages from the city of Riverside, its Chief of Police, and 30 police officers, based on 256 separate claims allegedly arising out of the police breakup of a single party. Prior to trial, 17 of the police officers were dismissed from the case on motions for summary judgment, and [plaintiffs] dropped their requests for injunctive and declaratory relief. More significantly, [plaintiffs] also dropped their original allegation that the police had acted with discriminatory intent. The action proceeded to trial, and the jury completely exonerated nine additional police officers. [Plaintiffs] ultimately prevailed against only the city and five police officers on various § 1983, false arrest and imprisonment, and common negligence claims. No restraining orders or injunctions were ever issued against [defendants], nor was the city ever compelled to change a single practice or policy as a result of [plaintiffs'] suit. The jury awarded [plaintiffs] a total of $33,350 in compensatory and punitive damages. Only about one-third of this total, or $13,300, was awarded to [plaintiffs] based on violations of their federal constitutional rights.

[O]n the basis of some of the statements made by the District Court in this case, I reluctantly conclude that the court may have attempted to make up to [plaintiffs] in attorney's fees what it felt the jury had wrongfully withheld from them in damages.

But a district court, in awarding attorney's fees under § 1988, does not sit to retry questions submitted to and decided by the jury. If jurors are reluctant to make large awards against police officers, this is a fact of life that plaintiffs, defendants, and district courts must live with, and a district court simply has no business trying to correct what it regards as an unfortunate tendency in the award of damages by granting inflated attorney's fees.

I agree with the plurality that the importation of the contingent-fee model to govern fee awards under § 1988 is not warranted by the terms and legislative history of the statute. But, [compensating] [n]early 2,000 attorney-hours spent on a case in which the total recovery was only $33,000, in which only $13,300 of that amount was recovered for the federal claims, and in which the District Court expressed the view that, in such cases, juries typically were reluctant to award substantial damages against police officers, is simply not "reasonable" . . . .

NOTES

1. The Lodestar Approach. *Rivera* makes clear that the District Court has a large measure of discretion to fix the amount of an attorney's fee award. Justice Powell, whose vote was necessary to make a majority, made much of this point. Whether hours should be compensated is thus generally left to the discretion of the District Court. Justice Brennan also makes clear in *Rivera* that declaratory and injunctive relief will likewise support fee awards under § 1988(b). *See also Blanchard v. Bergeron*, 489 U.S. 87, 95 (1989) ("It is clear that Congress 'intended that the amount of fees awarded . . . be governed by the same standards which prevail in other types of equally complex Federal litigation . . . and not be reduced because the rights involved may be non-pecuniary in nature.' "). Thus, hours devoted to winning prospective relief qualify for lodestar treatment on the same terms as those spent winning money damages.

The first question under the lodestar analysis is temporal; how much time was reasonably necessary to win the case? Assuming that a plaintiff wins all of the relief sought — whether damages, an injunction, or a declaratory judgment — he or she would ordinarily be entitled to compensation for most of the hours expended. Should the plaintiff win less than what was sought, the hours and resulting fees are often, *see, e.g., Farrar v. Hobby*, 506 U.S. 103, 105 (1992) (discussed in Note 3, *infra*), though not always, reduced. Indeed, *Rivera* is testament to the fact that the District Court can still fully compensate a plaintiff's lawyer who wins less than what was originally demanded. Where a plaintiff prevails only against some of the defendants or on only some of its claims, the District Court will usually attempt to separate those hours that should be compensated from those that should not. Justice Brennan also noted in *Rivera* that " '[c]ounsel for a prevailing party should make a good-faith effort to exclude from a fee request hours that are excessive, redundant, or otherwise unnecessary, just as a lawyer in private practice ethically is obligated to exclude such hours from his fee submission.' " *See* footnote 9. In the end, the plaintiff is entitled to an award of attorney's fees if it prevailed on "any significant issue" and achieved "some of the benefit" sought. *Texas State Teachers Association v. Garland Independent School District*, 489 U.S. 782 (1989). The plaintiff's victory need not be on a "central issue" or achieve "primary" relief to support an award of attorneys' fees.

The next matter is one of reasonable rate. In *Rivera*, Justice Brennan noted that "in determining an appropriate hourly rate for a lawyer's services, 'the rates charged in private representations may afford relevant comparisons.' " *See* footnote 9. Along these same lines, the Court in *Blum v. Stenson*, 465 U.S. 886 (1984), observed that the reasonableness of an attorney's hourly rates should be gauged by the rates commonly charged in the local legal community. Lower courts have thus tended to focus on the prevailing rates charged by local attorneys in similar cases, *see, e.g., Paschal v. Flagstar Bank*, 297 F.3d 431 (6th Cir. 2002) (observing in a Title VII case that the court should look to similar cases to assess the reasonableness of the fee), as well as the particular attorney's experience and expertise. Local rates provide the bounds of reasonableness, with the litigating lawyer's experience — both generally and in the civil rights field — acting to adjust the rate within this range. Because "few practitioners regularly defend the disadvantaged by billing on an hourly basis," James K. Green & Barbara Kritchevsky, *Litigating Attorney's Fees: Running the Gauntlet*, 37 URB. LAW. 691, 699 (2005), courts commonly look to antitrust and securities cases for comparable hourly rates. *Id.* The result is that rates awarded in civil rights cases tend to mirror the rates actually charged in sophisticated business cases. In *Marisol A. v. Guiliani*, 111 F. Supp. 2d 381 (S.D.N.Y. 2000), for example, the District Court set a fee of $375 per hour for the lead counsel in the case, since he had extensive experience. It then set a reasonable rate of $300 per hour for co-counsel who had more than ten years' experience, and $230–250 per hour for co-counsel who had more than seven years' experience. The rates awarded in § 1983 cases are thus ordinarily much higher than rates commonly charged in the realm of public service.[19] The Judicial Conference of the United States, for example, has established a base hourly rate of $113 under the federal Criminal Justice Act (CJA), 18 U.S.C. § 3006A. *See, e.g., Hadix v. Johnson*, 398 F.3d 863 (6th Cir. 2005) (observing that the CJA rate established by the Judicial Conference is $113). And many District Courts cross the country routinely pay less to court-appointed counsel. *See, e.g., Johnson v. Daley*, 339 F.3d 582 (7th Cir. 2003) (finding that the local hourly rate under the CJA is only $90).

---

[19] *But see Yahoo!, Inc. v. Net Games*, 329 F. Supp. 2d 1179 (N.D. Cal. 2004) (stating that the aim of fee-shifting is to facilitate plaintiff's obtaining "reasonably competent counsel" and thus limiting fees under § 1988(b) to $190 per hour in the San Francisco Bay area).

2. Record Keeping. Justice Brennan noted in *Rivera* that "[a] fee applicant should 'maintain billing time records in a manner that will enable a reviewing court to identify distinct claims.'" *See* footnote 4. In *Hensley v. Eckerhart*, 461 U.S. 424 (1983), the Court explained that an attorney "is not required to record in great detail how each minute of his time was expended," but the attorney should "at least" identify the subject matter of the time expended. "Billing records should be considered adequate if they contain the 'date, the number of hours spent, and a short but thorough description of the services rendered.'" James K. Green & Barbara Kritchevsky, *Litigating Attorney's Fees: Running the Gauntlet*, 37 URB. LAW. 691, 694 (2005). Along these lines, Green and Kritchevsky recommend that time records be kept "in blocks of tenths of an hour." *Id.* "[C]ourts have found that time records using half-hour or quarter-hour time increments are unacceptable." *Id.* Courts have also rejected records that reflect "terse listings," such as "library research," "analyzing documents," "reading background documents," and "phone interviews." *Id.* (citing *Walker v. U.S. Department of Housing & Urban Development*, 99 F.3d 761 (5th Cir. 1996)). Rather than reject fee applications outright, some courts have instead imposed percentage reductions on fee requests that are too vague or otherwise inadequate. *See id.* at 694 (citing *Kirsch v. Fleet St., Ltd.*, 148 F.3d 149 (2d Cir. 1998)). The better practice, Green and Kritchevsky report, is for lawyers "[i]n addition to the contemporaneous itemization of tasks" to "summarize their overall time by activity." *Id.* at 695.

3. Nominal Damages. In *Farrar v. Hobby*, 506 U.S. 103 (1992), the Supreme Court addressed "whether a civil rights plaintiff who receives a nominal damages award is a 'prevailing party' eligible to receive attorney's fees under 42 U.S.C. § 1988." The plaintiffs, Joseph and Dale Farrar, owned and operated a private school for delinquent, disabled, and disturbed teens. After a student died in 1973, a local grand jury returned a murder indictment charging Joseph Farrar with willful failure to administer proper medical treatment and failure to provide timely hospitalization. State authorities then temporarily closed the school. After the criminal charges were dismissed, the plaintiffs sued several state and local officials under § 1983 for monetary and injunctive relief. Their complaint alleged deprivations of liberty and property without due process by means of conspiracy and malicious prosecution aimed at closing their school. Later amendments to the complaint dropped the claim for injunctive relief, and increased the request for damages to $17 million.

A jury found that all of the defendants, except one (Lieutenant Governor William Hobby), had conspired against the plaintiffs, and that Hobby had "committed an act or acts under color of state law that deprived Plaintiff Joseph Davis Farrar of a civil right." The jury also concluded, however, that neither the conspiracy nor Hobby's conduct was a proximate cause of any injury suffered by the plaintiffs. The District Court thus ordered that "Plaintiffs take nothing, that the action be dismissed on the merits, and that the parties bear their own costs." Based on the jury's conclusion that Hobby had violated plaintiffs' civil rights, however, the Fifth Circuit ordered entry of judgment against Hobby for nominal damages not to exceed $1. On remand, the District Court then awarded the plaintiffs attorney's fees in the amount of $280,000. In reversing the fee award, Justice Thomas wrote for the Court:

> [A] plaintiff who wins nominal damages is a prevailing party under § 1988. When a court awards nominal damages, it neither enters judgment for defendant on the merits nor declares the defendant's legal immunity to suit. To be sure, a judicial pronouncement that the defendant has violated the Constitution, unaccompanied by an enforceable judgment on the merits, does not render the plaintiff a prevailing party. Of itself, "the moral satisfaction [that] results from any favorable statement of law" cannot bestow prevailing party status. No material alteration of the legal relationship between the parties occurs until the plaintiff becomes entitled to enforce a judgment, consent decree, or settlement against the defendant. A plaintiff may demand payment for nominal damages no less than he may demand payment for millions of

dollars in compensatory damages. A judgment for damages in any amount, whether compensatory or nominal, modifies the defendant's behavior for the plaintiff's benefit by forcing the defendant to pay an amount of money he otherwise would not pay.

Although the "technical" nature of a nominal damages award or any other judgment does not affect the prevailing party inquiry, it does bear on the propriety of fees awarded under § 1988. Once civil rights litigation materially alters the legal relationship between the parties, "the degree of the plaintiff's overall success goes to the reasonableness" of a fee award. . . . Indeed, "the most critical factor" in determining the reasonableness of a fee award "is the degree of success obtained." In this case, [the Farrars] received nominal damages instead of the $17 million in compensatory damages that they sought. This litigation accomplished little beyond giving [them] "the moral satisfaction of knowing that a federal court concluded that [their] rights had been violated" in some unspecified way. We have already observed that if "a plaintiff has achieved only partial or limited success, the product of hours reasonably expended on the litigation as a whole times a reasonable hourly rate may be an excessive amount." Yet the District Court calculated [the Farrars'] fee award in precisely this fashion, without engaging in any measured exercise of discretion. "Where recovery of private damages is the purpose of . . . civil rights litigation, a district court, in fixing fees, is obligated to give primary consideration to the amount of damages awarded as compared to the amount sought." Such a comparison promotes the court's "central" responsibility to "make the assessment of what is a reasonable fee under the circumstances of the case." Having considered the amount and nature of damages awarded, the court may lawfully award low fees or no fees without reciting the 12 factors bearing on reasonableness [cited in *Rivera*], or multiplying "the number of hours reasonably expended . . . by a reasonable hourly rate."

In some circumstances, even a plaintiff who formally "prevails" under § 1988 should receive no attorney's fees at all. A plaintiff who seeks compensatory damages but receives no more than nominal damages is often such a prevailing party. As we have held, a nominal damages award does render a plaintiff a prevailing party by allowing him to vindicate his "absolute" right to procedural due process through enforcement of a judgment against the defendant. In a civil rights suit for damages, however, the awarding of nominal damages also highlights the plaintiff's failure to prove actual, compensable injury. Whatever the constitutional basis for substantive liability, damages awarded in a § 1983 action "must always be designed 'to compensate injuries caused by the [constitutional] deprivation.'" When a plaintiff recovers only nominal damages because of his failure to prove an essential element of his claim for monetary relief, the only reasonable fee is usually no fee at all.

Justice O'Connor, whose fifth vote was necessary to make a majority opinion,[20] concurred with the following remarks:

[T]he Court properly holds that, when a plaintiff's victory is purely technical or *de minimis*, a district court need not go through the usual complexities involved in calculating attorney's fees. As a matter of common sense and sound judicial administration, it would be wasteful indeed to require that courts laboriously and mechanically go through those steps when the *de minimis* nature of the victory makes the proper fee immediately obvious. Instead, it is enough for a court to explain why the victory is *de minimis* and announce a sensible decision to "award low fees or no fees" at all.

---

[20] Justices White, Blackmun, Stevens and Souter dissented.

Indeed, § 1988 contemplates the denial of fees to *de minimis* victors through yet another mechanism. The statute only authorizes courts to award fees "as part of the costs." As a result, when a court denies costs, it must deny fees as well; if there are no costs, there is nothing for the fees to be awarded "as part of." And when Congress enacted § 1988, the courts would deny even a prevailing party costs under Federal Rule of Civil Procedure 54(d) where the victory was purely technical. Just as a Pyrrhic victor would be denied costs under Rule 54(d), so too should it be denied fees under § 1988.

In the context of this litigation, the technical or *de minimis* nature of Joseph Farrar's victory is readily apparent: He asked for a bundle and got a pittance. While we hold today that this pittance is enough to render him a prevailing party, it does not by itself prevent his victory from being purely technical.

That is not to say that *all* nominal damages awards are *de minimis*. Nominal relief does not necessarily a nominal victory make. But, . . . a substantial difference between the judgment recovered and the recovery sought suggests that the victory is in fact purely technical. Here that suggestion is quite strong. Joseph Farrar asked for 17 million dollars; he got one. It is hard to envision a more dramatic difference.

The difference between the amount recovered and the damages sought is not the only consideration, however. [A]n award of nominal damages can represent a victory in the sense of vindicating rights even though no actual damages are proved. Accordingly, the courts also must look to other factors. One is the significance of the legal issue on which the plaintiff claims to have prevailed.

Given that Joseph Farrar got *some* of what he wanted — one seventeen millionth, to be precise — his success might be considered material if it also accomplished some public goal other than occupying the time and energy of counsel, court, and client. Section 1988 is not "a relief Act for lawyers." Instead, it is a tool that ensures the vindication of important rights, even when large sums of money are not at stake, by making attorney's fees available under a private attorney general theory. Yet one searches these facts in vain for the public purpose this litigation might have served.

Lower courts have often looked to Justice O'Connor's concurring remarks in *Farrar* to guide them in the context of attorney's fees and nominal damages. Where litigation that results in only nominal damages is viewed as serving some "public purpose" beyond compensating the plaintiff and paying the lawyers, courts have awarded substantial attorney's fees notwithstanding the fact that only nominal damages were recovered. *See, e.g., Lippoldt v. Cole*, 468 F.3d 1204 (10th Cir. 2006) ("To determine whether the plaintiff achieved technical success only, we apply three factors from Justice O'Connor's concurrence in *Farrar*: (1) the "difference between the amount recovered and the damages sought;" (2) the "significance of the legal issue on which the plaintiff claims to have prevailed;" and (3) the "accomplishment of some public goal other than occupying the time and energy of counsel, court, and client."); *Mercer v. Duke University*, 401 F.3d 199 (4th Cir. 2005) (awarding substantial attorney's fee in a Title IX case even though only nominal damages were recovered).

4. Fee Enhancement. Following *Rivera*, successful plaintiffs' lawyers operating on a contingent basis often sought (and received) fee enhancements, commonly known as multipliers, under § 1988. The Supreme Court rejected this practice in *City of Burlington v. Dague*, 505 U.S. 557 (1992). That case involved a successful challenge under the Solid Waste Disposal Act (SWDA) and the Federal Water Pollution Control Act (Clean Water Act (CWA)), both of which have fee-shifting provisions similar to that found in § 1988(b). The question presented to the Court was whether an award of attorney's fees could be enhanced "above the 'lodestar' amount in order to reflect the fact that the party's attorneys were retained on a contingent-fee basis and thus assumed the risk of receiving no payment at all for their services." Per Justice Scalia, the Court ruled that fee enhancement based on the relative risk of the case is not permissible:

> Fees for legal services in litigation may be either "certain" or "contingent" (or some hybrid of the two). A fee is certain if it is payable without regard to the outcome of the suit; it is contingent if the obligation to pay depends on a particular result's being obtained. Under the most common contingent-fee contract for litigation, the attorney receives no payment for his services if his client loses. Under this arrangement, the attorney bears a contingent risk of nonpayment that is the inverse of the case's prospects of success: if his client has an 80% chance of winning, the attorney's contingent risk is 20%.
>
> The "lodestar" figure has, as its name suggests, become the guiding light of our fee-shifting jurisprudence. We have established a "strong presumption" that the lodestar represents the "reasonable" fee, and have placed upon the fee applicant who seeks more than that the burden of showing that "such an adjustment is necessary to the determination of a reasonable fee." . . . Dague argues here[] that a "reasonable" fee for attorneys who have been retained on a contingency-fee basis must go beyond the lodestar, to compensate for risk of loss and of consequent nonpayment. Fee-shifting statutes should be construed, he contends, to replicate the economic incentives that operate in the private legal market, where attorneys working on a contingency-fee basis can be expected to charge some premium over their ordinary hourly rates. Petitioner Burlington argues, by contrast, that the lodestar fee may not be enhanced for contingency.
>
> We note at the outset that an enhancement for contingency would likely duplicate in substantial part factors already subsumed in the lodestar. The risk of loss in a particular case (and, therefore, the attorney's contingent risk) is the product of two factors: (1) the legal and factual merits of the claim, and (2) the difficulty of establishing those merits. The second factor, however, is ordinarily reflected in the lodestar — either in the higher number of hours expended to overcome the difficulty, or in the higher hourly rate of the attorney skilled and experienced enough to do so. Taking account of it again through lodestar enhancement amounts to double counting.
>
> The first factor (relative merits of the claim) is not reflected in the lodestar, but there are good reasons why it should play no part in the calculation of the award. It is, of course, a factor that always exists (no claim has a 100% chance of success), so that computation of the lodestar would never end the court's inquiry in contingent-fee cases. Moreover, the consequence of awarding contingency enhancement to take account of this "merits" factor would be to provide attorneys with the same incentive to bring relatively meritless claims as relatively meritorious ones. Assume, for example, two claims, one with underlying merit of 20%, the other of 80%. Absent any contingency enhancement, a contingent-fee attorney would prefer to take the latter, since he is four times more likely to be paid. But with a contingency enhancement, this preference will disappear: the enhancement for the 20% claim would be a multiplier of 5 (100/20), which is quadruple the 1.25 multiplier (100/80) that would attach to the 80% claim. Thus, enhancement for the contingency risk posed by each case would encourage meritorious claims to be brought, but only at the social cost of indiscriminately encouraging nonmeritorious claims to be brought as well. We think that an unlikely objective of the "reasonable fees" provisions. "These statutes were not designed as a form of economic relief to improve the financial lot of lawyers."
>
> Instead of enhancement based upon the contingency risk posed by each case, Dague urges that we adopt the approach [that inquires whether] the party seeking contingency enhancement [could] "establish that without the adjust-

ment for risk [he] 'would have faced substantial difficulties in finding counsel in the local or other relevant market.' " [This] would forbid enhancement based "on an assessment of the 'riskiness' of any particular case." But since the predominant reason that a contingent-fee claimant has difficulty finding counsel in any legal market where the winner's attorney's fees will be paid by the loser is that attorneys view his case as too risky (i.e., too unlikely to succeed), these two propositions, as a practical matter, collide.

A second difficulty with th[is] approach . . . is that it would base the contingency enhancement on "the difference in market treatment of contingent fee cases as a class." To begin with, for a very large proportion of contingency-fee cases — those seeking not monetary damages but injunctive or other equitable relief — there is no "market treatment." Such cases scarcely exist, except to the extent Congress has created an artificial "market" for them by fee shifting — and looking to that "market" for the meaning of fee shifting is obviously circular. Our decrees would follow the "market," which in turn is based on our decrees. But even apart from that difficulty, any approach that applies uniform treatment to the entire class of contingent-fee cases, or to any conceivable subject-matter-based subclass, cannot possibly achieve the supposed goal of mirroring market incentives. As discussed above, the contingent risk of a case (and hence the difficulty of getting contingent-fee lawyers to take it) depends principally upon its particular merits. Contingency enhancement calculated on any class-wide basis, therefore, guarantees at best (leaving aside the double-counting problem described earlier) that those cases within the class that have the class-average chance of success will be compensated according to what the "market" requires to produce the services, and that all cases having above-class-average chance of success will be overcompensated.

An attorney operating on a contingency-fee basis pools the risks presented by his various cases: cases that turn out to be successful pay for the time he gambled on those that did not. To award a contingency enhancement under a fee-shifting statute would in effect pay for the attorney's time (or anticipated time) in cases where his client does not prevail.

5. Contingent Fees. Although judicially imposed multipliers are not authorized under most modern fee-shifting statutes (including § 1988), contingent fee arrangements remain common in § 1983 litigation. These arrangements, for the most part, are governed by contract law and local codes of professional responsibility. Still, federal fee-shifting questions have emerged from privately negotiated contingent contracts.

Blanchard v. Bergerson, 489 U.S. 87, 88 (1989), addressed "whether an attorney's fee allowed under 42 U.S.C. § 1988 is limited to the amount provided in a contingent-fee arrangement entered into by a plaintiff and his counsel." The plaintiff (Blanchard) recovered compensatory and punitive damages totaling $10,000 on his § 1983 claim. The District Court awarded $7,500 in attorney's fees and $886.92 for costs and expenses under § 1988. The Court of Appeals reduced this fee award to $4,000, because petitioner had entered into a contingent-fee arrangement with his lawyer under which the attorney was to receive 40% of plaintiff's damage award. Justice White, speaking for a unanimous Court, held that the contingent agreement did not limit the award of fees available under § 1988:

> The . . . contingency-fee factor is simply that, a factor. The presence of a pre-existing fee agreement may aid in determining reasonableness. "The fee quoted to the client or the percentage of the recovery agreed to is helpful in demonstrating the attorney's fee expectations when he accepted the case." But as we see it, a contingent-fee contract does not impose an automatic ceiling on an award of attorney's fees, and to hold otherwise would be inconsistent with the statute and its policy and purpose.

Should a fee agreement provide less than a reasonable fee calculated in this manner, the defendant should nevertheless be required to pay the higher amount. The defendant is not, however, required to pay the amount called for in a contingent-fee contract if it is more than a reasonable fee calculated in the usual way.

[Bergerson] cautions us that refusing to limit recovery to the amount of the contingency agreement will result in a "windfall" to attorneys who accept § 1983 actions. Yet the very nature of recovery under § 1988 is designed to prevent any such "windfall." Fee awards are to be reasonable, reasonable as to billing rates and reasonable as to the number of hours spent in advancing the successful claims. Accordingly, fee awards, properly calculated, by definition will represent the reasonable worth of the services rendered in vindication of a plaintiff's civil rights claim.

The contingent-fee model, premised on the award to an attorney of an amount representing a percentage of the damages, is thus inappropriate for the determination of fees under § 1988. The attorney's fee provided for in a contingent-fee agreement is not a ceiling upon the fees recoverable under § 1988.

Venegas v. Mitchell, 495 U.S. 82, 83-84 (1990), addressed "whether § 1988 invalidates contingent-fee contracts that would require a prevailing civil rights plaintiff to pay his attorney more than the statutory award against the defendant." The plaintiff (Venegas) and his lawyer (Mitchell) signed a contingent-fee contract providing that Mitchell would represent Venegas at trial for a fee of 40% of the gross amount of any recovery. The contract gave Mitchell "the right to apply for and collect any attorney fee award made by a court," prohibited Venegas from waiving Mitchell's right to court-awarded attorney's fees, and allowed Mitchell's intervention to protect his interest in the fee award. The contract also provided that any fee awarded by the court would be applied, dollar for dollar, to offset the contingent fee. Venegas won over $2 million in damages, and the District Court awarded him $75,000 in fees under § 1988 based on the work done by Mitchell. Mitchell then sought to collect ½ of 40% of the judgment ($406,000) — the other half being due his co-counsel — from Venegas based on their contingent-fee agreement. The Supreme Court, per Justice White, unanimously ruled that § 1988 does not displace contingent-fee agreements:

> [T]here is nothing in [§ 1988] to regulate what plaintiffs may or may not promise to pay their attorneys if they lose or if they win.
>
> It is true that in construing § 1988, we have generally turned away from the contingent-fee model to the lodestar model of hours reasonably expended compensated at reasonable rates. . . . But it is a mighty leap from these propositions to the conclusion that § 1988 also requires the District Court to invalidate a contingent-fee agreement arrived at privately between attorney and client.
>
> [Section] 1988 controls what the losing defendant must pay, not what the prevailing plaintiff must pay his lawyer. What a plaintiff may be bound to pay and what an attorney is free to collect under a fee agreement are not necessarily measured by the "reasonable attorney's fee" that a defendant must pay pursuant to a court order. Section 1988 itself does not interfere with the enforceability of a contingent-fee contract.

6. Double Recovery? The lawyer in *Venegas* agreed to use any shifted fee under § 1988(b) to offset his 40% contingent fee. He thus could not recover *both*. Assuming he had not so agreed, does § 1988(b) allow attorneys to recover a shifted fee *as well as* a contingent fee? Lower courts have found that federal fee-shifting statutes, like § 1988(b), do not preclude attorneys from recovering contractually imposed contingent fees as well as statutorily shifted fees. *See, e.g., Gobert v. Williams*, 323 F.3d 1099 (5th Cir. 2003) (holding that an attorney was entitled to recover a 35% contingent fee —

totaling $17,419 — as well as a shifted fee of almost $37,000 in a successful Title VII action). Is this sort of double recovery ethical? *Cf. Quint v. A.E. Staley Mfg. Co.*, 84 Fed. Appx. 101 (1st Cir. 2003) (stating that court will alter a "fee agreement only in those 'exceptional circumstances' where the fee assessed by counsel is 'unethically excessive' ").

7. Pro Bono Representation. The Court has stated on several occasions that plaintiffs who are represented by non-profit legal services organizations or pro bono attorneys are nonetheless entitled to fee awards under § 1988(b). *See, e.g., Blanchard v. Bergeron*, 489 U.S. 87, 95 (1989) ("That a nonprofit legal services organization may contractually have agreed not to charge any fee of a civil rights plaintiff does not preclude the award of a reasonable fee to a prevailing party in a § 1983 action, calculated in the usual way."). Thus, the fact that a contract between the plaintiff and its lawyer states that the legal services are *pro bono* does not defeat the plaintiff's right to recover attorney's fees under § 1988(b). Of course, because attorney's fees due under § 1988(b) belong to the client, *see, e.g., Evans v. Jeff D.*, 475 U.S. 717 (1986) (excerpted in Section D., *infra*), the attorney must obtain an assignment from the client or otherwise negotiate an enforceable contract to establish a right to the shifted fee.

8. Time Expended by Law Clerks and Paralegals. The Supreme Court in *Rivera* noted that the District Court also awarded fees for the time of two law clerks, though the rate awarded was below the customary rate. The Court in *Missouri v. Jenkins*, 491 U.S. 274 (1989), in an opinion by Justice Brennan, ruled that it is proper to award fees for time expended by law clerks and paralegals at the market rate:

> We . . . take as our starting point the self-evident proposition that the "reasonable attorney's fee" provided for by statute should compensate the work of paralegals, as well as that of attorneys. The more difficult question is how the work of paralegals is to be valued in calculating the overall attorney's fee.
>
> We reject the argument that compensation for paralegals at rates above "cost" would yield a "windfall" for the prevailing attorney. Neither petitioners nor anyone else, to our knowledge, has ever suggested that the hourly rate applied to the work of an associate attorney in a law firm creates a windfall for the firm's partners or is otherwise improper under § 1988, merely because it exceeds the cost of the attorney's services. If the fees are consistent with market rates and practices, the "windfall" argument has no more force with regard to paralegals than it does for associates.
>
> Nothing in § 1988 requires that the work of paralegals invariably be billed separately. If it is the practice in the relevant market not to do so, or to bill the work of paralegals only at cost, that is all that § 1988 requires. Where, however, the prevailing practice is to bill paralegal work at market rates, treating civil rights lawyers' fee requests in the same way is not only permitted by § 1988, but also makes economic sense. By encouraging the use of lower cost paralegals rather than attorneys wherever possible, permitting market-rate billing of paralegal hours "encourages cost-effective delivery of legal services and, by reducing the spiraling cost of civil rights litigation, furthers the policies underlying civil rights statutes."
>
> Such separate billing appears to be the practice in most communities today. In the present case, Missouri concedes that "the local market typically bills separately for paralegal services," and the District Court found that the requested hourly rates of $35 for law clerks, $40 for paralegals, and $50 for recent law graduates were the prevailing rates for such services in the Kansas City area. Under these circumstances, the court's decision to award separate compensation at these rates was fully in accord with § 1988.[21]

---

[21] Professional Fees paid to expert witnesses in § 1983 actions are not subject to shifting either as part of

The Chief Justice authored the lone dissent: "Because law clerks and paralegals have not been licensed to practice law in Missouri, it is difficult to see how charges for their services may be separately billed as part of 'attorney's fees.' And since a prudent attorney customarily includes compensation for the cost of law clerk and paralegal services, like any other sort of office overhead — from secretarial staff, janitors, and librarians, to telephone service, stationery, and paper clips — in his own hourly billing rate, allowing the prevailing party to recover separate compensation for law clerk and paralegal services may result in 'double recovery.' "[22]

9. Tax Consequences of Attorney's Fees. When a prevailing plaintiff's attorney is paid a fee — whether from the plaintiff or the defendant — that attorney has clearly realized income for purposes of the Internal Revenue Code. *See* 26 U.S.C. § 61 (income "from whatever source derived" is gross income). But what about the client? Does the payment of a contingent fee from a judgment directly to the plaintiff's lawyer still result in taxable income to the plaintiff? Does a fee paid by a losing defendant, pursuant to court order, directly to a plaintiff's lawyer constitute taxable income to the plaintiff? The Supreme Court in in *C.I.R. v. Banks*, 543 U.S. 426 (2005), unanimously (per Justice Kennedy) ruled that in both instances the fees paid to the prevailing plaintiff's lawyer constitute taxable income to the client.[23]

After the Supreme Court granted review in *Banks*, the American Jobs Creation Act of 2004 was signed into law on October 22, 2004. Section 703 of this Act, entitled "Civil Rights Tax Relief," amended the Internal Revenue Code to allow taxpayers to subtract from their gross income "attorneys fees and court costs paid by, or on behalf of, the taxpayer in connection with any action involving a claim of unlawful discrimination." 26 U.S.C. § 62(a)(19). "Unlawful discrimination," in turn, includes any "act that is unlawful under" a long list of state and federal laws, including 42 U.S.C. §§ 1981, 1983 and 1985. *See* 26 U.S.C. § 62(e). Consequently, awards of attorney's fees under § 1988(b) that are premised on § 1983 claims are no longer taxable as income to prevailing plaintiffs. Nor are fees paid to successful § 1983 lawyers under contingent fee arrangements. "Still, tax problems can arise in § 1983 litigation when non-exempt state-law damage claims — including those for defamation, intentional infliction of emotional distress, . . . unfair competition, and personal injuries giving rise to punitive damages — are joined with exempt federal claims." Mark R. Brown, *A Primer on the Law of Attorney's Fees Under § 1988*, 37 URB. LAW. 663, 687 (2005). "The key . . . is separating attorney's fees

---

costs or attorney's fees. *See West Virginia University Hospitals v. Casey*, 499 U.S. 83 (1991). *Compare L&W Supply v. Acuity*, 475 F.3d 737 (6th Cir. 2007) (observing that the "Eighth and Third Circuits [have] allowed for the taxation of expert witness fees in the court's discretion when the expert's testimony was indispensable to the determination of a case," but disagreeing and noting that those precedents antedate *Casey* and *Arlington Central School District Board of Education v. Murphy*, 548 U.S. 291 (2006) (which disallowed expert fees under the federal Disabilities Education Act)). Expert fees in § 1983 litigation are thus properly governed by 28 U.S.C. § 1821, which limits fees to $40 per day, plus expenses for common carriage and/or private vehicles, and daily subsistence allowances when overnight stays are needed. *See L&W Supply v. Acuity*, 475 F.3d 737 (6th Cir. 2007). Actions under 42 U.S.C. §§ 1981 or 1981a, however, may result in an award of expert witness fees under 42 U.S.C. § 1988(c).

[22] Paralegal fees are treated differently under the federal EAJA; they are subject to shifting, but only as "expenses" rather than "attorney's fees." *See, e.g., Richlin Security Service Co. v. Chertoff*, 472 F.3d 1370 (Fed. Cir. 2006). Thus, they are only shifted at cost and not at the market rate. *Id.*

[23] Due to a corresponding deduction for amounts expended in the collection of income, *see* 26 U.S.C. § 67(a), this problem can prove trivial when attorney's fees are small. However, the intricacies of the Internal Revenue Code can reduce the value of deductions. *See* 26 U.S.C. §§ 55(b)(2), 56(b)(1)(A)(i); *Barlow v. C.I.R.*, 210 F.3d 1346, 1347 n.3 (11th Cir. 2000) (noting that "[t]he deduction for attorneys' fees and costs which the IRS allowed was less favorable to the taxpayer than the exclusion-from-income approach . . . because of the operation of technical tax rules such as the alternative minimum tax"). Note also that § 104(a) of the Internal Revenue Code excludes from gross income damages for physical injuries. To the extent an attorney's fee is drawn from (or related to) an award for physical injury, it too may be excluded from the client's gross income under § 104(a). *See Banks v. C.I.R.*, 345 F.3d 373 (6th Cir. 2003), *rev'd on other grounds*, 543 U.S. 426 (2005).

collected for these non-exempt state-law claims from fees earned for the exempt § 1983 claims. As suggested by the Court in *Banks*, judgments and settlements that do not adequately distinguish their federal legal bases could still give rise to tax difficulties for clients." *Id.* In the end, therefore, "it would appear wise for plaintiffs' lawyers to structure their contingency agreements, arguments, and settlements so as to best preserve their clients' newly created tax shelters." *Id.* at 688.

10. Attorney's Fees in Prisoner Litigation. Section 1997e(d) of title 42, part of the Prison Litigation Reform Act (PLRA), amends § 1988(b) to limit the attorney's fees that are due prisoners who successfully sue under § 1983. Section 1997e(d)(1) states, in relevant part, that a successful prisoner's[24] attorney's fee must be "directly and reasonably incurred in proving an actual violation of the [prisoner's] rights,"[25] and "proportionately related to the court ordered relief . . . or directly and reasonably incurred in enforcing the relief." Section 1997e(d)(2) effectively reduces the inmate's[26] recovery in a case where "a monetary judgment is awarded," stating that "a portion of the judgment (not to exceed 25 percent) shall be applied to satisfy the amount of attorney's fees awarded against the defendant." This same section then states: "If the award of attorney's fees is not greater than 150 percent of the judgment, the excess shall be paid by the defendant." Although this language is a bit confusing, most courts have ruled that it limits the amount a losing defendant can be required to pay a prevailing inmate's lawyer to 150% of the judgment, less the 25% paid out of the inmate's judgment. *See Johnson v. Daley*, 339 F.3d 582, 583 (7th Cir. 2003) (concluding that § 1997e(d)(2) limits attorney's fees attributable to monetary relief to "150% of the damages"); *Riley v. Kurtz*, 361 F.3d 906 (6th Cir. 2004) (same).[27] Lower courts uniformly agree that these limits on attorney's fees survive constitutional scrutiny. *See, e.g., Johnson v. Daley*, 339 F.3d 582 (7th Cir. 2003) (upholding § 1997e(d)(2)); *Walker v. Bain*, 257 F.3d 660 (6th Cir. 2001) (same).

Section 1997e(d)(3) restricts the hourly rate used in the lodestar calculation of a prisoner's attorney's fee awards — whether for monetary or non-monetary relief — to no more than "150 percent of the hourly rate established under section 3006A of Title 18

---

[24] Section 1997e(d)(1) limits attorney's fee awards in "any action brought by a prisoner." Does this apply to § 1983 actions brought by inmates to redress constitutional violations that occurred outside the prison context? Section 1997e(a), requires exhaustion only on behalf of prisoners who challenge "prison conditions." *See* Chapter 8.A.[3], *infra*. Is § 1997e(d) likewise limited to prison conditions litigation? *Contrast Robbins v. Chronister*, 402 F.3d 1047 (10th Cir. 2005) (holding that § 1997e(d)'s limitation on attorney's fees does *not* apply to an inmate's action against a police officer for excessive force), *with Jackson v. State Bd. of Pardons and Paroles*, 331 F.3d 790 (11th Cir. 2003) (holding that limitations on attorney's fees found in § 1997e(d) are not limited to suits challenging prison conditions). What about prison conditions that harm inmates who are subsequently released? Are former prisoners still subject to the attorney's fees limitations found in § 1997e(d)? *See Morris v. Eversley*, 343 F. Supp. 2d 234 (S.D.N.Y. 2004) (holding that a former prisoner who successfully sued for prison abuse was *not* limited by § 1997e(d)). Does § 1997e(d) limit the attorney's fees due inmates who successfully proceed under statutes other than § 1983? *See Armstrong v. Davis*, 318 F.3d 965 (9th Cir. 2003) (holding that § 1997e(d) does not limit a prisoner's attorney's fee award under the federal ADA and Rehabilitation Act).

[25] Does this mean that attorney's fees incurred in recovering attorney's fees under § 1988(b), so-called "fee-on-fees," are not recoverable under § 1997e(d)? *See Volk v. Gonzalez*, 262 F.3d 528 (5th Cir. 2001) (holding that fees-on-fees can be recovered under § 1997e(d) but that they are subject to the same caps).

[26] The attorney's fee limitations spelled out in 42 U.S.C. § 1997e(d)(1) apply only to an "action brought by a prisoner who is confined to any jail, prison, or other correctional facility." What qualifies as a "jail, prison, or other correctional facility" for purposes of § 1997e(d)? *See Christina A. ex rel. Jennifer v. Bloomberg*, 315 F.3d 990 (8th Cir. 2003) (holding that a state's juvenile training school qualified for treatment under § 1997e(d)).

[27] What if the prisoner seeks only prospective relief? Does this subsection apply to suits seeking non-monetary relief? *See Dannenberg v. Valadez*, 338 F.3d 1070 (9th Cir. 2003) (holding that § 1997e(d)(2)'s 25% and 150% limits do *not* apply to prisoner suits that result in both monetary and injunctive relief).

[the Criminal Justice Act (CJA)], for payment of court-appointed counsel."[28] *See, e.g., Hadix v. Johnson*, 398 F.3d 863 (6th Cir. 2005) (finding that permissible rate under PLRA is 150% of $113, or $169.50); *Johnson v. Daley*, 339 F.3d 582 (7th Cir. 2003) (finding that the hourly rate under the CJA was $90 and thus limiting a successful lawyer in prisoner litigation to $135 per hour).[29] *See* David Rudovsky, *Running in Place: The Paradox of Expanding Rights and Restricted Remedies*, 2005 U. ILL. L. REV. 1199, 1243–44 (discussing limitations on attorney's fees following adoption of the PLRA).

Johnson v. Daley, 339 F.3d 582 (7th Cir. 2003), provides an apt illustration of how lower courts have applied these limitations. The inmate (Johnson) in *Daley* sued the medical director of the prison (Daley) where he was detained for violations of the Eighth Amendment. Johnson recovered $10,000 in compensatory and $30,000 in punitive damages. The Seventh Circuit concluded that § 1997e limited Johnson's § 1988(b) attorney's fee award to $46,451.50: "as we read subsection (2), attorney's compensation comes *first* from the damages, as in ordinary tort litigation, and only if 25% of award is inadequate to compensate counsel fully may defendant be ordered to pay more under § 1988." Hence, Johnson was required to pay 25% of his judgment, $10,000,[30] toward a maximum fee award of $60,000 (150% of the $40,000 judgment). Because of the cap on hourly rates found in § 1997e(d)(3), however, the Seventh Circuit concluded that Johnson's attorneys were entitled to a total lodestar award of only $46,451.50 — which the court arrived at by multiplying 525 hours by various rates that were below the $135 ceiling. Hence, Daley was held responsible for $36,451.50 of the fee award. Had § 1997e(d) not been in place, the attorney's fee award would have totaled $79,800.

C. SETTLEMENTS AND CONSENT DECREES

One thing is clear following *Buckhannon*: a simple agreement on behalf of a defendant not to enforce a challenged rule is not sufficient to support an award of attorney's fees. *Buckhannon* was adamant that the plaintiff must win some sort of juridical relief. So long as an agreement is extra-judicial, the plaintiff cannot claim that it is a prevailing party within the meaning of § 1988(b). The *Buckhannon* Court also noted, however, that a settlement incorporated into a court order, like that in the case that follows, may form the basis of a fee award.

---

[28] Section 1997e(d)(4) preserves a prisoner's ability to enter "into an agreement to pay an attorney's fee in an amount greater than the amount authorized under this section, if the fee is paid by the individual rather than by the defendant pursuant to section 1988."

[29] The Judicial Conference of the United States has established a base hourly rate of $113 under the CJA. Many districts and circuits across the country, however, routinely pay less to court-appointed counsel. The Tenth Circuit, for example, pays counsel appointed under the CJA only $90 per hour. Which is the appropriate base rate for purposes of the PLRA? Some courts have concluded that the appropriate base rate is that established by the Judicial Conference. *See, e.g., Hadix v. Johnson*, 398 F.3d 863 (6th Cir. 2005) (finding that the permissible rate under PLRA is 150% of $113, or $169.50). In contrast, "it appears that the majority of courts have adopted the policy of using the established rate for that jurisdiction, [which] allows for regional difference in rates normally charged by attorneys." *Skinner v. Uphoff*, 324 F. Supp. 2d 1278 (D. Wyo. 2004).

[30] Is the 25% figure mandatory, or does it reflect only a ceiling on what the successful prisoner can be required to pay? "Some courts read Section 1997e(d)(2) as giving them the discretion to set the percentage at less than 25%. Other courts have concluded that 25% is not a ceiling, but an automatic percentage applied in every case." *Farella v. Hockaday*, 304 F. Supp. 2d 1076, 1080 (C.D. Ill. 2004) (concluding that courts have discretion to charge less than 25% to the prisoner's judgment and finding that 10% was appropriate).

MAHER v. GAGNE
Supreme Court of the United States
448 U.S. 122 (1980)

Mr. Justice Stevens delivered the opinion of the Court.

In an action brought under 42 U.S.C. § 1983, the court, in its discretion, may allow the prevailing party to recover a reasonable attorney's fee as part of the award of costs. The question presented by this petition is whether fees may be assessed against state officials after a case has been settled by the entry of a consent decree, without any determination that the plaintiff's constitutional rights have been violated.

[Maher] is responsible for the administration of Connecticut's Aid to Families with Dependent Children (AFDC), a federally funded public assistance program. [Gagne] is a working recipient of AFDC benefits. Under state and federal regulations, the amount of her benefits depends, in part, on her net earnings, which are defined as her wages minus certain work-related expenses. In 1975 [Gagne] filed a complaint in the United States District Court for the District of Connecticut alleging that Connecticut's AFDC regulations denied her credit for substantial portions of her actual work-related expenses, thus reducing the level of her benefits. Her complaint alleged that these regulations violated . . . the Social Security Act and the Equal Protection and Due Process Clauses of the Fourteenth Amendment to the United States Constitution.[31]

A few months after the action was commenced, while discovery was underway, [Maher] amended the AFDC regulations to authorize a deduction for all reasonable work-related expenses. After an interval of almost a year and a half, [Gagne] filed an amended complaint alleging that actual expenses in excess of certain standard allowances were still being routinely disallowed.

Thereafter, a settlement was negotiated and the District Court entered a consent decree that, among other things, provided for a substantial increase in the standard allowances and gave AFDC recipients the right to prove that their actual work-related expenses were in excess of the standard.[32] The parties informally agreed that the question whether [Gagne] was entitled to recover attorney's fees would be submitted to the District Court after the entry of the consent decree.

Following an adversary hearing, the District Court awarded [Gagne's] counsel a fee of $3,012.19. The court held that [Gagne] was the "prevailing party" within the meaning of § 1988 because, while not prevailing "in every particular," she had won "substantially all of the relief originally sought in her complaint" in the consent decree. The court also rejected [Maher's] argument that an award of fees against him was barred by the Eleventh Amendment in the absence of a judicial determination that [Gagne's] constitutional rights had been violated. Relying on the basic policy against deciding constitutional claims unnecessarily, the court held that [Gagne] was entitled to fees under the Act because, in addition to her statutory claim, she had alleged constitutional claims that were sufficiently substantial to support federal jurisdiction under the reasoning of *Hagans v. Lavine*, 415 U.S. 528 (1974).

We . . . find no merit in [Maher's] suggestion that [Gagne] was not the "prevailing party" within the meaning of § 1988. The fact that [Gagne] prevailed through a settlement rather than through litigation does not weaken her claim to fees. Nothing in the language of § 1988 conditions the District Court's power to award fees on full

---

[31] [n.5] In her complaint [Gagne] alleged [that] Defendants' practice and policy constitute an invidious discrimination against persons whose work-related expenses exceed the allowances set forth in [federal guidelines] and violate the Equal Protection Clause of the Fourteenth Amendment . . . .

[32] [n.9] As is customary, the consent decree did not purport to adjudicate [Gagne's] statutory or constitutional claims. Rather, it explicitly stated that "[n]othing in this Consent Decree is intended to constitute an admission of fault by either party to this action."

litigation of the issues or on a judicial determination that the plaintiff's rights have been violated. Moreover, the Senate Report expressly stated that "for purposes of the award of counsel fees, parties may be considered to have prevailed when they vindicate rights through a consent judgment or without formally obtaining relief."

[Maher's] second argument is that, regardless of Congress' intent, a federal court is barred by the Eleventh Amendment from awarding fees against a State in a case involving a purely statutory, non-civil-rights claim. [Maher] argues that Congress may empower federal courts to award fees against the States only insofar as it is exercising its power under § 5 of the Fourteenth Amendment to enforce substantive rights conferred by that Amendment. Thus, [Maher] contends that fees can only be assessed in § 1983 actions brought to vindicate Fourteenth Amendment rights or to enforce civil rights statutes that were themselves enacted pursuant to § 5 of the Fourteenth Amendment.

In this case, there is no need to reach the question whether a federal court could award attorney's fees against a State based on a statutory, non-civil-rights claim. For, contrary to [Maher's] characterization, [Gagne] did allege violations of her Fourteenth Amendment due process and equal protection rights, which the District Court and the Court of Appeals both held to be sufficiently substantial to support federal jurisdiction under *Hagans v. Lavine*. Although [Maher] is correct that the trial judge did not find any constitutional violation, the constitutional issues remained in the case until the entire dispute was settled by the entry of a consent decree. Under these circumstances, [Maher's] Eleventh Amendment claim is foreclosed by our decision in *Hutto v. Finney*, 437 U.S. 678 (1978) [discussed in Chapter 3.B., *supra*].

We agree with the courts below that Congress was acting within its enforcement power in allowing the award of fees in a case in which the plaintiff prevails on a wholly statutory, non-civil-rights claim pendent to a substantial constitutional claim or in one in which both a statutory and a substantial constitutional claim are settled favorably to the plaintiff without adjudication. As the Court of Appeals pointed out, such a fee award "furthers the Congressional goal of encouraging suits to vindicate constitutional rights without undermining the longstanding judicial policy of avoiding unnecessary decision of important constitutional issues." It is thus an appropriate means of enforcing substantive rights under the Fourteenth Amendment.

JUSTICE POWELL, with whom THE CHIEF JUSTICE and MR. JUSTICE REHNQUIST join, concurring in the judgment.

I see no reason to . . . apply today's ruling in *Maine v. Thiboutot*, 448 U.S. 1 (1980). That decision holds that plaintiffs may win attorney's fees under § 1988 when they bring an action under 42 U.S.C. § 1983 without any constitutional claim whatever. For the reasons given in my dissenting opinion in *Thiboutot*, I believe that decision seriously misconceives the congressional purpose behind § 1983. In this case, however, the complaint included a substantial constitutional claim which "remained in the case until the entire dispute was settled by the entry of a consent decree." Since Congress has made plain its intent that fees be awarded to "prevailing" parties in these circumstances, we have no occasion to look behind the settlement agreement to evaluate further the constitutional cause of action.

NOTES

1. Attorney's Fees and the Eleventh Amendment. In rejecting Maher's Eleventh Amendment defense, the Court in *Maher* relied on its prior decision in *Hutto v. Finney*, 437 U.S. 678 (1978). *Hutto*, which is discussed in Note 2 following *Edelman* in Chapter 3.B., *supra*, held that Congress abrogated the states' Eleventh Amendment immunity when it enacted § 1988. In so holding, *Hutto* relied on the long tradition of awarding costs "without regard for the States' Eleventh Amendment immunity." "The Court has never viewed the Eleventh Amendment as barring such awards, even in suits between States and individual litigants." The *Hutto* Court also pointed to language in the House and Senate Reports accompanying § 1988(b), which clearly evinced a congressional intent that attorney's fee awards be paid by States when State employees were sued in their official capacities for prospective relief. The Court quoted a statement in the Senate Report indicating that "it is intended that the attorney's fees, like other items of costs, will be collected either directly from the official, in his official capacity, from funds of his agency or under his control, or from the State or local government (whether or not the agency or local government is a named party)," as well as a footnote in the House Report stating that "[o]f course, the 11th Amendment is not a bar to the awarding of counsel fees against state governments."

Although *Hutto*'s reliance on legislative history does not survive more recent Supreme Court precedent demanding a "clear statement" in the legislation itself in order to abrogate the states' Eleventh Amendment immunity, *see Atascadero State Hospital v. Scanlon*, 473 U.S. 234 (1985) (which is excerpted in Chapter 3.C., *supra*), the Court reaffirmed *Hutto*'s result in *Missouri v. Jenkins*, 491 U.S. 274 (1989): "the Eleventh Amendment has no application to an award of attorney's fees, ancillary to a grant of prospective relief."

2. Attorney's Fees for Statutory Violations. The § 1983 claims in *Maher* were both constitutional and statutory. Because a substantial constitutional claim was found to exist, the *Maher* Court did not have to address the question whether a state could be ordered to pay attorney's fees under § 1988(b) for a purely statutory violation. In the seminal case of *Maine v. Thiboutot*, 448 U.S. 1 (1980), which was issued on the same day as *Maher*, the Supreme Court ruled that federal statutory violations — there, claims under the Social Security Act — could form the basis for claims under § 1983. Although *Thiboutot* has been limited by more recent holdings, *see* Note 3 following *Golden State* in Chapter 1.E., *supra*, federal statutory claims can still support claims under § 1983.

Assuming a *Thiboutot*-type claim is properly brought for prospective relief against state officials acting in their official capacity, can the state be forced to pay attorney's fees under § 1988(b)? Does the Fourteenth Amendment's enforcement provision (§ 5) allow Congress to override a state's Eleventh Amendment immunity (and force open its treasury to pay attorney's fees) in a non-constitutional setting? The Court, per Justice Brennan, held that it did in *Maine v. Thiboutot*, 448 U.S. 1 (1980). Although subsequent Supreme Court cases have cast doubt on Thiboutot's broad view of both Congress's § 5 powers and its cramped view of the Eleventh Amendment, *see, e.g., Seminole Tribe v. Florida*, 517 U.S. 44 (1996) (excerpted in Chapter 3.A., *supra*), ordering states to pay to prevailing plaintiffs their attorney's fees for statutory violations still does not violate the Eleventh Amendment. This is because *Hutto* held in the alternative that "costs and attorney's fees" — which it concluded constituted prospective relief — were never protected by the Eleventh Amendment in the first place. Thus, it would seem that Congress is free under § 1988(b) to force states to pay attorney's fees regardless of the nature of the underlying cause of action.

3. Settlements. *Maher* makes clear that *consent decrees* will support fee awards under § 1988(b) regardless of whether they contain an admission or finding of liability. So long as there is a substantial federal question within the meaning of *Hagans v. Lavine* — that is, so long as the federal claim is not "so insubstantial, implausible, foreclosed by prior decisions of [the Supreme Court] or otherwise completely devoid of merit, as not to involve a federal controversy" — fees can be awarded to the plaintiff as a result of a settlement that is incorporated into a judgment as part of a consent decree.

What about simple *settlements* that are not incorporated into judgments? Before *Buckhannon*, lower courts used the catalyst theory to award attorney's fees based on settlements, even if the settlement was not incorporated into a judgment. After *Buckhannon*, this is no longer permissible. "Most circuits recognize that some settlement agreements, even though not explicitly labeled as a 'consent decree' may confer 'prevailing party' status, if they are sufficiently analogous to a consent decree." *Bell v. Board of County Commissioners of Jefferson County*, 451 F.3d 1097 (10th Cir. 2006). *Contrast Christina A. v. Bloomberg*, 315 F.3d 990 (8th Cir. 2003) (holding that the extension of prevailing party status is limited to those who have "receive[d] either an enforceable judgment on the merits or a consent decree"). The question is how much judicial involvement is needed to treat a settlement as the equivalent of a consent decree. "[I]f a court does not incorporate a private settlement into an order, does not sign or otherwise provide written approval of the settlement's terms, and does not retain jurisdiction to enforce performance of the obligations assumed by the settling parties, the settlement 'does not bear any of the marks of a consent decree' and does not confer prevailing party status on the party whose claims have been compromised." *Bell*, 315 F.3d 990. *But see Carbonell v. INS*, 429 F.3d 894 (9th Cir. 2005) (holding that a settlement supports attorney's fees so long as it is a "legally enforceable instrument").

Consider the Fourth Circuit's application of *Bell*'s principles in *Smyth v. Rivero*, 282 F.3d 268 (4th Cir. 2002):

> A consent decree has elements of both judgment and contract, a dual character that "result[s] in different treatment for different purposes." *Local No. 93, Int'l Assn. of Firefighters, AFL-CIO v. Cleveland*, 478 U.S. 501 (1986) (describing the "hybrid nature" of consent decrees). Thus, a consent decree embodies an agreement of the parties and . . . is an agreement that the parties desire and expect will be reflected in, and be enforceable as, a judicial decree that is subject to the rules generally applicable to other judgments and decrees.
>
> The parties to a consent decree expect and achieve a continuing basis of jurisdiction to enforce the terms of the resolution of their case in the court entering the order. Because it is entered as an order of the court, the terms of a consent decree must also be examined by the court. In other words, a court entering a consent decree must examine its terms to ensure they are fair and not unlawful.
>
> By contrast, a private settlement, although it may resolve a dispute before a court, ordinarily does not receive the approval of the court. Nor is a private settlement agreement enforceable by a district court as an order of the court unless the obligation to comply with its terms is "made part of the order of dismissal — either by separate provision (such as a provision 'retaining jurisdiction' over the settlement agreement) or by incorporating the terms of the settlement agreement in the order." *Kokkonen v. Guardian Life Ins. Co. of Am.*, 511 U.S. 375 (1994).
>
> Although the district court's order below did not describe its disposition of the case as a "consent decree" (or a "consent order" or "consent judgment"), that does not necessarily end the inquiry. We doubt that the Supreme Court's guidance in *Buckhannon* was intended to be interpreted so restrictively as to require that the words "consent decree" be used explicitly. Where a settlement agreement is embodied in a court order such that the obligation to comply with its terms is court-ordered, the court's approval and the attendant judicial oversight (in the form of continuing jurisdiction to enforce the agreement) may be equally apparent.
>
> [But] [t]he obligation to comply with a settlement's terms must be expressly made part of a court's order for jurisdiction to enforce the settlement after dismissal of the action to exist. Either incorporation of the terms of the agreement or a separate provision retaining jurisdiction over the agreement will suffice for this purpose. Where a court merely recognizes the fact of the parties' agreement and dismisses the case because there is no longer a dispute before it,

the terms of the agreement are not made part of the order and consequently will not serve as a basis of jurisdiction.

We have no trouble concluding that the district court's order in this case does not meet th[is] test . . . . The district court's mention of the . . . agreement in its final order . . . does not make the obligation to comply with the terms of that agreement part of the order.

See also Oil, Chemical & Atomic Workers, International Union AFL-CIO v. Department of Energy, 288 F.3d 452 (D.C. Cir. 2002) (holding that a "Stipulation and Order of Dismissal" stating that the government had provided "substantial amounts of material" requested by the plaintiff under the federal Freedom of Information Act and dismissing the claims with prejudice did not constitute a judicially enforceable agreement).

D. BARGAINING OVER FEES

Rather than risk the vagaries of *Buckhannon*, can the parties simply agree on the attorney's fees that will be paid in lieu of an award under § 1988(b)? What are their (and their attorneys') incentives in the bargaining process?

MAREK v. CHESNY
Supreme Court of the United States
473 U.S. 1 (1985)

CHIEF JUSTICE BURGER delivered the opinion of the Court.

[T]hree police officers, in answering a call on a domestic disturbance, shot and killed [Chesny's] adult son. Chesny, in his own behalf and as administrator of his son's estate, filed suit against the officers in the United States District Court under 42 U.S.C. § 1983 and state tort law.

Prior to trial, [the police officers] made a timely offer of settlement "for a sum, including costs now accrued and attorney's fees, of ONE HUNDRED THOUSAND ($100,000) DOLLARS."[Chesny] did not accept the offer. The case went to trial and attorney's was awarded $5,000 on the state-law "wrongful death" claim, $52,000 for the § 1983 violation, and $3,000 in punitive damages.

[Chesny] filed a request for $171,692.47 in costs, including attorney's fees. This amount included costs incurred after the settlement offer. [The police officers] opposed the claim for postoffer costs, relying on Federal Rule of Civil Procedure 68, which shifts to the plaintiff all "costs" incurred subsequent to an offer of judgment not exceeded by the ultimate recovery at trial. [They] argued that attorney's fees are part of the "costs" covered by Rule 68. The District Court agreed with [the police officers] and declined to award [Chesny] "costs, including attorney's fees, incurred after the offer of judgment." The parties subsequently agreed that $32,000 fairly represented the allowable costs, including attorney's fees, accrued prior to [the police officers'] offer of settlement.[33]

Rule 68 provides that if a timely pretrial offer of settlement is not accepted and "the judgment finally obtained by the offeree is not more favorable than the offer, the offeree must pay the costs incurred after the making of the offer." The plain purpose of Rule 68 is to encourage settlement and avoid litigation. The Rule prompts both parties to a suit to evaluate the risks and costs of litigation, and to balance them against the likelihood of success upon trial on the merits. This case requires us to decide whether the offer in this case was a proper one under Rule 68, and whether the term "costs" as used in Rule 68 includes attorney's fees awardable under 42 U.S.C. § 1988.

---

[33] [n.1] The District Court refused to shift to [Chesny] any costs accrued by [the police officers]. [They] do not contest that ruling.

The first question we address is whether [the police officers'] offer was valid under Rule 68. [Chesny] contends that the offer was invalid because it lumped [the police officers'] proposal for damages with their proposal for costs. [Chesny] argues that Rule 68 requires that an offer must separately recite the amount that the defendant is offering in settlement of the substantive claim and the amount he is offering to cover accrued costs. Only if the offer is bifurcated, he contends, so that it is clear how much the defendant is offering for the substantive claim, can a plaintiff possibly assess whether it would be wise to accept the offer. He apparently bases this argument on the language of the Rule providing that the defendant "may serve upon the adverse party an offer to allow judgment to be taken against him for the money or property or to the effect specified in his offer, with costs then accrued."

We do not read Rule 68 to require that a defendant's offer itemize the respective amounts being tendered for settlement of the underlying substantive claim and for costs.

The critical feature of this portion of the Rule is that the offer be one that allows judgment to be taken against the defendant for both the damages caused by the challenged conduct and the costs then accrued. In other words, the drafters' concern was not so much with the particular components of offers, but with the judgments to be allowed against defendants. If an offer recites that costs are included or specifies an amount for costs, and the plaintiff accepts the offer, the judgment will necessarily include costs; if the offer does not state that costs are included and an amount for costs is not specified, the court will be obliged by the terms of the Rule to include in its judgment an additional amount which in its discretion it determines to be sufficient to cover the costs. In either case, however, the offer has allowed judgment to be entered against the defendant both for damages caused by the challenged conduct and for costs.

Accordingly, it is immaterial whether the offer recites that costs are included, whether it specifies the amount the defendant is allowing for costs, or, for that matter, whether it refers to costs at all. As long as the offer does not implicitly or explicitly provide that the judgment not include costs, a timely offer will be valid.

Contrary to [Chesny's] suggestion, reading the Rule in this way does not frustrate plaintiffs' efforts to determine whether defendants' offers are adequate. At the time an offer is made, the plaintiff knows the amount in damages caused by the challenged conduct. The plaintiff also knows, or can ascertain, the costs then accrued. A reasonable determination whether to accept the offer can be made by simply adding these two figures and comparing the sum to the amount offered.

Curiously, [Chesny] also maintains that [the police officers'] settlement offer did not exceed the judgment obtained by [Chesny]. In this regard, [Chesny] notes that the $100,000 offer is not as great as the sum of the $60,000 in damages, $32,000 in preoffer costs, and $139,692.47 in claimed postoffer costs. This argument assumes, however, that postoffer costs should be included in the comparison. The . . . postoffer costs merely offset part of the expense of continuing the litigation to trial, and should not be included in the calculus.

The second question we address is whether the term "costs" in Rule 68 includes attorney's fees awardable under 42 U.S.C. § 1988. By the time the Federal Rules of Civil Procedure were adopted in 1938, federal statutes had authorized and defined awards of costs to prevailing parties for more than 85 years. Unlike in England, such "costs" generally had not included attorney's fees; under the "American Rule," each party had been required to bear its own attorney's fees. The "American Rule" as applied in federal courts, however, had become subject to certain exceptions by the late 1930's. Some of these exceptions had evolved as a product of the "inherent power in the courts to allow attorney's fees in particular situations." But most of the exceptions were found in federal statutes that directed courts to award attorney's fees as part of costs in particular cases.

The authors of Federal Rule of Civil Procedure 68 were fully aware of these exceptions to the American Rule. . . . Against this background of varying definitions of "costs," the drafters of Rule 68 did not define the term; nor is there any explanation whatever as to its intended meaning in the history of the Rule.

In this setting, given the importance of "costs" to the Rule, it is very unlikely that this omission was mere oversight; on the contrary, the most reasonable inference is that the term "costs" in Rule 68 was intended to refer to all costs properly awardable under the relevant substantive statute or other authority. In other words, all costs properly awardable in an action are to be considered within the scope of Rule 68 "costs." Thus, absent congressional expressions to the contrary, where the underlying statute defines "costs" to include attorney's fees, we are satisfied such fees are to be included as costs for purposes of Rule 68.

Here, [Chesny] sued under 42 U.S.C. § 1983. Pursuant to . . . § 1988, a prevailing party in a § 1983 action may be awarded attorney's fees "as part of the costs." Since Congress expressly included attorney's fees as "costs" available to a plaintiff in a § 1983 suit, such fees are subject to the cost-shifting provision of Rule 68.

[W]e do not believe that this "plain meaning" construction of the statute and the Rule will frustrate Congress' objective in § 1988 of ensuring that civil rights plaintiffs obtain "effective access to the judicial process." Merely subjecting civil rights plaintiffs to the settlement provision of Rule 68 does not curtail their access to the courts, or significantly deter them from bringing suit. Application of Rule 68 will serve as a disincentive for the plaintiff's attorney to continue litigation after the defendant makes a settlement offer. There is no evidence, however, that Congress, in considering § 1988, had any thought that civil rights claims were to be on any different footing from other civil claims insofar as settlement is concerned. Indeed, Congress made clear its concern that civil rights plaintiffs not be penalized for "helping to lessen docket congestion" by settling their cases out of court.

Moreover, Rule 68's policy of encouraging settlements is neutral, favoring neither plaintiffs nor defendants; it expresses a clear policy of favoring settlement of all lawsuits. Civil rights plaintiffs — along with other plaintiffs — who reject an offer more favorable than what is thereafter recovered at trial will not recover attorney's fees for services performed after the offer is rejected. But, since the Rule is neutral, many civil rights plaintiffs will benefit from the offers of settlement encouraged by Rule 68. Some plaintiffs will receive compensation in settlement where, on trial, they might not have recovered, or would have recovered less than what was offered. And, even for those who would prevail at trial, settlement will provide them with compensation at an earlier date without the burdens, stress, and time of litigation. In short, settlements rather than litigation will serve the interests of plaintiffs as well as defendants.

To be sure, application of Rule 68 will require plaintiffs to "think very hard" about whether continued litigation is worthwhile; that is precisely what Rule 68 contemplates. This effect of Rule 68, however, is in no sense inconsistent with the congressional policies underlying § 1983 and § 1988. Section 1988 authorizes courts to award only "reasonable" attorney's fees to prevailing parties. . . . In a case where a rejected settlement offer exceeds the ultimate recovery, the plaintiff — although technically the prevailing party — has not received any monetary benefits from the postoffer services of his attorney. This case presents a good example: the $139,692 in postoffer legal services resulted in a recovery $8,000 less than [the police officers'] settlement offer. Given Congress' focus on the success achieved, we are not persuaded that shifting the postoffer costs to [Chesny] in these circumstances would in any sense thwart its intent under § 1988.

JUSTICE BRENNAN, with whom JUSTICE MARSHALL and JUSTICE BLACKMUN join, dissenting.

For a number of reasons, "costs" as that term is used in the Federal Rules should be interpreted uniformly in accordance with the definition of costs set forth in [28 U.S.C.] § 1920 [which defines the costs that are generally taxable in federal litigation and does not include attorney's fees]:

First. The limited history of the costs provisions in the Federal Rules suggests that the drafters intended "costs" to mean only taxable costs traditionally allowed under the common law or pursuant to the statutory predecessor of § 1920.

Second. The Rules provide that "costs" may automatically be taxed by the clerk of the court on one day's notice, Fed. Rule Civ. Proc. 54(d) — strongly suggesting that "costs" were intended to refer only to those routine, readily determinable charges that could appropriately be left to a clerk, and as to which a single day's notice of settlement would be appropriate.

Third. When particular provisions of the Federal Rules are intended to encompass attorney's fees, they do so explicitly. Eleven different provisions of the Rules authorize a court to award attorney's fees as "expenses" in particular circumstances, demonstrating that the drafters knew the difference, and intended a difference, between "costs," "expenses," and "attorney's fees."

Fourth. With the exception of one recent Court of Appeals opinion and two recent District Court opinions, the Court can point to no authority suggesting that courts or attorneys have ever viewed the cost-shifting provisions of Rule 68 as including attorney's fees. Yet Rule 68 has been in effect for 47 years, and potentially could have been applied to numerous fee statutes during this time. "The fact that the defense bar did not develop a practice of seeking" to shift or reduce fees under Rule 68 "is persuasive evidence that trial lawyers have interpreted the Rule in accordance with" the definition of costs in § 1920.

Fifth. We previously have held that words and phrases in the Federal Rules must be given a consistent usage and be read in pari materia, reasoning that to do otherwise would "attribute a schizophrenic intent to the drafters." Applying the Court's "plain language" approach consistently throughout the Rules, however, would produce absurd results that would turn statutes like § 1988 on their heads and plainly violate the restraints imposed on judicial rulemaking by the Rules Enabling Act. For example, Rule 54(d) provides that "costs shall be allowed as of course to the prevailing party unless the court otherwise directs." Similarly, the plain language of Rule 68 provides that a plaintiff covered by the Rule "must pay the costs incurred after the making of the offer" language requiring the plaintiff to bear both his postoffer costs and the defendant's postoffer costs. If "costs" as used in these provisions were interpreted to include attorney's fees by virtue of the wording of § 1988, losing civil rights plaintiffs would be required by the "plain language" of Rule 54(d) to pay the defendant's attorney's fees, and prevailing plaintiffs falling within Rule 68 would be required to bear the defendant's postoffer attorney's fees.

Had it addressed this troubling consequence of its "plain language" approach, perhaps the Court would have acknowledged that such a reading would conflict directly with § 1988, which allows an award of attorney's fees to a prevailing defendant only where "the suit was vexatious, frivolous, or brought to harass or embarrass the defendant," and that the substantive standard set forth in § 1988 therefore overrides the otherwise "plain meaning" of Rules 54(d) and 68. But that is precisely the point, and the Court cannot have it both ways. Unless we are to engage in "schizophrenic" construction, the word "costs" as it is used in the Federal Rules either does or does not allow the inclusion of attorney's fees. If the word "costs" does subsume attorney's fees, this "would alter fundamentally the nature of" civil-rights attorney's fee legislation.

Although the Court's opinion fails to discuss any of the problems reviewed above, it does devote some space to arguing that its interpretation of Rule 68 "is in no sense inconsistent with the congressional policies underlying § 1983 and § 1988."

The Court is wrong. Congress has instructed that attorney's fee entitlement under § 1988 be governed by a reasonableness standard.

Rule 68, on the other hand, is not "sensitive" at all to the merits of an action and to antidiscrimination policy. It is a mechanical per se provision automatically shifting "costs" incurred after an offer is rejected, and it deprives a district court of all discretion with respect to the matter by using "the strongest verb of its type known to the English language — 'must'."

Of course, a civil rights plaintiff who unreasonably fails to accept a settlement offer, and who thereafter recovers less than the proffered amount in settlement, is barred under § 1988 itself from recovering fees for unproductive work performed in the wake of the rejection. This is because "the extent of a plaintiff's success is a crucial factor in determining the proper amount of an award of attorney's fees"; hours that are "excessive, redundant, or otherwise unnecessary" must be excluded from that calculus. To this extent, the results might sometimes be the same under either § 1988's reasonableness inquiry or the Court's wooden application of Rule 68.

But the results under § 1988 and Rule 68 will not always be congruent, because § 1988 mandates the careful consideration of a broad range of other factors and accords appropriate leeway to the district court's informed discretion. . . . It is clear, however, that under the Court's interpretation of Rule 68 a plaintiff who ultimately recovers only slightly less than the proffered amount in settlement will per se be barred from recovering trial fees even if he otherwise "has obtained excellent results" in litigation that will have far-reaching benefit to the public interest. Today's decision necessarily will require the disallowance of some fees that otherwise would have passed muster under § 1988's reasonableness standard, and there is nothing in § 1988's legislative history even vaguely suggesting that Congress intended such a result.

Rule 68 "is a 'one-way street,' available only to those defending against claims and not to claimants." Interpreting Rule 68 in its current version to include attorney's fees will lead to a number of skewed settlement incentives that squarely conflict with Congress' intent. To discuss but one example, Rule 68 allows an offer to be made any time after the complaint is filed and gives the plaintiff only 10 days to accept or reject. The Court's decision inevitably will encourage defendants who know they have violated the law to make "low-ball" offers immediately after suit is filed and before plaintiffs have been able to obtain the information they are entitled to by way of discovery to assess the strength of their claims and the reasonableness of the offers. The result will put severe pressure on plaintiffs to settle on the basis of inadequate information in order to avoid the risk of bearing all of their fees even if reasonable discovery might reveal that the defendants were subject to far greater liability. Indeed, because Rule 68 offers may be made recurrently without limitation, defendants will be well advised to make ever-slightly larger offers throughout the discovery process and before plaintiffs have conducted all reasonably necessary discovery.

Other difficulties will follow from the Court's decision. For example, if a plaintiff recovers less money than was offered before trial but obtains potentially far-reaching injunctive or declaratory relief, it is altogether unclear how the Court intends judges to go about quantifying the "value" of the plaintiff's success.[34] And the Court's decision

---

[34] [n.48] For example, a plaintiff who is unable to prove actual damages at trial and recovers only nominal damages of $1, but who nevertheless demonstrates the unconstitutionality of the challenged practice and obtains an injunction, is surely a "prevailing party" within the meaning of § 1988. If the plaintiff had earlier rejected an offer of $500 to "get rid" of the controversy, the damages portion of his suit will fall within Rule 68 as interpreted by today's decision. Yet we previously have emphasized that "a plaintiff who failed to recover damages but obtained injunctive relief, or vice versa, may recover a fee award based on all hours reasonably

raises additional problems concerning representation and conflicts of interest in the context of civil rights class actions.[35]

NOTES

1. Plaintiff's Responsibility for Defendant's Fees. In footnote 1, the Court in *Marek* states that it is not concerned with whether a prevailing § 1983 plaintiff can be forced to pay the costs and attorney's fees incurred by a losing defendant under Rule 68 following a rejected settlement offer. Rather, the Court only holds that the losing defendant need not pay the plaintiff's costs and attorney's fees incurred after the plaintiff rejects the defendant's offer. Justice Brennan in dissent insists that losing § 1983 defendants cannot recover their post-offer attorney's fees from prevailing plaintiffs under Rule 68. Is the dissent correct? *Compare Hughes v. Rowe*, 449 U.S. 5 (1980) (holding that prevailing § 1983 defendants are entitled to attorney's fees under § 1988(b) only if the plaintiff's claims were frivolous, meritless or vexatious) (discussed in Section A., *supra*). Lower courts have tended to agree with Justice Brennan. In *Crossman v. Marcoccio*, 806 F.2d 329 (1st Cir. 1986), for example, the court concluded that a § 1983 plaintiff who had refused a Rule 68 offer of judgment, and then failed to obtain a more favorable judgment at trial, was not obligated to pay the losing defendant's post-offer attorney's fees. *See also Payne v. Milwaukee County*, 288 F.3d 1021 (7th Cir. 2002) (same); *O'Brien v. City of Greers Ferry*, 873 F.2d 1115 (8th Cir. 1989) (same). Instead, for § 1983 plaintiffs, the reversible costs include only those spelled out in 28 U.S.C. § 1920: "(1) Fees of the clerk and marshal; (2) Fees of the court reporter for all or any part of the stenographic transcript necessarily obtained for use in the case; (3) Fees and disbursements for printing and witnesses; (4) Fees for exemplification and copies of papers necessarily obtained for use in the case; (5) Docket fees under § 1923 of this title; [and] (6) Compensation of court appointed experts, compensation of interpreters, and salaries, fees, expenses, and costs of special interpretation services under § 1828 of this title." *Cf. Jordan v. Time, Inc.*, 111 F.3d 102 (11th Cir. 1997) (holding under the federal Copyright Act, which has a fee-shifting provision similar to § 1988(b), that a prevailing plaintiff who rejected a Rule 68 offer of judgment, only to recover less at trial, can be required to pay a losing defendant's post-offer attorney's fees).

2. *Marek*'s Impact on the Bargaining Process. Consider the remarks of Professor Julie Davies:

> After *Marek* was decided, commentators predicted that Rule 68 would provide a strong incentive for plaintiffs to accept settlement offers in civil rights cases. The plaintiffs would be placed in the position of having to assume the cost of post-offer fees even if they prevailed, so long as the amount of the award did not exceed the Rule 68 offer. Thus, plaintiffs might potentially be deterred from prosecuting claims that had the potential to expand civil rights protection when such claims were not clearly going to prevail or to result in a predictable monetary award. In addition, Rule 68 offers might be made at such an early date

---

expended if the relief obtained justified that expenditure of attorney time." Although courts must therefore evaluate the "value" of nonpecuniary relief before deciding whether the "judgment" was "more favorable than the offer" within the meaning of Rule 68, the uncertainty in making such assessments surely will add pressures on a plaintiff to settle his suit even if by doing so he abandons an opportunity to obtain potentially far-reaching nonmonetary relief — a discouraging incentive entirely at odds with Congress' intent.

[35] [n.49] [T]these difficulties can be expected to create substantial problems in administering class actions. . . . [A]s the Advisory Committee recently has cautioned, in the class-action context "[an] offeree's rejection would burden a named representative-offeree with the risk of exposure to heavy liability [for costs and expenses] that could not be recouped from unnamed class members. . . . [This] could lead to a conflict of interest between the named representatives and other members of the class." Moreover, Rule 23(e) requires the court's approval before a class action is compromised . . . . Yet Rule 68 does not mesh with such careful supervision.

in litigation that plaintiffs might be led to make uninformed settlement decisions. Thus, the consensus was that Rule 68's primary effect would be to give defendants litigating under many civil rights statutes leverage that they would not have under other statutes.

Despite Rule 68's potential to reduce attorneys' fees and induce settlements, in reality, it does not appear to be a major factor in the practices of the civil rights lawyers I interviewed, whether they represent plaintiffs or defendants. Many plaintiffs' attorneys were surprised that they had not received more Rule 68 offers and could count the number of times they had on one hand. Defense attorneys like Rule 68 in theory, but most do not use it frequently in practice.

The attorneys offered a variety of explanations. First, it is often difficult for defense counsel to evaluate a case, including plaintiffs' attorneys' fees, to derive an offer that is serious enough to get the plaintiff's attorney's attention. One defense attorney hesitates because he believes even if plaintiffs receive an award that is less than the amount of a Rule 68 offer, their attorneys may inflate their fees so as to exceed the amount of the offer, and the court would not detect the inflation if the amount was not egregious. Both plaintiff and defense attorneys responding noted that at times it is difficult to get a defense client to give permission to make a realistic settlement offer at an early date, even if that offer carries a strategic benefit. Also, Rule 68 offers are public records, so defendants concerned about the confidentiality of offers may be reluctant to use them. In addition, some defendants, particularly public entities, may believe that they have an excellent chance of winning at trial even if the conduct of their employees was wrong.

Julie Davies, *Federal Civil Rights Practice in the 1990's: The Dichotomy Between Reality and Theory*, 48 HASTINGS L.J. 197, 222–24 (1997).[36] If Professor Davies is correct, Rule 68 changes little in the context of attorney's fees under § 1988(b). Perhaps this is the reason legislative attempts to overrule *Marek* have proved unsuccessful. *See* Edward F. Sherman, *From "Loser Pays" to Modified Offer of Judgment Rules: Reconsidering Incentives to Settle with Access to Justice*, 76 TEX. L. REV. 1863, 1896 n.94 (1998) (describing legislative efforts to overturn *Marek*). For an excellent round-table discussion on Rule 68, *see* Symposium, *Revitalizing FRCP 68: Can Offers of Judgment Provide Adequate Incentives for Fair, Early Settlement of Fee-Recovery Cases?*, 57 MERCER L. REV. 717 (2006).

EVANS v. JEFF D.
Supreme Court of the United States
475 U.S. 717 (1986)

JUSTICE STEVENS delivered the opinion of the Court.

[A group of emotionally and mentally disabled children filed a class action seeking an injunction to correct deficiencies in the educational and health care services provided to them by Idaho state officials. The District Court appointed an Idaho Legal Aid Society attorney, Charles Johnson, to represent them. Because the Idaho Legal Aid Society was prohibited from representing clients who are capable of paying their own fees, it made no agreement requiring that any of the plaintiffs pay for the costs of litigation or the legal services it provided through Johnson. One week before trial, Evans presented the group with a settlement proposal that "offered virtually all of the injunctive relief [they] had sought in their complaint." The offer, however, also provided for a waiver of any claim to attorney's fees or costs. Johnson ultimately determined that his ethical

---

[36] Copyright © 1997 by University of California, Hastings College of Law and Julie Davies. Reprinted from 48 HASTINGS L.J. 197 (1997) by permission.

obligation to his clients mandated acceptance of the proposal. Because the case was certified as a class action, the parties conditioned the waiver on approval by the District Court pursuant to Rule 23 of the Federal Rules of Civil Procedure.]

In this case, we consider the question whether attorney's fees must be assessed when the case has been settled by a consent decree granting prospective relief to the plaintiff class but providing that the defendants shall not pay any part of the prevailing party's fees or costs. We hold that the District Court has the power, in its sound discretion, to refuse to award fees.

Rule 23(e)[37] [of the Federal Rules of Civil Procedure] wisely requires court approval of the terms of any settlement of a class action, but the power to approve or reject a settlement negotiated by the parties before trial does not authorize the court to require the parties to accept a settlement to which they have not agreed. Although changed circumstances may justify a court-ordered modification of a consent decree over the objections of a party after the decree has been entered, and the District Court might have advised petitioners and respondents that it would not approve their proposal unless one or more of its provisions was deleted or modified, Rule 23(e) does not give the court the power, in advance of trial, to modify a proposed consent decree and order its acceptance over either party's objection. The options available to the District Court were essentially the same as those available to [the plaintiffs]: it could have accepted the proposed settlement; it could have rejected the proposal and postponed the trial to see if a different settlement could be achieved; or it could have decided to try the case. The District Court could not enforce the settlement on the merits and award attorney's fees anymore than it could, in a situation in which the attorney had negotiated a large fee at the expense of the plaintiff class, preserve the fee award and order greater relief on the merits. The question we must decide, therefore, is whether the District Court had a duty to reject the proposed settlement because it included a waiver of statutorily authorized attorney's fees.

That duty, whether it takes the form of a general prophylactic rule or arises out of the special circumstances of this case, derives ultimately from the Fees Act rather than from the strictures of professional ethics. Although [the plaintiffs] contend that Johnson, as counsel for the class, was faced with an "ethical dilemma" when [Evans] offered him relief greater than that which he could reasonably have expected to obtain for his clients at trial (if only he would stipulate to a waiver of the statutory fee award), and although we recognize Johnson's conflicting interests between pursuing relief for the class and a fee for the Idaho Legal Aid Society, we do not believe that the "dilemma" was an "ethical" one in the sense that Johnson had to choose between conflicting duties under the prevailing norms of professional conduct. Plainly, Johnson had no ethical obligation to seek a statutory fee award. His ethical duty was to serve his clients loyally and competently.[38] Since the proposal to settle the merits was more favorable than the probable outcome of the trial, Johnson's decision to recommend acceptance was consistent with the highest standards of our profession. The District Court, therefore, correctly concluded that approval of the settlement involved no breach of ethics in this case.

The defect, if any, in the negotiated fee waiver must be traced not to the rules of ethics but to the Fees Act.[39] Following this tack, [the plaintiffs] argue that the statute

---

[37] Rule 23(e) states: "A class action shall not be dismissed or compromised without the approval of the court, and notice of the proposed dismissal or compromise shall be given to all members of the class in such manner as the court directs."

[38] [n.14] Generally speaking, a lawyer is under an ethical obligation to exercise independent professional judgment on behalf of his client; he must not allow his own interests, financial or otherwise, to influence his professional advice.

[39] [n.15] Even state bar opinions holding it unethical for defendants to request fee waivers in exchange for relief on the merits of plaintiffs' claims are bottomed ultimately on § 1988. For the sake of completeness, it

must be construed to forbid a fee waiver that is the product of "coercion." They submit that a "coercive waiver" results when the defendant in a civil rights action (1) offers a settlement on the merits of equal or greater value than that which plaintiffs could reasonably expect to achieve at trial but (2) conditions the offer on a waiver of plaintiffs' statutory eligibility for attorney's fees. Such an offer, they claim, exploits the ethical obligation of plaintiffs' counsel to recommend settlement in order to avoid defendant's statutory liability for its opponents' fees and costs.

The question this case presents, then, is whether the Fees Act requires a district court to disapprove a stipulation seeking to settle a civil rights class action under Rule 23 when the offered relief equals or exceeds the probable outcome at trial but is expressly conditioned on waiver of statutory eligibility for attorney's fees.

The text of the Fees Act provides no support for the proposition that Congress intended to ban all fee waivers offered in connection with substantial relief on the merits. On the contrary, the language of the Act, as well as its legislative history, indicates that Congress bestowed on the "prevailing party" (generally plaintiffs) a statutory eligibility for a discretionary award of attorney's fees in specified civil rights actions. It did not prevent the party from waiving this eligibility anymore than it legislated against assignment of this right to an attorney, such as effectively occurred here. Instead, Congress enacted the fee-shifting provision as "an integral part of the remedies necessary to obtain" compliance with civil rights laws, to further the same general purpose — promotion of respect for civil rights — that led it to provide damages and injunctive relief. The statute and its legislative history nowhere suggest that Congress intended to forbid all waivers of attorney's fees — even those insisted upon by a civil rights plaintiff in exchange for some other relief to which he is indisputably not entitled — anymore than it intended to bar a concession on damages to secure broader injunctive relief. Thus, while it is undoubtedly true that Congress expected fee shifting to attract competent counsel to represent citizens deprived of their civil rights, it neither bestowed fee awards upon attorneys nor rendered them nonwaivable or nonnegotiable; instead, it added them to the arsenal of remedies available to combat violations of civil rights, a goal not invariably inconsistent with conditioning settlement on the merits on a waiver of statutory attorney's fees.[40]

In fact, we believe that a general proscription against negotiated waiver of attorney's fees in exchange for a settlement on the merits would itself impede vindication of civil rights, at least in some cases, by reducing the attractiveness of settlement. Of particular relevance in this regard is our recent decision in *Marek v. Chesny*, 473 U.S. 1 (1985). In that case, which admittedly was not a class action and therefore did not implicate the court's approval power under Rule 23(e), we specifically considered and rejected the contention that civil rights actions should be treated differently from other civil actions for purposes of settlement.

To promote both settlement and civil rights, we implicitly acknowledged in *Marek v. Chesny* the possibility of a tradeoff between merits relief and attorney's fees when we upheld the defendant's lump-sum offer to settle the entire civil rights action, including any liability for fees and costs.

---

should be mentioned that the bar is not of one mind on this ethical judgment.

[40] [n.22] Indeed, Congress specifically rejected a mandatory fee-shifting provision, a proposal which the dissent would virtually reinstate under the guise of carrying out the legislative will. Even proponents of nonwaivable fee awards under § 1988 concede that "one would have to strain principles of statutory interpretation to conclude that Congress intended to utilize fee non-negotiability to achieve the purposes of section 1988." This conclusion is buttressed by Congress' decision to emulate the "over fifty" fee-shifting provisions that had been successful in enlisting the aid of "private attorneys general" in the prosecution of other federal statutes that had been on the books for decades. No one has suggested that the purpose of any of those fee-shifting provisions has been frustrated by the absence of a prohibition against fee waivers.

In approving the package offer in *Marek v. Chesny*, we recognized that a rule prohibiting the comprehensive negotiation of all outstanding issues in a pending case might well preclude the settlement of a substantial number of cases.

Most defendants are unlikely to settle unless the cost of the predicted judgment, discounted by its probability, plus the transaction costs of further litigation, are greater than the cost of the settlement package. If fee waivers cannot be negotiated, the settlement package must either contain an attorney's fee component of potentially large and typically uncertain magnitude, or else the parties must agree to have the fee fixed by the court. Although either of these alternatives may well be acceptable in many cases, there surely is a significant number in which neither alternative will be as satisfactory as a decision to try the entire case.[41]

The adverse impact of removing attorney's fees and costs from bargaining might be tolerable if the uncertainty introduced into settlement negotiations were small. But it is not. The defendants' potential liability for fees in this kind of litigation can be as significant as, and sometimes even more significant than, their potential liability on the merits. This proposition is most dramatically illustrated by the fee awards of district courts in actions seeking only monetary relief. Although it is more difficult to compare fee awards with the cost of injunctive relief, in part because the cost of such relief is seldom reported in written opinions, here too attorney's fees awarded by district courts have "frequently outrun the economic benefits ultimately obtained by successful litigants." Indeed, in this very case "[c]ounsel for defendants view[ed] the risk of an attorney's fees award as the most significant liability in the case." Undoubtedly there are many other civil rights actions in which potential liability for attorney's fees may overshadow the potential cost of relief on the merits and darken prospects for settlement if fees cannot be negotiated.

The unpredictability of attorney's fees may be just as important as their magnitude when a defendant is striving to fix its liability. Unlike a determination of costs, which ordinarily involve smaller outlays and are more susceptible of calculation, "[t]here is no precise rule or formula" for determining attorney's fees. Among other considerations, the district court must determine what hours were reasonably expended on what claims, whether that expenditure was reasonable in light of the success obtained, and what is an appropriate hourly rate for the services rendered. Some District Courts have also considered whether a "multiplier" or other adjustment is appropriate. The consequence of this succession of necessarily judgmental decisions for the ultimate fee award is inescapable: a defendant's liability for his opponent's attorney's fees in a civil rights action cannot be fixed with a sufficient degree of confidence to make defendants indifferent to their exclusion from negotiation. It is therefore not implausible to anticipate that parties to a significant number of civil rights cases will refuse to settle if liability for attorney's fees remains open, thereby forcing more cases to trial, unnecessarily burdening the judicial system, and disserving civil rights litigants. [The plaintiffs'] own waiver of attorney's fees and costs to obtain settlement of their . . . claims is eloquent testimony to the utility of fee waivers in vindicating civil rights claims. We conclude, therefore, that it is not necessary to construe the Fees Act

---

[41] [n.23] It is unrealistic to assume that the defendant's offer on the merits would be unchanged by redaction of the provision waiving fees. If it were, the defendant's incentive to settle would be diminished because of the risk that attorney's fees, when added to the original merits offer, will exceed the discounted value of the expected judgment plus litigation costs. If, as is more likely, the defendant lowered the value of its offer on the merits to provide a cushion against the possibility of a large fee award, the defendant's offer on the merits will in many cases be less than the amount to which the plaintiff feels himself entitled, thereby inclining him to reject the settlement. Of course, to the extent that the merits offer is somewhere between these two extremes the incentive of both sides to settle is dampened, albeit to a lesser degree with respect to each party.

as embodying a general rule prohibiting settlements conditioned on the waiver of fees in order to be faithful to the purposes of that Act.[42]

The question remains whether the District Court abused its discretion in this case by approving a settlement which included a complete fee waiver. As noted earlier, Rule 23(e) wisely requires court approval of the terms of any settlement of a class action. The potential conflict among members of the class . . . fully justifies the requirement of court approval.

[The plaintiffs], and various amici supporting their position, however, suggest that the court's authority to pass on settlements, typically invoked to ensure fair treatment of class members, must be exercised in accordance with the Fees Act to promote the availability of attorneys in civil rights cases. Specifically, [they] assert that the State of Idaho could not pass a valid statute precluding the payment of attorney's fees in settlements of civil rights cases to which the Fees Act applies. From this they reason that the Fees Act must equally preclude the adoption of a uniform state-wide policy that serves the same end, and accordingly contend that a consistent practice of insisting on a fee waiver as a condition of settlement in civil rights litigation is in conflict with the federal statute authorizing fees for prevailing parties, including those who prevail by way of settlement. Remarkably, there seems little disagreement on these points. [Evans] and the amici who support [him] never suggest that the district court is obligated to place its stamp of approval on every settlement in which the plaintiffs' attorneys have agreed to a fee waiver. The Solicitor General, for example, has suggested that a fee waiver need not be approved when the defendant had "no realistic defense on the merits," or if the waiver was part of a "vindictive effort . . . to teach counsel that they had better not bring such cases."

We find it unnecessary to evaluate this argument, however, because the record in this case does not indicate that Idaho has adopted such a statute, policy, or practice. Nor does the record support the narrower proposition that [Evans'] request to waive fees was a vindictive effort to deter attorneys from representing plaintiffs in civil rights suits against Idaho. [The plaintiffs] have not offered to prove that [Evans'] tactics in this case merely implemented a routine state policy designed to frustrate the objectives of the Fees Act. Our own examination of the record reveals no such policy.

What the outcome of this settlement illustrates is that the Fees Act has given the victims of civil rights violations a powerful weapon that improves their ability to employ counsel, to obtain access to the courts, and thereafter to vindicate their rights by means of settlement or trial. For aught that appears, it was the "coercive" effect of [the plaintiffs'] statutory right to seek a fee award that motivated [Evans's] exceptionally generous offer. Whether this weapon might be even more powerful if fee waivers were prohibited in cases like this is another question,[43] but it is in any event a question that

---

[42] [n.30] The Court is unanimous in concluding that the Fees Act should not be interpreted to prohibit all simultaneous negotiations of a defendant's liability on the merits and his liability for his opponent's attorney's fees. We agree that when the parties find such negotiations conducive to settlement, the public interest, as well as that of the parties, is served by simultaneous negotiations. This reasoning applies not only to individual civil rights actions, but to civil rights class actions as well. Although the dissent would allow simultaneous negotiations, it would require that "whatever fee the parties agree to" be "found by the court to be a 'reasonable' one under the Fees Act." The dissent's proposal is imaginative, but not very practical. Of the 10,757 "other civil rights" cases filed in federal court last year — most of which were 42 U.S.C. § 1983 actions for which § 1988 authorizes an award of fees — only 111 sought class relief. Assuming that of the approximately 99% of these civil rights actions that are not class actions, a further 90% would settle rather than go to trial, the dissent's proposal would require district courts to evaluate the reasonableness of fee agreements in several thousand civil rights cases annually while they make that determination in slightly over 100 civil rights class actions now.

[43] [n.34] We are cognizant of the possibility that decisions by individual clients to bargain away fee awards may, in the aggregate and in the long run, diminish lawyers' expectations of statutory fees in civil rights cases. If this occurred, the pool of lawyers willing to represent plaintiffs in such cases might shrink, constricting the

Congress is best equipped to answer. . . . In this case, the District Court did not abuse its discretion in upholding a fee waiver which secured broad injunctive relief, relief greater than that which plaintiffs could reasonably have expected to achieve at trial.[44]

JUSTICE BRENNAN, with whom JUSTICE MARSHALL and JUSTICE BLACKMUN join, dissenting.

[T]he proper question is whether permitting negotiated fee waivers is consistent with Congress' goal of attracting competent counsel. It is therefore necessary to consider the effect on this goal of allowing individual plaintiffs to negotiate fee waivers.

Permitting plaintiffs to negotiate fee waivers in exchange for relief on the merits actually raises two related but distinct questions. First, is it permissible under the Fees Act to negotiate a settlement of attorney's fees simultaneously with the merits? Second, can the "reasonable attorney's fee" guaranteed in the Act be waived?

[S]ince simultaneous negotiation and waiver may have different effects on the congressional policy of encouraging counsel to accept civil rights cases, each practice must be analyzed independently to determine whether or not it is consistent with the Fees Act. Unfortunately, the Court overlooks the logical independence of simultaneous negotiation and waiver and assumes that there cannot be one without the other. . . . An independent examination leads me to conclude: (1) that plaintiffs should not be permitted to waive the "reasonable fee" provided by the Fees Act; but (2) that parties may undertake to negotiate their fee claims simultaneously with the merits so long as whatever fee the parties agree to is found by the court to be a "reasonable" one under the Fees Act.

[I]t does not require a sociological study to see that permitting fee waivers will make it more difficult for civil rights plaintiffs to obtain legal assistance. It requires only common sense. Assume that a civil rights defendant makes a settlement offer that includes a demand for waiver of statutory attorney's fees. The decision whether to accept or reject the offer is the plaintiff's alone, and the lawyer must abide by the plaintiff's decision. See, e.g., ABA, Model Rules of Professional Conduct 1.2(a) (1984). As a formal matter, of course, the statutory fee belongs to the plaintiff, and thus technically the decision to waive entails a sacrifice only by the plaintiff. As a practical matter, however, waiver affects only the lawyer. Because "a vast majority of the victims of civil rights violations" have no resources to pay attorney's fees, lawyers cannot hope to recover fees from the plaintiff and must depend entirely on the Fees Act for compensation.[45] The plaintiff thus has no real stake in the statutory fee and is

---

"effective access to the judicial process" for persons with civil rights grievances which the Fees Act was intended to provide. That the "tyranny of small decisions" may operate in this fashion is not to say that there is any reason or documentation to support such a concern at the present time. Comment on this issue is therefore premature at this juncture. We believe, however, that as a practical matter the likelihood of this circumstance arising is remote.

[44] [n.36] Although the record in this case does not provide us with any information concerning the amount of money that had been expended on costs, it is appropriate to note that costs other than fees may also be a significant item in class-action litigation. . . . The interest in recovering costs already expended by a class representative may justify a refusal to accept a settlement including only prospective relief and, conversely, the interest in avoiding the additional expenditures associated with continuing the litigation may also justify accepting an otherwise doubtful settlement.

[45] [n.10] Nor can attorneys protect themselves by requiring plaintiffs to sign contingency agreements or retainers at the outset of the representation. Amici legal aid societies inform us that they are prohibited by statute, court rule, or Internal Revenue Service regulation from entering into fee agreements with their clients. Moreover, even if such agreements could be negotiated, the possibility of obtaining protection through contingency fee arrangements is unavailable in the very large proportion of civil rights cases which, like this case, seek only injunctive relief.

unaffected by its waiver. Consequently, plaintiffs will readily agree to waive fees if this will help them to obtain other relief they desire.[46]

And, of course, once fee waivers are permitted, defendants will seek them as a matter of course, since this is a logical way to minimize liability. Indeed, defense counsel would be remiss not to demand that the plaintiff waive statutory attorney's fees.

The fact that fee waivers may produce some settlement offers that are beneficial to a few individual plaintiffs is hardly "consistent with the purposes of the Fees Act," if permitting fee waivers fundamentally undermines what Congress sought to achieve. Each individual plaintiff who waives his right to statutory fees in order to obtain additional relief for himself makes it that much more difficult for the next victim of a civil rights violation to find a lawyer willing or able to bring his case.

The Court's decision in no way limits the power of state and local bar associations to regulate the ethical conduct of lawyers. Indeed, several Bar Associations have already declared it unethical for defense counsel to seek fee waivers. Such efforts are to be commended and, it is to be hoped, will be followed by other state and local organizations concerned with respecting the intent of Congress and with protecting civil rights.

In addition, it may be that civil rights attorneys can obtain agreements from their clients not to waive attorney's fees.[47] Such agreements simply replicate the private market for legal services (in which attorneys are not ordinarily required to contribute to their client's recovery), and thus will enable civil rights practitioners to make it economically feasible — as Congress hoped — to expend time and effort litigating civil rights claims.

NOTES

1. Judicial Review of Bargaining. *Evans* establishes that a defendant can bargain for a plaintiff's waiver of fees under § 1988(b). During settlement negotiations, the parties can also simultaneously bargain over the amount of attorney's fees to be paid to the plaintiff in lieu of an award under § 1988(b). None of this is subject to judicial supervision or approval, *see, e.g., Smalbein ex rel. Estate of Smalbein v. City of Daytona Beach*, 353 F.3d 901 (11th Cir. 2003) (stating that a court has "no basis under § 1988(b) for ignoring the provisions that the parties bargained for in an arms-length transaction"),[48] with the result that confidentiality is not uncommon in civil rights settlements. *See* Minna J. Kotkin, *Secrecy in Context: The Shadowy Life of Civil Rights Litigation*, 81 CHI.-KENT. L. REV. 571, 586 (2006) (stating that with the advent of simultaneous negotiations and lump sum settlements "confidentiality became an easily obtained concession").

Of course, the court may subsequently be called on to determine whether a waiver occurred. In this regard, "silence in a settlement agreement does not equal a waiver of a claim for attorney's fees." *Ellis v. University of Kansas Medical Center*, 163 F.3d 1186 (10th Cir. 1998). *See also Muckleshoot Tribe v. Puget Sound Power & Light Co.*, 875 F.2d 695 (9th Cir. 1989) (same); *Jennings v. Metropolitan Government of Nashville*, 715 F.2d 1111 (6th Cir. 1983) (same). "Absent express language in the

---

[46] [n.11] This result is virtually inevitable in class actions where, even if the class representative feels sympathy for the lawyer's plight, the obligation to represent the interests of absent class members precludes altruistic sacrifice.

[47] [n.20] Since Congress has not sought to regulate ethical concerns either in the Fees Act or elsewhere, the legality of such arguments is purely a matter of local law.

[48] *Smalbein* was an "odd" case, according to the court, because it involved a settlement that fixed only damages, and required a judicial hearing on whether the plaintiff's claim had "merit" justifying an award of attorney's fees under § 1988(b). The court ruled that this settlement was enforceable, and thus the District Court would have to hold the hearing.

settlement agreement waiving the right to recover attorneys' fees, the intent of the parties governs." *Brown v. General Motors Corp.*, 722 F.2d 1009 (2d Cir. 1983).[49]

Where the parties enter into consent decrees, or otherwise agree that their settlements should be incorporated into judgments, the court will necessarily be called on to review the terms of the settlement. *Id.* Where the case has been certified as a class action, moreover, any settlement must be approved by the court under Rule 23(e) of the Federal Rules of Civil Procedure.

2. Exceptions. After *Evans*, under what circumstances can the court refuse to approve a class action settlement because it waives attorney's fees? Because it pays the lawyers representing the class too little? Compare footnote 36 to the majority opinion, which suggests that an inordinate expenditure on costs by the named representative (and its attorney) may justify the court's rejection of a settlement affording only prospective relief. What about individual actions under § 1983? Is there room to argue that waivers violate § 1988(b)? Justice Stevens in *Evans* cautioned that a state's blanket policy barring the payment of attorney's fees in settlement agreements might contradict the purpose behind § 1988(b) and be invalid. He also observed that there was no evidence that the state's settlement in *Evans* reflected "a vindictive effort to deter attorneys from representing plaintiffs in civil rights suits," nor was there proof that fee waivers have had the effect, "in the aggregate and in the long run," of shrinking "the pool of lawyers willing to represent plaintiffs in such cases." *See* footnote 34. What if the state had adopted or implemented a blanket policy requiring fee waivers, or otherwise sought to deter civil rights lawyers from taking cases? In *Bernhardt v. Los Angeles County*, 339 F.3d 920 (9th Cir. 2003), the court concluded that Los Angeles's policy barring the payment of attorney's fees in civil rights settlements violated § 1988(b): "a County policy that requires the waiver of statutory attorney's fees in all civil rights cases . . . may unduly interfere with the method — i.e., the availability of statutory attorney's fees — that Congress has chosen to encourage representation of individuals whose civil rights have been violated, and thereby violate the Supremacy Clause." "[L]ump sum settlement offer[s]," the court concluded, are "the kind of fee preclusion that — if embodied in a uniform policy or practice — might [violate] *Evans*." The court therefore issued a preliminary injunction "barring the County from offering to settle [the plaintiff's] civil rights case . . . in a way that inhibits, interferes with, or prohibits her counsel from applying for attorney's fees under 42 U.S.C. § 1988, including but not limited to 'lump sum including all attorney's fees' settlements."

3. Mitigating the Risk of Waivers. Plaintiffs' lawyers have several devices at their disposal to circumvent the risk of fee waivers under *Evans*. First, where allowed by local rules of professional responsibility, lawyers can include a provision in retainer agreements preventing clients from waiving fees. *See* Paul R. Tremblay, *Acting "A Very Moral Type of God": Triage Among Poor Clients*, 67 FORDHAM L. REV. 2475, 2532 n.195 (1999) (citing a California bar opinion endorsing this approach). Second, in actions seeking money damages, clients can be made responsible for contingency fees. *See* Minna J. Kotkin, *Invisible Settlements, Invisible Discrimination*, 84 N.C. L. REV. 927, 940–41 (2006) (observing that plaintiffs' lawyers in civil rights cases have commonly extracted contingency agreements from their clients after *Evans*). Third, where the expected monetary judgment is small, or where only prospective relief is sought, clients can be made contractually responsible for paying lodestar fees, regardless of the outcome of the case. Knowing that they will have to pay either a percentage of their

---

[49] Should a settlement be incorporated into a judgment, *see* Section C., *supra*, whether the question of silence constitutes a waiver remains an important issue. After all, consent decrees of this nature qualify the plaintiff as a prevailing party under § 1988(b) and would entitle the plaintiff to an award in the absence of a waiver. On the other hand, if the settlement is not somehow incorporated into a judgment, silence over waiver would seem immaterial after *Buckhannon* (excerpted in Section A., *supra*). After all, such a settlement would not render the plaintiff a prevailing party under § 1988(b), and there would therefore be no fee entitlement to waive.

judgment or a lodestar figure to their attorneys, clients will be less willing to waive their right to a shifted fee under § 1988(b). Fourth, lawyers can "exercis[e] caution in client selection and . . . educat[e] clients about the importance of fees in a civil rights practice to prepare clients in the event of a settlement offer contingent on a waiver." Julie Davies, *Federal Civil Rights Practice in the 1990's: The Dichotomy Between Reality and Theory*, 48 HASTINGS L.J. 197, 214 (1997). Professor Davies concludes that these tactics have proved largely successful; a majority of plaintiffs' lawyers report that "requests for fee waivers were not much of a problem in their practice." *Id. See also* Samuel R. Bagenstos, *The Perversity of Limited Civil Rights Remedies: The Case of "Abusive" ADA Litigation*, 54 UCLA L. REV. 1, 19 (2006) ("attorneys have largely avoided such coercive settlements by simply making clear at the outset of the lawyer-client relationship that their agreement to represent the plaintiff is conditioned on the plaintiff's agreement not to accept a settlement that waives the right to recover attorneys' fees"). *But see* Louis S. Rulli & Jason A. Leckerman, *Unfinished Business: The Fading Promise of ADA Enforcement in the Federal Courts Under Title I and Its Impact on the Poor*, 8 J. GENDER, RACE & JUST. 595, 637 (2005) (arguing that *Evans* "has profoundly affected settlement behavior by strengthening the leverage of defendants and converting settlement negotiations into the functional equivalent of personal injury negotiations, employing lump sum offers as the rule. This has led to the under-compensation of plaintiffs' lawyers, especially where damages are not the primary objective of the litigation or where the measure of damages is not large enough to support a reasonable attorney's fee.").

4. Public Interest Organizations. Although public interest law firms are eligible to receive fee awards under § 1988(b), *see, e.g., Blanchard v. Bergeron*, 489 U.S. 87 (1989), they are placed at a bargaining disadvantage by tax laws. In order to maintain their tax-exempt status, public interest law firms are generally prevented from directly charging fees to their clients. This "makes non-profit law firms less able to protect themselves from waivers than private attorneys." Davies, *supra*, at 214 n.94. Does the risk of fee-waiver discourage public interest organizations from taking important civil rights cases? *See, e.g., Panola Land Buying Association v. Clark*, 844 F.2d 1506 (11th Cir. 1988) ("Legal Services tells us: 'Prior to *Evans*, competent federal litigators in Alabama were refusing to accept civil rights cases because of the great professional and personal costs. Post *Evans*, the likelihood of recovering fees is further diminished; thus, black groups like plaintiff will often be unable to obtain counsel for important civil rights litigation.'"). *See also* Randal S. Jeffrey, *Facilitating Welfare Rights Class Action Litigation: Putting Damages and Attorney's Fees to Work*, 69 BROOKLYN L. REV. 281, 330 (2003) ("These decisions [*Evans* and *Buckhannon*] make it even more difficult for nonprofit attorneys to pursue welfare rights litigation.").

5. Legal Service Programs. The plaintiff's lawyer in *Evans* worked for the Idaho Legal Aid Society, an organization funded, in part, by the federal government. *See Legal Services Corp. v. Velazquez*, 531 U.S. 533 (2001) (describing the federal Legal Services Corporation program that distributes federal funds to local organizations that serve the poor). At the time *Evans* was decided, these legal service programs, though not allowed to charge clients, could recover fees under federal fee-shifting statutes, like § 1988(b). Today, legal service programs are not only prohibited from directly charging clients, but are also precluded from using federal and state fee-shifting statutes. *See* 45 C.F.R. § 1642.3 (1999); Davies, *supra*, at 214 n.94. Indeed, legal service program attorneys today experience numerous practical and legal constraints on their ability to prosecute constitutional claims. *See* Alan W. Houseman, *Civil Legal Assistance for the Twenty-First Century: Achieving Equal Justice for All*, 17 YALE L. & POL'Y REV. 369, 379–80 (1998). *But see Legal Services Corp. v. Velazquez*, 531 U.S. 533 (2001) (striking down under the First Amendment federal restrictions on legal aid lawyers' ability to challenge the constitutionality of welfare laws).

6. Ethical Obligations of Defense Lawyers. Are defense lawyers ethically prohibited from asking plaintiffs to waive fees?

At the time *Evans* was decided, a number of bar ethics opinions prohibited defense attorneys from conditioning settlement offers on plaintiff's waiver of attorneys' fees. After *Evans*, the New York City and Maine Bar Association's opinions [prohibiting the practice] were withdrawn. However, some other bar associations [most notably Los Angeles] took a contrary position to the practice approved in *Evans*. In 1989 the D.C. Bar modified its previous 1985 opinion prohibiting conditional settlement offers, stating that conditioned settlement offers are not per se unethical, but could be unethical when (1) a lump-sum settlement including attorneys' fees is achievable or (2) the defendant has no legitimate defense on the merits and is merely using the threat of further litigation to force the plaintiff to waive her statutory right to attorneys' fees.

Edward F. Sherman, *From "Loser Pays" to Modified Offer of Judgment Rules: Reconsidering Incentives to Settle with Access to Justice*, 76 TEX. L. REV. 1863, 1879 n.93 (1998).[50]

---

[50] © 1998 by Texas Law Review Association and Edward F. Sherman. All Rights Reserved.

APPENDIX

    Constitution of the United States
      Civil Rights Statutes
42 U.S.C. § 1981.   Equal rights under the law
42 U.S.C. § 1981a.   Damages in cases of intentional discrimination in employment
42 U.S.C. § 1982.   Property rights of citizens
42 U.S.C. § 1983.   Civil action for deprivation of rights
42 U.S.C. § 1985.   Conspiracy to interfere with civil rights
42 U.S.C. § 1986.   Action for neglect to prevent
42 U.S.C. § 1988.   Proceedings in vindication of civil rights
42 U.S.C. § 1997e.   Suits by prisoners
      Jurisdictional Statutes
28 U.S.C. § 1251.   Original jurisdiction
28 U.S.C. § 1254.   Courts of appeals; certiorari; certified questions
28 U.S.C. § 1257.   State courts; certiorari
28 U.S.C. § 1291.   Final decisions of district courts
28 U.S.C. § 1292.   Interlocutory decisions
28 U.S.C. § 1331.   Federal question
28 U.S.C. § 1332.   Diversity of citizenship; amount in controversy; costs
28 U.S.C. § 1341.   Taxes by States
28 U.S.C. § 1342.   Rate orders of State agencies
28 U.S.C. § 1343.   Civil rights and elective franchise
28 U.S.C. § 1344.   Election disputes
28 U.S.C. § 1367.   Supplemental jurisdiction
28 U.S.C. § 1391.   Venue generally
28 U.S.C. § 1441.   Actions removable generally
28 U.S.C. § 1443.   Civil rights cases
28 U.S.C. § 1446.   Procedure for removal
28 U.S.C. § 1447.   Procedural after removal generally
28 U.S.C. § 1658.   Time limitations on the commencement of civil actions arising under Acts of Congress
28 U.S.C. § 1738.   State and Territorial statutes and judicial proceedings; full faith and credit
28 U.S.C. § 1821.   Per diem and mileage generally; subsistence
28 U.S.C. § 2201.   Declaratory Judgments
28 U.S.C. § 2202.   Further Relief
28 U.S.C. § 2283.   Stay of State court proceedings
28 U.S.C. § 2403.   Intervention by United States or a State; constitutional question
      Criminal Statutes
18 U.S.C. § 241.   Conspiracy against rights
18 U.S.C. § 242.   Deprivation of rights under color of law
      Miscellaneous Statutes
47 U.S.C. § 555a.   Limitation of franchising authority liability

Federal Rules of Civil Procedure

Rule 4.	Summons
Rule 8.	General Rules of Pleading
Rule 9.	Pleading Special Matters
Rule 12.	Defenses and Objections — When and How Presented — By Pleading or Motion — Motion for Judgment on Pleadings
Rule 14.	Third-Party Practice
Rule 18.	Joinder of Claims and Remedies
Rule 20.	Permissive Joinder of Parties
Rule 21.	Misjoinder and Non-Joinder of Parties
Rule 23.	Class Actions
Rule 24.	Intervention
Rule 25.	Substitution of Parties
Rule 49.	Special Verdicts and Interrogatories
Rule 56.	Summary Judgment
Rule 60.	Relief from a Judgment or Order
Rule 65.	Injunctions
Rule 68.	Offer of Judgment
Rule 69.	Execution

CONSTITUTION OF THE UNITED STATES

PREAMBLE

WE THE PEOPLE of the United States, in Order to form a more perfect Union, establish Justice, insure domestic Tranquility, provide for the common defence, promote the general Welfare, and secure the Blessings of Liberty to ourselves and our Posterity, do ordain and establish this CONSTITUTION for the United States of America.

Article I.

Section 1. All legislative Powers herein granted shall be vested in a Congress of the United States . . . .

Section 8. The Congress shall have Power To lay and collect Taxes, Duties, Imposts and Excises, to pay the Debts and provide for the common Defence and general Welfare of the United States; . . .

To regulate Commerce with foreign Nations, and among the several States, and with the Indian Tribes; . . .

To make all Laws which shall be necessary and proper for carrying into Execution the foregoing Powers, and all other Powers vested by this Constitution in the Government of the United States, or in any Department or Officer thereof.

Section 9. . . . The Privilege of the Writ of Habeas Corpus shall not be suspended, unless when in Cases of Rebellion or Invasion the public Safety may require it. . . .

Section 10. No State shall . . . pass any Bill of Attainder, ex post facto Law, or Law impairing the Obligation of Contracts, or grant any Title of Nobility. . . .

Article II.

Section 1. The executive Power shall be vested in a President of the United States of America. . . .

Article III.

Section 1. The judicial Power of the United States shall be vested in one supreme Court, and in such inferior Courts as the Congress may from time to time ordain and establish. The Judges, both of the supreme and inferior Courts, shall hold their Offices during good Behaviour, and shall, at stated Times, receive for their Services a Compensation, which shall not be diminished during their Continuance in Office.

Section 2. The judicial Power shall extend to all Cases, in Law and Equity, arising under this Constitution, the Laws of the United States, and Treaties made, or which shall be made, under their Authority; — to all Cases affecting Ambassadors, other public Ministers and Consuls; — to all Cases of admiralty and maritime Jurisdiction; — to Controversies to which the United States shall be a Party; — to Controversies between two or more States; — between a State and Citizens of another State; — between Citizens of different States; — between Citizens of the same State claiming Lands under Grants of different States, and between a State, or the Citizens thereof, and foreign States, Citizens or Subjects.

In all Cases affecting Ambassadors, other public Ministers and Consuls, and those in which a State shall be Party, the supreme Court shall have original Jurisdiction. In all the other Cases before mentioned, the supreme Court shall have appellate Jurisdiction, both as to Law and Fact, with such Exceptions, and under such Regulations as the Congress shall make.

The Trial of all Crimes, except in Cases of Impeachment, shall be by Jury; and such Trial shall be held in the State where the said Crimes shall have been committed; but when not committed within any State, the Trial shall be at such Place or Places as the Congress may by Law have directed. . . .

Article IV.

Section 1. Full Faith and Credit shall be given in each State to the public Acts, Records, and judicial Proceedings of every other State. And the Congress may by general Laws prescribe the Manner in which such Acts, Records and Proceedings shall be proved, and the Effect thereof.

Section 2. The Citizens of each State shall be entitled to all Privileges and Immunities of Citizens in the several States.

A Person charged in any State with Treason, Felony, or other Crime, who shall flee from Justice, and be found in another State, shall on Demand of the executive Authority of the State from which he fled, be delivered up, to be removed to the State having Jurisdiction of the Crime.

No Person held to Service or Labour in one State, under the Laws thereof, escaping into another, shall, in Consequence of any Law or Regulation therein, be discharged from such Service or Labour, but shall be delivered up on Claim of the Party to whom such Service or Labour may be due. . . .

Article VI.

All Debts contracted and Engagements entered into, before the Adoption of this Constitution, shall be as valid against the United States under this Constitution, as under the Confederation.

This Constitution, and the Laws of the United States which shall be made in Pursuance thereof; and all Treaties made, or which shall be made, under the Authority of the United States, shall be the supreme Law of the Land; and the Judges in every State shall be bound thereby, any Thing in the Constitution or Laws of any State to the Contrary notwithstanding.

The Senators and Representatives before mentioned, and the Members of the several State Legislatures, and all executive and judicial Officers, both of the United States and of the several States, shall be bound by Oath or Affirmation, to support this Constitution; but no religious Test shall ever be required as a Qualification to any Office or public Trust under the United States. . . .

Amendment I [1791]

Congress shall make no law respecting an establishment of religion, or prohibiting the free exercise thereof; or abridging the freedom of speech, or of the press; or the right of the people peaceably to assemble, and to petition the government for a redress of grievances.

Amendment II [1791]

A well regulated militia, being necessary to the security of a free state, the right of the people to keep and bear arms, shall not be infringed.

Amendment III [1791]

No soldier shall, in time of peace be quartered in any house, without the consent of the owner, nor in time of war, but in a manner to be prescribed by law.

Amendment IV [1791]

The right of the people to be secure in their persons, houses, papers, and effects, against unreasonable searches and seizures, shall not be violated, and no warrants shall issue, but upon probable cause, supported by oath or affirmation, and particularly describing the place to be searched, and the persons or things to be seized.

Amendment V [1791]

No person shall be held to answer for a capital, or otherwise infamous crime, unless on a presentment or indictment of a grand jury, except in cases arising in the land or naval forces, or in the militia, when in actual service in time of war or public danger; nor shall any person be subject for the same offense to be twice put in jeopardy of life or limb; nor shall be compelled in any criminal case to be a witness against himself, nor be deprived of life, liberty, or property, without due process of law; nor shall private property be taken for public use, without just compensation.

Amendment VI [1791]

In all criminal prosecutions, the accused shall enjoy the right to a speedy and public trial, by an impartial jury of the state and district wherein the crime shall have been committed, which district shall have been previously ascertained by law, and to be informed of the nature and cause of the accusation; to be confronted with the witnesses against him; to have compulsory process for obtaining witnesses in his favor, and to have the assistance of counsel for his defense.

Amendment VII [1791]

In suits at common law, where the value in controversy shall exceed twenty dollars, the right of trial by jury shall be preserved, and no fact tried by a jury, shall be otherwise reexamined in any court of the United States, than according to the rules of the common law.

Amendment VIII [1791]

Excessive bail shall not be required, nor excessive fines imposed, nor cruel and unusual punishments inflicted.

Amendment IX [1791]

The enumeration in the Constitution, of certain rights, shall not be construed to deny or disparage others retained by the people.

Amendment X [1791]

The powers not delegated to the United States by the Constitution, nor prohibited by it to the states, are reserved to the states respectively, or to the people.

Amendment XI [1798]

The Judicial power of the United States shall not be construed to extend to any suit in law or equity, commenced or prosecuted against one of the United States by citizens of another state, or by citizens or subjects of any foreign state.

Amendment XIII [1865]

Section 1. Neither slavery nor involuntary servitude, except as a punishment for crime whereof the party shall have been duly convicted, shall exist within the United States, or any place subject to their jurisdiction.

Section 2. Congress shall have power to enforce this article by appropriate legislation.

Amendment XIV [1868]

Section 1. All persons born or naturalized in the United States, and subject to the jurisdiction thereof, are citizens of the United States and of the state wherein they reside. No state shall make or enforce any law which shall abridge the privileges or immunities of citizens of the United States; nor shall any state deprive any person of life, liberty, or property, without due process of law; nor deny to any person within its jurisdiction the equal protection of the laws.

Section 2. Representatives shall be apportioned among the several states according to their respective numbers, counting the whole number of persons in each state, excluding Indians not taxed. But when the right to vote at any election for the choice of electors for President and Vice President of the United States, Representatives in Congress, the executive and judicial officers of a state, or the members of the legislature thereof, is denied to any of the male inhabitants of such state, being twenty-one years of age, and citizens of the United States, or in any way abridged, except for participation in rebellion, or other crime, the basis of representation therein shall be reduced in the proportion which the number of such male citizens shall bear to the whole number of male citizens twenty-one years of age in such state.

Section 3. No person shall be a Senator or Representative in Congress, or elector of President and Vice President, or hold any office, civil or military, under the United States, or under any state, who, having previously taken an oath, as a member of Congress, or as an officer of the United States, or as a member of any state legislature, or as an executive or judicial officer of any state, to support the Constitution of the United States, shall have engaged in insurrection or rebellion against the same, or given aid or comfort to the enemies thereof. But Congress may by a vote of two-thirds of each House, remove such disability.

Section 4. The validity of the public debt of the United States, authorized by law, including debts incurred for payment of pensions and bounties for services in suppressing insurrection or rebellion, shall not be questioned. But neither the United States nor any state shall assume or pay any debt or obligation incurred in aid of insurrection or rebellion against the United States, or any claim for the loss or emancipation of any slave; but all such debts, obligations and claims shall be held illegal and void.

Section 5. The Congress shall have power to enforce, by appropriate legislation, the provisions of this article.

Amendment XV [1870]

Section 1. The right of citizens of the United States to vote shall not be denied or abridged by the United States or by any state on account of race, color, or previous condition of servitude.

Section 2. The Congress shall have power to enforce this article by appropriate legislation.

Amendment XIX [1920]

The right of citizens of the United States to vote shall not be denied or abridged by the United States or by any state on account of sex.

Congress shall have power to enforce this article by appropriate legislation.

Amendment XXIV [1964]

Section 1. The right of citizens of the United States to vote in any primary or other election for President or Vice President, for electors for President or Vice President, or for Senator or Representative in Congress, shall not be denied or abridged by the United States or any state by reason of failure to pay any poll tax or other tax.

Section 2. The Congress shall have power to enforce this article by appropriate legislation.

Amendment XXVI [1971]

Section 1. The right of citizens of the United States, who are 18 years of age or older, to vote, shall not be denied or abridged by the United States or any state on account of age.

Section 2. The Congress shall have the power to enforce this article by appropriate legislation.

CIVIL RIGHTS STATUTES

42 U.S.C. § 1981. Equal rights under the law

(a) Statement of equal rights

All persons within the jurisdiction of the United States shall have the same right in every State and Territory to make and enforce contracts, to sue, be parties, give evidence, and to the full and equal benefit of all laws and proceedings for the security of persons and property as is enjoyed by white citizens, and shall be subject to like punishment, pains, penalties, taxes, licenses, and exactions of every kind, and to no other.

(b) "Make and enforce contracts" defined

For purposes of this section, the term "make and enforce contracts" includes the making, performance, modification, and termination of contracts, and the enjoyment of all benefits, privileges, terms, and conditions of the contractual relationship.

(c) Protection against impairment

The rights protected by this section are protected against impairment by nongovernmental discrimination and impairment under color of State law.

42 U.S.C. § 1981a. Damages in cases of intentional discrimination in employment

(a) Right of recovery

(1) Civil rights

In an action brought by a complaining party under section 706 or 717 of the Civil Rights Act of 1964 (42 U.S.C. § 2000e-5) against a respondent who engaged in unlawful intentional discrimination (not an employment practice that is unlawful because of its disparate impact) prohibited under section 703, 704, or 717 of the Act (42 U.S.C. §§ 2000e-2 or 2000e-3) and provided that the complaining party cannot recover under section 1981 of this title, the complaining party may recover compensatory and punitive damages as allowed in subsection (b) of this section, in addition to any relief authorized by section 706(g) of the Civil Rights Act of 1964 from the respondent.

(2) Disability

In an action brought by a complaining party under the powers, remedies, and procedures set forth in section 706 or 717 of the Civil Rights Act of 1964 (as provided in section 107(a) of the Americans with Disabilities Act of 1990 (42 U.S.C. § 12117(a)), and section 794a(a)(1) of Title 29, respectively) against a respondent who engaged in unlawful intentional discrimination (not an employment practice that is unlawful because of its disparate impact) under section 791 of Title 29 and the regulations implementing section 791 of Title 29, or who violated the requirements of section 791 of Title 29 or the regulations implementing section 791 of Title 29 concerning the provision of a reasonable accommodation, or section 102 of the Americans with Disabilities Act of 1990 (42 U.S.C. § 12112), or committed a violation of section 102(b)(5) of the Act against an individual, the complaining party may recover compensatory and punitive damages as allowed in subsection (b) of this section, in addition to any relief authorized by section 706(g) of the Civil Rights Act of 1964 from the respondent.

(3) Reasonable accommodation and good faith effort

In cases where a discriminatory practice involves the provision of a reasonable accommodation pursuant to section 102(b)(5) of the Americans with Disabilities Act of 1990 or regulations implementing section 791 of Title 29, damages may not be awarded under this section where the covered entity demonstrates good faith efforts, in consultation with the person with the disability who has informed the covered entity that accommodation is needed, to identify and make a reasonable accommodation that would provide such individual with an equally effective opportunity and would not cause an undue hardship on the operation of the business.

(b) Compensatory and punitive damages

(1) Determination of punitive damages

A complaining party may recover punitive damages under this section against a respondent (other than a government, government agency or political subdivision) if the complaining party demonstrates that the respondent engaged in a discriminatory practice or discriminatory practices with malice or with reckless indifference to the federally protected rights of an aggrieved individual.

(2) Exclusions from compensatory damages

Compensatory damages awarded under this section shall not include backpay, interest on backpay, or any other type of relief authorized under section 706(g) of the Civil Rights Act of 1964.

(3) Limitations

The sum of the amount of compensatory damages awarded under this section for future pecuniary losses, emotional pain, suffering, inconvenience, mental anguish, loss of enjoyment of life, and other nonpecuniary losses, and the amount of punitive damages awarded under this section, shall not exceed, for each complaining party—

(A) in the case of a respondent who has more than 14 and fewer than 101 employees in each of 20 or more calendar weeks in the current or preceding calendar year, $50,000;

(B) in the case of a respondent who has more than 100 and fewer than 201 employees in each of 20 or more calendar weeks in the current or preceding calendar year, $100,000; and

(C) in the case of a respondent who has more than 200 and fewer than 501 employees in each of 20 or more calendar weeks in the current or preceding calendar year, $200,000; and

(D) in the case of a respondent who has more than 500 employees in each of 20 or more calendar weeks in the current or preceding calendar year, $300,000.

(4) Construction

Nothing in this section shall be construed to limit the scope of, or the relief available under, section 1981 of this title.

(c) Jury trial

If a complaining party seeks compensatory or punitive damages under this section—

(1) any party may demand a trial by jury; and

(2) the court shall not inform the jury of the limitations described in subsection (b)(3) of this section.

(d) Definitions

As used in this section:

(1) Complaining party

The term "complaining party" means—

(A) in the case of a person seeking to bring an action under subsection (a)(1) of this section, the Equal Employment Opportunity Commission, the Attorney General, or a person who may bring an action or proceeding under title VII of the Civil Rights Act of 1964 (42 U.S.C. § 2000e et seq.); or

(B) in the case of a person seeking to bring an action under subsection (a)(2) of this section, the Equal Employment Opportunity Commission, the Attorney General, a person who may bring an action or proceeding under section 794a(a)(1) of Title 29, or a person who may bring an action or proceeding under title I of the Americans with Disabilities Act of 1990 (42 U.S.C. § 12101 et seq.).

(2) Discriminatory practice

The term "discriminatory practice" means the discrimination described in paragraph (1), or the discrimination or the violation described in paragraph (2), of subsection (a) of this section.

42 U.S.C. § 1982. Property rights of citizens

All citizens of the United States shall have the same right, in every State and Territory, as is enjoyed by white citizens thereof to inherit, purchase, lease, sell, hold, and convey real and personal property.

42 U.S.C. § 1983. Civil action for deprivation of rights

Every person who, under color of any statute, ordinance, regulation, custom, or usage, of any State or Territory or the District of Columbia, subjects, or causes to be subjected, any citizen of the United States or other person within the jurisdiction thereof to the deprivation of any rights, privileges, or immunities secured by the Constitution and laws, shall be liable to the party injured in an action at law, suit in equity, or other proper proceeding for redress, except that in any action brought against a judicial officer for an act or omission taken in such officer's judicial capacity, injunctive relief shall not be granted unless a declaratory decree was violated or declaratory relief was unavailable. For the purposes of this section, any Act of Congress applicable exclusively to the District of Columbia shall be considered to be a statute of the District of Columbia.

42 U.S.C. § 1985. Conspiracy to interfere with civil rights

(1) Preventing officer from performing duties

If two or more persons in any State or Territory conspire to prevent, by force, intimidation, or threat, any person from accepting or holding any office, trust, or place of confidence under the United States, or from discharging any duties thereof; or to induce by like means any officer of the United States to leave any State, district, or place, where his duties as an officer are required to be performed, or to injure him in his person or property on account of his lawful discharge of the duties of his office, or while engaged in the lawful discharge thereof, or to injure his property so as to molest, interrupt, hinder, or impede him in the discharge of his official duties;

(2) Obstructing justice; intimidating party, witness, or juror

If two or more persons in any State or Territory conspire to deter, by force, intimidation, or threat, any party or witness in any court of the United States from attending such court, or from testifying to any matter pending therein, freely, fully, and truthfully, or to injure such party or witness in his person or property on account of his having so attended or testified, or to influence the verdict, presentment, or indictment of any grand or petit juror in any such court, or to injure such juror in his person or property on account of any verdict, presentment, or indictment lawfully assented to by him, or of his being or having been such juror; or if two or more persons conspire for the purpose of impeding, hindering, obstructing, or defeating, in any manner, the due course of justice in any State or Territory, with intent to deny to any citizen the equal protection of the laws, or to injure him or his property for lawfully enforcing, or attempting to enforce, the right of any person, or class of persons, to the equal protection of the laws;

(3) Depriving persons of rights or privileges

If two or more persons in any State or Territory conspire or go in disguise on the highway or on the premises of another, for the purpose of depriving, either directly or indirectly, any person or class of persons of the equal protection of the laws, or of equal privileges and immunities under the laws; or for the purpose of preventing or hindering the constituted authorities of any State or Territory from giving or securing to all persons within such State or Territory the equal protection of the laws; or if two or more persons conspire to prevent by force, intimidation, or threat, any citizen who is lawfully entitled to vote, from giving his support or advocacy in a legal manner, toward or in favor of the election of any lawfully qualified person as an elector for President or Vice President, or as a Member of Congress of the United States; or to injure any citizen in person or property on account of such support or advocacy; in any case of conspiracy set forth in this section, if one or more persons engaged therein do, or cause to be done, any act in furtherance of the object of such conspiracy, whereby another is injured in his person or property, or deprived of having and exercising any right or privilege of a citizen of the United States, the party so injured or deprived may have an action for the recovery of damages occasioned by such injury or deprivation, against any one or more of the conspirators.

42 U.S.C. § 1986. Action for neglect to prevent

Every person who, having knowledge that any of the wrongs conspired to be done, and mentioned in section 1985 of this title, are about to be committed, and having power to prevent or aid in preventing the commission of the same, neglects or refuses so to do, if such wrongful act be committed, shall be liable to the party injured, or his legal representatives, for all damages caused by such wrongful act, which such person by reasonable diligence could have prevented; and such damages may be recovered in an action on the case; and any number of persons guilty of such wrongful neglect or refusal may be joined as defendants in the action; and if the death of any party be caused by any such wrongful act and neglect, the legal representatives of the deceased shall have such action therefor, and may recover not exceeding five thousand dollars damages therein, for the benefit of the widow of the deceased, if there be one, and if there be no widow, then for the benefit of the next of kin of the deceased. But no action under the provisions of this section shall be sustained which is not commenced within one year after the cause of action has accrued.

42 U.S.C. § 1988. Proceedings in vindication of civil rights

(a) Applicability of statutory and common law

The jurisdiction in civil and criminal matters conferred on the district courts by the provisions of titles 13, 24, and 70 of the Revised Statutes for the protection of all persons in the United States in their civil rights, and for their vindication, shall be exercised and enforced in conformity with the laws of the United States, so far as such laws are suitable to carry the same into effect; but in all cases where they are not adapted to the object, or are deficient in the provisions necessary to furnish suitable remedies and punish offenses against law, the common law, as modified and changed by the constitution and statutes of the State wherein the court having jurisdiction of such civil or criminal cause is held, so far as the same is not inconsistent with the Constitution and laws of the United States, shall be extended to and govern the said courts in the trial and disposition of the cause, and, if it is of a criminal nature, in the infliction of punishment on the party found guilty.

(b) Attorney's fees

In any action or proceeding to enforce a provision of sections 1981, 1981a, 1982, 1983, 1985, and 1986 of this title, title IX of Public Law 92-318, the Religious Freedom Restoration Act of 1993, the Religious Land Use and Institutionalized Persons Act of 2000, title VI of the Civil Rights Act of 1964, or section 13981 of this title, the court, in its discretion, may allow the prevailing party, other than the United States, a reasonable attorney's fee as part of the costs, except that in any action brought against a judicial officer for an act or omission taken in such officer's judicial capacity such officer shall not be held liable for any costs, including attorney's fees, unless such action was clearly in excess of such officer's jurisdiction.

(c) Expert fees

In awarding an attorney's fee under subsection (b) of this section in any action or proceeding to enforce a provision of section 1981 or 1981a of this title, the court, in its discretion, may include expert fees as part of the attorney's fee.

42 U.S.C. § 1997e. Suits by prisoners

(a) Applicability of administrative remedies

No action shall be brought with respect to prison conditions under section 1983 of this title, or any other Federal law, by a prisoner confined in any jail, prison, or other correctional facility until such administrative remedies as are available are exhausted.

(b) Failure of State to adopt or adhere to administrative grievance procedure

The failure of a State to adopt or adhere to an administrative grievance procedure shall not constitute the basis for an action under section 1997a or 1997c of this title.

(c) Dismissal

(1) The court shall on its own motion or on the motion of a party dismiss any action brought with respect to prison conditions under section 1983 of this title, or any other Federal law, by a prisoner confined in any jail, prison, or other correctional facility if the court is satisfied that the action is frivolous, malicious, fails to state a claim upon which relief can be granted, or seeks monetary relief from a defendant who is immune from such relief.

(2) In the event that a claim is, on its face, frivolous, malicious, fails to state a claim upon which relief can be granted, or seeks monetary relief from a defendant who is immune from such relief, the court may dismiss the underlying claim without first requiring the exhaustion of administrative remedies.

(d) Attorney's fees

(1) In any action brought by a prisoner who is confined to any jail, prison, or other correctional facility, in which attorney's fees are authorized under section 1988 of this title, such fees shall not be awarded, except to the extent that—

(A) the fee was directly and reasonably incurred in proving an actual violation of the plaintiff's rights protected by a statute pursuant to which a fee may be awarded under section 1988 of this title; and

(B) (i) the amount of the fee is proportionately related to the court ordered relief for the violation; or

(ii) the fee was directly and reasonably incurred in enforcing the relief ordered for the violation.

(2) Whenever a monetary judgment is awarded in an action described in paragraph (1), a portion of the judgment (not to exceed 25 percent) shall be applied to satisfy the amount of attorney's fees awarded against the defendant. If the award of attorney's fees is not greater than 150 percent of the judgment, the excess shall be paid by the defendant.

(3) No award of attorney's fees in an action described in paragraph (1) shall be based on an hourly rate greater than 150 percent of the hourly rate established under section 3006A of Title 18, for payment of court-appointed counsel.

(4) Nothing in this subsection shall prohibit a prisoner from entering into an agreement to pay an attorney's fee in an amount greater than the amount authorized under this subsection, if the fee is paid by the individual rather than by the defendant pursuant to section 1988 of this title.

(e) Limitation on recovery

No Federal civil action may be brought by a prisoner confined in a jail, prison, or other correctional facility, for mental or emotional injury suffered while in custody without a prior showing of physical injury.

(f) Hearings

(1) To the extent practicable, in any action brought with respect to prison conditions in Federal court pursuant to section 1983 of this title, or any other Federal law, by a prisoner confined in any jail, prison, or other correctional facility, pretrial proceedings in which the prisoner's participation is required or permitted shall be conducted by telephone, video conference, or other telecommunications technology without removing the prisoner from the facility in which the prisoner is confined.

(2) Subject to the agreement of the official of the Federal, State, or local unit of government with custody over the prisoner, hearings may be conducted at the facility in which the prisoner is confined. To the extent practicable, the court shall allow counsel to participate by telephone, video conference, or other communications technology in any hearing held at the facility.

(g) Waiver of reply

(1) Any defendant may waive the right to reply to any action brought by a prisoner confined in any jail, prison, or other correctional facility under section 1983 of this title or any other Federal law. Notwithstanding any other law or rule of procedure, such waiver shall not constitute an admission of the allegations contained in the complaint. No relief shall be granted to the plaintiff unless a reply has been filed.

(2) The court may require any defendant to reply to a complaint brought under this section if it finds that the plaintiff has a reasonable opportunity to prevail on the merits.

(h) Definition

As used in this section, the term "prisoner" means any person incarcerated or detained in any facility who is accused of, convicted of, sentenced for, or adjudicated delinquent for, violations of criminal law or the terms and conditions of parole, probation, pretrial release, or diversionary program.

JURISDICTIONAL STATUTES

28 U.S.C. § 1251. Original jurisdiction

(a) The Supreme Court shall have original and exclusive jurisdiction of all controversies between two or more States.

(b) The Supreme Court shall have original but not exclusive jurisdiction of:

(1) All actions or proceedings to which ambassadors, other public ministers, consuls, or vice consuls of foreign states are parties;

(2) All controversies between the United States and a State;

(3) All actions or proceedings by a State against the citizens of another State or against aliens.

28 U.S.C. § 1254. Courts of appeals; certiorari; certified questions

Cases in the courts of appeals may be reviewed by the Supreme Court by the following methods:

(1) By writ of certiorari granted upon the petition of any party to any civil or criminal case, before or after rendition of judgment or decree;

(2) By certification at any time by a court of appeals of any question of law in any civil or criminal case as to which instructions are desired, and upon such certification the Supreme Court may give binding instructions or require the entire record to be sent up for decision of the entire matter in controversy.

28 U.S.C. § 1257. State courts; certiorari

(a) Final judgments or decrees rendered by the highest court of a State in which a decision could be had, may be reviewed by the Supreme Court by writ of certiorari where the validity of a treaty or statute of the United States is drawn in question or where the validity of a statute of any State is drawn in question on the ground of its being repugnant to the Constitution, treaties, or laws of the United States, or where any title, right, privilege, or immunity is specially set up or claimed under the Constitution or the treaties or statutes of, or any commission held or authority exercised under, the United States.

(b) For the purposes of this section, the term "highest court of a State" includes the District of Columbia Court of Appeals.

28 U.S.C. § 1291. Final decisions of district courts

The courts of appeals (other than the United States Court of Appeals for the Federal Circuit) shall have jurisdiction of appeals from all final decisions of the district courts of the United States, the United States District Court for the District of the Canal Zone, the District Court of Guam, and the District Court of the Virgin Islands, except where a direct review may be had in the Supreme Court. The jurisdiction of the United States Court of Appeals for the Federal Circuit shall be limited to the jurisdiction described in sections 1292(c) and (d) and 1295 of this title.

28 U.S.C. § 1292. Interlocutory decisions

(a) Except as provided in subsections (c) and (d) of this section, the courts of appeals shall have jurisdiction of appeals from:

(1) Interlocutory orders of the district courts of the United States, the United States District Court for the District of the Canal Zone, the District Court of Guam, and the District Court of the Virgin Islands, or of the judges thereof, granting, continuing, modifying, refusing or dissolving injunctions, or refusing to dissolve or modify injunctions, except where a direct review may be had in the Supreme Court;

(2) Interlocutory orders appointing receivers, or refusing orders to wind up receiverships or to take steps to accomplish the purposes thereof, such as directing sales or other disposals of property;

(3) Interlocutory decrees of such district courts or the judges thereof determining the rights and liabilities of the parties to admiralty cases in which appeals from final decrees are allowed.

(b) When a district judge, in making in a civil action an order not otherwise appealable under this section, shall be of the opinion that such order involves a controlling question of law as to which there is substantial ground for difference of opinion and that an immediate appeal from the order may materially advance the ultimate termination of the litigation, he shall so state in writing in such order. The Court of Appeals which would have jurisdiction of an appeal of such action may thereupon, in its discretion, permit an appeal to be taken from such order, if application is made to it within ten days after the entry of the order: *Provided, however*, That application for an appeal hereunder shall not stay proceedings in the district court unless the district judge or the Court of Appeals or a judge thereof shall so order. . . .

(e) The Supreme Court may prescribe rules, in accordance with section 2072 of this title, to provide for an appeal of an interlocutory decision to the courts of appeals that is not otherwise provided for under subsection (a), (b), (c), or (d).

28 U.S.C. § 1331. Federal question

The district courts shall have original jurisdiction of all civil actions arising under the Constitution, laws, or treaties of the United States.

28 U.S.C. § 1332. Diversity of citizenship; amount in controversy; costs

(a) The district courts shall have original jurisdiction of all civil actions where the matter in controversy exceeds the sum or value of $75,000, exclusive of interest and costs, and is between—

(1) citizens of different States;

(2) citizens of a State and citizens or subjects of a foreign state;

(3) citizens of different States and in which citizens or subjects of a foreign state are additional parties; and

(4) a foreign state, defined in section 1603(a) of this title, as plaintiff and citizens of a State or of different States.

For the purposes of this section, section 1335, and section 1441, an alien admitted to the United States for permanent residence shall be deemed a citizen of the State in which such alien is domiciled.

(b) Except when express provision therefor is otherwise made in a statute of the United States, where the plaintiff who files the case originally in the Federal courts is finally adjudged to be entitled to recover less than the sum or value of $75,000, computed without regard to any setoff or counterclaim to which the defendant may be adjudged to be entitled, and exclusive of interest and costs, the district court may deny costs to the plaintiff and, in addition, may impose costs on the plaintiff.

(c) For the purposes of this section and section 1441 of this title—

(1) a corporation shall be deemed to be a citizen of any State by which it has been incorporated and of the State where it has its principal place of business, except that in any direct action against the insurer of a policy or contract of liability insurance, whether incorporated or unincorporated, to which action the insured is not joined as a party-defendant, such insurer shall be deemed a citizen of the State of which the insured is a citizen, as well as of any State by which the insurer has been incorporated and of the State where it has its principal place of business; and

(2) the legal representative of the estate of a decedent shall be deemed to be a citizen only of the same State as the decedent, and the legal representative of an infant or incompetent shall be deemed to be a citizen only of the same State as the infant or incompetent.

(d) The word "States", as used in this section, includes the Territories, the District of Columbia, and the Commonwealth of Puerto Rico.

28 U.S.C. § 1341. Taxes by States

The district courts shall not enjoin, suspend or restrain the assessment, levy or collection of any tax under State law where a plain, speedy and efficient remedy may be had in the courts of such State.

28 U.S.C. § 1342. Rate orders of State agencies

The district courts shall not enjoin, suspend or restrain the operation of, or compliance with, any order affecting rates chargeable by a public utility and made by a State administrative agency or a rate-making body of a State political subdivision, where:

(1) Jurisdiction is based solely on diversity of citizenship or repugnance of the order to the Federal Constitution; and,

(2) The order does not interfere with interstate commerce; and,

(3) The order has been made after reasonable notice and hearing; and,

(4) A plain, speedy and efficient remedy may be had in the courts of such State.

28 U.S.C. § 1343. Civil rights and elective franchise

(a) The district courts shall have original jurisdiction of any civil action authorized by law to be commenced by any person:

(1) To recover damages for injury to his person or property, or because of the deprivation of any right or privilege of a citizen of the United States, by any act done in furtherance of any conspiracy mentioned in section 1985 of Title 42;

(2) To recover damages from any person who fails to prevent or to aid in preventing any wrongs mentioned in section 1985 of Title 42 which he had knowledge were about to occur and power to prevent;

(3) To redress the deprivation, under color of any State law, statute, ordinance, regulation, custom or usage, of any right, privilege or immunity secured by the Constitution of the United States or by any Act of Congress providing for equal rights of citizens or of all persons within the jurisdiction of the United States;

(4) To recover damages or to secure equitable or other relief under any Act of Congress providing for the protection of civil rights, including the right to vote.

(b) For purposes of this section—

(1) the District of Columbia shall be considered to be a State; and

(2) any Act of Congress applicable exclusively to the District of Columbia shall be considered to be a statute of the District of Columbia.

28 U.S.C. § 1344. Election disputes

The district courts shall have original jurisdiction of any civil action to recover possession of any office, except that of elector of President or Vice President, United States Senator, Representative in or delegate to Congress, or member of a state legislature, authorized by law to be commenced, wherein it appears that the sole question touching the title to office arises out of denial of the right to vote, to any citizen offering to vote, on account of race, color or previous condition of servitude.

28 U.S.C. § 1367. Supplemental jurisdiction

(a) Except as provided in subsections (b) and (c) or as expressly provided otherwise by Federal statute, in any civil action of which the district courts have original jurisdiction, the district courts shall have supplemental jurisdiction over all other claims that are so related to claims in the action within such original jurisdiction that they form part of the same case or controversy under Article III of the United States Constitution. Such supplemental jurisdiction shall include claims that involve the joinder or intervention of additional parties.

(b) In any civil action of which the district courts have original jurisdiction founded solely on section 1332 of this title, the district courts shall not have supplemental jurisdiction under subsection (a) over claims by plaintiffs against persons made parties under Rule 14, 19, 20, or 24 of the Federal Rules of Civil Procedure, or over claims by persons proposed to be joined as plaintiffs under Rule 19 of such rules, or seeking to intervene as plaintiffs under Rule 24 of such rules, when exercising supplemental jurisdiction over such claims would be inconsistent with the jurisdictional requirements of section 1332.

(c) The district courts may decline to exercise supplemental jurisdiction over a claim under subsection (a) if—

(1) the claim raises a novel or complex issue of State law,

(2) the claim substantially predominates over the claim or claims over which the district court has original jurisdiction,

(3) the district court has dismissed all claims over which it has original jurisdiction, or

(4) in exceptional circumstances, there are other compelling reasons for declining jurisdiction.

(d) The period of limitations for any claim asserted under subsection (a), and for any other claim in the same action that is voluntarily dismissed at the same time as or after the dismissal of the claim under subsection (a), shall be tolled while the claim is pending and for a period of 30 days after it is dismissed unless State law provides for a longer tolling period.

(e) As used in this section, the term "State" includes the District of Columbia, the Commonwealth of Puerto Rico, and any territory or possession of the United States.

28 U.S.C. § 1391. Venue generally

(a) A civil action wherein jurisdiction is founded only on diversity of citizenship may, except as otherwise provided by law, be brought only in (1) a judicial district where any defendant resides, if all defendants reside in the same State, (2) a judicial district in which a substantial part of the events or omissions giving rise to the claim occurred, or a substantial part of property that is the subject of the action is situated, or (3) a judicial district in which any defendant is subject to personal jurisdiction at the time the action is commenced, if there is no district in which the action may otherwise be brought.

(b) A civil action wherein jurisdiction is not founded solely on diversity of citizenship may, except as otherwise provided by law, be brought only in (1) a judicial district where any defendant resides, if all defendants reside in the same State, (2) a judicial district in which a substantial part of the events or omissions giving rise to the claim occurred, or a substantial part of property that is the subject of the action is situated, or (3) a judicial district in which any defendant may be found, if there is no district in which the action may otherwise be brought.

(c) For purposes of venue under this chapter, a defendant that is a corporation shall be deemed to reside in any judicial district in which it is subject to personal jurisdiction at the time the action is commenced. In a State which has more than one judicial district and in which a defendant that is a corporation is subject to personal jurisdiction at the time an action is commenced, such corporation shall be deemed to reside in any district in that State within which its contacts would be sufficient to subject it to personal jurisdiction if that district were a separate State, and, if there is no such district, the corporation shall be deemed to reside in the district within which it has the most significant contacts.

(d) An alien may be sued in any district.

. . .

28 U.S.C. § 1441. Actions removable generally

(a) Except as otherwise expressly provided by Act of Congress, any civil action brought in a State court of which the district courts of the United States have original jurisdiction, may be removed by the defendant or the defendants, to the district court of the United States for the district and division embracing the place where such action is pending. For purposes of removal under this chapter, the citizenship of defendants sued under fictitious names shall be disregarded.

(b) Any civil action of which the district courts have original jurisdiction founded on a claim or right arising under the Constitution, treaties or laws of the United States shall be removable without regard to the citizenship or residence of the parties. Any other such action shall be removable only if none of the parties in interest properly joined and served as defendants is a citizen of the State in which such action is brought.

(c) Whenever a separate and independent claim or cause of action within the jurisdiction conferred by section 1331 of this title is joined with one or more otherwise non-removable claims or causes of action, the entire case may be removed and the district court may determine all issues therein, or, in its discretion, may remand all matters in which State law predominates.

(d) Any civil action brought in a State court against a foreign state as defined in section 1603(a) of this title may be removed by the foreign state to the district court of the United States for the district and division embracing the place where such action is pending. Upon removal the action shall be tried by the court without jury. Where removal is based upon this subsection, the time limitations of section 1446(b) of this chapter may be enlarged at any time for cause shown.

(e) The court to which such civil action is removed is not precluded from hearing and determining any claim in such civil action because the State court from which such civil action is removed did not have jurisdiction over that claim.

28 U.S.C. § 1443. Civil rights cases

Any of the following civil actions or criminal prosecutions, commenced in a State court may be removed by the defendant to the district court of the United States for the district and division embracing the place wherein it is pending:

(1) Against any person who is denied or cannot enforce in the courts of such State a right under any law providing for the equal civil rights of citizens of the United States, or of all persons within the jurisdiction thereof;

(2) For any act under color of authority derived from any law providing for equal rights, or for refusing to do any act on the ground that it would be inconsistent with such law.

28 U.S.C. § 1446. Procedure for removal

(a) A defendant or defendants desiring to remove any civil action or criminal prosecution from a State court shall file in the district court of the United States for the district and division within which such action is pending a notice of removal signed pursuant to Rule 11 of the Federal Rules of Civil Procedure and containing a short and plain statement of the grounds for removal, together with a copy of all process, pleadings, and orders served upon such defendant or defendants in such action.

(b) The notice of removal of a civil action or proceeding shall be filed within thirty days after the receipt by the defendant, through service or otherwise, of a copy of the initial pleading setting forth the claim for relief upon which such action or proceeding is based, or within thirty days after the service of summons upon the defendant if such initial pleading has then been filed in court and is not required to be served on the defendant, whichever period is shorter.

If the case stated by the initial pleading is not removable, a notice of removal may be filed within thirty days after receipt by the defendant, through service or otherwise, of a copy of an amended pleading, motion, order or other paper from which it may first be ascertained that the case is one which is or has become removable, except that a case may not be removed on the basis of jurisdiction conferred by section 1332 of this title more than 1 year after commencement of the action.

(c) (1) A notice of removal of a criminal prosecution shall be filed not later than thirty days after the arraignment in the State court, or at any time before trial, whichever is earlier, except that for good cause shown the United States district court may enter an order granting the defendant or defendants leave to file the notice at a later time.

(2) A notice of removal of a criminal prosecution shall include all grounds for such removal. A failure to state grounds which exist at the time of the filing of the notice shall constitute a waiver of such grounds, and a second notice may be filed only on grounds not existing at the time of the original notice. For good cause shown, the United States district court may grant relief from the limitations of this paragraph.

(3) The filing of a notice of removal of a criminal prosecution shall not prevent the State court in which such prosecution is pending from proceeding further, except that a judgment of conviction shall not be entered unless the prosecution is first remanded.

(4) The United States district court in which such notice is filed shall examine the notice promptly. If it clearly appears on the face of the notice and any exhibits annexed thereto that removal should not be permitted, the court shall make an order for summary remand.

(5) If the United States district court does not order the summary remand of such prosecution, it shall order an evidentiary hearing to be held promptly and after such hearing shall make such disposition of the prosecution as justice shall require. If the United States district court determines that removal shall be permitted, it shall so notify the State court in which prosecution is pending, which shall proceed no further.

(d) Promptly after the filing of such notice of removal of a civil action the defendant or defendants shall give written notice thereof to all adverse parties and shall file a copy of the notice with the clerk of such State court, which shall effect the removal and the State court shall proceed no further unless and until the case is remanded.

(e) If the defendant or defendants are in actual custody on process issued by the State court, the district court shall issue its writ of habeas corpus, and the marshal shall thereupon take such defendant or defendants into his custody and deliver a copy of the writ to the clerk of such State court.

(f) With respect to any counterclaim removed to a district court pursuant to section 337(c) of the Tariff Act of 1930, the district court shall resolve such counterclaim in the same manner as an original complaint under the Federal Rules of Civil Procedure, except that the payment of a filing fee shall not be required in such cases and the counterclaim shall relate back to the date of the original complaint in the proceeding before the International Trade Commission under section 337 of that Act.

28 U.S.C. § 1447. Procedure after removal generally

(a) In any case removed from a State court, the district court may issue all necessary orders and process to bring before it all proper parties whether served by process issued by the State court or otherwise.

(b) It may require the removing party to file with its clerk copies of all records and proceedings in such State court or may cause the same to be brought before it by writ of certiorari issued to such State court.

(c) A motion to remand the case on the basis of any defect other than lack of subject matter jurisdiction must be made within 30 days after the filing of the notice of removal under section 1446(a). If at any time before final judgment it appears that the district court lacks subject matter jurisdiction, the case shall be remanded. An order remanding the case may require payment of just costs and any actual expenses, including attorney fees, incurred as a result of the removal. A certified copy of the order of remand shall be mailed by the clerk to the clerk of the State court. The State court may thereupon proceed with such case.

(d) An order remanding a case to the State court from which it was removed is not reviewable on appeal or otherwise, except that an order remanding a case to the State court from which it was removed pursuant to section 1443 of this title shall be reviewable by appeal or otherwise.

(e) If after removal the plaintiff seeks to join additional defendants whose joinder would destroy subject matter jurisdiction, the court may deny joinder, or permit joinder and remand the action to the State court.

28 U.S.C. § 1658. Time limitations on the commencement of civil actions arising under Acts of Congress

(a) Except as otherwise provided by law, a civil action arising under an Act of Congress enacted after the date of the enactment of this section may not be commenced later than 4 years after the cause of action accrues.

(b) Notwithstanding subsection (a), a private right of action that involves a claim of fraud, deceit, manipulation, or contrivance in contravention of a regulatory requirement concerning the securities laws, as defined in section 3(a)(47) of the Securities Exchange Act of 1934 (15 U.S.C. § 78c(a)(47)), may be brought not later than the earlier of—

(1) 2 years after the discovery of the facts constituting the violation; or

(2) 5 years after such violation.

28 U.S.C. § 1738. State and Territorial statutes and judicial proceedings; full faith and credit

The Acts of the legislature of any State, Territory, or Possession of the United States, or copies thereof, shall be authenticated by affixing the seal of such State, Territory or Possession thereto.

The records and judicial proceedings of any court of any such State, Territory or Possession, or copies thereof, shall be proved or admitted in other courts within the United States and its Territories and Possessions by the attestation of the clerk and seal of the court annexed, if a seal exists, together with a certificate of a judge of the court that the said attestation is in proper form.

Such Acts, records and judicial proceedings or copies thereof, so authenticated, shall have the same full faith and credit in every court within the United States and its

Territories and Possessions as they have by law or usage in the courts of such State, Territory or Possession from which they are taken.

28 U.S.C. § 1821. Per diem and mileage generally; subsistence

(a) (1) Except as otherwise provided by law, a witness in attendance at any court of the United States, or before a United States Magistrate Judge, or before any person authorized to take his deposition pursuant to any rule or order of a court of the United States, shall be paid the fees and allowances provided by this section.

(2) As used in this section, the term "court of the United States" includes, in addition to the courts listed in section 451 of this title, any court created by Act of Congress in a territory which is invested with any jurisdiction of a district court of the United States.

(b) A witness shall be paid an attendance fee of $40 per day for each day's attendance. A witness shall also be paid the attendance fee for the time necessarily occupied in going to and returning from the place of attendance at the beginning and end of such attendance or at any time during such attendance.

(c) (1) A witness who travels by common carrier shall be paid for the actual expenses of travel on the basis of the means of transportation reasonably utilized and the distance necessarily traveled to and from such witness's residence by the shortest practical route in going to and returning from the place of attendance. Such a witness shall utilize a common carrier at the most economical rate reasonably available. A receipt or other evidence of actual cost shall be furnished.

(2) A travel allowance equal to the mileage allowance which the Administrator of General Services has prescribed, pursuant to section 5704 of title 5, for official travel of employees of the Federal Government shall be paid to each witness who travels by privately owned vehicle. Computation of mileage under this paragraph shall be made on the basis of a uniformed table of distances adopted by the Administrator of General Services.

(3) Toll charges for toll roads, bridges, tunnels, and ferries, taxicab fares between places of lodging and carrier terminals, and parking fees (upon presentation of a valid parking receipt), shall be paid in full to a witness incurring such expenses.

(4) All normal travel expenses within and outside the judicial district shall be taxable as costs pursuant to section 1920 of this title.

(d) (1) A subsistence allowance shall be paid to a witness when an overnight stay is required at the place of attendance because such place is so far removed from the residence of such witness as to prohibit return thereto from day to day.

(2) A subsistence allowance for a witness shall be paid in an amount not to exceed the maximum per diem allowance prescribed by the Administrator of General Services, pursuant to section 5702(a) of title 5, for official travel in the area of attendance by employees of the Federal Government.

(3) A subsistence allowance for a witness attending in an area designated by the Administrator of General Services as a high-cost area shall be paid in an amount not to exceed the maximum actual subsistence allowance prescribed by the Administrator, pursuant to section 5702(c)(B) of title 5, for official travel in such area by employees of the Federal Government.

(4) When a witness is detained pursuant to section 3144 of title 18 for want of security for his appearance, he shall be entitled for each day of detention when not in attendance at court, in addition to his subsistence, to the daily attendance fee provided by subsection (b) of this section.

(e) An alien who has been paroled into the United States for prosecution, pursuant to section 212(d)(5) of the Immigration and Nationality Act (8 U.S.C. § 1182(d)(5)), or an alien who either has admitted belonging to a class of aliens who are deportable or has been determined pursuant to section 240 of such Act (8 U.S.C. § 1252(b)) to be deportable, shall be ineligible to receive the fees or allowances provided by this section.

(f) Any witness who is incarcerated at the time that his or her testimony is given (except for a witness to whom the provisions of section 3144 of title 18 apply) may not receive fees or allowances under this section, regardless of whether such a witness is incarcerated at the time he or she makes a claim for fees or allowances under this section.

28 U.S.C. § 2201. Declaratory Judgments

(a) In a case of actual controversy within its jurisdiction, except with respect to Federal taxes other than actions brought under section 7428 of the Internal Revenue Code of 1986, a proceeding under section 505 or 1146 of title 11, or in any civil action involving an antidumping or countervailing duty proceeding regarding a class or kind of merchandise of a free trade area country (as defined in section 516A(f)(10) of the Tariff Act of 1930), as determined by the administering authority, any court of the United States, upon the filing of an appropriate pleading, may declare the rights and other legal relations of any interested party seeking such declaration, whether or not further relief is or could be sought. Any such declaration shall have the force and effect of a final judgment or decree and shall be reviewable as such.

(b) For limitations on actions brought with respect to drug patents see section 505 or 512 of the Federal Food, Drug, and Cosmetic Act.

28 U.S.C. § 2202. Further Relief

Further necessary or proper relief based on a declaratory judgment or decree may be granted, after reasonable notice and hearing, against any adverse party whose rights have been determined by such judgment.

28 U.S.C. § 2283. Stay of State court proceedings

A court of the United States may not grant an injunction to stay proceedings in a State court except as expressly authorized by Act of Congress, or where necessary in aid of its jurisdiction, or to protect or effectuate its judgments.

28 U.S.C. § 2403. Intervention by United States or a State; constitutional question

(a) In any action, suit or proceeding in a court of the United States to which the United States or any agency, officer or employee thereof is not a party, wherein the constitutionality of any Act of Congress affecting the public interest is drawn in question, the court shall certify such fact to the Attorney General, and shall permit the United States to intervene for presentation of evidence, if evidence is otherwise admissible in the case, and for argument on the question of constitutionality. The United States shall, subject to the applicable provisions of law, have all the rights of a party and be subject to all liabilities of a party as to court costs to the extent necessary for a proper presentation of the facts and law relating to the question of constitutionality.

(b) In any action, suit, or proceeding in a court of the United States to which a State or any agency, officer, or employee thereof is not a party, wherein the constitutionality of any statute of that State affecting the public interest is drawn in question, the court shall certify such fact to the attorney general of the State, and shall permit the State to intervene for presentation of evidence, if evidence is otherwise admissible in the case, and for argument on the question of constitutionality. The State shall, subject to the applicable provisions of law, have all the rights of a party and be subject to all liabilities of a party as to court costs to the extent necessary for a proper presentation of the facts and law relating to the question of constitutionality.

CRIMINAL STATUTES

18 U.S.C. § 241. Conspiracy against rights

If two or more persons conspire to injure, oppress, threaten, or intimidate any person in any State, Territory, Commonwealth, Possession, or District in the free exercise or enjoyment of any right or privilege secured to him by the Constitution or laws of the United States, or because of his having so exercised the same; or

If two or more persons go in disguise on the highway, or on the premises of another, with intent to prevent or hinder his free exercise or enjoyment of any right or privilege so secured—

They shall be fined under this title or imprisoned not more than ten years, or both; and if death results from the acts committed in violation of this section or if such acts include kidnapping or an attempt to kidnap, aggravated sexual abuse or an attempt to commit aggravated sexual abuse, or an attempt to kill, they shall be fined under this title or imprisoned for any term of years or for life, or both, or may be sentenced to death.

18 U.S.C. § 242. Deprivation of rights under color of law

Whoever, under color of any law, statute, ordinance, regulation, or custom, willfully subjects any person in any State, Territory, Commonwealth, Possession, or District to the deprivation of any rights, privileges, or immunities secured or protected by the Constitution or laws of the United States, or to different punishments, pains, or penalties, on account of such person being an alien, or by reason of his color, or race, than are prescribed for the punishment of citizens, shall be fined under this title or imprisoned not more than one year, or both; and if bodily injury results from the acts committed in violation of this section or if such acts include the use, attempted use, or threatened use of a dangerous weapon, explosives, or fire, shall be fined under this title or imprisoned not more than ten years, or both; and if death results from the acts committed in violation of this section or if such acts include kidnapping or an attempt to kidnap, aggravated sexual abuse, or an attempt to commit aggravated sexual abuse, or an attempt to kill, shall be fined under this title, or imprisoned for any term of years or for life, or both, or may be sentenced to death.

MISCELLANEOUS STATUTES

47 U.S.C. § 555a. Limitation of franchising authority liability

(a) Suits for damages prohibited

In any court proceeding pending on or initiated after October 5, 1992, involving any claim against a franchising authority or other governmental entity, or any official, member, employee, or agent of such authority or entity, arising from the regulation of cable service or from a decision of approval or disapproval with respect to a grant, renewal, transfer, or amendment of a franchise, any relief, to the extent such relief is required by any other provision of Federal, State, or local law, shall be limited to injunctive relief and declaratory relief.

(b) Exception for completed cases

The limitation contained in subsection (a) of this section shall not apply to actions that, prior to such violation, have been determined by a final order of a court of binding jurisdiction, no longer subject to appeal, to be in violation of a cable operator's rights.

(c) Discrimination claims permitted

Nothing in this section shall be construed as limiting the relief authorized with respect to any claim against a franchising authority or other governmental entity, or any official, member, employee, or agent of such authority or entity, to the extent such claim involves discrimination on the basis of race, color, sex, age, religion, national origin, or handicap.

(d) Rule of construction

Nothing in this section shall be construed as creating or authorizing liability of any kind, under any law, for any action or failure to act relating to cable service or the granting of a franchise by any franchising authority or other governmental entity, or any official, member, employee, or agent of such authority or entity.

FEDERAL RULES OF CIVIL PROCEDURE

Rule 4. Summons

. . .

(j) Service Upon Foreign, State, or Local Governments.

(2) Service upon a state, municipal corporation, or other governmental organization subject to suit shall be effected by delivering a copy of the summons and of the complaint to its chief executive officer or by serving the summons and complaint in the manner prescribed by the law of that state for the service of summons or other like process upon any such defendant.

Rule 8. General Rules of Pleading

(a) Claims for Relief. A pleading which sets forth a claim for relief, whether an original claim, counterclaim, cross-claim, or third-party claim, shall contain (1) a short and plain statement of the grounds upon which the court's jurisdiction depends, unless the court already has jurisdiction and the claim needs no new grounds of jurisdiction to support it, (2) a short and plain statement of the claim showing that the pleader is entitled to relief, and (3) a demand for judgment for the relief the pleader seeks. Relief in the alternative or of several different types may be demanded.

(b) Defenses; Form of Denials. A party shall state in short and plain terms the party's defenses to each claim asserted and shall admit or deny the averments upon which the adverse party relies. If a party is without knowledge or information sufficient to form a belief as to the truth of an averment, the party shall so state and this has the effect of a denial. Denials shall fairly meet the substance of the averments denied. When a pleader intends in good faith to deny only a part or a qualification of an averment, the pleader shall specify so much of it as is true and material and shall deny only the remainder. Unless the pleader intends in good faith to controvert all the averments of the preceding pleading, the pleader may make denials as specific denials of designated averments or paragraphs or may generally deny all the averments except such designated averments or paragraphs as the pleader expressly admits; but, when the pleader does so intend to controvert all its averments, including averments of the grounds upon which the court's jurisdiction depends, the pleader may do so by general denial subject to the obligations set forth in Rule 11.

(c) Affirmative Defenses. In pleading to a preceding pleading, a party shall set forth affirmatively accord and satisfaction, arbitration and award, assumption of risk, contributory negligence, discharge in bankruptcy, duress, estoppel, failure of consideration, fraud, illegality, injury by fellow servant, laches, license, payment, release, res judicata, statute of frauds, statute of limitations, waiver, and any other matter constituting an avoidance or affirmative defense. When a party has mistakenly designated a defense as a counterclaim or a counterclaim as a defense, the court on terms, if justice so requires, shall treat the pleading as if there had been a proper designation.

(d) Effect of Failure to Deny. Averments in a pleading to which a responsive pleading is required, other than those as to the amount of damage, are admitted when not denied in the responsive pleading. Averments in a pleading to which no responsive pleading is required or permitted shall be taken as denied or avoided.

(e) Pleading to be Concise and Direct; Consistency.

(1) Each averment of a pleading shall be simple, concise, and direct. No technical forms of pleading or motions are required.

(2) A party may set forth two or more statements of a claim or defense alternately or hypothetically, either in one count or defense or in separate counts or defenses. When two or more statements are made in the alternative and one of them if made independently would be sufficient, the pleading is not made insufficient by the insufficiency of one or more of the alternative statements. A party may also state as many separate claims or defenses as the party has regardless of consistency and whether based on legal, equitable, or maritime grounds. All statements shall be made subject to the obligations set forth in Rule 11.

(f) Construction of Pleadings. All pleadings shall be so construed as to do substantial justice.

Rule 9. Pleading Special Matters

(a) Capacity. It is not necessary to aver the capacity of a party to sue or be sued or the authority of a party to sue or be sued in a representative capacity or the legal existence of an organized association of persons that is made a party, except to the extent required to show the jurisdiction of the court. When a party desires to raise an issue as to the legal existence of any party or the capacity of any party to sue or be sued or the authority of a party to sue or be sued in a representative capacity, the party desiring to raise the issue shall do so by specific negative averment, which shall include such supporting particulars as are peculiarly within the pleader's knowledge.

(b) Fraud, Mistake, Condition of the Mind. In all averments of fraud or mistake, the circumstances constituting fraud or mistake shall be stated with particularity. Malice, intent, knowledge, and other condition of mind of a person may be averred generally.

(c) Conditions Precedent. In pleading the performance or occurrence of conditions precedent, it is sufficient to aver generally that all conditions precedent have been performed or have occurred. A denial of performance or occurrence shall be made specifically and with particularity.

(d) Official Document or Act. In pleading an official document or official act it is sufficient to aver that the document was issued or the act done in compliance with law.

(e) Judgment. In pleading a judgment or decision of a domestic or foreign court, judicial or quasi-judicial tribunal, or of a board or officer, it is sufficient to aver the judgment or decision without setting forth matter showing jurisdiction to render it.

(f) Time and Place. For the purpose of testing the sufficiency of a pleading, averments of time and place are material and shall be considered like all other averments of material matter.

(g) Special Damage. When items of special damage are claimed, they shall be specifically stated.

. . .

Rule 12. Defenses and Objections — When and How Presented — By Pleading or Motion — Motion for Judgment on Pleadings

. . .

(b) How Presented. Every defense, in law or fact, to a claim for relief in any pleading, whether a claim, counterclaim, cross-claim, or third-party claim, shall be asserted in the responsive pleading thereto if one is required, except that the following defenses may at the option of the pleader be made by motion: (1) lack of jurisdiction over the subject matter, (2) lack of jurisdiction over the person, (3) improper venue, (4) insufficiency of process, (5) insufficiency of service of process, (6) failure to state a claim upon which relief can be granted, (7) failure to join a party under Rule 19. A motion making any of these defenses shall be made before pleading if a further pleading is permitted. No defense or objection is waived by being joined with one or more other defenses or objections in a responsive pleading or motion. If a pleading sets forth a claim for relief to which the adverse party is not required to serve a responsive pleading, the adverse party may assert at the trial any defense in law or fact to that claim for relief. If, on a motion asserting the defense numbered (6) to dismiss for failure of the pleading to state a claim upon which relief can be granted, matters outside the pleading are presented to and not excluded by the court, the motion shall be treated as one for summary judgment and disposed of as provided in Rule 56, and all parties shall be given reasonable opportunity to present all material made pertinent to such a motion by Rule 56.

. . .

(h) Waiver or Preservation of Certain Defenses.

(1) A defense of lack of jurisdiction over the person, improper venue, insufficiency of process, or insufficiency of service of process is waived (A) if omitted from a motion in the circumstances described in subdivision (g), or (B) if it is neither made by motion under this rule nor included in a responsive pleading or an amendment thereof permitted by Rule 15(a) to be made as a matter of course.

(2) A defense of failure to state a claim upon which relief can be granted, a defense of failure to join a party indispensable under Rule 19, and an objection of failure to state a legal defense to a claim may be made in any pleading permitted or ordered under Rule 7(a), or by motion for judgment on the pleadings, or at the trial on the merits.

(3) Whenever it appears by suggestion of the parties or otherwise that the court lacks jurisdiction of the subject matter, the court shall dismiss the action.

Rule 14. Third-Party Practice

(a) When Defendant May Bring in Third Party. At any time after commencement of the action a defending party, as a third-party plaintiff, may cause a summons and complaint to be served upon a person not a party to the action who is or may be liable to the third-party plaintiff for all or part of the plaintiff's claim against the third-party plaintiff. The third-party plaintiff need not obtain leave to make the service if the third-party plaintiff files the third-party complaint not later than 10 days after serving the original answer. Otherwise the third-party plaintiff must obtain leave on motion upon notice to all parties to the action. The person served with the summons and third-party complaint, hereinafter called the third-party defendant, shall make any defenses to the third-party plaintiff's claim as provided in Rule 12 and any counterclaims against the third-party plaintiff and cross-claims against other third-party defendants as provided in Rule 13. The third-party defendant may assert against the plaintiff any defenses which the third-party plaintiff has to the plaintiff's claim. The third-party defendant may also assert any claim against the plaintiff arising out of the transaction or occurrence that is the subject matter of the plaintiff's claim against the third-party plaintiff. The plaintiff may assert any claim against the third-party defendant arising out of the transaction or occurrence that is the subject matter of the plaintiff's claim against the third-party plaintiff, and the third-party defendant thereupon shall assert any defenses as provided in Rule 12 and any counterclaims and cross-claims as provided in Rule 13. Any party may move to strike the third-party claim, or for its severance or separate trial. A third-party defendant may proceed under this rule against any person not a party to the action who is or may be liable to the third-party defendant for all or part of the claim made in the action against the third-party defendant. The third-party complaint, if within the admiralty and maritime jurisdiction, may be in rem against a vessel, cargo, or other property subject to admiralty or maritime process in rem, in which case references in this rule to the summons include the warrant of arrest, and references to the third-party plaintiff or defendant include, where appropriate, a person who asserts a right under Supplemental Rule C(6)(b)(i) in the property arrested.

(b) When Plaintiff May Bring in Third Party. When a counterclaim is asserted against a plaintiff, the plaintiff may cause a third party to be brought in under circumstances which under this rule would entitle a defendant to do so.

Rule 18. Joinder of Claims and Remedies

(a) Joinder of Claims. A party asserting a claim to relief as an original claim, counterclaim, cross-claim, or third-party claim, may join, either as independent or as alternate claims, as many claims, legal, equitable, or maritime, as the party has against an opposing party.

(b) Joinder of Remedies; Fraudulent Conveyances. Whenever a claim is one heretofore cognizable only after another claim has been prosecuted to a conclusion, the two claims may be joined in a single action; but the court shall grant relief in that action only in accordance with the relative substantive rights of the parties. In particular, a plaintiff may state a claim for money and a claim to have set aside a conveyance fraudulent as to that plaintiff, without first having obtained a judgment establishing the claim for money.

Rule 20. Permissive Joinder of Parties

(a) Permissive Joinder. All persons may join in one action as plaintiffs if they assert any right to relief jointly, severally, or in the alternative in respect of or arising out of the same transaction, occurrence, or series of transactions or occurrences and if any question of law or fact common to all these persons will arise in the action. All persons (and any vessel, cargo or other property subject to admiralty process in rem) may be joined in one action as defendants if there is asserted against them jointly, severally, or in the alternative, any right to relief in respect of or arising out of the same transaction, occurrence, or series of transactions or occurrences and if any question of law or fact common to all defendants will arise in the action. A plaintiff or defendant need not be interested in obtaining or defending against all the relief demanded. Judgment may be given for one or more of the plaintiffs according to their respective rights to relief, and against one or more defendants according to their respective liabilities.

(b) Separate Trials. The court may make such orders as will prevent a party from being embarrassed, delayed, or put to expense by the inclusion of a party against whom the party asserts no claim and who asserts no claim against the party, and may order separate trials or make other orders to prevent delay or prejudice.

Rule 21. Misjoinder and Non-Joinder of Parties

Misjoinder of parties is not ground for dismissal of an action. Parties may be dropped or added by order of the court on motion of any party or of its own initiative at any stage of the action and on such terms as are just. Any claim against a party may be severed and proceeded with separately.

Rule 23. Class Actions

(a) Prerequisites to a Class Action. One or more members of a class may sue or be sued as representative parties on behalf of all only if (1) the class is so numerous that joinder of all members is impracticable, (2) there are questions of law or fact common to the class, (3) the claims or defenses of the representative parties are typical of the claims or defenses of the class, and (4) the representative parties will fairly and adequately protect the interests of the class.

(b) Class Actions Maintainable. An action may be maintained as a class action if the prerequisites of subdivision (a) are satisfied, and in addition:

(1) the prosecution of separate actions by or against individual members of the class would create a risk of

(A) inconsistent or varying adjudications with respect to individual members of the class which would establish incompatible standards of conduct for the party opposing the class, or

(B) adjudications with respect to individual members of the class which would as a practical matter be dispositive of the interests of the other members not parties to the adjudications or substantially impair or impede their ability to protect their interests; or

(2) the party opposing the class has acted or refused to act on grounds generally applicable to the class, thereby making appropriate final injunctive relief or corresponding declaratory relief with respect to the class as a whole; or

(3) the court finds that the questions of law or fact common to the members of the class predominate over any questions affecting only individual members, and that a class action is superior to other available methods for the fair and efficient adjudication of the controversy. The matters pertinent to the findings include: (A) the interest of members of the class in individually controlling the prosecution or defense of separate actions; (B) the extent and nature of any litigation concerning the controversy already commenced by or against members of the class; (C) the desirability or undesirability of concentrating the litigation of the claims in the particular forum; (D) the difficulties likely to be encountered in the management of a class action.

(c) Determination by Order Whether Class Action to be Maintained; Notice; Judgment; Actions Conducted Partially as Class Actions.

(1) As soon as practicable after the commencement of an action brought as a class action, the court shall determine by order whether it is to be so maintained. An order under this subdivision may be conditional, and may be altered or amended before the decision on the merits.

(2) In any class action maintained under subdivision (b)(3), the court shall direct to the members of the class the best notice practicable under the circumstances, including individual notice to all members who can be identified through reasonable effort. The notice shall advise each member that (A) the court will exclude the member from the class if the member so requests by a specified date; (B) the judgment, whether favorable or not, will include all members who do not request exclusion; and (C) any member who does not request exclusion may, if the member desires, enter an appearance through counsel.

(3) The judgment in an action maintained as a class action under subdivision (b)(1) or (b)(2), whether or not favorable to the class, shall include and describe those whom the court finds to be members of the class. The judgment in an action maintained as a class action under subdivision (b)(3), whether or not favorable to the class, shall include and specify or describe those to whom the notice provided in subdivision (c)(2) was directed, and who have not requested exclusion, and whom the court finds to be members of the class.

(4) When appropriate (A) an action may be brought or maintained as a class action with respect to particular issues, or (B) a class may be divided into subclasses and each subclass treated as a class, and the provisions of this rule shall then be construed and applied accordingly.

(d) Orders in Conduct of Actions. In the conduct of actions to which this rule applies, the court may make appropriate orders: (1) determining the course of proceedings or prescribing measures to prevent undue repetition or complication in the presentation of evidence or argument; (2) requiring, for the protection of the members of the class or otherwise for the fair conduct of the action, that notice be given in such manner as the court may direct to some or all of the members of any step in the action, or of the proposed extent of the judgment, or of the opportunity of members to signify whether they consider the representation fair and adequate, to intervene and present claims or defenses, or otherwise to come into the action; (3) imposing conditions on the representative parties or on intervenors; (4) requiring that the pleadings be amended to eliminate therefrom allegations as to representation of absent persons, and that the action proceed accordingly; (5) dealing with similar procedural matters. The orders may be combined with an order under Rule 16, and may be altered or amended as may be desirable from time to time.

(e) Dismissal or Compromise. A class action shall not be dismissed or compromised without the approval of the court, and notice of the proposed dismissal or compromise shall be given to all members of the class in such manner as the court directs.

(f) Appeals. A court of appeals may in its discretion permit an appeal from an order of a district court granting or denying class action certification under this rule if application is made to it within ten days after entry of the order. An appeal does not stay proceedings in the district court unless the district judge or the court of appeals so orders.

Rule 24. Intervention

(a) Intervention of Right. Upon timely application anyone shall be permitted to intervene in an action: (1) when a statute of the United States confers an unconditional right to intervene; or (2) when the applicant claims an interest relating to the property or transaction which is the subject of the action and the applicant is so situated that the disposition of the action may as a practical matter impair or impede the applicant's ability to protect that interest, unless the applicant's interest is adequately represented by existing parties.

(b) Permissive Intervention. Upon timely application anyone may be permitted to intervene in an action: (1) when a statute of the United States confers a conditional right to intervene; or (2) when an applicant's claim or defense and the main action have a question of law or fact in common. When a party to an action relies for ground of claim or defense upon any statute or executive order administered by a federal or state governmental officer or agency or upon any regulation, order, requirement, or agreement issued or made pursuant to the statute or executive order, the officer or agency upon timely application may be permitted to intervene in the action. In exercising its

Rule 25. Substitution of Parties

(a) Death.

(1) If a party dies and the claim is not thereby extinguished, the court may order substitution of the proper parties. The motion for substitution may be made by any party or by the successors or representatives of the deceased party and, together with the notice of hearing, shall be served on the parties as provided in Rule 5 and upon persons not parties in the manner provided in Rule 4 for the service of a summons, and may be served in any judicial district. Unless the motion for substitution is made not later than 90 days after the death is suggested upon the record by service of a statement of the fact of the death as provided herein for the service of the motion, the action shall be dismissed as to the deceased party.

(2) In the event of the death of one or more of the plaintiffs or of one or more of the defendants in an action in which the right sought to be enforced survives only to the surviving plaintiffs or only against the surviving defendants, the action does not abate. The death shall be suggested upon the record and the action shall proceed in favor of or against the surviving parties.

(b) Incompetency. If a party becomes incompetent, the court upon motion served as provided in subdivision (a) of this rule may allow the action to be continued by or against the party's representative.

(c) Transfer of Interest. In case of any transfer of interest, the action may be continued by or against the original party, unless the court upon motion directs the person to whom the interest is transferred to be substituted in the action or joined with the original party. Service of the motion shall be made as provided in subdivision (a) of this rule.

(d) Public Officers; Death or Separation from Office.

(1) When a public officer is a party to an action in his official capacity and during its pendency dies, resigns, or otherwise ceases to hold office, the action does not abate and the officer's successor is automatically substituted as a party. Proceedings following the substitution shall be in the name of the substituted party, but any misnomer not affecting the substantial rights of the parties shall be disregarded. An order of substitution may be entered at any time, but the omission to enter such an order shall not affect the substitution.

(2) A public officer who sues or is sued in an official capacity may be described as a party by the officer's official title rather than by name; but the court may require the officer's name to be added.

Rule 49. Special Verdicts and Interrogatories

(a) Special Verdicts. The court may require a jury to return only a special verdict in the form of a special written finding upon each issue of fact. In that event the court may submit to the jury written questions susceptible of categorical or other brief answer or may submit written forms of the several special findings which might properly be made under the pleadings and evidence; or it may use such other method of submitting the issues and requiring the written findings thereon as it deems most appropriate. The court shall give to the jury such explanation and instruction concerning the matter thus submitted as may be necessary to enable the jury to make its findings upon each issue. If in so doing the court omits any issue of fact raised by the pleadings or by the evidence, each party waives the right to a trial by jury of the issue so omitted unless before the jury retires the party demands its submission to the jury. As to an issue omitted without such demand the court may make a finding; or, if it fails to do so, it shall be deemed to have made a finding in accord with the judgment on the special verdict.

(b) General Verdict Accompanied by Answer to Interrogatories. The court may submit to the jury, together with appropriate forms for a general verdict, written interrogatories upon one or more issues of fact the decision of which is necessary to a verdict. The court shall give such explanation or instruction as may be necessary to enable the jury both to make answers to the interrogatories and to render a general verdict, and the court shall direct the jury both to make written answers and to render a general verdict. When the general verdict and the answers are harmonious, the appropriate judgment upon the verdict and answers shall be entered pursuant to Rule 58. When the answers are consistent with each other but one or more is inconsistent with the general verdict, judgment may be entered pursuant to Rule 58 in accordance with the answers, notwithstanding the general verdict, or the court may return the jury for further consideration of its answers and verdict or may order a new trial. When the answers are inconsistent with each other and one or more is likewise inconsistent with the general verdict, judgment shall not be entered, but the court shall return the jury for further consideration of its answers and verdict or shall order a new trial.

Rule 56. Summary Judgment

(a) For Claimant. A party seeking to recover upon a claim, counterclaim, or cross-claim or to obtain a declaratory judgment may, at any time after the expiration of 20 days from the commencement of the action or after service of a motion for summary judgment by the adverse party, move with or without supporting affidavits for a summary judgment in the party's favor upon all or any part thereof.

(b) For Defending Party. A party against whom a claim, counterclaim, or cross-claim is asserted or a declaratory judgment is sought may, at any time, move with or without supporting affidavits for a summary judgment in the party's favor as to all or any part thereof.

Rule 60. Relief from a Judgment or Order

(a) Corrections Based on Clerical Mistakes; Oversights and Omissions. The court may correct a clerical mistake or a mistake arising from oversight or omission whenever one is found in a judgment, order, or other part of the record. The court may do so on motion or on its own, with or without notice. But after an appeal has been docketed in the appellate court and while it is pending, such a mistake may be corrected only with the appellate court's leave.

(b) Grounds for Relief from a Final Judgment, Order, or Proceeding. On motion and just terms, the court may relieve a party or its legal representative from a final judgment, order, or proceeding for the following reasons:

(1) mistake, inadvertence, surprise, or excusable neglect;

(2) newly discovered evidence that, with reasonable diligence, could not have been discovered in time to move for a new trial under Rule 59(b);

(3) fraud (whether previously called intrinsic or extrinsic), misrepresentation, or misconduct by an opposing party;

(4) the judgment is void;

(5) the judgment has been satisfied, released or discharged; it is based on an earlier judgment that has been reversed or vacated; or applying it prospectively is no longer equitable; or

(6) any other reason that justifies relief.

(c) Timing and Effect of the Motion.

(1) Timing. A motion under Rule 60(b) must be made within a reasonable time—and for reasons (1), (2), and (3) no more than a year after the entry of the judgment or order or the date of the proceeding.

(2) Effect on Finality. The motion does not affect the judgment's finality or suspend its operation.

(d) Other Powers to Grant Relief. This rule does not limit a court's power to:

(1) entertain an independent action to relieve a party from a judgment, order, or proceeding;

(2) grant relief under 28 U.S.C. § 1655 to a defendant who was not personally notified of the action; or

(3) set aside a judgment for fraud on the court.

(e) Bills and Writs Abolished. The following are abolished: bills of review, bills in the nature of bills of review, and writs of coram nobis, coram vobis, and audita querela.

Rule 65. Injunctions

(a) Preliminary Injunction.

(1) Notice. No preliminary injunction shall be issued without notice to the adverse party.

(2) Consolidation of Hearing With Trial on Merits. Before or after the commencement of the hearing of an application for a preliminary injunction, the court may order the trial of the action on the merits to be advanced and consolidated with the hearing of the application. Even when this consolidation is not ordered, any evidence received upon an application for a preliminary injunction which would be admissible upon the trial on the merits becomes part of the record on the trial and need not be repeated upon the trial. This subdivision (a)(2) shall be so construed and applied as to save to the parties any rights they may have to trial by jury.

(b) Temporary Restraining Order; Notice; Hearing; Duration.

A temporary restraining order may be granted without written or oral notice to the adverse party or that party's attorney only if (1) it clearly appears from specific facts shown by affidavit or by the verified complaint that immediate and irreparable injury, loss, or damage will result to the applicant before the adverse party or that party's attorney can be heard in opposition, and (2) the applicant's attorney certifies to the court in writing the efforts, if any, which have been made to give the notice and the reasons supporting the claim that notice should not be required. Every temporary restraining order granted without notice shall be indorsed with the date and hour of issuance; shall be filed forthwith in the clerk's office and entered of record; shall define the injury and state why it is irreparable and why the order was granted without notice; and shall expire by its terms within such time after entry, not to exceed 10 days, as the court fixes, unless within the time so fixed the order, for good cause shown, is extended for a like period or unless the party against whom the order is directed consents that it may be extended for a longer period. The reasons for the extension shall be entered of record. In case a temporary restraining order is granted without notice, the motion for a preliminary injunction shall be set down for hearing at the earliest possible time and takes precedence of all matters except older matters of the same character; and when the motion comes on for hearing the party who obtained the temporary restraining order shall proceed with the application for a preliminary injunction and, if the party does not do so, the court shall dissolve the temporary restraining order. On 2 days' notice to the party who obtained the temporary restraining order without notice or on such shorter notice to that party as the court may prescribe, the adverse party may appear and move its dissolution or modification and in that event the court shall proceed to hear and determine such motion as expeditiously as the ends of justice require.

(c) Security.

No restraining order or preliminary injunction shall issue except upon the giving of security by the applicant, in such sum as the court deems proper, for the payment of such costs and damages as may be incurred or suffered by any party who is found to have been wrongfully enjoined or restrained. No such security shall be required of the United States or of an officer or agency thereof.

The provisions of Rule 65.1 apply to a surety upon a bond or undertaking under this rule.

(d) Form and Scope of Injunction or Restraining Order.

Every order granting an injunction and every restraining order shall set forth the reasons for its issuance; shall be specific in terms; shall describe in reasonable detail, and not by reference to the complaint or other document, the act or acts sought to be restrained; and is binding only upon the parties to the action, their officers, agents, servants, employees, and attorneys, and upon those persons in active concert or participation with them who receive actual notice of the order by personal service or otherwise.

Rule 68. Offer of Judgment

At any time more than 10 days before the trial begins, a party defending against a claim may serve upon the adverse party an offer to allow judgment to be taken against the defending party for the money or property or to the effect specified in the offer, with costs then accrued. If within 10 days after the service of the offer the adverse party serves written notice that the offer is accepted, either party may then file the offer and notice of acceptance together with proof of service thereof and thereupon the clerk shall enter judgment. An offer not accepted shall be deemed withdrawn and evidence thereof is not admissible except in a proceeding to determine costs. If the judgment finally obtained by the offeree is not more favorable than the offer, the offeree must pay the costs incurred after the making of the offer. The fact that an offer is made but not accepted does not preclude a subsequent offer. When the liability of one party to another has been determined by verdict or order or judgment, but the amount or extent of the liability remains to be determined by further proceedings, the party adjudged liable may make an offer of judgment, which shall have the same effect as an offer made before trial if it is served within a reasonable time not less than 10 days prior to the commencement of hearings to determine the amount or extent of liability.

Rule 69. Execution

(a) In General.

Process to enforce a judgment for the payment of money shall be a writ of execution, unless the court directs otherwise. The procedure on execution, in proceedings supplementary to and in aid of a judgment, and in proceedings on and in aid of execution shall be in accordance with the practice and procedure of the state in which the district court is held, existing at the time the remedy is sought, except that any statute of the United States governs to the extent that it is applicable. In aid of the judgment or execution, the judgment creditor or a successor in interest when that interest appears of record, may obtain discovery from any person, including the judgment debtor, in the manner provided in these rules or in the manner provided by the practice of the state in which the district court is held.

TABLE OF CASES

[References are to pages]

A

Aaron v. Target Corp.	415
Abbott v. Village of Winthrop Harbor	224
ACLU of Ohio v. Taft	361
Addiction Specialists, Inc. v. Township of Hampton	383
Adickes v. S. H. Kress & Co.	24, 25; 327
Adler v. Duval County School District	362
Administrator of (see name of estate)	
Agostini v. Felton	426
Alabama v. Pugh	165
Alabama Public Service Commission v. Southern Railway	390
Albright v. Oliver	28; 50; 483
Alden v. Maine	131; 146; 176
Alexander v. Fulton County	362
Alexander v. Riga	321
Alexander v. Sandoval	71, 72
Allen v. McCurry	421, 422; 428; 434
Allen v. Wright	338
Almand v. DeKalb County	14
Almand in Griffin v. City of Opa-Locka	18
Almond v. Kent	259
Alyeska Pipeline Service Co. v. Wilderness Society	145; 497, 498
American Trucking Ass'ns v. Scheiner	202
American Trucking Ass'ns v. Smith	202
AmerisourceBergen Corp. v. Roden	408; 420
Amerson v. Iowa	419
Amy v. Supervisors	77
Anderson v. Cornejo	265
Anderson v. Creighton	110, 111; 114, 115; 118; 124; 127
Anderson v. Green	350
Anderson v. Romero	110
Ankenbrandt v. Richards	390; 408; 419; 453
Antoine v. Byers & Anderson, Inc.	99
Arizonans for Official English v. Arizona	349; 356; 386
Arlington Heights v. Metropolitan Housing Dev. Corp.	35
Armstrong v. Asarco, Inc.	501
Armstrong v. Davis	518
Arnold v. Duchesne County	264
Ashafa v. City of Chicago	264
Ashcroft v. Iqbal	124; 194

Askew v. Hargrave	384
Asociacion De Subscripcion Conjunta Del Seguro De Responsabilidad Obligatorio v. Galarza	431
Association of Data Processing Service Organizations v. Camp	336
AT&T Communications of Southwest v. City of Austin	355
Atascadero State Hospital v. Scanlon	136; 159; 162; 171, 172; 522
Atlanta Retail, In re	425
Auer v. Robbins	147
Austin v. Hopper	113
Auto Workers v. Hoosier Cardinal Corp.	256
Avery; United States v.	311

B

Bad Frog Brewery Inc. v. New York State Liquor Authority	385
Baker v. City of Hamilton	126
Baldwin v. Chesapeake & Potomac Tel. Co.	495; 497
Bank of the United States v. Deveaux	186; 192
Bannum, Inc. v. City of Fort Lauderdale	190
Barbour v. Washington Metropolitan Area Transit Authority	164; 172
Barlow v. C.I.R.	517
Barlow v. Collins	336
Barna v. City of Perth Amboy	18
Barnes v. Wright	310
Barney v. Pulsipher	232
Baron v. Suffolk County Sheriff's Department	217
Barr v. Matteo	101
Barrett v. Orange County Human Rights Commission	246
Barron v. Mayor of Baltimore	185
Barry v. Barchi	64
Bastien v. Office of Senator Ben Nighthorse	79, 80
Bates v. Township of Van Buren	426
Bauman v. Ross	284
Baze v. Rees	468
Beattie v. Madison County School District	216
Becerra v. Asher	19
Behrens v. Pelletier	127, 128
Belcher v. Norton	34; 41, 42
Bell v. Burson	29
Bell v. Clackamas County	328
Bell v. Fowler	264

TABLE OF CASES

[References are to pages]

Bell v. Maryland 26
Bellotti v. Baird 383
Bernhardt v. Los Angeles County 537
Bethesda Lutheran Homes & Services, Inc. v.
    Leean 225
Bibbs v. Newman 224
Biggs v. Meadows 174
Bilida v. McCleod 428
Bisbal-Ramos v. City of Mayaguez 320
Bishop v. Wood 32
Bivens v. Six Unknown Named Agents of Federal
    Bureau of Narcotics 72; 158; 189, 190; 335
Blake v. Katter 261
Blanchard v. Bergeron 508; 516; 538
Blankenship v. Blackwell . . . 351, 353, 352; 414, 415
Blatchford v. Native Village of Noatak . 131; 136; 144
Blazar v. Perkins 285
Blessing v. Freestone 70
Blum v. Stenson 509
Blum v. Yaretsky 27; 360
BMW of North America v. Gore 318
Board of Comm'rs v. Aspinwall 184
Board of County Commissioners v. Umbehr 79
Board of County Commissioners of Bryan County v.
    Brown 194; 232–234
Board of Regents v. Roth . . . 28; 32; 54; 62; 195; 248
Board of Regents v. Tomanio . 256; 258; 260, 261; 264
Board of Trustees v. Garrett 177, 178
Bob Jones University v. United States 27
Boerne, City of v. Flores 177
Bogan v. Scott-Harris 75; 218
Bolden v. City of Topeka 250
Boneberger v. Plymouth Township 18
Booth v. Churner 443; 447
Bordanaro v. McLeod 232
Borough of (see name of borough) . . . .
Boston Chamber of Commerce v. Boston 279
Boulahanis v. Board of Regents 71
Boyce v. Fernandes 111
Bradley v. Fisher 81, 82; 85
Bradley v. Richmond School Board 499
Brand v. Lewis 447
Brandon v. Holt 174
Brandt v. Board of Education of City of Chicago . 303
Branti v. Finkel 20
Bray v. Alexandria Women's Health Clinic . 9, 10; 26
Brentwood Academy v. Tennessee Secondary School
    Athletic Association 21; 27
Brewster v. Shasta County 224
Brewster; United States v. 79
Bright v. Westmoreland County 60–62
Brillhart v. Excess Insurance Co. 398
Briscoe v. LaHue 26; 99
Briscoe v. Potter 59

Brokaw v. Mercer Co. 10; 112
Brooks v. Vassar 69; 355
Brosseau v. Haugen 109; 123; 127
Brotherton v. Cleveland 225
Brower v. Inyo County 50
Brown v. Board of Education 24; 190; 374
Brown v. Bryan County 242
Brown v. Chote 353; 361
Brown v. Commonwealth of Pennsylvania, Department
    of Health Emergency Medical Services Training
    Institute 246
Brown v. Felsen 421
Brown v. General Motors Corp. 537
Brown v. Grabowski 251
Brown v. Hotel Employees 406
Brown v. Illinois 482
Brown v. Legal Foundation of Washington 431
Brown v. Muhlenberg Township 34
Brown v. Socialist Workers '74 Campaign
    Committee 367
Brown v. Western R. Co. of Alabama . 268; 271, 272;
    274
Brown II 190
Browning-Ferris Industries of Vermont, Inc. v. Kelco
    Disposal, Inc. 318
Bruce v. Beary 231
Bruno, and Aldinger v. Howard 188; 248; 254
Buckhannon Bd. & Care Home, Inc. v. W. Va. Dep't of
    Health & Human Res. 492
Buckley v. Fitzsimmons 90; 307
Buckley v. Fitzsimmons 91
Bunting v. Mellen 109; 354
Burch v. Appalachee Community Mental Health
    Services, Inc. 42
Burford v. Sun Oil Co. 388; 412
Burlington, City of v. Dague 512
Burnett v. Grattan 256, 257; 269
Burns v. Reed 92; 94, 95; 307
Burton v. Richmond 112
Burton v. Wilmington Parking Authority 26, 27
Bush v. Lucas 72
Bush v. Schiavo 456
Bushnell v. Rossetti 292
Butts v. County of Volusia 250
Butz v. Economou 88, 89; 91; 98, 99; 101; 103

C

C.I.R. v. (see name of defendant) . . . .
Cain v. Darby Borough 297
Califano v. Sanders 451; 453
California v. Grace Brethren Church 374
Cameron v. Johnson 403
Campbell v. Haverhill 256; 259

TABLE OF CASES

[References are to pages]

Cannon v. University of Chicago 71
Canton, City of v. Harris 217; 227; 241, 242
Caplin & Drysdale v. United States 339
Carbonell v. INS 523
Carey v. Piphus 262; 266; 300; 302; 472; 475
Carlson v. Green 72; 266, 267; 312
Carpenters, Local 610 v. Scott 10
Carrasca v. Pomeroy 311
Carringer v. Rodgers 267
Carswell v. Borough of Homestead 232
Carter v. Greenhow 68, 69
Casey and Arlington Central School District Board of Education v. Murphy 516
Castle Rock, Town of v. Gonzales 62; 388
Cedar Shake and Shingle Bureau v. City of Los Angeles 385
Celotex Corp. v. Catrett 126
Central Virginia Community College v. Katz . . . 177
Cervantes v. Jones 99
Chandler v. Roudebush 440
Chapman v. Houston Welfare Rights Organization . 259
Chardon v. Fernandez 265
Chase Brexton Health Services v. Maryland . 392; 399
Chattanooga Foundry & Pipe Works v. Atlanta . . 256
Chavez v. Martinez 51
Chemical Producers and Distributors Ass'n v. Helliker 345
Cherry, State ex rel. v. Burns 288
Chevron Oil Co. v. Huson 202; 209
Chicago, City of v. International College of Surgeons 458
Chisholm v. Georgia 132; 134; 139
Christiansburg Garment Co. v. EEOC 491
Christy v. Pennsylvania Turnpike Commission . . 148
Church v. City of Huntsville 338; 361
Church of Scientology of Cal. v. United States . . 342
Ciraolo v. City of New York 327
City and County of (see name of city and county) . .
City of (see name of city) . . . .
Clark v. Barnard 159; 162
Clark v. Burger King Corp. 366
Clarke v. Securities Industry Association 336
Classic; United States v. 4; 11
Clay v. Sun Insurance Office, Ltd. 386; 392
Clay v. United States 425
Clay Regional Water v. City of Spirit Lake 399
Cleveland Board of Education v. LaFleur . . 182; 206
Cleveland Board of Education v. Loudermill . 66; 431
Cleavinger v. Saxner 89
Clinton v. Jones 106
Coalition for Basic Human Needs v. King 502
Codd v. Velger 32
Cody v. Hillard 503
Cohens v. Virginia 140, 141

Coleman v. Kaye 224
Coleman v. Thompson 443
College Savings Bank v. Florida Prepaid Postsecondary Education Expense Board 164
Collins v. Harker Heights 57
Colorado River Water District v. United States . . 390
Columbia Basin Apartment Association v. City of Pasco 385
Commonwealth of (see name of commonwealth) . . .
Communities for Equity v. Michigan High School Athletic Association 71
Comprehensive Drug Testing, Inc.; United States v. 366
Connally v. General Construction Co. 122
Cooey v. Strickland 265; 329; 468
Cook County v. United States ex rel. Chandler . . 191; 326
Cooper v. Pate 463
Cooper Industries, Inc. v. Leatherman Tool Group, Inc. 318
Coopers & Lybrand v. Livesay 358
Corbitt v. New Jersey 290
Cordi-Allen v. Conlon 62
Correctional Services Corp. v. Malesko 72
Cort v. Ash 71
County of (see name of county) . . . .
Covington v. City of New York 488
Cowles v. Mercer County 186; 192
Cozzo v. Tangipahoa Parish Council-President Government 48
Craig v. Boren 61
Crane v. Texas 224
Crawford-El v. Britton 12; 124–126; 282
Crete v. City of Lowell 241
Cross v. New York City Transit Authority 328
Crossman v. Marcoccio 529
Crowder v. Housing Authority of City of Atlanta . 351
Crowe v. Bolduc 203
Cruz v. Farquharson 360
Cunningham v. Gates 479
Curley v. Klem 127
Curley v. Village of Suffern 246, 247
Currie v. Group Insurance Commission 388
Currier v. Doran 124
Curtis v. Loether 277, 278; 283; 288
Cuyler v. Sullivan 21

D

D.H.L Associates v. O'Gorman 345
D.T. v. Independent School District 19
Dababnah v. West Virginia Bd. of Medicine 411
DaimlerChrysler Corp. v. Cuno 339, 340; 375
Dang Vang v. Vang Xiong X. Toyed 15, 16

TABLE OF CASES

[References are to pages]

Daniels v. Williams 34; 41; 282
Dannenberg v. Valadez 518
Davidson v. Cannon 37
Davis v. Michigan Department of Treasury 202
Davis v. Monroe County Board of Education 71
Davis v. Passman 72
Davis v. Rennie 320
Davis v. Schifone 475
Davis v. United States 397
Davison v. City of Minneapolis 216
Dawes v. Walker 373
Deakins v. Monaghan 416; 488
Dean v. Olibas 319
DeFunis v. Odegaard 333; 362
Delaware State College v. Ricks 265
Delgado v. Jones 126
Dellmuth v. Muth 171; 175
Dennis v. Higgins 69; 437
Dennis v. Sparks 24
Deposit Bank v. Frankfort 427
Deposit Guaranty Nat. Bank v. Roper 358
DeShaney v. Winnebago County Dep't of Social Servs. 53
Diamond "D" Const. Corp. v. McGowan 411
Diffenderfer v. Central Baptist Church of Miami, Inc. 342
Dill v. City of Edmond 224
DiMarco-Zappa v. Cabanillas 127
Dionne v. Bouley 361
Dirrane v. Brookline Police Department 190
District of Columbia Court of Appeals v. Feldman . 454
District of Columbia Hosp. Ass'n v. District of Columbia 426
DLX, Inc. v. Kentucky 432
Doe v. Bolton 400
Doe v. Taylor Independent Schools 19, 20
Doe v. McMillan 80
Doe v. Stincer 366
Doe v. Tangipahoa Parish School Board 375
Dombrowski v. Pfister 394
Donovan v. City of Dallas 397
Doran v. Salem Inn, Inc. 337; 401; 403; 405
Dotson v. Chester 218
Double Oak Construction Co. v. Cornerstone Development 491
Douglas v. California 339; 402
Dow Jones, Inc. v. Kaye 349
Dowd, Anderson ex rel. v. City of Boston 304
Dubuc v. Green Oak Township 503
Duke Power Co. v. Carolina Environmental Study Group 336
Dupasseur v. Rochereau 427
Duvall v. County of Kitsap 224
Dykes v. Hosemann 34

E

E.W. Audet & Sons v. Firemen's Fund Ins. 426
Eastland v. United States Servicemen's Fund 80
Eaton Vance Corporation Securities Litigation, In re 360
Edelman v. Jordan 148; 159–161; 163; 165; 167
Edmonson v. Leesville Concrete Co. 26, 27
Educadores Puertorriquenos en Accion v. Hernandez 124
Edwards v. Balisok 302; 475; 490
EEOC v. Commercial Office Products Co. 443
Eggar v. City of Livingston 224
Eidson v. State of Tennessee Department of Children Services 488; 490
Elder v. Holloway 126
Elk Grove Unified School District v. Newdow . . 338
Elkins v. Moreno 388
Elliott v. Perez 123
Ellis v. University of Kansas Medical Center . . . 536
Ellison v. Garbarino 42
Elrod v. Burns 336
Employees of the Department of Public Health & Welfare v. Department of Public Health & Welfare 163, 164
England v. Louisiana Board of Medical Examiners 386; 428; 432; 433
Engquist v. Oregon Department of Agriculture . . . 62
Erie Railroad Co. v. Tompkins 263; 271; 274
Estate of (see name of party) . . . .
Estelle v. Gamble 35; 51
Evans v. Jeff D. 492, 493; 516; 530
Ewing v. Mytinger & Casselberry, Inc. 29
Ewolski v. City of Brunswick 246
Ex parte (see name of relator) . . . .
Ex rel. (see name of relator) . . . .
Executive Arts Studio, Inc. v. City of Grand Rapids 415
Exxon Mobil Corp. v. Allapattah Services, Inc. . . 251
Exxon Mobil Corp. v. Saudi Basic Industries Corp. 419; 425; 454
Exxon Shipping Co. v. Baker 318

F

Fagan v. City of Vineland 246
Fahey v. Mallonee 29
Fair Assessment in Real Estate Ass'n v. McNary . 373; 438
Fairfax Covenant Church v. Fairfax County School Board 203
Fairley v. Luman 247
Farber v. City of Paterson 10
Farella v. Hockaday 519
Farmer v. Brennan 51; 114; 120, 121; 231; 465

TABLE OF CASES

[References are to pages]

Farrar v. Hobby 303; 493; 509, 510
Fay v. Parker 315
FDIC v. Meyer 72
Federal Maritime Commission v. South Carolina State Ports Authority 146
Federation of African-American Contractors v. Oakland 250
Felder v. Casey 267
Feltner v. Columbia Pictures Television, Inc. . 277–279; 282
Fenner v. Boykin 394
Fields v. Office of Eddie Bernice Johnson 79
Finley v. United States 251
First English Evangelical Lutheran Church of Glendale v. County of Los Angeles 284
Fitzpatrick v. Bitzer . . . 159; 166, 167; 170; 186; 192
Flagg Bros. v. Brooks 25
Flast v. Cohen 339
Florida Department of Health & Rehabilitative Services v. Florida Nursing Home Association 162
Florida Public Interest Research Group Citizen Lobby, Inc. v. EPA 426
Ford Motor Co. v. Department of Treasury . 149, 150; 152; 154; 162; 165
Foreman v. Dallas County 501
Fornaris v. Ridge Tool Co. 392
Forrester v. White 79; 88; 91
Forty-One News, Inc. v. County of Lake 415
Forum for Academic and Institutional Rights v. Rumsfeld 366, 367
Fountain v. Talley 121
Fox v. DeSoto 490
Francis v. City of Columbus 438
Franklin v. Gwinnett County Public Schools 71
Freedom Baptist Church of Delaware County v. Township of Middletown 73
Frew v. Hawkins 156, 157
Friends of Earth, Inc. v. Laidlaw Environmental Services (TOC), Inc. 494; 500
Friends of the Earth, Inc. v. Chevron Chemical Co. . 368
Friery v. Los Angeles Unified School District . . . 387
Frontier Insurance Co. v. Blaty 267
Fuentes v. Shevin 25; 29
Fumero Soto 257; 264
Fund Democracy, LLC v. S.E.C. 368
Fusari v. Steinberg 343

G

Galbraith v. County of Santa Clara 124
Garcetti v. Ceballos 53
Garcia v. San Antonio Metropolitan Transit Authority 171; 176
Gardner v. New Jersey 162
Garner v. Memphis Police Department 225

Gates v. Collier 116; 121
Gauger v. Hendle 489
General Atomic Co. v. Felter 397
Georgia; United States v. 179
Gernetzke v. Kenosha Unified School District No. 1 190
Gerstein v. Pugh 357; 361
Gertz v. Robert Welch, Inc. 300
Gibson v. Berryhill 404; 406; 447
Gibson v. City of Chicago 247
Gibson v. Superintendent of New Jersey Department of Law and Public Safety Division 52; 311
Gilbert v. Homar 32
Gilbrook v. City of Westminster 492
Glazner v. Glazner 203
Gobel v. Maricopa County 224
Gobert v. Williams 515
Gold v. City of Miami 242
Goldberg v. Kelly 32; 64; 151
Golden State Transit Corp. v. Los Angeles 66
Goldin v. Bartholow 351; 356
Goldstein v. Long Beach 98
Gomez v. Toledo 103; 123
Gonzaga University v. Doe 70
Gonzalez v. Crosby 468
Gonzalez v. Kokot 297
Goodson v. McDonough Power Equipment, Inc. . . 427
Goss v. Lopez 64; 190
Government & Civic Employees Organizing Committee, C.I.O. v. Windsor 429
Graham v. Connor 49; 111; 123; 490
Graham v. Richardson 151
Grand Rapids, School District of City of v. Ball . 340
Gratz v. Bollinger 359
Gravel v. United States 79, 80; 102
Gray v. Laws 10
Gray-Hopkins v. Prince George's County 129
Great Lakes Dredge & Dock Co. v. Huffman . . . 397
Grech v. Clayton County 224
Green v. County School Board 188
Green v. Mansour 155, 156
Greenholtz v. Inmates of Nebraska Penal and Correctional Complex 33
Gregoire v. Biddle 103
Gregory v. Louisville 51
Gregory v. Shelby County 319
Gregory v. Thompson 84
Grier v. Galinac 251
Griffey v. Lindsey 352
Griffin Industries v. Irvin 61
Griffith v. Kentucky 202
Griggs v. Duke Power Co. 442
Groh v. Ramirez 122, 123

Gros v. City of Grand Prairie 241
Guaranty Trust Co. v. York 271, 272; 274
Gulfstream Aerospace v. Mayacamas 385
Gurley; United States v. 426
Gutierrez-Rodriguez v. Soto 320
Gutter v. Seamandel 270

H

Hadix v. Johnson 509; 519
Hafer v. Melo 173, 174
Hagans v. Lavine 520
Hager v. City of West Peoria 376
Haines v. Kerner 463
Halbert v. Michigan 339; 402
Hall v. Ochs 297
Hall v. Unum Life Insurance Company of America . 352
Hamilton v. City of Overland Park 261
Hamilton v. Leavy 129
Hampton v. Chicago 93
Hanrahan v. Hampton 493; 499
Hans v. Louisiana 132; 135, 136; 141
Hansen v. Soldenwagner 112
Hardeman v. City of Albuquerque 320
Hardin v. Straub 264
Hare v. City of Corinth 231
Harlow v. Fitzgerald 93; 100; 113
Harper v. Public Service Commission of West
  Virginia 390; 409; 416; 459
Harper v. Virginia Department of Taxation 202
Harper, Harper ex rel. v. Poway Unified School
  District 350
Harris v. Coweta County 50; 129
Harris v. District of Columbia 201
Harris v. Ford Motor Co. 425
Harris v. McRae 55
Harrison v. NAACP 383
Hartman v. Moore 52; 304; 489
Harvey v. Harvey 42
Hathaway v. Worcester City Hosp. 190
Hawaii Housing Authority v. Midkiff . . 285; 403; 406
Haywood v. Drown 276
Heart of America Grain Inspection Serv., Inc. v.
  Missouri Dep't of Agriculture 69
Heck v. Humphrey . 264, 265; 278; 282; 306; 402; 420;
  469; 482
Hein v. Freedom of Religion Foundation, Inc. . 340; 375
Henderson v. Stalder 375; 377, 378
Hensley v. Eckerhart 493; 510
Hensley v. Municipal Court 460
Hess v. Port Authority Trans-Hudson Corp. 147
Hessel v. O'Hearn 303
Hewitt v. Helms 33

Hi Tech Trans LLC v. New Jersey 385; 411
Hiatt v. County of Adams 363
Hibbs v. Winn 178, 179; 373
Hicks v. Miranda 403
Hill v. McDonough 329; 467
Holmberg v. Armbrecht 265; 329
Holmes v. Crosby 89
Holmes v. Pension Plan of Bethlehem Steel Corp. . 360
Home Tel. & Tel. Co. v. City of Los Angeles . 2; 13; 153
Honda Motor, Ltd. v. Oberg 318
Honig v. Doe 338; 362
Hope v. Pelzer 112; 205
Hopkins v. Andaya 246
Houghton v. Shafer 463
Houston Chronicle Publishing Co. v. City of League
  City 355
Houston, City of v. Hill 337; 383; 387
Howard v. Grinage 231
Howard v. Lawton 449
Howard, Howard ex rel. Estate of v. Bayes 65
Howlett v. Rose 276; 329; 428; 458
Hubbard v. Taylor 351
Hudson v. City of New Orleans 224
Hudson v. Hudson 65
Hudson v. McMillian 114; 120
Hudson v. Michigan 498
Hudson v. Palmer 11; 33
Huffman v. Pursue, Ltd. 402; 406; 408
Hughes v. Rowe 491; 529
Hulen v. Yates 129
Hulin v. Fibreboard Corp. 203
Hunt v. Washington State Apple Advertising
  Comm'n 364; 367
Hurley v. Kincaid 284
Hutchinson v. Proxmire 80
Hutto v. Finney . . 154, 155; 157; 165; 167; 174; 521

I

IBEW v. Public Service Commission 378; 412
Imbler v. Pachtman 91; 93–95; 97, 98; 266; 291
In re (see name of party) . . . .
Ingraham v. Wright 33; 35; 44
Instructional Systems, Inc. v. Computer Curriculum
  Corp. 430
International College of Surgeons v. City of
  Chicago 48; 251; 385; 416; 448
International Ground Transportation v. Mayor and City
  Council of Ocean City 247
Interoceanica Corp. v. Sound Pilots, Inc. 428
Irby v. Sullivan 70
Ismail v. Cohen 251
Ivy Club v. Edwards 430

TABLE OF CASES

[References are to pages]

J

J.I. Case Co. v. Borak	71
Jackson v. Leavitt	352
Jackson v. State Bd. of Alabama State Tenure Commission	70
Jackson v. State Bd. of Pardons and Paroles	518
Jacobsen; United States v.	26
James B. Beam Distilling Co. v. Georgia	203
Jefferson v. City of Tarrant	267
Jeffes v. Barnes	216; 224
Jeffries v. Harleston	218
Jenkins v. City of New York	428
Jennifer, Christina A. ex rel. v. Bloomberg	518; 523
Jennings v. Metropolitan Government of Nashville	536
Jett v. Dallas Independent School District	9; 216, 217; 250; 254
Jett v. Dallas Independent School District	216
Jinks v. Richland County	459
JMM, Corp. v. District of Columbia	415
Jocks v. Tavernier	18
Johnson v. Board of Regents of University of Georgia	304
Johnson v. California	51
Johnson v. City of Lincoln Park	246
Johnson v. Daley	509; 518, 519
Johnson v. Fankell	127; 276
Johnson v. Georgia Highway Express, Inc.	504, 505
Johnson v. Jones	128
Johnson v. Outboard Marine Corp.	174
Johnson v. Railway Express Agency, Inc.	260
Johnson v. Zerbst	164
Jones v. Alfred H. Mayer Co.	9
Jones v. Allen	329
Jones v. Bock	124; 447
Jones v. City of Los Angeles	338
Jones v. Cunningham	460
Jones v. Hildebrant	267
Jones v. Loving	76
Jones v. R.R. Donnelley & Sons Co.	263
Jones v. Reynolds	60
Jones v. Taber	292
Jordan v. Fox, Rothschild, O'Brien Frankel	107
Jordan v. Time, Inc.	529
Juidice v. Vail	406; 408; 418

K

Kalina v. Fletcher	97–99; 282
Karcher v. May	347; 349–352
Kawananakoa v. Polyblank	144
Kawaoka v. City of Arroyo Grande	218
Kaylor v. Fields	419
Kelly v. Serna	266
Kennecot Copper Corp. v. State Tax Commission	162
Kennedy v. City of Ridgefield	60
Kenosha, City of v. Bruno	183; 188; 190
Kentucky v. Graham	173, 174
Kilbourn v. Thompson	76
Kimel v. Florida Board of Regents	177, 178
King v. One Unknown Federal Correctional Officer	266
King v. Smith	152
Kirsch v. Fleet St., Ltd.	510
Klein; United States v.	370
Koblan; United States v.	352
Kohl v. United States	284
Kokkonen v. Guardian Life Ins. Co.	252; 493; 523
Kolstad v. American Dental Association	328
Kontrick v. Ryan	425
Koulta v. Merciez	60
Kowalski v. Tesmer	339; 402, 403
Kremer v. Chemical Construction Corp.	428; 439
Kutschbach v. Davies	363

L

L&W Supply v. Acuity	516
Lake Country Estates, Inc. v. Tahoe Regional Planning Agency	76; 79; 146, 147
Lance v. Dennis	426; 456
Lanier; United States v.	11; 16; 18; 110; 114, 115; 117
Lanzetta v. New Jersey	122
Lapides v. Board of Regents	162; 172; 458
LaRouche v. Kezer	501
Larson v. Snow College	264
Lawrence v. Blackwell	362
Leatherman v. Tarrant County Narcotics Intelligence & Coordination Unit	123
Lee v. Edwards	319
Legal Services Corp. v. Velazquez	538
Leon; United States v.	122
Leonard v. Robinson	309
Lewis v. Casey	372
Lewis v. Continental Bank Corp.	501
Libertarian Party of Ohio v. Blackwell	361, 362
Lincoln County v. Luning	146; 186; 192; 384; 453
Lingle v. Chevron U.S.A.	434; 436
Lindsey v. Normet	55
Linkletter v. Walker	202
Lippoldt v. Cole	512
Livingstone v. North Belle Vernon Borough	297
Local No. 93, Int'l Assn. of Firefighters, AFL-CIO v. Cleveland	523
Logan v. Zimmerman Brush Company	47
Lombardi v. Whitman	58; 60, 61
Lorillard v. Pons	277
Los Angeles v. Heller	243
Los Angeles, City of v. Lyons	191; 311; 329

TABLE OF CASES

[References are to pages]

Los Angeles County v. Rettele 109
Los Angeles Police Protective League v. Gates . . 191
Louisiana Acorn Housing v. LeBlanc 321
Louisiana Debating and Literary Ass'n v. City of New Orleans 385
Louisiana Power & Light Co. v. City of Thibodaux . 392
Louisville R. Co. v. Letson 186; 192
Lugar v. Edmondson Oil Co. 13; 21; 327
Lujan v. Defenders of Wildlife 63; 335
Lyes v. City of Riviera Beach 10
Lynch v. Baxley 338; 361
Lynch v. City of Alhambra 297
Lynch v. Johnson 84
Lytle v. Doyle 232

M

M'Cluny v. Silliman 259
Maestri v. Jutkofsky 88
Maher v. Gagne 493, 494; 520
Maine v. Thiboutot 68, 69; 259; 263; 521, 522
Malley v. Briggs 91; 93; 95; 99; 109; 119
Manders v. Lee 243
Mansfield, C. & L. M. R. Co. v. Swan 495
Marbury v. Madison 395
Marek v. Chesny 524; 532
Markman v. Westview Instruments, Inc. . 278; 280; 283; 287
Marsh v. Alabama 27
Marsh v. Butler County 110
Marshall v. Columbia Lea Regional Hospital . . . 311
Marshall v. Marshall 425
Martin v. Heckler 501
Martin v. Stewart 390
Martin v. Wilks 428
Martinez v. California 39; 41; 55; 60; 269; 273
Martinez v. City of Albuquerque 481
Massachusetts Board of Retirement v. Murgia . . . 61
Massachusetts, Personnel Administrator of v. Feeney 61
Mathews v. Crosby 51
Mathews v. Eldridge 44; 447
Mathie v. Fries 320
Maynard v. Wooley 428
McAlester v. Brown 83
McCardle, Ex parte 372
McCarthy v. Madigan 447
McCarthy; State v. 245
McClaine v. Rankin 256
McGautha v. California 290, 291
McKart v. United States 447
McKay v. Hammock 262

McKesson Corp. v. Division of Alcoholic Beverages and Tobacco, Fla. Dept. of Business Regulation 141; 146; 437
McKinley v. City of Mansfield 51
McKinley v. Kaplan 356
McLaughlin v. City of Canton 225
McMann v. Richardson 352
McMann v. Ross 352
McMillian v. Monroe 147; 218
McNair v. Allen 265
McNamara v. City of Rittman 34; 42
McNeese v. Board of Education 257
Meachum v. Fano 33
Meals v. City of Memphis 49
Mellen v. Bunting 354
Memphis Community School Dist. v. Stachura . . 278; 282; 299; 303; 322; 372
Memphis Light, Gas & Water Div. v. Craft 64
Memphis, Tennessee Area Local American Postal Workers Union, AFL-CIO v. Memphis 18
Mercer v. Duke University 512
Mesquite, City of v. Aladdin's Castle, Inc. . . 341; 344
Meyer v. Grant 361
Meyers v. Texas 162
Michau v. Charleston County 448
Michigan High School Athletic Association v. Communities for Equity 71
Middlesex County Ethics Committee v. Garden State Bar Ass'n 410
Middlesex County Sewage Authority v. National Sea Clammers 70
Migra v. Warren City School Dist. Bd. of Education 421; 458
Miller v. Davis 89
Miller v. French 368; 426; 443
Milliken v. Bradley 154; 156; 186
Mills v. Electric Auto-Lite Co. 499
Mink v. Suthers 97
Minneapolis & St. Louis R.R. Co. v. Bombolis . . 288
Minnesota Dog Clubs v. City of Minneapolis . . . 225
Minnesota Rate Cases 153
Miranda Violations. Violations of Miranda v. Arizona 51; 205
Mireles v. Waco 88
Mismash v. Murray City 261
Missouri v. Jenkins 175; 516; 522
Mitchell v. Donchin 264
Mitchell v. Forsyth . 97; 106; 109, 110; 114; 124; 127; 148; 276
Mitchell v. W. T. Grant Co. 25; 44
Mitchum v. Foster 78; 167, 168; 257; 378; 404
Mobil Oil Corp. v. Rocky River 407

TABLE OF CASES

[References are to pages]

Monaco v. Stone 362, 363
Monaghan v. Deakins 419
Monell v. New York City Dept. of Social Services . 165; 167, 168; 182
Monessen Southwestern R. Co. v. Morgan 271
Monroe v. Pape . 1; 165; 167; 181; 257–259; 278; 282; 459
Monterey, City of v. Del Monte Dunes, Ltd. . . 276; 431
Moor v. County of Alameda 183; 188; 250
Moore v. Ogilvie 353; 361
Moore v. Sims 406; 408
Moose Lodge v. Irvis 27
Morales v. TWA, Inc. 419
Morel v. Giuliani 363
Morris v. Crawford County 241
Morris v. Eversley 518
Morros; United States v. 383
Morse v. Frederick 107
Moses H. Cone Memorial Hospital v. Mercury Construction Co. 385; 390
Mt. Healthy City School District Board of Education v. Doyle 52; 146; 303
Muckleshoot Tribe v. Puget Sound Power & Light Co. 536
Mueller v. Allen 374
Muhammad v. Close 465; 476
Mullane v. Central Hanover Trust Co. 29
Munsingwear, Inc.; United States v. 343; 346
Murphy v. Fort Worth Independent School District . 351
Murray v. Wilson Distilling Co. 160
Murtagh v. County of Berks 438

N

N.Y. State Bd. of Elections v. Lopez Torres 366
NAACP v. Alabama ex rel. Patterson 364; 367
Nader v. Keith 415, 416
Nantahala Power & Light Co. v. Thornburg 412
National Black Police Association v. District of Columbia 356
National Collegiate Athletic Association v. Tarkanian 27
National League of Cities v. Usery . 164; 176; 186; 192
National Private Truck Council v. Oklahoma Tax Commission 373; 438
Nectow v. Cambridge 287
Neinast v. Texas 376
Nelson v. Campbell 266; 465
Nelson v. Jashurek 481
Nerness v. Johnson 448
Nevada v. Hall 132, 133
New Directions Treatment Services v. City of Reading 363
New Orleans Public Services, Inc. v. Council of City of New Orleans 378; 388; 409; 411; 450; 458

New York, Ex parte 136
Newman v. Piggie Park Enterprises, Inc. 499
Newport, City of v. Fact Concerts . 203; 258; 312; 320; 322
Newton v. Merrill, Lynch, Pierce, Fenner & Smith, Inc. 358
Newton v. Rumery 289
Nicholson v. Scoppetta 385; 388
Nix v. Norman 191
Nixon v. Fitzgerald 101; 103; 106
Nixon v. Herndon 301
Nobby Lobby, Inc. v. City of Dallas 191
Norita v. Northern Mariana Islands 148
Norman v. Reed 361
North American Cold Storage Co. v. Chicago 29
Northeastern Florida Chapter of Associated General Contractors of America v. City of Jacksonville . 311; 336; 341; 356; 500
Northern Insurance Co. v. Chatham County . 146, 147
Norwood v. Bain 303
Norwood v. Harrison 26
Novitsky v. City of Aurora 126
Nydam v. Lennerton 320

O

O'Bannon v. Town Court Nursing Center 63
O'Brien v. City of Greers Ferry 529
O'Connor v. Donaldson 45
O'Shea v. Littleton 330
O'Sullivan v. Felix 259
Office of Senator Mark Dayton v. Hanson 79
Ohio Adult Parole Authority v. Woodard 33
Ohio Bureau of Employment Services v. Hodory . 383; 406
Ohio Civil Rights Commission v. Dayton Christian Schools 337; 404
Oil, Chemical & Atomic Workers, International Union AFL-CIO v. Department of Energy 524
Oklahoma City, City of v. Tuttle 192; 207; 226
Ort v. White 113; 116; 120
Oscar Mayer & Co. v. Evans 443
Outdoor Media Group v. City of Beaumont 500
Ove v. Gwinn 475
Overstreet v. Lexington-Fayette Urban County Government 425
Owen v. City of Independence 170; 195
Owens v. Okure 263

P

Pace v. Bogalusa City School Board . . 164; 172; 175
Pacific Mutual Life Insurance Co. v. Haslip 317
Padelford; United States v. 370
Padgett v. Nicholson 352

TABLE OF CASES

[References are to pages]

Palazzolo v. Rhode Island 431
Panola Land Buying Association v. Clark 538
Papasan v. Allain 156
Parden v. Terminal Railway 163
Parham v. Southwestern Bell Telephone Co. . . 494, 495
Parker v. Williams 15; 223
Parklane Hosiery Co. v. Shore 427
Parratt v. Taylor 28; 63; 431; 435
Parsons v. Bedford 278
Paschal v. Flagstar Bank 509
Patsy v. Board of Regents . . 162, 163; 271; 275; 329;
    406; 410; 435; 443; 452; 469; 471
Patterson v. Balsamico 318; 320, 321
Patterson v. McLean Credit Union 9
Patterson v. Von Riesen 89
Paul v. Davis 20; 32
Paul v. Virginia 189
Payne v. Milwaukee County 529
Peacock v. Thomas 252
Pearson v. Callahan 109
Pembaur v. City of Cincinnati 206
Pennhurst State School and Hospital v.
    Halderman 157; 160; 175; 383; 452, 453
Pennsylvania v. Delaware Valley Citizens' Council for
    Clean Air 145
Pennsylvania v. Union Gas Co. 170; 176
Pennsylvania Psychiatric Society v. Green Springs
    Health Services, Inc. 366
Pennzoil Co. v. Texaco, Inc. 383; 408
Perez v. Ledesma 397
Perez v. Oakland County 51
Perry v. Sindermann 64; 195
Peters v. Village of Clifton 437
Peyton v. Rowe 461
Philip Morris USA v. Williams 318
Pierce v. Society of Sisters 338
Pierson v. Ray 82; 87; 91; 99; 105; 258
Pinder v. Johnson 60
Planned Parenthood of Dutchess-Ulster v.
    Steinhaus 385
Plaut v. Spendthrift Farm, Inc. 369
Plaut and Hayburn's Case 369
Polite v. Diehl 258
Polk County v. Dodson 20; 99
Port Authority Trans-Hudson Corp. v. Feeney . . . 162
Porter v. Nussle 443
Potomac Electric Power Co. v. Sachs 419
Pottgen v. Missouri State High School Activities
    Association 501
Powell v. Alexander 174
Powers v. Hamilton County Public Defender
    Commission 362; 478
Preiser v. Rodriguez 403; 459; 475
Prigg v. Pennsylvania 184

Princeton Univ. v. Schmid 342; 344, 345
Principality of Monaco v. Mississippi 136; 146
Procunier v. Navarette 104
Propper v. Clark 383
Provost v. City of Newburgh 321
Pruitt v. City of Chicago 362
Public Util. Comm'n of Ohio v. United Fuel Gas
    Co. 389
Public Works v. Columbia College 424
Puerto Rico Aqueduct & Sewer Authority v. Metcalf &
    Eddy, Inc. 147, 148
Pujol v. Shearson/American Express, Inc. 426
Pulliam v. Allen 89; 290; 361

Q

Quackenbush v. Allstate Insurance Co. . . 389; 392; 419;
    451
Quern v. Jordan 155; 160; 165; 201
Quint v. A.E. Staley Mfg. Co. 516
Quintanilla v. City of Downey 246

R

Railroad Com. of Texas v. Pullman Co. . . 381; 428; 432
Rancho Palos Verdes, City of v. Abrams . . . 70; 263
Randall v. Brigham 81
Rayburn Office Building; United States v. 80
Raygor v. Regents of the University of Minnesota . 453;
    459
Regents of the University of California v. Doe . . 147
Regents of University of Michigan v. Ewing 48
Region 8 Forest Service Timber Purchasers Council v.
    Alcock 368
Remus Joint Venture v. McAnally 354; 426
Rendell-Baker v. Kohn 27
Revere, City of v. Massachusetts Gen. Hospital . 48; 51;
    228; 338
Reynolds v. Giuliani 191
Reynolds v. Sims 498
Reynolds; United States v. 279; 284
Reynoldsville Casket Co. v. Hyde 203
Rhodes v. Chapman 114; 118
Rhodes v. Stewart 500
Richardson v. McKnight 106, 107
Richlin Security Service Co. v. Chertoff 517
Richman v. Sheahan 89
Richmond v. J.A. Croson Co. 329; 500
Riley v. Kurtz 518
Rio Grande Community Health Center, Inc. v.
    Rullan 408; 414
River City Capital v. Board of County
    Commissioners 42
Rivera v. La Porte 18
Rivers v. McLeod 419

TABLE OF CASES

[References are to pages]

Riverside v. Rivera	504
Riverside, County of v. McLaughlin	361
Rizzo v. Goode	187; 194; 331
Robbins v. Chronister	518
Robertson v. Wegmann	260, 261; 266; 273
Robinson v. Kansas	411
Robinson v. Moore	246
Rochin v. California	48; 55
Rockstead v. City of Crystal Lake	431
Roe v. Humke	19
Roe v. Wade	31; 48; 358; 360, 361; 367; 400
Romero-Barcelo v. Hernandez-Agosto	80
Rooker v. Fidelity Trust Co.	452; 454
Rosado v. Wyman	152
Rosario v. Rockefeller	361
Ross v. Bernhard	288
Rossi v. Gemma	399; 420
Rothstein v. Wyman	149–151
Royal Towing, Inc. v. City of Harvey	458
Ruckelshaus v. Monsanto Co.	435
Ruggiero v. County of Orange	443
Runyon v. McCrary	9; 256; 259

S

Sacramento County v. Lewis	48; 58; 108; 287
Saldana-Sanchez v. Lopez-Gerena	328
Salerno; United States v.	206
Samuels v. Mackell	393; 397
San Francisco Arts & Athletics, Inc. v. U.S. Olympic Committee	27
San Remo Hotel L.P. v. City and County of San Francisco	47, 48; 430; 432; 437
Sandin v. Conner	33; 465
Santa Fe Independent School District v. Doe	367
Santini v. Connecticut Hazardous Waste Management Services	432
Saucier v. Katz	108; 111; 113, 114; 118
Scarborough v. Principi	491
Scarbrough v. Morgan City Board of Education	217
Scheuer v. Rhodes	101; 105, 106
Schindler, Schiavo ex rel. v. Schiavo	457
Schneider v. Colegio de Abrogadas de Puerto Rico	386
Schweiker v. Chilicky	72; 157
Scott v. Harris	49; 109; 129
Scott-Harris v. City of Fall River	218
Screws v. United States	4; 6; 11
Select Milk Producers v. Johanns	349; 502
Seminole Tribe of Fla. v. Florida	131; 136–138; 153; 157, 158; 161; 170; 175, 176; 522
Shamaeizadeh v. Cunigan	488
Shelley v. Kraemer	26
Shelton v. Tucker	367
Siegert v. Gilley	32; 108; 123; 125
Sierra Club v. Glickman	352
Simon v. Eastern Kentucky Welfare Rights Organization	360
Skinner v. Uphoff	519
Skoog v. County of Clackamas	310
Slagenweit v. Slagenweit	349
Smalbein, Smalbein ex rel. Estate of v. City of Daytona Beach	536
Smith v. Allwright	27
Smith v. City of Enid	69
Smith v. Colorado Department of Corrections	34
Smith v. Holtz	488
Smith v. Jackson	475
Smith v. Reeves	136
Smith v. Robinson	70
Smith v. Wade	262; 300; 311
Smyth v. Rivero	502; 523
Sniadach v. Family Finance Corp.	25
Soldal v. Cook County	25
Sole v. Wyner	503
Sorrels v. McKee	126
Sosna v. Iowa	163; 357; 359; 406
South Dakota v. Dole	164
Southern California Gas Co. v. City of Santa Ana	69
Spalding v. Vilas	101
Spallone v. United States	77
Spencer v. Kemna	476, 477; 485
Springfield v. Kibbe	214; 226
Springfield, City of v. Kibbe	226
St. George v. Pinellas County	126
St. Louis v. Praprotnik	210; 215; 242; 282
Staley v. Harris County	352
Stanton v. District of Columbia Court of Appeals	428
State v. (see name of defendant)	
State ex rel. (see name of relator)	
State Farm Mutual Automobile Insurance Co. v. Campbell	318
State of (see name of state)	
Steagald v. United States	207
Steffel v. Thompson	337; 399; 405
Stewart v. North Carolina	162
Stone v. Powell	423; 477; 484, 485
Stone v. Wall	385
Storer v. Brown	361
Strickler v. Waters	224
Stroman Realty v. Martinez	403; 410; 415
Stump v. Sparkman	80
Suitum v. Tahoe Regional Planning Agency	435
Sullivan v. Little Hunting Park, Inc.	257; 262
Summers, In re	83
Sumner v. Philadelphia	186
Supreme Court of Virginia v. Consumers Union	79, 80; 98

TABLE OF CASES

[References are to pages]

Suster v. Marshall 353
Suter v. Artist M. 70
Sutton v. Rasheed 109
Swann v. Charlotte-Mecklenburg Bd. of Educ. ... 248
Swiecicki v. Delgado 489
Swift v. Tyson 263
Szabla v. City of Brooklyn Park 232; 241, 242

T

Tacoma v. Taxpayers of Tacoma 426
Taliaferro v. Darby Township Zoning Board 402
Teague v. Lane 202
Teamsters v. Terry 278
Tellier v. Fields 127
Telluride; United States v. 265
Temple v. Marlborough Division of District Court . 34
Tennessee v. Garner 13; 50; 123; 206; 232
Tennessee v. Lane 179
Tenney v. Brandhove 76–79; 166
Tesmer v. Granholm 403
Texas v. Lesage 304; 311; 321; 337
Texas Association of Business v. Earle 419
Texas State Teachers Association v. Garland Independent School District 509
Thomas v. Washington Gas Light Co. 441
Thompson v. Duke 224
Thornhill v. Alabama 394
Time Warner Cable v. Doyle 458
Torromeo v. Town of Fremont 436
Tory v. Cochran 351
Tower v. Glover 10; 91; 99; 418
Town of (see name of town) ....
Townes v. City of New York 233
Township of (see name of township) ....
Trainor v. Hernandez 406; 408
Trevino v. Gates 303
Trop v. Dulles 114
Troxel v. Granville 48
Tull v. United States 277
Turner v. Upton County 218
Turquitt v. Jefferson County 224

U

U.S. Bancorp Mortg. Co. v. Bonner Mall Pshp. . 346; 501–503
Uboh v. Reno 488
Ulrich v. City and County of San Francisco . 216, 217
Union & Planters' Bank v. Memphis 424
Union Oil Company of California v. City of Los Angeles 438
United Airlines, Inc. v. McDonald 358, 359
United Food and Commercial Workers Union Local 751 v. Brown Group, Inc. 357; 364

United Mine Workers v. Gibbs .. 248; 384; 450, 451
United States v. (see name of defendant) ....
United States Parole Commission v. Geraghty . 353; 357
University of Tennessee v. Elliott 439; 458, 459
Urban Developers LLC v. City of Jackson 431

V

Vacca v. Barletta 251
Vakilian v. Shaw 99
Valdez v. City & County of Denver 89
Valero Terrestrial Corp. v. Paige 350
Vallone v. Lee 297
Van Wie v. Pataki 349; 351
Venegas v. Mitchell 515
Village of (see name of village) ....
Virginia v. Rives 168
Virginia; United States v. 51
Virginia, Ex parte 2; 78; 168
Volk v. Gonzalez 518

W

W.T. Grant Co.; United States v. 344
Walker v. Bain 518
Wallace v. Kato . 53; 264; 265; 309; 420; 478; 481; 488
Walling v. James Reuter, Co., Inc. 346
Washington v. Davis 52; 61; 442
Washington v. Summerville 488
Washington v. Washington State Commercial PassengerFishing Vessel Ass'n 426
Washington Legal Foundation v. Legal Foundation of Washington 431
Watkins v. Bowden 52
Watkins v. Mabus 349; 353
Watson v. County of Riverside 503
Wayte; United States v. 52; 308
Weber v. Dell 218
Weiner v. San Diego County 224
Weinstein v. Bradford 362
Wells v. Bonner 481
West v. Atkins 20; 27
West Virginia University Hospitals v. Casey 516
Wexler v. Lepore 415
White v. McKinley 10
White, Grazier ex rel. v. City of Philadephia ... 232
Whitley v. Albers 51; 114; 118
Whren v. United States 311
Wilkie v. Robbins 72
Wilkinson v. Austin 33
Wilkinson v. Dotson 479
Will v. Michigan Department of State Police . 172, 173; 191; 202; 373; 437
Williams v. City of Carl Junction 310

TABLE OF CASES

[References are to pages]

Williams v. Kaufman County 319; 321
Williams v. United States 6
Williamson County Regional Planning Commission v. Hamilton Bank 47; 431, 432
Willowbrook, Village of v. Olech 61
Wilson v. City of Chicago 252; 328
Wilson v. Garcia 255; 272; 459
Wilson v. Layne 110
Wilson v. New York 76
Wilton v. Seven Falls Co. 398
Wilwording v. Swenson 463
Wisconsin v. Yoder 407
Wise v. Fiberglass Systems, Inc. 246
Wolf v. Colorado 5
Wolff v. McDonnell 33
Wood v. Strickland 103; 106, 107; 198
Woodford v. Ngo 444; 465
Wooley v. Maynard 402
Worcester County Trust Co. v. Riley 165
Worth v. Jackson 345
Wright v. Roanoke Redevelopment and Housing Authority 68; 70
Wyatt v. Cole 25; 105–107

Y

Yahoo!, Inc. v. Net Games 509
Yang v. City of Chicago 253
Yarris v. County of Delaware 51; 310
Yee v. Escondido 433, 434; 436
Yick Wo v. Hopkins 55; 61
Ying Jing Gan v. City of New York 224
Young v. City of Providence ex rel. Napolitano . 232; 242; 247
Young v. Harper 33
Young, Ex parte . 150; 152, 153; 166; 328; 393; 397; 453
Youngberg v. Romeo 40; 51
Younger v. Harris . . 98; 339; 378; 388; 392; 454; 462

Z

Zinermon v. Burch 42
Zwickler v. Koota 400

INDEX

[References are to pages.]

A

ATTORNEY'S FEES
American rule . . . 491
Bargaining over fees . . . 524
Consent decrees . . . 519; 522
Contingent fees . . . 514
Eleventh Amendment . . . 521
Enhancements of fee . . . 512
Fee-shifting . . . 492
Law clerks, time expended by . . . 516
Lodestar approach . . . 508
Mootness and . . . 345; 500
Nominal damages and, awarding of . . . 510
Paralegals, time expended by . . . 516
Preliminary injunctions . . . 501
Prevailing parties
    Generally . . . 492
    Nominal damages, awarding of . . . 510
Pro bono representation . . . 516
Public interest organizations . . . 538
Reasonableness of fees . . . 504
Settlements . . . 519; 522
Statutory violations, for . . . 522
Tax consequences of fee shifting under § 1988(b) . . . 517
Waiver of . . . 537

F

FEDERAL ABSTENTION IN FAVOR OF STATE PROCEEDINGS
Anti-Injunction Act . . . 378; 404
Burford abstention . . . 388
Certification to state courts . . . 386
Colorado River Water District abstention . . . 390
Declaratory relief . . . 397
Forcing state court proceedings . . . 383
Legislative and executive state action . . . 411
Money damages, § 1983 claims for . . . 416
Pending state proceedings, deference to . . . 392
Pullman abstention
    Generally . . . 381
    Appeal . . . 385
    Preclusion . . . 428
    Younger abstention comparison with . . . 404
Subsequently filed charges . . . 403
Supplemental jurisdiction . . . 384
Threatened prosecution . . . 399
Younger abstention
    Generally . . . 392
    Administrative proceedings, extension to . . . 410
    Appeal . . . 411
    Bad faith exception . . . 403
    Civil cases, extension to . . . 408

FEDERAL ABSTENTION IN FAVOR OF STATE PROCEEDINGS—Cont.
Younger abstention—Cont.
    Damages action, application to . . . 419
    Grand jury proceedings, applicability to . . . 419
    Inadequate state forum exception . . . 404
    Patently unconstitutional exception . . . 403
    Pullman abstention comparison with . . . 404
    Waiver . . . 411

I

IMMUNITIES, OFFICIAL
Absolute immunity
    Judicial immunity (See subhead: Judicial immunity)
    Legislative immunity (See subhead: Legislative immunity)
    Prosecutorial immunity (See subhead: Prosecutorial immunity)
Injunctive actions
    Judicial immunity . . . 89
    Legislative immunity . . . 80
    Prosecutorial immunity . . . 98
    Qualified immunity . . . 107
Judicial immunity
    Generally . . . 80
    Derivative judicial immunity . . . 89
    Functional approach . . . 88
    Injunctive actions, from . . . 89
    Judicial acts exception . . . 88
    Jurisdiction, clear absence of . . . 87
Legislative immunity
    Generally . . . 75
    Derivative legislative immunity . . . 80
    Functional approach . . . 79
    Injunctive actions, from . . . 80
Municipal immunity
    Generally . . . 195
    Punitive damages and . . . 326
Presidential immunity . . . 106
Prosecutorial immunity
    Generally . . . 90
    Functional approach . . . 98
    Injunctive actions, from . . . 98
    Other actors in judicial process . . . 98
    Scope of . . . 97
Qualified immunity
    Generally . . . 100
    Appeal of denial of . . . 127
    Burden of proof . . . 123
    Clearly established rights, defining . . . 109
    Discovery . . . 124
    Extraordinary circumstances exception . . . 108
    Injunctive actions, from . . . 107
    Pleading requirements, heightened . . . 123
    Presidential immunity . . . 106

[References are to pages.]

IMMUNITIES, OFFICIAL—Cont.
Qualified immunity—Cont.
    Private parties . . . 106
    Special functions exception . . . 106
Sovereign immunity (See SOVEREIGN IMMUNITY)

INJUNCTIONS
Immunity from injunctive actions (See IMMUNITIES, OFFICIAL)

J

JURY TRIAL
Right to . . . 276
Waiver of . . . 288

L

LOCAL LIABILITY
Ad hoc policies
    Generally . . . 206
    Deliberate indifference . . . 225
    Final authority analysis . . . 206
Collection action against local governments . . . 253
Hiring, improper . . . 241
Historical antecedents . . . 181
Innocent agents
    Generally . . . 242
    Criminal proceedings . . . 245
    Tort law . . . 246
Municipal immunity
    Generally . . . 195
    Punitive damages . . . 326
"Person" for state liability, bifurcated meaning of . . . 191
Respondeat Superior . . . 192
State laws
    Local government, using state attribution principles to reach . . . 248
    Pendent party jurisdiction over state claims . . . 251
Supervisor liability . . . 194
Training, inadequate . . . 242

N

NOTICE-OF CLAIM
Generally . . . 267

O

OFFICIAL LIABILITY FOR CONSTITUTIONAL WRONGS
Constitutional violations of . . . 66
Deprivation of rights, privileges or immunities . . . 1
Fifth Amendment takings claim . . . 47
Implied constitutional causes of actions . . . 72
Implied statutory causes of actions . . . 71
Miranda violations . . . 51
Private party as state actor . . . 21
Procedural due process claims . . . 28
State action
    Generally . . . 13
    Private party as state actor . . . 21
    Public function theory . . . 27
State inaction . . . 53
Statutory violations . . . 66

OFFICIAL LIABILITY FOR CONSTITUTIONAL WRONGS—Cont.
Substantive due process claims . . . 48
Unauthorized conduct not violative of Constitution . . . 28
"Under color of" state law . . . 1

P

PRIOR AND PARALLEL STATE PROCEEDINGS
Appealing adjudicative agency action . . . 448; 458
Criminal proceedings, pending . . . 488
Exhaustion under § 1983 . . . 443
Fifth Amendment takings claim . . . 431
Fourth Amendment excessive force claim . . . 481
Full and fair opportunity . . . 427
Full Faith and Credit Clause . . . 427
Habeas corpus and exhaustion requirement . . . 459
Preclusion . . . 421; 474
Prisoners, exhaustion requirement for state . . . 465
State agencies, decisions by . . . 438
Statute of limitations . . . 459
Title VII, litigating issues under . . . 442

R

RELEASE-DISMISSAL AGREEMENTS
Generally . . . 289

REMEDIES
Causation . . . 303
Compensatory damages . . . 299
Municipal immunity and punitive damages . . . 326
Nominal damages . . . 302
Presumed damages . . . 303
Punitive damages
    Generally . . . 311
    Actual injuries, without . . . 321
    Constitutional constraints . . . 318
    Municipal immunity . . . 326
    Nonconstitutional constraints . . . 320
State and local officials, prospective relief against
    Anti-Injunction Act . . . 378; 404
    Article III limitations
        Associational standing . . . 364; 365
        Capable of repetition yet evading review . . . 360
        Class certification . . . 359; 362
        Mootness . . . 328; 340
        Ripeness . . . 328
        Standing . . . 328
        Third party standing . . . 338
        Threatened injuries . . . 337
    Congressional power . . . 372
    Injunctive relief, statutory limitations on . . . 368
    Prison Litigation Reform Act, limitations in . . . 372

S

SOVEREIGN IMMUNITY
Abrogation
    Generally . . . 165
    Article I powers, under Congress' . . . 175
    Civil rights statutes, applicability to other . . . 174
    Clear statement rule for . . . 171

[References are to pages.]

SOVEREIGN IMMUNITY—Cont.
Eleventh Amendment . . . 131
Express waiver by state law . . . 162
Federal jurisdiction, waiver by affirmative invocation of
. . . 162
Implied waiver . . . 163; 164
Individual capacity suit distinguished from official capacity suit . . . 173
Introduction . . . 131
Official capacity suit distinguished from individual capacity suit . . . 173
"Persons", states as . . . 172
Prospective injunction suits filed against state officials
    Generally . . . 148
    Retrospective injunctions distinguished from
        . . . 154
Waiver
    Generally . . . 159
    Express waiver . . . 162
    Federal jurisdiction, by affirmative invocation of
        . . . 162
    Implied waiver . . . 163; 164

STATE AND FEDERAL LAW IN § 1983 LITIGATION
Accrual rules . . . 264
Jury trial, right to . . . 276; 288
Notice-of-claim requirements . . . 267
Release-dismissal agreements . . . 289
Section 1988(a) . . . 255
Statute of limitations
    Generally . . . 255; 263
    Tolling rules . . . 264
Survivorship rules . . . 266
Wrongful death suit . . . 266

STATUTE OF LIMITATIONS
Generally . . . 255; 263; 459
Tolling rules . . . 264

SURVIVORSHIP RULES
Generally . . . 266